The People:

A History of Native America

The People:
A History of Native America

R. David Edmunds
University of Texas at Dallas

Frederick E. Hoxie
University of Illinois–Urbana-Champaign

Neal Salisbury
Smith College

HOUGHTON MIFFLIN COMPANY   Boston   New York

Publisher: Patricia A. Coryell
Senior Sponsoring Editor: Sally Constable
Senior Development Editor: Jeffrey Greene
Editorial Assistant: Uzma Burney
Senior Project Editor: Bob Greiner
Editorial Assistants: Katherine Leahey and Cassandra Gargas
Art and Design Manager: Gary Crespo
Senior Art and Design Coordinator: Jill Haber Atkins
Composition Buyer: Chuck Dutton
Associate Manufacturing Buyer: Brian Pieragostini

Cover Image: Detail from *Kiowa Mother and Papoose* by Stephen (Qued Koi) Mopope
(1898–1974). Courtesy of the Archives and Rare Books Library, University of Cincinnati.

Printed in the U.S.A.

Library of Congress Catalog Number: 2004114378

Instructor's exam copy
ISBN-10: 0-618-73138-5
ISBN-13: 978-0-618-73138-1

For orders, use student text ISBNs:
ISBN-10: 0-669-24495-3
ISBN-13: 978-0-669-24495-3

2 3 4 5 6 7 8 9-CRS-10 09 08 07

Contents

Preface   *ix*

1
American History Begins: Indian Peoples Before the Advent of Europeans   *1*

The Peopling of America   *2*
Farmers in the Desert Southwest   *6*
   Indian Voices: *Akimel O'odham Speaker (1775)*   *7*
   People, Places, and Things: *Pueblo Bonito, Chaco Canyon*   *9*
Farmers in the Eastern Woodlands   *11*
Villagers of the Far West   *18*
Band Societies of the Western Interior and Far North   *22*
Conclusion   *25*
Suggested Readings   *26*

2
Strangers in Indian Homelands, 1490–1600   *27*

Indian-Spanish Encounters Beyond North America, 1492–1536   *28*
Southeastern Chiefdoms Confront Imperial Adventurers   *31*
   Indian Voices: *A Timucua Chief Defies De Soto, 1539*   *34*
Encounters in the American West   *41*
   People, Places, and Things: *Spaniards Entering the Southwest: A Navajo View*   *44*
Early Contacts in the Northeast   *45*
Conclusion   *51*
Suggested Readings   *51*

3
Native Peoples and the Founding of European Colonies, 1600–1660   *53*

Struggling for Power in the Northeastern Interior: The Iroquois vs. New France   *55*
   Indian Voices: *Kiotseaeton, Mohawk Iroquois Diplomat, 1645*   *60*
Coastal Indians and Early European Settlements   *64*
   People, Places, and Things: *Powhatan's Mantle*   *73*
Confronting Spanish Expansion in the Southeast and Southwest   *75*
Conclusion   *79*
Suggested Readings   *79*

4
Worlds in Upheaval, 1660–1720   *81*

The Northeast: Iroquois Power and European Expansion   *83*
   People, Places, and Things: *Onondaga Iroquois Artifacts Made from European Metals*   *85*
The Southeast: Slaves, Confederacies, and War   *95*
West of the Mississippi: Native Resistance and Cultural Transformation   *102*
   Indian Voices: *Pedro Naranjo, San Felipe Pueblo, 1681*   *104*
Conclusion   *108*
Suggested Readings   *109*

5
Native Americans in Peace and War, 1716–1754   *110*

Indians and Empires: The East   *113*
Exiles in Their Own Homelands: Indians in the English Colonies   *119*
Native Americans and French Expansion in the Mississippi Valley   *124*
   Indian Voices: *Stung Serpent, Natchez, 1723*   *126*

Horses and Guns on the Plains   *129*

People, Places, and Things: *Spanish Slave-Raiding Expedition, c. 1720*   *131*

Conclusion   *133*
Suggested Readings   *133*

6
Native Peoples and Imperial Crises, 1754–1821   *135*

Eastern Indians and the Seven Years' War, 1754–1761   *137*
Eastern Indians and the American Revolution, 1761–1783   *141*

Indian Voices: *Joseph Brant (Mohawk), 1789*   *150*

Struggles for Power in the Southern Plains and Southwest, 1754–1810   *151*
Neophytes, Gentiles, and Colonizers on the Pacific, 1769–1833   *155*

People, Places, and Things: *Ohlones Gambling at Mission Dolores, 1816*   *159*

Conclusion   *162*
Suggested Readings   *162*

7
The Defense of the Trans-Appalachian Homelands, 1795–1815   *164*

The Struggle for Autonomy   *166*

People, Places, and Things: *Captives*   *169*

American Indian Policy   *175*
Revitalization Movements   *179*

Indian Voices: *Tecumseh Demands That the British Honor Their Promises!, 1813*   *183*

Conclusion   *186*
Suggested Readings   *187*

8
Western Tribes Meet the Long Knives, 1800–1820   *189*

Indian Voices: *A Piegan (Blackfoot) Describes the Arrival of Horses*   *190*

Before Lewis and Clark   *192*
The Tribes Encounter Lewis and Clark   *194*

People, Places, and Things: *Mandan Earth Lodges*   *199*

The Western Fur Trade   *204*
Conclusion   *211*
Suggested Readings   *212*

9
Indian Removal, 1820–1845   *213*

Indian Country in the New Republic   *214*

People, Places, and Things: *Native American Women as Entrepreneurs*   *219*

Jacksonian Indian Policy   *220*
Indian Removal: The Southeast   *222*

Indian Voices: *Cherokee Leaders Denounce the Injustices of Removal*   *229*

Indian Removal: The Old Northwest   *230*
Fighting Removal: Armed Resistance   *233*
Conclusion   *238*
Suggested Readings   *238*

10
Strangers Invade the West, 1845–1861   *241*

Indian Territory   *243*

People, Places, and Things: *The Cherokee Female Seminary*   *248*

Texas   *250*
California   *253*

Indian Voices: *William Joseph (Nisenam Tribesman) Describes a Lynching*   *258*

The Northwestern Tribes   *260*
The Southwest   *263*
Conclusion   *266*
Suggested Readings   *267*

11
Indian People in the Civil War Era, 1850–1868   *268*

Civil War in Indian Territory   *269*

Reconstruction in Indian Territory   *272*
Eastern Indians in the Civil War   *276*
Violence in the West   *277*
The Desert Southwest   *280*

   Indian Voices: *Herrero (Navajo Headman) Testifies
   About Conditions at Bosque Redondo*   *285*

The Plains Tribes During the Civil War Era   *286*

   People, Places, and Things: *Teepees: "Exceedingly
   Picturesque and Beautiful"*   *291*

Conclusion   *292*
Suggested Readings   *293*

12
Warfare in the West, 1867–1886   *295*

Cultural Change on the Plains   *296*
The Warfare Continues   *298*
The Northern Plains, 1868–1881   *301*

   Indian Voices: *Two Moons (Cheyenne War Chief)
   Recounts the Battle of Little Big Horn*   *305*

Rebellions Against Reservation Life   *308*
The Apaches, 1865–1886   *315*

   People, Places, and Things: *Lozen: Shield to Her
   People*   *318*

Conclusion   *320*
Suggested Readings   *320*

13
"Kill the Indian, Save the Man": Survival in a Shrinking Homeland, 1878–1900   *322*

Assaults on Indianness   *322*
"Raising Up" the Indians: Schools, Missionaries,
   and Government Agents   *331*
Prophets, Inventors, and Writers: Indian Resistance
   in an Age of Oppression   *336*

   People, Places, and Things: *Teton Lakota Parasol*
   342

   Indian Voices: *Sarah Winnemucca*   *343*

Conclusion   *345*
Suggested Readings   *345*

14
Survival and Renewal, 1900–1930   *347*

Finding New Places to Be Indian   *347*
The Native American Church   *348*

   People, Places, and Things: *Monroe Tsa Toke
   (1904–1937)*   *349*

   Indian Voices: *Charles Eastman Criticizes
   "Civilization"*   *351*

Fighting for the Indian Cause   *357*
Facing Economic Hardship   *365*
Conclusion   *371*
Suggested Readings   *372*

15
Reorganization and War, 1930–1945   *373*

PRESSURES MOUNT FOR DRASTIC CHANGE   *374*

   Indian Voices: *D'Arcy McNickle Reveals His Hopes for
   Indians in the Future*   *376*

   People, Places, and Things: *Crow Indian Round Hall*
   389

World War II   *390*
Conclusion   *394*
Suggested Readings   *396*

16
Fighting to Be Indians, 1945–1970   *397*

Indians on the Move   *398*

   People, Places, and Things: *Chicago American Indian
   Center*   *402*

Termination Takes Shape   *406*
Battling Back   *410*

   Indian Voices: *Alice Jemison Speaks Out Against
   Termination*   *411*

Gaining Recognition   *415*
New Voices   *421*
Conclusion   *423*
Suggested Readings   *423*

17
Acting Sovereign, 1970–1990   *425*

Red Power   *426*

> Indian Voices: *Russell Means Advocates Reviving Indian Traditions*   431

Victories in Congress and the Courts   *435*

Sovereignty on the Ground   *444*

> People, Places, and Things: *Indian Governments at Work*   451

Conclusion   *452*

Suggested Readings   *452*

18
Indians in the New Millennium   *454*

> Indian Voices: *Joy Harjo Writes About Indian Life*   457

Tribe or Nation?   *459*

Indian Health   *462*

Struggling Economies   *464*

Who Is an Indian?   *470*

> People, Places, and Things: *National Museum of the American Indian*   472

Conclusion   *473*

Suggested Readings   *473*

Appendix A: Chronology   *475*

Appendix B: State and Federally Recognized Tribes   *481*

Appendix C: Most Populous Tribes   *488*

Appendix D: Largest Landholding Tribes   *489*

Appendix E: Suggested General Reference Works   *490*

Appendix F: Films and Videos   *492*

Appendix G: List of Tribal Gaming Operations   *495*

Photo Credits   *501*

Index   *503*

Preface

When translating their names for themselves into English, most Indian communities prefer to call themselves, "the people." This simple term is remarkably revealing. It does not refer to a specific race or political ideology. It does not tie a community to a single event or location. It indicates instead that the central connection binding members together is their humanity. This book is a history of "the people" in North America.

Few books offer readers an opportunity to trace the sweep of Native American history from the pre-contact era to the present. Fewer still attempt to tell this story from the perspective of Indian people themselves. *The People* attempts both tasks. The book's narrative begins with the peopling of North America and ends with the twenty-first century. Our primary focus is on events that occurred in what is now the United States after 1492, but we have tried to ground our narrative in an understanding of the cultures and traditions that evolved in North America over the thousands of years when the continent had no sustained contact with the Eastern Hemisphere. Throughout this book we have used an ethnohistorical approach to our subject. That is, we have drawn on the insights of anthropology (including the fields of ethnography, archaeology, and folklore) to develop and articulate a Native American perspective on events. We have looked beyond traditional historical sources as well as to scholarship in many other fields to craft a narrative that assesses events from the point of view of the Indian communities that are at the center of our tale. In this text, Indians are actors in history; they are not simply acted upon.

While we keep our focus on the experiences of Native Americans, we recognize that the many stages of the European invasion—from the early travels of explorers to the establishment of European settlements and, later, the United States—profoundly influenced the lives of Indian peoples. *The People* describes the events and new peoples who disrupted and remade the American environment over the past 500 years, but it also explains how Native actions affected that same environment. Conflicts between Indians and non-Indians inevitably are one focus of the text, but we also illuminate areas of cooperation and places where Native people worked autonomously to create new

traditions and institutions. One caveat: While *The People* describes religious leaders and religious change, it generally avoids descriptions of community religious life. We believe that Native American community leaders are best equipped to explain that dimension of their lives when and where they deem it appropriate.

THEMES

The People describes a vast array of people and events but we hope not to bury our readers beneath an avalanche of disjointed information. Instead, we hope to assist and orient those readers by keeping a series of themes before them throughout the text. These themes include:

1. *The Struggle to Defend Homelands and Preserve Community Autonomy* Intensely attuned to local environments and traditions, Indian peoples have exhibited a continuous allegiance to their territories and to the goal of governing their homelands without interference. This outlook was evident in disputes that occurred prior to the arrival of Europeans and it persisted through the era of European settlement as well as in modern times.
2. *Shifting Identities* American Indians have adapted to new conditions and taken advantage of new opportunities from their first days in North America. As a consequence "being Indian" has meant different things at different times. We will demonstrate that Indian identities have never stopped changing.
3. *Cultural Persistence* As a counterweight to their adaptability, Native Americans have been determined to sustain the traditions that have defined their communities for thousands of years. Communities have continuously balanced tradition and change and insisted, even when external conditions have brought devastating damage, they remain "Indian."
4. *Distinctive Views of Family and Gender* Despite the cultural variety that exists within Native American traditions, it is clear that most Indian communities based group allegiance on a sense of kinship and shared traditions. Indian

communities were (and are) not rooted in ideology and coercion but rely upon the mutual responsibilities created by human relationships. These relationships may include ties to family, allies, spiritual beings, and the environment. As a consequence of these many relationships, Indian communities have developed traditions of gift-giving and social roles that are different from those of non-Indian communities.

5. *Diversity* It is not surprising that a cultural tradition rooted in local environments, family loyalties, and social traditions would express itself in hundreds of local variants. American Indian communities created thousands of languages and dialects, hundreds of distinctive tribal traditions, and dozens of ways of making a living from the land around them. No text can fully represent this diversity, but *The People* attempts to indicate its dimensions throughout the narrative.

While each chapter has its own conclusion, one story runs through all: an epic drama of *survival* in the face of dispossession and horrific cruelty, and courageous *persistence* in the face of colonization and oppression. While studying these events is often upsetting, it is ultimately inspiring and uplifting. The survival of Native American peoples into the modern world and their dynamic presence in contemporary society not only demonstrates the heroism of uncounted people, but the benefits all citizens enjoy from the active participation of American Indians in a modern, democratic society. Their participation has shaped the United States in the past and will continue to shape it in the decades and centuries to come.

ORGANIZATION

The People is organized into eighteen chapters. Each chapter addresses a major period of history and illuminates many of the themes outlined above. Deciding how to define these eighteen "major periods" was one of the most difficult tasks associated with writing this book. In the end our decisions regarding the coverage of chapters were governed by our commitment to telling our story from a Native American perspective. Despite the wide geographical sweep of our chapters, we believe they each describe a distinctive moment in the history of Native Americans. These chapters cover periods that we believe would have made sense to the Indian people who experienced them. Here is a summary of our chapters and their contents.

Chapter 1: American History Begins: Indian Peoples Before the Advent of Europeans offers a concise history of Native Americans over the thousands of years before the arrival of Europeans. It draws on archaeology and other scholarship to outline the emergence and development of regional cultures, contextualizing the peoples whom Europeans would encounter in the coming centuries.

Chapter 2: Strangers in Indian Homelands, 1490–1600 focuses on the often-overlooked period between the initial arrival of Europeans in the Americas and the beginnings of sustained colonization north of present-day Mexico after 1600. It examines the earliest recorded encounters of Indians with Europeans. It points to both the successes and failures of Europeans in interacting with Native peoples, and to the catastrophic impact of epidemic diseases on Indian societies.

Chapter 3: Native Peoples and the Founding of European Colonies, 1600–1660 concerns interactions between Indians and the new French, English, and Spanish colonies from the St. Lawrence to the Rio Grande. In just six decades, a series of tiny European outposts expanded into several formidable colonies.

Chapter 4: Worlds in Upheaval, 1660–1720 discusses the intensification of warfare involving Indians and Europeans from 1660 to 1720, a period during which the regional conflicts of the early seventeenth century gradually merged with the imperial rivalries of Britain, France, and Spain. A central feature of this warfare was the dislocation of massive numbers of Native Americans as refugees, slaves, and adopted captives.

Chapter 5: Native Americans in Peace and War, 1716–1754 examines Native Americans and their interactions with Europeans across the vast region between the Atlantic Ocean and the Rocky Mountains. These interactions transformed both the landscape and the membership of many Native communities.

Chapter 6: Native Peoples and Imperial Crises, 1754–1821 spans the years from the onset of the Seven Years War to the independence of Mexico, weaving together several struggles over imperial authority. Native Americans were involved in each of the conflicts and were critically affected by the outcomes. From an Indian perspective, the Seven Years War and American Revolution were virtually a single, continuous conflict in the East. In the West, Spanish efforts to subjugate Native Americans met with considerable success in California but had little impact on the rising power of the Comanches and other groups on the southern Plains.

Chapter 7: The Defense of the Trans-Appalachian Homelands, 1795–1815 focuses on the tribes' attempts to maintain political autonomy after the American Revolution. The chapter also examines federal efforts to formulate and administer a comprehensive Indian policy, and the role that missionaries played in the government's efforts to encourage cultural change among the tribes. Finally, the chapter discusses the rise of Native American revitalization movements led by Handsome Lake and Tenskwatawa, the Shawnee prophet, and how Tecumseh utilized the Shawnees prophet's teachings in an attempt to unite the tribes against the Americans.

Chapter 8: Western Tribes Meet the Long Knives, 1800–1820 provides a brief survey of tribal migrations onto the Plains before tracing their locations at the time of the Lewis and Clark expedition to the Pacific in 1804–1806. This chapter also examines the interaction of Native people and non-Indians in Alaska, focusing upon the relationship of the Aleuts and Tlingits with Russians, British, and Americans. Finally, this chapter explores Native American participation in the western fur trade.

Chapter 9: Indian Removal, 1820–1845 examines cultural change among tribes both south and north of the Ohio, focusing upon the Cherokees as the primary example of a southern tribe with many members who adopted and adapted to American ways. The chapter then turns to the Midwest and illustrates that many Native people had adopted cultural patterns from the Creole French, and that people of mixed lineage (métis) prospered in the Indian trade in this region. The chapter concludes by describing and discussing the removal of both northern and southern tribes to lands in the west.

Chapter 10: Strangers Invade the West, 1845–1861 examines the eastern tribes' arrival in the West, their interaction with tribes indigenous to the region, and efforts of the Five Southern Tribes to establish new homes and governments in Indian Territory. The chapter also surveys the tribes of Texas and their relationship with the Lone Star Republic. The focus then shifts to the Far West and the tribes of California, Oregon, and Washington and the Pueblo-dwelling people in New Mexico. By mid-century, the United States had become the dominant non-Indian political and military power in the region.

Chapter 11: Indian People in the Civil War Era, 1850–1868 illustrates first that the conflict was disastrous for the tribes in Indian Territory. Yet the chapter shows that in the decades that followed the war many of the tribes rebuilt their homes and reestablished viable governments. Finally, the chapter examines the interaction of Indians and white emigrants on the Great Plains during this era, and describes the major treaty negotiations that took place at Fort Laramie and elsewhere in an effort to bring an end to conflicts with settlers and miners.

Chapter 12: Warfare in the West, 1867–1886 focuses upon the struggles of western tribes to defend their homelands and to remain free of federal control. The chapter investigates the events that led to the battle of the Little Big Horn, the Red River War on the Southern Plains, the tragedy of Captain Jack and the Modocs, the flight of Chief Joseph and the Nez Percé, and conflicts between the government and the Paiutes, Bannocks, and Utes. The chapter also surveys the Apache-U.S. warfare in the 1870s and 1880s and analyzes the government's difficulty in suppressing and controlling Geronimo. Finally, the chapter examines the appeal of Plains Indians and why stereotypes of Plains warriors have been romanticized in the popular media.

Chapter 13: "Kill the Indian, Save the Man": Survival in a Shrinking Homeland, 1878–1900 describes the widespread assault on Indian lifeways launched in the wake of the American conquest of the trans-Mississippi West. This chapter also describes the many tactics Native Americans devised to protest the assimilation effort or to turn it to their own advantage.

Chapter 14: Survival and Renewal, 1900–1930 describes an era when Indians were being portrayed as a "vanishing race." While many of the assaults on tribal cultures continued in the twentieth century, this chapter focuses on a remarkable array of Native men and women who struggled to preserve their communities and their freedoms at a time when indigenous people were becoming a tiny minority in a rapidly industrializing United States. This cultural and political struggle was often successful, despite the continuing invasion of tribal lands by non-Indians who sought to "develop" (and profit from) Indian resources.

Chapter 15: Reorganization and War, 1930–1945 traces the Native American experience during two dramatic moments in twentieth-century American history: the New Deal and World War II. During the 1930s, the upsurge of activism among federal agencies made it possible for many of the efforts launched earlier in the century to bear fruit. Similarly, World War II offered American Indians—citizens since 1924—opportunities to demonstrate both their patriotism at home and their valor in battle. The war years offered both men and women the chance to participate successfully in the American economy and to live in dignity beyond the control of reservation agents and missionaries.

Chapter 16: Fighting to Be Indians, 1945–1970 focuses primarily on the remarkable movement of Native people to new homes in cities and towns across America in the decades immediately after World War II. The migrations of these years were unprecedented and they demonstrated once again the adaptability of Indian people and the extent to which their tribal and community identities both persisted and changed in response to new conditions.

Chapter 17: Acting Sovereign, 1970–1990 begins by recounting the history of the Red Power movement of the 1970s and traces the legacy of that period of activism for the ensuing decade. Red Power brought together a broad coalition of Indian men and women from reservations and cities across the nation in a campaign to win political autonomy, cultural respect, and economic support for Native communities.

Chapter 18: Indians in the New Millennium focuses on five difficult issues that confronted Native Americans as the twenty-first century began.

Lawyers and political leaders sought practical definitions of Indian sovereignty: where did the rights of tribes end and the rights of states and the federal government begin? Communities across the country struggled as well to find the answer to persistent health problems that plagued Indians of all ages. A parallel discussion focuses on Indian poverty. How could the resources seized and exploited in earlier times be restored? And how should tribal wealth best be managed—by individuals or by the group as a whole? Many commentators looked to a small but growing group of prosperous Indian-run casinos to solve the economic problems of Native communities. Finally, as Native people migrated to cities and intermarried in growing numbers with non-Indians, community leaders asked, "Who is an Indian?" How would tribal membership be defined in the decades to come? These difficult questions mark the end of this extraordinary story of survival, adaptation, renewal, and growth.

We have organized each chapter around a strong interpretive theme so that readers will be able to grasp the distinctive pattern of events at each moment in our story. This attention to organization and theme is also reflected in the way each chapter is broken into a series of three or four major subsections, each with its own clearly marked divisions. Readers will be able to grasp the central points of each chapter by reviewing the section and subsection headings, either before or after they read through the text.

FEATURES

In each chapter, there are two features that underscore the themes discussed and provide a focus for discussion and reflection. "People, Places, and Things" documents a person or object rather than a written text. Photographs of these objects and people—buildings, works of art, and tribal leaders—provide a tiny, two-dimensional museum display that illustrates some aspect of the time period covered in the chapter. "Indian Voices" are texts generated by Indian people. These documents bring Indian voices into our narrative and, we believe, deepen the interpretations offered in each chapter.

An annotated list of suggested readings accompanies each chapter. We assembled these lists with an eye to recent and widely available titles. They provide readers with pathways to continue exploring many of the topics addressed in the text.

Three final points: Throughout *The People*, the terms "Native American" and "Indians" (and "American Indians") are used interchangeably. In addition, we use the popular term "mixed blood" only occasionally with quotation marks. In general we avoid this term. In discussions of mixed ancestry, we use the French *métis*, a term used commonly in Canada and the Spanish *mestizo*. Finally, *The People* avoids the term "white," especially as a noun. Instead the authors use "Euro American," "non-Indian," or "the majority culture."

TEACHING AIDS

To help in teaching this course, we are offering an Instructor's Resource Manual and a Test Bank. They are both written by Jennifer Guiliano and Melissa Rohde of the University of Illinois at Urbana-Champaign.

The Instructor's Resource Manual includes for each chapter: a summary, themes, suggested lecture topics, class discussion topics, and print and non-print resources. The Test Bank includes identification items, multiple-choice questions, and essay questions.

ACKNOWLEDGMENTS

Because each of the authors of *The People* has been teaching and writing in the field of Native American history for many years, our debts to teachers and colleagues are literally beyond measure. Each of us began work in this area at a time when the historical establishment had little interest in indigenous histories, but we were each encouraged to pursue our interests by extraordinary mentors at the three institutions where we studied: Donald J. Berthrong at the University of Oklahoma, Mor-

ton Keller at Brandeis University, and Gary Nash at UCLA.

For this project we have drawn on materials we have each assembled in the course of our professional careers, but we have had special assistance from a number of people. These include Elizabeth Carney, Brian Ingrassia, Ann Lattinville, Stacy Schlegel, and Paula Wagoner. We are also grateful to those who reviewed the text:

Ned Blackhawk, University of Wisconsin (Madison)
Clyde Ellis, Elon University
Gregory Evans Dowd, University of Michigan
Colin Fisher, University of San Diego
Brian Hosmer, Newberry Library
Jess A. Levine, Brookdale Community College
Claudio Saunt, University of Georgia
Nancy Shoemaker, University of Connecticut

and to Lucy Eldersveld Murphy of The Ohio State University at Newark, who also reviewed the text, assigned portions of it to her students, and offered us several valuable suggestions. We have also benefited from the support of our home institutions—the University of Texas at Dallas, the University of Illinois at Urbana/Champaign, and Smith College—and to the Newberry Library that has, at different times for each of us, been a source of research material and intellectual stimulation. Finally, this book is dedicated to three extraordinary Native American intellectuals, D'Arcy McNickle, Alfonso Ortiz, and Vine Deloria, Jr., who wrote and taught about the themes running through this book and who lived lives that demonstrated that "the people" will endure.

R.D.E.
F.E.H.
N.S.

The People:

A History of Native America

American History Begins: Indian Peoples Before the Advent of Europeans

In the late 1880s an Eastern Cherokee Indian in North Carolina named Swimmer told a story to an ethnologist from the Smithsonian Institution. The ethnologist, James Mooney, was recording Eastern Cherokee songs, stories, and other traditions related to him by Swimmer and other informants. One of Swimmer's stories, which Mooney titled the "Origin of Disease and Medicine," began by recalling "the old days [when] the beasts, birds, fishes, insects, and plants could all talk, and they and the people lived together in peace and friendship." But thereafter people grew in numbers and spread over the earth, trampling on the smaller creatures while hunting down the larger ones for meat and hides. Various groups of animals then held councils to devise means of retaliating. First, the bears met but were unable to agree on a workable plan. As a result of the bears' failure, "the hunter [since then] does not even ask the Bear's pardon when he kills one." Next, the deer met and decided "to send rheumatism to every hunter who should kill one of them unless he took care to ask their pardon for the offense." For that reason, "no hunter who has regard for his health ever fails to ask pardon of the

Deer for killing it." Then, the fish and reptiles agreed to send terrible dreams of slithering snakes and rotting fish, which continue to haunt people to this day. Finally, the other animals sent people all the diseases that still afflict them. Hearing about the diseases, the many plants of the earth rallied to the humans' defense. As Mooney recorded it, "each tree, shrub, and herb down even to the grasses and mosses agreed to furnish a cure for some one of the diseases." With the aid of the plants, humans were able to overcome the suffering inflicted on them by resentful animals.

The Cherokee story tells how humans learned the hard way that, despite their considerable physical powers, they inhabited a spiritual world in which animals and plants were also conscious beings with powers of their own. None of Earth's creatures could dominate the others; rather, all depended on and interacted with one another to survive. Together they constituted a kind of community that was central to human existence.

The story also refers to a number of significant historical episodes—the rise of human hunters, the origins of hunting rituals, the spread of diseases, and the advent of remedies for those diseases—

that figure in the histories of most Native American peoples. These were significant events in Cherokee history as well as in the formulation of Cherokees' spiritual beliefs. In telling and retelling such episodes—and the lessons they convey—over many centuries, Cherokee storytellers helped their people to sustain a collective sense of their history and to forge a cultural identity that served them especially well in times of upheaval and travail.

The Cherokees' depiction of different kinds of interactions between beings also represents the ways in which Indians idealized relations among humans. Over many millennia, Native Americans created communities based on members' ties to one another of kinship and interdependence. At the heart of kinship and interdependence lay the ideal of reciprocity, in which both human and other-than-human beings gave gifts with the expectation of appropriate reciprocity. Just as hunters ritually thanked the deer for the gift of sustenance, Indians reciprocated among themselves for gifts of utilitarian or spiritually powerful goods, access to hunting or fishing grounds, new technical or spiritual knowledge, and countless other benefits. Reciprocal exchanges constituted the glue linking not only near neighbors but diverse Indian peoples separated by long distances. Even as disparities emerged within and between Native communities, the principle of reciprocity underlay relations between people of different social ranks and between groups that were unequal in power. The result was hundreds of distinct but overlapping histories that together unfolded over thousands of years, entirely apart from developments in the Eastern Hemisphere. Together these diverse histories constituted the long, complex history of America that preceded the arrival of European and other outsiders.

THE PEOPLING OF AMERICA

Exactly how and when the first American Indian communities appeared is a subject of great controversy. Once they were established, most observers would agree, American Indians lived in small communal bands whose members procured food by hunting game, fishing, and gathering wild plants and seeds in their varied ecological settings. Through kinship and reciprocal exchanges, these communities established distinctive identities of their own while interacting with outsiders. In the process they created the foundations of the regional and cultural diversity that would characterize Native American life for thousands of years thereafter.

The First Americans

A controversy surrounding the earliest Americans pits Native American oral traditions against the theories and findings of academic scholars, both Indian and non-Indian. Traditional Native peoples have always relied on oral traditions to explain how their ancestors arrived in the homelands they inhabit. For example, Pueblo Indians and their neighbors recount how the first human beings originated far underground and passed upward through three worlds before emerging on the earth's surface in the Southwest. According to the Iroquois and most of their neighbors in the Northeast, a pregnant woman fell from the sky toward a watery planet. Ducks gathered and spread their wings to soften her fall, and a muskrat gathered earth from beneath the water, piling it atop a turtle's back so that she and the people after her would have a place to live.

Most scholars, on the other hand, postulate that human beings gradually expanded into the Western Hemisphere from northeastern Asia by traveling either over or along the coast of a thousand-mile-wide expanse of land that filled the Bering Strait for long intervals during the last Ice Age (ca. 75,000–10,000 BCE [Before the Common Era]). (Temperatures were so cold that much more water than at present was frozen into glaciers, thus lowering the sea level.) No doubt searching for food, the newcomers probably lived for long periods on the now-vanished land (often called, misleadingly, a "land bridge") and would have had no reason to think that they had entered a different continent. Because surviving evidence is so sparse, scholars have disagreed among themselves over the timing of the newcomers' movements and the routes they followed. Many now postulate that as sea levels rose precipitously near the end of the Ice Age, the earliest Americans began moving southward from the Arctic regions. With much of the Pacific Northwest coast free of ice and supportive of plant and animal life, these people apparently moved by watercraft, settling various coastal and interior locales as far south as Monte Verde, in southern Chile, a site dating to ca. 12,500 BCE. Other, more skeptical scholars continue to doubt that the earliest Americans moved south of the Arctic Circle before about 9000 BCE, when an ice-free corridor opened along the eastern edge of the Rocky Mountains, through which people passed and dispersed across the North American interior.

At the heart of the controversy between Indians' oral traditions and academics' accounts of the earliest Americans is the issue of historical authority. Which accounts—and which group of people—are most reliable when it comes to ascertaining the historical truths about Native Americans' origins? The issue is complicated by the fact that the two kinds of accounts serve very different purposes. For one thing, Native American origin accounts refer to specific tribal nations whereas scholars try to understand when and how members of the human species to which all people belong first reached the Americas. Most scholars who study the subject doubt that any historically known Native American cultures and peoples can be traced directly to the beginnings of human history in the Western Hemisphere. Furthermore, academic scholars are concerned with dating events as precisely as possible in linear, calendrical time. In Native traditions, on the other hand, the chronology of a people's origins is significant only for having occurred at the beginning of their existence, before which there was no time. In that sense, Indian accounts parallel the book of Genesis in the Hebrew and Christian bibles more nearly than they resemble academic findings and hypotheses regarding the first Americans. Just as Genesis constitutes the basis on which believers have built religious traditions and group identities over thousands of years, so indigenous American origin accounts have served as foundations for tribal nations' understandings of the universe, their systems of values, and their sense of themselves as distinct peoples. Not surprisingly, then, Native peoples insist on the fun-

damental truth of their accounts and reject scholars who claim that scientific evidence contradicts, or is otherwise insufficient to support, Indian oral traditions. Over the past five centuries, these stories have continued to sustain Indian peoples in the face of efforts by non-Indians to impose Christianity and other alien value systems on them.

Because the assumptions and concerns underlying the two approaches differ so fundamentally, some archaeologists and Native authors maintain that they do not overlap at all and therefore cannot directly contradict one another. Some go so far as to suggest that a number of Native oral traditions are compatible with scholarly accounts of the earliest Americans. For example, Pawnee scholar Roger C. Echo-Hawk points to a Cheyenne account that refers to the first people as coming from a country "where great waters were all around them." Numerous origin stories, including that of the Iroquois, resemble the Arikara belief that the original humans found "wide, thick ice and deep water" until a diving bird or animal brought soil on which they could walk. Many stories recall large mammals, monsters, or "hairy people" with whom the first humans shared the earth. Despite their mythological features, Echo-Hawk argues, such stories also record some of the experiences of the earliest Americans as they passed through Arctic environments, hunted mammoths and other large mammals, and moved south either by water or through the narrow interglacial corridor. Even the "cave worlds" described by the Hopis and other Pueblos allude to conditions that undoubtedly confronted some of the first Americans.

Although the precise details of the earliest Americans' origins will never be ascertained with precision, it is clear that they were a diverse lot from the beginning. Except for the speakers of languages in the Athapaskan and Aleut-Inuit language families (discussed later in the chapter), the ancestors of all other contemporary Indians were among the very earliest Americans. Linguists have ascertained that ten other distinct language families were represented among the first Americans, from which descended the hundreds of Indian languages spoken when Europeans began arriving.

Creating American Habitats

The earliest Paleo-Indians supported themselves by exploiting as many species of plants and animals in their environments as was practicable. As with all small hunting-gathering societies observed and described by outsiders over the past five centuries, men were almost certainly responsible for hunting while women, whose roles as mothers required them to remain closer to the camps, would have been in charge of gathering wild plant products. Central to the food supplies of the earliest Paleo-Indians were large mammals such as mammoths, mastodons, bison, and caribou that thrived in the absence of predators. Numerous archaeological sites show evidence of Paleo-Indians having hunted the large mammals with various weapons, but most frequently with the combination of an atlatl—the Aztec word for throwing stick—and a spear. Rather than simply hurling spears at their prey with their bare hands, Paleo-Indian hunters threw them with an atlatl, giving the spear sufficient range for hunters to stand back and avoid detection and enough velocity that the point would pass through the mammals' thick skins.

The points themselves were also critical to the spears' effectiveness. Representing the earliest known, distinctively American technological advance, Paleo-Indians' projectile points have been uncovered at sites from Canada to Guatemala, dating at least as far back as 10,000 BCE. They were three to six inches long and skillfully flaked on both sides. They were distinguished from contemporaneous projectile points made in Asia and Alaska by the way their makers "fluted" them, that is removed a long flake at the base on both sides, parallel to the edges, apparently to facilitate the wounded animal's bleeding. One of the most commonly found types of fluted point is termed "Clovis," for the New Mexico town where modern researchers first observed some in the 1930s. The effectiveness of Clovis and other fluted points is apparent from the many that have been found embedded in or lying next to the skeletons of large mammals. Eight points, five of them in the chest area, accompanied the remains of one mammoth found near Naco, Arizona. Thirteen Clovis points and eight butchering tools lay near the skeletal remains of nine young mam-

Clovis Points Paleo-Indians throughout North America crafted "fluted" points like these and used them when hunting large mammals.

moths at Lehner Ranch Arroyo in New Mexico. Hunters often separated the younger mammoths from the herd before attacking them.

Although most Paleo-Indian "kill sites," as archaeologists call them, feature mammoth bones, the remains of bison, caribou, and even a mastodon and a giant sea tortoise have also been found. Most kill sites were near water sources, suggesting that the hunters stalked and attacked the animals as they gathered to drink. Once an animal was slain, band members joined in taking the carcass to a base camp where the women prepared the meat for all to share.

By about 9000 BCE, the era of hunting large mammals ended as mammoths, mastodons, and several other species of large mammals became extinct. According to a tradition among Northwest Coast Indians, a legendary giant turned the monsters that once roamed that region into stone. Perhaps the giant is a representation of Paleo-Indian hunters. Nevertheless the big mammals were doomed by the continuation of post–Ice Age climatic warming, which depleted the food chain on which they depended, as well as by the hunters' effectiveness.

While mammoths and other large mammals failed to adapt to climatic and environmental changes, Paleo-Indians succeeded by shifting their hunting efforts toward other animals. Throughout the Great Plains, for example, the changing climate gave rise to an arid land of short grass in which bison, or buffalo, thrived. As they shifted to bison, Plains Paleo-Indians developed new hunting strategies. While they killed most bison individually, they often obtained many at once. At the Bonfire Shelter site in Texas, archaeologists have found the bones of about 120 buffalo from three different herds, each of which was stampeded over the cliff. Elsewhere, Paleo-Indians captured bison by driving them into box canyons and steep-sided sand dunes, and between icy embankments. As with Bonfire Shelter, the Indians used many of these locales repeatedly. The most remarkable kill site found on the Plains is the Olsen-Chubbock site in eastern Colorado where, in about 8200 BCE, hunters drove about 200 buffalo into a narrow, steep canyon and killed them all. While the hunters and their families ate some of the meat at the time and preserved more of it by drying it in the sun, they left nearly a quarter of it on the bones. The Olsen-Chubbock site is one of a handful of Paleo-Indian sites at which vast amounts of waste were left behind. Clearly, the hunters' less-than-precise hunting methods occasionally yielded more meat than they could transport, even after processing.

Far fewer Paleo-Indian kill sites have been found east of the Mississippi than in the West. Most of those that have been identified show caribou as the mammal of choice. Like their mammoth-hunting forebears, the caribou hunters often captured their prey at the shores of lakes and ponds where the animals had stopped to drink.

Rather than being permanent, Paleo-Indian campsites were places where bands stopped for a few weeks or months during the course of a long annual circuit, or "round." Bands generally occupied exclusive hunting territories that varied enormously in size, depending on the populations of both the bands themselves and their prey. A band's annual round within its territory consisted of movements between favored hunting spots and quarries. In their encampments, band members processed meat and hides and worked stone, bone, and wood for tools, weapons, and other implements. Based on archaeological evidence from campsites, Paleo-Indians appear to have lived in bands consisting of a few families and numbering anywhere between twenty and fifty people altogether. Larger bands remained together only during spring and summer, splitting into smaller parties during winters, when hunting was more difficult.

Although economically self-sufficient, Paleo-Indian bands interacted regularly with their neighbors. Archaeological evidence indicates that 150 to 200 people participated in the processing and consumption of the meat at the Olsen-Chubbock site. The large figure means that several bands came together and cooperated in the enterprise. But bands did not cooperate solely for purposes of hunting. To judge from the practices of modern hunting bands, rules requiring wives to marry outside their own bands was a primary motive for neighboring groups to get together. In turn, marriages created kinship networks that reinforced interband ties, helping to resolve any conflicts between groups that might arise. Marriage and other joint ceremonies strengthened the common beliefs and identities of neighboring groups. Such meetings were also occasions for sharing ideas, goods, techniques, and stories based on experiences within one's own territory and contacts with other neighbors. It was almost certainly through such gatherings that the technology of fluted points spread so widely among Paleo-Indians.

The most extensive evidence of interband activity comes from the Lindenmeier site in northern Colorado, dating to about 8800 BCE. Of the vast amount of stone and other material used for tools, weapons, and other artifacts at Lindenmeier, none is local. Instead it shows that Lindenmeier attracted Paleo-Indians from widely dispersed places. For example, the obsidian on one side of the camp comes from central New

Mexico while that on the other side originated in the Yellowstone area of northwestern Wyoming. These encounters of different peoples introduced elements of change and innovation to local Paleo-Indian cultures and provided band members with access to a larger world of people and ideas.

FARMERS IN THE DESERT SOUTHWEST

In two very different environments—the arid Southwest and the humid Eastern Woodlands—Indian peoples drew on women's long experience harvesting wild plants, as well as on techniques introduced from outside, to make farming their principal mode of procuring food. The challenges to farming were especially formidable in the Southwest because of that region's dry climate. Yet over time, many southwestern societies produced considerable agricultural surpluses, enabling some of them to flourish as politically powerful centers of long-distance trade. Despite these successes, aridity continued to challenge southwestern Indians and eventually contributed to the decline of the most centralized societies.

The Advent of Farming in the Southwest

After 8000 BCE, the southwestern climate grew not only warmer but also more arid, and the population of large mammals in the region sharply declined (except for bison in the eastern portion of the region, adjoining the Plains). The role of women, who had long foraged for wild plants and helped hunt rabbits and other small mammals, became more critical to the sustenance of southwestern Indians. In dozens of caves and rock shelters, archaeologists have found the remains of grinding tools, organic matter, and other evidence that point to the elaborate gathering, shelling, roasting, and storing of large quantities of seeds.

After 2000 BCE, the trend toward increased aridity in the Southwest ended and reversed enough to allow new species to grow. Sometime around 1500 BCE, women at Bat Cave, New Mexico, and other highland locations in the region acquired some new plant seeds from neigh-

bors to the south. The seeds were maize, or corn, which had been cultivated as early as 5000 BCE in areas of central Mexico. Although maize had become a major food source for people in Meso-america, southwestern Indians for several centuries treated it as another plant product to be roasted and ground like the wild grass seeds they collected on their annual rounds.

Gradually, domestic plants assumed greater importance in the lives of southwestern Native Americans. Sometime after 1000 BCE, they learned about the cultivation of two additional Mexican crops, squash and beans. More than just another source of food, beans greatly enriched southwesterners' diets for two reasons. First, when eaten in combination with maize, beans greatly increase the nutritional value of maize by releasing lysine, an amino acid required by humans. Second, bean plants release nitrogen into the soil, thereby compensating for maize's depletion of nitrogen from soil.

Over time southwestern Indians acquired and further developed new strains of maize that better withstood the hot, dry conditions of the region. After about 200 CE (Common Era), some farming peoples began gathering into permanent villages where they lived in pit-houses, systematically irrigated their crops, and used clay to make pots for cooking and storing food. In most of these villages one house was set aside for ceremonial purposes; it was the forerunner of the kiva that is still the central sacred space of every southwestern pueblo. Because of the heavy physical labor required to construct and maintain irrigation works and because fields were often located at some distance from villages, southwestern men joined women as producers of crops.

Hohokam Culture

By 500 CE, villagers at Snaketown and other locales in the Gila and Salt valleys of southwestern Arizona were constructing irrigation canals as long as ten miles and producing two successive crops of corn, beans, and squash per year. These developments marked the beginning of a new regional culture known as Hohokam, meaning "those who have gone" in the language of their Akimel O'odham (Pima) descendants.

INDIAN VOICES   Akimel O'odham Speaker (1775)

Like the history of America after Europeans arrived, earlier American history was characterized by change over time. Just as they did in the Cherokee story that begins this chapter, Indian peoples conceived of historical developments in terms of stories that were usually personal and conveyed a moral lesson.

In 1775 the Akimel O'odham headman of the village of Uturituc, now Cuk Su:dagi (Black Water), told the following story to Pedro Font, a Spanish missionary. It tells how earlier Hohokam peoples confronted the challenges posed by their desert environment as they built their major center at Casa Grande and as they first tried to grow crops. But it recounts these experiences as those of a single "Bitter Man." Bitter Man's "ill nature and harsh rule" override the reciprocity that Akimel O'odhams and other Indians saw as fundamental to relationships among humans as well as between humans and nonhumans. Finally Bitter Man is obliged to search for the Wind and Clouds, whose assistance he had thought he could do without, in order to resume reaping "great harvests."

As with many Indian oral narratives recorded by non-Indians, the assumptions and values of those doing the recording sometimes creep into a story. Such instances remind us that oral evidence, like any other kind of evidence, needs to be critically evaluated. In this case, Font clearly inserted the Christian God into the part of the story where Bitter Man calls for spiritual assistance in cutting and transporting the timbers for Casa Grande. In all other respects, the story appears perfectly consistent with Akimel O'odham tradition.

Archaeologists have also recorded the emergence of Casa Grande and Hohokam farming as well as Casa Grande's later abandonment. But they recount these developments in terms of what they can verify scientifically from the surviving archaeological evidence. While the two accounts are fundamentally different in narrative construction and underlying assumptions, their content is complementary rather than contradictory.

A long time ago there came to that country a man who was called The Bitter Man because of his ill nature and his harsh rule. This man was old, but he had a young daughter. And there came in his company a young man who was not a relative of his or of anybody else, and married the daughter, who was very pretty as he was handsome. And this old man brought as servants the Wind and the Clouds.

When the old man began to build that great house he ordered his son-in-law to go and look for timber with which to roof it. The young man went a long distance, but since he had no ax or anything with which to cut the trees, he was gone many days, and he finally returned without bringing any timbers. Now the old man was very angry, and he said that the son-in-law was good-for-nothing, and he would show him how he would bring the timbers. And so the old man went away to a sierra where there are many pines, and, calling on God to aid him, he cut many pines and brought many timbers for the roof of the house.

When this Bitter Man came, there were no trees in the country, nor any plants, but he brought seeds of all kinds and reaped very large harvests, with the aid of his two servants, the Wind and the Clouds, who served him. But because of his ill nature he became angry with the two servants, and discharged them, and they went a long way off. And then, for lack of servants, he was not able to reap the harvests, so he ate all that he had raised, for he was now dying of hunger. He then sent his son-in-law to call the two servants and bring them back, but he could not find them no matter how much he looked for them. Then the old man went to look for them, and having found them he took them again into his service, and with their aid he again reaped many great harvests. And so they continued to live for many years in that country, but after a long time they went away, and they have heard nothing more about them.

Source: Herbert Eugene Bolton, ed. and trans., *Anza's California Expeditions*, vol. 4: *Font's Complete Diary of the Second Anza Expedition* (Berkeley: University of California Press, 1930), 38–39. Reprinted with permission of The University of California Press.

As in several other regions of North America, the organization of labor for food production—in the Hohokam case, the construction and maintenance of elaborate irrigation works—fostered more formal and complex ties among communities. Beginning in the mid-sixth century, some of the larger villages, numbering one hundred or more residents, extended their irrigation canals to smaller villages located farther from sources of water. The primary villages in the resulting networks featured platform mounds and ball courts where people from throughout the network gathered for ceremonies, games, and other public events. Such gatherings reinforced the unity of the networks and the dominant role of the larger villages. The larger villages, along with a new center at Casa Grande, also forged and dominated Hohokam networks' exchange relations with northern Mexico. Mexican influences were apparent in the canals, pottery, carved stone artifacts, turquoise mosaics, rubber balls, copper bells, macaws, and iron pyrite mirrors found at Hohokam sites. Hohokam peoples also participated in trade networks extending from the Great Plains to the southern California coast, the latter of which provided thousands of sea shells that artisans used in crafting jewelry, mosaics, and other objects of beauty.

Anasazi Culture and Chaco Canyon

Under the influence of Hohokam culture, other southwestern peoples expanded their farming during the sixth century. At numerous places in what is now eastern Arizona and western New Mexico, bands settled in villages consisting of one or two dozen pit-houses where they grew maize, squash, and beans and made pottery to cook and store their food. Although these later farmers did not build irrigation canals, they resembled the Hohokam in that trade with Mexico was the foundation of networks that united neighboring communities.

Initially these later farmers represented two distinct cultural traditions, the Mogollon, located above the Hohokam near the headwaters of the Gila and Salt rivers, and the Anasazi, situated in and around the tributaries of the San Juan River. The two traditions merged after about 900, with Mogollon being largely absorbed by a changing Anasazi culture. At this time, summer rainfall began to increase markedly, enabling Anasazi peoples (modern Pueblo ancestors) to spread into previously uncultivated areas of the Southwest. In so doing, they abandoned their pit-houses for multistoried apartments built of clay or adobe. Besides farming, they hunted with bows and arrows, raised turkeys, and grew and wove cotton. Evidence from rock art makes clear that the Anasazi carefully observed the movements of the sun, especially noting the winter and summer solstices. They considered these solar observations spiritually significant as well as useful in making calculations for farming and other seasonally based practices.

Anasazi villages spread over much of the Colorado Plateau and surrounding areas. In a few

PEOPLE, PLACES, AND THINGS

Pueblo Bonito, Chaco Canyon

Pueblo Bonito, Chaco Canyon, New Mexico Pueblo Bonito illustrates the richness and grand scale of Anasazi architecture.

Pueblo Bonito was the largest town in the powerful Anasazi center that flourished at Chaco Canyon, in what is now New Mexico, from the tenth to twelfth centuries. As with the other large towns in the canyon, its eight hundred rooms and dozens of circular kivas (ceremonial centers) were all enclosed within a single multistory structure. While elite leaders lived in a few apartments, most of the rooms served to store food and other goods. Similar kivas are still found in Southwestern Indian pueblos to this day.

choice locations, major centers arose to coordinate trade and religious rituals. The largest and most notable Anasazi center was at Chaco Canyon, which emerged during the tenth century to dominate a much larger network of pueblos on the San Juan River in northwestern New Mexico. About three thousand people lived at its center in twelve large towns on the north side of the canyon and in more than a hundred small villages on the south. Each town consisted of a vast enclosure consisting of a few apartments, hundreds of storage rooms for food and for trade and ceremonial goods, plus several small kivas and one "great kiva" for spiritual observances. As opposed to the small, simple rooms of the villages, town apartments had finely veneered masonry walls supported by log beams that Anasazi men had cut and hauled from upland areas as far as fifty miles away. The few hundred Chaco Canyon town residents appear to have been elite administrators who coordinated the collection and distribution of water as well as trade and religious ceremonies. In contrast, the approximately three thousand villagers farmed and made goods of turquoise for local and long-distance trade.

In about 1100, Chaco Canyon reached the height of its power and grandeur. The canyon itself constituted only the core of a vast network of communities numbering about fifteen thousand people. The network consisted of at least 70 additional towns and 5,300 villages, located up to sixty-five miles away in all directions. Linking the villages to the towns and the towns to the canyon was a system of perfectly straight roads that became stairways or footholds when crossing cliffs and other obstructions, and dozens of signaling stations at which messengers lit fires to communicate information. Although the reason that the roads went straight over, instead of circumventing, all obstacles is not altogether clear, it undoubtedly had a religious dimension. The array of goods and materials recovered at Chaco Canyon—timbers, turquoise beads, copper bells, macaw feathers, sea shells, and other imports—indicates that its trade networks extended southward through Mexico to Central America and westward to the Pacific coast.

During the thirteenth century, Chaco Canyon collapsed as a regional center and then was abandoned altogether. Underlying this abandonment was a new cycle of drought. The drought rendered the canyon towns' control of rainwater runoff meaningless and their agricultural surpluses inadequate. As a result, the beliefs upholding the elites' power were apparently undermined, and they lost their control of production and regional trade. By the end of the thirteenth century, Chaco Canyon and other large concentrations of Anasazi peoples had dispersed.

Selected Native American Tribal Nations, ca. 1500

New Societies in the Southwest

Most Anasazi refugees formed new, smaller pueblos (villages or towns) where they would eventually be known collectively as the Pueblo Indians. Seeking more reliable sources of water, some moved only short distances to become the Hopis, while many more moved south and east to join or form what became Ácoma, the Zunipueblos, and the Eastern pueblos on the Rio Grande and Pecos River. Their relocation to new communities with new environments and new neighbors apparently

provoked a spiritual crisis among the refugees. Pueblo communities developed a complex of beliefs, art, and ceremonies centering on katsinas—spirits thought to have influence in fostering rain as well as cooperation among villagers. As they settled in their new locations and as ecological stability was restored, the katsinas played a central role in the religious life of the Pueblos.

The same drought that undermined Anasazi societies led to the dispersal of Hohokam centers to the south. Hohokam refugees became the Akimel O'odham (Pima) and Tohono O'odham

(Papago) Indians of what is now southwestern Arizona. The Akimel O'odhams were centered in the river valleys of the Gila and its tributaries while the hunting-gathering Tohono O'odhams dispersed to drier uplands. Although living in smaller villages than before, the Akimel O'odhams continued to irrigate their crops and, like the Pueblos, produced regular surpluses. Akimel O'odham women, also like their Pueblo counterparts, wove cotton blankets and made coiled baskets. They traded these products to the Tohono O'odhams for meat and for the fruit of saguaro cactus, which the Tohono O'odhams were especially successful at harvesting. The Tohono O'odhams also continued to participate in long-distance exchanges linking California, northern Mexico, and the Pueblos.

The emergence of new Pueblo and O'odham societies coincided with the arrival in the Southwest of Athapaskan-speaking Apaches and Navajos (Diné), descendants of subarctic Dene Indians, who had migrated south over the Great Plains (discussed later in this chapter). The Apaches and Navajos settled in the mountains and deserts of the Southwest, often in areas recently abandoned by Anasazi peoples. (*Anasazi* is a Navajo word meaning "the old ones.") While eastern Apache men hunted buffalo on the Plains, western Apache and Navajo men shifted to deer, elk, and smaller mammals. Apache and Navajo women continued to gather berries, piñon nuts, and seeds.

With their differing cultures and foods, Athapaskan speakers and the Pueblos had much to offer one another. The Apaches and Navajos were adept hunters and had trade connections with peoples on the Plains. The Pueblos were highly productive farmers, potters, weavers of cotton, and importers of goods from Mexico and California. By the end of the fifteenth century, Apache and Navajo hunters were carrying meat and hides to the pueblos and exchanging them for corn, cotton blankets, obsidian, turquoise, and ceramics. The eastern Apaches in particular carried bison meat and skins from the Plains to semi-annual trade fairs at Taos, Pecos, and other pueblos. In turn, the Apaches exchanged many of the durable goods they received from the Pueblos with peoples on the Plains, and then returned to the Pueblos with shells and other exotic goods

from the east. The result was a vast extension of indigenous trade across what is now the southern rim of the United States, linking the lower Mississippi Valley and Gulf coast with northern Mexico and the Pacific through the southwestern pueblos. Spanish explorers in the sixteenth century saw Gulf Coast and Pacific shells in the Southwest while others on the lower Mississippi River saw pottery and woven cotton from the Southwest. Pueblo trade and social ties with Apaches and Navajos fostered social and cultural changes among Native peoples, most notably in the Navajos' adoption of Pueblo farming practices. These ties would also affect Spanish colonizing efforts after 1600 (see Chapters 3–6).

FARMERS IN THE EASTERN WOODLANDS

Native Americans in the humid Eastern Woodlands, extending from the Mississippi Valley to the Atlantic coast, also incorporated farming into their ways of life. Unlike in the Southwest, the abundance and diversity of food sources enabled Indians in eastern North America to increase their numbers and, in many cases, to coordinate trade and religious activity over wide areas long *before* agriculture became their principal mode of food production. But once farming did become central, some eastern societies—similarly to the Anasazi in the Southwest—became highly centralized and flourished for several centuries before their members dispersed and resumed the smaller-scale village life of their ancestors.

Early Nonfarming Societies

The remarkable abundance and diversity of foods in the humid Eastern Woodlands enabled Indians there to satisfy their dietary needs within increasingly small territories. This trend is most apparent at the Koster site on the Illinois River, where archaeologists have found fourteen distinct occupation levels, dating from 7500 BCE to 1200 CE. In 6500 BCE, Koster was a campsite of three-fourths of an acre that was occupied for part of each year by a band of about twenty-five people. The occupants ate white-tailed deer, various small mammals, fish, mussels, pecans, and hickory nuts. They ground the nuts as well as seeds and other plant foods, they crafted objects of wood and leather, and they made baskets. After being abandoned for about a thousand years, Koster reemerged as a village with permanent houses in which the inhabitants spent much of each year. The houses, which were eight to ten feet wide and twenty to thirty-five feet long, were supported by posts eight to ten inches in diameter. By 3500 BCE, after a long spell in which it was occupied only intermittently, Koster had become a year-round village. Although the villagers ate virtually the same foods as had their predecessors three thousand years earlier, they had become far more effective in capturing, preparing, and storing food, and especially in smoking fish, for wintertime consumption.

As elsewhere in North America, Indian women in the Eastern Woodlands had long gathered and prepared wild plants and seeds. As societies became even less mobile and more sedentary, hunting declined and women's roles as food producers became more prominent. By 1500 BCE, eastern women cultivated numerous plants, including gourds, squashes, pumpkins, sunflowers, sumpweed (or marsh elder), goosefoot, knotwood, and maygrass, for vegetables or seeds. At the same time, women began baking clay, carving soft stones such as steatite and sandstone, and fashioning bottle gourds into containers for storing surplus foods. Because of their weight, gourds would have been impractical for mobile bands, but they enabled village-based Native Americans to store and preserve food surpluses for extended periods.

Despite the advantages of their more sedentary lives, the diminishing of their annual rounds actually left some eastern Indians more dependent than before on outsiders for certain specialized items. Many communities could obtain materials such as flint or foods such as fish only by trading with other communities for them. As a result, local and long-distance trade multiplied, entailing larger quantities of exotic materials that circulated hundreds and often thousands of miles from their points of origin. Archaeologists have found copper and hematite from Lake Superior, sea shells from the Gulf and Atlantic coasts, galena

(lead sulfide) from the upper Mississippi Valley, obsidian from the High Plains, jasper from eastern Pennsylvania, and other rare minerals throughout the region, both in raw form and as finished points, tools, jewelry, and religious articles.

As among their Paleo-Indian ancestors thousands of years earlier, neighboring Indian communities in the East (and elsewhere) gathered regularly to exchange goods and information, celebrate marriages and visit with relatives, and observe religious ceremonies. Heeding the principle of reciprocity, individuals and communities gave away goods to demonstrate their generosity and obligate the recipients to reciprocate. The idea was that each presentation further strengthened the mutual obligations felt by each party.

For most of North American history before the arrival of Europeans, the societies that exchanged goods were relatively equal in strength and resources. But in some parts of the Eastern Woodlands, as the redistribution of food surpluses and the coordination of exchanges and ceremonies became more complicated, they came under the control of certain prominent families. Archaeological evidence of such distinctions is apparent at several sites in the Ohio Valley, dating to between 3000 and 2000 BCE, and especially at Indian Knoll in western Kentucky. About 4 percent of those buried at Indian Knoll were interred with nearly all of the finely crafted, imported goods of conch shell and copper found at the site.

The evidence also points to gender roles at Indian Knoll. Men are associated with tools for working wood, flint, and leather and for fishing, and women with stones and pestles for cracking and grinding nuts. Most men and some women owned knives, scrapers, and drills. And men and women in equal proportions possessed medicine bundles, turtle shell rattles, bone flutes, and other objects used by medicine people. These patterns indicate that most subsistence and craft activities were divided by gender, but also that some women used tools usually associated with men. It also shows that both women and men served as religious healers.

The shell artifacts at Indian Knoll originated on the Gulf coast of Florida while copper goods came from the Great Lakes. Those who lived far from these sources only received the materials through exchange and thereby came to place higher value on them. Indian Knoll's unusual wealth appears to have been based on its control of the movement of goods *between* these two regions as well as of the local distribution of each within the Ohio Valley.

Few eastern Indian societies at the time drew the stark social distinctions found at Indian Knoll. Archaeological evidence indicates that relatively egalitarian communities, such as Koster, were the norm. Yet there were other exceptions, most notably after 1000 BCE at a Louisiana site known as Poverty Point. Like Indian Knoll, Poverty Point was a regional trade center, receiving goods from throughout eastern and central North America and distributing them to local communities. But it was distinguished from all other Native American societies until then by its mammoth earthworks—several large mounds and a series of concentric ridges surrounding a central plaza—that aided solar observations and probably served other religious as well as defensive purposes. From the scale of the construction at Poverty Point, it is clear that surrounding communities contributed labor to the project; it is not clear, however, whether that labor was voluntary or coerced and how it was organized. Nevertheless, the earthworks do seem to symbolize Poverty Point's domination of a large network of communities bound together by trade and religion as well as collective labor.

Poverty Point also follows Indian Knoll in its social ranking. The rarest and clearly most valued objects—red jasper beads, stone pipes, and certain pendants with animal figures on them—are found exclusively in the western embankments near the largest mound, indicating the quarters of elites. Concentrations of finely crafted spear points, made from a variety of flint found only in the upper Midwest, and of decorated baked clay objects suggest the presence of men and women, respectively, of a middling status. A wide variety of other objects are more universally distributed throughout Poverty Point.

The complex society that arose around Poverty Point flourished for about three centuries and then dissolved around 700 BCE. Archaeologists have been unable to determine what happened and why, but it is clear that the center at Poverty Point lost its ability to dominate regional exchanges. Such domination was not apparent

again in the East until a new cultural fluorescence, known as Adena, arose several centuries later in the Ohio Valley.

Although Adena culture began simply, by 100 BCE more than three hundred large mound centers were linked by common rituals and beliefs centering on commemorations of the dead and by exchanges of finely crafted objects used in these ceremonies. Among the objects uncovered at Adena sites are intricately crafted stone pipes, sheets of mica imported from North Carolina, jewelry and talismans of copper from Lake Superior, and engraved stone tablets.

During the first century BCE, Adena culture merged with another exchange-based culture arising in the Illinois Valley to form Hopewell, the most complex and extensive culture yet to appear in North America. Each of the larger Hopewell ceremonial centers spread over several hundred acres and consisted of two to three dozen mounds averaging 30 feet in height, 100 feet in diameter, and 500,000 cubic feet in volume. Hopewell exchange networks were even more far-flung than those of their Adena predecessors. Besides copper from Lake Superior and the Southeast, Hopewell centers imported mica, chlorite, and quartz crystal from the southern Appalachians; obsidian from the Yellowstone region; conch and turtle shells, shark and alligator teeth, and barracuda jaws from Florida; galena from the Mississippi Valley; a variety of flint found only in Indiana; a type of quartz from North Dakota; and silver from the upper Great Lakes. Artisans at the centers used all these materials to make an array of fine objects, primarily for consumption by elites.

Adena and Hopewell cultures appear to represent the transformation of regional exchange networks into a combination of religious systems based on shared beliefs and ceremonies and economic systems in which certain centers controlled the movement of raw materials and the production and distribution of finished products. The role of elites in coordinating all these activities gave them a degree of political power unprecedented in North America at the time.

Hopewell influences spread over much of eastern North America, and even into the eastern Plains, between the first century BCE and the fourth century CE. Nevertheless, like earlier regional cultures in the Eastern Woodlands, Ohio and Illinois Hopewell declined in the fifth and sixth centuries. The causes are not entirely clear, but the presence of many small arrow points at some sites seems to confirm the likelihood of violence in those instances. At several centers, the inhabitants had built defensive enclosures and some of these centers were subsequently burned. The advent of the bow and arrow coincided with the decline of Hopewell, and may have provided rebels or external enemies the advantage they needed to overpower the centers. In the Southeast, on the other hand, Hopewell survived and eventually fused with local exchange networks.

The Turn to Agriculture

From the seventh to tenth centuries, women cultivators in the Eastern Woodlands developed a new strain of maize, known today as "northern flint." Better adapted to the short growing season of the East than the southwestern varieties used previously, northern flint corn led easterners to depend primarily on cultivated crops—maize, squash, and (somewhat later) beans—as their primary source of food. This dependence was furthered by a breakthrough in pottery. By tempering clay pots with shell, women were able to make larger but thinner-walled vessels for storing surplus food crops. By 1000 CE cultivated maize, beans, and squash were the most important food staples in most of the Eastern Woodlands.

The labor and productivity connected with farming varied greatly, depending on environmental factors. The first eastern farmers were inhabitants of the Mississippi floodplain where annual flooding renewed the soil's fertility. Compared to Indians elsewhere, they did relatively little clearing and other preparation of fields and could count on remaining in the same locations indefinitely. In uplands and more heavily wooded areas, on the other hand, cultivation was more complicated. To clear their fields, Indians in southern New England set fires that enabled them to clear the underbrush and plant among the dead trees still standing. When the trees finally fell, they contributed to the village's wood supply. Because regular flooding did not renew upland soil, intensive cultivation eventually deprived it of nutrients. For

that reason, as well as because they depleted nearby wood supplies, most farming peoples rotated their villages among several favored sites every five to ten years.

Even while farming intensively, eastern North Americans continued to hunt, fish, and gather wild plants within specific boundaries. They simply added farming to the long summer phase of their annual subsistence cycle, combining it with other spring and summer village-based activities. The Ojibwes (Anishinaabeg, Chippewas) of the upper Great Lakes region became especially adept at harvesting wild rice. Native peoples along the Atlantic coast from New England to Florida added sea fish, shellfish, and aquatic plants to their diets.

Coastal Indians at the northern and southern extremes of the Woodlands did little farming. Abenakis north and east of the Merrimac River in New England sometimes planted maize when summering in large groups near the coast. But they did not depend on crops because they knew that the growing season that far north could be cut short. Although the Calusa Indians of the lower Florida peninsula abandoned farming after trying it briefly during the late tenth century, the extraordinary abundance of their environment supported a large centralized chiefdom that was tied through trade to highly productive farming societies in both the southeastern interior and the West Indies. More than one thousand people inhabited the central Calusa village of Calos at the end of the fifteenth century.

As women became the primary producers of food and the most constant presence in Woodlands villages, many eastern farming societies shifted from earlier patterns by recognizing the families of mothers rather than of fathers as the basis for reckoning kinship, residence, and identity. This meant that husbands moved into the households of their wives' families when getting married and that a mother's brother had more authority over her children than their father.

The dependence on agriculture also affected the religious beliefs and ceremonies of eastern North Americans. Although varying in detail, new rituals throughout the region marked spring planting, the fall harvest, and—most important of all—the appearance of soon-to-ripen green corn in early summer. The green corn ceremony celebrated and gave thanks for the assurance that the crops the women had planted would sustain the community for another year. Among Mississippian societies (discussed in the next section), the sun was regarded as not only the source of fertility but of the community itself. For the Narragansett Indians of southern New England, fertility was embodied in a supernatural being named Cautantowwit who lived to the southwest, the general direction from which crops had in fact come to them.

While many Woodlands communities simply incorporated farming into their earlier hunting, fishing, and gathering patterns, others undertook more radical transformations. The most notable were the Mississippian societies of the Midwest and Southeast.

Mississippian Societies

In the Mississippi Valley and the Southeast, Native Americans' adoption of agriculture and ceramic pottery led to the emergence of a new culture known as Mississippian. Mississippian peoples built on earlier Adena and Hopewell patterns of exchange, large-scale earthworks, specialized production of artifacts, and powerful, highly visible elites, but the scale of their endeavors dwarfed those of their predecessors.

Hundreds of Mississippian communities, large and small, participated in the production, exchange, and consumption of raw materials and finished goods. As in earlier networks, much of the trade consisted of ornamental objects that artisans had made from copper, mica, and other exotic materials. Marine shells were especially common. Shell objects appear at virtually every Mississipian site, often with engravings of human or animal figures. Mississippians also traded for two items linked to their dependence on farming. Local craftsmen fashioned chert (an impure variety of quartz) obtained from southern Illinois into stone hoes used by women farmers across much of the middle Mississippi Valley. Salt also came into demand among Mississippians as maize became their primary food, giving communities near major salt deposits a valuable trade commodity.

Some major centers eventually became urban "supercenters," dominating several smaller cen-

ters, dozens of surrounding "suburbs," and exchange networks that extended hundreds of miles. Regional centers were built around large public plazas with platform burial mounds, religious temples, and the ornate palaces of hereditary chiefs. The chiefs were distinguished by the vast quantities of food and artifacts that they collected as tribute from throughout their networks. Although Mississippians' beliefs about the sources of chiefly power varied, all considered it superhuman. The Natchez, closely observed by French colonizers in the early eighteenth century, were typical. They believed that their chiefs mediated between themselves and the source of agricultural fertility, the sun. Within the temple at each Mississippian center, there burned a sacred fire, which the inhabitants believed had been lit by the sun and maintained through elaborate ceremonies conducted by religious leaders. The fire marked the center of the sacred universe for all peoples connected to that center.

The largest, most extensive Mississippian center was Cahokia, situated just below the confluence of the Mississippi and Missouri rivers near modern East St. Louis, Illinois. Cahokia was first settled in the seventh century by farming peoples attracted to its rich floodplains. It was transformed into a major center during the late eleventh century when a sudden influx of newcomers arrived on Cahokia's outskirts. A new cluster of communities emerged along a north-south axis, with Cahokia at the center, and featured several circular structures that permitted solar observations. These observations enabled the people to maintain a calendar for scheduling the phases of the planting season and major ceremonies. At its peak in the early thirteenth century, Cahokia was an urban complex numbering about twenty thousand people and contained over 120 mounds within a five-square-mile area. Nine smaller mound centers and dozens of farming villages surrounded Cahokia, producing its food and managing its river-borne commerce with other Mississippian centers in the Midwest and Southeast.

Cahokia developed an even more elaborate social structure than had its Adena and Hopewell predecessors. Unskilled workers built the mounds and other public works; specialized craftsmen fashioned products from shell, copper, clay, and

Mississippian Ceremonial Vessel Besides making ceramic pottery for everyday use, Mississippian peoples produced finely crafted pieces like this one for use in religious ceremonies.

other materials obtained both locally and from elsewhere; managers coordinated work and exchange; and hereditary chiefs obtained tribute from non-elites in the form of food and manufactured goods. The religious ceremonies conducted in support of planting and harvesting foods appear also to have entailed the presentation of tribute and reinforcement of chiefs' powers.

The archaeological evidence indicates that Cahokia reached the peak of its power and prominence in the early thirteenth century and thereafter declined. Several interlocking factors apparently caused this decline. For one thing, a combination of drought and spiraling demand led to severe crop shortages in which outlying farming communities could no longer feed both themselves and Cahokia. (The drought was the same one that had led to the dispersal of centralized societies in the Southwest.) For another, the city had depleted nearby forests in its quest for firewood and building materials. In so doing, it also depleted many wild plants and drove away animals on which people depended for meat. Moreover, Cahokia's exchange networks collapsed, and it was under

siege from enemies, internal or external. Tensions are evident from the fact that fortifications had been constructed around the city's center during the twelfth century; now those fortifications were weakening. Clearly, some combination of environmental and political pressures was undermining Cahokia, leading in turn to the undermining of beliefs or ideologies that had reinforced the earlier unity and chiefly power.

These pressures continued into the fourteenth century, finally resulting in the complete abandonment of Cahokia. At the same time, related centers at Kincaid on the Ohio River and Aztalan in Wisconsin momentarily flourished and were then likewise abandoned. The inhabitants of these centers dispersed over the surrounding prairies to become farmers living in independent villages. Instead of paying heavy tribute to a regional center and its powerful chief, they traded occasionally with neighbors on a reciprocal basis. While they still valued exotic materials like marine shells and mica for burials, they did not attempt to amass vast quantities of these items. Thus the Mississippian legacy in the upper Midwest was a selective one. While the inhabitants abandoned political and religious centralization, they retained innovations they could incorporate into the kind of village life that had prevailed before the centralizing impulse took hold.

Although Cahokia and other Mississippian societies of the upper Midwest dispersed, their counterparts in the southeastern interior continued to flourish as the sixteenth century began. Southeastern Mississippian urban centers were smaller than Cahokia, usually numbering below ten thousand people, but were no less densely populated. They, too, were built around large public plazas where religious and other ceremonies took place, although their public structures were less elaborate than the most spectacular ones at Cahokia. Major centers such as Moundville, Cofitachequi, and Coosa (see Chapter 2) resembled Cahokia in that they dominated several smaller centers that in turn held sway over smaller neighbors. Likewise, they produced massive food surpluses, enabling them to exempt some people from farming to work as full-time artisans crafting jewelry and other fine objects for export.

Southeastern coastal peoples were likewise organized in extensive chiefdoms. From the Pensacolas on the Gulf coast to the Calusas on the Florida peninsula to the Guales and Powhatans on the Atlantic, hereditary chiefs and other elites oversaw societies numbering in the thousands. Except for the Apalachees, coastal peoples are not considered Mississippian because they were less densely clustered and did not manufacture large quantities of trade goods. Nevertheless they were tied to Mississippians through trade, alliances, and mutual cultural influences. Most coastal chiefdoms produced substantial food surpluses even though some, like the Calusas and Guales, enjoyed such abundance of wild food sources that they did little or no farming.

The Northeast reflected even less in the way of direct Mississippian influence. During the eleventh and twelfth centuries, warfare intensified in the Northeast as rising populations put pressure on available supplies of farmland, wood, and meat. The subsequent collapse of Cahokia and related exchange networks may have heightened competition among Indians for control of long-distance trade. In any event, the consequences of war are apparent in the archaeological evidence at many northeastern sites. Iroquoian speakers in what is now upstate New York took protective measures by excavating trenches and erecting palisades around their villages. Eventually, the Iroquois consolidated their villages into larger population centers and moved them to more defensible bluff-top locations. Although some small hamlets remained, most villages numbered more than fifteen hundred people and covered more than five acres. To coordinate their larger populations and increased military activity, residents formed village councils and distinguished sharply between war chiefs and peace chiefs. Over time, these villages and towns coalesced as five distinct nations— the Mohawk, Oneida, Onondaga, Cayuga, and Seneca. Probably during the fourteenth century, these nations grouped themselves into a single Iroquois Confederacy, or Haudenosaunee (whole house).

Among the Iroquois, a confederacy council consisted of fifty sachems (chiefs), each representing a hereditary clan at a major Iroquois village. At annual meetings, the sachems reenacted a

Huron War Leader Huron and Iroquois warriors wore wooden armor to protect them from arrows. This French engraving dates from the early seventeenth century.

ceremony prescribed by the spiritual prophet, Deganawidah (Peacemaker), whose vision and message led the five Iroquois nations to cease fighting among themselves and form their confederacy. In the ceremony, the sachems exchanged solemn "words of condolence" that conveyed their peaceful frame of mind and intentions. Then they aired any differences and grievances that had arisen among them during the preceding year and, following the advice of his clan's matrons, replaced any sachem who had died. The chiefs did not hand down orders but functioned more like a modern arbitration board than like an executive. The power of their rulings depended on the shared adherence of all Iroquois people to the principles of peace laid out by Deganawidah. That shared adherence was basic to the sense of collective identity and purpose that made the Iroquois the most formidable military and diplomatic power in the Northeast.

By the sixteenth century, the Iroquois and a second confederacy, the Huron (Wendat), were important centers of power in the Northeast. The Hurons maintained fruitful ties of exchange with hunter-gatherers to the north, with whom they exchanged farm produce for meat and animal skins. For their part, the Iroquois turned to coastal peoples in lower New England and Long Island to obtain wampum shells, highly valued marine shells that they strung in belts. They made wampum belts for use in sacred tribal and confederacy ceremonies, in diplomatic exchanges, and in historical recordkeeping. The Iroquois and Hurons, while closely related by language and culture, became bitter rivals. The exclusion of the Iroquois from major inland trade networks was apparently a factor in the hostility between them and some of their neighbors, including the Hurons and other peoples on the St. Lawrence River, the upper Great Lakes, and the Ohio Valley. These patterns of exchange and rivalry would continue after the arrival of Europeans in the Northeast.

Algonquian-speaking Indians along the Atlantic coast north of Chesapeake Bay maintained exchange ties, while sometimes fighting, with the Iroquois and other inland neighbors. These ties exposed them to new agricultural techniques and other developments in the interior

regions but distanced them from the most violent upheavals there. While consolidating some villages and forging close alliances with one another, peoples such as the Wampanoags, Narragansetts, and Delawares (Lenni Lenape) did not form institutionalized confederacies like that of the Iroquois. Farther south, some Algonquian speakers near Chesapeake Bay, situated closer to the Mississippian centers, united in confederacies with powerful hereditary leaders known as weroances. Among the Powhatans, this process would accelerate with the advent of European colonizers.

VILLAGERS OF THE FAR WEST

For most Native Americans outside the Eastern Woodlands and the Southwest, farming was impossible or impractical because water was scarce, temperatures were extreme, or the land was unsuitable. Yet just as some eastern peoples established complex societies and networks before relying primarily on domesticated crops for their food, so the peoples of California, the Northwest Coast, and the Columbia Plateau established highly elaborate political systems without adopting agriculture. The secret of their successes lay in their effective use of the abundant resources available in these regions.

California

By about 3000 BCE, coastal Californians were exploiting shellfish, land mammals, seeds, seals, and numerous species of fish to great effect. Thereafter, Indians of California's coasts and valleys focused especially on gathering and processing acorns. To maximize production, bands established permanent villages near large oak groves. After harvesting the crops, Indian women ground the acorns, leached the bitter tannic acid from them with water, and baked, boiled, or roasted them. They then stored the acorn meal that was not needed immediately. Over time, California Indians refined the mortars and pestles with which they ground acorns and the various baskets in which they carried, processed, and stored the precious food. Although they were familiar with ceramic techniques, as evidenced by the clay balls they used in baking acorns, they preferred their lighter waterproof baskets to clay pots as containers. In acorn production lie the origins of the fine basketware for which California Indians are now famous.

During the one thousand years after 500 CE, the Indians of California extended these patterns of food production inland to the western slope of the Sierra Nevada Mountains. Villagers carefully coordinated mixed subsistence strategies based on the harvesting and storing of acorns and other plant products, hunting, and fishing. Groups living on the coast and offshore islands added various fish, mammals, and plants of the sea to this range of foods.

The abundance of food in California contributed to the growth of its indigenous population. The intense competition for acorns and other resources led to the formation of ranked village societies in which hereditary chiefs coordinated internal and external affairs. Their adoption of the bow and arrow and the harpoon after the sixth century added to California Indians' food-producing efficiency and, thereby, to even more rapid population growth. Immigration augmented this natural increase in northern California, where

Algonquian-speaking Wiyots and Yuroks and Athapaskan-speaking Tolowas and Hupas arrived between the tenth and thirteenth centuries. By the fifteenth century, California was one of the most densely populated regions of North America, with villages along the southern coast often numbering 1,000 people and averaging 10 or more inhabitants per square mile. Sherburne Cook, the most thorough scholar of California's Indian population, estimates that approximately 310,000 people lived in the future state (minus its eastern desert) in 1492.

The Chumash Indians of the Santa Barbara coast and nearby islands exemplify the abundance enjoyed by Californians. Chumash men hunted deer as well as smaller mammals and fished for tuna and 125 other species of fish in plank canoes. Chumash women harvested vast quantities of acorns as well as walnuts, pine nuts, yucca, abalone and other shellfish, and numerous wild seeds whose growth the Chumash encouraged by controlled burning. The Chumash also hunted seals and sea lions and ate the meat of whales stranded during their annual migrations through the Santa Barbara Channel.

Although located at the extreme western edge of the continent, California Indians were integral to the larger history of Native Americans. Coastal groups like the Chumash maintained close ties

Chumash Baskets Central to the diets of the Chumash and most other California Indians were the acorns that women harvested, processed, and stored in finely crafted containers such as these baskets.

with inland Californians that in turn linked them to the North American interior. Inland Indians carried obsidian, quartz, and other valued materials to coastal allies when joining them in fishing. The inland Indians returned home with olivella and other sea shells, many of which they traded to Indians farther east, so that the shells found their way to Chaco Canyon and other Anasazi and Hohokam centers in the Southwest, and to bands throughout the Great Basin and western Plains.

Northwest Coast

By about 3000 BCE, Indians of the Northwest Coast produced surpluses of salmon, shellfish, walrus, and other foods. Among the innovations making possible such abundance were polished slate and bone knives and other pointed tools, and the use of carved wood for houses and boats as well as for tools and utensils. The concentration of exploitable foods enabled Northwestern Indians, like many of their contemporaries in the Eastern Woodlands and Columbia Plateau (see the next section), to live in permanent villages. They began constructing longhouses of cedar planks and otherwise increased their use of wood. By 1500 BCE, the Northwest Coast was a region of master woodworkers who built houses, seagoing dugout canoes, tools, and utensils from the region's abundant supply of timber. Some also carved masks and other ritual objects, beginning the remarkable artistic traditions that flourished on the Northwest Coast when Europeans began arriving more than three thousand years later.

The most important of the new food-production activities in the Northwest Coast were possible only because entire villages worked together at certain critical times. During spawning season, members caught, dried, and stored as many salmon as possible. After killing a whale, seagoing crew members processed and stored the meat and especially the oil. Heads of leading families coordinated these communal tasks and distributed food, fuel, and other products of that labor within each village. Over time, the leading family in each village developed into a political dynasty. The emergence of elite families was marked by the appearance of carved crests ("totem poles") and

legends that purportedly demonstrated the families' descent from spiritual beings, a sure claim to their superior status.

In the Northwest Coast, as in California, elite village families further consolidated their power after the sixth century in the face of growing populations, increased production of food surpluses, and intensified trade and warfare between groups. The richness of life in the Northwest Coast during the centuries before Europeans arrived is vividly revealed at Ozette, a Makah village that was buried in a mudslide in the sixteenth century. Excavators at Ozette in the 1970s found the wood and other organic materials of four cedar plank longhouses to be remarkably well preserved. Scores of boxes and baskets contained woodworking tools, harpoons and other weapons, and carved objects, including a representation of a whale's fin inlaid with shells and more than seven hundred sea otter teeth. Many of the decorated objects show that the Makahs had close trade and artistic ties to other Nootkan-speaking peoples on western Vancouver Island and to Coast Salish groups in Puget Sound.

The societies of the Northwest Coast, especially from Puget Sound northward, were strictly divided into three ranks—elites, commoners, and slaves captured in wars. The head of the leading family in a village was its chief, meaning that he presided over social and ceremonial activities, and the chief of the most important village was also leader of the whole tribe. As elsewhere in North America, however, the chief's political authority was limited; real authority over individuals lay with the male head of each lineage or extended family. This man coordinated the family's economic activities, managed its fishing and other territories, settled internal disputes, and led the family to join others in the event of war with outsiders.

The major ceremony in the social and political life of the village was the potlatch. Elite (and sometimes common) families staged a potlatch when a member got married, received her or his name, ascended to the chieftainship, or otherwise made a change regarded as significant to the family's social position. The male head of the family invited the entire community to be his guests for several days. The potlatch began with speakers reciting the history of the family to show the legitimacy and importance of the event being celebrated. After the host showered his guests with food and gifts, including canoes, shell beads, and carved artwork, more ceremonies alternated with feasting and socializing. In hosting a potlatch, a family and its leader publicly flaunted their status and their wealth and placed an obligation on their guests to reciprocate with either a potlatch of their own or at least an acknowledgment of the host's hospitality. In the process, much of the surplus wealth garnered by one family was redistributed to less prosperous ones, reinforcing the ideals of reciprocity and communal interdependence.

Salmon Fishers of the Columbia Plateau

To the east of the Northwest Coast, Indians in the Columbia Plateau had early on learned the migratory patterns of the salmon that, with the warming climate, began swimming up the Fraser, Columbia, and Snake rivers each year to spawn. By around 6000 BCE, the Milliken site on the Fraser and The Dalles on the Columbia were the sites of permanent salmon fishing stations. Thereafter the Plateau Indians based their way of life on salmon. By preserving much of their rich salmon harvests for wintertime consumption, Indians of the Plateau needed to leave only for short foraging expeditions. By 500 CE, they concentrated in large, sheltered villages near the major rivers from fall through early spring. For the rest of the year, they traveled in small bands while hunting and gathering. During the long winters between spring and fall fishing, villagers lived off the salmon, meat, and wild plants they had procured, dried, and stored during the preceding warm season. Villages shared hunting territories and gathered each year for fishing and trading, but were politically independent of one another. The families in each village were considered equal in status and, rather than inheriting their positions, political and religious leaders were chosen by the men of the village on the basis of their abilities.

Ties between many Plateau and coastal peoples were rooted in language. In the northern Plateau, Salishan speakers such as the Okanagons,

Kalispels, and Spokanes were related to the Coast Salish and Bella Coolas on the Northwest Coast. To the south and east, the Sahaptin or Penutian languages linked the Nez Percé, Yakamas, Wishrams, and Wascos with the Chinooks, Cayuses, Umatillas, and other coastal peoples in Oregon and northern California.

Plateau peoples were linked to one another and to outsiders by trade as well as by language. For several centuries before the arrival of Europeans, the major center for exchange and social interaction in the Plateau region was The Dalles (Chinookan for "trading place"), a narrow stretch of rapids located on the Columbia where the dry Plateau meets the more humid rainforest of the Northwest Coast. Here (and at comparable rapids elsewhere) Plateau Indians built platforms projecting from canyon walls over the water from which they speared salmon. The Dalles, then, was a choice site for fishing and was located on a major waterway at the interface of two ecological zones. At this ideal spot, the Wishrams on the north side of the river and the Wascos on the south hosted a trade fair each fall. Among the items exchanged were buffalo robes and pemmican from the Plains, fish oil and shells from the Northwest and California coasts, obsidian and other minerals as well as seed and plant foods from the interior. Late in the nineteenth century a Haida slate carving from the Northwest Coast was found in the medicine bundle of a Crow warrior on the Plains. Most likely it had passed through The Dalles sometime during the preceding centuries in the course of its long eastward journey.

While gathering at The Dalles, artists from various locales also displayed their traditions in rock art, much of which survives to this day. Northwest Coast rock artists carved what are called petroglyphs, most often representing masks or human faces similar to those on "totem poles." Plateau artists, on the other hand, painted rocks in what are known as pictographs. They usually depicted game animals and human hunters. But artists in and around The Dalles eventually developed new ideas that were influenced by both traditions. The most notable example of such an artistic synthesis is the carving of a grinning face, called Tsagigalal, which was repeated or emulated many times over in The Dalles region but appears nowhere else.

BAND SOCIETIES OF THE WESTERN INTERIOR AND FAR NORTH

Environmental constraints precluded Native Americans of the Great Basin, Plains, and Arctic regions from transforming themselves as thoroughly as Indian peoples did elsewhere. For this reason, their societies reflected most clearly the Paleo-Indian heritage of all Native Americans. Nonetheless, they continued to make significant innovations in their ways of life as their environments modified over time and, in some areas, as new ideas or peoples arrived from elsewhere.

Hunters and Farmers on the Plains

When we think today of Plains Indians, we point most often to Sioux men on horses hunting buffalo or confronting enemies while adorned with spectacular war bonnets. But such images bear no relation to life on the Plains before the arrival of Europeans. As late as 1600 CE, there were no horses and no elaborately feathered war bonnets on the Plains. All this would come later (see Chapter 5).

The one component of the popular image of Plains Indians that does hold for the precolonial period is the hunting of buffalo, or bison. For millennia, the meat of choice for Plains people had been bison. The tightly organized bands of Paleo-Indian times remained little changed as late as the sixth century CE. Plains hunters still frequented sites first used by Paleo-Indians, such as Olsen-Chubbock, Medicine Lodge Creek, and Head-Smashed-In, in western Alberta. To be sure, environmental change brought them, like peoples elsewhere, a greater range of choices, so that they now ate deer, mountain sheep, and other animals in addition to bison, and they increasingly supplemented meat with plants and seeds gathered and processed by women. Yet not only environmental changes but also the arrival of peoples from elsewhere would change the way people lived on the Plains.

One group of newcomers to the Plains consisted of hunters from the north who spoke several related languages of the Athapaskan family. Archaeologists and linguists agree that Athapaskan speakers arrived in North America from Siberia sometime after the Paleo-Indians had dispersed throughout the Western Hemisphere. Until the beginning of the Common Era, the Athapaskans lived in southern Alaska, but thereafter bands began to disperse, particularly southward into western Canada. In about 720 CE, a massive volcano erupted near the upper White River in Alaska, spreading ash over most of what is now southwestern Yukon Territory. The memory of that volcano survives in oral traditions among the Athapaskan-speaking Dene Indians of western Canada who fled the devastated area, and it probably accounts for their dispersion to widely separated parts of North America and the diversification of their languages. The Mountains, Hares, Yellowknifes, Chippewyans, and Slaveys were among the refugees who fled to the Mackenzie Valley and adjacent regions of Canada. According to a Hare tradition, the many coal mines atop the mountain caught fire, causing the rocks to explode: "The mountain disappeared and there remained only a large plain occupied by people who no longer understood one another, and who did not know what they were saying to one another." Some of the refugees went much farther, not stopping until they found homelands they could enjoy uncontested. These were the ancestors of the Apaches and Navajos of the Southwest and the Tolowas and Hupas of northern California (discussed earlier in this chapter).

Within a century or two of the blast on the White River, bands of Athapaskan-speaking hunters who had migrated south entered the northwestern Plains and settled in the Black Hills region of what is now South Dakota. Soon the Athapaskans were trading with village-dwelling neighbors on the Missouri River who brought them artifacts from throughout the continent. To this day the Kiowa Apaches of Oklahoma tell stories of their days in the northern Plains.

Besides the immigrants from the north, new peoples from the east influenced Plains-dwelling peoples. During the fifth century, some Hopewell village-mound centers arose in the northeastern Plains. The inhabitants combined the bison-hunting culture of their ancestors with the new culture being introduced from the East. More eastern Indians arrived after the tenth century as intensified agriculture created shortages of good farmland in portions of the East. The newcomers established permanent villages in most of the river valleys of the eastern Plains from the Dakotas southward. Planting the hardy northern flint corn developed east of the Mississippi, Plains village women produced surplus crops that they stored for winter and traded to nonfarming hunting bands. At the same time, men shifted to hunting buffalo with bows and arrows. Like their Plains Hopewell predecessors, these villagers combined Plains and Woodlands cultures. For example, instead of using the wooden and stone tools of eastern farmers, Plains women used the lighter, more effective bison scapula (shoulder bone) for weeding and digging.

The development of farming in the eastern Plains was disrupted in the thirteenth century by the same drought that had ravaged the Southwest and Midwest. The search by growing numbers of people for what was probably a diminishing amount of arable land led to competition and often violence. As with the Iroquois and Hurons far to the east, the disruption of Mississippian trade networks may also have contributed to the conflicts. And like the Iroquoian speakers, Missouri River people surrounded their villages with moats and located them atop ridges and bluffs from which they could be easily defended.

By the end of the fifteenth century, the Missouri River valley was once again stable. The Siouan-speaking Mandans and Hidatsas inhabited the Dakota portion of the river from the east and the Caddoan-speaking Arikaras arrived from the south. These highly successful farmers built on the local trading of crop surpluses to become the focal points of a vast interregional network. Archaeologists working at one village site in South Dakota have found shells from the Atlantic, Pacific, and Gulf of Mexico coasts as well as freshwater snail shells from the Tennessee River. These centers would continue to flourish after the arrival of European fur traders.

On the central Plains, where the drought was more severe, it scattered the Caddoan-speaking ancestors of the Pawnees, with one group moving north and the other south. During the fifteenth

century, most of the Pawnees returned and reestablished their villages on the Loup and Platte rivers. But the Pawnees were sharply divided between the Skidis, whose Arikara relatives remained on the Missouri, and the Kawarahkis, who had lived among the Wichitas to the south. Nearby Siouan-speaking peoples such as the Kansas, Otos, Missouris, Poncas, and Omahas were immigrants from east of the Mississippi.

Southern Plains peoples, such as the Wichitas and Jumanos, responded to the drought by shifting their focus westward where bison herds moving down from the north began appearing in larger numbers. In so doing, they came into contact with many of the Black Hills Athapaskan speakers who followed the migrating herds. These newcomers, forerunners of the Apaches and Navajos, established trade ties with the Pawnees, the Wichitas and, through the latter, with the Mississippian Caddoan confederacy. In so doing, they became rivals of the Jumanos for control of exchange networks between the Mississippian Southeast and the Pueblo Southwest. The newcomers' position as

Crow Medicine Shield Plains warriors carried shields laden with spiritual medicine to protect them when fighting with enemies. This nineteenth-century shield shows the moon, which had given the shield to its bearer during a vision. Attached to it are a crane's head and eagle's feathers—additional sources of spiritual power.

trade intermediaries between the Plains and the Southwest would become critical after the Spanish began to colonize the Southwest.

As the Athapaskan speakers moved south along the eastern edge of the Plains, other migrating peoples arrived to hunt buffalo in the regions they left behind—Blackfeet above the Missouri River, Crows in the Yellowstone region, Cheyenne and Arapahos on the branches of the Platte River. This new configuration of peoples was still taking shape when European horses and guns arrived on the Plains late in the seventeenth century.

The Great Basin

Further west, from the Rockies to the Pacific coastal range, where neither farming nor significant amounts of hunting was possible, the trend toward seed processing and consumption was most pronounced. As early as 8200 BCE, the occupants of Fort Rock Cave in eastern Oregon were making stone tools for grinding seeds, while those at Danger Cave in northern Utah were making twined baskets for collecting, storing, and cooking seeds by 7700 BCE. Pickleweed seeds were the major food of those frequenting Hogup Cave in northern Utah, followed by bison, and then by several additional species of flora and fauna. As the centuries passed, peoples in the Great Basin developed increasingly elaborate material cultures, including hemp nets, hide thongs, bone awls and pipes, sheep-horn wrenches, rabbit-fur robes, and wooden shafts, fire drills, and digging sticks. Archaeologists excavating one site have even found a noisemaker, probably used in rituals or festivals. The increased importance of seed gathering and processing in the Indians' food economies reflects the growing importance of Great Basin women in food production.

Material life in the Great Basin changed little until about 500 CE, when Native people in what is now Utah began growing maize and building pit-houses. Yet in the thirteenth century, the same drought that plagued farmers and undermined societies in the Eastern Woodlands, the Plains, and the Southwest ended farming in the Great Basin. Archaeologists have been unable to determine what happened to the Great Basin farmers, but they were supplanted by Numic-speaking

forebears of the Utes and Shoshones who were already expanding slowly eastward from a homeland in eastern California. Subsequently, the easternmost Shoshones moved out of the Great Basin to the northwestern Plains in Wyoming. There they hosted an annual trade rendezvous that attracted peoples from the Plains, the Great Basin, and Columbia Plateau regions. Like the movements of peoples in other North American regions, those of Indians in the Great Basin remind us that the configurations of tribes and cultures observed by the earliest Europeans in the region were not set in stone and that Indian history had always been in flux.

Inuit and Aleut Hunters of the Far North

By 3000 BCE, most descendants of earlier immigrants to North America had left the Arctic regions of northwestern North America for warmer climes and Siberian newcomers known as Aleuts (Unangans) and Inuits (Eskimos) had taken their place. The newcomers were ethnically and linguistically related hunting peoples who had begun to diverge before crossing the Bering Sea to Alaska. The most basic linguistic division was between Aleut, spoken by the people who settled the Aleutian Islands and the western Alaska Peninsula, and Inuit, the language of the Inuits, who moved to the Alaska mainland. Inuit later divided into Yupik, spoken in southwestern Alaska, and Inupik, spoken by Inuits elsewhere in North America.

The Aleuts and Inuits developed means of surviving and even flourishing amidst the harsh environments they encountered. Living on small islands, the Aleuts turned to the mammals, fish, birds, and plants of the sea for their food. The earliest Alaskan Inuits adopted a seasonal rotation; they spent summers at small coastal encampments hunting sea mammals and fishing for salmon, and lived during winters in sod houses while hunting caribou, musk oxen, birds, and small mammals. Among the Aleuts' and Inuits' most significant contributions to life in North America were harpoons for hunting sea mammals. Early Inuit winter houses were square or round in shape, with the floors dug slightly below the surface of the ground outside. People entered through a long tunnel.

Although there was only a single room, the inhabitants slept, cooked, and manufactured their implements in distinct parts of it. Summer campsites consisted of three to six small tents. At the center of each tent was a fire in which the inhabitants burned seal bones and fat as well as wood.

As they perfected their ways of life in Alaska, some Inuits began moving eastward and southeastward. By about 2000 BCE, Inuit peoples had established communities across what is now northern Canada and in Greenland. During later cold intervals, when the timber line moved south, Inuit groups occupied areas around Hudson Bay and in Newfoundland, only to retreat when the trees moved north again.

During the five centuries before Columbus, Inuit peoples developed an even more sophisticated hunting technology. Inuits on both the Siberian and Alaskan shores of the Bering Sea perfected intricately carved ivory harpoon heads that could pass through the skin and blubber and into the muscle of whales and sea lions in such a way that nothing could dislodge them. They also perfected a large skin boat known as the *umiak*, in which crews of four to seven men hunted whales, as well as one-man kayaks and sleds pulled by teams of domesticated dogs. Eventually, they followed migrating whales, seals, or caribou with their boats and sleds. Besides mining copper locally, they obtained iron from the residue of a widespread meteor shower in northeastern Greenland, and from Siberian Inuits to the west and—beginning in the tenth century— from Norse explorers, traders, and settlers arriving from the east.

Norse colonization was concentrated primarily in two areas of southwestern Greenland, where as many as seven thousand Scandinavians settled by the fourteenth century. From there these first Europeans in the Western Hemisphere frequented what is now the coast of northeastern Canada in search of trade, plunder, timber, and additional settlement sites. Both archaeology and Norse sagas provide evidence for one settlement in this region, Vinland, located at L'Anse aux Meadows in northern Newfoundland. About six hundred colonists lived at Vinland for a year or two in the eleventh century gathering wood to ship to Greenland and launching explorations further south.

Norse relations with the "Skraelings," as they termed the Inuits and the Beothuk Indians of Newfoundland, ranged from friendly to hostile. The Native people acquired metal goods, such as iron knife blades and bronze bowls as well as woolen cloth from the Europeans in exchange for animal skins and ivory. Evidence of what must have been a friendly contact is a figurine carved in the traditional Thule style on Baffin Island in the thirteenth century. It depicts a European bishop, presumably one of the Catholic bishops stationed there. Norse writings indicate that some settlers abandoned their countrymen to live among the Inuits.

Despite these friendly encounters, Inuit-Norse disputes arose over trade and over Norse attempts to occupy areas where Inuits did not want them. The colonists held attitudes of cultural superiority similar to those of later Europeans but, unlike the later immigrants, were unable to gain any military, economic, or demographic advantages over the Native people they encountered. The cooler temperatures of a "Little Ice Age" that began in the fourteenth century further undermined their colonial effort. At the end of the fifteenth century, just as other Europeans were expanding into the Atlantic, the Norse abandoned their Greenland settlements to Inuits who occupied them as hunting camps. Other Europeans, arriving elsewhere, would begin Europeans' sustained efforts to colonize North America and its indigenous peoples.

CONCLUSION

By the time Europeans began arriving, human history had been unfolding in North America for as long as it had in all but a few areas of the globe. Over many thousands of years, Native American peoples had developed a wide range of cultures across a highly varied landscape. In hundreds of languages, Native societies preserved their diverse histories and reaffirmed their group identities. They constructed these identities not in isolation from one another but through constant intergroup contacts and exchanges. Building on common foundations of kinship and reciprocity, Native Americans met periodically for trade and ceremonies, often forging alliances and occasionally institutionalizing their relationships in hierarchical chiefdoms or extensive confederacies. The evidence for long-distance trade makes clear that neither geographic distance nor linguistic barriers limited the spread of materials, techniques, beliefs, and peoples. Yet in some instances, Indians were forcibly reminded that human knowledge and power were limited. Just as the Cherokees in the story of disease and medicine discovered that they could not kill as many animals as possible with impunity, so the peoples of Chaco Canyon and Cahokia suffered the consequences of ignoring environmental constraints during the widespread drought of the late thirteenth century.

In short, North America was the site of a diverse range of complex, overlapping, and ongoing histories long before outsiders set foot on its soil. By 1500, according to the most carefully considered estimates, between seven million and ten million Indians lived north of present-day Mexico. Over the ensuing centuries, they would confront the greatest challenges yet to their ways of life, their values, and their identities.

SUGGESTED READINGS

Claassen, Cheryl, and Joyce, Rosemary A., eds. *Women in Prehistory: North American and Mesoamerica.* Philadelphia: University of Pennsylvania Press, 1997. This collection of essays by archaeologists constitutes the best introduction to issues of gender in precolonial North America.

Echo-Hawk, Roger C. "Ancient History in the New World: Integrating Oral Traditions and the Archaeological Record in Deep Time," *American Antiquity* 65, no.2 (2000): 267–290. A Pawnee scholar's provocative argument for the usefulness of oral traditions as historical sources, especially for pre-Columbian Native Americans.

Fagan, Brian M. *Ancient North America: The Archaeology of a Continent.* 3rd ed. London and New York: Thames and Hudson, 2000. A useful, highly detailed introduction to North American archaeology.

Kehoe, Alice Beck. *America Before the European Invasions.* London and New York: Longman, 2002. An excellent brief overview of Native American history as known through archaeology.

Krech, Shepard, III. *The Ecological Indian: Myth and History.* New York: W. W. Norton, 1999. A controversial but learned examination of the relations between pre-Columbian Indians and their environments.

Nabokov, Peter. *A Forest of Time: American Indian Ways of History.* Cambridge: Cambridge University Press, 2002. An excellent, highly insightful study of Native Americans' many ways of reckoning and representing the past.

Perry, Richard J. *Western Apache Heritage: People of the Mountain Corridor.* Austin: University of Texas Press, 1991. An anthropological-archaeological history that traces the Western Apaches from their subarctic beginnings and long migration to the Southwest through the twentieth century.

Shaffer, Lynda Norene. *Native Americans Before 1492: The Moundbuilding Centers of the Eastern Woodlands.* Armonk, NY: M.E. Sharpe, 1992. A very readable survey of the rise, flourishing, and decline of the major sites and networks.

Struever, Stuart, and Holton, Felicia Antonelli. *Koster: Americans in Search of Their Prehistoric Past.* Prospect Heights, IL: Waveland Press, 2000. An engaging account of the excavations and interpretation of a remarkable archaeological site.

Sullivan, Lawrence E., ed. *Native American Religions: North America.* New York: Macmillan, 1989. A useful set of essays, introducing the spiritual beliefs, practices, and traditions of Indian peoples.

Thomas, David Hurst. *Skull Wars: Kennewick Man, Archaeology, and the Battle for Native American Identity.* New York: Basic Books, 1999. A stimulating, judicious discussion of the major controversies within archaeology and the tensions between archaeologists and Native Americans.

Zolbrod, Paul G. *Diné Bahane': The Navajo Creation Story.* Albuquerque: University of New Mexico Press, 1984. An excellent translation of a major work of oral history and literature.

Strangers in Indian Homelands, 1490–1600

Because it was a dry spring at Hawikuh and the other five Zuni pueblos in 1539, the Zunis were preparing to conduct ceremonies calling on the katsinas to bring rain (see Chapter 1). Suddenly several couriers arrived with a message and a gift for Hawikuh's headman. The couriers reported that a stranger named Esteban, regarded by some of the Zunis' southwestern Indian neighbors as a "black katsina," was approaching the pueblo, planting crosses along his route, and vowing to "establish peace and heal" the Zunis. The couriers then presented Hawikuh's headman with a gourd rattle adorned with red and white feathers and small bells. Instantly recognizing the bells as Spanish-made, the headman threw the gourd to the ground, exclaiming, "I know these people, for these jingle bells are not in the shape of ours. Tell them to turn back at once, or not one of their men will be spared."

Who was Esteban and how did he come to be on the outskirts of Hawikuh in 1539? Why did the Zunis reject his proffered gift and threaten him? What happened thereafter? Esteban had been born a Muslim in Azamar, Morocco, where he was captured during a Spanish raid and enslaved. Sometime thereafter his captor sold him as a slave and, probably after more such transactions, he became the property of Andrés Dorantes, a military offi-

cer. Dorantes took Esteban to the West Indies and then, in 1528, on a voyage to explore and colonize Florida. After becoming separated from their ships, members of the expedition sailed in rafts to the Texas Gulf Coast. By 1534 Esteban, Dorantes, and the two other surviving Spaniards left the Gulf Coast, wandering thousands of miles for another two years before meeting Spanish slave hunters in northern Mexico. Although Esteban and his companions did not meet the Zunis directly, they heard fabulous tales of the Zuni pueblos during their travels nearby. Word of the Zunis' supposed wealth excited Spanish officials in Mexico who, in 1539, dispatched an expedition to the pueblos with Esteban as its guide (discussed later in this chapter).

To prevent Esteban from entering Hawikuh and polluting its ceremonies, the Hawikuh elders ordered that a line of corn meal be spread across the road, indicating the boundary between their sacred space and the rest of the world. Esteban defiantly crossed the line anyway, was detained, and told his captors that many white katsinas were following close behind him. The Zunis already distrusted Esteban because he represented the Spanish in Mexico, who were known to enslave and spread death among Native Americans instead of honoring the principles of reciprocity and respecting Indians and their sacred traditions. Now the black katsina's words confirmed that he was indeed a witch as well as a Spanish agent. Accordingly, the elders ordered his execution.

While reciprocity remained the norm underlying political, economic, and social relations, even among Indian societies of unequal wealth and power (see Chapter 1), such was no longer the case in Europe at the end of the fifteenth century. To be sure, reciprocity had long governed Europe's local economies and feudal hierarchies. But a new quest for wealth and power—informed by a sense of divine mission and superiority to non-Europeans and non-Christians—would dominate the early campaigns of Spanish, French, and English monarchs to colonize the Americas and their indigenous peoples. Ignoring or defying norms of reciprocity, some Spanish campaigns achieved spectacular conquests in portions of the Western Hemisphere south of the present United States. However, would-be conquerors undertaking similar efforts north of Mexico and the Caribbean largely failed to achieve their goals before 1600 even as other European visitors to the same regions who did not try to dominate Native Americans enjoyed more successful interactions.

For better or worse, all these interactions introduced Indians as well as Europeans to a "new world" of peoples, technologies, and values. Over time and to widely varying degrees, Indians, Europeans, and enslaved Africans such as Esteban modified their diets, their clothing, their modes of producing food and waging war, and sometimes even their cultural values and identities. Such modifications defied the rigid distinctions that Europeans drew between "civilized" and "savage" peoples, especially when individuals from one side of the divide crossed over to join a community on the other side.

Most ominously, the earliest Indian-European encounters also exposed Native Americans to a range of unfamiliar diseases that shattered Indian lives and communities over much of the Eastern Woodlands and the Southwest. Smallpox would prove to be the greatest single cause of Native American mortality during the sixteenth century (and the three centuries that ensued), followed by other imported diseases including measles, influenza, and several varieties of plague. While these diseases cost many lives in the Eastern Hemisphere,

long experience had enabled Europeans, Africans, and Asians to develop immunities that significantly limited the effects. The peoples of the Western Hemisphere, on the other hand, had never been exposed to such deadly epidemics. (The Norse colonizers who had interacted earlier with Inuits and Beothuks, as discussed in Chapter 1, had arrived from lands beyond the reach of most epidemics.) Epidemic diseases undoubtedly afflicted Native Americans before Europeans arrived; indeed the evidence is strong, though not absolutely certain, that Indians introduced a form of syphilis to Europe via some of Christopher Columbus's sailors. But there was no precedent in the Americas for the scale of mortality among Native Americans that ensued. Lacking sufficient antibodies to ward off many of the deadly diseases introduced by Europeans and their African slaves after 1492, American Indians died in massive numbers, with communities sometimes losing three-fourths or more of their populations.

The strange encounter of Esteban and the Zunis at Hawikuh was but one of dozens that unfolded over the course of the sixteenth century in those portions of the Eastern Woodlands, the Southwest, and the California coast where Europeans dared to tread. Even Indians who lived well beyond the limits of Europeans' travels encountered the newcomers indirectly, often fatally, through diseases, trade goods, and reports by those who had met some of the strangers. Although they established only two tiny outposts before 1600, in Florida and New Mexico, Europeans figured in the lives and deaths of many Native Americans.

INDIAN-SPANISH ENCOUNTERS BEYOND NORTH AMERICA, 1492–1536

The earliest Indian-European encounters occurred not within the present United States but in regions to the south—in the West Indies, Mexico, Central America, and South America. Several of these southerly encounters, in particular, would reinforce the assumptions and expectations of Europeans when they intruded later into the homelands of Indians farther north. One was the vast range and abundance of potential wealth the invaders found in the Americas in the form of material resources and of indigenous people's labor. A second was the astonishingly high mortality rates of Native Americans in the face of European-introduced epidemic diseases, especially smallpox. Deadly epidemics enabled small forces of Europeans to overcome the resistance offered by even the largest, most powerful Indian societies. Underlying Europeans' expectations, of course, were their assumptions that they were a superior people who had God on their side and that the world was theirs for the taking. The early encounters that most directly shaped Europeans' later attempts to subjugate Indians within the present United States were those of Spanish colonizers with Tainos in the West Indies, the Aztec empire in Mexico, and the Inca empire in the Andes Mountains of South America.

The Tainos Meet Columbus, 1492

The first indigenous Americans to encounter the new European colonizing spirit were the Tainos, who inhabited several Caribbean island chains—the Bahamas, the Virgin Islands, and the Greater Antilles (Cuba, Jamaica, Hispaniola [modern Haiti and the Dominican Republic], and Puerto Rico). Over about one thousand years before 1492, the Tainos had developed a highly complex society, with villages numbering between a few hundred to 2,000 inhabitants built around ball courts and other public structures. They farmed some maize but specialized in growing root crops such as cassavas and sweet potatoes. Powerful male and female hereditary chiefs each dominated several villages and the trade networks that linked them to other Tainos. Trade and war parties traveled in large canoes that carried up to 150 people, and Tainos from adjacent portions of eastern Hispaniola and Puerto Rico visited each other daily. Religious ceremonies centered on *zemis*, wooden and stone images of spiritual figures. Altogether the Tainos may have numbered as many as 6 million people by 1492.

Into the Taino world in that year came three ships sailing for the king and queen of Spain under the command of Christopher Columbus. Thinking he was in the "Indies" off the coast of Asia, Columbus had actually reached Guanahaní (which he renamed San Salvador) in the Bahamas and called the Tainos he met there "Indians." Columbus and his fellow Europeans would later extend his mistaken term to other indigenous Americans, thereby bestowing on them a single identity they had not previously possessed. Columbus's mistake was not only in the name he gave the people he met but also in the stereotypes he used to describe them. Of his first encounter with the Tainos, he wrote:

> [T]hey are so guileless and so generous with all that they possess, that no one would believe it who has not seen it. They refuse nothing that they possess, if it be asked of them; on the contrary, they invite any one to share it and display as much love as if they would give their hearts.

Without realizing it, Columbus was describing the workings of an economy in which people sought not to possess and accumulate material goods but to give them away in order to obligate the recipients to give them gifts in return. Like other Europeans who scorned reciprocity, Columbus saw such values as childish and the people who held them as inferior to Europeans. Moreover, in Columbus's view, the Tainos lacked the metal technology, the private property, and the state sovereignty characteristic of Europeans. Such inferior peoples were to be subordinated to the Spanish monarchy, converted to Christianity and European "civilization," and put to work for the Spanish. If they resisted these beneficial measures, they would be forcibly suppressed and enslaved.

Columbus returned to the Caribbean in 1493 with plans to colonize the Tainos and their land. Having seen evidence of gold, he planned to use Tainos to mine the precious metal as well as to work on sugar plantations like those operated by Spanish planters in the Canary Islands. But the Tainos began dying in great numbers from smallpox, often exacerbated by other European-borne diseases, overwork, and Spanish violence.

Within thirty years, all but about thirty thousand of the six million Tainos had died, and their chiefdoms, trade networks, villages, and other social and political institutions had disappeared. The

Spanish found little gold in Taino lands, but sugar production proved profitable. As Tainos perished, Spanish planters turned elsewhere for laborers, first to Native Americans in adjacent lands and eventually to enslaved Africans. Meanwhile, the terrible experience of the Tainos was being replicated, with variations, elsewhere in the Americas.

Aztecs and Incas, 1519–1536

The first American empires were based not in Europe but in the Western Hemisphere itself. Formed during the fifteenth century, the Aztec and Inca empires dominated large expanses of territory in Mexico and South America, respectively, and were still expanding when invaded by Spanish conquistadors.

The Aztecs had arrived in the Valley of Mexico from the north during the thirteenth century. At first they were incorporated as subjects to one of the several Indian states in the area. These states were hierarchical societies with bureaucracies that had supplanted the more personal rule of chiefdoms. In 1428, the Aztecs overthrew their rulers and proceeded to subject most of the peoples of central Mexico in a far-flung empire.

Nearly a century later, while Columbus's successors enjoyed modest prosperity in the West Indies, other Spanish elites searched for the ultimate source of wealth, gold. In 1519, Hernán Cortés, accompanied by six hundred troops, landed on the coast of Mexico at the outer edge of the Aztec empire, where he encountered many discontented subjects and enemies of the Aztecs. Shrewdly cultivating their support, Cortés marched on the sumptuously wealthy Aztec capital of Tenochtitlan and confronted the emperor, Moctezuma. With fabulous gifts, Moctezuma welcomed the Spanish through a remarkable Mayan-born woman, Malinche (whom the Spanish called Doña Marina), who became Cortés's interpreter and mistress. Craving the city's great wealth, the invaders spurned Moctezuma's offer. They raided the pyramids and other great buildings, smashing and melting religious icons and artistic treasures to extract the gold from them.

The Aztecs resisted and were on the verge of expelling the Spanish when they suddenly began dying. As in the West Indies, smallpox had struck, enabling Spanish troops to overpower the Aztecs

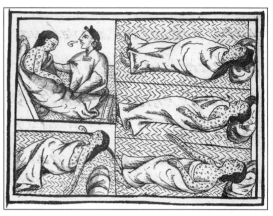

Smallpox in the Conquest of Mexico   Originally published in a sixteenth-century Spanish account, these illustrations depict the painful and deadly impact of smallpox on the Aztecs and other Indians during Cortés's invasion.

and their allies. Spain now ruled central Mexico, giving the European nation an enormous source of wealth and a mainland American base from which to further its expansion. As one Aztec lamented,

> Broken spears lie in the roads;
> We have torn our hair in grief.
> The houses are roofless now. . . .
> And the walls are splattered with gore. . . .
> We have pounded our hands in despair
> Against the adobe walls.

Cortés's seizure of Aztec wealth inspired some of his countrymen to try and duplicate his feat. One, Francisco Pizarro, did so in 1532–1536, when his expedition crushed the Inca empire in the Andes Mountains of South America. Like the Aztecs, the Incas had established their empire only recently, in 1438. Here, too, a powerful emperor reigned from a central capital, Cuzco (in modern Peru), over subjects representing a variety of languages and cultures. Among the keys to the Inca empire's power was its ability to overcome the obstacles posed by the Andes with terraced, irrigated croplands and an elaborate network of roads and bridges. Like the Aztecs, the Incas collapsed when smallpox struck, enabling Pizarro's troops to seize control of their empire and its wealth, including vast deposits of gold and silver.

The Spanish conquests in the West Indies, and especially in Mexico and Peru, convinced many Europeans that with little effort they could find great wealth, seize vast territories, and subject large numbers of Indians anywhere in the Americas. For the remainder of the sixteenth century, these assumptions shaped European efforts to colonize more northerly lands.

The early conquests had a more direct impact on early Spanish colonial efforts in the Southeast and Southwest. Most of these efforts originated in Cuba or Mexico; their leaders and soldiers were veterans of the early conquests; and they usually included some enslaved Africans as well as large numbers of Tainos, Aztecs, and other Indians from previously colonized regions. For these Indians, serving the Spanish was often their only or best hope for survival in the new imperial world.

SOUTHEASTERN CHIEFDOMS CONFRONT IMPERIAL ADVENTURERS

In light of the competition and rivalries that frequently divided southeastern chiefdoms, it is not surprising that Indians of the region cast wary eyes on the Spanish and other Europeans who began entering their homelands in the early sixteenth century. But Indians' wariness often turned to either overt or covert resistance when Europeans ignored reciprocity and attempted to force Native peoples to submit to their authority—most frequently by paying tribute in the form of food (regardless of the Indians' own food needs), other gifts, and labor. Some Indians attempted to establish trade and military partnerships with colonizers in order to benefit from the newcomers, but none of these relationships lasted longer than a few months. As a result, Europeans failed to establish lasting colonies in the sixteenth-century Southeast beyond a small military outpost at St. Augustine, Florida. Nevertheless, by their mere presence they inflicted massive casualties on Native Americans through epidemic diseases, transforming the human landscape of the Southeast and facilitating the colonial efforts of those who would come later.

Rebuffing Spanish Entradas in Florida, 1513–1528

The Calusas of southern Florida were the first Southeastern Indians to experience the effects of Columbus's colonizing activities. As Spanish enterprises expanded in the Caribbean and the Tainos died in heavy numbers, slave traders looked for laborers on the nearby mainland. Even before Spain's first recorded entrada (entrance) into Florida in 1513, some of these slave hunters had engaged in skirmishes with the Calusas and other Indians of the Florida peninsula. In 1513 and again in 1521, Juan Ponce de León, a member of Columbus's second expedition who had colonized Puerto Rico, led attempts to establish a colony called La Florida among the Calusas. The Calusas resisted these efforts and mortally wounded Ponce de León during his second invasion.

Coastal Indians north of the peninsula were the next to confront Europeans. Despite Ponce de León's failure, Spanish and French explorers during the 1520s made several forays along the Atlantic coast, frequently kidnapping Indians in the process. Although the Spanish transported most of their captives to Caribbean plantations, they carried a few to the royal court in Madrid, expecting to impress them with Spanish wealth and power and then persuade them to assist Spain's colonizing efforts in their homelands. One such Indian was a Catawba speaker, captured near Winyah Bay in South Carolina, whom the Spanish named Francisco de Chicora. After Chicora regaled the Spanish court with descriptions of his homeland's abundance, Spanish officials sent him home with a colonizing expedition. As soon as the expedition arrived in 1526, Chicora and other Indian captives fled into the interior, leaving the Spanish without guides and interpreters. He was the first but by no means last Indian to use such a ruse to escape European captors. Without guides and interpreters, the six hundred Spanish soldiers and officials and the enslaved Tainos and Africans moved south and established a town on the Georgia coast. But their inability to live off the land and an unusually cold winter led to 450 deaths, so the survivors abandoned the colony after three months.

Indians of the Florida Gulf Coast were the next to confront a Spanish challenge when in 1528 an expedition led by Pánfilo de Narváez landed near

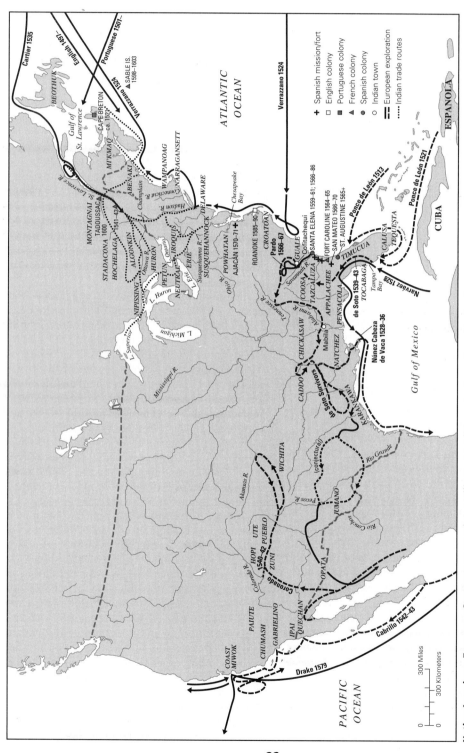

Native American–European Contacts: 1497–1600. Military expeditions, trade ventures, and religious missions were the primary means by which Europeans made contact with Native Americans before 1600. *Source maps from The Cambridge History of the Native Peoples of the Americas vol. 1: North America, ed. Bruce G. Trigger and Wilcomb E. Washburn (Cambridge, U.K.: Cambridge University Press, 1996), part 1, 341, 345, 346.*

Tampa Bay. A veteran of the Taino and Aztec conquests, Narváez hoped to find bullion (gold and silver) in the quantities he had seen in Mexico. But with the reputation of Spanish slave traders firmly established on the Gulf Coast, local Tocobagas were anxious to rid themselves of these unwanted guests. Accordingly, they persuaded Narváez that he would find the gold and other wealth he sought in the Apalachee chiefdom to the northwest.

While his ships sailed along the Gulf Coast, Narváez led three hundred troops overland to the Apalachee capital of Anaica. Relations were cordial until the Spanish seized a prominent Apalachee chief as hostage. Hostilities erupted and the Apalachees easily gained the upper hand because their warriors' arrows penetrated Spanish armor. Withdrawing, the Spanish troops' miseries were compounded when they were unable to locate their ships. Finally, the desperate survivors built five rafts and sailed west along the coast in hopes of reaching Mexico. It would be ten years before the Apalachees and their neighbors would see another Spanish expedition.

Mississippians Confront de Soto, 1539–1543

Until the late 1530s, coastal chiefdoms, primarily on the Florida peninsula, bore the burden of confronting Spanish colonizers, slavers, and others in the Southeast. Thereafter the Mississippian chiefdoms of the interior likewise had to deal with an intensified Spanish effort to conquer the Southeast.

Reports that Narváez had heard of gold, along with the fabulous riches they had seized during the recent Inca conquest, redoubled and extended Spain's efforts to find bullion in North America. Leading these efforts was Hernando de Soto, who had already found wealth as one of Pizarro's senior officers in Peru. In 1537 the Spanish king appointed de Soto governor of Cuba and commissioned him to conquer "La Florida," which on Spanish maps at the time embraced all the territory south of Delaware Bay and east of the Texas Plains. With about 700 Spanish, African, and Indian men, 250 horses, and 300 pigs, he landed in 1539 at Tampa Bay, where Narváez had disembarked eleven years earlier. Soon after landing, the Spanish encountered Juan Ortiz, a member of Narváez's expedition whom the Apalachees had captured in 1528. Ortiz had become a fluent speaker of Muskogean, the most widely spoken language in the Southeast. De Soto purchased the Spanish captive and, over the next two years, made much use of his bilingualism and his familiarity with the region and its peoples.

Despite the advantages afforded by Ortiz's knowledge, memories of Narváez and de Soto's own conduct made Indians wary of the invaders. Traveling northward, the Spanish found that the Native Americans they encountered were only superficially cooperative or avoided contact with the invaders altogether. But one Timucua chief resolutely defied the Spanish (see Indian Voices), and the Apalachees, who had fought Narváez eleven years earlier, likewise resisted de Soto's invasion of their country. Unlike Narváez, de Soto was able to drive the Apalachees from Anaica. His troops wintered at the capital, but the Apalachees kept up constant attacks on them as Spanish food supplies ran dangerously low.

During the following spring, the expedition moved northeastward to a wealthy Mississippian center called Cofitachequi. From a hilltop near modern Camden, South Carolina, the Spanish looked down upon the largest concentration of Native Americans north of Mexico that any Europeans had yet seen. More than twelve hundred residences, housing six to ten thousand people, surrounded a large temple and plaza. The invaders soon learned that Cofitachequi was the seat of a chiefdom that included at least five other large towns and extended from the South Carolina piedmont region to the mountains of western North Carolina.

After the Spanish assured a Cofitachequi delegation that their intentions were peaceful, their female chief, a woman whom Spanish chroniclers called "the Mistress of Cofitachequi," came forward and welcomed de Soto. Both leaders sat in chairs borne by attendants and conducted themselves with grave formality. Whereas the "Mistress" appeared willing to explore the possibilities of friendship, de Soto was interested in just two commodities—corn to feed his people and bullion. Cofitachequi could provide neither. Cofitachequi's own food supplies were low because it had lost many residents to a destructive epidemic, undoubtedly originating with a recent Spanish expedition on the Carolina coast. And the chief denied that her people had any gold or silver.

INDIAN VOICES   A Timucua Chief Defies de Soto, 1539

During the sixteenth century, southeastern Indians responded in many different ways, both direct and indirect, to the arrival of Spanish invaders in their homelands. Few were more direct than the "Cacique Acuera," as the Spanish called this Timucua chief. In 1539, having arrived in the territory of the Acuera Timucuas, de Soto sent a message to the chief, inviting him to subordinate himself and his people to Spanish authority. While he did not seek to harm the Timucuas, de Soto warned, "my men can cause much damage to your vassals and your lands," should the Indians fail to submit. In his translated reply, printed here, the chief repudiated all Spanish claims to authority over him and his people and reminded de Soto that the Timucuas were already experienced with Castilian (meaning Spanish) invaders. While de Soto professed surprise at the chief's "arrogance," he continued to persuade him to surrender peacefully. After the chief refused to receive several more of his messages, de Soto moved his followers on toward the interior in their search for gold.

The Cacique Acuera's reply to the Governor's message was insolent. "I have long since learned who you Castilians are," he said, "through others of you who came years ago to my land; and I already know very well what your customs and behaviors are like. To me you are professional vagabonds who wander from place to place, gaining your livelihood by robbing, sacking, and murdering people who have given you no offense. I want no manner of friendship or peace with people such as you, but instead prefer mortal and perpetual enmity. Granted that you are as valiant as you boast of being, I have no fear of you, since neither I nor my vassals consider ourselves inferior to you in valor; and to prove our gallantry, I promise to maintain war upon you so long as you wish to remain in my province, not by fighting in the open, although I could do so, but by ambushing and waylaying you whenever you are off guard. I therefore notify and advise you to protect yourselves and act cautiously with me and my people, for I have commanded my vassals to bring me two Christian heads weekly, this number and no more. I shall be content to behead only two of you each week since I thus can slay all of you within a few years; for even though you may colonize and settle, you cannot perpetuate yourselves because you have not brought women to produce children and pass your generation forward."

In reply to what was said about his rendering obedience to the King of Spain, the Cacique continued: "I am king in my land, and it is unnecessary for me to become the subject of a person who has no more vassals than I. I regard those men as vile and contemptible who subject themselves to the yoke of someone else when they can live as free men. Accordingly, I and all of my people have vowed to die a hundred deaths and maintain the freedom of our land. This is our answer, both for the present and forevermore."

Then apropos of the subject of vassalage and the Governor's statement that the Spaniards were servants of the Emperor and King of Castile, for whose empire they now were conquering new lands, the Cacique retorted: "I should congratulate you warmly, but I hold you in even less esteem now that you have confessed that you are servants and that you are working and gaining kingdoms so that another may rule them and enjoy the fruits of your labor. Since in such undertaking you are suffering hunger, fatigue and other hardships as well as risking your lives, it would be more to your honor and advantage to acquire things for yourselves and your descendants rather than for someone else. But being so contemptible and as yet unable to rid yourselves of the stigma of servitude, you should never at any time expect friendship from me, for I could not use my friendship so basely. Furthermore, I do not wish to know what your sovereign demands, for I am well aware of what has to be done in this land, and of what manner I am to use in dealing with you. Therefore, all of you should go away as quickly as you can if you do not want to perish at my hands."

Source: Garcilaso de le Vega, *The Florida of the Inca*, trans. John Grier Varner and Jeannette Johnson Varner (Austin: University of Texas Press, 1951), 118–119. Copyright © 1951. Courtesy of the Unversity of Texas Press.

Interpreting this news as defiance, de Soto abandoned the pretense of reciprocity and ordered his troops to ransack the city. Although they saw large amounts of freshwater pearls as well as European goods, which Cofitachequi had obtained through trade with coastal Indians, the Spanish found no bullion. In hopes of pressuring Cofitachequi's tributaries to provide them with corn, the Spanish seized the "Mistress," along with many pearls, and moved on. But the captive chief soon escaped, leaving the Spanish to their own devices.

From Cofitachequi the Spanish traveled westward to the Tennessee Valley and then southward through Coosa, one of the largest chiefdoms in the Southeast. The Coosa chiefdom extended from the Great Smoky Mountains in what is now eastern Tennessee, through northwestern Georgia, and into Alabama. Within this expanse was the principal center at Coosa itself and at least four other major towns, each of which was surrounded by a cluster of smaller towns. The clusters in turn were surrounded by vast expanses of uninhabited land. Whether this arrangement was designed to facilitate hunting or protect town-dwellers from enemies is unclear. Moving through the chiefdom, the Spanish enslaved Coosa men to carry their supplies and women to provide sexual favors. They killed, tortured, or amputated the hands and noses of any Indians who resisted. After the Spanish chief captured the paramount chief at Coosa's center, Indian anger mounted still further and there were several instances of violent resistance.

With his Coosa captives, de Soto moved further south into the Mississippian chiefdom of Tazcaluza, where his reputation preceded him. The Choctaw-speaking Indians of Tazcaluza were prepared to resist being treated like those of Cofitachequi and Coosa. After an elaborate welcoming ceremony in which the principal chief feted de Soto, the would-be conquistador proclaimed the chief his vassal and all people of Tazcaluza his subjects. Seeming to cooperate, the chief accompanied de Soto south to the allied town of Mábila (modern Mobile, Alabama). On a prearranged signal, the Indians attacked the Spanish. With the advantages provided by their guns, swords, armor, and horses, the Spanish killed 2,500 to 3,000 Indians while losing only 22 of their own men. Nevertheless the battle was a disaster for the Spanish because they lost many of their horses and much of their food and supplies. After a difficult winter in Mississippi, an attack by Chickasaws in March 1541 inflicted even greater damage on the expedition, ending its ability to threaten Indian peoples militarily. The diminished expedition continued its search for gold, crossing the Mississippi into Arkansas and Texas and wandering two more years before abandoning its effort in 1543. (De Soto himself died in 1542.)

Southeastern Indians at Midcentury

A measure of southeastern attitudes toward the Spanish at midcentury can be seen in the fate of a religious mission that Luis Cáncer de Barbastro, a Dominican friar, attempted to establish among the Calusas and neighboring Indians in 1549. Cáncer intended to settle without troops and in a spirit of pure Christian love. But the Calusas now distrusted all Spaniards and seized three men whom Cáncer had sent ahead as he approached. When Cáncer went ashore to ascertain their fate, the Calusas killed him.

Despite the bitterness left by would-be conquistadors, some southeastern Indians became familiar with Europeans and their culture in less hostile settings. From early in the century, Spanish and other European ships were wrecked in storms and washed up on the shores of the Atlantic and the Gulf of Mexico. Indians scoured the wrecks for metal, which they fashioned into arrowheads, knives, tools of various kinds, and items of apparel. Especially in Florida, Indians often made statues and ornaments from gold and silver salvaged from Spanish ships. Coastal Indians frequently exchanged such objects with Native Americans of the interior, along with information about the Europeans themselves. In this way, Indians across the Southeast became acquainted with aspects of European culture before ever meeting European people. On the other hand, Europeans who arrived later and saw some of the gold assumed that it originated in the Southeast, which often drove them to act more aggressively toward Indians.

Expeditions and shipwrecks yielded not only European goods but also European and other non-Indian people. From early in the sixteenth century, Indian societies incorporated deserters, shipwrecked sailors, and captives, of whom Juan Ortiz was only the most prominent. For several centuries, Mississippian chiefdoms had absorbed captives into their societies to bolster populations and to work, but suddenly increased death rates from European diseases probably heightened Indian demand for captives. (Unbeknownst to anyone at the time, captives furthered the spread of epidemics while being better prepared than Indians to survive them.) Virtually every expedition to the coast or interior of the Southeast encountered Europeans, Africans, or Caribbean Indians who had been left behind and now belonged to some local Native American community. The single largest such group consisted of some two hundred Spanish soldiers stranded in south Florida after their ship was wrecked in a storm in 1549. The Calusas rounded up the sailors and distributed them to their allies as inferior laborers. When a Spanish expedition arrived among the Calusas in 1565, it found that most of the captives were still alive.

Coastal Chiefdoms and Colonial Endeavors, 1562–1601

Although southeastern Indians had repeatedly discouraged Spain's colonizing efforts, they confronted new colonial strategies by Spain as well as by that country's French and English rivals after 1560. The Timucuas of Florida's east coast were the first Native Americans to feel the effects of this heightened European rivalry. After an initial foray in 1562, a French effort began in earnest two years later when René de Goulaine de Laudonnière led several ships of soldiers, Huguenot (Protestant) settlers, and adventurers to the mouth of the St. John's River, where they erected Fort Caroline. Laudonnière initially allied with a nearby Timucua chiefdom headed by Saturiwa against a more westerly Timucua chiefdom led by Utina. But as he saw increasing quantities of gold, silver, and other metals, Laudonnière became convinced that they originated in the interior mines de Soto had sought. (In fact the metal came entirely from Spanish shipwrecks on the Florida coast.) To get at the mines, the French leader reasoned that he could not afford to offend Utina, who controlled the route into the interior. Indeed, by allying with Utina, the French entered an exchange network that extended as far west as the anti-Spanish Apalachees on the Gulf Coast.

The alliance between Utina and the French was characterized by mutual suspicion. Utina recognized the power of French firearms and persuaded the French to support two raids on a rival chiefdom, all the while telling them that he would later lead them to the "mountains" where they would find gold and silver. But after two battles in which the rival suffered high casualties, Utina insisted that they withdraw while the French protested that the enemy had not been totally destroyed. The division of opinion reflected the difference between Indian and European approaches to war. Indians would claim victory when they had demonstrated their military superiority while avoiding unnecessary casualties, whereas the Europeans sought to conquer and subdue an enemy with no regard for the enemy's humanity.

As with earlier European expeditions, the French discovered the limits of their success during spring 1565 when they ran out of food. They appealed to Utina, but his people refused to sell the

Utina and the Timucuas The powerful chief, shown here surrounded by Timucua warriors, successfully led his people in resisting both French and Spanish efforts to subject them during the 1560s.

French what little corn they had because they needed it for seed. Recognizing their advantage, the Timucuas offered the French some fish and acorns, but sold these "at such a high price that in no time at all they got . . . all" the expedition's remaining supplies of trade goods. The French then seized Utina, but this tactic did little to relieve the French plight. The Timucuas alternately negotiated with and attacked the French until the latter released Utina without ever receiving any food.

The Timucuas obtained assistance in expelling the French from an unlikely source in 1565 when a Spanish expedition under Pedro Menéndez de Avilés arrived in Florida with orders to do just that. After violently crushing the French, however, Menéndez sought to incorporate the Timucuas and other powerful chiefdoms of the coastal Southeast into the structure of Spanish authority. His efforts came to grief because the Indians resisted the imposition of Spanish authority.

By 1568, attacks by Timucuas and neighboring Indians had forced the Spanish to abandon most of their bases on the Florida peninsula, except for San Mateo, on the site of Fort Caroline. Because the Timucuas' priority was to rid themselves of whichever outsiders most directly threatened their autonomy, they supported in that year a French effort to retake the fort. Although the Spanish managed to hold the fort, the Timucuas' refusal even to cooperate led Spain to abandon San Mateo two years later.

The Calusas brought Menéndez further grief. Suspicious of one another from the beginning, Menéndez and the Calusa chief, Carlos, each maneuvered to dominate the other. In accordance with Calusa custom, Carlos insisted that Menéndez marry his sister in order to seal their alliance. Realizing that to decline would risk an attack by the powerful Calusas, Menéndez consulted with his officers, one of whom was his own wife's brother, and with their approval he consented. But after sleeping on their wedding night with his new wife, whom the Spanish called Doña Antonia, Menéndez avoided her, all the while making excuses so as not to alienate the Calusas. But the Spanish intrusion had already upset the delicate balance of political forces in southern Florida upon which Carlos's power rested. Neighboring Indians stopped paying tribute to the Calusas, fearing that it would go to Spain, while Carlos's cousin, whom the Spanish called Don Felipe, challenged the chief's claim to his position. In 1567 the Spanish assassinated Carlos, who was then succeeded by Don Felipe. But the Calusas so thoroughly resented what was obviously a Spanish-inspired coup that the Spanish, fearing a full-scale uprising, abandoned their fort in June 1569. Doña Antonia, along with a few other Christian converts, accompanied them to Havana, where she died a few years later.

Timucua and Calusa resistance led Spanish officials to shift their colonizing efforts in Florida northward to the Guale Indians of what is now coastal Georgia and South Carolina. They hoped to win over the Guales by dispatching Franciscan missionaries to convert them to Catholicism. Arriving in 1573, the Franciscans established a chain of missions among the Guales, but their presence was never secure. Spanish civil officials insisted that the Indians deliver canoe-loads of corn while missionaries demanded that the Guales give up their religious traditions and become Christians. In 1576 such demands prompted a violent reaction that spread quickly throughout the three Guale chiefdoms. Although the Spanish burned twenty Guale villages in 1579 and the Franciscans withdrew, the rebellion continued. The Spanish moved their capital and all settlers from the Guale homeland to St. Augustine because of attacks from land by the Guales and from sea by English privateers.

Franciscan efforts flagged until a new corps of friars arrived among the Guales in 1595, when the patterns of the preceding decades reappeared. Spanish demands for food, the arbitrary violence inflicted on even cooperative Indians by Spanish soldiers, and the missionaries' denunciation of Guale culture fanned the smoldering flames of Indian resentment. In 1597 a Guale chief's son, whom the Spanish called Don Juanillo, led an uprising by most of the Guale villages. Although considering himself a Christian, Don Juanillo rebelled after a missionary ordered him to abandon all but one of his wives. He refused because the kin connections afforded by multiple wives were essential to exercising the powers of a chief, which he was soon to become. He rallied other Guales to his cause by pointing out how the Spanish "deprive us of every vestige of happiness which our ancestors obtained for us, in exchange for which they hold out the hope of the joys of heaven." In a carefully coordinated assault, the Guales killed five missionaries before the Spanish launched a violent crackdown. By 1601 Spanish troops had finally crushed the revolt and either killed its leaders in battle or executed them. Other prisoners were enslaved. But while avenging the revolt, the Spanish had gained neither the loyalty nor the submission of the Guales.

Coosa, Spain, and the Southeastern Interior, 1559–1600

Although peninsular and Atlantic coastal Indians bore the brunt of European colonizing efforts in the Southeast, Indian peoples of the interior confronted renewed Spanish activity in the second half of the sixteenth century. The Tazcaluzas, Chickasaws, and other Mississippians who had resisted de Soto had permanently dashed Spanish dreams of conquering the interior as they had Mexico. Spain also needed support against its English and French rivals, and the only sources of such support in the Southeast were Indian. Accordingly Spain abandoned the failed strategy of massive, overwhelming conquest and instead planned to establish alliances with key Mississippian chiefdoms, particularly Coosa, which de Soto had tried to subjugate.

Spain launched its new effort in 1559 when Tristán de Luna y Arellano arrived at Ochuse (modern Pensacola) with one thousand colonists, including soldiers and their wives, missionaries, Mexican Indian laborers, African slaves, and a Coosa woman whom de Soto had captured twenty years earlier. Luna expected to establish a base at Ochuse, proceed northward and erect a second base at Coosa, and then build a road eastward to the Spanish town of Santa Elena on the Atlantic coast.

At Ochuse, the local Pensacola Indians fled on the approach of the Spanish, whose ships carrying their food and supplies had just been destroyed by a hurricane. On the basis of their past experience with Spanish intruders, the Pensacolas took their food with them. Moving north, the expedition entered the Tazcaluza chiefdom and soon reached the town of Nanipacana, whose warriors had joined in the battle against de Soto at Mábila nearly twenty years earlier. The Tazcaluzas, too, wanted no dealings with the Spanish and actually burned their own towns and gardens before fleeing, hoping thereby to discourage the colonizers from remaining. Nevertheless the Spanish wintered at Nanipacana.

In the following spring, Luna sent a contingent of troops northward to obtain food from Coosa. As they entered the territory of the Coosa chiefdom, Indians for the first time freely offered the Spanish food and even men to carry their goods. In exchange, the soldiers gave the Indians ribbons, cloth, beads, and other items. Nevertheless, the Indians in each town tried to hurry the troops along to the next town as quickly as possible to minimize the loss of food.

At Coosa itself, Spanish officers scored a rare diplomatic triumph. The Coosa chief told them that if they could help Coosa recover tribute owed it by the nearby Napochie Indians, there would be enough corn for all of them. The Napochies had formerly been tributaries of Coosa but broke away when Coosa's power declined as the result of an epidemic, probably introduced by de Soto's expedition. As Coosa and Spanish forces approached a Napochie town, a Spanish soldier shot and killed a Napochie man from a great distance. Astonished, the Napochies quickly surrendered and offered to resume their tributary status.

Despite the Napochies' submission, the Spanish failed to secure enough food for the one thousand colonists. Meanwhile, Indians to the south harassed the hungry Spaniards and Luna himself grew mentally unstable. He and all the colonists finally withdrew during the fall of 1560 but Spanish officials remained hopeful that the alliance with Coosa would be the basis for future colonization.

For the next six years, Indians of the southeastern interior had reason to hope that Luna's withdrawal signaled an end to Spanish colonizing efforts in their homelands. Those hopes were dashed in 1566 when Spanish troops led by Juan Pardo arrived to build a string of forts that would extend from Santa Elena to Zacatecas, Mexico (a distance the Spanish greatly underestimated). Departing Santa Elena in December 1566, Pardo traveled north through Cofitachequi, which had been fatally weakened by epidemics after de Soto sacked it twenty-three years earlier. The expedition halted for the winter in a neighboring chiefdom, Joara, formerly a tributary of Cofitachequi, and established friendly ties by assisting the chief in collecting corn and other tribute from several neighboring towns.

Building on his alliance with Joara, Pardo continued westward in September 1567. Near Coosa, some Indians informed him of a plot by some Coosa tributaries to ambush the Spanish, to prevent them from seizing the Indians' corn. The informants' subsequent disappearance seemed to confirm the plot, so Pardo turned back toward Santa Elena, building four more forts along the way. But the new forts proved useless. The few soldiers left at each one were in no position to command either the obedience or the friendship of surrounding Indians, who soon either killed or adopted them. In the meantime, Spain abandoned its efforts to colonize the southeastern interior.

As in coastal Florida, Spain profoundly affected Native American life in the southeastern interior during the sixteenth century in spite of its repeated failures to colonize there. Those failures are even more glaring in light of the fact that the region's Indians died in great numbers as a result of direct or indirect contact with the intruders. The principal factor in this depopulation was epidemic diseases, the effects of which were political as well as demographic. Except among the Natchez Indians of what is now Louisiana, the highly concentrated Mississippian chiefdoms of the Southeast dissolved as population losses soared to 75 percent or more. Survivors of the epidemics left the large temple mound centers, regrouping in villages, some of which joined together in confederacies. The principal difference between the chiefdoms and the confederacies was the decentralization of political power in the latter. As survivors came together to form new local communities, they were in no position to produce the enormous quantities of food and craft goods that Mississippians had exchanged and which were the foundation of chiefs' and elites' power. Even in local communities, the ties of kinship and familiarity that had formerly bound peoples must have been more fragile at first.

Several of the confederacies even brought together peoples of different languages and ethnicities. Coosa, the focus of so much Spanish activity, was a confederacy of five smaller chiefdoms at the outset of the sixteenth century. However, after the visits of de Soto, Luna, and Pardo (and, perhaps, after experiencing epidemics originating elsewhere), depopulated Coosa consisted of a single town. By the end of the century Coosa was joining other devastated communities of survivors to form a less centralized confederacy, which later Europeans would know as the Creeks. A comparable process occurred to the west, where survivors of the Mississippian chiefdom centered at Moundville, on the Black Warrior River in Alabama, regrouped as the Choctaw confederacy. Similarly, the Chickasaw, Cherokee, and Catawba confederacies emerged as less centralized but nevertheless highly integrated successors to Mississippian chiefdoms.

Roanoke Indians and England's "Lost Colony," 1584–1590

Although most Indians in the Southeast were organized in chiefdoms when the sixteenth century began, a number of Algonquian-speaking tribes on the Outer Banks and the adjoining coast of what is now North Carolina were an exception. As with Algonquian speakers to the north as far as New England, the Roanokes, Croatoans, and other tribes in the area consisted of anywhere from one to eighteen villages. While the tribes often grouped themselves in alliances or confederacies, they did not form highly centralized chiefdoms like their neighbors to the south. Like most of their more northerly counterparts, they relied for food primarily on the corn, beans, and squash produced by women, supplemented by game, wild plants, and the abundance of marine life found in the sounds separating the mainland from the Outer Banks.

For most of the sixteenth century, the Indians of the northern Carolina coast had less acquaintance with Europeans than their neighbors to the south and north. The dangerous seas around the Outer

Banks constituted one major barrier for maritime invaders. The Secotan Indians saved one Spanish crew in 1558, helping its members fashion a boat so they could return to Florida. This and numerous other shipwrecks introduced the Indians to European-made materials and finished objects, particularly of metal, which they often refashioned as tools, weapons, and jewelry. The Indians were also well aware of hostilities between their Powhatan neighbors and Spanish colonizers at nearby Chesapeake Bay during the early 1570s (see Powhatan Resistance on the Lower Chesapeake later in this chapter).

All this changed in 1584 when an English explorer, Arthur Barlowe, arrived among the Roanokes at Roanoke Island and was immediately entranced. The island, in his words, was a place where "the earth bringeth forth all things in abundance . . . without toil or labor," and the Roanoke Indians were "most gentle, loving, and faithful, . . . such as live after the golden age." After trading congenially with the Roanokes and their chief, Wingina, Barlowe returned to England with two young Roanoke men, Manteo and Wanchese.

Barlowe's descriptions of natural abundance and Indian conviviality led his employer, Sir Walter Raleigh, to imagine that English colonists could thrive at Roanoke without working. In the following year Raleigh dispatched a company of settlers and soldiers to the island. Anglo-Roanoke relations began amicably. Two Englishmen, Thomas Hariot and John White, recorded details of Roanoke culture in words and watercolors, respectively. But when a chief, with whom they had concluded a friendly meeting, failed to turn over a missing cup and its alleged thief, the English burned his village and its corn stores to the ground. Thereafter most Roanokes distrusted the English, who in turn viewed all meetings and travel by Indians as evidence of a conspiracy against them. As English food supplies ran low that winter, the colony's military commander, Ralph Lane, tried with limited success to force the Roanokes and neighboring Indians to provide the English with food. In June 1586 Lane called for a peace conference during which, by prearrangement, English troops assassinated Wingina and other Indian leaders. But the plan proved to be shortsighted because it left the English more isolated from potential Native American allies than ever. When another Englishman,

Roanoke Indian Town, 1585 Based on a watercolor by John White, one of the English colonists at Roanoke, this engraving shows agricultural fields, houses, and a ceremonial complex (foreground).

Sir Francis Drake, arrived with supplies a week later, most of the colonists, along with Manteo and another friendly Roanoke, clambered aboard.

In 1587 Raleigh sent White, who had consistently urged a more peaceful approach to Indian relations, at the head of a third expedition to Roanoke. The expedition consisted of 110 colonists plus the two friendly Indians. The colonists arrived to discover that most Indians in the area remained hostile to them and had already routed a small garrison sent ahead by Raleigh. Feeling a need to establish their authority and avenge the soldiers' deaths, they attacked a nearby Croatoan Indian village on Cape Hatteras. Only after killing many Croatoans did the colonists realize that they had mistakenly attacked the one group of Indians that was, until then, still friendly to them.

Isolated and fearing that their English suppliers might neglect them, the colonists sent White back to England to muster support for their beleaguered community. Events in England, particularly the battle of the Spanish Armada in 1588, prevented White from returning until 1590. Finally reaching Roanoke, he found the English colony abandoned. The only clue to the whereabouts of the colonists, including his own daughter and granddaughter, was the word "Croatoan" carved into a wooden post. White never found the colonists and their fate has remained a mystery. Presumably, they were absorbed into Croatoan society, with some, like Spanish refugees and captives in Florida, dispersed among neighboring Indian communities. It is quite likely that the Roanoke English, like the Croatoans themselves, were among the forebears of the Lumbee Indians of North Carolina.

ENCOUNTERS IN THE AMERICAN WEST

Many fewer Indians west of the Mississippi Valley encountered Europeans during the sixteenth century than was the case in the Eastern Woodlands. Yet there was more cultural diversity among those western Indians who did interact with the newcomers than among their eastern contemporaries. Even the hunting-gathering Indians of the Texas and California coasts had little in common with one another in terms of political organization, material culture, and language, and neither even superficially resembled the Pueblo Indians of the Rio Grande and nearby parts of the Southwest, who lived in densely populated farming communities. Despite the differences among Indians across the West, visiting Europeans found ample evidence of the extensive exchange networks that linked them to one another. The Pueblo Indians' position at the heart of these networks contributed to their wealth and power as well as to rumors among Spaniards in early sixteenth-century Mexico that some of the pueblos were fabled cities of gold. Even after these rumors proved false, the Rio Grande remained the focus of most early colonial efforts in the West.

Stragglers' Entrada: Cabeza de Vaca, 1528–1536

Native Americans in the American West first encountered Europeans not as ambitious conquistadors but as defeated, desperate strangers struggling just to survive. After Narváez withdrew from Florida (see Rebuffing Spanish Entradas in Florida, 1513–1528, earlier in the chapter), ninety starving, thirsty survivors of his expedition landed in 1528 among the Karankawa Indians on the Gulf of Mexico coast. The Karankawas lived between Galveston Bay and Corpus Christi Bay in what is now Texas. Although the climate was too dry for farming, nine bands of several hundred Karankawas each ranged annually over well-defined territories to hunt, fish, and harvest wild plants. Initially suspicious, the Karankawas treated the castaways well, but both peoples suffered over the following winter, during which several dozen Spaniards along with half the Karankawas died. Over the next six years, eight more Spaniards and many more Karankawas perished, mostly from Spanish-borne illnesses, the effects of which were exacerbated by a drought then ravaging the southern Plains. Under these conditions, one of the Spanish survivors, Alvar Nuñez Cabeza de Vaca, acquired a reputation among the Karankawas and neighboring Indians as a trader and formidable healer with spiritual powers. Ironically, his supposed putative powers derived in part from his ability to treat typhoid, dysentery, and other Spanish-borne diseases. In 1534 Cabeza de Vaca and the other remaining survivors—two Spaniards and the enslaved African, Esteban—set out by land for New Spain (Mexico). As they crossed the southern Plains, they encountered Jumanos and other Indians who had been blinded by hunger-induced trachoma. The travelers cured this blindness, probably with copper sulfate, a technique that Esteban would have learned in his North African homeland. They also carried buffalo hides and other trade goods as they traveled from one community to another.

Turning toward the Southwest, the four traded and healed wherever they went, eventually reaching the Pima-speaking Ópatas of northern Sonora. Here they saw coral and shells from the Pacific as well as trade goods from central Mexico and from the Pueblo peoples to the north. The Ópatas told them how they obtained turquoise and some of their other fine goods from a place to the north called Cíbola, their term for one of the Zuni pueblos in present-day New Mexico.

Ópata guides accompanied the four travelers as they headed southward toward Mexico. In July 1536, eight years after landing with Narváez in Florida, they encountered Spanish slave traders on what was then the northern frontier of New Spain. The Ópatas could not believe that the four men they had come to know so well could have anything in common with the cruel people they had occasionally encountered in Mexico. As Cabeza de Vaca later characterized their reaction, "We [he and his companions] healed the sick, they [slave traders] killed the sound; we came naked and barefoot, they clothed, horsed, and lanced; we coveted nothing but gave whatever we were given, while they robbed whomever they found." Reluctantly the Ópatas allowed their companions to leave them and continue on with the slave catchers. Cabeza de Vaca pleaded with the "Christian slavers," as he termed them, to cease their activities but to no avail.

Southwestern Indians and Spanish Gold-Seekers, 1538–1542

Word of Cabeza de Vaca's travels also directly inspired Spanish exploration in the Southwest. The viceroy of New Spain, Antonio Mendoza, was particularly eager to find Cíbola, as described by the Ópatas. Although there were only six Zuni pueblos, the Spanish assumed that they must be the seven "golden cities" that had long been rumored to lie in some unknown part of the world. In 1538, Mendoza commissioned a Franciscan priest, Fray Marcos de Niza, a veteran of the Inca conquest, to lead a small expedition from Mexico City to find Cíbola. When none of the three Spanish survivors of Cabeza de Vaca's party agreed to accompany the expedition, Mendoza purchased Esteban, the enslaved African, to serve as his guide.

Unfazed by Esteban's death at the hands of the Zuni in Hawikuh, de Niza returned to Mexico and claimed to Mendoza that, standing on a nearby mountaintop, he had seen Cíbola, which he pronounced "the greatest and best of the discoveries." Convinced of the city's vast wealth, the viceroy in 1540 commissioned Francisco Vásquez de Coronado, with de Niza as a guide, to lead three hundred Spanish soldiers and more than one thousand Mexican Indians on an expedition to conquer Cíbola. At the same time, he dispatched Hernando de Alarcón with three ships to sail up the Gulf of California and try to meet up with Coronado at some point to the west of the Rio Grande.

Arriving at Hawikuh, Coronado was disillusioned to find a pueblo with about one hundred families. His disillusionment reflected the different notions of wealth held by Spanish elites and southwestern Indians. To the Ópatas, Hawikuh was a wealthy center, rich in valuable goods, but it could never live up to Spanish expectations—fueled by de Niza's wild exaggerations—of a "golden city." After angrily sending de Niza back to Mexico, Coronado seized and occupied Hawikuh and then dispatched his forces in several directions to continue the search. Following another report of seven cities to the northwest, one party found the Hopi pueblos. Having heard of the Spanish treatment of the Zunis, the Hopis refused to welcome the invaders, who thereupon seized one of the pueblos. Another party traveled as far west as the Grand Canyon and found a message from Alarcón.

Coronado decided to winter on the Rio Grande among the densely clustered pueblos there. During the harsh months that followed, Spanish soldiers took food and clothing from the Indians at will and harassed and raped Pueblo women. Finally the pueblos rebelled in what was the first of several attempts over the next two and a half centuries to rid themselves of Spanish invaders. After the Spanish smoked out the inhabitants of one pueblo, capturing and burning suspected rebels at the stake, many Pueblo Indians moved from harm's way by temporarily abandoning their homes. By the time the Spanish moved on in the spring of 1541, they had destroyed thirteen pueblos and killed several hundred Indians.

Guided by a Plains Indian they called "the Turk," Coronado moved eastward, encountering Jumano and Apache bands and Pawnee and Wichita villages as they searched for the fabled cities. Finally, upon reaching the Arkansas River, the Turk admitted that he had deliberately tried to lead them where, as Coronado put it, "we and our horses would starve to death." After killing the Turk, the Spanish returned to the Rio Grande. During the following winter, Coronado suffered a severe head injury while riding. Leaving behind some Mexican Indians and African slaves, he returned to Mexico with the rest of his entourage in the spring of 1542. As with de Soto in the Southeast, a combination of Indian resistance and Spanish arrogance and incompetence had defeated an invasion of Native American homelands, but only after the loss of many Indian lives.

Pueblo Indians and a "New Mexico," 1581–1600

For nearly four decades after Coronado's ignominious exit, the Pueblo Indians slowly recovered from the damages inflicted by his expedition. In time only the elders could recall the invasion directly, but the Pueblos would have known through their extensive trade connections that would-be Spanish colonizers remained within striking distance to the south. In 1581, their anxieties were realized when a Franciscan missionary, Father Agustín Rodríguez, accompanied by two other Franciscans and seven soldiers, arrived in the Rio Grande valley. After exploring widely, Rodríguez and another missionary remained behind to proselytize among the Pueblos while their companions returned to Mexico. In the next year, Antonio de Espejo led an expedition that was to reinforce the Franciscans. Although finding that the two missionaries had been killed, Espejo returned to Mexico and reported hearing of great wealth in the land of the Pueblos.

To the great peril of the Pueblos, Espejo's description revived Spanish dreams of wealth in the Southwest. In 1590 Gaspar Castaño de Sosa led an unauthorized expedition of 170 prospective colonists into Pueblo country. (By then a series of royal ordinances had formally outlawed unlicensed colonizing and the military conquest of new lands, calling instead for missionary-led pacifications.) Reviving the methods of the conquistadors, Castaño intended to take over the Rio Grande pueblos and turn them over to Spanish authorities who, he expected, would forgive him for his legal violations. Accordingly, when the Pecos Indians resisted his assertions of authority over them, he sacked their village. Thereafter he went from one pueblo to another, planting crosses at each to symbolize his authority. But Spanish officials, who were serious about

PEOPLE, PLACES, AND THINGS

Spaniards Entering the Southwest:
A Navajo View

For thousands of years before Europeans arrived, rocks constituted the "canvas" on which Indian artists painted and drew visual images. This striking example depicts mounted Spanish colonizers, including soldiers and a missionary.

Navajo View of Spanish Colonizers
This pictograph—a painting or drawing on rock—was sketched in the early colonial period in Cañon del Muerto, Arizona.

outlawing unauthorized conquests, dispatched troops to stop Castaño's activities. The soldiers arrested Castaño at Santo Domingo pueblo and informed the Indians that the Spanish king was their friend and would punish anyone who abused them, even his own countrymen. As the Spanish withdrew yet again from the Southwest, the Pueblos must have been relieved yet wary, wondering when they would next be visited by one of the unpredictable parties that came every so often from the south.

That visit came in 1598 when Don Juan de Oñate led an authorized colonizing party to New Mexico. Arriving in Santo Domingo, Oñate assured thirty-one leaders from nearby pueblos that he had been sent by the king of Spain to bring them the benefits of Spanish rule and Christianity. The Indians at Santo Domingo and several other pueblos submitted readily to Spanish authority. In keeping with Pueblo teachings about the importance of social harmony, they wanted to avoid violence with intruders they thought would, like those who came before, soon leave anyway. As it turned out, the intruders remained. As winter set in, Spanish soldiers and colonists seized food and clothing from the Indians, often physically and sexually abusing them in the process. Finally Indians at Ácoma pueblo re-

volted by attacking a party of Spanish soldiers and killing eleven. Considering the revolt a violation of Ácoma's oath of obedience to the king, Spanish troops brutally attacked the pueblo, killing eight hundred men, women, and children and condemning those captured either to twenty years of servitude or to having a foot severed. As the sixteenth century ended, the Pueblo Indians faced an uncertain future.

First Encounters in California, 1542–1595

Some Indians in coastal California also encountered Europeans hoping to establish colonial bases during the sixteenth century. The first were Ipai (Digueño) Indians who met Juan Rodriguez Cabrillo, a veteran of Cortés's expedition to Mexico, when he arrived at San Diego in the fall of 1542. Cabrillo and his men found that even though no Europeans had ever been there before, the Ipais fled on seeing the Spaniards and then shot arrows at them during the night. When the Spanish were finally able to communicate with some Ipais, they learned that "men like us were traveling about, bearded, clothed, armed . . . killing many native Indians, and . . . for this reason they were afraid."

The Ipais were almost certainly referring to Alarcón's expedition on the lower Colorado River, as reported on by the Quechan (Yuma) Indians there, who spoke a related language and maintained close trade ties with the Ipais.

Sailing north, Cabrillo wintered among the Gabrielino Indians at Santa Catalina Island. He died soon thereafter following an altercation with the Gabrielinos. Nevertheless his expedition remained and apparently left its mark, for six decades later another group of Spanish visitors to the island reported that many of the Gabrielino children were "white and blonde."

Indians in California saw few if any Europeans for at least two decades after Cabrillo's men left. During the 1560s, as Spain was seizing control of the Philippine Islands, it established a regular trade route between Acapulco, on the Pacific coast of Mexico, and the new port of Manila. Ships known as "Manila galleons" returned from Asia via the Japanese currents, turning southward upon reaching the California coast. After the long voyage, many of the ships would stop for a few days at California for fresh water and food. Crew members interacted with Pomos, Miwoks, Ohlones (Costanoans), Chumash, and other coastal peoples but left little record of these encounters and their effects on Indians.

All this Spanish activity drew the attention of the English explorer and privateer, Sir Francis Drake, who in 1579 arrived in Miwok territory, just north of San Francisco Bay. (The exact location of his landing is disputed.) Drake proclaimed the region an English colony and named it "New Albion." Over the course of their thirty-eight-day stay, Drake and his crew traded extensively with local Coast Miwoks. According to a highly plausible Miwok tradition, some English sailors abandoned the voyage to live among the Miwoks. As a result of events in England and a shift in English imperial priorities, no one ever returned from that country to colonize New Albion.

The Manila galleons, and perhaps other ships, including Drake's, left behind portions of their cargo that archaeologists later found at a Miwok site. Alongside Miwok artifacts of bone, stone, and shell were pieces of European metal, Southeast Asian stoneware, and Ming porcelain from China, all dating to the late sixteenth century. The Asian materials were destined for wealthy consumers in Spain's Latin American colonies and in Europe. As did the Indians on the Atlantic coast who scoured shipwrecks during the sixteenth century, Miwoks fashioned many of the foreign objects into tools for cutting, scraping, and other utilitarian purposes.

Thanks to Europeans having shifted their full attention to the Atlantic and adjacent lands, Indian-European contacts in California were intermittent at best over the next century and a half. In addition to material objects and some children of mixed heritage, the Spanish and English visitors of the 1500s appear to have communicated some deadly diseases among coastal Indians, at least some of which probably spread to interior peoples. (The crews of the Manila galleons were in notoriously poor health on their return voyages.) But the legacy of the earliest Europeans was gradually obscured as Indians in California recovered from the epidemics and resumed living on their own terms. The permanent impact of disease and colonization would begin in California more than a century and a half later (see Chapter 6).

EARLY CONTACTS IN THE NORTHEAST

As in the Southeast and West, Indians in parts of the Northeast confronted Europeans seeking economic, political, or religious gains during the sixteenth century. Here, too, outsiders introduced lethal epidemic diseases that spread quickly among Native peoples, causing enormous catastrophes in affected communities. As a consequence, the demographic and political map of the region bounded by the St. Lawrence River valley, Appalachian Mountains, and Chesapeake Bay was transformed during the sixteenth century.

Despite broad similarities across the Eastern Woodlands in the impact on Indians of early contacts with Europeans, Indian-European relations in the Northeast often followed a different course from those in the Southeast. In the Southeast, Mississippian chiefs presiding over extensive tributary networks typically confronted Spanish military officers. While Indian chiefs' powers among tributaries were sustained by reciprocity and those of military officers by their unquestioned authority over subordinates, prominent leaders stood at the head of each side in most southeastern encounters. In the Northeast, on the other hand, village and tribal leaders represented leading families but depended on consensus among their people in making decisions and maintaining their positions. The French traders with whom northeastern Native leaders typically interacted appeared in small parties that, while armed, were not organized as military units of their home countries. Unlike Spanish officers who sought to subordinate Indians in the Southeast, French traders in the Northeast recognized that establishing solid trade relations required them to observe the norms of reciprocity that governed exchanges among Native Americans. Northeastern encounters, then, centered less on power and status and more on the content of exchanges than those in the Southeast.

These regional distinctions did not mean that there was less violence in the Northeast than in the Southeast during the sixteenth century. Trading with Europeans often proved as disastrous for northeastern Indians as resisting Spanish authority was for their southern contemporaries. Exchanges with the newcomers from across the Atlantic fostered competition, frequently deadly, among northeastern Indians as they sought to increase their production of furs for the commercial market and to control trade between neighboring Indians and visiting Europeans. Whereas the large-scale violence of the sixteenth-century Southeast was largely a result of Indian-European hostilities, the lower level of violence in the Northeast was more often inflicted by Native Americans on one another.

Hostility and Reciprocity, 1490–1524

The trade that came to characterize Indian-European relations in the Northeast during the sixteenth century emerged only gradually. The earliest northeastern Indians to encounter strangers from across the Atlantic were nonfarming Beothuks of Newfoundland, Mi'kmaqs (or Micmacs) around the Gulf of St. Lawrence and the adjacent coast, and Abenakis of what is now coastal Maine. As during the fifteenth century, European fishing crews increased their activity in the North Atlantic. By the 1490s, as the Norse withdrew from Greenland, a

few English and Portuguese fishing vessels were venturing near Newfoundland where some of them undoubtedly interacted with the indigenous Beothuks. In 1497 John Cabot, making an official voyage for England, reported sighting Newfoundland and its Beothuk inhabitants. Thereafter fishermen, whalers, and explorers from Spain, Portugal, the Basque country, Brittany, and England frequented the coast between Newfoundland and New England.

Early Indian-European contacts on the northeastern coast varied from hostile to friendly. From the Indians' perspective, the outcome depended on whether the newcomers observed the obligations of reciprocity that traditionally governed intergroup relations. During the first quarter of the sixteenth century, Spanish and Portuguese explorers kidnapped dozens of Beothuks, Mi'kmaqs, and Abenakis for sale into slavery. Not surprisingly, these peoples quickly developed deep-seated suspicions of Europeans. The wary Beothuks often disappeared into the Newfoundland interior whenever unfriendly Europeans approached too closely. The Eastern Abenakis of Maine took a different approach. When a French expedition led by Giovanni de Verrazzano arrived at the Maine coast in 1524, the local Abenakis allowed the visitors to trade but only on certain conditions. The French had to remain in their boats without landing while the two parties passed their trade goods back and forth by rope. The Abenakis would accept only knives, fishhooks, and other sharp metal objects. Clearly, they appreciated certain European artifacts but wished to avoid direct contact with Europeans themselves.

Other early contacts proceeded on more friendly terms. Shortly before meeting the Abenakis, Verrazzano and his crew had sailed into what is now Narragansett Bay in Rhode Island. In contrast to the icy reception accorded them by the Abenakis, the French were welcomed with enthusiasm and rejoicing by the Narragansetts and Wampanoags whose villages lined the bay. These Indians spurned utilitarian objects in favor of what Europeans thought of as "trinkets"—copper bells, glass beads, mirrors, and, in Verrazzano's words, "other toys to hang in their ears and about their necks." To the Narragansetts and Wampanoags, these "trinkets" were the equivalents of the copper, mica, quartz, and other minerals long valued by Native Americans for their spiritual qualities. For thousands of years, Native Americans had traded across vast distances for such materials and made artifacts from them. The exchanges themselves were ceremonial occasions in which groups affirmed mutual friendship and reciprocity. The Narragansetts and Wampanoags had either never seen Europeans or had had only peaceful encounters with them. Verrazzano and his men appeared to them as bearers of spiritual power to be honored rather than as threats to be avoided. Yet there were dangers that these Indians did not yet understand, for Verrazzano like Columbus regarded them as naive and inferior to Europeans for preferring "trinkets" to metal tools, silk cloth, and gold.

Stadacona, Hochelaga, and French Colonizers on the St. Lawrence, 1534–1543

Like the Mississippi and the Rio Grande, the St. Lawrence River is a major waterway along whose banks Native Americans erected towns and villages to facilitate farming and trade. At the outset of the sixteenth century, the most prominent towns on the St. Lawrence were Stadacona and Hochelaga, near the modern cities of Quebec and Montreal, respectively. Closely related by language and culture to the Huron and Iroquois peoples (see Chapter 1 and Trade and Upheaval in the St. Lawrence–Great Lakes Interior, 1580–1600, later in this chapter.), the Stadacona and Hochelaga Indians were the first Indians of the northeastern interior to encounter and deal with Europeans.

The occasion for these encounters was a series of French expeditions to the St. Lawrence, beginning in 1534. The French hoped that the river would provide a northwest passage to Asia. With intelligence provided by European fishermen and previous explorers, Jacques Cartier arrived in 1534, leading an expedition with ample supplies of glass beads and other trade goods to facilitate his securing Indian trade partners, allies, and guides.

Cartier's first dealings were with some Mi'kmaqs near the mouth of the St. Lawrence, who were eager to trade with the French. Thereafter, he sailed upriver to Stadacona. French-Stadacona relations proceeded amicably until, having gained the Indians'

confidence, the French seized two sons of the chief, Donnacona, and took them back to France.

Under questioning, the Stadacona captives told Cartier that he could sail far up the St. Lawrence to a vast sea (undoubtedly the Great Lakes). Thinking that this sea must be the Pacific Ocean or linked to it, Cartier returned to Stadacona the following year with the captives. The people of Stadacona were relieved at the two young men's return and ready to forgive the French. But Cartier alienated them again when, without their permission, he established his camp next to their town and then defied their insistence that he not sail upriver to the larger town of Hochelaga. In so acting, Cartier violated Stadacona's autonomy and undermined its control of downriver trade with its larger neighbor. The Hochelaga Indians welcomed the French for their goods, but the French distrusted them and quickly returned to Stadacona.

During the winter of 1535–1536, an epidemic, perhaps of smallpox, broke out in Stadacona while the nearby French suffered from an outbreak of scurvy. Although the French kept the Stadaconas at a distance, the Indians told them how to cure scurvy by drinking a brew made from cedar fronds. Cartier also heard tales of a land of fabulous wealth in the interior beyond Hochelaga. To gain support in France for an expedition to this land, Cartier kidnapped Donnacona and nine other Stadaconas so that King Francis I could hear firsthand reports of its wealth.

Favorably impressed, the king sought first to establish France's claim to the St. Lawrence with a colony there, and appointed Jean-François de la Rocque, sieur de Roberval, as its viceroy. It was 1541 before Roberval sent Cartier back to the St. Lawrence with several hundred colonists. The one surviving Stadacona captive was left behind in France. The Stadaconas as well as previously friendly Indians in the area were now united in opposition to the French. Over the course of the winter, they killed thirty-five settlers, leading the French to return home. Roberval himself led a final attempt to settle the St. Lawrence in 1543. But when their own food supplies ran out, the French stole from the Indians while also contracting scurvy. Finally, realizing that the St. Lawrence would never carry them to the Pacific anyway, they gave up and returned to France.

Coastal Indians and European Traders, 1540–1600

As the sixteenth century wore on, northeastern Indians encountered European explorers, fishermen, whalers, seal hunters, fur traders, privateers, and would-be colonizers with increasing frequency. As they acquired experience with Native Americans, some of these Europeans made a point of carrying metal and glass goods for trade with coastal Indians in exchange for hospitality and furs. Eventually, the quantity of furs brought back by fishermen induced some Europeans, particularly the French, to mount specialized fur trading expeditions. Although such ventures were only occasional rather than regular at first, one French ship acquired more than one thousand furs from Indians at Chesapeake Bay in 1546.

The fur trade began slowly, then escalated abruptly. By 1580 a demand for beaver hats among the emergent middle classes of western Europe led traders to concentrate primarily on securing beaver pelts. The process by which Indians prepared the pelts for trading was an intricate one. Native hunters trapped beavers in their dens during winters, when the fur was thickest, and skinned them.

Indian women scraped the inner side of the pelts so as to loosen the roots of the longer, harder "guard" hairs covering the softer fur, then cut the pelts into rectangles and stitched several such pelts together into robes. They and other Indians wore the robes for up to a year and a half, during which time the guard hairs fell out, and the remaining fur became even softer and more pliable—and more desirable for European consumers.

In return for such prepared pelts, Indian traders most often received iron tools, copper kettles, and glass beads from their French (and occasionally, English) counterparts. While keeping some trade goods for themselves, coastal Indians exchanged the rest with neighboring peoples, especially those with access to even thicker pelts from subarctic regions to the north. In this way, some favorably situated villages and tribes on the coast emerged as powerful brokers in the movements of goods between two continents.

Although most Indian-European trading encounters were friendly, some were hostile. In 1574 a skirmish between Spanish Basque whalers and Montagnais (Innu) on the Labrador coast marred what had been a record of peaceful dealings between the two groups for several decades. In 1580

Beavers and Indians A French engraving depicts beavers at work and Indians hunting them for pelts.

an English party raided a Penobscot Abenaki village and stole three hundred pelts. Three years later local Mi'kmaqs rebuffed a French attempt to establish a permanent trading post and religious mission on the Bay of Fundy.

Because of their location on Cape Breton Island and the Gulf of St. Lawrence, the Mi'kmaqs had the most frequent contacts of all northeastern Indians with European traders, primarily French. Before the end of the sixteenth century they were altering their subsistence patterns to accommodate the trade, hunting longer during winters and then trading with the French during summers instead of fishing and gathering. In addition to metal and glass goods, they received food to replace what they no longer produced for themselves. They also traded some of their European goods to Indians in southern New England for corn.

As elsewhere in sixteenth-century North America, contacts with Europeans brought deadly epidemic diseases to the Northeast. During the century as a whole, the Mi'kmaq population declined from about twelve thousand to about three thousand. In 1610 the Mi'kmaq sachem Membertou sadly recalled when his people were "as thickely planted there as the hairs upon his head."

Trade and Upheaval in the St. Lawrence–Great Lakes Interior, 1580–1600

The 1580s also marked the beginning of regular exchanges in the St. Lawrence Valley between Indians and French traders. Tadoussac, at the junction of the St. Lawrence and Saguenay rivers, became the center of this trade, serving as a major rendezvous point for Indians as far west as the Ottawa River and lower Great Lakes. What before 1580 had been a trickle of finished European products into inland communities was becoming a small but steady flow, mostly of axes, knives, and glass beads. Twentieth-century archaeologists found some of these goods in burials, indicating that Indians must have valued them for their spiritual qualities. But Native Americans also appreciated the practical uses of metal, often flattening brass and copper pots into tools for cutting, scraping, and digging and into fine ornaments of apparel. As a result, northeastern Indians' production of stone

tools declined and the manufacturing of some objects changed. For example, after fashioning metal carving tools, Iroquois men began carving their pipes from wood instead of stone.

Although European goods remained few in number at the end of the sixteenth century, they affected the lives of northeastern Indians in significant ways. As had been the case for centuries and even millennia, a community's or tribe's power was enhanced if it controlled the movement of exotic or spiritually powerful goods through exchange networks—particularly if it had direct access to the sources of those goods. By the same token, its position was weakened if it lacked access to such goods, directly or through allies. The Algonquian-speaking Montagnais and Algonkins controlled access to Tadoussac and appear to have excluded the Mohawks and other nations of the Iroquois Confederacy from access to French trade while including the Iroquois' Huron rivals. Situated between the Huron and Iroquois were other Iroquoian-speakers, including the Stadaconas and Hochelagas, whom Cartier had visited and described in the 1530s. These communities were dispersed sometime in the middle or late sixteenth century, probably because of Iroquois-Huron conflict over access to the French (and possibly from an epidemic as well). Whether Stadacona and Hochelaga supported one side against the other or were divided internally is unclear, and archaeologists are at odds with one another on the matter. Ceramic evidence from pottery does indicate that women potters from the two St. Lawrence towns and a third one in what is now Jefferson County, New York, went to live among both the Iroquois and Hurons. Most likely they went to one side as captives and to the other as refugees.

Besides absorbing people from the St. Lawrence, the Hurons responded in other ways to the changing trade patterns. The more southerly Huron villages moved north during the 1580s to be nearer the villages that had long stood in Simcoe County, Ontario. From here the Hurons produced even larger surpluses of corn than before to trade with nonfarming Algonkins, who in turn supplied them with European goods as well as meat. Thus new Huron-Algonkin-French trade links represented a modification of earlier exchange relations, into which the Indians now absorbed the French and their goods.

These links excluded the Hurons' neighboring rivals, the Five Nations Iroquois. Archaeological evidence indicates that, in their quest for trade contacts with Europeans, the Five Nations turned toward their Susquehannock and Erie Indian neighbors, some of whom were moving from their interior homelands to the northern Chesapeake Bay. There the Susquehannocks and Eries competed with each other to dominate the flow of goods, not only between Indians and Europeans but also between coastal and interior Indians. In addition to European metal and glass goods, Susquehannock and Erie traders offered interior Indians substantial quantities of sacred wampum (see Chapter 1) and other marine shells that they had obtained from Indians at Chesapeake Bay.

As the sixteenth century came to a close, the Iroquois were being excluded from direct access to European traders on the St. Lawrence and, as we just saw, in the upper Chesapeake. The rivalries and alliances growing out of late sixteenth-century trade patterns would do much to shape the history of Indians and Europeans in the region during the seventeenth century.

Powhatan Resistance on the Lower Chesapeake

The sixteenth-century experiences of Algonquian-speaking Indians living on the western shore and adjacent tidewater valleys of Chesapeake Bay reflected their proximity to changes occurring in both the Northeast and Southeast. Although archaeologists and other scholars differ over precise causes and chronologies, most agree that the emergence of centralized chiefdoms among the Powhatans, Pamunkeys, and other Indians of the region was at least partially a response to the effects of intensified trade that involved both interior Indians, such as the Susquehannocks and Eries, and visiting Europeans.

Recognizing both the opportunities that such trade offered them and the potential threats that Indian outsiders posed to their autonomy, clusters of tribes in the densely populated region appear to have solidified their ties to one another, especially by strengthening kin connections among elite families. Gradually powerful weroances (chiefs) emerged, consolidating their power through multiple marriages throughout their chiefdoms. As in the South-east, Chesapeake-area chiefs eventually presided over extensive trade networks that were rooted in elaborate religious ceremonies. Although there is no archaeological evidence bearing directly on the impact of previously unknown epidemic diseases, the repeated visits of Europeans most likely took their toll in Indian lives, thereby reinforcing the tendencies of communities and tribes to consolidate.

By the mid-sixteenth century, some European traders in the Northeast had extended their activities southward along the Atlantic coast, often as far as Chesapeake Bay. The number and volume of French and English ships trading at the bay soon alarmed Spanish officials concerned with consolidating their position in Florida. In addition, the Spanish (like other Europeans) believed that one of the Chesapeake's tributary rivers might lead to the "Northwest Passage," connecting the Atlantic directly to the Pacific and Asia, which they wanted to control.

In 1561 Pedro Menéndez (discussed in the section Coastal Chiefdoms and Colonial Endeavors, 1562–1601) explored the lower Chesapeake looking for such a passage and captured a young boy, the son of a Powhatan weroance. The boy spent the next nine years in Spain, Cuba, and Mexico, during which time he was converted to Catholicism and renamed Don Luis de Velasco, for the Viceroy of New Spain. In 1570 Menéndez sent Don Luis, now a young man, back to his home on the James River with eight Jesuit missionaries and a Spanish boy. The party went ashore without soldiers in hopes that an unthreatening approach and the sight of Don Luis would reconcile the Powhatans to the Spanish presence. Although the Powhatans welcomed Don Luis's return with astonishment, relations with the poorly provisioned Jesuits soured when the missionaries established their quarters apart from the Indians' village and then demanded food. The Powhatans had little food to spare because they were emerging, in the words of one Jesuit, from "six years of famine and death." Indeed, some Powhatans had left the region in search of food. Repudiating the missionaries, Don Luis returned to his people and resumed his traditional customs and beliefs, scandalizing the Jesuits who condemned what they considered his sexually promiscuous behavior. Finally Don Luis led an attack on the Jesuits in which all eight were killed; only the Spanish boy was spared.

In the following year some Powhatans attacked a Spanish vessel bringing supplies to the mission. The Spanish seized several of the Powhatans, taking them to Havana and telling Spanish authorities there about the Jesuits' fate and the surviving boy. With one of the Powhatan captives in tow, Menéndez led an expedition to the Chesapeake in 1572 to rescue the boy and to capture and punish Don Luis for treacherously murdering the missionaries. Although the Powhatans returned the boy, Don Luis eluded the Spanish. In retaliation, the Spanish captured and hanged eight other Powhatans, including the weroance, an uncle of Don Luis. It was probably after this incident that a young man, himself named Powhatan, assumed the position of weroance of what would be known in the seventeenth century as the Powhatan Confederacy. By then Europeans as well as Indians would recognize Powhatan as one of the leading figures in colonial America (see Chapter 3).

CONCLUSION

By the end of the sixteenth century, Indians and Europeans in several parts of America north of Mexico were no longer strangers to one another. Over the course of the century, Native Americans had made clear that massive conquest as carried out by Cortés and Pizarro would not bring comparable rewards among Indians to the north. Indians there had no gold in the first place, but neither would they offer food or hospitality on command. Because would-be conquistadors threatened to diminish rather than augment the power of Native communities, chiefdoms, and confederacies, Indians generally rejected their presence. Meanwhile dozens of traders in the Northeast were discovering that honoring the principles of reciprocity yielded what Indians had to offer more readily and at far less cost. European trade goods offered Indian consumers new sources of spiritual power as well as practical, technological advantages over some of the tools, pots, and other objects that Native people used in their everyday lives.

Another sixteenth-century development—epidemic diseases—also affected the daily lives of many Indians. Whether the motives of the Europeans who spread them were friendly or hostile, epidemics severely diminished and traumatized Indian communities, leading to the formation of new, composite communities of survivors and new ties of exchange and tribute between communities both old and new. As the seventeenth century began, Indians responded to the crises and upheavals resulting from Europeans' presence as they had to earlier ones originating within North America. But it remained unclear whether Indians would be able to continue their recovery or whether expansion-minded Europeans would take further advantage of Indians' vulnerability to their microbes.

By 1600 more than a century had elapsed since Columbus's first American landfall among the Tainos in 1492—approximately 20 percent of the period between 1492 and the present. Yet in spite of the enormous upheavals that had occurred in several parts of North America across this expanse of time, Native Americans had successfully resisted Europeans' many attempts to control them and colonize their lands. After 1600, however, Europeans would undertake new, more lasting efforts to colonize what was to them a "new world," thereby presenting Indian peoples with even more formidable challenges.

SUGGESTED READINGS

Bradley, James W. *Evolution of the Onondaga Iroquois: Accommodating Change, 1500–1655.* Syracuse: Syracuse University Press, 1987.   An analysis and interpretation of the archaeological evidence bearing on one tribal nation's early interactions with Europeans.

Calloway, Colin G. *One Vast Winter Count: The Native American West Before Lewis and Clark.* Lincoln and London: University of Nebraska Press, 2003.   Chapter 3, "Sons of the Sun and People of the Earth," offers an excellent introduction to sixteenth-century Indian-European encounters between the Mississippi and the Rio Grande.

Crosby, Alfred W., Jr. *The Columbian Exchange: Biological and Cultural Consequences of 1492.* Westport, CT: Greenwood, 2003.   Originally published in 1972, the volume remains a classic examination of the environmental and epidemiological implications of Indian-European interactions.

Galloway, Patricia. *Choctaw Genesis, 1500–1700*. Lincoln and London: University of Nebraska Press, 1995. Combining documentary, cartographic, and archaeological evidence, this comprehensive study shows how several Mississippian peoples forged a new national and cultural identity during the sixteenth and seventeenth centuries.

Hudson, Charles, *Knights of Spain, Warriors of the Sun: Hernando de Soto and the South's Ancient Chiefdoms*. Athens: University of Georgia Press, 1997. An authoritative, meticulous account of de Soto's expedition and its encounters with Native peoples.

Hudson, Charles, and Carmen Chaves Tesser, eds. *The Forgotten Centuries: Indians and Europeans in the American South, 1521–1704*. Athens and London: University of Georgia Press, 1994. An excellent collection of essays by historians and archaeologist-anthropologists on early Indian-European interactions and their consequences across the Southeast.

Milanich, Jerald T. *Florida Indians and the Invasion from Europe*. Gainesville: University Press of Florida, 1995. An authoritative history of indigenous peoples in Florida, beginning with Paleo-Indians but emphasizing the sixteenth and seventeenth centuries.

Thornton, Russell, *American Indian Holocaust and Survival: A Population History Since 1492*. Norman and London: University of Oklahoma Press, 1987. The leading study of the impact of epidemics and other factors on the numbers of Native Americans.

Thomas, David Hurst, ed. *Columbian Consequences*. 3 vols. Washington: Smithsonian Institution Press, 1989–1991. Nearly one hundred essays by anthropologists, historians, and other scholars discuss aspects of Spanish interactions with Native peoples, primarily in North America.

Weber, David J. *The Spanish Frontier in North America*. New Haven and London: Yale University Press, 1992. A history of Spanish colonial endeavors within the present United States that pays particular attention to relations with Native Americans.

Native Peoples and the Founding of European Colonies, 1600–1660

It was a most unusual wedding. On April 5, 1614, the tiny colonial outpost of Jamestown, Virginia, hosted the marriage of Pocahontas, daughter of the most powerful Indian leader in the region, and John Rolfe, a minor English gentleman recently arrived to seek his fortune. The wedding was remarkable not only for the couple's ethnic and cultural differences but because, until a few weeks before, the Powhatans and Virginia had been at war. How did this unlikely couple come together under such circumstances? What motivated the newlyweds and others on both sides who sanctioned their marriage? What did the wedding mean for Anglo-Indian relations in Virginia?

Pocahontas was born in about 1597. Her father was Powhatan, weroance of the Powhatan chiefdom that reigned supreme on the lower Chesapeake Bay. Her mother, whose name went unrecorded, was one of Powhatan's wives of the time. (As a chief who consolidated his authority by establishing kin ties in every community under his power, Powhatan had several dozen wives over the course of his half-century reign.) Pocahontas had drawn the colonists' attention soon after they arrived in 1607 as the two, mutually suspicious sides cautiously assessed one another. In December 1607,

the Powhatans captured Virginia's military leader, John Smith. Smith's later claim that the ten-year-old Pocahontas dramatically rescued him after Powhatan ordered his execution is doubtful because no account written at the time, including Smith's own, confirms it. More likely, Powhatan was trying only to intimidate Smith and the Virginians. Nevertheless, the weroance's daughter favorably impressed the English captain, who wrote shortly thereafter how "for feature, countenance, and proportion, [she] much exceedeth any of the rest of [her father's] people." After hostilities between the two sides resumed a few months later, Powhatan sent his daughter with a diplomat to Jamestown to secure the release of several Powhatan prisoners. The mission succeeded and Pocahontas was thereafter a frequent and popular visitor to the capital, seeming to transcend the antagonisms generally dividing Powhatans and English.

The depth of these antagonisms became apparent in 1610 when full-scale war erupted between the two sides (see Powhatans and the Rise of Virginia on the Chesapeake later in this chapter). With epidemics also ravaging Indian communities, the English gradually gained the advantage. The war's turning point came in April 1613, when the Virginians captured Pocahontas and placed her in an English household. They hoped to use their prize captive as a bargaining chip with her father, but negotiations with him quickly collapsed. Meanwhile Pocahontas met Rolfe, ten years her senior, who began instructing her in Christianity and English customs. A mutual attraction developed, and soon the couple became engaged. Powhatan only learned of his daughter's engagement on the eve of the wedding. Calculating that the marriage would bring an end to his people's exhaustion from sickness and war, the old weroance consented and sent several representatives to the wedding.

For the widowed Rolfe's part, Pocahontas was a most attractive prospect. Only a handful of English women, most of them destitute servants beneath his class, lived in Virginia in 1614. Once she was baptized, Pocahontas was by far the colony's highest-ranking single woman. Rolfe sought approval of the marriage from Virginia's governor, Thomas Dale. Above all, Rolfe wanted to quell whisperings among some colonists that he was marrying above his social class and that his motives were less than pure. He loved Pocahontas, Rolfe insisted, despite the facts that her "education hath been rude, her manners barbarous, her generation accursed, and so discrepant in all nurture from myself." Dale readily approved; to him the wedding symbolized Virginia's victory over not only Powhatan power but over Indian culture and identity in the lower Chesapeake. The subsequent birth of the couple's son, Thomas, only solidified the new political relationship.

Emphasizing her father's position, colonial officials termed Pocahontas a "princess" and proudly displayed her in polite society, including the royal court, when she, her family, and several other Powhatans traveled to England in 1616. The tour was a triumph because the "princess" carried herself throughout with the bearing and dignity of royalty. When she died the next year from a contagious disease while about to sail home, the romance of her life became a tragedy.

Was Pocahontas a helpless female victim, passively manipulated first by her father and then by Rolfe and other Englishmen? Or was she an unusually shrewd, fully active participant in the events surrounding her life? The answer is less simple than either alternative suggests. One telling episode illustrates the complexity of Pocahontas's perspective. Shortly before her scheduled return from England, John Smith paid a visit. Immediately upon seeing her first English admirer, Pocahontas left the room and refused for several hours to speak with him. Finally returning, she roundly chastised the usually domineering Englishman for not visiting earlier, for deceiving and mistreating her father, and because "your Countriemen will lie much." Not only had Smith failed in his social obligations to her, he had failed her father, and his people had failed hers. Not even an invitation from the king to return had made her an English-woman.

We will never know what would have happened had Pocahontas lived to return to Virginia. In her absence, the Powhatans and English fought two more wars over a quarter of a century before the colonists crushed the Indians' ability to challenge them militarily. Back in Virginia, Rolfe gained wealth and more fame before dying in 1627.

Although neither Pocahontas nor Rolfe typified their societies, their union reflected a new kind of Indian-European relationship, one that emerged after 1600 as Europeans began establishing permanent American colonies. From the St. Lawrence to the Rio Grande—and particularly in the Northeast—European traders, officials, soldiers, missionaries, and farmers used the advantages afforded by epidemics and the attractiveness of their trade goods to insert themselves into indigenous, regional economic and political networks. For their parts, Native Americans either resisted such encroachments overtly or tried to use the newcomers to enhance their own regional power. Acting according to principles of reciprocity, Indians often accepted the presence of Europeans and some of their material and religious offerings, seeing them as especially useful in a world now shared with the newcomers. But once colonizers had achieved some degree of success, they attempted to assert authority over Indians without regard for reciprocity, in some cases forcing Native Americans to forsake their distinctive identities and values. On such occasions, even the most willingly bicultural Indians, such as Pocahontas, reaffirmed their allegiance to their people and their people's values.

STRUGGLING FOR POWER IN THE NORTHEASTERN INTERIOR: THE IROQUOIS VS. NEW FRANCE

Some of the most complex and ferocious struggles of the early and mid-seventeenth century were waged across a broad expanse of the St. Lawrence and Hudson valleys and around lakes Champlain, Ontario, and Erie. These struggles grew out of regional rivalries originating before Europeans arrived and during Indians' earlier exchanges with visiting European traders (see Chapters 1 and 2).

After 1600, a diverse range of Indian nations and confederacies played central roles in the region's conflicts. One source of their diversity was language. Speakers of languages in the Iroquoian family flourished west of Lake Champlain in two powerful confederacies, the Five Nations Iroquois and the Hurons, and in several nations on Lake Erie and the eastern shore of Lake Huron. Meanwhile, the Mahicans of the Hudson River valley spoke languages of the Algonquian family, as did the Montagnais (Innu) and Algonkins in the St. Lawrence River valley east of Lake Champlain.

In addition to language, other differences characterized the Indians of the northeastern interior. One difference had to do with subsistence economies, arising from the environmental divide that permitted the Iroquois, Hurons, and Mahicans to practice farming while shorter growing seasons limited or altogether prevented the Montagnais and Algonkins from doing so. The peoples of the region could also be distinguished by political organization. For all of them, political power lay at the level of the band or village. Closely related bands and villages had grouped themselves in tribes that kept the peace among them and advanced their common interests. Several groups of Iroquoian speakers, most notably the Iroquois and the Hurons, went further and formed powerful intertribal, or international, confederacies. Unlike Mississippian chiefdoms, these confederacies were not hierarchical or centralized political formations. Instead of a single paramount chief, a council of chiefs oversaw them. As the principal centers of power in the northeastern interior, the Iroquois and Hurons had been, for at least two centuries

prior to the establishment of European colonies, economic and diplomatic rivals (see Chapters 1 and 2).

In the first decade of the seventeenth century, two European nations—France and the Netherlands—stepped into the interior Northeast's welter of alliances and rivalries. The French and Dutch founded colonies in order to accumulate wealth and expand territorially at a time when imperial rivalries among western European nations were intensifying. Toward these ends, they sought access to the region's abundant sources of beaver and other animal pelts by forging alliances with Indians who appeared best positioned to assist them. The struggles involving Indians and Europeans took many forms, but rarely simply pitted Indians against Europeans. More typically, an alliance or coalition of Indians confronted a comparable combination of European and Indian peoples. Seeking to trade while also spreading Christianity through Jesuit missionaries, France sought to secure its own position while limiting the power of the Five Nations Iroquois Confederacy. While the French worked through their Indian allies, the Iroquois dominated their European partner, the Dutch. The contest between these two very different coalitions had widespread effects among northeastern Indians.

The Hurons: Power and Crisis, 1600–1648

As the new century began, France acted to strengthen its traders' position on the St. Lawrence River against encroachments by European rivals, particularly the English and Dutch. The initial beneficiaries of the new policy were France's Montagnais, Algonkin, and Huron trade partners who sought protection from attacks by the feared Mohawks of the Five Nations Iroquois Confederacy. In 1608 Samuel de Champlain established a trade-military post at Quebec, on the site of the abandoned town of Stadacona. In 1609 and again in 1610, he and several armed French soldiers, accompanied by Montagnais, Algonkin, and Huron warriors, decisively defeated Mohawk war parties on Lake Champlain and the Richelieu River, respectively. Iroquois warriors had until then been virtually invincible because their wooden shields had protected

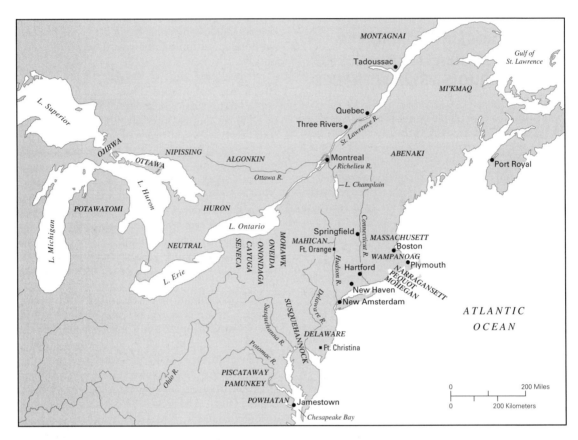

Native Peoples and European Colonies in the Northeast, 1645 Europeans of several nationalities occupied Indian homelands across much of the Northeast during the first half of the seventeenth century. *Source:* The Cambridge History of the Native Peoples of the Americas, *vol. 1: North America, Part 2, ed. Bruce G. Trigger and Wilcomb E. Washburn (Cambridge, U.K.: Cambridge University Press, 1996), 416.*

them against arrows, even those with metal tips fashioned from European objects. The victory thus represented a significant shift in the military balance of power in the Northeast. For while Europeans had used guns against Indians in the Southeast and Southwest during the sixteenth century, these two battles marked their first use as military weapons in the Northeast.

After the joint attacks on the Mohawks in 1609 and 1610, the key to French economic and political power on the St. Lawrence was the Huron confederacy. Realizing the size and extent of the Hurons and their trade connections, Champlain and some of his troops joined them in an attack on an Oneida Iroquois village in 1615. Although the

French were disappointed that they did not destroy the village, the Hurons considered the attack a major victory. The two assessments reflected the differences between French and Huron military goals. Rather than completely defeating the Iroquois, the Hurons were satisfied because they had avenged earlier Huron deaths at Oneida hands and because the French now considered the Hurons their most important ally.

During the 1620s, the Huron-French axis extended its power north of the St. Lawrence. Of the twelve thousand to twenty-two thousand pelts exported annually from New France, the majority had reached French traders via the Hurons. In return metal knives, axes, awls, arrowheads, and ket-

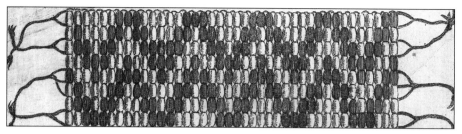

Wampum Strings and Belt Iroquois and other northeastern Indians used sacred purple and white shell beads (wampum) to express their peaceful intentions toward one another and to record their histories.

tles as well as glass beads flowed to the Hurons. Although Huron hunters exhausted the beaver population in their own land by 1630, the trade was barely affected. Huron men exchanged goods obtained from the French and corn grown by Huron women for furs with Ottawas, Neutrals, and other neighbors in present-day Ontario. These neighbors, in turn, traded with still more distant Indians as far north as Hudson Bay and as far west as Lake Superior. The Hurons also increased their trade with Indian peoples to the south for Chesapeake Bay shells used to make sacred wampum beads. As had been the case in the sixteenth century, European traders helped to stimulate the exchange of their own goods as well as those made by Indians. In the early years of their alliance, the arrival of the French enhanced rather than threatened Huron power and identity.

After a short-lived English occupation, the French returned to Quebec in 1632 and renewed their alliance with the Hurons. But the French now insisted that, as a condition of the alliance, the Hurons accept Jesuit missionaries in their villages. In 1634 three priests and some French workers entered Huron country, and others soon followed. The missionaries' arrival coincided with that of a smallpox epidemic that had broken out among New England Indians and the Iroquois during the preceding year (also discussed in The Rise of the Iroquois, 1600–1648, later in this chapter). For the Hurons, the outbreak was only the beginning of what proved to be a sequence of deadly diseases that swept through their communities over the next six years. Smallpox, measles, influenza, and other diseases contributed to a population decline of

more than half—from about twenty-one thousand to about ten thousand—during this brief period.

Like Europeans of the same period, the Hurons believed that spiritual forces hostile to humans caused most diseases and that the most destructive illnesses were due to witchcraft. But after accusing some of their own people, many Hurons began blaming the Jesuits. The missionaries' celibacy, their immunity from most illnesses, their mysterious ceremonies, and the fact that the sick people they baptized then died led the Hurons to see the Jesuits as practitioners of deadly witchcraft. If not for French threats to discontinue trading and to stop protecting them from the Iroquois, the Hurons would have killed the Jesuits or driven them from their country. Huron suspicions led most surviving converts to renounce Christianity in a traditionalist revival in 1639–1640. When the epidemics finally receded the next year, the Hurons assumed that they had triumphed over the alien force that had invaded their land and the bodies of many of their people.

The damage to their reputation prompted the Jesuits to take a new approach in their work among the Hurons. Since trade was the basis for the Hurons' connection with the French, they worked with French officials to offer inducements that would attract Huron traders to Catholicism. Beginning in 1643, Huron traders who were baptized paid lower prices for European goods than did non-Christian Indians. Unlike their countrymen, Christian Hurons were allowed to purchase guns, powder, and ammunition along with other goods. With these incentives, about five hundred Hurons converted to Catholicism over the next three years, forming a small but powerful minority.

At the Jesuits' urging, the converts abandoned their traditional religious beliefs and activities. Huron Christians kept their European trade goods for themselves and their families, rather than displaying the traditional generosity on which Hurons prided themselves and by which they provided for one another. They also declined to participate in ceremonies such as the Feast of the Dead in which all Hurons periodically gathered the bones of their recent dead for a mass reburial, a powerful means of renewing their group identity. The better-armed Christians even refused to fight alongside their non-Christian countrymen, a refusal that badly weakened Huron society in the face of Iroquois attacks.

The Christians' withdrawal from communal affairs resulted in severe, bitter factionalism among the Hurons. Fearing that the Jesuits were reviving their witchcraft and destroying Huron society, traditionalists ridiculed, threatened, and bribed Christians, expelled them from their wives' or mothers' longhouses, and even tried to seduce them. The disputes sometimes turned violent. By the late 1640s, Huron society was in crisis.

The Rise of the Iroquois, 1600–1648

As the Huron-French alliance developed on the St. Lawrence, the Hurons' Iroquois rivals established a European alliance of their own with the Netherlands, or Dutch Republic. Having recently overthrown Spanish rule, the Dutch were eager to join the European competition for wealth in North America and other continents. In 1609 an Englishman, Henry Hudson, led a Dutch expedition up the Hudson River. Although his contacts with local Munsee Indians at the mouth of the river were hostile, Hudson had a more satisfying encounter upriver with the closely related Mahican Indians. Dutch documents and a Munsee-Mahican oral account recorded in the eighteenth century both tell how the Dutch got some Mahicans drunk on alcohol, which they had never before tasted. Word of the beaver and otter skins Hudson obtained from the Mahicans attracted dozens of Dutch trading vessels over the next several years. In 1614 the Dutch West India Company established a trading post in Mahican country and concluded an agreement in which the Mahicans allowed the Mohawk

Iroquois and those Munsees living nearby to trade there. So began the colony of New Netherland.

Conflict between Mohawks and Mahicans erupted in the Mohawk-Mahican War (1624–1628) after the Mahicans invited the anti-Iroquois Montagnais and Algonkins, who were momentarily disaffected with the French, to trade at Fort Orange, as the Dutch post was now called. The Montagnais and Algonkins threatened the Mohawks' trade ties with the Dutch because the two Canadian tribes offered unusually thick beaver pelts originating in subarctic regions, which were far more desirable to European consumers than the thinner ones originating in Iroquois country. Resenting the invitation extended by the Mahicans, the Mohawks quickly and forcefully reacted, even capturing some Dutch troops trying to support the Mahicans. In no position to challenge the Mohawks, the Dutch withdrew from the conflict. By 1628, the Mohawks had soundly defeated the Mahicans. At Mohawk insistence, the Dutch barred all Indians except the Mohawks and Mahicans from trading directly at Fort Orange. Friendly Indians like the Munsees would have to furnish furs to Mohawk or Mahican intermediaries in exchange for Dutch goods, while enemies of the Mohawks or Mahicans would be denied access altogether.

The Mohawk-Mahican War is unusual because victorious Native Americans were not trying to expel Europeans, instead insisting that the Europeans remain but on the Indians' terms. In part, the war's outcome reflected the fact that while the Dutch were a maritime and commercial power, they were not a formidable military power and no match for Mohawk and other Iroquois warriors. The Mohawk-Dutch agreement that settled the conflict reflected Iroquois efforts to incorporate the Dutch into their web of reciprocal political relationships. Although no written record survives, later Iroquois speakers at treaty councils would refer to their earliest agreements with the Dutch, including that of 1628, as "covenants" binding the two peoples together with rope.

Like the Hurons, the Iroquois lost about half their people in the cycle of epidemics that swept through northeastern Indian societies, beginning with the smallpox outbreak of 1633. By 1640 the Iroquois, too, numbered only about ten thousand persons. In the face of such devastation, the Iroquois engaged in "mourning wars"—raids conducted against enemies for the express purpose of obtaining captives. Although mourning wars were a traditional means of replacing dead family members, their scale was now far greater than earlier raids that had netted one or a few captives. In 1634, for example, the year after the first epidemic, some Senecas returned from a raid with more than one hundred Huron prisoners. While some of the captives were ritually tortured and killed, most were adopted into families to replace those who had died.

Iroquois mourning wars escalated after 1639, when the Dutch West India Company opened Fort Orange to private traders, and particularly after 1643, when the Mohawks and Dutch signed their first formal treaty. Replacing their less formal agreements made of rope, the two peoples referred to their new alliance as a "chain" made of iron. Under its terms, the Mohawks pledged to assist the Dutch in their conflicts with coastal Munsee Indians (discussed in Munsees, Delawares, and Dutch later in this chapter). In exchange, the colonists added substantial quantities of guns, powder, and ammunition to the trade goods they sent via the Mohawks to all the Five Nations. Particularly effective in this regard was Arent van Curler, whom the Iroquois affectionately dubbed "Old Corlaer." Van Curler had arrived two years earlier as chief trading agent for the Dutch West India Company with a mandate to keep the company competitive with private traders. In 1642 he traveled to the three major Mohawk towns, at each stop presenting gifts like a prestigious chief rather than driving hard bargains. Although Van Curler's superiors complained that he was too generous with company assets, that very generosity raised the Dutch in Iroquois eyes and paved the way for the treaty of 1643. By placing reciprocity over profits when dealing with the Five Nations, "Old Corlaer" became a model with whom the Iroquois would compare later colonial agents and governors.

Iroquois Triumph, Huron Collapse, 1648–1660

Van Curler's generosity and the proliferation of other traders gave the Iroquois a distinct advantage over the Hurons among whom, as noted earlier, only Christians could buy guns. Over the course of the 1640s, guns became commonplace among the Iroquois, and many warriors became experts in shooting and repairing them. By 1648, the Iroquois had over 500 guns while the Hurons had no more than 120. With their advantage in weapons, the Iroquois escalated their raids into attacks on Huron settlements and trade flotillas. In one attack outside the walls of Montreal in 1643, armed Mohawks captured twenty-three Hurons, killing thirteen and returning home with the other ten. As in other such raids, they also seized "robes of Beaver without number," which they traded to the Dutch for more guns and other goods. In 1647, as the toll from the epidemics continued to mount, the Five Nations united for a series of massive assaults on the major Huron population centers. Said a Jesuit who had been a captive of the Mohawks: "So far as I can divine, it is the design of the Iroquois to capture all the Hurons, . . . put the chiefs and a great part of the nation to death, and with the rest to form one nation and one country."

The Iroquois assaults on the Hurons coincided with a deepening of the division within Huron society between traditionalists and Christians. With so many of their people being carried away by Iroquois or, as Christians, withdrawing from communal undertakings, the Hurons feared that their society was becoming irreparably split. Recognizing this, the Iroquois tempted the Hurons with peace offerings, appealing to those wishing to be reunited with captured relatives, to be secure from Iroquois attacks, and to be rid of the Jesuits' witchcraft. In April 1648 some Huron traditionalists tried to force the issue on their people by murdering a French missionary assistant and then demanding at a confederacy council meeting that the Jesuits be expelled. In this way they hoped to arouse French hostility toward the Hurons, giving their people no choice but to ally with the Iroquois. But while most Hurons opposed the Jesuits, they opposed the Iroquois even more resolutely. Accordingly, the council decided to pay reparations to the French for the death of their countryman, thereby maintaining the diplomatic status quo.

The Hurons' rejection of the proposed Iroquois alliance was a major victory for the Jesuits. Already the missionaries had begun easing requirements for Huron baptisms in order to effect mass conversions. Seeing no alternative to Iroquois attacks,

INDIAN VOICES   Kiotseaeton, Mohawk Iroquois Diplomat, 1645

Throughout history, nations have conducted diplomatic relations according to commonly accepted norms and protocols that are based on shared political and cultural values. When Indian and European nations began negotiating with one another, diplomats on each side encountered practices and values they found utterly strange. Not surprisingly, they never fully fathomed one another. Yet while "mutual misunderstanding," to use historian Richard White's term, characterized Indian-European diplomacy and often led to failure and intensified hostilities, diplomacy sometimes succeeded. It did so because, despite their differing practices and assumptions, each party recognized that the practice of diplomacy was rooted in ritual and symbols, the ruthless and successful manipulation of which was the key to success.

Among Native Americans, the Iroquois Confederacy employed perhaps the most elaborate protocols. The confederacy itself was the result of a peace treaty established among five previously warring nations by the prophet Deganawidah, who also instructed them in the presentation of wampum (sacred shell beads symbolizing one's peaceful intentions) in regularly renewing their confederacy (see Chapter 1). Subsequently the Iroquois broadened their diplomatic efforts to include neighboring Indians and then European colonizers. One of the most brilliant practitioners of Iroquois diplomacy during the mid-seventeenth century was a Mohawk named Kiotseaeton. In this selection, Kiotseaeton arrives at Three Rivers, in what is now Quebec, during a brief truce in the bitter conflict pitting the Iroquois against the Huron and Algonkin allies of New France. The French governor had convened the conference in hopes of making the truce permanent. A Jesuit missionary who was present recorded, through an interpreter, what was not simply a speech but a remarkable performance. Note how Kiotseaeton uses rhetoric and physical gestures, underscored by gifts of wampum belts, to impress the French with his people's generosity and desire for peace, all the while implying that the Hurons and Algonkins were deficient in these respects.

When all had assembled and had taken their places, Kiotseaeton, a tall man, rose to his feet and regarded the sun. He then cast his eyes over the whole company, took a wampum in his hand, and began to speak in a loud voice. "Onontio, lend me your ear. I am the mouth for the whole of my country. You listen to all the Iroquois in hearing my words. There is no evil in my heart. I have only good songs in my mouth. We have a multitude of war songs in my country, but we have cast them all to the ground. We no longer have any but songs of rejoicing."[1] Thereupon he began to sing, and as his countrymen responded, he walked about the great space as if on the stage of a theater. He made a thousand gestures, looking up to heaven, gazing at the sun, rubbing his arms as if he wished to draw from them the strength that moved them in war. After he had sung awhile, he said that the present that he held in his hand thanked Monsieur the governor for having saved the life of Tokhrahenehiaron when, last autumn, he pulled him from the fire and from the teeth of the Algonquins. But he complained gracefully that he had been sent back all alone to his own country. "If his canoe had been upset, if the winds had caused it to sink, if he had been drowned, you would have waited long for the return of the poor injured man, and you would have accused us of a fault which you yourselves have committed." When he had said this, he fastened his wampum at the appointed spot.

Drawing out another [wampum belt], he tied it to the arm of Guillaume Couture, saying aloud: "It is this collar that brings you back this prisoner. I would not have said to him, while he was still in our country: 'Go, my nephew. Take a canoe and return to Quebec.' My mind would not have been at rest. I would have been thinking over and over again to myself, 'Is he not lost?' In truth, I would have no sense, had I acted in that way. He whom you have sent back had all the difficulties in the world on his journey." . . . He took a stick, placed it on his head like a bundle, then carried it from one end of the square to the other, representing what that prisoner had done on the rapids and the fast-flowing waters. Arriving at these points, he had transported his baggage, piece by piece. [Kiotseaeton] went backward and forward, showing the portages and returns of the prisoner. He ran against a stone, retreating more than he advanced in his canoe, because alone he could not maintain it against the current. He lost heart and then regained his strength. . . . "And yet," said he, "if you had helped him to pass the rapids and the bad roads, and then if, while stopping and smoking, you had watched him from afar, you would have greatly consoled us. But I know not where your thoughts were, to send a man back quite alone amid so many dangers. I did not do that. 'Come, my nephew,' I said to him whom you see before your eyes, 'follow me, I wish to take you back to your country, at the risk of my life.'" That is what was said by the second wampum, which he tied next to the first.

The third [belt] bore witness that they had added something of their own to the presents that Monsieur the governor had given to the captive whom he had sent back to their country, and that those presents had been distributed to the nations who are allied to them, to arrest their hatchets and to cause the weapons and paddles to fall from the hands of those who were embarking to go to war. He named all those nations.

The fourth present was to assure us that the thought of their people killed in war no longer affected them, that they cast their weapons under their feet. "I passed by the place where the Algonquins massacred us last spring," he said. "I saw the spot where the fight took place in which they captured these two prisoners here. I passed by quickly, for I did not wish to see the blood that had been shed by my people. Their bodies still lie in that place. I turned away my eyes for fear of exciting my anger. Then, striking the earth and listening, I heard the voice of my ancestors massacred by the Algonquins. When they saw that my heart was capable of seeking vengeance, they called out to me in a loving voice: 'My grandson, my grandson, be good; do not get angry. Think no longer of us, for there is no means of bringing us back from death. Think of the living—that is the important thing—save those who still live from the sword and fire that pursue them. One living man is better than many dead ones.' Having heard those voices, I passed on, and I came to you, to deliver those whom you still hold."

The fifth [belt] was given to clear the river and to drive away enemy canoes, which might impede navigation. He made use of a thousand gestures, as if he had collected the waves and had caused a calm, from Quebec to the Iroquois country. . . .

The tenth [belt] was given to bind us all very closely together. He took hold of a Frenchman, placed his arm within his, and with his other arm he clasped that of an Algonquin. Having thus joined himself to them, he said, "Here is the knot that binds us inseparably. Nothing can part us." This belt was extraordinarily beautiful. "Even if the lightning were to fall upon us, it could not separate us, for if it cuts off the arm that holds you to us, we will at once seize each other by the other arm." And thereupon he turned around and caught the Frenchman and the Algonquin by their two other arms and held them so closely that he seemed unwilling ever to leave them.

The eleventh invited us to eat with them. "Our country is well stocked with fish, with venison, and with game. It is everywhere full of deer, elk, beaver. Give up," said he, "those striking hogs that run among your houses, that eat nothing but filth. Come and eat good meat with us. The path is clear. There is no longer any danger." He accompanied his discourse with appropriate gestures.

He lifted the twelfth belt to dispel the clouds in the air, so that all might see quite plainly that our hearts and theirs had nothing hidden, that the sun and the truth might spread their light everywhere.

The thirteenth was to remind the Hurons of their goodwill. "Five days ago," he said (and by this he meant five years), "you had a sack filled with wampum and other presents, all ready to come and seek for peace. Who made you change your minds? That sack will upset, the presents will fall out and break, they will be lost, and you will lose your nerve."

The fourteenth was to urge the Hurons to speak without delay, not to be bashful like women, and that they should resolve to go to the Iroquois land, passing by way of the country of the Algonquins and the French.

The fifteenth was to show that they had always desired to bring back Father Jogues and Father Bressani. They had thought that Father Jogues had been taken from them and they turned over Father Bressani to the Dutch because that was what he wanted.[2] "If he had been patient, I would have brought him back. How can I know now where he is? Perhaps he is dead, possibly drowned. It was not our intention to put him to death. If Francois Marguerie and Thomas Godefroy had remained in our country," he added, "they would have been married by this time, we would be but one nation, and I would be one of you."[3] (Father Jogues listened to this speech, then told us with a smile: "The stake was all prepared; had not God preserved me, they would have put me to death a hundred times. This good man says whatever he pleases." Father Bressani told us the same thing on his return.)

The sixteenth was to welcome them to this country when they came here and to protect them from the hatchets of the Algonquins and the cannons of the French. "When we brought back your prisoners some years ago, we thought that we would be your friends, but we heard arquebus and cannon shots whistling by on all sides. That frightened us and we withdrew, but we are brave in war, and so we decide to give proof of our courage the following spring. We made our appearance in your territory and captured Father Jogues, together with some Hurons."

The seventeenth present was the very beaded necklace that Honatteniate wore in his country. This young man was one of the two prisoners last captured. . . .

When this great Iroquois had said all that is mentioned above, he added: "I am going to spend the remainder of the summer in my country in games, in dances, in rejoicing for the sake of peace, but I fear that, while we dance, the Hurons will come to taunt and annoy us."

[1] Iroquoian- and Algonquian-speaking Indians in the Northeast referred to the governor of New France, Montmagny, as Onontio (Big Mountain), a literal Algonquian translation of his surname.

[2] Jogues and Bressani were Jesuit missionaries who had been captured separately by Mohawks while traveling near Huron country and were later released to the Dutch in New Netherland.

[3] Marguerie and Godefroy were French interpreters and traders whom the Mohawks had briefly held as prisoners in 1641.

Source: Abridged from *Jesuit Relations: Natives and Missionaries in Seventeenth-Century North America*, edited by Allan Greer. Copyright © 2000 by Bedford/St. Martin's. Reproduced by permission of Bedford/St. Martin's.

more Hurons began to convert. During the summer of 1648, 20 percent of the nation was Christian, and a year later fully half were converted. But whereas earlier converts were animated by the commercial incentives offered by the Jesuits, the new ones were motivated largely by fear. Having believed earlier that the Jesuits practiced witchcraft, they now expected that the priests' "magic" would somehow rescue them from the Iroquois.

Emboldened by the Indians' seeming passivity, the Jesuits sought to extend their reformation of Huron society even further. In the village of Ossossané, where Christians were now a majority, they persuaded the council to name a French priest as headman and completely eliminate all non-Christian ceremonies and behavior. Traditionalists had the choice of obeying or leaving the community. Such exercise of hierarchical, arbitrary authority was entirely foreign to Huron culture.

The Jesuits were prevented from executing their plans at Ossossané by the further escalation of Iroquois attacks. The mass conversions were occasioned by the destruction of several Huron towns. On a cold winter night in March 1649, 1,000 Iroquois warriors surprised the sleeping inhabitants of one town, also the site of a Jesuit mission, killing 390 of its 400 inhabitants. From there they launched attacks on several more Huron settlements in the surrounding countryside. By the time the Iroquois finally withdrew, they had slain 700 Hurons, successfully prevented most Huron women from planting their fields, and carried away hundreds of Huron captives.

Feeling powerless in the face of forces they could not control, starving Huron survivors erupted in panic and scattered. Some simply moved to secluded areas and hid. Others joined neighboring Indians such as the Algonkins, Petuns, or Neutrals (so-called because they had never taken sides in the Huron-Iroquois rivalry). Still others voluntarily moved into Iroquois society, often rejoining relatives captured earlier by the Iroquois. Finally, a significant number of Hurons remained with the Jesuits, but without adequate food, clothing, and shelter, many of them died during the winter of 1649–1650. In 1650 many remaining Huron Christians decided to join their kin among the Iroquois while the Jesuits led the remainder to Lorette, on the outskirts of Quebec City, where they established a community of their own.

Having destroyed the Huron Confederacy, the Iroquois went on to eliminate all remaining Huron resistance and to expand their own hunting territories. Accordingly, they extended their attacks to include neighboring groups with whom Hurons had sought refuge. By the mid-1650s they had dispersed the Petuns, Neutrals, Nipissings, and Eries, absorbing them and the Hurons into their own ranks or driving them out of their homelands. As a result, the Iroquois could now hunt beaver in the lands north of lakes Erie and Ontario.

The Beaver Wars (1648–1657), as the Iroquois wars against their Indian neighbors to the north are often called, also dealt a severe blow to New France's economy, based as it was on trade with the Hurons. As a result, the French were amenable to peace with the Iroquois. For their part the Iroquois were so eager to reconcile the many Huron Christians now living among them to life in the Five Nations that they agreed, in 1656 and 1657, to permit the Jesuits to establish missions in two of their nations, the Onondaga and Mohawk.

New Iroquois-French tensions quickly doomed the agreements. With the Hurons gone, Ottawa, Potawatomi, and Ojibwa Indians from the upper Great Lakes took over the transporting of furs from the Canadian interior to French traders in Montreal. Determined to halt this traffic, the Iroquois raided the Ottawas and their allies. The French now concluded that the Five Nations sought nothing less than to monopolize the fur trade in Canada as well as on the Hudson. Abandoning the Jesuit-inspired restrictions they had imposed on the Hurons, they provided their new Indian allies with enough guns, powder, and ammunition to protect themselves effectively against Iroquois attacks. Iroquois resentment against the French for arming their Indian enemies was compounded when an epidemic originating in the Jesuits' Mohawk mission spread among the Iroquois. Fearing the consequences of Iroquois hostility, the Jesuits abandoned their Iroquois missions in 1658 and returned to Canada.

The political and physical landscape of the northeastern interior was altered considerably during the first sixty years of the seventeenth century. The French had established themselves as a major colonial power and most of their Indian allies had suffered some loss of power. The most formidable source of resistance to the French were the Iroquois, who perhaps had adapted most successfully to the new colonial realities in the Northeast. Athough victorious, the Iroquois, like the allies of the French, paid a heavy price for French colonization.

COASTAL INDIANS AND EARLY EUROPEAN SETTLEMENTS

Several hundred thousand Indians inhabited the Atlantic coast and lower river valleys between the St. Lawrence River and Chesapeake Bay in 1600. Except for some recently arrived, Iroquoian-speaking Susquehannocks and Eries in the upper Chesapeake, all of them spoke one or another Algonquian language. As in the interior, short growing seasons prevented the most northerly Indians—in this case, Mi'kmaqs and most Abenakis—from cultivating the extensive food crops produced by Indians to the south. Coastal northeastern Indians also differed among themselves when it came to political organization. Around Chesapeake Bay, tribes and confederacies such as the Piscataways, Chickahominies, and Powhatans had consolidated considerable political authority in the hands of chiefs. By contrast, these chiefs' northern counterparts ruled more by persuasion than command and were more frequently ousted by their followers.

Northeastern coastal Indians confronted a different kind of colonial challenge than that faced by their contemporaries in the interior. Although traders and, in some cases, missionaries were present in seaboard colonies, their efforts were eventually subsumed by the desire of massive numbers of Dutch and, especially, English colonists to possess Native Americans' land.

Indians and the Emergence of New England

At the outset of the seventeenth century, Indians in what would become known as "New England" were more receptive to French than to English colonizers. As with the Montagnais on the St. Lawrence, the French moved in the first decade of the seventeenth century to strengthen earlier trade ties with the coastal Mi'kmaqs (see Chapter 2). In 1605 they established a permanent base at Port Royal, on the Bay of Fundy, near a Mi'kmaq village headed by Membertou, renowned as a spiritual, military, and political leader. Membertou used his people's relationship with the French to control trade between them and neighboring Indians. When in 1608 Abenakis to the south attempted to trade directly with the French and English, Membertou's Mi'kmaqs and their allies attacked an Abenaki village. The battle was decided when Mi'kmaqs armed with French muskets killed ten Abenakis, including two sachems. As in the battle of Lake Champlain (discussed earlier in this chapter), guns helped to determine the balance of military power on the Atlantic.

Meanwhile English expeditions were attempting to establish bases among coastal Abenakis and other Indians as far south as Cape Cod. English explorers generally alienated the Indians by fortifying themselves apart from their Native hosts, by refusing to exchange gifts with them, or by attempting to coerce them. At least seven English expeditions kidnapped Indians and took them to England. As with Spanish expeditions in the Southeast during the preceding century, such kidnappings had one of two purposes, either to gain slaves for sale to Caribbean planters or to so impress the captives with European power that they would assist and promote colonization in their homelands. As with earlier expeditions, most English kidnappings of Indians backfired.

The most serious setback for the English came in 1607 with the failure of a colony called Sagadahoc, established near some Abenakis. The Abenakis might have welcomed trade with the English, but they were dissuaded by two members of their community whom English explorers had forcibly carried to England two years earlier. At the urging of the returned captives, the Abenakis attacked the tiny outpost, killing eleven Englishmen. After enduring a harsh winter, the isolated, helpless colonists returned home. Equally damaging to the English reputation was the seizure in 1614 of about twenty-seven Wampanoags at Plymouth Bay and on Cape Cod. One of the Wampanoags, Squanto, would later return and aid the English colony of Plymouth.

While the English blundered, French traders met with success in eastern New England and, by 1614, were exporting thousands of pelts annually. But French trade brought disastrous results to the region's Indians. First the Mi'kmaqs, resenting the Abenakis for resuming trade with the French, attacked in 1615 and inflicted heavy casualties on the Abenakis, including their most revered sachem, Bashaba. In the following year a massive epidemic, probably a strain of plague, devastated coastal Indian societies allied to the French, indicating that French traders probably introduced the disease unwittingly. Many Indian communities, such as the Wampanoag village at Plymouth Bay, were vacated and others were reduced from several hundred people to a few dozen, including refugees from abandoned towns. Most estimates indicate that 90 percent of the coastal Indian population perished in this epidemic. The massive devastation from European diseases that had already been experienced by Indians in several other American regions had now reached the Northeast. An English observer, arriving at Plymouth Bay six years later, was astonished that even then he could see overgrown cornfields covered with the "bones and skulls" of the unburied dead.

In the aftermath of the epidemic, Mi'kmaqs from the north and Narragansetts from the west subjected surviving Abenakis, Massachusett Indians, and Wampanoags to raids for tribute. In this context, Wampanoags watched in November 1620 as about one hundred English colonists, later called "Pilgrims," arrived at Plymouth Bay aboard the *Mayflower*. After half the English died during the ensuing winter, the Wampanoags allied with the equally devastated newcomers. Relations went smoothly at first because the recently returned captive, Squanto, showed the settlers how to fertilize corn with fish. But the English regarded what the Wampanoags assumed was a relationship based on reciprocity as submission to the authority of Plymouth and the English crown. When some Indians balked at paying tribute in the form of corn, the colony collected it by threatening violence. Although the colonists in the fall of 1621 invited some Wampanoag leaders to celebrate the colonists' first successful harvest (in what has been misleadingly called the first Thanksgiving), other Wampanoags openly scorned Squanto and the leading Wampanoag sachem, Massasoit.

Meanwhile New Netherland extended its trading activities from the Hudson River eastward to Cape Cod. These activities intensified after 1622 when the Dutch learned of the high demand for wampum among interior Indians, especially the Iroquois. Thereafter they began supplying steel drills to coastal Indians from the Connecticut to the Delaware rivers in order to speed up the transformation of purple and white shells into the sacred beads. While keeping some wampum for their own ceremonies, burials, and exchanges, coastal Indians traded most of it to the Dutch, who included it among the goods they supplied to their inland Indian trade partners. Here as elsewhere Indian-European trade enhanced the exchange of indigenous products among Indians as well as their adoption of European items. In southernmost New England the Narragansetts and Pequots emerged as the groups controlling the exchange of goods between Dutch traders and Indian wampum producers.

Wampum spread to eastern New England in 1627 when the Dutch began selling it to Plymouth's traders. Plymouth hoped that wampum would give it a monopoly on European-Indian trade on the coast north of Cape Cod. But growing numbers of English fishers, traders, and farmers settled there during the late 1620s. Some of these groups incurred Indian hostility that was then directed at Plymouth while others established lucrative trade ties that threatened the colony's own trade. In 1629 a new era in the region's history began with the founding of a much larger Puritan-dominated colony, Massachusetts Bay.

The approximately one thousand settlers reaching Massachusetts in 1630 overwhelmed the two hundred Massachusett Indians who had survived the epidemic of the late 1610s. But the Indians' concerns were partially laid to rest after the Mi'kmaqs, fearing English retaliation, ceased their raids in 1631. English settlers began trading cloth and metal tools to the Massachusett Indians in exchange for corn, land, labor, and furs. But tensions arose because free-roaming English livestock invaded Indian cornfields, and because the colony expected Indians to obey its laws while avoiding social contacts with colonists. In 1633 the smallpox epidemic that swept the Northeast, striking the Huron and Iroquois, was particularly devastating for the Massachusetts, who had never recovered from the epidemic of 1616. The epidemic left the Massachusetts with just a few dozen survivors; among the casualties were their major sachems.

Although the epidemic made still more land available to the English, many colonists remained dissatisfied with the farming and commercial opportunities around Boston and turned their attention southward and westward. In so doing, they encountered, not the empty "wilderness" of Puritan writings, but dozens of Indian communities engaged in trading furs and wampum. But the trade was generating tensions, especially because of resentment among the Narragansetts and other Indians over Pequot attempts to control Indian-Dutch trade. In 1632, Massachusetts introduced a new factor into the regional balance of power by allying with the Narragansetts through their common ally, the Massachusett Indians. Soon thereafter the Narragansetts, along with the Mohegans and other Indians from the region, were at war with the Pequots. In order to control the violence among its clients, the Dutch established a post on the Connecticut River with the explicit proviso that all Indians could trade freely there. Like the Mohawks at Fort Orange a decade earlier, the Pequots attempted in 1634 to prevent rival Indians from dealing directly with Dutch traders at the post. On this occasion, however, Dutch troops were better prepared and pursued the Pequots, killing their charismatic sachem, Tatobem.

Already alarmed by the Dutch presence in territory they claimed for themselves, the English view of the Connecticut Valley had abruptly shifted after the smallpox epidemic of 1633–1634. A Dutch report estimated that 950 out of 1,000 residents of one village there had died. Whereas they had previously considered the Connecticut Valley too heavily populated by Indians, the English now saw it as ripe for settlement. In 1636, 800 settlers established a new colony, Connecticut, and a settlement–trading post stood at Springfield in western Massachusetts. In the same year, the Puritan dissenter Roger Williams forged an agreement with the Narragansetts and founded Rhode Island. With settlers still pouring into Massachusetts, New England's colonization now reached into Indian homelands far beyond the seaboard. (Approximately 20,000 English colonists would arrive by 1642.)

Anglo-Pequot tensions rose after English traders were murdered in two separate incidents. Although evidence of Pequot complicity was lacking, the English insisted that the Pequots turn over the perpetrators. The Pequots defied the English and appealed to their recent enemies, the Narragansetts, to join them, saying that the English "were strangers and began to overspread their country, and would deprive them thereof in time, if they were suffered to grow and increase." But the Narragansetts, whose rivalry with the Pequots in the wampum trade had become bitter, rejected the proposal. Meanwhile the Mohegans and their sachem, Uncas, discontented tributaries of the Pequots, broke with that tribe and reached an accommodation with the English. While the English ostensibly sought to avenge the two traders' deaths, their larger goal was to break Pequot power on the lower Connecticut River so as to give their settlers and

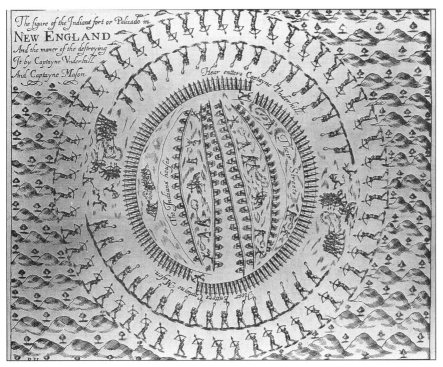

Attack on Pequot Village, 1637 In a print accompanying an English account of the time, English troops, backed by Mohegan and Narragansett allies, have surrounded the fortified village and are shooting at Pequot warriors. Shortly thereafter, the soldiers would burn the village and most of its civilian inhabitants.

traders a free hand there. With the Narragansetts and Mohegans nursing grievances of their own against the Pequots and eager to supplant them in the regional wampum trade, English diplomacy effectively deprived the Pequots of potential allies while securing significant Indian support for their expansion.

During the Pequot War (1637), English troops, along with Mohegan, Narragansett, and Massachusett warriors, advanced into Pequot country. The war's turning point was a predawn surprise attack on a fortified Pequot village at Mystic. Three hundred to eight hundred people, mostly noncombatant women, children, and elders, occupied the village at the time. Entering the village, the English set it afire and then cut down the astonished Pequots as they emerged from their wigwams. Narragansetts surrounding the outer palisade killed all but a dozen of those who escaped the village itself.

A new type of warfare, entailing massive casualties among noncombatants, which Europeans had introduced earlier to Indians in other regions, had now arrived in the Northeast.

Pequots who were not at Mystic, including their sachem, Sassacus, fled westward hoping to escape the English and find allies. Although the English and Mohegans hunted down and killed or captured most of them, Sassacus and about forty others crossed the Hudson River to seek refuge and support from the Mohawk Iroquois. But the Narragansetts had already secured Mohawk allegiance with a large gift of wampum. So the Mohawks attacked the Pequots and killed most of them, including Sassacus.

The Treaty of Hartford (1638), imposed by Connecticut, declared the Pequot nation to be dissolved and dispersed its surviving members among the victors. Those sent to the English were enslaved, some entering local households and others being sold to English slave traders bound for the West Indies. The remaining Pequots lived in two villages, one paying tribute to the Mohegans, the other to the Narragansetts.

Almost immediately the victorious alliance became divided as Mohegans and Narragansetts competed for allies among Indians in the Connecticut Valley and on Long Island Sound and for the support of the English colonies. While the Narragansetts won the support of most New England Indians, the Mohawks, and the dissident colony of Rhode Island, the other English colonies (Massachusetts, Connecticut, Plymouth, and New Haven) favored the Mohegans.

Although war nearly broke out between the two sides on several occasions during the next quarter century, peace always prevailed because elite English traders were among those who depended on the Narragansetts and their allies—coastal Indians who produced wampum and interior Indians who produced furs. Indian women in coastal communities gathered the special purple and white shells used for wampum beads during the fall gathering season. With steel drills provided by the traders, they spent winters drilling and stringing the beads. Coastal Indians traded some wampum to the Narragansetts who in turn gave some of what they collected to the Mohawks, whose support they valued as a discouragement to English attacks. They sold other wampum to traders, such as Springfield's William Pynchon, in exchange for European metal goods, cloth, and glass beads. The traders took the wampum and included it with the European goods they exchanged with interior Indians for beaver pelts.

The result of these many transactions was a heightened interdependency of Indians and English. The fur and wampum trade provided capital for the colonies and material goods for participating Indians. Despite these changes, Native Americans in southern New England retained their distinct way of life. Instead of participating fully in the English economy, they used the wampum and goods they acquired for their own purposes. With cloth, needles, and scissors, they fashioned new clothing styles. New England Indians used wampum in ceremonies and to strengthen alliances, particularly with the Mohawks, which offset their dependence on the English. And they included all these items as grave goods to accompany them in their journeys to Cautantowwit's house, where the souls of the dead were thought to dwell.

On the coast, the few dozen remaining Massachusett Indians were surrounded by thousands of settlers. In 1644 their sachems agreed to place the Massachusetts and their lands under Massachusetts' jurisdiction. Two years later the colony banned traditional religious practices and authorized a Puritan minister, John Eliot, to "civilize" and Christianize the Massachusetts. Eliot recognized that the Massachusetts' world had been utterly transformed as newcomers streamed in and their own people died off, as new material goods replaced traditional ones, and as the English pressured them to give up more land. While Eliot secured Native communities against English encroachments by designating those dominated by Christians as "praying towns," he also attempted to enforce religious and cultural conformity within the praying towns. The missionary denounced the Indians' traditional powwows (medicine men) as ineffective charlatans and their traditional beliefs and practices as sinful and "savage." By confessing their sins and repudiating their pasts, Eliot maintained, Indians could start new lives.

Many Massachusett Indians listened to Eliot's teachings and some professed their allegiance to Christianity. Having seen the destruction of much of their traditional world, these so-called "praying" Indians concluded that they had to build entirely new lives by recognizing the Christian God's grace and confessing to their sins. Many cited the effects of the epidemics on their decisions. "I see God is angry with me for all my sins," confessed Robin Speen, a former Massachusett powwow, "and he hath afflicted me by the death of three of my children." But others were skeptical. One sachem charged that Eliot's warnings about hell were designed "to scare us out of our old Customs, and bring us to stand in awe of" the English.

The Puritans' Christian message had particular implications for Indian men and women who were married. One Massachusett Indian woman, Sarah Ahhaton, grew dissatisfied when her Christian husband began insisting that she obey him without question and beating her when she did not. The husband had taken to heart Christian notions of patriarchy in household governance. Finally, Ahhaton left him for a non-Christian Indian man, an action that would have been unremarkable before the advent of English colonization. Her husband thereupon complained to the praying town's Indian magistrate, who charged Ahhaton with the new crime of adultery. For reasons that are unclear, Ahhaton soon had second thoughts, returned to the town, and threw herself on the mercy of the court. After serving several months in prison, she returned to her Christian husband.

Although the Ahhatons appear to have adopted Anglo-Christian norms, the praying towns often reinforced rather than undermined the Indians' old ways. Because most colonists remained hostile toward all Indians regardless of their religion, the towns were isolated from English influences other than the missionaries. Given the opportunity to elect magistrates who would dispense justice in each town, praying Indians usually chose the sachems who already exercised such powers. Instead of living in the towns and farming year-round, residents retained their "wandering ways," as the English termed their mobile subsistence patterns, and their contacts with non-Christian Indians. Praying Indians traded many of the tools and other goods they received for their "civilization" to non-Christians or took them to their graves. Rather than following Eliot's formula unquestioningly, they drew selectively from his message in reconstituting their communities and their culture in a world now dominated by the English. In this way they retained their Indian identities even while adopting many of the innovations introduced by the newcomers.

Munsees, Delawares, and Dutch

South of New England, between the lower Hudson and lower Delaware valleys, was the homeland of the closely related Munsee and Delaware Indians. Across this area, an estimated ten thousand people lived in about forty communities, most of them along rivers or the shores of bays and smaller coastal inlets. Although Munsees and Delawares were closely tied together as peoples through language, ethnicity, and culture, their villages were autonomous and not politically unified like those of the Iroquois and the Chesapeake Bay chiefdoms. Consequently, neither Munsees nor Delawares pursued a single policy in dealing with the Dutch.

Whereas inland Munsees living near Mahican country were enveloped in the tumult surrounding the Mohawk-Mahican War discussed earlier, Indian-Dutch relations nearer the Atlantic coast were initially harmonious. A Dutch trading post on the lower Delaware River, established at about the same time as Fort Orange, developed lucrative ties with nearby Delaware villages while Dutch traders flocked to Munsee communities on the lower Hudson and western Long Island. These ties deepened in 1622 after wampum production gave an added dimension to Dutch-Indian trade. The trade intensified still further in 1626 when Munsees at Canarsee (modern Brooklyn) ceded Manhattan Island to New Netherland in exchange, not for the useless "trinkets" of popular legend, but for cloth, copper, iron tools, and steel drills for making wampum beads. The colony soon established its new capital of New Amsterdam on the island. By drawing the Dutch close to their village, the Canarsee Munsees enhanced their position in regional networks through which both indigenous and European goods circulated. Over the next several years these networks broadened as Munsees around Manhattan provided maize as well as pelts to Dutch traders.

During the 1630s Munsee-Dutch harmony gave way to tensions. Contributing to the tensions were a sharp rise in the number of land-seeking immigrants to New Netherland, a decline in the beaver population due to the Indians' commercial overhunting, and Munsee population losses from epidemics. Seizing on their vulnerability, Governor Willem Kieft pressured the Munsees to sell large parcels of land and imposed a heavy tax on them. The colony's efforts to collect the tax by force led some Munsees to resist violently. Deciding to extirpate coastal Munsees altogether, the governor launched Kieft's War (1643–1645). The war began with a surprise massacre of two separate Munsee groups that had camped near New Amsterdam, seeking Dutch protection from Mohawks, on whom Kieft had called for assistance under terms of the treaty of 1643 (discussed earlier). Recognizing the fate in store for them, other Munsees began attacking colonists and destroying their property. Soon no Dutch farm or village outside New Amsterdam was safe from Indian attacks. Peace was only restored after officials in the Netherlands became concerned that Kieft's actions were proving expensive and would render the colony unlivable

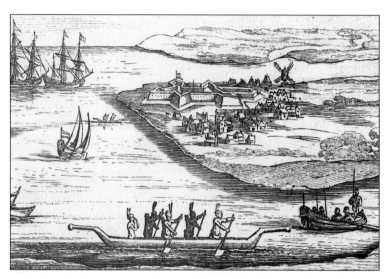

Indians at New Amsterdam During the early decades of the seventeenth century, Indian canoes as well as European ships were a regular presence at the Dutch settlement.

for Europeans. They recalled the governor in 1645, by which time the war had cost more than one thousand Munsees lives.

Although less pressured by immigrants than the Munsees near New Amsterdam, Delaware Indians expelled the Dutch traders from their post on the Delaware River in 1632. Six years later, they welcomed Swedish traders and farmers, rivals of the Dutch, who established the colony of New Sweden nearby (discussed in the next section).

In New Netherland, the end of Kieft's War proved to be a truce rather than a permanent peace. Dutch immigration, which halted during the conflict, resumed on an even larger scale thereafter. From a population of about fifteen hundred in 1640, New Netherland's population rose to four thousand in 1650 and to nine thousand by 1664. Most of the immigrants were farm families who occupied land on which Munsees still depended for hunting and gathering. Hostile encounters increased as hungry Indians stole Dutch livestock or robbed and assaulted colonists, often with guns bought from Dutch traders. Disputed land purchases, in which Munsees argued that they had not

been fully compensated, added to the tensions. The Peach War (1655) broke out after a colonist supposedly shot a Native woman who was picking peaches from his tree. Some Munsees seized several dozen Dutch hostages for use as diplomatic bargaining chips. The strategy paid off because the Dutch were themselves militarily vulnerable. Their troops had just exhausted most of their supplies while seizing New Sweden. Meanwhile English colonists on Long Island (part of New Netherland) refused to furnish troops because England and the Netherlands were now enemies. The result was a standoff in which the Munsees returned the hostages and some of the land they had seized and the colonists ceased harassing them.

The reduction in tensions did not extend upriver to the homeland of the Esopus Munsees, who resented encroaching Dutch settlers. After an Indian killed a Dutch farmer in 1658, Governor Peter Stuyvesant demanded that the Esopus cede half their land. The Esopus agreed to the demand, but expected gifts and consideration of their grievances in return. The bitter Esopus Wars (1658–1660 and 1663–1664) finally ended with the Dutch and their

Mohawk allies crushing the Esopus, but at enormous cost to the virtually bankrupt colony.

Piscataways and Susquehannocks in the Upper Chesapeake

South of the Delawares' homeland lay the Chesapeake Bay, a large body of water into which several major rivers flowed, linking thousands of Indians on its eastern and northern shores with interior Indians ranging from the Iroquois in the north to the Cherokees in the south. Although the Chesapeake by 1600 had become an important site of Indian-European trade, Anglo-Powhatan warfare in Virginia (discussed in the next section) isolated Native Americans in the upper bay from European traders until the late 1620s. Thereafter, Virginia's commercial success made the upper Chesapeake attractive to potential tobacco planters seeking land as well as to Indians and Europeans interested in trade. The result was deadly competition. At the center of this competition were two major Indian powers, the Algonquian-speaking Piscataways, a formidable chiefdom on the lower Potomac River, and the Iroquoian-speaking Susquehannocks, a confederacy of five nations situated along the Susquehanna River.

In 1627 Virginia traders began regular exchanges with the Piscataways and their neighbors on the western shore of the upper Chesapeake. This activity drew the attention of the inland Eries who had forcibly sought to control Indian-European trade in the area during the late sixteenth century (see Chapter 2). In similar fashion, the Eries attacked and killed about one thousand Piscataways in 1631, obliging the Piscataways to grant them access to the traders when they visited each spring.

Already weakened by the Erie attack, the Piscataways in 1634 confronted a group of English Catholics seeking permission to settle on their land. Unwilling to resist the newcomers directly, the wary Piscataway tayac (chief) Wannas told Governor Leonard Calvert that "he would not bid him goe, neither would he bid him stay, but that he might use his own discretion." Deciding that discretion was the better part of valor, Calvert took his followers downriver to land recently vacated by local Indians, where he founded the colony of Maryland.

As Maryland grew, some Piscataways, including Wannas's own brother, Kittamaquund, began to see the colony as a major source of European goods and as a potential source of protection from the Eries. When Wannas declined to accommodate the English, Kittamaquund assassinated his brother in 1636, succeeded him as tayac, and immediately made peace with the colonists. Although most Piscataways distrusted Kittamaquund, his support by the English discouraged opposition and enabled him to control trade between them and his people as well as with neighboring Indians. In 1639 an English Jesuit missionary, Andrew White, arrived in Maryland and quickly converted Kittamaquund, who gave up his multiple wives, sent his daughter to an English Catholic school, and otherwise adopted many of the trappings of "civilization." By 1642 White had baptized 130 Piscataways. Although the Piscataways retained their distinctive identity, they had lost much of the power and autonomy they had enjoyed as recently as a decade and a half earlier.

As Maryland established its trading primacy in the northern Chesapeake, it confronted the powerful Susquehannocks. The Susquehannocks had tried during the 1610s to trade with the Dutch on both the Hudson and the Delaware rivers, but they were excluded by their Mohawk, Mahican, and Delaware rivals. As with the Piscataways, the advent of English traders from Virginia in the late 1620s restored the Susquehannocks' direct access to European goods. But in 1638 Maryland barred both Virginians and Susquehannocks from trading in the upper Chesapeake and Delaware bays. Recognizing their common grievances against neighboring Europeans, the Susquehannocks and Delawares submerged their differences and jointly welcomed the establishment of New Sweden on the Delaware River in 1638. After Susquehannock-English tensions flared in 1642, Maryland troops routed some Susquehannocks merely by firing their guns. Turning to their Swedish trade partners, the Susquehannocks obtained guns of their own. When the next English expedition approached them, the newly armed Susquehannocks prevailed, capturing fifteen troops and two artillery pieces. The Susquehannocks then attacked and destroyed the Jesuit mission to the Piscataways. As a result of this victory, Susquehannocks and Swedes gained control of the trade in furs and European goods on the Susquehanna River.

While Swedish arms gave them advantages over coastal neighbors, the Susquehannocks were no match for the heavily armed Five Nations Iroquois to the north. After the Iroquois finished dispersing the Hurons and their neighbors in the Beaver Wars, a large Mohawk force attacked the Susquehannocks in the winter of 1651–1652. According to a Jesuit report, the victorious Mohawks carried off more than five hundred Susquehannock captives. To bolster their strength against the Iroquois, the Susquehannocks signed a treaty with their other enemies, the English of Maryland, who provided them with many more arms than could New Sweden. Besides furnishing Maryland's traders with beaver pelts, the Susquehannocks agreed not to contest Maryland's claims to land on Chesapeake Bay. The new alliance proved timely for the Susquehannocks when in 1655 the Dutch conquered New Sweden and annexed it to New Netherland, ally of the Iroquois.

Powhatans and the Rise of Virginia on the Chesapeake

On Chesapeake Bay south of the Potomac River, the powerful weroance Powhatan continued to expand his chiefdom of the same name as the seventeenth century began. After Roanoke's demise (see Chapter 2), as epidemic diseases took their toll among his own people and their neighbors, Powhatan had used intimidation and warfare to incorporate most Indians on the lower Chesapeake Bay other than the defiant Chickahominies and the Chesapeake Indians into a paramount chiefdom. Moreover, he had established firm alliances northward to the Potomac River and on the Chesapeake's eastern shore. As a result of his efforts, the depopulated Indians of the lower bay were a far more formidable force when confronting outsiders—European or Indian—than they would otherwise have been.

Besides Massachusetts, the other major English colony established during the early seventeenth century was Virginia, begun in 1607—the same year as the failed Sagadahoc colony on the Kennebec (see Indians and the Emergence of New England earlier in this chapter). The Powhatans initially welcomed the newcomers and furnished them with corn in exchange for copper, glass beads, and other goods. But as in so many early colonial efforts, Europeans' insistence that Indians supply them with food as well as submit to their political authority undermined this goodwill. By December, as their own supplies dwindled, the Powhatans and their allies stopped selling corn to the English. After the Powhatans captured John Smith and he met Pocahontas, Powhatan and Smith sealed an alliance, agreeing that Powhatan would be a "father" to the English. As a good father, he supplied his children with ample corn, enabling Virginia—unlike Sagadahoc—to survive its first winter.

Relations chilled the following year when the English attempted to reverse Smith's submission to Powhatan by staging a ceremony in which the weroance would defer to them. First Powhatan refused to go to the colony's capital at Jamestown for his "coronation," insisting that Christopher Newport, now Virginia's highest-ranking official, come to him. Once at Powhatan's village, the English tried to get the weroance to kneel so they could place a copper crown on his head and scarlet robe on his shoulders, and designate him a vassal of King James I. But Powhatan refused to kneel, clearly recognizing that to do so would be to submit to English authority over him and his people. Only after pushing him so that "he was a little stooped" did the English get the crown on his head. Powhatan finally accepted the crown and robe and reciprocated by presenting Newport with his cloak, or mantle (see People, Places, and Things), and what an Englishman termed "his old shoes."

Despite the appearance of reciprocity in the exchange, the Powhatans recognized and resented the colonists' insult. During the winter of 1608–1609, they tried to starve the English out by refusing to sell them corn. Smith went to several Indian villages and forced the residents at gunpoint to hand over corn, even though the harvest that year was poor. At one village they limited their demands because of the "complaints and tears from women and children." Virginia's third winter was harder still. Smith returned to England while more colonists arrived with inadequate food. By spring, 120 of the 220 English had died.

The balance of power shifted later in 1610 when more colonists, more food, and a new set of lead-

PEOPLE. PLACES, THINGS

Powhatan's Mantle

Powhatan's Mantle

During the complex diplomatic maneuvering by Powhatan leaders and Virginia officials in 1608, the weroance Powhatan presented a deerskin cloak, or mantle, to Captain Christopher Newport. Subsequently an English visitor to Virginia obtained the mantle and listed it in a catalogue, dated 1656, of "curiosities"—objects originating in "exotic" lands. Subsequently, another collector bought the mantle and donated it to Oxford University, which retains it to this day.

The mantle, about 7 feet 8 inches by 5 feet 3 inches, consists of four deerskins stitched together with sinew and adorned with figures consisting of tiny shell beads. Indians in the Chesapeake region called the shells roanoke while coastal and interior Indians to the north referred to similar beads they used as wampum. At the center stands a human figure, probably Powhatan himself. The figure is flanked on each side by a mammal, a wolf or mountain lion on the viewer's left and a deer to the right. Precisely what the animals represent is unclear, but they could either stand for clan totems or serve as reminders of these animals' special powers. The remaining thirty-four figures, in which the shells form round spirals, apparently stand for the tributary communities comprising Powhatan's chiefdom. The number corresponds to the figure recorded by English observers at the time. Although we cannot ascertain the meaning of all its details, the mantle stands as a record of Powhatan's power when first encountering the Virginians.

ers arrived in Virginia. After Powhatan refused to submit to the new governor and to return some English captives, an English expedition burned the village of Passapegh, killing most of the men, women, and children who lived there. Thus began the First Anglo-Powhatan War (1610–1614), during which the English continued to settle on the lands of the Powhatans and their tributaries while the Indians launched surprise raids on English farms and settlements. The war ended only when Powhatan agreed to the marriage of Pocahontas and John Rolfe, in effect, recognizing Virginia's independence from his chiefdom.

With the two sides at peace, Rolfe began a new direction for the colony by introducing a Caribbean strain of tobacco called Orinoco that had proven successful when grown as a cash crop. Rolfe and Pocahontas sailed in 1616 for England (where she would die in 1617), as aspiring planters swarmed to Virginia to grow the plant and get rich. More than 600 arrived in 1617. The settlers were so single-minded in pursuing the new crop that they relied on the Powhatans to provide them not only with corn but with drinking water (for they had polluted their own supply) and meat, which Indians procured with guns and powder furnished by the English. In 1619 the Virginia Company provided added incentives for prospective settlers, so that the number of immigrants began surpassing 1,000 per year (although diseases and malnutrition among indentured servants kept the English population at only 1,240 by the beginning of 1622).

Meanwhile Powhatan had died and leadership of the vast chieftainship and system of alliances passed to his younger brother, Opechancanough. Opechancanough initially favored the English, granting them additional land and encouraging the Anglican lay missionary George Thorpe, who preached to the Powhatans. Thorpe urged the Indians to live among the English and converted some to Christianity. But the influx of immigrants, their rapid expansion across the land, and their aggressive behavior concerned a growing number of Powhatans. The anti-English Indians were led by a medicine man named Nemattanew, whom the English called "Jack of the Feathers" for an elaborate costume he wore. Powhatan resentment toward the English crystallized after a settler shot and killed Nemattanew in the fall of 1621, but the Indians momentarily concealed their anger and awaited an opportunity to take revenge.

That opportunity came on the morning of March 22, 1622, when hundreds of Powhatans went unarmed into English yards and homes throughout the colony. Welcomed by the settlers as had become customary, the Indians picked up axes, knives, and whatever other weapons were at hand and attacked their hosts. But some Indians, especially Christian converts, refused to participate, and one of them had alerted the English. As a result only 347 colonists, over one-fourth of the total number, were killed. The remaining English launched a second Anglo-Powhatan War (1622–1632) with the goal of exterminating the Indians. Although they did not eliminate the Powhatans altogether, the colonists did drive them from the lower James and York rivers so that Virginia gained three hundred thousand additional acres for tobacco production. By 1634 the immigrant population (in spite of continued high servant mortality) was about 5,200.

Although Powhatan-Virginia hostilities formally ceased in 1632, tensions persisted, primarily because Virginia entered upon a tobacco boom in which the hunger for land was greater than ever. From 5,200 colonists in 1634, Virginia's non-Indian population rose to 8,100 in 1640. While the English formally purchased some Indian land, they simply claimed most of it as "empty." By 1644 English planters had expanded their production of tobacco to additional lands on the York as well as to the Rappahannock and Potomac rivers. Tensions

revived because the English made peremptory demands for food (which most tobacco planters still did not grow for themselves), because Indians sometimes stole from their more prosperous English neighbors, and because resentments on both sides sometimes resulted in violence and death.

In a last, desperate attempt to drive out the colonists, the Powhatan weroance, Opechancanough—now nearly one hundred years old and riding on a litter—led his people and their allies in a surprise uprising in April 1644. The Native Americans killed about four hundred English and took many prisoners before withdrawing to their villages. The Indians' withdrawal enabled the English to plan and organize their response. Militia companies dispersed over the countryside, mounting effective attacks on Powhatan, Weyanock, Nansemond, Pamunkey, Appamattuck, and Chickahominy villages. After refusing to talk peace with Virginia, Opechancanough was captured in March 1646 and taken to Jamestown where, in defiance of Governor William Berkeley's orders, a soldier shot and killed the elderly, disabled weroance. The Indians' defeat and Opechancanough's death marked the end of the Powhatan chiefdom, the dominant force among Indians on the lower Chesapeake for most of the preceding century.

In dealing with the defeated Indians, the English decided it would be convenient to have a single individual recognized as head of all Indians so that they could negotiate with that person alone rather than with various village heads. Thus the treaty of 1646 designated a Pamunkey weroance, Necotawance, as the "emperor" of all Virginia's Indians. Despite being an emperor, Necotawance was also a vassal of the king of England, a position that Powhatan had rejected during the mock coronation of 1608. Under the terms of the treaty, the Indians paid a tribute of twenty beaver skins per year, could sell land only with the colony's permission, and could not enter territory designated as settled. Like Necotawance, their succeeding emperors would be appointed by the colony. While the Indians had to turn over to the English all the prisoners and guns they had seized, the colonists kept their Native prisoners as servants or slaves.

Living close to English neighbors brought new difficulties for the Indians, especially as tobacco production continued to expand. When English livestock trampled on Indians' corn, the Indians complained or shot the offending animals. The free-ranging livestock, along with the English, who cleared the land and hunted down wild animals, deprived the Indians of vital sources of food. Although severely constricted, the surviving Powhatans, Pamunkeys, and other Indians recognized Necotawance as their new paramount chief, retained their older national identities, and generally persisted, contrary to English expectations that they would soon disappear.

CONFRONTING SPANISH EXPANSION IN THE SOUTHEAST AND SOUTHWEST

In 1600, Spain was the only European power with outposts on North American soil. But in the aftermath of the revolts by the Guales in Florida and Ácoma pueblo in New Mexico (see Chapter 2), Spain seriously considered abandoning its costly North American ventures. But before it could do so, the insistence and offers of subsidies by the Franciscan order of Catholic missionaries provided a means to maintain and expand the two colonies. At the same time, the emergence of a powerful English colony on the Chesapeake persuaded Spanish officials that they needed to colonize north of the West Indies and Mexico in order to protect their wealthy empire from European competitors.

Guales, Timucuas, and Apalachees in Florida

As the seventeenth century began in Florida, Spain finally crushed the Guale revolt. Traumatized and seeing no other hope for survival, the remaining Guales and their Timucua neighbors reaffirmed their loyalty to Spain and their desire for missionaries. From the end of the revolt in 1603, the mission system expanded rapidly across the Spanish colony. By 1616 twenty-one Franciscans ministered to the Guales, a figure that doubled by 1630, as the missionaries moved into Timucua country. The system expanded even more rapidly after 1633 as many

Apalachees began accepting baptism. By 1646 there were about fifty Franciscans actively working among the Guales, Timucuas, and Apalachees in Florida.

Although the Franciscans claimed thousands of converts by 1660, the reality of epidemics, forced labor, and Native uprisings limited their successes. During the 1610s alone, about half the sixteen thousand Guales in communities linked to missions died in epidemics. With their medicine men powerless to destroy the diseases and their chiefs unable to organize resistance to Spanish power, many Indians came to accept the missionaries for the spiritual powers they appeared to possess. Aside from Christian artifacts such as bibles and priests' vestments, virtually every material object as well as every item of food at the missions was produced by Indian labor. Indians grew wheat in the winter as well as corn in summer, presenting portions of the crops to the missionaries as offerings for the dead. The Franciscans consumed some of this grain themselves and Indians transported the rest to St. Augustine to supply the Spanish population there.

Most Indians found the Franciscans' moral strictures difficult to obey. The missionaries complained that even devout converts retained second and third wives, participated in traditional ceremonies, and continued to play a ball game called *pelota*. Varying versions of the game had been played for centuries in most Southeastern societies. The games and the ceremonies and festivities that accompanied them were major public events that reinforced group identity within chiefdoms. But the Franciscans saw them as pagan and tried to prohibit the Indians from holding them. Besides outlawing traditional practices, the Franciscans inflicted arbitrary and cruel punishments, refused to compensate Indians for the food they provided, and interfered in their private lives and their relations with non-Christian Indians, even relatives. Because of the harsh discipline meted out by Spanish missionaries and plantation owners, many Florida Indians fled to more remote, non-Christian villages where the Franciscans had not established missions.

Two byproducts of the Franciscan project were violence and factionalism among Indians. Native resentment turned violent in 1647 when traditionalist, anti-Christian Apalachees attacked the missions in their country and killed three of the eight friars. After defeating the first Spanish troops sent

Timucua Sporting Contests The Timucuas engaged in a variety of games and sports, including a game that resembled basketball. Because the contests had religious significance for the Timucuas, Spanish Franciscan missionaries banned them as "pagan."

against them, the traditionalists were suppressed by a second expedition that was aided by Apalachee Christians. Quickly recovering, the Franciscans dispatched more friars to Apalachee and reopened the devastated missions.

An even more serious uprising began among the Timucuas in 1656. The Timucuas had been suffering from a series of smallpox and other epidemics since 1649. Then in 1655 Governor Diego de Rebolledo ordered each Timucua to carry seventy-five pounds of maize to St. Augustine to relieve an acute shortage there. With sickness already limiting their food production and their capacity for hard labor, the Timucuas were hard pressed to honor the governor's order. Rebolledo also undermined the political structure of Indian communities and of the mission system itself by including the Timucua chiefs in his order. As in Spain and other European societies, Native heads of state in the Southeast did not perform hard labor. To demand that they do so was to demean them and challenge their authority. Even the Franciscans found Rebolledo's de-

mands too extreme and attempted to persuade the governor to modify his order. When he refused, eleven Timucua chiefs mobilized their people to defy him. The rebellious chiefs were captured by Spanish troops and executed by garroting. Authorities in Spain later punished Rebolledo for his cruelty, but his actions further undermined Timucua respect for colonial authorities at a time of great hardship.

By the end of the 1650s, colonization had cost thousands of Indian lives in Florida through repeated epidemics and violent, heavy-handed efforts to impose Spanish power, forced labor, and Catholic Christianity. While such efforts initially intimidated many Indians, most Native Americans deferred only temporarily. Spain remained unable to break the determination of Indians in Florida to remain politically and culturally independent. Nearly a century after founding St. Augustine (see Chapter 2), Spanish officials and missionaries had not found a way to neutralize Indians' resistance to colonization.

Pueblos, Apaches, and Navajos in New Mexico

During the early and mid-seventeenth century, the Pueblo Indians remained the focus of Spanish colonial efforts west of the Mississippi River. As in Florida and elsewhere, Spanish colonizers profoundly affected the lives of the indigenous peoples they sought to rule. But because Pueblos had not lived in an isolated world before Don Juan de Oñate and his followers arrived in 1598 (see Chapter 2), they were not the only Native peoples affected by the newcomers' presence. Pueblo Indians maintained elaborate exchange ties with Apache and Navajo hunter-gatherers whose territories spanned the dry uplands surrounding the Rio Grande valley. At the heart of these ties were, on the one hand, the Pueblos' abundant corn surpluses and, on the other, the considerable quantities of buffalo meat and hides offered by Apache and Navajo traders. Beyond these goods, the exchanges featured others, many of them from peoples living far beyond the Southwest on the Plains and in the Southeast, California, and other parts of northern New Spain. While tensions between trade partners sometimes erupted, occasionally even in violence, hostilities rarely persisted for extended periods. Instead each of the rivals would simply find a different trade partner. In that way, Pueblos, Apaches, and Navajos sustained the general interdependence that had arisen from their exchanges and had come to shape their respective ways of life. Almost inevitably, Spanish efforts to dominate the Pueblos had a ripple effect that extended to neighboring non-Pueblo Indians.

Having suppressed the Ácoma revolt in 1599, Oñate continued his tour of the New Mexico pueblos in order to secure their submission to the Spanish crown. While some Indians abandoned their pueblos to avoid surrendering their autonomy, most submitted in order to avoid the fate of the Ácomas. As in Florida, Spanish officials asserted their authority by levying tributes of corn from the pueblos to support the colonists. In New Mexico the tribute was collected monthly by soldiers who often ransacked villages and even took sacred seed corn. The tribute collection was especially hard in 1601, when Oñate sought to supply an expedition to the Plains despite a severe drought in the Southwest. The drought affected not only the Pueblos but also their Navajo and Apache trade partners. When the Apaches and Navajos did not receive the corn they expected, they raided the Pueblos as well as the Spanish for any food they could find. As a result, the Pueblos became dependent on the Spanish for protection from Apache and Navajo raids.

Not content with conquering the Pueblos, Oñate wanted to find the gold he believed was somewhere nearby. Accordingly he led expeditions to the southern Plains in 1601 and to the Colorado River in 1604–1605. Encountering many of the same lands and peoples as had Coronado sixty years earlier, Oñate likewise found no gold or other wealth. Having bankrupted the colony in his futile quest, Oñate resigned in 1607 and officials in Spain considered abandoning the colony altogether. They changed their minds after receiving reports from Franciscan missionaries in New Mexico indicating that Pueblo Indians in large numbers were accepting baptism.

Encouraged by these reports, the crown in 1609 dispatched a new governor, Don Pedro de Peralta, who sought to reconcile the Pueblos to Spanish rule. Peralta modified Spanish levies of Indian goods and labor and strengthened the colony's defenses against the Apaches and Navajos. Meanwhile the Franciscans poured money and labor into their conversion efforts. Although temporarily set back by revolts among the Zunis and at Jemez and Taos pueblos, they built twenty-seven churches and seventeen convents by 1626 and claimed with considerable exaggeration that sixty thousand Pueblo Indians were now within the Catholic fold.

The Franciscans' initial successes came about because they persuaded many Pueblos that they could control spiritual forces, especially rain and disease. The missionaries took credit for the unusually abundant rainfall of the 1610s and 1620s and appeared to cure deadly new diseases such as smallpox that Pueblo medicine men could not combat. Moreover, many Indians saw general parallels between the Catholic mass and baptism and their own ceremonies and did not, like the missionaries, view the two religious systems as mutually incompatible. Above all, the Pueblos' deep belief in harmony as the governing principle of the universe led them to avoid conflicts where possible.

Over time the Pueblo Indians' faith in the power and virtues of the Franciscans was undermined.

Taos Pueblo, North House Block, 1810 A view of Taos virtually identical to that seen by arriving Spaniards nearly three centuries earlier.

During the 1630s smallpox and drought brought mass starvation and death, casting doubt on the missionaries' supposedly superhuman powers. By 1638 the Pueblo population was about forty thousand, half of what it had been when Oñate arrived just four decades earlier. Conflicts between Spanish missionaries and civilian authorities, during which each accused the other of abusing the Indians, upset Pueblo ideals of harmony. When the Franciscans administered whippings and other humiliating punishments to Christian converts for disobeying their teachings, many Indians heeded the counsel of traditional religious leaders who saw the missionaries as causes of rather than cures for their troubles. Indians in several pueblos revolted by burning churches and killing priests, while other dissidents fled to live among the Apaches.

Pueblo grievances against the Spanish were not confined to the missions. Equally onerous were the legal devices colonists used to impose forced labor on Indians. Under a feudal institution called *encomienda*, privileged *encomenderos* were granted the right to collect tribute quotas from all Pueblos within a given area. The tribute was in the form of goods such as corn and cotton blankets, and the labor required to meet the quotas was generally burdensome. The colony also compelled Indian labor for public works projects through the *repartimiento*. The capital at Santa Fe, for example, was constructed largely by Indian men whose absence from home usually posed hardships for their families. Moreover, Spanish colonists regularly flouted royal policy governing both institutions by forcing Indians to work in private households as servants or laborers. Pueblo women working in these circumstances frequently suffered from sexual abuse at the hands of Spanish male employers.

Despite the Indians' many grievances, Spanish authorities maintained control through a combination of coercion, co-optation, and their ability to provide military protection against Apache and Navajo attacks. These tactics were all the easier to employ because the Pueblo Indians were not politically united. Although sharing a recent history as well as basically similar cultures and religions, Pueblo peoples spoke four distinct languages and lived in about forty separate, autonomous communities. While interacting constantly, they had no precedent for taking collective political or military action.

The drought of the 1630s led Apaches and Navajos, as well as Utes from the Great Basin, to conduct raids in New Mexico on Pueblos and colonists alike. The raiders seized corn as well as metal tools, weapons, and livestock—sheep, cattle, and horses. They began riding the horses themselves as well as trading some to Indians on the Plains and Great Basin. Some Navajos began growing corn and raising sheep, leaving off their mobile settlement patterns for a more sedentary way of life. In response to the raids, New Mexican authorities conducted counterraids, often utilizing Pueblo warriors, in which they captured Apaches, Navajos, and Utes whom, contrary to Spanish law, they sold as slaves to mine operators in Spanish provinces in Mexico. In all these ways, Spanish colonization affected the lives of Native Americans well beyond the lands they occupied.

During the 1650s, colonial officials discovered and halted plots for two interpueblo uprisings. In the more serious of the incidents, the residents of six pueblos agreed to turn local horse herds over to cooperating Apaches and Navajos, who would then attack Spanish settlements during Holy Thursday church services. The revolt was crushed and nine leaders executed, but only after two pueblos had already seized and released nearby horses. Although the cooperation of several pueblos, along with some Apaches and Navajos, indicated that anti-Spanish sentiment had united Indians across traditional political boundaries, Spanish authorities saw no reason to doubt that their control of New Mexico was secure.

CONCLUSION

By the end of the 1650s, early European outposts in the Northeast, Southeast, and Southwest had become formidable territorial colonies. The American landscape now featured places with alien names like New France, Jamestown, and Santa Fe in which European farms, forts, missions, and trad-ing posts thrived. Once formidable Indian polities such as the Hurons, Pequots, and Powhatans no longer intimidated their Indian or European neighbors. Even groups that remained powerful, such as the Iroquois, had suffered devastating losses to European diseases and the brutal warfare associated with colonization. Every Native American group that had engaged in sustained, as opposed to sporadic, relations with Europeans was in a weaker position in 1660 than in 1600. And there was every indication that European expansion thus far represented only the tip of an iceberg.

As extensive as they were, Europeans' accomplishments and future prospects in 1660 did not mean that Native American history was drawing to a close. In every colonial arena, tensions between Indians and Europeans were rising rather than abating in the face of expanded immigration, missionary activity, and imperial rivalries relating to commerce and territorial domination. Indian peoples who had accommodated themselves to colonization were having second thoughts and were reevaluating their relationships with the intruders. Far from an end, what followed would prove to be yet another chapter in an ongoing story.

SUGGESTED READINGS

Calloway, Colin G. *New Worlds for All: Indians, Europeans, and the Remaking of Early America.* Baltimore: Johns Hopkins University Press, 1997. Nine thematic chapters examine the astonishing variety of Indian-European interactions in colonial America.

Hann, John H. *A History of the Timucua Indians and Missions.* Gainesville: University Press of Florida, 1996.   An outstanding study of the Timucuas and their relations with Spanish colonizers.

Kupperman, Karen Ordahl. *Indians and English: Facing Off in Early America.* Ithaca, NY: Cornell University Press, 2000.   An insightful study of intercultural encounters in New England and the Chesapeake.

Richter, Daniel K. *Facing East from Indian Country: A Native History of Early America.* Cambridge, MA: Harvard University Press, 2001. A stimulating, highly original exploration of Indian perspectives on the colonial era.

Richter, Daniel K. *The Ordeal of the Longhouse: The Peoples of the Iroquois League in the Era of European Colonization.* Chapel Hill: University of North Carolina Press, 1992. An important study of the Iroquois people and the Five Nations Confederacy.

Rountree, Helen C. *Pocahontas's People: The Powhatan Indians of Virginia Through Four Centuries.* Norman: University of Oklahoma Press, 1990. An authoritative study of the Powhatans and their relations with colonists in early Virginia.

Salisbury, Neal. *Manitou and Providence: Indians, Europeans, and the Making of New England, 1500–1643.* New York: Oxford University Press, 1982. A history of relations between indigenous peoples and early European colonizers in New England.

Townsend, Camilla. *Pocahontas and the Powhatan Dilemma.* New York: Hill and Wang, 2004. A thoughtful, well written treatment of the life and times of the best known woman in early colonial North America.

Trelease, Allen W. *Indian Affairs in Colonial New York: The Seventeenth Century.* Reprint ed. Lincoln: University of Nebraska Press, 1997. A useful survey of Dutch relations with both coastal and interior Indians.

Trigger, Bruce G. *Natives and Newcomers: Canada's "Heroic Age" Reconsidered.* Kingston, Ont., and Montreal: McGill-Queen's University Press, 1985. A brilliant, panoramic view of Indian history in the St. Lawrence Valley and lower Great Lakes through the middle seventeenth century.

Worlds in Upheaval, 1660–1720

On May 26, 1713, a miniaturized international conference occurred at Kahnawake, a town populated primarily by Mohawk Iroquois who practiced Catholicism. A visiting English trader, John Schuyler, had taken a day away from his commercial affairs in Montreal and hired some Mohawks to row him to the small town on a nearby island in the St. Lawrence. Greeted by the two resident priests, Schuyler announced that he "proposed to know the reason why this poor captive should be married to an Indian, being [that she was] a Christian born. "

The "poor captive" was one Eunice Williams, seized at Deerfield, Massachusetts, in February 1704 when a French-Indian expedition attacked the town and the Indians captured 112 of its residents. Altogether, such raids had netted the Indian allies of the French about 370 white captives from New England during the sequence of Anglo-French-Indian wars between 1689 and 1713. The captors generally killed those, including Williams's mother and infant sister, who otherwise would have slowed the relentlessly paced return marches ahead of pursuing English troops. But most captives survived and were either adopted into Mohawk, Abenaki, and Huron families or sold by their captors to French purchasers. Some of the latter became servants or wives in French Canadian households,

while French officials returned the rest to the English in exchange for French prisoners or other concessions. Consequently, most English captives who wished to return home had done so by the time of Schuyler's visit. Like many other English colonists captured as young children, Williams had elected to remain among those who had adopted her.

Schuyler's mission was remarkable because Eunice Williams was unusual among English captives. To begin with, the Deerfield raid had been the most successful of all from the captors' viewpoint because of the extraordinary number of people seized there, nearly a third of the total taken during a quarter century of warfare. For the same reason, the raid was the most notorious and galling to white New Englanders. But more than that, Williams was the daughter of the best known of all English captives, John Williams, the town's Puritan minister. A prominent member of the New England elite, Williams was quickly redeemed by his countrymen and within three years had remarried, resumed preaching at Deerfield, and published a best-selling narrative of his experience. *The Redeemed Captive Returned to Zion* represented Deerfield as a Puritan outpost whose saintly inhabitants were martyred or otherwise suffered at the hands of Indian "savages" and French Catholic "papists. "Campaigning strenuously and publicly for his daughter's return, Williams had gained wide support among influential colonists in New England and New York. Throughout the campaign, Eunice Williams had refused to see her father or otherwise respond to his entreaties. But the news of her marriage to Arosen, a Catholic Mohawk, prompted the minister to ask Schuyler to intervene during his Canadian visit.

At Schuyler's request, the priests sent for Williams, who came quickly, accompanied by her husband. The merchant first addressed her in English, but her impassive demeanor confirmed rumors that she had forgotten her native tongue. In order to continue, he relied on one interpreter who spoke English and another who spoke French and Mohawk. Schuyler began by telling Williams what she already knew—that most of Deerfield's surviving captives, including her brother as well as her father, had returned and that family, friends, and especially her father earnestly desired her to reunite with them. But while clearly understanding Schuyler's words now, the sixteen-year-old newly-wed remained silent. Seeing that he was getting nowhere, Schuyler permitted one of the priests to make a more modest request—that Williams agree simply to visit her father and then, if she still wished, return to Kahnawake. Still she said nothing until, after nearly two hours, saying in Mohawk, "*jaghte ogthe*," which in English means "maybe not." Schuyler, now desperate, angrily condemned Williams for ruthlessly and callously betraying her father. In response Arosen interjected on his wife's behalf, observing "had her father not married again, she would have gone and seen him long [before] this time." Now recognizing the depths of Williams's resistance, Schuyler returned to Montreal empty handed.

While uttering few words, Williams and Arosen made clear that family and kinship obligations lay at the center of Williams's attitude toward her father. Like hundreds of other English captives before 1763 (see also Chapter 6), she had been adopted into a Native American family with its extended kin networks and relative autonomy for women and had embraced its cultural and spiritual values. But as Arosen made clear, his wife had done still more, breaking irrevocably with her father because he had remarried. Among white New Englanders, a normal family was one headed by a father-husband, assisted by a wife. Besides providing her own household labor, a wife bore and reared the children, who supplied additional labor and, in the case of sons, perpetuated the family line. Remarriages by widows and widowers were commonplace. But from his Mohawk daughter's standpoint, John Williams had sundered their relationship when he remarried. The Mohawks and other Iroquois—and most Native Americans in the Eastern Woodlands—reckoned kinship through one's mother's multigenerational family. In these Indian societies, a husband was basically a guest of his wife's family. In return for the family's admitting him, he was expected to be generous and kind, above all to his children. As a father, he exercised no authority over his children; that role was assumed by one of his wife's male relatives, usually her oldest brother.

Although adopted by a new family, Eunice Williams did not initially reject the family in which her mother had raised her. But then her father abandoned that family by joining the family of a woman to whom Eunice was unrelated. For John to ask his daughter to join this family was unthinkable for her, the more so now that her adopted family had welcomed Arosen as her husband. Eunice later underscored this view when, after her father died, she finally visited her brother and other maternal relatives in New England on four occasions. Other Kahnawake Mohawks with kin ties to Deerfield did the same, and even today some of their descendants regard the town as having a special place in their history.

Experiences of war, captivity, and dislocation were by no means limited to Eunice Williams and the other residents of Kahnawake. On the contrary, the later decades of the seventeenth century and the beginning of the eighteenth marked a period in which some or all of these experiences were shared by large numbers of Native Americans in the Eastern Woodlands and Southwest. As had been the case since Europeans arrived, epidemic diseases were not only the single greatest cause of Indian deaths but also left survivors especially vulnerable to the effects of war and other catastrophes.

Throughout the period, wars were either in progress or threatening to erupt in the East and Southwest. But the scope of wars broadened over time. From the 1660s through most of the 1680s, wars were regional conflicts in which European efforts to trade for furs and Indian slaves, to gain Indian lands, or to force Christianity on Native peoples were central ingredients. But after 1689, these regional wars fused with imperial competition between England or Britain on one hand and France and Spain on the other. (England and Scotland united in 1707 to form Great Britain.) To be sure, Indians defined and pursued their own priorities in choosing European allies and in strategizing militarily. Nevertheless European protagonists now figured even more prominently and the scale of warfare broadened both geographically and in intensity, particularly because of the wide availability to Indian participants of European weaponry.

As a result of the transformed scale and intensity of war, more Native American communities than ever were dispersed and more Indian people than ever were captured in raids and invasions by other Indians. Indian captives frequently joined other refugees to form new communities in new homelands, where the inhabitants drew on their varied tribal backgrounds, as well as on European influences, to refashion cultures and identities that reflected their new circumstances. In other words, they survived and adapted by reinventing themselves. Particularly in the Northeast, Europeans—primarily French traders and English captives such as Eunice Williams—added to the multicultural diversity of their new towns and villages. Their experiences confirm that Europeans were affected by Native peoples, as well as vice versa. By 1720, few Indians east of the Mississippi and on the upper Rio Grande and adjoining lands had avoided these transformations.

THE NORTHEAST: IROQUOIS POWER AND EUROPEAN EXPANSION

During the 1660s, the string of Five Nations Iroquois victories over Indian neighbors came to an end as some of those neighbors—especially ones allied with New France—acquired European weapons and retaliated against Iroquois attacks. Meanwhile, renewed tensions erupted in New England and the Chesapeake region, where expanding English colonies demanded additional land as well as political submission by Indians. These tensions

led to regional wars that ended with victorious colonies strictly limiting the autonomy of all Indians, friendly as well as hostile, solely on the basis of their being Indian.

In due time, English colonists and beleaguered Iroquois discovered their common interest in limiting the power of New France and its Indian allies. But the Five Nations defied their English allies in 1701 by declaring their neutrality in subsequent European wars and forging new ties of trade and peace among former French and Indian enemies. By 1715, the Iroquois and most other northeastern Indians were at peace, although war raged among the western Indian allies of New France. Iroquois power had waxed and waned over the preceding half century before stabilizing at a point at which the Five Nations could enjoy the benefits of peace with both England and France. But other Indians paid a price for the Iroquois' good fortune, especially those in some seaboard colonies whom the Iroquois helped to suppress or relocate.

Changing Iroquois Fortunes, 1660–1680

By the early 1660s, resentful Indian neighbors and expansion-minded Europeans were effectively challenging the power of the Five Nations Iroquois on several fronts. One challenge came from the Susquehannocks and the English of Maryland, who together sought to prevent the Dutch and Iroquois from dominating trade in the upper Chesapeake Bay. After several skirmishes, an Iroquois party of eight hundred Senecas, Cayugas, and Onondagas besieged a Susquehannock village in 1663. When the Susquehannocks defied the siege, the Iroquois dispatched twenty-five delegates to seek a truce. The Susquehannocks seized the delegates and, "without further delay, made [them] mount on scaffolds where, in sight of their own army, they were burned alive." The Susquehannocks had avenged their defeat by the Mohawks more than a decade earlier (see Chapter 3), and the Iroquois returned home thoroughly humiliated.

A second challenge to the Five Nations arose among former allies to the east. For a quarter century, Algonquian-speaking southern New England Indians had supplied wampum to the Iroquois (see Chapter 3). But by the early 1660s, wampum production far outstripped demand, so that Iroquois

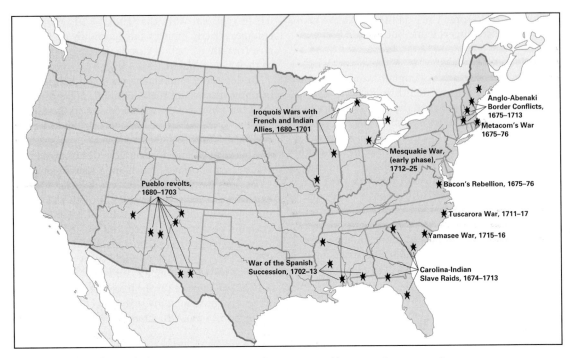

Major Armed Conflicts Involving Native Americans and Europeans, 1660–1725. *Source map:* Cambridge History of the Native Peoples of the Americas, *vol. 1:* North America, *part 2 (Cambridge, UK: Cambridge University Press, 1996), 190–191.*

Algonquian vs. Mohawk

consumers no longer sought the shell beads. At the same time, some southern New England Indians began supporting fellow (pro-French) Algonquian speakers in Canada in raiding, and defending against counterraids by, Mohawks. Retaliating for attacks on Mohawk villages, Mohawk, Seneca, and Onondaga warriors in 1663 and 1664 destroyed two large villages on the Connecticut River in western Massachusetts. Determined to avoid the fate of the Hurons, Algonquian speakers from the Hudson River to Boston were now, in the words of an English colonist, "at deadly feud with" the Mohawks.

Closer to home, a smallpox epidemic in 1664 wreaked what a Jesuit missionary called "a sad havoc," killing an estimated one thousand Iroquois. More Iroquois starved after deserting their villages and leaving behind unharvested crops. The Five Nations were further shaken in 1664 when the English conquered New Netherland, renaming it New York. The Iroquois suddenly found them-

selves without the vital but easily managed Dutch and instead dependent on an unfamiliar ally. In 1666 New York officials restored peace between the Mohawks and Mahicans at the behest of the once-domineering Mohawks, who pleaded, "we do not want to be killed by the" Mahicans. But New England Indians, many of whom were Christian and were backed by Massachusetts, remained hostile to the Mohawks.

Besides enemies to the south and east, the Five Nations faced a revitalized New France to the north. Recognizing the Iroquois as a direct threat to the colony and its Indian allies (see Chapter 3), the French government dispatched one thousand soldiers in 1665 with orders "totally to exterminate" the Five Nations. In order to secure peace on at least one front, the Oneida, Cayuga, Onondaga, and Seneca Iroquois quickly signed a treaty with the French and their Indian allies. After the Mohawks refused to go along, French troops launched an invasion of Mohawk country. Failing once, the

PEOPLE, PLACES, AND THINGS

Onondaga Iroquois Artifacts Made from European Metals (late seventeenth century)

As Indian-European trade developed over time, so did the skills and imaginations of Indian metalworkers. Among the Iroquois, these artisans—generally men—fashioned lead, pewter, brass, iron, and other metals into both utilitarian and spiritually significant objects. Among hundreds of artifacts that archaeologists have recovered from seventeenth-century Onondaga Iroquois sites are the two shown here. The first is an iron saw blade made from the trigger guard of a European, probably Dutch, musket. The blade may have been tied to a longer handle made of wood or metal.

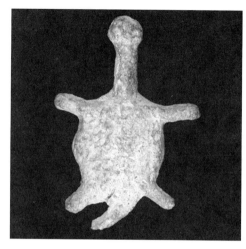

Onondaga Iroquois Artifacts Made from European Metals

The second artifact is an effigy of a turtle made from pewter, an alloy of tin and lead. Commonly used in European tableware of the period, pewter was especially favored by the Dutch, whose traders exchanged many pewter objects, among other things, to the Iroquois for furs during the seventeenth century. The turtle was and remains a common figure in Iroquois iconography. The traditional Iroquois creation account tells how Sky Woman fell toward a water-covered Earth and landed on the back of Turtle. There Muskrat, after diving repeatedly to the sea's bottom, had piled some soil so that she and, eventually, other people could thrive. Many Iroquois still refer to North America as Turtle Island. In addition, the Turtle clan is one of the three original Iroquois clans, said to have been established by one of Sky Woman's twin sons. Someone from the Turtle clan probably wore this effigy to make public his or her affiliation.

Taken together, the two objects remind us that Indian consumers of European goods did not simply accept goods made of alien materials but in fact used the new materials for their own purposes, which often differed from those intended by European producers and traders.

troops returned in September 1666, looting and burning most of the Mohawks' longhouses and destroying enough crops "to nourish all Canada for two entire years." Although warned in time to avoid casualties, the Mohawks were sobered by their extensive losses and by the friendly reception given the French by nearby New York colonists. In June 1667 they too made peace with the French.

As with the Hurons earlier, the French alliance obliged the Five Nations to allow Jesuit missionaries

Iroquois Funeral Under the impact of epidemics and wars, the Iroquois conducted burial ceremonies more frequently during the late seventeenth century than earlier. The practice of arranging the corpse in a flexed position prior to interment in a circular pit long antedated the arrival of Europeans.

to live in their villages and seek converts, leading to the rise of Christian and traditionalist factions. While some converts were attracted less to Christian doctrines than to the earthly rewards of peace with France, most of the approximately eighteen hundred Iroquois Catholics (20 percent of the total population) were former Hurons and other recent adoptees and their children. Jesuits had already baptized many of these outsiders in their former homes. Along with first-time converts, these Christians saw Catholicism as a way of asserting their tribal identities in the face of Iroquois pressures to assimilate. Following Jesuit instructions to repudiate "superstitions," they withdrew from traditional ceremonies and other expressions of solidarity with other Iroquois, attracting ridicule and hostility from non-Christians.

Like members of Iroquois minority factions before them, many Christians moved away from hostile neighbors to new villages—in this case, to "praying towns" at Kahnawake and La Montagne near Montreal. By 1680 the larger Kahnawake was

home to several hundred Indians, representing about twenty tribes. Some migrants sought improved hunting and farming prospects or Kahnawake's proximity to French traders. But most moved to distance themselves from the hostility of anti-Christian Iroquois and to practice their new religion unhindered. Indeed Catholicism became the basis of a powerful spiritual movement at Kahnawake during the late 1670s and 1680s. Yet while identifying as Catholic, most residents also identified themselves as Mohawk, maintaining their connection to the people they had left behind.

By far the best known of the émigrés is Kateri Tekakwitha, born in 1656 to a Christian Algonkin woman and her non-Christian Mohawk husband. Four years later young Tekakwitha lost both parents in a smallpox epidemic that left her skin severely pockmarked and her eyes unable to withstand bright light. Being disfigured and unable to work in the fields made her undesirable as a wife and, perhaps, especially responsive to the Jesuits' teachings. In 1676 she was baptized and moved to

Kahnawake, where she encountered a group of Indian women who had vowed to practice extreme penitence (atonement for sin). Their penitence took such forms as fasting, walking on hot coals, sleeping on beds of thorns, and whipping one another so as to approach the pain experienced by Jesus during his crucifixion. Although appearing on the surface to be a complete repudiation of Iroquois identity, the movement drew on Iroquois as well as Catholic traditions of physical self-denial and women's voluntary associations as means of empowerment. Penitence thus enabled the women to overcome stigmas rooted in gender, ethnicity, and—in Tekakwitha's case—physical disability and to assert a distinctive Iroquois Catholic female identity.

Tekakwitha proved to be the most extreme in her extreme group. At the age of twenty-four she died from severe malnutrition, made more life-threatening by injuries resulting from her self-sacrifices. Yet her death inspired those she left behind. For years to come, ill or injured Indians and French colonists alike would claim to have been spared from death after praying for her to intervene on their behalf. Her reputation as a worker of miracles endured, and in 1980 she became the first North American Indian to be beatified (the final step before sainthood) by the Roman Catholic Church.

New England: Metacom's War and the Covenant Chain, 1660–1677

Besides intensified hostilities with the Iroquois, Algonquian-speaking Indians in southern New England confronted continued English expansion. During the 1660s, a shift in the regional balance of power undermined the Anglo-Indian accommodations and interdependence achieved after the Pequot War (see Chapter 3). Native Americans' ability to produce furs they could trade to the English was curtailed as Indian hunters, having responded to commercial incentives, virtually eliminated the region's beavers through overhunting. Meanwhile the Native population was falling as a result of diseases such as smallpox and influenza. By 1675 southern New England's Indians numbered about eleven thousand, representing a decline of 90 percent over the preceding sixty years.

The environmental effects of English farming further weakened the Indians' position. Colonists' hogs invaded Indian women's cornfields and shellfish-gathering sites, devouring and otherwise destroying critical sources of food. Although Native Americans repeatedly complained to colonial officials, over time they were obliged to fence their fields because English custom allowed livestock to roam freely. Moreover, colonists' cattle devoured native grasses, permitting their replacement by English weeds and domesticated grasses that were adapted to intensive grazing. As expanding colonial farmers cleared forests for additional pasture (on a far larger scale than Indians had cleared), they destroyed wild berries and other species on which not only Indians but deer—their principal source of meat—depended. As early as 1642, a Narragansett sachem, Miantonomi, recognized the ecological dimension of the English threat:

> [O]ur fathers had plenty of deer and skins, our plains were full of deer, as also our woods, and of turkies, and our coves full of fish and fowl. But these English having gotten our land, they with scythes cut down the grass, and with axes fell the trees; their cows and horses eat the grass, and their hogs spoil our clam banks, and we shall all be starved.

A generation after Miantonomi's lament, when hunting and fur trading had become difficult, some Indians turned to hog farming themselves as one means of surviving in a colonial economy. Hog production by Wampanoag farmers was especially successful, leading several towns to ban them from common grazing lands and the Plymouth government to discourage them from carrying pork to Boston, where they undersold the colony's English producers. Thus an effort by Indians to adapt to colonial conditions was repudiated when it proved effective.

Rapid population growth, along with the emergence of land speculation as a form of investment, generated a powerful English demand for even more Indian land. With no furs to trade, Nipmucs, Pocumtucks, and other inland Indians became indebted to merchants, particularly John Pynchon of Springfield, who had formerly advanced them trade goods before each hunting season. Taking indebted

Indians' land as collateral, the merchants sold it to colonists seeking to establish new towns. Other longtime Indian allies of English colonies, such as the Wampanoags of Plymouth and the Narragansetts of Rhode Island, faced renewed pressures to sell land, beyond the extensive tracts their fathers had granted the first generation of immigrants. John Eliot and other Puritan missionaries compounded the pressures on Indians by seeking new converts among the Wampanoags and Nipmucs. The Christian Indians defied traditional sachems by refusing to pay them tribute and by selling land without the sachems' approval. Tensions reached a boiling point in 1671, when the colonies forced the Wampanoag sachem Metacom (called "King Philip" by the English) to submit formally to the colony, granting it direct authority over his people and their land.

Thereafter the question was no longer whether war could be avoided but rather when it would start. The answer came in June 1675 after the body of John Sassamon, a Christian, Harvard-educated Indian, was found floating in a pond. Formerly a counselor to Metacom, Sassamon had recently alleged to English officials that the Wampanoag sachem planned an intertribal war against the colonies. Another Christian Indian came forward to claim that he had seen three associates of Metacom beat Sassamon to death before leaving his body in the pond. A jury of twelve colonists and six Christian Indians found the three defendants guilty and sentenced them to hang. Whether or not the allegations were true, war was now inevitable.

Metacom's War (1675–1676) eventually pitted most Wampanoags, Nipmucs, Narragansetts, and Connecticut Valley Indians against the English colonies and their Indian allies—Massachusetts, Mohegans, Pequots, and minorities among the Wampanoags and Nipmucs. But many colonists advocated a racialized war against all Indians, and English vigilante groups attacked friendly Massachusetts and Nipmucs. To appease them, Massachusetts and Plymouth imprisoned friendly Indians on remote islands where, lacking adequate food and shelter, many died.

Meanwhile in December, an intercolonial force of nearly a thousand English troops and about 150 Mohegans and Pequots mobilized to attack a fort that the still-neutral Narragansetts were building

in western Rhode Island's Great Swamp. Rationalizing that some Narragansetts were protecting a few enemy Wampanoags, the English decided to destroy the entire Narragansett nation. Locating the fort with the aid of a frightened Narragansett captive, the soldiers twice mounted massive assaults only to be thrown back by well-armed Narragansett warriors. Unable to take the fort in battle, the troops emulated their New England forebears during the Pequot War (see Chapter 3) by burning the fort. As in the earlier attack, several hundred Indian women, children, and elders died along with about a hundred warriors. Several hundred more Narragansetts managed to escape and join other anti-English Indians.

After the battle, the English found evidence of their technological influence on their Indian neighbors. The stone-walled fort, modeled on English forts, had been built by a Narragansett mason known to his many English clients as Stonewall Jack. At the center was a forge in which a Narragansett blacksmith repaired damaged flintlock rifles, which the Narragansetts and other Indians owned in large quantities. Having learned their crafts by apprenticing among the English, both artisans had begun teaching their skills to younger Indian men.

Meanwhile, anti-English Indians launched devastating attacks on towns across central Massachusetts, killing and capturing colonists and destroying livestock, crops, and buildings. One such attack on Lancaster, Massachusetts, in February 1676, resulted in the capture of Mary Rowlandson, the war's best-known English prisoner, whose later memoir of her experience became a bestseller. After an attack on neighboring Medfield, pursuing English troops were startled to find a note in English on a bridge post. "The Indians that thou hast provoked to wrath and anger," it proclaimed, "will war this twenty one years. . . . You must consider the Indians lost nothing but their life; you must lose your fair houses and cattle." Clearly, the note had been written by a praying Indian, for missionaries only taught English literacy to a few Native converts. Like John Sassamon, the author had accepted English skills and beliefs but, unlike the slain Christian, he used his education to criticize the English and mock their attachment to material possessions.

The military tide turned in the colonists' favor in spring 1676, after Massachusetts and Plymouth turned to their imprisoned Indian allies for help. Once they began using friendly Indians to spy, scout, and fight, the colonies' fortunes improved. At great risk to their own lives, friendly Indians went among the anti-English forces, seeking out old acquaintances and pretending to be sympathetic so as to gather intelligence. Other friendly Indians showed the English how to move through the woods undetected, how to locate their enemies, and most importantly how to take the offensive against them.

A second critical source of Indian support came from the Mohawk Iroquois, who were eager to regain an advantage over their New England Indian rivals. Their opportunity came in January 1676, when Metacom led a large expedition westward to Hoosic, near the Hudson River, to seek the active support of Mahicans and other Algonquian speakers gathering there, some of whom had access to French guns. Learning of the meeting, some Mohawks informed New York's Governor Edmund Andros, who provided them with weapons to attack the gathering. Aided by an outbreak of disease that had already begun to disperse the participants, the Mohawks prevailed. Thereafter well-armed Mohawks pursued New England Indians in the Connecticut Valley, prompting many to surrender to the English so as to avoid capture by the Mohawks.

As the growing season began in spring 1676, Wampanoags and Narragansetts in western New England found themselves far from home and short of food. Moving southwestward, they broke into small groups to avoid starvation and epidemics as well as pursuing Mohawk and Anglo-Indian forces. One female Wampanoag sachem, Awashunkes, and her people abandoned Metacom in return for regaining their former homes and lands in Plymouth. As some Indians surrendered and joined pro-English ranks, attacks on remaining anti-English Indians grew more intense. An attack on some Narragansetts resulted in the death of 171 men, women, and children. Especially effective was a unit consisting largely of Awashunkes's warriors and commanded by Benjamin Church. In August 1676 they trapped Metacom himself, and a fellow Wampanoag fatally shot the sachem. Church ordered Metacom's body to be drawn and quartered and took his head back to Plymouth, where it was put on display as a warning to Indians and as a grisly message to colonists that racial extermination was the key to their security and cultural identity. Thus ended, ignominiously, the life of the man whose father had welcomed the first New England colonists.

Metacom's War was one of the deadliest conflicts in American history, killing about five thousand (40 percent) of the Indians and twenty-five hundred (5 percent) of the English, and leaving thousands of survivors on both sides homeless and without livelihoods. But while the English eventually reoccupied their sacked towns and resumed their expansion, the region's Native Americans never regained their prewar strength. While the English spared many combatants who, like Awashunkes's warriors, surrendered before the end, they executed or sold into slavery those who continued to resist or were deemed guilty of crimes, including Metacom's wife and nine-year-old son. Enslaved Indians ended up not only in New England but as far away as Virginia, Barbados (until the legislature there outlawed them as troublemakers), Europe, and even North Africa. Hundreds of other Native Americans fled to live among Abenakis in upper New England and at Catholic praying towns in New France, or at Schaghticoke, an intertribal village established by New York and the Iroquois. In time, most of these refugees would join the Abenaki allies of the French and seek opportunities to avenge expulsion from their homelands. Meanwhile, the relatively few Indians remaining in southern New England, including Christians and others who had supported the English, struggled to survive with diminished populations, lands, and political autonomy. Regardless of religious or political allegiances, all were relegated to an inferior status solely on the basis of being Native American.

The regional significance of the English victory became clear at Albany in April 1677 when representatives of New York, Massachusetts Bay, Connecticut, the Mohawks, and the Mahicans signed a treaty. With New York mediating, the Mohawks and Mahicans promised to extradite any Indian fugitives from New England that they caught and to cease raiding Indians living within the New England colonies' jurisdiction. For their part, the

New Englanders agreed to negotiate with the Mahicans and Mohawks only through New York officials. The effect was to elevate New York to a position of supremacy in Anglo-Indian relations and to formalize the role of the Mahicans and Mohawks (and, by extension, the other Iroquois nations) in subjecting coastal Indians to colonial rule. Although differences between Massachusetts and the Mohawks were not fully resolved until 1684, the treaty constituted the beginning of the Covenant Chain system of alliances, linking the Mohawks and other Iroquois with the English colonial system.

The Chesapeake: Bacon's Rebellion

As in New England, tensions flared around Delaware and Chesapeake bays as English settlers encroached on the lands of friendly Indians. During the early 1670s, the Susquehannocks resisted efforts by Maryland to displace them from the north end of Delaware Bay, prompting the English to make peace with the Susquehannocks' Iroquois enemies. Diplomatically isolated, the Susquehannocks complied when Maryland ordered them in 1675 to leave their homes and move south to an abandoned Piscataway village on the Potomac River.

The Susquehannocks soon discovered that English colonists, eager to produce tobacco, coveted their new homeland as well. Anglo-Indian tensions were complicated because of lucrative trade monopolies controlled by Maryland's proprietor, Lord Baltimore, and Virginia's governor, William Berkeley, and their cronies. These elite groups preferred to maintain peaceful trade ties with Susquehannocks, Doegs, and other neighboring tribes rather than pressure the Indians to sell their remaining lands and move away. Seeing themselves as unjustly deprived of land so that a few could profit, many ordinary colonists resented both the monopolists and, in the sarcastic words of Nathaniel Bacon, the dissidents' leader, the "protected and darling Indians." Yet the Indians hardly lived well. As in New England, English diseases continued to take their toll while the spread of English farming and grazing undermined the plants and animals on which Native Americans depended for subsistence.

Matters came to a head in 1675 after some Doeg Indians killed an Englishman in a dispute over money. Pursuing the Doegs into Maryland, Virginia militiamen killed not only several of them but also some recently arrived Susquehannocks. The Susquehannocks called for a peace parley and, when Virginia and Maryland troops arrived at their village, sent out five leading men to negotiate. The English promptly killed the Susquehannock leaders, whose followers avenged the treacherous murders by attacking some Virginians in January 1676. That attack, along with news of New England Indians' victories in Metacom's War, played into the hands of colonists who hoped to use the conflict to drive all Indians from Virginia. Led by Bacon, English vigilantes defied Berkeley and began attacking all Indians without regard for their conduct. Peaceful Pamunkeys, Occoneechees, Mattaponis, and other Indians already subject to Virginia's authority suffered heavy casualties. The English killed and enslaved Indian men, women, and children while looting their villages of valuable trade goods. In one attack on a Pamunkey village, for example, a militia unit seized, not only forty-five prisoners, but also "Indian matts, Basketts, matchcotes, parcells of wampampeag, and Roanoke (which is their money) in Baggs, skins, ffurs, Pieces of Lynen, Broad cloth and divers sorts of English goods. . . . "

Bacon's Rebellion, as the uprising came to be known, briefly expanded to a civil war when rebels drove Berkeley from Jamestown and burned the capital. But it ended abruptly after Bacon died of a fever in August 1676. A royal commission sent from England agreed that Virginia had wronged its tributary Indians and persuaded the assembly to conclude a new treaty with them. The Treaty of Middle Plantation (1677) recognized Cockacoeske, weroansqua (female chief) or "queen" of the Pamunkeys, as the supreme leader among Virginia's Indians and confirmed the Indians' status as English subjects. In this respect, the Pamunkeys regained their status, first acknowledged in 1646 (see Chapter 3) but later allowed to lapse, as the Indians' common broker in their dealings with Virginia officials. As in the earlier treaty, Anglo-Indian transactions were to be regulated by the governor, who would also resolve disputes between individual members of the two groups. To prevent livestock incursions, colonists were prohibited from settling within three miles of Native villages, while Indians had to obtain a magistrate's permission to leave their reservations in order to fish or gather wild plants. In other words, the two peoples were to live apart from one another, and the governor's authority to regulate relations between them was strengthened. But the true balance of intercultural power in Virginia is more accurately reflected in population figures. By 1700 Virginia numbered about forty-two thousand free colonists and seventeen thousand enslaved Africans (most of whom arrived after 1676), compared to about one thousand Indians. Having divided its population into three exclusive categories, Virginia further refined the kind of racial hierarchy that was also emerging in New England.

To the north, meanwhile, Susquehannocks fleeing Bacon's aggression returned to the upper Delaware Bay. In June 1676 New York's Governor Andros brokered a peace between them and their old enemies, the Five Nations Iroquois. With New York and the Iroquois promising to protect them from Maryland's aggression, most Susquehannocks accepted adoption into Iroquois villages, while the rest remained among their Delaware Indian neighbors. In June 1677 Maryland and Virginia signed a treaty with New York and the Iroquois under which they joined the Covenant Chain. The two colonies agreed not to pursue or deal independently with Susquehannocks or other Indians protected by the Iroquois. In return, the Iroquois pledged that the colony's settlements and tributary Indians would not be harassed or attacked by either the Iroquois themselves or by "foreign" Indians. The Susquehannocks themselves did not sign the treaty; the English and Iroquois signatories agreed that they were no longer an independent people.

The Middle Ground, 1660–1680

In waging the Beaver Wars, the Iroquois had driven thousands of Indians in the eastern Great Lakes and Ohio Valley from their villages (see Chapter 3). Although some of the displaced Indians moved to the Southeast (see the discussion of the Southeast slave trade later in this chapter), most fled westward and formed new villages at places like Chequamegon Bay, Sault Ste. Marie, Green Bay, and Michilimackinac in the upper Great Lakes, as

well as the Kaskaskia village near Starved Rock on the Illinois River. These interethnic refugee communities included Algonquian-speaking Mesquakies (or Foxes), Ojibwes, Potawatomis, Kickapoos, Miamis, Ottawes, and Illinois, as well as Iroquoian-speaking Hurons and Petuns and local Siouan-speaking Ho-Chunks (Winnebagos). Numbering anywhere from one thousand to twenty thousand, the inhabitants intended their communities to be large enough to repel Iroquois attacks. To ensure sufficient food supplies, they located the towns adjacent to ample farmland and to lakes or rivers abundant with fish. With their different tribal backgrounds, community members had to work out compromises among themselves in many of their customs, including rules and obligations of kinship and of political authority, the resolution of disputes, and exchanges of goods.

Besides intermarriage and adoption, the most important basis for harmony among the refugee Indians was the calumet, an elaborately adorned pipe used in ceremonial exchanges and peace talks. Originating among the Pawnees of the Great Plains, the calumet was a symbol of the bearer's peaceful intentions and imposed an obligation on anyone presented with it to cease hostilities. In the words of a French missionary, it was the Indians' "God of peace and war, the arbiter of life and death. It suffices for one to carry and show it to walk in safety in the midst of enemies who in the hottest fight lay down their weapons when displayed." Although the calumet rarely halted fighting with either their Iroquois or Sioux enemies, it did help to resolve internal differences that arose as they learned to live with one another.

The emergent refugee communities quickly attracted traders and missionaries from New France. To the Native Americans, the French were strange beings who offered protection from diseases and Iroquois attacks as well as powerful and useful new goods. One Jesuit noted that the Indians often invited French guests for meals "not so much for the sake of eating as of obtaining through us either recovery from their ailments or good success in their hunting and war." But Native Americans would reject missionaries who insisted that their God was superior to the Indians' manitous (spiritual powers) or traders whose greed became overbearing. The Indians called Montmagny, the governor of New France, Onontio (literally, big mountain), characterizing him as a (metaphorically) towering figure who generously gave presents to those around him. In their view, their treating him as such obligated him to play that part. After Montmagny left Canada, the Indians called whoever served as governor of New France by that name.

Unlike the English in the Atlantic coastal colonies, for example, the French were in no position to impose either their authority or their values on the Indians of the upper Great Lakes. Nor could the Indians dictate terms of trade to the Europeans, as the Iroquois had to the Dutch in the 1620s. Rather Indians and French alike, most of them far from their original homelands, needed one another for trade and for support against the Iroquois. Over time they worked out ways of getting along by creating what historian Richard White calls a "middle ground." The middle ground, White writes, is not a place where people share values or goals, or even understand one another very well. Instead Indians and French, from their very different cultural perspectives "misinterpret and distort both the values and practices of those they deal with, but from these misunderstandings arise new meanings and through them new practices—the shared meanings and practices of the middle ground."

Through such misunderstandings, Jesuit missionaries and Christian converts found one another as did French traders and Indian hunters. Indians and French built on such relationships to advance their interests among their own people as well as with one another. In 1694 an Illinois sachem, Rouensa, proposed to seal a trade connection by marrying off his seventeen-year-old daughter, baptized Marie Rouensa, to a French trader. Marie stridently objected, citing her Christian beliefs and Jesuit accusations that the would-be groom was a "libertine." While gaining Jesuit support by invoking Christianity, she also reasserted Illinois women's traditional control of their own sexuality, a control that her father proposed to override. Only after both her parents as well as the trader agreed to be baptized as Catholics did she consent to the marriage. Such were the concessions and compromises of the middle ground.

Comparable relationships unfolded among English traders and Indians north of the Great Lakes. Although England and France were at peace until 1689, the commercial rivalry between the two empires had been sharpening for three decades. To

Huron Woman The woman's cloth dress, glass beads, and iron hoe reflect the impact of trade with the French, while her infant's cradleboard demonstrates the persistence of indigenous practices.

counter France's virtual monopoly on the Canadian fur trade, a new English trading company, the Hudson's Bay Company, established a series of posts on Hudson and James bays beginning in 1670. In this way the English hoped to intercept the thick pelts of beavers and other mammals that flourished in the subarctic region of central Canada. The new posts attracted Algonquian-speaking Western Crees and Siouan-speaking Assiniboines, formerly linked to the French trade only indirectly via the Ottawas. As allies of the English, the Western Crees and Assiniboines gained more direct access to English goods, including firearms and ammunition. They used the weapons to advantage in contests over hunting territories with French allies near the upper Great Lakes, especially Ojibwes and Sioux, and with

Gros Ventres and Blackfeet on the northern Plains. By the 1680s, one historian estimates, virtually every adult male Assiniboine and Western Cree owned a gun. In this way, Anglo-French competition in the fur trade propelled an arms race among Indians that spread guns and deadly violence westward to the heart of the continent.

Although nominally at peace with the French, the Iroquois grew suspicious of French ties with the refugees, particularly after the French built a series of fortified trading posts on the Great Lakes and the Mississippi River. When fully operative, the Iroquois feared, the posts would facilitate imports of trade goods and exports of furs via the Mississippi River and Gulf of Mexico, bypassing Iroquois country. These suspicions played into the hands of the English, especially New York's Governor Andros, who consistently reiterated offers of support to the Five Nations to strengthen their English ties with the Covenant Chain. By 1680 French influence among the Iroquois was waning along with hopes that peace would last.

The Iroquois: From War to Peace, 1680–1701

As with the earlier Beaver Wars, a combination of demographic and economic factors finally led the Five Nations to lash out at their rivals. Besides being threatened with exclusion from the western fur trade, the Iroquois population was once again declining as a result of diseases, culminating in a devastating smallpox epidemic in 1679. Well armed with English guns, the Five Nations undertook a new round of mourning wars. In 1680, they attacked the Miamis and Illinois, killing thirty and seizing about three hundred captives. They continued their assaults, including one in 1682 that brought seven hundred captives to the Onondaga nation alone. One French observer estimated that the Iroquois "have strengthened themselves, in this and the preceding years, with more than nine hundred men armed with muskets." Although the Five Nations were losing as many people through disease and warfare as they were gaining through their attacks, the comment underscores Iroquois military power and effectiveness.

Recognizing that the Iroquois offensive threatened their trading interests, the French declared war on the Five Nations. In 1687 French troops and some western Indian allies invaded Seneca country, killing only twenty Senecas but burning four villages and more than a million bushels of food, and desecrating and looting Seneca graves. In retaliation Iroquois warriors attacked Montreal and destroyed several French fortified posts in the Great Lakes.

The conflict widened in 1689 when England and France began a new European war, the War of the League of Augsburg, known in the English colonies as King William's War (1689–1697). The expanded war proved disastrous for the Five Nations. While the English in New York largely ignored the Iroquois, the French armed and worked closely with their own Indian allies—Abenakis and other Indians from eastern Canada and New England, western Indians from the Great Lakes, and even the Iroquois' Catholic relatives in Kahnawake and other Canadian villages—in attacking and defending against the Five Nations. The Five Nations suffered a series of devastating assaults, including two French-led invasions deep into their homeland and an Ojibwe offensive that drove them from Canadian hunting territories seized during the Beaver Wars. Thousands of Iroquois were driven from their homes and many starved. By war's end, the Five Nations had lost at least 500 of their 2,150 warriors and 2,000 of their total population of 8,600. Not surprisingly, factionalism revived among the survivors as many, questioning the wisdom of an exclusive alliance with the English, favored a return to the French cause or outright neutrality.

While under attack from the east, north, and west, the Five Nations Confederacy was undermined diplomatically from the south. In 1681 Quaker colonizer William Penn received a charter to settle the Delaware Valley. With Penn prepared to trade with Native Americans and vowing to purchase title before settling any Indian lands, the Delawares became close allies of the colony and grew more independent of the Iroquois. After the French invasion of 1687, the Five Nations tried to shame the Delawares into supporting their war effort, saying "you delaware Indians doe nothing but stay att home and boil your potts, and are like women, while wee Onondages and Senekas goe abroad and fight against the enemie." With Pennsylvania's backing, the Delawares rebuffed the

Iroquois. Soon thereafter, some Susquehannocks who had been forced to live among the Senecas fled to their former homeland, now within Pennsylvania, where they became known as Conestogas. In 1701 the Conestogas and Pennsylvania agreed to trade freely with one another and the colonists pledged not to take or sell Conestoga land.

Although King William's War ended in 1697, the Iroquois conflict with France continued. But pro-French and neutralist factions among the Iroquois increased their influence as growing numbers of Iroquois sought to end the war and redefine the Five Nations' relations with the two European powers. In 1699 the Canadian Iroquois reached their own peace with the Five Nations and worked to bring about a French-Iroquois accord. Over the next two years Iroquois delegates conducted negotiations simultaneously with the French and the English. The end result was a delicately balanced set of agreements known as the Grand Settlement of 1701. Negotiating separately with England and France, the Iroquois served notice that they would remain neutral in the event of war between the two European nations. They also agreed with the French to make peace with the latter's Indian allies in exchange for access to hunting lands and trade goods as far west as France's new post of Detroit. While maintaining a special relationship with the English through the Covenant Chain and their trade privileges at Albany, the Grand Settlement promised the Iroquois neutrality, peace with their neighbors, and freedom to hunt and trade over a wide area without fear of conflict. On the brink of destruction, the Iroquois had fashioned a means of surviving in a new imperial world.

The Northeast in an Era of Iroquois Neutrality, 1701–1720

The Grand Settlement was put to an immediate test when Anglo-French hostilities resumed as the War of the Spanish Succession (1702–1713), called Queen Anne's War in North America. Many Iroquois feared that the English would draw them into the New England front of this war against Abenakis and Canadian Indians, including their own Catholic relatives at Kahnawake. Both European powers dispatched diplomats, missionaries, and gunsmiths to Iroquois villages in hopes of gaining their loyalty. But while a few Iroquois joined the English cause for a time, most shared the sentiment of the Iroquois delegate who in 1705 told Onontio: "We regard you and the English alike. We exhort you both to make peace together."

Iroquois neutrality was reinforced when the Five Nations developed means of profiting from peace as well as from the rise of Detroit. As the treaties of 1701 were being signed, the French had encouraged their Great Lakes Indian allies to settle at the new post and forge close ties with its French resident traders. Within five years, six thousand Hurons, Petuns, Ottawas, Ojibwes, Miamis, and others—no longer fearing Iroquois attacks—had abandoned the refugee centers and moved to Detroit. At first the Iroquois feared that so large a concentration of French allies might threaten their newly won hunting and trading rights in the area. But in 1703, a Mohawk delegation escorted some Hurons and Miamis to Albany to trade with the English, and by 1707 Iroquois guides regularly led parties of Indians from Detroit to Albany. The Detroit Indians' preference for trading at Albany did not signal dissatisfaction with Onontio or the middle ground but simply their preference for the wider range of high-quality, low-priced trade goods offered by English traders there.

Detroit was also problematic for the French because they failed to anticipate the intensity of ethnic tensions among some of the Native Americans they had invited there. As early as 1706 Ottawa-Miami violence in Detroit led the Miamis to return to their homeland on the Maumee River. An even more serious conflict erupted after 1710, when Mesquakies (Foxes) began arriving from west of Green Bay. Competition generated by the fur trade had recently led the Mesquakies into wars with the French-allied Ottawas and Ojibwes, as well as with the powerful Sioux to the west. In these conflicts, the French seemed to favor the Mesquakies' enemies. But the Mesquakies hoped that Detroit would afford them access to European goods and a chance to enhance their ties to the Iroquois. These hopes were dashed by Mesquakie antagonisms with Ottawas, Hurons, and other Detroit Indians plus French suspicions that the Mesquakies would ally themselves with the Five Nations and Britain. In 1712 open warfare erupted between the Mesquakies, Mascoutens, and Kickapoos on one side and the French and most other western Indians on the other. Thus began the "Fox wars" that would rage for a generation in the Great Lakes (see Chapter 5).

On the borderlands between New France and New England, the Abenakis sought to maintain their independence from both the French and the English. During the late seventeenth and early eighteenth centuries, their homeland was transformed both by imperial conflict and by an influx of Native American and European outsiders. Following Metacom's War, Indian refugees from southern New England transformed western Abenaki villages in what is now Vermont and Quebec province into interethnic refugee centers, comparable to those on the Great Lakes. Thereafter, still more refugees arrived from the Hudson River center at Schaghticoke, where nearby English settlements had rendered hunting difficult. French traders and missionaries lived in several eastern Abenaki communities, although they and the Abenakis also traded with the English and sought to remain neutral until the outbreak of imperial war in 1689 obliged them to choose sides. As a Jesuit missionary who knew them well put it, no Abenaki community "will patiently endure to be regarded as under subjection to any [European] Power whatsoever; it will perhaps call itself an ally, but nothing more."

All the Abenaki communities sided with the French during the wars of 1689–1713 because English settlements encroaching on their lands threatened them more directly than did French traders. Along with Mohawks and Hurons from the praying towns of Kahnawake and Lorette, respectively, Abenakis attacked outlying English settlements from Maine to the upper Connecticut Valley. In these attacks, they seized captives whom they could adopt, sell to the French in Canada, or offer to return to the English during peace negotiations. The war produced hundreds of English captives who further enriched ethnic interaction and diversity in the Northeast. John Gyles, captured by eastern Abenakis as a youth, returned to English society and used his knowledge of Abenaki language and culture as interpreter, diplomat, and trader on the Maine frontier. Two English children who remained with their captors eventually married and bore a son, Joseph Gill, later a prominent Abenaki sachem. The most renowned English captive was Eunice Williams, daughter of the Puritan minister of Deerfield, Massachusetts, who spurned her family's well-publicized efforts to redeem her and married a Catholic Mohawk from Kahnawake (discussed earlier in this chapter).

THE SOUTHEAST: SLAVES, CONFEDERACIES, AND WAR

For a century after the major Spanish expeditions of the mid-sixteenth century, the southeastern interior existed in a power vacuum occasioned by the collapse of a number of major Mississippian chiefdoms and by Spain's withdrawal to the eastern coast and Florida peninsula (see Chapter 2). This vacuum proved beneficial to interior Indians, enabling them to recover both demographically and politically before English and French colonizers, along with Indian refugees, entered the region in the late seventeenth century.

Following a century of relative peace and population recovery, the Southeast was plunged into greater turmoil than ever during the late seventeenth and early eighteenth centuries. At the heart of the turmoil was the Indian slave trade, which shaped not only relations among Indians and between Indians and Europeans but even the imperial competition among Europeans.

Initially, English slave traders in the Carolinas sought Indians for one of two reasons, either as slaves to sell abroad or as armed allies to bring them such slaves. The primary targets of English-allied Indians were the large populations of Native Americans in Florida, living at or near Franciscan missions. The infusion of guns and other English trade goods sparked an expansion of the slave trade, especially after the powerful Creek Confederacy became involved. As in the Northeast, conflicts among Indians over trade fused with the imperial competition emerging among Europeans, especially after French colonists established Louisiana in 1699 and allied with the Choctaws. Eventually, however, the trade in Indian slaves declined. Nevertheless, Carolina colonists remained interested in Indians—especially in their land. The result was a new round of Anglo-Indian conflicts along the Carolina seaboard during the first decade and a half of the eighteenth century. By 1720, the Southeast was a region as turbulent and war-torn as the longer-colonized Northeast.

Rise of the Indian Slave Trade, 1660–1685

The single most disruptive feature of expanded colonization in the Southeast was the Indian slave trade. The enslavement of Native Americans was not unknown in the region before Europeans arrived, but indigenous practices differed fundamentally from those introduced by the newcomers. Indians enslaved by other Indians had usually been captured during raids or skirmishes with rivals. Whereas northeastern Indians such as the Iroquois generally adopted war captives into their lineal families, southeastern chiefdoms often excluded captives from full membership in families. As in all Native American societies, one's identity in the Southeast depended on one's having kinship connections within a community; without such connections outsiders had no identity of their own and were therefore considered of inferior status. While some southeastern captives may have functioned as laborers, most served chiefs and other elites as retainers, burden-bearers, and in other capacities where they publicly reinforced the power and prestige of their masters and their masters' societies. As chiefdoms declined in the Southeast during the sixteenth century, indigenous slavery also receded.

Upon arriving in the Southeast, the Spanish and then the English imposed their own forms of enslavement. Spanish explorers such as de Soto had arbitrarily seized Indians, forcing them to labor under onerous conditions and often subjecting them to sexual abuse and extreme violence. English colonists in Virginia enslaved Indians captured during wars and acquired through trade with friendly Indians, and forced them to work as laborers on tobacco plantations. Like most Africans by 1660 (and unlike white indentured servants), enslaved Indians in Virginia had no contracts providing for their eventual freedom. Instead they were considered the personal property of their owners and as such could be bought and sold.

By the time English colonizers reached the southeastern interior, then, European slavery differed from its indigenous American counterpart in at least three fundamental ways. First, a slave's status derived from his or her continent of origin rather than from a lack of kin connections. More specifically that status was based on the hierarchy that Europeans created to distinguish themselves as superior to Africans and Native Americans. Second, slaves were commodities whose owners could buy, sell, and exploit them for no purpose other than to maximize their personal profits. Third, as in West Africa, slave traders actively encouraged some indigenous peoples to enslave others, particularly by supplying them with firearms.

Following the defeat of the Powhatan Confederacy in 1646 Virginia's traders extended their activities to dozens of Indian communities south and west of the colony. Native villages located on principal trade routes became known for "always entertaining Travellers, either English, or Indian." But three decades later, the Virginians faced competition from a new English colony, South Carolina, established in 1670, and its Westo Indian allies.

The Westos consisted of about four thousand Erie Indians who had migrated from their Great Lakes homeland to Chesapeake Bay during the sixteenth century to trade with visiting Europeans and, later, Virginia traders. As Virginia expanded its land base, the Westos moved farther south to land once occupied by the Mississippian chiefdom of Cofitachequi and now by scattered villages of Yamasees and other groups. South Carolina initially supported the local Indians, whom the Westos had terrorized with guns acquired from the Virginians. But in 1674 some Westo delegates approached Carolina trader Henry Woodward and proposed that the two peoples replace their hostilities with peaceful trade. An interested Woodward traveled with the delegates to the Westos' clustered towns near modern Augusta, Georgia, where he was greeted by a fifty- to sixty-gun salute. During the speeches that followed, Westo leaders emphasized their people's prowess and desire for trade. In a ceremonial demonstration of their sincerity, Woodward recounted, his hosts "oiled my eyes and joints with bears oil" and showered him with gifts and food.

Over the next five years, the Westos used English guns, powder, and ammunition to capture hundreds of Indians, primarily coastal Guales, who either lived in mission towns in Florida or fled to them for protection when the Westos attacked. But the Westos also raided Indians as far away as the Chickasaws in what is now northern Mississippi. They exchanged their captives with the Carolinians for European goods, including cloth, metal kettles and tools, and glass beads as well as more weaponry. The English traders in turn sold some enslaved Indians locally and in other mainland colonies but sent the vast majority to the West Indies, primarily to Barbados where most traders had lived before moving to South Carolina. With their profits, the traders hoped to establish large plantations that would perpetuate their wealth and power once the region was emptied of Indians. They also recognized that in weakening their Indian and Spanish neighbors, the slave trade could facilitate South Carolina's future expansion.

By 1680 the South Carolina traders had concluded that the Westos were no longer of value to them. Because they had alienated most other Native Americans in the region, the Westos were depriving the English of potential Indian allies who, together, could bring them many more captives than could the Westos alone. Accordingly, the English in 1680 ceased trading with the Westos and began arming another group of Beaver War refugees. The new allies were Shawnees from the Ohio Valley known as Savannahs, who had first moved to the Gulf Coast before approaching the English in South Carolina. Regarded now by the English as their "good Friends and useful Neighbours," the Savannahs attacked the Westos, whose diminishing supplies of powder, ammunition, and working guns rendered them vulnerable. Over the next three years, Savannah warriors captured most of the Westos who did not die or escape, destroying the tribe as a political and military entity. Once in English hands, the Westos became, like the Indians they had once captured and traded, slaves in the English West Indies. The English thereupon invited the Savannahs to remain where the Westos had lived, even changing the name of the river there from the Westo to the Savannah. At the same time, they invited Yamasees who had been displaced by the Westos to resettle downriver from the Savannahs.

As demands for slaves by English sugar planters in the island colonies continued to grow during the 1680s, the Carolinians' new Yamasee allies undertook slave raids on Guales and Timucuas living in Spanish mission towns in Florida. Spanish officials lacked large supplies of guns and in any case were reluctant to arm Indians who had often rebelled against them. Although they were able to move some Indians to missions beyond the Yamasees' range, they were unable to prevent thousands of the Guales and Timucuas from being captured and sold as slaves in South Carolina. When Florida accused the English of instigating the Yamasee raids,

South Carolina's governor replied that the Yamasees are "a people who live within our bounds after their own manner, taking no notice of our Government." Unconvinced, the Spanish sent their own troops to attack South Carolina settlements, initiating a rivalry that, like the one between England and France in the Northeast, would become intertwined with divisions among the region's Native Americans. The Spanish counterattack did little to restrain either the Yamasees or the English, and in 1685 Florida abandoned all its missions in what would later become coastal Georgia. Remaining Guales and Timucuas fled to find new homes among the Apalachees, among coalescing Muskogean speakers (discussed in the next section), and even among the Yamasees themselves.

The Emergence of Southeastern Indian Confederacies, 1685–1700

Having seen to the Westos' defeat, South Carolina's traders spread inland, exchanging guns and other goods for skins and slaves with Native groups from the piedmont to the Mississippi Valley. The traders soon discovered that several groups of closely tied Indian communities were emerging as formidable confederacies. The most tightly knit and effective confederacies replicated, in less centralized form, the Mississippian chiefdoms of earlier times. In the Carolina piedmont, several Siouan-speaking peoples came together and confederated with the Catawbas under the latter's name. In the mountains farther west, Iroquoian-speaking Cherokees formed clusters of towns, some of which moved south into what would later become northwestern Georgia and eastern Tennessee. In modern western Alabama and eastern Mississippi, Choctaw speakers converged in villages to form the Choctaw Confederacy. Although no longer organized as a Mississippian chiefdom, the Chickasaws reemerged as a powerful village-based confederacy in the Mississippi delta homeland where they had defeated de Soto more than a century earlier. Most remarkable of all the new polities were several clusters of closely linked towns in what later became western Georgia and eastern Alabama. The Indians of these towns would soon become known as the Creeks.

In all the confederacies, older loyalties to kin and town remained primary. The matrilineal (mother's) extended family and the clan provided the kinship connections that defined one's personal identity. The village or town was not simply a place of residence but the basis for distributing land and material wealth and for the religious ceremonies and communal games through which people expressed a local group identity. Particularly among the Creeks and Cherokees, clusters of towns within the larger confederacy usually acted in concert, functioning much as each of the Five Nations did within the Iroquois Confederacy. Through common ceremonies, southeastern confederacies kept the peace among constituent towns and coordinated matters such as trade and war. But also like the Iroquois, gatherings of chiefs did not dictate courses of action for all towns to follow. Although southeastern Indians remained locally oriented, the shared institutions, ceremonies, and customs of each confederacy gave rise to a shared culture and identity that overlay, without displacing, those of kinship and town.

Among those showing interest in trading with the English were the Creeks, some of whom had already resisted Spanish efforts to colonize them. As early as 1679 Franciscans from Florida had tried to counter English expansion by establishing a mission among Muskogean-speaking Creeks living on the Chatahoochee River. But the Indians there, led by the powerful mico (headman) of the talwa (town) of Coweta, expelled the missionaries and in 1685 built a trading post for the English. Although Spanish troops burned the post and four nearby talwas, English trade continued to grow. After Spanish soldiers built a fort on the upper Chatahoochee in 1689, English-armed Creeks drove them away. Meanwhile several talwas moved eastward to Ochese Creek, near present Macon, Georgia, to be closer to English traders.

The expansion of English trade and the move eastward reinforced the growing power of the Creeks. Dispersed along well-traveled trade routes across the southeastern interior, these Muskogean speakers strengthened ties not only among themselves but also with neighboring non-Muskogean speakers. Clusters of talwas on each river functioned as magnets for Yuchis, Apalachees, and other Indians who, preferring to enslave others rather than be enslaved themselves, arrived from throughout the Southeast. Even some surviving

Creek Square Ground and Council Fire The ceremonial center of a Creek talwa (town).

Westos regrouped and began a new town on the Chatahoochee. The English began referring to the peoples of the Ochese Creek talwas as "Creeks," and as the political ties among the several polities grew stronger, the term came to be applied to the entire group. (Those on the Coosa, Alabama, and Tallapoosa rivers were often called Upper Creeks while those on the Chatahoochee and eastward were deemed Lower Creeks.) By then Creek talwas extended from the Alabama River to the Savannah, making the Creeks the most powerful and widespread Indians in the Southeast.

The incorporating of new communities into the Creek Confederacy contrasted with comparable processes among the Iroquois. The Iroquois invited or, along with the English, coerced non-Iroquois refugees into relocating to the margins of Iroquois country and deferring to the league's authority in matters of war and peace (see Chapter 5). Indian communities affiliating with the Creeks, on the other hand, did so of their own free will and were treated equally.

French Louisiana and Indian-Imperial War,
1700–1712

The intensified Anglo-French rivalry that pushed the Netherlands out of the imperial picture in the Northeast likewise shoved Spain to one side—but not out altogether—in the Southeast. French interest in the Southeast focused on the lower Mississippi Valley, from which it hoped to circumvent northeastern trade routes threatened by the Iroquois (discussed earlier), contain the English colonies' westward expansion, and launch an invasion of New Spain. Through expeditions by Father Jacques Marquette and Louis Jolliet (1673) and by René Robert Cavelier, sieur de La Salle (1682), the French became familiar with the valley and many of its Native inhabitants. La Salle claimed the Mississippi Valley and adjacent territory for France and named it Louisiana. The French began colonizing there in 1699 when they established a post at Biloxi Bay on the Gulf coast.

Among Native Americans, the French sought to establish trade ties by capitalizing on Indian exhaustion from English-subsidized slave raids. In 1702 they established a post at Mobile, site of de Soto's defeat, and soon thereafter hosted leaders of the warring Choctaws and English-allied Chickasaws. French negotiators learned that ten years of warfare had resulted in more than eighteen hundred Choctaws killed and five hundred captured for sale as slaves, while more than eight hundred Chickasaws had also been killed. Sympathizing with the Choctaws, the French condemned the Chickasaws for "foolishly follow[ing] the advice of the English," but they nonetheless persuaded the two confederacies to make peace with one another and trade exclusively with the French. Each delegation received gifts of "200 pounds of powder, 200 pounds of bullets, 200 pounds of game-shot, 12 guns, 100 axes, 150 knives, some kettles, glass beads, gunflints, awls, and other hardware."

The French gifts soon proved counterproductive to French interests when the Choctaws used theirs to avenge raids by the Upper Creeks. The Choctaw counterraids undermined delicate French efforts to establish trade ties with the Upper Creeks who, alienated by abusive English traders, were receptive to French overtures. Instead the Creeks turned back to the English for more guns.

Further French efforts to make peace with interior Indians were sidetracked by the outbreak of the War of the Spanish Succession, or Queen Anne's War (1702–1713). The war pitted France and Spain against England; in the Southeast, it intensified existing rivalries among Indians and colonists. The war basically consisted of two theaters. The turning point in eastern Florida came in 1702 when South Carolina's Governor James Moore led fifty Carolina troops and more than a thousand Lower Creek, Yamasee, and Savannah warriors in a devastating expedition against Spanish mission centers. Over the next four years they destroyed all the Apalachee and remaining Timucua missions (thirty-two in all) and returned to South Carolina with more than four thousand enslaved Indians. In western Florida and Louisiana, the Upper Creeks besieged but failed to hold both a new Spanish fort at Pensacola and the French post at Mobile. Nevertheless they and the Chickasaws captured and enslaved thousands of Choctaws and other French-allied Indians over the course of the war. Although the English and their allies captured the vast majority of Indian slaves, the French (whose West Indian planters also demanded slaves) and Choctaws engaged in the practice as well.

Although the War of the Spanish Succession did not officially end until 1713, fighting stopped in the Southeast a year earlier. By then the exhausted Spanish, their chain of Indian missions destroyed, held little more than St. Augustine and Pensacola. But the main reason the war ended early was a decision by the Creeks and their allies to break with Britain and make peace with France. Besides growing weary of war, the Creeks were responding to overtures from French and Spanish traders and to abuses inflicted on them by English traders. The abuses usually originated when traders, like their fur-trading counterparts in New England (discussed earlier in the chapter), attempted to collect debts from Indians to whom they had advanced goods on credit. Once the slave-raiding Indians had obliterated the Florida missions, the availability of Indians to capture and sell as slaves dwindled, leaving a growing number of Creeks and other allies of the English unable to pay their debts. To compensate themselves, English creditors would steal from and often beat Indians, or enslave them or their relatives. While the creditors followed a strict commercial logic, their actions flew in the face of the way that Creeks, following Indian customs of hospitality and reciprocity, expected friends and allies to treat one another. An incident in 1712, in which an English trader captured and carried away several relatives of a prominent Upper Creek man, was merely the latest in a long string of incidents that the Creeks had come to resent deeply. When the French that year proclaimed "a general peace among the savages," it marked the achievement, unwittingly facilitated by the English, of the goal they had first pursued at Mobile a decade earlier.

Anglo-Indian Conflict in the Carolinas, 1700–1717

The Creeks were not the only Indians who chafed under abuses by South Carolina traders. A quarter century after being welcomed by the colonists and encouraged to destroy the Westos, the Shawnee Savannahs were experiencing similar abuses as well as encroachments by colonists on their lands. The Savannahs also angered colonial officials by taking some of their captives northward and selling them directly to colonists in Virginia, Maryland, and Pennsylvania, bypassing the Carolina traders. In 1707, after being attacked by English-armed Catawbas, the Savannahs began fleeing westward to live among the Creeks or northward to Pennsylvania, a colony that welcomed Indians on its frontier and was near the Shawnees' Ohio Valley homeland. Despite English efforts to prevent their departure, most Savannahs left the colony by 1712.

Colonial expansion generated even more serious conflict in North Carolina, where over 700 Swiss and German immigrants, led by Baron Cristoph von Graffenreid, established a town called New Bern adjacent to the Iroquoian-speaking Tuscaroras in 1710. Already suffering from smallpox and locked in trade disputes with Virginia, the Tuscaroras were now crowded by colonists and their livestock as well. As tensions rose, the Tuscaroras attempted in 1711 to expel the newcomers with a surprise blow. Although they killed 120 in their

first attack and several dozen more over the next few days, New Bern held out until the arrival from South Carolina and Virginia of reinforcements, including Cherokees, Yamasees, and other Indians. Over the next two years, about 1,400 Tuscaroras were killed, more than 1,000 were enslaved, and many of their towns and farms were destroyed. North Carolina established a reservation for the surviving 1,500 to 2,000 Tuscaroras but by 1717, most of them had abandoned the colony and moved north to live among the Iroquois.

In 1722 the Iroquois made the Tuscaroras the sixth nation of their confederacy, which was known thereafter as the Six Nations. Unlike other Indian communities that had recently affiliated with the Iroquois, the Tuscaroras enjoyed full membership in the confederacy and were given land on which to build villages near Onondaga, at the political and geographic center of Iroquois country. But while Tuscarora sachems participated in confederacy affairs, the Iroquois did not admit them to formal membership in the council of chiefs.

Although the Yamasees supported the English against the Tuscaroras, they too found themselves mistreated and crowded by expanding colonists in South Carolina. Living on the coastal plain, their supplies of deerskins were depleted as a result of overhunting while the availability of Indian slaves to trade had ended with the collapse of the Florida missions. Their English creditors threatened to gain satisfaction by enslaving the Yamasees themselves. At the same time English livestock overran Yamasee land, destroying crops and further discouraging deer. In 1715, the Yamasees decided to follow the Tuscarora strategy of waging a preventive attack. Unlike the Tuscaroras, the Yamasees enjoyed wide support among southeastern Indians. They were closely aligned with the powerful Creeks as well as with the Catawbas, piedmont Indians who feared that they would be next in the expanding colony's path. The Yamasees also received indications of support from the Cherokees while, farther west, the French and the Choctaws saw that a Yamasee uprising would advance their interests.

In May 1715, the Yamasees rose and attacked South Carolina settlements while the Creeks and Catawbas drove English traders from their villages. Indian enemies, one panicked colonist wrote, "Surround us on Every Side but the Sea Side. . . . [W]e have not one Nation for us." By summer's end,

Tuscarora Uprising During their surprise attack on North Carolina colonists in 1711, the Tuscaroras seized both black and white captives.

Yamasees had slain about four hundred colonists, driven many more from their farms and plantations, and generally paralyzed the colony.

The tide turned against the Yamasees in January 1716 when the Cherokees unexpectedly entered the war against the Creeks, depriving the Yamasees of their most powerful supporters. While friendly with the Yamasees, the Cherokees had long resented Creek slave raids and hoped to supplant the Creeks as South Carolina's principal trade partner. In a surprise move, Cherokees killed Creek delegates who were seeking support at the Cherokee town of Toogaloo and then launched attacks on Ochese Creek and Yamasee towns. The conflict with the Cherokees diverted the Creeks from substantially assisting the Yamasees in their conflict with the colonists.

A comparable diversion occurred when the Iroquois undertook a new round of mourning wars against the Catawbas, the Yamasees' other major ally. The Catawbas were also undermined when traders from Virginia, an important source of guns, stopped dealing with them. While the Yamasees and their allies ran short of guns and ammunition, their Indian and English foes enjoyed ample supplies of both. In the face of this imbalance, the Ochese Creeks left South Carolina for their former villages on the Chatahoochee while the Yamasees fled to Florida, where Spanish officials had finally changed their mission-based policy and begun seeking Indian allies without insisting they become subjects and Christians.

Only with the support of the Cherokees and Iroquois was South Carolina able to survive the Yamasee War. Although the colony had "won" the conflict, nearly a decade would pass before its substitution of enslaved Africans for Indians would provide it with an economic foundation—the production of rice for large-scale export—that did not depend primarily on Native Americans.

The Southeast in an Age of Turmoil: The Human Toll

Although precise statistics do not exist on the slave trade and on Indian populations in the Southeast, a careful study by historian Alan Gallay estimates that between thirty thousand and fifty thousand Native Americans were captured and sold as slaves between 1670 and 1715. If we place these figures against estimates of the total (declining) Indian population during this period, it appears that between 23 and 40 percent of the total Indian population in 1685 was enslaved and that during the half century from 1670 to 1720, the Indian population in areas primarily affected by the slave trade declined by as much as two-thirds. Of course, other factors in addition to the exodus of enslaved Indians contributed to the decline—epidemic diseases, warfare, emigration, and the health-related effects of upheaval and dislocation. Meanwhile, the combined population of whites and blacks between 1685 and 1715 increased nearly tenfold, from about four thousand to nearly forty thousand.

The Indians who became English-owned slaves went in many directions. Some remained in South Carolina as plantation laborers, some were sold to other English mainland colonies as far north as Massachusetts, but most were shipped to Barbados, Jamaica, and other English colonies in the West Indies. The island colonies kept few records of their Indian slave imports so as to avoid paying taxes on them to British imperial officials. Most probably died in the lethal disease environment and plantation regimen of the tropics, where even most Africans met early deaths. Evidence of the number and conditions of enslaved Indians shipped to other mainland colonies is also scant. Most of those sent to Virginia worked on plantations on the upper York River. Colonists in the North, from Pennsylvania to Massachusetts, initially turned to Indian slaves from Carolina because they were far cheaper than Africans. But the number remained small because most northern colonies barred further imports after the Tuscarora and Yamasee wars, fearing that the slaves would arouse nearby Indians to join an uprising against the English. As with English-owned Indian slaves, most of the much smaller number captured by Indian allies of Louisiana were shipped to French sugar plantations in the West Indies.

WEST OF THE MISSISSIPPI: NATIVE RESISTANCE AND CULTURAL TRANSFORMATION

Although the East witnessed most of the upheaval associated with European imperial and colonial efforts in the late seventeenth and early eighteenth centuries, those areas west of the Mississippi River where Europeans intruded were by no means immune. Parallel to developments in New England and the Chesapeake, rising Pueblo-Spanish tensions

in New Mexico led to the outbreak of large-scale violence. In contrast to Indians in the English colonies, the Pueblos actually expelled their rulers—indeed the entire Spanish population of New Mexico—for a time. When Spanish power was eventually restored in the province, it was on decidedly milder terms than in the seventeenth century. Along with increased European activity on the Mississippi and Great Plains, the Spanish return to New Mexico was a sign that European expansion and imperial competition would soon expand beyond the Eastern Woodlands.

Pueblo Revolts

For the first two-thirds of the seventeenth century, Pueblo Indians lived in uneasy tension with Spanish colonists in New Mexico. While many Pueblos had converted to Christianity, others were ambivalent or rejected the new religion altogether because of the Franciscan missionaries' forceful tactics. Many Pueblos spoke Spanish, raised livestock, or married colonists. Yet even Pueblos who were receptive to aspects of Spanish culture resented encomenderos' harsh treatment of Indian laborers, laws prohibiting them from trading with non-Pueblo Indians, and many colonists' general disdain for Indians. They reconciled themselves to Spanish colonization for the time being because Christianity seemed to protect them from droughts and because the Spaniards provided vital protection from raids by other Indians.

As the century wore on, Pueblos grew increasingly impatient with Spanish rule. The turning point in Pueblo-Spanish relations was a sequence of consecutive droughts between 1666 and 1671. With most farm crops failing, Pueblos starved in large numbers while also becoming more vulnerable to epidemic diseases. The Apaches and Navajos, also short of food, resumed raiding Indian pueblos with frightening effectiveness. In the face of all these factors, six pueblos were abandoned during the late 1660s and early 1670s, and the total Pueblo population fell to seventeen thousand—just 20 percent of what it had been when New Mexico was established in 1598.

These catastrophes, and Spanish inability to prevent or halt them, fostered a spiritual crisis in which many Indians turned to traditional religious leaders who claimed that Christianity was destroying, rather than enriching, the Pueblos and their culture. Increasingly, Pueblos saw Spanish rule and Catholicism as violating their sacred attachment to the land and their deeply rooted beliefs in the importance of social balance and harmony. In these ways, the Spanish and particularly the Franciscans were threats to Pueblo spiritual order.

A new governor, Juan Francisco Treviño, arrived in 1675 and supported the Franciscans in suppressing the revival. Compared to their fellow Catholics, the Jesuits, the Franciscans were far less tolerant of indigenous religious practices and placed more emphasis on Indians' obeying religious authority, even employing force and violence when they deemed it necessary. Now Franciscans in New Mexico entered the sacred kivas in each pueblo, destroying sacred objects and publicly flogging religious leaders, not simply to punish them but also to humiliate them in front of their followers. Then soldiers sacked kivas throughout the colony and arrested forty-seven religious leaders for "idolatry" and "sorcery." After three of the arrested Indians were executed and a fourth committed suicide, the rest were sentenced to slavery. In an unprecedented act, several dozen Pueblo warriors stormed the governor's palace in Santa Fe and demanded the prisoners' release. With most Spanish troops mobilized away from the capital for defense against the Navajos and Apaches, Treviño capitulated.

Although releasing the religious leaders, Spanish authorities and missionaries continued efforts to prevent them from preaching. But the Pueblo warriors' action had proven that, despite their traditional autonomy, their linguistic differences, and the geographic distances between them, the pueblos could act together and prevail over Spanish power. A group of the most determined religious and political leaders secretly gathered at Taos Pueblo and planned the expulsion of the colonizers. The group reflected the breadth of anti-Spanish sentiment among New Mexico's pueblos. They included traditionalists such as El Saca, their Taos host, and Popé, one of those arrested and released by Treviño, as well as Christian converts with baptismal names such as Luis Tupatú, Pedro Naranjo (see Indian Voices), and Antonio Malacate. Some Christians were of Mexican Indian, Spanish, or even African as well as Pueblo ancestry. Despite long-held antagonisms between Pueblos and

Entrance to Kiva, Pecos Pueblo As the centers of traditional Pueblo religious practice and anti-Catholic resistance, the kivas were prime targets of the Franciscan missionaries.

Apaches, the revolt's leaders successfully cultivated the support of several Apache bands.

The leaders planned several uprisings against the Spanish but postponed them when one or more pueblos declined to participate. Then in 1680 Popé had a vision in which three figures, "emit[ting] fire from all the extremities of their bodies," told him how and when to plan an uprising in which each pueblo would attack local colonists on an appointed day. He was to make a knotted cord of maguey, a local plant, each knot signifying "the number of days they must wait before the rebellion." Messengers began carrying the cord to each pueblo, but, after Indians loyal to the Spanish warned the authorities, the Indians at Taos and some Apache allies acted two days in advance. On August 10, after attacking and killing all but two colonists at Taos, they marched to Santa Fe, summoning Indians from other pueblos. Within a week more than twenty-five hundred Pueblos surrounded the capital, separating the one thousand Spanish there from the colony's widely scattered troops.

For the first time in nearly a century, the Pueblo Indians controlled their Rio Grande Valley homeland. On August 21 they allowed the colonists in Santa Fe, mostly women and children, to leave, saying, "we are at quits with the Spaniards and the persons whom we have killed; . . . now we shall live as

INDIAN VOICES   PEDRO NARANJO, SAN FELIPE PUEBLO, 1681

The Pueblo Revolt in New Mexico was the most successful Indian uprising in American history, driving out Spanish colonizers for twelve years and preventing the complete resumption of their rule for two decades. Most of the revolt's Pueblo Indian supporters were disillusioned Catholic converts who sought to return to indigenous religion and self-government. As in many subsequent Native American uprisings, they were inspired by a visionary prophet-leader, in this case Popé, a San Juan Pueblo. In the revolt's earliest stage, before the Pueblos expelled the Spaniards from New Mexico, colonial authorities conducted hearings on how and why the revolt began by soliciting testimony from Spanish and Indian witnesses, including some captured rebels. One of the captives, eighty-year-old Pedro Naranjo, from the pueblo of San Felipe, was particularly forthcoming in describing Popé and his visions and in providing an "insider's" account of participants' sentiments and actions.

Like all the hearing transcripts, this one was recorded by a Spanish clerk and thereby subject to errors based on mistranslation and on cultural or religious bias. But in general Naranjo's descriptions of Popé's vision and other details are consistent with other accounts of Pueblo beliefs. And unlike most Indian witnesses at the hearings, Naranjo testified in fluent Spanish rather than through an interpreter who might have further garbled his words. Pueblo and non-Pueblo scholars alike regard his testimony as one of the most useful records of the revolt's origins and beginnings.

It happened that in an estufa of the pueblo of Los Taos there appeared to the said Popé three figures of Indians who never came out of the estufa.[1] They gave Popé to understand that they were going underground to the lake of Copala. He saw these figures emit fire from all the extremities of their bodies, and that one of them was called Caudi, another Tilini, and the other Tleume; and these three beings spoke to the said Popé. . . . They told him to make a cord of maguey fiber and tie some knots in it which would signify the number of days that they must wait before the rebellion. He said that the cord was passed through all the pueblos of the kingdom so that the ones which agreed to it [the rebellion] might untie one knot in sign of obedience, and by the other knots they would know the days which were lacking; and this was to be done on pain of death to those who refused to agree to it. As a sign of agreement and notice of having concurred in the treason and perfidy[2] they were to send up smoke signals to that effect in each one of the pueblos singly. The said cord was taken from pueblo to pueblo by the swiftest youths under the penalty of death if they revealed the secret. Everything being thus arranged, two days before the time set for its execution, because his lordship had learned of it and had imprisoned two Indian accomplices from the pueblo of Tesuque, it was carried out prematurely that night, because it seemed to them that they were now discovered; and they killed religious, Spaniards, women, and children. This being done, it was proclaimed in all the pueblos that everyone in common should obey the commands of their father whom they did not know, which would be given through El Caydi or El Popé. This was heard by Alonso Catití, who came to the pueblo of this declarant to say that everyone must unite to go to the villa to kill the governor and the Spaniards who had remained with him, and that he who did not obey would, on their return, be beheaded; and in fear of this they agreed to it. Finally the señor governor and those who were with him escaped from the siege, and later this declarant saw that as soon as the Spaniards had left the kingdom an order came from the said Indian, Popé, in which he commanded all the Indians to break the lands and enlarge their cultivated fields, saying that now they were as they had been in ancient times, free from the labor they had performed for the religious and the Spaniards, who could not now be alive. He [Naranjo] said that this is the legitimate cause and the reason they had for rebelling, because they had always desired to live as they had when they came out of the lake of Copala. . . .

Asked for what reason they so blindly burned the images, temples, crosses, and other things of divine worship, he stated that the said Indian, Popé, came down in person, and with him El Saca and El Chato from the pueblo of Los Taos, and other captains and leaders and many people who were in his train, and he ordered in all the pueblos through which he passed that they instantly break up and burn the images of the holy Christ, the Virgin Mary and the other saints, the crosses, and everything pertaining to Christianity, and that they burn the temples, break up the bells, and separate from the wives whom God had given them in marriage and take those whom they desired. In order to take away their baptismal names, the water, and the holy oils, they were to plunge into the rivers and wash themselves with amole, which is a root native to the country, washing even their clothing, with the understanding that there would thus be taken from them the character of the holy sacraments. . . .

Asked what arrangements and plans they had made for the contingency of the Spaniard's return, he said that what he knows concerning the questions is that they were always saying they would have to fight to the death, for they do not wish to live in any other way than they are living at present; and the demons in the estufa of Taos had given them to understand that as soon as Spaniards began to move toward this kingdom they would warn them so that they might unite, and none of them would be caught.

[1]The passage from the four worlds below this one, through which Pueblos believe their ancestors passed before emerging in the Fifth World via Lake Copala.
[2]Undoubtedly, the Spanish clerk's terms.

Source: *Revolt of the Pueblo Indians of New Mexico and Otermín's Attempted Reconquest, 1680–1682*, Coronado Cuarto Centennial Publications, ed. George P. Hammond (Albuquerque: University of New Mexico Press, 1942), vol. 9, 246–248.

we like and settle in this villa and wherever we see fit." Heeding the three fiery figures in his vision, Popé toured the pueblos, ordering Indians to repudiate Christianity by destroying the churches and all Christian paraphernalia, terminating marriages sanctioned only by the priests, and erasing the effects of baptism by washing themselves in rivers with amole, a native root. Christian Indians who resisted his message were killed. At each pueblo, he urged the inhabitants to rebuild kivas and resume traditional ceremonies, especially the katsina dances that would bring rain and restore the "abundant health and leisure" they had known before the Spanish lured them away from "the law of their ancestors."

Meanwhile, the Spanish refugees, along with several hundred Christian Indians, fled south to El Paso, from which they attempted without success to retake New Mexico the following year. Their position was further weakened as Pueblo refugees at El Paso itself threatened to rebel in 1684 at Spanish failure to protect them from Apache attacks and as news of the revolt inspired similar uprisings among Janos, Sumas, Piros, and other missionized Indians across what is now northern Mexico. Until the end of the century, New Spain's northern frontier was in a state of upheaval.

Much of the turmoil in New Mexico was among Indians themselves. Despite having eradicated Christianity and restored the traditional ceremonies, the Pueblos were desperately short of food and vulnerable to diseases due to the persistence of drought throughout the 1680s. Popé and other leaders blamed one another for the continued adversity while pueblos raided one another for corn and livestock. Popé's influence declined as Picurís, Tewas, and Tanos, led by Luis Tupatú, went to war against a loose coalition of Indians from Taos, Pecos, and several other pueblos. Meanwhile Apaches, Navajos, and Utes, who had collected most of the horses and many of the guns left by the fleeing Spanish, raided the pueblos with near impunity. Several pueblos were abandoned, and some Indians left the Rio Grande Valley altogether to live among the Ácoma Pueblos, Hopis, Apaches, and Navajos.

By the late 1680s, the Spanish at El Paso were ready to try and regain New Mexico. After expeditions in 1688 and 1689 destroyed the pueblos of Santa Ana and Zia, respectively, they mounted a more serious effort in 1692 under the command of a new governor, Diego de Vargas. Upon entering Santa Fe, Vargas promptly sent messengers to the pueblos, shrewdly promising to pardon all Indians, even rebel leaders, who surrendered peacefully and pledged loyalty to Spain. Among the first to respond were Domingo Naranjo and Luis Tupatú, whom Vargas formally recognized as *caciques* (governors or chiefs) of the Tesuques and of the Tewas and Tanos, respectively. Accompanied by Tupatú and three hundred more Indian troops, plus about one hundred Spanish soldiers and several priests, Vargas toured the pueblos, offering peace and baptism to all. Although many Indians hid and refused to surrender, most participated in ceremonies formally reinstating Spanish rule. Once the Rio Grande pueblos were secured, Vargas traveled west and obtained pledges of loyalty from the Ácomas, Zunis, and Hopis.

Vargas failed to realize that many Pueblo Indians, caught off guard by his tactics while bitterly divided among themselves, did not consider their ceremonial surrenders as submission to Spanish rule. While the governor recruited soldiers and settlers in El Paso, rumors spread among the Indians that he planned to avenge the deaths of all colonists slain in 1680. While some pueblos welcomed his return in October 1693, others resisted, particularly some Tanos who had occupied Santa Fe since 1680. When the Spanish arrived in December with little food, the Tanos refused to admit them to the city, forcing them to camp on the outskirts in the cold. After two weeks, the desperate Spanish successfully stormed the city, executing seventy Tanos and enslaving four hundred more.

Over the next year, Spanish troops fought and finally subdued the resisting pueblos. Attempting to quell rebelliousness, the Franciscans resumed some of the harsh punishments and abuses of traditional religion that had fueled the revolt of 1680. In 1696 a new rebellion broke out when Indians simultaneously murdered missionaries at five pueblos. Although not all Pueblos joined the uprising, most fled to the mountains in fear of Spanish retaliation. As in 1692, Vargas finally restored peace in the Rio Grande Valley by pardoning many rebels. Two more years passed before the Ácomas, Lagunas, and Zunis made peace. Only the Hopis successfully resisted the reimposition of Spanish rule. In 1701 anti-Spanish Hopis attacked and dispersed the lone Christian Hopi pueblo, Awatovi, and then repelled Spanish troops sent to subdue them. The Hopis thereafter remained independent of Spanish rule. A short-lived uprising among the Zunis in 1703 marked the final end of nearly a quarter century of Pueblo revolts.

The revolts were enormously costly to the non-Hopi pueblos. Besides failing to rid themselves of the Spanish, they lost about three thousand of their seventeen thousand people between 1680 and 1700. Nevertheless the Spanish victory remained limited; Spain did not restore the most odious aspects of its earlier rule, so the Pueblos exercised more autonomy in the eighteenth century than in the seventeenth. While the Franciscans resumed preaching and converting, they were forbidden from entering the kivas or otherwise interfering with Indians practicing traditional religion. Indeed many Pueblos participated in both Catholic services on Sundays and traditional ceremonies at other times. While the Spanish appointed governors of the pueblos, the Indians followed their traditional leaders, recognizing the governors as intermediaries between them and the Spanish rather than as authority figures. The Spanish abolished the encomienda so that, while many Indians continued to work for colonists as servants and in other menial positions, they did not do so as forced laborers.

The process whereby Pueblos simultaneously cooperated with the Spanish while controlling life inside their communities has been termed "compartmentalization" by one anthropologist. Looked at more broadly, it reflects the recognition by both Pueblos and settlers in New Mexico of their interdependence. Nowhere was this more apparent than in the colony's armed forces in which Pueblos after 1700 served faithfully and which protected both them and the colonists from outside attack. Although the two populations remained distinct, with elite Spanish monopolizing political power, they became increasingly familiar with one another and with one another's customs and habits. As the late Tewa Pueblo anthropologist Alfonso Ortiz put it, "during the eighteenth century, the increasingly native Hispanics and the undeniably hispanicized Pueblo peoples learned to live and let live."

Indians on New Mexico's Periphery

Over the course of the seventeenth century, Pueblo-Spanish interactions affected southwestern Indians living outside New Mexico itself. Through raiding, trading, and absorbing Pueblo captives and refugees, the Navajos, Apaches, Southern Utes, Jumanos, and other neighboring Indians acquired horses, domestic livestock, guns, axes, knives, and cloth in addition to the maize, cotton, and other Pueblo products with which they were already familiar. Horses in particular rendered Indians far more effective in hunting buffalo, raiding rivals, and resisting Spanish slaving expeditions. The influx of European goods accelerated when the Pueblo Revolt of 1680, which many Navajos and Apaches actively supported, forced the Spanish to withdraw from their colony for twelve years. Navajos, Apaches, and Southern Utes captured thousands of horses left behind by the fleeing colonists as well as acquiring livestock and other goods. New Mexico's Indian neighbors not only used the new goods themselves but also traded them to other Native Americans. By the beginning of the eighteenth century, raids by mounted Navajos, Apaches, Southern Utes, and the latter's Comanche allies to the north were effectively containing the colony's expansion.

The Native Americans most affected by Spanish-Pueblo contacts were the Navajos. During the era of the revolts, hundreds of Pueblos sought refuge among the Navajos, and many chose to remain rather than return and live under Spanish rule. The influence of the Pueblo refugees on Navajo life and culture was profound. From the Pueblos, Navajo women learned the ways of sheep. While Navajo men farmed, hunted, and cared for horses, women managed vast herds of sheep, which became critical sources of both meat and cloth. In quest of grazing land and security from outside attack, the Navajos spread into many previously unoccupied canyons of the San Juan River drainage. They also incorporated Pueblo ceremonies and beliefs into their own religion and adapted pottery-making and other techniques from the newcomers. Navajos continued to raid New Mexico for horses, sheep, and other goods until increasing depredations by Utes and Comanches, as well as by Pueblo-Spanish forces, led them to make peace with New Mexico in 1716.

European Encroachments and Cultural Change on the Plains

For the most part, Europeans exercised influence on Native Americans between the Mississippi and Rio Grande by trading horses and other goods rather than by directly colonizing them, leaving Indians free to select and use the new items as they saw fit. But slowly the growing European competition for domination of North America affected the West more directly. Following his descent of the Mississippi River (discussed earlier in this chapter), the French explorer La Salle established a small colony at Matagorda Bay in 1684 among the Karankawas after failing to find the river's mouth. Over the next three years, Native Americans of the southern Plains periodically encountered both the French, as they searched for the river, and Spanish soldiers sent to find and expel the French. The colony collapsed in 1687 due to starvation, sickness, infighting (which cost La Salle his life), and Karankawa attacks.

Attempting to establish a foothold in the region before the French returned, the Spanish in 1690 dispatched traders and missionaries to establish a new province, Tejas (or Texas), among the powerful Caddos. But the Franciscans' scorn for Caddo religious traditions, two deadly epidemics, and the repeated destruction of crops by Spanish livestock alienated the Caddos. In 1693 they ordered the Spanish to leave on pain of death. Far from rebellion-plagued New Mexico and without adequate military support, the would-be colonizers complied.

French traders proved more effective than the Spanish at establishing a presence among the Caddos. Dispatched from the new colony of Louisiana, Quebec-born Louis Juchereau de Saint-Denis in 1700 established lasting ties with the Caddo villages on the Red River. The outbreak of the War of the Spanish Succession temporarily turned the commercial alliance into a military one in which some Natchitoches Caddos, returning with Saint-Denis to Louisiana, joined the French war effort in the Southeast. With the war over in 1713, Saint-Denis, with the Natchitoches, returned to the Red River and established a French-Caddo trading post. With twelve French and thirty Caddos, Saint-Denis then traveled overland, trading with various Native groups on the southern Plains, until reaching the Spanish post of San Juan Bautista on the lower Rio Grande in July 1714. The expedition's trading successes and uncontested intrusion into their territory alarmed Spanish officials who, fearing the loss of their Indian allies, acted to counter French influence by preparing to reestablish Texas.

Meanwhile French traders operating from Illinois and a post at the mouth of the Arkansas were expanding contacts with Mississippi Valley and central Plains Indians. Pawnees, Wichitas, Osages, and other peoples of the region were acquiring guns, horses, and other goods from them, from the Spanish at trade fairs held at Taos and other New Mexico pueblos, and from other Indians through either trade or force. Before 1700, French traders had explored the lower Missouri and recognized both the trade potential of the river's inhabitants and its importance as a link to still more distant regions. North of the Missouri, few Indians had horses, but many had acquired guns from French or English traders in exchange for furs or for helping the French fight the Iroquois and the Mesquakies (discussed earlier).

CONCLUSION

The late seventeenth and early eighteenth centuries constituted a tumultuous time for Native Americans throughout the East and in the colonized portion of the Southwest. Indians in these areas were obliged to respond to the challenges raised by Europeans either by resisting, accommodating, or otherwise creatively throwing back challenges of their own to the newcomers. No matter how successfully they responded, disease and war took many Indian lives and depleted many Indian societies. The survivors gathered to form new communities, often representing multiple tribal and cultural backgrounds. Although physical survival was their most immediate priority, they also adapted and reshaped their cultural identities, redefining who they were in relation to one another, to other peoples, and to the spiritual forces animating the universe. The ability of Indian peoples to reinvent themselves under radically transformed circumstances was perhaps their most remarkable accomplishment during this highly charged period.

SUGGESTED READINGS

Cronon, William. *Changes in the Land: Indians, Colonists, and the Ecology of New England.* New York: Hill and Wang, 1983. A classic study of the environmental implications of Indian-European relations in one colonial region.

Drake, James D. *King Philip's War: Civil War in New England, 1675–76.* Amherst: University of Massachusetts Press, 1999. The best one-volume study of Metacom's War.

Gallay, Alan. *The Indian Slave Trade: The Rise of the English Empire in the American South, 1670–1717.* New Haven: Yale University Press, 2002. A pathbreaking discussion of the trade in enslaved Indians and its impact on the Southeast.

Greer, Allan. *Mohawk Saint: Catherine Tekakwitha and the Jesuits.* Oxford, UK: Oxford University Press, 2005. A brilliant biography, studded with insights into the multiple cultures and historical contexts that shaped Tekakwitha's life.

Haefli, Evan, and Kevin M. Sweeney. *Captors and Captives: The 1704 French and Indian Raid on Deerfield.* Amherst: University of Massachusetts Press, 2003. A model of borderlands history, providing a fully rounded study of the raid and subsequent captivities, and identifying most Indian, French, and English participants, how and why they came to be at Deerfield that day, and what happened to them afterward.

Kessel, John L. *Spain in the Southwest: A Narrative History of Colonial New Mexico, Arizona, Texas, and California.* Norman: University of Oklahoma Press, 2002. A richly detailed, informative history that emphasizes Spanish-Indian relations.

Knaut, Andrew L. *The Pueblo Revolt: Conquest and Resistance in Seventeenth-Century New Mexico.* An excellent discussion of the revolt and its historical context, with attention to relations between Pueblos and ordinary as well as elite colonists.

Lepore, Jill. *The Name of War: King Philip's War and the Origins of American Identity.* New York: Alfred A. Knopf, 1998. A nuanced discussion of how the protagonists and later Americans have remembered and interpreted the war and its brutality.

Merrell, James H. *The Indians' New World: Catawbas and Their Neighbors from European Contact Through the Era of Removal.* Chapel Hill: University of North Carolina Press, 1989. Outstanding historical account of one Indian nation, created out of the chaos and dislocations of the late seventeenth and early eighteenth centuries.

Richter, Daniel K. *The Ordeal of the Longhouse: The Peoples of the Iroquois League in the Era of European Colonization.* Chapel Hill: University of North Carolina Press, 1992. A masterful account of the Five Nations in a time of upheaval.

White, Richard. *The Middle Ground: Indians, Empires, and Republics in the Great Lakes Region, 1650–1815.* Cambridge, UK: Cambridge University Press, 1991. A classic study of Indian-European relations and their transformation over time in a contested borderland.

Native Americans in Peace
and War, 1716–1754

In about 1700, a daughter named Coosapona-keesa was born in the Lower Creek town of Coweta to a prominent Creek woman (like most Indian women, never named in European documents) and Edward Griffin, an English trader. Coosaponakeesa spent the first seven years of her life with her mother's extended family in Coweta, where she spoke the Muskogee language and was immersed in a culture and history that long pre-dated the arrival of Europeans. Then her father placed her with an English family in Carolina, where she spoke, read, and wrote English; practiced Christianity; and acquired a second name—Mary. At the age of sixteen, Coosaponakeesa/Mary stood on the verge of adulthood, steeped in the cultures of two peoples who alternately cooperated and competed over a wide area of the Southeast. In 1716 she was back in Coweta where her maternal uncle Brims, the mico (headman) of the town and the most powerful Creek political leader, was negotiating an end to the Yamasee War with the Carolinians. To help seal the agreement, Brims agreed with John Musgrove, one of the Carolina peace commissioners, that Coosaponakeesa/Mary would marry Musgrove's son, also named John. Like his

new wife, John Musgrove Jr. spoke Creek and (apparently) had a Creek mother.

The Musgroves' married life reflected their bicultural backgrounds. For nearly a decade they remained among the Creeks, who considered Mary and possibly John members of the Creek Nation by virtue of maternal descent. After living among the English for sixteen years, the couple settled among the Yamacraw Creeks at the mouth of the Savannah River in 1732. Their move proved well timed when, less than a year later, James Oglethorpe arrived there to found the new British colony of Georgia. The Musgroves quickly became Georgia's leading source of deerskins and principal suppliers of provisions. In the process, Coosaponakeesa/Mary rose to political prominence as a trusted interpreter, adviser, and diplomatic mediator both to Oglethorpe and to her cousins Chekilli and Malachi, who had succeeded Brims in leading the Creeks. She continued her bicultural role even after John Musgrove, Jr., and a second husband died and she married an Englishman named Thomas Bosomworth in 1744.

Coosaponakeesa/Mary's complex identity as a forceful Anglo-Creek woman posed obstacles as well as opportunities for exercising power and influence on an unstable intercultural frontier. For her services to her own people, the Creeks had granted her extensive tracts of land near Savannah and on three nearby offshore islands. But English law did not allow Mary as a married woman to own property, and it prohibited her as an Indian from selling her land directly to any colonists, even to pay off debts to other colonists. Instead, the English asserted, she had only a "limited right" to sell land to the British crown. For three decades, beginning in the late 1730s, Mary petitioned the British government for reimbursement of expenses incurred in enabling Georgia to survive its early years and for full title to the lands granted her by the Creeks. After Oglethorpe departed in 1743, Georgia officials successfully weakened her influence among the Creek micos for a time, but she quickly recovered her prestige by giving shrewd diplomatic advice to the micos on several occasions. In 1759 the Bosomworths and a new Georgia governor finally reached a compromise on their land dispute in which Mary and Thomas retained one island while they granted Mary's remaining lands to the colony, which promised to turn over to her the proceeds from the sale of the land. Satisfied with this resolution, Coosaponakeesa/Mary resumed her role as Anglo-Creek mediator, serving until her death in 1765.

The life of Coosaponakeesa/Mary illuminates a critical era in Native American history, during which several powerful, favorably located tribes and confederacies proved to be diplomatically astute when it came to dealing with Europeans. The Creeks, Iroquois, and others exploited colonists' needs and played off competing colonies and empires against each other to their own advantage. The intricacies of Indian-European diplomacy afforded prominent roles to those individuals who had the knowledge (including linguistic) and experience to mediate between communities and interest groups on both sides of the cultural divide. The ranks of intercultural brokers included both Native American and European traders, diplomats, and others. Among the most successful brokers were those whose forebears were both Indian and European, people called "mixed-bloods" in English, "*métis*" in French, and "*mestizos*" in Spanish. Very few women emerged as intercultural brokers; Coosaponakeesa/Mary was the best known of those who did. Native Americans and

Europeans alike made little room for women in public life, although matrilineal Indian societies like the Creeks enabled women to exercise power behind the scenes. Coosaponakeesa/Mary drew on her position in Creek society, her marriages, and her bicultural heritage to wield more overt political power than almost any North American woman of her time. Yet she never ceased to struggle against British-imposed barriers of gender and race, against British efforts to subjugate all Indians—even their own allies—to their own authority, and against British claims to sovereignty over Native American lands and peoples.

For most of the period from the end of the Yamasee War in 1716 to the outbreak of the Seven Years War in 1754, Europe's empires were at peace with one another in North America, abetted in part by the refusal of many Indian nations to support their imperial wars. The interval of peace marked not a cessation of Europeans' imperial rivalries and colonizing activities but a shift in approach. Instead of focusing on highly coordinated military efforts, France, Britain, and Spain concentrated on broadening their trade and diplomacy with Indian people and, in some areas, establishing and expanding colonies on Indian lands.

Native peoples exercised the greatest power and autonomy where European goods circulated but where Europeans themselves were not permanently present. Such was the case with the Sioux, the Comanches, and the Osages on the prairies and Plains west of the Mississippi, where Indian-European trade spread during the eighteenth century. At the other extreme were Indians in areas where Europeans' presence was overwhelming, most notably within the oldest British colonies on the Atlantic coast. Overrun by waves of disease and by colonists seeking their land, coastal tribes such as the Narragansetts in Rhode Island and Pamunkeys in Virginia were cut off from outside sources of Indian or European support. In between these extremes, most Indian people followed a variety of calculated strategies for maximizing autonomy on the one hand while interacting reciprocally with Europeans on the other. The Six Nations Iroquois and the Creeks, for example, coordinated competing factions within their own ranks to play off European powers against one another. Among the Choctaws, on the other hand, competing factions fatally

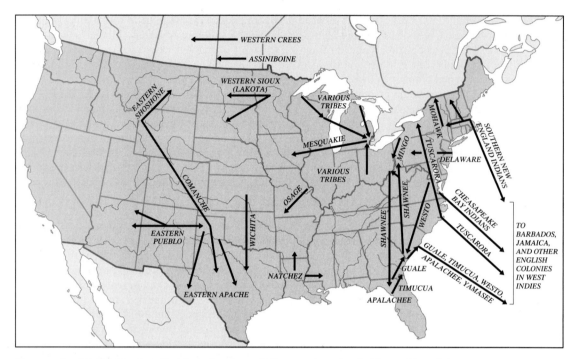

Movements of Native American Peoples, 1675–1750. Native peoples relocated for a wide variety of reasons. Some were forcibly carried as captives or slaves, others moved as refugees or under pressure from Europeans or other Indians, and still others sought access to horses or to European trade goods. *Source map:* Cambridge History of the Native Peoples of the Americas, *vol. 1:* North America, *part 2 (Cambridge, UK: Cambridge University Press, 1996), 190–191.*

divided into civil war. Other Native groups successfully pursued long-standing alliances with one or another empire, such as the Chickasaws with Britain and the Pueblo Indians with Spain. Such alliances were crucial to suppressing anti-European resistance by peoples like the Mesquakies and many Delawares. To avoid a similar fate, other anti-European groups such as the Shawnees relocated so as to limit European ties to the strictly commercial.

For many Native Americans, involvement with colonizing Europeans brought fundamental change in their everyday lives. The mass migrations, both forced and self-initiated, of Indians that had begun earlier (see Chapter 4) escalated still further after 1720. New Indian refugee villages across the East, particularly in the Ohio Valley, augmented older ones in New France and New York. Farther west, Native peoples such as the Sioux and Comanches moved to the Plains from very different environ-

ments, using their military prowess to take advantage of trade opportunities among both Indians and Europeans. Native American farmers adjusted their annual subsistence rounds to produce surpluses of animal and farm products for Europeans while adopting an astonishing array of new material goods, including cloth and blankets; metal tools, dishware, and jewelry; glass containers and beads; guns, ammunition, and gunpowder; horses and other livestock; and alcohol. In the course of interacting with Europeans, Native communities significantly modified their material cultures, gender and other social patterns, and political ties with both Europeans and one another. Yet these modifications were just that—modifications—that built on rather than erased older ways of life. Several generations of trade and alliance, even the adoption of Christianity, failed to divorce most Indians from their cultural identities.

INDIANS AND EMPIRES: THE EAST

The multifaceted alliances and rivalries among Native Americans and European empires in the Eastern Woodlands centered on a long swath of land stretching from Mi'kmaq and Abenaki homelands on the Atlantic coast through Iroquois country and along the crest of the Appalachian Mountains to the Gulf of Mexico. The imperial rivals in this region were, first, Great Britain with its unprecedented colonial population and global economic power; second, France, the most powerful, centralized monarchy in Europe; and third, Spain, now a second-rate European power but one that still wielded influence in the Southeast. In the face of imperial competition, the overriding goals of most eastern Indians were to take advantage of the economic and technological benefits of European trade while retaining their political independence and their distinct cultural identities. In so doing they hoped to avoid becoming casualties in Europe's wars and becoming excessively dependent on—and therefore subordinate to—any European empire. Above all, they wanted to avoid the fate of Indians in the British seaboard colonies whose lands were being overrun by European settlers. In pursuing this common goal, different Indian communities and tribes followed different strategies, depending on such factors as their relative political and economic power, their geographic position, and their ties with Indian and European outsiders.

Abenakis, Mi'kmaqs, and Anglo-French Colonization

The restoration of Anglo-French peace in 1713 heightened rather than reduced tensions among Indians situated between New France and New England. While most Mi'kmaqs and Abenakis had close ties to French traders and missionaries, they preferred to remain neutral in conflicts between the two European powers. But the Treaty of Utrecht awarded the French colony of Acadia, where many Mi'kmaqs lived, to the British, who renamed it Nova Scotia. The treaty left ambiguous a New England–New France boundary that ran through Abenaki lands. As soon as the treaty was signed, Indians from Nova Scotia to the upper Connecticut River confronted encroaching English officials and colonists. While attempting to counter French influence by offering presents, British authorities in Massachusetts and Nova Scotia simultaneously alienated Native Americans by insisting that they submit to English rule. "I have my own kings and governors, my chief and my elders," a Penobscot Abenaki leader told a British delegation in 1714, "I do not wish . . . that any stranger erect any fort or establishment on my land . . . . I am [strong] enough to occupy the land on my own."

Anglo-Indian tensions continued thereafter as French Jesuit missionaries among the Abenakis and Mi'kmaqs, along with French Acadians in Nova Scotia, joined in resisting British rule. Full-scale Anglo-Indian war finally broke out in 1722. The conflict in Maine and Nova Scotia is often called Râle's War, after a French missionary, or Dummer's War, after a British official. Bands of Mi'kmaqs periodically seized English fishing boats and attacked British towns in Nova Scotia, but they were unable to inflict lasting damage on the colonists. In Maine fierce fighting between Abenakis and the English culminated in 1724 when the English attacked and burned Norridgewock, killing many inhabitants, including Râle. Farther west, the conflict is usually termed Grey Lock's War. Born in Woronoco, on the Connecticut River in western Massachusetts, a young Grey Lock had fled with his entire town as English colonists encroached on their land in 1673. His anti-English militancy and that of his fellow refugees never wavered thereafter. In 1723 he rallied the Western Abenakis, along with supporters from Indian refugee towns at Schaghticoke, New York, and Kahnawake, New France. Attacking English settlements and military patrols with impunity, Grey Lock and his warriors rolled back English colonization on the upper Connecticut River.

By 1725, the Penobscot Abenakis, recognizing the futility of resisting English colonization without French military support, signed a peace treaty with the British. Over the next two years, they persuaded other Eastern Abenakis and the Mi'kmaqs to ratify the treaty. While the Indians acknowledged English sovereignty, they did so not as separate nations but as a united Wabanaki alliance in hopes that they would constitute a stronger force for dealing with both Britain and France in the future.

Although the Western Abenakis did not sign the treaty, they too ceased their attacks in 1727.

For nearly two decades peace reigned across the northeastern borderlands. Mi'kmaqs and Abenakis regularly traded with both British and French and became familiar sights in English towns. British Protestants made some efforts to convert Indians, but they were unable to compete with New France's Jesuit Catholics. The interval of peace demonstrated above all that Native Americans could live on friendly terms with neighbors of both European nationalities. Nevertheless renewed English expansion generated tensions that erupted when Britain and France once again went to war.

With the widening in 1744 of the War of the Austrian Succession (1740–1748) to North America, where it was called King George's War, Mi'kmaqs and Abenakis openly allied with the French, recognizing that English advances were the greater danger to their independence. Although the Western Abenakis expelled most English colonists from the upper Connecticut River valley and the French and Mi'kmaqs together nearly drove the British from Nova Scotia, the Treaty of Aix-la-Chapelle (1748), agreed to by diplomats in Europe, nullified these accomplishments. As a result, tensions in the region remained high at midcentury.

Iroquois Diplomacy in an Imperial Age

To the south and west of Abenaki country, the Five Nations Iroquois Confederacy (after 1722, the Six Nations; see Chapter 4) worked carefully to play off England against France even though the Treaty of Utrecht formally recognized the Iroquois as British subjects and they maintained their special Covenant Chain system of alliances with the English colonies. Simultaneously pursuing alliances with both European empires, the Confederacy transformed itself from a military to a diplomatic power in eastern North America.

One example of this policy is the Iroquois Confederacy's relations with Native peoples and English colonies to the south. Early in the eighteenth century, smallpox resumed taking Iroquois lives, so Iroquois warriors once again resorted to mourning wars (see Chapter 3) as a means of replenishing their ranks. Having made peace with their former Indian enemies to the west, pro-French members of the Confederacy expanded long-standing animosities with Catawbas and Cherokees into full-scale raids, often joined by other pro-French Indians. The British wished to halt the violence between their northern and southern Indian allies as well as to prevent traveling warriors from approaching colonial towns. But they proceeded cautiously lest they drive the Iroquois into an alliance with the French. In addition, some Iroquois were again helping the English to move other Indians off lands coveted by colonists in Pennsylvania (discussed further in this section). For these reasons, the British needed the Iroquois as much as the Iroquois needed them. Accordingly, Virginia, Pennsylvania, and the Iroquois agreed in 1722 on a boundary line separating the north-south "warriors' path" from English neighborhoods. In so agreeing, the two colonies tacitly accepted the raids' legitimacy. For the next several decades, Iroquois raids on the Catawbas and Cherokees continued with little English interference.

Although they maintained their neutrality, the Iroquois could not prevent Britain and France from expanding at Iroquois expense. Throughout the seventeenth century, the Five Nations had prevented Europeans from establishing permanent posts on their lands. But after the Grand Settlement of 1701 (see Chapter 4), both empires sought direct access to greater numbers of Indians with fur to trade. Accordingly, the French constructed Fort Niagara on Seneca land in 1726, and the British erected Fort Oswego in Onondaga country the next year. While many Iroquois opposed one or both projects, the confederacy's chiefs consented in order to balance factions within their own ranks as well as to appease the two colonial powers. Not only did European traders and soldiers now occupy Six Nations Iroquois territory but also, with the forts easily accessible to the Great Lakes Indians and Canadian Iroquois, the confederacy no longer monopolized links between Indians and European traders.

Even more threatening to the Iroquois than Anglo-French rivalry was the rapid influx of land-hungry European immigrants to the English colonies, especially to Pennsylvania where thousands of Scots-Irish and German immigrants flooded the upper Delaware and Susquehanna valleys. But the Delaware Indians there—refugees who had moved to the valleys so that the Iroquois would protect them (see Chapter 4)—attempted to rebuff Pennsylvania's efforts to buy their land. The colony overcame Delaware resistance with the help of the Iroquois. On several occasions between the late 1720s and early 1740s, the Six Nations claimed authority over the Delawares and sold tracts of their land to Pennsylvania. In the largest and most notorious such sale, known as the Walking Purchase, colony officials produced a blatantly forged "treaty," indicating that the Delawares had agreed in 1700 to sell land extending west from the Delaware River as far as a man could walk in a day and a half. Over the protests of Delaware elders, none of whom remembered such a treaty, the colony in 1734 hired two men to walk as the document stipulated. After rehearsing, the men walked sixty-four miles west, resulting in Pennsylvania's "purchase" of nearly twelve hundred square miles of Delaware land. When the Delawares refused to recognize the sale's validity and threatened any colonists who moved in, members of the Iroquois forcibly escorted the Delawares to the upper Susquehanna River, adjacent to Iroquois territory. The Iroquois thereby placed Pennsylvania in its political debt while establishing the Delawares as buffers between its own homelands and land-hungry colonists.

The Iroquois claimed authority to speak for the Delawares because, in placing themselves under Iroquois protection, the Delawares had become "women." Like actual Native American women, the Delawares could not, according to the Iroquois, speak for themselves in public settings. Instead their Six Nations protectors would speak for them. Once a term of honor, signaling a community's peacefulness and behind-the-scenes influence, the term *women* was acquiring in Anglo-Iroquois diplomacy the connotations of subordination it had for Europeans. At the same time, the British invoked their claims to sovereignty over the Iroquois to claim the lands for themselves, claims that went undisputed so long as British and Iroquois aims were compatible.

As the eighteenth century reached its midpoint, the easternmost Mohawks faced growing encroachments by English colonists while at the same time they became increasingly isolated from the main currents of Six Nations Iroquois diplomacy. While the other nations of the Iroquois Confederacy dealt independently with the English colonies and with other Indians, the Mohawks remained oriented toward New York and the Covenant Chain system of alliances that had bound English and Iroquois (see Chapter 4). During the War of the Austrian Succession, most Mohawks abandoned neutrality to fight against the French, hoping thereby to restore their standing among their own people and the British. But after suffering heavy losses when sent to attack Montreal, they grew resentful that the British took them for granted. At a conference with New York officials in 1753, Theyanoguin, a Mohawk sachem known to the British as Hendrick, pronounced the Covenant Chain dead, concluding "so brother, you are not to expect to hear of me any more and brother we desire to hear no more of you." Both Six Nations Iroquois unity and the Covenant Chain lay shattered.

Indian Refugees in the Ohio Country

Many of the Delawares forced from their Pennsylvania homelands to the upper Susquehanna Valley subsequently declared their independence from the Six Nations by moving to the upper Ohio Valley. They were but one part of a larger repopulating of the Ohio River and its tributaries, a region largely emptied of Native Americans during the Beaver Wars (see Chapter 3). During the 1720s and 1730s, Indians entered "the Ohio country," as the area was called, from all directions. Besides the Delawares came Shawnees, Iroquois (primarily Senecas), Abenakis, Mahicans, and members of other eastern nations. From the north, a band of Hurons and Petuns known as Wyandots left Detroit to begin a new village at Sandusky, while the Miamis migrated from Michigan to the Wabash and Maumee valleys. Smaller numbers of Cherokees arrived from the south, as did some Mascoutens and Kickapoos from the west.

While most Indians moved to the Ohio country to improve their hunting and farming prospects, they also sought to avoid the authority of Britain, France, the Six Nations Iroquois, and even—in some cases—their own nations. Shawnee, Delaware, and Wyandot refugees all spurned leaders in their home communities when they moved, as did the Ohio Iroquois, who became known as Mingos. In breaking with outside political authorities, the Indians in Ohio entered into new political and social relationships with one another. The new peopling of the Ohio Valley represented an expansion of the middle ground from the upper Great Lakes (see Chapter 4). Refugees in this region gathered in interethnic villages to ensure their survival as well as their independence. Kuskuski, Logstown (so named for the log cabins of its residents), and other new towns emerged as centers of economic and political power, their inhabitants courted by outsiders seeking to influence developments in the region. The new communities were often headed by prominent migrants who had not previously been leaders, such as Orontony, an anti-French dissenter who led some Wyandots from Detroit; Aliquippa, a Mingo woman; and Peter Chartier, a Shawnee sachem whose father had been a French-Canadian trader.

Although politically independent, the Ohio Indians eagerly traded with Europeans. For nearly a century, France had maintained a vast network of allies north of the Ohio River through the abundance of "presents" (as European gifts to Indians were now usually termed) it gave them in return for furs and for military services against the British and Six Nations. But the advent of British traders in the Ohio country, beginning in the late 1730s, undermined the French monopoly. The British traders were successful because of the superior quality and lower prices of their wares and because of the active support of their colonial governments. Struggling to compete with these commercial advantages, the French had to sacrifice commercial profits for diplomatic necessity in bestowing gifts on Ohio country Indians. Unable to match England's massive colonial population and its ability to manufacture large volumes of trade goods cheaply, France could hope to maintain its North American empire only by securing the loyalty of Indian allies.

The outbreak of the War of the Austrian Succession only magnified France's disadvantages. A British naval blockade prevented most French goods from reaching North America, raising French prices still further. Yet while offering less than before in the way of presents, French officials insisted that their Indian allies give back more by actively supporting the French war effort. Many Indians saw French conduct as arrogant and in violation of the reciprocity that was the proper foundation of all alliances. As the Wyandot leader Orontony put it, the French "would use [the Indians] as their own people; that is like slaves; and their goods were so dear that they, the Indians, could not buy them." Some Indians refused to pay the prices demanded by the French, others attacked French traders, and a few, such as Orontony's Wyandots and a breakaway Miami town at Pickawillany, led by Memeskia (also known as La Demoiselle and Old Briton), openly allied with Pennsylvania and the Six Nations Iroquois. The widespread Indian resistance to French domination led one official to fear a "general conspiracy" of Indians against the French.

Following the war, Anglo-French competition for control of the Ohio country intensified. With both Virginia and Pennsylvania asserting claims, Captain Pierre-Joseph Cèleron de Blainville led a French expedition through the Great Lakes–Ohio region in 1749. Attempting to intimidate Indians with his show of force, Cèleron erected lead plates proclaiming French territorial authority at key locations. While some Great Lakes Indians returned to the French fold, others—along with nearly all those in Ohio—remained defiant. The focal point for much of this anti-French sentiment was Memeskia, who attracted broad support from former French allies as far west as the Illinois River and north to the upper Great Lakes. Despite this consensus, a smallpox outbreak and internal dissension weakened Memeskia's movement, and in 1752 he was killed and his followers routed by a French-recruited force of Ottawas and Ojibwes. Memeskia's adversaries were as much a product of the middle ground as he was; their leader, Charles Langlade, came from a leading *métis* family. Meanwhile French troops chased British traders out of the Ohio Valley.

At the moment when the French were crushing Memeskia's movement, Ohio Indians faced a diplomatic threat from the English. At a treaty conference at Logstown in 1752, Virginia's delegates insisted that the Mingos, Delawares, and Shawnees confirm their colony's claim to an extensive tract of land at the Ohio Forks. The Delawares and Shawnees boycotted the conference, leaving some Mingos, led by Tanaghrisson, to negotiate with the Virginians. Although he attempted to limit Virginia to just enough land for a fort, Tanaghrisson finally consented to the entire cession after Virginia implicitly threatened his people's "trade and security."

The agreement served only to undermine Tanagh-risson's standing among the Ohio Indians, especially the Delawares whose lands he sold and whose painful memories of the Walking Purchase the cession recalled.

England and France were headed for a showdown. During 1753, French forces began building a fort-lined road from Lake Erie to the Ohio Forks. Seizing a small Virginia post at the Forks in April 1754, the French expanded it and named it Fort Duquesne. In response, Virginia's George Washington assembled militia units and prepared to drive the French from Ohio. An imperial war over the Ohio country loomed.

Creeks and Cherokees

Emerging from the wars of 1702–1716 as the most powerful and independent Indian nation in the Southeast were the Creeks. Creek power was based on the extraordinary national unity of the multilingual, multiethnic Creek Confederacy; the Creeks' ability to play off English Carolina, French Louisiana, and Spanish Florida; and the skillful leadership of the Lower Creek mico Brims in reconciling Creek factions favoring each of the European powers. In the aftermath of war, the Alabama Creeks allowed the French to build Fort Toulouse among them, the Ochese Creeks admitted Spanish traders to their towns on the Chatahoochee, and the Lower Creeks resumed trade ties with Carolina in the treaty leading to the marriage of Coosapon-akeesa to John Musgrove, Jr. But the Creeks also defied Carolina by refusing both to make peace with the Cherokees and to stop their Yamasee and Apalachee allies from raiding the English colony. Although the European nations each hoped for an exclusive alliance with the Creeks, they were obliged to accept an arrangement whereby the Creeks traded with all and were committed militarily and diplomatically to none.

The Creeks' successes among the English came at the expense of the Cherokees. The Cherokees had hoped that their critical contributions to Carolina's victories in the Tuscarora and Yamasee wars would enhance their relations with that colony and its powerful traders. They were bitterly disappointed when Carolina resumed ties with the Creeks, failed to halt or aid the Cherokees against Creek and Six Nations Iroquois attacks, and failed to prevent abuses by British traders. Unlike the Creeks, the Cherokees could not easily turn to the French, with whom they had no direct contact or mutual allies and who, like the English, backed their Indian enemies.

Cherokee discontent with South Carolina (now separate from North Carolina) was tapped in 1730 when Sir Alexander Cuming, a Scottish gentleman acting on his own, toured Cherokee country as a self-proclaimed royal representative. Employing elaborate pomp and circumstance, Cuming at each stop led toasts to King George II that, he later asserted, included Cherokee acknowledgment of English sovereignty over them and their lands. He crowned an ambitious pro-English leader, Moytoy, "emperor" of the Cherokees and took seven Cherokees with him to England to formalize the new relationship. The Cherokees interpreted the crowning of Moytoy as English recognition of their nationhood (the title "emperor" matched that which the English and French applied to the Creeks' Brims) and not as their submission to English authority.

Cuming's actions appealed to some Cherokees, but growing numbers of them preferred a more independent diplomatic course. After Moytoy died in 1741, Chota, the oldest of all Cherokee towns, with roots in the Mississippian era, emerged as the center of an anti-English bloc. Led by Connecorte and Attakullaculla (also known, respectively, as Old Hop and Little Carpenter), Chota in 1745 made peace via pro-French Creeks with the French and their Indian allies. Chota's influence rose further as English traders, seeking to collect debts, abused Cherokee clients and as repeated English efforts to achieve a lasting Creek-Cherokee peace failed. In 1750 a deadly Creek attack destroyed pro-English Cherokee towns, driving them into the Chota-led faction. Inviting Shawnee and Mingo warriors to join them, anti-English Cherokees launched widespread attacks on English traders through 1751.

Meanwhile, the influence of Spain and France among the Creeks grew still more limited. The Creeks recognized the extent of Spain's weakness in 1728, after English troops raided and destroyed Yamasee villages in Florida with impunity. And they became disillusioned with the French after Louisiana dispersed the Creeks' Natchez allies in

Creek Delegation in London, 1734 Trade and diplomatic ties between the Creeks and Georgia were solidified when some Creek leaders accompanied Governor James Oglethorpe to meet the colony's trustees in London. On the same trip, the delegation met with King George II and the Archbishop of Canterbury.

1729 (discussed later). Finally, the inability of France and Spain to provide ample quantities of high-quality, low-priced trade goods undermined Creek towns with which those nations had cultivated ties. After Brims died (ca. 1730), English trade so predominated among the Creeks that most of them, following Coosaponakeesa, welcomed the founding of Georgia as a fourth trading option, to be played off against South Carolina, Florida, and Louisiana.

As among the Cherokees, however, many Creeks grew wary of their nation's dependence on the British and the latter's demands on them. The limits of their enthusiasm became evident in 1739

when England and Spain went to war. Seeking Creek military support for an invasion of Florida, Georgia recruited only a few warriors, despite Coosaponakeesa/Mary's efforts to find more. When the Anglo-Spanish war widened into an all-European war, the Creeks were badly divided. Anti-English sentiment grew among the Yamacraws and Lower Creeks after Oglethorpe returned to England and Georgia refused to address repeated complaints that its colonists were usurping Creek land. At the same time, the British navy's squeeze on the supply of French trade goods undermined Creek support for the French.

In the end, the Creeks and Cherokees made peace on their own. With both nations now more antagonistic toward the British than toward one another, they met in 1752 and "smoked in the hunting grounds," ending more than four decades of conflict. Although the governors of both South Carolina and Louisiana later claimed to have brokered the agreement, the two nations ended hostilities by themselves with Coosaponakeesa playing a leading role among the Creeks.

By banding together, the Creeks and the Cherokees achieved a remarkable feat, without assistance from any Europeans. But tensions in the Ohio country to the north had made inevitable the imperial war they and other Indians had tried so hard to avoid.

EXILES IN THEIR OWN HOMELANDS: INDIANS IN THE ENGLISH COLONIES

Whereas Native Americans in the eastern interior asserted their power vis-à-vis one another and Europeans through trade, diplomacy, and military action, Indians east of the Appalachians had long since lost these options and were even more vulnerable than before to the effects of British demographic and economic growth. From a population of about 250,000 in 1700, the English colonies' free and slave population doubled or more in each quarter century thereafter—to 500,000 in 1725, to more than 1 million in 1750, to about 2.5 million in 1775. Overwhelming in numbers alone, this influx had an even greater impact on Native Americans because it directly threatened their land. Most white colonists owned or worked on land for agricultural production, and most enslaved Africans were imported to work on farms and plantations. These immigrants had overrun many coastal Indians by the end of the Yamasee War in 1716. Thereafter Indians in piedmont regions—between coastal lowlands and the Appalachians—likewise found themselves surrounded by colonists, minorities on lands they had once had to themselves.

By the middle of the eighteenth century, Native Americans living in English colonies had been reduced to a tiny, impoverished minority. They lacked the political autonomy that Indians elsewhere struggled to assert, and they served to remind other Indians of what lay in store should the English gain the upper hand in their homelands. Yet Native Americans in the English colonies also symbolized what it meant to be Indian. In the face of unimaginably daunting conditions, they found ways to perpetuate their distinct cultural identities, affirming their survival and defying English assumptions that their histories had ended.

The Ravages of Colonization

Throughout the English colonies, Indians faced a host of challenges, including massive losses of population and land, poverty, and racism. Alongside the phenomenal growth in the numbers of non-Indians, eastern Indians continued to experience sharp declines in their own populations. Wampanoags on the island of Nantucket off the Massachusetts coast had numbered about 2,500 when they first encountered Europeans at the dawn of the seventeenth century. After one hundred years of exposure to European diseases, they numbered only 800. By 1763, there remained 358 Nantucket Wampanoags, a figure that declined by half after a yellow fever epidemic in the following year. Over the same period, the Catawbas of South Carolina declined from 5,000 to 500. The once-powerful Pamunkeys in Virginia still counted 150 male family heads after Bacon's Rebellion (see Chapter 4), but that number fell to just 10 by 1730 and 7 by 1748.

As in the sixteenth and seventeenth centuries, the principal causes of such sharp declines were diseases brought to America by outsiders. Smallpox and measles continued their ravages, joined by influenza, dysentery, diphtheria, tuberculosis, pneumonia, yellow fever, and others. Throughout the mid-eighteenth century, for example, the Catawbas experienced at least one "national Distemper" each year. Native Americans in areas dominated by colonists were especially vulnerable to these maladies not only because they lacked adequate immunities but also because of chronic malnutrition, exposure, alcoholism, and other factors associated with extreme poverty and racist policies.

The warfare of the period proved especially lethal because of the diseases it helped spread. During Britain's wars with France, more colonial soldiers—and wildly disproportionate numbers of eastern Indians fighting on the English side—died from diseases that rampaged through crowded, unsanitary quarters than from wounds received on the battlefields. Unsuspecting Native soldiers returned to their communities with these diseases, infecting people of all ages and both genders. Nevertheless, men in particular suffered disproportionately from war-related diseases as well as casualties in southern New England, where Native American participation in colonial militias was greatest. Although the numbers of Massachusett Indian women and children in the town of Natick held firm between censuses conducted in 1698 and 1749, the number of adult men in the community declined during that period from 59 to 34. Wars involving only Native Americans could be just as lethal. For most of the eighteenth century, the Catawbas' wars with the Six Nations Iroquois and other Indian enemies meant that their towns were regularly under siege and their people in danger. "Our Enemies are so thick about us we cannot go from Home," they lamented to South Carolina's governor in 1750. To defend themselves, they fortified their four villages and closely clustered them, unknowingly accelerating the spread of deadly microbes in the process.

The sharp decreases in Native populations were compounded, for the survivors, by equally drastic losses of land. During the eighteenth century, the English colonies confined Indians within their jurisdictions to ever-smaller reservations, rationalizing their actions by pointing to Indians' diminishing numbers and shifting locations as evidence of their "disappearance" or "extinction." Even Native Americans who had fought against other Indians on behalf of the colonies, such as the Mashantucket Pequots of Connecticut, struggled to resist English efforts to take their remaining lands. In 1712 Connecticut seized a tract that Mashantucket Pequot women had left fallow. By the 1720s the Pequots were opposing several efforts to take more of their land. In 1732, they protested "that the inhabitants of the town of Groton are continually cutting down and carrying away their timber and firewood . . . and make pretence to lay out to themselves, and fence and improve certain valuable parts thereof." Connecticut's General Court (legislature) responded with a decree enabling, over Pequot objections, the Groton farmers to continue their encroachments.

Finally in 1761, the court granted the disputed tract to Groton outright. The town's initiative was well timed. Pequot protests were effectively muted because most Mashantucket men had recently died fighting for the English against France and its Indian allies during the Seven Years War (see Chapter 6) and because the women and children left behind on the reservation were starving.

Piedmont Indians such as the Catawbas of South Carolina enjoyed some respite from encroaching colonists early in the eighteenth century but, by 1750, they too confronted the new threat. Although not yet losing land on the scale of Native Americans in colonies to the north, they encountered newcomers who cleared and fenced fields, filling them with new crops (and weeds) and with grazing livestock. Besides houses and barns, the colonists built roads, bridges, mills, and dams. As a result, the deer, fish, and many of the other species on which Catawbas had depended for sustenance (and in the case of deer, for trade) were diverted or depleted, and Catawbas' economic and subsistence options narrowed considerably. The Catawbas could hardly go anywhere in their homelands now without encountering the English newcomers, with whom they shared a mutual distrust. Like their counterparts up and down the English colonies, they found themselves living in an alien world without ever having left their homelands.

Resisting English Authority

Although Native Americans in the colonies protested efforts to defraud and otherwise deprive them, the fragmentation and dispersal of their communities, along with the close scrutiny of English authorities, discouraged intercommunal attempts to resist. The most notable exception occurred on Maryland's Eastern Shore in 1742 when Nanticokes, Choptanks, Pocomokes, Assateagues, and other Indians gathered at a swamp with some visiting Shawnees. Men, women, and children had left their reservations to attend, leading Maryland authorities to fear a violent uprising. They quickly dispatched troops who disarmed the Indians and arrested twenty of their leaders. The prisoners' explanations of the gathering varied, some affirming that it was an anti-English conspiracy, others maintaining that the Indians sought merely to hunt and "to make a new emperor" among them. Even if only attempting "to make a new emperor," the Indians clearly sought to consolidate their limited power vis-à-vis that of the colonizers. Sensing the potential threat, Maryland quickly forced each community to sign a new treaty, reaffirming its submission to the colony's authority.

The alien quality, both material and cultural, of their environments led some Native Americans to leave their communities and, often, their homelands altogether. Like Native refugees moving to the Ohio Valley, Indians under direct colonial rule often moved to escape colonial pressures and to achieve a measure of economic autonomy. Piscataways, Susquehannocks, Conoys, Nanticokes, and other Indians left Maryland to join displaced Delawares in the upper Susquehanna Valley, where they became tributaries of the Six Nations Iroquois. Nottaways and Meherrins left Virginia to follow their Tuscarora allies when the Tuscaroras moved north to become the sixth nation of the Iroquois Confederacy in 1722 (see Chapter 4). Members of other depopulated Indian nations, from the Nipmucs of Massachusetts to the Nansemonds of Virginia, fled their reservations—or the lands on which dissolved reservations had formerly stood—for nearby lands less attractive and less visible to English farmers and planters.

Surviving Colonization

Throughout the early and middle eighteenth century, small groups of Native Americans were like islands in a sea of colonizing Europeans and enslaved Africans. Cut off from most of the mammals, fish, wild plants, and farmland on which they had traditionally subsisted, Indians turned to the English market economy. But lacking land, capital, and white skin, they were poorly positioned to take advantage of that economy. One of the most characteristic conditions of Native peoples in the seaboard colonies was chronic indebtedness. Obtaining debt relief was one reason Indians sold land to whites. In 1748, after their English neighbors had been cutting and hauling away their timber for years, the Pamunkeys sold an eighty-eight-acre tract so that surviving members could pay off debts for "Medicines, Doctors attendance, Corn, Clothing, and other Necessarys."

For Indians without land, debt led often to slavery or servitude. During the seventeenth century, slavery and servitude had been primarily punishments meted out to Native Americans by colonial authorities for violating colonial laws or resisting the English in war. By the eighteenth century, bonded Indian labor had acquired an economic dimension that greatly facilitated its expansion.

As with Africans, race was a factor distinguishing Native Americans' bonded labor from that of whites. Despite laws prohibiting the practice, colonists in southern New England deliberately drew hundreds of Indians into debts they could not hope to repay, then obliged them to pay off the debts as indentured servants. In 1747 a Wampanoag man, Paul Quaabe, described for the Massachusetts General Court how an English whaler, assisted by a constable and two other men, had forced him out of his own house, on to the back of a horse, and then aboard a whaling ship. Just six weeks later a group of Christian Wampanoags complained to the court that forced labor interfered with their religious observances. "How," they asked, "can we serve God or . . . worship him on the Sabbath days or any time when our masters lead us to darkness and not in light[?]."

Farther south, where enslaved Africans were becoming the primary source of forced labor, Native American slaves and servants became fewer than in New England. In South Carolina, where an Indian slave trade had flourished before and during the Yamasee War (see Chapter 4), a growing influx of African-born slaves was accompanied by a steady decline in the number and proportion of enslaved Indians. In St. Thomas Parish, for example, the number of Africans rose from eight hundred in 1720 to one thousand just eight years later, while the number of Indian slaves fell from ninety to fifty.

Other Native Americans were able to avoid coerced labor and work on their own. One of their most common occupations was making baskets and brooms, crafts that drew on deep-rooted cultural traditions, for sale to colonists. A Natick Massachusett woman's experience demonstrates the possibilities as well as the limits of such an occupation. Widowed in 1745, Abigail Speen Moheag two years later sold her family's remaining land to pay off her crushing debts. For the next fifteen years she provided for herself "by her industry in the business of making brooms, baskets, and horse collars." But eventually she grew too old and infirm for such work and, with most of her relatives already dead, faced a grim future. When she died in 1771 at the age of about seventy, an official English inventory of her possessions declared that she had none of any monetary value.

As noted above, Native American men in southern New England often turned to English military service in order to sustain themselves and their families. Special Indian militia units fought Eastern Abenakis and Mi'kmaqs in Maine and Acadia during successive border conflicts after 1689. For those Indian soldiers who survived their experiences, military service brought sorely needed cash as well as an opportunity to maintain warrior traditions without opposing the English. But many Native militiamen sacrificed more than they gained. After a bullet smashed the wrist of William Jeffry, a Wampanoag serving in Maine, he depended for the next twenty years on a small annual allotment from Massachusetts. Many returning Indian soldiers found their entire military pay absorbed by medical bills, which they could only pay off by selling land or indenturing themselves as servants.

As late as the 1720s and 1730s, a few Catawba men in South Carolina still hunted and traded deerskins. But with the deer population depleted, most were directly serving colonists by driving teams of packhorses, rowing river boats, working fields, catching runaway slaves, tanning hides, and—like their New England counterparts—helping the colony fight its wars. As with their peers to the north, the work they sought was so unsteady that they moved often from one place to another.

"Indianisme"

As treacherous as life in the English colonies was for Indians, they not only survived but continually reaffirmed their Native American cultural identities. Paradoxically, one of the factors reinforcing their sense of themselves as Indians was their systematically racist treatment by the colonies. On one hand, restrictions on the rights of all Indians to travel outside their communities, to practice certain occupations, and to serve in militia units with whites contributed to high rates of Native American mortality and poverty. Yet these same rules kept Indians together in their communities in the face of pressures to fragment, while reinforcing their sense of themselves as distinct from the English. Abusive behavior by white colonists, such as illegally taking Indians' land or subjecting them to forced labor, had similar effects, especially when condoned or perpetrated by colonial authorities.

Considered fundamentally Indian by themselves and outsiders, Native Americans did not alter that identity in the course of adapting to their new, more constricted circumstances. Even changes that on the surface appeared to move them closer to the English could in fact affirm what Massachusetts colonist Samuel Sewall called their "Indianisme." By the early eighteenth century, for example, most Powhatans in Virginia wore clothes made from such imported fabrics as linen and cotton, which they made using scissors, needles, and other items obtained from the English. Yet they cut the cloth into the same breechcloths, aprons, and matchcoats they had formerly made from leather. At the same time, they took advantage of the variations afforded by cloth and favored certain red and blue colors disdained by the colonists. All the while they wore leggings and moccasins that were unchanged since the arrival of Europeans. Neither strictly traditional nor strictly English, the Powhatans and most other colony Indians were unmistakably Native American in their appearance.

Indian peoples' creative blending of old and new styles in their wardrobes was part of a larger cultural pattern. Just as traditional clothing materials had become scarce and, for many garments, less desirable than cloth, so too familiar food sources, building materials, and other components of an older material culture grew scarce or vanished altogether from Indians' environments. In their place Native Americans turned increasingly to English replacements but utilized them with a distinctively Indian touch.

Spirituality

What Sewall called "Indianisme" was by no means confined to the material world. Spirituality, or religion, was the means by which Native Americans, like all peoples, understood and interacted with the larger forces shaping their existence and their environment. As the world on which traditional spirituality had been founded was broken by the invasion of European peoples, animals, and microbes, new beliefs and practices arose to compete with older ones in the minds of Native peoples. For Wampanoags on Cape Cod and Martha's Vineyard, Christianity had become so basic to community life during the shock of initial colonization that it remained at the heart of their spirituality during the eighteenth century. On the other hand, after incoming colonists took over the former Massachusett praying town of Natick, and its church, Christianity receded as the focal point of Massachusett Indian identity. Other eastern seaboard Native Americans consistently resisted missionaries. When in 1717 a Virginia official tried to persuade some Saponis to be instructed in Christianity and English culture, "they thought it hard," as one Englishman put it, "that we should desire them to change their manners and customs, since they did not desire us to turn Indians." Forty years later, a South Carolina Catawba replied to similar efforts, gruffly informing a Presbyterian minister that "old Indian make no Sabbath and young Indian make no Sabbath."

Many more Indians turned to Christianity with the advent in the 1740s of the Protestant revivals among colonists known as the Great Awakening. The revivals placed greater emphasis on emotions and less on firsthand familiarity with the Bible than did Puritan and other early missionaries. And unlike their predecessors, many revivalists welcomed all people who came to hear them, regardless of class or color, and did not expect potential converts to adopt English culture before accepting Jesus as their savior. Most importantly, New Light Christianity, as revivalist teachings were called, often emphasized a heavenly justice that would reward those who had experienced divine grace but suffered injustice in their lives. Such an emphasis understandably appealed to the poor, to Africans and African Americans, and to Native Americans.

One of the most notable early converts was a young Mohegan from Connecticut named Samson Occom, who became a Christian at the age of sixteen. Along with several other Indians youths, he undertook rigorous studies in reading, writing,

Samson Occom, Mohegan Christian Clergyman Converted during the Great Awakening, Occom preached Christianity and became a prominent leader among Native Americans in southern New England.

and Christian theology with Eleazar Wheelock, a New Light preacher. Thereafter he preached and taught among the Montauks on Long Island. From there his fame spread far and wide, among the English because Wheelock publicized his work, and among Indians because of his powerful preaching, his effectiveness as a teacher of English language and reading, and his concern for their material and spiritual welfare. Through his efforts and those of subsequent pupils of Wheelock, Indians across Connecticut and Long Island were introduced to New Light Christianity.

New versions of Christianity likewise resonated among the dispossessed and dispersed eastern Delawares. Some Delawares were drawn to the Moravians, a German religious group that in 1746 founded Gnadenhütten, a town for Delaware converts. Delaware motives for accepting Moravian baptism and moving to Gnadenhütten varied. Moravian beliefs in universal salvation and the solemnity of Moravian religious ceremonies offered spiritual certainty in the face of deadly diseases and the alcohol made readily available by

English traders. Likewise, the Moravians were highly skilled farmers and artisans whose knowledge and skills appealed to Indians whose traditional pursuits no longer sustained them. Finally, the Moravians represented a useful political ally, one with wealth and influence, who did not try to dominate Indians.

Other eastern Delawares responded to the Brainerd brothers, David and John, New Light revivalists who were likewise active in the 1740s and 1750s. The Brainerds focused on the discovery of divine grace within, a spiritual rebirth that appealed to those experiencing spiritual and cultural disorientation. Like the Moravians, they emphasized the importance of spiritual discipline in resisting the temptations of alcohol and other forms of self-destructive behavior. One of the Brainerds' most notable Delaware converts was Tunda (Moses) Tatamy, an independent farmer and prominent interpreter and mediator in Anglo-Delaware diplomatic exchanges.

Brainerd and the Moravians faced competition for religious followers from several Delaware religious prophets. These prophets were not strict traditionalists, instead offering their audiences a blend of ideas that were old and new, Indian and European. David Brainerd encountered one such prophet (unnamed) who resembled a Christian in some respects but not in others. He had formerly lived in ignorance, the prophet told Brainerd, until becoming distressed and going to the woods to live alone. "At length," Brainerd related, "God comforted his heart, and showed him what he must do. And since that time, he had known God and tried to serve him, and loved all men . . . as he never did before." Brainerd and the prophet found that they shared many of the same goals, including dissuading Indians from alcohol and persuading them to worship a single God. Yet the prophet directly contradicted Christian teachings by denying the existence of a devil on the grounds that "there was no such creature known among the Indians of old times," and claiming like his forebears "that departed souls all went southward."

Like so many of their Indian contemporaries along the eastern seaboard (and across the continent), the Delaware prophets had crafted hybrid identities for themselves without becoming any less Indian in the process, defying English assumptions that Native American history would soon end.

NATIVE AMERICANS AND FRENCH EXPANSION IN THE MISSISSIPPI VALLEY

As Indians in easternmost North America confronted British colonization, those in the Mississippi Valley dealt primarily with the French. Despite intensive efforts, France failed to attract significant numbers of European colonists to its American territories. Although small colonies emerged in Louisiana and Illinois, they alone would never enable the French to control the Great Lakes–Mississippi passageway and halt English expansion westward, prerequisites in French eyes for erecting a formidable colonial empire of their own. Instead France relied on a vast network of Indian allies, including Choctaws, Illinois, Ojibwes, and its many allies at Detroit to achieve its ends. Although yielding some rewards, France's policy was costly and dangerous. Where the French sought to expand their territorial domain, as among the Natchez, they risked alienating Indians. Elsewhere, such allies of the British as the Chickasaws threatened either to draw off or menace France's allies. Some French allies at the Great Lakes deliberately excluded other Indians, such as the Mesquakies and the Dakota Sioux, from enjoying direct access to French goods, setting off bitter conflicts. The French suppressed all these peoples with a violence that rivaled anything implemented by the English, belying France's reputation for greater benevolence toward Indians.

The Natchez Uprisings

After peace returned to the lower Mississippi Valley in 1713, France's Louisiana colony accelerated its effort to procure deerskins from Indian suppliers. In so doing, the colony alienated the Natchez, a Mississippian people who for some years had controlled trade between the French and Indians upriver. In 1715, Louisiana's governor, Antoine de la Mothe Cadillac, sailed past the principal Natchez town without stopping for the customary smoking of the calumet. Interpreting the governor's action as a declaration of war, some Natchez attacked a nearby French warehouse, killing four French traders and seizing the trade goods stored there. The French responded by dispatching an envoy along with thirty-five troops to de-

Indian-French Trade in Louisiana Native Americans gather around French goods. The Mesquakie woman (lower left) and African child are enslaved.

mand that the Natchez turn over the heads of the raiders who killed their traders. Unsatisfied when the Natchez Sun (grand chief) offered only three heads, the French troops seized and killed four additional Indians who were present. The intimidated Natchez settled the matter by allowing the French to erect a new fortified post, Fort Rosalie, on Natchez territory. But Natchez resentment against French assaults on their people and their sovereignty lingered.

Matters only worsened during the following decade. Expanding French tobacco plantations worked by enslaved Africans slowly encroached on the Natchez homeland. The spread of smallpox, influenza, and other deadly diseases had reduced a Natchez population that had numbered about thirty-five hundred in 1700 by about half. Older Natchez lamented the obsession of the young with French goods, while many French decried the casual social ties developing among Europeans, Africans, and Native Americans around Fort Rosalie.

Natchez-French tensions escalated in 1728 after the French appointed an Indian-hating commandant at Fort Rosalie while a new Sun, whose kinsman had recently been slain by the French, assumed

leadership of the Natchez. Deciding to build a plantation on the site of a Natchez town, the commandant ordered the local Sun to move his people. As the Natchez discussed their response, one asked, "Is not death preferable to slavery?" Agreeing, the Natchez devised an elaborate plan to kill all the French in their homes, one that paralleled the Powhatans' strategy in Virginia in 1622 (see Chapter 3). On a morning in November 1729, they went among the French as if to trade. At a prearranged signal, they drew their weapons, killing over two hundred colonists and capturing about three hundred Africans and fifty European women and children. The French retaliated by calling on their Choctaw allies, who besieged the Natchez town until February 1730, when the Natchez gave up their remaining hostages. The Natchez then slipped out of the town and crossed the Mississippi River. French troops pursued them, eventually capturing about five hundred, mostly women and children, whom they sold as slaves to French planters in the West Indies. Like many of their counterparts in British colonies, the remaining Natchez abandoned their homeland to land-hungry colonists.

INDIAN VOICES   Stung Serpent, Natchez, 1723

The early alliance of Natchez Indians and French colonists in Louisiana had deteriorated badly by 1723. In that year, about six hundred French troops and allied Indians stormed into the principal Natchez village and demanded that the Indians turn over the severed heads of six young men and the body, dead or alive, of an escaped African slave who had taken refuge there. The French accused the Indians of stealing livestock and produce from them and the African of joining in some of the raids. Although reluctantly complying, the Natchez grew even more embittered at the French, perhaps none more so than Stung Serpent, a war chief and brother of the Great Sun (paramount chief), who had negotiated the humiliating agreement. When a French author and former friend asked Stung Serpent why he now ignored the Frenchman, the Natchez leader gave the following angry reply. Note that one of his complaints is that of a Natchez man who is upset with the impact of French trade goods on Natchez women's willingness to work.

Why did the French come into our country? We did not go to seek them. They asked land of us, because their country was too little for all the men that were in it. We told them they might take land where they pleased, there was enough for them and for us; that it was good the same sun should enlighten us both, and that we should walk as friends, in the same path, and that we would give them of our provisions, assist them to build, and to labor in their fields. We have done so; is not this true? What occasion, then, had we for Frenchmen? Before they came, did we not live better than we do, seeing we deprive ourselves of a part of our corn, our game, and fish, to give a part to them? In what respect, then, had we occasion for them? Was it for their guns? The bows and arrows, which we used, were sufficient to make us live well. Was it for their white, blue and red blankets? We can do well enough with buffalo skins which are warmer; our women wrought feather blankets for the winter, and mulberry mantles for the summer; which indeed were not so beautiful, but our women were more laborious and less vain than they are now. In fine, before the arrival of the French we lived like men who can be satisfied with what they have; whereas at this day we are like slaves, who are not suffered to do as they please.

Source: Colin G. Calloway, ed., *The World Turned Upside Down: Indian Voices From Early America* (Boston: Bedford Books of St. Martin's Press, 1994), 91.

Civil War Among the Choctaws

Many Natchez refugees found new homes among the Chickasaws, formidable enemies of both the French and the Choctaws. Supplied with guns and other trade goods by English traders from Carolina, Chickasaw and Natchez raiders harassed both of these enemies with deadly effectiveness during the 1730s. Unable to match either the quantity or quality of English goods, the French encouraged Choctaw retaliation against the Chickasaws. Above all, the French feared that if the Choctaws made peace with the Chickasaws, the two Indian nations together might turn on the French. These fears rose further in the late 1730s when French troops, along with enslaved Africans and Choctaw, Illinois, and other northern Indian allies, were defeated in all-out efforts to crush the Chickasaws.

In time many Choctaws concluded that the French were using them and that their only rewards were increased casualties, shortages of food and other necessities, and enemy attacks. The hazards of a steadfast French alliance first became apparent to one of the Choctaws' outstanding young warriors, Shulush Houma (known to Europeans as Red Shoes). As early as the 1720s, Shulush Houma's feats made a distinct impression not only on his fellow Choctaws but on the French, to whom he brought large quantities of enemy scalps (to exchange for bounties) and captives after every battle. Eventually he became a war captain and was honored by the French as "Chief of the Red Warriors." During the 1730s, however, Shulush Houma and his large warrior following pursued a more independent course, moving back and forth between English traders in South Carolina and their French counterparts in Louisiana. In that way, Shulush Houma hoped to maximize the flow of trade goods to the Choctaws, preserve Choctaw independence, and consolidate his own power among his people.

To counter Shulush Houma's growing influence among the Choctaws, a new French governor, Philippe de Rigault de Vaudreil, worked closely with the hereditary Choctaw civil chiefs in the early 1740s. The chiefs resented Shulush Houma as an upstart who had usurped their power and received a French medal, an honor previously reserved for them. After isolating Shulush Houma, Vaudreil planned to make peace with the Chickasaws. In retaliation, Shulush Houma boldly approached English authorities in Charleston, South Carolina, and the "Blind King" of the Chickasaws. To the English he proposed that they supply trade goods to the Choctaws. To both he outlined an Anglo-Choctaw-Chickasaw peace that, contrary to the French effort, would exclude the civil chiefs.

Badly divided over which course to follow, the Choctaws plunged into full civil war. With the Carolinian traders providing Shulush Houma's followers with ample supplies of guns, ammunition, and powder, the war captain isolated the civil chiefs and was on the verge of leading the Choctaws into an alliance with the English. But eyeing the French offer of a bounty for Shulush Houma's head, a young warrior assassinated the remarkable captain in 1747. Uncertain of what the Choctaws would do without their leader, the English in Carolina halted their aid while the rejuvenated French in-

creased their rewards for the scalps of anti-French Choctaws. As a result, many warriors returned to the French fold, which finally led to a victory for pro-French Choctaws in 1750. Thereafter, the Choctaws remained closely tied to the French until the latter's colonial rule ended in 1762. Shulush Houma's hopes for a Choctaw nation free of ties to a single European power were dashed.

The Mesquakie Wars

Along with the Chickasaws, the major obstacles to French control of the Mississippi–Great Lakes passageway were the Mesquakie (Fox) Indians. In the aftermath of their earlier conflict with the French and their Indian allies at Detroit (see Chapter 4), most Mesquakies had returned to homes in what is now Wisconsin. In 1725, Charles de la Boische de Beauharnois, newly appointed governor of New France, began a campaign to break Mesquakie power. Beauharnois began by threatening to withhold trade and attack the Dakota Sioux, Sauks, Winnebagos, Kickapoos, Miamis, Mascoutens, and Potawatomis if they insisted on remaining allied with the Mesquakies. In the absence of other Europeans with whom to trade, these Indians cooperated with the French, leaving the Mesquakies by 1730 without allies on the Mississippi.

Among the Mesquakies' few remaining sympathizers were the Seneca Iroquois, with whom they had forged ties while at Detroit. Although the Seneca homeland lay hundreds of miles to the east and could be reached only by traveling through enemy territory, many Mesquakies were convinced that their only hope for survival lay in moving there. In June, 900 of them began the long trek. Two months later, a combined force of Illinois, Kickapoos, Potawatomis, and Mascoutens, along with some French troops, caught up with the Mesquakies in Illinois and besieged their fortified encampment. The Mesquakies withstood the siege for over a month, until their food supplies ran low. During an exceptionally stormy night in September 1730 about 500 Mesquakies slipped out of the encampment in hopes of continuing their journey, but by morning both they and those remaining in the encampment had been overpowered. About half the migrating Mesquakies were killed and most of the rest captured. Fewer than 100 survivors made their way back to Wisconsin, joining the 350 Mesquakies who had remained behind in a single town under the leadership of a war chief named Kiala.

After the French twice sent heavily armed Indians to attack the Mesquakies' one remaining village, Kiala surrendered with his people at Green Bay in 1733. He, his wife, and a few other Mesquakies were taken to Montreal to negotiate with Governor Beauharnois. Even while meeting with Kiala, Beauharnois ordered French troops to seize the Mesquakies remaining at Green Bay and to kill those they could not capture. But the Mesquakies, along with some Sauk allies, fended off the French and escaped to the country of the Iowa Indians, who permitted them to establish two villages on the west bank of the Des Moines River. A vengeful Beauharnois ordered Kiala and his wife sold as slaves in the French plantation colony of Martinique. But the Mesquakies' reputation for rebelliousness was so widespread that no French planter would buy the prisoners, fearing that they would foment rebellion among the planters' African slaves. Finally, French slave traders took Kiala and his wife to the shore of Venezuela where they either found a buyer or simply left the couple to perish.

Failing to capture the surviving Mesquakies in Iowa country, Beauharnois was ready to make a genuine peace. Several of the governor's Indian allies, particularly those with kin ties to the Mesquakies, persuaded him that the Mesquakies no longer threatened French interests. Moreover, the French faced too many competing diversions, particularly the war with the Chickasaws, a growing conflict between the Ojibwes and the Dakotas (discussed in the next section), and British encroachments in the Ohio country. Soon thereafter, Beauharnois was recalled and a new Onontio agreed that the Mesquakies could have their own town at the junction of the Rock River with the Mississippi. By the fall of 1750, most surviving Mesquakies had relocated to their new home, made peace with most of their Indian neighbors, and allied especially closely with the Sauks.

The Dakota Sioux and the Struggle for French Trade

Like the Mesquakies, the Sioux in what is now Minnesota had traded beaver pelts for French goods since the mid-seventeenth century but lacked direct contact with French traders. Instead they sent and received commodities via other Indians, mostly Ojibwes living at the western end of Lake Superior. By the end of the seventeenth century, a combination of trade-related factors was making life difficult for the Sioux. The commercial overhunting of game animals, deadly epidemic diseases among both people and animals, and intensified warfare among Native Americans seeking advantages in hunting and trading induced the more westerly Teton, Yanktonai, and Yankton Sioux to move west during summer hunting seasons. By the end of the century, growing numbers of these western Sioux were relocating permanently on the Plains (discussed later in this chapter).

During the 1720s, those Sioux who did not move, the Dakotas, allied with the Mesquakies in an attempt to weaken the Native allies of the French who controlled French-Indian trade on the upper Mississippi. Mesquakie defeats plus the opening of three posts on the Mississippi by 1730 finally brought the Sioux the direct ties with the French they had sought. But the Dakotas quickly discovered that the French continued to trade far more guns to their Ojibwe, Western Cree, and Assiniboine enemies than to the Sioux themselves. The arrival of the son of a leading French official, Pierre Gaultier de Varennes, Sieur de la Vérendrye, with a Western Cree war party in 1733, seemed to confirm Dakotas' fears that the French planned, as with the Mesquakies and Natchez, to eliminate them as a people. To prevent such an outcome, a Sioux war party in 1736 attacked a French gathering at the Lake of the Woods, killing all twenty-four who were present, including the younger La Vérendrye. The Dakotas followed this action with several raids on the Ojibwes and Winnebagos, leading these tribes and the French in 1737 to withdraw entirely from the upper Mississippi.

After 1740, the Dakota Sioux sought to make peace and restore ties with the French. Besides suffering deadly attacks by Ojibwes, Ottawas, Western Crees, and Assiniboines, the Dakotas were missing out on some profitable commerce. In 1742 Beauharnois convened a conference of all these nations and secured a treaty binding them to respect one another's hunting territories and guaranteeing the Dakotas some traders and posts at their villages. By 1750, French traders resided in most Dakota villages on the Mississippi and Minnesota rivers, often solidifying their ties by marrying Sioux women. But the Dakotas' promising future was dampened just three years later. Another son of La Vérendrye, whose family had long-standing ties with the Ojibwes and who remained embittered about his brother's death, became France's military commandant in the west. The new commandant urged the Dakotas' enemies to attack them and expelled the French traders from the Sioux villages.

By 1754, most Native peoples in the Mississippi Valley were engaged in relations with French colonizers, but on sharply varying terms. After several decades of war and enormous losses, the Mesquakies were finally at peace with the French. On the other hand, recently harmonized relations between the Dakota Sioux and the French were once again in turmoil. Choctaw and Illinois Indians, reduced by diseases, internal strife (in the case of the Choctaws), and warfare with the English-allied Chickasaws, now depended on the French for military protection but received substantial trade benefits in return. The Chickasaws remained the greatest Indian threat to French control of the vast region. Despite the expense and violence entailed in suppressing Native resistance, the French not only secured the Mississippi Valley from European rivals but expanded their trade and colonizing efforts westward.

HORSES AND GUNS ON THE PLAINS

From early in the eighteenth century, the impact of French activity in the Mississippi Valley extended to Native Americans on the Great Plains, the vast expanse of arid land stretching to the base of the Rocky Mountains. The advent of horses, mostly originating in New Mexico, and guns, arriving primarily from French and British traders to the east and north, transformed the Plains as a human habitat. Village-dwelling farmers in the river valleys incorporated the new items into their own material cultures and into the inventories of goods they exchanged with other Indians. Some of the villagers, particularly the Osages, became formidable powers. Horses and guns also drew more mobile hunting-oriented peoples to the Plains. Using horses to

pursue buffalo and guns to raid and defend against enemies, the newcomers—particularly the western Sioux and the Comanches—rose from obscurity to become regional powers. Altogether, the balance of power on the Plains was completely overturned during the first half of the eighteenth century.

The Northern Plains

To the north of the Dakota Sioux, Anglo-French trade competition prompted Indian groups to try and maximize their own beaver harvests while minimizing those of their enemies. This multifaceted competition moved swiftly westward across what is now Canada. In 1691 an English trader, Henry Kelsey, led an expedition to the Plains near the Saskatchewan River, farther west and north of the Missouri River than any European had yet traveled. There he encountered newly arrived Assiniboines and Western Crees hunting buffalo for hides to supplement the diminishing quantities of beaver pelts around the Great Lakes.

On the Saskatchewan, the Western Crees and Assiniboines were soon supplying neighboring Blackfeet and Gros Ventre Indians with French-made goods, including guns, in exchange for buffalo hides at a mark-up of about 300 percent. The guns arrived none too soon for the Blackfeet and Gros Ventre, upon whose hunting territories Eastern Shoshones were encroaching from the south. One day in about 1730, some Eastern Shoshones attacked some Blackfeet with large animals "on which they rode swift as a deer," as one Blackfeet elder recalled many years later. The startled—and badly defeated—Blackfeet had seen their first horses. The Blackfeet quickly turned to their Cree and Assiniboine friends, who provided them with ten guns and about thirty rounds of ammunition for each warrior. Now it was the Shoshones' turn to be startled. Armed with the novel weapons, the Blackfeet more than avenged their previous losses, killing fifty Eastern Shoshones. Soon the Blackfeet had ample supplies of both horses and guns and were a force to be reckoned with among Indians on the Northern Plains.

The Eastern Shoshone attack on the Blackfeet demonstrates how far north horses had spread among Native peoples on the western periphery of the Plains by the 1730s. The Eastern Shoshones' shocking victory drew the attention of Indians throughout the Northern Plains, upper Great Basin, and Eastern Plateau. Crows, Yakamas, Nez Percés, Coeur d'Alenes, and other Native peoples across this vast region began seeking horses for hunting and for raiding rivals. For a time, the Eastern Shoshones remained so feared militarily that when La Vérendrye approached their homeland in 1743, his Native guides balked at proceeding any farther. Nevertheless the French established several new trading posts on the Assiniboine and Saskatchewan rivers, enabling well-armed Blackfeet, Assiniboine, and Western Crees to halt the Shoshones' northward thrust.

Farther south, as already mentioned, the Teton, Yanktonai, and Yankton Sioux began moving westward from the upper Mississippi and Minnesota valleys during the late seventeenth century. Well armed through trade with the French, these western Sioux pushed the Omaha, Oto, Missouri, Iowa, and Cheyenne peoples south and west from their prairie homelands toward the Missouri Valley. Having occupied these lands, the Tetons, Yanktonais, and Yanktons became the dominant hunters and traders of the region, exchanging not only their own furs but also those received from Native Americans farther west for European goods. Their meetings with French traders took place at annual spring ceremonies hosted by the Dakota Sioux on the Mississippi. Although most of the furs they traded were beaver pelts, the western Sioux had begun turning to buffalo as a prime source of food. From early in the eighteenth century, they acquired horses for pursuing buffalo herds during summers (but not, at this time, for fighting enemies).

As the western Sioux continued to pressure local beaver populations, the Tetons and Yanktons moved still farther west in search of untapped sources. Eventually reaching the upper Missouri River valley, they encountered Native Americans who were very different from the prairie peoples they had so easily displaced. The Arikaras, Hidatsas, and Mandans were village-based farming peoples whose communities were centers of long-distance trade for several centuries before Europeans reached the Americas. While on a mission for Beauharnois in 1738, La Vérendrye visited the Mandan villages. Although his hosts had never seen Europeans, they possessed substantial quantities of guns, axes, kettles, cloth, and other European commodities, obtained largely from the Assiniboines to the north. With larger numbers of people, guns, and horses, and with heavily fortified villages consisting of earth lodges, the three village nations successfully resisted and retaliated against Sioux raids. The Sioux finally established themselves on the Missouri only by allying with the Arikaras, from whom they obtained corn and other farm products as well as support in hostilities against the Mandans and Hidatsas. By the mid-eighteenth century, the Algonquian-speaking Cheyennes had also arrived on the Missouri. Like the Sioux, they did not establish permanent villages but instead followed a wide-ranging annual subsistence cycle that included trapping beaver and hunting buffalo on horses.

The Southern Plains and the Southwest

South of the Missouri River, Osage, Pawnee, Wichita, Oto, Kansa, and Caddo peoples straddled the ecological boundary between the prairie grasslands of the Mississippi Valley and the arid Plains. By the outset of the eighteenth century, they were acquiring European commodities, including guns, horses, and other livestock, from the French to the east, from the Spanish in New Mexico, and from other Indian groups. Like villagers on the upper Missouri, prairie-plains peoples lived in permanent towns and combined farming and other familiar subsistence practices with summer buffalo hunts on horseback. Some of them used guns to great advantage in raiding Apache and Spanish settlements to the west and southwest. To counter such raids, a New Mexican expedition traveled to the upper Platte River in 1720 but was routed by a force of Pawnees and Otos.

The most powerful people on the prairie-plains borderland south of the Missouri River were the Siouan-speaking Osages. Originally obtaining guns to defend themselves against raids by armed rivals, the Osages turned the new weapons against their Pawnee, Wichita, and Caddo neighbors. Gaining control of most French-Indian exchange between the Mississippi and the Central Plains, the Osages rose to dominate the prairie-plains borderland as far south as the Red River valley.

In recognition of Osage power, a French company established a post, Fort Orleans, on the lower Missouri River in 1723. From here French traders

PEOPLE, PLACES, AND THINGS

Spanish Slave-Raiding Expedition, ca. 1720

Human beings were among the prizes most eagerly sought after by Indian and Spanish raiding parties in the Southwest and Southern Plains. This painting on buffalo hide, probably made by a Spanish missionary, depicts a party of mounted Spanish and allied Indian raiders attacking a palisaded Apache encampment. While Apache warriors confront the raiders outside the palisade, women and children take cover behind it. After the battle, the captured Apaches were probably sold into slavery in Mexico.

Buffalo hide painting, depicting Spanish slave raiding expedition, ca. 1720.

fanned out to Osage towns, acquiring deerskins, beaver pelts, and buffalo hides. Ironically, the Osages even supplied the French with horses, obtained both by raiding and trading with Indians to the west and by raiding Spanish colonists in New Mexico. The Osages also sold war captives to the French. Whereas they had formerly killed or adopted those they seized in battle, the Osages now raided enemies to obtain captives they could sell. The French sold the captive Indians as slaves, first to work on Louisiana plantations, and later to exchange with French West Indian planters for enslaved Africans. In addition, some French traders, acting on their own, sold captive Indians to English slave traders in South Carolina, who in turn shipped them to the British West Indies.

While welcoming French traders to Osage towns, the Osages prevented the traders from traveling farther west to make direct contact with other Native Americans. While they could not prevent the French from ascending the Missouri, the Osages did keep them off the Arkansas and other rivers to the south. Although the French resented this interference, they complied so as not to alienate the Osages, who were their most important trade partners below the Missouri. Osage power remained unchallenged until the rise of the Comanches in the early 1750s.

Having separated from the related Eastern Shoshones on the western edge of the northern Plains, the Comanches had moved to the southern Plains to hunt buffalo in place of more restricted sources of food in their homelands. Europeans made no record of the Comanches until 1706, when the governor of New Mexico listed them as one of several nations of *indios bárbaros* (wild Indians) menacing his colony. Comanches had undoubtedly been joining their Southern Ute allies in raids on New Mexico since the aftermath of the Pueblo Revolt. These raids provided them with the horses that facilitated their traveling eastward to trade with the Wichitas for French-made guns. The Comanches also seized captives, both Indian and Hispanic, for adoption and for trading to others. By the 1720s the Comanches had effectively incorporated horses, guns, and captives into a way of life based on hunting and raiding. Besides the Spanish and the Pueblo Indians, the Comanches' principal targets were the Lipan, Jicarilla, and Mescalero Apaches—often referred to collectively as the Eastern Apaches—who themselves had raided New Mexico from the colony's earliest days.

Increasingly subject to attacks by well-armed Comanches and their Southern Ute and Wichita allies, the Eastern Apaches moved southward and directed their own raiding at the newer Spanish colony of Texas. Through the 1730s and 1740s the Apaches raided San Antonio for the goods they could no longer obtain at French forts and at Pueblo trade fairs in New Mexico. But the Comanches and Wichitas pursued the Apaches into

Texas and harassed them there while Spanish troops also retaliated. During the 1740s beleaguered Apaches began making peace with Texas officials, and Spanish missionaries at San Antonio even drew a few of them to Christianity. In August 1749, most Eastern Apaches who had not done so already made peace with Texas officials at an elaborate ceremony in San Antonio. Into a large pit participants from both sides placed a live horse along with many weapons. In a peacemaking ritual conducted by Apache and Spanish leaders, the entire assembly helped fill the pit, burying the weapons and the unfortunate horse. Although peace now prevailed, some Apaches, still doubting Spanish ability to protect them from the Comanches, moved farther south.

As the Apaches retreated, the Comanches spread across the southern Plains, dominating the area between Osage country and the Spanish colonies. Comanches' relations with colonists and Pueblo Indians in New Mexico alternated between hostilities and uneasy truces. The parties usually reached truces so that they could all attend the annual trade fairs at Taos Pueblo, where they exchanged horses and other livestock, captives, and both Indian and European goods while participating in the ceremonies and sociability of these occasions. But the festivities typically ended when Comanches' resentment over high prices or some discourtesy led them to attack the offending party, prompting Spanish-Pueblo retaliation. The usual outcome was losses on both sides, further fanning their mutual desires for revenge. The cycle of violence only heightened after a Comanche–Southern Ute rupture in the early 1730s led the Utes to support the Spanish and Pueblos against the Comanches.

Hoping to stop the violence, Spanish officials in 1746 barred the Comanches from attending the Taos fair altogether. The Comanches responded to the ban by directing even more trade toward the French-allied Wichitas and Pawnees to the east. But the Comanches were no more willing to allow the French than the Spanish to control Indian-European trade on the southern Plains. When a French trading expedition from Louisiana headed toward New Mexico in 1750, Comanches intercepted it, seizing most of the traders' goods and destroying their papers before allowing them to proceed.

Pleased that the Comanches had discouraged the French from visiting his colony, New Mexico's

Comanche Warriors The Comanches were the dominant power in what is now Texas during the late eighteenth century.

Governor Tomas Vélez Cachupín invited the Comanches back to Taos in 1751. The fair itself proceeded smoothly but afterward a Comanche band attacked Pecos Pueblo. Vélez Cachupín himself headed a retaliatory expedition that trapped the band in a box canyon, killing many Comanches before persuading the survivors that Spain's intentions were peaceful. The survivors in turn persuaded most other Comanches to make peace with New Mexico, and in 1754 the Comanches returned to Taos.

Meanwhile Vélez Cachupín had also invited Apaches, Southern Utes, Navajos, and Pueblos—all current or former enemies of one another as well as of the Comanches—to that year's fair. The fair proceeded peacefully, and Vélez Cachupín's diplomacy seemed destined to bring lasting peace to the

Southwest and southern Plains. But already the Spanish viceroy in Mexico City had dispatched a new governor, Francisco Marín del Valle, to New Mexico. Although Marín del Valle tried to maintain the delicate balance of forces, the Comanches and other Indians and colonists soon resumed the earlier pattern of hostilities alternating with intervals of peaceful trading.

By the mid-eighteenth century, Indians of the prairies and Plains were distributing horses, guns, and other European goods as far west as the Rocky Mountains, in the process transforming their own cultures and homelands. Utilizing European materials, some of them achieved extraordinary heights of political power while fashioning new ways of life entirely independent of European control. The major European beneficiary of these developments was France, which appeared poised in 1754 to dominate the westward expansion of European power across the North American continent.

range of human interactions. Enclaves of Indian survivors in the British seaboard colonies generally included peoples from several tribes as well as a few Africans or Europeans. The inhabitants of refugee communities between the Appalachians and the Mississippi often represented as many as a dozen or more tribal backgrounds and two or three European nations. Treaty conferences in the East and trade fairs in the West likewise attracted peoples from a wide range of cultural and geographic backgrounds. Present in most of these venues were individuals who were themselves descended from multiple backgrounds. The transformed cultures and new identities that emerged in eighteenth-century Native American communities were the products of multiple interactions across cultures, communities, and nationalities. While the lines of descent had by no means been sundered, Indian America in 1750 was a very different place than Indian America in 1450.

CONCLUSION

The period from the 1710s to the 1750s marked the high point of European colonization in North America. From the English colonies on the Atlantic to Native American villages on the upper Missouri River, colonization entailed Indians interacting with Europeans. Some did so as powerless subjects, enduring poverty and discrimination, or as slaves on plantations in America or elsewhere. Other Indians dealt with European traders at their posts, during traders' visits to their villages, or at trade fairs. Indians also interacted with the newcomers at treaty conferences and on battlefields. Many of these interactions resulted in new patterns of alliance and rivalry among Native peoples and helped transform Indians' material cultures and physical environments. Relations with Europeans led some Indians to modify cherished spiritual concepts and induced others to move a few or several hundred miles to new homelands. Like Coosaponakeesa/ Mary, some Native Americans became adept at functioning in both Indian and European worlds and at mediating between them.

Colonization not only brought Native Americans and Europeans together, it facilitated a wider

SUGGESTED READINGS

Brooks, James F. *Captives and Cousins: Slavery, Kinship, and Community in the Southwest Borderlands.* Chapel Hill: University of North Carolina Press, 2002.   A pathbreaking exploration of the meanings of captivity and enslavement as practiced by indigenous and colonizing peoples in the Southwest.

Calloway, Colin G. *One Vast Winter Count: The Native American West Before Lewis and Clark.* Lincoln: University of Nebraska Press, 2003.   Provides an excellent introduction to developments in the Southwest and Plains.

Edmunds, R. David, and Peyser, Joseph L. *The Fox Wars: The Mesquakie Challenge to New France.* Norman: University of Oklahoma Press, 1993.   A detailed but lively narrative of the long-running conflict.

Grumet, Robert S., ed. *Northeastern Indian Lives, 1632–1816.* Amherst: University of Massachusetts Press, 1996.   An excellent collection of short biographies of Native Americans, focusing on the various ways they confronted colonialism and helped shape historical developments in the Northeast.

Merrell, James H. *The Indians' New World: Catawbas and Their Neighbors from European Contact Through the Era of Removal*. Chapel Hill: University of North Carolina Press, 1989. The leading study of a single tribal nation's experience with British colonial expansion in the eighteenth century.

———. *Into the American Woods: Negotiators on the Pennsylvania Frontier*. New York: W. W. Norton, 1999. An outstanding study of the individuals—Indian, European, and Euro-Indian—who served as diplomatic and intercultural brokers and their experiences in times of peace and war.

Merritt, Jane P. *At the Crossroads: Indians and Empires on a Mid-Atlantic Frontier, 1700–1763*. Chapel Hill: University of North Carolina Press, 2003. A penetrating study of Christian Indian communites struggling to survive in eastern Pennsylvania.

Perdue, Theda. *Cherokee Women: Gender and Culture Change, 1700–1835*. Lincoln: University of Nebraska Press, 1998. An excellent discussion of the ways that Cherokee women contributed to the refashioning of Cherokee culture in the face of colonization.

Sleeper-Smith, Susan. *Indian Women and French Men: Rethinking Cultural Encounter in the Western Great Lakes*. Amherst: University of Massachusetts Press, 2001. The best study of the roles of Native American women in shaping Indian-French relations on the middle ground.

Usner, Daniel H., Jr. *Indians, Settlers, and Slaves in a Frontier Exchange Economy*. Chapel Hill: University of North Carolina Press, 1992. Demonstrates brilliantly how the colony of Louisiana emerged from the interactions, both peaceful and hostile, of Indians, Africans, and Europeans.

Native Peoples and Imperial Crises, 1754–1821

In the summer of 1781, Saukamappee led a Piegan Blackfeet attack on an enemy Shoshone camp in what is now southern Alberta. The Blackfeet ripped through the Shoshone tents with daggers, Saukamappee later recalled, but then "our war whoop instantly stopped, our eyes were filled with terror; there was no one to fight with but the dead and dying, each a mass of [bodily] corruption." Concluding that the Good Spirit had abandoned the camp to the Bad Spirit, the Blackfeet plundered some "clean and good" Shoshone possessions and returned home. A few days later, the Bad Spirit reached Saukamappee's own camp, spreading "from one tent to another. . . . We had no belief that one man could give it to another, any more than wounded man could give his wound to another." Only a third of those in Saukamappee's camp died, but in other Piegan camps, "there were tents where everyone died." Once he and other survivors were able, he continued, "we moved about to find our people, . . . no longer with the song and the dance but with tears, shrieks, and howlings of despair for those who would never return to us." To stop the spread of the deadly malady, the Blackfeet and their neighbors made offerings. "What little we could spare we offered to the Bad Spirit to

let us alone and go to our enemies. To the good Spirit we offered feathers, branches of trees, and sweet smelling grass."

Saukamappee later learned from British traders that white people called the terrible disease "smallpox." He also learned that it had spread well beyond his people and their neighbors, though even his informants did not realize just how far. Indeed, between 1780 and 1782, thousands of Indians across western North America, including many living in areas yet unexplored by Europeans, succumbed to smallpox. During that brief period, more than five thousand Native Americans, mostly Pueblos and Apaches, died in New Mexico. On the Plains, smallpox carried away about four thousand Comanches; thirty-five hundred Crows; thirty-five hundred Sioux; thirteen thousand Mandan, Hidatsa, and Arikara villagers on the Missouri River; and ten thousand northern Plains Indians, including Saukamappee's Blackfeet. At the same time, approximately twenty-five thousand Northwest Coast Indians also perished.

How did smallpox victimize so many Native Americans in so short a time? As Indians in the East had long since discovered, their forebears' utter lack of prior exposure to the virus made them far

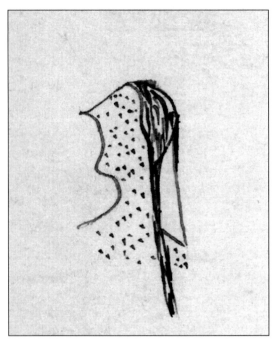

"Many Died of Smallpox," 1780–1781 A Lakota man's winter count—a pictorial record depicting a major event for each year—marks the impact of smallpox on his people.

more vulnerable than were most Europeans. "Although many Spaniards die," observed a Jesuit missionary during an earlier epidemic, "smallpox kills incomparably more Indians." When smallpox struck Indian communities, many who survived the disease perished nevertheless because no one was able to provide basic care in the form of water, food, and warmth. As among the Piegans, the few survivors only began to recover about two weeks after the epidemic struck, by which time most of their kin and neighbors had died.

Where did the epidemic come from and how did it spread? Although epidemics are difficult for historians to track across vast distances, this one left some suggestive clues scattered in the writings of Europeans who either witnessed its effects or recorded the memories of survivors and witnesses. There are also references to epidemics in winter counts (pictorial records that illustrate a significant event for each year) kept by some Plains Indians.

The Comanches may have contracted smallpox from French traders traveling out of New Orleans on the Red River near the end of 1780. Otherwise, they caught it from Pueblos or Apaches who, along with colonists in New Mexico, were directly or indirectly exposed to hundreds of travelers annually on the royal highway that linked Mexico City with Santa Fe. Mexico City had suffered a major outbreak in late 1779 and early 1780. The Mexico City outbreak closely followed one in New Orleans, by then a major Spanish seaport, so that either way the New Orleans outbreak was the most likely source of the western epidemic.

Given both Pueblos' and Comanches' active trading and—in the Comanches' case—mobility and raiding, the virus traveled swiftly. As Sauka-mappee and his party discovered only too late, the virus could even spread via objects only touched by an infected victim. Reinforcing its rapid spread was the fact that the virus incubates in a new human carrier for twelve days before its painful symptoms begin to appear, meaning that the person could travel far and infect many others before realizing that he or she was sick. Also like Sauka-mappee, those lacking experience with or knowledge of smallpox spread it still further before realizing that it was communicable.

The epidemic of 1780–1782 appears to have traveled via the Comanches to Plains Indians farther north and, through them, to Indians across what is now central Canada as far east as Hudson Bay. The Comanches also probably communicated it to their Shoshone relatives, who in turn carried it to friends and enemies in the northern Plains and Great Basin regions and to trade partners along the Columbia River, by which route it reached Indians in the Northwest Coast.

Behind this massive catastrophe lay the epidemic that erupted in New Orleans in 1779. The virus could have arrived there from any number of places in the Atlantic world. The likeliest possibilities are Spain's colonies in the West Indies and the southern battlefields of the American Revolution, where soldiers on both sides and their Indian allies were infected.

Regardless of its exact origin, the epidemic's significance lies in the way it suddenly and catastrophically deepened the links between western Indians and an imperial world reaching to all corners of the Atlantic Ocean and beyond. Previously, those links had consisted of economic exchanges, military and diplomatic alliances, labor systems, and missionary enterprises that affected Indians while sustaining Europe's American empires. But as the land and water routes linking the West with the outside world became more heavily traveled, epidemics emerged as a more lethal form of interaction.

Just as smallpox, by now familiar to eastern Indians, solidified connections between western Native Americans and the Atlantic world, Europe's North American empires were coming to an end, transforming those links in other ways. First, the vast French empire in America collapsed with the conclusion of the Seven Years War in 1763. Then thirteen rebellious colonies from New England to Georgia completed their secession from the British Empire in 1783. Finally, Mexico, including the provinces of New Mexico, Texas, and California, secured its independence from Spain in 1821. Only in British Canada did Europeans still rule in North America.

These successive imperial crises disrupted and often terminated long-established Indian-European arrangements of exchange and diplomacy. As balances of power shifted, Native Americans scrutinized non-Indian players for their trustworthiness, their ability to deliver on promises, and their long-term goals vis-à-vis Native Americans' land and distinctive cultural identities. Accommodating new, more menacing political forces while surviving physically and culturally would prove to be the greatest challenge facing many Indians in this uncertain period.

EASTERN INDIANS AND THE SEVEN YEARS WAR, 1754–1761

The simmering rivalry between France and Britain again erupted in violence with the outbreak in 1754 of the Seven Years War (1756–1763 in Europe). The prospect of all-out imperial war was fraught with peril for eastern Indians for, instead of the two European powers competing for Native Americans' commerce and loyalty, a victory by either would likely lead the winner to assert imperial mastery over Indians and their homelands. For as long as possible after 1754, Indians of the eastern interior

sought to avoid such a fate by preventing either European power from being defeated altogether. At the same time, Native Americans placed the highest priority on protecting their populations, homelands, sovereignty, and distinct cultural identities while maintaining reciprocity in their exchanges with Europeans. Pursuing these priorities, some Native communities embraced or abandoned neutrality or switched sides, often more than once, during the war. Such conduct led Europeans to brand Native Americans as disloyal and untrustworthy, failing to acknowledge that Indians' goals differed sharply from their own.

Crucible of Conflict: The Ohio Valley

War began in 1754, when Virginia dispatched two hundred troops under George Washington to seize Fort Duquesne, recently built by the French at the Ohio Forks (see Chapter 5). Although outnumbered by the French, the twenty-two-year-old Washington expected to make up the discrepancy by recruiting Indian allies. But Washington's expectations did not match those of Indian people. The Catawbas and Cherokees rejected Britain for being allied with their Iroquois enemies, and the Cherokees suspected the British of seeking territorial gain at their expense. Among Indians, only about forty Mingos and a few Delawares led by the sachem Tanaghrisson (see Chapter 5) joined the expedition. Although they scoffed when Washington claimed that his only motive in seizing the fort was "to put [the Indians] in possession of those lands which the French had taken from them," Tanaghrisson and his followers calculated that a destructive imperial war might encourage both European sides to quit the region. After French troops attacked and the Virginians began to retreat, Tanaghrisson abandoned Washington, complaining that the young officer "would by no means take advice from the Indians." Washington surrendered to the French on July 4, 1754.

Despite their disgust with the British, most Shawnees, Delawares, and Mingos remained neutral and a few even leaned toward Britain, calculating that France's heightened military presence was now the greater threat to their autonomy. But British officials ignored Indians' motives and in 1755 sent several thousand troops to North

America to crush the French. A force of twenty-five hundred British and colonial soldiers led by General Edward Braddock was to begin the campaign by capturing Fort Duquesne. Before setting out from Fort Cumberland, Maryland, Braddock contemptuously dismissed about fifty Mingos who offered their assistance. Along the way, some other Ohio Indians led by Shingas, a Delaware sachem, proposed joining Braddock's forces. But when Shingas asked the general what terms the Indians might expect from a victorious Britain, Braddock replied "that no savage should inherit the land." Shingas retorted that his people would not fight for land they could not keep, to which Braddock "answered that he did not need their help." With that haughty repudiation, Braddock lost the support of all but about a half dozen Indians—not enough to provide his forces with adequate scouting.

Snaking toward Fort Duquesne on July 9, 1755, the advance British column of 1,450 troops walked into an ambush. About 600 Ottawas, Potawatomis, Abenakis, Shawnees, Delawares, Mingos, and other Indians—plus 250 French and Canadian troops—had caught the British by surprise, forcing them to fall back in chaos. Within three hours, Braddock and about 900 of his men lay dead. The general "was a bad man when he was alive," an Oneida chief said. "He looked upon us as dogs, and . . . that was the reason a great many of our warriors left him and would not be under his command."

Although the military balance had shifted even more decisively toward the French, most Ohio Indians found more to fear in Braddock's statements. For the next three years, Shawnees, Delawares, and Mingos—aided by French arms and other presents supplied from Fort Duquesne—attacked Anglo-Americans in western Pennsylvania, Maryland, and Virginia, killing hundreds of colonists while capturing and (usually) adopting others, mostly women and children. Besides driving back non-Indians' encroachments on their lands, the attacks prevented the three colonies from supporting Britain against France. Despite their support of the French, however, the Ohio Indians' ultimate goal remained freedom from all colonizers. As a Delaware speaker summed up his people's strategy, the British were "such a numerous people" that the Indians needed French help to remove them. Thereafter, he continued, "we can drive the French away when we please."

Native Peoples and the Anglo-French War in the North

In the aftermath of Braddock's defeat, even Britain's most loyal allies, the Mohawk Iroquois, grew disillusioned with the British. About a hundred Mohawks joined one British expedition, only to see it aborted when colonial troops, dispirited by the news from Fort Duquesne, deserted. Other Mohawks joined British troops who encountered more, better equipped French forces at Lake George in September 1755. The French contingent included six hundred Indians, about half of them pro-French, non-Confederacy Mohawks from Kahnawake, the Catholic praying town near Montreal. With the Confederacy Mohawks in the British vanguard, the Kahnawake Mohawks and some French and Canadians ambushed them, killing ninety. Although the battle ended as a military standoff, Britain's loss was greater because Confederacy Mohawk women elders, appalled by the destructive fighting between Mohawks, persuaded their people to withdraw from the war.

While the Mohawks became neutral, other Confederacy Iroquois moved from neutrality to active support of the French. These Iroquois were especially alarmed because eleven hundred British soldiers had recently joined those at Fort Oswego in preparation for an attack on France's Fort Niagara. For three decades, the Six Nations had allowed the two posts to coexist in their homeland so that they could trade conveniently at both. Preempting British action, several hundred Iroquois and other Indians in August 1756 joined three thousand French and Canadian troops in overwhelming Fort Oswego and capturing sixteen hundred survivors. In the aftermath of victory, Iroquois Confederacy leaders thanked the French commander, Montcalm, for restoring their people "in a place that was their property" and promised "to make [the Mohawks] recover their lost senses" and join the French cause.

Unfortunately for these Iroquois, their enthusiasm for the French came just as France's willingness and ability to provide for its Native allies was waning. Montcalm displayed less interest than had earlier French commanders in drawing on Indians for support and rewarding them with presents. Receiving no gifts from him at Fort Oswego, warriors plundered the English prisoners, including the wounded, for goods and scalps and killed those who resisted. A similar result followed the French-Indian capture of Britain's Fort William Henry in 1757. Such actions angered Montcalm who, like Braddock and other officers on both European sides, disdained Indians. In accordance with European military ideals, the officers would have preferred to fight exclusively with trained, disciplined troops who would obey their commands unquestionably. Resenting Montcalm's haughty attitude, most of the Indians returned home with no plans to fight for the French again. As one of them put it, "I make war for plunder, scalps, and prisoners. You are satisfied with a fort, and you let your enemy and mine live. I do not want to keep such bad meat for tomorrow. When I kill it, it can no longer attack me."

The resentful Indian's statement pointed to the fact that Native Americans' military aims, like their diplomatic aims, differed from those of Europeans. Throughout the war France's Indian allies consistently sought prisoners, goods, and trophies, but the results varied depending on the circumstances of each battle. When, after the victory at Lake George, the French pressed their attack against the main English camp, their Native allies refused to join, having already won what they considered a great victory. The Native Americans, for whom a minimum of casualties in their own ranks was a high priority, were especially astonished when the French commander ordered a head-on bayonet charge, knowing that his troops would suffer heavily. (They did; about one-third of the French died in the unsuccessful assault.) Whereas on that occasion the Indians obtained their objectives early in the fighting, the French refusal at forts Oswego and William Henry to treat them as equal allies led Native Americans to inflict many more casualties on their enemies to achieve their aims.

The Indians' withdrawal from the war in the North led to the more conventional kind of fighting preferred by most Europeans. "Now war is established here on the European basis," enthused a victorious French officer. But the officer's enthusiasm would prove to be misplaced, for France was more greatly disadvantaged by the loss of Native support than was Britain with its vastly larger colonial population. Beginning in the winter of 1757–1758, moreover, the British navy blockaded French ports, preventing French ships from carrying troops, supplies, and presents for Indian allies to America.

Delaware Diplomacy and the War's Turning Point

The shift in military fortunes also affected the war in Pennsylvania and the Ohio country. Lacking gifts, French officers tried instead to impose direct authority over Native Americans, only further alienating them. Meanwhile as Native men went off to war, their communities suffered because they ran short of meat and fish. When they did return, they brought the smallpox that infected people on all sides but as usual affected Native Americans most drastically. Many Ohio Indians noted that French victories came as Indians suffered more misfortune, leading them to question their continued support for France. One group of Miamis, for example, proclaimed that "they were now resolved to turn the hatchet against" the French.

Although they had suffered many abuses from colonists, even the western Delawares were receptive to talking peace with the British. In July 1758 Shingas, who had questioned Braddock three years earlier, now queried a Pennsylvania negotiator, Christian Frederick Post, just as sharply:

> Why don't you and the French fight in the old country, and on the sea? Why do you come to fight on our land? This makes everybody believe that you want to take the land from us by force and settle it.

Although not fully persuaded of Britain's good intentions, the western Delawares sent a delegate to a treaty conference at Easton, Pennsylvania, in October 1758.

The Easton conference drew representatives from the eastern and western Delawares, the Six Nations Iroquois, the colonies of Pennsylvania and New Jersey, and the British Empire. The parties agreed to unite in the struggle against France. Accordingly, western Delaware warriors abandoned Fort Duquesne, leaving the fewer than five hundred remaining French troops so vulnerable that they withdrew. A larger British force promptly occupied the post and renamed it Fort Pitt.

While welcoming the French departure, the western Delawares made clear that they expected the British to leave soon as well. "Brother," said one of their sachems, "I would tell you in a most soft, loving, and friendly manner to go back over the mountain [Appalachians] and stay there." If the British would agree, the western Delawares promised to enlist the Shawnees and "all the Indians settled to the westward" in a regional league of peace. They envisioned the league supporting neither Britain nor France militarily.

The western Delawares' ambitions were constrained by a second outcome of the Easton conference, the revival by the British and Six Nations Iroquois of the Covenant Chain, long an instrument used by the two to seize land from and otherwise dominate non-Iroquois Indians, including the Delawares. To secure an agreement with the British, the western Delawares reluctantly agreed to rejoin the Covenant Chain on terms that ostensibly allowed them to negotiate for themselves but would require Iroquois approval of any diplomatic agreements or treaties. But then, with Iroquois consent and over strident Delaware objections, the British kept two hundred troops at Fort Pitt. Any remaining Indian hopes for a complete British withdrawal collapsed in September 1759, when British troops captured Quebec. One year later, as the British prepared to seize Montreal, France surrendered all of Canada. Except in Spanish Florida, Britain was now the sole imperial power in eastern North America.

Creeks, Cherokees, and the War in the Southeast

As war approached on the Ohio, the Creeks and Cherokees strengthened their recently concluded peace agreement (see Chapter 5) and sought to play Britain and France against one another diplomatically. In May 1755, as Braddock planned his march to Fort Duquesne, several Creek headmen agreed to trade with the French in Louisiana, hoping thereby to gain more favorable trade concessions from the British in South Carolina. The Carolinians responded but demanded a steep price: the Creeks must permit the British to build a fort among the Upper Creeks (where French traders were most active) and must actively aid the Chickasaws in their ongoing war with the French-allied Choctaws. Creek negotiators at Charleston accepted the terms, but not a single Creek town ratified the treaty because their inhabitants feared that the British

wanted their land. At the same time, however, most Creeks repudiated a pro-French faction that urged them to rally all Indians south of the Ohio and east of the Mississippi to the French cause. Although differences among the Creeks continued, the competing factions and viewpoints neutralized each other and enabled the Creeks to withstand British and French pressures to take sides.

Comparable sentiments and tensions flourished among the Cherokees, but instead of trying to keep the various colonizers out of their homelands, the Cherokees invited Virginia, South Carolina, and Louisiana each to build a fort among its more westerly Overhill towns. The Cherokees hoped to enjoy the benefits of trade with each colony while citing the proximity of British and French troops as an excuse to fight for neither. Virginia in 1754 built a fort but abandoned it after the Cherokees refused to join Washington's assault on Fort Duquesne. South Carolina in 1756 built Fort Loudoun and furnished it with a large garrison. Cherokee women from nearby towns brought farm products and men carried deerskins to exchange with the troops for cloth and other English goods. Running short of imports for themselves and Indian allies, the French in Louisiana declined the Cherokee invitation.

France's weakness as a counterweight encouraged Britain to press the Cherokees harder for military support. In 1757, English officials, promising scalp bounties and presents, recruited some Cherokee warriors for a successful attack on Shawnees in Ohio. Afterward, a neutral Cherokee headman complained that what had formerly been a "free path" to his town, "clean and neat, without any danger," was now, because of Shawnee anger, "dirty and bloody, and very dangerous." In the following year the British sought Cherokee assistance in recapturing Fort Duquesne and the Ohio country. Most Cherokees resisted these pressures after hearing that their Iroquois enemies would participate and because their medicine men predicted that fighting would bring "sickness and death to many [Cherokees] and vast fatigue to the whole."

Despite popular sentiments, about three hundred pro-British Cherokees, led by Attakullakulla (Little Carpenter), joined the expedition—and came to regret it. After treating Attakullakulla as a subordinate rather than an ally, British General John Forbes briefly imprisoned the prestigious headman

Outacite, Cherokee War Leader Outacite was a Cherokee who for a time cooperated with the British, as evidenced by the gorget that hangs from his neck (ca. 1762) displaying the royal arms of King George III.

for trying to leave the expedition. Returning home in small parties, other Cherokees were attacked by quasi-official mobs from the colonies they had just defended.

In fall 1759, as Britain's military advantage became decisive, South Carolina's governor William Lyttleton decided that it was time "to humble our perfidious [Cherokee] enemy." Mobilizing fifteen hundred troops, the colony seized as hostages twenty-eight peace-seeking Cherokees who had traveled to Charleston. Thereafter, retaliating Cherokees harassed British troops and struck hard at western colonists. The Cherokees eventually forced the surrender of Fort Loudoun when Cherokee women ceased delivering food to the hungry garrison.

Thereafter, most Cherokees were prepared to make peace with Britain but the British commander, General Jeffrey Amherst, was determined to punish the Cherokees. In the spring and summer of 1761, an expedition of twenty-eight hundred regular troops, colonial militiamen, and Native allies, primarily Catawbas, Chickasaws, Mohawks, and Stockbridge Mahicans, attacked and burned several Middle Cherokee towns, along with cornfields and peach orchards. (The Cherokees, like other eastern Indians, had begun growing peaches after obtaining them from British traders.)

Despite the extensive damage to their homes and crops, the Cherokees avoided heavy casualties. Nevertheless, without significant outside support, the war was enormously burdensome and the prospects for expelling the British virtually nil. In December 1761 the Cherokees agreed with South Carolina and Virginia to exchange prisoners and to establish a clear boundary line between Cherokee and English settlements. The Cherokees also returned Fort Loudoun to the British and permitted them to build other forts in their country.

EASTERN INDIANS AND THE AMERICAN REVOLUTION, 1761–1783

France's surrender undermined the foundations of eastern Native Americans' strategies for dealing with Europeans. Mounting a fierce movement of resistance, Indians in the Ohio Valley and around the Great Lakes forced Britain to make concessions, especially to protect their lands and peoples from unscrupulous outsiders. But Britain's concessions to Indians challenged the authority and land claims of colonial governments, adding further to the list of grievances leading the colonies toward revolution. When revolution came, most eastern Indians either supported Britain, recognizing that an independent United States directly threatened their sovereignty, or tried to remain neutral in hopes of ensuring their survival. In the end, white Americans' contempt for neutral Indians drove nearly all Native Americans between the Appalachians and the Mississippi to support the British.

Tensions Among the Victors, 1761–1763

Native Americans in 1761 faced a victorious Britain whose leaders considered them subjects rather than allies of distinct, sovereign nations. Indians were to be commanded and, if obedient, rewarded, said General Amherst. But, he continued, "when men of [any] . . . race behave ill, they must be punished." Accordingly, Amherst stationed British troops in the former French military-trade posts (and several newly built ones) across the Ohio–Great Lakes region. In February 1761 he ordered that Anglo-Indian trade be confined to the forts and decreed an end to giving presents to Indian allies. From now on, Indians would pay—usually with furs—market value for whatever goods they obtained at the posts. Because the policy covered gunpowder and ammunition, it prevented Native hunters from providing enough meat to feed their hungry families. Yet at the same time, Amherst allowed white Virginians to hunt on Indians' land.

As the implications of the new policies became clear, Indians living near the forts grew apprehensive. When British forces occupied Detroit in late 1760, Indians there protested that "this country was given by God to the Indians." Papoonan, an eastern Delaware religious leader, articulated Native Americans' grievances against what they perceived as Britain's arbitrary raising of prices for trade goods. "God," he said, "cannot be pleased to see the price of one and the same thing so often altered and changed." Another Delaware pleaded with Pennsylvania's traders to lower their prices "that we may live and walk together in one brotherly love and friendship as brothers ought to live." The Delawares were reiterating Native Americans' time-honored understanding that people exchanged goods not only for material advantages but to affirm mutual respect and strengthen alliances. To demand more in an exchange than was customary or than the other party could afford was insulting.

Another point of Anglo-Indian contention was Amherst's insistence that Indians return all Anglo-American captives living among them. Native families had long adopted prisoners seized in raids to compensate for kin killed in battle and to replenish their communities' numbers. The fierce fighting of the Seven Years War resulted in the capture of hundreds of colonists—especially western Pennsylvanians—by Delawares, Shawnees, and Mingos.

Indians generally developed strong emotional ties with their Anglo-American kin. In about 1763 the two Seneca sisters of young Mary Jemison, captured several years earlier in Pennsylvania, took her to Fort Pitt to be redeemed, but they panicked at the last minute and turned back. "So great was their fear of losing me," Jemison later recalled, "they never stopped rowing till they got home," about eighty miles away. In another instance, an Indian man known to the English as Jimmie Wilson returned his Pennsylvania-born wife to her birth family because she requested it, "notwithstanding he loved her." Dividing his worldly possessions with her, Wilson bought her a horse and escorted her himself.

Most captives adopted as children forgot the families, languages, and cultures into which they had been born and eventually married Indians. Some male captives became traders, diplomats, translators, or even political leaders of their adoptive communities. Like Eunice Williams six decades earlier (see Chapter 4), these children often resisted returning to their biological parents. One boy, John McCullough, had to be tied to his British father's horse for the journey home from Fort Pitt but soon escaped and returned to his Indian family. He was recaptured a year later and sent back to the fort, this time under "strong guard." British observers were repeatedly astonished at the grief expressed by both Native Americans and their white captives when forced to part. Despite the mutual hatreds dividing Native Americans and colonists, Indians and their former captives often maintained contacts for years after the captives returned to white society.

Word of the Treaty of Paris (1763), in which France ceded its territorial claims east of the Mississippi River to Britain, marked a turning point in Anglo-Indian relations. According to one officer, the reports struck the Indians around Fort Pitt "like a thunderclap." After recovering from the shock, the Shawnees proclaimed that because "they were never Conquered by any nation, the French had no right to give away their Country." The British, they continued, were now "too great a People." For two years, Ohio Indians' anti-British resistance had been coupled with the expectation that France would return to the region, enabling them to resume exploiting the imperial rivalry to their own advantage. The dashing of that expectation reinforced the spread among Indians of more radical ideas, already being espoused by Neolin, also known as the Delaware Prophet.

Neolin and Pontiac's Rebellion, 1763

Although they were radical, Neolin's ideas were not entirely new. Like earlier Native prophets, he described having visions that revealed a spiritual solution to his people's problems. When preaching, Neolin displayed "a kind of map on a piece of deerskin," according to a Delaware-speaking missionary. The map depicted "the white people" as having blocked the Indians' path to "the heavenly regions," leaving them confined to a land where the ground was dry, food was scarce, and "the evil spirit . . . transformed men into horses and dogs, to be ridden by him and follow him in his hunts and wherever he went." The solution, he continued, was "to make sacrifices, . . . to put off . . . the customs which you have adopted since the white people came among us, [and] return to that former state, in which we lived in peace and plenty, before these strangers came to disturb us." In particular, Indians must cease drinking "their deadly *beson* [alcohol], which they have forced upon us, for the sake of increasing their gains and diminishing our numbers." Instead he advocated a collective ritual practiced by southeastern Indians in which participants brewed, drank, and vomited an emetic known as "black drink." By so doing, they would, in Neolin's words, "purge out all they got of the White peoples ways & Nature." By so transforming their lives, the prophet concluded, the Indians would gain the strength to drive out the invaders and "recover the passage to the heavenly regions."

Neolin's preaching resonated powerfully with Indians from Pennsylvania to Detroit. They shared a range of recent experiences—sickness, death, poverty, hunger, drunkenness, bitter divisions among themselves, violence at the hands of whites, separation from homelands—that seemed likely to worsen unless the causes were removed. By repudiating Europeans and everything associated with them and by living once again simply as Indians, Neolin asserted, Native Americans would regain the health, prosperity, and independence they had enjoyed before the onset of colonization.

Neolin's message became especially potent in the hands of a charismatic Ottawa war leader named Pontiac. Pontiac fused Neolin's prophecy with Great Lakes and Illinois Indians' persistent nostalgia for the French into a militantly anti-British call to arms. In spring 1763 Pontiac led the intertribal community at Detroit in a siege of the British post there, an action quickly emulated by groups of Indians near most of the other British forts. Native Americans destroyed three of the forts, but the other sieges either failed at the outset or were soon broken by the British, who were aided in some cases by loyal Indians.

Three other sieges—at Fort Pitt, Fort Niagara, and Detroit—proved less easy for the British to break. They finally regained Fort Pitt through the earliest recorded use of biological warfare in American history. Since 1492 Europeans had gained most of their American territory and won many of their military victories over Indians because of Natives' extreme vulnerability to epidemic diseases. The recent development of a form of inoculation against smallpox enabled the British to manipulate the disease with little risk to themselves. In June 1763, after discussing possible peace terms with a Delaware delegation, British officers at Fort Pitt gave their departing guests some presents, including "two Blankets and an Handkerchief out of the Small Pox Hospital." These "presents" were no anomaly; even as they were being distributed, Amherst and other senior officers encouraged local commanders to use smallpox blankets as weapons. By August, several dozen Delawares, Shawnees, and Mingos near Fort Pitt had died of the disease, enabling a British rescue force to relieve the fort.

Meanwhile, after inflicting heavy casualties on British troops, the Seneca Iroquois lacked adequate provisions for maintaining the siege of Fort Niagara and withdrew in July. Divisions among Pontiac's followers, along with British determination, forced a lifting of the siege at Detroit in October.

A New British Indian Policy, 1763–1768

Although Britain had regained control of the forts, officials recognized that imperial authority would remain tenuous without significant concessions to Native Americans. British authority was being

Indian-British Diplomacy in the Ohio Country, 1764 A Native American spokesman holds a wampum belt while addressing British officials.

challenged not only by Indians but also by colonial governments and by speculators, squatters, hunters, unsavory traders, outlaws, and other colonists who invaded Indian homelands, heightening Anglo-Indian tensions.

The heart of the new British policy was set forth in the Proclamation of 1763, issued by King George III in October. A "Proclamation Line" along the crest of the Appalachian Mountains set limits to the colonies' western land claims. The proclamation recognized tribes' title to their unceded lands west of the line, although their sovereignty remained subordinate to that of the British, and required that any sales of that land by Indians be approved by one of two Superintendents of Indian

Affairs. The proclamation also empowered the superintendents to license traders west of the line and barred other non-Indians from crossing the line without the superintendents' permission. In other words, British officials would directly oversee all Anglo-Indian transactions, thereby avoiding the abuses of Native Americans by colonial agents and private individuals that had fueled Indians' anti-British sentiments.

The new regulations incurred the wrath of colonists who resented British authority, whether exerted in the form of taxes or of constraints on colonial expansion. From 1763 until colonists' resentments exploded in revolution twelve years later, British policymakers walked a tightrope between the conflicting interests of Native Americans and expansion-minded Anglo-Americans.

To enforce the proclamation's mandates, the London government appointed John Stuart and William Johnson as superintendents for the southern and northern districts, respectively. In addition, it recalled Jeffrey Amherst as its senior military commander in North America, citing his poor leadership as the principal cause of the uprising. Although the proclamation did not recognize Native American sovereignty in the affected areas, the Indians had nevertheless succeeded in forcing the empire to adjust its policy to reflect their concerns.

In the South, Stuart summoned leaders of the Cherokees, Upper and Lower Creeks, Choctaws, Chickasaws, and Catawbas along with the governors of the four southernmost British colonies to meet at Augusta, Georgia, in November 1763. The tribes' long-standing grievances against British traders and trespassing colonists had recently led them to consider following Pontiac's lead at forts in their region. Over the next two years, Stuart deftly persuaded the Cherokees, Catawbas, and Lower Creeks that colonists from Virginia, the Carolinas, and Georgia would honor the Proclamation Line while convincing the Upper Creeks, Choctaws, and Chickasaws to ignore the Spanish and trade exclusively with the British.

Britain appointed Johnson as superintendent in the North on the basis of his experience as a trader and imperial official with close ties to the Six Nations Iroquois, especially the Mohawks. In that capacity he had consistently upheld the Six Nations in their claims, through the Covenant Chain, to exercise authority over non-Iroquois Indians in the Northeast.

Johnson's most immediate challenge came from Indians in the Wabash and Illinois valleys, who had never fallen under the Covenant Chain and who now rallied behind Pontiac. Failing to recognize that Indians at Detroit had largely discredited Pontiac, Johnson and other British officials imagined the Ottawa war leader as an intertribal "king" through whom they could extend their authority over all Indians in the region, much as the Six Nations Iroquois supposedly did farther east through the Covenant Chain.

Unfortunately for Pontiac, he could not resist Johnson's tempting offer. Even as negotiations proceeded, many western Indians feared that Pontiac had become a slave of the British and would sacrifice their interests. Although Pontiac persuaded the British to restore gift giving and to recognize a limited Indian sovereignty, he promised Johnson in 1766 to give the British "every thing you have desired of us, and . . . nothing but what is good." A virtual outcast in most Indian communities after this submission, Pontiac retreated to Illinois, where local Indians assassinated him in 1769.

The Collapse of British Policy, 1768–1775

Even before Pontiac's assassination, British imperial officials were feeling the financial pinch from colonists' rejections of the various revenue measures they had tried to impose over the preceding six years. Short of funds, London returned control of Anglo-Indian trade to the colonies, reduced the number of troops at its forts, scaled back its gift giving to Indians, and cut Stuart's and Johnson's budgets. British officials also began pressuring Indians to sell lands to colonial governments, settlers, and speculators, many of whom had already seized the lands illegally. In this way, officials who, under the Proclamation of 1763, were supposed to protect Indians' interests acted to undermine Native Americans' landholdings.

As in earlier periods, Britain—now represented by William Johnson—colluded with the Six Nations Iroquois and used the Covenant Chain to deprive non-Iroquois Indians of their land. By recognizing Iroquois sovereignty over other Indians' land, the British satisfied themselves that "purchases" of that land from the Iroquois would be legitimate. In the Treaty of Fort Stanwix (1768), the Iroquois—claiming to speak for Cherokees, Delawares, and Shawnees—ceded to Britain several million acres of those tribes' lands south of the Ohio River. The treaty extended southwest to the Tennessee River, far beyond what British officials had instructed Johnson to acquire. The Cherokees, Delawares, and Shawnees were not even notified in advance of the Iroquois-British negotiations. Besides upholding the façade of British authority, Johnson had appeased squatters and speculators already active in the area; among the speculators was Johnson himself.

The Treaty of Fort Stanwix prompted the formation of a new resistance movement led by some

Shawnees among Indians in the Ohio country. Even before the treaty conference broke up, these Shawnees urged non-Iroquois Indians to "unite and attack the English" and followed up by sending delegations to Detroit and other communities. Iroquois delegates, armed with gifts supplied by Johnson, persuaded a few communities to reject the call for war. Countering them were young Shawnee, Delaware, and other warriors who boldly challenged the authority of village chiefs who accepted Iroquois gifts. Like rebellious colonists to the east, Indians in the Ohio country defied official authority, thereby threatening to bring on another all-out war.

Tensions exploded in May 1774 after two white Virginians murdered eight to ten Mingos in cold blood at Yellow Creek on the Ohio River. Among the victims was the family of Logan, a war leader previously friendly to whites. Already angered by some murders of local Indians, Logan and other aggrieved Mingos and Shawnees could not be placated. After leading a war party in the retaliatory murders of thirteen white Virginians, Logan declared that he had obtained his revenge. But Virginia's royal governor, Lord Dunmore, used the occasion to declare all-out war on the Shawnees, recruiting twenty-four hundred volunteers with promises of plunder. As the Virginians prepared to attack a cluster of Shawnee towns on the Scioto River, some pro-peace Shawnee chiefs negotiated a cease-fire. They agreed to give up Shawnee land south of the Ohio River, as dictated by the Treaty of Fort Stanwix, on the condition that a formal peace conference be called to confirm the cession. Ignoring the condition, many of the dispersing troops scouted for real estate in Shawnee country.

In the Southeast, colonists undid Stuart's careful diplomacy among the Cherokees and Creeks. In the Treaty of Augusta (1773), Georgia cynically played the two Indian nations against one another, persuading them to sell tracts of one another's land so as to cancel their debts to white traders. In all, Georgia acquired nearly six million acres of Indian land during the decade prior to the outbreak of the American Revolution. British officials and speculators also pressured the Cherokees to sell off Ohio Valley lands, some of which belonged to the Shawnees, in several secret deals, culminating in the notorious Henderson's Purchase (1775). In this deal, speculator Richard Henderson, having already sold claims to hundreds of colonists, obtained about twenty-seven thousand square miles of Cherokee land in violation of both English and Cherokee law. Although a few Indian leaders had consented to these cessions in return for trade goods, most Creeks and Cherokees resented the illegal sales of lands on which they lived and depended.

As colonists poured across the Proclamation Line onto Indian lands, British troops in April 1775 fired on colonists in Lexington and Concord, Massachusetts. The outbreak of the American Revolution introduced a new dynamic into the struggles of eastern Native Americans to retain their lands, sovereignty, and way of life.

The American Revolution as an Imperial War, 1775–1783

The defeat of France by Britain and its American colonies thirteen years earlier had deprived Native Americans of their ability to play the two imperial powers against one another. While the outbreak of hostilities *between* Britain and the colonies might seem to have offered Indians comparable opportunities, in fact few Indians west of the Proclamation Line were prepared to support colonists who would, upon winning the war, move immediately to seize their land. While Britain had betrayed many of the tribes on more than one occasion, the empire now depended on Indian military support and would be in no position to take Indians' land if victorious. The only dilemma for most Indian communities was whether supporting Britain or remaining neutral would better ensure their goals of survival, autonomy, and retaining land.

The ranks of the Six Nations Iroquois Confederacy, once a united, powerful military and diplomatic force, were badly divided. Although the Iroquois and British had revived the Covenant Chain when signing the Treaty of Fort Stanwix in 1768, Britain's continued decline thereafter left the system of alliances a weak instrument. While most Iroquois hoped to play the two sides off one another and avoid the ravages of war and internal disunity, a minority favored one side or the other. A rising young Mohawk leader, the English-educated Joseph Brant, found support among the Mo-

Joseph Brant The brilliant young Mohawk led his and other Iroquois nations who allied with the British against the American colonists.

hawks, Onondagas, Cayugas, and Senecas for sustaining the Covenant Chain and opposing the colonies. But the Oneidas and most Tuscaroras were among the few Indians favoring the Americans, thanks to the influence of the missionary Samuel Kirkland.

With Iroquois unity already collapsing, an epidemic struck the Onondagas in January 1777. So devastating was the sickness that the Onondagas could not maintain the confederacy's central council fire, allowing it to go out for the first time since the confederacy was formed more than three centuries earlier (see Chapter 1). The loss of the ceremonial and symbolic heart of the confederacy removed the last restraint on active Iroquois participation on both sides. Within a year, Iroquois warriors were fighting face to face, slaying one another and burning one another's homes.

Indians in the Ohio country were initially divided between pro-British and neutralist factions. Not wishing to provoke "a general Indian War" of all Ohio Indians against the new republic, rebel officials in 1776 and early 1777 declined to retaliate

for several Shawnee attacks on white Virginians. But the tide soon turned when some Virginians, declaring that all Indians were their enemies, murdered the Shawnee leader Cornstalk under a flag of truce. At that point, most neutral Shawnees joined the anti-American effort. Similarly, when white Americans in 1778 murdered the Delaware chief White Eyes, who had signed a peace treaty with the United States, many neutral Delawares sided with Britain. After white Pennsylvanians attacked and massacred the inhabitants of two neutral Delaware towns in 1782, few neutral Delawares remained.

The war similarly divided the Cherokees. In spring 1776 a delegation of Ottawas, Mohawks, and Shawnees arrived at the Cherokee town of Chota to urge support for Britain. The delegation's Shawnee speaker presented a belt of wampum, nine feet long and, in the words of a British witness, "strewed over with vermilion," symbolizing war. The speaker pointed out that whereas "red people . . . were once masters of the whole country," now they "hardly possessed ground enough to stand on." The "Virginians," as many Ohio and southeastern Indians referred to all white colonists, had "an intention to extirpate them, and . . . he thought it better to die like men than to dwindle away by inches." Already blamed for the recent sales of Cherokee lands, older Cherokee leaders stood still, but Dragging Canoe, the most prominent of a group of younger militants, stepped forward and accepted the belt. After Dragging Canoe spoke, another Cherokee led his people in a "war song and all the Northern Indians joined in the chorus." Remaining silent, however, were "the principal chiefs of the Cherokees, who were opposed to the measure," including Dragging Canoe's own father, Attakullakulla.

After the Chota conference, Dragging Canoe and the militants overshadowed the older Cherokee headmen. For the remainder of 1776, Cherokee warriors launched deadly raids on encroaching settlers in Georgia, the Carolinas, and Virginia. But by year's end they ran short of ammunition while the states mobilized. During 1777, five thousand militiamen raided and destroyed most Cherokee towns east of the Blue Ridge Mountains, including their homes, fields, livestock, and stored food. Several thousand Cherokees fled to the Appalachians and survived on whatever wild foods they could find. Hoping to relieve their people's suffering, the older headmen submitted in 1777 to Georgia and South Carolina in the Treaty of DeWitt's Corner and to North Carolina and Virginia in the Treaty of Long Island of the Holston. Together the two treaties resulted in the loss of another eighty-two hundred square miles of Cherokee land. But the militants, led by Dragging Canoe, rejected the treaties and defied the headmen. Regrouping in the Tennessee Valley as the Chickamaugas, they procured British arms and resumed their attacks on rebels.

The Anglo-American rush for Cherokee lands created a spiral effect, driving otherwise peaceable Cherokees into the ranks of the Chickamaugas to fight the Americans. Retaliating American troops destroyed several peaceful Cherokee towns and killed many innocent Cherokees, and so the spiral continued. As the war drew to a close, the divisions among Cherokees remained as deep as those between them and their non-Indian neighbors.

Farther south, the Creeks were also divided into pro-British and neutralist factions. Pro-British sentiment was strongest in several Upper Creek towns that had strong trade ties with Britain and among whom some Shawnees had lived since the seventeenth century. The most prominent militant, Emistisigno, promised British Superintendent John Stuart in November 1776 that "if the red warriors to the northward would hold a red stick to the Virginians there, I would hold one against them here." But neutralist sentiment among other Upper Creeks and most Lower Creeks, among whom American and Spanish influence was stronger, restrained the militants until 1778, when they began joining Chickamauga raiding parties.

Besides the towns of the Creek Confederacy itself, several towns made up of Lower Creek emigrants had formed in northern Florida over several decades before the Revolution. The founders of these towns had moved in order to distance themselves from British traders, settling on lands vacated by Apalachees, Timucuas, and other peoples dispersed during earlier Indian slave raids (see Chapter 4). By the 1760s, the immigrants had acquired a distinct identity as Seminoles. Like their Creek relatives, the Seminoles were divided. Although Spain had withdrawn from Florida in 1763, southern Seminoles traded with Spaniards in Cuba via Spanish fishing boats and their own canoes.

After an American offensive forced Stuart and other British officials to flee to St. Augustine, Florida, in 1776, the northern Seminoles actively joined the British cause.

Although Britain suffered some costly early defeats, its ability to field large numbers of troops and maintain commerce with Indians initially contrasted with the Continental Army's absence from areas near Native communities. Accordingly, Britain won a number of significant victories in 1778 with the help of Indian allies it supplied with arms and other trade goods. Pro-British Iroquois, some led by Brant, conducted devastating raids on Anglo-Americans living near Iroquois homelands, driving out families while depriving the Continental Army of crucial food supplies. In the lower Ohio Valley, Miamis, Potawatomis, and other Indians assisted British forces in capturing the key town of Vincennes from American troops. While Chickamaugas and some Creeks kept up their raids on white southern Americans, other Creeks along with Chickasaws and Choctaws assisted the British in defending key southern positions.

As stunning as these and other Indian victories were, several of them were reversed by the end of 1779. Besides maturing as a military force, the United States had gained the critical support of France and Spain while Britain's strained finances limited its military effort and made the war unpopular at home. The consequences of these shifts were severe for some pro-British Indians. American forces under John Sullivan retaliated for the Iroquois invasions by destroying homes and burning cornfields at forty villages, causing more than five thousand Iroquois to flee to Canada to avoid starvation and exposure. On the lower Ohio, George Rogers Clark persuaded some Indians to withdraw their support of the British at Vincennes and then recaptured the town. Upriver, Kentucky militiamen burned Shawnee villages while American troops burned Delaware and Mingo towns. After John Stuart died in 1779, Britain's relations with its southern Indian allies broke down, leading the Creeks and Choctaws to withdraw from Augusta, Pensacola, and other key posts. Without the support of their Native allies, Britain lost these posts to the Americans.

Only in the Ohio–Great Lakes region did the Indians and their British allies regain the offensive. In Kentucky, the Shawnees simply rebuilt their burned villages in nearby locales. In late 1779, they joined an attack on a convoy bringing supplies for Ohio Valley settlers from New Orleans. Forty white Americans were killed and the rest taken captive. In the following spring, British troops armed with cannons and allied Indians attacked two key settlements and seized three hundred additional captives. Before long much of the settler population in Kentucky had fled to Virginia. When the war ended, Indians and their British allies controlled the Ohio–Great Lakes region.

Success in the west was not sufficient to revitalize the British cause. The independence of the new United States was certified in the second Treaty of Paris (1783). Under the treaty, Britain transferred all its territorial claims east of the Mississippi River to the United States. (In a separate treaty, Britain ceded East and West Florida to Spain.) As in the first Treaty of Paris twenty years earlier, the new agreement made no explicit reference to Native Americans, leaving Indians to deal on their own with a victorious nation that claimed sovereign authority over them and their lands. And like France's Indian allies in 1763, Indians were shocked and outraged at Britain's abandonment of them. One Creek chief was certain that the news was "a Virginia lie." Joseph Brant, speaking for the pro-British Iroquois, demanded that Canada's governor tell him "the real truth, whether . . . [the Iroquois] are not partakers of that Peace with the King and the Bostonians," as northern Indians termed all white Americans. Alexander McGillivray, who had emerged as principal leader of the Creeks, protested that "to find ourselves & Country betrayed to our Enemies & divided between the Spaniards & Americans is Cruel & Ungenerous." American officials seized on such sentiments, telling the Shawnees that the British had treated them "like Bastards." Simultaneously, they reinforced Indians' worst fears, bragging to the Iroquois, "We are now Masters of this island, and can dispose of the Lands as we think proper or most convenient to ourselves."

In the wake of the American victory, Native peoples sought to rebuild their shattered communities while positioning themselves as favorably as possible vis-à-vis the new republic and its non-Indian population. The Six Nations Iroquois Confederacy remained divided after the war. With their homeland surrounded by victorious settlers, most Mohawks remained with Brant in Canada without hope of returning. British officials rewarded them with two tracts purchased from Mississauga Indians in what is now Ontario. Nearly all remaining Mohawks and smaller numbers of other Iroquois and allied non-Iroquois joined Brant's followers at the new Grand River and Tyendinaga reserves, where their descendants live today. Meanwhile the Oneidas, most Senecas and Tuscaroras, and some Onondagas and Cayugas returned to homelands in what is now upstate New York. But whether fleeing or returning to their homes, Iroquois people faced equally daunting challenges of starting over with diminished numbers and resources.

The return of peace brought an upsurge in the land rush of settlers to the Ohio Valley. From the war's outbreak until 1790 some eighty thousand whites moved to Shawnee lands alone. As far as Congress was concerned, the region's Indians bore complete responsibility for the war and owed compensation to American citizens in the form of land. Native Americans had a different perspective. An intertribal delegation told the Spanish governor at St. Louis how the newcomers "extend[ed] themselves like a plague of locusts" in the Ohio Valley.

They treat us as their cruelest enemies are treated, so that today hunger and the impetuous torrent of war which they impose upon us with other terrible calamities, have brought our villages to a struggle with death.

As they faced the future, Ohio Indians saw little reason to hope that these conditions would change soon.

Thomas Jefferson termed the independent American republic an "empire of liberty." By "liberty," he meant the liberty of individual white men (and any Indian men willing to break entirely with their people and culture) to own private property in land. By "empire of liberty," he referred to a nation-state that would secure land for as many property-seeking men as wanted it. Native peoples whose traditions, sovereignty, and identities were rooted in lands claimed by the United States confronted yet another empire of antagonistic non-Indians. From the Indians' perspective, the struggle against empires had not ended.

INDIAN VOICES   Joseph Brant (Mohawk), 1789

By the late eighteenth century, decades of destructive warfare had led many Native Americans, particularly in the East, to grow weary of Europeans and the supposed superiority of their "civilization." While the best-known Indian critics of Europeans, such as Neolin, had always rejected all things European, others had once embraced "civilization" and criticized it on the basis of this experience.

One such critic was Thayendanegea, a Mohawk military and political leader better known by his English name, Joseph Brant. Brant was born into a family of Mohawk Catholics in 1742. The family became prominent in 1759 when Brant's sister, Molly, married William Johnson, the British trader and diplomat. Through his kin ties with Johnson, Brant gained admission to the leading Protestant school for Indians in North America, acquiring first a facility with the English language and culture and then a position of leadership among his people.

After the outbreak of the American Revolution, Brant traveled to London to confer with British officials and became popular with the press and public. On his return, he commanded Iroquois forces against the rebelling colonists and, after the British defeat, led his people to a new homeland in Canada. In 1789, a magazine writer asked Brant for his thoughts on the "civilization" in which he was steeped and whether it was more or less conducive to liberty than Indian "savagery." Brant's reply reflects not only the bitterness and disillusionment of his later years but also a widespread sentiment among Native Americans.

> I was, sir, born of Indian parents, and lived while a child, among those you are pleased to call savages; I was afterwards sent to live among the white people, and educated at one of your schools; since which period, I have been honoured, much beyond my deserts, by an acquaintance with a number of principal characters both in Europe and America. After all this experience, and after every exertion to divest myself of prejudice, I am obliged to give my opinion in favour of my own people. . . . I will not enlarge on an idea so singular in civilized life, and perhaps disagreeable to you; and will only observe, that among us, we have no law but that written on the heart of every rational creature by the immediate finger of the great Spirit of the universe himself. We have no prisons—we have no pompous parade of courts; and yet judges are as highly esteemed among us, as they are among you, and their decisions as highly revered; property, to say the least, is as well guarded, and crimes are as impartially punished. We have among us no splendid villains, above the controul of that law, which influences our decisions; in a word, we have no robbery under the colour of law—daring wickedness here is never suffered to triumph over helpless innocence—the estates of widows and orphans are never devoured by enterprising sharpers. Our sachems, and our warriors, eat their own bread, and not the bread of wretchedness. No person, among us, desires any other reward for performing a brave and worthy action, than the consciousness of serving his nation. Our wise men are called fathers—they are truly deserving the character; they are always accessible—I will not say to the meanest of our people—for we have none mean. But such as render themselves so by their vices.

…We do not hunger and thirst after those superfluities of life, that are the ruin of thousands of families among you. Our ornaments, in general, are simple and easily obtained. Envy and covetousness, those worms that destroy the fair flower of human happiness, are unknown in this climate.

The palaces and prisons among you, form a most dreadful contrast. Go to the former places, and you will see, perhaps, a deformed piece of earth swelled with pride, and assuming airs, that become none but the Spirit above. Go to one of your prisons—here description utterly fails!—certainly the sight of an Indian torture, is not half so painful to a well informed mind. Kill them [the prisoners], if you please—kill them, too, by torture; but let the torture last no longer than a day. . . . Those you call savages, relent—the most furious of our tormentors exhausts his rage in a few hours, and dispatches the unhappy victim with a sudden stroke.

But for what are many of your prisoners confined? For debt! Astonishing! and will you ever again call the Indian nations cruel?—Liberty, to a rational creature, as much exceeds property, as the light of the sun does that of the most twinkling star: but you put them on a level, to the everlasting disgrace of civilization. . . . And I seriously declare, that I had rather die by the most severe tortures ever inflicted by any savage nation on the continent, than languish in one of your prisons for a single year. Great Maker of the world! And do you call yourselves christians? . . . Does then the religion of him whom you call your Saviour, inspire this conduct, and lead to this practice? Surely no. It was a sentence that once struck my mind with some force, that "A bruised reed he never broke." Cease then, while these practices continue among you, to call yourselves christians, lest you publish to the world your hypocrisy. Cease to call other nations savage, when you are tenfold more the children of cruelty, than they.

Quoted in Isabel Thompson Kelsay, *Joseph Brant* (Syracuse: Syracuse University Press, 1984), pp. 534–535, citing *American Museum* 6 (September 1789): 226–227.

STRUGGLES FOR POWER IN THE SOUTHERN PLAINS AND SOUTHWEST, 1754–1810

While empires fell in eastern North America, the Apaches, Comanches, and Navajos defied Spanish power on the southern Plains and in the Southwest. These tribal nations had developed ways of life based in part on extensive trading with, and raiding of, Spanish colonists and other Indians. In the late eighteenth century, Spain undertook extensive reforms in its northern provinces, including Texas and New Mexico, as part of a larger effort to revitalize its empire. These reforms included a vastly strengthened military presence, one that would be coordinated with the civil administrations of the provinces. One major goal of the new policy was to force Apaches, Comanches, and Navajos to submit to Spanish authority and to cease their raiding activities.

While Spain expended considerable effort to impose its authority over the raiding tribes at the cost of considerable suffering on all sides, the most significant change in the balance of power in the southern Plains–Southwest during the second half of the eighteenth century was the continued rise of the Comanches at the expense of the Apaches. While the Spanish helped to shape this outcome, they were but secondary players in a conflict among Native Americans. Far more challenging for Native Americans than Spanish power were Spanish diseases, material goods, and captives.

"Gran Apachería"

The most immediate challenge to Spanish colonial power in the northernmost provinces of Mexico was the group of tribes known as Apaches. The Apaches were mobile hunter-gatherers who, when the Spanish first arrived, lived in five tribes spread across what eventually became west Texas, New Mexico, and Arizona. The Lipans, Jicarillas, and Mescaleros, sometimes referred to together as Eastern Apaches, lived on the southern Plains of eastern New Mexico and Texas. (A fourth Eastern Apache tribe, the Kiowa Apaches, lived in the northern Plains with the separate Kiowa Indians.) West of the Rio Grande were the Chiricahuas and Western Apaches, who lived in highland environments. All the Apaches acquired horses early and used them to enhance their mobility in hunting and in raiding Pueblo Indians and Spanish colonists.

By the second half of the eighteenth century, Apache bands were spread across what is now southwestern Texas, southern New Mexico and Arizona, and the northern portions of the states of Coahuila, Nueva Vizcaya, and Sonora—a vast expanse that the Spanish termed "Gran Apachería." This Apache diaspora was a recent historical phenomenon. Having been pushed southward and westward by both Spaniards and Comanches (see Chapter 5), the Eastern Apaches were no longer able to hunt buffalo. They now focused—along with the Chiricahuas and Western Apaches—on raiding widely dispersed Spanish ranches for horses, mules, and cattle as well as for other provisions and captives.

In retaliation for these raids, Spanish troops launched ferocious attacks on the Apaches. Although Spaniards routinely accused the Apaches of cruelty, at least one Spanish officer recognized that when an Apache "avenges himself it is for just satisfaction of his grievances." The officer was thinking of fellow officers, such as the one who bragged how he cut off the head of an Apache war chief "before the eyes of the enemy, then . . . charged the Apache line single-handed, with the head stuck on his lance."

For all their cruelty, Spanish soldiers failed to limit Apache power. Unable to field enough troops for the task, the troops struck sporadically and rarely attempted to pursue Apache war parties after a skirmish. Moreover, Spanish rancheros (ranch owners), unable to count on the military for protection, frequently violated Spanish regulations by trading guns, corn, and other goods to the Apaches. In part they did so to gain the return of captured livestock, but often the exchanges went so far as to entail full-scale alliances. The foundation for such alliances was the presence among the Apaches of many Spaniards whom the Apaches had seized, often as children, and adopted into their communities.

As with many eastern Indians, the Apaches' primary motive in seizing captives was to augment their population, which had been devastated by European-borne diseases and the effects of war with Spanish and Indian enemies. The same motive led them to absorb non-Apache Indians, both refugees and captives, into their ranks. But Spanish children offered additional advantages. They spoke Spanish and, from a young age, most had acquired experience in herding livestock. One boy, recaptured by Spanish soldiers in Coahuila in 1776, reported that his Lipan band had included people of Spanish and African as well as Indian descent. The most prominent Spanish-descended Apache was Josecillo El Manco ("One-handed Joe"). Speaking fluent Spanish, Josecillo cultivated close ties with Spanish towns in northern Coahuila that included not only the exchange of goods but of warnings of both Apache raiders and Spanish military patrols. As in much of eastern North America, "Indian" communities were often multiethnic groupings of refugees and captives who cooperated as often as they fought with their colonizing neighbors.

The withdrawal of so many Apaches from Texas left the Comanches, supported by their Wichita and Caddo allies (termed collectively the *norteños*—northerners—by Spaniards), the most powerful commercial and military coalition on the southern Plains. The end of French sovereignty in North America in 1763 did not affect the norteños' trade for European goods because Spain retained the long-established French traders at their posts in order to withstand the growing competition of British traders from east of the Mississippi. (In 1764 French traders even established a new center, St. Louis, at the conjunction of the Mississippi and Missouri rivers.) Subsequently, the Comanches enhanced their commercial and military primacy by trading as well with the Anglo-Americans who encroached on the southern prairies and Plains.

Pack Train at Taos Pueblo Attracting Indians and Europeans from throughout the Southwest and southern Plains, the annual trade fairs at Taos were critical to those regions' commerce.

Trading and Raiding in New Mexico

The Comanches' vast array of trade items appealed not only to Indians but also to Spanish colonists in New Mexico, who were largely isolated from European commercial networks. A Spanish friar attending the trade fair at Taos in 1776 listed the goods offered by Comanche traders. On their own, they produced "buffalo hides, 'white elkskins', horses, mules, buffalo meat, pagan Indians [captives whom the Spanish shipped south to work in mines]." In addition, their Wichita allies, whose contacts included both French and English traders, had supplied the Comanches with "guns, pistols, powder, balls [bullets], tobacco, hatchets, and some vessels of yellow tin." In return for all these items the Comanches obtained corn as well as locally manufactured Spanish goods. Under the fixed rate of exchange during the 1770s, for example, another friar observed that if the Comanches "sell a pistol, its price is a bridle."

Although Spanish policymakers recognized the value of trade with the Comanches, they wished to gain the upper hand in relationships with the Comanches and other Indians who raided colonists in Texas and New Mexico. Consciously emulating French policy prior to the Seven Years War, Spain during the 1770s began pouring trade goods into the region, hoping to draw anti-Apache and friendly Indians into ties of dependence on the Spanish colonies. At the same time, Spanish officials sent additional troops and undertook the strategic relocation of most presidios to pressure Indians into actively supporting them against the

Apaches. They hoped as a result to utilize the dependent Indians as allies in a coordinated, systematic war of extermination against the Apaches.

The plan quickly succeeded in Texas. Officials there established formal ties with the Wichitas and Caddos, who then persuaded eastern Comanche bands to join the new alliance. The greater challenge was in New Mexico, where Navajos and Utes as well as Apaches and western Comanches regularly raided Spanish ranches and villages, the colony's Pueblo Indian allies, and one another.

New Mexico's only certain allies were the Pueblos. Unlike their Indian neighbors, the Pueblos resided in villages that predated the arrival of not only the Spaniards but also the Navajos and Apaches (see Chapter 1). This continuity of place strongly reinforced indigenous traditions and identities at each pueblo despite nearly two centuries of Spanish colonization. Catholic missions operated either in or adjacent to most of their villages, but indigenous religion flourished and the Christianity that attracted many Pueblos distinctively combined Catholic and traditional beliefs and practices. Traditional religious leaders, along with clan elders, oversaw a way of life based on common ownership of lands and an emphasis on harmony and communal values. Although marriages between Hispanics and Pueblos were frequent, most people of mixed heritage lived and identified with the Native population.

To be sure, there were limits on the independence of the Pueblos. The governor of New Mexico collected an annual tribute in money or crops from each pueblo, an obligation that many Indians sorely resented. Spain had also imposed a system of government under which elected or appointed *alcaldes* (magistrates) presided over each community. Finally, Spanish military officials organized Pueblo warriors into military units to help colonial troops defend the colony from hostile Indian raiders. Yet the warriors retained their own traditions, remaining distinct from Spanish soldiers. And, often with Spanish assistance, they defended their own communities as well as those of colonists. Pueblos' military as well as trade ties to New Mexico helped to sustain their communities' autonomy.

With Pueblo support assured, New Mexico's Governor Juan Bautista de Anza in 1779 turned his attention to the western Comanches, who had until then resisted his peace offers. He personally led Spanish troops in a surprise attack on a Comanche camp that resulted in the death of a leading war chief, Cuerno Verde. Cuerno Verde's stunned followers offered to make peace, but Anza insisted that all western Comanche bands had to submit to him at once. In so doing, he promoted an unprecedented political centralization among the Comanches. Finally in February 1786, western Comanche leaders signed a treaty with Anza that brought an end to the long hostilities between their two peoples.

Having reached an agreement with the Comanches, the governor sought to quash raiding by the Navajos. Like the closely related Apaches, the Navajos (Diné) had raided Spanish settlements since the early seventeenth century. Following the Pueblo Revolt, many Pueblo Indians had taken refuge with the Navajos, helping the Navajos expand their economic base beyond hunting and gathering to include farming and the herding of goats, sheep, and horses. Thereafter, Navajo raids on colonists and Pueblo Indians focused above all on livestock. Owned by women, goats provided milk and sheep were a source of meat as well as clothing. Navajo women wove woolen blankets featuring bold patterns in earth tones, indigo, and bright red, the yarn for which they obtained from Spanish traders. Navajo clothing included traditional leather as well as wool and cotton, which likewise came from Spanish as well as Pueblo sources. Navajo men owned the horses. Young men in particular sought prestige by pilfering livestock that they could give away to other Navajos.

While partaking liberally but selectively from the material cultures of their neighbors, the Navajos retained control of their cultural and political affairs. Although Spanish Catholic missionaries remained hopeful that they would eventually "spread the blessed water of conversion" among the Navajos, the tribe remained impervious to Christianity. Beginning in the 1750s, the Navajos took action to ensure the continuation of their relative prosperity and political autonomy. Having acquired so many sheep and horses, they had become targets themselves of raids by better armed Utes and Comanches. In addition, Spanish colonists were encroaching on their lands from the east. To insulate themselves from these developments, the Navajos gradually migrated southwestward from their homeland, "Old Dinetah," centered in the Chama Valley of north central New Mexico. They finally settled in a more isolated locale, bordered on the east by Mt. Taylor and the Chuska Mountains, on the west by Black Mesa in what is now Arizona, and on the north by the San Juan Valley. Having established their new homeland, the Navajos sought to enhance their security by agreeing in the late 1780s to a truce with New Mexico.

The Navajo–New Mexico truce enabled the colony to focus on its last Indian enemy, the Apaches. During the 1790s, Spanish officials showered their coalition of old and new Indian allies with gifts, including firearms, in order to hasten the end of Apache independence. They rewarded soldiers and Indian allies who brought them pairs of Apache ears. Instead of sending Apache prisoners to Mexico, from which many had previously escaped and returned, they now shipped them to Spanish colonies in the Caribbean. The few Apache prisoners who survived the diseases and wretched conditions that beset them en route spent what remained of their lives as slaves.

Surrounded by well-armed and coordinated enemies, Apache bands across the region agreed with Spanish authorities to cease hostilities. Colonial officials sent Apaches who submitted voluntarily to "peace establishments," where soldiers distributed weekly rations of food and tobacco as well as instructions in farming, ranching, and other ways of "civilization." They offered similar rewards to western Comanches in hopes of distracting them from resuming their raids on colonists once the Apache threat was quashed. Forerunners of the reservations that the United States would later impose, the peace establishments were a mixed success. Many Apaches and Comanches, concluding that peace was less costly and destructive than war, reconciled themselves to the establishments, at least for the time being. But others, finding the food supplies inadequate or the supervised, confined existence too stultifying, left and resumed raiding. Similarly, many Navajos resumed their raids for Spanish-owned horses. Although raiding once again co-existed with more peaceful interactions, an unparalleled peace characterized the two decades following the mid-1790s in New Mexico and Texas.

NEOPHYTES, GENTILES, AND COLONIZERS ON THE PACIFIC, 1769–1833

Indians in California also confronted the revival of Spanish imperial expansion in the late eighteenth century. Having recently colonized the area around the Gulf of California, Spanish officials termed it Baja (Lower) California and the new colony to the north Alta (Upper) California (hereafter California). Military officials and Franciscan missionaries founded California at San Diego in 1769 but soon extended it northward to San Francisco Bay.

Spanish colonization posed enormous challenges to Indians in California. Compared to Native Americans elsewhere, they lacked some of the more proven means of countering colonial power. Although populous, Indian towns in coastal California—like southwestern pueblos in 1598—were politically autonomous and not organized in confederacies or other translocal groupings with precedents for concerted military action. Moreover, California Indians lacked recent, sustained contact with Europeans, their trade goods, and their livestock, so that the significant quantities of guns and horses used in other Indian resistance movements had not yet fallen into their hands. Nor—unlike in much of eastern North America—were there European competitors of Spain whose traders or officials could offer Indians alternative sources of support, be it economic, diplomatic, or military.

Instead Native peoples in California suffered heavily from diseases while Franciscan missionaries, backed by secular authorities, confined them to mission compounds where they were forced to work, taught to renounce their Native identities, and suffered appalling mortality rates from a range of diseases introduced by colonists. In order to survive physically and culturally, Indians drew on their familiarity with the land when escaping and on their mission educations when resisting overtly. As Spanish imperial authority waned, and particularly after California became a province of Mexico, mission Indians used their Spanish military training and weapons and their skills as artisans and cowboys to sustain resistance that contributed to the ultimate demise of the mission system.

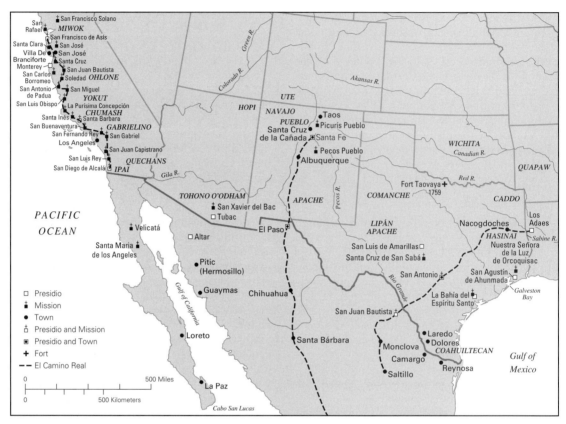

Native Peoples and Spanish Colonizers in California and the Southwest in the Late Eighteenth Century. Spain expanded its presence among Indians in California and the Southwest through religious missions, military forts, and civilian settlements.

Quechans and the Spanish Road to California

Although the first Spaniards to enter California arrived by sea, Spanish officials believed that an overland route would more effectively encourage immigration by colonists from Mexico. Accordingly, they dispatched four expeditions in the mid-1770s to explore the territory between California and New Mexico, discover the best east-west route, and secure that route by initiating peaceful relations with nearby Native people. The explorers learned the lay of the land and the trails that traversed it from Mohaves, Utes, and other Indians of the region as well as from a Gabrielino Indian who had fled one of the new Franciscan missions

in California (see the discussion in the next section). At the Hopi pueblos, two expeditions learned only that the Hopis were no more receptive to Spaniards and, especially, Christianity than they had been three-quarters of a century earlier at the conclusion of the Pueblo Revolt (see Chapter 4). Hopis at Oraibi refused to meet with Spanish emissaries at all, while some male dancers at Walapi entertained a missionary with a "horrifying spectacle" in which "the only part of their bodies that was covered was the face, and at the end of the member it is not modest to name they wore a small and delicate feather."

On the basis of reports from these expeditions, Spanish officials decided that the best route between California and New Mexico would cross the

Colorado River at its junction with the Gila River in the homeland of the Quechan (Yuman) Indians. The approximately three thousand Quechans lived in about a half dozen settlements, or rancherias, consisting of several hundred people each. Political decisions in each rancheria resulted from consensus, but headmen usually exercised considerable influence on the outcome. Elders in each rancheria chose headmen based on membership in a leading family, on experience and competence, and above all on the power of his dreams as he reported them in oral testimony. Headmen from the Quechan rancherias met periodically as a council to deal with issues relating to the tribe as a whole. A war leader and a civil leader were the only tribal officials.

In 1776 the Quechan civil leader Olleyquote-quiebe befriended members of a Spanish expedition headed by Juan Bautista de Anza, the future governor of New Mexico. Anza took the Quechan leader to Mexico City, where he was baptized Salvador Palma and feted with elaborate ceremonies and gifts. Concluding that Spaniards were a generous people, Palma invited them to settle among the Quechans. By 1779 two small, fortified Spanish villages had been established, one on each side of the Colorado, near the site of modern Yuma, Arizona.

Spanish demands soon led the Quechans to forget the colonizers' earlier generosity. Driving thousands of cattle and horses to California, prospective colonists destroyed the wild and domestic plants on which Quechans depended for food while demanding food anyway and inflicting corporal punishment when the Indians failed to comply. Even Salvador Palma felt betrayed. Finally, while the two Spanish villages celebrated mass on June 17, 1781, the Quechans arose and attacked without warning, killing four missionaries and many soldiers. Reinforcements eventually arrived, ransoming Spanish prisoners and inflicting some casualties on the Quechans. But Spain declined to try to rebuild its villages. Thereafter, people and provisions reached California either by sea or overland via Baja California.

California Indians and the First Missions

As with the Quechans and other "settled" Indians in its colonies, Spain took a two-pronged approach to dealing with Native peoples in California. Fran-ciscan missionaries would attempt to persuade Indians to become Christians and to accept "civilization" and Spanish rule peacefully. Should any Indians resist these peaceful efforts, however, Spanish soldiers would subdue them forcefully.

Franciscan persuasion met with little success at first. During the first five years of colonization (1769–1774), only a few dozen of the several thousand Indians living near the five established missions accepted baptism. Although wary in approaching the newcomers, no Native Americans violently resisted initial Spanish incursions into their homelands. But Spanish missionaries, soldiers, and civilians quickly alienated the Indians by stealing their food, sexually abusing Indian women, and employing military force and corporal and capital punishment to establish their authority.

Despite having limited means, some Indians found ways to resist the invaders. One way was to flee, as did a Gabrielino couple, Sebastián Tarabal and his wife (name unknown), in 1773 when they left Mission San Gabriel. After his wife died in the Sonora desert, Tarabal encountered a Spanish expedition there, guided it to the Quechan communities on the Colorado and then to his southern California homeland. Tarabal apparently thought that the Spaniards he met would prove more congenial than the missionaries. A more pointed challenge to Spanish rule arose the following year when Ipai Indians, whose forebears had met Cabrillo two and a half centuries earlier, burned Mission San Diego and killed its resident missionary.

Life and Death in the Missions

Despite such resistance, the mission system expanded steadily in the years that followed. By the time that the first head of the Franciscan effort, Junípero Serra, died in 1784, nine missions housing about 4,650 Indians lined the California coast from San Diego to San Francisco. While the number of Indians employed by presidios and civilian enterprises declined, the number of missions and of Indians residing at them continued to grow—to eighteen missions with 13,500 Natives in 1800 and then to twenty-one missions with more than 21,000 Native Americans by 1823. This growing population was the foundation of colonial California's economy, producing not only its own food and other necessities but also supplying virtually all the needs of the small Spanish population (about 3,500 in 1821) and producing goods for export.

As impressive as these numbers and accomplishments are, they conceal a monumental catastrophe. Another set of figures suggests the bare outlines of that catastrophe. From the beginning of Spanish colonization in 1769 until 1821, when California joined the rest of Mexico in declaring its independence from Spain, the total number of Indians in the colony dropped from about 310,000 to about 200,000. Along the coast where Spanish missions, presidios, and towns were concentrated, the indigenous population of 72,000 fell by 75 percent to 18,000 in 1830. At one mission—San Carlos, at Monterey—whose records have survived, an Indian population of 2,800 in 1770 declined to about 875 in 1795 and 300 in 1825. Noting the high mortality among mission Indians, one Franciscan admitted that they "live well free but as soon as we reduce them to a Christian and community life, . . . they fatten, sicken, and die." Why did Indians in California die in such large numbers under Spanish rule?

Far more than in other parts of North America, large numbers of Native Americans died from venereal diseases in California. Spanish soldiers, along with Indian men they brought from Baja California (where Spaniards had spread the disease), introduced syphilis and gonorrhea. Although a few Spanish men married single Indian women in Catholic ceremonies, the majority forced themselves on Indian women, including many with Indian husbands. Lamenting the soldiers' impact on his work, Serra complained that "a plague of immorality had broken out" among them.

The impact of venereal diseases on Indians' bodies ran far beyond those women who contracted diseases directly from Spanish carriers. Infected Indian women unknowingly spread the diseases to their husbands and children, both living and unborn. Living children became ill when nursing or being cleaned with an infected blanket or cloth. If not stillborn, Native children infected before birth began life with anemia, jaundice, cranial palsies, and damaged bones and organs. Not surprisingly, most such children did not live long. Many Indian women deliberately aborted infected fetuses or strangled ill newborns, especially the products of unwanted pregnancies, while others were unable

to bear any more children. By striking down so many children and women of childbearing age, venereal diseases contributed not only to high death rates among Indians but to lower birth rates in subsequent generations.

Spanish colonists brought other diseases to California that also claimed Indians' lives in disproportionately high numbers. Among these were dysentery, diphtheria, measles, typhoid, smallpox, malaria, pneumonia, and tuberculosis. Sherburne Cook, a pioneering student of California Indian demography, estimated that Spanish-introduced diseases contributed directly to 45 percent of the Indian population decline during the mission period and that the resulting lower birth rate caused an additional 15 percent of the decrease.

Despite the high death rates among Indians, the numbers of those living at the missions continued to grow. Ties of ethnicity, language, and trade facilitated the spread of epidemics from neophytes—as missionaries termed baptized Native Americans—to indigenous communities nearby and in valleys and low-lying mountains to the east. While many neophytes fled to the interior to escape the missionaries' authoritarianism, even more gentiles—as the Franciscans called unbaptized Indians—entered the missions. With their own communities diminished by diseases, the new mission Indians were motivated less by a desire to find Christianity than to seek sustenance and the company of those with whom they shared a cultural identity.

Once inside the missions, neophytes found themselves in a society that was utterly unfamiliar. To begin with, on joining a mission and being baptized, neophytes were completely subordinated to priestly authority and could not return to their old homes even if they changed their minds. To travel outside the mission, a neophyte was required to carry a pass signed by a missionary. The Franciscans enforced a rigid code of discipline covering all aspects of neophytes' lives. Central to the new regimen was labor that contributed to the missions' economic productivity. Missionaries and other colonists ignored or dismissed Native Americans' complex, seasonally based food production and other work, viewing them as wild and in need of the discipline necessary to become "civilized" Christians. Accordingly, missionaries gathered neophytes into mission compounds where Indian men tended Spanish grains and other crops, herded livestock, and built the missions and other buildings, while Native women sewed and washed clothing and prepared food. Over time, male neophytes learned specialized skills and supplemented their basic tasks as carpenters, shoemakers, tanners, masons, gunsmiths, and blacksmiths. Men and women worked together in producing cloth. In return they were fed, housed, instructed in Catholic Christianity, and occasionally given a new set of clothes.

Missionaries established rigid work schedules and communicated them through the mission's bells, which sounded times for work, meals, and prayers. The neophytes worked five to eight hours per day, five to six days per week. They did not work on Sundays or on the several dozen religious holidays then observed by Catholics. The arbitrarily timed, externally imposed mission schedule was alien to California Indians, who customarily based their work routines on the familiar requirements of specific tasks such as hunting, fishing, or acorn gathering and processing.

The missions were intended to transform the tribal identities of Native Americans to those of Spanish Christians. By Spanish governmental decree, the education of Indians in colonies was to be administered in Spanish while indigenous languages were to be eradicated as quickly as possible. Although many missionaries disagreed with this rule, most gave religious instruction in Spanish and at least tried to require neophytes to communicate with one another in Spanish. The Franciscans' ef-

forts were reinforced by the fact that so many of the material goods and spiritual concepts that were central to mission life had no direct equivalents in indigenous languages. Nevertheless while many Indians learned at least some Spanish, others did not, reported one Franciscan, because of "their frequent communication and intercourse with their relatives and countrymen, both Christian and heathen."

Critical to the exercise of authority in each mission were several elected Indian officials. In 1778 the governor of California, Felipe de Neve, ordered that neophytes at each mission elect one or two alcaldes ("captains") and one or two regidores (councilors). Neve was acting in accordance with Spanish policy and in hopes of preventing a repeat of the Ipai uprising of 1775. Serra and the other Franciscans initially resisted the order, but they gave in after Neve allowed them to control the elections, particularly by limiting the suffrage to previous officeholders and by approving lists of candidates. Instead of being freely chosen by their own people and empowered to act independently of the missionaries, most alcaldes and regidores were hand-picked subordinates of the Franciscans. As a later governor noted, "although [the alcaldes] are granted some powers, they are necessarily dependent on the missionaries, without whose direction they would not be able to exercise them." Writing in the 1830s, Pablo Tac, a devout Luiseño Catholic, observed how the head alcalde at his mission, a former chief, "dressed like the Spanish,

PEOPLE, PLACES, AND THINGS

Ohlones Gambling at Mission Dolores, 1816

Franciscan missionaries produced volumes of writings representing most California Indian neophytes as pious Catholics who had abandoned their "pagan" ways, alongside a minority who required the friars' strict discipline. Yet an abundance of evidence indicates that Native resistance to the Franciscans' strictures was widespread. Although resistance sometimes took the form of escape or overt rebellion, Indians more often simply found time and space within mission compounds for pursuing traditional practices, both religious and secular, that missionaries had banned. In this watercolor Louis Choris, a visiting artist, depicts Ohlone men openly playing a game of chance at Mission Dolores (originally Mission San Francisco) despite regulations outlawing gambling.

always remaining captain, but not ordering his people about as of old." Instead, he continued, the captain and other alcaldes simply communicated the missionary's pronouncements to the neophytes.

Besides communicating orders, alcaldes assisted missionaries in supervising neophytes' labor, explaining Catholic beliefs and practices in Native languages, administering corporal punishment, and keeping unmarried men and women apart. Ohlone Indians at Mission San Francisco complained of one alcalde, Valeriano, who, for example, forced one neophyte to work when he was sick and hit another "with a heavy cane for having gone to look for mussels at the beach." The alcaldes also reported any crimes committed by neophytes to military officials.

Rebellion at the Missions

Many alcaldes and other neophytes chafed under the rigorous discipline of the missions and took steps to resist it. The Indians had entered the missions primarily to survive. In accepting Christian baptism, they signaled their acceptance of the missionaries' offer of a new form of spiritual power that, they hoped, would sustain them in the face of so much sickness. But many rebelled when forced by painful, humiliating corporal punishment to conform strictly to the rules of an imposed way of life and to repudiate and abandon every facet of their familiar customs and deeply felt beliefs.

Baltasar, an alcalde among Ohlones and Esselens living at Mission San Carlos, was one such Indian. Baltasar was discharged from his position and expelled from the mission after fathering a child by his wife's sister. Baltasar was exercising a prerogative that enabled chiefs among California Indians (always men) to have enough wives to host lavish feasts and to produce many children to strengthen their families, but the Franciscans condemned his behavior as sinful. After his expulsion, Baltasar continued to act as a chief, gathering other disaffected ex-neophytes around him in the nearby mountains, from where they lured still more neophytes away from the mission.

Baltasar's resistance from outside the mission walls was hardly unique. The close ties between neophytes and nearby gentiles often helped strengthen neophyte opposition to missionary authority. In 1785 a neophyte at Mission San Gabriel,

Nicolas José, had grown resentful because the missionaries prohibited him from continuing to practice traditional Gabrielino religion. Deciding that all Spaniards had to be driven from the Gabrielinos' homeland, he enlisted the help of a gentile medicine woman, Toypurina, in organizing an uprising of Indians from eight neighboring villages. The rebellion failed because word reached the local presidio before it began, enabling Spanish troops to capture the rebels. During the inquisition that followed, Toypurina scorned her captors, saying, "I hate the padres and all of you for living here on my native soil . . . for trespassing upon the land of my forefathers and despoiling our tribal domains." Nicolas José and two other male leaders were sentenced to hard labor and their followers were whipped. Toypurina was placed in solitary confinement until accepting Catholic baptism sixteen months later and then exiled to Mission San Carlos three hundred miles to the north.

Other neophytes acted more quietly. In 1812, fourteen Ohlones at Mission Santa Cruz plotted to kill Father Andrés Quintana. Already resentful of the missionary's harsh discipline and punishments, they decided to act before he could use his newest whip, one laced with barbed wire. Among the conspirators were some of Quintana's most devoted neophytes, including one of his alcaldes, his page, his cook, and his gardener. When the men faltered at one point, the gardener's wife threatened to accuse them publicly unless they carried through with the plan. After capturing Quintana one night as he walked between buildings, the conspirators strangled and castrated him and placed his body in his bed. Then they summoned the unmarried women and men for an all-night party, something that Quintana had forbidden. When Spanish officials found the missionary's body the next day, they assumed that he had died of natural causes. Only when a participant's son told the story many years later did the actual cause of Quintana's death come to light.

The Chumash Revolt, 1824

The deadliest of all mission uprisings erupted among the Chumash Indians in 1824, although its seeds had been planted much earlier. In 1801, when many Chumash were suffering and dying from pneumonia and pleurisy, an unnamed Native woman reported a vision of the Chumash female deity Chupu. Chupu told the woman that all baptized Chumash were destined to die unless they ritually washed their hands with special water called "tears of the sun." Although the missionaries thought they had suppressed the devotions to Chupu soon after hearing about them, the movement continued without their knowledge. Then in 1818, as Spanish power in California was eroding and colonists feared foreign invaders, missionaries at Santa Barbara and a second Chumash mission, La Purísima, organized their male neophytes into infantry units, arming them with bows, machetes, and lances and drilling them in European formations. In the years that followed, Chumash men manufactured bows and other weapons and became adept at European modes of warfare.

While the missionaries assumed that "their" male neophytes had become loyal soldiers, the Chumash continued to honor Chupu while chafing under Spanish rule. Their resentment finally erupted in February 1824 after a Chumash neophyte from La Purísima was flogged while visiting a relative imprisoned at Santa Ynéz. In what was clearly a preplanned response, well-drilled, well-armed neophyte infantries seized control of the two missions. Although the Chumash alcalde at San Buenaventura immediately condemned the uprising, Andrés, his counterpart at Santa Barbara, commanded rebellious neophytes there. After resisting an effort by Mexican soldiers to seize the mission, the Santa Barbara Chumash hid in the nearby hills and later fled farther inland to the homeland of some friendly Yokut Indians. (Mexico had seceded from Spain in 1821.)

Four weeks later, the governor of California sent a large military force to suppress the uprising at La Purísima, which recently had been reinforced by some Santa Barbara Chumash and a few Yokuts. The Indians made a bold stand, even using the mission's cannons and its store of muskets. But inexperienced in using firearms and outgunned by the Mexican troops, they were crushed. Sixteen Chumash died and many more were wounded, compared with just three Mexican casualties. Mexican authorities sentenced seven leaders of the rebellion to death and twelve others to terms of hard labor.

In June the governor dispatched another force in pursuit of the Santa Barbara Chumash who had fled inland. Offered a pardon by the troops, about half of the Chumash fugitives, including Andrés, returned while the rest fled even deeper into Yokut country. The refugees found work on Spanish ranches by drawing on skills they had acquired in the missions. Abandoning Christianity, they resumed open sexual relations among unmarried men and women, modified their traditional gambling game to include Mexican currency and playing cards, and restored many traditional religious practices. Upon receiving a message from the missionary at Santa Barbara, offering forgiveness and imploring them to return, the Chumash replied that they would "maintain ourselves with what God will provide us in the open country. Moreover, we are soldiers, stonemasons, carpenters, etc., and will provide for ourselves by our work."

Horses and Rebellion: The Rise of Estanislao

The close ties between neophytes and interior Indians were evident not only in neophytes' rebellions but in the growing role of horses in the lives of California Indians. From soon after the first missions were established, escaped neophytes raided the missions for horses, which they supplied to gentiles along with knowledge (acquired in the missions) of riding and caring for the animals. Roughly paralleling Native Americans in the colonial Southwest, horse-mounted Indians hunted antelope and elk while continuing to raid the missions for horses. Horses captured at missions, presidios, and ranches on the Pacific coast often mingled in the intermountain West with others arriving via Southwestern and Plains Indians. Spanish and Mexican efforts to recover horses stolen in California met with only limited success. One Spanish military expedition, dispatched to northern California in 1819, recovered forty-nine horses from a band of interior Miwoks, but only after a fierce battle in which twenty-seven Miwoks and five Spaniards were killed. This effort remained notable for many years because no others approached its success.

During the 1820s, the trade in horses attracted even more neophytes, especially Miwoks and Yokuts, whose gentile kin were the principal purveyors of horses to points east of California. In 1827 more than four hundred neophytes from both tribes fled Mission San José en masse. A year and a half later, some Yokuts from that mission sparked the last major rebellion of California neophytes. In November 1828 a trusted group of Yokuts, permitted by the Franciscans to visit kinfolk on the Stanislaus River, sent back a message instead of returning. Their leader, Estanislao, an experienced *vaquero* (cowboy) and former alcalde, announced that they had summoned neophytes from three other missions to flee with horses and join them in open rebellion. As for any Mexican troops that might try and stop them, Estanislao continued, "they are few in number, are very young, and do not shoot well."

Estanislao's defiant message proved to be well founded. A small Mexican expedition sent to capture the Yokuts at the end of the year returned quickly after a skirmish in which three soldiers died and five more were wounded. In May 1829 a larger force, including three artillerymen, nine cavalrymen, and seventy neophyte auxiliaries, confronted the renegades. After a wheel on the Mexicans' artillery piece broke, their commanding officer called for a cease-fire and met with Estanislao to try to persuade the Yokut leader to surrender peacefully. But Estanislao refused, avowing that he would rather die in his homeland. After a three-hour battle in which two Mexicans died and eight, along with eleven Indian auxiliaries, were wounded, this expedition, too, withdrew.

Mexican authorities dispatched a third, more formidable expedition two weeks later under a promising twenty-one-year-old officer, Mariano Vallejo. Many of the one hundred Mexicans (joined by fifty Indian auxiliaries) under Vallejo wanted above all to avenge the deaths of two soldiers in the preceding expedition whom the rebels had captured and executed. After one encounter in which the Yokuts drove the troops back from a fortified position, the Mexicans surrounded and stormed the position only to find the Yokuts gone. Proceeding to a nearby Yokut village, the soldiers set it afire and then shot Indians who tried to escape. Although they found a few rebels both dead and alive, neither Estanislao nor the other prominent rebel leader, Cipriano, was among them. Vallejo returned to his presidio at San Francisco with eighteen recovered horses and no Indian rebels.

The aftermath of Vallejo's expedition confirmed that the balance of power in California was too precarious for Mexican authorities to use force to assert their authority. Learning that Mexican troops had shot and killed Indian noncombatants, the governor ordered an investigation, although in the end just one soldier was convicted. At the same time, reasoning that "it is easier to control [neophytes] when they are present than when they are absent," he offered to pardon any rebels who would return to their missions and display their repentance through "Christian and industrious conduct." Many rebels, including Estanislao, took up the offer while others, among them Cipriano, refused it. Cipriano was slain in battle later that year; Estanislao died of smallpox at Mission San José eight years later. As with George Washington in the Ohio Valley seventy-five years earlier, Vallejo's early failure did not prevent him from going on to a distinguished military and political career.

Even as Estanislao returned to San José and Cipriano met his death, California's missions were on their way to being "secularized," that is, becoming regular parish churches whose lands were transferred to private hands. At the same time, a small but rapidly growing number of Anglo-Americans were settling in California. For neophytes and gentiles alike, the coming decades would bring tragedies even more enormous than those already experienced (see Chapter 10).

CONCLUSION

In different ways, the imperial upheavals of the late eighteenth and early nineteenth centuries had important consequences for Native Americans. Before the Seven Years War, Indians from the Atlantic to the western Plains had played French traders and officials against their British and Spanish rivals. The collapse of France's American empire drove Native Americans from the Appalachians to the Plains to modify these strategies, and many were successful. But the colonists' triumph soon thereafter in the American Revolution left eastern Indians vulnerable to the undisguised land hunger and spirit of white supremacy that had helped motivate the movement for independence.

To the west, a revitalized Spanish colonial administration, no longer seriously threatened by

French and British rivals on the Mississippi, made formidable efforts to subjugate southern Plains and Southwestern Indians to Spanish authority. But Indians in these regions recognized how weak Spain was and continued to thrive. Despite its weaknesses, Spain extended its reach to coastal California, subjugating Native Americans through a chain of religious missions. Indians had to find space within this authoritarian system to survive and maintain their cultures and identities until after the Mexican Revolution, when their concerted resistance helped to undermine the entire mission system.

As the republics of the United States and Mexico emerged to replace Europe's empires, Indians struggled to survive, to maintain their autonomy, and when necessary to find new ways of "being Indian" in worlds turned upside down.

SUGGESTED READINGS

Anderson, Gary Clayton. *The Indian Southwest, 1580–1830: Ethnogenesis and Reinvention.* Norman: University of Oklahoma Press, 1999. Focuses on the transformation of Indian societies confronting Spanish colonization on the southern Plains.

Calloway, Colin G. *The American Revolution in Indian Country: Crisis and Diversity in Native American Communities.* Cambridge, UK, and New York: Cambridge University Press, 1995. An excellent account of the Revolution's impact on Native Americans, with in-depth examinations of eight Indian communities.

Dowd, Gregory Evans. *A Spirited Resistance: The North American Indian Struggle for Unity,* *1745–1815.* Baltimore: Johns Hopkins University Press, 1992. A pathbreaking study of Indian spirituality and resistance in eastern North America.

Fenn, Elizabeth A. *Pox Americana: The Great Smallpox Epidemic of 1775–82.* New York: Hill and Wang, 2001. Traces the epidemic through Indian country in the West and the battlefields of the American Revolution in the East.

Hackel, Steven W. *Children of Coyote, Missionaries of St. Francis: Indian-Spanish Relations in Colonial California, 1769–1850.* Chapel Hill: University of North Carolina Press, 2005. A major study that explores the complexities of Native resistance and accommodation in the missions.

Hinderaker, Eric. *Elusive Empires: Constructing Colonialism in the Ohio Valley, 1673–1800.* Cambridge, UK, and New York: Cambridge University Press, 1997. Examines and compares French, British, and American efforts to colonize Native peoples and lands in the Ohio country.

John, Elizabeth A. H. *Storms Brewed in Other Men's Worlds: The Confrontation of Indians, Spanish, and French in the Southwest, 1540–1795.* Lincoln: University of Nebraska Press, 1975. A meticulously detailed account of developments in New Mexico and Texas.

Sandos, James A. *Converting California: Indians and Franciscans in the Missions.* New Haven: Yale University Press, 2004. Along with Hackel (above), the most informative of the new histories of Native Americans in the California missions.

The Defense of the Trans-Appalachian Homelands, 1795–1815

It was the first fireworks display that many of the Indians had ever seen. On July 4, 1795, after providing the five hundred Indians who had already assembled at Greenville, Ohio, with a feast of mutton, bread, and wine, General Anthony Wayne, the American military commander in the west, ordered his men to ignite a small display of skyrockets, fountains, and pinwheels to celebrate the nineteenth anniversary of his country's declaration of independence. The Indians (Delaware, Ottawas, Potawatomis, Ojibwes, Miamis, and other tribes) were duly impressed with the fireworks, although they complained that they much preferred pork over mutton and that the government's wine bottles were too small, "like snuff boxes." According to Le Gris (Crippled Ankles or "the Gray One"), a Miami chief, the tribespeople needed a little more wine, since the weather had been cool and the wine would "warm them" against the rain that had plagued the camp during the past week.

Other Indians were concerned about more serious matters. Little Turtle, also a Miami chief, had arrived at Greenville on June 23, hoping to serve as the spokesman for the assembled Indians in their negotiations with the government, but to his dismay he found that many of the tribes had not yet

arrived at Wayne's camp, and those who had assembled were divided in their attitudes toward the Long Knives (the Americans). The Indians' lack of unity particularly bothered Little Turtle, for he knew that the tribes were vulnerable to American influence. One year earlier, in August 1794, Wayne had defeated a multitribal Indian army at the Battle of Fallen Timbers, and Little Turtle feared that the Americans would use the victory to dictate the terms of a peace treaty and demand a series of land cessions from the tribes.

Little Turtle's fears were valid. Small parties of Indians continued to arrive at the treaty site for the next two weeks, and the formal treaty negotiations did not begin until July 16. Although the Indians wished to retain their lands in Ohio, Wayne was determined to acquire much of the territory for the government. Moreover, it became apparent to Little Turtle that the tribes were split in their response to Wayne's demands. Some leaders remained opposed to any land cessions and had refused to attend the proceedings; others seemed willing to barter away almost all of Ohio in exchange for American promises of peace and annuities (annual payments of cash or trade goods). Little Turtle's position was somewhere in between. He hoped to

The Treaty of Greenville This painting depicts Little Turtle speaking to Anthony Wayne, William Henry Harrison, and other American officials. During the treaty negotiations the northwestern tribes ceded much of Ohio to the United States.

make peace with the Americans and obtain generous annuity payments. He also was eager for the tribes to retain their political autonomy. He strongly opposed the American claims to lands north of the Ohio and east of the Mississippi since they had defeated the British in the American Revolution. Little Turtle pointed out to Wayne that none of the tribes had ever ceded the Ohio lands to anyone. How could the Americans claim them?

But in the end, Wayne was successful. He played the tribes against each other and eventually forced the Indians to accept the government's terms. The Treaty of Greenville, signed on August 3, 1795, provided that the tribes would give up all claims to the southeastern two-thirds of Ohio as well as to a small slice of lands in southeastern Indiana. The Indians also gave the government permission to construct military posts at several strategic locations (Chicago, Fort Wayne, Michilimackinac, and others) in the Great Lakes region or the Midwest.

In exchange, the government promised the Indians annuities and assured them that the remaining lands north of the Ohio and east of the Mississippi would belong to the tribes. The Indians could "enjoy them, hunting, planting, and dwelling thereon so long as they please, without any molestation from the United States."

Little Turtle eventually signed the treaty, but he remained apprehensive. The Americans were an unpredictable lot. Indeed, their army had defeated the warriors at Fallen Timbers, but the new federal government exercised only minimal power in the west. Promises made by officials in Washington often went unfulfilled in the west, and like traditional tribal chiefs, federal officials seemed unable to control their own people, particularly frontiersmen who regularly trespassed on Indian lands. Yet Little Turtle knew that the contest for the trans-Appalachian west would continue. Like the other tribes residing between the Appalachians and the

Mississippi, the Miamis were determined to defend their autonomy. They had no desire to be part of the new American nation.

THE STRUGGLE FOR AUTONOMY

In the three decades following the American Revolution, the Native American people living in the trans-Appalachian west struggled to maintain control over their lives and their homelands. Initially unsure of their relationship with the emergent American nation, tribal leaders adopted a series of political, military, and economic strategies designed to maximize Native Americans' autonomy. Some refused to participate in federal programs and urged their people to minimize all contact with the Americans. Others crossed the Mississippi into Spanish territory. Attempting to preserve their independence, some leaders attempted to form broad political coalitions, seeking alliances with other Native Americans or with European powers. A minority attempted to cooperate with the Americans. Convinced that they could survive only by learning to live as small yeoman farmers, these people hoped to assure some degree of autonomy by living peacefully with their new white neighbors. Initially, most of these "cooperators" were unsuccessful, not because they failed to adjust to American social and economic patterns, but because they continued to reside on lands desired by non-Indians. And finally, some Indian people sought a religious deliverance from the changes that seemed to be swirling around them. Like other Native Americans who both preceded and would follow them, they relied upon religious revitalization movements to meet the challenges of a white man's world.

While Native Americans attempted to defend their lands and autonomy, the federal government labored to develop a comprehensive set of Indian policies designed to integrate Native American people into the new nation. Unsure of its control over the trans-Appalachian west, the government balanced its claims to the region against competing claims from both the tribes and the individual states. Meanwhile, federal agents experimented with programs designed to control the commerce between Indians and other Americans and to strongly encourage Indians to become small yeomen farmers. The programs also championed the orderly transfer of Native American land to the United States. Most of these programs would prove unsuccessful, from both a Native American and a non-Indian point of view, but the government was new, inexperienced, and unsure of itself. Its formulation and implementation of federal Indian policy reflected such uncertainty.

The Ohio Country

For Native American people, the War of the American Revolution never ended. The Treaty of Paris, signed by the British and the United States and its allies in 1783, brought a formal cessation of hostilities between the Europeans and the Americans, but the tribes had not been a party to the treaty negotiations and most Indian people were shocked by the agreement. In the treaty the British gave up their hegemony over their former colonies, including their control over lands claimed by the colonies in the trans-Appalachian west. In contrast, the new United States now claimed the trans-Appalachian lands as far west as the Mississippi River, the eastern border of Spanish Louisiana. Discounting territorial claims to the region by the individual states, the Articles of Confederation government desperately needed funds from the sale of the lands to pay its daily operating expenses. The government still needed to discharge debts incurred during the Revolution, and it hoped to persuade unpaid veterans of the Continental Army to accept western "bounty lands" in Ohio in lieu of unpaid wages. Consequently, American officials argued that in addition to exercising political control over the region, the United States actually owned the land as public property; since the majority of the tribes had supported the British during the recent conflict, their claims to ownership of land in the region were invalid.

Most of the tribespeople were dumbfounded. The Cherokees had been forced to relinquish much of their territory in South Carolina and settlers now occupied former Cherokee lands along the Watauga and Nolichucky rivers, but west of the mountains, near modern Chattanooga, Dragging Canoe and the Overhill people (Chickamaugas) still remained effectively outside American control. The Creeks continued to claim large sections of modern Georgia and Alabama, while Choctaw and Chickasaw villages spread across Mississippi and western Tennessee. In the north, Sullivan's campaign had devastated the Iroquois and eventually forced Joseph Brant and many pro-British Iroquois to flee to Canada, but the tribes in the Old Northwest had successfully defended the Ohio River as the southern border of their homeland, and during much of the Revolutionary War they had carried the conflict to Kentucky, creating havoc for American settlements in the Bluegrass Region. Indeed, from the perspective of the Shawnees, Wyandots, and Miamis, tribes of the Ohio country and the Wabash Valley, they had not lost the war, and they were unwilling to relinquish their claims to lands north of the Ohio River.

Seeking Native American acquiescence to the government's claims, American officials sent messages to the northwestern tribes, explaining that although the Indians now were a "conquered people," the Americans were "disposed to be kind" to their "red children" and would allow the Ohio tribes to occupy small reservations within their former homeland. In 1784, under some duress, the Iroquois signed the Second Treaty of Fort Stanwix, relinquishing their claims to all lands west of New York and Pennsylvania. In 1785 (at Fort McIntosh) and 1786 (at Fort Finney) government officials pressured small delegations from several Ohio tribes to give up large tracts of land in southern and eastern Ohio, but these treaties were denounced by most other Indians, who declared that all of Ohio remained Indian country and that "the Ohio River shall be the boundary between them and the Long Knives." When settlers attempted to clear lands and build cabins north of the Ohio, they were attacked by Shawnee war parties. Other warriors ambushed emigrants on flatboats as they descended the river toward Louisville. In retaliation, Benjamin Logan led five hundred Kentuckians up the Great Miami River, where he burned seven Shawnee villages, but the Indians remained intransigent and the warfare continued.

Native American resistance was encouraged by the British at Detroit. At the Treaty of Paris the Crown had agreed to withdraw from Detroit and Michilimackinac, posts held by British troops when the Revolutionary War ended. But in the postwar years the British, citing the American failure to pay debts incurred to British creditors, vowed to retain the western posts until the debts were paid. While it was true that the Americans had defaulted on their debts, the primary reason for the British intransigence was the lack of American military power. In the immediate postrevolutionary years, the entire standing army of the United States consisted of less than 625 men, most of whom were garrisoned at scattered posts on the eastern seaboard.

Since Detroit remained the focal point for the western Great Lakes fur trade, Native American hunters and trappers brought their pelts to the post, where they purchased British trade goods. Both British officials and merchants encouraged the tribespeople to resist the Americans. Although British officials admitted that the Crown had relinquished political control over Ohio, they assured the Indians that their British father had not given the tribespeople's lands to the Long Knives; the Indians still owned their lands. Intent on retaining the loyalty of the tribes, British officers supplied the warriors with guns, ammunition, and promises; and while officials in Canada may have been guarded in their assurances of assistance, British Indian agents who lived among the tribes were not. Trader-agents such as Matthew Elliott and Alexander McKee were married to Shawnee women. They interacted with Indian people on a daily basis and lived for extended periods within the tribal villages. Of Scots or Irish descent, many of these local agents disliked their English superiors and identified with the tribespeople. They told the Shawnees and their neighbors what the Indians wanted to hear: that the British would provide them with sufficient military assistance (including troops) to defend their lands against the Long Knives.

Buttressed by such promises, delegates from the northwestern tribes met at Detroit in 1786. Attempting to form a united front against American expansion in Ohio, the nascent confederacy sent a letter to Congress denouncing the treaties of Fort Stanwix, Fort McIntosh, and Fort Finney and asking that government surveyors withdraw from lands illegally ceded in these agreements. Asserting that "the interests of any one nation should be the interests of us all, the welfare of the one should be the welfare of all the others," the tribesmen requested that American officials negotiate with the confederacy, not with individual tribes.

Yet political union was difficult for a people traditionally divided by a multiplicity of loyalties, and American officials continued their policies of "divide and conquer." More vulnerable to American military power, tribes such as the Senecas, Wyandots, and Delawares, communities on the eastern fringe of the confederacy, were willing to compromise. Rather than risk an immediate confrontation with the Americans, they proposed to cede lands east of the Muskingum River, and they enjoyed some support from Potawatomis and Ottawas from Lake Michigan, who had no claims to the region and were not threatened by land cessions in eastern Ohio. In contrast, the Shawnees, Miamis, and Kickapoos believed any surrender of lands was an immediate threat to their control of western Ohio and the Wabash Valley; they adamantly opposed any concessions.

Eager to obtain the confederacy's acceptance of the earlier treaties, in 1788 Arthur St. Clair, the governor of the Northwest Territory, met with delegates from some of the tribes at Fort Harmar, near the mouth of the Muskingum River. Few prominent Native American leaders attended the conference. John Heckewelder, the Moravian missionary to the Delawares, commented that the signatures on the treaty did not contain "the name of even one Great Chief," while George Morgan, an American Indian agent, admitted:

> Few of the natives attended and none was fully represented; here the treaty was negotiated and speeches and explanations to the Indians made by our superintendent in the French language through a Canadian interpreter who had to guess at his meaning for he can neither write or speak the language [so] as to make himself understood in any manner of that importance.

After being browbeaten by St. Clair, the assembled Indians reluctantly signed the Treaty of Fort Harmar (January 1789), which reconfirmed the huge land cessions previously made at Forts McIntosh and Finney, but the majority of Native Americans in the Old Northwest were incensed by St. Clair's demands and refused to abide by the agreement.

Encouraged by the treaty, American settlement spread up the river valleys from the northern bank of the Ohio, but the Shawnees struck back with a vengeance and warfare increased rather than diminished. In 1789 several expeditions of Kentuckians that attempted to attack Indian towns along the Wabash achieved only nominal success. The Miamis rebuffed American peace overtures, and in April 1790, a large war party attacked a flotilla of military supply boats on the Ohio, killing five soldiers and taking eight prisoners. In response, Secretary of War Henry Knox ordered General Josiah Harmar and St. Clair to organize an expedition to "extirpate, utterly, if possible, the (Indian) banditti" responsible for the attacks.

Harmar and St. Clair spent the late summer of 1790 organizing a force of 320 regulars and over 1,100 Kentucky militia at Fort Washington (Cincinnati), while Major John Hamtramck mustered and then led a force of mounted Kentuckians up the Wabash Valley against Wea and Kickapoo villages. In October, Hamtramck proceeded no further north than the mouth of the Vermilion, before his ill-disciplined Kentucky militia refused to go any further. They returned to Vincennes without encountering any Indians.

Harmar was less fortunate. He left Fort Washington on September 30, 1790; arrived at Kekionga, the Miami town at modern Fort Wayne, on October 15; and found the village in ashes. Aware of Harmar's plans, Little Turtle had sent his women and children down the Maumee Valley toward Lake Erie, and then burned his village. Assuming that his enemy had fled, Harmar experienced difficulty in controlling the militia who scattered throughout the surrounding forest searching for plunder.

On October 19, when Colonel John Hardin led a mixed force of militia and regulars down the Maumee in pursuit of a handful of fleeing Indians, they were ambushed by Little Turtle and a large war party of Miamis, Shawnees, Ottawas, and Potawatomis. Hardin lost about 100 men. Two days later Little Turtle lured another mixed force of regulars and militia into a similar ambush, killing an additional 183 Americans. With approximately one-fourth of his force now dead or missing, Harmar had had enough. On October 22, he broke camp and retreated back toward Fort Washington.

Elated over the victories, the warriors boasted that "there should not remain a smoke [settler's cabin] on the Ohio by the time the Leaves put out." Those tribes which had been willing to compromise

PEOPLE, PLACES, AND THINGS

Captives

A Miami Indian Called Ken-Tuck

Sarah Cooke and Rachel Ramadhyani, eds., *Indians and a Changing Frontier: The Art of George Winter* (Indianapolis: Indiana Historical Society, 1993), plate 52.

One of the most pervasive myths of American history and folklore is the horrible fate of non-Indians taken captive by Native Americans. Both literature and the popular media are replete with accounts and images of white captives being assaulted, tortured, and even burned alive. Indeed, the "save the last bullets for the women and children" syndrome, supposedly to keep helpless civilians from falling into Indian hands, was a standard scenario in western movies and pulp fiction throughout the first three-quarters of the twentieth century.

The reality of life for captives taken by Indians was usually quite different. Unquestionably, some captives were mistreated, assaulted, and even killed, but many others suffered relatively little physical abuse (frequently less than Indians captured by whites) and were either held for ransom or adopted into Indian communities. The ransom or adoption of captives was more common in the East, where many of the tribes previously had participated in the warfare between the colonial powers. It was less common on the Plains or in the desert Southwest, but even in the West many captives were ransomed or adopted.

The ransom and adoption of white captives was common in the Northeast and Ohio Valley. Both Eunice Williams, taken from Massachusetts and adopted by Canadian Mohawks, and Mary Jemison, captured by the Senecas, married Indian men, refused repatriation, and spent their lives within their adopted communities. In the postrevolutionary period, tribes such as the Miamis, Shawnees, and Potawatomis, who opposed American expansion into Ohio, also took many captives who were either ransomed or adopted.

Frances Slocum

Sarah Cooke and Rachel Ramadhyani, eds., *Indians and a Changing Frontier: The Art of George Winter* (Indianapolis: Indiana Historical Society, 1993), plate I.

Featured here are three Miami captives whose careers illustrate the permeability of cultural and political borders separating Indian and American communities in the Ohio Valley. Ken-Tuck, a Miami warrior painted by George Winter circa 1837, was taken captive as a child in Kentucky and retained little memory of his white family. He spoke no English, had been integrated completely into the Miami tribe, and identified himself as a Miami, not a white man. Mono-con-a-qua, or Frances Slocum,

PEOPLE, PLACES, AND THINGS

(continued)

also painted by Winter, had been captured as a child by the Delawares from the Wyoming Valley in Pennsylvania. Adopted and raised by the Miamis, she had married Deaf Man, a prominent Miami chief who lived on the Mississinewa River. Mono-con-a-qua spoke both Miami and English and remembered her white family, but she preferred to remain a Miami. When her family members from Pennsylvania attempted to repatriate her, she refused their pleas, choosing to remain among her grown Miami children. William Wells, also taken as a child in Kentucky, had been adopted by the famous Miami chief Little Turtle and had fought with the Miamis at both Harmar's and St. Clair's defeats. Wells then returned to the Americans, however, and served as a scout for Anthony Wayne. Following the treaty of Greenville, he was employed as an Indian agent at Fort Wayne, but he retained his ties to Little Turtle and the Miamis and participated in the Indian trade in northern Indiana. Although the Miamis evidently accepted his role as an intermediary between the tribe and the government, other Indians mistrusted him, and in August 1812 he was killed by hostile Potawatomis.

William Wells This miniature is the only likeness of William Wells, Indian agent and Little Turtle's son-in-law. The uniform indicates that it was probably made between 1805 and 1810.

Source: Harvey Leis Carter, *The Life and Times of Little Turtle* (Urbana: University of Illinois Press, 1987), 225. Reproduced by permission of the Chicago Historical Society. Object X0269.

If so many non-Indian captives lived comfortably among the Native American tribes, and often refused repatriation, why did the myth that such captivity was "a fate worse than death" become accepted as true by much of the American public? What purposes did such a myth serve?

---

with the Americans now joined with the militants, and in January 1791 a large war party besieged Dunlap's Station, only eighteen miles north of Fort Washington. Other war parties attacked settlers on the Ohio or in northern Kentucky. During the following summer mounted Kentuckians destroyed Wea towns on the central Wabash, but the majority of the tribespeople remained defiant, refusing to negotiate with the Long Knives.

Embarrassed by Harmar's defeat, the federal government launched another campaign against the Maumee villages. In September 1791, St. Clair led about 2,300 men, including two small regiments of regular infantry, north across Ohio toward Kekionga. With the exception of two small regiments

of regular infantry, the remainder of this mélange again consisted of poorly trained volunteer and militia units. In an outstanding display of poor judgment, St. Clair allowed about 200 women, mostly prostitutes and camp followers, to join the expedition; even worse, some of the women were accompanied by their children.

Aware that the Long Knives were coming, Little Turtle and Blue Jacket of the Shawnees had recruited almost 1,000 warriors. Boasting that their numbers were "like fireflies in the forest," early in the morning on November 4, 1791, they quietly surrounded St. Clair's camp of about 1,400 men (900 had already deserted) in a small clearing surrounded by dense forest on the headwaters of the

Wabash River. When they attacked shortly after dawn, the militia units panicked. Firing from the cover of the surrounding forest, the warriors found the Americans, huddled around the baggage carts, to be easy targets. The battle raged until about nine thirty that morning, with the Americans suffering horrendous casualties. Finally St. Clair and the survivors broke through Indian ranks on the eastern perimeter and fled south toward Fort Washington. In their panic, the Americans abandoned many wounded comrades and almost all their equipment.

St. Clair's defeat was the greatest Indian victory over an American military force in all of American history. The United States suffered 647 men killed and hundreds wounded. The number of women and children killed is unknown. The confederacy lost fewer than 150 warriors.

Bolstered by success, the confederacy sent messages to Congress demanding that the federal government relinquish all claims to lands north or west of the Ohio River. In response, the government offered the tribes additional trade goods and annuities, agreed to give up claims to much of Ohio, but refused to renounce its hegemony over lands already sold to settlers or to military posts ceded by the British following the Revolution. Supremely confident, the Indians rejected the government's compromise and suggested that government officials distribute the money offered to the Indians to those settlers who had purchased lands in the region, for:

> we are persuaded that they would most readily accept it, in lieu of the lands you sold them. If you add also the great sums you must expend in raising and paying armies, with a view to force us to yield you our country you will certainly have more than sufficient for the purpose of repaying these settlers for all their labor and their improvements.

With the collapse of negotiations, both sides again moved toward war. The confederacy was much encouraged by Lord Dorchester, the governor of Quebec, and John Graves Simcoe, the governor of Upper Canada, who both assumed that the United States would soon join its old ally France in a war against Great Britain. In February 1794, Dorchester assured the Indians of British support and ordered Simcoe to build Fort Miamis, a new

British post at the rapids of the Maumee, just upstream from modern Toledo, Ohio. The construction of the new post, completed in July 1794, so heartened the Indians that even Joseph Brant, who earlier had championed compromise with the Americans, now urged the western confederacy to continue their resistance.

While the British built forts, the Americans prepared for war. In April 1792 officials appointed General Anthony Wayne as the new commander of American troops in the west. Nicknamed "Mad Anthony" by his troops because of his strict discipline, Wayne recruited an army and then drilled his men mercilessly, imposing harsh punishments for desertion, drunkenness, or sleeping on duty. During 1793 he reinforced Fort Jefferson, built by St. Clair near modern Greenville, Ohio, then erected Fort Greenville and Fort Recovery at the site of St. Clair's defeat. By the summer of 1794, Wayne commanded a disciplined, well-equipped force of 2,000 men, augmented by about 1,500 mounted Kentucky volunteers. His army marched from Fort Greenville on July 28, 1794.

The Indian confederacy was aware of Wayne's intentions, and by mid-June approximately 2,000 warriors had assembled on the Maumee. Unlike Wayne's army, however, they were subject to no single commander. Against the advice of Little Turtle and British Indian agents, on June 30 the warriors attacked Fort Recovery, an American supply depot near the headwaters of the Wabash. The attack failed, and arguments over captured horses caused many of the Ottawas, Potawatomis, and Ojibwes to abandon the campaign and return to their villages. Little Turtle also left the hostile camp. By mid-August he had become convinced that the British would not assist the Indians, and he advised the confederacy to negotiate a compromise. When Wayne reached the Maumee Valley, the Indian army had shrunk to 1,300 warriors.

The remaining warriors chose to meet Wayne at Fallen Timbers, a location on the northern bank of the Maumee River where storm-felled trees formed a natural barricade. The tangle of fallen trees and underbrush was less than three miles upstream from newly constructed Fort Miamis, where the Indians believed the British would provide sanctuary if they were forced to retreat. On August 18, Wayne approached within four miles of the Indian position, then stopped and spent two days

Defending the Trans-Appalachian West

Source: Gregory E. Dowd, A Spirited Resistance: American Indian Struggle for Unity, 1745–1815 *(Baltimore: Johns Hopkins University Press, 1992), 92. Reprinted with permission of The Johns Hopkins University Press. Also see maps in Ray Allen Billington,* Westward Expansion: A History of the American Frontier *(New York: Macmillan Co., 1960), 229; Francis Paul Prucha,* Atlas of American Indian Affairs *(Lincoln: University of Nebraska Press, 1990), 113, 115.*

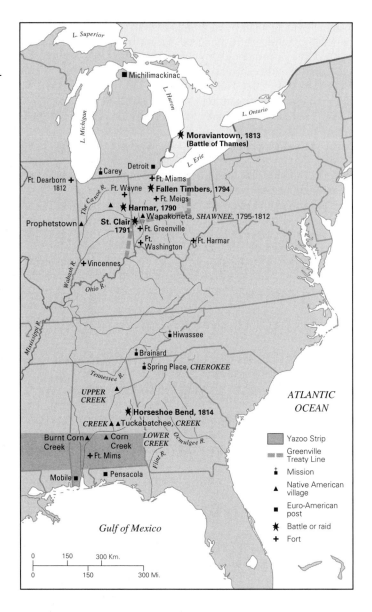

constructing a small fortified supply depot. On the evening of August 19, after a thunderstorm swept through the region, many of the warriors left Fallen Timbers and returned to the British fort for provisions. On the morning of August 20, with his adversaries distracted, Wayne attacked. The warriors who were present fought valiantly, but Wayne's more numerous, well-disciplined troops forced

them from their positions. Undaunted, many of the warriors retreated willingly, planning to make another stand, with their British allies, behind the walls of Fort Miamis. They were sorely disappointed. As the retreating warriors approached the fort, Major William Campbell, the commander of the post, closed the stockade's doors and refused them sanctuary. The Crown was willing to furnish arms and ammunition to the confederacy, but it was not willing to risk a direct confrontation with the United States. Demoralized, the warriors retreated toward Detroit.

Wayne spent the next few days exchanging notes and insults with Campbell, then burned the neighboring Indian towns and destroyed their cornfields. He then marched back to Fort Defiance, a new post at the mouth of the Auglaize. Both sides had suffered similar casualties (Wayne lost forty-four killed and eighty-nine wounded, while Indian losses were approximately fifty warriors), but Fallen Timbers was an American victory. The failure of the British to provide armed support or even sanctuary to the confederacy devastated Indian morale, and many tribesmen never forgot the British infidelity. Nineteen years later, in September 1813, when the British again seemed intent on deserting their Indian allies, the Shawnee war chief Tecumseh bitterly reminded British officers that he and other warriors still remembered "when the gates were shut against us."

During the autumn and early winter of 1794 the confederacy disintegrated. Tribal leaders met with American officials and negotiated separate armistice agreements. In the spring Indian leaders learned that Jay's Treaty had been signed and that the British had agreed to surrender the western posts to the Americans. Convinced that they had no choice, the former leaders of the confederacy met with Wayne, and after two weeks of American pressure they signed the Treaty of Greenville on August 3, 1795. The agreement reflected how far the balance of power had shifted since 1792, when the Indians had refused American offers of compromise. In return for trade goods and annuities ranging from $500 to $1,000 per tribe, the Indians ceded all their lands in eastern or southern Ohio. They also agreed to allow the federal government to erect military posts at strategic points throughout the northwest (Fort Wayne, Fort Dearborn at modern Chicago, and other places). Indian leaders also promised that their people would remain at peace. In return, federal officials agreed that the tribesmen could hunt in the ceded regions until such time as the region was settled by farmers. The Ohio country was lost; and the Long Knives now had footholds in the heart of the remaining tribal homelands.

The Southeast

In the South, Native American attempts to defend their autonomy and unite politically also suffered setbacks. Although several southern tribes, including the Choctaws and Chickasaws, were threatened by American expansion in the decades immediately following the American Revolution, the brunt of this aggrandizement was born by the Cherokees and Creeks. As in the territory north of the Ohio, the new national government exercised only minimal control over settlers in the trans-Appalachian south, but in this region Native American attempts to control their own lands and lives also were contested by southern states, such as Georgia, or pseudo-states such as Franklin. Moreover, in this region, as in the Great Lakes, European colonial powers continued to exert considerable influence in both tribal and international politics.

In the two decades following the Peace of Paris, the ranks of the southern tribes were split by disagreements over the structure of tribal governments and the accumulation of material wealth. Native Americans, white southerners, and African Americans all had borrowed from each other's cultural adaptations, but within some tribal communities, this exchange engendered opposition. The focus of tribal politics remained in the autonomous villages, but by the 1780s the old ways were being challenged by a growing number of tribespeople of mixed lineage who had embraced cultural patterns from European or American settlers who entered the region in growing numbers. Many tribespeople of mixed lineage wished to centralize political power within tribal councils that transcended the traditional village councils. These new leaders believed that village-based chiefs and governments were more vulnerable to corruption by non-Indians and that only a united tribal government could safeguard tribal homelands. In addition, they championed a system of internal order based on social compacts or statutory laws, rather than relying on the clan justice of their forefathers. And finally, many of these less traditional tribespeople envisioned accumulated capital as a source of honor and power; they were much less interested in following older patterns of generosity and reciprocity.

The conflicts within Creek society during these decades offer interesting insights into these changes.

When the American Revolution ended, the British withdrew from the South, but they were eager to divide the American-French-Spanish coalition that had opposed them during the war and they signed separate treaties with the Americans and Spaniards. The British ceded all of Florida—including West Florida, which stretched to the Mississippi—to Spain in a treaty setting the northern border of West Florida at 32°28' north latitude. In a separate treaty, the British ceded the rest of the trans-Appalachian west to the United States, but placed the southern border of American territory at the thirty-first parallel. Obviously the ceded territories overlapped, and the "Yazoo Strip," the contested region, contained over 39,000 square miles. The region was also claimed by Georgia through the state's old colonial land claims. More importantly, however, most of the eastern half of the strip was occupied by the Creeks.

By 1783 the Creek Confederacy, comprising about 20,000 individuals in fifty towns, was divided into two amorphous divisions, the Lower Creeks and the Upper Creeks. The Lower Creeks lived primarily in western Georgia, while the Upper Creeks resided along the Coosa and Tallapoosa rivers in Alabama. The Upper Creeks were led by Alexander McGillivray, the son of a British trader and a Creek woman. McGillivray was not a clan leader or mico (traditional village chief), but he enjoyed the support of many less traditional Creeks who had adopted many European cultural patterns, and he was eager to consolidate and centralize political power in the Creek confederacy.

Working through the Creek National Council, an informal and previously ineffective gathering of town chiefs, McGillivray hoped to counterbalance the American, Spanish, and Georgian claims to the Yazoo Strip and to defend Creek interests in the region. In 1784 he met with Spanish officials and signed the Treaty of Pensacola, in which he promised Creek military support in return for Spanish guarantees of Creek lands in Spanish Florida. The Spaniards agreed to furnish the Creeks with merchandise and to permit Panton and Leslie, a British trading firm, to supply the Creeks with arms, ammunition, and other trade goods. McGillivray profited personally from the agreement. He received a Spanish pension, and he also was made a silent partner in Panton and Leslie, the British firm that was allowed to monopolize trade

with the tribe. In return, McGillivray assured the Spaniards that the Creeks would fight against the Americans or Georgians if either invaded Spanish Florida.

McGillivray's attempts to centralize power and his accumulation of personal wealth created resentment among those Creeks still tied to the old ways. In an attempt to strengthen the influence of the National Council, McGillivray and his allies established a group of Creek "constables," who were recruited primarily from McGillivray's clan. The constables attempted to enforce the council's decisions, but their efforts alienated those Creeks who preferred the old political structure that vested decision making in autonomous villages. Moreover, as Panton and Leslie prospered and McGillivray accumulated more possessions (plantations, slaves, trade goods), his failure to redistribute wealth to less fortunate members of the tribes also engendered animosity. More traditional Creeks saw McGillivray as an opportunist whose bid for power reflected foreign values and whose support came from outsiders, not from within the traditional Creek political structure.

In response, Hoboithle Mico and Eneah Mico, village chiefs among the Lower Creeks, ignored the National Council's authority, and between 1783 and 1786 they signed three treaties with Georgia in which they relinquished Creek claims to lands in that state. Not surprisingly, when settlers from Georgia attempted to occupy the lands, warriors loyal to the National Council pushed them back so successfully that Spain became alarmed that the Creeks might seize the offensive and invade central and eastern Georgia. Wary that Creek aggression might entangle her in a war with the United States, Spain reduced her supplies to the Creeks and ordered McGillivray to make peace with the Georgians. Meanwhile, the Nootka Sound Crisis (1789), a naval confrontation between Spanish and British warships off the coast of modern British Columbia, seemed to threaten war between Spain and Britain, and McGillivray realized that if such a conflict occurred, all supplies from Panton and Leslie, the British trading firm in Spanish Florida, would be terminated.

Aware that Spanish influence in the Southeast was waning, McGillivray decided to seek new friends in his struggle with Georgia. He knew that federal officials were eager to enhance the power of the new federal government while limiting the powers of the states, and he was far more concerned about Georgia's claims to the region than those of a distant government housed in Philadelphia. Consequently, in 1790 McGillivray and his followers signed the Treaty of New York, which ceded several eastern portions of the Creek homeland to the United States but placed the Creeks "under the protection of the federal government" and stated that settlers who intruded onto remaining Creek lands would "forfeit the protection" of the United States. The Creeks also agreed to not hold any treaty with an "individual State." In return, the Creeks received a large quantity of trade goods and a perpetual annuity of $1,500; secret provisions appointed McGillivray to the rank of brigadier general in the U.S. Army with a salary and pension commensurate to his rank and allowed him to annually import, duty free, goods worth $60,000 for sale and distribution within the Creek Nation.

Spanish officials were alarmed by the treaty, but since the agreement technically did not violate the earlier Treaty of Pensacola, they were unsure how to respond. Georgia protested that her claims to the Yazoo Strip had been ignored, but the recently ceded land on her western frontier now was open for settlement. Nevertheless, the treaty ultimately weakened the Creek Confederacy. McGillivray's assurances to federal officials that his constables would punish Creek "bandits" who stole horses from American settlements angered traditional Creeks, who interpreted such enforcement as a further infringement on clan justice, while their resentment over high prices charged by Panton and Leslie increased their determination to return to more traditional ways. By 1792 Hoboithle Mico led a faction of Lower Creeks active in the National Council who openly opposed many of McGillivray's initiatives, while William Bowles, an American adventurer married to a Creek woman, proclaimed that he, not McGillivray, was the "Director-General of the Creek Nation" and espoused a return to a decentralized, town-based political structure based on clan justice and reciprocity.

In February 1793 McGillivray died of natural causes and was buried in the garden of the Panton and Leslie trading post in Pensacola. With his passing, the Creek political system reverted once more to a political structure based more on the towns than on the National Council. Many of the less tra-

ditional Creeks (often of mixed lineage) continued to amass personal fortunes, and their refusal to follow age-old obligations of reciprocity still made them objects of suspicion among rank-and-file tribespeople.

The Creek experience during these years offers a microcosm of political and cultural change in other southern tribes. Among the Chickasaws, George Colbert, a "Chickasaw chief," also amassed a personal fortune, and like McGillivray he, too, urged his kinspeople to adopt a political structure that incorporated Euro-American values. Choctaw families such as the LeFlores, Folsoms, and Pitchlynns owned and grazed large herds of cattle on tribal lands and also served as agents of change within their tribal communities, while Cherokees such as James Vann and Charles Hicks built personal fortunes by trading in houses, land, and slaves and urged their people to adopt many changes. Yet traditional tribespeople still clung to the old ways and remained suspicious of these younger men's leadership. Cultural change continued in these tribal societies, but traditional Creeks, Chickasaws, Choctaws, and Cherokees wished to control its pace, and they were wary of new kinsmen, many of mixed lineages, who lived amidst plenty but sometimes refused to share with their relatives. New laws that were designed to protect property and that undermined clan obligations held little appeal for these traditional tribespeople. In the 1820s the wealthy Indian planters and merchants would eventually gain legitimacy as tribal leaders but only after they stepped forward to protect the homeland (and their plantations) from American encroachment.

AMERICAN INDIAN POLICY

While Native American people struggled to develop strategies for coping with the onrush of western settlement, federal officials attempted to formulate a coherent national Indian policy that would provide a program for interaction between Native Americans and non-Indians. In addition, federal officials were eager to devise a systematic process to encourage and regulate the transfer of Indian lands to the federal government. And finally, although most of the Founding Fathers were ethnocentric and believed that traditional tribal cultures were far inferior to those of western Europeans or non-Indian Americans, they did believe that Native Americans might adapt to Euro-American ways and become members (perhaps even citizens) of the new republic. Consequently, they labored to develop policies that would facilitate this transformation and convert Indians into a "new red yeomanry" that would take its place in American society.

In addition to Indian resistance to these policies, federal officials faced problems of their own. Policies formulated in Philadelphia or Washington often went unheeded by frontiersmen, and federal agents encountered considerable difficulty in regulating Indian trade or the trespass of non-Indians onto tribal lands. Moreover, programs designed by policymakers in Washington (although sometimes philanthropic in intent) were often developed in ignorance of the traditional tribal cultures that they wished to transform.

Land and Trade Regulations

Conflicts engendered by American citizens settling on Indian lands sparked the Indian Trade and Intercourse Acts, a series of laws passed at two- or three-year intervals between 1790 and 1834. These acts echoed earlier British Indian policy, particularly the Proclamation of 1763. The laws were designed to maintain law and order in the Indian country, regulate trade, and promote government-sponsored "civilization programs." Legislation passed in 1790, for example, prohibited states or individuals from purchasing Indian lands, regulated Indian traders, and provided for the punishment of whites committing crimes against Indians on Indian land. In contrast, Trade and Intercourse Acts passed in 1793 and 1796 focused on white settlers who trespassed on Indian territory; they prohibited all unauthorized people from hunting or grazing their livestock on Indian land.

Other legislation focused on equitable justice. The Trade and Intercourse Act of 1790 judged crimes by whites against Indians as similar to those against fellow whites, and in 1796 Congress specifically decreed that any American citizen convicted of murdering an Indian in Indian country would be eligible for a death sentence, as would Indians committing similar crimes against whites. Additional legislation provided for compensation for property stolen by either side. In contrast, federal officials were willing to allow the Native American communities to solve their own problems. Until the mid-nineteenth century Congress made no provisions for the punishment of offenses by Indians against each other (unless their warfare disrupted neighboring white communities), and tribespeople were encouraged to administer justice in accordance with their own laws or traditions. Tribes would rely on this legislation as they struggled with states over land title in the twentieth and twenty-first centuries.

Eager to wean Native Americans from the influence of British or Spanish traders, George Washington and others championed a series of government trading posts designed to provide goods to the Indians at a small profit, undercut foreign merchants, and "engross their [the Indians'] trade, and fix them strongly in our interest." In 1795, just prior to the Treaty of Greenville, Congress established the first federal trading houses or "Indian factories" among the Creeks, Cherokees, and Chickasaws, and the factory system was soon extended to other tribes. The factories were stocked with an assortment of goods that the tribespeople supposedly needed, and the president appointed "factors," or merchants, and clerks to manage the establishments. The factors and clerks could accept furs, skins, maple sugar, corn or other agricultural produce, and even Indian-smelted lead from the tribespeople but were forbidden to accept any trade goods, cooking utensils, or any commodity that the Indians previously had received from non-Indians.

Between 1800 and 1820 the factory system expanded, but it never achieved the success its proponents had promised. Government factories may have offered goods that Indians agents believed tribespeople *needed*, but they often were not the goods that tribespeople *wanted*. Northern and western factories were profitable prior to the War of 1812, but the southern posts, which traded extensively for deerskins, often registered losses. The factory system suffered during the War of 1812, when the British and Indians seized goods at several factories, and although it rebounded following the conflict, government factors were hard-pressed to compete with private traders. Entangled in bureaucratic snarls, the factory system endured until

1822 when Congress succumbed to pressure from the American Fur Company and abolished all the government trading posts.

The "Civilization" Program

While the federal government struggled to mediate disputes between Indians and frontiersmen, it also initiated a program designed to "civilize" Native Americans and integrate them into the larger mainstream of American society. In his message to Congress in October 1791, George Washington championed "rational experiments" designed to provide the Indians with the "blessings of civilization." Two years later the Intercourse Act of 1793 appropriated $20,000 to purchase domestic animals, farm equipment, and other merchandise "in order to promote civilization among the friendly Indian tribes." In addition, the president was authorized to appoint agents, farmers, and blacksmiths to assist the tribes in this "civilization" process.

The government's civilization program blossomed under Thomas Jefferson. Heavily influenced by the Enlightenment, Jefferson believed that while Indians were not necessarily the "noble savages" so idealized by French philosophers, they were "in body and mind equal to the whiteman." They had not achieved European levels of "civilization" because of their isolation in the New World. Subscribing to a linear view of civilization in which mankind progressed from more primitive stages toward "civilization," Jefferson believed that while Native Americans simply were at a lower stage than Europeans, they had the potential to quickly ascend the ladder until they reached the Euro-American level.

Jefferson believed that small yeoman farmers epitomized the ideal American, and he envisioned a United States in which extended Indian families would be transformed into nuclear farm families. These new Indian families would "meet [with non-Indians] and blend together, to intermix, and become one people." Indian men would plant small farms, while Indian women would become spinners and weavers, emulating Anglo-American women of the late eighteenth century. He chose to ignore the important role that women already played in tribal agriculture and instead championed "education" as the "key" to the Indians' "progress."

In 1802 Jefferson advised a delegation of western tribesmen visiting Washington:

> to cultivate the earth, to raise herds of useful animals and to spin and weave for their food and clothing. These resources are certain, they will never disappoint you, while those of hunting may fail. . . . We will with pleasure furnish you with implements of the most necessary arts, and with persons who will instruct you how to make and use them.

Yet the apparent altruism of Jefferson's Indian policy hid a darker side. Although Jefferson envisioned a future in which Native Americans and European Americans would be joined, he believed that Native Americans had no future as "Indians." Indian people could be assimilated into white society only if they made rapid and radical changes. More importantly, most of those changes could be accomplished only if they sold their remaining homelands and settled down as small farmers. Of course, the transfer of Indian land to the government also would facilitate America's westward expansion and the development of an American landscape that Jefferson espoused. Moreover, for all of his reputed benevolence, Jefferson was willing to adopt devious methods to attain such goals. In 1803 he wrote to William Henry Harrison, the governor of Indiana Territory:

> We wish to draw them to agriculture, to spinning and weaving . . . , to the culture of a small piece of land. They will perceive how useless to them are their extensive forests, and will be willing to pare them off . . . in exchange for necessaries for their farms and families. To promote this disposition to exchange lands . . . we shall push our trading houses (Indian factories), and be glad to see the good and influential individuals among them run in debt, because we observe that when these debts get beyond what the individuals can pay, they become willing to lop them off by a cession of lands.

Missionaries Among the Tribes

Under Jefferson's leadership the government emphasized instruction in agriculture and the "domestic arts" but relied on missionaries or federally employed farmers, carpenters, or blacksmiths rather than on any formal school system. Many Protestant missionaries readily embraced this marriage of church and state and encapsulated Christianity within the government's civilization program. For most missionaries, the agricultural skills and domestic arts espoused by the government were part of God's plan for mankind, and they supported federal goals transforming the Indians into communities of small farm families. Moreover, the missionaries believed that not only would literacy in English enable Indians to read and understand the Bible, it also would facilitate their acceptance of American values.

By 1800 Moravian missionaries were active among the Cherokees, Creeks, and Delawares, and they soon were joined by Quakers, Congregationalists, and other Protestants. The missionaries taught Indian adults through practical, "hands-on" daily activities and through example, but they also established schools for Indian children. In 1804 the Moravians opened a day school among the Cherokees at Springplace in northwestern Georgia, and one year later the Presbyterians organized a boarding school among the same tribe at Hiwasse in eastern Tennessee. In 1816 the American Board of Foreign Missions established another mission among the Cherokees at Brainerd, near modern Chattanooga, and in 1818 Congregationalist Cyrus Kingsbury opened a mission and school among the Choctaws. North of the Ohio, Moravian, Quaker, and Baptist clergy continued to labor among the tribes of Ohio and Indiana, and like their southern brethren, they too augmented their efforts with mission schools.

The missionaries initially reported some success. In Georgia and Alabama many Creek and Cherokee warriors still hunted, fished, and traded in deerskins, but others, men who previously had sought status on the warpath or in ballgames, now turned to domestic animals, raising small herds of hogs and cattle. Meanwhile a small but emerging class of mixed-lineage planters, the product of white men and Cherokee or Creek women, cleared larger tracts of land, increased the number of their slaves, and emulated their white neighbors by participating in a mixed-crop plantation economy. Cherokee women, long adept at raising plentiful harvests of corn and vegetables, added cotton, and by 1805 many sought instruction in spinning and weaving

from missionaries or from white women in neighboring communities.

North of the Ohio several communities of Shawnees, Miamis, and Delawares also subscribed to the government's programs, and assisted by Moravian or Quaker missionaries, they constructed "log houses with chimneys," cleared and fenced land, and raised crops of corn, cabbages, turnips, and potatoes. By 1808 Shawnee villagers at Wapakoneta, Ohio, had cultivated over four hundred acres, planted orchards, and erected a sawmill. White Ohioans, impressed by these Shawnees' "sobriety and good behavior," reported that they were making "rapid progress toward industry and civilization."

Yet federal policy during these decades achieved only limited success. Certainly an elite corps of nontraditional planters among the Cherokees, Creeks, Choctaws, and Chickasaws subscribed to the federal programs, and they readily adopted many (but not all) of the socioeconomic values of the white planter class in the South. But many other members of the southern tribes still followed traditional ways. North of the Ohio some Miamis, Delawares, and Shawnees also attempted to "walk the white man's road," but their commitment to becoming small yeoman farmers was even less than that of the southern tribes. Moreover, opposition to government programs, loss of land, and deteriorating socioeconomic conditions gave rise to nativistic, religious revitalization movements in both regions, which during the War of 1812, blossomed into armed resistance to the United States.

The missionaries themselves inadvertently contributed to the civilization program's lack of success. Many were well-intentioned individuals, but they were ethnocentric and demanded that Native Americans adopt and adhere to European cultural norms. Almost none of the Moravians, Presbyterians, and Congregationalists who proselytized among the southern tribes learned the Cherokee, Creek, or Choctaw languages, and prior to the War of 1812 they described the Indians' network of kinship and extended families as "confusing, immoral, and repugnant." Others commented that Cherokee dress was "comical," that Cherokees lived in "filthy, smoky huts," and that Cherokee people were devoid of any culture.

The mission schools reflected the clergy's inflexibility. The institutions followed a daily schedule and curriculum similar to other American schools of the early nineteenth century and were poorly suited for Native American children. Most Indian children were raised in families or communities in which discipline or social controls differed markedly from European or American systems. Although white visitors in tribal villages sometimes complained about undisciplined "wild little Indians," most Native American villages were orderly communities, despite the fact that controls over individual behavior were nonhierarchical. Children were conditioned not to "mind" a parent but to subscribe to family or community mores, which were encouraged by a broad spectrum of peers and family members. Moreover, they were "raised" to participate in societies in which power was neither hierarchical nor authoritarian and in which cooperation or consensus was valued more than individualism.

In contrast, the mission schools mirrored the strict regimen of public schools during this period, and Indian students were subjected to values and methods of instruction alien to their home communities. Teachers championed individualism, and students were expected to compete against each other in class. The schools enrolled both boys and girls, who were expected to follow rigid and repetitive schedules and to parrot the instructions of their masters. At Carey, a Baptist mission near modern Niles, Michigan, the Reverend Isaac McCoy proudly boasted that his Indian students were "not allowed to be idle." According to McCoy, "in taming the wild man, we conceived that instruction in manual labor was as necessary as instruction in letters." McCoy's Potawatomi and Miami students were awakened by a bugle at four in the morning and marched to the school for religious services. They then worked at agricultural and domestic "chores" necessary to maintain the mission. Shortly after sunrise they ate breakfast and then faced a daily round of classes, manual labor, and religious instruction. The evening meal was served at six o'clock, and following religious instruction and "vespers," the students retired to their beds. According to McCoy's own estimates, most students spent approximately half of the daylight hours in the "manual arts," or working for the mission. Not surprisingly, many Native American students rebelled against such regimentation, and after 1825 both McCoy's mission and his school declined.

During the early 1820s federal Indian policy seemed to follow a similar pattern. Discouraged that most Indian people seemed to reject the federal programs, officials began to search for alternatives to the civilization program. If Indian people refused to become "civilized," what would happen to them? White settlers, who continued to pour into the trans-Appalachian west, settled on Indian lands in the region. New state and territorial governments encouraged such usurpation. From the American perspective, Indians could not be allowed to remain in their old homelands. During the 1820s new policies would be formulated to solve the government's "Indian problem," but the solution would not bode well for Native Americans.

REVITALIZATION MOVEMENTS

Much of the failure of American Indian policy in the three decades following the American Revolution resulted from the federal government's inability to enforce laws and control its own citizens. Throughout the trans-Appalachian west tribes faced an invasion of illegal hunters and squatters, and although the Treaty of Greenville delineated a boundary between Indian and American lands in Ohio and Indiana, frontiersmen repeatedly trespassed onto Indian lands, hunting deer and setting trap lines. In 1802 Delaware and Shawnee leaders pleaded with Indian agents to "stop your people from killing our game. At present they kill more game than we do," and William Henry Harrison admitted:

> The people of Kentucky . . . make a constant practice of crossing over onto Indian lands . . . to kill deer, bear, and buffalo—the latter from being in great abundance a few years ago is now scarcely to be met with. One white hunter will destroy more game than five of the common Indians.

South of the Ohio, Cherokee, Creek, and Choctaw hunters faced similar competition, and Creek leader Hoboithle Mico complained to Jefferson that white hunters were trespassing on Creek lands, setting fire to the forest, killing deer, and cutting down "bee trees" (trees in which bees made their hives) to gain access to the honey. Yet state and federal officials seemed powerless to stop the trespass, and poaching continued.

Many Americans on the frontier also "squatted" permanently on Indian lands. After 1805, white Georgians ignored treaty lines and moved west of the Ocmulgee River, settling on rich bottom lands along the Flint Valley. Creek leaders complained, but local officials ignored their protests and the settlers received open encouragement from state officials in Georgia. Similar encroachment occurred in Ohio, Indiana, and Illinois. Ignoring the Greenville Treaty Line, white settlers spilled into the Auglaize and Sandusky valleys, advanced up the Wabash watershed, or scattered their cabins along the road that stretched from Vincennes, across southern Illinois, to St. Louis.

Frontier courts also reflected the settlers' disdain for Native Americans. White juries routinely convicted Indians accused of committing crimes against settlers, but they regularly acquitted Americans accused of similar offenses against tribespeople. Frontiersmen stole Indian livestock, pilfered Indian camps, and even murdered Native Americans with impunity.

Federal officials in Ohio admitted that Indian people were being subjected to "injustices and wrongs of the most provoking character, for which [we] have never heard that any person was ever brought to justice and punishment . . . they are abused, cheated, robbed, plundered, and murdered at pleasure," but when Native American leaders traveled to Washington and protested, officials were either unwilling or unable to cope with the problem.

They also were unable to stop the liquor trade. In 1802 Congress authorized the president to "prevent and restrain" the sale of alcohol to Indian people, but the law did not apply to traders operating on ceded lands where states or territories had jurisdiction. The liquor trade was so lucrative that whiskey continued to flow into the Indian country. The problem was particularly acute in the Ohio Valley where Shawnees, Delawares, and Potawatomis consumed the fiery liquid by the barrel. Tribal villages sometimes degenerated into scenes of drunken violence. Both men and women drank heavily, brawls erupted, and even those tribespeople who abstained suffered injuries. The bacchanalia sorely tested the political and social cohesion of the Indian communities. Some Indians blamed witches for their misfortunes; others blamed the Americans.

Ironically, frontier lawlessness, coupled with the whiskey trade, facilitated Jefferson's Indian policy. Most tribespeople had little interest in becoming small yeoman farmers, but the decline in hunting and trapping, coupled with their demand for alcohol, seriously depleted the Indians' economic base. No longer able to support their families, the tribes were forced to sell parts of their remaining homelands to pay off their mounting debts.

Between 1800 and 1810 federal officials negotiated twenty-seven separate treaties with tribes both north and south of the Ohio. The Indians surrendered over forty million acres, including most of Illinois and huge tracts of Indiana, Ohio, Michigan, Tennessee, and Alabama. Revenue from the land sales brought a temporary respite, but the tribes were forced to relocate onto their remaining lands, which created even greater demands on the surviving homelands' resources. In turn, tribespeople became ever more dependent on federal annuities, and this left them more vulnerable to federal influence.

Not surprisingly, the deterioration of their old way of life, combined with frustration over federal Indian policy, alcohol, and the loss of their homelands sparked a period of religious revitalization. Envisioning no political, economic, or military solution to their dilemmas, many Native Americans, either deliberately or inadvertently, sought a religious deliverance. Senecas living on a reservation adjoining the Allegheny River in western New York were one of the first groups to experience this phenomenon.

Handsome Lake and the Senecas

Like many other members of the Iroquois League, the Senecas were ripe for such transformation. In the decade following the American Revolution, the Iroquois League had lost its position of leadership among the northeastern tribes. Their support of the British during the war had been costly, and following the war a portion of the Iroquois, particularly the Mohawks and Cayugas led by Joseph Brant, had fled to Ontario where they established Brantford, a new settlement on the Grand River.

In the postwar period western tribes such as the Shawnees, Wyandots, and Miamis gave lip service to Brant's leadership, but they believed the Mohawk was too willing to compromise with the Americans. The western tribes also were angered by Iroquois land cessions at the Second Treaty of Fort Stanwix (1784), in which the Iroquois gave up their claims to western Pennsylvania and Ohio, and by the Seneca chief Cornplanter, who had cooperated with the Americans. Indeed, after 1795, the once proud Iroquois held little influence outside their homeland.

The Iroquois homeland itself had become diminished. Between 1784 and 1797 Iroquois leaders signed six treaties through which they relinquished most remaining Iroquois land and agreed to occupy a series of small reservations located in New York and northwestern Pennsylvania. In some of these treaties Iroquois leaders such as Cornplanter accepted "presents," bribes, and the title to tracts of land that were set aside for their private ownership. Although Cornplanter and other leaders shared their wealth and lands with their followers, the land cessions still engendered bitterness.

Many Seneca women were particularly wary of the changes taking place in Iroquois society. In 1799 the Senecas were scattered over eleven reservations in western New York, while the Allegheny Band occupied a tract adjacent to the Pennsylvania border. Other members of the band had moved onto Cornplanter's square-mile tract just south of the Allegheny reservation in Pennsylvania. The two communities were plagued with problems, including poverty and alcoholism, but Seneca women continued to form the economic backbone of Seneca society. Although Quaker missionaries active in these communities advocated that Seneca men assume the role of farmers and that women be relegated to domestic chores, the women resisted. Moreover, Seneca women also opposed Quaker proposals that the Senecas form small, male-dominated nuclear families, similar to those embraced by non-Indians. They continued to prefer the extended families and traditional longhouses organized around matrilineal clans. Seneca women also wished to share their agricultural labor with their mothers and sisters, rather than work alone in separate, isolated households.

The emergence of Handsome Lake, Cornplanter's half-brother, accelerated some of the changes that the Seneca women opposed. In June 1799 Handsome Lake experienced the first of a series of visions in which spiritual messengers informed him that the tribe should renounce alcohol and return to traditional seasonal rituals. In subsequent visions Handsome Lake claimed to have visited heaven and hell, to have met with George Washington and Jesus, and to have been provided with a code forbidding sexual promiscuity, gambling, and spousal abuse. He remained a strong proponent of traditional Seneca religious beliefs, and the modern Iroquois Longhouse religion has been shaped by his efforts. None of these admonitions threatened Seneca women, but Handsome Lake also taught that the Senecas should adopt selected aspects of the white man's culture, including small, male-dominated, nuclear households. He also urged the Senecas to farm like white people and to send their children to school, and warned against the interference of Seneca mothers in their daughters' daily lives.

Handsome Lake's religion attracted many adherents, and in the long run it provided a viable alternative to the total acculturation urged by the American Indian agents and missionaries. The new faith allowed the Senecas and other Iroquois to adopt certain non-Indian social and economic patterns, while they still retained much of their old religious faith. But Handsome Lake's teachings did weaken the role of women in Iroquois society. Although few Seneca men embraced agriculture, women's role in this economic activity contracted and they began to focus on secondary activities such as the manufacture of crafts, trade, or even domestic service in nearby non-Indian communities. Some continued as active behind-the-scenes negotiators in tribal politics, but their previous role as powerful leaders of a political structure dominated by matrilineal clans diminished.

The Shawnee Prophet and Tecumseh

Other revitalization programs were not so successful. Like the Iroquois, the Shawnees also had suffered from land loss, alcoholism, and white injustice, but in 1805, when an alcoholic, ne'er-do-well Shawnee medicine man experienced a series of visions, the short-term impact was profound. Born in 1774 as one of a set of triplets, Lalawethika (the "Noisemaker") was a younger brother of Tecumseh (a Shawnee war chief) who had been abandoned by his Creek mother during the American Revolution. His childhood spent amidst the tumultuous years of the Revolution and border warfare, Lalawethika was never a warrior, but following Fallen Timbers he lived in a small village of conservative Shawnees led by his older brother, Tecumseh.

In 1805 Lalawethika fell into a trance so profound that other Shawnees believed he had died. He emerged after several hours and reported that he had visited heaven and hell, where he was shown the rewards for the virtuous, but also the tortures awaiting sinners, particularly alcoholics like himself. Subsequent visions provided Lalawethika with additional spiritual guidance and he admonished the Shawnees to abandon alcohol, respect their elders, strengthen traditional family ties, and return to the old ways. He also changed his name from Lalawethika to Tenskwatawa, or "the Open Door."

In contrast to Handsome Lake, Tenskwatawa (known to non-Indians as "the Shawnee Prophet") did not urge cooperation with the Americans. According to Tenskwatawa, the Indians (and the British and French) had been created by the Master of Life, the primary force for good in the universe, but the Americans were the children of the "Great Serpent," the Shawnee embodiment of evil. The Prophet urged his followers to shun American food, clothing, and other goods and condemned those Indians who adopted American technology and culture as "witches." In March 1806, he condemned some Moravian converts among the Delawares in Indiana as "witches," and the Delawares burned five of the accused converts (including one woman) at the stake. Moravian missionaries appealed to American Indian agents for assistance, and in response William Henry Harrison, governor of Indiana Territory, challenged the Prophet to prove his supernatural power by causing "the sun to stand still—the moon to alter its course—the rivers to cease to flow—or the dead to rise from their graves."

On June 16, 1806, Tenskwatawa predicted a total eclipse of the sun, and following the eclipse, his influence spread like wildfire throughout the Great Lakes and Ohio Valley. The Prophet and Tecumseh established a new village, Prophetstown, near the juncture of the Tippecanoe and Wabash

Tenskwatawa, the Shawnee Prophet Tenskwatawa survived the War of 1812 and sought refuge in Canada, but he eventually returned to the United States. He died in Kansas in 1836.

rivers in western Indiana, and Tecumseh used his brother's religious movement as the basis for uniting Indians in the Midwest. In 1809 and 1810 Tecumseh traveled throughout the region, arguing that no more lands be ceded to the government and that people from all tribes should unite under his leadership.

The Shawnee Prophet and Tecumseh were opposed by traditional village chiefs such as Little Turtle, whose influence was threatened by their movement. In September 1809, after Harrison purchased over 3,000,000 acres of Illinois and Indiana from friendly chiefs at the Treaty of Fort Wayne, Tecumseh strengthened his ties with the British and then journeyed to the South, attempting to bring the warriors from the southern tribes into his confederacy. He met with little success among the Choctaws and Chickasaws, but he received a favorable reception among the Upper Creeks, who also had produced several anti-American prophets. Unfortunately for Tecumseh, while he was in the South, Harrison marched against Prophetstown and in the resulting Battle of Tippecanoe (November 7, 1811) killed at least fifty

INDIAN VOICES — Tecumseh Demands That the British Honor Their Promises!

Although Native Americans are often stereotyped as a stoic, taciturn people, they possess a rich oral tradition that has enabled them to retain traditional stories that illustrate their cultural values. Many tribal languages are replete with an abundance of descriptive terms that empower Native American speakers with the ability both to persuade and inspire their audiences. Native American history is filled with stirring speeches (some actual, some apocryphal) by Indian orators that have been preserved through the eyewitness accounts, but unquestionably one of the most eloquent addresses ever delivered by a Native American leader was delivered by Tecumseh, the great Shawnee war chief, on September 18, 1813, as the British army was preparing to abandon its post at Amherstburg and flee from the Americans.

During the summer of 1813 the British and Indians had suffered several defeats by the Americans, most notably Commodore Oliver Perry's defeat of the British fleet on Lake Erie on September 9. Afraid that Americans might land an army in his rear, cutting off his supply routes and any opportunity to retreat, Colonel Henry Proctor prepared to abandon Amherstburg, (opposite Detroit) and withdraw toward Lake Ontario. Envisioning the British flight as disgraceful, Tecumseh delivered an impassioned speech, denouncing the British as cowards and pleading with them either to stand and face the Americans or surrender their weapons to the Indians. The British interpreters who heard the original oration, delivered in the Shawnee language, were so frightened by Tecumseh's comments that they feared the Indians in the audience might rise up and attack the British officers. Although the English translation presents only a tempered, more moderate version of Tecumseh remarks, the speech remains inspirational; its more powerful impact in its original form can only be imagined. To what was Tecumseh referring when he complained that "when we retreated to our father's fort . . . the gates were shut fast against us"?

> FATHER, listen to your children! You have them now all before you. The war before this, our British father gave the hatchet to his red children, when our chiefs were alive. They are now dead. In that war our father was thrown on his back by the Americans, and our father took them by the hand without our knowledge; and we are afraid that our father will do so again this time.
>
> Summer before last, when I came forward with my red brethren, and was ready to take up the hatchet in favor of our British father, we were told not to be in a hurry, that he had not yet determined to fight the Americans.
>
> Listen! When war was declared, our father stood up and gave us the tomahawk, and told us that he was then ready to strike the Americans; that he wanted our assistance and that he would certainly get us our lands back, which the Americans had taken from us.
>
> Listen! You told us, at that time, to bring forward our families to this place; and we did; and you promised to take care of them, and that they should want for nothing, while the men would go away and fight the enemy. That we need not trouble ourselves about the enemy's garrison; that we knew nothing about them,

Tecumseh.

Tecumseh Based on a sketch by Pierre Le Dru, this engraving of Tecumseh is considered by most historians to be the most accurate likeness of him.

and that our father would take care of that part of the business. You also told your red children, that you would take care of your garrison here, which made our hearts glad.

Listen! When we were last at the Rapids, it is true we gave you little assistance. It is hard to fight people who live like ground hogs.

Father listen! Our fleet has gone out; we know they have fought; we have heard the great guns; but we know nothing of what has happened to our father with one arm. Our ships have gone one way and we are astonished to see our father tying up everything and preparing to run away the other, without letting his red children know what his intentions are. You always told us to remain here and take care of our lands; it made our hearts glad to hear that was your wish. Our great father, the king, is our head, and you represent him. You always told us you would never draw your foot off British ground; but now, father we see you are drawing back, and we are sorry to see our father doing so without seeing the enemy. We must compare our father's conduct to a fat animal [camp dog], that carries its tail upon its back, but when affrighted, he drops it between its legs and runs off.

Listen Father! The Americans have not yet defeated us by land; neither are we sure that they have done so by water; we, therefore, wish to remain here, and fight our enemy, if they should make their appearance. If they defeat us, we will then retreat with our father.

At the battle of the Rapids last war, the Americans certainly defeated us; and when we retreated to our father's fort at that place the gates were shut against us. We were afraid that it would now be the case; but instead of that we now see our British father preparing to march out of his garrison.

Father! You have got the arms and ammunition which our great father sent for his red children. If you have an idea of going away, give them to us and you may go and welcome. For us, our lives are in the hands of the Great Spirit. We are determined to defend our lands, and if it be his will we wish to leave our bones upon them.

Source: Speech of Tecumseh, September 18, 1813, in Logan Esarey, ed., *Messages and Letters of William Henry Harrison,* 2 vols. (Indianapolis: Indiana Historical Commission,1922), vol. 2, 541–543.

---

of Tecumseh's followers, burned Prophetstown, and destroyed the Indians, accumulated stores of food and ammunition. The Shawnee Prophet survived the battle, but his religious influence was much diminished.

Tecumseh returned to the Midwest in mid-January 1812 and immediately began to rebuild his confederacy. In early July he met with British agents at Amherstburg in Canada and learned that war had broken out between the British and Americans. The conflict split most of the midwestern tribes into pro-British and pro-American factions, and Tecumseh assumed command of those who favored the Crown. He led a large party of warriors who assisted British forces in the capture of Detroit, while other war parties defeated the garrison at Fort Dearborn (Chicago), captured Fort Michilimackinac in Michigan, and besieged Fort Wayne in Indiana. During 1813, however, the war turned in the Americans' favor. Two British and Indian attempts to capture Fort Meigs, an American post near Toledo, Ohio, proved unsuccessful, as did a subsequent assault against Fort Stephenson, a small post on the Sandusky River.

After Captain Oliver Perry defeated the British fleet on Lake Erie on September 10, 1813, the Americans gained the initiative and the British prepared to abandon Amherstburg and flee toward Toronto. Angered by the British withdrawal, Tecumseh met with Major Henry Proctor, the British commander, and denounced the British for their vacillation, weakness, and lack of courage (see Indian Voices). The British still retreated, but

goaded by Tecumseh, they finally stood against the approaching Americans at the Thames River on October 5, 1813. In the resulting battle the British fled after firing only three volleys, while Tecumseh and about 700 warriors were left to face 3,200 Americans. In the subsequent fighting Tecumseh was killed and the Indians were defeated. With Tecumseh's death, his attempt to unite the western Indians and preserve an autonomous Indian territory ended. In the aftermath of the War of 1812, Indian lands in the Ohio Valley and Great Lakes region eventually would be gobbled up by the government, and the tribes would lose both their homelands and their autonomy.

Creeks and Red Sticks

Although few southern tribespeople had rallied to Tecumseh's cause, his mission to the Creeks accelerated a growing rift within the Creek Confederacy and contributed to a Creek civil war, which was heightened by the subsequent participation of the Americans. In 1796 Benjamin Hawkins had been appointed as the Indian agent among the Creeks and he had gained considerable influence among the Lower Creeks in Georgia, many of whom began to subscribe to the government's "civilization" programs. Most Upper Creeks rejected Hawkins's efforts, but they quarreled among themselves. Some followed Big Warrior, a village chief from Tuckabatchee who disliked Hawkins but who personally profited from ferries, taverns, and other commercial ventures along the federal road that bisected the Creek homeland. Other Upper Creeks opposed Big Warrior, resented his personal gains, and were wary of his ties to nontraditional Cherokees and Chickasaws. These more traditional Upper Creeks may have nurtured a nascent religious revitalization movement prior to 1811, but after Tecumseh visited their villages, the movement gained momentum.

Several Creek prophets emerged, including Josiah Francis, Captain Isaacs, and Peter McQueen, most of whom were of mixed lineage. Early in 1813 the prophets quarreled among themselves. They then turned on those village chiefs who had cooperated with either Big Warrior or Hawkins, killing several and forcing others to flee for their lives. Since the prophets' followers carried red war clubs as a mark of identification, they became known as "Red Sticks."

Hawkins denounced the Red Sticks as "rebels," and in July 1813 frontier militia or "irregulars" attacked a party of Red Sticks at Burnt Corn Creek in southern Alabama as these Creeks returned home from Spanish Florida. In retaliation, one month later the Red Sticks assaulted Fort Mims, a poorly defended, half-finished stockade on the Alabama River where many of the irregulars, including some Creeks who opposed the Red Sticks, and their families had sought sanctuary. The Red Sticks overwhelmed the fort and killed all those irregulars or other Creeks who either defended the post or had taken refuge in it.

Their victory at Fort Mims proved disastrous for the Red Sticks. Alarmed by the attack, the states of Georgia and Tennessee and the territory of Mississippi sent troops into the Creek homeland, and what had been a civil war among the Creeks now became a war between the Red Sticks and the Americans. Assisted by many Lower Creeks along with some Cherokees and Choctaws, the Americans laid waste to the Red Stick towns, killing men, women, and children. The warfare ended on March 27, 1814, when Andrew Jackson led 1,500 Americans, 500 Cherokees, and 100 pro-American Lower Creeks against Tohopeka, a heavily fortified Red Stick town built at a horseshoe bend on the Tallapoosa River. The remaining Red Sticks fought well but were overwhelmed. The Americans killed over 800 warriors and captured 350 Creek women and children. All the Creek prophets were either killed or fled the Creek homeland.

On August 9, 1814, Andrew Jackson forced the Creeks to sign the Treaty of Fort Jackson, which transferred over twenty million acres of southern Georgia and central Alabama to the United States. Ironically, most of this land was claimed and occupied by Lower Creeks friendly to the United States, many of whom had fought *with* Jackson *against* the Red Sticks. Nevertheless, the ceded territory held potentially good farmland and was more desirable to American settlers than the region occupied by the Red Sticks. The treaty provided a portent of things to come. Not even Indian people who befriended the Americans would be immune from their land hunger. Tribes could not rely on the goodwill of the government. The future would be full of empty promises.

CONCLUSION: THE END OF THE BEGINNING

The American victories over Tecumseh's coalition and the Red Sticks in Alabama marked a major turning point for the tribes east of the Mississippi. In most of their previous military confrontations with the colonial powers or with the new American republic, the tribes could rely on military, or at least logistical, assistance from other Europeans. If Native Americans attacked the British, the French furnished arms and ammunition; or if warriors fought to keep the Long Knives from the Ohio Country, the British sent muskets and gunpowder. Moreover, the tribes themselves often had attempted to balance the fulcrum in the European contests for North America, playing the British against the French or the Spaniards against the Americans. But following the Treaty of Ghent, which ended the War of 1812, the British no longer supported Indian resistance to the Americans and Spanish political hegemony over Florida was tenuous at best; the Spaniards dared not anger the Americans by providing arms and ammunition to the tribes. Consequently, the eastern tribes, soundly defeated during the War of 1812, were left on their own. They no longer could rely on outside assistance.

In response, those tribes who remained east of the Mississippi searched for other, nonmilitary methods to protect their remaining lands and political autonomy. Their options were limited. Some clung to the ways of their fathers, attempting to eke out an existence within a shrinking land base, while others adopted selected cultural patterns from the Europeans or Americans who now surrounded them. In choosing the second path, many tribespeople partially subscribed to the government's "civilization" programs. They accepted the assurances of both Indian agents and missionaries that their compliance with the government's agenda of changing land tenure and new gender roles would enable them to retain their homelands and maintain some semblance of political autonomy. They would learn, however, that neither the Indian agents nor the missionaries spoke for frontier settlers, who soon would infest their lands like fleas on a camp dog. American demands for fertile agricultural lands cast an ominous shadow over the remaining tribal territory east of the Mississippi. The tribes would be hard-pressed to retain their homes.

The opening decades of the nineteenth century also signaled another turning point in the relationship between Native Americans and non-Indians. Since the eastern Mississippi Valley was now open to white settlement, the government shifted its focus toward the trans-Mississippi west. In 1803 the American government had acquired the Louisiana Territory from France, and one year later President Thomas Jefferson had dispatched Lewis and Clark up the Missouri River to meet with the western tribes. Any significant extension of American influence into the region had been interrupted by the War of 1812, but by 1815, the war had ended. Tribespeople in the trans-Mississippi west soon would face the same incursion of outsiders that had earlier plagued and overwhelmed their brothers and sisters east of the river.

SUGGESTED READINGS

Berkhofer, Robert. *Salvation and the Savage: An Analysis of Protestant Missions and the American Indian Response.* New York: Atheneum Press, 1972. An excellent analysis of the Protestant missionary efforts and their impact on tribal communities.

Calloway, Colin G. *Crown and Calumet: British-Indian Relations, 1783–1815.* Norman: University of Oklahoma Press, 1987. This volume provides a good survey of the continued British influence among the tribes, particularly among the Indians of the Old Northwest.

Dowd, Gregory. *A Spirited Resistance: The Native American Struggle for Unity, 1745–1815.* Baltimore: Johns Hopkins University Press, 1992. The author argues persuasively that the Indian confederacy of the 1790s and Tecumseh's efforts to unify the tribes were part of a larger attempt by tribes in the Old Northwest to form politically centralized confederacies.

Edmunds, R. David. *The Shawnee Prophet.* Lincoln: University of Nebraska Press, 1983. The volume illustrates that Tecumseh's attempt to unify the tribes grew out of his brother's religious revitalization movement.

————. *Tecumseh and the Quest for Indian Leadership.* Boston: Little, Brown and Co., 1984. This biography of Tecumseh separates the man from the myth and analyzes Tecumseh's lasting appeal to non-Indians.

Martin, Joel. *Sacred Revolt: The Muskogee Struggle for a New World.* Boston: Beacon Press, 1991. The volume examines Creek cosmology and its role in the coming of the Red Stick War, 1812–1813.

McLoughlin, Charles. *Cherokees and Missionaries, 1789–1832.* New Haven: Yale University Press, 1984. An excellent survey of the interaction between Cherokees and missionaries and the impact of the missionary effort on Cherokee culture during these years.

Prucha, Francis Paul. *The Great Father: The United States Government and the American Indian,* 2 vols. Lincoln: University of Nebraska Press, 1984. This detailed, comprehensive survey of American Indian policy constitutes the best volumes ever published on this subject. An excellent reference work.

Saunt, Claudio. *A New Order of Things: Property, Power, and the Transformation of the Creek Indians, 1733–1816.* Cambridge: Cambridge University Press, 1999. An excellent study of the evolution of Creek society in the decades following the American Revolution.

Schultz, George A. *An Indian Canaan: Isaac McCoy and the Vision of an Indian State.* Norman: University of Oklahoma Press, 1972.   This volume offers an interesting case study of Protestant mission efforts among the tribes of Michigan and Indiana.

Sheehan, Bernard. *Seeds of Destruction: Jeffersonian Philanthropy and the American Indian.* New York: W. W. Norton and Co., 1973.   This scholarly analysis of Jefferson's Indian policies and other "civilization" programs argues that although they were well-intentioned, they ultimately had a negative impact on the tribes.

Sugden, John. *Blue Jacket: Warrior of the Shawnees.* Lincoln: University of Nebraska Press, 2000.   A detailed biography of a Shawnee war chief that offers a good account of Indian resistance to the government during the border wars following the American Revolution.

Wallace, Anthony F. C. *The Death and Rebirth of the Seneca.* New York: Alfred A. Knopf, 1970.   A classic study of cultural change and religious revitalization among the Senecas in New York and Pennsylvania.

Western Tribes Meet
the Long Knives, 1800–1820

The expedition of Americans did not intimidate them. On the evening of September 24, 1804, Brulé Lakota leaders Black Buffalo, the Partisan, and Buffalo Medicine gathered with their advisers around council fires in their village near the mouth of the Bad River in modern South Dakota. They were concerned about the flotilla of keel boats and pirogues that had ascended the Missouri River past the Otoe-Missouria and Omaha villages, but the Brulés had often browbeaten traders from St. Louis who paddled up the river and they expected the new party of Americans to pay them a heavy tribute in trade goods and other materials. The Brulé leaders were angered, however, by reports that this much larger party of Americans had met with other Indian people, urging them to trade directly with American merchants and had offered them political alliances that threatened Lakota interests. During the past half century the Lakotas had used their superior numbers and military power to dominate the middle Missouri Valley, and the Brulés had no intention of sharing their position with these newcomers.

On the following morning, the Brulé leaders and about one hundred of their warriors met on an island near the mouth of the Bad River with Meriwether Lewis, William Clark, and other members of their expedition. The meeting did not go well. Both sides postured, parleyed, and exchanged gifts (the Lakotas offered buffalo meat; the Americans, medals, clothing, and small amounts of whiskey), but Black Buffalo and the Partisan remained suspicious of the Americans' intentions, and on several occasions the two sides almost came to blows. The talks continued for six days, with the Americans periodically firing several small cannons in a futile attempt to impress the Lakotas, while the Indians invited Lewis and Clark into their village, served them a feast of roasted buffalo meat and boiled dog (a great delicacy), and then held a dance in their behalf.

Yet the two sides continued to distrust each other. Although Lewis and Clark advised the Brulés that they lived in a territory now belonging to the United States, the admonition meant little to the Indians. From the Brulés' perspective, the Americans were interlopers in their domain. Like other Native American people in the trans-Mississippi west, they were part of a larger political and economic system of their own making. The Americans were from a different world. Treaties signed in eastern states or in Europe had little meaning to these Indians. The West remained Indian country, where

INDIAN VOICES

A Piegan (Blackfoot) Describes the Arrival of Horses

The arrival of both horses and Europeans onto the northern Plains brought profound changes for the tribes living in the region. While horses generally arrived from the south or west, firearms were traded onto the Plains from the north or east, first by Creole-French and later by British traders. The arrival of horses revolutionized bison hunting on the northern Plains and led to a material abundance undreamed of by earlier pedestrian buffalo hunters. No longer were hunters forced to scour the Plains on foot, hoping to drive small herds of bison over cliffs at kill-sites. The acquisition of horses enabled tribespeople to find the herds, kill the animals they needed, and transport surplus hides and dried meat that could then be traded for other items. Some historians have argued that horses were a mixed blessing for the Plains tribes since they altered the ecology of the Plains and changed the economic structure of some tribes. How? Why? The following account focuses on a Piegan's (Blackfoot's) recollection of the arrival of horses among his tribe and of how the animals and trade goods transformed the life of one Piegan leader.

The first horses we ever saw came from west of the mountains. A band of Piegans were camped on Belly River, at a place that we call "Smash the Head" [Head Smashed-In World Historic Site, near Calgary, in Alberta, Canada] where we hunted buffalo.

We had made a big drive, and had run a great lot of buffalo over the cliff . . . when suddenly the Kutenai [Kootenai, a tribe living in northern Idaho and southern British Columbia], on his horse, followed by his wife and children on theirs, rode over a hill nearby. When they saw them all the Piegans were astonished and wondered what this could be. None of them had ever seen anything like it, and they were afraid. They thought it was something mysterious. The chief of the Piegans called out to his people, "This is something very strange. I have heard of wonderful things that have happened from the earliest times, but I never heard of anything like this."

As it drew nearer, they could see that it was a man coming, and that he was on some strange animal. The Piegans wanted their chief to go toward the man and speak to him. The chief did not wish to do this; he was afraid; but . . . when he got near to him the Kutenai made signs that he was friendly, and patted his horse on the neck. The Kutenai rode into the camp and were received as friends.

The Kutenai stayed with the Piegans for some time, and the Kutenai man told the chief that he had more horses at his camp up in the mountains, and that beyond the mountains there were plenty of horses. He asked the Kutenai to bring in the rest of his horses; and the next day [he] came back driving all his horses before him, and they came to camp, and all the people saw them and looked at them and wondered. . . .

When they first got horses, the people did not know what they fed on. They would offer the horses pieces of dried meat, or they would take a piece of back-fat and rub their noses with it, to try to get them to eat it. Then the horses would turn away and put down their heads, and begin to eat the grass on the prairie. . . .

> White people had begun to come into the country, and Many Horses' [a Piegan chief] young men wanted ropes and iron arrow-points and saddle blankets, and the people were beginning to kill furs and skins for trade. Many Horses began to trade with his own people for these things. He would ask the young men of the tribe to kill skins for him, and they would bring them to him and he would give them a horse or two in exchange. Then he would send his relations in to Hudson's Bay post to trade. . . .
>
> At length, one winter, these white men packed their dog sleds with goods and started to see Many Horses. They took with them guns. When these came to Many Horses' camp, they asked where Many Horses' lodge was. . . . The whites went to this lodge and began to unpack their things—guns, clothing, knives, and goods of all kinds.
>
> Then these white men began to distribute the guns, and with each gun they gave a bundle of powder and ball. At the same time, the young men received white blankets and the old men black coats. Then we first got knives, and the white men showed us how to use knives; to split down the legs and rip up the belly—to skin for trade.
>
> Source: Nabakov, Peter, ed., *Native American Testimony*, rev. ed. (New York: Penguin Books, 1999), 42–44. (Taken from George Bird Grinnell, *Story of the Indian* [New York: Appleton Publishing Company, 1895].)

tribal people and their ways still held sway. On September 29, 1804, when Lewis and Clark left their encampment and proceeded on up the Missouri to the Arikara villages, the Lakotas were glad to see them go. The Americans were a nuisance, but the Brulés still dominated the trade on the river.

The Brulé Lakota response to Lewis and Clark reflected the political and economic reality of the Great Plains and Rocky Mountain regions in 1800. During the previous century new tribes and new technologies had moved onto the Plains, displacing earlier residents or forcing them to alter their ways of life (see Chapter 5). The introduction of horses changed the Plains from an undesirable, windswept region with plentiful bison but little wood, water, or other necessities to a region that attracted newly mounted tribes who could traverse the vast distances, harvesting bison and trading with each other.

The primary beneficiaries of the horses were women. Prior to the introduction of horses, most food, clothing, or other commodities were carried by women or packed on camp dogs, and women could never stockpile large amounts of food or clothing because only a limited quantity of goods could be carried. But horses revolutionized their lives. Since horses now could carry heavy loads of food, clothing, and other materials, women could prepare surplus quantities of these commodities and easily transport them. Moreover, horses enabled Plains nomads to enlarge the size of their teepees, since the animals could carry much longer teepee poles and larger lodge-skins. Clothing, buffalo robes, and other material things now filled the enlarged teepees, and the quality of the nomads' lives improved dramatically.

Throughout the West, tribes vied with one another for control over hunting grounds, for pelts for the fur trade, and for the distribution of European or American trade goods. By 1800 Indian people had become more dependent on European and American technology, but Euro-American political influence in the region remained minimal; most of the tribes retained their political autonomy. Americans or Europeans venturing into the region entered a realm where Indian people still conducted their lives according to their own motives, not as pawns or in response to the whims of American or European politics. The Great Plains, Rocky Mountain region, and much of the Pacific Northwest remained Indian country, but it was poised on the brink of change. In 1803 the United States purchased Louisiana from the French, and it was eager to explore and exploit its new purchase. The political and economic autonomy of the western tribes soon would be threatened. A floodtide of change was coming, and it did not bode well for Native Americans.

BEFORE LEWIS AND CLARK

While Indian people east of the Mississippi fought to retain their lands and adjusted to federal Indian policies, the intertribal balance of power was changing on the northern Plains. Prior to the American Revolution sedentary village dwellers along the central and upper Missouri River valley had dominated intertribal trade, but the entrance of the Lakotas (Sioux) onto the Plains destroyed this dominance and engendered a series of tribal migrations that altered demographic patterns in the region.

The western Lakotas were separated into three large divisions: the Tetons, the Yanktons, and the Yanktonais. In turn the Tetons (the most westerly of the group) were split into seven smaller components or bands: the Oglalas, Brulés, Hunkapapas, Minneconjous, Sans Arcs, Two Kettles, and Sihaspas. Each band, in turn, divided into smaller hunting villages of extended family groups. In the mid-eighteenth century Lakota hunters, who obtained firearms from French and British traders, advanced out of the upper Midwest onto the prairies of western Iowa and Minnesota, where they gradually pushed Omaha, Otoe, and Iowa hunters west of the Missouri River. Meanwhile, the Lakotas themselves were pushed westward by the Ojibwes, who expanded into eastern Minnesota.

With newly acquired horses, the Lakotas moved onto the Plains, but their westward march initially was blocked by Arikara, Mandan, and Hidatsa tribespeople who lived in sedentary villages along the Missouri River, in modern North and South Dakota. These village tribes resisted the Lakota advance, but their large, earthen-house villages made them particularly vulnerable to disease. In the late eighteenth century, smallpox spread up the Missouri Valley as far as the Blackfeet Confederacy in Montana. The village tribes were decimated. Jean Baptiste Truteau, a trader among the Arikaras, reported that by 1795 the Arikaras' population had dropped from almost 20,000 to 3,000, and the Mandans and Hidatsas also suffered significant losses. Even the Omahas, living in northeastern Nebraska, shrank from 700 to 300 warriors during these decades. Less vulnerable were the more nomadic Lakotas, whose widely dispersed camps were not located on the Missouri corridor. They suffered some losses, but they enjoyed a high birth rate and their ranks were swelled by additional immigrants from Minnesota. Raids by the more numerous Lakotas forced the Mandans and Hidatsas into a defensive alliance, while the Lakotas crossed the Missouri and ranged as far west as the Black Hills. By 1800 they were the dominant military power on the northern Plains, and their hunters ranged as far west as the mouth of the Yellowstone.

Lakota expansion on the northern Plains sparked a dispersal of other tribes. The Kiowas, who had resided near the Black Hills, migrated south to the Wichita Mountains in southwestern Oklahoma. The Crows retreated westward into southern Montana. The Cheyennes and Arapahos formed a loose alliance, then split into two bi-tribal divisions: the southern Cheyennes and Arapahos, who relocated to western Kansas and eastern Colorado; and the northern Cheyennes and Arapahos, who remained in eastern Wyoming and allied themselves with their new Lakota neighbors. By the 1820s the Lakota-Cheyenne-Arapaho alliance (led by the Lakotas) dominated the northern Plains from the lower Yellowstone and Missouri rivers as far south as Nebraska. They pushed the Pawnees, another earth-lodge people, from their former hunting grounds along the Loup River, and the Pawnees were forced to regroup south of the Platte, where they sought new alliances with other people, including the Americans.

While the Lakota emergence created a new balance of power on the northern Plains, similar changes were taking place south of the Arkansas River. Prior to the American Revolution the southern Plains had been dominated by an alliance between the Wichitas, a Caddoan-speaking people, and the Comanches. The Wichitas, who resided in heavily thatched, grass houses along the Red River and headwaters of the Brazos and Trinity, were a semisedentary people who not only grew gardens of vegetables but also hunted buffalo on the Plains. In contrast, the Comanches prospered in the "livestock business." The Comanches were a Shoshonean-speaking people from the Great Basin and were closely related to the Shoshones, or Snakes, of central Wyoming (the movement for both tribes in Plains sign language is a wavy horizontal movement of the hand and lower arm). Attracted to the southern Plains by the large herds of bison and wild horses and by the considerable number of horses and mules available near the Spanish settlements, the Comanches were described

Indian Women Moving Camp, by Charles Russell Although horses enabled men to hunt bison more efficiently, they also greatly increased the quality of women's lives. With horses, women could transport food, clothing, and lodge poles for larger teepees much more easily.

as short, stocky, ungainly people afoot, but as superb horsemen. Allied with the Wichitas, they had pushed the Lipan and Jicarilla Apaches into the desert Southwest, and although they too had suffered from a smallpox epidemic, their dispersed population had protected them from heavy losses. By 1800 the Comanches numbered between 15,000 and 20,000 people. Moreover, the Comanche language had become the lingua franca of the region.

After 1790 the Kiowas, who emigrated from the Black Hills region to Oklahoma, joined the Wichita-Comanche alliance. The Kiowas were closely associated with a small band of Apaches (Kiowa-Apaches) who generally followed the Kiowa leadership and who became secondary members of the Wichita-Comanche-Kiowa coalition. Although the Kiowa population rarely exceeded 2,000, they exerted an influence disproportionate to their numbers. Described by early American observers as "large, athletic, fine-looking people" who were "admirably equipped" and who dressed "in a style surpassing in richness and elegance" all the other

tribes on the southern Plains, the Kiowas were extroverted people who amassed large herds of horses. They settled in the Wichita Mountains in southwestern Oklahoma and joined with the Wichitas to defend their newfound homeland from the Osages, who hunted into the region from western Missouri.

The southern Cheyennes and Arapahos were the final tribes to enter the southern Plains. Tall, slender, graceful people, the Cheyennes and Arapahos both spoke Algonquian languages loosely related to those spoken by many tribes of the Great Lakes region. They hunted across western Kansas, southeastern Colorado, and northwestern Oklahoma. During the 1830s many traded regularly at Bent's Fort, a trading post on the Arkansas River in Colorado. In the early 1800s the southern Cheyennes numbered 300 lodges, or 1,500 people, while the more numerous southern Arapahos counted slightly over 2,000. Their southern migration initially was opposed by the Kiowas and Comanches, who resented their bison hunting in the Texas and

Oklahoma panhandles, but both sides eventually made peace and the Cheyennes and Arapahos established new villages in northwestern Oklahoma.

If the Lakotas dominated the northern Plains, the Comanches played a similar role south of the Arkansas. Both tribes served as intermediaries in an extensive trade system that exchanged bison hides, horses, and other commodities for trade goods manufactured by Europeans and Americans. Unlike the Lakotas, the Comanches and their trading partners focused their activities on the Spanish frontier, which served as the source of part of their merchandise (horses and mules) and also as an outlet for hides and livestock obtained from other locations. On both the northern and southern Plains, tribal people participated in highly integrated political and economic networks that maintained an evolving (if sometimes precarious) political balance and facilitated the flow of goods and livestock. Few of the major participants envisioned the need for any major American presence. Both the Lakotas and Comanches (and their allies) preferred to keep the Americans on the periphery of their world, as a distant customer or as a source of trade goods, not as an active participant in Plains trade or politics.

THE TRIBES ENCOUNTER LEWIS AND CLARK

American influence on the Plains had been limited prior to 1803. The region had been claimed first by Spain, then by France, but in 1803 American agents purchased Louisiana from France. Thomas Jefferson was eager to learn more about the region's topography, plants and animals, and inhabitants. He believed that British traders threatened American control of the area, and he hoped to bind the tribes of the northern Plains to American merchants along the Missouri and Mississippi. In 1803 he instructed Meriwether Lewis and William Clark to ascend the Missouri River, find a passage over the Rocky Mountains, and descend the Columbia River to the Pacific. In addition the explorers and their party were ordered to establish good relations with all the tribes along their route, but "particularly . . . because of their immense power . . . to make a favorable impression" on the Teton Lakotas.

The Plains Tribes

On May 14, 1804, accompanied by about forty-five men—including George Drouillard, a mixed-lineage Shawnee who served as the expedition's chief hunter and scout, and York, Clark's African-American slave—the expedition left Wood River, Illinois, and ascended the Missouri. On August 3 they reached Council Bluffs, where they were welcomed by a delegation of Otoe and Missouria leaders. The Otoes and Missourias were eager to obtain inexpensive trade goods but were unimpressed when Lewis announced that their homeland now was part of the United States. The Indians promised to live in peace with the Omahas, who lived nearby but were hunting buffalo on the Plains, but Lewis was disappointed that they seemed so indifferent to an American political alliance, and the expedition continued up the Missouri to the mouth of the James, where they met with the Yankton Lakotas. The Yanktons also were friendly, but they too preferred trade goods to political ties to the United States.

On September 23, 1804, the expedition reached the mouth of the Bad River, near modern Pierre, South Dakota, where they encountered the Brulé band of the Teton Lakota (see the opening discussion in this chapter). The Brulés did not relish the prospect of either the United States or merchants from St. Louis developing direct ties with neighboring tribes, and they envisioned the expedition as a threat to their dominance of the middle Missouri Valley. Although Lewis and Clark repeatedly asked Black Buffalo and the Partisan to guarantee safe passage for American traders through their territory, the Brulé leaders warily refused. On September 28, as the expedition left camp and set sail up the river, the Brulés and Americans almost came to blows, and only Black Buffalo's intercession kept the Partisan and his followers from firing on the expedition's vessels. The Brulés remained defiant, and writing in his journal, Clark denounced them as "the pirates of the Missouri." The expedition reached the Arikara villages clustered around the mouth of the Grand River in northern South Dakota in early October. Lewis and Clark believed the Arikaras were victims of Lakota aggression and assumed that the Arikaras would welcome a political and economic alliance with the United States, but their presumptions were naive and reflected their ignorance of tribal politics.

A sedentary village people, the Arikaras, like the Mandans and Hidatsas who resided further upstream, lived in large earthen lodges and grew extensive crops of corn, beans, and squash. They supplemented their agriculture by hunting buffalo on the Plains, and during the fall Arikara hunters often were absent for weeks at a time securing meat and hides for the winter. But the Arikaras maintained a symbiotic relationship with their Lakota neighbors, purchasing meat and manufactured goods from the Lakotas in exchange for agricultural products and horses, which the Arikaras procured from the Cheyennes, Kiowas, and tribes to the southwest. Indeed, during August and September the Arikara villages were the scene of a trade fair where the Arikaras met with Lakotas, Cheyennes, and other tribes to barter products much in demand in the intertribal trade. Moreover, the Arikaras and Lakotas often joined together to make war on the Mandans and Hidatsas, whose trading activities rivaled the Arikara-Lakota axis.

Although the Arikaras were friendlier to Lewis and Clark than the Lakotas, they were skeptical of the American proposals and had an agenda of their own. Lewis and Clark hoped to detach the Arikaras from the Lakotas as well as to negotiate a peace among the Arikaras, the Mandans, and the Hidatsas, eventually turning the Arikara, Mandan, and Hidatsa villages into expanding centers of American commerce and influence on the northern Plains. Arikara leaders rejected this proposal; they were unwilling to alienate their Teton Lakota allies in exchange for American promises. In addition, they distrusted the Mandans, with whom they had warred for decades. From the Arikara perspective, the American proposal was a pipe dream that would only bring ruin and Lakota retaliation. They treated the Americans hospitably, and one of their chiefs agreed to accompany Lewis and Clark to the Mandan and Hidatsa villages, but the Arikaras remained noncommittal; they believed the Lakotas were more powerful than the Americans.

On October 12, 1804, the expedition left the Arikara villages and proceeded up the Missouri into modern North Dakota. They arrived at two Mandan and three Hidatsa villages located near the juncture of the Knife and Missouri rivers two weeks later. Lewis and Clark met with Mandan and Hidatsa leaders on October 28, promoting their familiar agenda of American political influence, economic ties to St. Louis traders, an Arikara alliance, and in this case, an end to the Mandan-Hidatsa reliance on British traders. Since the Mandans and Hidatsas already were at war with the Lakotas and had nothing to lose, they seemed more receptive. They gave lip service to Lewis's promotion of an Arikara alliance, although they still distrusted their southern neighbors, but the Hidatsas, in particular, were reluctant to sever all their ties with the British Northwest Company.

Lewis and Clark spent the winter of 1804–1805 camped near the Mandan and Hidatsa villages, and their journals tell us much about the Mandan, Hidatsa, and Arikara way of life. All of these tribes spent much of their year residing in large earth-covered houses that were arranged in large, sometimes palisaded, villages along the bluffs overlooking the Missouri or its tributaries. A sedentary people, these Missouri River tribes relied heavily on farming. Using hoes fashioned from bison scapulae, village women cleared and cultivated fields of corn, beans, squash, tobacco, and sunflowers, which were planted in the river bottoms. After harvest, surplus crops were stored in food caches sunk into the ground. All three tribes supplemented their horticulture through hunting on the Plains, although by the late eighteenth century such activity was becoming more precarious as the result of the increased Lakota presence. Surprisingly, although they lived along the river, neither the Arikaras nor the Mandans and Hidatsas utilized fish, turtles, or shellfish as a significant part of their diet. They did construct bull-boats (round willow frames about six feet in diameter and covered with buffalo hide) to cross the river, but the washtub shaped vessels, propelled by a single paddle, were unwieldy and were not used for fishing or travel up and down the Missouri.

Even more than the Arikaras, the Mandans and Hidatsas were heavily involved in intertribal trade. Described as "the central market place of the northern plains," the Mandan and Hidatsa villages served as the focal point for a trade network stretching westward to the Cheyennes, Arapahos, and Crows. In exchange for agricultural products and manufactured goods, these Plains tribes brought horses, meat, and highly decorated leather garments. Meanwhile, from the north and northeast came Crees, Assiniboines, and Northwest Company traders from the Red River valley and southern Saskatchewan who carried firearms,

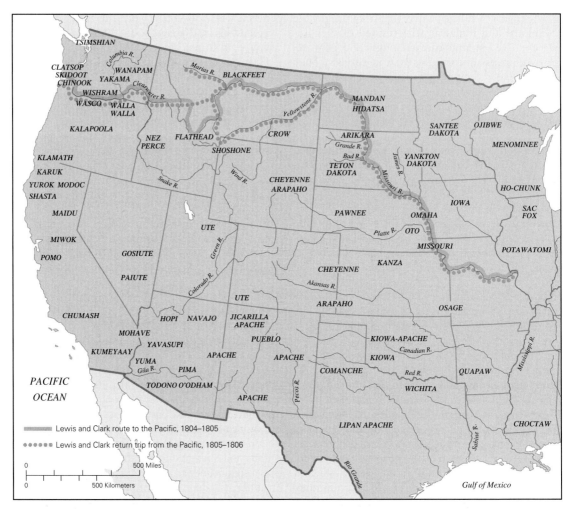

The Western Tribes in 1805. Based on A. M. Gibson, *The American Indian: Prehistory to the Present* (Boston: D. C. Heath, 1980), 63. *Reprinted with permission of Houghton Mifflin Company.*

ammunition, and other trade items. The Crows, Assiniboines, and Crees often were forced to run a Lakota gauntlet to reach the upper Missouri, but the highly attractive goods available in the Mandan and Arikara villages seemed worth the risk.

Mandan and Hidatsa politics bewildered the Americans. The two Mandan villages each were led by a separate chief and there is little evidence to indicate that either man exercised much influence outside his village. Unquestionably, Le Borgne, or

One Eye, was the most prominent chief among the three Hidatsa villages, which were joined through a twelve-member "tribal" council that met irregularly to discuss issues of war or defense. Yet most Hidatsas identified primarily with their family or kinship group, and any pretense of tribal unity disintegrated in personal, clan, or village rivalries that confused and irritated the Americans. Although Lewis and Clark promoted Black Cat of the Mandans and Le Borgne as the keystones on which to build a pro-American Arikara-Mandan-Hidatsa economic and political alliance, contesting Mandan and Hidatsa leaders attempted to use the American officers as pawns in their efforts to increase their own personal influence.

The Mandans and Hidatsas lived within structured societies that provided their members with a strong sense of group identity. The Mandans and Hidatsas were divided into a series of clans that transcended different villages, and by the middle decades of the nineteenth century even integrated members from both tribes. In theory the clans were exogamous (members could not marry within the clan) and when Lewis and Clark visited the villages marriage between clan members was forbidden, but later in the century, as the Mandan and Hidatsa populations declined, some of these bans were relaxed. Clan members provided each other with economic, social, and political assistance. Clans also owned certain medicine bundles and associated rituals, which always were connected with their kinship group and which were passed down through the generations to younger members of the clan.

In addition to clans, the Mandans and Hidatsas were members of age-graded societies that transcended clan lines and added cohesion to the communities. Divided by gender and age, these societies provided certain services and set standards of behavior for tribal members as they passed through various stages of their lives. For example, both the Mandans and the Hidatsas possessed warrior societies comprised of young men in the physical prime of their lives who were expected to form the vanguard in military action against the Lakotas or other enemies. When these young men reached middle age, however, they might join the Black Mouths, a society consisting of mature, responsible, middle-aged men who provided a limited, informal police function, particularly during the extended bison hunts. Women also joined societies based on their age and experience, and as they matured, they too passed from one society to the next.

The Mandan and Hidatsa clans and societies exerted effective, if informal social control over their members. They also engendered a strong sense of community. For most Mandans and Hidatsas, to achieve personal gain at the expense of other members of one's family, clan, or society was unthinkable, and the competitive individualism espoused by the Americans seemed both immoral and ill-conceived. Moreover, unlike the Americans, who lived within a society governed by statutory laws and who supported a formal, hierarchical political structure designed to enforce such regulations, the tribespeople existed in a society in which almost everyone shared a sense of what was expected of them, and peer pressure to conform to such expectations was intense. The Mandans and Hidatsas needed no written laws; the disapproval of one's friends and relatives loomed as an important social control, for to be shunned or excluded by members of one's kinship group was a horrible punishment.

Their lives also were filled with ceremonies. As with many other Native Americans, religion permeated Mandan and Hidatsa life, and the tribespeople believed that their ceremonies would assure a continuation of their existence. Because the ceremonies were seasonal, and in some cases very sacred and private, Lewis and Clark did not witness many of them.

The Okipa Ceremony, the most elaborate and unquestionably the most sacred of the Mandan celebrations, lasted four days and was associated with the summer bison hunt. It usually was sponsored by a Mandan warrior whose clan provided a series of feasts and distributed a quantity of goods to tribal members. The Okipa dramatized the Mandan's beliefs about their origins and beliefs embraced by many Plains tribes that the general well-being of the community was enhanced by the personal suffering or sacrifice of a few of its individuals. Part of the ceremony incorporated self-torture by young Mandan warriors who were suspended from the rafters of a ceremonial lodge by thongs under the skin of their backs or chests. Although the Mandans believed that such activity assured a good bison hunt and a bountiful harvest, American and European observers were shocked by the ceremony and often described it in sensational terms in their reports and journals.

Lewis, Clark, and other non-Native American observers who visited the Mandan, Hidatsa, and Arikara villages during the first third of the nineteenth century observed these societies in decline. They remained prosperous, viable communities, but they struggled to survive. The introduction of horses permanently altered the balance of power on the Plains. The pedestrian bison hunters who previously had been forced to stalk single bison while wearing the skins of wolves, or who had risked their lives attempting to drive bison herds over cliffs, readily adopted horses and became the new masters of the Plains. But the Mandans, Hidatsas, and Arikaras fared less well. Although they adopted horses and used them to transport meat and hides back from their annual bison hunts, the village tribes remained tied to their sedentary way of life. Their earthen lodges seemed too spacious and their gardens of corn, beans, and other vegetables too plentiful to risk in exchange for a new, nomadic life on the Plains. Too comfortable, too conservative, too set in their ways, the Mandans, Hidatsas, and Arikaras watched their former economic and political dominance fade as newly mounted and well-armed nomads contested their ability to hunt bison on the Plains or swept in to raid their villages. By the 1780s the balance of power on the northern Plains had changed, and it had not changed in the village tribes' favor.

Their sedentary villages also made the Mandans, Hidatsas, and Arikaras much more susceptible to smallpox. In October 1804, when Lewis and Clark visited the Arikaras, they complained that Arikara politics was plagued by a plethora of "captains without companies," since the chiefs of so many former villages had been forced to consolidate their surviving people into the three remaining Arikara settlements near the mouth of the Grand River. During the 1780s several epidemics had swept along the Missouri, taking significant tolls among both the nomads and the sedentary tribes, but in these early plagues the Arikaras, Mandans, and Hidatsas suffered the most casualties. Prior to 1780 the Arikaras had numbered over ten thousand, while the Mandan and Hidatsa villages probably numbered about six thousand to seven thousand apiece. When Lewis and Clark visited their villages, the Arikaras numbered twenty-five hundred; the Mandans, slightly over fifteen hundred; the Hidatsas, about twenty-one hundred. Yet the pestilence wasn't finished. Between 1804 and 1837 the Arikara, Mandan, and Hidatsa villages were visited by a growing number of Americans and Europeans—including artists Karl Bodmer and George Catlin, whose sketches and paintings provide a vivid visual record of the village tribes' life. Indeed, by the early 1830s the Mandan and Hidatsa villages had become popular stopping spots for both traders and other travelers along the Missouri, and although the Mandans and Hidatsas were often besieged by the Lakotas, they remained hospitable to Americans.

Perhaps they were too hospitable. In June 1837, the *St. Peter's*, an American Fur Company steamboat, arrived in the Mandan villages en-route to Fort Union, a fur company post at the mouth of the Yellowstone. The vessel carried several passengers who were infected with smallpox, and the disease soon spread through the Mandan and Arikara villages. Although the Mandans burned cedar, danced, and chanted to protect themselves from infection, entire households succumbed to the malady, and their relatives, overwhelmed with grief at the loss, then committed suicide rather than face life without the support of their friends and kinspeople. The disease raged through the Mandan and Arikara villages until September, when it began to subside, but it then spread to the Hidatsas, many of whom previously had been absent hunting bison. Frightened by news of the epidemic, some of the Hidatsas remained out on the Plains and they suffered fewer losses than the Mandans, but by the spring of 1838, when the disease had run its course, the effects were devastating. The Arikara population had been halved to about twelve hundred, the Hidatsas numbered approximately one thousand, and the Mandans had shrunk to twenty-three men, forty women, and about sixty-five children!

The smallpox epidemic of 1837–1838 also took a toll among the nomadic tribes of the northern Plains. The Assiniboines, Crees, Blackfeet, and Lakotas all suffered from the plague, but their scattered, nomadic populations and well-ventilated teepees did not facilitate the spread of the disease as did the sedentary, earth-lodge villages. Less scathed, the Lakotas and other nomads redoubled their attacks on the village tribes, and in 1845 the Mandans and Hidatsas joined together to form a new village named Like A Fishook (because of its configuration on a bluff overlooking the Missouri) near the American Fur Company post at Fort Berthold, opposite the mouth of Beaver Creek in modern McLean County, North Dakota. The Arikaras joined them in 1862, and the three tribes have lived together or in close proximity on the Fort Berthold Indian Reservation (established in 1870) since that time.

PEOPLE, PLACES, AND THINGS

Mandan Earth Lodges

Interior of the Hut of a Mandan Chief,
by Karl Bodmer

In 1804, as Lewis and Clark ascended the Missouri, they spent their first winter camped near the Mandan and Hidatsa villages in modern North Dakota. Like other Europeans or Americans who visited these communities in the early nineteenth century, the explorers were impressed by the Mandans' large earth lodges. Indeed, these lodges were among the largest and most substantial Native American residences north of Mexico, and they provided admirable shelter for people facing the climatic extremes of the central and northern Great Plains. Artists Karl Bodmer and George Catlin later visited these villages, and their sketches and paintings provide a rich visual portrayal of the houses.

Built on bluffs overlooking the Missouri or its tributaries, villages usually were protected on two flanks by steep river bluffs. They were often palisaded on the sides facing the open prairie. Larger villages, arranged around a central plaza, originally had contained over one hundred lodges, but by 1804 the villages visited by Lewis and Clark probably contained no more than eighty individual residences. Each unit, however, housed an extended matrilineal family, sometimes numbering over twenty people.

Although men assisted in setting central support posts, much of the construction was performed by women who "owned" the residences. After a shallow pit, forty to sixty feet in diameter (sometimes larger) was excavated, four support posts were erected in the center of the pit and interlaced with crossbeams. Smaller branches radiated out from the center to a ring of short posts raised vertically around the perimeter of the excavation, and the entire structure was overlain with smaller sticks, grass, and reeds, then covered with soil or sod. The finished structure was substantial, well insulated, and spacious. Smoke from a central hearth escaped through a hole in the roof. The lodges were well built; children scampered over the rooftops, and in the summer family groups often sat on the grassy roofs and conversed with their neighbors.

Many of the lodges were divided into separate living areas by bison-hide curtains, and some were large enough that horses could be housed within them during inclement weather. The houses held storage areas, large root cellars for dried vegetables, low willow platforms with sleeping robes, food preparation areas, and smaller sweat lodges. Lodges were entered through a doorway that extended through a narrow log hallway to the outside, and buffalo hides were hung across both ends of the hall to keep out wind or cold temperatures. European visitors often commented on the cleanliness and orderly appearance of the houses' interiors and the lodges' comfortable furnishings.

George Catlin's depiction of a summer evening in a Mandan village portrays the affability of the Mandan people and their use of rooftops for social activities. Indeed, although contemporary American artists usually portray the nomadic Plains tribes as the stereotypical "Plains Indians," prominent European or American artists who visited the region in the early nineteenth century focused much more on the earth-lodge people. Why? What made them so attractive to artists such as Bodmer and Catlin?

Sakakawea and the Rocky Mountain Tribes

Lewis and Clark left the Mandan and Hidatsa villages in early April 1805 and proceeded up the Missouri River toward its three forks in southwestern Montana. Accompanying their party was Sakakawea ("Bird Woman"), a former Shoshone captive taken by the Hidatsas near the forks of the Missouri and married to Touissant Charbonneau, a Canadian trader who had been residing in the Hidatsa villages. Like many other Native Americans in American history, Sakakawea has been enshrouded in considerable myth. Some historians have erroneously claimed that the expedition relied on her as their primary guide on the upper Missouri. Such was not the case, although she did periodically reaffirm that the expedition was headed in the right direction. More important, however, was Sakakawea's role as an interpreter and mediator with the Shoshonean-speaking tribes whom Lewis and Clark would encounter in the Rocky Mountains and plateau region. In addition, her presence on the expedition, accompanied by her infant son, did much to convince many of the Native American people whom Lewis and Clark encountered that the expedition was not a war party, for as Clark recorded in his journal, Sakakawea "reconsiles [sic] all the Indians, as to our friendly intentions. A woman with a party of men is a token of peace." She accompanied the expedition to the Pacific, returned with Lewis and Clark to the upper Missouri, and evidently died of a fever at Fort Manuel in modern South Dakota on December 20, 1812.

Lewis and Clark were particularly reliant on Sakakawea's fluency in Shoshone, since they needed to purchase horses from this tribe in order to cross the Rocky Mountains. They proceeded up the Missouri to its forks and then ascended the Jefferson, where they encountered the Shoshones, or Snakes, in mid-August. Originally a people of the Great Basin or Inland Plateau, the Shoshones traditionally had hunted deer, mountain sheep, and other smaller game. They had relied on the yearly runs of salmon up the Snake River for much of their food. With the advent of horses, however, some bands had migrated westward into Wyoming and had begun to hunt bison on the Plains. These Eastern Shoshones, many of whom would later reside in the Wind River Basin in Wyoming, rapidly adopted many of the cultural patterns of the Plains nomads. Other Shoshones, such as the band that Lewis and Clark encountered in southwestern Montana, remained a transitional people, spending part of their year west of the Continental Divide in Idaho feasting on salmon and then crossing over into Montana to hunt bison in the late summer and fall.

The Shoshones whom the party met in the Lemhi Pass region of southwestern Montana were familiar with European trade goods, but most had never seen white men, and they were much taken by the Americans. Good relations were assured, however, when Sakakawea recognized Cameahwait, the leader of the band, as her older brother. The Shoshones' previous access to trade goods stretched through a circuitous route to Spanish merchants in Mexico, and they were eager to acquire American items, particularly guns and ammunition. While hunting bison on the Plains, they encountered hostile parties of Blackfeet, Crows, Lakotas, and other enemies, and the poorly armed Shoshones needed firearms. They offered the Americans horses in exchange for guns, but Lewis and Clark had few weapons to spare and countered with offers of other merchandise and promises of political alliances. The Americans assured the Shoshones that American traders who would follow in their wake would eventually provide the tribe with all the firearms they needed. But the Shoshones were shrewd traders, and the Americans were forced to barter a significant number of firearms. In return, the Shoshones provided horses, but many were older, lame animals, hardly fit to travel. A Shoshone guide named "Old Toby" agreed to lead them to the Columbia.

Old Toby led the expedition over Lemhi Pass to the Bitteroot Valley, where in early September they camped for a brief period with a Salish-speaking tribe, whom whites called Flatheads. The Salish were a hospitable people who, like the Shoshones, utilized both salmon and bison. The Americans remained with the Salish for three days, purchased additional horses, then, following Old Toby, they spent the next two weeks negotiating the arduous Lolo Trail over the Bitterroot Mountains. On September 22 they reached a Nez Percé village on the Clearwater River in Idaho.

Like the Shoshones and Salish, the Sahaptian-speaking Nez Percés also welcomed the strangers and provided the Americans with feasts of dried salmon, berries, and camas bulbs on which Lewis,

Clark, and their followers gorged, and from which they suffered debilitating cases of diarrhea. The Nez Percés also followed a transitional way of life, utilizing both salmon and bison hunting east of the mountains, but since their villages were more accessible from the Pacific, Lewis and Clark noticed that they possessed kettles, beads, and other items that had originally come from British traders near the mouth of the Columbia. Like their eastern neighbors, the Nez Percés cared little for American alliances but wanted firearms, since their hunting expeditions on the Plains were bitterly opposed by the Blackfeet.

Leaving their horses with the Nez Percés, the Americans constructed dugout canoes, and on October 7 left the Nez Percé villages and descended the Clearwater en-route to the Pacific. Two Nez Percé guides replaced Old Toby, and nine days later the expedition reached the confluence of the Snake and Columbia. There they encountered Wanapam and Yakama Indians, fishing people who depended on the great salmon runs that surged up the Columbia on a regular basis. Unlike the Plains tribes, these Sahaptian-speaking people resided in multifamily lodges constructed of poles and woven mats, and they dried large quantities of salmon on racks along the river bank. The Wanapams, Yakamas, and neighboring Walla Wallas received the Americans hospitably, but on October 19, as the expedition reached Umatilla settlements near the mouth of the river bearing that name, they found the Umatillas to be suspicious since many had never encountered Europeans.

The Pacific Tribes

On October 24 Lewis and Clark reached The Dalles of the Columbia, where steep cliffs forced the river through a narrow passage between rapids and boulders. The Dalles marked a cultural boundary between the plateau tribes and the Indian people of the lower Columbia. For centuries it had served as a great marketplace to which the Nez Percés, Yakamas, and tribes located on the upper reaches of the Columbia and its tributaries carried bison meat, skin clothing, and other products to be traded for items brought upstream from the lower river. The Wishram people occupied the north bank at The Dalles, the Wascos resided on the opposite side of the river, and both tribes prided themselves on their trading acumen and their role as intermediaries between the plateau tribes and the people of the lower Columbia.

Both tribes lived in large wooden plank houses, common among the people of the Pacific Northwest, and although the trading season had just ended, Clark estimated that the Wishrams still had almost five tons of dried salmon stored for future bartering. Both tribes also possessed extensive trade goods of European manufacture, as clothing, metal items, beads, and blankets had passed up the Columbia to their villages. These trading tribes were wary that the Americans might pose a potential economic threat, endangering their position as intermediaries on the river, and when Wishram, Wasco, and other warriors assisted the expedition to portage around The Dalles' rapids, they pilfered part of the expedition's trade goods.

Tribespeople living downstream from The Dalles were even more suspicious. Skilloot, Chinook, and other fishing tribes saw the expedition as trading rivals, and although they offered no armed resistance, they also helped themselves to objects from the American camp at every opportunity. Finally, in mid-November Lewis and Clark reached the Pacific, then moved back up the Columbia, and established a permanent winter camp, named Fort Clatsop near modern Astoria, Oregon.

The Indian people who interacted with Lewis and Clark during the winter of 1805–1806 differed markedly from the Mandans and Hidatsas who had hosted the expedition during the previous winter. Unlike the village people of the upper Missouri, the Clatsops and other Chinookan-speaking people of the lower Columbia maintained regular contact with maritime traders who frequently visited their villages. Consequently, the Clatsops and their neighbors were not fascinated by this new group of Americans who had arrived overland from the east; Europeans with large stores of trade goods often were present at the mouth of the Columbia. Indeed, the Clatsops' extensive experience bartering sea otter pelts and other fur to the mariners had taught them to be shrewd traders, and they commonly demanded what Lewis and Clark considered to be exorbitant prices for the commodities (primarily food) that they bartered to the Americans. Their relationship with the Americans was not social; it was commercial.

Russell's painting depicts Sakakawea negotiating with tribesmen in an approaching canoe. Sakakawea's presence convinced many of the tribes that Lewis and Clark's expedition was peaceful and that it was not a war party. While generally accurate, it is unlikely that the dugout canoes the explorers carved with the aid of the Nez Percés were as beautifully decorated as the craft in the painting.

The lack of social contact between the two peoples was further diminished by the Americans' isolation in a separate camp and by their belief that the Clatsops and their neighbors could not be trusted. Annoyed at the Indians' disregard for private property, which they had experienced at The Dalles, Lewis and Clark issued orders on January 1, 1806, that all Indians who entered the fort must be carefully watched, and if they trespassed into the private quarters of the garrison, they were to be expelled outside the palisade. In addition, all Indians were to be removed from the post at sunset unless they were granted permission to remain "by the Commanding Officers."

And finally, sitting in their soggy quarters, short of supplies in a world enshrouded by clouds and rain, Lewis, Clark, and other members of the expedition believed themselves to be at the ends of the earth, separated by half a continent from the people and culture they valued. Much of their early "sense of adventure" had vanished, and they spent a miserable winter waiting for spring and a return to their homes. Consequently, their appraisal of the Clatsops and neighboring people reflected their disgruntlement. Unlike the Plains tribes, the Chinookan people of the lower Columbia were a short, stocky people whom Lewis described as "low in stature and illy shapen, possessing thick broad flat feet, crooked legs, large nostrils, and black coarse hair." Some of the Americans were repulsed by the tribespeople's practice of flattening the front and occipital regions of their children's heads, and they complained that the Chinookan language was impossible to learn and sounded like poultry calling. In comparison to the less sophisticated Plains tribes, the hard-bargaining Clatsops demanded high prices for their products, and the hungry Americans accused them of harboring "avaricious all grasping dispositions."

The Americans' unfavorable characterization of the lower Columbia tribes is more a reflection of their own ethnocentrism than any just appraisal of the Clatsops and their neighbors. Desirable physical characteristics are culturally defined, and the Americans probably seemed as "badly clad and illy made" to the Chinookan-speaking people as did the Clatsops to Lewis and Clark. Moreover, American complaints about Clatsop bartering practices seem hypocritical from a culture that championed the hard bargaining and questionable economic methods of its own "Yankee traders." And although the Americans described the Chinookans as "thievishly inclined" people and accused them of pilfering items from the expeditions' baggage packs, in March 1806 Lewis and Clark authorized the theft of a canoe from the Clatsop village to begin their return voyage up the Columbia.

Yet Lewis and Clark's journals also indicate that the Clatsops and their neighbors were a prosperous people, well adapted to a coastal way of life. It is regrettable, but not surprising, that the Americans stole a Clatsop canoe, for the Clatsops and other Chinookan-speaking people handcrafted beautiful vessels, admirably designed for both the rugged seas at the mouth of the Columbia and for transporting merchandise up the river for intertribal trade.

Retracing the Path of Empire

In March 1806 Lewis and Clark left Fort Clatsop and began their journey home. They ascended the Columbia and Snake rivers, then journeyed overland to the Clearwater, where snow-packed passes in the Bitterroot Mountains forced them to remain for almost a month among the Nez Percés. The Nez Percés, long known for their hospitality, treated the Americans well, but the extended visit severely strained the Nez Percés' food supplies. The Americans had so exhausted their supply of trade goods that they had only limited items to barter for dried salmon, camas bulbs, or the village dogs, which the Nez Percés did not regard as food but which the Americans ate with relish. Nez Percé leaders met repeatedly with Clark and politely listened to his admonitions for intertribal peace, but they informed the Americans that they had been repeatedly attacked by the Blackfeet and pleaded with

Lewis and Clark to send traders who would supply their warriors with firearms. Yet the Nez Percés and their visitors seemed to genuinely enjoy each other's company, and a friendship developed that would last until the tragic flight of Chief Joseph toward Canada six decades later.

On June 10 the Americans left their camp, and assisted by Nez Percé guides, they crossed over the Bitterroots, where the party split; Clark led most of the expedition to the Three Forks of the Missouri, then overland to the Yellowstone, where he descended to the Missouri. Meanwhile Lewis led a smaller party overland to the "Great Falls of the Missouri," then up the Marias, where he intended to contact the Blackfeet. Lewis hoped to convince the Blackfeet and their Atsina (Gros Ventre) allies to make peace with the surrounding tribes and to wean them from British influence.

He failed on both counts. The Nez Percé scouts turned back, warning Lewis that the Blackfeet were hostile, and in July 1806 when he encountered a camp of young Blackfeet men near the junction of the Two Medicine and Marias rivers, he found the Nez Percé warnings to be valid. By the first decade of the nineteenth century the Blackfeet and their allies were the dominant military power on the Plains of Montana and Alberta. Comprised of three Blackfeet tribes (the Piegans; Bloods; and Siksikas, or Blackfeet proper), the Blackfeet alliance also included the Atsinas, or Gros Ventres, and the Sarsis, a smaller tribe of Athapaskan-speaking people who resided on the upper Saskatchewan River. Although smallpox had decimated the Blackfeet in 1781, their losses were fewer than those of their neighbors, and by 1800 the three Blackfeet tribes numbered over 5,000, with at least 1,400 warriors. The Gros Ventres contributed another 4,000 souls and 900 fighting men to the alliance, while the Sarsis probably numbered 500, including 120 warriors.

Located on the northern borders of the Plains, the Blackfeet gained access to British traders in Canada, and fierce competition between the Hudson's Bay Company and the North West Company enabled the Blackfeet to obtain firearms at reasonable prices. Well armed with trade muskets, they drove the Shoshones south into Wyoming and pushed the Flatheads westward over the mountains. Although the British traders initially hoped that the Blackfeet would trap the abundant beaver that populated the watershed of the northern Rockies, the

Blackfeet and their allies ran few trap lines, preferring instead to trade in dried meat, buffalo robes, or horses, which they obtained in considerable numbers through their raids on their southern and western neighbors. Since merchants at Fort Vermilion and Rocky Mountain House, British posts along the Clearwater and Saskatchewan rivers, readily purchased these commodities, the Blackfeet were a prosperous people, and they were determined to maintain their hegemony over the northern Plains. They did not welcome the advent of Americans and American traders among their enemies. On July 26, 1806, Lewis spoke with a group of Blackfeet near the junction of the Two Medicine and Marias rivers. When Lewis informed the Blackfeet that the Shoshones, Nez Percés, and other Blackfeet enemies already had become friends of the Americans and would be supplied by American traders, the Blackfeet were astounded. They had no intention of relinquishing their British trading ties for American promises, but more importantly, they did not want the Americans arming their enemies. The two groups separated for the night, but early in the morning of July 27 a few of the young Piegan men who had met with Lewis and his party on the previous day attempted to steal their firearms and horses. The Americans reacted angrily, killing two of them. Both sides rapidly withdrew, and Lewis and his party fled south to the Missouri, where they rejoined Clark and the rest of the expedition. The Americans then descended the river to the Mandan, Hidatsa, and Arikara villages, where they again attempted to entice these village people into a closer relationship with the American government. Late in August the expedition left the Arikara village at the mouth of the Grand River in South Dakota. They arrived in St. Louis on September 23, 1806.

The Lewis and Clark expedition provided American officials with valuable information about the Native American population of the Missouri Valley and the Pacific Northwest. It also introduced many of the northern Plains tribes, plateau peoples, and Northwest Coast villagers to official emissaries of the United States and provided opportunities for both Indians and whites to interact over a period of weeks or months. Yet the Americans were strangers in an Indian land. Intertribal alliances, trading agreements, and warfare were the institutions and issues that governed people's lives in the region, and regardless of Lewis and Clark's grand promises and pronouncements, most tribal leaders viewed the American government and its emissaries as weak intruders, peripheral to their daily lives. Yet with few exceptions, most Indian people treated the Americans hospitably. Although they were indifferent to political alliances, they obviously were open to friendship, interested in economic ties, and eager to access American technology. Most tribes of the upper Missouri, Rocky Mountains, or plateau region had been exposed to trade goods through long and circuitous intertribal trade routes, but their appetite for these items had only been whetted by the limited number of trade goods that previously had reached their villages. The Mandans and Hidatsas wanted knives, kettles, trade cloth, and whiskey. The Nez Percés, Shoshones, and Salish wanted American firearms. Indeed all of these people, geographically isolated from ready sources of trade goods, were more desirous of well-stocked trading partners than promises of political alliances. If the Americans could supply these commodities, they indeed would be welcome in the tribal villages. The Americans' political ambitions and promises of alliances had little appeal.

THE WESTERN FUR TRADE

The fur traders and mountain men who followed in Lewis and Clark's wake brought the trade goods that the tribal people so desperately wanted. By 1800 the fur trade had declined east of the Mississippi. Both Indian and white trappers had depleted many of the valuable fur-bearing animals, and following the War of 1812 most traffic was conducted in raccoon, muskrat, and other less valuable pelts. Yet the demand for fur continued, and in the postwar period the focus of the fur trade shifted west of the Mississippi, eventually centering on the Rocky Mountain region and the Pacific Northwest.

Aleuts and Inuits

At first, much of this trade centered in the Pacific Northwest. Chinook, Makah, and Nootka hunters had taken seal and especially sea otter pelts for centuries, but the skins had been used only for personal clothing or traded, in limited quantities, to

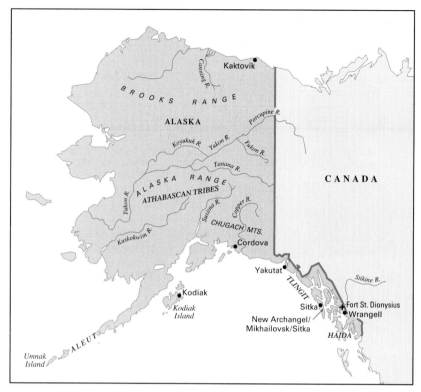

Alaska. *Compiled from Claus-M. Naske and Herman E. Slotnick,* Alaska: A History of the 49th State *(Normal: University of Oklahoma Press, 1987), xvi–xvii. Reprinted with permission of Oklahoma University Press.*

the tribes of the interior. Sea otter pelts had long been in much demand in East Asia, and British and American mariners found that otter pelts purchased for trade goods worth less than six pence on the Oregon or Washington coast could be exchanged in China for merchandise worth almost one hundred dollars. In Alaska, Russian fur traders literally forced Aleut hunters to slaughter thousands of these marine mammals, while Native American hunters from southern Alaska to California, armed with bows and trade muskets, also harvested otters, whose pelts were traded to European or American merchants for manufactured goods and alcohol.

Initially the Russians seemed to hold an advantage. By 1750 they had penetrated the Aleutian Islands, where lawless traders or *promyshlenniki* virtually enslaved Aleut villagers, seizing women

and children and forcing their husbands and fathers to secure pelts while their families were held for ransom. Embittered, Aleut hunters cooperated, but they also fought back, killing isolated traders and pilfering their warehouses. In 1761, when the Russians attempted to seize Aleut women at Unmak, in the central Aleutians, villagers resisted and the Russians were forced to flee for their lives. One year later Aleuts attacked and burned five Russian trading ships that attempted to anchor off their villages, and for four years, between 1762 and 1766, the Aleuts regained their independence and held off the Russian onslaught.

The Russians returned with a vengeance. In 1766 Ivan Solovief, a trader from Okhotsk, in eastern Siberia, led several hundred *promyshlenniki* in heavily armed ships eastward into the Aleutians where they destroyed Aleut villages and slaughtered

Aleuts The Aleut hunter portrayed in this nineteenth-century illustration wears a waterproof parka used for hunting. The Aleut woman has been converted to Christianity by Russian Orthodox missionaries.

thousands of men, women, and children. Although the Aleuts again resisted, they were forced back under the Russian yoke, and since the central Aleutian Islands now had been depopulated of otters, the Russians pushed eastward, establishing small trading stations on Kodiak Island and at other locations amid the hundreds of bays and inlets that blanket the southern Alaskan coastline. Forced aboard Russian trading ships in the spring, Aleut hunters were deposited at locations along the Alaskan coast where, separated from their families, they were obligated to secure otter, seal, and other pelts during the summer. They were then returned to their captive wives and children in the autumn. In theory, Aleuts were entitled to a share of their pelts, but the *promyshlenniki* forced them to purchase supplies at such high prices that they remained at the Russians' mercy.

In 1784 Gregory Shelikov established a permanent Russian settlement on Kodiak Island, and in 1790 he formed the United American Company, which dominated the Alaska trade. Assigning the management of the Alaskan operations to Alexander Baranov, Shelikov traveled to St. Petersburg,

where he met with the czar. In 1799 the government granted Shelikov a monopoly over the Alaskan fur trade and he organized a new firm, the Russian-American Company. The company was given control over Russian affairs in Alaska similar to the rule of the British East Indian Company on the Indian Subcontinent. Its hegemony proved disastrous for the Aleut villagers. In Alaska, Baranov divided the region into sixteen districts and forced many of the Aleuts to leave their old villages and relocate on islands off the Alaskan panhandle. While Aleut hunters were transported to even more remote regions, their women and children were "employed" by the company, working endless hours processing pelts, hides, and other animal products. Some were forced into prostitution to feed their families, while others were required to dry or smoke fish or to collect and preserve edible roots and other forest foods for use during the long winters. For the Aleuts, their half century of contact with the Russians proved catastrophic. British traders employed by the Hudson's Bay Company estimated that the Aleut population had declined by almost 90 percent between 1750 and 1800.

Despite Baranov's efforts, the small Russian and Aleut populations both consistently suffered from food shortages. Russian peasants eventually were imported from Siberia, and attempts were made to grow potatoes, cabbages, and turnips, but the crops often failed, and in 1805 the Russian and Aleut settlements in Alaska faced starvation. Baranov earlier had purchased quantities of foodstuffs from American and Spanish merchants who carried wheat and cattle north from California, but he was forced to pay in otter pelts or by allowing "his" Aleut hunters to secure pelts for the Americans, and in either case the foodstuffs were expensive. To remedy their perennial shortages, in 1812 officials of the Russian-American Company transported ninety-five Russians and about eighty Aleuts to Bodega Bay, just north of modern San Francisco, where they built Fort Ross, a post designed to foster a Russian agricultural station at that location and to tap the seal and otter trade along the northern California coast.

The transplanted Aleuts had no agricultural traditions and were entirely unfamiliar with the plants and animals of California, so most were employed on the Fallarone Islands, thirty miles off the coast, where they fished, hunted seals, and gathered sea bird eggs. In turn, the Russians attempted to rely on the local Pomo tribespeople, a coalition of coastal hunter-gatherers who traditionally subsisted on acorn meal, salmon, and the bountiful shellfish available along the shore. But the Pomos also had few agricultural inclinations. Unlike the tribespeople to the south, they had not been incorporated into the Spanish mission system and had little desire to supply labor for the Russian fields. At first the Pomos grudgingly cooperated, but during the harvest, when the Russians demanded fourteen-hour work days, the Pomos abandoned the fields and returned to their villages. The Russians then turned to conscription, but the Pomos fled into the Coast Range and agricultural productivity plummeted. Some Pomos eventually acquiesced to the Russian authority, but others retaliated by burning crops and killing livestock. The agricultural station struggled on, but it never produced sufficient harvests to provision the trading posts in Alaska. Meanwhile, the Pomos contracted Eurasian diseases to which they had no natural immunity. Russia abandoned Fort Ross in 1841, but by then the Pomo population had diminished by one-third, from approximately nine thousand to six thousand.

Russia's exploitation of Alaska's native peoples did not go unnoticed. In 1793 Catherine the Great issued a directive that ordered Russian Orthodox priests to Alaska, and three years later missionaries established a church on Kodiak Island. Priests began to proselytize among the Aleuts, where they received a mixed reception. Nonetheless, some tribespeople were converted and the Russian mission system limped along until 1824, when Ivan Veniaminoff arrived from Siberia and revitalized the church's efforts. The surviving Aleuts respected Veniaminoff, who learned the Aleut language and interceded in their behalf with the Russian-American Company. Moreover, Veniaminoff and the priests who followed him extended their efforts into the interior, where they established missions among the Athapaskan people. They also sought converts among the Inuit people of the far north. Veniaminoff established schools at Sitka and other locations where native students were provided with the rudiments of a Russian education, after which a few were sent (at the Russian-American Company's expense) to St. Petersburg for further instruction. Most of the young men who journeyed to academies in Russia were of mixed lineage, and many were educated to fill positions within the company's ranks. Some, however, returned to Alaska to serve as intermediaries between the company and their people, perhaps ameliorating the company's impact on their less fortunate kinsmen. Meanwhile Veniaminoff and other priests continually protested to St. Petersburg regarding the abuse of Alaska's native people, but the Russian court remained far distant from Sitka, and for many Indians in Alaska, the hardships continued.

The Tlingits

The Tlingits fought back. Occupying the Alaskan coastline from the eastern shores of Prince William Sound south to Prince of Wales Island, the Tlingit people remained fiercely independent and resisted the Russian advance. Residing in substantial plank houses, which contained extended matrilineal families, the Tlingits, like the neighboring Haidas, Tsimshians, and several other northwestern coastal tribes, incorporated elaborately carved tree trunks as supports for their dwellings. The heavy posts were fashioned by skilled wood carvers into designs that often reflected the lineage of the residents; others were carved into images symbolic of the family's clan affiliation. During the Russian period most of these highly decorated posts were incorporated in the construction of houses and other buildings, but by the late nineteenth century they had evolved into the freestanding "totem poles" that today symbolize Northwest Coast cultures.

Skilled mariners, the Tlingits used great cedar logs to fashion canoes capable of carrying fifty passengers, and traveled in these vessels amid the myriad channels and islands that interlaced their homeland. The Tlingits hunted seals, whales, and other marine mammals, but they also relied heavily on halibut and salmon. Like the Aleuts, the Tlingits hunted otters, which they traded to British and American merchants who occasionally visited their villages, but they resented the intrusion of Baranov and the Aleut hunters into their homeland. Moreover, Tlingit warriors were well armed with heavy clubs and knives. They also carried spears and arrowheads tipped with iron or native copper. In addition, they readily purchased other weapons, including firearms, from British and

Tlingit Women Weaving This painting by Langdon Kihn portrays women in a large Tlingit plank house weaving the Chilkat blankets (made from goats) for which they were famous.

American traders. Numerous and well organized, they were a formidable foe for the Russian traders.

Trouble emerged in 1799, after Baranov established Mikhailovosk, a post near modern Sitka in the heart of Tlingit territory. Although neighboring Tlingits traded with the Russians, they resented the newcomers' assumptions of superiority and their disdain for tribal women. Described by Europeans as "the keepers of the family treasures," Tlingit women closely monitored the fur trade and had the power to veto an exchange negotiated by male relatives if they believed their male relatives were not receiving sufficient trade goods for their pelts. Russian traders believed that they were demeaning themselves by bargaining with women, and they resented that Tlingit women were "far keener at [trading] than the men, and much more difficult to cheat." In June 1802, after Russian traders attempted to force themselves on Tlingit women, the Tlingits attacked and destroyed Mikhailovosk, killing 20 Russians and 130 Aleuts and seizing several thousand otter pelts. A few Russians and Aleuts managed to escape to a British trading vessel anchored offshore, whose captain carried them to Kodiak Island and then demanded

a ransom before releasing them to Baranov. Meanwhile, other Tlingits harassed or ambushed Russian and Aleut hunting parties, and the fur trade was much disrupted.

Incensed by the attacks, in 1804 Baranov returned to Sitka where he utilized the cannons from a Russian warship to bombard and destroy a Tlingit village. Landing a contingent of 120 Russians and almost 1,000 Aleuts, he rebuilt the former Russian settlement and christened it New Archangel. But the Tlingits were not finished. They continued to attack Russian and Aleut fur hunters, and the residents of the rebuilt village often feared for their lives. In 1805 Tlingit warriors overran a Russian settlement at Yakutat, killing most of the residents, and one year later they besieged New Archangel in such numbers that the desperate commander of the settlement was forced to distribute most of the Russian-American Company's trade goods at the post before the Tlingits would return to their villages. Throughout the remainder of Russia's occupancy of the Alaskan coast, the Tlingits and Russians maintained a "cold war" of armed truces, general suspicion, periodic acts of violence, and occasional armed conflict.

Baranov was forced to resign as chief manager of the Russian-American Company in 1818, but the Russian officials who followed in his wake were so short of men and resources that they could never mount an effective campaign against the Tlingit villages. In 1834 Governor Baron von Ferdinand Wrangell, one of Baranov's successors, established Fort St. Dionysius among the Tlingit communities on modern Wrangell Island and tenuously extended Russian authority into the region, but traders at the fort could not compete with merchants from the British Hudson's Bay Company and the post was abandoned six years later. Meanwhile the Tlingits continued their fiercely independent ways, sometimes quarreling among themselves but never acquiescing to the Russians. In 1855, just a decade prior to Alaska's purchase by the United States, the Tlingits at Sitka again attacked neighboring New Archangel, captured the chapel, and so threatened this center of Russian government in Alaska that the governor was forced to placate them with payments before he could make peace.

After 1867, Tlingit relations with American merchants followed a similar, if initially less hostile pattern. Since Baranov had been forced to purchase grain, livestock, and other foodstuffs from American merchant ships that sailed north from California, American traders were keenly aware of the plentiful supply of pelts amassed by Tlingit hunters and trappers, and they readily traded for them. In return, the Tlingits purchased a broad spectrum of American goods, including firearms, which Americans willingly made available. Although the Tlingits could not purchase muskets for all their warriors and usually suffered from shortages of lead and powder, their acquisition of firearms enabled them to meet the Russians on even terms, except when the Russians brought large naval vessels into coastal waters. Baranov and other officials complained about the arms trade to American emissaries, but the Yankees disavowed any responsibility for the commerce of their citizens.

After 1824 the British Hudson's Bay Company displaced the Americans as the primary merchant for Tlingit and other tribal goods, and the Tlingits' prosperity increased. Better stocked and more highly organized, Hudson's Bay Company traders established trading posts on the Stikine and Taku rivers and later visited Athapaskan-speaking peo-ple in the Yukon and Porcupine river valleys of the interior. Some of these initial British posts later were abandoned, but company trading vessels such as the *Beaver* continued to visit Tlingit villages along the coast on a regular basis.

The Tlingits and their neighbors rapidly developed a taste for European or American products. Furs were traded for firearms, clothing, brass and copper kettles, metal utensils, beads, and alcohol. They also acquired a taste for European foods, including tea, coffee, sugar, and flour. The Tlingits had always lived among relative abundance, but the acquisition of these Euro-American trading goods accentuated a tribal hierarchy, which in turn created a surplus of wealth for Tlingit families. The Tlingits accumulated blankets, weapons, utensils, food products, and other commodities. In turn, this wealth enlarged the value of goods distributed at potlatches (see Chapter 1), the Tlingits' ceremonial distribution of gifts, that celebrated a family's rank and generosity. The expanded potlatches thus increased the emphasis on reciprocity.

The new wealth and technology also encouraged the expansion of slavery among the Tlingits. Tlingits always had practiced slavery, but armed with new weapons, they became more aggressive and many families either captured or purchased tribespeople from other northwestern tribes or from people living in the interior. Ordinarily the slaves were treated with moderation, but Tlingit warriors exercised life-and-death control over their captives, and the latter occasionally were killed for ceremonial and other purposes.

The acquisition of iron and later steel cutting utensils markedly enhanced the Tlingits' ability as woodworkers. They continued to build massive canoes with which they plied the waterways of their world, but they also enlarged both their splendid cedar plank houses and the tall totem poles, symbolizing family lineages and clan affiliations, that stood before many of the structures. Indeed, access to keen, hard-edged European or American cutting instruments (adzes, axes, chisels, etc.) generated a flowering of Tlingit and other Northwestern tribes' artistic expression that resulted in a stunning display of intricately carved and elaborately painted ceremonial masks, utensils, storage containers, and other objects. For the Tlingits, the middle decades of the nineteenth century were a time of plenty.

Relatively immune from meaningful Russian control and well supplied by Hudson's Bay Company traders, the northern Tlingits remained the unchallenged masters of their realm. To the south, British gunboats from Vancouver Island threatened southern Tlingit independence, but even here, most Tlingit villages retained their autonomy.

The Northern Rockies

The tribes of the northern Rockies also prospered in the fur trade, but their prosperity was less universal and shorter-lived. During the late eighteenth century, Spanish traders from St. Louis had opened trading posts among the Osages in western Missouri. Spanish attempts to engage the tribes of the upper Missouri, however, had been turned back by the Arikaras, who were supplied by British traders from Canada. The Arikara-Dakota trading alliance was clearly evident to Lewis and Clark during their ascent of the Missouri in 1804, but on their return to St. Louis their reports of abundant beaver and tribes hungry for trade goods sparked an ingress of American traders into the Upper Missouri valley that had a dramatic impact on the Indian people of the region.

In 1807 Manuel Lisa led a group of American traders and trappers from St. Louis up the Missouri, where they encountered resentment and some hostility from both the Arikaras and Assiniboines. The Americans proceeded on, turned up the Yellowstone, and then reached the mouth of the Big Horn, where they prepared a fortified camp that Lisa modestly christened "Fort Manuel." In contrast to the downriver tribes, the Crows immediately welcomed Lisa and his comrades. They were eager to trade beaver and other pelts for Yankee trade goods, particularly firearms for defense against the Lakotas and Blackfeet. John Colter and other "mountain men" spent the winter visiting Crow, Shoshone, and Salish camps, cementing good relations between these northern mountain tribes and the Americans. During the next three years these tribes received the Americans into their midst, readily bartering for American trade goods and welcoming their military assistance against the Blackfeet. In contrast, Blackfeet warriors bitterly resented the American intrusion into the region. Carrying arms obtained from British traders, they attacked the Americans and their newfound allies. In April 1810, when the Missouri Fur Company (Lisa's company) attempted to

build a post at the Three Forks of the Missouri, a Blackfeet war party overran the fort, killing many of its inhabitants and destroying the company's property. Two months later the Americans abandoned the site and retreated to Fort Manuel, where they sought solace among the Crows and Shoshones.

Blackfeet opposition and lack of capital caused the Missouri Fur Company to withdraw from the northern Rockies, but it was immediately supplanted by John Jacob Astor's American Fur Company, which also aspired to control the fur trade in the region. Astor planned to construct a series of posts from the northern Missouri Valley across the mountains and plateau to the Pacific coast, and in 1810 he established Astoria, a fur trading post at the mouth of the Columbia River. Yet competition from the Hudson's Bay Company and the War of 1812 forced Astor to abandon his namesake post, and during the war trade between the tribes and the Americans diminished. In contrast, British traders, unopposed by American merchants or authority, ranged freely across the plateau, readily supplying the Blackfeet and even offering trade goods to the Crows and Shoshones.

The British monopoly did not last. Following the war, the Americans came back, and Crow, Shoshone, and Salish warriors preferred to trade with their former friends rather than barter with the "king's men" who also supplied their enemies. Still wary of the Blackfeet, the new American trade offensive focused on a more southerly route, attempting to penetrate the northern Rockies from the Platte River valley. Led by Jedediah Smith, during the mid-1820s American traders and trappers reestablished themselves among the Crows in the Wind River valley and then crossed South Pass into the Green River valley, which they found teeming with beaver and separated from the Blackfeet by the formidable Absaroka and Madison ranges. There friendly villages of Shoshones and neighboring Nez Percés and Bannocks helped the trappers establish base camps, then joined with them to set traps throughout the region. Many trappers married women from these tribes, and the women proved indispensable to their husbands' success. In addition to processing the pelts secured by their husbands, the wives were members of extended kinship groups, which facilitated their husbands' friendly access to distant villages.

Many of the friendly Crows, Shoshones, and Nez Percés preferred to hunt bison rather than beaver, but they too possessed horses, foodstuffs, and other commodities also needed by the trappers. Moreover, rather than establishing a series of trading posts, the new Rocky Mountain Fur Company opted to host yearly trading fairs, or "rendezvous," at which both Native Americans and trappers, or "mountain men," could barter their pelts, hides, and horses for merchandise carried overland by pack trains from St. Louis.

The Rendezvous

The rendezvous, which flourished during the late 1820s and 1830s, were held at several sites along the Cache, Snake, Green, and Wind rivers in northern Utah, southeastern Idaho, and western Wyoming. These trading fairs, often lasting for weeks, attracted large numbers of Native American men and women in addition to Anglo trappers, *métis* or Creole merchants from the upper Mississippi and Great Lakes, Mexican traders from the southwest, and a potpourri of travelers, adventurers, stray missionaries, and other curious onlookers. For Indian families in attendance (mostly Shoshones, Salishes, Bannocks, and Nez Percés—but also a scattering of Crows, Lakotas, Arapahos, and even a few Delaware and Iroquois hunters employed by the fur companies), the festivities represented a bacchanalia of Mardi Gras proportions. Since the rival Rocky Mountain and American Fur companies often vied for customers, Nez Percé warriors bartered Appaloosa horses for muskets and gunpowder, while their wives traded dried salmon for bright trade cloth, metal utensils, and other items that caught their fancy. Shoshone trappers from the Wind River region offered beaver trapped on the headwaters of the Popo Agie, while Salish from the Bitterroot country traded beaver, ermine, and other pelts from the streams that bordered their homelands. Meanwhile all the revelers participated in both foot and horse racing, vied against each other in wrestling and shooting matches, shared each others' food and campfires, and partook of the frontier whiskey carried to the site by the fur companies. Friendships were made and broken, marriages were arranged, and children were sired in a festive atmosphere. In 1832 a large party of Blackfeet and Gros Ventres even tried to join the festivities at Pierre's Hole in eastern Idaho, but they were driven away by the revelers, who could

neither forgive nor forget their enemy's consistent hostility to American fur traders and their Indian allies on the upper Missouri. The northern Rocky Mountain fur trade and associated rendezvous unquestionably reinforced the dependency of several tribes on American manufactured trade goods. Moreover, it initiated friendships, family ties, and political alliances between the Americans and tribes such as the Shoshones, Crows, Salish, Bannocks, and Nez Percés that lasted for decades until increased white settlement threatened Bannock and Nez Percé lands in Idaho. But the fur trade and associated rendezvous were relatively short-lived. By the 1840s most of the beaver had been trapped from the streams east of the plateau and Great Basin, and the vagaries of fashion dictated that silk should replace beaver as the primary substance of gentlemen's hats. In later decades, bison hides would replace beaver pelts as a commodity to be harvested from the American West, and white men's appetite for bison hides would have even more devastating consequences for the western tribes. A rich culture based on the hunting of bison still flourished on the Plains, but its death knell was ringing.

CONCLUSION: THE BEGINNING OF THE END

The contacts that developed between Native American residents of the Great Plains, Rocky Mountains, and Pacific Northwest that were initiated by Lewis and Clark must have seemed innocuous enough to Indian people living along the Missouri and Columbia rivers and in the surrounding regions. Tribal people in the region participated in a way of life that had evolved over the centuries, and although it more recently had been changed by the advent of horses and the introduction of European trade goods, the parameters of that life were still governed primarily by interaction with other Indians, not with Americans. Undoubtedly all had heard of, and most had seen, the pale-skinned, hairy-faced men who now occupied lands far to the east, but prior to 1805 these strangers had never entered the region in significant numbers. Indian trade networks and Indian politics dominated the mountains and plains, and the Americans had remained on the periphery.

After the Lewis and Clark expedition, things changed. Although American political hegemony was slow to permeate the region, American traders followed in the wake of the expedition, and their ready supply of firearms and other trade goods broke earlier tribal and British monopolies, providing arms to the Crows, Nez Percés, Shoshones, and other people who previously had been dominated by better armed enemies. Moreover, the penetration of American traders into the interior and the growing abundance of merchandise created an increased dependency on these trade goods by tribal peoples, a dependency that would eventually make them much more susceptible to American political pressure. And finally, as American trappers, traders, and merchants became more familiar with the Great Plains, Rocky Mountains, and Pacific Northwest, they returned to the Mississippi Valley with vivid stories of great rivers, lush valleys, and unbounded natural resources that would excite and entice an American population eager to exploit the "new lands in the West." Neither Lewis and Clark nor the fur trappers envisioned themselves as the harbingers of change, but they opened the spigot that eventually became a floodtide of American settlement onto Native American lands west of the Mississippi.

SUGGESTED READINGS

Anderson, Gary C. *The Indian Southwest, 1580–1830: Ethnogenesis and Reinvention*. Norman: University of Oklahoma Press, 1999.   The volume contains a comprehensive discussion of tribal migrations and shifting political patterns on the southern Plains.

Dening, Edwin Thomson. *Five Indian Tribes of the Upper Missouri*. Edited by John C. Ewers. Norman: University of Oklahoma Press, 1961.   Good ethnographic accounts of the Lakotas, Arikaras, Crows, Crees, and Assiniboines.

Ewers, John C. *The Blackfeet: Raiders on the Northern Plains*. Norman: University of Oklahoma Press, 1958.   Still the best survey of Blackfeet history in the first half of the nineteenth century. Written by the late, leading authority on Blackfeet history and culture.

Gibson, James R. *Imperial Russia in Frontier America: The Changing Geography of Supply and Demand*. New York: Oxford University Press, 1976.   This volume provides an adequate discussion of Russian policies toward the Alaskan tribes.

Hinckley, Ted C. *The Canoe Rocks: Alaska's Tlingit and the Euroamerican Frontier, 1800–1912*. Lanham, Md.: University Press of America, 1996.   An excellent survey of the Tlingits' struggle to maintain their tribal autonomy.

Josephy, Alvin M., Jr. *The Nez Percé Indians and the Opening of the Northwest*. New Haven: Yale University Press, 1965.   A good survey of Nez Percé tribal history and culture.

Meyer, Roy. *The Village Indians of the Upper Missouri*. Lincoln: University of Nebraska Press, 1977.   The best single-volume survey of Mandan, Hidatsa, and Arikara history and culture in the nineteenth and twentieth centuries.

Ronda, James. *Lewis and Clark Among the Indians*. Lincoln: University of Nebraska Press, 1987.   A prize-winning account of the expedition's encounters and interaction with Indian people on their voyage to the Pacific and back. The volume assesses the expedition's impact on the tribes and contains good discussions of tribal cultures.

Ruby, Robert H., and John Brown. *The Chinook Indians: Traders on the Lower Columbia*. Norman: University of Oklahoma Press, 1976.   The volume contains an excellent account of the Clatsops and other Chinookan-speaking tribes of the Columbia Valley and illustrates their participation in the widespread trading network of the region.

White, Richard. "The Winning of the West: The Expansion of the Western Sioux in the Eighteenth and Nineteenth Centuries." *Journal of American History* 65 (September 1978), 319–343.   An excellent article tracing Lakota expansion on the northern Plains and the impact of that expansion on other tribes.

Wishart, David. *The Fur Trade of the American West, 1807–1840*. Lincoln: University of Nebraska Press, 1979.   This volume contains the best survey of the fur trade in the trans-Mississippi west.

Indian Removal, 1820–1845

On May 31, 1825, shortly before four in the morning, over 150 Creek warriors surrounded the large two-story house built at Acorn Bluff, a plantation overlooking the rain-swollen Chattahoochee River and belonging to William McIntosh, a mico, or chief, among the Lower Creek towns in Georgia. Led by Menawa, a chief among the Upper Creeks from eastern Alabama, the warriors watched as a small party of their kinsmen piled dry brush against the house's outer walls, then lit the brush with embers they had concealed in metal containers. The fire soon spread to the house, and as McIntosh's two wives and children fled the burning structure, they were seized by the warriors, stripped of part of their clothing, and humiliated. McIntosh, accompanied by Etomme Tustennuggee, a close friend and political ally, remained inside and fired at the besiegers through shattered windows, but within twenty minutes the heat became unbearable. When McIntosh opened the front door, a fusillade of rifle shots struck Etomme Tustennuggee, who fell dead inside the residence. McIntosh then retreated upstairs, where he held out for another ten minutes before the flames forced him down the stairs and out the front door onto the porch.

As he staggered through the doorway McIntosh was struck by several rifle balls, then dragged by his attackers into the yard, where he attempted to rise. Dismounting from a horse, one of the Creek warriors walked to where McIntosh lay, drew a long dagger, and buried it in McIntosh's chest. The Creeks then killed McIntosh's hogs, burned his crops and the rest of the buildings on the plantation, and seized his slaves, horses, and cattle.

From the attackers' perspective, McIntosh's death was appropriate; justice had been served. Although McIntosh sincerely believed that the government's plans to remove the tribes into the west was inevitable and had warned his fellow tribespeople that unless they sold their lands in Georgia and removed west of the Mississippi they would "be left to wander the earth without homes and be beaten like dogs," he was opposed by the majority of Creek tribespeople. In 1821 the Creek National Council had decreed that any Creek who sold tribal lands to foreigners without the permission of the council would be put to death. But McIntosh, who previously had supported the decree, evidently changed his mind. In February 1825, persuaded by a bribe of almost $40,000, he and his followers signed the nefarious Treaty of Indian Springs, which ceded a large tract of land to the United States. In response, Menawa and his followers delivered Creek justice. In addition to McIntosh and Etomme Tustennuggee, the council executed two

William McIntosh, by McKenney & Hall In 1825 McIntosh was executed by the Creek National Council for illegally selling tribal lands to the United States in the Treaty of Indian Springs.

those tribespeople who had adopted many facets of non-Indian culture and those who remained tied to more traditional ways. Among other tribes, such as the Cherokees, Creeks, or Choctaws, the divisions over removal cut across cultural boundaries, and both camps (opponents and proponents of removal) embraced a broad spectrum of both those tribespeople who favored cultural changes and "traditionalists" who wished to retain many of the old ways. McIntosh's execution was not atypical. The intratribal schisms were both deep and bitter; quarrels that emerged in the removal period would follow the tribes into the West and would plague tribal politics for decades to come.

This chapter examines the tribes' attempts to retain their autonomy and homelands during an era of American expansion after the War of 1812. Ironically, during the first four decades of the nineteenth century both the adolescent United States and many of the tribal peoples within its boundaries developed a growing sense of nationalism. The federal government was eager to exercise its hegemony over Indian people; at the same time, many of the tribes also began to refer to themselves as "nations" and argued that they retained sovereignty over their homelands and people. Although most tribal people east of the Mississippi faced similar pressures from American expansion, the chapter focuses on several tribes whose experiences exemplify the broader patterns of the Native American experience in these decades.

INDIAN COUNTRY IN THE NEW REPUBLIC

While tribespeople along the Missouri and Columbia rivers or in Alaska became more familiar with Americans and Europeans, Native Americans east of the Mississippi struggled to adapt to the growing numbers of white people who surrounded or invaded their remaining homelands. In the decades between 1815 and 1840, five states in the trans-Appalachian region entered the union, and as their population burgeoned, Indian people in this region found themselves surrounded. Since the American Revolution, many eastern tribespeople had adopted selected tenets of European or American culture,

of McIntosh's sons-in-law who also had participated in the treaty.

The Creek quarrel resulting in McIntosh's death illustrates the intratribal bitterness that characterized the Indian Removal period. As the non-Indian population of the United States spread across the Midwest and Gulf Plains, pressure mounted for tribes east of the Mississippi to relinquish their lands and remove west of the river. Many tribes split into factions that either adamantly opposed removal or argued that emigration was inevitable and that the tribes should negotiate with the government for the best possible terms, then cross the Mississippi and begin a new life in the West. Among some tribes, such as the Sauks and Foxes or the Ho-Chunks (Winnebagos), the schisms seemed to form between but the patterns and extent of their adaptation varied among different tribes, and even differed markedly within individual tribal communities.

Nowhere was this process of adaptation more apparent than among the tribes of the southeastern United States. There, cultural changes that had occurred in the decades following the American Revolution accelerated after the War of 1812. These changes produced new economic patterns, kinship systems, and political structures, transforming many tribespeople's lives. Although the region held relatively few beaver, hunters among the Cherokees, Choctaws, Creeks, Chickasaws, and other tribes had scoured the forests for deer, since deerskins were in great demand for the manufacture of leather goods in Europe. By 1815, however, most of the deer herds had been depleted, and many of the former hunters had begun to raise cattle and hogs, letting the animals forage in the forests before gathering them in the fall and selling them at frontier markets. The herding activities seemed to be a natural extension of the warriors' old hunting patterns, but since the free-ranging livestock were owned by individual Indians, this livestock business marked a major shift away from the communal sharing of economic assets (the deer herds) toward private ownership.

Closer to the villages, Indian women continued to do most of the farming, particularly the tedious, repetitive hoeing of the crops to keep weeds from invading the fields. Although men often assisted in the initial clearing and plowing, they avoided most daily agricultural activity, which they described as "women's work" and below the dignity of warriors. Meanwhile, women also cared for the children, stitched clothing from trade cloth, and prepared food for the family. More traditional Cherokee or Choctaw families continued to follow these gender-related patterns, but by the 1820s some of the more successful cattlemen purchased slaves, and with the boom in upland cotton, they began to carve out small plantations. The acquisition of slaves enabled wealthier Indian women to leave the fields and devote their time to supervising household duties and pursuing the "domestic arts," as did the wives of non-Indian planters. Meanwhile their husbands turned from rounding up livestock in the forests to overseeing their slaves' production of corn and cotton. Many of these Native American planters were of mixed Native American–white ancestry (usually British or Scots-Irish), and although their numbers were not large, they sought positions of leadership within the tribes. Initially, their political ambitions were limited by many traditional tribespeople's distrust of their mixed lineage, their adherence to European or American values, and their acquisition of private property. Yet many of these people of mixed lineage also possessed the rudiments of a frontier education and were better prepared to negotiate with American Indian agents. By the 1820s more traditional tribespeople among the Cherokees, Choctaws, Creeks, and Chickasaws relied on these mixed-lineage planters to protect the tribal homelands from white settlers.

Cadres of mixed-lineage planters exerted considerable leadership within all the southern tribes, but nowhere had this process of cultural change advanced as far as among the Cherokees. By 1800 the Cherokees had inaugurated what one scholar has termed a "Renascence" within the American republic, instituting changes that profoundly altered the way of life of many members of the tribe.

Protestant missionaries served as catalysts for some of this change. In 1800, Moravian missionaries intent upon spreading the gospel arrived within the tribe, but Cherokee leaders were more eager for their children to learn English and to acquire an education than to be converted. After rival Presbyterian missionaries opened schools on the Hiwassee River and at Richard Fields's plantation on Sale Creek in southeastern Tennessee, the Moravians countered with a school at Spring Place, near Cherokee David Vann's plantation in northwestern Georgia. The enrollment at all the mission schools was limited almost entirely to the children of the emerging planter-elite, and few Cherokees embraced Christianity. In fact, the Moravians gained no converts until 1809, and although Baptist, Methodist, and Congregationalist ministers peddled their spiritual wares for the next two decades, by the 1830s, when the Cherokees were removed to the West, only about 8 percent of the adult population had officially converted to Christianity.

But the missionaries' promotion of early-nineteenth-century American Christianity, presented as a curious amalgam of religion and cultural values, did much to change the Cherokee Nation. Convinced that true Christianity also embraced the cultural values of nineteenth-century America, the missionaries enshrouded their religion with concepts of hard work, thrift, sobriety, and the importance of private property. These sermons appealed to the planter-elite, who supported the missionaries and sent their children to mission schools.

Cherokee students attending the Brainerd Mission near modern Chattanooga, Tennessee, enrolled in classes in mathematics, reading, writing, spelling, and geography. Girls were instructed in the "domestic arts," including sewing and needlepoint, while boys learned the rudiments of Anglo-American agriculture, or even trades such as blacksmithing. Much of the instruction was heavily infused with nineteenth-century Christian values, and the students were required to attend daily religious services. Students also were strongly discouraged from participating in traditional Cherokee dances, ball games, or other ceremonies that the missionaries believed would retard their "progress" toward "civilization."

The teachers "trained" Cherokee students to enter a rapidly changing world. By the 1830s almost all Cherokee men had abandoned hunting as a major economic activity, and most had adopted agriculture. Many traditional Cherokee men initially plowed their fields in the spring, but they then relied on the women of their family to provide much of the labor associated with the production of crops. In contrast, more assimilated men "managed" their farms, both large and small, and tended their growing herds of cattle, hogs, and horses. Emulating neighboring white planters, members of the planter-elite established plantations and purchased slaves. Others owned grist- or sawmills, managed retail establishments, or operated inns or ferries along the public roads that stretched throughout the Cherokee Nation.

Although the Cherokee elite accounted for no more than 10 percent of the tribe, by the 1830s their ideas dominated much of the nation. Traditional Cherokee values still persisted, but the changing economic, political, and social values championed by the elite shaped a tribal economy that made the Cherokees self-subsistent and independent of government payments to provide for their people. The 15,000 Cherokees living east of the Mississippi owned large herds of hogs, almost 8,000 horses, and over 22,000 cattle. They raised extensive crops of corn and cotton and operated

62 blacksmith shops, 31 gristmills, 14 sawmills, 9 saltpeter works, and 18 ferries. Most families, both traditional and those who embraced change, owned plows, spinning wheels, and looms, and most tribespeople dressed entirely in clothing made of either handwoven cloth or dry goods. Traditional people still fashioned their clothing after the loosely fitting styles of their parents, but the elite wore clothing that resembled the daily attire of surrounding white southerners.

Tribal government reflected the Cherokees' willingness to embrace political change. Between 1797 and 1810 the Cherokee National Council passed a series of written laws designed to replace the older unwritten laws and practices that had guided earlier generations. The new statutes shifted much of the responsibility for maintaining order away from the Cherokee clans and created new institutions and procedures. For example, in 1797 the tribe established the Cherokee Light Horse, a national police force, and subsequent legislation empowered this force to arrest Cherokees accused of crimes (particularly homicide). The new police force replaced the age-old practice of retribution by vendetta or the "law of blood," which in earlier years had been exacted by the victim's clan members. New laws focused on the protection of private property and enabled Cherokee men to bequeath their property to their wives and children, a practice that weakened the traditional matrilineal clans and strengthened the Cherokee transition to male-dominated families.

Other legislation shifted the focus of government away from the towns and toward the National Council. In 1817 the National Council enacted legislation providing that only the council could cede Cherokee land; during the next decade additional acts strengthened the executive power of the council, established a formal judiciary, and provided that representatives to the National Council would be elected from specific geographic districts within the nation. In 1827, the Cherokees adopted a written constitution providing for a bicameral national legislature, an elected chief, and a judicial system resembling that of the United States.

Perhaps the group that suffered most from these changes was Cherokee women. The tribe's adoption of Anglo-American values undermined the prominent place that women originally held within Cherokee society. Traditionally, Cherokee women were the backbone of the matrilineal clan system around which much of Cherokee society was organized, and all Cherokees gained their identity from their mother's kinship group. Cherokee households had consisted of an extended clan grouping, encompassing an older woman, her daughters, and their husbands. The women had lived in an extended household and had cooperated to produce corn and other crops. Matrilineal clans shared the lands they farmed, and the right to utilize these particular fields was associated with these women and their kinship group. Agriculture was the realm of women, and their production of corn was essential to the tribe's economy. Moreover, women played a major role in Cherokee politics. Internal order within the tribe was maintained through the interaction of these clans, and crimes such as murder or rape were punished or "balanced" through clan-based vendettas. If an individual Cherokee was wronged, he or she could rely on his or her clan to seek vengeance or gain satisfaction, but since the clans were matrilineal, mothers, sisters, and daughters exercised considerable influence in clan-based decisions and exerted significant power in tribal politics.

Within the new, evolving Cherokee society the power of women diminished. As families were restructured into nuclear, hierarchical, male-dominated households, the role of the matrilineal clans dwindled. Many women still worked in the fields, but their labor was less communal, since their sisters and daughters no longer labored at their side. They now worked in separate fields associated with their husbands' land holdings. Indeed, among the Cherokee elite, agricultural labor was performed by slaves or white laborers, who completely replaced Cherokee women in the important role of food production. Moreover, as the Cherokees turned toward a market economy, males controlled the marketing of tribal products, such as livestock, crops, and home-loomed cloth, even though the latter two commodities were produced by women. In addition, while changing economic patterns provided new opportunities for Cherokee men (traders, innkeepers, blacksmiths, etc.), these activities generally were not accessible to women. Gender roles borrowed from non-Indian neighbors emphasized the role of women as wives and mothers, not as agricultural laborers and businesswomen.

Finally, the Cherokees' new political institutions also minimized women's influence. As the tribe cre-

ated a National Council and written statutes, it diminished the role of matrilineal clans. Women did not serve on the National Council, and they now were forced to rely on abstract laws, rather than on closely related male clan members, to protect their interests. New laws of inheritance allowed men to leave private property to their wives and children, but they also assured that private property would be redistributed though patterns that reinforced a growing reliance on a family's male line. The Cherokee matriarchies of the past seemed obsolescent.

Although the tribe's adoption of Anglo-American cultural patterns was selective and uneven, and most Cherokees remained more traditional than the planter-elite, the values of the elite (like their counterparts in white southern society) guided the evolution of Cherokee society. Not all Cherokees were successful planters who owned slaves, nor were they all businessmen and innkeepers, but the tribe had become reliant on white technology. By 1830 most Cherokees lived in nuclear households dominated by males and devoted (to a greater or lesser degree) to the acquisition and protection of private property. The Cherokee political system also had evolved toward the federal model, and growing numbers of Cherokees spoke English, if only as a second language.

Many Cherokees were literate in their native language. In 1821 Sequoyah (George Gist or Guess), a traditional Cherokee of mixed lineage from eastern Tennessee, devised the Cherokee syllabary, which provided symbols for the eighty-six syllables that comprise the Cherokee language. Because the syllabary was easy to learn, much of the Cherokee tribe became literate in a matter of months. The syllabary was a source of great pride for the tribe and did much to foster Cherokee nationalism. Following its adoption, the literacy rate of the Cherokee Nation—in either Cherokee or English—was similar to, or even surpassed, that of the white South.

Not all Cherokees embraced the changes taking place in northern Georgia or eastern Tennessee. During the 1790s a party of Cherokees led by "the Bowl" had crossed the Mississippi to occupy lands in northeastern Arkansas. During the War of 1812 they moved to the northwestern corner of the state, where they were joined by other Cherokees who opted for a more traditional hunting existence in the west over the changes that were transforming Cherokee society back in their former homeland. These western Cherokees clashed with the Osages, but assisted by other emigrant Indians (Delawares, Shawnees, Kickapoos, etc.), they gradually extended their territory into modern northeastern Oklahoma. Since game was plentiful and non-Indians were relatively few, they were able to pursue a more traditional lifestyle, but even in the west the tide of change began to transform their culture. By 1830 the 2,000 Western Cherokees, or "Old Settlers," also had established a code of written laws and had centralized their tribal government.

By almost any standard, the Cherokees in both Georgia and Arkansas were making good, if somewhat uneven, "progress toward civilization." Tribespeople living in both regions encompassed a broad spectrum of cultural changes. They were hardly the "uncivilized savages" described by frontier politicians who clamored that they could never become part of the new American nation.

Cultural changes also took place north of the Ohio River, but in this region it followed a different pattern. Unlike the southern tribes who had associated with British trader-farmers and then American planters, northern tribes such as the Potawatomis, Miamis, and Ottawas had interacted primarily with the French. French *coureurs de bois* who initially entered the Great Lakes region had been skilled traders, but with the exception of a relatively few Creole-French settlers in southern Michigan or in the American Bottom, opposite St. Louis, they had little interest in agriculture. In contrast to southern tribesmen who envisioned white farmers or planters as role models for cultural change, many northern tribespeople admired the French or Creole traders in their midst. The traders prospered within the fur trade, but like the Native American hunters and warriors with whom they bartered, most did not farm.

In the North, Native Americans intermarried extensively with their white neighbors. French or Creole traders often married Indian women, either in formal Catholic ceremonies or more commonly *a la façon du pays* ("in the fashion of the country"—according to tribal custom) since marriage ties to powerful kinship groups greatly facilitated the trade. As in the South, these marriages produced a growing population of *métis*, or people of mixed lineage, but from the federal government's

perspective, these northern people seemed less "civilized" and retained more of their traditional values. Anglo-American evaluations of the lack of cultural change among the northern tribes were heavily influenced by American prejudice against the Creole-French population. Since many of the French rejected the idealized role of small yeomen farmers so strongly championed by the government, American officials considered the Creoles to be almost as "uncivilized" as the Indians. Any cultural change by Indians toward the Creole-trader role was unacceptable. According to Indian Agent Lewis Cass, both the Creoles and the *métis* were "unacquainted with the laws of the civilized world" and unacceptable for assimilation into American society.

Ironically, however, the sophistication and prosperity of many of the *métis* traders in the Great Lakes and Wabash Valley did much to refute Cass's appraisal. Many spoke French, English, and several tribal languages; managed trading empires that stretched across the upper Midwest; and balanced ledgers that remain complicated even to modern accountants. Most *métis* traders lived in houses similar to or more spacious than those of white frontiersmen. *Métis* housewives lived amid imported furniture, crystal, china, and silverware, while their husbands sometimes kept servants or employed less-acculturated tribal members to hunt for their family. In addition, as the *métis* began to acquire lands adjoining their trading establishments, they employed non-Indian agricultural laborers to produce the limited crops needed for livestock and other purposes.

Many *métis* were more prosperous than most frontier whites. They lived in comfortable log cabins surrounded by split rail fences and numerous outbuildings. Many dressed in clothing fashioned from silks, satins, and other expensive trade cloth, and their costumes combined highly decorated leggings, turbans, and comfortable moccasins with Anglo-American ruffled shirts, vests, and frock coats. Women wore long blouses, skirts, and leggings, and carried blankets or shawls when they left their homes. Many Miami and Potawatomi *métis* raised and traded fine horses, and traders such as Miamis François Godfroy and Jean Baptiste Richardville prospered. Godfroy's estate, Mt. Pleasant, located at the juncture of the Wabash and Mississinewa rivers, held a well-furnished two-story

PEOPLE, PLACES, AND THINGS

Native American Women as Entrepreneurs

D-Mouche-kee-kee-awh, by George Winter

Many Americans assume that Native American entrepreneurs are a modern phenomenon, but many Indian people have long prospered in trade and commerce, and Native American women often played key roles in organizing and administering these activities. Women were particularly active among many of the midwestern and Great Lakes tribes, and during the first half of the nineteenth century they played key roles in business ventures among the Mesquakies, Ho-Chunks, and Potawatomis. Mesquakie and Ho-Chunk women controlled much of the production and marketing of lead from the rich mines near modern Dubuque, Iowa. Although their mixed-lineage husbands often "fronted" for the women in the sale of lead ore and ingots to Euro-Americans, the women used kinship networks to promote the mining and distribution of lead among the tribal communities.

In northern Indiana and southwestern Michigan, Potawatomi women such as Kakima and Mouto (Madeline Bertrand) played pivotal roles in their husbands' far-flung trading activities. Married to William Burnett, Kakima's kinship ties to prominent Potawatomi village chiefs enabled her husband to pass freely among the Potawatomi communities in the region, and he admitted that "she had done her part in the trading very, very well." Madeline Bertrand, who also was active in the trade, spent considerable time promoting Roman Catholicism within the Potawatomi villages.

During the late 1830s, frontier artist George Winter painted Potawatomi and Miami women whose families were active in trade, and his portraits illustrate the wealth and sophistication these women enjoyed. D-Mouche-kee-kee-awh (pictured here), the wife of Abram Burnett, Kakima's adopted son, posed

Massaw, by George Winter

for Winter adorned in trade silver. Massaw, another Potawatomi businesswoman pictured here, wears a cape and silver earrings. In addition, Massaw has a shawl of expensive imported silk draped over her shoulders. Massaw was an entrepreneur who owned and operated an "inn and gambling house" on the Michigan Road in modern Fulton County, Indiana. A "chieftess" of some political influence, Massaw not only provided food and lodging, she also maintained a "card room" on the upper floor of her large, two-story log residence, where travelers reported that "she was in fact a gambler of no ordinary ability . . . an adroit expert [at euchre and poker], often raking men of experience."

PEOPLE, PLACES, AND THINGS

(continued)

Ironically, even after removal, Potawatomi women continued their business activities in Kansas. During the 1850s, many reestablished inns and restaurants to market food and lodging to American emigrants traveling west. Like Massaw's hotel in Indiana, these Kansas roadhouses also offered travelers games of chance and an opportunity to sample frontier dining. Not all travelers were smitten with the cuisine, however. In 1859, after dining at the Red Vermillion, an inn owned by a Potawatomi woman in St. Mary's, Kansas, Horace Greeley, an American journalist, complained that his stomach was rebelling against the "the worst half-dollar dinner I have ever consumed."

Until recently, historians have ignored the important role that tribal women played in the economic systems that developed in the Great Lakes and Upper Mississippi Valley regions. Why?

---

frame house, a trading post, and numerous barns and other outbuildings. Richardville established trading posts at both ends of the Wabash-Maumee portage, controlled the traffic between the streams, and was reputed to be the richest man in Indiana when the region became a state in 1816.

Unlike their counterparts among the Cherokees, many women among these northern tribes benefited from the acculturation process. Women had always grown corn, beans, and squash to supplement the game or fish supplied by their husbands, but they also had traded surplus crops, maple sugar, or other products in the intertribal trade. When this commerce was expanded by the French demand for furs, they had continued to participate in it. In addition, Mesquakie women in the Dubuque region mined lead, which they traded to both neighboring tribes and non-Indians. Consequently, unlike their sisters among the Cherokees, who lost political power and were forced to accept the diminished role that American women played in trade and politics, many Potawatomi, Miami, Ottawa, and other northern women continued to enlarge their trading activities, utilizing kinship networks and other traditional associations to buttress their businesses.

As in the South, cultural change among the northern tribes remained uneven. A few northern tribesmen, such as Black Hoof's Shawnees in western Ohio, unsuccessfully attempted to "walk the corn road" (become small yeomen farmers). Other northern people, especially those living in remote parts of Michigan and Wisconsin, continued to follow the traditional ways of their fathers. But most northern Indians had begun to adopt selective aspects of the white man's culture. They too had changed, and while they preferred to model themselves after the lifestyles of Creole traders rather than American farmers, they had embraced a process of cultural change that was markedly altering their lives. Yet even these changes would not guarantee that tribal people, both north and south, would continue to occupy their homelands.

JACKSONIAN INDIAN POLICY

The decade and a half (1815–1830) following the War of 1812 brought profound changes to American politics. The Founding Fathers—American icons such as Washington, Adams, or Jefferson—were not averse to forcing an alien culture onto the tribes and purchasing their lands, but their Indian policies were based on the assumption that Native Americans eventually would disappear or be assimilated into the United States. Indeed, the government's "civilization" program, epitomized by the Indian Intercourse Acts and the reliance on both missionaries and federal Indian agents to transform the tribesmen into small yeomen farmers, bears active testimony to these goals; and since small yeomen farmers needed less land than hunters and gatherers, then the Indians' surplus lands would be opened up to white settlement.

The Jacksonians, who emerged in the 1820s, were politicians of a different mettle. Historians still argue over the origins and significance of the Jacksonian Democrats, but by all accounts they represented a new "rough and tumble" approach to American politics. Like Andrew Jackson, many of his followers were white frontiersmen, and they were eager to open the trans-Appalachian west to economic development. Jackson had sprung to political prominence through his campaigns against the Creeks and his victory at the Battle of New Orleans. He believed that the western tribes were barriers to the American settlement of valuable farmlands. Although he knew that the southern Indians had made significant strides toward "civilization," he remained doubtful that they would ever join American society. He also argued they were being degraded by many of the whites with whom they were in contact. Moreover, Jackson was an inveterate Anglophobe; as a veteran of the War of 1812, he was convinced that the western tribes were a fertile medium for British intrigue. In addition, the opening of Indian land to western settlers would further strengthen the growing power of Jackson's new Democratic Party. If Indians could not fit into American society, they must be removed to new homes in the west.

Other factors strengthened Jackson's hand. Between 1816 and 1828 (the year in which Jackson was elected president) six new states joined the union, all of which (except Maine, which was admitted in 1820) were located in the Mississippi Valley. Eager to attract population, these new states petitioned the federal government to purchase the remaining Indian lands within their borders and to remove the tribes west of the Mississippi. State and local officials flooded Washington with exaggerated reports of Indian decadence, "barbarism," and hostility. In addition, Thomas McKenney, the head of the recently established (1824) Bureau of Indian Affairs, reported that the government's civilization program was failing. According to McKenney, the western tribespeople were not becoming small farmers; instead, they continued to "catch fish, and plant patches of corn; dance, paint, hunt, get drunk, when they can get liquor, fight, and often starve." To save Indian people from complete debauchery, McKenney recommended that they be removed beyond the Mississippi, where they could be protected from whiskey traders and other evil influences.

Some missionaries, who believed that the Indians were being tempted by "the devil's minions" in the East, also argued for removal. Clergymen such as Baptist Isaac McCoy complained bitterly that Potawatomis and Miamis in his congregation were falling prey to whiskey peddlers who swarmed around the tribes "likes crows to a carcass." In the proverbial battle between God and Mammon, Mammon was winning, and only if the tribes could be removed to the "pristine" trans-Mississippi west could the missionaries protect them from corruption. McCoy became such a proponent of Indian removal that he conducted "exploring parties" from many tribes to lands west of the Mississippi where they supposedly would select locations for their future homes. Indeed, by the 1830s Baptist Isaac McCoy spent more time guiding Indians to Kansas than to "glory"; he functioned more as a removal agent than as a missionary.

The Indian Removal Act, passed by Congress and signed by the president in May 1830, formalized Jacksonian Indian policy. It stipulated that in exchange for the cession of the tribes' remaining homelands east of the Mississippi, the president would set aside lands in the west "not included in any organized state or territory and to which the Indian title has been extinguished" as a future home for those eastern Indians who could be persuaded to remove. The United States would "forever secure and guaranty" the new lands in the west to the emigrant Indians and their heirs, and if they were forced to leave homes, farms, or other businesses on their old eastern homelands, the government would pay them for such "improvements." The government also promised to pay the cost of removing the eastern Indians into the west, and to support them for one year after they arrived in their new homes. In addition, the act stipulated that government agents would protect the emigrants "at their new residence, against all interruptions or disturbance from any other tribe or nation of Indians, or from any other person or persons."

INDIAN REMOVAL: THE SOUTHEAST

Like the Western Cherokees, portions of many tribes had removed voluntarily prior to 1830, but following the passage of the Removal Act, the process accelerated. In 1802, Jefferson had promised Georgia that in exchange for relinquishing its claims to lands in the old Yazoo Strip (see Chapter 7), the federal government eventually would extinguish Indian title to lands in the region. By 1830 white planters were eager to gain access to additional cotton lands in Georgia, Alabama, and Mississippi. Encouraged by the Removal Act, officials in these states attempted to extend control over Indian lands within their borders. Even if the tribespeople remained in their homeland, they would be subjected to discrimination by state and local governments.

The Choctaws

In 1820 the Choctaws had signed the Treaty of Doak's Stand in which they exchanged part of their lands in Mississippi for lands in modern Arkansas and Oklahoma. Although many traditional Choctaws planned to remain in Mississippi, they were willing to exchange those regions in which the deer herds had been depleted for more bountiful hunting lands in the west. Yet Choctaw herdsmen and planters with growing herds of cattle and nascent cotton plantations were determined to retain the remainder of the tribe's Mississippi homeland, since it held valuable pastures and cotton fields. The region also was desirable to whites, and during the 1820s white squatters moved onto these lands, while the state of Mississippi passed legislation outlawing the Choctaw tribal government. State and local officials in Mississippi refused to protect the Choctaws and their property, and when the Choctaws appealed to the federal government, Jackson's Indian agents declined to intervene.

Government demands for their removal engendered splits within the tribe, and leaders of the Choctaw planter-elite argued among themselves over the proper response to the American demands. One faction led by the Pitchlynn family favored cooperation with state and local officials, while others, including David Folsum and John Garland, supported by many of the more traditional tribes-people, opposed removal. In September 1830, Choctaw leaders met with federal agents and signed the Treaty of Dancing Rabbit Creek. The Choctaws ceded all tribal lands in Mississippi in exchange for further guarantees to their western lands in modern Oklahoma; a twenty-year tribal annuity (a yearly payment) of $20,000; and funds for schools and the education of Choctaw children. To secure the agreement of Indians still determined to remain in Mississippi, the government promised that those Choctaws who refused to remove would be given individual allotments of land (some received one square mile or 640 acres, but most received less) from the recently ceded territory. The allotments would belong to an individual Indian in fee simple: he or she would possess a title to the acreage not as tribal land, but as private property. These Choctaws could then remain within their old homeland, but they would be subject to all the laws of the state of Mississippi and local counties or towns in which they might reside. They also would be separated from the majority of the tribe in the west and could organize no tribal government.

About five thousand Choctaws, or one-fourth of the tribe, decided to remain in Mississippi, but dishonest Indian agents failed to register their individual allotments with the local land office. The acreages were then lost to speculators. In consequence, many of the Choctaws who had remained in Mississippi became landless and impoverished, then eventually drifted westward where they joined their relatives in Oklahoma. A few members of the Choctaw elite retained their large allotments, but eventually many of these individuals also left for the west. Those Choctaws who still remained in Mississippi (fewer than one thousand) retreated into small isolated communities in the pine barrens or swamplands. There they eked out an existence by hunting, fishing, and subsistence agriculture. The federal government ignored them until 1918, when an Indian Agency was opened at Philadelphia, Mississippi. They received a reservation along the Pearl River in Mississippi in 1944.

Those Choctaws who agreed to remove to the west also suffered. The Treaty of Dancing Rabbit Creek stipulated that the Choctaws would remove in three parties between 1831 and 1833. Federal officials had little experience in organizing Indian removals, but in 1831 Secretary of War John Eaton allocated considerable funds to ship the Choctaws, via steamboat, into central Arkansas, where they would disembark and travel by wagons to Indian Territory. Since Eaton wished to encourage other southern Indians to remove, he initially allocated considerable funds for provisions and transportation. But Eaton left office before the removal began, and Lewis Cass, his bumbling successor, did much to negate Eaton's benevolence. Moreover, local removal agents quarreled among themselves, and the removal disintegrated into bureaucratic chaos. In October 1831 about 4,000 Choctaws left Mississippi for Oklahoma, but en route across Arkansas they encountered one of the worst blizzards of the nineteenth century. Roads became impassable, provisions were depleted, and agents were forced to purchase food, blankets, and other supplies at inflated prices. By March 1, 1832, after considerable suffering, 3,749 Choctaws reached Oklahoma.

The additional food, clothing, and other equipment purchased by the removal agents saved many Choctaw lives, but the cost of this first large-scale Indian removal, almost three times what the government originally had allocated, staggered federal officials. In consequence, in 1832, Secretary of War Cass dismissed all civilian removal agents and ordered the army to remove the Choctaws. The second removal was more tightly organized, but it also encountered disaster. About 5,800 Choctaws started west from Mississippi in October 1832; most walked since funds for teams and wagons had been reduced considerably by the War Department. When they reached Memphis and Vicksburg, they found that steamboats chartered to carry them to Rockroe on the White River in Arkansas had not arrived; instead, these river towns were full of cholera. The disease spread through the Choctaw ranks, and as they trudged westward across the muddy roads of Arkansas, many sickened and died. In February 1833, about 5,400 Choctaw emigrants arrived in Oklahoma, but many of their kinspeople lay buried in Arkansas. Federal officials prided themselves that this second removal had remained "within budget," but it had been costly in terms of Choctaw lives and suffering.

The third party, which went west in October 1833, contained only 813 Indians. One of the steamboats chartered to carry these Choctaws into Arkansas exploded as it approached the dock at Memphis, but after another boat was secured, the removal proceeded more smoothly, and in December this final contingent of the "official" Choctaw removal also arrived in Oklahoma.

The Chickasaws

The Chickasaw land cessions and removals went more smoothly. The smallest of the Five Southern Tribes (about 4,800 in 1830), the Chickasaws were closely related to the Choctaws and occupied lands in northern Mississippi, northwestern Alabama, and western Tennessee. Like the Choctaws and Cherokees, the Chickasaws also were led by a coterie of planters and businessmen, particularly the Colbert family, but among the Chickasaws the planter-elite were perhaps the most socially and politically influential of all those in the southern tribes. In 1816 and 1818 the Chickasaws had ceded their lands in Alabama and Tennessee, but they continued to occupy northern Mississippi. Following the passage of the Indian Removal Act, however, many Chickasaw leaders believed that removal was inevitable. In 1830 they met with Andrew Jackson at Franklin, Tennessee, and signed a provisional treaty relinquishing their claim to lands east of the Mississippi. They agreed to remove west providing they found acceptable lands in the Indian Territory. However, the Chickasaws rejected the lands initially set aside for them, and the treaty never was ratified.

The Choctaw treaty at Dancing Rabbit Creek put additional pressure on the Chickasaws, and in 1832 a new treaty was negotiated at the Chickasaw council house at Pontotoc Creek. The new treaty reaffirmed the aborted land cession of 1830, and also called for Chickasaw approval of western lands prior to any removal; but Chickasaw leaders shrewdly negotiated a government promise that the ceded lands would be surveyed immediately and sold at a fair market price, the proceeds to be placed in a general fund to be at the Chickasaws' disposal. In addition, each adult Chickasaw received an allotment where his or her family might reside until the removal took place. These allotments were to be owned by individual Chickasaws and the proceeds from their sale also would go directly to the Indians. A tribal commission was established to protect less acculturated Chickasaws from fraud. Obviously, the sophisticated Chickasaws had learned from the Choctaw experience.

In 1837 the Chickasaws agreed to purchase the western portions of the Oklahoma lands assigned to the Choctaws, and between 1837 and 1840 most of the tribe removed to Indian Territory. First, however, they sold their individual allotments for an additional profit, and as the tribe moved west to Oklahoma, many Chickasaws were more financially secure than members of other tribes. Many Chickasaws suffered during the removal process, but they probably fared better than the other southern tribes.

The Creeks

Things did not go so well for the Creeks. Following the War of 1812, Creek attempts at political unity again were stymied by old intratribal animosities, and Creek divisiveness played into the hands of the Americans. In 1818 and 1821 Creek leaders friendly with politicians in Georgia ceded two tracts of lands in southern and central Georgia, which caused the Creek National Council to forbid any further land cessions and to prescribe the death penalty for any tribe member who negotiated such a treaty with the Americans. Yet William McIntosh, who was related by marriage to Governor George Troup of Georgia, was offered a bribe of $40,000 to cede additional lands in that state. Convinced that removal was inevitable, in 1825 McIntosh and a handful of his allies signed the Treaty of Indian Springs, which relinquished Creek claims to much of western Georgia. The Creek National Council subsequently executed McIntosh (see the discussion at the beginning of the chapter), and Creek leaders protested that the treaty was illegal. It was ratified by the Senate, but when President John Quincy Adams learned of the circumstances surrounding the agreement, he refused to sign the document. Meanwhile, white frontiersmen in Georgia flooded onto the lands in question, and pressure to legalize the acquisition of the region heightened. In addition, McIntosh's relatives and friends (mostly Lower Creeks) threatened retaliation against those responsible for his death (mostly Upper Creeks), and the Creek Nation appeared to be on the brink of a new civil war.

Finally, cooler heads prevailed. Federal troops were dispatched to Georgia to protect white settlers from the Creeks (and vice versa), and new ne-

gotiators worked to achieve a compromise. The United States abrogated the Treaty of Indian Springs, and on January 24, 1826, the Creeks signed a new agreement, the Treaty of Washington, in which they relinquished their remaining lands in Georgia for additional payments, federal acknowledgment of their remaining lands in Alabama, and renewed guarantees that the federal government would protect them against local officials and settlers in Alabama. Warfare with Georgia had been avoided, and both the Creeks and the Adams administration believed they had made the best of a bad situation.

But Adams lost the election of 1828, and Andrew Jackson's administration refused to honor Adams's guarantees. Crowded onto their remaining lands in Alabama, the Creeks watched in dismay as the state of Alabama initiated a series of legal actions similar to those previously exercised by Georgia. When Alabama's Extension Act of 1829 declared that Alabama's laws "extended" over Creek lands within the state, the Creeks protested to Washington, asking the federal government to honor its promises, but Andrew Jackson replied:

> My white children of Alabama have extended their law over your country. If you remain in it, you must be subject to that law. But if you wish, you can escape that law by removing to the west where you will be free from the troublesome laws of white men. There you can live as you please, by your own laws, in the care of your father, the President, as long as the grass grows and the water flows, in peace and plenty.

Regardless of the government's previous promises, it would not protect the Creeks in Alabama.

Led by Opothle Yaholo, an Upper Creek chief, the Creeks continued to protest, but in 1832 they signed a treaty giving up their remaining lands east of the Mississippi in exchange for lands in Oklahoma. Similar to the Choctaw removal agreement, the treaty provided that those Creeks wishing to remain in Alabama would receive individual allotments. Although the government encouraged the Creeks to remove and promised to pay their removal expenses, Article XII of the treaty stipulated that the government would not "compel any Creek Indian to emigrate, but they shall be free to go or

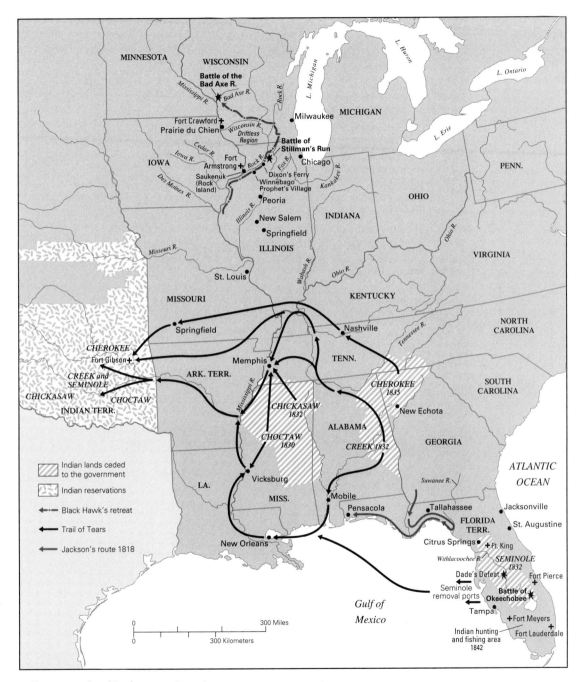

Indian Removal and Resistance, 1819–1845

to stay, as they please." Those who stayed would be subject to the laws of Alabama and eventually would be citizens of the state.

Less than 700 of the almost 20,000 Creeks remaining in Alabama initially chose to go west, and when officials in Alabama learned that of the five million acres recently ceded at the Second Treaty of Washington, almost two million acres would be assigned as Creek allotments, they were incensed. With the state's blessing, white settlers immediately intruded onto the unsurveyed Creek lands, staking claims on sections containing Creek farms and cabins. Creeks applying for legitimate land allotments were assigned sections of pine barrens or swamplands, while land agents readily accepted the "sale" of Creek lands by white imposters posing as Indians. Federal officials assigned to protect Creek interests cooperated in the fraud, and the Creeks again found themselves overwhelmed.

By 1836 Creek resentment had reached such a pitch that bloodshed broke out between Creeks and state militia units in both Alabama and western Georgia, where some Creeks had fled to escape the turmoil. Meanwhile, Creek resistance crystallized around Eneah Mico, a headman from the towns along the western tributaries of the Chattahoochee. Federal troops were sent to Georgia and Alabama; Opothle Yaholo, Eneah Mico, and most of their followers were arrested; and "the 1836 Creek War" ended.

During the summer of 1836 federal troops removed the Creeks from Alabama. The recently "hostile" Creek warriors, handcuffed, chained, and guarded by soldiers, were marched out of Fort Mitchell early in July, while their women and children followed in wagons. Other hostiles were shipped by steamboat to Mobile, then to New Orleans and up the Mississippi and Arkansas rivers. Contingents of "friendly" Creeks followed in both parties' wakes. A few Creeks remained in southern Alabama and the Florida panhandle, but by late fall 1836 almost 15,000 new Creek refugees had arrived in the Indian Territory. There they merged with members of the McIntosh party, who had removed earlier on their own accord. The two parties, McIntosh's followers and the recent émigrés, joined to form a new Creek Nation, but the political divisions engendered by the Treaty of Indian Springs and the execution of William McIntosh remained. These schisms would plague the Creeks in the west.

The Cherokees

The Cherokees also were divided by the removal process. In 1817 and 1819 the Cherokees had ceded tracts of land east of the Mississippi in return for lands in Arkansas, and in 1828 they exchanged most of these Arkansas lands for a large tract in northeastern Oklahoma and a narrow strip of land known as the "Cherokee Outlet" that stretched westward from northern Oklahoma and provided the Cherokees with access to "buffalo lands" on the Great Plains. The Western Cherokees, or "Old Settlers," resided on these western lands, but the majority of the tribe continued to live on its remaining territories in northern Georgia and southeastern Tennessee. Like other tribes, the Cherokees intended to remain in their homeland, and since their lands in the foothills of the Smoky Mountains were considered less fertile than neighboring Creek territories, at first the pressure for their removal was not intense. But in 1829 gold was discovered along the Chestatee River in Georgia, and whites flooded onto the southeastern section of the Cherokee Nation, where they opened mines, seized Cherokee livestock, and occupied Cherokee farms and plantations. Cherokee protests were ignored by state officials, and between 1829 and 1831 the state's legislature enacted a series of "extension laws" designed to place the Cherokees and their territories under Georgia's jurisdiction. The acts forbade the Cherokee government to meet, barred the Cherokees from mining gold, and demanded that any white person living in the Cherokee Nation take an oath of allegiance to the State of Georgia.

The Cherokee response resulted in two court cases that still exert significant influence on American jurisprudence. When officials arrested a Cherokee who had been accused of killing another tribesman within the Cherokee Nation, the tribal government brought a suit against Georgia, claiming that the tribe was an independent nation over which the state government had no legal jurisdiction. The case, *Cherokee Nation* v. *Georgia*, reached the Supreme Court, where Chief Justice John Marshall admitted, "If courts were permitted to indulge their sympathies . . . a case better calculated to excite them can scarcely be imagined." However, he declared that the tribe was not an independent "foreign" nation, but a "domestic dependent nation." The court obviously was sympathetic to the Cherokees, and the tribe was determined to seek further legal recourse against Georgia.

It wasn't long in coming. The Georgia statute requiring whites who lived among the Cherokees to take an oath of allegiance to the state had been aimed at missionaries, whom Georgia envisioned as "outside agitators" responsible for the Cherokees' refusal to remove to the west. If the missionaries signed the oath and then counseled against removal, they could be arrested for violating the laws of Georgia; if they refused to sign the oath, they could be arrested for residing illegally within the Cherokee Nation. Samuel Worcester, a Congregationalist minister, refused to sign the oath and was arrested, tried, and convicted by the state. Worcester appealed through the federal court system, and his case reached the Supreme Court in 1832. In *Worcester v. Georgia*, Marshall ruled in the Cherokees' favor. He declared that the laws of Georgia were invalid within the Cherokee Nation and that "the citizens of Georgia have no right to enter" Cherokee territory without the tribe's permission. In addition, he ordered state courts in Georgia to reverse their conviction and release Worcester. When Andrew Jackson heard of Marshall's decision, he supposedly replied, "Well, John Marshall has made his decision; let him enforce it," and refused to comply with the Supreme Court's directive. Since the judicial branch of the federal government had no police power and was forced to rely on the executive branch to enforce its decisions, Jackson's inaction meant that Marshall's decision in the case would be ignored. In the late twentieth century however, *Worcester v. Georgia*, with Marshall's interpretation that tribes retain considerable sovereignty in relation to the states that surround their reservations, emerged as a cornerstone in the growth and sovereignty of modern tribal governments.

Encouraged by Jackson's inaction, Georgia increased its pressure on the Cherokees. Both Jackson and officials in Georgia falsely claimed that the majority of the tribe was willing to remove but was being dissuaded by the planter-elite, who were interested only in protecting their plantations. Accordingly, in 1834 officials in Georgia seized the plantations of Cherokee leaders such as John Ross, the Ridge family, Joseph Vann, and others. One year later Georgia surveyed the Cherokee lands and

established a state lottery through which Cherokee farms and homesteads would be raffled off to white Georgians. In 1835 the Georgia militia invaded the Cherokee capital at New Echota, occupied the Cherokee National Council House, and then smashed the printing press used to print the *Cherokee Phoenix* (the tribal newspaper), charging that the paper had printed editorials opposing removal. Cherokee protests to Jackson again brought only admonitions that the federal government could provide no assistance and that the Cherokees should remove to the west.

Continued pressure by both Georgia and the federal government created a split within the Cherokee ranks. Prior to Jackson's refusal to enforce the *Worcester v. Georgia* decision, most Cherokees remained opposed to removal, but by 1833 their solidarity had eroded. A minority of the planter-elite, led by Major Ridge, his son John Ridge, and Elias Boudinot, the editor of the *Cherokee Phoenix*, decided that removal was inevitable. They argued that the tribe should negotiate a favorable removal treaty and move to the west. The vast majority of the tribe, however, led by John Ross, the elected chief, denounced this Treaty Party as government collaborators. Although Ross and the Cherokee National Council refused to attend the proceedings, the Treaty Party met with federal agents in December 1835 and signed the Treaty of New Echota in which the Treaty Party ceded all Cherokee lands east of the Mississippi for $5 million. The treaty also awarded the Cherokees additional lands in the west and promised that the western lands would never be included within the jurisdiction of any state or territory. In return, the Treaty Party pledged that the Cherokees would leave Georgia within two years of the treaty's ratification.

The treaty brought a storm of protest from the Cherokees. Although less than two hundred members of the Treaty Party had attended the treaty proceedings, over fifteen thousand Cherokees flooded Congress with petitions claiming that the agreement was illegal. Many Cherokee women were particularly vocal in their opposition to the treaty. Led by Ross, the Cherokees sent delegations to Congress who argued that the Treaty Party did not represent the majority of the tribe and urged the Senate not to ratify the agreement. Ross was able to garner considerable support from northeastern

Trail of Tears   The forced removal of the Cherokee people caused much suffering. Most historians estimate that about four thousand people, or approximately one-fifth of the Cherokee Nation, died during the removal process. *Buffalo Bill Historical Society.*

Senators (Whigs), who disliked Jackson and feared that the removal of the Cherokees and their slaves would extend slavery into the west. Nevertheless, on May 18, 1836, the Senate ratified the Treaty of New Echota by a single vote. The Cherokees' fate was sealed.

Led by the Ridge family, the Treaty Party and their followers (about 2,000 tribespeople) quickly emigrated west, but Ross and the remaining 16,000 Cherokees vowed to remain in Georgia. Between 1836 and 1838 Ross repeatedly petitioned the federal government and sought public support for the tribe's plight. Although their lands were overrun by white Georgians, the Cherokees refused to budge. Federal troops sent into Georgia and Alabama to maintain the peace were sickened by their assignments, and their officers generally sided with the Cherokees, but when they arrested whites trespassing on Cherokee lands, local courts promptly freed the intruders and charged the officers with "usurping the powers" of state and local governments. Finally, in May 1838, General Winfield Scott and a contingent of federal troops reluctantly rounded up the Indians and escorted them to "em-

igration camps" where they were forcibly enrolled for removal.

The intolerable conditions in the emigration camps and the subsequent Cherokee suffering as they were removed over the Trail of Tears have become an indelible part of both Cherokee and American history. Herded like cattle into crowded camps, the Cherokees suffered from tainted food and intolerable sanitary conditions. Latrines were open slit trenches within the camp, devoid of any privacy except for loosely hung blankets. Dysentery became epidemic, and children, the weak, and the elderly sickened and died. The first contingents of Cherokees, accompanied by federal removal agents, left the camps in mid-July, but their trek was plagued by a prolonged heat wave and drought. They suffered such deprivation that Ross convinced federal officials to postpone any further departures until September and to allow the Cherokees to conduct the remainder of the removals themselves. During July and August, Cherokee leaders scrambled to provide adequate food and shelter for the people in the camps, and in late August, when the drought ended, the removal began

INDIAN VOICES   Cherokee Leaders Denounce
the Injustices of Removal

Most scholars agree that the Cherokee Trail of Tears, like the forced removal of other tribes during the Jacksonian Era, was one of the most shameful episodes in American history. Modern Cherokees still remember the suffering of their ancestors during this period, and bitter memories of the removal experience continue to permeate the work of contemporary Cherokee artists and writers. Indian removal in the South has received considerable attention from historians, but excerpts from the two letters below, written by Cherokee leaders swept up in these events, provide dramatic documentation of both the chicanery of frontier whites and the suffering of the Cherokee people. The first letter, written by George Hicks, a Cherokee leader in charge of a removal party that has just departed for the west, complains about frontier whites who continue to steal Cherokee livestock. The second letter, written by Chief John Ross soon after the Cherokees arrived in the west, comments on the quality of the food supplied to the Indians during and after their removal. Despite the suffering of many other tribes during their removal experiences, why have historians and the American public often focused primarily on the plight of the Cherokees and the Trail of Tears?

George Hicks writes:

We are now about to take our final leave and kind farewell to our native land the country that the Great Spirit gave our Fathers, we are on the eve of leaving that Country that gave us birth. It is the land of our [page torn] and it is with [sorrow?] that we are forced by the authority of the white man to quit the scenes of our childhood. Since we have been on the march many of us have been stopped and our horses taken from our teams for the payment of just and unjust demands, yet the government says we must go, and its citizens say you must pay me, and if a debtor has not the means, the property of his next friend is levied on and yet the Government has not given us our spoilations [payments] as promised. Our property has been stolen and robbed from us by white men and no means given us to pay our debts, when application is made to, as we think the proper authority, the agents of government, and the commanding officers of the military, the one says we have no jurisdiction over any thing, only such as happens in their own sight, or in the mile square about the agency, and the other says our hands are tied. . . . They give us no assistance, yet they have the power to force us off.

They may not think it necessary to delay any time to recover our property robbed of us in open day light and in open view of hundreds. And why are they so bold. They know that we are in a defenseless situation, dependent upon the Government for protection, who all know have denied us that protection. Therefore we will have to leave our property in the hands of whosoever may have the conscience to rob us of it. And those appear to be plenty, since protection has been denied.

And from Chief John Ross we hear:

From the many complaints daily made to me by Cherokees who have been recently removed into this country, of their suffering, from the want of being properly subsisted with provisions, I am constrained to address you this hasty letter. It is reported that, apart from the scantiness of the ration allowed under the contract made on the part of the United States Government . . . the contractors were only required to furnish one lb. of fresh beef, three pints of corn, and four quarts of salt to every 100 pounds of beef—or if they (the contractors) choose they might furnish in lieu of beef, ¾ lb. salt pork or bacon provided the Indians will receive it. The beef being poor and not considered wholesome this time of year, the Cherokees have generally objected to and refused to receive it, and have insisted on being furnished with salt pork or bacon, yet it seems that the contractors have refused to comply with their demand; saying that they were bound to furnish only beef rations.

The health and existence of the whole Cherokee people who have recently been removed to this distant country demands a speedy remedy for the inconveniences and evils complained of, and unless a change in the quantity and kind of rations as well as the mode of issuing the same, be made from that which has heretofore been granted and observed, the Cherokees must inevitably suffer. Therefore, to avoid hunger and starvation, they are reduced to the necessity of calling upon . . . the U. S. Govt. . . . to take immediate steps as will ensure the subsistence of the Cherokees who have been recently removed here.

Source: From George Hicks to John Ross, November 4, 1838, in Gary E. Moulton, ed., *The Papers of Chief John Ross*, 2 vols. (Norman: University of Oklahoma Press, 1985), vol. 1, 687–688; from John Ross to George Arbuckle, April 23, 1839, 704–706. Reprinted with permission of the University of Oklahoma Press.

anew. Separate parties of Cherokees (usually 1,000 to 1,200 individuals) started west, and by early December 1838, the removal camps were emptied.

The trek west (the Trail of Tears) mirrored the Choctaw experience, but with even greater suffering. Although Ross and other Cherokee leaders tried valiantly to provide for their people's welfare, they were plagued by private contractors who failed to supply the promised provisions or charged exorbitant prices for fodder, food, and blankets. Some of the removal parties were transported west by steamboats, but others made the entire journey overland, following circuitous routes through Tennessee, Kentucky, southern Illinois, and Missouri. Winter arrived before the Cherokees reached Indian Territory, and many people struggled westward through freezing rain and snow. Most of the removal parties were forced to camp in the open, and many Cherokees sickened and died. John Ross's wife, the kindly Quatie, contracted pneumonia after giving her blanket to a feverish child.

She died and was buried in Arkansas. Tragically, many other Cherokees suffered a similar fate. The last removal parties reached Fort Gibson, in Indian Territory, in March 1839. Historians still argue over the final death toll on the Trail of Tears, but most scholars agree that at least 4,000 Cherokees, about one of every four persons originally imprisoned in the emigration camps, perished before they reached Indian Territory.

INDIAN REMOVAL: THE OLD NORTHWEST

The displacement of Native Americans north of the Ohio River followed a similar pattern. Like the western Cherokees, some bands from the northern tribes voluntarily removed westward, fleeing white settlement. Bands of Delawares, originally resident in Pennsylvania, had moved to Ohio during the mid-eighteenth century. They had then migrated to Indiana, southern Illinois, and finally Missouri, where they relocated to the Cape Girardeau and St. Genevieve regions of Spanish Louisiana during the revolutionary period. In 1779 part of the Shawnees followed the Delawares to Missouri, where they were joined by Kickapoos from Illinois and most of the remnant of the Illinois Confederacy (Peorias, Kaskaskias, Cahokias, and others), who also crossed the Mississippi in the years preceding the War of 1812. Other tribespeople from the eastern states voluntarily removed to Wisconsin. By the 1830s Stockbridge Indians from Massachusetts and members of the Munsee band of Delawares, who previously had fled to Ontario, had settled near Green Bay. Meanwhile some Oneidas from upstate New York had established new homes in eastern Wisconsin on lands purchased from the Menominees.

The Menominees retained their land base in Wisconsin, but its size was much diminished. The Menominees had lived in Wisconsin longer than any other tribe. Traditionally they had occupied the Green Bay region and neighboring territories as far west as the Wolf, Wisconsin, and Yellow rivers. Succumbing to federal pressure, between 1831 and 1836 Menominee leaders sold most of their lands adjacent to Green Bay and Lake Winnebago, where federal agents resettled the Stockbridges, Munsees, and Oneidas. The Menominees initially retained their lands between the Fox and Wolf rivers, but in two subsequent treaties (1848 and 1854) most of their remaining territory was exchanged for a reservation of 234,000 acres in modern Menominee County.

Although communities of Ottawa and Ojibwe people in northern Michigan, Wisconsin, and Minnesota were forced to give up their claims to lands in the southern parts of these states, they fared better than many of their Indian neighbors. Because their remaining lands were located in arboreal forests that blanketed the northern counties of these states, the Americans demanded that they retreat to small reservations north of desirable farmland. Despite their struggle to maintain hunting and fishing rights, conflicts over fishing rights would reemerge in the twentieth century. Even so, most of the Ottawas and Ojibwes remained on reservations in their homeland.

The Ho-Chunks (Winnebagos) were less fortunate. In 1825, at the Treaty of Prairie du Chien, Ho-Chunk leaders agreed to occupy a tract of land in northern Illinois and west-central Wisconsin. Two years later, however, after white miners abused Ho-Chunk villagers, a small party of Ho-Chunk warriors led by Red Bird attacked a keel boat on the Mississippi and then killed five settlers near Prairie du Chien. Federal troops quickly crushed the "Red Bird Uprising," Red Bird and several followers voluntarily surrendered, and Red Bird died before going to trial. The other Ho-Chunks were convicted of murder and lesser crimes. Since the Ho-Chunks had been provoked, President John Quincy Adams pardoned most of the convicted tribesmen, but pressure mounted on the tribe to surrender its lands in Illinois and Wisconsin. Between 1829 and 1832 Ho-Chunk leaders signed treaties relinquishing most of their remaining lands in these two states, but the treaties did not mention removal and most of the tribe continued to reside in Wisconsin until 1837, when a delegation of Ho-Chunk chiefs visited Washington and signed a confusing removal agreement (the government stated that the tribe must move west in eight *months*—the Ho-Chunks thought it stated eight *years*). In response, government agents prepared to move the tribe from Wisconsin.

The 1837 treaty divided the Ho-Chunks into two opposing parties. Part of the tribe (the "Treaty Winnebagos") moved first to Iowa, then to Minnesota, and then—in 1862 following the eastern Sioux uprising in that state (see Chapter 11)—they were removed to South Dakota. They initially settled on a barren reservation at Crow Creek, but in 1863 almost 500 Treaty Winnebagos died of disease and starvation, and many of the survivors sought refuge among the Omahas in northeastern Nebraska. Others returned to Wisconsin, where they joined with the Non-Treaty Ho-Chunks, who occupied scattered camps in the forests and pine barrens in the central and western parts of the state. In 1865 the Treaty Winnebagos (about 1,200 individuals) accepted a new reservation in northeastern Nebraska, just north of the Omahas. The Wisconsin Ho-Chunks formed several communities near Baraboo and Black River Falls, but their tribal government did not receive federal recognition until March 1963.

The primary target of federal land agents in the Old Northwest were the Potawatomis and Miamis, tribes who held title to the deep, rich prairies encompassing the northern half of Illinois and Indiana and a wide corridor of potentially fertile farmland stretching across southern Michigan and Wisconsin. Both state and federal agents found that negotiating with either tribe presented considerable difficulties.

The Potawatomis were a numerous people (often intermarried with the Ottawas and Ojibwes) whose domain extended from west-central Wisconsin as far south as Lake Peoria in Illinois. They also claimed much of northern Indiana and all of southern Michigan from the St. Joseph Valley to modern Detroit. Their political structure was so decentralized that federal attempts to associate individual villages with certain geographic regions (Prairie band, Wabash band, etc.) was useless, since individual Indians often moved from village to village or claimed membership in more than one band.

To the government's dismay, most of the Potawatomi "bands" were led by sophisticated *métis* such as Billy Caldwell and Alexander Robinson or shrewd traditional chiefs such as Topinbee and Waubansee, leaders who forced the government to negotiate thirteen separate major treaties before they relinquished their lands and agreed to remove to the west. In addition, in many of these treaties they persuaded federal agents to assign individual sections of land from within the ceded region to leading members of the tribe as personal reservations, resulting in myriad small individual reservations that often contained valuable fords or ferries at river crossings or commercial sites at heavily traveled crossroads. Unlike similar land assignments in the South, most Potawatomi *métis* did not fall victim to local officials or land agents and retained their acreages, which they later sold at a profit to non-Indian settlers.

Yet like many of the southern tribes, the Potawatomis suffered during the removal process. The first Potawatomi removal party left Logansport, Indiana, in April 1833. Other removals followed over the next five years, but the government seemed unsure of the Potawatomis' final destination. Some were sent to Kansas, others to northwestern Missouri, while many Potawatomis from northern Illinois were removed to a new reservation near Council Bluffs, Iowa.

In Indiana, Potawatomi removal was complicated by frontier merchants who attempted to either keep the Indians in the east or secure lucrative government contracts to furnish provisions for their trek west. Removal also was opposed by local priests who encouraged Catholic Potawatomis to remain in the state and argued that "civilized, Christian Indians" could easily be assimilated into frontier society. Federal agents denounced these clergymen as "intriguing papists, foreigners, and British agents," but the priests were only acting on the Indians' behalf.

In 1836, when Menominee, a Catholic chief from Twin Lakes, Indiana, refused to enroll for removal, federal officials bribed other Potawatomis to sell Menominee's small village reservation. Indiana militia then surrounded the old chief's village and forced Menominee and his eight hundred followers west toward Kansas at gunpoint. Suffering from tainted food, typhoid fever, and exposure, about fifty tribespeople died on this two-month Trail of Death. Although the casualty rates were smaller, other Potawatomi removal parties suffered similar fates. By the early 1840s, however, most Potawatomis had been removed or had fled to northern Wisconsin or Canada. Finally, in 1846, all the disparate Potawatomi bands in the west were consolidated at a new reservation on the Kansas River near modern Topeka.

Like the Potawatomis, the Miamis also signed a series of treaties that ceded most of their lands in Indiana. The Miamis, too, were led by sophisticated leaders such as Jean Baptiste Richardville, Francis Godfroy, or Meshingmesia, who obtained large personal reservations that they shared with other members of the tribe. By 1840 the Miami population had dropped to just over 500 individuals. Although almost all Miamis resided on the reservations set aside for their leaders, Hoosiers were eager to expel all Indians from their state. The Miamis also had become heavily indebted to local traders, and federal officials used these merchants' influence to obtain a removal agreement. In 1846, 323 Miamis were removed via canal boats to Cincinnati, then by steamboat to eastern Kansas. The remaining Miamis continued to reside on the small personal reservations in Indiana, but following the removal, federal officials refused to recognize the Indiana refugees as having any status within the Miami tribe. Ironically, however, following the removal, many of the western Miamis returned to Indiana, and although they have no federal recognition, the modern Miami community in Indiana now numbers about 2,800. About 1,500 Miamis still live in the west.

In addition to the large communities of tribal people in northern Michigan and Wisconsin, smaller communities also remained in the Midwest. Refugee Potawatomi, Delaware, and Shawnee people formed new communities in southwest Ontario, particularly on Walpole Island, near the eastern shore of Lake St. Clair. Small communities of Potawatomis remained on the Huron River in eastern Michigan, on the St. Joseph River in western Michigan, and in the Green Bay region. Remnant Shawnee communities remained scattered across southern and western Ohio, while other Native Americans, living in either family groups or as individuals, resided on the fringe of white society or adopted white men's clothes and mannerisms. To use their own words, they "hid in plain sight."

The Senecas in New York also retained small reservations in their homeland. In the mid-1820s Seneca leaders signed two treaties with the Ogden Land Company, but the Senate had refused to ratify the agreements since the lands had not been sold to the United States. In 1838 a group of Seneca chiefs negotiated another land cession and removal agreement with federal officials, but these documents were so muddled by bribery and complications that both President Martin Van Buren and the Senate were reluctant to support them. Amended versions of the latter agreements eventually were ratified, but the Senecas refused to abide by them and remained in New York.

FIGHTING REMOVAL: ARMED RESISTANCE

Almost all the tribes who were forcibly removed to the west opposed their relocation and took actions to thwart or slow the government's removal procedures. Most of this resistance was manifested in refusals to assemble at removal camps, flight into remote regions of their old homeland, legal challenges, or general procrastination. In contrast, two tribal groups—the Sauks and Foxes (Mesquakies),

and the Seminoles—mounted an armed resistance to the removal process that resulted in open warfare with the federal government.

The Black Hawk War

The Sauk and Fox tribes had lived in close proximity since the colonial period, but by the early nineteenth century they occupied lands in northwestern Illinois, southwestern Wisconsin, and eastern Iowa. In 1804 a delegation of Sauk leaders had signed a treaty relinquishing their claims to land east of the Mississippi, but their territory was far to the north of most initial white settlement in Illinois and their homes were not threatened.

Many Sauks, led by the war chief Black Hawk, had supported Tecumseh and the British during the War of 1812, but others, led by Keokuk, had remained neutral or pro-American. In the postwar period the rivalry between Black Hawk and Keokuk continued. Black Hawk's followers, a minority of the tribe, were known as the "British Band," but since American officials favored Keokuk and funneled presents and annuities through his camp, the aging Black Hawk's influence diminished. During the late 1820s, after white miners swarmed to the lead deposits in the Dubuque region, American demands for the Sauk and Fox lands in Illinois increased. In response, Keokuk led about 2,500 Sauks across the Mississippi during 1829 to settle permanently on the Iowa River. In contrast, Black Hawk remained at Saukenuk, his ancestral village at Rock Island, Illinois, until late June 1831, when Illinois militia and volunteers forced Black Hawk and 1,000 followers reluctantly to retreat to Iowa.

Camped along the Iowa River, Black Hawk and his followers spent a miserable winter of 1832–1833. They had arrived too late to plant any crops, and they were short of food and blankets. During the winter, Neapope, one of the old chief's ill-chosen advisers, traveled to Canada, then returned and falsely reported that the British would support the Sauk and Fox return to Illinois. Also encouraged by rumors that the Ho-Chunks and Potawatomis would assist him, Black Hawk led about 1,000 Sauks and Foxes, including 600 women and children, back across the Mississippi on April 6, 1832. They planned to reconnoiter with a village of

Black Hawk, by McKenney & Hall Painted in 1837, this portrait of Black Hawk captures the pride and independence of the Sauk war chief.

Ho-Chunks led by Wabokioshiek ("the Winnebago Prophet") on the Rock River and then to reoccupy Saukenuk.

Rumors of their intentions flooded the frontier, and federal troops commanded by General Henry Atkinson were dispatched from St. Louis. Meanwhile, Governor John Reynolds of Illinois also sent the Illinois militia north to apprehend the "hostiles." By May 1, 1832, Black Hawk's followers had swollen to almost 2,000 Indians as other Sauks and Foxes, and even a smattering of Kickapoos and dissident Potawatomis, joined his ranks. But the show of force by the Americans frightened most other Indians; the Winnebago Prophet offered no support; and the Potawatomis warned Black Hawk not to approach their villages.

On May 14, while Potawatomi leaders met with Black Hawk and advised him to return to Iowa, they were interrupted by scouts who reported that a force of mounted militia was rapidly approaching Black Hawk's camp on the Rock River. Now aware that he

had no allies, Black Hawk led about thirty warriors out to meet the Americans. He intended to surrender and lead his people back to Iowa.

Things did not go as planned. As he rode to meet the militia, Black Hawk dispatched half a dozen warriors, carrying a white flag, in advance of his party. The Illinois volunteers, poorly disciplined, but spoiling for a fight, were led by Major Isaiah Stillman. When they discovered the advance party of Sauks and Foxes, the volunteers ignored the white flag, seized three of the warriors, then fired upon the others. The survivors, now pursued by Stillman's entire command (350 men), fled back toward a small grove of trees where Black Hawk and the remainder of his party were concealed. When the pursuing Americans came within range, Black Hawk's two dozen warriors fired from the shelter of the underbrush, killing eleven Americans. The other Americans fled, panic stricken, back toward Dixon's Ferry, twenty miles in their rear, where they proffered exaggerated claims that they had been attacked by Black Hawk and 1,000 warriors.

The Battle of Stillman's Run, a skirmish initiated by the Americans, spread panic through the settlements, and in response, the government committed more troops to the campaign. Cut off from Saukenuk, Black Hawk led his followers up the Rock River, then turned west across the rugged "Driftless Region" of southwest Wisconsin, attempting to return to Iowa. Desperately short of food and other supplies, the Sauks and Foxes made several attempts to surrender, but their offers were either ignored or misinterpreted. Meanwhile, skirmishes between Indians and whites broke out across northern Illinois and Wisconsin. Ultimately, about 160 Americans, both civilians and militia, were killed in the fighting.

On August 2, 1832, the pursuing army came upon the retreating Sauks and Foxes at the mouth of the Bad Axe River, where the Indians were preparing to cross the Mississippi back into Iowa. The Sauks and Foxes again attempted to surrender, then fled onto small sandy islands in the river, but they were caught between the troops on the bank and grapeshot fired from the armed steamboat *Warrior*, which had steamed upriver from Prairie du Chien. The Battle of the Bad Axe lasted almost eight hours, and according to Indian agent James Street, the backwaters of the Mississippi were "perceptively tinged with the blood of the Indians." When the fighting stopped, over two hundred Indians, including many women and children, lay dead on the islands or in the water. Many of the Sauks and Foxes who successfully crossed the river were then attacked by the Sioux shortly after they reached the western bank. Of the 1,000 Sauks and Foxes who originally had accompanied Black Hawk across the Mississippi in April, about 200 safely returned to Iowa.

Black Hawk escaped the slaughter, later surrendered, and following a short imprisonment was taken east and shown the power of the Great White Father. After touring Washington and several other eastern cities, he returned to the west and was released. He died in Iowa in 1838.

Following the war, federal officials purchased the tribe's remaining lands in Iowa. In 1842 the Sauks and some Foxes were removed to Kansas, but many Foxes, or Mesquakies (the tribe's name for themselves), refused to leave and scattered in small groups along the upper Raccoon, Des Moines, and Skunk rivers. Federal attempts to capture and remove these refugees failed, and during the 1850s the Mesquakie population was augmented by kinsmen who returned from Kansas. Finally, in 1857 Mesquakie leaders purchased eighty acres of bottomland along the Iowa River near Tama, which became the nucleus of the modern Mesquakie settlement. Today the settlement incorporates 430 acres of federally recognized Indian land and contains a population of over 600 Mesquakies.

The Seminole Wars

Seminole resistance to removal was more effective. Descendants of Native American tribes who had occupied Florida during the colonial period and of refugees from the Creek Confederacy who had fled into the region following the American Revolution, the Seminoles resided in loosely affiliated villages stretching from the Florida panhandle south through most of the peninsula. Separate Seminole villages spoke different languages but shared a culture that utilized the rich flora and fauna of Florida. Augmenting their hunting and gathering with horticulture, by the 1820s most Seminoles dressed in loose-fitting garments fashioned from trade cloth

and sought shelter in log cabins similar to those of frontier whites, although they often spent the hot summer months residing in "chickees," open sided platforms raised two to three feet above the ground and covered with a thatch roof. Because Florida was not valued as cotton land and seemed inaccessible to overland travel, demands for Seminole territories remained minimal prior to the 1820s. Moreover, during the decades following the Treaty of Paris, Florida remained in Spanish hands and Americans were not welcome in the colony.

Unfortunately, Florida attracted American attention for other reasons. The region served as a magnet for African-Americans fleeing bondage in the lower South. If escaped slaves could reach Florida, they were free (in theory, at least), and although Spanish officials exercised only minimal control over the peninsula's interior, they were quick to take affront at Americans who entered the region without their permission.

Escaped slaves also were given haven by the Seminoles. The relationship between the Seminoles and the runaways is difficult to categorize, since it varied among different Seminole communities, and even within the same village, but the Seminoles certainly were more receptive to African-Americans than southern whites and most other southern Indians. In some instances African-Americans were integrated into Seminole communities, while at other locations they formed separate communities that lived in proximity to a Seminole settlement. A few Seminoles purchased African-Americans from white southerners, but they treated them more like tenant farmers than slaves.

The autonomy of both Seminoles and slaves deteriorated rapidly after the War of 1812. American demands for the return of runaway slaves increased and professional "slave-catchers" repeatedly crossed into Spanish or Seminole territory, seizing any African-American they encountered. In November 1817 an American military force attacked a Seminole village in southwestern Georgia when neighboring planters charged that it was a haven for runaways. Neighboring Seminoles retaliated, ambushing a military column in northern Florida and firing on American supply boats on the Apalachicola River. In response, during March 1818 Andrew Jackson led an American military force into Florida, where he burned several Seminole and African-American villages, seized a Spanish fort near modern Tallahassee, and then captured Pensacola. He also executed two British traders whom he accused of conspiring with the Indians against the United States. By June, Jackson was back in Georgia and the First Seminole War was over, but the invasion of northern Florida demonstrated the region's vulnerability to American military power. One year later, in the Adams-Onis Treaty, Spain ceded Florida to the United States.

The Adams-Onis treaty did not bode well for the Seminoles. Southern planters seemed poised to expand into the panhandle, and in response, many Seminoles abandoned the northern part of Florida and retreated to the south. Yet American demands for lands continued unabated, and in 1823 Seminole leaders signed the Treaty of Moultrie Creek, which opened both Florida coastlines to white settlement but retained the interior of the peninsula for the tribe. Yet difficulties continued. Both Indians and whites trespassed on each other's territory, and since the Seminoles refused to surrender all former slaves living in their villages, white southerners clamored for their removal. Most Seminoles were determined to remain in Florida, but in 1832 a group of tribal leaders met with federal officials at Payne's Landing, on the Ocklawaha River, and signed a treaty agreeing to remove from Florida within three years. The treaty also provided that an exploring party of Seminoles would tour Oklahoma to select a site for their new homes.

The treaty was fraught with controversy. The Seminoles believed that the treaty allowed them to remain in Florida for twenty years and that the exploring party had the option of rejecting Oklahoma as a final removal site. Unbiased American observers reported that the government bribed an interpreter $200 to misrepresent the treaty's terms, and army officers in Oklahoma also admitted that the agent who conducted the Seminole exploring party to the west forced the party to sign another document, the Treaty of Fort Gibson, before allowing them to return to Florida. When the party arrived back in Florida, the Seminoles rejected the western lands, but the Treaty of Fort Gibson, forwarded to Washington, indicated that they approved of the region. In 1834 the Senate ratified both treaties. The Seminoles refused to abide by either agreement.

Federal efforts to enforce the treaties resulted in the Second Seminole War. During 1834, General Wiley Thompson of the Georgia militia met repeatedly with Seminole leaders in a futile attempt to procure their removal. During these meetings Osceola, a younger leader, rose to prominence. In June 1835, when Thompson summoned Seminole leaders to Fort King and presented them with a removal agreement, an angry Osceola reputedly drew a large knife and pinned Wiley's copy of the removal agreement to the treaty table. Although the event is undocumented, it still is celebrated by modern Seminoles. In response Thompson imprisoned Osceola and other antiremoval chiefs, releasing them only after they signed an agreement to remove by January 1836.

The removal did not occur. Claiming the agreement was invalid since it had been signed under duress, the Seminoles stockpiled arms, executed a proremoval chief, and stole livestock. When federal troops pursued the raiders, the Indians retreated into the swamps, from which they attacked isolated patrols and supply trains. Florida militia sent as reinforcements proved as ineffective as federal troops in apprehending the warriors.

On December 28, 1835, the warfare escalated. During the morning a large war party led by Micanopy, Jumper, and Alligator ambushed Major Francis Dade and 107 officers and men north of Tampa Bay, killing all but 3 of them. The Seminoles lost only 3 killed and 5 wounded. Later in the same afternoon, Osceola led a separate attack on the Indian Agency at Fort King, killing Wiley Thompson and 6 other Americans.

Fearing American retaliation, many Seminoles withdrew to the Wahoo Swamp on the Withlacoochee River, where they defeated an American expedition that had followed them. Two months later a large war party of Seminoles and ex-slaves ambushed and turned back another expedition of 1,100 regulars and volunteers near modern Citrus Springs. During January 1836 General Winfield Scott arrived to assume command of all troops in Florida, but his efforts to locate and engage the Seminoles proved ineffective. Warriors led by Osceola, Micanopy, and Alligator attacked settlements as far north as St. Augustine, while Scott's forces trudged through the swamps and hummocks but found few Indians. In May 1836 Scott was replaced as commander by Governor Richard Call of Florida, who also achieved little success, and in December, Call was succeeded by former quartermaster general Thomas S. Jesup. By early 1837 Jesup had over 8,000 troops

United States Marines Penetrating the Everglades, by John Clymer Familiar with the forests and swamps in Florida, the Seminoles used their knowledge of the terrain to mount a determined defense of their homeland.

in the field, but he still couldn't pin the Seminoles down. Familiar with the tangle of waterways that laced Florida's interior, the Seminoles struck at will, then retreated into the swamplands.

Yet by 1837 the war had taken a toll on the tribe's women and children. Although they eluded the troops, the Seminoles could plant no crops and were hard-pressed to feed and clothe their families. In March 1837 Micanopy, Jumper, and Alligator met with Jesup and signed a preliminary armistice in which they agreed to assemble at Tampa, where federal ships would transport them across the Gulf of Mexico and on to Oklahoma. Osceola, described by white observers as "care-worn, gloomy and thin," did not sign the armistice, but he reluctantly agreed to its terms. Yet when the Seminoles arrived at Tampa, white slave owners attempted to seize the tribe's African-American allies; in response, the Seminoles, led by Osceola, abandoned the removal camp and fled back into the interior.

Augmented by additional troops, Jesup renewed his military campaign. In October 1837, after Osceola informed Jesup that the Seminoles would accept a reservation in southern Florida but would not leave the peninsula, the commander invited Seminole leaders to meet and negotiate an agreement. Jesup concealed federal troops at the negotiation site, violated the flag of truce, and seized Osceola, 75 warriors, and 6 women. The warriors were imprisoned at Fort Marion in St. Augustine. During November, Wildcat and eighteen other prisoners escaped, but the malaria-stricken Osceola could not accompany them. Federal officials then transferred Osceola to Fort Moultrie, South Carolina, where he died on January 30, 1838.

Following Osceola's capture, the Seminole resistance disintegrated. In December 1837 troops led by Colonel Zachary Taylor attacked a large Seminole village near Lake Okeechobee, and during the following spring Jesup seized 675 Seminoles after first promising them he would let them remain in Florida, then informing them that his superiors had countermanded his request. Micanopy also was seized under a flag of truce, and the war dragged on until 1842 when President John Tyler offered the Seminoles the option of removing to Oklahoma (which the government strongly encouraged) or of remaining in Florida, where they could occupy an isolated reservation west of Lake Okeechobee. No formal peace treaty was signed, but for all practical purposes the Second Seminole War was over. About 600 Seminoles remained in Florida.

They remained at peace until 1855, when a series of skirmishes between Seminoles and troops near Lake Okeechobee eventually spread to isolated homesteads as far north as Tampa. This "Third Seminole War" continued intermittently until March 1858, when the last hostiles, led by Billy Bowlegs, surrendered and were shipped to Oklahoma. The remainder of the Seminoles retreated into the Everglades and remained in Florida. All hostilities ceased, but in theory the tribe remained at war with the United States until 1956 when a formal peace was signed with the government.

Although the Seminoles lost the Second Seminole War, they mounted an impressive resistance. For seven years, fewer than 1,300 Seminole and African-American warriors fought valiantly against as many as 9,000 troops and hundreds of allied Indians. Perennially short of arms and ammunition, the Seminoles suffered several hundred casualties, but 1,600 white Americans died in the contest. Eventually, the United States removed about 4,400 Seminoles to Oklahoma, but the cost was at least $20 million, or $4,545.45 per Indian, a staggering sum in the 1840s. Moreover, Jesup's decision to ignore flags of truce in the capture of Osceola, Micanopy, and other Seminoles was a clear violation of military protocol. It was not the army's finest hour.

CONCLUSION: CHANGING HOMELANDS

By 1850 the United States had removed almost all organized Indian communities from agricultural lands east of the Mississippi and had either carried them west or forced them to take refuge in less desirable regions on the fringes of white society. Significant numbers of Ojibwes, Ottawas, Menominees, and other tribespeople still resided on small reservations in the thinly soiled, arboreal forests of the Great Lakes region; while remnant groups of Choctaws, Cherokees, Seminoles, and other southern Indians sought refuge in the Appalachians or Everglades. Communities of Iroquois people (Oneidas, Onondagas, Mohawks, Senecas, Cayugas, and Tuscaroras) persisted on small tracts of land in upstate New York or Pennsylvania, but their reservations were isolated islands of "Indianness," surrounded by a spreading sea of settlement. Most of the vast tracts of land between the Appalachians and the Mississippi that tribal people had possessed at the beginning of the nineteenth century now belonged to white people. The fertile Indian lands were gone.

Those tribes who moved west would face new challenges. Many would attempt to reconstruct their lives and communities in new environments, and they would be forced to defend their new homes from American settlers who seemed to follow in their wake. In addition, the newcomers to the west would not find an empty landscape. Other Indian people already lived in the region, and many would contest the newcomers' arrival. And for these older residents of the prairies and plains, the emigration of the eastern tribes brought changes and challenges similar to those the emigrants themselves had faced in their old homelands.

SUGGESTED READINGS

Beck, David. *Siege and Survival: A History of the Menominee Indians, 1634–1856.* Lincoln: University of Nebraska Press, 2002. This volume includes a good description of the Menominees' loss of land in Wisconsin during the removal period. It also illustrates their ability to remain in Wisconsin while other tribes were being forced west.

Carson, James T. *Searching for the Bright Path: The Mississippi Choctaws from Prehistory to Removal.* Lincoln: University of Nebraska Press, 1999. This volume analyzes cultural change among the Choctaws and discusses their struggle against the government during the removal period.

Edmunds, R. David. *The Potawatomis: Keepers of the Fire*. Norman: University of Oklahoma Press, 1978.   The volume discusses cultural change among the Potawatomis and offers a good case study of the loss of tribal lands and the subsequent removal process in the Midwest.

Green, Michael. *The Politics of Indian Removal*. Lincoln: University of Nebraska Press, 1982.   An excellent case study of the interaction of state and federal governments and its impact on Creek removal in the South.

Indians and a Changing Frontier: The Art of George Winter. Indianapolis: Indiana Historical Society, 1993.   This "coffee-table" volume featuring portraits and camp scenes by a nineteenth-century Indiana painter offers vivid visual images of acculturation patterns among Indians in Indiana and Michigan. Analytical essays by scholars also are included.

Jackson, Donald, ed. *Black Hawk: An Autobiography*. Urbana: University of Illinois Press, 1964. This autobiography, originally dictated by Black Hawk to Antoine LeClaire, a métis government interpreter, presents the events of Black Hawk's life, including the Black Hawk War, from the old chief's perspective.

Mahon, John. K. *History of the Second Seminole War, 1835–1842*. Gainesville: University of Florida Press, 1967.   This remains the most comprehensive and balanced account of the warfare between the Seminoles and the government during these years.

McLaughlin, William G. *Cherokee Renascence in the New Republic*. New Haven: Yale University Press, 1986.   An excellent analysis of cultural change within the Cherokee Nation in the half century following the American Revolution.

Murphy, Lucy E. *A Gathering of Rivers: Indians, Métis, and Mining in the Western Great Lakes, 1737–1832*. Lincoln: University of Nebraska Press, 2000.   The volume examines the evolution of gender roles among Native American and *métis* women in Wisconsin, Iowa, and Illinois and illustrates the degree to which Americans saw Native Americans much differently than they did the Creole-French.

Nichols, Roger. *Black Hawk and the Warrior's Path*. Arlington Heights: Harlan Davidson, 1992.

A concise biography of Black Hawk that illustrates how out of step his militancy was with the cultural changes accepted by many Sauks and Foxes.

Perdue, Theda. *Cherokee Women: Gender and Culture Change, 1700–1835*. Lincoln: University of Nebraska Press, 1998.   An excellent analysis of the changing role of women within Cherokee society in the late eighteenth and nineteenth centuries.

———. *Slavery and the Evolution of Cherokee Society*. Knoxville: University of Tennessee Press, 1979.   The volume discusses the Cherokees' acceptance of African-American slavery and compares slavery within the Cherokee Nation to the institution's development and impact in the white South.

Prucha, Francis Paul. "Andrew Jackson's Indian Policy: A Reassessment." *Journal of American History* 56 (December 1969): 527–539.   This essay argues that Jackson's decision to remove the tribes was based on his Anglophobia and his belief that the tribes could not be protected from unscrupulous whites in the East. A controversial and thought-provoking essay.

Satz, Ronald. *American Indian Policy in the Jacksonian Era*. Lincoln: University of Nebraska Press, 1975.   By far the most detailed and balanced account of American Indian policy during this period.

Sleeper-Smith, Susan. *Indian Women and Catholic Men: Rethinking Cultural Encounters in the Western Great Lakes*. Amherst: University of Nebraska Press, 2001.   The volume analyzes the previously ignored role that Indian and *métis* women played in the economic development of the region and illustrates their importance in both the fur trade and the production and marketing of agricultural products.

White, Richard. *The Roots of Dependency: Subsistence, Environment, and Social Change Among the Choctaws, Pawnees, and Navajos*. Lincoln: University of Nebraska Press, 1983.   The first five chapters of the book contain an excellent analysis of cultural change among the Choctaws and illustrate how the acquisition of private property and the subsequent defense of their plantations enabled members of the mixed-lineage Choctaw planter-elite to attain positions of political leadership in the tribe.

Strangers Invade the West, 1845–1861

On the morning of November 29, 1847, when Narcissa Whitman entered the kitchen of her home at the Waiilatpu Mission among the Cayuse Indians in southeastern Washington, she found the room crowded with angry Indians. Retreating back into the sitting room, she informed her husband, Marcus, of the intrusion, then hurried to dress several of her stepchildren. Marcus Whitman confronted the warriors, who demanded that he provide them with medicine, and when Whitman hesitated, Tomahas, a Cayuse warrior, struck him in the head with a tomahawk while other warriors shot both Whitman and John Sager, his sixteen-year-old stepson, with their rifles. Ten other people, including mission employees, the schoolmaster, the gristmill operator, and several emigrants en route to Oregon who had stopped at the mission, also were slain. When Narcissa opened the front door of her home, she too was struck by a rifle ball. Severely wounded, she fell back into the house, but later in the day, she was forced from her home and also murdered. The Cayuses then looted the mission, burned the buildings, and took about forty-five other emigrants or children attending the mission school as captives.

The events culminating in the "Whitman Massacre" in southeastern Washington exemplify the multifaceted relationship of Native Americans with the expanding American nation in the two decades prior to the Civil War. Eager to exploit good farm lands in Oregon, gold in California, or trade opportunities in the Southwest, Americans hurried westward, often heedless of native peoples long resident in these regions. In response, Native Americans sometimes greeted the newcomers with friendship, developing symbiotic economic or political relationships with the emigrants, or, as in the Indian Territory, sequestered themselves apart in autonomous regions, yet maintained economic ties with the larger society that surrounded them. This chapter focuses on the diverse strategies utilized by Native American people residing west of the Mississippi in their responses to an advancing tide of newcomers (both Native Americans and non-Indians) who began to establish permanent residences in tribal homelands in the two decades preceding the Civil War. It also looks at how some of these newcomers (in this case, Native Americans themselves) created a new homeland for themselves in the Indian Territory. Ironically, some of those Native Americans living immediately west of the Mississippi (in the Great Plains) would not be as threatened by this initial invasion. Although their territories would be traversed by immigrants traveling west, their homelands would not attract permanent non-Indian residents until the post–Civil War period. The interaction of these Plains tribes with white immigrants will be discussed in Chapter 11.

Native Americans residing in Texas, California, the Pacific Northwest, and New Mexico were less fortunate. Although they warily accepted the first Americans onto their lands, their hospitality waned as the initial trickle of strangers grew to a flood of emigrants who threatened their homeland and its resources. Moreover, as the floodtide of empire surged across their valleys, mesas, and canyons, many Native Americans in the west found that friendships formed with the first settlers slowly diminished. Isolated settlers newly resident in Indian country felt vulnerable to Native American retribution and treated their Indian neighbors with tolerance and respect. But as their numbers increased, even many of the affable newcomers grew less tolerant of Native Americans and their ways, and Indian people felt threatened in their own homeland.

The Whitmans and their mission provide an excellent example. In 1836, when they first arrived among the Cayuses, the Whitmans were eager to spread the gospel and befriended Indians as potential converts. But they continued to scorn Cayuse ways, and although Narcissa grudgingly permitted Indian people to enter her kitchen and "Indian room," she refused them access to other parts of her house. She described the Cayuses as "filthy, lazy, and insolent." By the mid-1840s, as growing numbers of white emigrants passed through the mission station en route to the Oregon country, the Whitmans spent more time "ministering" to the emigrants than to the Indians. Among these travelers were several Delawares who warned the Cayuses that the Americans already had forced many eastern Indians from their homelands. The Cayuses and neighboring tribes became more suspicious of the rapidly increasing newcomers. In 1847, when measles broke out at the mission station, the Cayuses suspected the missionaries of spreading the disease. After several emigrants who contracted the disease recovered but many Cayuses died, the Cayuses believed that the missionaries were withholding medicine from Indian people. Coupled with their growing resentment over the flood of emigrants, the measles epidemic spurred them to action. They attacked the mission, killing the Whitmans and ten other Americans. In contrast, friendly Nez Percés warned neighboring missionaries of the uprising and shielded them from hostile Indians.

Similar patterns (sometimes hostile—sometimes friendly) characterized Indian-American interactions in other parts of the West during these decades. At first Anglo-Americans were welcomed amidst the Cherokee villages in Texas or the pueblos along the Rio Grande, but as the years passed, relationships between Native Americans and Anglo-Americans generally deteriorated. The trans-Mississippi west remained a vast region with a relatively sparse population, but its capacity to accommodate both Indians and whites was rapidly diminishing.

Many tribes in the trans-Mississippi west also resented the arrival of the emigrant Indians. The government's removal policy was based on the assumption that western lands were essentially empty. Such was not the case. Many federal officials knew that the western territories already were occupied, but they argued that the newcomers would serve as more "civilized" role models for the Plains tribes. In contrast, the western tribespeople bitterly opposed the emigrant Indians. Many were traditional enemies against whom they had fought for decades.

The violence escalated. In Iowa, officials attempted to establish a "Neutral Ground" between the Sauks and Foxes and the Dakotas, but warfare between the two sides continued. Potawatomis who had temporarily resettled at Council Bluffs complained of Dakota raids, while farther south, in western Missouri and eastern Kansas, warfare between the Osages and the Cherokees intensified. Allied with Shawnee and Delaware emigrants, the Cherokees forced the Osages from southern Missouri, but the Osages struck back, attacking parties of eastern tribesmen who hunted bison on the Plains.

Forced westward, the Osages found themselves "caught between the hammer and the anvil": pressed on the east by emigrant Indians, but blocked on the west by the Comanches, Kiowas, and Wichitas. Well armed by Creole traders such as Pierre and Auguste Chouteau, the Osages initially held their own, striking back at the Cherokees and Creeks and creating havoc in the Wichita and Kiowa villages. In 1833 federal officials (the Stokes Commission) negotiated a series of compacts in which emigrant tribes in Missouri, Arkansas, and Indian Territory agreed to boundaries between their new tribal lands, but the Osages, led by Black Dog and Clermont, denounced the pacts and charged that the government was stealing Osage land.

Two years later prospects for peace brightened when Osage chiefs and leaders from the other southern Plains tribes met with emigrant Indians on the South Canadian River in Indian Territory. Mushalatubbee of the Choctaws urged that "there be no more killing of each other," while Roley McIntosh of the Creeks added, "we must have peace . . . we are all of one color." The Osages and other Plains tribes agreed. The Camp Holmes Treaty provided for free passage of all tribes through each other's territories and promised federal arbitration of all intertribal quarrels. The treaty contributed to peace, but the western tribes were forced to recognize the government's right to settle eastern Indians on their homelands. Difficulties between the "Civilized Tribes" and the "wild Indians" would continue.

Although the Plains tribes have been stereotyped as the preeminent Indian "warriors," the emigrant tribesmen held their own in military clashes between the two sides. The Plains warriors were better horsemen, but the emigrant Indians were far better armed, and many had extensive military experience in the East. In addition, the emigrant Indians fought as coordinated military units rather than as individuals. Plains war parties raided emigrant Indian settlements, but in July 1848, when a mixed party of Potawatomis and Sauks hunting bison on the headwaters of the Kansas River was attacked by a large force of Pawnees, the emigrants readily defeated their assailants, taking a toll of Pawnee killed and wounded. Five years later another party of about 200 Potawatomis and Sauks were attacked by almost 800 Cheyennes, Arapahos, Comanches, and Kiowas on the Smoky Hill River in western Kansas. Dismounting, the emigrant warriors formed ranks, and in the best European military tradition, repulsed their attackers with coordinated volleys. The emigrants suffered four killed and one wounded; the Plains tribes lost over 100 warriors.

INDIAN TERRITORY

In Indian Territory, the political schisms engendered by removal posed a greater threat than any invasion of outsiders. Within the Cherokees, Creeks, and Choctaws, internecine bickering and violence plagued tribal politics during the immediate postremoval period, while the Chickasaws and Seminoles struggled to establish and maintain separate nations. Meanwhile, these tribal societies continued to evolve. The cultural bifurcation between the planter-elite and more traditional tribespeople continued, but the gap narrowed in the decades prior to the Civil War. American missionaries, educators, and cultural institutions continued to permeate Indian Territory, slowly transforming tribal life in the region.

Prior to the Trail of Tears, the Old Settlers, or Western Cherokees, had established a constitutional government in Arkansas and Indian Territory. In 1835, when the Treaty Party fled westward, they had joined the Old Settlers, participating in their government. Four years later, when John Ross and the Anti-Removal Party arrived, they outnumbered the Old Settlers and their Treaty Party allies and were reluctant to join their government. Disagreements over the distribution of annuity payments added to the tension, while the Keetowahs, a Cherokee secret society opposed to removal, denounced the Treaty Party as traitors. On June 22, 1839, the resentment boiled over when the Keetowahs and their supporters executed (assassinated) three Treaty Party leaders, including Major Ridge; his son, John Ridge; and Elias Boudinot, the former editor of the *Cherokee Phoenix*. Stand Watie and other Treaty Party members also were targeted for death, but they escaped assassination. The deaths brought the Cherokees to the brink of civil war before federal troops intervened and restored order. Although the executions were carried out by Ross's supporters, he evidently had no previous knowledge of their plans.

The executions plagued Cherokee politics for the next seven years. "Revenge murders" continued until at least 1846, when all factions agreed to a general amnesty that prevented any retribution. Meanwhile, Ross's followers gained control of the Cherokee government and implemented the constitution that had governed the tribe in Georgia. Resentment between the factions continued, however. In January 1846 the Old Settlers and the remaining members of the Treaty Party petitioned the federal government to divide the Cherokee lands into three regions, assigning a portion to each faction. Ross and his followers opposed the resolution, and fortunately the petition became

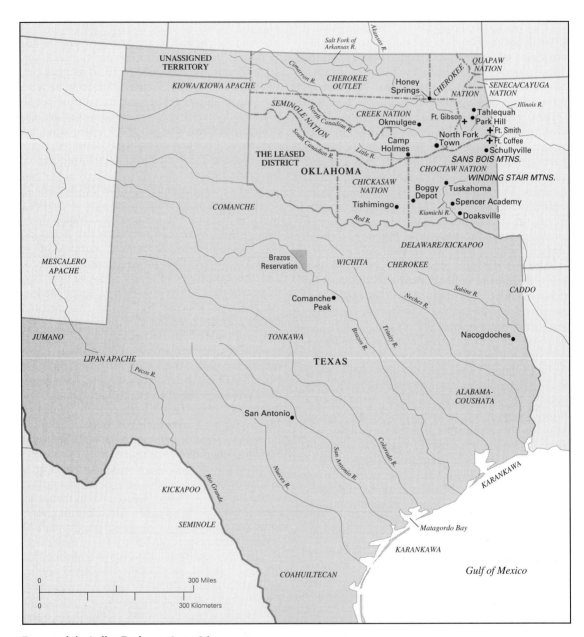

Texas and the Indian Territory, 1840–1860.

sidelined during the Mexican War. Meanwhile Ross and cooler heads on both sides championed reconciliation, and although the old schisms remained, they somewhat diminished.

Creek politics also was plagued by removal-era divisions. When the Creeks moved west, the Lower Creeks, primarily from southern Georgia and southeastern Alabama, settled in the northeastern part of the new Creek Nation, while the Upper Creeks, people from central and northern Alabama, settled in the southern region of Creek lands. Roley McIntosh, a brother of the slain William McIntosh, led the Lower Creeks. He was generally recognized by federal officials as the official spokesman for the tribe, but Opothle Yaholo, who had led the Creek resistance to removal, continued as the leader of the Upper Creeks. Old quarrels still split the tribe, causing most political decisions to be made at the town or local level until the Civil War.

The Choctaws and Chickasaws faced a different set of political problems. In 1834, the Choctaws adopted a new government in Indian Territory. It sanctioned many traditional Choctaw laws, but also protected private property and insured that wealthy planters would continue to dominate Choctaw affairs. By the late 1850s, however, many rank-and-file Choctaws believed that the planter-elite exercised too much power. They also objected to a new constitution proposed by the planter-elite, which they feared would lead to the Choctaw Nation being incorporated into the United States. Political parties representing both sides quarreled and almost came to blows, and in 1860 federal agents intervened and negotiated a compromise. The new Choctaw Constitution of 1860 strengthened the central government, but it also retained traditional Choctaw political nomenclature and symbols, as well as the tribe's communal ownership of the land.

When the Chickasaws signed the 1837 Treaty of Doaksville, they accepted membership within the Choctaw Nation, although they still retained control over their financial affairs and received all payments for the sale of remaining lands in the East. The Choctaws assigned the Chickasaws to a separate district on the western border of the Choctaw Nation, but since that area abutted Comanche and Kiowa lands and was vulnerable to their incursions, few Chickasaws settled in the region. Scattered throughout the Choctaw Nation, the Chickasaws were marginalized in both Choctaw politics and the mainstream of Choctaw life. Meanwhile, the traditional Chickasaw tribal government, loosely organized around Ishtehotopa, a hereditary "king," and *iksas*, or clans, vied with the planter-elite for the distribution of funds from the sale of the eastern lands and annuities.

By the mid-1840s many of the planter-elite had settled on the eastern side of the "Chickasaw District" within the Choctaw Nation, and in 1855 they joined with the traditionalists to purchase the district from the Choctaws. Here they established a new, separate Chickasaw Nation. The new Chickasaw Constitution was modeled after that of the United States, but it still retained certain traditions of the old kinship system. For example, blood revenge was outlawed, but the nation maintained no jails; people accused or convicted of crimes were expected to voluntarily attend their own trials and submit for punishment, even execution if convicted. Failure to do so was seen as demeaning to one's honor and the honor of one's family, and most Chickasaws readily complied. Although the new national government was led by the Colbert and Harris families, wealthy planters, they were sympathetic to many of the traditionalists' interests and enjoyed broad support throughout much of the tribe.

The Seminole arrival in the West was marked by controversy. Since the Seminoles were removed piecemeal through the late 1830s and 1840s, part of the tribe originally settled within the Creek Nation, while others remained on Cherokee lands near Fort Gibson. Disagreements between the Seminoles and the Creeks over the location of the Seminole villages and the status of African-Americans living within the Seminole communities caused friction, but in 1845 the Seminoles finally agreed to consolidate their settlements on the Little River, in modern Seminole and Pottawatomie counties, Oklahoma. Led by Micanopy, Alligator, and Wildcat, the Seminoles retained their traditional decentralized form of government. An intervillage council comprised of headmen met sporadically, but little centralization occurred, and any decisions supposedly were subject to the Creek National Council. Most Seminoles strongly defended their separate Seminole identity and refused to cooperate with the Creeks, while the latter regarded the Seminoles as lawless "country cousins" and a potential threat to peace and progress.

Angered over his treatment by the Creek majority, and fearing that Creek and Cherokee slaveholders might attempt to seize the African-Americans in their midst, in 1845 Wildcat led between three hundred and four hundred Seminoles and African-Americans from Oklahoma to northern Mexico, where they were joined by Kickapoos, some Wichitas, and remnants of other tribes and established themselves in Coahuila. Agitation between the Creeks and Seminoles over the status of African-Americans continued; nevertheless, in 1855 federal officials negotiated an agreement under which the Seminoles received the relatively small tract of land they occupied and became a separate Seminole Nation, free of any attachment to the Creeks.

As political conditions within the Five Southern Tribes stabilized, the socioeconomic divisions that had characterized life in the East resurfaced. Most Native Americans were small farmers whose material surroundings resembled those of frontier whites in Arkansas or Missouri. Many women still worked in the fields, and even though rainfall in Oklahoma was sporadic, most tribespeople enjoyed a rude, if rustic plenty. Land was plentiful and livestock were allowed to range free in the forests. Most people subsisted on much of what they grew, herded, or hunted, and their limited surpluses were traded for materials that they could not manufacture themselves. Most lived in one- or two-room log cabins, the latter separated by a covered, open "dog-trot" or "breezeway." Cabins featured either puncheon or dirt floors, and furniture was sparse. Women cooked over an open hearth, which also provided heat during the winter. Although moccasins were commonly used for footwear, almost everyone dressed in trade cloth clothing. Many families owned a horse or mule, but prior to the Civil War, most traditional families did not own wagons. Although many people had some knowledge of English, most people used tribal languages in their everyday conversation. Moreover, almost everyone still celebrated the old ceremonies, regularly assembling (to the missionaries' and Indian agents' chagrin) for Green Corn Festivals, Stomp Dances, and other traditional occasions.

Women's political and economic influence continued to decline. Matrilineal clans still functioned, but as the acculturation process accelerated, their roles diminished. In Oklahoma, much more than in their former homelands, tribespeople lived scattered across the land, rather than in closely knit communities. Consequently, communal economic activities among women and their sisters, daughters, or other female relatives became more difficult, and although women still helped in the fields, men began to assume a larger proportion of the agricultural labor. Most traditional tribesmen had little interest in amassing wealth, but they did assume the dominant culture's assumptions that they were responsible for their crops and their livestock. Unlike white women, however, women in the Cherokee, Choctaw, and Chickasaw Nations continued to hold property separate from their husbands. Moreover, they could easily divorce their spouse, and they often retained control over their children.

The planter-elite lived much differently. While never amounting to more than 10 to 15 percent of tribal membership, these planters managed to dominate tribal politics and set the standards (at least in their own minds, and in the opinion of neighboring whites) for "fashion and gentility" in tribal society. Emulating wealthy planters in Arkansas or Louisiana, the planter-elite maintained farms or plantations incorporating substantial fields of corn, hemp, cotton, and tobacco. Choctaw and Chickasaw plantations along the Red River in the southern regions of their nations were usually the largest, but some Cherokees also operated plantations of from 600 to 1,000 acres. Although most plantations were smaller, many planters owned considerable herds of livestock, including fine thoroughbred horses.

Almost all the Indian planters owned slaves. By 1860 Cherokee planters and businessmen owned about 2,500 African-Americans; the Choctaws, 2,350; Creeks, 1,500; and the Chickasaws, about 1,000. Most planters owned no more than a handful of slaves, but others rivaled large slave owners throughout the antebellum South. Robert Love, a Chickasaw planter on the Red River, housed over 200 slaves on his two plantations, while Lewis Ross, a Cherokee planter and businessman, reputedly owned 300. With the exception of the Seminoles, all these nations adopted strict slave codes, which provided severe penalties for runaways and banned the teaching of abolition.

Many of the planter-elite diversified their economic activities. Some ran businesses, operated mills, owned lead mines and salt works, or practiced law. Others, such as Cherokees Lewis Ross and John Martin, bought and sold slaves or traded in hides or horses. John Ross owned a dry goods and general merchandise store at Park Hill. Robert Jones, a Choctaw planter, owned a fleet of steamboats that traveled the Red River between Kiamichi Landing and New Orleans.

The elite's economic success was reflected in their material possessions. Wealthy Cherokee, Choctaw, Chickasaw, and Creek planters and businessmen lived in large, frame, clapboard houses furnished with carpets, books, fine china, and furniture, all brought upriver from New Orleans or Memphis. Men wore frock coats and top hats on formal occasions. Women wore calico or gingham dresses on a daily basis, but they dressed more elegantly when the occasion demanded. The wives and daughters of planters did not labor in the fields; they sewed or crocheted, did fine needlework, or sometimes even painted with watercolors. John Ross traveled between his home at Park Ridge and the Cherokee capital at Tahlequah by carriage, complete with a liveried driver and attendant, while the aristocratic Peter Folsum, a Choctaw planter and district chief, transported his family in "an elegant barouche . . . a black coachman sat out in front and a well-dressed servant sat in the boot, while the lady within had one or two maids to give her attention; the old chief rode in front upon a splendid saddle horse." Most other planters traveled less pretentiously, but they did "live in style."

Although life in the Indian Nations retained its rural tone, towns or trading centers flourished. Tishimingo, the nation's capital, prospered among the Chickasaws. Doaksville, Boggy Depot, and Skullyville served large markets among the Choctaws, while Creek farmers and merchants exchanged commodities at North Fork Town, northeast of modern Eufaula, or at Honey Springs, near modern Tulsa. In 1850, Tahlequah, the Cherokee capital on the Illinois River, numbered 1,600 inhabitants and boasted that it contained the tribe's legislative building, supreme court, office of the *Cherokee Advocate* (the tribal newspaper), a post office, eight general merchandise stores, five hotels, three blacksmith shops, a tailor shop, a saddlery, a tannery, a shoemaker's shop, a dentist, several law offices, and a brick Masonic Temple. Park Hill, which was located three and one-half miles southeast of Tahlequah and served as the center of Methodist and Congregational missionary activity in the nation, was favored by Chief John Ross and many of the wealthier merchants as a place of residence. Although smaller than Tahlequah, Park Hill fancied itself the "cultural center" of the Cherokee Nation and was locally famous for its seminaries, fine shops, social life, and stately residences.

Missionaries active among the tribes prior to their removal followed them into the west, and although their success in converting the tribes to Christianity remained mixed, their impact on education was obvious. Mission schools, supported by the tribes' national councils, opened in all of the Indian Nations, but they flourished most successfully among the Choctaws and Cherokees. In 1825, while still in Mississippi, the Choctaws had set aside funds for the establishment and maintenance of the Choctaw Academy, a boarding school for Choctaws and other Native American boys at Great Crossing, Kentucky. Ironically, the school was sponsored by Colonel Richard M. Johnson, whose previous claim to fame was that he personally had killed Tecumseh at the Battle of the Thames (1813). The academy functioned primarily as a manual training school, and by the late 1830s the school enrolled more non-Choctaws than students from that tribe. In response, during 1843 the Choctaws withdrew their support from the Kentucky school and focused their funds on elementary schools, academies, and other secondary institutions that emerged within the Choctaw Nation.

Choctaw education was buttressed by the efforts of missionary Cyrus Byington. During the 1830s Byington reduced the Choctaw spoken language to written form, then published a Choctaw grammar and other readers. Other missionaries produced a Choctaw-English dictionary and then organized both adult education programs, held in conjunction with Sunday schools, and weekend camp meetings that did much to eradicate illiteracy in the Choctaw Nation. The Choctaw National Council generously supported their efforts, and in 1844 it opened Spencer Academy, a secondary school for "advanced study" by "young Choctaw gentlemen," near Doaksville. Meanwhile, the New Hope Academy, a school for young Choctaw women near Fort Coffee, and several other institutions opened

PEOPLE, PLACES, AND THINGS

The Cherokee Female Seminary

Students at the Cherokee Female Seminary, 1854

Although the degree of cultural change embraced by the Cherokees after their arrival in the west varied considerably among different communities and individuals within the tribe, many members of the tribes' planter and merchant elite championed an Anglo-American ethos and urged that their children be provided with a formal education that transmitted the values associated with upper-middle-class American society. Nowhere were these values encouraged more than at the Cherokee Female Seminary at Tahlequah, Oklahoma, a finishing school for young Cherokee women.

Housed in a large wooden structure at neighboring Park Hill, the first female seminary opened in 1852, provided classrooms and living accommodations to about one hundred students (four classes of twenty-five students each), and was financed by the Cherokee National Council. The school was disbanded during the Civil War, but reopened in 1872 and continued to operate until 1909. The original school building, which burned in 1887, was replaced by a larger structure that housed the seminary until the institution was absorbed into Northeastern Oklahoma State College.

Students arrayed in "their Sunday best" posing in the seminary parlor, circa 1900. The parlor was off-limits to students except when they had visitors, cleaning duty, or a "photograph" session.

The school was modeled after similar female academies in the Northeast (its curriculum was patterned after Mount Holyoke Seminary) and was designed to provide young Cherokee women with a classic mid-nineteenth-century formal education while instilling within them "an appreciation for the better things of life" (good manners, thrift, cleanliness, Protestant Christianity, etc.). Students enrolled in classes such as arithmetic, penmanship, reading, grammar, composition, and history. As they progressed through the curriculum, the girls also studied geometry, trigonometry, botany, geology, French, and German. They also took courses in logic, "mental philosophy," zoology, and surveying. In addition they were instructed in gardening, sewing, "household chemistry (cooking)," "the art of handling a broom," and the "science of the dust cloth." Students also were encouraged to participate in glee clubs, dramatic productions, and musical performances. Teachers and principals such as Florence Wilson, who supervised the seminary from 1876–1902, took pains to insure that students conducted themselves as "ladies" and closely chaperoned picnics, parties, or cotillions to which young men were invited.

PEOPLE, PLACES, AND THINGS

(continued)

Most of the students attending the institution were from mixed-lineage, rather well-to-do families. The seminary offered no courses focusing on traditional Cherokee culture, and no classes were taught in the Cherokee language. Indeed, traditional Cherokee ways were discouraged at the school, and many darker-complexioned students, or students from more traditional families, sometimes faced discrimination from both the faculty and other students. Still, most of the young women who graduated from the seminary cherished their matriculation at the institution, and many graduates played leading roles in both the Cherokee Nation and the new state of Oklahoma.

The photographs on page 248 picture the seminary students circa 1854 and students posing in the seminary parlor circa 1900. Compare the cultural changes that seem to have taken place between 1854 and 1900. Why did the seminary discourage young Cherokee women from identifying with and retaining traditional Cherokee cultural patterns? How did such policies reflect American concepts of "progress" in the decades following the Civil War?

throughout southeastern Oklahoma. After 1847 promising graduates from these institutions were provided with scholarships to attend colleges and universities in the East. By the Civil War, a small but influential cadre of Choctaw scholars had graduated from Dartmouth, Yale, and other institutions.

Cherokee educational efforts mirrored those of the Choctaws, but they featured a system of tribal elementary schools that enrolled more students than those sponsored by religious denominations. By 1859 almost 1,500 students were enrolled at thirty schools throughout the nation; moreover, by 1859 only two teachers in the Cherokee public school system were non-Cherokees.

Many of these teachers, as well as other well-educated young Cherokees, were products of the planter-elite's educational pride and joy: the Cherokee seminaries. Opened in 1850, the Cherokee Male Seminary at Tahlequah and the Female Seminary at Park Hill were each imposing three-story brick structures that housed classrooms, dormitories, a kitchen and dining facilities, and a formal parlor. The buildings were designed to house 100 students, and twenty-five were admitted each year into the four-year course of study. The Cherokee National Council provided teachers, tuition, textbooks, food, and lodging. Students furnished their own linen, clothing, and other expenses. Admission was supposedly open to any member of the tribe, but in reality the student bodies were comprised primarily of children of the planter-elite. Fluency in English was a prerequisite for admission.

Critics charged that the institutions resembled "finishing schools" more than institutions reflecting traditional Cherokee values. Indeed, the curricula of the institutions were designed by leading educators from the East: the Male Seminary was modeled after the Boston Latin School and the Lawrenceville Academy in New Jersey. In addition, many of the students reflected the class-consciousness of their parents and sometimes made disparaging remarks about the minority of darker-skinned, less sophisticated, more traditional full-blood students who were enrolled in their classes. Still, many graduates attended colleges in the East, and in the decades to come they formed much of the leadership that would guide the Cherokee Nation. Others, both men and women, played leading roles in Oklahoma after the new state was founded in 1907.

A. M. Gibson, a renowned historian of Oklahoma, has referred to the period between removal and the Civil War as the Five Southern Tribes' "golden years." Removed from the immediate threat of white encroachment and left to their own devices, the Cherokees, Choctaws, Chickasaws, Creeks, and (to a much lesser degree) Seminoles came to terms with their new homes, ran their own affairs, and generally prospered. Of course, not all members of these tribes shared equally in such prosperity, and accelerating cultural change among the planter-elite created a widening divide in these tribes' class systems. Yet most people did live comfortably, and even within the more traditional communities cultural change continued. "Being Indian" in eastern Oklahoma began to encompass a broader spectrum of cultural experiences than in most Native American communities in other parts of the United States.

TEXAS

Conditions were different in Texas. This vast area, the size of modern France, had originally been claimed by Spain. After 1820, it became part of the Republic of Mexico. An isolated land, Texas had remained on the northern periphery of both Spain's and Mexico's boundaries, and officials in Mexico had exercised limited control over the region's population. The loose Spanish or Mexican hegemony was a mixed blessing: it proved advantageous to some tribes who had remained outside Spanish or Mexican control, but it was disastrous for others, who needed protection from the aggression of Spanish, Mexican, or American citizens.

The Texas Tribes

The two tribal groups who initially suffered the most from the expansion of Spanish, Mexican, or American settlement were the Coahuiltecans and Karankawas. Coahuiltecan-speaking hunter-gatherers had lived in small groups and had resided amidst the grasslands and brush country of South Texas for generations. By 1820 most had lost their separate identity and had been absorbed into the Spanish-speaking population in the region.

East of the Coahuiltecans, among the lowlands, bays, and barrier islands of the Texas coast, the Karankawas also lived as hunter-gatherers, but they remained outside both Spanish and Mexican hegemony, stealing Spanish cattle from settlers and eluding Spanish or Mexican military expeditions. In 1820, after Anglo-Americans began to colonize the region, Stephen F. Austin and other Anglo *empresarios* (large land owners) considered the Karankawas to be "barbarians and canibals [sic]" and conducted a campaign of extermination against them. Armed with six-foot bows and cane arrows, the Karankawas fought back, but by 1836 they had retreated from their lands north of Matagorda Bay. Many survived this displacement by working periodically for Spanish-speaking ranchers. After Texas's independence from Mexico, however, increased American settlement forced the Karankawas from many of their fishing and gathering sites, and the loosely organized bands suffered from lack of food and from European diseases. Many hunted the cattle (both feral and domestic) that grazed in the coastal prairies, provoking additional American retaliation. The remnants of the tribe fled south to Mexico or sought refuge among the Tonkawas. By the mid-1850s, the once-proud Karankawas had ceased to exist as a separate people.

The Tonkawas, a people who in 1820 lived in the Hill Country and the Edwards Plateau, earlier had ranged from southern Kansas to the Rio Grande. A nomadic people, they not only hunted bison but also gathered a considerable amount of plant foods and were not as dependent on the bison herds as were tribes such as the Comanches and Kiowas. Never large in numbers, the Tonkawas comprised several smaller groups who had coalesced during the colonial period. They walked a political tightrope, attempting to maintain their independence through shifting alliances with the Spaniards, Caddos, Wichitas, Comanches, and Lipan Apaches. When the Anglo-Americans settled in Texas, initial relations between the *empresarios* and Tonkawas were friendly. The Tonkawas traded horses and hides to the Americans, who saw the Tonkawa settlements along the Brazos and Colorado rivers as a barrier against Comanche and Wichita raids. Some Tonkawas supported the Texans during the Texas War of Independence, and following the war they readily served as scouts for Texan military expeditions against the Comanches.

The Tonkawas' service to the Republic of Texas, and later as scouts to the American military, however, earned them the disdain of other southern Plains tribes, who denounced them as "government Indians" and even accused them of cannibalism. The Tonkawas remained in Texas, occupying a reservation with the Caddos and Wichitas on the Brazos River until 1859, when they were removed to southwestern Indian Territory.

The Caddos, a loose confederacy of tribes (Hasanai, Kadohadachos, Natchitoches, etc.) who lived in the Piney Woods of eastern Texas and adjoining regions of modern Louisiana and southern Arkansas, had descended from the pre-Columbian Mississippian culture. Sedentary village dwellers, the Caddos raised extensive gardens of corn, beans, and squash, which they supplemented by hunting and fishing. By the 1820s they had acquired horses and periodically hunted bison on the Plains. When Texas gained its independence, President Sam Houston pursued a policy of friendship with the Caddos and other tribes living in the eastern portions of the Lone Star Republic, but Houston's successor, Mirabeau B. Lamar forced the Caddos north from Texas into the Indian Territory. In 1843, after Houston was reelected to the presidency of Texas, the Caddos, accompanied by some Delawares, returned to Texas and established new villages along the Brazos River about twenty miles downstream from Comanche Peak. The Caddos and Delawares served as peacemakers between the Texans and the more hostile Comanches and Wichitas. In 1846, after Texas entered the union, federal commissioners met with the Caddos, Delawares, Tonkawas, Comanches, and Wichitas at Council Springs and signed a general treaty of peace and friendship.

The peace did not last. Although the federal government "officially" assumed responsibility for the Indian tribes in Texas, the unique provisions governing Texas's entrance into the union created significant problems. Unlike other states, Texas retained ownership of all public lands in the state, so the lands on which the Indians lived were exempt from the federal protection supposedly accorded to tribes in other states; federal agents could not intercede on the Indians' behalf. In consequence, Native Americans were forced to rely on the Texas Rangers, an organization long known for its enmity to tribal people.

Following the Treaty of Council Springs, the Caddos and Delawares on the Brazos were joined by a portion of the Wichitas and the Penateka Comanches, who also erected villages nearby. Robert Neighbors, the federal Indian agent in north Texas, labored diligently to protect the Indians and maintain the peace, but both he and the tribespeople were helpless against white Texans who continued to harass the tribes, seizing lands and murdering Indians. In response, most of the Wichitas and Comanches withdrew to Oklahoma, from which they retaliated in kind, raiding white ranches and stealing livestock. Although the Caddos did not participate in these raids, the Texans accused them of complicity and called for their removal. Finally, at Neighbors's suggestion, in 1854 the state of Texas established a new reservation (the Brazos Reserve) for the Caddos, Delawares, and some of the Wichitas in modern Young County. Between 1855 and 1859 Caddo and Wichita men cleared fields there, planted and harvested crops, built log houses, and tended livestock. In 1858 a Methodist mission school opened, and the new teacher reported that the Caddos and Wichitas were well on the road to "civilization."

The prediction proved far too optimistic. Late in 1858 the Comanches renewed their raids on white ranches. Although the Caddos and Wichitas took no part in the attacks and suffered themselves from Comanche depredations, the Texans blamed all Indians. Wichita and Caddo scouts assisted the Texas Rangers in recovering stolen livestock, but in May 1859 a white mob led by John Baylor invaded the Brazos Reserve, killed several elderly Caddos, and stole much of the tribe's livestock. Baylor's mob was driven off by the Caddos, Wichitas, and the few federal troops assigned to protect them, but federal officials believed that the Caddos could no longer remain in Texas. In August, the Caddos and Wichitas were removed to Indian Territory. One month later Robert Neighbors, who had defended these tribespeople and had supervised their removal, returned to Texas to conduct some private business. On September 14, 1859, he was killed by a shotgun blast in the back as he walked along the main street of Belnap, Texas. Edward Cornett, his assailant, was never prosecuted.

The Wichitas partially shared in the Caddos' fate. Close relatives of the Caddos (both spoke dialects of the Caddoan language group), the Wichitas were composed of several bands, often referred to as "Black Pawnees" or "Pawnee Picts"

A Wichita Grass House The thatched grass houses of the Wichitas were unique among tribes on the southern Plains.

because of their dark complexions and their habit of heavily tattooing their faces and bodies. During the colonial period the Wichitas had ranged across the southern Plains from southern Kansas into northern Texas, and like the Caddos, the Wichitas also were farmers. Since they lived in the more arid "cross-timbers" region, they planted smaller gardens and relied more heavily on bison hunting. By the early nineteenth century they were closely allied with the Comanches, trading horses and mules taken from Spanish or Mexican ranches to Creole-French or Anglo-American traders from the Mississippi Valley. The Wichitas were hard-pressed by the Osages, but following the Camp Holmes agreement in 1835, their warfare with their northern neighbors diminished. After Texas achieved independence, most of the Wichitas, with the exception of about 250 tribespeople who settled with the Caddos on the Brazos Reserve, abandoned their villages along the upper Trinity and Brazos rivers and retreated into Indian Territory. Prior to the Civil War they remained closely associated with the Comanches and Kiowas, but following the war they were assigned a separate agency at Anadarko, which they shared with the Caddos.

Emigrant Indians in Texas

Emigrant Indians also fared poorly in Texas. In the first decade of the nineteenth century small groups of eastern Indians had moved into the region, flee-

ing the advancing Americans. Alabamas and Coushatas, Muskogean-speaking people from the state of Alabama, settled on the Neches River, south of Nacogdoches, while a handful of Choctaws and Chickasaws also crossed over into Spanish territory and established small, scattered settlements in the pine forests west of the Sabine River. More important, however, were 300 Western Cherokees, accompanied by about 200 Delawares, Shawnees, and Kickapoos, who settled near the Caddos in the Piney Woods region. Led by Duwali ("The Bowl") and Tahchee ("Dutch"), these refugees represented less acculturated members of the Cherokee community who had fled the wars with the Osages. Spanish officials had welcomed the newcomers as allies against the Comanches, and after 1820 Mexico initially envisioned the emigrant Indians as a buffer against illegal American settlement in the region. In 1822–1823 Cherokee emissaries traveled to Mexico City in a futile attempt to secure an official land grant for the tribe.

Unfortunately for the emigrants, their requests were ignored by Mexican officials more interested in attracting Anglo-American *empresarios* as colonists into the region than in cultivating Indian allies. The officials erroneously assumed that in return for lands, the *empresarios* would remain loyal to the Republic of Mexico and support the government against American attempts to annex the region. Moreover, after 1825, Mexican officials became wary of the Cherokee plans to recruit large numbers of additional Indians from Arkansas and Indian Territory to Texas, since they believed that Native American emigrants would be more volatile and less likely to generate trade and tax revenue than Anglo-Americans.

Although the Cherokees and their allies continued to occupy lands in the region, many of their villages were located on large land grants eventually awarded to Anglo-American *empresarios*, and conflicts between the two sides emerged. In 1836, discouraged by Mexico's reluctance to provide them with clear land grants, a minority of the Texas Cherokees led by Robert Field agreed to support ex-*empresario* Haden Edwards's ill-fated scheme to withdraw east Texas from Mexico and establish the "Republic of Fredonia." Mexico quickly crushed the Fredonian Revolt, and Field's verbal support of the revolt cost the Cherokees dearly. Duwali and Gatuwundi ("Big Mush"), another

Cherokee chief, ordered Field's execution, but Mexican officials remained suspicious.

The Cherokees now found themselves caught between two unfriendly forces. The Mexican government distrusted them because of Field's flirtation with Edwards, while the *empresarios* resented the Cherokees' occupation of lands they claimed as their own. Yet Duwali and other Cherokee leaders knew that tensions were growing between the *empresarios* and the Mexican government, and they hoped to use the antagonism to their advantage. By 1836 the ranks of emigrant Indians in east Texas had swollen to almost 3,000 as additional Cherokees, Choctaws, Creeks, Shawnees, and Kickapoos had either joined Duwali's people or settled nearby. Illegal American emigration also had increased, and the English-speaking population numbered almost 9,000.

In 1836, at the outbreak of the Texas Revolution, Duwali negotiated a treaty with Sam Houston in which the Republic of Texas promised to set aside land for the Cherokees and their allies in return for Cherokee neutrality in the war against Mexico. But when the Texas legislature refused to ratify the treaty, the Cherokees and other Indians met with Mexican emissaries who also promised lands in return for their support. Duwali remained neutral, but a minority of the Cherokees and most of the 700 Kickapoos living in east Texas accepted the Mexican offer. Meanwhile, Texans intercepted other Mexican emissaries and publicized their plans for an alliance with the Indians. Most Cherokees and other emigrant Indians took no part in the conflict, but when the Texans won their independence, they turned their suspicions on all Indians remaining in the region.

In 1838, Mirabeau B. Lamar replaced Houston as the president of the Lone Star Republic. A former resident of Georgia and a protégé of Georgia governor George M. Troup, who had advocated Indian removal in the Southeast, Lamar championed a similar policy in Texas. In July 1838 Lamar issued an ultimatum that the Cherokees and other emigrant Indians leave Texas. When Duwali asked for more time to consider the ultimatum, General Thomas Jefferson Rusk and a force of Texas militia marched on the Indian villages. Between July 15 and July 17, 1838, a series of skirmishes and battles occurred, and in the fighting, Duwali was killed and the tribespeople were defeated. Most of the Cherokees retreated back to Indian Territory where they were reluctantly received by the Cherokee Nation.

Not all the emigrant Indians returned to Oklahoma. A small party of Cherokees, accompanied by part of the Shawnees and Delawares, fled to Tamaulipas and Coahuila, just across the Rio Grande, in Mexico. In 1849 they were joined by Wild Cat and Gopher John, two Seminole chiefs and their followers, who fled the Seminole Nation in Oklahoma because they resented the attempts by Creek and Cherokee slaveholders to seize African-Americans associated with the tribe. Following the Mexican-American War, the Mexican government encouraged the settlement of these Seminoles and other Indians, particularly the Kickapoos, along its northern border as a barrier against further American aggrandizement in the region. In addition, Mexico enlisted the Seminoles, Kickapoos, and other American émigrés against the Comanches and Apaches, who continued to raid the region in the mid-nineteenth century.

Like earlier Seminole towns in Florida, the Mexican Seminole and Kickapoo settlements attracted runaway slaves from South Texas. Settlers in the region also accused the Seminoles and Kickapoos of crossing the river to steal livestock. In 1855 a force of Texas militia invaded Mexico, intent on attacking Wild Cat's village, but the Seminoles defeated the Texans and drove them back into the United States. Wild Cat's village remained a center of anti-American activity until 1857, when Wild Cat died of smallpox. In the same year, the establishment of a separate Seminole Nation free of Creek domination in Indian Territory enticed most of the Mexican Seminoles to return to the United States. In contrast, many of the Kickapoos remained in Mexico, where they resided until late in the twentieth century.

CALIFORNIA

Like Texas, California also remained on the periphery of both Spanish and Mexican political control, and Native Americans in the region frequently interacted with Hispanic officials or landowners, who often acted independently of the central government. Mexico became independent in 1820, and

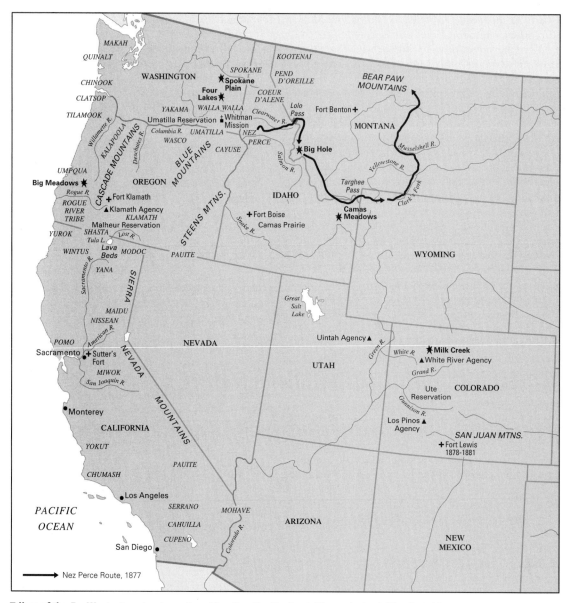

Tribes of the Far West. *Based on Joann Levy,* They Saw the Elephant: Women in the California Gold Rush *(Hamden, CT: Archon Books, 1990), 12–13; and Robert Ruby and John Brown,* Indians of the Pacific Northwest *(Norman: University of Oklahoma Press, 1981), 39, 69, 100.*

during the next decade the Mexican government secularized the missions, forcing economic and social changes on the Indian population. Many tribespeople adapted admirably to these changes, but a floodtide of European and American immigrants

during the gold-rush period proved disastrous since the newcomers were unfettered by any institutional restraints and readily exploited Indian people. Not surprisingly, the Native American population plummeted, leaving California with a fraction of its formerly large Indian population. Some fled to adjacent states, but others remained, adopting a series of strategies designed to ensure that the Indian presence in California would continue.

The California Tribes

In California, Spanish and Mexican settlement had been concentrated along the coast and to a lesser extent in the great interior valleys of the San Joaquin and Sacramento rivers. Near the coast, Christian Indians (neophytes) had been partially integrated into the mission system, and some Native American leaders had served as alcaldes (magistrates) or regidores (councilmen) within the mission communities. But in August 1833 the Mexican government secularized the California missions and decreed that about half the mission lands, livestock, and farming equipment were to be given to the neophytes. The former mission communities were to be converted into self-governing, secular pueblos where mission priests could perform their religious duties but were forbidden to participate in the villages' government. Unfortunately, the plan was poorly administered and most of the lands supposedly set aside for neophytes fell into the hands of former lay administrators associated with the missions.

Many of the former "mission Indians" settled near Mexican towns or presidios at Monterey, San Diego, and Los Angeles. Others clustered in Catholic communities at Pala, Temecula, and Santa Ysabel. At Los Angeles, Anglo observers remarked that Native Americans, both ex-neophytes and gentiles (non-Christians), performed much of the labor taking place in the settlement, and by 1844 the town contained almost 650 Indians, many of whom were recent arrivals from former missions along the southern California coast. They resided in communities along the Los Angeles River, worked at seasonal jobs for low pay, and gathered acorns and other natural foods in the surrounding foothills. The Mexican population complained that these new workers were unreliable and often left employers "for no reason," but they were an integral part of the Los Angeles community.

Other Indians worked on Mexican ranches. After secularization, many of the ex-neophytes remained near their former homes. As the mission lands passed into Mexican hands, communities of Native Americans transferred their focus from the missions to ranches created in their wake. Since entire communities often made this transition together, they retained their former cohesiveness. Similar to their role at the missions, Indians herded cattle and sheep, raised crops, built and maintained buildings, and served as tanners, carpenters, cooks, and maids. In turn, the ranch owner provided them with housing, small plots for gardens and animals, and minimal wages. Although the ranch owner exercised less religious and social control than had the padres at the missions, he did regulate their economic well-being and often mediated their disputes. In essence, the large ranch replaced the mission as a focal point for these Indians' existence.

Not all ex-neophytes settled in towns or on ranches. During the 1820s, even before the missions were secularized, many neophytes fled Mexican authority and took refuge in the San Joaquin Valley. After these "wild Indians" raided Mexican ranches, military expeditions eventually destroyed their villages. Farther south other tribal people remained autonomous of Mexican control, pursuing their own interests and sometimes providing services to ranches in the region. In the San Bernardino Valley, Cooswootna (Juan Antonio) led several bands of Cahuilla people, who remained independent but were associated with the Lugo family and protected their ranches against livestock thieves. During the mid-1840s ex-neophyte Antonio Garra organized the Cupeños into a significant force in the region east of modern Escondido, where they provided similar services to other ranchers.

To the north, in the Sacramento and American river valleys, other tribespeople labored for non-Hispanics. Several hundred American or European immigrants lived in the region, and they also depended on a portion of the 20,000 Indians living near their farms and ranches for labor. John Sutter, the Swiss land baron who owned New Helvetia, a massive estate on the American River, employed large numbers of Miwoks, Nisenans, and other Indians, hiring as many as 600 just to assist with his wheat harvest. Other Native Americans worked in Sutter's distillery, hat factory, blanket works, and gristmill. They hunted deer and caught salmon, which were then salted and shipped in barrels to the coast. Some tribesmen sailed Sutter's launch from his estate downstream to San Francisco Bay,

Luiseño Women These Luiseño women were part of the Native American population residing at the Catholic mission at San Luis Rey.

while others, dressed in surplus Russian military uniforms, garrisoned his fort and protected his estate from trespassers and horse thieves. Indeed, Sutter employed such numbers of Indians that he "hired them out" to other ranchers during slack periods at New Helvetia.

The employment of Indian workers by Sutter and other ranchers provided them with food, lodging, and income, but it had a negative effect on many tribal communities. Since the ranches hired far more men than women, it drained men from the villages, disrupting traditional family life, lowering the birth rate, and making the villages vulnerable to attacks by outsiders. In contrast, there were few ranch jobs for women. Some, who worked as servants, often developed relationships with or "married" Anglo or Mexican overseers. When the workers, both men and women, returned to their villages, they often carried diseases contracted from Hispanics or Americans; in conse-

quence, during the 1840s the Indian population continued to fall, a pattern that would accelerate in the next half century.

The American and European employers differed from the Mexican employers in other ways. Although the Mexicans undoubtedly exploited Indian labor, they still envisioned Native Americans as a permanent part of their society, and the Catholic Church, regardless of the abuses of the mission system, considered tribal people as part of its greater congregation. But the new, non-Hispanic employers were a portent of things to come. They were willing to "marry" Indian woman and temporarily exploit Indian labor, but they considered Native Americans to be people "of a lesser race," and they would readily abandon both wives and workers when they no longer needed them. In the mad scramble for riches that characterized the newly emerging American California, there would be little place for Indian people.

The Gold Rush

The discovery of gold at Sutter's Mill in February 1848 was catastrophic for the California tribes. The Treaty of Guadalupe Hidalgo, which officially transferred California to the United States, was signed in the same month. News of the discovery spread throughout California, and many Native Americans participated in the initial rush to stake claims or seek employment in the gold fields. Throughout 1848 and 1849 many Indians panned or dug for gold, and as late as Christmas 1848, American officials estimated that over half of the 4,000 miners seeking gold in the Sierras east of the Sacramento River were Native Americans. Yet more than 100,000 gold seekers arrived in California in 1849, and by 1852 the number of new immigrants approached 250,000. Although they came from all over the world, most were from either Oregon or the eastern states, and unlike the Hispanic gold seekers who readily accepted the Indian miners, most of the new arrivals considered all Indians to be "savages." Many were outraged that potentially rich claims already were occupied by Indians while they were forced to prospect in less productive regions.

Violence against Native Americans flared as early as 1849. In March prospectors from Oregon kidnapped and raped several Maidu women near the American River, then murdered their male relatives who tried to rescue them. The Maidus retaliated by killing five miners, but prospectors then attacked some Miwoks and Nisenans near Weber's Creek, summarily executing seven of them although they were not connected to the previous violence. Meanwhile after two ranchers raped and abused Pomo women near Clear Lake, the Pomos killed both men. In response, federal troops and militia units attacked the Pomo village, killing 160 Pomos at the Bloody Island Massacre. Similar acts of violence flared throughout the gold fields as poverty-stricken miners, angered that the pipe dreams of instant riches were not immediately fulfilled, turned their frustration on the Indians. Populated primarily by young males between the ages of eighteen and thirty-five, the mining camps were social tinder boxes easily sparked to violence. Isolated from wives, families, churches, or other ameliorating institutions, most prospectors considered Indians to be less than human and believed "that

extermination of the red devils will have to be resorted to before the country will be safe."

By 1850 racism and the exploitation of Indian labor in California had been institutionalized into state and local statutes. In Los Angeles, Indian prisoners in the local jail were "auctioned off to the highest bidder . . . when the city has no work in which to employ them." During the same year the state of California passed "An Act for the Government and Protection of Indians," which historian Albert Hurtado has wryly described as legislation that "protected them very little, and governed them quite a lot." The act prohibited non-Indians from compelling Native Americans to work against their will, yet able-bodied Indians could be arrested for loitering or "strolling about," and if designated a "vagrant," he or she could be hired out to the highest bidder for up to four months. Moreover, any Indian fined by a court for any offense was liable to work for the white person paying the fine until the value of the Indian's labor matched the fine payment. Non-Indians who paid the fines were required to feed and clothe Indians working for them, but since the bill also provided that "in no case shall a white man be convicted of any offence on the testimony of an Indian," any allegations of abuse by Indians were summarily dismissed.

Indian Women and Children

Indian women and children may have suffered the most. Although miners commented that Native American women were the antithesis of Victorian standards of female beauty ("degraded beings . . . dwarfish creatures . . . repugnant in all ways"), such unfavorable descriptions did not prevent American miners from aggressive sexual behavior toward them. Part of the problem resulted from the shortage of women in the mining camps. In 1852 there were seven men for every woman in California, and the ratio was higher in the mining country. Moreover, in 1850 there were 7,000 non-Indian women and about 40,000 Indian women in the state. Although many non-Indian women entered California during the 1850s and the number of Indian women declined, Native American women still remained a significant and vulnerable part of the state's population.

INDIAN VOICES   William Joseph (Nisenan Tribesman) Describes a Lynching

Anglo-American exploitation of Indian people in California reached a crescendo during the Gold Rush. Although there are numerous descriptions of these abuses from government documents and frontier newspapers, the Native American population in California declined so precipitously that few Indian accounts were recorded and preserved. One of the best, a narrative by William Joseph, a Nisenan tribesman from the foothills of the Sierras about forty miles east of modern Sacramento, describes the lynching of an Indian boy who pilfered some cash from a miner's cabin and the subsequent usurpation of an Indian mining site by Anglo-American miners. Why were Anglo-American miners more prone to violence toward Native Americans than Hispanic, Asian, or European miners?

On the west side of Mt. Oakum two white men had their home in a small log cabin. From there they used to go to work at the river every day. The door of their house being left open, an Indian boy who was hunting around, felt hungry and went to that house to eat. When he had finished eating, he saw two buckskin sacks full of gold and silver money on the table. He took [the money], put [it] in his pocket, and went off.

When the two men came home from work they missed the . . . money. They followed the Indian's tracks. They tracked (him) to the Indian's camp. They saw (him) playing cards and putting down sackfuls of gold. The white men took him right there. They took back all the money. But they took him all the same to a little valley on the west side of Mt. Oakum.

The white men gathered. From there, afterwards, they summoned all the Indian chiefs. They kept him there all day waiting for one chief. When it was about three o'clock, they put a rope around (his) neck.

(The white people) said to the mule, "Get Up!" (The mule) pulled (him) up by the rope and hanged (him). All the Indians hollered and cried. When (he) was dead, (they) let (him) back down. They gave (him) to the Indians. The Indians took the body along and burned (it).

After that the Indians did not burgle or steal anything belonging to white people. "That is the way (they) will treat us if they catch (us)," they said. "Those white men are different men, they are not our relatives," they said. "They will hang you without mercy," they said. All the chiefs preached that. The Indians were very much afraid of those whites in the early days. That is what was done, the whites were bad in the old days, those who prospected for gold.

About a year after that hanging (an Indian boy) found gold in a creek while he was hunting a deer. . . . He looked around for a tree to hang it on. He saw this gold. He took the deer along instead of hanging it up. When he brought it into camp he told his relatives, "There is a lot of this gold, let us go tomorrow," he said.

That morning at dawn they went. . . . They all brought a lot of gold. They took (it) to town to exchange (it) five or six times to that town, the same fellows.

The white men talked about (it) "Those Indians bring in a lot of gold from somewhere," said the storekeeper. "Let us watch those Indians, where is it they are always going?" they said. They saw those fellows go, the white men tracked (them) that way. From the hills they saw them at work. When the sun was from the west the Indians went back from work.

The whites gathered and went there. When the Indians tried to go to work, they found the whites there. They sneaked away. "That is those fellows, those who hanged that boy," they said. That way those whites stole their prospecting place. The whites named that [place] Indian Digging.

From: Hans Jorgen Uldall and William Shipley, eds., *Nisenan Texts and Dictionary*, vol. 46 of the University of California Publication in Linguistics (Berkeley: Regents of the University of California, 1966), 177–181. Reprinted with permission of The University of California Press. (Excerpt also quoted in Albert L. Hurtado and Peter Iverson, eds., *Major Problems in American Indian History* [Lexington: D. C. Heath and Co., 1994], 291–292).

Some Indian women married miners, but their new husbands often abandoned them after a relatively short time. Others, however, were the victims of rape, and newspapers from the period are full of accounts in which violence between Indians and whites was triggered by such assaults. Since Indians had little legal recourse, rapists generally were immune from prosecution, And since many of the miners considered the California tribes to be less than human, the stigma associated with rape in more civilized regions was rarely applied in the mining districts. In addition, as Native American economic resources were depleted, some Indian women turned to prostitution to help feed their families. Accordingly, venereal diseases spread through both mining camps and tribal communities.

Children also fell victim to the gold rush maelstrom. Labor shortages in the Mexican period had fostered the clandestine kidnapping of Indian children, but the 1850 act contained articles that provided for the apprenticeship and indenture of Indian children, legalizing the removal of these children from their families. Supposedly, children could not be apprenticed without a parent's or relative's approval, but the laws were abused and professional "apprenticers" systematically kidnapped Indian children, obtained them through the collusion of local law enforcement agents, or followed in the wake of frontier vigilantes who killed the children's parents, then seized the children as "orphans." Boys usually were apprenticed

until they reached twenty-five years of age (sometimes thirty); girls were held until they reached twenty-one. Prices for the children ranged between $30 and $200, but most were marketed for around $50. A darker side of the trade provided young children for sexual purposes. By the Civil War the practice had created such abuses that public outrage, coupled with concerns over its similarity to slavery, caused the state legislature to repeal the 1850 act, and the apprenticeship program slowly faded away; yet historians estimate that between 1850 and 1860 well over 4,000 children fell victim to the program's brutality.

Anti-American sentiment spread throughout most of the California tribes, but the separate communities were unable to unite against the newcomers. In 1851 Antonio Garra, who had united many of the Cupeños, attempted to enlist neighboring tribes (Cahuillas, Luiseños, Ipais, and Quechans) against the Americans in southern California. The Indians resented American indignities, particularly taxes, yet other tribal leaders remained suspicious of Garra's political ambitions. The Cupenos attacked some isolated ranches, and in response white posses and militia units retaliated against other Indians. The Garra uprising failed when Cahuilla leaders seized Garra and turned him over to the Americans. He was found guilty of murder and executed at San Diego on January 10, 1852.

Attempting to exert control over an increasingly chaotic situation, federal commissioners in 1851 negotiated a series of treaties that proposed the creation of eighteen reservations to serve as home-lands for almost 25,000 tribespeople. Unfortunately, when the treaties arrived in Washington, politicians from California argued that the agreements set aside too much land for Native Americans and the Senate refused to ratify them. In response, during the next seven years, federal agents established several smaller reservations within the state, and by 1860 about 10,000 Native Americans resided on reservation land. At first they raised crops and seemed to be interested in the government's programs, but when funding for their support was slashed during the Civil War, the agricultural programs diminished. Moreover, several reservation administrators were charged with corruption or malfeasance, and by the end of the 1850s, most of the reservations were abandoned. More menacing, however, was the continued opposition by non-Indians to any continued Native American presence in the state. Some state politicians called for the removal of all remaining Indians from California (over the Sierras, into Nevada); others pointed out that the California tribes could never be "domesticated." Since their labor no longer was in demand, both federal officials and the public increasingly described tribespeople as "a dying race and a public nuisance" whose extinction was inevitable.

Tragically, census returns from California seemed to support their claims. The Native American population undoubtedly had declined during the Spanish and Mexican periods, but by the late 1840s one American remembered that when he first arrived in California, the state "had been densely populated with Indians." Yet thirty years later they were "all gone and that is the end of it." The decline was precipitous. In 1846 the Indian population of California was estimated at 150,000; by 1870 it was 30,000.

Many Indians succumbed to alcohol, disease, and other plagues introduced by the Americans. Others died from exposure and starvation as the newcomers and their livestock depleted the formerly abundant California environment. Salmon streams were polluted by placer mining, miners slaughtered the deer herds, and settlers' hogs roamed the oak groves, both fouling and consuming the acorn crops. Other tribespeople fell victim to violence. Journals, newspaper accounts, and other written records indicate that between 1848

and 1880 at least 4,500 California Indians were killed by Americans: the true number killed can only be speculated. Some Native Americans fled the state, seeking refuge in Oregon or Nevada. Others were absorbed into the Spanish-speaking population. Scattered remnants of the California tribes endured, however, and late in the nineteenth century the federal government established additional small reserves, or rancherias, for the survivors. Despite this, the population decline continued. In 1900 the official U.S. census listed only 15,377 Native Americans living in California; 90 percent of the population residing in the state only fifty years earlier had vanished. Ironically, those who remained persisted, and in the twentieth century California's Native American population had rebounded. In 2000 over 330,000 Native Americans resided in California, more than in any other state.

THE NORTHWESTERN TRIBES

Native Americans still held their homelands in the Pacific Northwest, but there, too, their lands were threatened. During the first third of the nineteenth century most tribal people in Washington, Oregon, and Idaho had exchanged furs and other commodities with British and American merchants. The fur traders, primarily from the British Hudson's Bay Company, maintained a symbiotic relationship with the Indians, establishing trading posts but never threatening to displace the tribes. In contrast, Americans settlers who invaded the region in the 1840s and 1850s had little use for tribal people and were determined to occupy their homelands permanently. Moreover, they spilled into the fertile river valleys where many Indian people resided. Indians in the Northwest now found themselves the target of ambitious politicians, eager to foist controversial treaties on the tribes in an attempt to further their own careers and to acquire tribal homelands. In addition, although the gold rush focused on California, miners also spilled into modern Washington and Oregon, seeking additional gold fields. For the first time, Indian people in the Northwest were seriously threatened by outsiders.

During the late 1820s Catholic Iroquois, loosely attached to the Hudson's Bay Company, visited Nez Percé villages and informed the western tribespeople of the white man's gospel. In response, during 1831 four Nez Percé tribesmen accompanied a party of fur traders to St. Louis where they supposedly asked for missionaries to "show them the road to heaven." Such a request (real or not) sparked a wave of evangelism among both Catholic and Protestant clergy, and in 1841 Salish and Pend d'Oreille tribespeople in western Montana welcomed Pierre Jean de Smet and other Jesuits into their villages. During the next five years the Jesuits established additional missions in tribal communities across the Idaho panhandle and into eastern Washington. The Jesuits modeled their stations after successful missions in Paraguay, but their Salish, Coeur d'Alene, and Spokane hosts were hunters and fishermen, not farmers, and the missions achieved only limited success. Some converts remained nominally Catholic, but they continued their traditional, seminomadic way of life.

The Protestants were even less successful. In 1836, two years after Methodists had established a mission among the Chinook people in the Willamette Valley in Oregon, American Board of Commissioners for Foreign Missions ("American Board") missionaries Henry and Eliza Spalding, along with Marcus and Narcissa Whitman, founded missions amid the Nez Percé villages (at Lapwai, Idaho) and among the Cayuses. When the Whitmans were killed (see the introduction to this chapter), the Oregon militia invaded the region, indiscriminately attacking both friendly and hostile Indians. In 1850 tensions temporarily were eased when five of the Cayuses who had led the attack voluntarily surrendered. These men believed a payment of trade goods and horses would "cover their crime," but they were hanged for murder. Their kinspeople were astonished at the severity of the punishment, and Indian resentment of the Americans increased.

The violence at the Whitmans' mission was a portent of things to come. Although American immigration to the Oregon Territory (modern Washington and Oregon) never matched the floodtide to California, it did threaten the 25,000 tribespeople in the region. Small communities of fishermen and gatherers lay scattered along the coast and adjacent river valleys from the northern boundaries of

California to the Olympic Peninsula. Speaking a potpourri of languages, small tribes like the Umpquas, Tilamoks, Clatsops (who had traded with Lewis and Clark), Quinalts, and Makahs had bartered with mariners and had suffered from introduced diseases, but they were less threatened by the American immigration than tribes in the Willamette, Columbia, and Snake river valleys. The Kalapoola people and associated tribes remained clustered in villages along the upper Willamette, while the remnants of the Wascos and Wishrams still occupied the Columbia Valley near The Dalles. East of The Dalles were Sahapatin-speaking Cayuses, Umatillas, Yakamas, Walla Wallas, and Nez Percés. To the north were Salish-speaking Spokanes, Coeur d'Alenes, Pend d'Orielles, and other people the whites called Flatheads. Although Christian missionaries had split many of these interior tribes into Christian and "pagan" factions, they remained more intact than the coastal communities. Their economic self-sufficiency had been compromised by the fur trade, but they still provided adequate food, clothing, and shelter for their families; moreover, many were well armed and well mounted.

During the 1850s tensions between the Oregon tribes and immigrants erupted in violence. In 1850 Congress passed the Oregon Donation Land Law, which ignored Indian title to land and granted 320 acres to any homesteader who cultivated the plot for four years. Meanwhile prospectors from northern California repeatedly trespassed on Indian land in the Rogue River valley in southwestern Oregon. In 1851 small parties of Coquille, Hani, and Miluk tribesmen struck back, harassing the intruders. Local militia and a small body of federal troops retaliated, but in 1853 Shasta tribesmen led by "Old John" raided farms and mining camps in southwestern Oregon, then fled into the Cascades. Pursued by the army and militia, the "Rogue River Tribes" were forced to sign the Treaty of Table Rock (September 1853) in which they relinquished claims to southern Oregon with the exception of a reservation along the Upper Rogue River.

The treaty brought little peace. The Rogue River tribes were so politically decentralized that many members of the loose coalition did not believe themselves obligated by the treaty agreement and refused to reside on the reservation. As additional settlers moved into the region the nonreservation tribespeople pilfered their livestock, and when militia units could not apprehend the perpetrators, the settlers focused their resentment on the reservation Indians. In October 1855 "volunteers" from nearby Jacksonville slaughtered twenty-three reservation Indians (almost all women and children), provoking a retaliatory raid that killed twenty-seven settlers along the Rogue River valley. Army officers attempted to negotiate a truce, but the "Rogue River War" continued until May 1856 when the Indians were defeated at the Battle of the Big Meadows. In the aftermath, the Rogue River tribes, both "friendly" and "hostile," were forced to abandon their homeland and resettle on the Grand Ronde and Siletz reservations near Kernville Oregon.

In the newly established (1853) Washington Territory, tribal people also fought for their homelands. During the winter of 1854–1855 Governor Isaac Stevens met with the Puget Sound tribes, negotiating a series of treaties in which the tribes ceded land west of the Cascades in exchange for small reservations and the right to continue their traditional fishing and gathering of shellfish. The tribes in eastern Washington were less amenable. In May 1855, when Stevens and Governor Joel Palmer met with leaders from the eastern Washington tribes, the leaders initially informed Stevens and Palmer that they would not sell their homeland. Nevertheless, after two weeks of negotiations, the chiefs reluctantly signed three land cession treaties. Jesuit observers commented that the tribesmen had no intention of abiding by the agreements and had put their marks on the documents only to be rid of Stevens and Palmer. Stevens then rode to northeastern Washington where he negotiated other questionable treaties with the Salish, Kutenais, and Pend d'Oreilles, then crossed the Rockies to meet with tribes in western Montana.

Ironically, while the Indians were meeting with Stevens, gold was discovered in northern Washington and a new gold rush sent prospectors scurrying across central sections of the territory. Kamiakin, a Yakama chief who had reluctantly signed one of the recent treaties, denounced the "Bostons" who now invaded his people's lands and argued that unlike "King George's Men" (Hudson's Bay Company traders), the newcomers intended to occupy the region permanently. While Stevens was still in Montana, Kamiakin enlisted the tribes of eastern and central Washington to drive the "Bostons" back into

Oregon. Even the Squaxon, Sisqually, and Puyallup people of Puget Sound, embittered over Stevens's treaties of the previous winter, promised assistance.

In August 1855 the Yakamas shot several prospectors who trespassed on their land, and one month later the Indians killed their agent when he attempted to investigate the attacks. When federal troops were sent to apprehend the "hostiles," Kamiakin and his warriors turned them back, inflicting casualties and capturing the expedition's howitzer and pack animals. In November, a subsequent American expedition found few Indians, but militia in northern Oregon violated a flag of truce, seized the Walla Walla chief Peo-Peo-Mox-Mox, shot the old man, then sent his scalp and ears back for display in the Oregon settlements. Meanwhile, the uprising spread to the Puget Sound region where it simmered throughout the winter before Squaxon, Nisqually, and Puyallup leaders made peace in the spring of 1856.

The fighting continued in central and eastern Washington. Stevens complained that federal troops seemed reluctant to attack Kamiakin and his allies, but General John Wool, the American military commander in the region, blamed the warfare on American settlers and countered that if "common justice and ordinary feelings of humanity" were extended to the Indians, they would "keep quiet and preserve the peace of the country." During the summer of 1856 federal troops and volunteers invaded the region and most tribespeople in southeastern Washington reluctantly made peace, but "hostile" Yakama and Walla Walla warriors, led by the intransigent Kamiakin, fled north to the Spokanes and Palouses. In September 1857, Kamiakin led warriors from these four tribes in a series of skirmishes (the battles of Four Lakes and Spokane Plain) against federal troops armed with new, long-range rifles. The Indians suffered heavy casualties, and the army captured and slaughtered over 1,000 Palouse horses. Kamiakin escaped to British Columbia, but later returned to Washington and died near Spokane in the mid-1870s.

In 1859 Congress finally ratified Stevens's treaties and the Washington tribes begrudgingly occupied their new reservations. The American invasion of their homeland had so angered them that they had overlooked tribal differences to unite against the "Bostons," but their direct confrontation with federal troops between 1855 and 1859

Indian Netting Salmon Many of the northwestern tribes depended on salmon as a food source. This painting by Langdon Kihn portrays a fisherman netting salmon at Celilo Falls, at The Dalles of the Columbia River. Many of the falls once used by theses tribes have been destroyed by modern dams and irrigation projects.

enabled the government to use its superiority in manpower and weaponry to crush their resistance. Unlike other regions where the tribes' reliance on guerilla tactics frustrated American military commanders, the pitched battles of the Pacific Northwest probably played into American hands.

THE SOUTHWEST

During the first half of the nineteenth century, the pueblo-dwelling people of New Mexico faced a different set of problems. Unlike the tribes in California or the Pacific Northwest, they welcomed few Americans into their midst, and those who arrived initially were often integrated into the Pueblo communities. But after 1820, Pueblo people, like other residents of New Mexico, suffered from both the negligence and oppression of a distant Mexican government, and their attempts to seek redress were betrayed and defeated. In the 1840s the Pueblos uncertainty over a new American regime also led to bloodshed, but the Americans crushed the Taos Revolt, and the Pueblos were defeated. Yet like the mountains and mesas that surround their villages, the Pueblos remained, and they persisted.

If the tribes of California and the Pacific Northwest were inundated by a flood of American newcomers, the Pueblo people in New Mexico faced only a trickle, and at first they seemed to absorb it rather well. In 1800 New Mexico remained an economic and administrative backwater of New Spain, isolated from Mexico City and supporting a population of about 9,500 Pueblo tribespeople and fewer than 19,000 non-Indians. Only five villages or towns numbered more than 1,000 residents. The eastern Pueblos had adapted admirably to the Spaniards (see Chapter 6), and colonial officials imposed a Spanish system of local government on the Pueblo villages, yet much of the daily life within the pueblo was governed by traditional priests and clan elders; the Pueblo people still owned their lands in common, grew their traditional crops, performed many of the old ceremonies, and followed a rhythm of life that emphasized harmony and communal values. The old ways still persisted.

After 1820, when Mexico became independent, things changed. In 1821, in a surge of liberal idealism, Mexico granted full "citizenship" to all Indians within its borders—they would no longer be "Indians," they would be "Citizens of Mexico." As in California, all Catholic missions were to be disbanded and communally held lands were to be divided into small plots and then parceled out to individual Indians, assuring that as a political and economic class, "Indians" would cease to exist. Yet laws passed in Mexico City were altered and diffused when applied in Albuquerque, and although mission lands were seized, communally held Pueblo lands initially were left intact. Still, the specter of unwanted land reform loomed on the horizon, and the instability of the new Mexican government created a sense of uncertainty and foreboding among the Pueblos along the Rio Grande.

During the late 1820s, conditions deteriorated. After Spanish troops were withdrawn from the presidios, Navajo, Apache, and Comanche raids increased. Strapped for funds, the new Mexican government attempted to garrison the posts, but the troops were ill equipped, ill paid, and few in number. Spanish officials had relied on native New Mexicans to fill many local posts, but the new government appointed bureaucrats from Mexico City or other distant venues, individuals less attuned to the particular needs of the Pueblo people. In addition, by the late 1820s growing numbers of Anglo-Americans began to arrive via the Santa Fe Trail. Settling in Taos, Santa Fe, and the pueblos, these newcomers brought a wealth of new trade goods, but they disrupted the harmony of the Pueblo communities.

Violence erupted in 1837. One year earlier Santa Ana had seized power in Mexico, centralizing the government, limiting local autonomy, and imposing new taxes. Resentful, wealthy Hispanics led by Manuel Armijo, a citizen of Albuquerque, informed the Pueblos that taxes soon would be raised so high that officials would "pluck eggs from the nests as quickly as the hens laid them." In August 1837, when the alcalde of Santa Cruz pueblo refused to allow officials to collect debts in his village, Alboni Perez, a governor appointed from Mexico, ordered the man arrested. Angered, a large party of Pueblos, supported by some poorer Hispanics, seized power and freed the alcalde. The revolt then spread to other pueblos, including Taos, where the rebels issued a statement that they were good Christians and loyal to the Republic of Mexico but would pay no more taxes. When Perez enlisted about 150 Pueblo warriors from the Santa Fe region to accompany his small garrison north to suppress the rebellion, the Pueblos accompanying him deserted and went over to the rebels. Perez then retreated toward Albuquerque but was intercepted by other Pueblos, killed, and decapitated.

Learning of the revolt, Manuel Armijo attempted to assume command of the rebels, but the Pueblos rejected him and turned to José Gonzalez, a capable and popular leader at the Taos Pueblo. Gonzales assembled the leaders from the northern pueblos and, assisted by some Hispanics, drafted a list of grievances, established a provisional government, and again pledged his support of Mexico. But Armijo, angered over his rejection, returned to Albuquerque and raised a force of Hispanics against the rebels. Returning to Santa Fe, Armijo declared himself provisional governor of New Mexico, and supported by 200 recently arrived Mexican dragoons, he marched against the northern Pueblos. Gonzalez and his followers met the army at Pojoaque, a pueblo about twenty-five miles north of Santa Fe; the two sides clashed and the Pueblos were defeated. In the aftermath, Gonzalez surrendered, but Armijo promptly executed him, along with four other Pueblo leaders. Temporarily subdued, the Pueblos returned to their villages and took refuge in their communities. Yet their rebellion achieved some success. Mexican tax collectors rarely ventured into

Pueblo villages, and the Pueblos continued to control the pace of their daily existence.

Although Armijo charged that the Pueblo revolt had been encouraged by Anglo-Americans, there is scant evidence to support such a claim. Nevertheless, during the Mexican period growing numbers of Americans arrived in the Pueblo villages. Since New Mexico was so isolated from Mexico City, manufactured goods remained scarce, and both Pueblos and Hispanics were eager for such commodities. In response, in 1821 William Becknell arrived in Santa Fe with a pack train of trade goods from Missouri, exchanged his merchandise for Mexican specie, and after returning to Missouri launched the Santa Fe trade, which flourished for the next two decades.

Initial contacts between Indians and Anglos in New Mexico generally were positive. Missouri traders arriving in Santa Fe or Taos were welcomed by neighboring Pueblos who purchased manufactured products, then carried them eastward to the Comanches, trading the goods for hides and horses. Indeed, these *Comancheros* (mostly people of mixed Pueblo-Hispanic ancestry) prospered during the middle decades of the nineteenth century, purchasing livestock that the Comanches had obtained from ranches in Texas or Mexico and supplying the Comanches with guns, ammunition, and other manufactured goods.

The Santa Fe trade also increased contacts between Native Americans and Anglos on the southern Plains. The heavily laden freight wagons made tempting targets for Comanches, Kiowas, and other Plains nomads, and although large, heavily armed wagon trains generally were secure against attacks, smaller caravans or isolated wagons were vulnerable. Yet the influx of Americans also spurred a clandestine trade in livestock in which the Americans participated. Comanche, Kiowa, and Pawnee warriors soon learned that while American traders were loathe to lose their own livestock, they asked few questions about the origins of animals that the Indians offered for sale. In response war parties swept the settlements in Texas and Mexico; they even sold horses and mules taken from other wagon trains.

By 1830 the Comanches, Kiowas, and Southern Cheyennes and Arapahos had become so proficient at procuring livestock from the northern provinces of Mexico that traders such as William Bent (who was married to Owl Woman, a Cheyenne) built permanent trading posts near the Santa Fe Trail and along the northern borders of New Mexico to

Taos North Building in the Nineteenth Century The multi-storied adobe village at Taos remains one of the classic Pueblo communities.

tap the burgeoning trade in bison hides, contraband, and horses. To their credit, Mexican officials attempted to patrol their northern boundaries, but political instability and a lack of resources severely hampered their efforts.

Some of the Americans who arrived in New Mexico stayed. By the mid-1820s significant numbers of Anglos were both trading and living in the Pueblo villages. Like their sisters among the northern tribes who formed liaisons with mountain men in Wyoming and Montana, some Pueblo women also welcomed fur trappers into their villages, where the Anglos settled down (some permanently, others less so), and the couples produced children. The Pueblo wives assisted their husbands in preparing hides and pelts, and the wives' kinship networks also facilitated the exchange of commodities. By the late 1820s so many Anglo trappers were operating in the Taos region that they depleted the beaver population and the Mexican government attempted to ban the foreigners; local officials, however, were powerless to enforce the measure and trapping continued.

Conditions changed during the 1840s. In 1846 the United States declared war on Mexico, and Colonel Stephen W. Kearney led an expeditionary force of about 2,000 men from Missouri toward the Southwest. In New Mexico, Governor Manuel Armijo initially mustered about 3,000 Mexican citizens, including a contingent of Pueblo warriors, in defense of the province, but in August, as the Americans approached Santa Fe, Armijo fled and the resistance disintegrated. After occupying Santa Fe, Kearney met with delegations from the surrounding pueblos, listened to their complaints about Navajo and Apache raids, and promised them that the Americans would protect them and bring about a general peace. In September 1846 Kearney departed for California, but his successor, Colonel Alexander Doniphan invaded the Navajo homeland and made at least a temporary peace with the Navajos (see Chapter 11).

The Pueblos found their American "protectors" to be more annoying than the Navajos and Apaches. The American soldiers who occupied the region were suspicious of all Indians, and unlike the Spaniards or Mexicans who envisioned the Pueblos as comrades in both suffering and arms against the Navajos and Apaches, the Americans disdainfully considered "all Indians to be the same." In addition, under Spanish law, the Pueblos had been given grants to about twelve square miles of land surrounding their villages, and these grants had been continued under the Mexican regime. But when Pueblo leaders asked Kearney, Doniphan, and other American officials for assurances that they would retain their property, the Americans gave ambiguous and unsatisfactory answers. Moreover, Mexico had awarded the Pueblos "citizenship," but many Pueblos now were uncertain about their status under the Americans. Former Mexican officials also added to the problem. Disgruntled over their failure to secure appointments within the new provisional American government, these bureaucrats informed the Pueblos that the Americans intended to seize their property and occupy their homes. They suggested that if the Pueblos would join Hispanics and rise against the Americans, they could recapture New Mexico.

The Americans learned of the conspiracy, but before they could capture the disgruntled officials, the latter fled to Mexico. In contrast, in January 1847 the Pueblos at Taos, assisted by part of the Hispanic population, rose against the Americans; killed Charles Bent, the newly appointed territorial governor and several of his associates; and then attacked other Americans in Taos and neighboring Arroyo Hondo. In response, an American force commanded by Colonel Sterling Price marched north from Santa Fe, fought off a Pueblo attack at Santa Cruz, and then besieged the rebels at the Taos Pueblo. The Indians and a handful of Hispanic supporters took refuge in the pueblo's church, but Price opened fire with artillery and killed many of the church's defenders. After losing almost 150 members of their pueblo, including many women and children, the Indians at Taos surrendered. Six Pueblos accused of killing Bent and other civilians were tried and executed. Subsequent violence flared at Mora and Las Vegas, but for all practical purposes, the Taos Revolt had ended.

CONCLUSION: A NEW POWER IN THE WEST

By the 1850s Native Americans across the trans-Mississippi west realized that their homelands now were threatened by new people and a new government. Unlike the British, who essentially had ruled the Oregon Country with a loose hand through the Hudson's Bay Company, and the Spanish and Mexican regimes whose control of California and the Southwest had been limited by isolation and few resources, the new intruders arrived in growing numbers, and they pursued policies far more dangerous to the tribes. In those regions in which federal officials initially exercised minimal control (Texas, California, and Oregon) Indian people struggled to cope with local, territorial, or state governments that reflected the newcomers' antipathy toward the tribes. In other areas, such as New Mexico, sedentary tribes found that troops representing the federal government were formidable opponents who readily applied military force to bring tribal people under federal hegemony. The potential for violence escalated.

More important, however, was the Indians' changing relationship to these newcomers and their society. Both the Hispanic regimes in the Southwest and the British traders in Oregon readily integrated Native American people into their societies and economies. Spanish and Mexican ranches as well as Catholic missions in California and the Southwest may have exploited Indian labor, but there was a place for Native Americans in their institutions. Indeed, Indian people were necessary for the well-being of both California and the Southwest. Similarly, tribespeople in Washington and Oregon traded readily with Hudson's Bay Company merchants, providing the traders with furs and other commodities that sustained the economy of the region. The traders needed the tribespeople; their economic system could not function without them.

But the Americans were intruders of a different sort. Primarily miners or farmers, the Americans had little use for Native Americans and had no interest in integrating them into their political or economic systems. In contrast to the earlier regimes, the Americans thought of Native Americans as a barrier to the transformation of the region, not as necessary components of its development. Like the citizens of the eastern states who clamored for the removal of the eastern tribes to new "homes" in the West, the American miners or farmers who flocked to Texas, California, or Oregon only wished for Indians to disappear; they had no intention of integrating them into their new frontier societies.

For Native Americans, the initial American expansion into the Southwest and the Pacific states in the decades prior to the Civil War was a precursor of things to come. The usurpation of lands and the exploitation of Indians and their resources in Texas and California would spread throughout the West. The Native American response would take many forms. Like many of the California tribes, some western Indians would seek an accommodation. Others would rise in armed resistance. But for the western tribes, the bell had begun to toll, and it was tolling for them.

SUGGESTED READINGS

Brooks, James F. *Captives and Cousins: Slavery, Kinship, and Community in the Soiuthwest Borderlands.* Chapel Hill: University of North Carolina Press, 2001. This sweeping study contains a perceptive analysis of cultural change in New Mexico during the eighteenth and nineteenth centuries.

Champagne, Duane. *Social Order and Political Change: Constitutional Governments Among the Cherokees, the Choctaws, the Chickasaws, and the Creeks.* Stanford: Stanford University Press, 1992. A good discussion of how Indian nations rebuilt their governments after arriving in Indian Territory.

Everett, Diane. *The Texas Cherokees.* Norman: University of Oklahoma Press, 1990. This volume contains the best survey of the Cherokee residency in Texas.

Foreman, Grant. *The Five Civilized Tribes.* Norman: University of Oklahoma Press, 1970 (reprint). An old standard, but still a valuable reference work for the establishment of tribal societies and governments in Indian Territory.

Hurtado, Albert. *Indian Survival on the California Frontier.* New Haven: Yale University Press, 1988. An excellent survey of the interaction of Native Americans and non-Indians in California from the Mexican period through 1860. Contains a good discussion of the important role Indians played in the region's economy.

Lancaster, Jane. *Removal Aftershock: The Seminoles' Struggle for Survival in the West, 1836–1866.* Knoxville: University of Tennessee Press, 1994. This volume features the most balanced survey of the Seminoles' efforts to maintain their tribal autonomy in Oklahoma and Texas during the antebellum period.

LaVere, David. *Contrary Neighbors: Southern Plains and Removed Indians in Indian Territory.* Norman: University of Oklahoma Press, 2000.

This volume contains good accounts of the military conflicts between the two sides and the emigrant tribes' attempts to reach an accommodation with and "civilize" the southern Plains tribes.

———. *The Texas Indians.* College Station: Texas A&M University Press, 2004. This volume offers the best survey of the Native American people (both indigenous and immigrant) of the region.

McLoughlin, William. *After the Trail of Tears: The Cherokee Struggle for Sovereignty, 1839–1880.* An excellent, scholarly account of the Cherokees' attempts to establish a new government and society in Indian Territory.

Mihesuah, Devon. *Cultivating the Rosebuds: The Education of Women at the Cherokee Female Seminary, 1851–1909.* Urbana: University of Illinois Press, 1993. Provides interesting insights into acculturation patterns and attitudes among the daughters of the Cherokee planter and merchant elite.

Miller, Susan A. *Coacoochee's Bones: A Seminole Saga.* Lawrence: University Press of Kansas, 2003. Written from a Seminole perspective, this volume chronicles the Seminole experience in Texas and Mexico.

Rawls, James. *The Indians of California: A Changing Image.* Norman: University of Oklahoma Press, 1984. Vividly illustrates how Americans manipulated the public image of the California tribes to further their own economic objectives.

Ruby, Robert H., and John A. Brown. *Indians of the Pacific Northwest.* Norman: University of Oklahoma Press, 1981. By far the best survey of the history and culture of the northwestern tribes, this volume contains valuable information regarding the cultures and histories of both the Pacific coast and inland plateau tribes.

Smith, Todd F. *The Caddos, Wichitas, and the United States.* College Station: Texas A&M University Press, 1995. The best survey of these tribes' relationship with the Republic of Texas and the federal government during these years.

Weber, David. *The Mexican Frontier, 1821–1846: The American Southwest Under Mexico.* Albuquerque: University of New Mexico Press, 1982. Undoubtedly the best survey of Mexican Indian policy in the region during the Mexican regime.

Indian People in the Civil War Era, 1850–1868

The younger warriors were elated. Shouting high-pitched war cries, they raced their horses back and forth in front of the burning buildings. Other Lakotas, older, more sedate, sat smiling astride their mounts and watched the wind carry plumes of smoke into the cloudless Montana sky. But they, too, were glad to see Fort C. F. Smith, the northernmost of the government's posts along the Bozeman Trail, go up in smoke. One week later, in early August 1868, the warriors burned Fort Phil Kearney on the eastern fringes of the Bighorn Mountains, then watched from the distance as the army also abandoned Fort Reno on the Powder River. Satisfied that the government indeed would withdraw its Blue-Coat soldiers from the Powder River country, on November 6, 1868, Red Cloud and several other Lakota chiefs made their marks on the treaty that had been negotiated at Fort Laramie during the previous spring. The Lakotas had forced the government to abandon the Bozeman Trail, and federal officials had guaranteed that the Lakotas could occupy their homelands in the western Dakotas and eastern Wyoming. In addition, Indian agents promised to protect the Lakotas within their newly designated homeland and to provide those tribespeople who re-

mained close to the agencies with rations and farm equipment.

Yet many Lakotas remained suspicious of the government's intentions. The 1868 Treaty of Fort Laramie had reduced the Lakota hunting grounds. It also established reservations where officials hoped to "concentrate" the Lakotas and other tribes. Red Cloud and some of his followers were willing to accept these limitations. Other Lakotas were less certain.

In the two decades between 1850 and 1870, tribal people living on the Plains and in the Southwest, regions that earlier had been largely bypassed by American expansion, found their homelands threatened by growing numbers of settlers. Many resisted these incursions, and because they were well-armed, formidable opponents, the government was reluctant to engage them in prolonged (and expensive) military confrontations. In response, federal officials attempted to purchase tribal regions that held good farmland or valuable mineral resources and to isolate the tribes from settlers, on smaller tracts within their remaining homelands. Federal officials argued that this policy of "concentration" would minimize hostile contacts between Indians and whites and allow the tribes to assimilate into American society.

Tragically, however, the government lacked both the determination and the resources to protect the tribes. Indeed, during the 1860s the federal government was engaged in a great civil war of its own. It had little time or money to spend on Indian people in the West. Indian policy was left to military officers and local officials, men who agreed that tribal people should be concentrated in smaller regions, but who had little commitment to honor federal promises of support and protection.

This chapter examines the eastern tribes' role in the Civil War and how the Reconstruction period that followed forced tribes in Indian Territory to surrender some of their land and sovereignty while enabling them to rebuild and transform their societies. It also surveys the 1862 Santee Dakota rebellion in Minnesota. The chapter then focuses on American attempts to exert control over Apache and Navajo peoples in the Southwest and on how these two tribes employed different strategies to meet this American challenge. In addition, the chapter centers on the Plains tribes, people whose lands had been crossed by Americans in the antebellum period, but who previously had remained autonomous in the face of American political hegemony. The chapter discusses their interaction with immigrants who crossed their homelands and how their resistance to American military units during the war years forced the federal government to abandon established military posts and to (temporarily, at least) accommodate federal policies to some of the Plains tribes' positions. Although the focal point of this chapter remains within the Civil War period, events occurring prior to the 1850s and 1860s that relate to the Navajos, Apaches, and Plains tribes are discussed in order to provide a proper historical perspective.

THE CIVIL WAR IN INDIAN TERRITORY

Following the Mexican War, Americans quarreled over whether slavery should be extended into the western territories. After the passage of the Kansas-Nebraska Act (1854), both North and South funneled settlers into Kansas, attempting to gain a majority of voters in the territory. Many of these immigrants settled in eastern Kansas, forcing emigrant tribes, who recently had been removed to the region, to move south into Indian Territory. The government's inability to protect the Indians in Kansas alarmed the Cherokees, Creeks, and other tribes in Indian Territory. These tribes believed that the federal officials' failure to honor their commitments in Kansas was indicative of what might happen to the emigrant Indians in Oklahoma. Moreover, Kansas Territorial Governor Robert J. Walker's public statement that "the Indian treaties [to acquire lands in Oklahoma] will be no obstacle, no more than similar treaties in Kansas" did little to assuage their apprehensions.

By 1861, as the country moved toward war, other factors pushed the Oklahoma tribes toward the Southern camp. The planter-elite among the Cherokees, Choctaws, Chickasaws, and Creeks held slaves and were sympathetic to Southern culture; moreover, many tribal members disliked the Republican support of small homesteaders, whom the Indians identified as a threat to their homelands. Most of the Indian agents active among the tribes in Oklahoma were Southerners, and they openly espoused the Southern cause; moreover, Arkansas, Texas, and southern Missouri, regions adjoining Indian Territory, brimmed with white Confederates. In addition, with war imminent, the federal government withdrew the Union Army from all of its posts in Indian Territory. From the Indians' perspective, the Confederate tide was rising while the Union seemed to be in disarray.

The South was eager for the Indians' support. In 1860 the combined population of the Five Southern Tribes reached almost 100,000, and Indian troops could provide a buffer against any Union campaign against Texas. In addition, the Indian Nations held large numbers of horses, mules, and other livestock, and lead mines in northeastern Indian Territory were estimated to hold sufficient deposits to supply musket balls and bullets for the entire Confederate army.

In the spring of 1861 Confederate forces from Texas and Arkansas occupied the abandoned Union posts in Indian Territory, and Albert Pike, a Confederate Indian commissioner from Arkansas, offered the Five Southern Tribes treaties that annexed Indian Territory to the Confederacy but guaranteed Indian title to tribal domains. In addition, the Confederacy pledged to protect the Indian

Nations from invasion; to assume all annuity obligations formerly incurred by the United States; and to arm, equip, and pay for troops raised by the tribes. In response, the Creeks and Seminoles agreed to raise a regiment of troops; the Chickasaws and Choctaws another. Hoping to keep the Cherokees out of the conflict, John Ross initially advised them to remain neutral, but large numbers of the planter-elite, plus members of the Old Settlers and Treaty Party, were pro-Confederate and formed a regiment of mounted "Cherokee Rifles" under the command of Stand Watie. Finally, in October, as Union fortunes waned, Ross reluctantly signed the Confederate treaty; better to keep the Cherokees united than to foster policies that might spread the Civil War to the Cherokee Nation.

Pike also met with leaders from the Wichitas, Caddos, and several Comanche bands who promised to refrain from attacking Texas. Pike was less successful among part of the Creeks, where Opothle Yaholo, now in his eighties, refused to join the Confederates. Although he too held slaves, Opothle Yaholo announced that he would remain neutral, and established a new town on the Deep Fork River late in the summer of 1861. He invited other neutral Indians from all tribes to assemble there and withdraw from the warfare. By September over 6,000 had collected at the village, and although they reasserted their neutrality, they were viewed with suspicion by pro-Confederate tribesmen and by Confederate military leaders.

Opothle Yaholo's settlement was particularly resented by pro-Confederate Creeks who had supported the removal of the tribe from Alabama. The Confederate Creeks were led by Motey Kennard and by Daniel and Chilly McIntosh, sons of the slain William McIntosh, whom Opothle Yaholo's followers had executed in 1825. Obviously, bitterness engendered by the removal crisis still simmered; for many Creeks, the Civil War would provide opportunities to settle old grievances.

In November 1861 nine hundred Confederate Indians, including Creeks and Seminoles commanded by the McIntoshes, joined with 500 Texans and marched against Opothle Yaholo, intent on driving "him and his party from the country." Aware of the Confederate plans, the old Creek chief and his followers retreated north toward Kansas, but their flight was slowed by their families and their large herds of livestock and wagons full of personal possessions. The Confederates first encountered the refugees on November 19 near modern Yale, Oklahoma, but Opothle Yaholo's followers repulsed their attack, set fire to the prairie, and escaped in the smoke and confusion.

Reinforced by a reluctant regiment of pro-Ross Cherokees led by Colonel John Drew, the Confederates caught the retreating refugees on December 9 on Bird Creek near modern Tulsa. Many of the newly arrived Cherokees either deserted to Opothle Yaholo or fled back to Tahlequah, and the Confederates again were repulsed, but new contingents of Cherokees, including Stand Watie's pro-Confederate Cherokee Rifles, arrived, and on December 26, 1861, they soundly defeated the neutral Creeks, capturing most of their baggage and livestock. Those Creeks who survived the Battle of Chustenahala fled north through a raging blizzard. They spent the remainder of the winter in exposed camps in Kansas, and Union surgeons were forced to amputate frostbitten feet from over 100 of the survivors, including many women and children. Not surprisingly, many of these former "neutral" Indians now enlisted in the Union cause.

The mixed performance of Cherokee regiments in the Creek campaign reflected the continued turmoil within the Cherokee Nation. Wounds inflicted in the removal crisis had never healed, and the Civil War brought these rifts to the forefront. In 1846 delegates from the Ross Party, the Treaty Party, and the Old Settlers had signed a treaty supposedly settling their disagreements, but the Treaty Party, comprised primarily of large planters and businessmen led by Stand Watie and Elias Boudinot, distrusted Ross and strongly supported slavery. Although Ross owned a plantation and slaves, his commitment to slavery was tenuous. Ross remained suspicious of the federal government, but his distrust of Watie and the Removal Party precluded any continued alliance with them. Moreover, most of his supporters were traditional tribespeople with little or no affinity for slavery, and he needed their support if he wished to continue in Cherokee politics.

To add to the intrigue, during the 1850s each of the rival groups had formed secret societies. The Knights of the Golden Circle (also called the Southern Rights Party) was a fraternal organization that limited its membership to supporters of slavery pledged to "assist in capturing and punishing any and all abolitionists." In contrast, the Keetowah

Society, or "Pins" (their symbol was crossed straight pins on the lapels of their jackets), limited their membership to "full-bloods" (actually more traditional tribesmen), advocated neutrality in any conflict between North and South, and blamed the planter-elite for most of the Cherokee problems. While not openly advocating abolition, the Keetowahs' membership included few slaveholders. In essence, the two organizations were split along social, economic, and cultural lines.

In March 1862 a Union army decisively defeated a combined force of Confederate white and Indian troops at the Battle of Pea Ridge in northern Arkansas. Stand Watie's Cherokee Rifles fought well, capturing Union artillery and covering the Confederate retreat, but the Confederate defeat opened the Cherokee Nation to a Union invasion, and northern troops, accompanied by two brigades of refugees from Opothle Yaholo's followers, invaded northeastern Oklahoma. In July 1862 Stand Watie's Cherokee Rifles and other Confederate forces were defeated at the Battle of Locust Grove, and Union forces occupied Tahlequah. Ross surrendered and many of his followers joined the occupying army. Ross, his immediate family, and much of his personal property were safely transported to Washington, where he met with federal officials and convinced them that the Cherokee Nation had been forced into a Confederate alliance by circumstances outside its control. Ross then moved to Philadelphia, where he spent the remainder of the war supporting the Union.

Tragically, however, Ross's fears of a civil war within the Cherokee Nation proved to be well grounded. When the Union army retreated to Kansas, both Ross's followers and Confederates led by Stand Watie established opposing governments. Violence flared across the Cherokee and Creek nations. Union forces reoccupied Tahlequah, captured Fort Smith, and forced Confederate forces south of the Arkansas River. The Confederates struck back, attacking Union forces, supply depots, and sympathizers. The guerilla warfare soon deteriorated into a melee of thievery and bloodshed, and both sides used the broader conflict of the Civil War to settle old quarrels. Irregular units, both Indian and white, committed depredations on both sides, and many individuals notorious in American history (William Quantrill, Frank and Jesse James, the Younger

Stand Watie The most successful Confederate leader in the trans-Mississippi west, Stand Watie led the Cherokees and other tribespeople in Indian Territory during the Civil War. He was the last Confederate general to surrender (at Doaksville, Choctaw Nation, June 23, 1865).

Brothers, and others) emerged from this border warfare.

In marked contrast to the ill-disciplined bands of cutthroats and renegades, Stand Watie's Cherokee Rifles and other Indian troops under his command focused on military objectives. Watie continued to harass Union garrisons and supply lines along the Arkansas River and seized northern livestock, food, and other supplies, which he then distributed to pro-Confederate tribespeople who had been forced to abandon their homes and flee south of the Canadian River. In June 1864 he captured the *J. R. Williams*, a Union steamboat en route to Fort Gibson, confiscating uniforms, food, and other supplies, a feat that earned him a promotion to brigadier general. Three months later he surprised and seized almost 300 wagons full of Union supplies worth $1,500,000 at Cabin Creek, on the

Grand River, which he also distributed to pro-Confederate refugees. Meanwhile, as Watie's forces raided Union posts in the Cherokee and Creek nations, Choctaw, Chickasaw, and Caddo troops led by Colonel Tandy Walker patrolled the region south of the Canadian, protecting the Red River frontier from any further Union incursions. Although Robert E. Lee surrendered to Ulysses S. Grant at Appomattox Courthouse on April 9, 1865, hostilities did not immediately end in Indian Territory. Stand Watie fought on and was the last Confederate general to surrender. He signed a document of capitulation at Doaksville, in the Choctaw Nation, on June 23, 1865.

The devastation in much of the Indian Nations was overwhelming. Cherokee, Creek, and Seminole homelands were particularly ravaged by the warfare. Farms and homesteads had been burned, crops had been destroyed, livestock had been stolen, and many of the institutions (schools, churches, and businesses) that had flourished prior to the conflict were closed or suspended. Armed bands of outlaws continued to roam the highways, making overland travel dangerous. By the war's end, one-third of all married Cherokee women had been widowed and one-quarter of all Cherokee children were orphans. One-third of all Cherokees and Seminoles had died from violence, starvation, or war-related illness during the conflict, and Creek losses, though less certain, probably were similar in number. A total of 3,503 Indians from Indian Territory had fought for the North in the war; of these, 1,018 had died during the conflict—a casualty rate higher than that of any other state or region in the Union. Reconstructing the Indian Nations would not be easy.

RECONSTRUCTION IN INDIAN TERRITORY

The reconstruction plan for Indian Territory was the brainchild of James Lane and Samuel Pomeroy, two U.S. senators from Kansas who were eager to remove Indians from Kansas into Indian Territory and to open the region to white settlement. In 1866 federal officials met with delegates from the Five Southern Tribes in Washington and signed a series of treaties in which the tribes agreed to relinquish part of their lands, free their former slaves, and provide for the construction of railroads across their nations. Ironically, however, the terms of the treaties did not reflect the tribes' relationship to the federal government during the conflict. The Choctaws and Chickasaws, nations that had been unanimous in their support of the Confederacy, suffered the least. Their joint treaty, signed with the government in April 1866, forced them to free their slaves and to cede the "Leased District" (southwestern Oklahoma) to the federal government, in return for which they received $300,000 for the lands. They agreed to the construction of railroads through their lands, but shared in the sale of lands for rights of way. No tribes from Kansas or elsewhere were settled within their boundaries. In the postwar period, railroad construction and coal mining spurred the Choctaw economy, while the Chickasaws leased much of their grazing lands to non-Indian ranchers. Both nations rebuilt and enlarged their school systems, and the Choctaw and Chickasaw nations progressed through the Reconstruction period with fewer difficulties than their former Confederate companions.

The Seminoles, Creeks, and Cherokees fared less well. Although significant numbers of Seminoles had accompanied Opothle Yaholo to Kansas and had fought with the Union, the tribe was forced to sign a treaty in April 1866 in which they sold *all* their lands in Oklahoma to the government for fifteen cents per acre and then were assigned 200,000 acres on the western fringe of the Creek Nation, for which they were charged $100,000. They erected cabins, cleared fields, and planted crops, but then learned that federal agents had mistakenly placed them on lands adjacent to, but not part of, their purchase. As a consequence, in 1867 the Seminoles were forced to purchase the 175,000 acres they already had planted and improved from the Creeks for an additional $175,000. In the immediate postwar period the Seminoles remained split into southern and northern factions, but by 1880 the animosity between the two groups had diminished and the Seminoles elected a national governor (chief), codified their laws, and established a permanent capital at Wewoka. Because of their past history, the Seminoles more ably integrated freedmen into their society, but they remained the least prosperous of the Five Southern Tribes.

The Creeks also faced many problems. In 1866 they agreed to free former slaves and sell "the west half of the Creek domain [three and one-quarter million acres at thirty cents per acre]" to the government "to be used as homes for other civilized Indians." The Creeks also were forced to sell railroad rights of way across their nation to "any company duly authorized by Congress," including a strip of land three miles wide adjoining the right of way if such lands had not been specifically purchased by individual Creeks; in consequence, the much diminished Creek Nation soon was crisscrossed by narrow strips of real estate owned by non-Indians.

The political schisms that had divided the Creeks during the Civil War continued, but former Confederate Creeks (the McIntosh-Checote-Perryman faction) dominated the government. Former pro-Union Creeks, supported by Creek traditionalists, initially refused to participate in Creek politics, but under the leadership of Oktarsars Harjo Sands, they eventually ran slates of candidates in opposition to the Confederates. Violence between the two sides flared throughout the late 1860s and 1870s, culminating in the Sands Rebellion (1870–1872), in which Sands and his followers seized and occupied the National Council House at Okmulgee. Sands died in 1877, but the traditionalist cause was taken up by Isparhechar, and four years later the Green Peach War, another series of skirmishes between the two factions, erupted. Because of the violence, federal troops repeatedly interceded within the Creek Nation.

Despite this turmoil, the Creeks slowly recovered. Schools were rebuilt, farms and plantations were reestablished, and railroads brought a growing, if uneven prosperity. Moreover, Okmulgee emerged as a center for pantribal activity, as many Creeks believed that all the tribes of Oklahoma should join in a united front to protect their remaining lands from further white aggrandizement. In 1870 representatives from many tribes met in Okmulgee to form the General Council of the Indian Territory. This organization, supported by Commissioner of Indian Affairs Enoch Hoag, championed the admission of Indian Territory into the union as a separate Native American state. The plan failed, but the council drafted the "Okmulgee Constitution," asking Congress to reaffirm the federal government's commitment to guaranteeing treaty rights and the sovereignty of the Five Southern Tribes. Congress ominously declined.

The Cherokees also remained split in the immediate postwar period. Both sides sent delegates to Washington during the spring of 1866, and Ross's opponents were determined to divide the Cherokee lands into two separate Cherokee nations. By 1866 John Ross's health was rapidly failing, but he adamantly opposed the former Confederates' plans. The Cherokees agreed to free their slaves and they relinquished their claim to southeastern Kansas and to the Cherokee Strip, a narrow span of land two and one-half miles wide immediately north of the Oklahoma border extending westward to the one-hundredth meridian. They also agreed to permit "friendly Indians" to settle on unoccupied lands in the Cherokee Outlet, the strip of land extending westward from the northern districts of the nation. Railroad rights of way were granted, but they were much narrower than among the other tribes. The treaty acknowledged John Ross as "principal chief of the Cherokees" but extended amnesty to all members of the tribe for "crimes and misdemeanors" committed against other Cherokees or against the United States. Still, Stand Watie was so discouraged over the treaty that he returned to Indian Territory before it was finalized, and none of his allies signed the final agreement. On July 19, Ross's supporters signed the document, but Ross was so ill that he was confined to his bed at a hotel in Washington. He died two weeks later on August 1, 1866.

The Cherokee Nation remained "united," but most of the former Confederates established new residences in the extreme southwestern corner of the nation and initially refused to participate in Cherokee politics. Ross's leadership was assumed by his nephew, William Potter Ross, and other die-hard anti-Confederates, but their bitter partisanship alienated many of the Keetowahs and traditionalists, who formed a new, moderate Union Party, which continued to dominate the Cherokee government in the decades following the Civil War.

Cherokee attempts to rebuild their economy were hindered initially by the lack of capital. Because many whites were convinced that all of the Indian Nations soon would be dissolved, they were reluctant to invest in Indian enterprises. Although the Cherokees obtained annuity payments that the government had "frozen" during the war and received funds from the sale of lands in the Cherokee Outlet, the Cherokee Nation remained in debt. In response the Cherokees attempted to tax Texas cattle drovers who pastured their herds in the Cherokee Outlet en route to Kansas, but levies were easier to assess than to collect. Moreover, while the construction of two railroads across the nation in the early 1870s contributed to economic growth, they also cost dearly in terms of Cherokee timber, slaughtered livestock, and the railroads' incessant attempts to limit the authority of the Cherokee government.

The railroads also brought in outsiders who added to the Indians' woes. Surveyors, engineers, laborers, whiskey peddlers, gamblers, and prostitutes all flocked to the railroad camps, then spilled out into the nation. Lawlessness mushroomed as the Cherokee justice system struggled to cope with the rising tide of thievery, fraud, and violence. Cherokee attempts to enforce their laws also brought conflicts with state and federal officials, particularly in Arkansas and Kansas.

Still, the Cherokees recovered. Fields were replowed, farms replanted, and homesteads rebuilt. By 1870 tribespeople again grazed growing herds of livestock. Cherokee entrepreneurs launched or reopened many small businesses, and eventually they prospered. The cultural life of the nation, though devastated by the war, also recovered. The Keetoowahs rekindled traditional dances, while the cultural change that had characterized much of the planter-elite population in the antebellum period also continued. The *Cherokee Advocate* resumed publication in 1867, and schools were rebuilt throughout the nation; by 1875 there were sixty-five public schools (fourteen for the children of freedmen) financed by the tribal government. The children of the planter-elite enrolled more regularly than traditionalists, although many of the latter attended when they were not needed for chores at their homes or farms. The Male and Female Seminaries reopened during the early 1870s, and Tahlequah reemerged as a center of education in both the Cherokee Nation and Indian Territory. In 1870, the Cherokees sponsored the first of successive annual fairs, also held in Tahlequah, which showcased the nation's agricultural and industrial progress and attracted visitors from other tribes and outside the territory.

By the middle 1870s the Indian Nations in Oklahoma had reemerged as "islands of civilization" on a "middle border" infamous for its coarseness, savagery, and excess. Railroads that crisscrossed the nations enabled the tribes to ship their products to neighboring states, but they also afforded avenues of penetration for non-Indians eager to share in the potential wealth of the region. Fertile farmlands and rich natural resources attracted young men of ambition into the territory, and if they married an Indian woman, they were eligible to farm land in the nations and to send their children to tribal schools. For poor white males in frontier Arkansas, Missouri, or Kansas, marriage to a Cherokee or Choctaw woman afforded a "step up" the socioeconomic ladder. The intermarriage of Indians and whites in the region shaped both politics and the population in Oklahoma for decades to come. In the twenty-first century, many modern Oklahomans remain proud of their Indian ancestry.

New Tribes Arrive in Indian Territory

Federal officials were eager to use the land acquired from the Five Southern Tribes as a home for other Indians, and the ink had hardly dried on the treaties before these new removals began. In 1867 Indian agents "settled" about 1,000 Delawares and 700 Shawnees from Kansas within the Cherokee Nation. Although both groups were accorded citizenship by the Cherokee Nation, they retained their own tribal identities. The "Registered Delawares" relocated to the northwestern corner of the Cherokee Nation (modern Nowata County), while the "Loyal Shawnees" established a community near modern White Oak.

Former Cherokee lands in the old Cherokee Outlet were set aside for other tribes. In 1871 and 1872, almost 1,500 Osages moved back from Kansas to Oklahoma, where they received a new reservation of about 1.5 million acres of rolling, broken grazing lands between the western border of the Cherokee Nation and the Arkansas River (modern Osage County). In 1872 the Kansa, or Kaws, accepted 100,000 acres in the northwestern corner of the Osage Reservation as a reservation of their own, and one year later, after federal agents confiscated Pawnee lands in Nebraska, the Pawnees

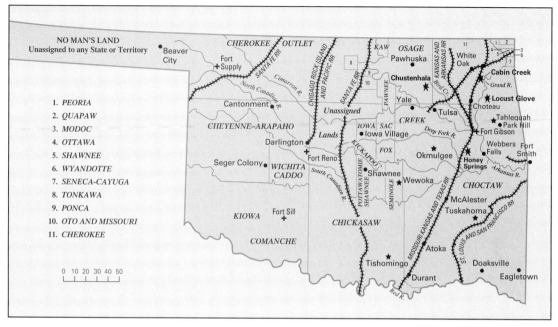

Indian Territory, 1860–1889. *Source: map based on John W. Morris, Charles Goins, and Edwin C. McReynolds,* Historical Atlas of Oklahoma *(Norman: University of Oklahoma Press, 1976), maps 27 and 33. Also see Alvin M. Josephy, Jr.,* The Civil War in the American West *(New York: Alfred A. Knopf, 1991), 320–321.*

retreated to a reservation south of the Osages, between the Arkansas and Cimarron rivers. In the early 1880s the Otoes and Missourias also moved from their former reservation astride the Kansas-Nebraska border to a 130,000-acre tract along the Arkansas River, just west of the Pawnees. Eventually, other Cherokee Outlet lands were utilized as a temporary (1874–1885) homeland for the Nez Percés, and later as a reservation for the Tonkawas and Poncas (see Chapters 10 and 12).

Lands taken from the Creeks and Seminoles also were used as new reservations for other tribes. Although more traditional Sauks and Foxes who followed Mokohoko initially remained in Kansas, Moses Keokuk led the "progressive" faction of these combined tribes to a new reservation between the North Canadian and Cimarron rivers, just west of the Creek Nation. In the 1870s they were joined by about 200 Iowas who were eventually awarded a reservation of their own, immediately west of the

Sauks and Foxes. In 1867 "Citizen Band Potawatomis" living in Kansas agreed to cede their lands and resettle on 575,000 acres west of the Seminole Nation, but when they arrived they found Absentee Shawnees, who had lived in Oklahoma and Texas for decades, residing along the Deep Fork River within their assigned lands. Initially, the two tribes jointly occupied the tract, but eventually the Shawnees moved to the northern parts (near modern Shawnee) while the Potawatomis settled in the region that bordered the South Canadian River. In 1874 the Potawatomis and Shawnees were joined by about 350 Kickapoos from northern Mexico, who after raiding into Texas, were followed into Mexico by the U.S. Army and then forced to abandon their homes and to relocate into Indian Territory. The Kickapoos were assigned a 200,000-acre reservation just north of the Shawnees and Potawatomis, between the Deep Fork and North Canadian rivers.

In addition to the tribes settled on lands taken from the Five Southern Tribes, remnants of other tribes were deposited on lands taken from the Quapaws, Senecas, and Loyal Shawnees. The small Quapaw, Seneca, and Shawnee reservations originally had occupied the extreme northeastern corner of modern Oklahoma, but in the postwar period, it also became the home for communities of Ottawas, Wyandots, Peorias, Miamis, Piankashaws, Cayugas, and Modocs who also were displaced from Kansas, Missouri, and California.

Obviously, in the decades following the Civil War, Oklahoma had become the government's primary depository for Native American tribes from states east of the Mississippi River. Tribes indigenous to the region (Osages, Wichitas, Kiowas, Comanches, Cheyennes, and Arapahos) were forced to share their homelands with large numbers of newcomers who occupied reservations in the eastern half of the region. Most of these Indian emigrants developed a growing attachment to their new homes and were determined to retain them. But as their new homelands prospered, their success attracted white Americans poised on their borders. Greedy eyes again would be turned on the lands of the Indian Nations. The tribes would be hard-pressed to defend their new homelands.

EASTERN INDIANS IN THE CIVIL WAR

Eastern tribes also participated in the Civil War. Over one hundred Ottawas, Ojibwes, and other tribesmen from Michigan and adjoining regions served in Company K of the 1st Michigan Sharpshooters. Similarly, Company D of the 132nd New York State Volunteers, known as the Tuscarora Company, consisted of Senecas, Onondagas, and Tuscaroras from western New York, while Oneidas and Stockbridges from Wisconsin served with the 37th Wisconsin Volunteers. Pequots and Mohegans from southern Connecticut fought for the Union cause, but since some of these soldiers were of mixed Native American–African lineage, they often were enrolled in "colored" regiments. Farther south, in Virginia, Pamunkey tribespeople guided units of the Union army after the latter in-

vaded the state. They also assisted the captains on Union vessels in navigating the rivers, bays, and estuaries of the Virginia Tidewater region.

Lumbee support of the Union, while less focused, was more pronounced and prolonged. Of mixed Native American, white, and African-American ancestry, the Lumbee people had been classified by the state of North Carolina as "free persons of color" and inhabited a heavily forested, swampy lowland region in modern Robeson County. In 1862, after state officials conscripted Lumbee men for labor battalions, Lumbees led by Henry Lowrie raided neighboring plantations. In response, the North Carolina Home Guard destroyed Lumbee farms and executed several Lumbee elders, but the Lowrie band received assistance from other Indians and many African-Americans. In 1864, when General William Tecumseh Sherman's army invaded North Carolina, Lumbee scouts guided the Yankees through swamps along the Lumber River. Skirmishes between the Lowrie band and local militia units continued, and by the end of the Civil War Henry Lowrie had emerged as a champion to the Lumbee community. Unfortunately, local politicians convinced the occupying Union army that Lowrie was a criminal, and in the postwar period he was forced to live as an outlaw. Nevertheless he received clandestine support from many Lumbees, poor whites, and African freedmen. He died in 1872, but he remains a folk-hero to the Lumbee people.

In addition to the warriors who fought in the ranks or who served the North as scouts or irregulars, one prominent Iroquois leader became a member of Ulysses S. Grant's general staff. Ely S. Parker, a Tonawanda Seneca, was well educated, had studied law, and had worked as an engineer during the 1850s. In 1863 he was commissioned as a captain and joined Grant's personal staff as assistant adjutant general. After Grant assumed command of the Union armies, Parker served as the commander's personal secretary. He was present when Robert E. Lee surrendered at Appomattox, and in the postwar period the friendship between Parker and Grant continued. In 1867 Grant served as Parker's best man when the latter married, and two years later President Grant appointed Parker as the first Native American commissioner of Indian Affairs. Parker became discouraged over the failure of Grant's Peace Pol-

Ely Parker Seneca Ely Parker served as a secretary to General Ulysses S. Grant during the Civil War. He later served as commissioner of Indian Affairs during the Grant administration (1867–1871).

icy (see Chapter 12), but he continued in office until 1871, when he resigned amid allegations of corruption that plagued the Grant administration.

Other Native Americans east of the Mississippi fought for the Confederacy. In South Carolina, many Catawbas, who had suffered discrimination from their white neighbors, hoped to distance themselves from African-Americans by volunteering for the Confederate army. They were joined by the Eastern Cherokees. Prior to the Cherokee removals of the late 1830s, some Cherokees had separated from the Cherokee Nation and had sought sanctuary in North Carolina on the eastern slopes of the Great Smoky Mountains. These Cherokees, who asserted that they were citizens of North Carolina, resided at Quallatown on land owned by William Holland Thomas, a white man who had been raised by members of this Cherokee community. Thomas, who was fluent in the Cherokee lan-

guage, owned a store that provided credit to tribal members and generally served as a *patron* to the Cherokee community. He also supported the Confederacy.

In 1861 Thomas organized the Eastern Cherokees into Thomas's Legion of Indians and Highlanders, a military unit that also enlisted Appalachian whites. The Cherokees patrolled the mountain passes between Tennessee, Virginia, and North Carolina; guarded strategic bridges; and scoured the countryside for northern sympathizers and southern deserters. In September 1862 they repulsed a Union thrust through the Cumberland Mountains, but their scalping of some of the Union dead engendered considerable criticism from northern newspapers. One year later, after Union forces captured Chattanooga, Thomas's Legion fought a series of skirmishes that prevented Union troops from occupying their homeland. The Thomas Legion laid down its arms on May 6, 1865, the last Confederate force east of the Mississippi to surrender.

The Eastern Cherokees' support of the southern cause eventually worked in their favor. In 1866 North Carolina's General Assembly gratefully affirmed their right to remain in the state "so long as they may see proper to do so." Two years later the federal government officially recognized their tribal status, and commonly owned tribal lands around Quallatown became the Qualla Boundary (Eastern Cherokee) Reservation. Although North Carolina still denied them the right to vote and their privately held lands seemed vulnerable to white-dominated local courts, the Eastern Cherokees were assured of a homeland.

VIOLENCE IN THE WEST

During the 1850s and 1860s, as most Anglo-Americans' attentions were focused on the struggle between the North and South, other Americans continued to move west, where they came in contact with the western tribes. Since federal officials in Washington were primarily concerned with problems of secession, the Civil War, or Reconstruction, they had little time or resources to devote to implementing Indian policy in the West.

Consequently, the administration of such policy was left to local officials or military officers. Some were conscientious and concerned for tribal people's welfare, but many others were not. Not surprisingly, the 1860s were bloody years for many of the western tribes.

The Santee Dakota Rebellion

During the early 1860s the Santees or eastern Dakotas (Sioux) of Minnesota seethed under the rule of government agents and traders whom they believed were dishonest. They had good cause. In 1851 the Santees had signed federal treaties exchanging most of their lands in Minnesota for two narrow reservations stretching along the Minnesota River. The Upper Agency (Upper Reservation) extended from the modern South Dakota border downstream to the mouth of the Yellow Medicine River, while the Lower Agency (Lower Reservation) spanned the Minnesota River valley from the Yellow Medicine to the mouth of Little Rock Creek, about eight miles northwest of New Ulm. The Wahpeton and Sisseton bands of Santees occupied the Upper Agency, while the Mdewakanton and Wahpekute bands resided on the Lower Agency.

Both the Upper and Lower Santees were unhappy with the treaties. The Upper Santees asserted that they had been tricked into signing a "traders' paper" that awarded more than one-third of their land payment to traders who claimed that amount for unpaid trade goods. The Lower Santees were angered that the U.S. Senate had amended their treaty, reducing their reservation's size and denying them access to woodlands. In addition, in 1858 Santee leaders from both agencies felt they had been coerced into additional cessions, which further limited the acreage of their reservations and confined Indians at both agencies to lands along the river's southern bank. Moreover, Congress failed to appropriate the funds to pay for these additional cessions until 1860, when money again was deducted to pay the alleged claims of traders.

Other events increased the tension between the two sides. In 1857 a small band of renegade Wahpekutes led by Inkpaduta ("Scarlet Point") killed forty-seven settlers in northwestern Iowa and southern Minnesota in a series of attacks known as the Spirit Lake Massacre. Although Inkpaduta was de-

nounced by the reservation Santees, he escaped to South Dakota and white resentment toward all Santees increased. Yet the success of Inkpaduta and his subsequent escape, coupled with the withdrawal of many troops from Minnesota at the beginning of the Civil War, also seemed to indicate that the government's power was waning. Meanwhile, in 1862 the Santees' annuity payment, usually dispersed in the spring, failed to arrive until August. The hungry Santees eventually broke into government warehouses and seized provisions to feed their families. They also asked nearby traders to provide them food on credit until their annuities arrived, but the traders refused. Indeed, one of the traders, Andrew Myrick, disdainfully advised them to go and "eat grass" like animals if they were hungry.

The spark that ignited the conflagration was supplied by four young Wahpeton warriors married to women at the Lower Agency. On August 17, while hunting near their reservation, they discovered a nest of eggs laid by a hen from a neighboring farm. Their debate over whether to take the eggs descended into a series of dares and counter-dares over who was afraid to seize a white man's property. To prove their bravado, they eventually attacked the farmhouse and killed five settlers before fleeing to their village. After meeting through the night, the Lower Santees decided that they undoubtedly would be punished. Better to seize the initiative and strike before the Americans could muster their forces. Little Crow, the most influential chief, initially opposed any hostilities, but he finally agreed to lead the attack on the settlements.

Shortly after daybreak on August 18 a large war party of Lower Santees surprised the government settlement at the Lower Agency. They first attacked the traders' stores, killed the traders (Myrick momentarily escaped but was captured, killed, and had his mouth stuffed with grass) and their clerks, then fell upon government employees. Twenty traders, Indian agents, or members of their families were killed, and ten were captured. Many others escaped across the Minnesota River, then fled to Fort Ridgley, about twelve miles to the east. The fort's garrison had been depleted by the Civil War, but a force of forty-seven infantrymen marched to the agency where the Santees ambushed them at the ferry crossing, killing twenty-four while losing only one warrior.

When news of the attack reached the Santees at the Upper Agency, some militants joined in the up-

Santee Women These Santee women and children were photographed protecting their cornfields from birds and other pests in August 1862, just days before the Santee Dakota uprising.

rising, and on August 18 they sacked and burned trading posts attached to the Upper Agency. Other Upper Santees (primarily Christian converts) led by John Other Day counseled against violence and warned nearby whites that an attack was imminent. When the assault took place, Other Day protected sixty-two whites who took refuge in the government's brick warehouse. On the following morning Other Day led them to safety.

The war soon spread to the surrounding area. Tragically, many of the settlers attacked by the Indians were recent German emigrants who had contributed little to the Santees' woes. Although two separate Santee attacks on New Ulm were repulsed after heavy fighting, the residents abandoned the frontier village and fled to Mankato on August 24. Meanwhile, Little Crow launched two unsuccessful assaults on Fort Ridgley.

Frontier residents of Minnesota were terrified, and Governor Alexander Ramsey dispatched Colonel Henry Sibley and 1,400 troops to put down the uprising. Sibley arrived at Fort Ridgley on

August 26, but a party of troops dispatched to bury the dead near the Lower Agency was surprised near Birch Coulee by Gray Bird and about 350 warriors, who killed 13 soldiers and wounded 47 others. Meanwhile Little Crow launched attacks against Forest City and Hutchinson, and the Santees also besieged Fort Abercrombie on the Dakota border in mid-September.

Yet the Santees' inability to capture Fort Ridgley and invade regions downstream sealed their fate. In mid-September Sibley marched up the Minnesota Valley with an additional 1,600 troops and on September 23 defeated Little Crow and almost 1,000 warriors near Wood Lake. In the aftermath, many Santees who had opposed the war escorted captives whom they had protected into the Americans' camp. To Sibley's surprise, friendly Santees had harbored almost 270 captives. Many were of mixed lineage, but 107 were white, almost all women and children.

These jubilant ex-prisoners had been sheltered by friendly Santees at considerable danger to themselves. Although many praised the kindness of their "captors," white Minnesotans clamored for vengeance. About 2,000 Santees were arrested, and almost all Indians accused of participating in the warfare were brought to trial. Confusion over names and contradictory testimony created judicial chaos (some trials lasted no more than five minutes), but when the proceedings ended, the court had sentenced 303 Indians to death. Ironically, several of the condemned were "friendlies" who had risked their own lives to save white captives. President Lincoln eventually commuted the sentences or pardoned all but 39 of those who were convicted of rape or murder. On December 26, 1862, those 39 were publicly hanged at the largest mass execution in American history. When the gallows platform fell, the crowd cheered their approval. Officials later learned that three of the men who were hanged were victims of mistaken identity: they had assisted white captives, not harmed them.

Following the executions, the surviving Santee Dakotas were shipped to new reservations in Nebraska and in North and South Dakota. Little Crow, Shakopee, and several other leaders initially escaped to Canada, but Little Crow was shot and killed in July 1863 when he returned to Minnesota. Shakopee was kidnapped in Canada and illegally returned to Minnesota, where he was hanged in November 1865.

The Great Sioux Uprising was a tragedy for all concerned. Subjected to questionable treaties, broken promises, and avaricious traders, the Santee Dakotas lashed out at neighboring settlers who had contributed little to their suffering. Certainly the subsequent trials were a travesty of justice, and only intervention by Lincoln brought any semblance of order to the proceedings. Moreover, the infusion of embittered Santee refugees from Minnesota into western Lakota communities on the Great Plains did not bode well for the United States. Bitter lessons learned in Minnesota would be remembered.

THE DESERT SOUTHWEST

While massive Union and Confederate armies clashed in the east, smaller forces of troops from both sides wrestled for control of the American Southwest. Apache and Navajo tribespeople in the region who previously had remained unfettered by Spanish or Mexican hegemony were confronted by new armies of Americans. Union troops soon gained the upper hand, and after driving Confederate forces back into Texas, they turned their attention toward Native peoples. The Civil War years brought profound changes for both the Apaches and the Navajos.

The Apaches

Spread in a wide arc from west Texas across southern New Mexico, Arizona, and adjoining provinces of Mexico, the Apaches' band membership remained fragmented (see Chapter 6). Political leadership was based primarily on personal magnetism, and band or village leaders exercised only limited authority during the best of times. Most Apaches continued to reside in brush-covered wickiups, although eastern bands such as the Lipans, Mescaleros, and Jicarillas utilized smaller versions of the skin-covered teepees so popular on the Plains. Camps moved frequently to utilize different natural foods and to minimize the band's vulnerability to enemy raids. Possessions were carried in skin bags or baskets. Few Apaches kept large numbers of sheep or cattle, although they grazed herds of horses, which they traded to other tribes or to Spanish settlements (other than those settlements from which the horses had been "obtained," of course).

Most Apaches dressed in some combination of buckskin and trade cloth: the men wore long breechcloths tucked into a belt and a skin or trade cloth shirt in the cooler months; women wore a skirt that extended past the knees and a loose shirt that fell almost to their hips. Both sexes wore moccasins and sometimes leggings that covered the legs below the knees as protection from cacti and other thorny underbrush. Apache women rarely wove cloth themselves. Women's garments originally were made of deerskin, but after trade cloth became available, women utilized brightly colored cottons and woolens. Men hunted, while women were responsible for gathering the wide variety of fruits, tubers, roots, and other natural foods that comprised much of the Apache diet.

The Apaches generally had remained outside the realm of Spanish hegemony, and with Mexican independence in 1820, their antipathy toward the

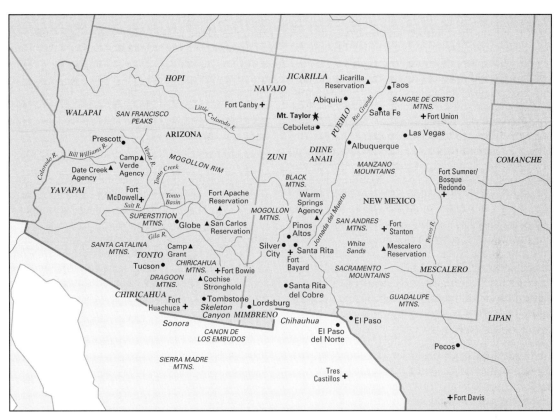

Apaches and Navajos, 1820–1888. *Source: map based on Francis Paul Prucha,* Atlas of American Indian Affairs *(Lincoln: University of Nebraska Press, 1990), 121.*

new regime increased. Raids on Mexican ranches continued. By 1830 the road from El Paso to Albuquerque had become so dangerous that Mexicans labeled it *Jornada de Muerto*, and Mexican officials reported that since 1820 the Apaches had killed at least 5,000 settlers in the region. In a desperate (and despicable) attempt to stem the tide, state governments in both Sonora and Chihuahua during the mid-1830s offered bounties for Apache scalps: 100 pesos for a warrior, 50 for a woman, 25 for a child. Tragically the bounties only exacerbated the situation since frontier cutthroats, many of whom were Anglos, indiscriminately slaughtered Indians of any tribe in a mad scramble to turn a profit. The senseless brutality of the bounty system was best exemplified in 1837, when a party of Mexican and Anglo miners lured friendly Mimbreno Apaches to a feast near Santa Rita del Cobre,

in southwestern New Mexico, then massacred them with grapeshot from a hidden cannon. Apache retaliation, led by Mangas Colorado, was so fierce that the perpetrators were forced to abandon both their mines and their settlement.

When American troops arrived in the Southwest during the Mexican War, the Apaches initially welcomed them as allies against a mutual enemy, but by 1850, after growing numbers of American miners infested the region, relations between the two sides had deteriorated. In the autumn of 1851, after drunken miners seized and beat the Mimbreno chief Mangas Colorado, Mimbreno war parties attacked several wagon trains and a mail station. Peace with the Americans was restored through the efforts of Indian Agent William Steck and Cochise, a Chiricahua leader, but the Apaches refused to relinquish their war against Mexico.

In 1853, after the United States acquired southern Arizona in the Gadsden Purchase, the Butterfield Stage Company organized a route through the region. The Apaches tolerated the stage traffic, even selling firewood to several stage stations, but trouble erupted anew in January 1861 when an army officer newly arrived from the East falsely accused Cochise and the Chiricahuas of holding white hostages. Although Cochise denied the charges, the officer attempted to arrest him. Cochise escaped, but other Apaches were taken, violence flared, and the Butterfield Stage Company abandoned all its stage stations in the region. Meanwhile, the approaching Civil War caused the army to reassign troops to the east, and the Apaches believed that the government's power was waning.

Confederate forces from Texas invaded New Mexico in 1861, but they didn't stay long. Colonel John R. Baylor initially seized control of former Union posts in southern New Mexico and declared himself governor of the region. Apache war parties raided his supply lines and in March 1862 he issued his infamous orders to lure all the Apaches and other Indians to Confederate camps, murder the adults, and sell their children into slavery. Fortunately, Confederate forces retreated from Texas before the orders could be implemented, and Jefferson Davis removed Baylor from his post, but the orders reflected the animosity many frontier Texans held toward Native Americans.

After Confederate attempts to occupy the Southwest failed, Union troops, led by James Carleton, left California, crossed southern Arizona, then advanced along the old Butterfield Stage route toward New Mexico. Still seething from the army's ill-advised attempt to arrest Cochise, Chiricahua and Mimbreno war parties raided Carleton's column, then fought a pitched, two-day battle at Apache Pass in southeastern Arizona, retreating only after Mangas Colorado was seriously wounded. In July 1862 Carleton constructed Fort Bowie at Apache Canyon, then occupied other posts in New Mexico and southwest Texas. Meanwhile, Apache raiders struck at his flanks, making travel and the transportation of supplies and livestock both expensive and hazardous.

Carleton earlier had campaigned against Native Americans in California, and he believed that negotiations with tribal people were pointless. After recruiting ten companies of New Mexican volunteers, Carleton launched a series of campaigns designed to "pacify" the Apaches and the Navajos. He enlisted the well-known trapper Kit Carson to command the New Mexican troops, instructing him that "there is to be no council held with the Indians nor any talks. The men are to be slain whenever and wherever they can be found. . . . If they beg for peace, their chiefs and twenty of their principal men must come to Santa Fe to have a talk here, but tell them fairly and frankly that you will keep after their people and slay them until you receive orders to desist."

Carleton first focused on the Mescaleros, who were fewer than the Mimbrenos or Chiricahuas, and whose villages were centered near Fort Stanton in southern New Mexico. After Carleton issued an ultimatum for them to assemble at the fort, some of the Mescaleros complied, but others fled into the Guadalupe and Sacramento mountains. In response, Carson's troops scoured the region, scattering Apache camps, cutting down their meager cornfields, and killing any who resisted. By March 1863 the Mescaleros had either been killed, had surrendered to Carson, or had fled to join other Apache bands in Arizona or northern Mexico. Meanwhile, Carleton established Bosque Redondo, a new reservation near Fort Sumner on the Pecos River in eastern New Mexico, which he envisioned as the future home for many Apaches and Navajos. The reservation contained little arable land, but Carleton forced the Mescaleros to settle there and begin farming. He promised to feed them until they could raise and harvest crops.

Carleton then turned his attention to the Chiricahuas and Mimbrenos. They proved to be more difficult adversaries. During late January 1863 Carleton sent troops commanded by Colonel J. R. West against the Mimbrenos, instructing West either to kill the Mimbrenos or force them to join the Mescaleros at Bosque Redondo. But the Mimbrenos scattered across their homeland, and the Americans found nothing but empty camps. In response, miners associated with West's forces seized Mangas Colorado under a flag of truce, then turned him over to West, who gave his tacit permission for the old chief to be murdered in a staged "escape" attempt. Following his death, army surgeons decapitated the Apache chief and sent his skull to a phrenologist in New York who assured his colleagues that the Apache's skull was "larger than that of Daniel Webster."

Mangas Colorado's death did not break the Mimbrenos' spirit. Accompanied by Chiricahuas, they lashed back at the Americans, attacking both troops and miners, who now flocked into the region from California. In 1864 Carleton launched a series of new campaigns, and government rations lured some Apaches onto reservations. But Cochise remained opposed to the Americans, and his people easily eluded Carleton's soldiers. The Apaches remained in their mountain strongholds, and miners prospected at their own peril. The Apache resistance, though diminished, would continue.

The Navajos

The Navajo resistance was less successful. Prior to the arrival of the Americans, the Navajos had prospered (see Chapter 6). Their earlier migration into western New Mexico and northern Arizona from "Old Dinetah" (northern New Mexico–southern Colorado) had increased Navajo conflicts with the Zunis and Hopis, who complained bitterly to the Spaniards. Spanish ranchers added their complaints, and although officials in New Mexico periodically had invaded the Navajos' new homeland, most of these campaigns, which killed small numbers of tribespeople or sought prisoners for the clandestine slave trade, achieved only limited success. In contrast, during the winter of 1804–1805 a Spanish military expedition swept through Canyon de Chelly, a Y-shaped, twenty-seven-mile-long canyon in northeastern Arizona, and killed large numbers of Navajo women and children who had sought refuge in a shallow rock shelter high in the canyon wall. The Navajos still call the place Massacre Cave.

The Navajo migration to the southwest also engendered a split within the ranks of the tribe. Led by a headman known as Joaquin, in 1818 a minority of Navajos settled near Ceboleta in the eastern shadow of Mt. Taylor. These *Dine Ana-aii* ("Alien Navajos") separated from their kinspeople and erected hogans close to the Pueblos at Zuni and Acoma. The Dine-Anaii still grazed sheep and horses, but like their Pueblo neighbors they were more sedentary and relied more on agriculture. They developed closer ties to the Spaniards, and unlike the Navajo majority who continued to raid Spanish ranches, the Dine-Anaii became known as

the white man's friends. After 1820, during the Mexican period, the Dine-Anaii's ties to white men increased, and led by Francisco Baca and Cebolla Sandoval, headmen of mixed Navajo-Mexican lineage, they periodically supported the Mexicans against other Navajos.

The first half of the nineteenth century was a prosperous period for the Navajo people. Wracked by internal turmoil, Mexico had neither the inclination nor the resources to address the problems on its northern frontiers. In contrast, the Navajos ranged across the western two-thirds of New Mexico, stealing horses and other livestock with impunity. Joking that they always left the Pueblos with enough mares and ewes to "reseed" their supply, the Navajos lived isolated from meaningful retribution. Flocks and herds thrived; small cornfields and peach orchards were bountiful; women wove blankets and other garments that they bartered for trade goods; ceremonial life flourished; and mutton filled the spits and cooking pots. The Blessing Way, the Navajos' ability to live in harmony with all things, brought prosperity and contentment. It was a good time to be Dine.

Things changed with the arrival of the Americans. In 1846 Navajo leaders, including Narbonna, Long Earrings, and Sandoval (from the Dine-Anaii) met with Colonel Alexander Doniphan in western New Mexico and promised to cease their raids, yet they exercised little control over younger warriors and the pilferage continued. In response the Americans sent an expedition to Canyon de Chelly that destroyed cornfields and hogans but encountered few Navajos. In 1851 federal officials built Fort Defiance as a symbol of American military power in eastern Arizona, but Navajo-American relations did not improve until two years later, when Henry L. Dodge was appointed Indian agent to the tribe. Dodge, called "Red Shirt" by the Navajo people, opened an agency near Fort Defiance, married a Navajo woman, and improved the relationship between the tribe and the government. His tenure as Indian agent marked a brief period of peace, but he was killed by Apaches in 1856 and conditions again deteriorated. In 1860 the Navajos unsuccessfully attacked Fort Defiance, and one year later, as the Civil War loomed, the government abandoned the fort amid jubilation among the Navajos. The Navajos mistakenly believed that the *Beleganas* were leaving their homeland.

Navajos at the Trading Post at Chinle Although this photo was taken in 1902, the Navajo men and women are dressed similar to the Navajo tribespeople during the 1860s and 1870s. *Palace of the Governors, New Mexico.*

Carleton's arrival in the Southwest disabused them of their optimism. When the Navajos learned of Carson's campaign against the Mescalero Apaches, they sent a delegation of chiefs to Santa Fe, where Carleton first refused to meet with them and then informed them that they too would have to remove to Bosque Redondo. When the Navajos refused, Carleton issued an ultimatum: after July 20, 1863, any Navajo who did not surrender for removal to Bosque Redondo "will be considered hostile and treated accordingly." He then constructed two new posts, Fort Wingate and Fort Canby, both within the Navajo homeland, to serve as bases for operations against the tribe.

During the autumn of 1863 troops led by Kit Carson scoured Navajoland, capturing considerable numbers of sheep and horses, but few Indians. Disappointed, Carleton ordered Carson to campaign throughout the winter, and in January 1864, guided by Ute scouts, Carson's men swept through Canyon de Chelly, destroying hogans, burning foodstores, and chopping down Navajo peach orchards. Facing starvation, many Navajos surrendered. By March about 8,000 Navajos, almost three-fourths of the tribe, had trudged in through the snow and bone-chilling cold to accept rations offered at Fort Wingate and Fort Canby, in Arizona. The remaining Navajos, led by Barboncito

and Manuelito, retreated into the mountains or to the vast mesas of north-central Arizona.

In March 1864 the Navajos began their "Long Walk" to Bosque Redondo. Separated into several contingents, they were forced to walk the four hundred miles from their homeland to the new reservation. Poorly fed, clothed, and cared for, many trekked eastward through spring blizzards and subsequent floods. Of the approximately 8,000 Navajos who had been assembled for removal in Arizona, almost 350 died before they reached Bosque Redondo.

The new reservation proved to be a "hellhole" on the Pecos. The Mescaleros already residing there resented the newcomers, who outnumbered them by almost twenty to one. In turn, the Navajos complained that the Mescaleros already occupied the few habitable locations and monopolized the scanty supply of firewood. Although both the Mescaleros and Navajos dug irrigation ditches, the water level of the Pecos was so uncertain that most of their crops failed. The corn, beans, and squash that survived perennial drought fell victim to insects. Housing was in such short supply that many Navajos initially were forced to live in burrows in the ground, covered with blankets. Meanwhile, Comanches raided the reservation stealing Apache and Navajo livestock, and even kidnapping children

INDIAN VOICES

Herrero (Navajo Headman) Testifies About Conditions at Bosque Redondo

The Navajo exile at Bosque Redondo (1864–1868) still engenders bitter memories for many Navajo people. Forced onto a barren, windswept reservation in eastern New Mexico, the Navajos were compelled to share the habitable areas with the Mescalero Apaches, their old enemies. Although General James Carleton initially envisioned the reservation as a location where the Navajos could be transformed into farmers, the experiment failed. The Navajos were herdsmen, not farmers. Despite this, federal officials limited the size of their herds and forced them to plant corn and other crops. Rations were sparse, irrigation systems failed, and the corn that reached maturity was attacked by army worms (which the Navajos found bitterly ironic). Impoverished, demoralized, and weakened by disease, many Navajos almost starved. Eventually some Navajo women were forced to prostitute themselves to feed their families. Although Bosque Redondo was abolished and the Navajos returned home in 1868, Herrero, a Navajo headman, supplied the following testimony to federal officials who investigated the short-lived reservation just prior to its closing. How have the location and resources of the modern Navajo reservation proven beneficial for the Navajo people in the post–Bosque Redondo era?

If we had the wool, we could make all the clothes for the tribe. All of us know how to cultivate by irrigation. There is plenty of land, but somehow the crops do not come out well. Last year the worms destroyed the crops. . . . There is plenty of pasture for all our stock. Some have 25, 30, or 40 [sheep], but more have none. None have a hundred.

We try and keep our sheep for their milk, and only kill them when necessary, when the rations are short or smell bad. We depend on the milk of the sheep to live and to give to our little children. We are honest and do not kill each other's sheep. We own our animals ourselves, and not in common.

Some officers at Fort Canby told us when we got here the government would give us herds of horses, sheep, and cattle, and other things we needed, but we have not received them. We had to lose a good deal of our property on account of the war, and the Utes stole the rest from us. . . . Before the war with the Utes and the Mexicans we had everything we wanted, but now we have lost everything. . . .

Some of the soldiers do not treat us well. When at work, if we stop a little they kick us or do something else. . . . We do not mind if an officer punishes us, but we do not like to be treated badly by the soldiers. Our women sometimes come to the tents outside the fort and make contracts with the soldiers to stay with them for a night. . . . But in the morning they take away what they gave them and kick them off. This happens most every day. In the night they [the soldiers] leave the fort and go to the Indian camps. . . . A good many of [these] women [now] have venereal disease.

We would rather prefer to be in our own country, . . . we have lost everything we want here. We are all of this opinion and would like to have you to send us back. And if you have any presents to give us we will distribute them among us. If we are sent back we promise never to commit an act of hostility.

Source: Peter Nabakov, ed., *Native American Testimony*, rev. ed. (New York: Penguin Books, 1999), 196–198. From *Conditions of the Indian Tribes*, Senate Report no. 156, 39th Congress, 2d sess. Washington, D.C.: Government Printing Office, 1867.

whom they held for ransom or sold into Mexico. In November 1865, after measles swept through the reservation, most Mescaleros fled to the mountains east of the Rio Grande. The Navajos remained behind, but in 1866 they too began to slip away and make their way back to their homeland.

By 1867 conditions at Bosque Redondo had reached such a crisis that the government intervened. Many citizens of New Mexico (hardly eastern "Indian lovers") were so appalled by conditions among the Navajos that they petitioned the government to allow the Navajos to return to their homeland. Carleton refused, but he was relieved of his command, and in 1868 the Navajos signed a new treaty with the United States and went home. Bosque Redondo was abandoned. Ironically, the isolation of the lands reserved for the Navajos in northern Arizona and northwestern New Mexico proved to be a blessing. Arid and seemingly devoid of precious metals, the region was undesirable to whites and provided the Navajos with a sanctuary in which to regroup and repopulate. Natural herdspeople, they tended their flocks and cared for their horses, and their livestock increased. New fields and peach orchards were planted in Canyon de Chelly. The Dine continued.

THE PLAINS TRIBES DURING THE CIVIL WAR ERA

While tribes in Oklahoma, in New Mexico, or on the West Coast fought to defend their autonomy, the Plains tribes initially faced intruders of a different sort: Americans who crossed through their homelands en route to other locations. American interest in California and Oregon had burgeoned during the 1840s. In 1847 about 4,500 emigrants traversed the Oregon Trail from Council Bluffs to Oregon. With the discovery of gold in California, however, the flow turned into a flood, and by 1852 the number of travelers reached 60,000 per year. Coupled with significant Mormon emigration to Utah, which also occurred during these years, the central Plains tribes and Indian people of the intermountain west found their homelands being crossed by growing numbers of strangers.

Contrary to the standard images in the popular media, contacts between Native Americans and Anglo-Americans on the Plains were usually marked by cooperation or trade rather than by violence. Although pulp fiction and western movies often depicted wagon trains desperately defending themselves from Indian attacks, such battles rarely occurred. In contrast, most Native Americans readily assisted emigrants, providing information about routes and water sources or serving as guides. Indians and emigrants actively traded with each other, exchanging hardware, firearms, clothes, and trinkets for horses, buffalo robes, moccasins, and freshly killed game. For the eastern Plains tribes (Pawnees, Otoe-Missourias, Kansa) or midwestern tribes newly removed to Kansas (Potawatomis, Shawnees, Delawares, etc.), the emigrants were a source of income. Pawnee tribespeople in Nebraska provided a variety of services (for a price), while shrewd Potawatomi merchants in Kansas established ferries, erected toll bridges, or sold fodder and other supplies to travelers at inflated prices.

If Native Americans threatened emigrants, it was manifested more in pilferage than in violence. The Americans carried large (at least from the Indians' perspective) amounts of goods, and tribespeople visiting their camps sometimes picked up and carried off items that were left unattended. Since tribal societies were communal and Indians did not hoard wealth (except for horses), the concept of strangers possessing a surplus when others were in need was difficult for Indians to understand. Small items of personal property left unattended obviously were not needed; why not put them to better use? Emigrants complained that Native Americans pilfered camp utensils, clothes hung out to dry, handkerchiefs, or harness snaps or other equestrian hardware. Some of this merchandise probably was just misplaced or simply "lost," or may have fallen victim to other emigrants within the camp, but tribesmen undoubtedly helped themselves to loose property owned by the travelers.

More serious, however, was the theft of livestock. Although Native Americans rarely "raided" organized wagon trains, livestock that strayed away from the encampment was deemed "fair game" and often taken. Horses, mules, and oxen were valuable commodities, and if Native Americans did not utilize the livestock themselves, they could readily sell the animals to other emigrants.

Moreover, the theft of horses already had been institutionalized in the warriors' code of coups and honor among many Plains tribes: to steal or acquire horses increased a warrior's wealth and prestige. Undoubtedly, considerable numbers of horses were taken, even when they had been tied to the owner's wagon at night, and one traveler commented that he believed the Pawnees could "steal a horse from under his rider" if the owner dozed off while in the saddle.

Horse thievery and other pilferage did lead to violence, but more whites were killed by Indians (or bands of white outlaws posing as Indians) west of the continental divide than by Indians on the Plains. Rumors of massacres circulated in the East, but between 1840 and 1860 only 362 emigrants (out of 300,000) were killed by Native Americans. In addition, a further examination of travel accounts, diaries, and the like, indicates that during the same twenty-year period emigrants murdered at least 462 Indians. Ironically, encounters between whites and Indians were more dangerous for Native Americans.

More damaging was the emigrants' destruction of the Plains environment. Livestock that accompanied the wagon trains overgrazed the pasturage along the Oregon, Santa Fe, and Colorado trails, creating long corridors denuded of forage. In addition, emigrant demands for firewood stripped the groves of trees that sheltered the rivers. Emigrants also readily slaughtered bison, deer, and other game, depleting these sources of food and clothing for the Plains Indians. As some historians have argued, the burgeoning herds of horses owned by the Plains tribes also may have contributed to the depletion of forage, and the demand for buffalo hides encouraged the Plains tribes to overhunt the herds. But the appearance of large numbers of emigrants on the Plains coincided with the depletion of these resources, and tribespeople associated the newcomers with increased shortages.

Fearful that growing contacts between emigrants and Native Americans might lead to increased bloodshed, federal negotiators met in September 1851 with the leaders of almost 10,000 tribespeople who assembled at Fort Laramie in eastern Wyoming. The Lakotas, Cheyennes, Arapahos, Crows, Gros Ventres, Assiniboines, Arikaras, and Shoshones tentatively agreed to end their intertribal warfare and to occupy regions that were removed from the Oregon Trail. In return for trade goods and annuities, the Lakotas promised to remain north of the Platte River and in the region roughly bordered by the Missouri River and Black Hills. The Gros Ventres and Assiniboines were to occupy the Missouri watershed north of the Lakotas, while the Crows were assigned to the Powder River and Big Horn Basin in northern Wyoming and southern Montana. The Cheyennes and Arapahos, in contrast, agreed to occupy the high Plains abutting the foothills of the Rockies in eastern Colorado or far western Kansas. All these regions located the tribes away from American travelers.

In July 1853 federal agents at Fort Atkinson in Kansas also met with the Comanches and Kiowas, who agreed to cease their attacks against Mexico and to allow wagons to pass unmolested along the Santa Fe Trail. Officials assumed that these southern Plains tribes would focus their hunting south of the Santa Fe route, also concentrating them in regions away from American travelers. Hopefully, contacts between Indians and emigrants would be minimized.

The plan failed. In the late 1850s gold was discovered in the Rocky Mountains in Colorado, and the government's attempt to separate Indians and emigrants disintegrated. Both prospectors and settlers swarmed up the Kansas, Smoky Hill, and Solomon river valleys, trespassing on the lands assigned to the Cheyennes and Arapahos, killing bison, cutting timber, and overgrazing pastures. The initial Cheyenne and Arapaho response was measured; they pilfered livestock or harassed the trespassers, but prior to the Civil War few people were killed on either side.

Conditions changed in 1861. When the Civil War began, Colorado's population had burgeoned to 30,000, but military leaders in the East recalled many of the regular troops stationed in the territory, and citizens of the region believed they were vulnerable to attacks both by Confederates and by Cheyennes and Arapahos. Officials in Washington initially blamed much of the Indians' hostility on the Coloradans and questioned the leadership of Territorial Governor John Evans, an ambitious entrepreneur eager to expel Indians from the territory.

In 1861 several peace chiefs among the southern Cheyennes and Arapahos met with federal officials at Fort Wise (later Fort Lyon) in southeastern

Colorado. In a very questionable treaty, they agreed to give up their claims to most of their hunting lands in exchange for a small reservation near the juncture of the Arkansas River and Sand Creek. The Senate ratified the treaty, but the chiefs who signed the pact later claimed that they believed that the new reservation was much larger than the lands delineated in the document and that Cheyenne and Arapaho lands still included the good buffalo lands on the headwaters of the Smoky Hill, Solomon, and Republican rivers. When they were informed that they would be limited only to the small tract of lands on the Arkansas, they refused to occupy the reservation. Meanwhile other southern Cheyenne and Arapaho bands, including the powerful and militant Dog Soldiers (originally a Cheyenne warrior society, but functioning as a semi-autonomous political band by the 1860s), who had refused to participate in the Fort Wise Treaty, denounced the proceedings. So did the northern Cheyennes and Arapahos, who continued to hunt on the lands between the Republican and South Platte rivers.

In September 1863 Evans again attempted to negotiate with the two tribes, but the Indians refused, and the Dog Soldiers raided isolated ranches and stage stations. In response, Colorado militia and "volunteers" led by John M. Chivington struck back indiscriminately at Cheyenne and Arapaho villages, achieving little success but spreading the conflict to previously peaceful Indians. Described by a superior as "a crazy preacher who thinks he is Napoleon Bonaparte," Chivington's ego matched that of Evans. Together, they were determined to rid eastern Colorado of its Indians.

By the summer of 1864 the war had widened. Cheyenne and Arapaho war parties ranged from the Platte to south of the Arkansas. In Colorado, Indian attacks made travel outside Denver so hazardous that freight companies could hardly supply goods to the city. In June, Evans demanded that all Cheyennes and Arapahos, including those who had not signed the Treaty of Fort Wise, go to the new reservation at Sand Creek; any Cheyennes or Arapahos not on the reservation would be attacked as "hostiles."

Eager to withdraw from the conflict, in September 1864 several of the older peace chiefs, including Black Kettle of the Cheyennes and Left Hand of the Arapahos, accepted Evans's offer. In September they journeyed to Denver, met with Evans and Chivington, and agreed to go to Sand Creek; but Evans seemed oddly evasive about guaranteeing their safety. Nonetheless, the Cheyennes and Arapahos settled down on the new reservation, supposedly under the government's protection.

Evans and Chivington betrayed them. Evans used his influence to facilitate the removal of Major Edward Wynkoop, the commander at Fort Lyon, who favored a peaceful approach to the "Indian difficulties." Meanwhile, Chivington mustered the Colorado militia, including the Third Colorado Cavalry (ignominiously known as the "Bloodless Third" because they previously had failed to kill any Indians), and in early November he led almost 600 troops to Fort Lyon. There he was joined by Major Scott Anthony, Wynkoop's replacement, who was "damned glad" to attack the tribespeople. Accompanied by about 125 rather reluctant regulars, and four twelve-pound howitzers, the combined force approached Black Kettle's and Left Hand's adjoining villages early in the morning on November 29, 1864.

The attack took place at dawn. When the Cheyennes and Arapahos saw the soldiers approaching, Black Kettle immediately raised an American flag on a long lodgepole, but the troops ignored the flag and began firing on the camp. As the howitzers rained grape shot down on the Indian village, the troops charged at the teepees, where Cheyenne and Arapaho warriors hurriedly mounted a defense. The Americans fired indiscriminately, killing men, women, and children, while the Indians sought shelter beneath the creek bank. Protected by handfuls of warriors, some "pockets" of Cheyennes and Arapahos held out till nightfall, then fled across the prairie. On the following morning the militia scoured the battlefield, killing the wounded and mutilating the bodies of the Cheyenne and Arapaho dead.

When the carnage ended, more than 150 Indians, two-thirds of whom were women and children, were slaughtered. (In his official report, Chivington claimed that his command killed over 400 "warriors.") Both Black Kettle and Left Hand survived the battle, although Left Hand eventually died from his wounds. The Coloradans lost 9 killed and 38 wounded, some of whom were shot by their drunken comrades in the wild, indiscriminate firing that took place in the attack. Following the massacre, Chivington's men carried Cheyenne and Arapaho bodies, pieces of bodies (particularly severed sex organs), and scalps back to Denver, where they were displayed in saloons and on street corners.

The aftermath of Sand Creek was not what Chivington and Evans had envisioned. Although Chivington initially was hailed as a hero in Denver, his exploits were questioned in the East, and a subsequent congressional investigation found that he had "planned and executed a foul and dastardly massacre which would have disgraced the veriest savage among those who were the victims of his cruelty." Yet by the time the investigation was completed, Chivington and all of his men had resigned from the military and escaped any prosecution for their actions. Chivington's political career had ended, however; needless to say, he was forced to resign his pastorate in the Methodist church.

Sand Creek did not crush the Cheyenne and Arapaho resistance. Incensed over the attack, both Northern and Southern Cheyennes and Arapahos joined with Lakotas and launched a series of raids that closed the Platte River Road for most of January 1865. They twice attacked Julesburg, Colorado, burning the town and forcing the inhabitants to take refuge in nearby Fort Rankin. Telegraph lines were destroyed for over eighty miles, and for over one month no stage, freight wagon, or telegraph message from the east arrived in Denver. Following the attacks, Black Kettle and part of the Southern Cheyennes retreated south of the Arkansas, where they sought refuge in Indian Territory. The other Cheyennes and Arapahos joined the Lakotas and retreated north to the Black Hills.

The Lakotas (Sioux) had an agenda of their own. They too had signed the 1851 Treaty of Fort Laramie, agreeing to remain north of the Platte River and to allow travelers to journey along the Oregon Trail. Generally, they abided by these terms, but in the mid-1850s tensions between the Lakotas and the army increased. In 1853, when the Lakotas assembled for their annuity payments at Fort Laramie, a dispute with an inexperienced officer led to a skirmish in which six Lakotas were killed. Only the intercession of mountain man Thomas Fitzpatrick kept hundreds of Lakotas from overrunning the fort. The annuities were distributed, but the Lakotas remained resentful.

In 1854, when the Lakotas again assembled for their annuities, Mormon emigrants accused them of killing a cow. Second Lieutenant John Grattan led thirty men from Fort Laramie to the Lakota camp and demanded the Lakotas surrender the "cow killer." They refused, and Grattan's men opened fire, killing Minneconjou chief Conquering Bear. In response, scores of Minneconjous, assisted by Brulés and Oglalas, fell upon Grattan's party, killing all but one soldier who fled back into the fort. The Lakotas then sacked several warehouses and withdrew toward the Black Hills. In the fall they attacked stages traveling along the Platte River Road, killing teamsters and stealing their cargo.

Although the Indian Bureau blamed the hostilities on the brash action of Grattan, the army was eager for retribution. In the late summer of 1855 troops led by Colonel William S. Harney attacked the Brulés at their village near the juncture of Blue Water Creek and the Platte, killing eighty-five Lakotas and capturing many others. In response, during March 1856 Lakota leaders met with Harney at Fort Pierre in North Dakota, where they agreed to a temporary peace. But by the early 1860s conditions had deteriorated. Santee refugees fleeing the aftermath of the uprising in Minnesota introduced embittered anti-American fugitives into the western bands, and in 1863, troops led by Brigadier General Alfred Sully invaded the Dakota territory and fought a pitched battle with the Lakotas, including many Santees led by the infamous Inkpaduta. The Lakotas lost almost 300 warriors, and over 250 women and children were captured, causing some Yankton and Blackfeet Lakota to ask for peace, but the losses angered other Lakotas and spurred their hostility toward the Americans. During the next summer, Sully established Fort Rice on the Missouri River, then fought another pitched battle with the Lakotas near the Killdeer Mountains in western North Dakota. Sully returned to Fort Rice in September 1864, but the Lakotas had learned a valuable lesson. They now realized that pitched battles with large, heavily armed military columns supported by artillery were futile. They would continue to defend their homeland, but they would pick and choose their battles.

The discovery of gold in Montana and the subsequent rush of miners and settlers across Lakota lands only inflamed the confrontation. In 1863 and 1864 Lakota warriors attacked miners journeying along the Bozeman Trail, a new track stretching north from Fort Laramie to Bozeman, Montana, and in 1865 federal officials made plans to transform the trail into the Powder River Road, a more formal and improved route, and to protect travelers on the road from Indians. The proposed road bisected Lakota hunting lands between the Black Hills and the Big Horn Mountains, and the Lakotas warned that they would oppose all surveyors, troops, or white travelers in the region.

Warfare also was renewed along the Oregon Trail. In July 1865, Lakota warriors joined with Cheyennes led by Roman Nose and attacked the Platte Bridge Station, about 130 miles west of Fort Laramie, killing twenty-nine soldiers, including Lieutenant Caspar Collins. The army answered, sending columns of troops into the Black Hills–Powder River country and another expedition into west-central North Dakota, but none of these campaigns achieved much success.

Still reeling from public outrage over the Sand Creek massacre and discouraged over costly, ineffective military expeditions, officials in Washington now turned, at least temporarily, to a policy of peace. In October 1865, Indian agents met with the southern Plains tribes (Cheyennes, Arapahos, Kiowas, Kiowa-Apaches, and Comanches) on the Little Arkansas River. In exchange for increased annuities, these tribal leaders again pledged to keep the peace, and because of the "gross and wanton outrages" committed at Sand Creek, the Southern Cheyennes and Arapahos received proportionately larger annuity increases than the other tribes. Meanwhile, nine bands of Lakotas met with Sully and Governor Newton Edmunds of the Dakota Territory at Fort Sully, near modern Pierre, and signed treaties similar to those negotiated on the Little Arkansas. Ironically, however, among the Lakotas who signed the pacts, only the aging Lone Horn held any prominence. Most of the war chiefs refused to attend the proceedings. They still saw themselves as being slowly strangled within a geographic noose tied by white men, and *washichus* ("white men") on the Bozeman Trail still trespassed on Lakota territory. The warfare wasn't over.

During the summer of 1866 the army built or regarrisoned three forts in the Powder River country. Fort Reno was located on the south fork of the Powder River, Fort Phil Kearney at the forks of Piney Creek, and Fort. F. C. Smith on the Bighorn River in southern Montana. Red Cloud, the Oglala war chief, had promised to chase all soldiers from the region and in late July Lakota, Cheyenne, and Arapaho war parties harassed travelers and made life miserable for soldiers who ventured outside the stockades. Pinned down in the forts, the troops could travel overland only in large, heavily armed parties; they provided little protection to civilians en route to Montana.

Among the reinforcements who arrived in the fall was Captain William J. Fetterman, a veteran of the Civil War, who had boasted that with eighty troopers he "could ride, roughshod, through the entire Sioux Nation." On December 21, 1866, he got his chance. Ordered to protect a wood-cutting party near Fort Phil Kearney, Fetterman was lured into an ambush by Crazy Horse, a relatively young, but already well-known war chief. In the ensuing firefight, Fetterman and eighty officers, troops, and civilians were killed by the Lakotas.

Red Cloud's War continued. The army remained on the defensive, protecting established locations but unable to carry the war to the Lakotas. In contrast, the proliferation of military posts and the increased traffic on the periphery of their territory offered tempting targets to Lakota, Cheyenne, and Arapaho raiding parties. Throughout much of 1867 they closed the Powder River Road to civilian traffic. In August 1, 1867, a large war party of Cheyennes, Arapahos, and Lakotas attacked a party of soldiers cutting hay near Fort F. C. Smith, but they were repulsed by the rapid fire of the troops' newly issued Springfield rifles. One day later, at the famous "Wagon Box Fight," another war party led by Red Cloud, Crazy Horse, and Hump also was turned back by similarly armed troops who were cutting wood near Fort Phil Kearney. The troops' morale improved, but in both raids the tribesmen captured considerable livestock and did not believe themselves to be defeated. Meanwhile, officials in Washington grew increasingly frustrated over the army's inability to take the war to the Indians.

Their frustration also was fueled by events in western Kansas. In April 1867 General Winfield Scott Hancock met with Roman Nose, the most famous of the Cheyenne War chiefs, but the chief was uncooperative, and the Dog Soldiers easily evaded Hancock's troops. Hancock burned several empty villages, then ordered Lieutenant Colonel George A. Custer and the Seventh Cavalry to pursue the fleeing Indians.

PEOPLE, PLACES, AND THINGS

Teepees: "Exceedingly Picturesque and Beautiful"

Teepees

No other dwelling is more stereotypically associated with Native American people than the teepees used by the Plains nomads. Non-Indian travelers on the Plains were attracted by the graceful lines of the conical bison-hide or canvas tents, and artist George Catlin described Crow teepees as constructed of buffalo hides dressed "almost as white as linen, and beautifully garnish(ed) with porcupine quills and paint . . . exceedingly picturesque and agreeable . . . exceedingly interesting."

Teepees also were "exceedingly" well adapted for a nomadic life on the Plains. Erected around a three- or four-pole base frame, which supported smaller poles and the hide or canvas covering, teepees on the northern Plains (where long, lodgepole pine poles were available for construction) sometimes towered eighteen feet high and were thirty feet in diameter. Large teepee covers could contain as many as thirty buffalo hides, although most were smaller. Women sewed the hides or canvas into a half circle, which was secured on the western side, then wrapped around the pole frame and laced together over the doorway (which almost always faced east). The bottom of the covering that extended onto the ground was weighted with large stones to anchor the structure and prevent wind from entering beneath the teepee shell. During cold months a liner was added to create a layer of dead air or insulation, and during the summer, the sides of the teepee could be lifted for better ventilation. A flap attached to a long pole opened the smoke hole at the top of the tent to allow smoke from the hearth to escape from the structure. Teepees were surprisingly warm; their A-frame construction kept warm air from escaping and provided for an efficient use of heat generated by a central hearth. Traditionally, the position on the west side, opposite the door, was a seat of honor reserved for elders or people of importance. In some tribes, women always sat on the south, while men sat on the north.

Large teepees took about an hour to erect, but in an emergency they could be dismantled and packed for travel in less than half that time. Since Plains tribes usually moved their camps several times during the warm months, teepees were equipped with light, flexible, easily transported furnishings. Clothing was carried in highly decorated parfleches (skin bags or large envelopes), and people usually sat on a carpet of bison hides and reclined against willow-frame backrests. Bison-hide robes also served as bedding. Other personal objects were stored in areas away from the fire or hung from tripods or teepee poles.

Both teepees and teepee liners often were highly decorated, displaying significant events from the residents' lives. Illustrations on the teepee cover or liner usually reflected religious symbols or personal exploits of the most prominent male member residing in the lodge, but the lodge cover and teepee poles (the lodge itself) belonged to the women in the family, who were responsible for their maintenance. Ironically, many ethnohistorians have argued that horses, more than bison, were responsible for the development of teepees and their furnishings. How? Why?

Custer never caught them. While Cheyenne and Arapaho war parties raided across eastern Colorado and western Kansas, Custer spent two months chasing dust trails on the high plains between the Platte and Smoky Hill rivers. He occasionally skirmished with small bands of warriors, but all the large, mobile villages eluded him. Plagued by desertions, he staggered into Fort Wallace on the Smoky Hill River in mid-July. Meanwhile, most of those Cheyennes and Arapahos who wished to remain at peace retreated south of the Arkansas River into western Indian Territory. Others defiantly remained in their homeland.

CONCLUSION: THE STRUGGLE FOR PEACE

The continued warfare along the Bozeman Trail, the failure of Hancock and Custer in Kansas, and the increased cost of military expenditures caused much second-guessing in Washington. Influenced by former abolitionists who now were turning their attention to Indian reform, many Congressmen favored a new policy of "concentration": confining the Plains tribes to smaller reservations on land unattractive to white Americans, but assigning the army to protect the tribes from frontier whites. They hoped that after being restricted to smaller areas, the Plains tribes eventually could be "civilized," would become farmers, and would accept membership in American society. The policy offered little that was new, except that the army would keep civilians off Native American lands. Tribespeople encountered off the assigned areas would be considered hostile.

In response, Congress appointed a new peace commission to convince the Plains tribes to accept smaller tracts of land north of the Platte and south of the Arkansas. Made up of four civilians and three military officers (including Chief of Staff General William Tecumseh Sherman and Generals William S. Harney and Alfred Terry), in October 1867 the commission met with representatives from the Comanches, Kiowas, Kiowa-Apaches, Southern Cheyennes, and Southern Arapahos at Medicine Lodge Creek in southern Kansas. After prolonged deliberations, the Indians accepted two large reservations: the Comanches, Kiowas, and Kiowa-Apaches agreed to occupy the southwest quadrant of the Indian Territory; the Cheyennes and Arapahos would live in the northwest quadrant. Unauthorized whites would be prohibited from the regions, and government agents would provide education and agricultural implements. The government also promised to furnish clothing and other "necessary goods" to the tribes for thirty years. In return the tribes agreed to remain within their designated lands. They could leave during the summer to hunt buffalo in lands south of the Arkansas River as long as the herds could be found in that region. They also pledged not to attack or harm railroads, military personnel, or any other whites whom they might encounter while off the reservation.

The Lakotas were more reluctant to accept the government's offers. In late April 1868, Spotted Tail and some of the other friendlier chiefs arrived at Fort Laramie and made their mark on the second treaty to bear this post's name. The treaty stated that almost all of modern South Dakota west of the Missouri River and adjoining regions in southeastern Montana, eastern Wyoming, and northwestern Nebraska would belong to the Lakotas. Whites would be forbidden to enter the area, and those Lakotas who wanted to walk the white man's road would receive clothing, plows, annuities, Indian agents, physicians, and teachers at reservations located between the Missouri River and the Black Hills. Lakotas who wished to live in the manner of their fathers (the "wild Sioux") could continue to hunt in the Powder River Country "so long as the buffalo may range thereon in such numbers as to justify the chase," and the government guaranteed that the Powder River country and Black Hills "shall be held and considered to be unceded Indian territory, . . . and no white person shall be permitted to occupy any portion of the same." And finally, federal officials also promised that within ninety days after all the Lakotas had signed the treaty, the army would close the Bozeman Trail and withdraw from all its forts along the route.

During the summer of 1868 copies of the treaty were sent to all the Lakota bands, but many were still reluctant to sign. Pierre Jean DeSmet, a Jesuit with considerable influence among the tribes of the upper Missouri, worked in the government's behalf, but even he could not persuade Sitting Bull to make his mark on the document. Only after troops withdrew from Forts Reno, Phil Kearney, and F. C. Smith and the posts were burned to the ground did Red Cloud sign, on November 6, 1868. Meanwhile, the peace commissioners contracted two more treaties, one with the Northern Cheyennes and Arapahos in which these two tribes agreed to remain at peace and to locate either within the Lakota reservation or to the new Southern Cheyenne and Arapaho lands in northwestern Oklahoma. On May 7, 1868, the Crows also signed a treaty pledging peace and friendship to the United States and agreeing to accept a large reservation in the Yellowstone Valley in Montana.

From the Lakota perspective, the second treaty of Fort Laramie (1868) was (at least temporarily) a victory. They promised to remain at peace, but the government agreed that the Lakotas could remain within their homelands. Those tribespeople who wished "to walk the white man's road" would be supported by federal agents and annuities, while those bands that wished to follow the old ways of their fathers would be permitted to do so. Blue-Coat soldiers would supposedly keep other *washichus* from trespassing on the remaining Lakota homelands, and the army even agreed to abandon its new forts in the Powder River country. Some Lakotas were cautiously optimistic, but others remained wary of the government's intentions. Still, all agreed to remain within the assigned lands. The Lakotas would wait and see if the *washichus* honored their promises.

Many federal officials also were encouraged. The Treaty of Medicine Lodge Creek and the Second Treaty of Fort Laramie were designed to concentrate the Plains tribes within smaller, more closely controlled locations where the army could supposedly protect them from frontier whites. Reformers hoped that the agreements would bring a lasting peace to the Plains and provide the Indians with an opportunity to "become civilized" and join mainstream American life. They were partially correct. Following the treaties, peace did return to the Plains. Unfortunately, in western Indian Territory it lasted only three weeks.

SUGGESTED READINGS

Anderson, Gary C. *Little Crow: Spokesman for the Sioux*. Minneapolis: Minnesota Historical Society, 1986. A biography of Little Crow that contains a good account of the circumstances leading to the Santee Dakota uprising of 1862.

Berthrong, Donald J. *The Southern Cheyennes*. Norman: University of Oklahoma Press, 1963. A scholarly, well-written account of Cheyenne life on the central and southern Plains during the prereservation period.

Debo, Angie. *The Rise and Fall of the Choctaw Republic*. Norman: University of Oklahoma Press, 1934. This old classic contains a good description of the Choctaws' efforts to reconstruct their government and society in the decades following the Civil War.

Hauptman, Laurence. *Between Two Fires: American Indians in the Civil War*. New York: The Free Press, 1995. An excellent survey of Native American participation in all theaters of the Civil War.

Iverson, Peter. *Diné: A History of the Navajos*. Albuquerque: University of New Mexico Press, 2002. This volume, written by the leading scholar of Navajo history, contains an excellent survey of the history of the tribe.

Josephy, Alvin M., Jr. *The Civil War in the American West*. New York: Alfred A. Knopf, 1991. This lively account contains well-written chapters on the tribes' participation in the Civil War, on Carleton's campaigns against the Apaches and Navajos, and on the Sand Creek massacre.

Larson, Robert. *Red Cloud: Warrior Statesman of the Lakota Sioux*. Norman: University of Oklahoma Press, 1996. This biography of a major Lakota leader contains a good account of the Powder River War.

Miner, H. Craig. *The Corporation and the Indian: Tribal Sovereignty and Industrialization in the Indian Territory*, Columbia: University of Missouri Press, 1976. An interesting analysis of the Five Southern Tribes' attempts to defend their lands from outside political and economic forces in America during Reconstruction and the Gilded Age.

Miner, H. Craig, and William Unrau. *The End of Indian Kansas: A Study of Cultural Revolution,*

1854–1871. Lawrence: The Regents Press of Kansas, 1978.   This volume examines the economic and political forces that uprooted the Kansas tribes and relocated them into Indian Territory in the decades following the Civil War.

Unruh, John D. *The Plains Across: The Overland Emigrants and the Trans-Mississippi West: 1846–60.* Urbana: University of Illinois Press, 1979.   This sweeping analysis of the emigrants' journeys across the Great Plains contains an excellent chapter illustrating that contacts between emigrants and Indians in the region were characterized more by cooperation and trade than by armed confrontations.

Utley, Robert. *Frontiersmen in Blue: The United States Army and the Indian, 1848–1865.* New York: Macmillan Publishing Company, 1967.   An excellent, detailed account of the army's interaction with Native American people during these decades. Although written from the army's perspective, the narrative is balanced and often sympathetic to Native Americans.

West, Elliott. *The Contested Plains: Indians, Gold-seekers, and the Rush to Colorado.* Lawrence: University of Kansas Press, 1998.   Focusing on the Cheyennes, this award-winning volume examines the relationship between Indians, American emigrants, and the ecology of the central Plains.

White, Christine Schultz, and Benton White. *Now That the Wolf Has Come: The Creek Nation in the Civil War.* College Station: Texas A&M University Press, 1996.   Written in an innovative style, the volume describes and discusses the impact of the Civil War on the Creeks in Indian Territory.

Warfare in the West, 1867–1886

They had lied! He had been told that he was going to meet with Colonel L. P. Bradley, the commander of the Blue-Coat soldiers at Fort Robinson, but as the Lakota war chief entered the log building he realized that they had taken him to the fort's guardhouse, intending to put him in a cell. Incensed, Crazy Horse drew a knife from beneath his shirt and lashed out at Little Big Man, once a trusted friend but now a servant of the *washichus,* who had grasped the war chief's arm and had led him into the guardhouse. The knife sliced into Little Big Man's wrist, and Crazy Horse leaped back through the door into the open twilight, but a squad of soldiers, bayonets fixed, had followed in his wake, and as he passed through the doorway their officer shouted, "Stab the son-of-a-bitch! Kill him! Kill him!" Meanwhile, Little Big Man regained his composure and seized Crazy Horse from behind, pinning his arms to his sides. Crazy Horse struggled to escape, but as he freed his arms a soldier thrust a bayonet into his abdomen. As he turned, another thrust entered his back and penetrated both kidneys. Mortally wounded, Crazy Horse sank to the ground. He was carried into the adjutant's office and placed on a cot, where the post's surgeon gave him morphine. His father was summoned, but in less than two hours, Crazy Horse, an Oglala holy man and the

most famous of the Lakota war chiefs, passed into the Great Mystery.

Crazy Horse's death on September 6, 1877, was emblematic of the final military struggles of the western tribes in defense of their homelands. Like many western tribes, the Lakotas had agreed to occupy a reservation in return for government pledges of assistance and protection; like other tribes the Lakotas found that federal officials did not honor their promises. In response, the Indians fought back in a last desperate attempt to defend their remaining homelands and their honor. They were overwhelmed, but their struggle often was heroic. Moreover, the war chiefs who led this resistance have emerged as significant figures in both American history and folklore.

In the two decades that followed the Civil War, the western tribes found their lands threatened by a floodtide of miners and settlers who poured into the West, eager to exploit the region's rich farmlands and mineral resources. As the tribes' fortunes deteriorated and they became more dependent on the very government and people who oppressed them, the tribal communities split into competing camps. Some, hoping "to make the best of a bad thing" or to secure positions of power within the reservation system, chose to cooperate with their oppressors. Others attempted to adhere to older tribal ways. In some instances, the "cooperators" condemned those kinsmen who continued to follow more traditional paths, describing them as malcontents whose intransigence endangered all members of the tribe and threatened their well-being. Indeed, among the Lakotas and Apaches, the two tribes most associated with military resistance during these years, cooperators and traditionalists became considerably estranged. Obviously, some Lakotas collaborated in Crazy Horse's death, and many Apaches eventually served as scouts for the army, guiding the troops to Geronimo.

This chapter examines the continued evolution of Indian life on the Plains and discusses the depletion of the buffalo herds as well as the growing dependency of the Plains people on products obtained from Americans. It also examines Grant's Peace Policy, the government's futile attempt to contain Native American people in isolated regions and protect them from white frontiersmen. The chapter focuses on the Lakotas, a tribe that fought against such containment, and also discusses other western tribes that used their military prowess to rebel against the strictures and broken promises of reservation life. Finally, the chapter examines why the stereotype of the "Plains warrior" has continued to appeal to the American public.

CULTURAL CHANGE ON THE PLAINS

By 1870 the Plains tribes were in the twilight of a golden age. Many still lived the lifestyle of their fathers, but the old ways were dying. Even as change swirled around them, the Plains tribes had adapted, both deliberately and unconsciously, to new products, patterns, and conditions.

Most Plains tribes were led by a combination of peace and war chiefs whose duties traditionally had reflected the dichotomy of tribal life. In the past the tribes usually had followed their peace chiefs: mature, seasoned men in their late forties or fifties whose broad experience and accumulated wisdom enabled them to guide the villages on a daily basis. Many of these peace chiefs had been successful warriors who had matured into diplomats and political leaders. Their followers relied on them to select village sites, lead the tribe to suitable buffalo grounds, or mediate disputes between the tribes or within the villages. In contrast, war chiefs were younger men, successful warriors in their thirties or early forties who led the tribe during periods of conflict. When the danger subsided, however, these younger war chiefs traditionally had relinquished their position of leadership to the peace chiefs, who again led the tribe on a daily, more regular basis.

Ironically, however, by the late 1860s the Lakotas, Cheyennes, Comanches, and other Plains tribes had lived for two decades in a state of almost constant warfare. Consequently, the role of the war chiefs, who originally had served as only temporary wartime leaders, had grown. They now surpassed the peace chiefs in influence.

The lives of the Plains people had changed in other ways. They still hunted buffalo, but the herds were rapidly diminishing. The immense herds that once had ranged the Great Plains from Texas well into Canada had fallen victim to the advancing frontier and to the demand for buffalo robes in the East and in Europe. At first, the tribespeople themselves had supplied most of the hides taken in the trade, but by the 1870s white buffalo hunters were scouring the Plains, killing large numbers of animals and leaving thousands of skinned carcasses rotting in the grasslands. As the number of buffalo diminished, the tribes found it harder to feed their families. Some grew more reliant on federal annuities and rations, particularly during the winter. Others remained aloof from their Great Father's largesse, but their kettles sometimes were empty and their resentment toward the white men increased. Even the part-time reservation dwellers who ate the government's beef during the winter disliked the confinement of the reservation system and looked forward to the summers when the treaties permitted them to leave the agencies and hunt in the Texas Panhandle or in the Black Hills and the Powder River Country.

As the buffalo herds dwindled, the southern Plains tribes, particularly the Comanches, augmented their economy with horses. The demands for horses increased as white settlement spread onto the eastern fringes of the Plains, and although settlers and ranchers complained bitterly about Comanche or Kiowa raiders who stole their livestock, they readily purchased other animals, "no

Bison Hides Awaiting Shipment The slaughter of the bison herds deprived tribal people of food and shelter. "Buffalo hunters" brought piles of bison hides to collection depots on the Plains. In 1874 over forty thousand hides were amassed by one shipper at Dodge City, Kansas.

questions asked," from horse traders who obtained the animals from the Indians. By 1870 the Comanches and Kiowas prospered in the livestock business. The size of their horse herds was phenomenal, often reaching a ratio of twelve to fifteen animals for every adult in the village. Some warriors owned more than one hundred horses.

All the Plains tribes purchased many things from Anglo or Hispanic traders. The tribespeople still preferred the circular teepees of their fathers, but they filled them with utensils or other objects manufactured by Americans or Europeans. Plains women packed and transported their families' possessions in parfleches (large, decorated leather cases), but they had replaced the skin bags or earthen pottery used by their grandmothers for cooking with brass or iron kettles. Steel knives, awls, or needles proved more durable than similar tools shaped from stone, bone, or antler. Clothing was still fashioned from both skins and trade cloth, but brightly colored trade beads now were used to decorate such items more often than the more traditional dyed porcupine quills. Cheyenne and Comanche women admired their reflections in glass

mirrors, adorned both everyday and special items with brass tacks or small bells, and ignited their campfires with flint and steel purchased from traders. Tortoise shell combs, woolen trade blankets, brightly colored facial paint, and silver clasps, pins, and other fasteners also adorned the clothing and accouterments of the women's households.

Trade muskets and growing numbers of breech-loading rifles and revolvers were replacing the more traditional bows, arrows, and lances of the warriors. Some men still carried war clubs or tomahawks, but the army's reliance on rapid-firing, breech-loading rifles made such close-range, hand-to-hand weapons less practical. Moreover, the nature of warfare on the Plains had evolved since the early decades of the nineteenth century. Conflicts between Plains tribes had never been the rather romanticized, coup-counting games and skirmishes sometimes portrayed by later writers and historians, but they had been characterized by small war parties, fights over horse herds, and ongoing but limited vendettas. By the 1870s, however, both the tribesmen opposed to the government and the army envisioned the warfare in much larger terms:

a desperate struggle involving a total commitment by both sides to decide who would control the region.

Within the context of their separate cultures, both sides were committed to total warfare, but they fought in different ways. The American troops were made up of professional soldiers who were unencumbered by families. Their training may have been inadequate, but they could rely on an expanding, rapidly industrializing nation for food, supplies, and armaments. Time and logistics were on their side. In contrast, the Indian people whom they fought were not an army, but a community at war. Unlike the federal troops, Indian warriors fought to protect their families, and their wives and children often were near the battlefields. Their attachment to families and homelands limited their mobility or their options in choosing when and where to fight. Indeed, sometimes Native American women took an active part in defending the villages. Moreover, unlike their enemies, Native Americans were faced with a growing logistical deficit. The Plains tribes encountered diminishing herds of buffalo, and they were forced to obtain arms and ammunition from the society that oppressed them. They fought valiantly, but their future held little promise.

THE WARFARE CONTINUES

Although federal officials hoped that the treaties signed at Medicine Lodge Creek (1867) and Fort Laramie (1868) would bring about peace on the Plains, they were mistaken. The warfare that had flared in the 1860s temporarily declined, but it came back with a vengeance.

The Southern Plains, 1867–1874

The Medicine Lodge Creek Treaties of 1867 had little meaning for many Cheyennes and Arapahos. Although peace chiefs such as Black Kettle remained in the reservation area in western Indian Territory, other members of both tribes continued their old patterns of hunting bison and stealing horses or raiding railroad construction camps that now extended into western Kansas. During the summer of 1868 Cheyenne Dog Soldiers created havoc along the headwaters of the Solomon and Smoky Hill rivers. When a party of about fifty civilian scouts attempted to track the raiders, they were surprised by over 600 Cheyennes, Arapahos, and Lakotas on the Arikara Fork of the Republican River. The scouts, led by Major George Forsyth, took shelter on an island in the river, but the warriors, led by Roman Nose and Bull Bear, besieged the Americans for a week. The sharp-shooting scouts turned back repeated charges, and they were relieved on September 25, 1868, by a column of Buffalo Soldiers (African-American troops serving in the Tenth Cavalry) from Fort Wallace. Although the Battle of Beecher Island resulted in relatively few casualties, the Cheyennes were disheartened by the death of Roman Nose, the most famous of their war chiefs, who was killed in the fighting. His kinsmen believed he was slain because he had violated his medicine when he inadvertently drank water from a metal vessel (a tin dipper).

For the Cheyennes and Arapahos, the death of Roman Nose was a portent of things to come. Convinced that troops could never catch warriors on the open plains, the army planned a winter campaign. It would attack when the tribes were more closely tied to their villages. After learning that many of the warriors responsible for the summer raids had retreated into Indian Territory, Colonel George A. Custer and 800 troopers from the Seventh Cavalry tracked some of the hostiles to Black Kettle's camp on the Washita River. Although Black Kettle had not participated in the raids, warriors from the summer war parties were in his camp, and on November 23, 1868, Custer's expedition swept in on the village. While the regimental band played "Gerry Owen," Custer's men fired indiscriminately, killing over 100 warriors (including Black Kettle) and unknown numbers of women and children. He also slaughtered over 800 Cheyenne horses. In response, neighboring Cheyennes, Arapahos, Comanches, and Kiowas counterattacked, and Custer retreated, arriving back at Fort Supply ten days later.

The Battle of the Washita opened the army's winter campaign, and for the next five months columns of troops pursued camps of Cheyennes, Arapahos, Comanches, and Kiowas across western Indian Territory. The troops established Fort Sill at the eastern end of the Wichita Mountains, and by spring many of the Indians rode into the fort and accepted the government's offer of rations. In contrast, the Dog Soldiers bolted for Kansas, joined some Lakotas, and resumed their raiding. In July 1869, however, they fought a pitched battle with an expedition of troops who were accompanied by "Indian scouts" Buffalo Bill Cody and Frank North along with about fifty Pawnee scouts who assisted the army against their old enemies. The Battle of Summit Springs, fought in northeastern Colorado, proved disastrous for the Dog Soldiers. Tall Bull, their leading war chief, was killed, many horses were killed or captured, and the Dog Soldiers were forced to split into two groups: one fled back to Indian Territory, the other sought sanctuary among the Lakotas in the Powder River Country.

Those Dog Soldiers who arrived back in Indian Territory found that the government had introduced new reforms. Elected president in 1868, Ulysses S. Grant championed a policy of reconciliation. Grant's Peace Policy advocated "conquest by kindness," and although the military still regarded all Indians who fled reservations as hostile, those who remained were to be treated equitably. In response to accusations of corruption in the Bureau of Indian Affairs, the Grant administration replaced many of the Indian agents with religious personnel, including Quakers, whom Grant and his advisers envisioned as honest men, interested in the Indians' welfare. A new National Board of Indian Commissioners, comprised of reformers and philanthropists, also was established to monitor Bureau of Indian Affairs activities.

Cheyenne defeats at the Washita, Beecher's Island, and Summit Springs had temporarily dampened the tribe's interest in warfare, and Quaker agents such as Brinton Darlington and John Miles generally were successful in keeping the southern Cheyennes and Arapahos at peace between 1868 and 1874. They were less successful, however, in preventing peddlers from Kansas and Missouri from selling illegal rotgut whiskey in the Cheyenne and Arapaho camps.

Lawrie Tatum, the Quaker agent to the Kiowas and Comanches, faced greater problems. The Kiowas and all the Comanches except for the Kwahadi band had settled in southwestern Indian Territory, where they drew rations at Fort Sill. Like the Cheyennes and Arapahos, the Kiowas and Co-

manches regularly left the reservation to hunt buffalo in the Texas Panhandle, but they, too, supposedly returned to Indian Territory following their summer hunts. Unfortunately, many Comanches and Kiowas also ranged southward across west Texas almost to Mexico, raiding ranches and stealing livestock. Texas Rangers periodically skirmished with the raiders, but at first Tatum excused his charges, blaming the raids on the Kwahadi Comanches, who still roamed free on the Staked Plains in eastern New Mexico. By 1871, however, he admitted that some reservation Indians had participated in the incursions.

The Red River War

In May 1871 a large Kiowa war party led by Satank, Satanta, and Big Tree clandestinely left the reservation and crossed the Red River, planning to raid along a wagon road that stretched southeast from Fort Sill to Jacksboro, Texas. Meanwhile, William Tecumseh Sherman, on an inspection tour of military posts, was traveling en route from Fort Richardson, near Jacksboro, to Fort Sill. As he passed along the wagon road, the Kiowas, unaware of his identity, initially prepared to attack his small party but let him pass unmolested when they learned that ten, lightly armed supply wagons were following some miles in his wake. Unaware of his narrow escape, Sherman traveled on to Fort Sill, but the Kiowas ambushed the wagon train, killed ten of the twelve teamsters, and seized their mules and cargo. A survivor of the attack staggered into Fort Sill where he informed both Tatum and Sherman of the raid.

On May 27, 1871, when the Kiowa chiefs appeared at the agency, Tatum confronted them. Arrogantly confident, Satanta boasted of the raid and demanded arms and ammunition. In response, Sherman and troops concealed nearby arrested the surprised Kiowa chiefs and sent them under military guard to Texas to be tried for murder. The aging Satank committed suicide en route, but Satanta and Big Tree were convicted of murder and sentenced to life imprisonment.

The imprisonment of their chiefs split the Kiowas into peace and war factions, but the warfare continued. The Comanches had not been cowed by the chiefs' fate, and joined by more

A Comanche Family Aptly termed "lords of the South Plains," the Comanches hunted, raided, and dominated intertribal political and military affairs from the southern Arkansas Valley to northern Mexico.

militant Kiowas, they renewed the raids on Texas. Hoping that appeasement might end the warfare, Commissioner of Indian Affairs Francis Walker offered to free Satanta and Big Tree if they pledged to remain on the reservation and the Kiowas ceased their raiding. The Kiowas agreed, and in October 1873 Satanta and Big Tree were paroled back to the reservation. Walker's leniency angered both Tatum and Sherman. Tatum resigned from the Indian Bureau while Sherman ordered Colonel Ranald Mackenzie, the commander of federal troops in west Texas, to pursue and attack all Indians found off the reservation.

During the winter of 1873–1874, conditions in the Indian camps deteriorated. Budgetary problems forced the government to reduce rations and the tribespeople went hungry. To add insult to injury, in the spring of 1874 when warriors went into the Texas Panhandle to hunt buffalo, they found few live animals, but thousands of rotting carcasses left by white hide hunters. Incensed, on June 27, 1874,

a large war party of Comanches, Kiowas, Cheyennes, and Arapahos attacked about thirty buffalo hunters at Adobe Walls, an old buffalo hunting post on the North Canadian River. The warriors vastly outnumbered their enemies, but the Americans were well armed and well protected. The tribesmen lost twenty warriors and many others were wounded, while the Americans suffered only two killed. After an eight-hour battle, the warriors withdrew. Some returned to the reservations; others rode south into Texas, seeking revenge and horses.

Convinced that the Peace Policy had failed, officials authorized the army to initiate a vigorous campaign against any "nonreservation" Indians on the southern Plains. By late summer 1874 about 1,800 Cheyennes and Arapahos, 2,000 Comanches, and 1,000 Kiowas (probably 1,100 warriors) remained in the Texas Panhandle or Staked Plains. In August columns of troops scoured the region, and after a series of skirmishes, some of those troops, led by Tonkawa scouts, converged on a large multitribal village in Palo Duro Canyon about twenty miles southeast of modern Amarillo, Texas. At dawn on September 28, 1874, troops led by Colonel Ranald Mackenzie surprised the camp and most of the Indians fled, abandoning their lodges, dried meat, and most of their horses. Mackenzie burned the camp and all Indian supplies, then slaughtered over 1,000 Indian horses.

Throughout the fall, troops pursued other villages of Comanches, Kiowas, Cheyennes, and Arapahos across the Staked Plains, and by winter the Indians were destitute and hungry. Most Kiowas, Cheyennes, and Arapahos surrendered in the late fall of 1874, but some of the Comanches held out until the following spring, when they also straggled into Indian Territory. Big Tree, temporarily imprisoned at Fort Sill, was released, but Satanta was sent back to prison in Texas, where he committed suicide. Seventy-four other "ringleaders" were shackled and conducted by Lieutenant Richard Pratt to Fort Marion in Florida. Some were released in 1878 and returned to Oklahoma; others voluntarily accompanied Pratt to Pennsylvania, where they enrolled at the newly established Carlisle Indian School. Pratt became the first director of the institution.

The Red River War was the final attempt by Native Americans on the southern Plains to mount an armed resistance. Isolated on their reservations, the tribes now would be forced to abandon the buffalo and "walk the corn road." It would prove hard for buffalo hunters to envision themselves as farmers. Yet new leaders would emerge as bridges between the buffalo days and the reservation. Some, like Quanah Parker of the Comanches, had achieved some fame as warriors, but their real service would come in the future as they helped their people keep many of the old ways, while learning the new.

THE NORTHERN PLAINS, 1868–1881

On the northern plains many Lakotas still lived free. At the 1868 Treaty of Fort Laramie they had agreed either to occupy agency lands between the Missouri River and Black Hills or to remain in unceded lands west of the Black Hills, stretching from the Yellowstone Valley, south through the Powder River Country to the Platte River, and eastward into northwestern Nebraska. The Fort Laramie treaties provided food and other supplies to the agency Sioux, but during the summers they often joined their "wild" kinsmen to hunt in the lands west of the Black Hills.

Not all these forays were limited to hunting. Allied with Northern Cheyennes and Arapahos, Lakota war parties periodically raided ranches on the western or southern fringes of their lands, and they bitterly resented the construction of the Union Pacific Railroad, which snaked westward along the Platte, and the Northern Pacific, which thrust like a dagger westward from Bismark, in modern North Dakota. In addition Lakota warriors regularly harassed the Poncas, Pawnees, Crows, Shoshones, and other tribes, spurring angry complaints from both these tribes and their agents. In response, the government built new forts on the periphery of the Lakota lands, but the posts failed to intimidate the Lakotas. The forts only confirmed their suspicions that the government wished to control them.

The Lakotas differed among themselves over their proper relationship with the government. None of the Lakota chiefs was allied with the government, but Red Cloud of the Oglalas and Spotted Tail of the Brulés maintained a dialogue with government agents and visited Washington, where they attempted to cajole the Great Father into establishing new agencies for their people in western Nebraska. At the other end of the spectrum, intransigents such as Sitting Bull of the Hunkpapas, or Crazy Horse of the Oglalas kept apart from the *washichus* and condemned those tribespeople who remained near the agencies as "Laramie Loafers" or "Hangs Around the Fort" idlers who "were slaves to a piece of fat bacon, hardtack, and a little sugar and coffee." Yet even the agency Sioux seethed with resentment over bad rations and federal attempts to foster agriculture. Meanwhile, members of the nonagency bands periodically visited the agencies, obtained food and ammunition, then slipped away to their villages. Most Indian agents had difficulty controlling their wards and discerning among those who were resident at the agencies and those who were only visitors.

American demands for access to the Black Hills added tinder to the coming conflagration. The army wanted a post in the hills as a base for campaigns against the "hostiles," and repeated rumors of gold deposits in the region continued to pique the public's interest. In response, during June 1874 Custer led over 100 troops, geologists, and mining engineers on a "scientific expedition" into the region. Before the expedition even returned, reports reached the press that gold was so thick it could be seen shining through the roots of the grass. Not surprisingly, a gold rush started, and by the summer of 1875 over 800 miners were panning for gold in the region.

It was a risky business. Lakota and Cheyenne warriors attacked the prospectors, attempting to drive them from the hills. Meanwhile, army patrols initially arrested trespassers, but frontier courts readily freed the culprits and the military gave up in frustration. During the summer of 1875 federal officials twice offered to buy the hills, but the Lakotas refused. They considered Paha Sapa (the Black Hills) to be the very heart of their remaining homeland. The region contained many holy sites and burial grounds, and it adjoined Bear Butte—a location particularly sacred to many Lakotas. Moreover, the Lakota chiefs reminded their agents that the government had guaranteed the region to the tribe only seven years earlier. The Black Hills were not for sale. The Lakotas would fight to keep them.

The Lakota intransigence frustrated federal officials. Obviously, the tribe had an indelible legal claim to the Black Hills, but officials were unwilling to take military action against the gold-seekers. Prospectors voted; the Lakotas did not. In addition, proponents of seizing the hills argued that the Lakotas had raided outside their assigned territories; they had opposed those monuments of nineteenth century progress, the railroads; and the "wild Sioux" continually returned to the agencies where they disrupted the progress of other members of the tribe. In November 1875 officials decided to withdraw all troops from the borders of the region; if the Black Hills filled with miners, so be it. One month later they issued an ultimatum that clearly violated the 1868 Treaty of Fort Laramie: all Lakotas, Cheyennes, and Arapahos must come to the established agencies by January 31, 1876. Any Indians remaining in the unceded region west of the Black Hills after that date would be deemed hostile, and federal troops would take action against them.

It was easy to make such an ultimatum; it was much more difficult to deliver it. The winter of 1875–1876 was so severe that some of the messengers sent out from the agencies could not find the camps to deliver the order. Moreover, the snow was so deep that it was impossible for the tribespeople to travel hundreds of miles to the agencies. More important, the "wild Sioux" had no intention of leaving their homeland. The 1868 treaty guaranteed their right to remain free, and they were determined to do so. Meanwhile, government rations were in short supply at many of the agencies on the Missouri. The hungry agency Sioux spent a miserable winter huddled in their lodges. In the spring of 1876, as soon as the grass was high enough to feed their horses, many left the agencies and fled to their kinsmen's camps in the Powder River Country.

When the "wild" Lakotas, Cheyennes, and Arapahos did not appear on the Missouri in January 1876, the army designed a three-part campaign to force them to the agencies. General George A. Crook planned to march north from Fort Fetterman, near modern Douglas, Wyoming, while General Alfred Terry would proceed west from Fort Abraham Lincoln, near modern Bismark. Colonel John Gibbon would lead troops east from Fort Ellis in Montana. The three columns hoped to converge on the Indians, who they believed were camped somewhere in northern Wyoming or southern Montana. In March, Crook led an initial foray to the Powder River where he skirmished with the Cheyennes, but heavy snow and subzero temperatures forced him back to Fort Fetterman.

The Road to Little Big Horn

Convinced that a winter campaign on the northern Plains was impossible, the commanders waited until spring, and in early June, Terry and Gibbon joined their forces on the Yellowstone, planning to march south against the Lakota camps. Meanwhile Crook again left Fort Fetterman and proceeded up the Powder River Road to a camp near modern Sheridan, Wyoming, where he was joined by over 350 Crow and Shoshone warriors eager to settle old scores with the Lakotas, who they believed had invaded part of their homelands.

There were plenty of opportunities. By mid-June 1876, the valleys of the Rosebud, Tongue, Bighorn, and Greasy Grass (Little Big Horn) teemed with Lakota, Cheyenne, and Arapaho tribespeople. In addition to the nonagency Indians who regularly lived in the region, those Lakotas who had fled the agencies due to inadequate food or other problems now filled the camps. Estimates of the Native American population in the region range from 10,000 to 15,000 people, but by all accounts they could muster from 2,500 to 3,000 warriors. Tribespeople who remembered the early summer of 1876 recalled those weeks as a sun-filled time of plenty. Cooking pots were full, families were together, and there were many ceremonies and celebrations. In mid-June the Hunkpapa Lakotas held a sun dance at which Sitting Bull had a profound vision. In his vision Sitting Bull saw soldiers, like many grasshoppers, falling headfirst from the sky into the Lakota village. It was powerful medicine.

In mid-June scouts reported that many soldiers had appeared on the upper Rosebud and were descending the stream toward the Oglala villages. On the morning of June 17 a combined force of Lakotas, Cheyennes, and Arapahos led by Crazy Horse attacked Crook's troops, Crows, and Shoshones who were marching north, intent upon eventually joining with Gibbon and Terry. The subsequent Battle of the Rosebud lasted six hours and cost Crook twenty-eight killed and fifty-six wounded. Stiff resistance by Crook's Crow and Shoshone allies kept American casualties from mounting higher.

SITTING BULL.

Copyrighted by O. F. Barry, 1885,
BISMARCK, DAK.

D. F. BARRY,   BISMARCK, DAKOTA.

Sitting Bull An inveterate opponent of American Indian policy, Sitting Bull was a Hunkpapa Lakota religious leader and war chief who most Americans believed was responsible for the Indian victory at the Little Big Horn.

The Lakotas and their allies suffered thirty-six killed and sixty-three wounded. The tribesmen eventually retreated, but Crook also withdrew to his base camp near modern Sheridan. The southern third of the Terry-Gibbon-Crook convergence had been turned back by Crazy Horse.

Unaware of Crook's retreat, Terry and Gibbon prepared to "trap" the Indians. Crow scouts reported that many Lakotas were camped along the Greasy Grass, so Terry ordered Gibbon to ascend the Big Horn valley and prevent the Indians from escaping to the north. He instructed Lieutenant Colonel George Custer, who had accompanied Terry from North Dakota, to swing around to the east and approach the Greasy Grass valley from the south, shutting off any Indian flight in that direction. In response, Custer led between 600 and 700 men, including Crow and Arikara scouts, to the lower Rosebud, then westward toward the Greasy Grass. At dawn on June 25, 1876, Custer observed the smoke and dust of a large Indian camp about fifteen miles in the distance. Afraid that he had been discovered by the Lakotas, who he feared would flee, he ordered his men forward toward the village site. By noon, his men and their exhausted horses (Lakota scouts reported that the soldiers' horses were so tired that their legs trembled) had reached a low hill about three miles southeast of the village.

Custer and his subordinates, Major Marcus Reno and Captain Frederick Benteen, could not actually see the village, but they knew they were near the settlement's southern end. Still fearing that the Indians would flee, Custer dispatched Benteen and 125 troopers to the southwest to prevent the Lakotas from escaping toward the Big Horn Mountains. Custer then ordered a small party to remain with the pack animals and sent Reno and 112 men to attack the southern end of the village, while he and about 210 men swung around some low bluffs that rose above the river on the east. The bluffs hid the village from view, but once around them he planned to descend on what he assumed was the northern end of the encampment.

Custer grossly miscalculated. The Indian village did not extend a mere mile and a half downstream; it ran for almost three miles along the western bank of the Greasy Grass. Moreover, instead of a narrow corridor of teepees strung along the river bank, the village spilled westward through the willows and cottonwoods, encompassing camps of Cheyennes and of Oglala, Hunkpapa, Minneconjou, Blackfeet, Sans Arc, and Brulé Lakotas.

Within the camp, people had been resting during the midday heat, but when scouts reported that Blue-Coat soldiers were approaching from the south, warriors ran for their weapons, while women and children fled toward the northern reaches of the village. Riders galloped north through the village shouting that soldiers on horseback had attacked the southern end of the encampment but had dismounted and were advancing on foot through a willow thicket. Hundreds of warriors rushed toward the camps on the south, where they forced Reno to retreat. The troops remounted, but as their horses recrossed the river and scrambled up the steep river bank Indian marksmen shot them from their saddles. By the time Reno reassembled his men on the east side of the river, he had lost almost half his command.

Reno's narrow escape back across the river was aided by reports that other soldiers had appeared on the bluffs just east of the village. Many of the warriors who had been pursuing Reno now turned and either rode or ran on foot toward where Custer had crossed over the bluffs, about one and a quarter miles downstream. To Custer's surprise, he had not reached the northern end of the village, and as growing numbers of warriors appeared on the opposite bank, he halted his descent toward the river, then evidently ordered his troops to retreat back up the bluffs where they dismounted and formed a loose skirmish line.

Meanwhile hundreds of Lakotas and Cheyennes, both on horseback and afoot, crossed the river to attack their adversaries. Many of the warriors who were not mounted crept up Medicine Tail Coulee, an arroyo that provided protection from the soldiers' rifles. Led by Crazy Horse and Gall, mounted warriors encircled the troopers, preventing any flight, then charged through the soldiers' lines, separating the Americans into two groups. Some troopers attempted to flee, but the warriors rode them down on the prairie. Others, including Custer, huddled together on a low ridge, while the Lakotas and Cheyennes tightened the circle around them. The battle of the Little Big Horn lasted less than one hour. By 3 p.m. the fight had ended. The Lakotas and Cheyennes were victorious. The bodies of Custer and 215 men lay scattered across the ridges and hilltops.

Some of the warriors then renewed their attack on Reno, who had joined with Benteen and the small force guarding the pack animals. These survivors frantically dug rifle pits, repulsed several Indian sorties, then watched in amazement as the huge village broke camp on June 26 and the tribespeople scattered over the prairie. Unknown to the troopers, Lakota scouts had brought reports that Terry and Gibbon were approaching the battle site from the north. When the relief column arrived on June 27, they hurriedly buried the fallen soldiers. In addition to the soldiers killed with Custer, Reno suffered 57 killed and 63 wounded. Approximately half of the Seventh Cavalry had suffered casualties.

Ironically, President Grant first received news of the Indian victory at Little Big Horn on July 4, 1876. He was in Philadelphia, attending the Centennial Celebration of the Declaration of Independence. The American military disaster spurred a quick response. On July 26 all Lakota agencies were placed under the control of military officers and fresh troops were rushed to the West. Meanwhile most hostile Cheyennes and Lakotas eluded Crook's troopers who followed them across Wyoming and Montana. One party of Minneconjou Lakotas, who were en route to surrender at the Spotted Tail Agency, were attacked in September by Crook and Captain Anson Mills at Slim Buttes in South Dakota. American Horse and several Lakotas were killed, but a large war party of Oglalas led by Crazy Horse again forced the army to retreat, and the surviving Minneconjous abandoned their surrender.

Although the government could not catch the hostile Cheyennes and Lakotas, it did force concessions from the agency Indians. Congress passed a resolution forbidding any further distribution of food or annuities to the Lakotas until they ceded the Black Hills and Powder River Country. In October 1876 Crook stripped Red Cloud of any "official" authority and appointed Spotted Tail as the "chief of all the Sioux." Federal commissioners then forced several agency chiefs to sign a new agreement relinquishing claims to the Black Hills and their right to hunt outside the newly defined "Great Sioux Reservation" (covering western South Dakota). Even so, Sitting Bull and other more traditional Lakota leaders rejected the document and still refused to go to the agencies.

But time was running out. The buffalo herds had shrunk, and the Cheyennes and Lakotas were hard-pressed to feed their families. Moreover, Crook and General Nelson Miles, the new American commander on the Yellowstone, mounted a winter campaign. Assisted by 400 Indian allies (primarily Pawnees, Shoshones, and Bannocks), in November 1876 Crook surprised a village of Cheyennes led by Dull Knife and Little Wolf near the Big Horn Mountains. The Cheyennes fought valiantly, but they lost forty warriors, and Crook captured most of their food and other supplies. Many suffered from the cold before finding refuge

INDIAN VOICES   Two Moons (Cheyenne War Chief) Recounts the Battle of Little Big Horn

Of all the military encounters between Native Americans and non-Indians, none has seized the imagination of the American public more than the Battle of the Little Big Horn. Custer's defeat on June 25, 1876, shocked the American public and engendered a plethora of literary accounts, lithographs, and paintings of the event. One of the paintings, Cassily Adams's "Custer's Last Fight"—a large, detailed, if highly speculative panorama of the closing moments of the battle—was one of the most widely distributed "works of art" in the United States at the beginning of the twentieth century. Yet until recently the battle site was officially known as the "Custer Battlefield," and only in 1991 was the site renamed the Battle of the Little Big Horn National Historic Site by the National Park Service. In addition to an older stone monolith that marks the mass grave of Custer and his troopers, a new memorial now honors the Native American warriors who also fell in the battle.

This changing focus, reflecting a new emphasis on the Native American perspective on these events, has led historians to reexamine earlier Indian accounts. The following narrative is by Two Moons, a Cheyenne war chief who fought in the battle. What are the many factors that have combined to create such a profound and ongoing interest in the Battle of the Little Big Horn in both American popular culture and among the American public?

About May (1876), when the grass was tall and the horses strong, we broke camp and started across the country to the mouth of the Tongue River. Then Sitting Bull and Crazy Horse and all went up the Rosebud. There we had a big fight with General Crook, and whipped him. Many soldiers were killed—few Indians. It was a great fight, much smoke and dust.

From there we went over the divide, and camped in the valley of the Little Horn. Everybody thought, "Now we are out of the white man's country. He can live there, we can live here." After a few days, one morning Sitting Bull, a Sioux messenger, rode up and said, "Let everyone paint up, cook, and get ready for a big dance."

I went to water my horses in the creek, and washed them off with cool water, then took a swim myself. I came back to the camp afoot. When I got near my lodge, I looked up the Little Horn towards Sitting Bull's camp. I saw a great dust rising. It looked like a whirlwind. Soon Sioux horsemen came rushing into camp shouting: "Soldiers are coming. Plenty white soldiers."

I ran into my lodge and said to my brother-in-law, "Get your horses; the white man is coming. Everybody run for horses."

After I had caught my horse, a Sioux warrior came again and said, "Many soldiers are coming." Then he said to the women, "Get out of the way, we are going to have a hard fight."

I rode swiftly toward Sitting Bull's camp. There I saw the white soldiers fighting in a line [Reno's men]. Indians covered the flat. They began to drive the soldiers all mixed up—Sioux, then soldiers, then more Sioux, and all shooting. The air was full of smoke and dust. I saw the soldiers fall back and drop into the river-bed like buffalo fleeing. They had no time to look for a crossing. The Sioux chased them up the hill where they met more soldiers in wagons, and then messengers came back saying the soldiers were going to kill the women, and the Sioux turned back. Chief Gall was there fighting, Crazy Horse also.

I then rode toward my camp and . . . I saw flags come up over the hill to the east. . . . Then the soldiers . . . formed into three bunches [squadrons in columns of fours] with a little ways in between. Then a bugle sounded, and they all got off their horses, and some soldiers led the horses back over the hill.

Then the Sioux rode up the ridges on all sides, riding very fast. The Cheyennes went up the left way. The shooting was quick. Some of the soldiers were down on their knees, some standing. Officers all in front. We circled all around them— swirling like water around a stone. We shoot, we ride fast, we shoot again. Soldiers drop, and horses fall on them. Soldiers in the line drop, but one man rode up and down the line—all the time shouting. He rode a sorrel horse. He was a brave man.

Indians keep swirling around and around, and the soldiers killed only a few. Many soldiers fell. At last all the horses were killed but five. Once in a while some man would break out and run for the river, but he would fall. At last about a hundred men and five horses stood on the hill all bunched together. All along the bugler kept blowing his commands. Then a chief was killed. I hear it was Long Hair [Custer], I don't know; then the five horsemen and a bunch of men, maybe forty, started for the river. The man on the sorrel horse led them. He wore a buckskin shirt and had long black hair and a mustache. He fought hard with a big knife. One man all alone ran down toward the river, then around up over the hill. I thought he was going to escape, but a Sioux fired and hit him in the head. He was the last man. He wore braid on his arms [a sergeant].

All the soldiers now were killed, and the bodies stripped. After that no one could tell which were officers. The bodies were left where they fell. We had no dance that night. We were sorrowful.

Next day four Sioux chiefs and two Cheyennes and I, Two Moon, went upon the battlefield to count the dead. There were thirty-nine Sioux and seven Cheyennes killed, and about a hundred wounded.

From: Wayne Moquin and Charles Dore, eds., *Great Documents in American Indian History* (New York: Praeger Publishers, 1973), 226–229. (Original from *McClure's Magazine*, September 1898.)

in Crazy Horse's village. In January 1877 a large Cheyenne and Lakota war party was defeated by Miles near the Wolf Mountains in southeastern Montana. Short of food and blankets, the Cheyennes and Lakota people spent a miserable winter dodging columns of troops and trying to feed their families. In the spring of 1877 Sitting Bull abandoned his homeland and led the Hunkpapa people north to refuge in Canada.

Discouraged, other Lakotas and Cheyennes slowly came to terms with the government. In March 1877, Spotted Tail visited the hostile villages with a government promise that if the Indians came to the agencies, they would be furnished with food and blankets. Initially, they would be forced to surrender their arms and horses, but both would be restored to them after a few weeks. Weakened by cold and hunger, most surrendered in April or

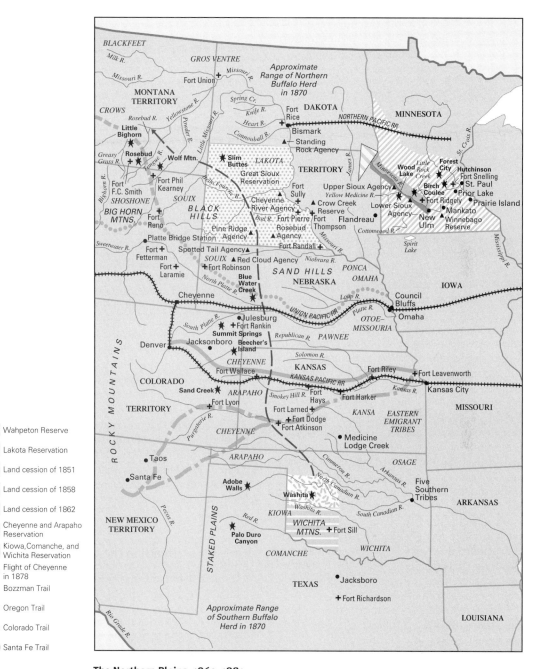

Legend:

- Wahpeton Reserve
- Lakota Reservation
- Land cession of 1851
- Land cession of 1858
- Land cession of 1862
- Cheyenne and Arapaho Reservation
- Kiowa, Comanche, and Wichita Reservation
- ← — Flight of Cheyenne in 1878
- Bozzman Trail
- •••• Oregon Trail
- Colorado Trail
- Santa Fe Trail

The Northern Plains, 1860–1881

May. Even Crazy Horse, the holy man of the Oglalas, rode into Red Cloud's Agency on May 6, 1877. A few bands, primarily Minneconjous led by Lame Deer and Red Star, held out, but they too surrendered later in the summer. The *washichus* claimed Paha Sapa. The Lakota war to save the Black Hills had ended.

REBELLIONS AGAINST RESERVATION LIFE

For the Plains tribes, the reservation days did not start well. Crazy Horse was murdered on September 6, 1877, and many Lakotas were stunned by his loss. The Cheyennes suffered a tragedy of their own. The Northern Cheyennes had requested a separate agency, but following their surrender, they were shipped to Indian Territory. Their southern kinsmen welcomed them, but they missed their former homeland, disliked the summer heat, and fell victim to a series of maladies that swept through the reservation camps. In response, during September 1878 Dull Knife, Little Wolf, and 300 of their tribespeople fled north from Indian Territory toward the Powder River Country. Troops followed in their wake or attempted to intercept them as they crossed western Kansas, but the Cheyennes eluded their pursuers, crossed the Platte, and vanished into the Sand Hills of northern Nebraska. There the fugitives split into two parties. Dull Knife and about 150 Cheyennes decided to surrender at nearby Fort Robinson, where they believed they would be given sanctuary by the Oglala Lakotas. Little Wolf and the remainder of the refugees refused to surrender, intending to make their way back to southern Montana.

Things did not go as planned. After surrendering, Dull Knife and his followers learned that the government previously had removed the Lakotas from Fort Robinson to new agencies at Rosebud and Pine Ridge. Captain Henry Wessells, the commander at Fort Robinson, informed the Cheyennes that they must return to Indian Territory. When they refused, Wessells confined them to an abandoned barracks and subsequently denied them any food, water, or firewood. Facing death from freezing or starvation, the Cheyennes broke through the barracks windows on the evening of January 9, 1879, killed several guards, and fled on foot through subzero temperatures toward freedom. The garrison of the fort followed in their wake, firing at the fugitives. Many were killed, but public opinion rallied on the survivors' behalf, and they were allowed to settle among the Lakotas at Pine Ridge. Little Wolf and the other Cheyenne refugees dodged army patrols until March, when they surrendered in southeastern Montana. Eventually (1884) both groups of refugees were assigned to a new reservation, adjacent to the Crow lands, near modern Lame Deer, Montana.

Sitting Bull remained in Canada, where he led a band of almost 4,000 Lakotas and about 100 Nez Percés who slipped away following Chief Joseph's surrender (discussed below). Camped between the Cypress Hills and Wood Mountain, about forty miles north of the border, they were tolerated by the Canadian government, which adopted a "live and let live" policy toward the Indians as long as the refugees remained at peace. Yet neighboring Canadian tribespeople (Crees, Assiniboines, and Blackfeet) were not happy to share their lands with the refugees, and the increased Indian population took its toll on game in the region. Sitting Bull initially rejected federal requests that he return to the United States, but in July 1881 he led his followers to Fort Buford, North Dakota, where he surrendered. His Hunkpapa followers were assigned to the Standing Rock Agency, while Sitting Bull was kept under house arrest for two years at Fort Randall.

Death in the Lava Beds

Captain Jack and the Modocs suffered a harsher fate. A relatively small tribe (about 700 people) that resided near Tule Lake and the Lost River in northern California, the Modocs were hunters, gatherers, and fishermen. Although they had skirmished with some of the early settlers, their lands were not threatened by miners and they remained on good terms with many of the ranchers and farmers near their homeland. In 1864 Modoc leaders including Captain Jack (Kintpuash) reluctantly signed a treaty agreeing to relocate to the Klamath reservation in southern Oregon. The Modoc and

Klamath languages were almost identical, but the Klamaths were much more populous, and the Modocs complained that they were treated like second-class citizens on the Klamath reservation. In 1865 Captain Jack led about 400 Modocs back to the Lost River valley, where they split into two groups. Captain Jack's followers occupied a small tract (approximately three miles long and one mile wide) that contained the tribe's fishing grounds along the river, while another party of Modocs, led by Hooker Jim, Scarface Charley, and Curley Headed Doctor (a medicine man), roamed the surrounding country. Ranchers accused the less sedentary band of stealing livestock, but Captain Jack's people often worked at odd jobs at nearby ranches and were praised as "good neighbors" by surrounding settlers.

General Edward Canby, the military commander in the region, praised the Modocs and supported their request for a small reservation encompassing their fishing grounds. He was opposed by Indian agents at the Klamath Agency who envisioned their flight and absence from the reservation as a threat to federal authority and demanded their return to the reservation. The Indian agents prevailed, and in November 1872 the army was ordered to collect the Modocs and bring them back to Oregon. At dawn on November 29, troops surrounded the villages of Captain Jack and Hooker Jim, who were camped on opposite sides of the river. Canby urged restraint, but a skirmish erupted; one Modoc, one soldier, and two civilian auxiliaries were killed. The Modocs fled from the river valley and took refuge amid lava beds near Lake Tule. En route to the lava beds, Hooker Jim's followers killed another fourteen settlers.

The lava beds were a formidable fortress. Described by ranchers as "hell with the fires out," the lava beds were undercut with fissures and broken into waves of steep ridges, great boulders, and innumerable hiding places: a rocky labyrinth well-known to the Modocs, but completely foreign to the army. While troops surrounded the periphery, the Modocs dug in and prepared their defense. By January 1873 the American troops numbered 400; the Modocs, 60 warriors.

The first American assault, mounted on the morning of January 16, proved disastrous. Mountain howitzers rained shells into the region, but the lava was impervious to the barrage, and when the

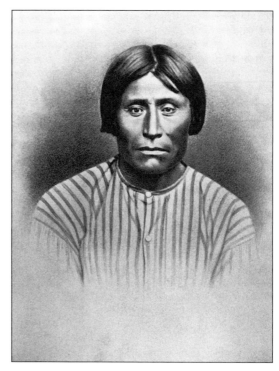

Captain Jack A reluctant leader of the Modoc resistance to American troops in the Lava Beds of northern California, Captain Jack was betrayed by other Modocs.

troops advanced into the maze they found the ridges and passages shrouded in a heavy ground fog. The Modocs immediately caught them in deadly crossfires and the confused troops huddled together until the fog lifted and they could withdraw. They suffered eleven killed and twenty-eight wounded. No Modocs were even seen by the soldiers, let alone killed or wounded.

Demoralized, government officials attempted to negotiate. Preliminary talks in February proved fruitless, and in March, Canby assumed control of the proceedings. Assisted by Winema, a Modoc woman related to Captain Jack and married to a white man, he offered the Modocs more generous terms, but he also reinforced the number of troops surrounding the Indians. Within the lava beds the Modocs split into peace and war factions, with Captain Jack leading those Modocs who wished to reach a negotiated settlement. He was opposed by Hooker Jim and Curley Headed Doctor, who vowed to fight till the end and denounced Captain Jack as a coward. Humiliated, Captain Jack foolishly succumbed to the bad advice of his rivals and agreed to kill Canby and the other American negotiators. Winema advised Canby that trouble was afoot, but he ignored her warning. The talks were conducted under a flag of truce, but on April 11, 1873 (Good Friday), Captain Jack and several other Modocs drew pistols and knives from under their clothing, then killed Canby and two other officials. Three other Americans escaped.

The Modoc treachery enraged most Americans, particularly Chief of Staff General William Tecumseh Sherman. He ordered additional troops to California and the army invaded the lava beds in force. Still defiant, the Modocs fought back, inflicting heavy casualties on the soldiers. By mid-May, however, troops converged on the center of the lava beds only to find that the Modocs were gone. Led by Captain Jack, they had slipped through their enemy's lines and fled from the lava beds to surrounding forests. Captain Jack and his followers continued to elude pursuers, but Hooker Jim and several other former intransigents defected to the army and offered to serve as scouts in return for amnesty. The government accepted their offer, and on May 29 Captain Jack and his family were captured near the Oregon border.

In the aftermath, Captain Jack and four of his men were tried and convicted of murder. They were hanged at Fort Klamath on October 3, 1873. Hooker Jim, Curley Headed Doctor, Scarface Charlie, and others who had actually fomented the murder plot were exonerated because they had become turncoats and helped the government. In the fall of 1873 they and the remaining 150 Modoc survivors of the conflict were exiled to the Quapaw Agency in Indian Territory. Most of the turncoat leaders died in Oklahoma, where the other Modocs remained in exile until 1909, when they were allowed to return to the Klamath Agency.

The Modoc War proved disastrous for everyone. The demands by Indian agents that the Modocs return to the Klamath Agency reflected the bureaucratic inflexibility of the Indian Office. Captain Jack and the Modocs mounted an admirable defense, but it was marred by their treachery in the deaths of Canby and the other negotiators. Perhaps the greatest condemnation should be saved for the turncoat Modoc leaders of the hostile faction who goaded Captain Jack into committing the murders, then shamelessly betrayed him. Needless to say, the affair did little to strengthen the public's faith in Grant's Peace Policy.

Chief Joseph and the Nez Percés

If the Modocs were widely condemned by non-Indians for their warfare, the Nez Percés attracted the public's admiration. They had enjoyed a long history of friendship toward Americans, had assisted Lewis and Clark, and in 1847 had sheltered the Spalding family when neighboring Cayuses attacked the Whitman mission. Between 1855 and 1863 part of the tribe had ceded large tracts of land near the juncture of Washington, Oregon, and Idaho, accepting a reservation in Idaho's Clearwater Valley. Several bands (nontreaty Nez Percés) continued, however, to reside in the Wallowa Valley of northeastern Oregon and were led by Chief Joseph ("Old Joseph"), who had refused to sign the 1863 reservation treaty. In 1871 Old Joseph died and was succeeded by his son, also known as Chief Joseph.

During the early 1870s the younger Chief Joseph argued so persuasively that his people should remain in their homeland that federal officials initially made plans to establish a new reservation in Oregon, but state officials protested and the federal government reneged. In 1875 the region was opened for settlement and the Nez Percés reluctantly decided to remain on public lands in Oregon and to attempt to live peacefully with their new white neighbors. General Oliver Howard, the military commander in the region, sympathized with the Nez Percés, but he could not stop the immigration into their homeland. He offered the Nez Percés additional payments to remove to Idaho, but the Indians still refused. Concerned that they might be influenced by followers of Smoholla and the Dreamer religion, an anti-American religious movement currently attracting many Indians in Washington, Howard met again with Joseph and other nontreaty chiefs in May 1877 and informed them that they had thirty days to remove to the Nez Percé reservation in Idaho. Although they believed the government had betrayed them, the Nez Percé leaders reluctantly agreed.

The removal did not go well. En route to Idaho the Nez Percés encountered difficulty in swimming their livestock across the swollen Snake River, where frontier ne'er-do-wells attempted to steal many of their fine Appaloosa horses. Embittered, Joseph's people made it across, then joined with other nonreservation Nez Percés to dig camas bulbs at Camas Prairie, just south of the reservation. But their young men were angry, and on June 13 several warriors from White Bird's village killed four settlers who recently had sold whiskey to the tribe. The nonreservation bands withdrew to White Bird Canyon to discuss their response. Joseph counseled caution, but many other Nez Percés believed they would be punished regardless of their subsequent actions.

On June 18 scouts reported the approach of a large body of troops and local volunteers toward the Nez Percé camp. Joseph sent out a party to negotiate with the Americans, but the volunteers fired on the Indians' white flag, touching off the Battle of White Bird Hill, in which the Americans lost thirty-four men and withdrew from the field much demoralized. Meanwhile Nez Percé raiding parties struck at neighboring ranches, killing an additional fourteen civilians.

While Howard awaited reinforcements, the Nez Percés slipped away into the mountain ranges separating the Snake and Salmon rivers, and in late June, an ill-advised army attack on Looking Glass's village only convinced this chief, who previously had remained neutral, to join the hostile camp. During July, Howard pursued the Nez Percés back and forth amidst the rugged mountains along the Snake and Clearwater rivers with little success. The Nez Percés, numbering about 300 warriors and 500 women and children, eluded their pursuers. After several skirmishes, in late July they crossed the treacherous Lolo Pass, bypassed a barricade in the Bitteroot Valley, and passed into western Montana, where they paused to rest, purchase supplies, and repair their lodges near the Big Hole River.

Although the Nez Percés had outdistanced Howard, they were unaware that other columns of troops were in the field, and at dawn on August 9, 1877, they were surprised by Colonel John Gibbon and 200 troops from Fort Missoula. Gibbon's attack initially drove the Nez Percés from their village, but the warriors regrouped in the forest and launched a counterattack that allowed their women

Chief Joseph One of the leaders of the Nez Percé retreat from Washington to the Bear Paw Mountains in Montana, Chief Joseph attracted the attention of writers, journalists, and the American public.

and children to gather their possessions and escape into the Lemhi Valley. Yet the Battle of the Big Hole had taken a heavy toll. Nez Percé marksmen had felled thirty soldiers, but Gibbon's surprise attack had killed ninety tribespeople, many of whom were women and children.

Still followed by Howard, who was now guided by friendly Nez Percé and Bannock scouts, Joseph's people turned east, slipped around another army barricade at Targhee Pass, and passed through modern Yellowstone Park. In September they descended the Clark's Fork onto the plains of Montana, repulsed an attack by Colonel Samuel Sturgis and the Seventh Cavalry, and crossed the Missouri River. On September 29, 1877, they camped near the Bear Paw Mountains, only forty miles from

Canada. Intent on joining Sitting Bull, they knew that neither Howard nor any of the other Blue-Coat soldiers following in their wake could catch them. Their women and children were tired, their horses were exhausted, and they desperately needed food. They planned to rest for two days, hunt, and then proceed on to Canada. A cold rain fell throughout the afternoon. They were hungry.

They were also in considerable danger. Unknown to the Nez Percés, Colonel Nelson Miles and about 400 fresh troops guided by Lakota and Cheyenne scouts had entered the chase from posts in southern Montana. At midmorning on September 30 they swept in on the Nez Percé camp, stampeding their horses and scattering people from their teepees. Now seasoned warriors, the Nez Percés took shelter on a heavily eroded ridge overlooking their camp and concentrated their fire against the officers. Most were killed or wounded and the troops withdrew from the village, but Miles opened fire with a Hotchkiss Gun (a small cannon). Tohoolhoolzote and several other prominent warriors were killed, but the Nez Percés remained on their ridge top, refusing to surrender. Late in the evening, however, a fall blizzard swept through the region, and the Nez Percés were cold and hungry. On October 4 Howard and additional troops arrived from the west, and after Miles promised that the Nez Percés could return to the reservation in Idaho, Joseph delivered his famous speech: "I am tired. My heart is sick and sad. From where the sun now stands, I will fight no more forever." The trek had ended. Joseph and about 400 tribespeople, mostly tribal elders, women, and children, surrendered. About 100 warriors and 200 women and children led by White Bird slipped through the soldiers' lines and escaped to join Sitting Bull in Canada.

Although Miles was sincere in his promises, they were not honored. Both Miles and Howard implored their superiors to return the Nez Percés to Idaho; instead the government shipped them first to Kansas, then on to Indian Territory, where they remained until 1884, when Joseph and the remaining members of his band were transferred to the Colville Reservation in Washington. Most of the Canadian Nez Percés gradually emigrated back to the Clearwater Reservation, but Joseph's people remained in Washington. The old chief journeyed to Washington, D.C., and repeatedly petitioned for his people to be returned to their beloved Wallowa

Valley, but his pleas went unanswered. He died on the Colville Reservation in 1904.

The epic flight of Chief Joseph and the Nez Percés rapidly became part of American history and folklore. It was an admirable achievement. Outnumbered, but never outfought, the Nez Percés had successfully retreated for 1,700 miles across some of the most difficult terrain in the United States. Although they killed about three dozen innocent settlers on their trek to the Bear Paw Mountains, these deaths were overshadowed by their brilliant retreats and hard-fought delaying tactics. Both Howard and Miles praised their fighting ability, and newspaper reporters who flocked to the campaign sent back stories of embattled "noble redmen." In addition, although Joseph may have not played a major role in the long trek to Montana, his leadership enhanced the Nez Percé image. A strikingly handsome man, a persuasive orator, and a leader sincerely interested in his people, he used his popularity to urge a return to the Wallowa Valley. The campaign struck a responsive chord among much of the eastern public, although it obviously did not play well in the state of Washington. Still, in the twenty-first century, Joseph is remembered as one of the foremost "Patriot Chiefs."

The Paiutes and Bannocks

While the epic of Chief Joseph and the Nez Percés has enjoyed a historical limelight, the struggles of the Paiutes and Bannocks have remained in the shadows. This obscurity resulted from the nineteenth-century American public's disdain for Indian people living in the Great Basin. In the nineteenth century, small bands of Shoshonean-speaking people traveled throughout the deserts and arid mountains of the Great Basin region. Derogatorily called "Diggers" by American emigrants to California, these hunter-gatherers lived within a centuries-old culture that was remarkably well adapted to a very harsh environment (see Chapter 1). Since the land could not support large numbers of inhabitants, the Paiutes and their neighbors lived in small, wide-ranging groups who utilized only simple, temporary, easily constructed shelters. The white Americans' condemnation of them as Diggers is more reflective of nineteenth-century American ethnocentrism than an accurate characterization of the Basin peoples' way of life.

During the 1840s and 1850s the Paiutes and their neighbors had periodically clashed with white emigrants, stealing each others' property and even killing isolated individuals, although the violence had been neither widespread nor particularly focused. In 1864, like the Modocs, a portion of the Paiutes relocated to the Klamath Reservation, but they too returned to their homelands, and one year later Paiute warriors led by Paunina (called "Pauline" by whites) raided isolated ranches and prospectors' camps. Federal troops dispatched to apprehend them proved ineffective, but in 1866 Lieutenant Colonel George Crook assumed command at Fort Boise in southern Idaho and launched a vigorous two-year campaign against the "hostiles." Guided by Shoshone scouts, Crook pursued the Paiutes, killed Paunina, and forced his followers to surrender. Eventually, many settled on a reservation on the Malheur River in southeastern Oregon, although others, now at peace, still roamed the desert. Crook's role in this venture initiated his career as a successful "Indian fighter."

The Paiutes and neighboring Bannocks remained at peace for a decade, but by the late 1870s both (particularly the Bannocks) had become resentful of settlers now threatening their homeland. In the spring of 1878, when Bannocks, Shoshones, Paiutes, and even a few Umatillas from Oregon arrived at Camas Prairie in southern Idaho where they always had harvested camas bulbs, they found much of the prairie uprooted by settlers' hogs. When they drove the hogs away, the settlers protested and the Bannocks shot and wounded two white men. Some of the Indians fled back to their reservations, but others, led by Buffalo Horn, a Bannock chief, raided westward across southern Idaho. Buffalo Horn was killed in the fighting, but the Indians crossed into Oregon, where they were joined by additional Paiutes from the Malheur River Reservation. In mid-June, numbering about 700 people, including more than 400 warriors, they established a temporary village near the Steene Mountains.

Fresh from his campaign against the Nez Percés, General Oliver Howard sent Sarah Winnemucca, the daughter of a friendly Paiute chief, to the Steene Mountains village, but resentment of the Americans so permeated the camp that Winnemucca and other friendly Paiutes in her party barely escaped with their lives. American troops responded by attacking their village on June 23, but the occupants escaped. Joined by some Klamaths, they retreated to the Blue Mountains in northeastern Oregon. On July 8, 1878, when troops under Howard's command attacked their camp on Birch Creek, the Paiutes and Bannocks fled to the nearby Umatilla Reservation. The Umatillas wanted no part of the fighting, and a party of Umatillas killed one of the Paiute chiefs and then delivered his scalp to the army.

Much disillusioned, the Paiutes scattered into small parties that retreated back toward the Malheur River Agency, where most surrendered. In contrast, the Bannocks, still defiant, crossed into southern Idaho, attempting to follow the Nez Percé trail through Yellowstone and on to Canada. Troops from western Wyoming and Idaho blocked their passage, and in early September large numbers also surrendered. Others fled to the Salmon Mountains in northern Idaho where they sought refuge among the Sheepeaters, a small band of mixed Bannock and Shoshone origins, whose rugged homeland kept them isolated from most other people, both whites and Indians. In May 1879, either refugee Bannocks or their Sheepeater hosts killed five prospectors on the Salmon River. In response, Howard dispatched about 100 troops and two dozen Umatilla scouts into the mountains in search of the perpetrators. The Sheepeaters and their Bannock allies numbered no more than forty warriors, but they knew the terrain and eluded their pursuers. In late July they ambushed one party of soldiers and captured their baggage, then attacked another party and disappeared into the mountains. The Sheepeater War dragged on until October, when most of the hostile Bannocks slipped away and returned to their reservation. The remaining Sheepeaters (less than one hundred people) surrendered on October 2, 1879. The army's "success" in the Sheepeater campaign was due more to the abilities of Umatilla scouts than to the military skill of its officers and men.

In the aftermath of this conflict the Bannocks were temporarily imprisoned, but in the spring of 1879 they were allowed to return to their reservation. The Malheur River Agency was closed, however, and in 1879 the 600 Paiutes residing there were transferred to the Yakama Reservation in

Washington. The Sheepeaters were deposited on the Fort Hall Reservation. The Paiute-Bannock War of 1878 remains overshadowed by the Nez Percé campaign, and unlike the latter it produced few heroes and relatively little press coverage. Yet for the residents of Idaho and eastern Oregon, both Native American and white, it was an event of considerable importance. In addition, lessons learned by Howard and other officers in pursuing the Nez Percés proved valuable against the Paiutes and Bannocks. Multiple columns of troops, dispatched from different directions, proved effective in locating and suppressing parties of hostile Indians. Moreover, in hostile terrain, regular troops needed the assistance of friendly Indian scouts if they ever hoped to locate small parties of their enemies: a lesson that both Indian agents and officers would later apply in their relations with the Apaches.

The Utes

The short-lived Ute War of 1879 illustrated the contest between the Bureau of Indian Affairs and the military in implementing federal Indian policy. Like the Nez Percés, the Utes, a people who inhabited the western slopes of the Colorado Rockies and eastern Utah, had a history of friendship with the Americans. Ute warriors had assisted Kit Carson in his campaigns against the Navajos, and Ute scouts had guided Crook's columns against the Lakotas and Cheyennes. Indeed, like the Crows and Pawnees, the Utes traditionally had warred with several neighboring tribes, and they had welcomed opportunities to assist the Americans against their mutual enemies.

In 1868 the Utes had given up their claims to lands in Utah and Colorado in return for a large reservation (about one-fourth of modern Colorado) encompassing much of Colorado's western slope. Five years later, to appease miners who were eager to exploit minerals in the region, they reluctantly had ceded another four million acres in the San Juan Mountains, but they planned no further cessions. By 1879 they were settled within two general areas on their reservation. The 800 Northern Utes clustered around the White River Agency, near modern Meeker, while about 3,000 Southern Utes lived farther south, at the Los Pinos Agency near modern Montrose and Durango. An additional band of about 400 Utes also lived on a small reservation in northeastern Utah.

The discovery of silver in the San Juan Mountains and the subsequent cession of Ute lands in the region were a portent of things to come. In 1876 Colorado was admitted into the Union, and politicians from the new state clamored for additional Ute cessions and the removal of the tribe to Indian Territory. Led by Ouray, an aging but influential chief from the Uncompahgres (one of the southern bands), the Utes reminded officials of their friendship and cooperation with the United States and refused to budge. Ouray was highly respected by Indian agents at the southern Ute agencies, and they generally supported his determination to remain in Colorado.

Indian agents among the Northern Utes, at the White River Agency, were less amenable. In 1878 Nathan Meeker, an ethnocentric utopian, was appointed as agent, and he was determined to force the Utes to become farmers. Two chiefs at the northern agency, Quinkent ("Douglas') and Nicaagat ("Jack"), opposed Meeker and were particularly angry when he plowed and fenced part of a rich tribal pasture in which the Utes traditionally had grazed their horses. Vowing to "elevate" the Utes to "an enlightened scientific and religious stage," Meeker threatened to seize Ute horses, withhold their rations, and "cut every Indian down to the bare starvation point."

After tolerating Meeker for a year, the Northern Utes became increasingly hostile. Fearing violence, Meeker appealed to the military for troops during the summer of 1879, but they considered him an eccentric and refused. Finally, in September 1879, after Meeker instructed a Ute to kill and eat all his horses, the warrior pushed Meeker off the agency building's front porch. In response, Meeker reported that the Indians had assaulted him, and troops were dispatched from southern Wyoming. When the Utes learned that troops were approaching, they feared the soldiers would kill their remaining horses and remove the tribe to Indian Territory.

In late September 1879, Major Thomas Thornburgh, with about 180 officers and men and thirty-three supply wagons, reached the northern edge of the reservation. Thornburgh left the wagons and sixty men there, then crossed Milk Creek, where he was confronted by Nicaagat and about one hundred warriors. Alarmed, Thornburgh deployed his cavalry in a skirmish line, which Nicaagat, who previously had served under Crook, interpreted as a hostile action. Shots were fired and the Utes charged at the troopers. Thornburgh's troops outnumbered their enemies, but Thornburgh was shot and killed and Captain Scott Payne led the troops back to the circled wagons, where his men dismounted and sought shelter. The Utes also dismounted and climbed neighboring creek bluffs. By nightfall they had killed ten soldiers, wounded twenty-three others, and either killed or wounded almost all the troops' horses and mules. During the night couriers slipped through the Ute lines, and on October 2 a small contingent of reinforcements arrived. The newcomers also sought questionable shelter behind the wagons, and the siege continued until October 5, when additional troops from Wyoming forced the Utes to withdraw. Meanwhile, other Utes at the White River Agency killed Meeker and nine agency employees and took Meeker's wife and daughter prisoners.

Embarrassed by the Battle of Milk Creek, the army rushed more troops into the region. Fortunately, cooler heads prevailed. Ouray sent messages to both federal officials and the hostiles, urging restraint and warning Nicaagat, Quinkent, and other Northern Utes that the southern bands would not support their warfare. Secretary of the Interior Carl Schurz also intervened and instructed agents to negotiate for the Meeker women's release. While military commanders in the field waited impatiently, both sides met and came to an agreement. In late October the Utes released their prisoners, and the government agreed that the Utes originally had not intended to fight. The warriors who took part in the Battle of Milk River were not punished, but twelve warriors deemed responsible for the death of the agency employees and the kidnapping of the women were charged with murder and other crimes.

Following the Ute War, however, the tribe was forced to cede most of its remaining lands in Colorado. The Northern Utes were deposited on a new, much smaller reservation in eastern Utah, while the southern bands at the Los Pinos Agency were to receive allotted lands in severalty along the Gunnison and La Plata rivers. Ouray died in 1880 and many of these promised allotments were not made. The Uncompahgre Utes and other followers of Ouray were then removed to another new reserva-

tion in Utah. The remaining Southern Utes were confined on small reservations in far southern Colorado, just north of the New Mexico border.

In retrospect, the misunderstandings, blunders, and mistakes of the Ute War seem almost like a tragicomedy—except that the Utes were hardly left laughing. Colorado's political pressure to remove the Utes to Indian Territory was hardly unique, but the appointment of the eccentric and bigoted Nathan Meeker as Ute agent was so ill advised it stands as a testimonial to the short-sightedness of both the Indian Bureau and the spoils system during the Gilded Age. Moreover, the military's alienation from the Indian Bureau and their initial reluctance to send military support to Meeker also reflects how far apart these two branches of government had become in their approach to Indian affairs during this period. In addition, Thornburgh's and Payne's failure to take the offensive, even when their troops outnumbered their enemies, hardly exemplified the aggressive military leadership that Sherman, Sheridan, and others expected. But the big losers were the Utes. Despite Ouray's efforts, most of their remaining lands in Colorado passed into the hands of the Americans.

THE APACHES, 1865–1886

The final chapter in the Apaches' defense of their homeland, while also tragic, was of longer duration. Although Carleton's campaigns had forced peace on the Navajos, it had not quelled the Apaches. During the late 1860s Apache war parties struck repeatedly at ranches and settlements across the American Southwest and in northern Mexico. Federal troops seemed incapable of stopping the raids. Most troopers, former residents from eastern states, considered their new posting in the Southwest as an "exile in Hell" and had no stomach for prolonged desert campaigning. By 1870 raiding had spread to the Yavapais and Walapais, people of mixed Apache-Mohave-Quechan ancestry who occupied the lower Colorado River Valley, and settlers in Arizona clamored for action.

Angered by the military's inaction, the "good people of Tucson" took matters in their own hands. On April 30, 1871, a mob of about 150 citizens from Tucson, including Anglos, Hispanics, and To-hono O'odhams (Papagos) attacked a sleeping village of Tonto Apaches led by Eskiminzin at Camp Grant, a small post on the San Pedro River. Ironically, Eskiminzin's people had remained at peace and were one of the few Apache rancherias that had attempted to farm, which made them more sedentary and more vulnerable to retribution. The onslaught was particularly vicious. Over 100 Apaches were killed, some raped then literally torn to pieces, and 29 children were seized and later forced into servitude. When federal troops brought charges against those responsible for the massacre, the accused were tried and promptly exonerated by juries of their peers.

The Camp Grant Massacre had important ramifications for Indian policy in the region. Shocked by the brutality, President Grant replaced General George Stoneman, the ineffectual military commander of the territory, with Lieutenant Colonel George Crook, fresh from his campaign against the Paiutes in Oregon. Still committed to his Peace Policy, Grant also dispatched Vincent Colyer, a civilian, and General Oliver Howard, who later would pursue Chief Joseph and the Nez Percés, to persuade the Apaches to resettle on new reservations near military posts, where they supposedly could be protected. Many Apache leaders met with Colyer and Howard during the winter and spring of 1872 and agreed to settle on the reservations, but Cochise and the Chiricahuas refused. In response, during September 1872 Howard personally journeyed to the Dragoon Mountains, spent eleven days with Cochise, and persuaded him to accept a new reservation in southeastern Arizona, just north of the Mexican border. Meanwhile additional reservations were established for other Apaches and Yavapais: Warm Springs in southwestern New Mexico; San Carlos in eastern Arizona; and smaller reservations at Camp Verde on the Verde River and at Date Creek, southwest of the Weaver Mountains. The Apaches and Yavapais settled down on the reservations, drew rations, and supposedly "set their feet on the white man's road."

It was a short journey. Apache political structure was so fluid that few chiefs maintained much control over their followers, and even Cochise admitted that his young men often "ran wild like winter horses." Bored by reservation life, warriors slipped away from the reservations seeking excitement, but in the process they took property and people's lives. Angered by the raids, in December 1872, Crook dispatched troops guided by friendly Apache scouts into the rugged Mogollon Rim–Tonto Basin country of east-central Arizona, where they killed about 75 fugitive Yavapais at Skull Cave. In March 1873 Crook's troops attacked "hostile" Apaches at Turret Creek, then pursued other Apaches across the Tonto Basin until most either surrendered or slipped back onto their reservations. By late summer the campaign had ended. Most of central Arizona was again (at least temporarily) at peace.

Things were more hectic along the Mexican border. The southern boundary of the Chiricahua reservation coincided with the U.S.-Mexican border, and although the Chiricahuas ceased their raids in Arizona, they turned south into Sonora and Chihuahua. Officials in Mexico complained, but Crook and white Arizonans, grateful that Apache hostility was channeled in another direction, did little to prevent the attacks. Then things changed. In 1874 Cochise died, and his sons Taza and Nachez exerted less effective leadership. One year later Crook was transferred to the northern Plains, and his successor, General August Kautz, quarreled incessantly with Tom Jeffords, the Chiricahua Indian agent (who had exercised considerable influence with Cochise), and with John Clum, the agent at San Carlos. Moreover, attempting to reduce "Indian expenses," officials decided to consolidate almost all the western Apaches, including the Chiricahuas at San Carlos, onto Clum's already crowded agency.

The plan proved disastrous. Some Warm Springs (Mimbrenos) and Chiricahuas accepted the government's decision, but others refused. Led by Juh and Geronimo, they fled south to the Sierra Madre Mountains in Mexico. Meanwhile, the disparate Apache bands and Yavapais now settled at San Carlos quarreled among themselves, and Clum, supported by his "Indian Police," was hard-pressed to keep the peace. Geronimo was captured in New Mexico and returned to San Carlos, but then Victorio, a Mimbreno leader, led a large party of his people off the reservation. Frustrated, Clum resigned from his post and moved to Tombstone, where he became the editor of the *Tombstone Epitaph*.

Victorio and his followers first returned to the Warm Springs and Mescalero reservations in New Mexico, but in September 1879 they bolted the Mescalero Reservation and raided across far west Texas, southern New Mexico, and Chihuahua, slipping back and forth across the Mexican border with impunity. In February, federal officials accused the Mescaleros of assisting Victorio and disarmed them, but the action only forced formerly peaceful Mescalero warriors into Victorio's camp.

Throughout the spring and summer of 1880 Victorio and his followers, now augmented by dissidents from San Carlos, skipped back and forth across the U.S.-Mexican border, skirmishing with troops from both countries. In October, however, Mexican troops surprised the "hostiles" near the Tres Castillos Mountains in Chihuahua, killing sixty warriors and eighteen women and children. Among the dead was Victorio, slain by a Tarahumara Indian serving with the Mexican army.

Geronimo

Victorio's mantle passed to Geronimo. During 1880 Geronimo had remained at San Carlos, where living conditions continued to deteriorate. Following Clum's resignation, the agency was rife with corruption and rations often were delayed, reduced, or stolen. The Apaches' attempts at farming were half-hearted at best, but conditions on the reservation were not conducive to agriculture. Meanwhile communities of farmers and miners emerged near the reservation's borders, and these non-Indian Arizonans intruded onto reservation lands. In addition, in 1881 Nakaidoklini, a medicine man from the former White Mountain Agency, began to preach a new doctrine promising to raise the dead and cleanse the land of white people. On August 30, 1881, when troops arrived at Nakaidoklini's village and arrested the medicine man, a skirmish ensued. Apache scouts accompanying the troops mutinied, joined with their kinsmen, and killed five soldiers. In the aftermath, the government tried and hanged three of the Apache scouts and sent two others to Alcatraz. Alarmed by the turmoil, Geronimo, Juh, Nachez, Chato, and seventy other Apaches fled to Mexico, where they joined with Nana and other former followers of Victorio.

They spent the winter of 1881–1882 in the Sierra Madre Mountains, but in April a war party led by Geronimo, Juh, Chato, and others returned to San Carlos, raided the subagency at Fort Goodwin, recruited Loco and about two hundred Mimbrenos and Chiricahuas, then returned to Mexico. Concerned about American troops who followed in their wake, the fugitives failed to send adequate scouts in advance, and on April 30, 1882, after crossing the border, they were ambushed by Mexican infantry who killed almost eighty Apaches and captured thirty-three women and children. The remainder fled into the Sierra Madre Mountains. During the winter of 1882–1883 they raided ranches in Sonora and Chihuahua, but in March, Chato and twenty-five warriors crossed the border and again struck at settlers in Arizona and New Mexico.

In response to the Apache attacks, the government reassigned General George Crook back to Arizona. Crook promptly recruited large numbers of Apache scouts, developed a system of paid Apache informers, and petitioned both American and Mexican officials for permission to pursue the Apaches south into Mexico. In response to Chato's raid, he crossed into Sonora and attacked Chato's camp in the Sierra Madres. The Apaches suffered only nine killed, but the American army's appearance in their mountain stronghold surprised them, and they accepted Crook's invitation to negotiate. In June 1883, Loco, Nana, and over 300 of their followers returned to San Carlos with Crook. Geronimo and most of the other Apaches promised to return in the fall when all their scattered camps could be assembled.

When news reached local authorities in Arizona that Crook had allowed Geronimo to remain in Mexico, they castigated Crook as a fool, but during the winter of 1883–1884, Geronimo, Nachez, Chato, and their followers returned to the reservation. Once again Indian agents encouraged them to become farmers, but not surprisingly, most still treated the suggestions with disdain. Meanwhile, local papers in Tucson accused the army of "mollycoddling" the former "hostiles" and demanded that Geronimo be arrested for murder. Other problems also festered. Although Indian agents forbade the

PEOPLE, PLACES, AND THINGS

Lozen: Shield to Her People

When historians write of the Apache resistance in the American Southwest, they usually describe the exploits of famous war chiefs such as Cochise, Victorio, or Geronimo. Often overlooked in this focus on Apache warriors is the important role women played within the Apache communities. In addition to providing their families with the majority of the food that the tribe consumed, women often served as important "medicine people," and they contributed significantly to the Apache military resistance to Mexican and American expansion into the region.

Many women accompanied their husbands on raids or into battle, sometimes participating in the combat, but by far the most famous and influential of these Apache "women warriors" was Lozen, the younger sister of Victorio, whose athletic ability, success as a warrior, and personal "medicine" made her

Prisoners of War, 1886
Renowned among her people, Lozen was highly respected as both a healer and a warrior. She is the third woman from the right, in the second row.

a legend among the Chiricahua Apaches, both past and present. Born between 1840 and 1845, Lozen excelled at athletic contests as a child, outrunning all the boys of her age and even outwrestling many of them. She was educated by her mother and aunts in the traditional ways of Apache women, but like many other Apache girls, she also became skillful with weapons and was an excellent horsewoman. While participating in the elaborate puberty ceremonies shared by all young Apache women in her teens, she received the "Power to Find the Enemy," a clairvoyant ability to sense when tribal enemies were near or approaching and to ascertain their location. She also was revered for her medical knowledge and often was sought to heal the sick or wounded. Although she regularly assisted her sisters and aunts in the gendered tasks associated with Apache women, she rejected several suitors and never married.

Skilled with a rifle, she often accompanied her brother into warfare and unlike other Apache women sat as a valued member of his war council. Victorio admitted that "Lozen is my right hand. As strong as a man, braver than most, and cunning in strategy; Lozen is a shield to her people," while Nana, Victorio's successor, reported that "though she is a woman, there is no warrior more worthy than the sister of Victorio." Indeed, Victorio was ambushed and killed by Mexican troops in 1880 while Lozen was absent assisting a woman with a difficult childbirth. Most Chiricahuas believed that if Lozen had been with her brother, she would have sensed the enemy, and her brother and his comrades would have escaped.

During the mid-1880s Lozen rode with Geronimo and was appointed by the aging chief to negotiate his surrender with the United States. Following Geronimo's surrender, Lozen was among the large number of Apaches who were imprisoned and shipped to Florida. The only known photograph of this remarkable woman was made at Nueces,

PEOPLE, PLACES, AND THINGS

(continued)

Texas, while the Apaches were assembled beside the train carrying them into exile. Lozen is sitting behind Geronimo, the second woman from the right in the second row. She is staring directly at the camera. Undaunted to the end, Lozen died of tuberculosis at Mount Vernon Barracks in Alabama in 1889. In recent years, interest in Lozen has increased. Why? How does this interest reflect an expansion of older, more traditional methods and fields of historical inquiry?

manufacture of tizwin, a fiery beverage distilled from mescal, the Apaches (particularly the recent arrivals from Mexico) continued to brew the drink, and they periodically drank it to excess. On May 17, 1885, after a dispute over the use of tizwin, Geronimo, Nana, Chihuahua, and Nachez, accompanied by thirty-eight men and about ninety women and children, again fled from San Carlos back into Mexico.

Although the American troops whom Crook sent after them this time pursued the Apaches for six months, they failed to catch them, and Crook's superiors began to question the loyalty of his Apache scouts. In March 1886 Geronimo and the other Apache leaders met with Crook at Canon de los Embudos in Sonora. Although they again promised to surrender, and Chihuahua, Nana, and about sixty of their followers complied, at the last minute Geronimo, Nachez, twenty men, and thirteen women reneged and fled into the Sierra Madres.

Geronimo's flight sealed Crook's fate. Criticized by his superiors for not seizing Geronimo when he had the chance, Crook resigned on April 1, 1886. He was replaced by General Nelson Miles. Never short of ambition, Miles launched a full-scale military campaign. Assisted by authorities in Mexico, Miles sent 5,000 troops, 500 Apache scouts, and large numbers of civilian auxiliaries into the field against Geronimo and his thirty-six followers. Miles's efforts were strongly supported by local businessmen in Arizona and New Mexico who envisioned Miles's campaign as an opportunity to profit from the sale of livestock, fodder, and other supplies. Ironically, it was also supported by local livestock dealers who previously had purchased ("no questions asked") stolen Mexican cattle from Victorio's and Geronimo's bands. Meanwhile, Miles

adopted a more ominous policy. Afraid that Chiricahua and Mimbreno people at San Carlos might again join the "hostiles," in August he loaded these Apaches in boxcars and shipped them to Florida.

The American and Mexican troops still couldn't catch Geronimo, but they forced him to move continually and by late August the Apaches were exhausted. Unaware that his kinsmen had been removed from San Carlos, Geronimo met with envoys from Miles on August 24 and agreed to surrender; however, eleven days later, when the formal capitulation took place at Skeleton Canyon in southeastern Arizona, Geronimo and his followers were informed that almost all the other Chiricahuas already were in Florida. If they wished to see their relatives, they too must go to Fort Marion, near St. Augustine.

Geronimo, Lozen (see People, Places, and Things), Nachez, and the others reluctantly agreed. In August they were loaded on a train and shipped to Florida. Ironically, the same train also carried many of the scouts who had helped the army track Geronimo. Since they also were Chiricahuas, the government no longer permitted them to live in the Southwest. The Apache warriors, both Geronimo's followers and the scouts, were initially imprisoned at Fort Marion while their families were sent to another location. Many sickened and died in the humid tropical climate, so in 1888 the men and their families were removed to Alabama. Six years later they were removed again to Fort Sill, in Indian Territory, where Geronimo died in 1909. In 1913 about two hundred Chiricahuas were returned to the Mescalero reservation in New Mexico. The remainder stayed behind in Oklahoma, where they currently are federally recognized as the "Fort Sill Apaches."

CONCLUSION:
AN IMAGE OF WARRIORS

The Apache surrender in September 1886 marked the end of the tribes' military struggle to defend their homelands and to remain free of federally imposed geographic boundaries. After 1886, at least in the contiguous forty-eight states, "Indian lands" became synonymous with "Indian reservations," and for the next quarter century most tribal people could not legally travel outside their reservation borders without the permission of Indian agents. Within the reservations themselves, individuals and communities would create their own "space" and develop strategies for coping with reservation life that enabled them to either resist or adapt to the "civilization" programs thrust on them by the federal government, but the old days, the "wild days," the days of freedom, had ended.

The tribes' military defense of Native American lands, which they had mounted against the Spanish, French, and British in the sixteenth and seventeenth centuries, had increased in the late eighteenth and early nineteenth centuries. Many of these earlier contests had been more critical in shaping the future course of the North American continent than the warfare following the Civil War.

Yet the tribes' final battles for the Great Plains and the desert Southwest received considerable press coverage and were closely followed by the American public. In the post–Civil War period most Americans lived in regions from which Native Americans already had been removed, and although they were fascinated by the warfare, it posed no immediate threat to them. In an era devoted to "progress," most Americans believed that the tribes' fate already had been sealed: Native Americans, like other "vestiges of the wilderness," were destined to be left behind. But most residents of the eastern United States, at least if they were honest with themselves, probably would have expressed a grudging admiration for these last valiant attempts by Native Americans to defend their homelands. Moreover, it was the war chiefs, those Native Americans who led the resistance, that were lionized in both the press and the dime novels of the period. Even in the twenty-first century, when asked to list the great chiefs of the past, most non-Indian Americans still mention Crazy Horse, Sitting Bull, Chief Joseph, or Geronimo.

Indeed, for most non-Indian Americans, the Plains warrior has become an icon for all tribes. Obviously, Native American people embraced a broad spectrum of cultures, but it was the last, desperate fights on the Plains that the public has remembered. Images of Plains warriors, bedecked in feathered splendor, hunting buffalo, still permeate American popular culture. It is not surprising that many Americans (and Europeans) still believe that most "Indians" lived in teepees, rode painted horses, and hunted buffalo. The stereotype of the Plains Indian lives on.

SUGGESTED READING

Ball, Eve. *Indeh: An Apache Odyssey*. Provo: Brigham Young University Press, 1980. This fascinating account of the Apache wars from the Apache perspective needs to be read in conjunction with a more traditional Western account, but the volume offers illuminating insights into the Apaches' memory of these events.

DeMallie, Raymond J., ed. *The Sixth Grandfather: Black Elk's Teachings Given to John Neihardt*. Lincoln: University of Nebraska Press, 1984. Edited by a preeminent scholar of Lakota history and culture, this volume offers excellent insights into a Lakota holy man's memories of Lakota life in the late nineteenth century.

Flores, Dan. "Bison Ecology and Bison Diplomacy: The Southern Plains from 1800 to 1850." *Journal of American History*, 78 (September 1991): 465–485. This well-written, but controversial essay argues that climatic changes, new hunting techniques, and a host of other factors already had depleted the bison herds and doomed the traditional lifestyle of the Plains tribes prior to the 1850s.

Greene, Jerome A. *Nez Percé Summer, 1977: The U.S. Army and the Nee-me-poo Crisis*. Helena: Montana Historical Society Press, 2000. A carefully researched, detailed, and well-written account of the Nez Percés' battles with the government and their flight toward Canada.

Haley, James. *The Buffalo War.* New York: Doubleday, 1976.   A popular but generally accurate account of the southern Plains tribes' participation in the Red River War of 1871–1874.

Hassrick, Royal B. *The Sioux: Life and Customs of a Warrior Society.* Norman: University of Oklahoma Press, 1964.   This older summary of Lakota culture offers a general discussion of Lakota life in the middle decades of the nineteenth century.

Murray, Keith. *The Modocs and Their War.* Norman: University of Oklahoma Press, 1959.   This volume remains the best scholarly study of these events.

Sandoz, Mari. *Cheyenne Autumn.* New York: Hastings House, 1953.   This gracefully written account of the Cheyennes' flight from Oklahoma and their return to the northern Plains empathetically portrays their hardships and struggles during the mid-1870s.

———. *Crazy Horse, the Strange Man of the Oglalas: A Biography.* New York: Alfred A. Knopf, 1942.   Although written over half a century ago, this account of Crazy Horse remains the best biography of this important Lakota leader.

Sprague, Marshall. *Massacre: The Tragedy at White River.* Lincoln: University of Nebraska Press, 1980.   This volume contains the best discussion of the Ute War of 1879.

Sweeney, Edwin R. *Cochise: Chiricahua Apache Chief.* Tucson: University of Arizona Press, 1991. This account of Cochise and the Chiricahua Apaches provides a detailed discussion of Apache history between 1850 and 1874.

Thrapp, Dan. *The Conquest of Apacheria.* Norman: University of Oklahoma Press, 1967.   Although this volume discusses Apache history in the decades following the Civil War, its primary focus is the interactions of Apaches and non-Indians in the 1870s and 1880s, particularly the Geronimo campaigns.

Utley, M. Robert. *Frontier Regulars: The United States Army and the Indian, 1866–1890.* New York: Macmillan Publishing Co., 1973.   Although written from the military's perspective, this is an excellent, detailed account of the interaction between the army and tribal people during these years.

———. *The Lance and the Shield: The Life and Times of Sitting Bull.* New York: Random House, 1994.   The most detailed biography of Sitting Bull and his times, this volume contains a good account of the Battle of the Little Big Horn.

"Kill the Indian, Save the Man": Survival in a Shrinking Homeland, 1878–1900

In the fall of 1879, an eleven-year-old Indian boy called Plenty Kill was playing near the Rosebud Agency in Dakota Territory. The agency was the home of Spotted Tail and other friendly Brulé Lakota chiefs. Noticing a crowd gathered around one of the buildings in the government compound, Plenty Kill drifted closer; a white man held out a stick of candy and beckoned him to approach. The white man explained that he was offering Lakota children a chance to go to a new school in Pennsylvania to "learn the ways of the white man." The boy later recalled that "he did not trust the white people very strongly," but he was attracted to the idea of visiting his enemy's country. He remembered thinking that "this chance to go East would prove that I was brave . . . So I said, 'Yes, I will go.'"

The next day Plenty Kill and a group of children about his own age piled into a wagon and began their journey to Carlisle, Pennsylvania. "Many of the little Indian boys and girls were afraid of the white people," Plenty Kill later wrote. The group journeyed on until, finally, in the middle of the night nearly a week after leaving home, they were told they had arrived at their destination, the newly es-

tablished Indian Industrial Training School, housed in what had originally been an army barracks. "Soon we came to a big gate in a great high wall," Plenty Kill reported. "The gate was locked, but after quite a long wait it was unlocked and we marched in through it. I was the first boy inside." These steps changed the course of Plenty Kill's life. When he returned home from Carlisle he had a new name—Luther Standing Bear—and could speak a new language. He was determined to use his new knowledge both to support himself and to help other young people adapt to the thousands of newcomers who were now arriving on the borders of his homeland.

ASSAULTS ON INDIANNESS

In the years between the 1877 murder of Crazy Horse at Fort Robinson, Nebraska, and the inauguration of Theodore Roosevelt as president of the United States in 1901, an unprecedented number of Native Americans would follow Plenty Kill's

The Carlisle Indian Industrial School When the Carlisle opened in 1879 it enrolled about 100 students drawn primarily from the Sioux reservations of the northern plains. By 1884, the year this picture was taken, the student body was larger and more diverse, but school administrators tried hard to force everyone into a common mold of "civilization."

journey to the land of his enemies. Some would travel voluntarily like Plenty Kill in search of new skills; others would be forced along this road and would reject the new customs they encountered. Still others would experience the young boy's odyssey in reverse as their communities attracted United States citizens who traveled to Indians' doorsteps in search of a new life.

Plenty Kill lived in an age of accelerating movement and migration. Just as the young boy was heading east, transcontinental rail lines were pushing west, carrying people and produce to places that had long been part of a distant "Indian country." In the decade after Plenty Kill traveled to Pennsylvania, isolated lands near what would soon become Gallup, New Mexico; Tacoma, Washington; Billings, Montana; and Ashland, Wisconsin, on the southern shore of Lake Superior, heard the whistle of steam locomotives for the first time. During the decades that followed, the numbers of new settlers on Indian lands exploded. Areas where the vast majority of Indian people lived—Indian Terri-

tory; the north woods of Minnesota, Wisconsin, and Michigan; the Northwest Coast; the Northern Plains; and the arid Southwest—lost their American Indian majorities and became majority-white territories. The change was most dramatic along the Missouri River and in the Northwest. There a tidal wave of new farmers, ranchers, miners, and merchants at the end of the century raised the population by 400 percent (from 447,000 to 2,014,000) and transformed the region from a thinly settled territory to the sovereign states of North and South Dakota, Washington, Idaho, Utah, Wyoming, and Montana.

As tens of thousands of Indians found their traditional territories surrounded by growing crowds of Americans, all of them were pressed to change their way of life. The results of that pressure varied widely. Some encounters—such as Crazy Horse's surrender at Fort Robinson—produced betrayal and death. For others, the last quarter of this tragic century caused intense but quiet suffering; for Plenty Kill and his more curious contemporaries, the 1880s and 1890s were decades during which they searched the white man's world for familiar values or caring people who might support their struggle to survive in this new world.

Indian people found the disruptions of these decades particularly difficult because they occurred at a time when America's white majority had concluded that there was no place for Native lifeways in an up-to-date country. Government officials, politicians, settlers, and educators insisted that the American Indians could only survive if they abandoned their old customs and followed the white man's road. Sometimes this insistence was practical—white settlers were transforming hunting lands into cultivated farms—and sometimes it was based on the majority's faith in the superiority of "civilization" over "backward" habits. One of the most outspoken advocates of both views was the Carlisle school's Captain Richard Henry Pratt—the man who beckoned to Plenty Kill in 1879—who urged the teachers at his school to attack all signs of Indianness in their students. He told them, "Kill the Indian and save the man." Wherever they traveled in the late nineteenth century, Native Americans encountered different versions of this same dispiriting message.

Capturing Indian Land and Resources

In the wake of the western Indian wars, American leaders were determined to "develop" the newly pacified tribal homelands. The "frontier"—an area of sparse Euro-American settlement still largely Indian in population and character—held an allure for easterners that was not satisfied by military victory alone. Some Americans saw the West as a source of future wealth, others saw it as a solution to urban crowding and crime, but all agreed that the nation's destiny lay in the "Indian country"; that territory could not be allowed to remain beyond the reach of "civilization."

Officials at the Indian Office and on Capitol Hill agreed that the best method for bringing Indian lands within the orbit of "civilization" would be to convert them to farms through a program known as "allotment." Under this program, federal officials would subdivide tribal lands into parcels that would then be distributed ("allotted") to individual tribal members.

Popular opinion among whites strongly supported allotment. To most Americans, it seemed obvious that owning and cultivating a plot of ground enabled citizens to escape the restrictions of class and ethnic background and become independent citizens. This faith recalled Thomas Jefferson's vision of America as a republic of yeoman farmers, but it also echoed more recent movements in support of homesteading and agrarian reform. Most observers also believed that the allotment of reservations into individual homesteads would instill new habits and inspire new social roles among Indians. They imagined that Indian men would plow and cultivate their land—thereby separating themselves from their tribes—and that Indian women would busy themselves with housekeeping and childrearing, adopting the majority's definitions of domesticity and proper women's roles. The new policy also seemed to insure that Indians would follow God's command to mankind to "earn their living by the sweat of their brow."

Scientists also weighed in to support the allotment concept. Most prominent among these was Lewis Henry Morgan, a student of Indian cultures who has often been called "the father of American anthropology." In *Ancient Society*, published in 1877, Morgan offered a universal theory of human progress: all peoples pass through the same stages of savagery, barbarism, and civilization. "Savages" did not own property, Morgan observed; "barbarians" owned property communally; only "civilized" people embraced individually held private property. When communities changed their practice of land ownership, they moved upward to a higher stage of culture. "It is impossible to overestimate the importance of property in the civilization of mankind," Morgan wrote. While Morgan urged caution in the application of allotment, he was convinced that individual land ownership was the only bridge between "barbarism" and "civilization."

Because the division of reservations into homesteads promised to break the power of the tribes and open Native American resources for white settlement, politicians were quick to support allotment. Representatives in Congress saw, for example, that giving a tribe such as the Crows of Montana (a group with no more than three thousand members in the 1880s) title to 200 acres each of their 5-million-acre reserve would require the allocation of only 600,000 acres of reservation land.

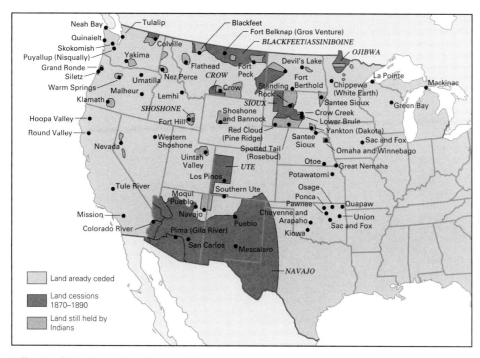

Indian Land Cessions and Major Agencies: 1870–1890

The "extra" 4.4 million acres of Crow property might then be declared "surplus" and opened for "development" by whites. Schemes of this sort had been proposed to dispossess tribes in the East and Midwest as early as the seventeenth century, but the additional support of reformers like Captain Pratt and scholars like Lewis Henry Morgan in the 1880s broadened allotment's appeal so much that policymakers began to consider it as *the* solution to the "Indian problem."

Massachusetts senator Henry Dawes spent most of the 1880s working for passage of a national allotment law. A stalwart Republican through both the Civil War and Reconstruction eras, Dawes understood that federal action was essential to the protection of minority populations. But Dawes was also aware that any new policy would require broad public support. Dawes and his allies won that support by proposing that allotment be applied nationally but implemented gradually. He suggested that reservations would be surveyed and allotted at "the President's discretion" rather than

all at once (tribes in Indian Territory and New York were declared exempt as special cases). Second, Dawes promised that Indians could choose their own homesteads. Heads of households would select 160-acre homesteads, while spouses and other adult family members would receive 80 acres each and children would get 40 acres. Only after refusing to choose an allotment for two years would individuals be assigned a farm. (Dawes used 160 acres as the portion for each adult male since that had been the standard homestead envisioned by eastern farmers when the survey of public lands was initiated at the beginning of the nineteenth century.) Third, Senator Dawes proposed that "surplus" lands—the tribal territory left over after all allotments had been made—would be purchased by federal authorities only if a sale was negotiated and ratified by tribal leaders. Finally, Dawes promised that all "allottees" (people receiving homesteads) would become American citizens.

Despite widespread support for allotment among whites and scattered support among small

At the same time that railroads and homesteaders were eager to claim land in Indian Territory, Indian families like these were attempting to adapt to a new life of farming and cattle ranching. Here a Southern Cheyenne man named Stump Horn is shown camped in what later became Oklahoma. While dressed in "civilized" attire, Stump Horn and his family still transport their goods with the traditional travois.

tribes who saw the proposal as a way to secure their land titles, most Indian leaders opposed Senator Dawes's proposal. The best-organized resistance arose in Indian Territory where prairie and Plains tribes had been resettled in the 1850s and 1860s on lands to the west of those held by the "Five Civilized Tribes" who had been forced out of the Southeast in the 1820s and 1830s. Both the "civilized" former eastern Indians and their new neighbors—Kiowas, Comanches, Southern Cheyennes, Osages, Pawnees, and others—believed that wholesale allotment would mean the end of their community existence. In March 1886, delegates from thirteen Indian Territory tribes gathered at Eufaula, capital of the Creek Nation, to organize their opposition. The convention adopted a "compact" that pledged uniform opposition to Senator Dawes's proposals and promised that "no Nation . . . shall, without the consent of all the other parties, cede or in any manner alienate to the United

States any part of their present territory." The Eufaula meeting sent copies of its resolutions to Washington, D.C., but without any elected representatives in the capital, the Indians were ignored. In February 1887 Congress approved the Dawes General Allotment Act, a measure that contained all the elements that the Massachusetts senator had proposed.

U.S. officials also ignored protests from individual tribes. Chief Jake of the Caddos and Standing Bear of the Kiowas, two leaders who had participated in the Eufaula conference, continued to voice their opposition once the Dawes Act became law. Over the objections of their agent, the two men traveled to Washington, D.C., to attempt to persuade Indian Commissioner John Atkins to oppose any new allotments. Jake later recalled that he told the commissioner that allotment would undermine the progress his community was making: "When my people are just now beginning to realize and accept

the benefits of knowledge how to work you are attempting to change our customs and entail ruin on
my people." Atkins turned these pleas aside and the
Kiowa and Caddo allotments moved forward.

Pressing for Land Sales

Despite the protests of Indian leaders, the evils of
the Dawes Act were not immediately obvious.
Dawes had promised that the law would be applied
slowly. Commissioner Atkins agreed that "too
great haste in the [allotment] matter should be
avoided." The commissioner initially restricted the
new policy to two dozen reservations, but within a
few years officials in Washington realized they
could not resist the pressure exerted by local settlers. Merchants, politicians, and land speculators
in the towns bordering western reservations insisted
that fragile settler communities required tribal land
for survival. Usually supported by railroad companies eager for new routes and new customers,
local "boosters" in the Northwest, the Plains, the
northern Great Lakes, and the states surrounding
Indian Territory reminded all who would listen that
allotment would open tens of thousands of acres
to white homesteaders. Allotment would also start
the process of making individual Indian homesteads part of the local tax base. (The Dawes Act
protected allotments from taxation for twenty-five
years.) As their settlements grew, white boosters
exerted growing political clout in Washington.
Congress had little choice but to accommodate
their wishes.

During the decade of the 1880s, the federal government negotiated land sale agreements calling for
a total cession of over 70 million acres of tribal
land with the Colorado Utes; the Minnesota Ojibwes; the western Sioux; the Crows, Blackfeet, and
Assiniboines of Montana; the interior Salish communities of eastern Washington; the Bannocks and
Shoshones of Idaho; and the Cherokees in Indian
Territory. For the Utes, land sales meant a retreat
to two relatively small reserves along the border
separating Colorado from New Mexico and the removal of several bands to Utah, thus ending a subsistence cycle that had sustained them for centuries.
The Crows' 1884 land sale confined them to the
prairies and grasslands along the Big Horn and Little Big Horn rivers and separated them from the

Rocky Mountain hunting grounds that had long
been an integral part of their annual movements.
For the Blackfeet, Gros Ventres, and Assiniboines,
the sale of 17.5 million acres of tribal lands in
northern Montana drove them from their now-
empty buffalo grounds along the upper Missouri
and forced them to settle near government agencies at Browning, Fort Belknap, and Fort Peck. Similar transactions created the Fort Hall and Colville
reserves in Idaho and Washington territories.

The most dramatic land cession took place in
Dakota Territory, where a relentless campaign by
white business interests eventually succeeded in
splintering the "Great Sioux Reserve" (created by
the 1868 Fort Laramie Treaty and running from
the Missouri River to the Black Hills) into five separate reservations. The dispossession of the Sioux
actually came in two stages. First, in the aftermath
of the Native American victory at the Little Big
Horn in 1876, Congress demanded the cession of
all lands west of the 103rd meridian (an area that
included the Black Hills). Second, territorial leaders in the 1880s pressed for the breakup of the remaining tribal lands. Sioux opposition continued,
but arguments in favor of expansion emanated
from struggling towns like Rapid City, Pierre, and
Bismarck. Together with the eagerness of regional
rail lines such as the Chicago and Northwestern
and the Chicago, Milwaukee and St. Paul, this desire for expansion worked relentlessly against the
Sioux.

Fittingly, in 1889, the year of South Dakota's
statehood, Major General George Crook—whose
forces had been turned back by the Sioux in 1876
at the Battle of the Rosebud—managed to make
enough threats and host enough feasts to win the
support of most tribal leaders for the sale of 9 million acres of Sioux land for $3 million. With In-
dian leaders like John Grass at the Standing Rock
Agency and American Horse at Pine Ridge grudgingly endorsing the agreement, Crook collected the
necessary signatures. When the argument reached
Congress, legislators ignored the general's promise
that the United States would support the tribes financially while they shifted from hunting to agriculture and ratified the pact while simultaneously
reducing appropriations for agency rations. (Legislators argued that Indians were better off fend-
ing for themselves than receiving food from the
authorities.) In the fall of 1889 homesteaders began

filing claims on the former Sioux lands as six new senators representing the states of Montana, North Dakota, and South Dakota prepared to take office. The "civilization" of the West was underway.

The Rush for Timber

In the Great Lakes, settlers eager to gain control of Indian forests pressed local tribes to alter their traditional dependence on fishing, hunting, and farming. Ojibwe communities that had ceded large tracts of land in the 1830s and 1840s in exchange for assurances that they would continue to hunt and fish outside their new reservation boundaries suddenly found that a wave of settlers had arrived with the new rail lines. The newcomers were inspired by dreams of delivering mountains of pine boards, fish, and other commodities to the rapidly expanding lakefront cities of Chicago, Milwaukee, Cleveland, and Detroit. Pressure from these settlers produced allotment drives on several reservations and the subsequent reduction of fishing and hunting grounds. In Minnesota, the Nelson Act (1889) forced most Ojibwe people to choose between relocating to the relatively large White Earth reservation in the northwestern part of the state or taking allotments near their former reservations. While many of the residents of the Mille Lacs, Red Lake, and Leech Lake Ojibwe reserves refused to move to White Earth, more than one thousand Ojibwe people ultimately chose to relocate.

Lumbermen were not particularly concerned with acquiring title to tribal land. Their goal was gaining access to the virgin pine that covered the northern tier of Michigan, Wisconsin, and Minnesota. They were successful first in 1882 when Secretary of the Interior Henry Teller permitted tribal members to sell timber on their property to non-Indian buyers. As a result, battalions of small timber-cutting outfits invaded the north woods and contracted with destitute Ojibwe landowners to take their pine forests off their hands. In 1888, 731 of these contracts were approved, funneling over 190 million board feet into the populous cities at the southern end of the lakes.

New settlements in the northern Great Lakes threatened other aspects of the native subsistence economy. Fewer trees meant smaller harvests of maple sugar; floating logs and steamer traffic on the region's lakes and waterways meant fewer stands of wild rice; and rising populations meant increased competition for fish, deer, and other resources. In addition to attracting farmers and lumbermen, the north woods also became a destination for summer visitors from "down below," who disembarked at steamship ports at Bayfield and Green Bay, Wisconsin, and Mackinac and Marquette, Michigan, and set out in search of the region's unspoiled lakes and streams. State officials paid scant attention to the tribes' claims to jurisdiction over water, fish, and wild rice, expecting the Indians to "progress" by becoming wage laborers in the region's new industrial and tourist economy.

Commercial Fishing Displaces Northwest Indians

In the Great Lakes, assaults on virgin pine forests often obscured the loss of game, but in the Pacific Northwest, the settlers' threat to the annual salmon harvest was a central feature of the white invasion. Intensive commercial fishing began in Washington and Oregon with the construction of the first salmon canneries on the Columbia River in 1866 and in Puget Sound in 1877. The canneries increased the annual salmon harvest, but Native fishers were not affected until well into the 1880s when improvements in salmon canning techniques and the arrival of the Northern Pacific Railroad vastly increased production and revolutionized the industry.

In 1885 the lone cannery on Puget Sound produced 12,000 cases of salmon, most of it caught by Native fishers and sold in the Northwest. By 1900 nineteen canneries on the sound produced nearly 500,000 cases of salmon, most of it caught by non-Indians and all of it destined for markets outside the Northwest. This level of output relied on non-Indians who introduced fish traps (permanently installed underwater fences that guided fish into nets) and purse seines (large bottom nets which scooped fish up into a bag) into Puget Sound. These techniques were mirrored on the Columbia River, where permanent fish wheels snatched millions of migrating salmon from the water, channeling them to nearby canneries.

Puget Sound Indian leaders, seeing that the advent of industrial fishing threatened their livelihood, urged the Office of Indian Affairs to intervene to limit the reach of non-Indian businesses. The Lummis, who fished along the Canadian border, declared in 1894 that they "were willing to have (the settlers) share with us," but noted that outsiders "have yearly made . . . obstructions to prevent our catching fish." When the Indian Office failed to act, the tribe hired its own attorneys to press its case. Federal authorities ultimately filed a lawsuit on the tribe's behalf, but the local courts saw little merit in the Lummi position. Claiming that there was adequate salmon for everyone and that the 1855 treaty with the tribe guaranteed only an "equal," not a "special" right to fish, the justices refused to intervene. It would be nearly a century before the Puget Sound tribes would gain another full hearing for their complaints.

Breaking Up Indian Territory

The frenzy for western "development" also reached Indian Territory, the area set aside in the 1830s as a permanent refuge for eastern tribes who had been evicted from their homelands in Georgia, Florida, Alabama, and Mississippi. Following the Civil War these groups had ceded large portions of their original Indian Territory land grants to the United States for the resettlement of smaller groups from the prairies of Kansas and Nebraska and the southern plains of Texas and Colorado. By 1885 only two areas in Indian Territory remained unoccupied by Indians: a centrally located two-million-acre territory and a long, western panhandle; both of these were officially the property of the Cherokees.

In 1889 Congress, acting over the objections of Cherokee leaders and other Indian Territory tribes, opened the first of these "unassigned" tribal lands to white homesteading. On April 22 of that year the two-million-acre central section previously claimed by the Cherokees was opened for settlement in the first of the famous Oklahoma land runs. In one day more than 50,000 settlers entered these previously closed lands and filed claims for homesteads. As the Indian leaders well knew, the arrival of white homesteaders was only the beginning of an attack on their governments and communities. In 1890 Congress recognized the white

settlers on reservation lands in Indian Territory as citizens of the new "Territory of Oklahoma."

As was the case in other parts of the West, opening one area for settlement simply inflamed the demand for Indian land. Oklahoma Territory's new white settlers pressed for the opening of other "unoccupied" lands as well as the rapid allotment of all tribal areas. In 1890 a congressional commission headed by former Michigan governor David H. Jerome negotiated eleven separate allotment agreements with the resettled tribes in the western half of the territory. These agreements brought more than fifteen million acres of "surplus" land onto the market for settlers. Working to overcome the opposition of stalwart tribal leaders like Quanah Parker of the Comanches, Jerome assured the tribes that he offered them better terms than they were likely to receive in the future. Jerome also negotiated the purchase of the Cherokees' six-million-acre western panhandle, setting the stage for the territory's largest land rush. On September 16, 1893, more than 100,000 new settlers surged onto these former grazing lands, transferring the entire tract from tribal to settler ownership in a single day.

With the western portion of the former Indian Territory coming quickly under the sway of Oklahoma Territory's growing population of white settlers, attention now shifted to the lands along the Arkansas border still controlled by the Five Civilized Tribes. Throughout the 1890s, local boosters and their congressional allies pressed the governments of these tribes to accept allotment and open their "surplus" lands to non-Indians. Commentators also complained that the Cherokees, Creeks, Seminoles, Chickasaws, and Choctaws were unable to control their territories and that squatters and other trespassers inspired an atmosphere of lawlessness and fear in the area.

In 1893 Congress created a special commission headed by the now-retired Massachusetts Senator Henry Dawes to press its case. In 1897 Dawes and his colleagues persuaded the Choctaws and Chickasaws to agree to a plan to allot their tribal lands and to open the "surplus" to non-Indian settlement. Similar negotiations extended allotment to the Seminoles (in 1898), the Creeks (in 1901), and the Cherokees (in 1902). These negotiations were also spurred on by the passage of the Curtis Act in 1898, a law that established a timetable for the dissolution of tribal governments and set these communities firmly on the path to official extinction.

The systematic dismemberment of Indian Territory had several unique features. First, it involved more land than in any other area. While large swaths of Montana, Washington, and the Dakotas were taken from Indian hands in this period, all of Oklahoma Territory was created from tribal holdings. Second, the outspoken tribal opposition to these land sales was frequently led by attorneys and sophisticated lobbyists paid for by tribal governments as well as by land and cattle interests who leased large tracts of Indian land for pasture and opposed any reduction of their privileges. Finally, several leaders in the Five Civilized Tribes spoke out in favor of allotment. Successful Native businessmen felt confident they would continue to prosper in an expanding territory filled with industrious farmers and eager new merchants. Men like Robert Owen and Elias Cornelius Boudinot, successful Cherokee attorneys with business ties to both whites and Indians, looked forward to what they believed was a prosperous new future for the region.

Indian Lands in the East

The quest for Indian land was not confined to the newly settled territories across the Mississippi. Western assaults on tribal resources found echoes in the East during the 1870s and 1880s, as settlers and entrepreneurs engulfed tribes in New England, the Mid-Atlantic States, and the Southeast. The United States Census for 1880 reported that only 5 percent of the nation's Indians—about 11,000 people—lived east of the Mississippi. These Eastern Indians lived largely in isolated, rural enclaves that had formed in New England, New York, Maryland, and across the South in the aftermath of the American Revolution and the removals that had followed in the 1830s and 1840s.

Assaults on Native American resources in the East involved small parcels of land and received little public attention, but they had devastating results. In Massachusetts, for example, the state legislature had designated the Mashpee lands on Cape Cod an "Indian township" in 1834 and had recognized the tribe's authority over its property and local affairs. In 1869 the legislature, acting over the protests of local tribes, revoked this clas-

sification and divided the tribe's property into individual parcels. Finding themselves "allotted"— even though state authorities did not use that term—tribal members struggled to fend off wealthy Bostonians who descended on them eager to buy up potentially valuable vacation real estate. As would soon prove to be true in allotted Native American communities in the West, the allure of ready cash proved too powerful to resist; large portions of the former Mashpee homeland rapidly changed hands. By century's end, much of the tribe had been reduced to dependency, eking out a living as seasonal laborers, sailors on fishing boats, and itinerant peddlers. In 1880 Rhode Island adopted a similar allotment policy with regard to the Narragansetts, eliminating state protection for their lands. Indians in Maine, most of whom had been dispossessed of their lands earlier in the century, sought to survive as fishermen and as wage laborers in the state's remote potato fields and logging camps.

Iroquois lands in New York also came under assault. The largest Native holdings were in the traditional Seneca country west of Rochester. Beginning in 1850, both the New York and Erie and the Atlantic and Great Western railways pushed their lines through Seneca country, establishing the town of Salamanca as a major terminus and bringing new settlers and new industries into the region. White settlers and merchants often acquired the use of tribal lands through illegal leases, many of which were retroactively ratified by Congress in special legislation approved by Congress in 1875 and 1890. The advent of the railroads and the expansion of commercial agriculture into tribal areas in New York also encouraged state and local officials to press for the allotment of all Indian land in the state. Indians in New York were exempted from the provisions of the Dawes Act, but in 1889 a special committee of the state legislature, headed by Assemblyman J. S. Whipple of Salamanca, called on Congress to extend the new program to their state. "These Indian children have been kept as wards long enough," the committee declared; "they should now be educated to be men, not Indians. . . ." Effective lobbying by Iroquois leaders prevented allotment from entering New York, but the debate raged on well into the twentieth century.

Despite their losses, Native Americans east of the Mississippi frequently developed innovative ways to hold off the settlers. For example, one of the largest and most resilient Indian communities along the Atlantic coast was in Robeson County, North Carolina, where a group designated by state authorities as "free people of color" lived apart from both their white and their black neighbors. Because these Indians did not hold any communal lands and lived largely as independent farmers on the margins of white society in a relatively isolated part of the state, they received little official notice. Fiercely proud of their Native heritage, a group headed by a local minister, W. L. Moore, petitioned the state legislature for recognition as "Croatan" Indians and exemption from all of the state's new segregation laws. In 1885 the North Carolina legislature accepted this petition and permitted the Croatans to create separate public schools for their children. This Indian group (who would be designated "Lumbees" in 1953) moved quickly to found common schools throughout the county and even to institute a normal school—later recognized as Pembroke State College for Indians.

A similar sequence of events took place in other segregated states. In 1881 the Delaware legislature recognized a group of Nanticoke Indians as an "Incorporated Body" and granted them the right to send their children to their own private schools rather than to schools for African-Americans. In the early twentieth century the legislature amended this action by designating the "Incorporated Body" as the official representative of the Nanticoke Indians in Delaware. South Carolina granted similar recognition to Catawbas and other groups in that state, and in 1900 Virginia's Pamunkey and Chickahominy Indians petitioned successfully for permission to ride in the "white" sections of the newly segregated railway cars. Following the ruling, Indians carried their own identity cards to insure respect for their status.

By 1900 every major area of Indian population outside Alaska had been penetrated by rail lines and "opened" to at least the beginnings of white settlement. The southwestern homes of the Navajos, Apaches, and Pueblos—largely arid areas in New Mexico and Arizona that did not attain statehood until the twentieth century—managed to elude allotment, but even there federal officials and a steady influx of newcomers conspired to draw local Indian communities into the orbit of wage labor and the cash economy. Across the continent, the scale of the assault on Indian autonomy and

freedom became clear. Families found they could no longer travel to traditional hunting and fishing grounds, and Native farmers and ranchers came to depend on distant markets for both supplies and income. Indian people might still control the daily routine that punctuated life in their villages and camps, but the economic resources they needed to sustain their communities were being torn from their grasp.

"RAISING UP" THE INDIANS: SCHOOLS, MISSIONARIES, AND GOVERNMENT AGENTS

In the fall of 1879, at about the same time that Plenty Kill and his friends were traveling to the Carlisle school in Pennsylvania, a Ponca chief named Standing Bear and three companions embarked on a similar eastward journey. But instead of traveling as students, ready to submit to the white man's lessons, Standing Bear and his companions embarked on a well-planned speaking tour. They arrived in Chicago, New York, and Boston as practiced advocates, eager to teach white audiences about the evils of the government's heavy-handed Indian policies.

Standing Bear had come to national attention the previous winter when he and his family left their reservation in Indian Territory and traveled north toward their traditional homeland in eastern Nebraska. The Poncas had been forced south in 1877 after their lands were inadvertently included in another tribe's reservation. The Indian Office hoped their new home would provide them with a chance to develop productive farms. Conditions in Indian Territory were intolerable, however, and the Ponca leader defied federal authorities and returned to Nebraska. To this point the chief's story sadly paralleled the experiences of removed tribes all across the West. Plateau tribes had been consolidated on the Umatilla reservation in the 1850s, the Navajos had been forced from their homelands in 1864, and Chief Joseph's Nez Percés had been one of many tribes that had been transported from their homeland to Indian Territory in 1877. But the Ponca's "plight" took an unexpected turn in April 1879, when Standing Bear filed a habeas corpus

Advocates for Their People Francis and Susette LaFlesche were outspoken Indian Office critics when they posed for this picture during the 1879 Standing Bear tour. Articulate and well-educated, they spoke feelingly about the government's stifling bureaucracy and high-handed methods.

suit in U.S. District Court. The chief argued that because he had not been charged with any crime, the court should order his release. On May 12, 1879, Judge Elmer Dundy stunned the Indian Office by declaring that the Indian Office had no power to hold Standing Bear against his will. "I cannot think that any such arbitrary authority exists in this country," Dundy declared.

Alerted by Omaha *Daily Herald* reporter Thomas Henry Tibbles, newspapers across the country published sympathetic stories about the Ponca chief. Standing Bear became an instant symbol of all the Indians who had been victimized by the military and heavy-handed government agents. According to Tibbles, the Ponca leader was also eager to abandon reservation life and enter American society as a self-sufficient individual. In the fall of 1879 audiences in Boston, New York, and Philadelphia cheered when Standing Bear cried, "We are bound, we ask you to set us free." Standing Bear's tour reached a mass audience. Mainstream religious leaders, former abolitionists, women's rights advocates, civil service activists, temperance advocates, and other government reformers could attach their larger concerns to "the Indian question." Civil service reformers focused on the evils of patronage in the Indian Office, while others stressed the goals of racial equality and moral uplift. In Boston, for example, a children's book author named Helen Hunt Jackson wrote to a former abolitionist friend after seeing the Ponca speaker, "I think I feel as you must have in the old abolition days." In Philadelphia, Amelia Stone Quinton, an official of the Women's Christian Temperance Union, began circulating petitions and speaking out on behalf of Indian causes.

In the wake of Standing Bear's tour, new "Indian reform" groups began to come forward. Middle class white women led the effort. In 1880 Amelia Stone Quinton established the Indian Treaty Keeping and Protective Association (later renamed the Women's National Indian Association) and in the following year Helen Hunt Jackson published *A Century of Dishonor*, a stinging manifesto that catalogued the American government's mistreatment of several major tribes: the Delawares, the Sioux, the Cheyennes, the Cherokees, and, of course, the Poncas. Bound with a special cover with this epigraph printed in red—"Look upon your hands! They are stained with the blood of your relation"— the book was delivered to every member of Congress. Jackson's book charged that America's treatment of Native Americans "convicts us, as a nation, not only of having outraged the principles of justice; . . . but of having made ourselves liable to all punishments which follow upon such sins."

Finally, the Indian Rights Association, founded in 1882 by Philadelphia activists Henry Pancoast and Herbert Welsh, offered itself as a general coordinating body for the Indian reformers. Financed by Welsh with the help of department store magnate John Wannamaker (who was also the publisher of the Philadelphia *Inquirer*), the IRA quickly established chapters in several eastern cities and hired a full-time Washington lobbyist. The organization also published a steady stream of reports on such subjects as the dissolution of Indian Territory and the future of Indian education.

Indian Education

The reformers supported allotment and a general reduction in Indian landholding, but in keeping with the religious motivation of many members, their great passion was a program to "raise up" Indian people to Christianity and American citizenship. The principal method of accomplishing that goal was education. In 1877, the year of Crazy Horse's death, the entire federal budget for Indian education was $30,000. Few Native American children were educated in school; most continued to live with their families and to be taught as their parents had been. By 1900 annual appropriations for education rose to nearly $3 million and nearly two-thirds of Native American children were attending classes. The result was a permanent change in Native life.

Richard Henry Pratt, the man who enticed Plenty Kill and his Sioux playmates to enroll at Carlisle in 1879, was one of the principal architects of this new system. He had first attracted public notice in 1877 at the end of the Red River war in Indian Territory when he escorted seventy-two Kiowa, Comanche, and Southern Cheyenne warriors to prison in Florida. Charged with overseeing their punishment, Pratt drew on his experience as a commander of African-American troops in the Civil War. He decided to organize a school and to instruct his prisoners to read and write. When his lessons appeared to succeed, the young officer began to lobby his superiors, arguing that education could provide the answer to the Indian's predicament. Civilization had "reached the heart of the continent," Pratt declared, and this change required that Native people prepare for the future: "the dawn of a great emergency has opened upon the Indian."

In April 1878 the Indian Office permitted Pratt to enroll his prisoners in Hampton Institute in Hampton, Virginia, a private coeducational school for African-Americans that had opened at the close of the Civil War. A few months after his arrival there, the captain learned that the Indian Office would support fifty more students (girls as well as boys) if they could be recruited in time for the fall term. Pratt was eager to bring women into his educational experiment on the theory that educated married couples would be the most effective agents for change in future reservation communities. Pratt quickly filled his quota (although only nine of the first forty-nine students were female) and the school year got underway.

The Hampton experiment proved successful—so successful that Indians would continue to attend the school until 1923—but Pratt wanted his own institution and he began searching for support in Washington. Through his friendship with First Lady Lucy Ware Webb Hayes, he succeeded in bringing the president and the secretary of the interior to Hampton's 1879 commencement, and he peppered legislators with letters and copies of sympathetic news stories. Pratt's lobbying paid off. The War Department offered him the use of an abandoned army barracks in Carlisle, Pennsylvania, and Secretary of the Interior Carl Schurz invited him to recruit up to 150 Indian children and bring them east to attend classes.

The Carlisle Indian Industrial Training School opened in the fall of 1879. Plenty Kill and his band of Sioux children were soon joined by groups of Navajos, Ojibwes, and Cheyennes. By 1900 the school's student body had swelled to nearly 2,000 and congressmen, who received the institution's paper, *The Red Man*, free of charge in their offices, were enthusiastic supporters. "Here is the solution of the vexed Indian problem," one legislator declared. "When we can educate the Indian children," he observed, "other kindred questions will naturally take care of themselves."

While classroom training was central to the Carlisle program, Pratt argued that his school could remake every aspect of an Indian child's life. He insisted that the school educate both boys and girls to adopt western gender roles and the prevailing Victorian moral and sexual codes. His school provided a comprehensive, twenty-four-hour experience. Boys in wool uniforms and girls in starched dresses were monitored from morning washing up to evening taps. Girls received instruction in "domestic science," and Sunday sermons stressed both the importance of female moral leadership and the responsibility of boys to provide for their families. Boys and girls sat together in the dining halls so that they could be trained to interact in a "civilized" manner. Boys could not eat until after the girls were served.

Pratt reinforced Carlisle's "life lessons" during summer vacations when students were placed in white farming households all along the Eastern Seaboard. Called "outing," this placement system was intended to expose boys and girls to mainstream life while relieving the school of the cost (and risk) of returning them to their parents during school breaks. Over time the summer program was supplemented by year-round placements with both rural and urban families. Students who accepted these voluntary assignments promised to obey their hosts and report regularly on their progress in learning the nuances of middle-class life. By 1900, more than 1,000 Carlisle students per year participated in the outing program.

Boarding Schools Proliferate

The apparent success of Carlisle generated support for similar schools in other parts of the country. By the end of the 1880s the Indian Office had opened boarding schools at Genoa, Nebraska; Lawrence, Kansas (Haskell Institute); Chemawa, Oregon; Albuquerque, New Mexico; Grand Junction, Colorado; and Chilocco, in the northern portion of Indian Territory. Seventeen more schools opened during the 1890s. All followed Pratt's model of co-educational instruction, and many imitated the outing system.

The new boarding schools followed a common routine. On arrival, students had their hair cut short and were issued uniforms and heavy work shoes. They lived in large dormitories and endured days organized around strict schedules filled with a mixture of classroom instruction and work in school gardens, kitchens, and workshops. Jobs and school tasks were strictly ordered by gender: boys learned vocational skills, while girls were taught sewing, cooking, and other domestic tasks. Students were generally forbidden to speak their tribal languages or to follow their traditional religions. Perhaps most humiliating, new arrivals were usu-

ally assigned "English names" to which they were expected to respond and which they were expected to keep for the rest of their lives. (Students generally attached an English given name to their father's name.) Plenty Kill, for example, was presented with a chalkboard covered with names. All the children were given a chance to choose one; when it came to his turn "Luther" was one of the few left. Combining his choice with his father's tribal name, the boy became "Luther Standing Bear."

Boarding school students were typically homesick, disoriented, and sad. The Yankton Sioux author Zitkala-Ša recalled that on her first day in school "two warm hands grasped me firmly, and in the same manner I was tossed high in midair." The friendly teacher who thought she was being playful suddenly discovered that the little girl, who had never been "a plaything," was terrified. "I began to cry aloud," Zitkala-Ša added. Struggling to adapt to a new name and a new language as well as to a new universe of rules and expectations, boarding school students learned to avoid anything that might attract attention to themselves or to arouse the curiosity of their instructors. At the same time, students quickly fell in with "gangs" led by older, more experienced students who promised to guide and protect them. Francis LaFlesche, who attended a boarding school near his Omaha reservation, recalled that "the boy who could not fight found it difficult to maintain the respect of his mates. . . ."

Students at boarding schools also faced an array of new diseases. Sleeping in crowded dormitories—sometimes sharing beds—and using common washrooms and toilets, children quickly passed colds, skin infections, lice, and more serious diseases among themselves. Attendance rules requiring reservation agents to send children to school even if they were contagious (a condition imperfectly understood in the nineteenth century) only exacerbated the problem. In time trachoma (an eye infection), tuberculosis, and influenza would prove particularly dangerous in the close quarters of a boarding school. It is impossible to estimate the death rate at these institutions, but each school's cemetery was as much a part of its architecture as its gymnasium or chapel. In addition, students frequently suffered from depression or other psychological problems. Luther Standing Bear remembered that students at Carlisle "had to get used to so many things that we had never known before that it worked on our nerves to such an extent that it told on our bodies."

By the turn of the century the Indian Office reported that nearly 20,000 Native American students attended government-supported schools. Twenty-five off-reservation boarding schools modeled on Carlisle accounted for more than 6,000 of that total. Another group of boarding schools were constructed at Indian agencies. These schools stretched across the country, from the Keam's Canyon School on the Hopi Reservation in Arizona to St. Francis at the Rosebud Agency in South Dakota. In 1900 these schools enrolled more than 8,000 students. Finally, the Indian Office operated more than 100 day schools on reservations and supervised missionaries who operated dozens more; together these schools that did not separate children from their parents accounted for approximately 5,500 students.

For the most part religious organizations and missionaries eagerly supported the government's "civilization" program and generally endorsed the harsh atmosphere at the government schools. Many tribes such as the Ojibwes of the Great Lakes and the Pueblos of New Mexico had been in contact with missionaries for centuries, but the end of the nineteenth century witnessed an unprecedented expansion of church activity among Native Americans. While not all missionaries were as optimistic as the Jesuit priest in Montana who promised in the 1880s to "turn the Crows into doves," they generally agreed with Richard Pratt and other reformers that the time had come for Indians to abandon their traditions.

Religious leaders applauded the goal of individual self-improvement that lay at the heart of the allotment policy and they offered to join the effort by signing contracts with the Indian Office to educate Indian children at mission schools. By 1890 nearly half a million federal dollars were being spent each year to educate Indian children in religious schools. Unfortunately for the churches, however, federal support for Indian education did not continue. During the 1880s anti-Catholic politicians and Protestant educators began a campaign to cut off funds to religious schools; by 1900 their efforts had ended the program.

Expansion of the Indian Office

A final element of the reformers' agenda was a campaign to transform the Indian Office from an instrument of political patronage to a bureau filled with high-minded civil servants. Corruption had been a hallmark of Indian affairs since the founding of the Republic. Treaties and other agreements had routinely been lubricated with liquor and cash, and Indian agencies, like post offices, were political treats handed out to the party faithful after each election. While it was illegal to profit directly from one's position as Indian agent, the cozy system of political appointment insured that supply contracts would go to friends and allies and that clerkships and other agency jobs would be reserved for family members and cronies. The system also guaranteed that local politicians would receive a sympathetic hearing when their white constituents sought access to tribal lands and resources.

Between 1880 and 1900 the addition of many new tasks to the Indian Office—education, agricultural instruction, the distribution of government rations, and the management of the allotment program—caused the agency staff to double in size. As the number of employees grew, activists led by Herbert Welsh urged the president to extend the recently passed Civil Service Act to the entire department. As it was, the prospect of maintaining so many patronage jobs was so attractive that progress was slow. In the spring of 1896 Grover Cleveland placed all Indian school administrators, teachers, clerks, physicians, and nurses under the protection of the civil service. While his action required competitive exams for all future appointments in these areas, it did not prevent his successor, William McKinley, from using patronage to fill most agents' positions. It was not until 1908 that the bulk of the Indian Office employees—agents as well as school personnel—were subject to civil service regulation. American Indian employees, who by 1900 accounted for nearly one-quarter of the Indian Office's staff, remained exempt from civil service regulations.

The rapid expansion of the Indian Office, together with the slow growth of civil service regulations, doomed individual agencies and schools to rule by inexperienced appointees. Agents rarely served for an entire presidential term, and the turnover among teachers and clerks was even more frequent. The Indian Office attempted to control this administrative chaos by issuing detailed orders to agency personnel. Circulars from Washington demanded that agents "induce Indians to labor in civilized pursuits" and warned that "no Indian should be idle for want of an opportunity to labor." Similar instructions required Indian children to attend school, prohibited traditional ceremonies such as the Sun Dance, and barred families from leaving the reservation to visit relatives or gather food. To enforce these orders, several agents created Indian police forces and tribal courts where those who violated reservation rules could be fined or sentenced to terms in the agency jail. By 1900 two-thirds of the Indian agencies featured these institutions of control.

The combination of weak staffs, strict orders from Washington, D.C., and Indian resistance created an environment in which the local agents felt embattled and isolated. Usually referred to with the honorary title "Major," agents were expected to monitor school attendance, police reservation boundaries, teach farming, and manage the tribe's finances. But they usually tackled these jobs alone. Agents issued commands and presided over general council meetings, but astute Native leaders understood that the government men had little power to force the tribes to obey them. Supported by a loyal local following, men like Manuelito among the Navajos, Red Cloud of the Sioux, or Washakie of the Wind River Shoshones could undercut an agent's authority and passively resist his orders. In time these tribal leaders would usually persuade their agents to take a milder—and mutually beneficial—approach. A well-placed gift of supplies or housing to the leaders' family could help preserve tribal tranquility. Or advice from a local leader on whom the agent should appoint to salaried positions on the reservation police force or at the agency school could produce faithful workers. "Gifts" to chiefs and elders could produce cooperation. Backed by the military, agents could overcome direct opposition when necessary, but when it came to everyday activities, cooperation with local leaders was far more productive, especially when army units were stationed at barracks hundreds of miles from the reservation headquarters.

Theoretically powerful but hemmed in by resourceful tribal leaders, geographical isolation, and sparse budgets, agents were often, as anthropologist Clark Wissler described them, "a little forlorn." The major features of Indian life in the late nineteenth century were structured by the government's ambitious allotment and education programs, but daily life continued to be shaped by local custom, tribal leaders, and the outcome of ongoing struggles between Native Americans and outsiders eager to "kill" their old way of life.

PROPHETS, INVENTORS, AND WRITERS: INDIAN RESISTANCE IN AN AGE OF OPPRESSION

The speed and scale of the late-nineteenth-century onslaught shocked the Indian people who experienced it. In less than a generation, most tribal communities in the United States found themselves surrounded by strangers and subjected to new and troubling regimes. Tribal leaders had little chance to escape the onrushing tide of American "civilization"; the government ignored their opposition to allotment. But Indians responded to the new conditions with something more than despair.

In every corner of the United States, chiefs, traditional religious leaders, and tribal elders struggled for ways to stem the rising tide of white settlement and to contain the lengthening reach of "civilization" programs. Amidst the bewildering changes taking place in the 1880s and 1890s, at least three forms of effective Native American resistance emerged. First, new religious movements inspired by visionary prophets caught the attention and the loyalty of people who had feared that their spiritual traditions had no meaning in a world of government agents and boarding schools. Second, a small but growing number of individuals in different parts of the country managed to find new activities—and even new identities—that allowed them to oppose the government's assimilation effort without giving up their Indian traditions. And third, a small group of educated Native Americans took up their pens and employed their new facility with English to attack American expansion. Together, these efforts provided a means by which later Indian leaders could critique—and even confront—the white people's smug assumption that only they held the keys to "civilization."

Prophets, East and West

The creation of reservations on the Columbia River plateau in the 1850s had forced a number of relatively small tribes—the Umatillas, Cayuses, Yakamas, Walla Wallas, Colvilles, Sanpoils, Nespelems, Okanagons, Nez Percés, Palouses, and others—to settle on four major reservations: Colville, Umatilla, Nez Percé, and Yakama. In the past these nonagricultural plateau communities had supported visionary leaders whose encounters with otherworldly beings allowed them to predict salmon runs, control the weather, and explain cataclysmic events. In the late nineteenth century, two men who were part of this prophetic tradition became particularly influential in the Pacific Northwest.

Smoholla came of age in the turbulent years of the 1840s, when American emigrants first disrupted the plateau world. A member of the tiny Wanapam tribe, he was born near present-day Walla Walla, Washington, and became a well-regarded shaman while still a young man. In 1855, when he was about thirty-five, the Indian Office ordered groups like the Wanapams to move to one of the area's new reservations in the central part of Washington Territory. Smoholla refused. He also refused to join the armed resistance that the Yakamas and others organized against the new reservations. Instead, Smoholla fell into a trance for several days. When he awoke, he began preaching the "Washani Creed." This creed was simple: the earth is literally the mother of all humankind; it must be owned communally and all people should live by hunting and gathering. According to the new prophet, no one—not even Indians—had the right to sell or farm the land. Smoholla's opposition to private property, Christianity, and agriculture horrified government officials. "Men who work cannot dream," the prophet said, "and wisdom comes to us in dreams."

Smoholla preached his message of passive resistance continuously from the 1850s until his death in 1895. He avoided direct confrontation with federal officials, thus avoiding arrest or imprisonment, and he won a loyal following to the Washani religion. His most famous disciple was Chief Joseph of the Nez Percés, who resisted resettlement on that tribe's Idaho reservation in the 1870s by referring to the teachings of Smoholla. Joseph's subsequent surrender and the growth of white communities in eastern Oregon and Washington did not deter Smoholla or his followers from continuing to argue against allotment and agriculture. Called "Dreamers," the prophet's followers were a presence on all of the area's reservations. They avoided cooperating with authorities whenever possible, and they insisted on exercising their treaty-protected right to leave their reserves to hunt and gather at their "usual and customary" places. (During major salmon runs as many as two thousand people would gather at Celilo Falls, one of the most important fishing sites on the Columbia River.) Associating regularly with one another beyond their reservation borders, these "Dreamers" often called themselves "Columbia River Indians," a new label that reflected a new common identity. By century's end the Washani faith and the "Columbia Indian" identity were widely recognized. Smoholla was revered by disciples and followers across the region. Many of these individuals quietly opposed the Dawes Act and refused to participate in the allotment process.

A more militant prophet emerged on Washington's Colville Reservation. Like Smoholla, Skolaskin fell unconscious for a period and then returned from the spirit world to deliver a message of opposition to the government's "civilization" programs. Unlike the Wanapam prophet, however, Skolaskin publicly condemned the government and its new policies. He urged his followers to refuse allotments and to keep their children from attending the government's schools. Skolaskin was also a more formidable opponent of local agents than Smoholla. He maintained a loyal following at the Colville Agency and kept his supporters in line by creating his own police force and jailing his critics. Skolaskin was also an outspoken opponent of political leaders such as the Columbia chief Moses, who cooperated with Indian Office officials in order to improve conditions at Colville. While Skolaskin never succeeded in stopping allotment, the Indian Office was worried enough about his activities to lock him up in the military prison on Alcatraz Island in San Francisco Bay, where he spent most of the time between 1889 and 1892 in solitary confinement. Skolaskin never surrendered, however; following his release from prison he continued to speak out against allotment.

Leaders fired by religious visions surfaced in other parts of Indian country as well. At the Crow

Agency in 1887, for example, a young man named Wraps Up His Tail told his followers that his powerful medicine would allow him to ride against the American soldiers without being harmed. Wraps Up His Tail led a raiding party against the Blackfeet—an action the Indian Office had specifically forbidden—and celebrated his victory by riding through the agency compound, shooting into buildings and frightening the staff. Troops were dispatched to Montana from as far away as Chicago, and the young rebel was captured and killed within the space of a month, but his opposition to "civilization" was unmistakable and inspiring.

The Keetowah band of Cherokees had organized in the 1850s to oppose the tribal government's growing friendship with southern slaveowners. Made up largely of descendants of the earliest Cherokee settlers in the West, the Keetowahs remained a center for dissident activity after the Civil War. In the 1880s, as outsiders urged tribal officials to sell and allot their lands, the Keetowahs took up the anti-allotment cause. Under the leadership of Redbird Smith, the group rallied tribe members with calls to revive traditional Cherokee "stomp dances" and reject the white man's "civilization."

The Ghost Dance and Wounded Knee

The most influential prophet of the early allotment era came from the Mason Valley in western Nevada. On New Year's Day 1889, a thirty-five-year-old Paiute man, Wovoka, fell into a trance. When he awoke he reported that he had visited heaven and heard that his people must love one another and cooperate with the whites. If they embraced peace and performed the traditional round dance, they would be rewarded in heaven. The new prophet's teachings won him a strong local following, but thanks to visitors who traveled by rail and wrote accounts that were later published in local newspapers, news of his vision soon reached reservations across the West. Delegations of Indian visitors began to appear in the Mason Valley, seeking an audience with the prophet. Wovoka's visitors included delegates from Paiute communities in Nevada and California, Shoshones from Idaho, and young Sioux leaders from the Plains.

The exact nature of Wovoka's message to the Plains tribes is still disputed, but most of his followers believed that performing the prophet's dance and following his call to peace would enable them to reunite with their dead ancestors in a world that would have no sickness or death—or white people. This message formed the core of a movement that became known across the Plains region as the Ghost Dance. Among the Pawnees, Shoshones, Kiowas, and others in the south, the Ghost Dance was the most recent in a series of visionary movements that provided Native people with a way of responding to the rapid changes going on around them. It became a part of tribal life, persisting among many groups into the twentieth century. But among the Sioux in the Dakotas, Wovoka's message appeared just as the hated 1889 land sale agreement was taking effect, and the prophet's call to unity became intertwined with the dramatic events surrounding the dismemberment of the Great Sioux Reservation.

Wovoka's principal disciple among the Sioux was a young man named Kicking Bear, who had traveled to visit the prophet early in 1890. Kicking Bear returned to South Dakota convinced the new dance could provide a solution to the tribe's difficulties. By spring he and his brother-in-law Short Bull were traveling among the Lakota communities, urging people to join the new dance and don "Ghost Shirts" made of white cotton and painted with symbols from Wovoka's teachings. Because their appeal came just as new settlers were arriving from the east to take up homesteads on what had only recently been tribal land, they won a ready audience. It was during precisely these months as well that the first Oklahoma land run took place and Sioux leaders learned that Congress had failed to support General Crook's promise to provide their people with cash for food and farming assistance. Facing the rapid erosion of their tribal land base and imminent starvation, many residents at the major Sioux agencies—Pine Ridge, Rosebud, Cheyenne River, and Standing Rock—decided they should join the Ghost Dancers.

Unfortunately, in the fall of 1890 the most important Sioux agency, Pine Ridge, was placed in the hands of Daniel Royer, a loyal Republican from Alpena, South Dakota, who had been nominated to the post by South Dakota's new U.S. senator. (Royer had hoped for a job in the land office.) Ignorant of Indian affairs, the new agent feared that the frustrated former warriors at Pine Ridge—

many of whom were veterans of the Little Big Horn—would soon launch an armed rebellion. Afraid that the prophet's message would inspire a general uprising, Royer cabled for help. Regular army troops began arriving at Pine Ridge on November 20. The Ghost Dance leaders and their followers responded by retreating to the desolate badlands on the reservation's northernmost boundary. As fall turned to winter, each side clung more firmly to the belief that their opponents were about to attack.

The tragic climax of this confrontation began to unfold in mid-December at the Standing Rock Agency in nearby North Dakota, where agent James McLaughlin presided over a restive community that included the famed warrior Sitting Bull. Sitting Bull's independent ways had long frustrated bureaucrats like McLaughlin. The aging hero of the Little Big Horn had never been defeated in battle, and he had nothing but contempt for allotment and the reservation "chiefs" who sought to compromise with the authorities. Sensing a chance to eliminate an "incorrigible" leader, McLaughlin ordered the agency police (backed up by a detachment of regular army troops) to arrest Sitting Bull on the pretense that imprisonment would prevent him from joining the Ghost Dancers.

The police surprised Sitting Bull at dawn on December 15. The chief rebuked the agency policemen, who quickly shot him at close range. News of Sitting Bull's death sped through the Sioux agencies, convincing many that the government was planning more arrests. Most band leaders were persuaded to remain at home, but one, Big Foot, head of the Minneconjous at neighboring Cheyenne River Agency, decided to flee to the Pine Ridge badlands and seek protection from the Ghost Dancers.

Elements of the Seventh Cavalry—Custer's command in 1876—apprehended Big Foot on December 28 just as his frightened and hungry group of refugees entered the Pine Ridge reservation from the north. The Ghost Dancers agreed to accompany the soldiers to their camp along Wounded Knee creek, about twenty miles from the agency headquarters. During the night, Colonel James Forsyth and the remainder of the Seventh Cavalry took up positions on the low hills that ringed the Indian captives. By dawn 500 Blue-Coats were peering down at the encampment of 350 Minneconjou men, women, and children. Forsyth's nervous commanders had instructed him to disarm his charges, so the colonel ordered his soldiers to approach the ranks of young Indian men.

Stiffly, the soldiers began to search and disarm each prisoner. Frightened about what would come next—and angry that their precious rifles were being taken unceremoniously from them—the Minneconjous began to protest. A holy man in the group, Yellow Bird, began to sing a Lakota Ghost Dance song. Tensions rose. Another young man, Black Coyote, raised his gun over his head and shouted that he should not have to surrender so valuable a possession. Soldiers grabbed him. A rifle went off.

At first the soldiers and Sioux warriors swirled about, firing at each other from close range; bullets that missed the Indians slammed through the tipis that stood behind them. One of the first shots killed Big Foot as he lay sick on his robes. In a few moments the groups separated and the Seventh Cavalry units ringing the camp poured rifle and artillery fire into the Sioux positions. The Minneconjous tried to escape down a nearby creek bed, but the soldiers pursued them, shooting at everyone dressed in buckskin or wrapped in a blanket. Because the fighting degenerated so quickly into chaos and murder, the number of Lakota dead and wounded could never be confirmed. At least 150 of Big Foot's band were killed; at least 50 more were wounded. Many of the Minneconjou casualties were women and children. The army counted 25 dead soldiers and 39 wounded as it pulled back to Pine Ridge village. Some of the soldiers appeared to have been caught in the confusion and shot by their own troops. The day turned cold and it began to snow; it would be New Year's Day 1891 before a burial party would venture out to Wounded Knee to cast the stiff and frozen bodies of Big Foot and his followers into a common grave.

Wounded Knee was a tragedy. It was not a defeat for the Sioux because Big Foot and his band had no objective other than to find refuge from the authorities. Nor was it a victory for the United States, despite the fact that 20 veterans of the killing were subsequently awarded the Congressional Medal of Honor for their actions. Instead the incident served as a graphic reminder of the cruelty and relentlessness of the American conquest of the continent. The United States was determined to assert its authority in every Native American community in the country and to crush all direct resistance. The massacre also demonstrated that despite the highly publicized efforts of Standing Bear, Captain Pratt, and others, a vast chasm still separated the reformers' slogans from the reality of Native American life. While many Indians had struggled to accommodate themselves to the demands of "civilization," most of their kinsmen were deeply suspicious of white people and their programs. Luther Standing Bear (formerly Plenty Kill, the first student to enter Carlisle) was a schoolteacher on the neighboring Rosebud reservation in 1890 when the killing took place at Wounded Knee. "It made my blood boil," he later recalled. "There I was, doing my best to teach my people to follow the white man's road . . . and this was my reward for it all!"

Cultural Inventors

A second group of Native Americans chose invention over resistance. This group avoided direct confrontations with the Americans. Rather they sought out new ways of expressing themselves so that they could bypass the agents and bureaucrats who surrounded them and communicate directly both with each other and with the American public. This group included performers, artists, and intellectuals. They tried to define themselves apart from the traditional Native American past as well as the cramped roles laid out for them by the moralistic reformers who wanted only to "lift them up" to "civilization."

Some of these new leaders performed versions of their traditional life or their history for white audiences. While Indians had been exhibited before white audiences since the age of Columbus, "show Indians" were a creation of the late nineteenth century. The most prominent among them were the people hired by William F. Cody (Buffalo Bill) to perform in his world famous Wild West Show. Cody, a scout and buffalo hunter, had spent most of his winters during the 1870s appearing in stiff, frontier melodramas on eastern stages. Performing alone or with other self-promoters like former sheriff Wild Bill Hickok, Cody had tried to bring the excitement of dime novels to life for urban audiences. His performances met with mild success until

1882, when he was asked to organize a grand procession of cowboys and Indians to celebrate the Fourth of July in his adopted hometown of North Platte, Nebraska. The celebration proved so successful that Cody decided to repeat it during the following summer in small cities across the Midwest. In May 1883, Cody and a band of thirty-six Pawnees performed before a wildly enthusiastic audience in Omaha; the event established the model for a show that would be performed before millions of people over the next two decades.

Cody repeated his successful tour with the Pawnees in 1884, but in 1885 he raised the visibility of his show dramatically when he hired Sitting Bull to join the troupe. The Indian Office had first rejected Cody's proposal to hire the famous war leader, but persistence—and the endorsement of General William Tecumseh Sherman—eventually carried the day. Sitting Bull opened with Cody in New York City in June 1885. He created a sensation.

Following the Sitting Bull tour, Cody traveled to Sioux country each spring to enlist up to a hundred people (mostly young men) for his show. The annual tours grew longer and more ambitious. Cody took his troop—including ninety-seven Indians—to London in 1887. He and his performers spent six months in Paris in 1889, before moving on to extended appearances in Spain and Italy. He returned to England in 1891, but his most profitable season would be 1893 when his show was a lead attraction at the World's Columbian Exposition in Chicago.

Indians in Wild West shows were obviously the employees of white people, but their participation in these displays ran completely counter to the government's assimilation efforts. The Indian Rights Association's Herbert Welsh, Carlisle's Captain Pratt, and many of the Indian Office's dedicated educators condemned the shows, charging that they degraded the performers and exposed them to the evils of city life. Congressman Darwin Rush James of New York even introduced a resolution in the House of Representatives denouncing the show as "the drama of savagery." Indian performers were repeatedly asked if they were being mistreated or held against their will, and usually they responded that they were very happy to be free of reservation rules. At one inquiry Black Heart, a young Sioux horseman, reminded the authorities that he, like

Indians in Venice While traveling with Buffalo Bill's Wild West extravaganza, these Native Americans not only brought Indian culture to people throughout the world, they also were able to explore foreign cultures in the company of fellow Indians.

they, should be free to work where he wished. "If [the] Indian wants to work at any place and earn money," he declared, "he wants to do so; [the] white man got [the] privilege to do the same—any kind of work that he wants." And the performers seemed to enjoy being themselves—dressing in traditional costumes and riding their horses. For example, when the Prince of Wales toured the Indian camp during the 1887 performances in London, he presented Red Shirt, a handsome Lakota man who had a prominent role in the performance, with a box of his private brand of cigars. Rather than thank his Highness, the performer immediately turned and passed them out among his fellow performers—demonstrating the obligations of Indian leadership.

Jostling over the appropriateness of Indians performing in Cody's show turned serious in the immediate aftermath of the Wounded Knee massacre. Cody was scheduled to leave for Europe early in 1891, but his troupe was short several dozen Indians. The Indian Office blocked him from recruiting on the troubled reservations, so the showman suggested something different: would the army permit him to hire some of the thirty Sioux "troublemakers" who had already been imprisoned at Fort Sheridan, near Chicago? General Miles agreed and within a few months twenty-seven Ghost Dance "ringleaders" were crossing the Atlantic with Buffalo Bill. Herbert Welsh and missionary leaders howled in protest, but by spring Kicking Bear and Short Bull, the Ghost Dance evangelists, were reenacting "the last Indian war" for enthusiastic European audiences.

Cody's "show Indians" said little about their adventures other than that they enjoyed traveling and making money. But they must have sensed the enthusiasm of white audiences for their portrayals of Indian life and they undoubtedly understood the difference between the authoritarian atmosphere

PEOPLE, PLACES, AND THINGS

Teton Lakota Parasol

Teton Lakota Parasol

Wonderfully capturing the Victorian style of the late nineteenth century and the colorful brilliance of Lakota bead and quillwork, this parasol is a stunning testimony to cultural persistence. The anonymous artist who conceived and executed this project (probably for sale to tourists) was clearly adapting to the shifting standards of her time and accommodating herself to the government's demand that she live a "civilized life." But her "civilized" accessory was constructed of traditionally tanned buckskin and decorated with floral patterns outlined by glass beads and dyed porcupine quills. These floral designs first appeared when Sioux people lived in the Great Lakes region and came into contact with French fur traders who favored their bright colors and stylish swirls.

of the reservation and the freedom of life on tour. Several performers were injured during the years the Wild West Show toured the world, and occasionally individuals became ill and even died, but the spring "sign ups" were always popular and Cody's employees generally gave him high marks for fairness and generosity. Significantly, as Cody grew more popular and Indian performances more commonplace, protests from reformers and Indian Office personnel declined. By 1900 public displays of "savage life" created hardly a stir.

During the last two decades of the nineteenth century, another arena of cultural survival opened among the Navajos of Arizona and New Mexico. The passage of a transcontinental rail line through the Southwest in 1880 brought two significant changes in tribal life. First, cheap cotton cloth became available, eliminating the need for Navajo weavers to make clothes and allowing them to turn their attention to weaving wool blankets and rugs. Second, the rail line enabled these same weavers to sell woven rugs to merchants and collectors from the East. As a consequence, the 1880s and 1890s witnessed a dramatic expansion of Navajo (and to a lesser extent Pueblo) weaving. Artists (including men, who had generally not been weavers in the past) experimented with new designs and bold new

colors. By 1900 Navajo rugs were a staple of American popular culture. Tourists also were drawn to the work of tribal silversmiths who increasingly worked with an eye to outside markets. Similar interest arose in other parts of the country as New York Iroquois beadwork, California basketry, and Pueblo pottery appeared with growing frequency in the parlors of American tourists.

Like Indian performers, Native craftspeople wielded little influence in the white man's vast industrial economy. They were dependent on traders for supplies and access to markets. Nevertheless these artists had located an arena where they could function outside the role that the Indian agents and schoolmasters had established for them. In the nineteenth century the dollar value of the rugs and silver sold to outsiders was relatively low, but in the decades to come this modest trade would grow into a national enterprise that would catapult Indian artists into the forefront of tribal life.

Finally, at the end of the nineteenth century a small number of American Indian intellectuals began to speak out in opposition to the government's assimilation programs and to defend tribal traditions. Only a few authors saw their work appear in print before 1900, but, as with tribal artists, these pioneers opened the way for others.

INDIAN VOICES   Sarah Winnemucca

This excerpt from the concluding pages of Sarah Winnemucca's autobiography includes a description of the Paiute woman's struggle to secure emergency food and shelter for her tribe. The passage includes her description of her community's response to the white man's failure to deliver the help that had been promised and her assessment of why this kind of disappointment occurred so regularly. She closes by calling into question the common claim that whites represented "civilization" and the Indians, "savagery."

When we got home we told our people to go to Lovelocks, and be ready to receive some tents that were to be sent there for them. They came from far and near to hear of the wonderful father we had seen, how he looked and all about him. While we were waiting we almost starved. I wrote to the Secretary of the Interior for God's sake to send us something to eat. He answered my letter telling me to take my people to the Malheur Agency [in Oregon]. Just think of my taking my people, who were already starving, to go three hundred miles through snow waist-deep. I told my people what the letter said. They all laughed and said:

"We are not disappointed. We always said that the Big Father was just like all the white people."

What could we say? We were only ashamed because we came and told them lies which the white people had told us.

"You must go make that up yourselves," they said, "for you have been to the white people's country, and all the white people say the Big Father at Washington never tells a lie."

My father rose and told his people he did not blame them for talking as they did.

"I say, my dear children, every word we have told you was said to us. Yes, they have said or done more than this. They have given us a paper which your mother will tell you of."

Then he called me and said,—

"Read the paper; your brother will interpret for you."

I did as I was told. I read very slowly. My brother did nicely, and after it was over my uncle, Captain John, rose and spoke, saying, "My dear people, I have lived many years with white people. Yes, it is over thirty years, and I know a great many of them. I have never known one of them do what they promised. I think they mean it just at the time, but I tell you they are very forgetful. It seems to me, sometimes, that their memory is not good, and since I have understood them, if they say they will do so and so for me, I would say to them, now or never, and if they don't, why it is because they never meant to do, but only to say so. These are your white brothers' ways, and they are a weak people."

Oh, for shame! You who are educated by a Christian government in the art of war; the practice of whose profession makes you natural enemies of the savages, so called by you. Yes, you, who call yourselves the great civilization; you who have knelt upon Plymouth Rock, covenanting with God to make this land the home of the free and the brave. Ah, then you rise from your bended knees and seizing the welcoming hands of those who are the owners of this land, which you are

> not, your carbines rise upon the bleak shore, and your so-called civilization sweeps inland from the ocean wave; but, oh, my God! leaving its pathway marked by crimson lines of blood, and strewed by the bones of two races, the inheritor and the invader; and I am crying out to you for justice,—yes, pleading for the far-off plains of the West, for the dusky mourner, whose tears of love are pleading for her husband, or for their children, who are sent far away from them.
>
> Source: Sarah Winnemucca Hopkins, *Life Among the Paiutes: Their Wrongs and Claims*, ed. Mrs. Horace Mann, with a Foreword by Catherine S. Fowler (Reno: University of Las Vegas Press, 1994), 224–225, 207. Reproduced with the permission of the University of Nevada Press.

The first was Sarah Winnemucca, a Paiute woman who was born in Nevada on the eve of the California gold rush. Winnemucca witnessed the violence and disruption that accompanied the early westward movement (Ch. 12). She learned English as a young girl while serving in a white household, and before long she was pressed into service by the army and the Indian Office as an interpreter. Winnemucca also sought allies for her community; she gave public speeches and sent letters to government officials complaining of corruption and false dealings. Winnemucca lobbied politicians in Washington, D.C., in 1880, and in 1883 and 1884 she delivered more than three hundred speeches to eastern Americans from Massachusetts to Maryland. In 1884 she published the first Native American woman's autobiography, *Life Among the Paiutes*. It was both a life story and a plea for understanding. It began: "I was a very small child when the first white people came into our country. They came like a lion, yes, like a roaring lion, and have continued so ever since. . . ." Winnemucca operated a bilingual school for Paiute children in Lovelock, Nevada, in the late 1880s, but financial and personal problems caused its demise. Winnemucca died in 1891 at the age of 46.

Simon Pokagon was a second pioneer critic. A member of a Catholic Potawatomi community in southern Michigan, he was born in 1830 just as settlers began to file for homesteads and clear farmland on former tribal lands. Pokagon believed Indians should accommodate themselves to American settlement, and he frequently spoke out in defense of both allotment and the government's "civilization" programs. White reformers frequently identified Pokagon as a role model for other Indians. But the Potawatomi leader was also deeply critical of modern American society. His calls for Indian "uplift" were usually paired with devastating attacks on the cruelty of outsiders.

Pokagon's most famous presentation occurred in 1893, when he spoke at the World's Columbian Exposition in Chicago, a fair organized to celebrate the four centuries of "progress" that had followed Columbus's original voyage to the New World. Pokagon told his audience that the continent's Native Americans "have no spirit to celebrate with you the great Columbian fair . . . No," he added, "sooner would we hold the high joy day over the graves of our departed than to celebrate our own funeral, the discovery of America." Pokagon went on to condemn western civilization for destroying the American forests and repeatedly betraying Indian people. He closed with a terrible image. America's native people, he said, were "chained hand and foot, while the incoming tide of the great ocean of civilization rises slowly but surely to overwhelm us."

Pokagon died in 1899, but his ideas continued to circulate and were picked up by others. His theme of support for accommodation mixed with criticism of government actions was echoed in Indian Territory, where tribal newspapers often gave voice to local critics. One of the most effective of these Oklahoma critics was Alexander Posey, a Eufaula newspaper editor, poet, and humorist. A member of a prominent Creek family of ranchers and farmers, Posey supported the allotment of tribal lands and criticized traditionalists who wanted to maintain a separate Creek government. But in editorials and poems Posey promoted the dignity of tribal traditions and praised those who resisted American expansion. A poem written in 1899, for example, defended Chitto Harjo, the conservative Creek leader, declaring:

A traitor, outlaw,–what you will
He is the noble red man still.
Condemn him and his kind to shame!
I bow to him, exalt his name!

Farther east, Francis LaFlesche, an Omaha anthropologist who had first risen to prominence as a member of Standing Bear's 1879 protest tour, compiled a memoir of his boarding school experiences in the 1870s. Published in 1900 as *The Middle Five*, the volume combined tales of youthful adventure with poignant comments on the school's authoritarian methods and cultural insensitivity. "The misconception of Indian life and character so common among the white people," La Flesche wrote, "has been largely due to an ignorance of the Indian's language, of his mode of thought, his beliefs, his ideals, and his native institutions." La Flesche worked as a scientist at Washington's Smithsonian Institution until his death in 1932, but he never retreated from these views.

CONCLUSION

In the 1920s an elderly Omaha man recalled the emotions that accompanied the white man's devastating conquest of his tribe's land and resources. "The face of all the land is changed and sad," he observed. "The living creatures are gone. I see the land desolate and I suffer an unspeakable sadness. Sometimes I wake in the night, and I feel as though I should suffocate from the pressure of this feeling of loneliness." The last two decades of the nineteenth century marked the moment when all remaining tribal lands in the United States came under the direct control of federal authorities. "Frontier" areas dominated by Indian people disappeared except in the most isolated areas of the Southwest or the Alaska Territory. Federal officials dominated the educational, the social, even the religious life of Indian people. Native Americans faced an unprecedented array of bureaucrats, regulations, and political enemies while community health deteriorated and tribal populations continued to decline.

There was "an unspeakable sadness" in Indian communities in the 1880s and 1890s as both physical conditions and well-meaning reformers conspired to "kill" the Native traditions that had sustained people for centuries. But these same years witnessed a spirit of resistance and a remarkable desire to support tribal cultures into the future. Tribal birthrates remained extraordinarily high (though death rates were even higher), new voices began to be heard, and new forms of cultural expression began to appear. In the survival of families and villages; in the spirit generated by prophets, dreamers, and artists; and in the biting words of those who had learned the white man's tongue lay the seeds of a new chapter in the continent's history.

SUGGESTED READINGS

Adams, David Wallace. *Education for Extinction: American Indians and the Boarding School Experience, 1875–1928.* Lawrence: University Press of Kansas, 1995. A history of boarding schools that traces both the development of school policies and the experiences of Native American children.

Hagan, William T. *Quanah Parker: Comanche Chief.* Norman: University of Oklahoma Press, 1993. A biography of the son of a white captive and a Comanche leader who fought against the United States and then became a community leader in the reservation era.

Hinsley, Curtis M. *Savages and Scientists: The Smithsonian Institution and the Development of American Anthropology, 1846–1910.* Washington, DC: Smithsonian Institution Press, 1981, 1994. A unique history of the Washington, D.C., scientific establishment's involvement with Indians as subjects for study and display in the late nineteenth century.

Hittman, Michael. *Wovoka and the Ghost Dance.* Lincoln: University of Nebraska Press, 1990. A modern anthropologist's retelling of the story of the origins of the Ghost Dance based on contemporary interviews as well as historical research.

Hoxie, Frederick E. *A Final Promise: The Campaign to Assimilate the Indians, 1880–1920,* 2nd ed. Lincoln: University of Nebraska Press, 2001. A history of Indian policymaking during the allotment era.

Lomawaima, Tsianina. *They Called It Prairie Light: The Story of Chilocco Indian School.* Lincoln:

University of Nebraska Press, 1994. A history of an Oklahoma boarding school by a Native American anthropologist who focuses primarily on the experiences of Native students.

Ostler, Jeffrey. *The Plains Sioux and U.S. Colonialism from Lewis and Clark to Wounded Knee.* New York: Cambridge University Press, 2004. A provocative study of the Lakota Sioux that emphasizes the Americans' relentless efforts to dominate and control the group; contains an excellent description of the Ghost Dance and Wounded Knee.

Standing Bear, Luther. *My People, The Sioux.* Boston: Houghton, Mifflin, 1928. The memoirs of one of the first Indian children to attend Carlisle, Standing Bear's narrative covers both his childhood and his later work with Buffalo Bill's Wild West Show and Hollywood producers.

Zanjani, Sally. *Sarah Winnemucca*. Lincoln: University of Nebraska Press, 2001. A full-length biography of a Nevada Paiute woman who served as an interpreter, diplomat, and national spokesperson for Indian people in the 1870s and 1880s.

Survival and Renewal, 1900–1930

The *New York Times* reported that it was "the greatest crowd that has ever been brought here" and no one who was present in Washington, D.C., on March 5, 1905, would have disagreed. The inauguration of the youngest man ever to serve as president of the United States generated unprecedented excitement. Theodore Roosevelt greeted guests, danced at the inaugural ball, and cheered lustily as 35,000 people marched down Pennsylvania Avenue in his inaugural parade. Marchers included students from Harvard, the president's alma mater, a detachment of Spanish American War "Rough Riders," and a battalion of students from the Carlisle Indian Industrial School. Riding at the head of the Carlisle students were six chiefs—Little Plume, a Blackfoot; American Horse and Buckskin Charley from the Sioux reservations in South Dakota; Quanah Parker, the Comanche leader from Indian Territory; and, most famous of all, "the once dreaded Geronimo." As they passed the reviewing stand "all of the chiefs turned in their saddles and waved their hands at the Great White Father, uttering whoops as they did so." Roosevelt stood and saluted them in return.

The appearance of Geronimo and his fellow chiefs in Theodore Roosevelt's inaugural parade reflects the odd predicament of American Indians in Progressive Era America. While Geronimo, Quanah Parker, American Horse, and the others had been conquered by the United States (Geronimo was technically still a prisoner of war), the chiefs had somehow become a crowd favorite, playing a central role in a national celebration.

In the first decades of the twentieth century, American Indians in every corner of the United States would find themselves in situations similar to the one faced by the six horsemen in Roosevelt's parade. Shackled by poverty and subdued by government regulations, Indians found that they were also immensely popular with the American public. And like the six chiefs, Native Americans adapted—drawing on the American public's sympathy and curiosity as they began the task of rebuilding their communities.

FINDING NEW PLACES TO BE INDIAN

In the late nineteenth century, missionaries and government agents worked hard to undermine traditional religious leaders and "kill" Indian culture. Some tribal religions were driven underground, but many others survived by adapting to new conditions. As a consequence, Indian people in the 1920s had many more religious rituals available to them than they could have imagined a generation before. Native communities also developed new ways of celebrating their distinctive identities that did not threaten the American majority. Finally, a growing cadre of resourceful individuals—from athletes to artists—managed to express a distinctive Indian presence in ways that won broad public support.

THE NATIVE AMERICAN CHURCH

Early in the 1880s the southern reaches of the Rio Grande valley became accessible by rail to the rest of the United States. Since well before the arrival of Columbus, south Texas had served as the place where peyote (*Lophophora williamsii*) had been cultivated and traded to neighboring tribes who used the mildly hallucinogenic fruit (called "buttons") from this cactus plant in religious rituals. The arrival of the railroad in south Texas meant that peyote buttons could now be shipped to every part of North America. The same rail cars that carried grapefruit and lettuce to St. Louis and Chicago could transport peyote to tribes in Indian Territory, Montana, and Wisconsin.

Precise dates are difficult to establish, but there is no doubt that by the end of the 1880s, Lipan Apache religious leaders from Texas were conducting all-night ceremonies focused on the use of peyote

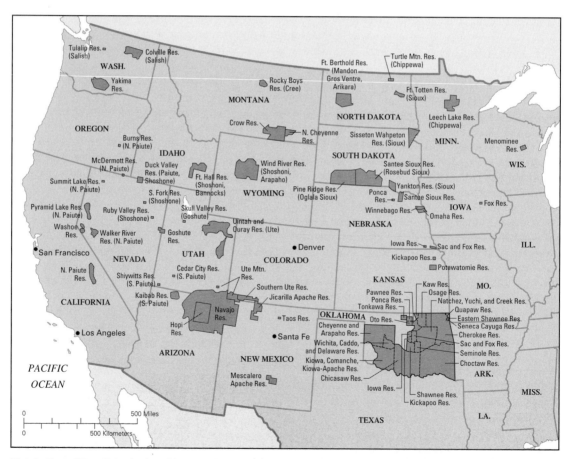

Distribution of Peyotists. In the mid-1980s, the reservation communities indicated here supported active Native American church groups. *Source: From Omer C. Stewart,* Peyote Religion: A History, *p. 149. Reprinted with permission of Oklahoma University Press.*

PEOPLE, PLACES, AND THINGS

Monroe Tsa Toke (1904–1937)

Tsa Toke's image of a young Kiowa performer communicates the pride and resilience of his tribal heritage as well as the beauty of the tribe's traditional dances.

One of the famed "Kiowa Five," Monroe Tsa Toke began drawing as a child. As a member of a talented group of Kiowa artists, Tsa Toke was encouraged to exhibit his works by an Anadarko schoolteacher, Susan Peters, and O. B. Jacobson at the University of Oklahoma. He painted murals in Oklahoma's state historical museum and exhibited his work across the United States, but Tsa Toke believed the message of his painting was at least as important as its medium. He wrote:

> To the average person the Indian is usually conceived and portrayed in his war paint and feathers, carrying the suggestion that nothing would be more pleasing to him...than to create war and bloodshed.... [D]id you know that behind the stoical mask there is a soul with the same impulses and longings, the same thirst for the higher things in life—probably with a more devout spiritual feeling than many of the white men?...By his art he strives to express his own concept of the divine creator. He has the ceremonies invoking the blessings of the only god he knows, all of which are expressed in his art.

Source: Copyright © 1957 by Leslie Van Ness Denman. Reprinted by permission of nac-art.com

among several of the southern Plains tribes that had been recently relocated to reservations in the western half of Indian Territory. Among the most active participants were groups of Comanches and Kiowas near Anadarko. During the 1890s, as pressure to allot tribal lands and "open" Indian Territory grew, the peyote ritual won a steadily increasing number of Native American adherents on these and neighboring reserves. "Road men" carried the peyote message. They taught that the plant was a conduit through which believers could gain access to the spirit world. Some believers reported speaking with Jesus or with dead ancestors during rituals; others simply appreciated the fellowship and spiritual well-being created at the peyote meetings. The new ritual was similar to many older tribal ceremonies. It was communal, and it relied on prayers in native languages and group singing and drumming to animate worship. Also, peyote meetings did not run by the clock; they began in the evening and lasted until dawn. Peyote meetings were egalitarian—there was no fixed priesthood—and they welcomed both male and female participants on an equal footing.

Rooted in these tribal values, the peyote ritual spread rapidly. Riding the nation's new rail lines, road men carried the ceremony north to the Omahas in Nebraska, the Ojibwes and Winnebagos in Minnesota and Wisconsin, and the Crows in Montana. They also traveled west along the Santa Fe line to the Pueblos and Navajos and then north to the Great Basin, where peyote was embraced by Utes and Shoshones.

Yet in certain fundamental ways, the peyote religion differed sharply from traditional tribal spiritual traditions. It was portable; peyote meetings could take place wherever a group of Indian believers gathered. It employed its own missionaries. Its followers insisted that faithful practitioners adapt to modern conditions by rejecting alcohol, practicing monogamy, and working as wage laborers.

Most whites opposed the new religion. State and federal officials tried to outlaw cultivation of the peyote plant, and the Indian Office struggled to seize the buttons wherever they appeared. In many communities tribal elders supported the government's efforts because they believed road men undermined local beliefs. Peyote leaders were quick to respond to their critics. The Comanche leader Quanah Parker observed, for example, that whites when in church "talk *about* Jesus" while the peyotist "talks *to* Jesus." Parker led the effort to defeat a state prohibition law, and in 1918 peyote leaders from across Oklahoma formed a new, nonprofit corporation, The Native American Church in Oklahoma, in order to "foster and promote" their religious beliefs and to teach "morality, sobriety, industry, kindly charity and right living." A successor organization, The Native American Church of the United States, was formed in 1944.

Other new religions spread through Indian country during the first few decades of the new century. In the Northwest, John Slocum, a Squaxon from Puget Sound, founded the Indian Shaker movement in 1882. He preached that Indians could heal themselves of the effects of alcoholism, poverty, and other effects of white civilization by participating in an elaborate series of ceremonies. Like the followers of the peyote ritual, the Shakers avoided politics. Instead they called on their fellow Indians to give up alcohol and gambling and to embrace the white man's work ethic. The Shaker program included group healing rituals aimed at removing sinfulness from believers and celebrations using candles, bells, crosses, and other Christian symbols. Despite opposition from reservation missionaries, the Shakers' "Indian Christianity" (which had no relation to the early nineteenth century New England sect) spread across the Northwest.

The Ghost Dance also survived into the twentieth century. Despite the damage caused by the massacre at Wounded Knee, Wovoka continued to inspire congregations in several Plains and Great Basin communities. The Paiute prophet met and corresponded with followers until his death in 1932.

Indian Christianity

In the course of the nineteenth century, most tribes had been exposed to the teachings of Christian missionaries. As a consequence, by 1900 communities of Christian Indians existed in every region of the country. One of these communities produced a remarkable twentieth-century Indian leader: Charles Eastman. Called Ohiyesa by his Santee Sioux kinsmen, Eastman was born in Minnesota in 1858 and

Dressed in traditional costume, Charles Eastman lectured to white audiences on the virtues and wisdom of Native American culture.

raised in the woods and on the prairies of Manitoba and the Dakotas. When Eastman was fourteen his father, a Christian convert, brought him to Flandreau, South Dakota, where Eastman entered the Santee Normal Training School. Eastman's outstanding scholarly record soon won him an invitation to study at Knox College in Illinois and later at Wisconsin's Beloit College and Dartmouth College. He graduated from the latter school in 1887 and, three years later, from Boston University Medical School.

Eastman became well known as a physician and writer, but he spent four years as a field secretary for the YMCA, organizing YMCA chapters in Indian communities. Eastman embraced the principles of Christianity, often pointing out that Jesus was so generous and kind that he had more in common with Indians than with contemporary white Americans. When he turned his office over to his successor, there were forty American Indian as-

INDIAN VOICES   Charles Eastman Criticizes "Civilization"

Charles Eastman devoted most of his writing and public speaking to idealized descriptions of his Santee Sioux childhood and the culture that shaped him before he left his tribe to be educated at mission schools and, ultimately, Dartmouth College. In the closing pages of his autobiography, however, he turned to comment on the world around him. His criticism of "civilization" closed the book on an ironic note. Titled, *From the Deep Woods to Civilization*, one would expect the autobiography to be a triumphant tale of a boy overcoming the "backwardness" of the woods so that he could enjoy the pleasures of "civilization." Ending as it does, however, the book causes readers to wonder—as Eastman himself must have—about the wisdom of his decision to leave his tribe and embark on the "white man's road."

Why do we find so much evil and wickedness practiced by the nations composed of professedly "Christian" individuals? The pages of history are full of licensed murder and the plundering of weaker and less developed peoples, and obviously the world to-day has not outgrown this system. Behind the material and intellectual splendor of our civilization, primitive savagery and cruelty and lust hold sway, undiminished, and as it seems, unheeded. When I let go of my simple, instinctive nature religion, I hoped to gain something far loftier as well as more satisfying to the reason. Alas! it is also more confusing and contradictory. The higher and spiritual life, though first in theory, is clearly secondary, if not entirely neglected, in actual practice. When I reduce a civilization to its lowest terms, it becomes a system of life based on trade. The dollar is the measure of value, and *might* still spells *right*; otherwise, why war?

Yet even in deep jungles God's own sunlight penetrates, and I stand before my own people still as an advocate of civilization. Why? First, because there is no chance for our former simple life any more; and second, because I realize that the white man's religion is not responsible for his mistakes. There is every evidence that God has given him all the light necessary by which to live in peace and good-will with his brother; and we also know that many brilliant civilizations have collapsed in physical and moral decadence. It is for us to avoid their fate if we can.

I am an Indian; and while I have learned much from civilization, for which I am grateful, I have never lost my Indian sense of right and justice. I am for development and progress along social and spiritual lines, rather than those of commerce, nationalism, or material efficiency. Nevertheless, so long as I live, I am an American.

Charles A. Eastman (Ohiyesa), *From the Deep Woods to Civilization: Chapters in the Autobiography of an Indian*. Introduction by Raymond Wilson (Lincoln: University of Nebraska Press, 1977), 194–195. Reprinted with permission.

sociations in the YMCA; by 1911 there were more than sixty.

In addition to the interdenominational YMCA, Indians belonged to a number of Protestant and Catholic lay organizations. These included the St. Joseph and St. Mary Societies among the Sioux. These groups of pious men and women first met at the Devil's Lake reservation in the summer of 1884 and then at congregations on the Pine Ridge, Rosebud, and other Plains reserves. Members of these two societies pledged to observe the Sabbath, to avoid polygamy and alcohol, and to work to convert their kinsmen. They would lead services when priests were not available in their communities, and each summer beginning in 1891 they would gather for a general "congress."

Among the Navajos, Hampton graduate Jacob C. Morgan won a significant following for the Christian Reformed Church. On the Crow reservation, a Baptist community that centered around a church and day school in the village of Lodge Grass grew up in the early twentieth century. In eastern Oklahoma, where most members of the Five Civilized Tribes had long been Christians, church activities frequently spilled over into social gatherings that featured hymn singing, visiting, and worship. East of the Mississippi the pattern was much the same. In Virginia, for example, the Chickahominy Indians organized the Samaria Indian Baptist Church in 1901. That institution became so important to the social and spiritual life of the Chickahominy community that local Indians came to equate their tribe's strength with the fortunes of the congregation.

Indian Christians were also deeply involved in education. In Indian Territory, the Baptist Cherokee Association proposed the creation of an Indian college in 1879; Bacone College opened a year later with the support of the Baptist Church's Home Mission Board and wealthy easterners (most prominently John D. Rockefeller). The school enjoyed strong support from Baptists across the United States and provided higher education to hundreds of Native Americans from Oklahoma and beyond. In 1922 the school enrolled 234 Indians from twenty-four tribes.

In 1921 an interdenominational group reported that twenty-six Protestant groups were supporting missions among tribal communities in the United States. They counted 597 Indian churches and 268 Native American ministers serving more than 110,000 people. The same report estimated that 336 Catholic missions and parishes served more than 61,000 Native American Catholics. These figures make clear that a generation after the massacre at Wounded Knee more than 50 percent of American Indians were nominally Christians.

Traditional Ceremonies and Powwows

Prior to 1900 government officials had suppressed elaborate ceremonies such as the Ghost Dance but paid little attention to smaller community celebrations. As Commissioner of Indian Affairs Hiram Price wrote in 1883, "the rules do not contemplate any interference with the social gatherings for the amusement of the Indians." On the Plains, for example, Indian people typically assembled on ration days or major national holidays to visit and share what food they had. Even the Sun Dance, an extended Plains ritual that involved individual sacrifice for the benefit of the community, could be obscured in a general gathering. As a consequence, the ritual survived among the Blackfeet, Sioux, Cheyennes, and Arapahos.

Social gatherings at Great Lakes reservations also became places where traditions were celebrated. In particular, visiting among Potawatomis, Ojibwes, and Menominees in the late nineteenth century produced a new dance performed to the accompaniment of a large, ceremonial drum. Called the Dream Dance or Drum Dance, this new ritual included sessions where dance leaders would urge participants to hold fast to communal values, to avoid alcohol, and to remember their tribal histories. While they avoided direct confrontation with government authorities, Dream Dancers played a major role in establishing "traditional" villages on several Great Lakes reserves. In Wisconsin these villages included Zoar on the Menominee preserve and the "Old Village" at Lac du Flambeau, both of which survived into the twentieth century.

The ceremonies that were best known among whites took place among the Pueblos of the Southwest. Often tied to the agricultural calendar, the Pueblo celebrations were both peaceful and picturesque. Since they occurred in communities close to the Atchison, Topeka, and Santa Fe Railway lines, these events were also accessible to tourists. The Hopi Snake and Antelope ceremony attracted more attention than any other. Performed in August to ensure abundant rainfall for the community's corn fields, the ceremony included a segment when priests handled live poisonous snakes. While frowned on by missionaries and government officials, the Snake Dance was vividly recorded by travel writers and anthropologists and actively promoted by tour guides. Nickelodeons at the 1893 Chicago World's Fair included a Snake Dance demonstration, and the 1904 fair in St. Louis even featured a Snake Kiva where visitors could witness daily reenactments of the ceremony in person (but with artificial snakes). Public enthusiasm eventually overwhelmed the Hopis' hospitality. The tribe gradually restricted photography at the ceremony during the 1920s and in later decades closed it entirely to outsiders.

Building on these surviving traditions, a new pan-Indian phenomenon began to spread through Indian communities in the first decades of the twentieth century, providing them with a new focus for cultural celebration and opening a new area where Native people could define themselves before the general public. While trade fairs and other intertribal gatherings had long been a part of Native American life throughout the continent (and the Algonquin word *pawauog* or "powwow"—meaning "medicine man" or "healer"—had been familiar to whites since the seventeenth century), the modern powwow originated among Plains tribes.

As part of the social dancing that agents and missionaries tolerated on western reservations in the late nineteenth century, many tribes performed "war dances" in which costumed men recalled the exploits of their youth. Called variously the Omaha Dance, the Crow Dance, or the Grass Dance, these performances (and their songs) became wildly popular and, by the turn of the century, were being held on different reservations at specific times each summer. It was these gatherings that local Indians called powwows. After the turn of the century these events began to appear in regional variations across North America. They were generally embraced by people who had continued to celebrate their tribal traditions, but they were clearly understood as a broad, "Indian" innovation. Dream Dancers in the Great Lakes, for example, took up the powwow and adopted what they called the Sioux Dance. In western Oklahoma Cheyennes, Kiowas, and others developed a flamboyant variation of the Plains dance that they called the Fancy Dance.

Powwows energized communities weighed down with poverty and despair. Planning and hosting one of these large gatherings required leadership and the cooperative participation of relatives and neighbors. Drums were frequently sponsored by Indian social clubs because each one required a large group of singers and musicians to fulfill the expectations of the crowd. The kinship generated by joining together to sing, dance, and give gifts could establish ties between isolated reservation communities while providing mutual support through times of poverty and displacement.

News of powwows traveled by newspaper and telegraph, and trains and automobiles made it possible for larger powwows to attract people from widely scattered tribes. In the East, where rail transportation was accessible first, these gatherings of Native Americans promoted the visibility of Indian culture. In 1901, Chickahominy people in tidewater Virginia began holding a fall "fish fry" to gather their community together and cement good relations with supportive white neighbors. The event evolved into a Virginia Indian "homecoming," and by the 1920s it was renamed the Fall Festival, complete with Native singing and powwow dancing. In New England, the Indian community at Mashpee began organizing an annual fall powwow in 1928. An extension of the tribe's annual summer homecoming (an informal event that families had held for decades), the new powwow attracted Native Americans from across the region and included religious services, baseball games, and a beauty contest. In a similar process Indians on Long Island gathered each summer to cement old ties and to celebrate their common past.

In the 1920s, as the transportation system in the West expanded, tribes in Oklahoma and on the northern Plains began to coordinate their powwows so that they formed a western "circuit" of events throughout the summer. When this schedule became well-known, powwows began to attract visitors from distant reservations. Kiowas from Oklahoma were regulars at the Crow gatherings in Montana. Canadian Ojibwes visited their kinsmen in Minnesota, Wisconsin, and Michigan, while Nez Percés visited old comrades east of the Rockies, and Plateau gatherings brought visitors from Oregon, Washington, and British Columbia.

Indians in Popular Culture

At the same time that powwow dancers were creating an arena where aspects of Native American life would be tolerated or even welcomed by officials, the general public was coming to appreciate outstanding individual Indians and even to adopt certain attractive elements of traditional Native cultures.

The first Indians to catch the public's eye in the twentieth century were male athletes associated with the Carlisle school. While health and fitness had been a part of the Carlisle curriculum from its inception, organized intramural sports did not begin there until the 1890s. During that decade, teams from various departments of the school played one another in football and baseball, and informal track and field competitions took place as a form of exercise and entertainment. Students welcomed this innovation. Not only did athletics provide a respite from the bleak discipline that characterized life at the boarding school, but it gave young Indian men and women a chance to continue an ancient Native tradition of physical competition. Tribes had not only developed and sustained the game of lacrosse across much of eastern North America, but they supported a great many local games, races, and contests.

College athletic competition among men had begun in the Ivy League in the 1870s; by the 1890s schools across the country had come to appreciate how sports could unite students and win support from the general public. Always eager to buff the school's public profile, administrators at Carlisle were eager to participate in this new phenomenon. Carlisle played a modest football schedule in the 1890s, taking on a variety of local colleges, club teams, and high schools, but public curiosity about the "Indian" team soon won them invitations from a wider circle of colleges. The high point of these early years was a night game in December 1896 at the Chicago Coliseum between Carlisle and the University of Wisconsin. The contest drew more than sixteen thousand fans to what was probably the first night football game ever played.

Eager to build on this success, Richard Pratt exempted team members from many of the school's rigid requirements, fed them at special tables in the dining hall, and encouraged coaches and teachers to recruit athletes from reservations and other boarding schools. His most dramatic action came in 1899 when he hired Glenn S. ("Pop") Warner to coach football, track, and baseball at the school. Warner quickly established a rigorous training schedule and his teams soared to national prominence. Playing for $10,000–$15,000 per contest (all money handled by Warner), Carlisle football teams took on opponents from the Ivy League and the Big Ten and scheduled contests in California and throughout New York and Pennsylvania. (Lacking a stadium, all of Carlisle's games were played on their opponent's home field.) In 1907 Carlisle won ten games and lost only one; in 1911 they won eleven of twelve. During these years several Carlisle students won All American honors, and the teams regularly appeared before huge crowds. Outstanding athletes also competed in intercollegiate track and baseball.

While men such as Bemus Pierce (Seneca), Jimmy Johnson (Stockbridge-Munsee), and Joe Guyon (Ojibwe) were celebrated football heroes during this era (and the Haskell school's John Levi won a spot on the All American team with Red Grange in 1923), the centerpiece of Carlisle's fame was Jim Thorpe. Thorpe was not a recruit; he was sent to Pennsylvania from his home on the Sauk and Fox reserve in Prague, Oklahoma, after running away from several Indian boarding schools. When he first arrived on campus, the young Oklahoman had no interest in sports, but he caught Warner's attention when he happened by the high jump arena one day during a meet and set a school record in his street clothes. Selected in 1950 by the Associated Press as the greatest male athlete of the first half of the twentieth century, Thorpe excelled at football, baseball, and track and field. He was named to three All American football teams, and by 1912, his final season, tales of his achievements were staples of the nation's sports pages. The most frequently repeated story during his last year came from the game against Army in which a 100-yard kickoff return by Thorpe was called back because of an offside violation. Thorpe received the ensuing kickoff and repeated his feat. Among the hapless cadets chasing him that day was future president Dwight Eisenhower.

Thorpe's greatest success came in 1912 when he won gold medals in both the pentathlon and decathlon at the Olympics in Stockholm. Shocking the European press and public with scores that far outdistanced the competition, Thorpe was celebrated by the King of Sweden as "the greatest athlete in the world." (He was reported to have replied, "Thanks, King.") The gold medalist returned to parades and celebrations, but early in 1913 American newspapers reported that Thorpe had played semiprofessional baseball in 1909, a technical violation of the American Athletic Union's (AAU) restrictions on amateur athletes. The AAU stripped Thorpe of his medals. This action set off a controversy that was not resolved until 1983 when the International Olympic Committee restored Thorpe's status as an amateur and presented his descendants with new medals. The controversy over Thorpe's gold medals did not lessen his fame in the United States. He played both professional football and professional baseball before adoring crowds well into the 1920s.

Other American Indians won acclaim in sports in the years before World War I. Louis Tewanima, a Hopi classmate of Thorpe's at Carlisle, participated in both the 1908 and 1912 Olympics, winning silver medals in the 5,000- and 10,000-meter races. Another Carlisle graduate, Charles Bender, an Ojibwe from Brainerd, Minnesota, pitched for the Philadelphia Athletics from 1903 to 1917; John Meyers, a Cahuilla from California who attended Dartmouth College, played catcher for the New York Giants and Brooklyn Dodgers baseball clubs between 1908 and 1918.

Perhaps more important, the fame of these Carlisle athletes inspired a surge in sports competition in Indian communities. Boarding schools and local clubs sponsored athletic teams that competed with each other as well as with non-Indians. The Catholic missions inaugurated a National Catholic Basketball Tournament, and one enterprising South Dakotan, William Conquering Bear, organized the Sioux Travellers, an exhibition basketball team that toured nationally and was occasionally matched up against the Harlem Globetrotters. Another Indian team gained fame as an early entry in the fledgling National Football League. The Oorang Indians competed in the NFL in 1922 and 1923, drawing enormous crowds with their stellar play and halftime shows featuring traditional dancing, tomahawk throwing contests, and bear wrestling.

White Americans also encountered Indians and their traditions in the lessons and folklore of two immensely popular organizations for young people: the Boy Scouts and the Camp Fire Girls. Formed in 1911 through a merger of the original organization founded in England and two American groups (the Woodcraft League and the Boy Pioneers), the Boy Scouts appeared at about the same time that Luther and Charlotte Gulick organized the Camp Fire Girls. The latter organization introduced adolescent girls to camping and activities that promoted good health and domestic skills. Both the scouts and the Camp Fire Girls emerged in the wake of the modern summer camp phenomenon, which drew thousands of boys and girls from their urban homes and exposed them to programs that featured "Indian" values such as environmental sensitivity and individual resourcefulness. The Camp Fire Girls and Boy Scouts repackaged these lessons for a national audience.

However distorted these romantic versions of Indian culture may have been, they represented a remarkable shift from the tales of frontier violence that had been presented to children only a generation earlier. The appealing image of "healthy" and virtuous Native Americans living in the woods assured middle-class citizens that "Indianness" was benign, not savage, and that Indian values—if not Indians themselves—could be incorporated into the national culture.

While American children were cultivating "healthy" tans at summer camp and joining the Boy Scouts and Camp Fire Girls, their parents were being exposed to artistic representations of Indian life that carried a similarly rosy view of tribal traditions. "Indian art" was not a category the American public would have recognized before 1900; by 1930 it was a burgeoning industry. In the nineteenth century, art collectors had taken little notice of the work of tribal artists. Widespread recognition came first to Indian weavers and potters. In the Southwest, the arrival of the Southern Pacific Railroad and, after 1900, the Fred Harvey Company tourist hotels and restaurants helped create a demand for Navajo blankets and Pueblo pottery. The latter category expanded dramatically in the early 1900s after Hopi potter Nampeyo (1860–1942) began producing exquisite polychrome water jars and bowls that were inspired by archaeological artifacts excavated at Sikyatki, a Hopi village abandoned in the seventeenth century. In a similar way, Maria Martinez (1887–1980), a young potter from San Ildefonso Pueblo, began to create pieces in an older style. Decorated by her husband Julian,

Maria Martinez and Her Husband Julian Maria Martinez was one of the most popular Pueblo potters of the early twentieth century. Working from her home village of San Ildefonso, New Mexico, Maria developed a signature, "black on black" style that combined glossy and matte finishes. Her work is treasured by collectors and museums around the globe.

Maria's pots were popular with tourists in Santa Fe and were featured attractions at the 1915 World's Fair in San Diego.

The popularity of Indian handicrafts whetted the public's appetite for other aspects of Native art. In 1917, New Mexican archaeologist Edgar Hewett began commissioning paintings of Pueblo ceremonial life from local artists and showing them to friends, particularly some of the artists and art collectors who had recently relocated to the Southwest. Within a few years these collectors, who included Mabel Dodge Luhan, Mary Austin, and Alice Corbin Henderson, had widened the circle of patronage and helped generate a market for the work of artists such as Fred Kabotie (Hopi), Otis

Polelonema (Cochiti Pueblo), and Awa Tsireh (San Ildefonso Pueblo). Hewett also played a central role in the creation of the first Santa Fe "Fiesta" in 1919, one of the earliest public events that brought together tourists and Indian artists.

While Hewett and his colleagues were encouraging Indian painters in New Mexico and Arizona, Susan Peters, a teacher at the Bureau of Indian Affairs' Anadarko boarding school in western Oklahoma, was organizing art classes for her Kiowa and Comanche students. By 1928 she had gained the attention of Professor O. B. Jacobson of the University of Oklahoma and had managed to enroll six of her best students in a special program at the university's college of art. There the six Kiowas, five men (Monroe Tsa Toke, Stephen Mopope, Spencer Asah, Jack Hokeah, and James Auchiah) and one woman (Bouge-te Smokey), developed a distinctive painting style that featured bold images and bright colors. Their work reached galleries in New York and Chicago at the same time as the work of the Pueblo potters and artists; together the two groups generated considerable enthusiasm for tribal arts.

During these same years American Indian writers were gaining a national audience for their work. Beginning in 1900, Gertrude Simmons Bonnin (1876–1938), a Yankton author who had been educated at Earlham College, published a series of autobiographical sketches in popular magazines such as *Atlantic Monthly* and *Harper's*. Taking the pen name Zitkala Ša, she celebrated her native heritage and poked fun at the white man's "civilization." As he grew disillusioned with his work for the Indian Office, physician Charles Eastman (1858–1939) also turned to literature. He published popular versions of traditional Sioux culture, such as *Old Indian Days* (1907) and *Wigwam Evenings* (1909), but his most enduring works were memoirs of his own life and career: *Indian Boyhood* (1902) and *From the Deep Woods to Civilization* (1916). In all, Eastman published nine books between 1902 and 1918. Other authors who published similar works for a mass audience included Pauline Johnson (Tekahionwake) (1861–1913), a Mohawk from Ontario whose most popular work was a collection of fictional portraits called *The Moccasin Maker* (1913); Christine Quintasket (1884–1936), a Salish woman who published the novel *Cogawea* in 1927 under the pen name Mourning Dove; and the former Carlisle student Plenty Kill who, as Luther

Standing Bear (1868–1939), published *My People, The Sioux* in 1928.

The newest popular medium—movies—also played an important role in communicating positive images of Native American life to the general public. Images of Indians had been featured in the first nickelodeons in the 1890s, so as feature films came to be produced in the first decades of the new century, Indian actors were quickly recruited to present themselves in Native costume and to portray positive aspects of their own culture. Many Indians were drawn to acting; among them was Carlisle graduate Luther Standing Bear, who left teaching and moved first to New York, and then, in 1910, to California where he went to work for film pioneer Tom Ince.

Mildred Bailey made a name for herself in jazz. Born Mildred Rinker in Tekoa, Washington, in 1907, this Coeur d'Alene woman entertained friends at local clubs before moving to Los Angeles in 1925. She was soon performing with Paul Whiteman. A childhood friend of Bing Crosby, she is credited with introducing the future crooner to Whiteman. Bailey went on to perform with Benny Goodman, Billie Holiday, and others, and to host her own show, *Mrs. Swing*, on CBS radio.

Rather than being "killed" as Captain Pratt had urged, Indian culture in the twentieth century seemed to be evolving into something new. Modern Indians mixed traditional activities with new media—novels, paintings, movies, popular music, even football games—to communicate with the American public. Whites controlled the sports teams, the art galleries, and the film companies, but Indians had found—and made—a Native place in each of these worlds.

FIGHTING FOR THE INDIAN CAUSE

As a political interest group, Native people had a great many liabilities. They were divided among dozens of tribes; few of them voted; and their most famous leaders were viewed as opponents of the United States and so had no influence over politicians in Washington or local state capitals. On the other hand, the missionaries who still hoped to eradicate their "heathen" cultures and the local set-tlers who sought access to their "undeveloped" lands were numerous and well organized. Not surprisingly, the first three decades of the new century were not a time of triumph for Indians, but they were a time when Native communities discovered ways of winning small victories and laying the groundwork for future success.

The End of Indian Territory

By 1900, the Dawes Commission that Congress had established to prepare final membership rolls for the Five Civilized Tribes was deeply engaged in its work. It reviewed applications from more than 300,000 people who claimed membership in the five tribes and assigned allotments to those who were eligible. Among those receiving homesteads from the commission were African-Americans who had been held as slaves by tribal members prior to 1863. By 1907 when it completed its work, the Dawes Commission had assigned 19.5 million acres of tribal land to 101,000 people.

The Indian Office also allotted all the reservations in the western portion of Indian Territory. Those reserves had been created in the nineteenth century as refuges for midwestern and western tribes and had gathered people from Illinois, Iowa, and Missouri. Other agencies were established for tribes from Nebraska, Kansas, and Colorado. The largest preserves (with the most land available for white homesteaders) attracted considerable interest from settlers and local politicians, and these lands were allotted quickly. By 1900 only a few reservations, most notably the one occupied by the Osages, remained undivided.

To complete the process of breaking up the territory's tribes, Congress approved a new law in 1901 that declared all Indians in Indian Territory to be U.S. citizens. This measure—adopted without consultation with Native Americans—placed the territory's Indians on the same legal footing as the white settlers who had organized "Oklahoma" in the nontribal areas in 1889. In theory the new citizenship made it possible for whites to claim that "Oklahoma" could someday include all of the people living on tribal lands in "Indian Territory." Indians were no longer citizens of the Cherokee or Creek nations because those nations no longer existed. For this reason, most tribal leaders opposed the citizenship law; instead they called for a separate legal status for Indians and a separate territorial government for the former Indian Territory. They hoped that this separate territory might enter the Union as an Indian state.

In November 1902, officials of the Creek Nation tried to rally Indian opposition to Oklahoma by sponsoring a general convention to discuss the future of the former Indian Territory. Meeting in Eufaula, the assembly passed resolutions calling for the creation of two territories, each eligible for statehood. One would be called Oklahoma and the other, called "Sequoyah," would encompass the former territories of the Five Tribes. Rebuffed by the authorities, the convention met again in 1905 and repeated its demands. At the 1905 meeting, the group also adopted a constitution for the proposed Indian state and asked that a referendum be held among all the residents of the Five Tribes' territory the following November. This vote took place, but despite the fact that it showed there was overwhelming support for the creation of Sequoyah, officials in Washington ignored it. The sentiment in Congress greatly favored a single, white-dominated territorial government, and Theodore Roosevelt personally rejected the idea of an Indian state in December 1905. Instead, the popular president proposed the admission of a single state called Oklahoma. An enabling act passed Congress the following summer, and the new state formally came into existence in September 1907.

The rejection of Sequoyah and creation of Oklahoma did not end resistance in Indian Territory. One elder recalled that his community "cried all night" on the eve of statehood. Others took more direct action. Among the Cherokees, Redbird Smith, a leader of the anti-allotment Keetowah Society, emerged in the first decade of the new century as an outspoken advocate of separate statehood for Indian Territory. Smith organized a new offshoot of the Keetowah Society, the Nighthawks, and refused to recognize the dissolution of the Cherokee government. After Smith's death in 1918, Frank Boudinot led the group, eventually calling for secession from the Cherokee Nation and the formation of a new tribal organization.

Chitto Harjo led a similar group among the Creeks. Called Crazy Snakes by federal authorities, Harjo and his followers refused to recognize the Creek government's dissolution. They formed their own secessionist government at Harjo's home village of Hickory Ground. There, Harjo and his followers attracted dissidents from other nearby tribes. In 1900 a U.S. cavalry unit was dispatched to arrest and disperse them. The rebels were quickly released with suspended sentences, but two years later continued obstruction from Harjo led to his rearrest and imprisonment at the federal penitentiary in Leavenworth, Kansas. Harjo never reconciled himself to Oklahoma statehood. After his return to Hickory Ground, he continued to advocate the revival of a tribal government and resistance to allotment.

In western Indian Territory, resistance took another form. Virtually every tribe subjected to the allotment process in the nineteenth century had members who tried to keep the reservation intact. This group was particularly fierce among the Kiowas. One Kiowa elder, a man called Lone Wolf, simply refused to cooperate with the government's new program. Called the Implacables by federal authorities, Lone Wolf's band held themselves aloof from Christian missionaries, allotting agents, and any federal official trying to arrange for the sale of tribal land. They grew more aggressive in their resistance after 1892 when a congressional commission chaired by former Michigan governor David Jerome completed an agreement that mandated the allotment and sale of all surplus lands. Lone Wolf charged that the Jerome agreement contained a number of irregularities (forged signatures, inaccurate statements) and that it violated the 1867 Medicine Lodge Treaty, which stipulated that all future land sales would require the approval of three-quarters of the adult males in the tribe. Lobbying by white allies—most prominently the Indian Rights Association—delayed congressional action, but in 1900 the key elements of the original Jerome agreement became law.

Determined to defend the authority of the 1867 Medicine Lodge Treaty, which had established the Kiowa reservation, Lone Wolf traveled to Washington, D.C., in the spring of 1901, accompanied by his nephew, former Carlisle student (and football star) Delos Lone Wolf. After consulting with William K. Springer, a sympathetic former Democratic congressman and federal judge, Lone Wolf filed suit in federal court to enjoin Secretary of the Interior Ethan A. Hitchcock from carrying out the Jerome agreement. In 1902, after lower courts had rejected his

Lone Wolf Lone Wolf (seated left), with a Kiowa delegation to Washington, D.C., in 1902. The group traveled to Washington to lobby members of Congress to block the allotment of their reservation and the sale of its "surplus" land.

petition, Lone Wolf and Springer appealed the Kiowa case to the Supreme Court. Despite continued help from the Indian Rights Association, Springer, and Hampton L. Carson, the attorney general of Pennsylvania, the Kiowas could not persuade the Court to honor the 1867 treaty. Early in 1903, in a decision that marked a crushing defeat for all tribes, the justices declared that congressional action could override the provisions of a ratified Indian treaty. "The power exists to abrogate the provisions of an Indian treaty," the jurists noted, "though presumably such power will be exercised only when circumstances arise . . . which may demand . . . that [the government] should do so."

Following Chitto Harjo's imprisonment at Fort Leavenworth and Lone Wolf's defeat before the Supreme Court, it was clear that for many Native Americans in Indian Territory, loyalty to one's tribes was stronger than their loyalty to the laws of the United States. Indians had organized conventions, held special elections, recruited white allies, lobbied Congress, and even carried their pleas to the Supreme Court—all in an effort to force the United States to live up to its eighty-year-old promise to protect the territory's relocated tribes in their new homeland.

The Black Hills

By 1900 the stout military resistance to white expansion on the northern Plains was a fading memory. Crazy Horse and Sitting Bull were dead, and white settlers were rapidly extending their ranching and farming operations across the Red, Missouri, and Yellowstone river valleys. Their homesteads drew ever closer to the tribal lands that were themselves being gradually eroded by allotments and land sales. Now that Montana, Wyoming, and the Dakotas were states, these settlers had eight new senators arguing their cause before Congress. The Indians had none.

Proving again that grim situations can get worse, the Supreme Court's *Lone Wolf* decision in 1903 removed the requirement that federal officials must gain tribal consent before opening treaty-protected lands to white settlement. As a consequence, allotment and land sale statutes were approved for the South Dakota Rosebud reservation, the Montana Crow and Flathead reservations, and North Dakota's Devil's Lake reserve within a year of the Supreme Court's ruling. Over the next ten years Congress acted to open all the remaining large reserves in the region—Pine Ridge in South Dakota, Standing Rock in North Dakota, and Blackfeet in Montana. By 1921, nearly 50 million acres of tribal land had passed to non-Indians, and more than two-thirds of the region's Native people had been given allotment certificates that covered 17.5 million acres of what had formerly been part of protected reservations.

As had been the case in western Oklahoma, individual leaders in several of these communities attempted to delay or derail the allotment process. The Crows were the most aggressive in this regard, hiring the Washington law firm of Kappler and Marillat to represent them before congressional committees and sending a series of delegations to lobby sympathetic legislators. One of their leaders in those years was Robert Yellowtail, an eloquent graduate of Sherman Institute, a boarding school in Riverside, California. Yellowtail told one committee that the Crow reservation was "a separate semisovereign nation" and that "no senator, or anybody else . . . has any right . . . to tear us asunder . . . simply because of our geographical proximity to his state." Unfortunately, none of these tactics or powerful words could stop the allotment process.

The Sioux and Cheyennes tried another tactic; they turned to the courts. The tribe's 1868 treaty with the United States, signed at Fort Laramie and ratified by Congress, had stated explicitly that no further land sales would be valid unless ratified by three-quarters of the tribe's adult males. But tribal elders remembered vividly the day in 1877 when the United States had seized their sacred Black Hills with an agreement that lacked this approval. (Note: Official treatymaking ended in 1871, but the 1877 "agreement" had the same legal force as a treaty.) The Pine Ridge agent reported as early as 1891 that groups of old men had begun meeting on the reservation to discuss the government's treaty violations, but no formal charge was made against the United States until the fall of 1903 when eighty-two-year-old Lakota Chief Red Cloud made his case to South Dakota Congressman Eben Martin. Saying the money the government had paid for the hills was "just a little spit out of my mouth," the old warrior demanded proper compensation.

Unlike Lone Wolf, Red Cloud sought compensation for the loss, not the reversal of a government's action. The Supreme Court's *Lone Wolf* decision therefore did not seem to cancel the Sioux claim. Congressman Martin ignored Red Cloud's plea, but in 1911 a gathering of more than one hundred representatives of all the Sioux and Cheyennes met at a reservation in central South Dakota and elected boarding school graduate James Crow Feather chairman of the Council of Nine Agencies, a group dedicated to press their complaint.

It seemed a hopeless effort, but in 1914 a Sioux delegation representing what was now called the Black Hills Council (led by neatly dressed "progressive" Indians) traveled to Washington, D.C., and managed to get a bill introduced in Congress that would authorize the U.S. Court of Claims to hear the tribe's complaint. The delegates argued for justice for the "Sioux Nation," an entity the Indian Office had theoretically destroyed when it divided the Sioux reserve into seven separate agencies back in 1889. Consideration of the Black Hills Council's bill was delayed by World War I, but the Indians persisted and gradually the Indian Office and a number of otherwise hostile South Dakota politicians came to support the measure. They believed a formal case would give the plaintiffs their "day in court" and put the matter to rest. In 1920 Congress finally approved turning the complaint over to the Court of Claims. Tribal attorneys filed the petition of "The Sioux Nation" versus the United States of America in May 1923.

Elaborate legal maneuvering and extensive research into the monetary value of the Black Hills delayed consideration of the Black Hills case for nearly two decades. Despite its frustrating length, this controversy provided a powerful forum for traditionalists who insisted that the Sioux Nation had not been dissolved, while offering white South Dakotans an ongoing history lesson. The claims court announced its verdict in 1942. Elaborating on its decision in *Lone Wolf* v. *Hitchcock*, the judges declared that Congress had the power to override the 1868 treaty and seize the hills. An appeal to the Supreme Court produced only a reaffirmation of the lower court's ruling.

It would take nearly forty more years and a small army of lawyers and lobbyists for the Black Hills claim to find its way back to the Supreme Court, but the Sioux and Cheyenne commitment to the issue never disappeared. Their struggle inspired other tribes to file similar lawsuits and generated new sympathy for Indians who had been victimized by greedy settlers and their political allies. When the Court finally acted in 1980, awarding the Sioux $110 million for the property taken from them, the symbolism of the tribe's former territory had become so powerful that its monetary value now seemed secondary. "The Black Hills Are Not for Sale" activists cried; the day when the tribe would simply accept money for the damages they suffered had passed. This new slogan overrode the desire in some quarters to take the federal dollars and put them to work for the benefit of the tribe. As a result, the case remains unresolved and interest on the tribe's reward has multiplied its value many times over.

Defending New Mexico Lands

In New Mexico, the "Indian Cause" was the protection of pueblo lands. Ever since the arrival of the Spanish in the sixteenth century, the boundaries of individual pueblo communities had been in dispute. Typically, these agricultural villages were surrounded by irrigated fields, grazing areas, and hunting grounds. Ordered as much by religious belief as by political authority, the limits of a particular pueblo's territory were rarely clear to outsiders. In the nineteenth century, the advent of aggressive new settlers from both the eastern United States and Mexico created additional confusion, particularly in the densely populated Rio Grande valley. Because the 1848 Treaty of Guadalupe Hidalgo had stipulated that all residents of what had been Mexico were now citizens of the United States, American officials had not concerned themselves with squatters who challenged the Indians' land titles. In their view, the tribes could enforce their titles in court like anyone else. Practically, however, this official indifference served as a green light to squatters, for the pueblos had little besides ambiguous and often contradictory Spanish land grants with which to defend themselves.

In 1913 the U.S. Supreme Court forced federal authorities to act. In a case involving the illegal sale of liquor to pueblo Indians (*U.S. v. Sandoval*) the High Court declared that, despite their American citizenship, these Native Americans were "backward" people who required the protection and supervision of the Indian Office. In the wake of the *Sandoval* decision, federal officials became more active on behalf of the Rio Grande tribes. Unfortunately for the pueblos, this search for justice began at a difficult time. New Mexico entered the Union in 1912. Suddenly—as in Montana and the Dakotas—the pueblos found themselves living in a state represented by a congressional delegation that had far more sympathy for non-Indian farmers and ranchers than for Native Americans who could not vote.

The New Mexico politicians' response to disputes over pueblo landownership appeared in 1922 in the form of a bill sponsored by the state's senator, Holm O. Bursum. Introduced with the support of Secretary of Interior (and former New Mexico senator) Albert Fall, the measure would have confirmed most of the non-Indian squatters' claims.

Bursum's bill quickly passed the Senate, but while the House of Representatives deliberated, New Mexico's Indian leaders began searching for a way to make their voices heard.

New Mexico's tribal leaders turned first to local Democratic politicians (Fall and Bursum were Republicans) and sympathetic whites. Among the latter were artists, writers, and intellectuals who had become active admirers of Indian art and culture. They included anthropologists such as Edgar Hewett, the patron of many early Indian artists and craftspeople, and writers such as Mary Austin and Willa Cather. Most prominent, however, was John Collier, a former New York City social worker who had recently become a college professor in California. In 1920 Collier and his family had spent the Christmas holiday in New Mexico as the guests of Mabel Dodge, an old friend from New York, and her Taos Pueblo husband, Antonio Luhan. Collier later recalled that the visit, during which his family witnessed a number of winter ceremonials at the Taos Pueblo, gave him "a new direction in life" and "a new . . . hope for the Race of Man."

Like the tourists who now filled the village square in Santa Fe or the Boy Scouts who camped in the Rockies each summer, Collier saw embedded in Native American culture the values that a rapidly urbanizing and industrializing United States was in danger of losing: respect for ancient traditions, a sense of community, and an appreciation for natural beauty. Following the Senate's approval of the Bursum bill, Collier and Antonio Luhan leaped into action. Soon a call went out to all Pueblo leaders to gather at Santo Domingo Pueblo for a general council in early November.

The first modern All-Pueblo Council met on November 3, 1922. There were 121 delegates from 19 pueblos (including Zuni Pueblo, which lay outside the Rio Grande valley) who spent two days and nights hearing explanations of the Bursum bill and discussing possible responses. On November 5 the pueblo representatives issued "An Appeal for Fair Play," which was quickly published in the Santa Fe *New Mexican* and reprinted in newspapers across the country.

The pueblos' 1922 "Appeal" echoed themes that had been heard in other tribal settings over the previous two decades. It declared: "The Pueblos existed in a civilized condition before the white man came to America. We have kept our old customs

All-Pueblo Council The governors of the All-Pueblo Council gather at New Mexico's Santa Domingo Pueblo in 1926. Originally organized in 1922 to fight the Bursum Bill, the council became a forum for discussing common concerns and voicing objections to unpopular or potentially damaging federal actions.

and lived in harmony with each other and with our fellow Americans. This bill will destroy our common life and will rob us of everything which we hold dear—our lands, our customs, our traditions." Tribal leaders repeated these themes in congressional testimony delivered in January 1923 and in a series of public presentations arranged by their allies in New York and Washington. These efforts—together with Secretary Fall's subsequent entanglement with Harding administration scandals—managed to scuttle the Bursum bill.

Pueblo leaders could not claim victory in their battle with the squatters, but they could take some solace in the fact that their general council and "Appeal," as well as the positive publicity they generated during their trip to Washington, D.C., had stopped Senator Bursum's juggernaut. They had established alliances with a number of powerful interests in the worlds of art and journalism and had shown that small embattled tribes could find support if they managed to capture the attention of the national press. They had also refined their message of Indian rights, asserting that attacks on their

lands and customs were not signs of "progress" but examples of America's "betrayal" of its responsibility to protect Native people. As with the Black Hills case, the Pueblo protests had defined a model others would emulate.

Making a Platform for an "Indian Voice"

Local conflicts with the surrounding non-Indian community often spurred Native Americans to form new organizations that would bring their case to the public. In Indian Territory, resistance to allotment, and Oklahoma statehood invigorated the Keetowah Society, while in South Dakota, the Black Hills Treaty Council became the group that coordinated the prosecution of the Sioux lawsuit in the U.S. Court of Claims. By the 1920s, similar organizations with local roots but with a common commitment to the defense of tribal interests had emerged in every corner of the United States.

One of the earliest regional organizations was formed in Alaska in 1912 by a small group of Tlingit and Tsimshian men who had attended the Presbyterian mission school in Sitka. In its first years the Alaska Native Brotherhood (ANB) was indistinguishable from the many Protestant lay societies that were typically affiliated with Indian missions. In fact, as was the case in most mission communities, a parallel women's organization, the Alaska Native Sisterhood (ANS), was founded almost immediately after the men's group came into being. But both groups developed a secular agenda—the "advancement" of Native people and opposition to "the narrow injustice of race prejudice." By the 1920s active chapters were functioning in all the major villages of southeast Alaska. One of its leaders was Carlisle graduate William Paul, a Tlingit who was elected to the Alaska territorial legislature in 1926. There he successfully challenged racial segregation in territorial schools and urged support for the unionization of Indian cannery workers.

In Washington State, members of Puget Sound bands and tribes established the Northwest Federation of American Indians (NFAI) in 1914. Like the ANB, the NFAI organized chapters at agencies and tribal communities across the area. The Washington group often focused its attention on defending tribal fishing rights. In New England, Cape Cod Indians formed the Wampanoag Nation in 1928. Initiated by Nelson Drew Simons, a graduate of Carlisle and Boston University Law School, and Eben Queppish, a former Wild West Show performer, the group's widely reported meetings mixed socializing with speeches by tribal leaders that celebrated tribal heroes like King Philip and called on whites to support the tribal cause.

In addition to the All-Pueblo Council formed to fight the Bursum bill, the Southwest witnessed the creation of the Navajo Tribal Council in 1922. The council was the first organization to bring together representatives from all of the widely scattered communities on the Navajo reservation. Ironically, the Tribal Council was initially organized by government officials who needed an official body to sign mineral leases with coal companies, but during the 1920s the group developed a tribal political agenda and a voice of its own.

The political organizations that articulated Native interests in the 1920s were nearly all local. The lone exception to this rule was the Society of American Indians (SAI), a group that formed on Columbus Day in 1911 on the campus of Ohio State University. Made up exclusively of educated Native men and women, the society cast itself as a national organization dedicated to working for "the advancement of the American Indian in enlightenment." The society announced that it was dedicated to providing a forum in which Indians could discuss "all subjects bearing on the welfare of the race," presenting "the true history of the race," promoting Indian citizenship, and exploring legal remedies for problems affecting Native Americans. It published a sophisticated magazine (The *Quarterly Journal*, 1913–1915; renamed *American Indian Magazine*, 1915–1920) and opened an office in Washington, D.C. The prominence and skill of its members won the organization quick attention, but internal disputes—over whether or not to oppose peyote use or advocate the abolition of the Indian Office—and a shrinking treasury led to its dissolution in the early 1920s.

The principal objective of the SAI was to reverse the public's view of Indians as backward and doomed. The first issue of its magazine reminded readers that George Washington had once said of the Indians, "They, poor wretches, have no press through which their grievances are related." The editors responded proudly: "We, 'poor wretches' have a press and the other side of the story may be told." Subsequent issues spoke out against the cruelty of the government's boarding schools and the paternalism of Indian Office bureaucrats. The SAI also endorsed court challenges like the Black Hills case and, despite the fact that most members were professed Christians, generally supported the right of tribes to conduct traditional ceremonies without interference.

The only other Native American to attempt to rally a national Indian audience in this period was Carlos Montezuma, a Yavapai physician based in Chicago. Montezuma had been captured as a child by a neighboring tribe and sold in 1871 to an itinerant Italian immigrant photographer named Carlos Gentile. Gentile named the boy after himself and the Aztec emperor and, after a few years of travel together, placed him in the care of a minister in Urbana, Illinois, home of the recently founded state university. Montezuma proved to be a remarkable young man. A brilliant student, he graduated with a degree in chemistry from the University of Illinois and went on to Chicago Medical

College, where he received his M.D. in 1889. Montezuma participated in the founding of the SAI in 1911, but he disapproved of the organization's friendly attitude towards the Indian Office and began publishing his own newsletter, *Wassaja*. Through his newsletter, Montezuma campaigned tirelessly for the extension of U.S. citizenship to Indians and the abolition of all government programs for Native people. "The sooner the government abolishes the Indian Bureau," he wrote, "the better it will be for Indians in every way." Montezuma had a loyal following, but he didn't have the time to build a political movement. Diagnosed with tuberculosis, he returned to Arizona in the 1920s. He died among his kinsman at Fort McDowell in January 1923. *Wassaja* died with him.

Indians Fight in the "War to End All Wars"

World War I offered Native Americans an unexpected opportunity to educate their fellow citizens about Indians and their history. When the United States entered the war in April 1917, Indians suddenly had a chance to be both patriotic and "Indian." The Indian Office established special draft boards at all agencies in the spring of 1917; by September nearly 12,000 young men had registered for service. Of these, 6,500 were called to arms. Indians seemed eager to respond. In addition to those drafted, another three to six thousand (the records are not clear) enlisted. Many of these enlistees were technically not U.S. citizens, but they signed up anyway. By war's end at least 12,000 Native Americans were in uniform. At the same time Indian women took the lead in organizing Red Cross fund raisers in their communities and volunteering to replace Indian Office staff who left for the front. Several Indian women served as army nurses in France. One of these, Lula Owl, became a battlefield supervisor and thereby gained notoriety as the only Eastern Cherokee officer in the war. This widespread participation produced a dramatic change in non-Indian perceptions of Native Americans.

Most of the outspoken new Indian organizations endorsed the war. In Indian Territory, a small group of Creeks at Chitto Harjo's old headquarters, Hickory Ground, threatened to resist the draft, but their protests were quickly overcome by a wave of local patriotism. The only prominent Indian

Plenty Coups and Marshall Foch Plenty Coups, the tradiional leader of the Crow Indians, participated in the dedication of the Tomb of the Unknown Soldier at Arlington Cemetery, outside Washington, D.C., in 1921. There he met Marshall Ferdinand Foch, the French commander during World War I, and invited him to visit the Crows' Montana homeland. Foch is pictured here in 1923 with the Crow chief and Joseph K. Dixon, an author of popular books about American Indian life.

leader to speak out against the war was Carlos Montezuma, who insisted Indians had no obligation to defend a nation that would not grant them citizenship or recognize their rights. "The Indian Office keeps us Indians from our rights," Carlos Montezuma wrote in *Wassaja*. "It tells the country that we are competent to be soldiers, but are not competent to be citizens." Despite Montezuma's eloquence, few joined him.

The war generated widespread popular support for Native Americans even though the public continued to view Indian people through racial stereotypes. Indians were not forced into segregated units as African-Americans were, but when they reported for duty, Native soldiers discovered that commanders believed they were "instinctive" warriors unsuited for command. Nearly two-thirds of Native Americans served in the infantry, and only 1 percent of them became officers. Military leaders also believed Indians possessed unique physical traits—night vision, speed, and a taste for "bloodthirsty" combat—and therefore possessed a special ability to scout enemy positions, serve as snipers, or deliver messages across difficult terrain.

Despite these misperceptions, Native American soldiers and nurses performed admirably in the war and won widespread praise for their contributions. Indians were members of the first units to reach France in July 1917, and they fought in every major engagement until the war ended in November 1918. A number of soldiers received battlefield commendations. Sergeant Otis Leader, for example, a Choctaw from Oklahoma, was decorated for his bravery at Chateau-Thierry, St. Mihiel, and the Argonne Forest, while a Sioux infantryman, Joe Young Hawk, won fame at the Battle of Soissons for escaping capture by killing three of his guards with his bare hands and capturing the other two. Robert Dodd, a Paiute, was a member of the famed "lost battalion," which fought alone in the Argonne Woods for six days in October 1918. The most highly decorated Indian soldier of the war was Joseph Oklahombi, another Choctaw, who was awarded a Silver Star by the Americans and the Croix de Guerre by the French for single-handedly rushing a German stronghold near St. Etienne in October 1918. In the course of the battle, Oklahombi captured a machine gun emplacement and took 171 prisoners.

Not surprisingly, perilous assignments produced high casualties. Overall an estimated 5 percent of Indian combat soldiers were killed in the war; only 1 percent of the American forces as a whole were lost. At home the sacrifices were less dramatic, but nearly as impressive. Indian communities bought war bonds at a record rate. By war's end, Native Americans owned $25 million of these bonds, the equivalent of $75 for every man, woman, and child. Ten thousand Indian women joined the Red Cross during the war, contributing time, money, and clothing to the war effort.

World War I was a turning point in the American public's view of Native Americans. The war provided Indians with a way to demonstrate a variety of admirable personal qualities—patriotism, intelligence, and bravery. Speaking at a meeting of the SAI in 1918, the Sioux educator Chauncey Yellow Robe declared: "The American Indian is not lacking in patriotism, he is not a disloyalist—a slacker or a traitor, but is a true patriot." When the war ended, it seemed logical that this patriotism should be repaid. Gertrude Bonnin put it simply: "The American Indian, too, made the supreme sacrifice for liberty's sake. He loves democratic ideals. What shall world democracy mean to this race?"

There were two answers to Bonnin's question. First, Congress approved a blanket extension of American citizenship to all Natives, first to veterans in 1919, and, in 1924, to all adults who had not previously been enfranchised. Citizenship did not bring all the blessings reformers had predicted—and some white politicians cynically advocated citizenship to reduce Indian Office expenditures—but the new legislation marked the first moment when the American government had declared all Native Americans to be *inside* the national political community.

The second response was more general. World War I gave American Indians the moral authority to insist on respect for their customs and lifeways. In November 1918, for example, the Hunkpapa community at Fort Yates, North Dakota, held a victory dance to celebrate the American victory over Germany. They sang traditional songs about the power of Sioux culture and the tribe's spiritual guardians. A disapproving local missionary reported that the dance had not been held "since the evening of the Little Big Horn battle" in 1876, but he could hardly object. Similar traditional ceremonies occurred on reservations across the nation; no whites protested. And while readjustment to civilian life presented problems for some, returning veterans were quick to point out that they would no longer tolerate the Indian Office's patronizing and authoritarian ways. Veterans became community leaders on their reservations and outspoken defenders of tribal interests. Among these were Choctaw Victor Locke, who became tribal chairman; the Seneca artist Jesse Cornplanter; Osage author John Joseph Matthews; George Jewett, a political leader from the Cheyenne River Sioux reservation; and Steve Spotted Tail, a Rosebud Sioux tribal councilman. For the first time since the beginning of the assimilation era, it was possible for assertive Indian leaders to be celebrated as heroic Americans.

FACING ECONOMIC HARDSHIP

In the early twentieth century, the struggle of Indian people for religious freedom, political independence, and public acceptance was heroic.

Confined to a narrow existence under the authority of the Indian Office and denigrated by politicians and missionaries, Native Americans faced powerful political enemies and a generally indifferent public. In the arenas of popular culture and politics Indians managed to create a public platform for their concerns and to win some modest victories. Their participation in World War I and the extension of citizenship that followed marked a remarkable shift in both public attitudes and the willingness of political leaders to recognize the rights and interests of Native people.

Events in the economic arena followed a far less hopeful path. Between 1900 and 1930 a sustained assault on Indian lands and resources stripped both tribes and individuals of the economic capital they might have used to build self-sustaining communities later in the century. As a result, Indians in 1930 were poorer than their parents had been in 1900.

Allotment at High Tide

When it became law in 1887, the General Allotment Act seemed to establish a roadmap for economic health and progress. Federal authorities promised the gradual extension of individual landholding to tribes that were ready to accept it, and they buttressed that pledge with the additional assurances that the Indians would be well compensated for "surplus" lands opened to white settlers. The Indian Office predicted that payments for "surplus" lands would support the purchase of tools, seed, and other materials necessary for the Indians' new life as farmers. Finally, the allotment act promised a period of federal "trust" supervision for individual Indian lands that would protect them from local taxation and the designs of unscrupulous businesspeople. These protective features of the original allotment program were largely in effect in 1900; by 1930 they had disappeared.

Beginning in 1903 with the Supreme Court's decision in *Lone Wolf* v. *Hitchcock*, all of the Dawes Act's legal protections were steadily undermined by congressional action and shifts in Indian Office policy. The *Lone Wolf* decision's announcement that tribal lands could be sold without regard to treaty guarantees was welcomed by Commissioner of Indian Affairs William Jones, who was an eager supporter of federal land acquisition. "If you wait for

[the tribe's] consent in these matters," Jones declared, "it will be fifty years before you can do away with the reservations." Federal officials like Jones accelerated the pace of allotment so that in the first decade of the twentieth century the total amount of allotted land rose nearly 500 percent, from 6.7 to 31 million acres; by 1920, 217,572 allotments had been made covering 35,897,069 acres. At that point nearly 75 percent of all Indian lands had been divided and distributed to individual tribal members.

The impact on Native Americans of this shift of tribal lands from communal property to individual allotments might have been cushioned if the Indians' new family homesteads had received the legal protections originally promised in the 1887 allotment law or if Native American landowners had received the agricultural training and financial assistance necessary to support a transition to commercial agriculture and stock raising. Unfortunately, neither training nor financial assistance materialized. Instead Congress acted to weaken, rather than strengthen, Indian landholding. First, in 1906 the Burke Act granted the commissioner of Indian affairs the power to extend the length of an allottee's trust patent or unilaterally declare Indian landowners "competent," fee-simple owners who were now responsible for all taxes owed on their lands.

Second, the Indian Office loosened the restrictions on the leasing of both individual allotments and tribal lands. Officials such as Teddy Roosevelt's commissioner of Indian affairs, Francis Leupp, argued that "primitive peoples" like the Indians failed to progress because they were "grossly wasteful" of their resources. Leupp and his successors thus looked with increasing favor on requests from ranchers, large commercial growers, and mining interests for leases on Indian lands. When World War I broke out, Commissioner Cato Sells demanded that tribes demonstrate their patriotism by granting leases to tribal grazing lands so large industrial farmers could support the war effort by raising wheat and other basic commodities. By 1920, 4.5 million acres of Indian "trust" land were being leased under this program.

Finally, Indian Office officials urged individual Indians to sell any allotments they could not farm. Such lands would include allotments assigned to people who had subsequently died, land belonging to the elderly or those considered "noncompetent," or land owned by minors who wished to raise cash for their education or some other worthy purpose. More than seventeen thousand allotments covering 2.1 million acres were sold under these policies between 1903 and 1920.

Throughout the pre–World War I period the Indian Office made only a modest effort to supply Indian allottees with farming instruction, supplies, and technical assistance. The staffs of local Indian agencies usually included "boss farmers," who acted as agricultural extension agents, but these officials operated with very limited budgets and tribal members rarely had the capital to invest in machinery or seed. Even skilled white farmers faced difficult market pressures in the early twentieth century. Facing uncertain markets and growing international competition, non-Indians turned increasingly to mechanized tractors and harvesting devices to increase the size and efficiency of their operations. Ironically, at this same moment, cash-strapped Indians (who were supposed to be imitating whites) were stuck in small, subsistence operations with little financial support and no training in new scientific farming methods. As a result the average size and productivity of Indian farms lagged far behind that of whites. In 1930 in South Dakota, for example, the average Native American farm was 287 acres, while the average white farmer in the state cultivated more than 445 acres. In this atmosphere, it became popular to declare that Native Americans were incapable of benefiting from government assistance. For example, Franklin Lane, Woodrow Wilson's secretary of the interior, recommended darkly that Indians "should be given their property and allowed to shift for themselves."

Relatively little allotment took place after 1920. By that date 35 million acres of tribal land had been divided and assigned; in the remaining fourteen years of the policy only 4 million more acres were allotted. In 1920 most of the desirable Indian land had either already passed to white ownership or was under lease to non-Indian farmers and ranchers. The only major tracts of tribal lands that had not been allotted lay in the arid Plains, the Southwest, and Alaska. In 1881 Native Americans had held title to 155 million acres of land; in 1933 that figure had shrunk to 52 million acres. Indians were no longer "land rich and cash poor"; by 1930 they were simply poor.

A Spirit of Enterprise

While allotment dealt Native Americans a devastating blow, the spirit of economic enterprise, deeply embedded in the cultural traditions of Indian people in every corner of the United States, managed to surface in a few reservation communities.

Some groups found commercial outlets for traditional products that they could produce locally. Most successful in this regard were the Navajos of Arizona and New Mexico, who greatly expanded their production of woven wool blankets in response to a growing demand from white consumers. Spurred by the construction of rail lines and the accompanying Fred Harvey tourist hotels, both male and female Navajo weavers saw their total annual sales rise from $50,000 in 1899 to $700,000 in 1917. By the mid-1920s Navajo blankets were being sold by national retailers such as Sears and Roebuck. The popularity of Navajo handicrafts also stimulated the production and sale of traditional silver jewelry, an art form that had only recently become popular among the Navajos. While less dramatic in their impact on both the tribes and the public, other Indian handicrafts caught the eyes of tourists who ventured close to reservations. Most of these products were created by women, who felt less pressure from educators and agents to become wage laborers.

Seneca women in New York, for example, sold beaded bags and moccasins to visitors to Niagara Falls; male Ojibwe carvers and female beadwork artists profited from the arrival of summer visitors to northern Michigan, Wisconsin, and Minnesota. In California, the tradition of female basket making was revived in communities where access to gathering areas and hunting grounds was becoming increasingly difficult. Profiting from the rapid rise of tourism in the state, California Indian women in both southern and northern tribal communities supported their families with expanding sales of reed baskets.

Other communities managed to create modern enterprises that were tribally owned and that could provide employment for large numbers of tribal members. Menominees in Wisconsin—led by boarding school graduates and traditional chiefs who gained the support of progressive senator Robert La Follette—managed to avoid opening their reservation to logging interests. In 1904 the tribe created a fifteen-man Menominee business committee to manage their timber resources and in 1908, with La Follette's help, managed to build a modern sawmill in the new reservation town of Neopit. Owned by the tribe but managed by Indian Office appointees, the sawmill employed more than two hundred tribal members. It opened in January 1909 with a production capacity of 40 million board feet of timber. Tribal members often criticized the Indian Office managers for confining Menominees to unskilled positions at the mill, but timber operations soon became a principal source of community income and social stability. By carefully managing their resources, the Menominees also avoided the deforestation and land loss that afflicted most Native communities in the Upper Midwest.

In South Dakota in the early twentieth century, white cattlemen rushed to lease grazing lands that had been allotted on the seven Sioux reservations that had been carved out of the tribal domain in 1889. In the words of one rancher, the region promised "free grass, no income tax, no county tax," and operating costs of $1–2 per head of cattle per year. The Newcastle Land and Livestock Company, for example, took up leases on 500,000 acres of the Pine Ridge reservation, while the Matador Land and Cattle Company sent a herd of 17,000 cattle to the Cheyenne River agency. These leases profited white cattlemen far more than Indian landowners, but the ranching business provided western Indian communities with a new business model.

If whites could profit from low-overhead cattle operations, tribal leaders reasoned, why can't we? As a consequence, Indian leaders across the West began to promote tribally owned stock operations on their remaining communal lands. Among the most successful of these were the Northern Cheyenne herd, which grazed the tribe's unallotted reservation in southeastern Montana, and the Hidatsas at Fort Berthold, North Dakota, who maintained a herd of nearly six thousand horses and cattle before World War I. Enterprising individuals also took advantage of the situation. At the White Mountain Apache reservation in northern Arizona, for example, a young Indian entrepreneur, Wallace Altaha, began in the 1890s with a small contract to supply beef to the local army post. Over the next thirty years Altaha used tribal land to build

his and his relatives' cattle herd to more than ten thousand head. The Apache rancher, who personally bought $25,000 worth of World War I liberty bonds, was celebrated as one of the wealthiest Native Americans of his day.

The Indians in Puget Sound struggled to continue their community fishing enterprise, but this proved nearly impossible in the face of state restrictions and competition from commercial fishers. In the early twentieth century large corporate entities such as the Alaska Packers Association took control of the small, independent canneries that had dominated the industry in previous decades. Alaska Packers introduced sophisticated machinery that could process and package thousands of cases of salmon each day. The number of Indians employed in the Washington State fishing industry fell dramatically during this period. Not only was it impossible for Native Americans in Puget Sound to compete with commercial fishers in large, well-equipped boats, but the huge rise in the annual salmon harvest reduced the number of fish that could reach the Indians' traditional fishing sites along the area's inland bays and river ways.

Excluded from the modern industry, Lummi and other Puget Sound fishers struggled to protect their treaty rights. In 1916 the Lummis began arresting commercial fishers who ventured into what they considered tribal waters. They also insisted on their right to fish from reservation land without regard to state-imposed seasonal regulations. While some fishing boats agreed to stay away from tribal waters, state officials generally ignored the tribe's actions. In fact, state officers arrested tribal members who violated state regulations and refused to rein in fish traps that blocked tribal members' access to their own fishing grounds. By the 1920s, the Puget Sound tribes were clinging desperately to their traditions and, like their counterparts in the Great Lakes, were being forced to support themselves with wage labor.

Probably the best known example of Indian success in the modern economy was the Oklahoma Osages, who gradually discovered that their reservation rested on one of the largest petroleum reservoirs in North America. Exploration teams had detected modest amounts of oil on Osage lands as early as the 1890s, but there was little interest in exploiting this resource until the first decade of the new century, when reservation production rose from 50,000 barrels to nearly 5 million barrels in a three-year period. Eager to capitalize on this production boom, tribal leaders insisted that the Osages should retain all subsurface mineral rights to their land—even after their reservation was allotted. When Osage allotment took place in 1906, the tribe retained this "underground reservation" of oil and it remained a source of group wealth long after individual tracts of land had been divided and sold.

On the eve of World War I tribal leaders lobbied to replace existing oil exploration leases with a system of open auctions. Supported by oil companies eager to break into the Osage fields, the tribe was successful; the competition sparked by these open auctions dramatically boosted oil production—and Osage wealth. In 1916, for example, one auction of 108 tracts of Osage land produced bonus payments of $2.3 million for the owners of the tracts being leased. As this new boom unfolded, a group of young councilmen led by Fred Lookout struggled to defend the tribe's interests by appointing a tribal inspector to verify the oil companies' production reports and turning away fraudulent applications from people trying to gain membership in the tribe. In 1924 Lookout also urged the FBI to investigate a series of unsolved murders among the tribe, murders that were later revealed as the work of local cattleman William K. Hale. It turned out Hale had ordered the killings to promote the interests of a nephew who had married into an extended Osage family.

The Osage's annual oil shares, called "headrights," rose to $13,000 per person in 1925. Large families reaped the income that came with several headright shares. They enjoyed a flow of cash that created temptation for hungry non-Indians and prosperity for all tribal members regardless of their education or business experience. This new wealth produced feature stories of "chiefs" who didn't even drive buying extravagant cars and building imposing homes on the Oklahoma prairie. At the same time whites appointed as "guardians" over the estates of uneducated Indians frequently mismanaged their affairs while local lawyers bilked their Native clients for needless and repetitive services. The most famous of these cases involved Jackson Barnett, a Creek man whose allotment rested atop a huge oil reserve. Victimized by unscrupulous guardians and a scheming wife, Bar-

nett, "the richest Indian in the world," lived in a Los Angeles mansion and was the subject of tabloid publicity until his death in 1934.

Indian leaders and eastern reformers fought against the widespread perception that all Indians were rich and wasteful. They also publicized the frauds and murders that so frequently characterized guardianship over wealthy Indian estates in Oklahoma. Most notably, SAI founder Gertrude Bonnin (Zitkala Ša) wrote *Oklahoma's Poor Rich Indians*, which the Indian Rights Association published in 1924. Although the report received broad press coverage, little could be done to alter the economic balance of power in the new state. An Osage attorney complained in 1927 that "the only business to speak of in [this] county is the Indian business."

Oil-rich Indians' wealth was dwarfed by the oil company profits that fueled the rise of the new Oklahoma towns of Bartlesville and Tulsa and spawned the region's mammoth new petroleum industry. Drawing oil from Indian lands, rising companies like Conoco and Phillips Petroleum extended their activities to production, refining, and distribution. These corporations launched major international enterprises from their Oklahoma headquarters, but for the Osages (and the few Creeks and Seminoles who found that they too had been allotted land on top of significant oil reserves) the prosperity was short-lived.

Poverty's Shadow

In the early twentieth century people in all parts of the United States began to be conscious of fellow citizens who lived in poverty. Often invisible in an older, rural America, poor people became a topic of national concern in the urban and increasingly middle-class society of the twentieth century. Robert Hunter's book *Poverty*, for example, published in 1904, shocked the public when it claimed that 10 percent of Americans were "poor." Muckraking journalists and researchers from the new discipline of sociology took up this theme, and books like Upton Sinclair's *The Jungle* (1906) created public sympathy for the dispossessed. During these years government investigators and congressional committees also began exploring social problems such as child labor and crime. In this atmosphere, the conditions associated with Native American poverty began to receive notice.

Indian health was the first focus of concern. Physicians had been assigned to Indian agencies since the late nineteenth century, but their performance and effectiveness were rarely reviewed. It was not until 1903 that Commissioner of Indian Affairs William Jones ordered a comprehensive study of sanitary conditions at Indian schools and agencies. While the report often blamed Indian "superstition" for the situation it uncovered, its grisly descriptions of tuberculosis, eye infections, malnutrition, and alcoholism caught the attention of Congress.

Congress made few appropriations for Indian health until 1912 when it funded the construction of new hospitals and a variety of public health campaigns. Among these special efforts were the Swat the Fly and Save the Babies campaigns aimed at better sanitation, increased reliance on Western medicine, and better nutrition. Unfortunately, even these strenuous efforts—which nearly doubled the Indian Office health budget by 1917—fell far short of what was needed. The outbreak of World War I ended budget increases for Indian health, and postwar congresses were reluctant to act. The war also decimated the Indian Office's already inadequate staff of physicians; by 1918 forty percent of these positions were vacant.

Over time, the Indian Office's education programs and the construction of Indian hospitals had an impact on Indian health. By 1926 there were 91 agency hospitals in operation, but Congress rarely made the large capital expenditures needed to build modern water delivery and storage facilities or expensive sewage treatment plants. As a result, infectious diseases and waterborne ailments continued to plague Native communities. The continuing crisis in Indian health was brought home most dramatically at the end of 1918 when the worldwide influenza epidemic, which took 15 million lives, struck the United States. Two percent of the country's Native Americans (6,270 people) died during the outbreak, a rate far higher than for any other group.

During the 1920s growing awareness of the problem of poverty in an affluent society and rising sympathy for Indian cultures fueled a concern for Native American welfare that occasionally placed the Indian Office on the defensive. In 1923

Secretary of the Interior Hubert Work appointed Society of American Indians activist Arthur Parker, a Seneca, to chair a Committee of One Hundred to review the government's Indian policy. Only sixty-six people actually convened for the committee's two-day official meeting in December. Among those gathered were Crow political leader Robert Yellowtail, author and physician Charles Eastman, and the Pueblo's defender John Collier. Unfortunately the group had neither the time nor the leadership to develop a forceful agenda. The committee passed a series of resolutions calling for better health care and larger congressional appropriations (and it delivered its recommendations to President Coolidge in a highly publicized ceremony), but its work was quickly forgotten.

Interest rose again in 1926 when the Board of Indian Commissioners, a government advisory group dominated by missionaries and supporters of the Indian Office, suggested that the Interior Department sponsor a systematic study of Native American life. The board hoped the study would focus public attention on the need for greater funding for Indian health and welfare. Secretary Work adopted the idea and turned to the Institute for Government Research, a private research group soon to become part of the Brookings Institution, to carry out the work. With financial support from John D. Rockefeller, Jr., the Institute appointed a staff researcher, Lewis Meriam, to direct the project. Meriam gathered a staff of nine specialists in the areas of law, economic conditions, health, education, agriculture, family life, and urban Indian life. Working with an "Indian adviser," educator Henry Roe Cloud, Meriam's team fanned out across the country to gather data. They delivered their report to Secretary Work on February 21, 1928.

The Meriam report marked a significant divide in public perceptions of Native Americans and of Indian affairs generally. Prior to its publication, advocates of assimilation could argue that education and allotment were bringing about the gradual improvement of Indian people. This improvement might be delayed by tight budgets or Indian resistance, officials argued, but Indians would eventually be incorporated into the American mainstream. The appalling statistics compiled in the Meriam report suggested that these predictions were a self-serving delusion.

"The overwhelming majority of the Indians are poor, even extremely poor," the report began. It went on to summarize conditions in a variety of areas.

Health. The health of the Indians as compared with that of the general population is bad. . . . [T]he death rate and the infant mortality rate are high. Tuberculosis is extremely prevalent. . . . Trachoma [an infectious eye disease] is a major problem. . . .

Living Conditions. The prevailing living conditions . . . are conducive to the development and spread of disease. . . . [T]he diet of the Indians is bad. . . . [T]he use of milk is rare, and it is generally not available, even for infants. . . . Sanitary facilities are generally lacking.

Economic Conditions. The income of the typical Indian family is low and the earned income extremely low. . . . [T]he number of real farmers is comparatively small . . . a considerable proportion engage more or less casually in unskilled labor. . . . Even the boys and girls graduating from government schools have comparatively little vocational guidance.

The report also spoke directly to the stereotype that Indians were somehow resigned to their poverty or that they were "happier in their idleness and irresponsibility." It noted that the project staff found "too much evidence of real suffering and discontent to subscribe to the belief that the Indians are reasonably satisfied with their condition. The amount of serious illness and poverty is too great to permit of real contentment."

When it turned to economic conditions, the report addressed another popular stereotype: that all Indians were somehow like the Osages who owned valuable property and had no need to work. The report countered that claim with statistics showing that nearly 70 percent of the Native American population lived in areas where the per capita value of their property was less than $2,000. The report of Indian incomes bordered on the surreal: 71 percent of Indians reported earning less than $200 per year from both individual labor and payments from their tribes. (When measuring individually earned income alone, this figure fell to $100.) "For several jurisdictions," Meriam and his colleagues reported, "the figures for income are reported so low as to be almost unbelievable."

Ironically, while the impetus for the Meriam report came initially from inside the government, its statistics were so distressing that critics charged that it was time for a complete overhaul of federal policy. As the critics gained support, it began to appear that Meriam's most important contribution might well have been the damage he inflicted on the Indian Office's credibility with Congress and the public.

CONCLUSION

At the end of the 1920s Charles Eastman retired from the Indian Service and built a cabin on the north shore of Lake Huron, not far from Sault St. Marie, Michigan. From 1928 until his death in 1939, the Sioux reformer and writer would spend most of each year at his cabin, leaving occasionally to deliver a public lecture or attend a Dartmouth College reunion. In the winter months he retreated to Detroit where he lived with his son. In these final years the prolific author stopped publishing and cut his ties to Indian reform groups. "When I reduce civilization to its lowest terms," he had written in 1916, "it becomes a system of life based upon trade." It seemed that by the end of the 1920s Eastman, one of the most accomplished Native Americans of his day, had had enough of civilization. He was happier in the woods.

Charles Eastman's final retreat symbolized the struggles of Native people during the first decades of the new century and the sense of failure that had spread across the world of Indian affairs at the end of the 1920s. Great energy and ingenuity on the part of individuals like Eastman had made individual success and tribal survival possible, but the pressures created by official indifference, economic dislocation, and public apathy had persisted and taken their toll. Eastman had made his way in this new world, but he had not been able to change the attitudes of the Indian Office or reverse the scales of political and economic power that weighed so heavily against Native peoples. His successors would turn to those tasks.

SUGGESTED READINGS

Britten, Thomas A. *American Indians in World War I: At War and at Home.* Albuquerque: University of New Mexico Press, 1997. A comprehensive treatment of Native Americans who fought in World War I as well as of the Indian home front during that conflict.

Child, Brenda J. *Boarding School Seasons: American Indian Families, 1900–1940.* Lincoln: University of Nebraska Press, 1988. A study of the impact of federal boarding schools on Native American families based primarily on letters between children and their parents. The author draws most of her examples from the Great Lakes region.

Dilworth, Leah. *Imagining Indians in the Southwest: Persistent Visions of a Primitive Past.* Washington, D.C.: Smithsonian Institution Press, 1996. A cultural historian's description of the rise of tourism in the Southwest in the early twentieth century.

Harmon, Alexandra. *Indians in the Making: Ethnic Relations and Indian Identities Around Puget Sound.* Berkeley: University of California Press, 1998. A history of Puget Sound tribes in Washington State that focuses on the shifting definitions of "Indian" and "tribe" in that region in the early twentieth century.

Hosmer, Brian. *American Indians in the Marketplace: Persistence and Innovation Among the Menominees and Metlakatlans, 1870–1920.* Lawrence: University Press of Kansas, 1999. A remarkable portrait of two Native American groups that successfully launched tribal enterprises during the Progressive Era.

Hoxie, Frederick E. *Parading Through History: The Making of the Crow Nation in America, 1805–1935.* New York: Cambridge University Press, 1995. A history of the Crow Indians of Montana that emphasizes the role of tribal leaders in the early reservation era.

Iverson, Peter. *Carlos Montezuma and the Changing World of American Indians.* Albuquerque: University of New Mexico Press, 1982. A biography of one of the founders of the Society of American Indians and the fiercest critic of the Bureau of Indian Affairs in the early twentieth century.

Jacobs, Margaret D. *Engendered Encounters: Feminism and the Pueblo Cultures, 1879–1934.* Lincoln: University of Nebraska Press, 1999. A study of the relationship between white feminists in the early twentieth century and the Indian communities that they tried to reform.

Meyer, Melissa L. *The White Earth Tragedy: Ethnicity and Dispossession at a Minnesota Anishinaabe Reservation, 1889–1920.* Lincoln: University of Nebraska Press, 1994. A history of the White Earth reservation and the transformation of its ecology and economy during the early years of the reservation era.

Robertson, Paul. *The Power of the Land: Identity, Ethnicity and Class Among the Oglala Sioux.* New York: Routledge, 2002. A community history of the Pine Ridge Sioux reservation that emphasizes the impact of early-twentieth-century land policies on contemporary social life.

Reorganization and War, 1930–1945

The rejection letter, dated April 6, 1929, was kind. "The story of an Indian wandering between two generations, two cultures; excellent," the editors wrote. They added, "[P]erhaps [it is] the beginning of a new Indian literature." Still, the answer was no. The twenty-five-year-old Native American author absorbed this disappointment as he rode New York's subways commuting from his editorial job in downtown Manhattan and his night class in American history at Columbia University. D'Arcy McNickle had dreamed of watching his tale of a young man on a western Indian reservation become a national bestseller. He had been working on stories like this one since his early student days at the University of Montana and was desperate to be a published author. Like other aspiring writers of his generation, McNickle had traveled for a time in Europe, haunted Paris bookstores and coffee houses, and returned to the United States with the dream of writing about his Native American relatives and presenting the public with a new picture of the American West. He wanted to celebrate people like his grandfather, the Cree hunter and trader Isidore Parenteau. He wanted to teach Americans about the struggles of Isidore's children and grandchildren: how they had endured the cruelty of boarding schools, the ignorance of government officials, and the heavy hand

of frontier injustice. But despite his long days at the New York Public Library, and the seemingly endless revisions, he would have to try again.

McNickle went back to work on his manuscript. After all, he had a unique view of the world around him. He wrote at the time that he shared little with those who believed in "loyalty to a boss, . . . being on time, . . . 'boosting' God, country and cowboy, . . . wearing a smile [and] . . . eschewing all mental activity that did not have to do with 'getting ahead.'" Eventually the struggle paid off. In December 1935, Dodd, Mead and Company agreed to publish the book under its most recent title, *The Surrounded*. Appearing alongside John Joseph Matthews's (Osage) *Sundown* (1934) and John Milton Oskinson's (Cherokee) *Brothers Three* (1935), McNickle's novel marked a vivid departure from earlier, romantic pictures of Indians. *The Surrounded* is a tragedy; at its end the protagonist, an educated young Indian man, is in shackles, and his agent declares, "You people never learn that you can't run away." The reviewer for the *New York Times* saw something new in McNickle's prose, noting, "This is a very modern, very youthful novel."

The appearance of *The Surrounded* in 1936 marked one of the first public achievements of a new generation of Native Americans. Born in the twentieth century, disillusioned with the government's promises of uplift and assimilation, and comfortable in both their traditional communities and in modern urban society, people like D'Arcy McNickle sought a way to be both Indian and modern. These individuals—writers, political figures, government officials, artists, and educators—were convinced that Native cultures offered crucial lessons for the American future.

PRESSURES MOUNT FOR DRASTIC CHANGE

By the end of the 1920s the Indian Office had surrendered much of its credibility as an organization capable of helping Indian people. The grim statistics in the Meriam report demonstrated that Native Americans were not making the "progress" government officials had long predicted. Missionaries and reformers who had traditionally supported the government now declared that years of inadequate budgets and staff cuts had all but destroyed the effectiveness of boarding schools and health agencies. To follow up on Meriam's findings, Congress authorized extensive hearings on conditions among individual tribes. Led first by Utah Senator William King and sustained by disgruntled legislators throughout the 1930s, these hearings provided Indian leaders with an ongoing public platform with which to attack the government's programs.

Even the Indian Office leadership seemed ready for a fundamental change. In 1929 Herbert Hoover chose Charles Rhoads, a former president of the Indian Rights Association, to be commissioner of Indian affairs. Quickly embracing the Meriam report, Rhoads called for a dramatic expansion of Indian education and urged his subordinates to consult with tribal leaders. He appointed Swarthmore professor W. Carson Ryan to oversee Indian education and applauded when Ryan began raising teaching standards, eliminating stifling rules, and creating cooperative ties between schools and Indian communities. The new commissioner seemed determined to eliminate the paternalism and authoritarianism that had long been a part of Indian Office culture.

During the New Deal era, Indian artists gained wide recognition. This poster reflects their growing popularity and illustrates how Native arts were no longer seen solely as artifacts of the past.

Unfortunately, Rhoads was only able to begin the extensive work necessary to reorganize the government's efforts. Just as he began to struggle against entrenched groups of employees and their congressional allies, the Depression hit and wiped away any talk of budget increases. Soon disappointed tribal leaders renewed their attacks on the government; they were quickly joined by a new, younger group of non-Indian activists who insisted that it was time to stop forcing Native Americans to abandon their cultures and traditions. Most prominent among these new critics was John Collier, the bespectacled former social worker who had earlier led the defense of New Mexico's Pueblos.

Initially concerned only with "saving" the Pueblos, Collier quickly became engaged in a wide array of Indian issues. Early in the decade the General Federation of Women's Clubs sponsored Collier's investigations, but in 1923 he and a group of eastern supporters formed a new organization, the American Indian Defense Association (AIDA). The board of the new group was dominated by artists and intellectuals; it included authors Mary Austin and Hamlin Garland, book publisher George Haven Putnam, and Chicago political reformers Harold Ickes and Carter Harrison. This disparate group shared a common admiration for traditional Indian cultures, as well as a distaste for heavy-handed government programs. Led by Collier, the group set out to improve Indian health care, promote the sale of arts and crafts, and modernize the government's education programs. Reflecting Collier's flamboyant style, the AIDA made no effort to work within the Indian Office; its favored tactics included highly publicized exposés of government incompetence and congressional investigations of official misconduct.

Attacked by what appeared to be a group of city-bred artists and intellectuals who knew little about the complexities of Indian affairs, government officials in the 1920s stuck to their guns. The Indian Office continued to support the allotment and sale of tribal lands and its leaders continued to argue that vocational education and wage labor were the only practical ways to deliver Native Americans from poverty. They saw little value in promoting traditional arts and crafts or relaxing the authoritarian atmosphere at government schools. Indians needed to learn to work, they insisted; tribal cultures and tribal councils did little to accomplish that end. Herbert Hoover's interior secretary (and former president of Stanford University) Ray Lyman Wilbur stated the position simply. He declared as he took office, "The red man's civilization must be replaced by the white man's."

But achieving "civilization" now seemed beside the point to many. The Great Depression had ushered in a period of unprecedented suffering and desperation. Overwhelmingly rural and lacking the financial infrastructure to alleviate community suffering, Native Americans faced falling farm prices, drought, and starvation. Their only sources of support were the Indian Office and the missionaries, both overwhelmed with demands from needy clients. In 1931 the Bureau of Indian Affairs (BIA) itself was forced to call on the American Red Cross and the U.S. Army to supply hungry Indians with winter rations. One Sioux leader caught the bitter irony of the situation. "We're all on the same level now," he noted, "the white man is in the same shape we are." A white homesteader from Wyoming recalled the Depression without this touch of humor. "Everyone was poor," he remembered, "but the Indians were poorer."

In addition to economic stress, most reservation communities were struggling to develop leaders who could be effective advocates with the public as well as with government bureaucracies. The nineteenth-century leaders who had claimed their positions on the strength of prereservation exploits or traditional clan affiliations had passed from the scene. In their place were competing groups of educated young men, middle-aged descendants of traditional "head men," and outspoken women, largely excluded from public leadership positions in the era of treaty "chiefs" and now empowered by education and contact with non-Indians to assert their interests and concerns.

Finally, tribes worried about the ongoing encroachment of non-Indian ranchers, farmers, and miners who sought access to Native resources. Tribal leaders were aware of the growing distance between their subsistence economies and the modern, mechanized farms and ranches that surrounded them, and they wondered how best to define and defend the boundaries between themselves and their white neighbors. How could they participate in the modern economy and political system while protecting their own communities? How could tribes manage their communal resources and hold the government to its treaty obligations to provide education and health care without sacrificing the individual rights of tribal members—all of whom were now American citizens?

A New Commissioner

Franklin Roosevelt's election in 1932 offered the prospect of change. After the frustration of Commissioner Rhoads's reforms, many tribal leaders and government critics hoped the new president would offer a new direction. Perhaps most enthusiastic was Crow leader Robert Yellowtail who, despite

INDIAN VOICES   D'Arcy McNickle Reveals His Hopes for Indians in the Future

Recruited by John Collier to develop better communications between the Indian Office and individual tribes, D'Arcy McNickle spent a good part of his tenure at the BIA traveling between Indian agencies and the commissioner's office. McNickle understood the gap between his boss's grand vision and the complex reality of reservation life, but he was convinced that the New Deal offered Native Americans an unprecedented opportunity to make a future for themselves as Indians and to insure in the process that Native values would live on into the future. This speech, delivered by McNickle to a non-Indian group in 1939, reveals some of the hopes the former boarding school student held out for both the Indian and the American futures.

When the present administration of Indian Affairs came into office in 1933, it was with the feeling that we had come into a ruined house. I don't mean that this feeling was entirely singular with the new administration. It was a feeling which was shared, I dare say, by all intelligent people who were at all familiar with Indian history. . . . The question was, and it overshadowed everything, every plan, and every hope—could the Indian be saved? Could he be pulled back short of final disaster? His land was all but gone. . . . the land remaining to him was fast playing out; his capital assets were dwindling so rapidly that it was only a question of a short time until they would be quite gone; his health was bad; his spirit was low; he had not been trained to take part in the enveloping white world—could he be rejuvenated?

And now, I say, comes the surprising realization that the Indian is not vanishing—not in physical numbers, not in capital assets, not in culture content. I do not say his position in our nation is lastingly assured. The Indian is still at the mercy of his conquerors, and will be for generations to come. But at least he is safe for the time.

Not in the Indian Service alone, but on the part of thinking people generally, there is probably an increasing tolerance toward culture habits other than our own—an increasing hesitancy to brand one civilization as superior to another. Except among those nations or individuals who must find some special devil upon which to load all the faults and shortcomings of their own thinking, no one with any conscience can believe today in the absolute superiority of one branch of mankind over another.

Aboriginal Indian life, as I need not tell you, was infinitely varied. It ranged from the almost formless, almost visionless, nomadic wanderings of the interior Athabaskan tribes of the far north, to the highly complicated and highly accomplished city states of Central America. This diversity has come down to our day. In Arizona we find the Hopi Indians living in the very same villages in which they lived before Columbus touched our shores. Their life is infinitely rich in ceremonialism, and in spite of almost 400 years of contact with European civilization, they live much as they have always lived; and so long as we abstain from breaking down the economy by which they have lived and the controls by which they keep

(continued)

their society toned, they will continue to function as any organism functions, yielding when necessary, changing when advantageous. . . .

In 1934 Congress undertook a fundamental revision of its Indian policy. It was spurred on to do this by the Meriam report . . . and by the persistent, courageous criticism of persons outside the Indian Service. Among the most persistent and the most courageous of these had been Mr. John Collier, who was to become Commissioner.

Basic legislation was needed to attack the problem, and Congress supplied this legislation in the Indian Reorganization Act, often called the Wheeler-Howard Act, which was approved on June 18, 1934. . . . [T]his new policy is based on two ideas: Tribal organization, and a fuller use of land. Out of organization will come greater participation in the management of property and domestic affairs; and out of land use, by which I mean to include the purchase of land for those who are landless and credit to carry on operations, will come better living conditions. Fundamental to the program is a recognition of the right of Indian culture to survive and enrich the daily life of the individual and the group. Not humanitarianism alone, but a belief that human beings are at their best when they are left at peace in those matters of conscience which come closest to them, prompts this attitude.

The Indian race generally has an infinitely rich nature upon which to build a future world. The Indian has the quality of belonging to the earth which, I suppose, at one time all peoples of the earth had and enjoyed. He belongs to the earth because he has never divorced himself from it. The whole trend of his existence has been, not to master the forces of the earth and so to raise himself above and to grow away from the things of nature; rather his desire has been to live in nature, to be a part of it, to worship it, and to endure in it. This is what we attempted in the past to break the Indian away from. We never wholly succeeded, but in so far as we did succeed we left individual Indians without vitality and without spirit. We left them bewildered and half destroyed. We have turned from that old course of doing. We have decided that an Indian, like an Anglo-Saxon, is entitled to believe in himself, in the strength of his past, and in the glory of his future.

D'Arcy McNickle, "The American Indian Today," *The Missouri Archaeologist 5* (September 1939): 1–10. Courtesy of The Missouri Archaeological Society, Inc.

his lifelong allegiance to the Republicans, persuaded two friends to drive with him from Montana to Washington, D.C., to attend the new president's inauguration. John Collier and his friends at the AIDA were also hopeful. They rejected the usual Indian Rights Association's nominees for the commissioner's post and actively promoted one of their own members for the job.

The AIDA leadership was thrilled when Roosevelt appointed one of the organization's board members, Harold L. Ickes, to be secretary of the interior. Ickes quickly named Collier to the post of

commissioner. While several missionary groups and western politicians objected, the Indian Office's most outspoken critic was confirmed and began moving swiftly to set a new course. Within weeks of assuming office he abolished the Board of Indian Commissioners, an advisory group long dominated by friendly missionaries and genteel reformers, and began recruiting anthropologists and other "experts" to assist him. Collier also assembled an eclectic young staff that included civil rights attorneys such as Nathan Margold (a protégé of Roosevelt's mentor, Supreme Court Justice

FDR and Chief Bird Rattler In August 1934, President Franklin Roosevelt visited Glacier National Park with his wife, Eleanor, and Secretary of the Interior Harold Ickes. During his visit, the president was ceremonially adopted into the Blackfeet tribe and presented with a traditional carved pipe by traditional leaders. On that occasion, one of the chiefs, Bird Rattler, posed for this photograph with Roosevelt.

Felix Frankfurter) and young Native Americans who had rarely been invited to help lead the agency. Among those whom Collier hired or promoted in his first years were Henry Roe Cloud, the Winnebago educator who had worked with Lewis Meriam on his study in the 1920s; Ben Reifel, a teacher at the Rosebud Sioux reservation; Robert Yellowtail; and Klamath leader Wade Crawford. In 1936 Collier discovered yet another talented young Indian: D'Arcy McNickle. The commissioner was confident he could use the services of this sophisticated young author from Montana's Flathead country.

Collier's rapid ascent from critic to commissioner amplified his administrative strengths and weaknesses. Having never served in a government post, Collier had no obligations to the existing bureaucracy or to the long-serving reservation superintendents who routinely resisted change. He would prove an innovative and flexible leader. On the other hand, Collier's sudden rise to power encouraged his sense that he understood Indian affairs better than any so-called expert. And ironically, despite his attacks on his predecessors for ignoring the Indians when making policy, Collier had limited experience in Native communities. Impatient and idealistic, he would frequently dismiss criticism from Indians as uninformed or naïve. In the end Collier trusted no one more than himself.

In his first months in office Collier maneuvered his agency into a position where it could take advantage of the rapidly expanding social welfare programs being created to carry out the New Deal. In June 1933, for example, he persuaded the new

Public Works Administration to create a separate "Indian desk" to channel federal relief funds to reservation construction projects. One of the agency's early projects was a "community center" in Window Rock, Arizona, which Collier envisioned as the new capital of the Navajo reservation. Later that first year Collier also persuaded the new Civilian Conservation Corps (CCC), an agency that hired unemployed workers for environmental projects, to create a special Indian section. The CCC-ID (Indian Division) eventually employed fifty thousand Native Americans planting trees, developing erosion control projects, and cultivating range lands on reservations in twenty-three states. Similar Indian programs operated in the Works Progress Administration, the Civil Works Administration, and the Resettlement Administration.

Collier also moved quickly to change the tone of the government's Indian programs. Within months of taking office he closed six boarding schools and made plans for expanding the day school program so that Native children could pursue their education close to home. Collier also ordered reservation superintendents to cancel any regulations that required compulsory attendance at Christian services or limited reservation residents' ability to participate in traditional ceremonies. The latter step provoked instant attacks from missionaries, but the commissioner ignored them in favor of traditional leaders who came to his defense. When told of the new rules, one such elder, Lakota Bert Kills Close to Lodge, declared in Lakota, "Well, I'll be damned."

In January 1934, Collier began the development of a broad new agenda for the Indian Office. He hosted a conference in Washington that brought together representatives from the major Indian reform groups (the Indian Rights Association, the American Indian Defense Association, and the newly reorganized Association on American Indian Affairs) and social welfare organizations (the General Federation of Womens Clubs, the American Civil Liberties Union) to formulate a plan of action. The group agreed on the need for an end to allotment, the consolidation of fragmented Indian resources, and the transfer of federal power to tribal governments. Almost simultaneously Collier issued an order to all reservation superintendents (the nineteenth-century term "agents" was no longer used), asking them to consult the commu-

nities within their jurisdiction about their views regarding self-government and enhanced powers for the tribes. The commissioner asked the superintendents to reply by February 15. Collier appeared to be building broad support for his next reform. Instead he acted alone.

The Indian Reorganization Act

On February 12, 1934, just days before input from the agencies was due, Collier's allies in the House and Senate introduced a massive legislative proposal to Congress that the commissioner and his staff had written on their own. The forty-eight-page bill was longer and more complicated than anything legislators had ever seen in the field of Indian affairs.

Collier's February proposal contained four sections. Section one set the procedures for tribes to establish their own governments. These new tribal authorities would have the power to operate their own courts, condemn and acquire land, manage Indian Office personnel, review federal budget requests affecting their homelands, and select which federal services they would accept in their communities.

Section two—devoted to education—promised federal employment to qualified Indians in all branches of the BIA bureaucracy, from law enforcement and bookkeeping to law and medicine. It also pledged to "promote the study of Indian civilization . . ." and to teach traditional Native history and culture at all government schools.

Section three of the commissioner's bill sought to reestablish Indian homelands by abolishing allotment, returning unsold tribal lands to community ownership, and granting both the new tribal governments and the secretary of the interior the power to return individual allotments to the tribes. The goal was to consolidate reservation lands so they could be managed by the new tribal governments for the good of the community.

Finally, Collier proposed the establishment of a national Court of Indian Affairs, comprised of seven judges appointed by the president and confirmed by the U.S. Senate. This national court would hear major criminal cases involving Indians and civil cases involving individual Native Americans, tribes, or tribal lands.

The scale of Collier's bill was breathtaking. It acted on the broad goals of ending allotment and supporting tribal development agreed to by the reformers who had met in Washington the previous January, but it pursued these ends further than almost anyone had imagined. White reformers questioned whether the new tribal governments should have the power to hire and fire Indian Office personnel. Tribal politicians worried about granting these governments the power to return individual allotments to community ownership (even if allottees were compensated), and mission groups questioned the document's unwavering support for the promotion of traditional art and culture. Congressional leaders wondered how a national Indian court could function within the federal system.

Collier defended his bill, but the congressional hearings on the proposal attracted a broad collection of critics. Legislators testified that the commissioner's ideas were too extreme a retreat from the government's assimilation efforts, and Indian leaders from a number of communities spoke out against his suggestion that tribal resources be managed communally. Joseph Bruner, a successful Creek businessman from Sapulpa, Oklahoma, told the Senate that Collier was trying to establish "Russian Communistic life in the United States." The Indian Rights Association leaders who had supported Collier's general goals in January also opposed the creation of strong tribal governments. They claimed that the administration was promoting "segregation" and fomenting a "revolutionary departure" in policymaking.

Attacked by people he believed should support him, Collier reverted to the tactics he had employed in the 1920s. He decided to go over the heads of his critics and launched a public relations campaign aimed at generating Indian support for his ideas. Collier had not been interested in gathering opinions from the reservations before he made his February proposal, but now, under fire, he decided to ask Indian leaders to offer their comments at a series of ten regional "congresses" where tribal leaders and agency personnel could discuss the proposed law with the commissioner and his staff. Convinced that he knew what was best for Indians, the commissioner was confident the tribes would endorse his plan.

The congresses, which took place in Oregon, Arizona, South Dakota, New Mexico, California,

Wisconsin, and Oklahoma, fell far short of Collier's expectations. Local leaders voiced a wide range of concerns that national legislation could not address and repeatedly emphasized that they were suspicious of all federal actions. People from the Pacific Northwest, for example, wanted Collier to address their struggle for fishing rights. People in the Southwest were concerned about water. The Navajos expressed their anger over the Indian Office's campaign to reduce their sheep herds. Leaders from several regions objected to granting tribal governments the power to acquire individual allotments and worried out loud that the new governments could come under the control of landless Indians who would outvote their more prosperous kinsmen and bankrupt the tribe.

By May 1, 1934, Collier realized he had failed to win the enthusiastic support of either his congressional allies or a majority of tribal leaders. His only hope lay in a congressional compromise. It was time to make a deal. Once again, the man who presented himself as an advocate of democracy and cultural sensitivity decided that he knew best and would act alone. Collier abandoned the new practice of consulting with tribal leaders and turned to the powerful chair of the Senate Committee on Indian Affairs, Burton K. Wheeler of Montana. A few weeks later Wheeler introduced a new, shortened version of the "Collier bill." With the blessing of Wheeler and his fellow western New Dealers, the bill quickly passed; President Roosevelt signed the Indian Reorganization Act into law on June 18, 1934.

The new statute—which like other New Deal reforms came to be known by its initials, IRA—contained no provision for a national Indian court, no statement of commitment to the principle of self-government, no declaration of support for traditional cultures, no tribal authority to acquire individual allotments from tribal members, and no tribal control over Indian Office budgets or personnel. Still, several elements of the commissioner's original bill survived:

1. *No Allotment.* The United States officially abandoned the policy of allotment.
2. *Tribal Governments.* Reservation communities were granted the right to organize governments that could manage local affairs, negotiate contracts, operate businesses, levy taxes, and exer-

Crow and Blackfeet Leaders at Rapid City Indian Congress, 1934 In 1934, while trying to win Native American support for his proposed reorganization act, John Collier organized public meetings in several parts of the country. This picture of Crows and Blackfeet was taken at the Rapid City Congress of tribal leaders from the northern plains.

cise "all powers vested in any Indian tribe . . . by existing law."

3. *Increased Appropriations.* The new law established a $10 million revolving loan fund for tribal enterprises and authorized $250,000 annually for educational programs.
4. *Indians in the BIA.* The law reaffirmed Indian exemption from Civil Service regulations.
5. *Tribal Consent.* The act would not apply to a tribe without its approval.

Undaunted by the defeat of his original proposal and unembarrassed by the manner in which the IRA was approved, Collier now began urging tribes to adopt the new law. And an obscure provision of the law gave him confidence that ratifications would be plentiful. When a vote was held, rejection would be difficult. A majority of a reservation's adult Indians would have to vote no in order to turn it aside. In a tribe with 500 adult members, for example, it would be necessary for 251 no votes to be cast in order to reject "reorganization." With a 500-person electorate, a vote of 100 yes to 150 no votes would not be enough to defeat the IRA because the no votes would be less than 50 percent of the tribal electorate. Only one ratifying vote was allowed per tribe; once a community had acted, no reconsiderations were possible.

The ratification rules were altered in 1935 to make acceptance dependent on a majority of the votes cast, but rejection of the law remained difficult. If only a small minority of a tribe turned out to vote, the plurality of those voting would decide the matter. With a 500-person electorate, for example, a vote of 50 yes and 25 no votes (with 425 people staying home) would constitute ratification. The ratification rules—both the original version and the revisions—confirmed the tribes' suspicion that Collier was trying to force his reforms on them. The commissioner dispatched special agents to reservations to campaign for approval of the IRA and, even though he never publicly threatened his opponents with punishment, he made it clear that those who rejected the act would not qualify for education or community development loans and would "drift to the rear of the great advance open to the Indian race." Despite continuing criticism, the ratification rules remained in place. By 1936, 181 tribes and communities had voted to accept the new law; 77 had rejected it.

The Indian New Deal

The Indian Reorganization Act was the centerpiece of what Collier quickly labeled the "Indian New Deal." The label was self-serving but fair. Despite its limitations, the IRA ended allotment and made tribal governments—however weak—the focus of Indian Office action. Collier stopped lecturing Indian people about the value of work and concentrated the bureau's efforts on the improvement of education, health care, and living conditions. For example, a new law, the Johnson-O'Malley Act, provided federal funds to public school districts that educated Indian children. Indian school attendance became universal. By 1938 approximately 65,000 Indian children were in school: 34,000 in public institutions, 14,000 in day schools, 10,000 in boarding schools, and 7,000 in institutions run by missionary groups.

At Collier's urging, Congress also approved the Indian Arts and Crafts Act (1935), which established a board to create standards of authenticity in tribal arts as well as to promote the production and marketing of these goods. The new board sponsored exhibits of Indian goods at the 1939 San Francisco World's Fair as well as at the Museum of Modern Art in New York City, in department stores, at national parks, and even at a sales office in the new Department of the Interior building in Washington, D.C. Collier was continuously on the lookout for economic opportunities. He promoted timber production on tribal lands and improved range management and reservation road construction. Finally, the commissioner expanded the number of Native employees in the BIA from a few hundred in 1933 to more than 4,500 by the end of the decade.

Collier's Indian New Deal mixed high-handed tactics with outreach to Native American leaders.

The commissioner's love of publicity and unwavering faith in his own wisdom undermined his idealistic image, but the IRA prevented Indian communities from being allotted to extinction and insured that reservations (and the communities inhabiting them) would be permanent features of American life. Well-intentioned but paternalistic, Collier remained isolated from the very people he wished to serve. The meaning of his reforms would not be known until they were implemented at Indian agencies across the country.

Tribes React to the New Deal

Just as John Collier's visionary ideas had shrunk and shifted course as they moved into the public arena, so the policy initiatives that began in Washington, D.C., during the New Deal years took different form as they reached reservation communities. Some communities welcomed the prospect of change while others found the government's new policies disruptive or even dangerous.

Tribal communities wrestled with conflicting views of their future as they confronted the task of accepting or rejecting the IRA. They questioned, for example, the extent to which the economic arrangements made possible by the act—tribal corporations, a revolving loan fund, the development of tribal resources—would offset the fact that each of these innovations required the approval of the Interior Department and cooperation with the BIA. The Oneidas in northern Wisconsin, for example, voted overwhelmingly in favor of the IRA in December 1934, largely in the hope that it would make possible the expansion of a tribal land base that had nearly disappeared during the allotment era. By 1939 the newly reconstituted Oneida Tribe of Wisconsin had purchased twelve thousand acres of land for its members, created two hundred new jobs with the help of the Works Progress Administration, and begun to build new frame houses for reservation residents. Similarly, at the San Carlos and White Mountain Apache agencies in Arizona and at the Lower Brulé Sioux agency in South Dakota, tribal councils established under the IRA set up tribal cattle herds, acquired new community pastures, and developed tribal housing projects. The Jicarilla Apaches in northern New Mexico used government and tribal resources to buy out a long-time white trader on their reservation and re-place him with a general store owned by the tribe. Along the Pacific Coast, the Swinomish in Wash-ington and the Pomos of Point Arena, California, also used their new status as "IRA tribes" to launch community enterprises.

Economic development programs could also cre-ate conflict. The Oregon Klamaths, for example, had long sought permission to lease their tribal tim-ber lands for the benefit of the entire community. This authority had been granted in 1929 and a Kla-math tribal council had operated since that date. Commissioner Collier argued that the IRA would give the tribe access to revolving loan funds and would place their council on a more modern foot-ing. But from the tribe's perspective, the IRA looked like more federal interference; they rejected the new law in 1935 by a vote of 666 to 56.

The Navajos Say No

Some of the most dramatic debates over the IRA and economic development took place among the Navajos. On the same day that the Klamaths voted in Oregon, bureau officials tabulated votes from more than 15,000 Navajo men and women at polling stations in Utah, Arizona, and New Mex-ico. The tribe narrowly rejected the new law by a vote of 7,992 to 7,608. Collier and his team had campaigned hard among the Navajos. They be-lieved the reserve's 1.3 million sheep and goats should be carefully managed by a modern govern-ment so that tribal incomes would rise and soil ero-sion would end. It also seemed clear to the BIA that the tribe's rapidly rising population (it had doubled in size from 20,000 to 40,000 between 1900 and 1933) would require expanded educational insti-tutions and extensive new business development. But like the Klamaths, the Navajos were suspicious of the government's programs. Tribal elders re-called that when they had been children in the 1860s the United States had nearly destroyed the Navajos by sentencing them to the "Long Walk" to eastern New Mexico that had separated them from their homelands for many years. Since those un-happy days, a procession of government men had promised many forms of assistance, but few of those promises had been fulfilled. Extended fami-lies of Navajos had developed growing herds of

sheep and cattle and had begun to trade handicrafts for cash. Their population was on the rise. The Navajos had established a tribal council in 1923; there seemed to be little need for the new law.

But the crucial factor among the Navajos was the commissioner himself. Collier was not contro-versial among the Navajos; he was actively disliked because he had so closely identified himself with the effort to reduce the size of the tribe's goat and sheep herds. As in other instances when he was sure he knew better than his critics, Collier did not ap-preciate the depths of the tribe's resentment of him. He first had called only for voluntary restrictions on tribal herds, but within a year of taking office he persuaded the tribe's leaders to order all Navajo stock owners to sell 10 percent of their sheep. When small herders organized active resistance to the order, Collier became even more forceful. He urged the tribal council to mandate the sale or de-struction of 150,000 goats and 50,000 sheep. When the council hesitated, Collier tried to make a deal. He promised that if the council acted he would deliver congressional approval of a pending land purchase. The council approved Collier's pro-posal, but the commissioner failed to secure the congressional action.

When Collier began campaigning for the IRA among the Navajos in late 1934, the tribal council was carrying out a coercive program to reduce tribal herds while accusing the commissioner of fraud. Tribal police accosted Navajo herders at wa-tering holes and dipping vats and forced them to sell up to 50 percent of their livestock for $1 per head. Sometimes owners were allowed to butcher their own animals and preserve the meat for their families, but on most occasions the animals were simply shipped away for slaughter or, worse, killed on site, doused with gasoline and set ablaze.

What Collier and his staff saw as a reasonable conservation measure—smaller herds meant less soil erosion—Navajo herders saw as a threat to their survival. The commissioner's critics were un-concerned with overproduction because they relied on their animals for food. They also rejected Col-lier's characterization of goats as unproductive and unprofitable. Navajo herders knew that goats were the hardiest animals on the range and provided a steady source of milk for both humans and or-phaned sheep. In addition, goats were largely owned by women, who viewed the animals as an

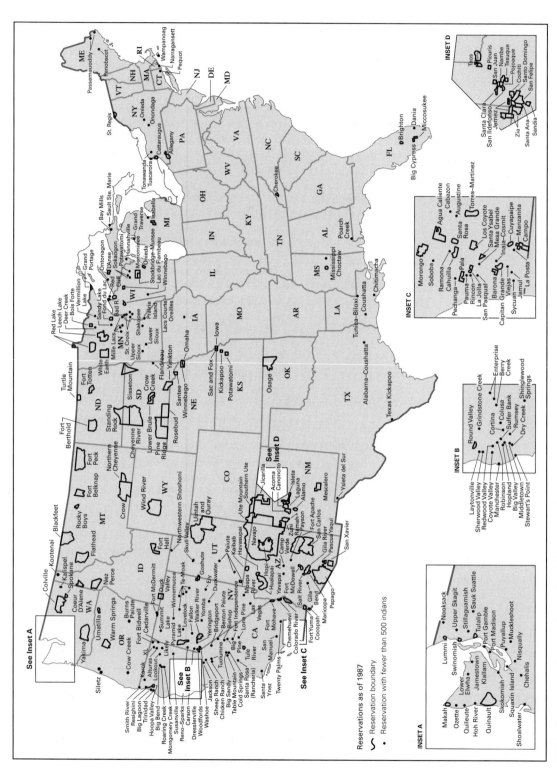

U.S. Indian Reservations as of 1987 (excluding Alaska).

Reservations as of 1987

⟩ Reservation boundary

• Reservation with fewer than 500 Indians

Jacob C. Morgan and His Family A principal critic of Collier, Jacob Morgan (third from left) is shown here with his wife, Zabrina Morgan; Thomas Jesse Jones; his granddaughter Vivienne Morgan; and his eldest son, Irwin Morgan in 1939. *Courtesy of the Navajo Nation Museum, Window Rock, Arizona.*

essential source of personal independence. Collier's animus towards goats thus won him special scorn from senior women in this matrilineal society.

Among tribal leaders, Collier's principal critic was Jacob Morgan, a boarding school graduate from Shiprock, New Mexico, who directed a Mennonite mission in the nearby town of Farmington, New Mexico. Pastor Morgan criticized stock reduction, but as a Christian missionary, he also disliked the new emphasis on traditional culture. He declared that the New Deal was nothing more than a "monkey show," intended to confine Navajos to the past.

The Navajos did strengthen their tribal council system in 1938, creating the office of tribal chairman and other tribal institutions, but they never embraced Collier's version of reservation development. The newly constituted Navajo tribal council took office in 1938 and moved into its impressive new headquarters in Window Rock—built with New Deal money—but the presiding officer, the first Navajo tribal chairman of the modern era, was Jacob Morgan, the man who had led the anti-IRA campaign.

The Divided Communities

In addition to wrestling with economic issues, a number of tribes in the New Deal era were also concerned with the promotion of reservation leadership. Some tribes like the Navajos saw no value in the IRA's system of centralized tribal councils. (Many Navajos, more comfortable with extended—and matrilineal—family groups, also doubted the wisdom of establishing a male-dominated government.) But to others, the IRA seemed modern and promising. On Montana's Flathead reservation, for example, the Confederated Salish and Kootenai tribes adopted the IRA in 1934, creating a tribal council that included both elected representatives from each community and tribal elders who were given permanent seats on the governing body. Similarly, most Pueblos adopted the IRA because its structure of centralized leadership generally fit with their traditions. The Santa Clara Pueblo, for example, ordered that council members must conduct their business in the Tewa language and that all reservation residents should fence their traditional gardens to avoid land disputes.

But opposition to a centralized council surfaced in several regions. The Montana Crows, for example, had established a tribal governance system in the early twentieth century based on the general tribal assemblies that had operated in the early days of their reservation. Crow councils approved leases of tribal pasture land and oil fields and appointed leaders to represent them in disputes with federal authorities. While the system was not perfect, the tribe was reluctant to change. As a consequence, the Crows rejected the IRA measure by a margin of more than 6 to 1. A month later, this same political dynamic produced a sweeping rejection of the IRA in upstate New York. In votes at six Iroquois agencies, the total vote in favor of ratification was 240 while 1,540 others expressed their opposition to Collier's law.

At the Klamath and Crow reservations and in New York, widely shared local opposition to centralized leadership schemes united tribes and doomed ratification. At other agencies, ongoing rivalries between reservation groups set off bitter debates over New Deal reforms. The Montana Blackfeet, for example, were among the first tribes to adopt the IRA, approving it by a vote of 832 to 171 in October 1934. Despite this wide margin, however, some Blackfeet—those who called themselves "full bloods" and who generally preferred subsistence farming and stock raising to large-scale agriculture—pointed out that nearly 800 tribal members had not voted in the election. The "full bloods," who favored a simple distribution of all tribal income instead of investment in large collective enterprises, called on the secretary of the interior to overturn the ratification vote. Secretary Ickes's refusal to do so insured that divisions within the Blackfeet tribe would continue into the future.

The Pine Ridge and Rosebud Lakota reserves in western South Dakota offer the most vivid example of how the Indian Reorganization Act so intensified local political divisions that the resulting tribal councils would be doomed to a marginal existence in deeply polarized communities. The combined population of nearly 15,000 at these adjoining agencies constituted the largest Indian population center outside the Southwest. There, the pro- and anti-IRA groups called themselves the "New Dealers" and the "Old Dealers." Their separate parties were the product of disputes over intermarriage with whites, the extent to which the children of nineteenth-century leaders deserved to be followed as "chiefs," and how to resolve the tribe's increasing division into groups of commercial and subsistence farmers and ranchers.

At Pine Ridge and Rosebud (as had been the case among the Navajos, the Oneidas, and the Blackfeet) individuals engaged in commercial agriculture, and many of those who had attended government schools tended to support the IRA. The "New Dealers" campaigned energetically for the new measure, and in October 1934 both communities voted their approval. Despite the nearly two-to-one margin in the voting at each agency, however, the "Old Dealers" challenged the outcome of the election. They pointed out that only about half of the electorate at each agency had gone to the polls and that this undisputed fact placed the IRA at odds with the revered Fort Laramie Treaty of 1868, which had stipulated that major decisions required the approval of three-quarters of the adult male members of the tribes.

Damaged by these political debates, Rosebud and Pine Ridge did not develop successful IRA governments. Community wrangling delayed approval of tribal constitutions, and once implemented, these new charters continued to provoke opposition. "Old Dealers" questioned the legitimacy of the new tribal councils and avoided involvement in the new economic development programs they sponsored. When conditions failed to improve, they blamed

Collier and Roosevelt for their poverty. At the same time "New Dealers" like Rosebud leader Sam Lapointe dismissed the opposition, calling them backward malcontents whose pride prevented them from seeing the benefits of cooperation with the Indian Office.

Help Arrives from Washington

Reactions to the New Deal were also affected by a group's sense of tribal identity. Clearly, Iroquois and Lakota traditionalists, Navajo subsistence sheepherders, and successful tribal politicians at the Crow or Klamath reservations were convinced that Collier's new scheme was not an important validation of their Indian culture. But in dozens of other communities, particularly those that had suffered the most land loss and government neglect, the New Deal offered a lifeline they were eager to grasp.

For example, when John Collier took office in 1933, Wisconsin's tiny Stockbridge-Munsee tribe had all but ceased to exist. Moving from the Midwest from the East in the early nineteenth century and allotted under the Dawes Act, the Stockbridge-Munsees had lost all of their tribal land. To make matters worse, most tribal members had lost their individual allotments to county taxes, sales to lumber companies, or creditors; in 1933 only a handful of individuals still retained title to their homesteads. Described in a BIA report as a group of "squatters and shackers," the Stockbridge-Munsees had nothing to hold their community together besides a shared heritage and a determination to rebuild. The tribe began this rebuilding process in 1931 when Carl Miller, a tribal leader who had attended Hampton Institute, called on the group to participate in a local township election and take control of its governing board. Following this success, the group formed a tribal business council and sought recognition from the Indian Office as the legal representative of the Stockbridge-Munsee people. The Hoover appointees in Washington rejected this initial request, but two years later, when he learned of Collier's appointment, Miller wrote again. Collier encouraged Miller and, as plans for the IRA took shape, he invited the Stockbridge-Munsees to ratify the new law and form a tribal council. In December 1934, the tribe accepted the

IRA with a vote of 166 to 1. Miller and his colleagues quickly drew up a constitution and applied for federal funds to support a program of land acquisition. By 1937 the Stockbridge-Munsees had assembled more than 15,000 acres of land and had become adept at finding federal agencies to support their employment training, farm development, and home construction projects.

In a similar vein, Washington State tribes along Puget Sound and the Olympic Peninsula viewed the Indian Reorganization Act as a vehicle for organizing themselves into groups that could take collective action to repair some of the damage caused by allotment. In the seven months between October 1934 and May 1935, seventeen separate Washington communities voted to accept the IRA and embrace the New Deal reforms. Unlike the Stockbridge-Munsees, the Puget Sound and Olympic Peninsula groups did not make significant land acquisitions. Instead, they used their new status to assert their political interests and to lobby for other forms of federal assistance. The Puyallups, for example, whose territory had been reduced by allotment to a mere sixty acres, reorganized themselves and established a variety of new community social welfare programs. Joe Hillaire, a leader of the Northwest Federation of American Indians, told Collier his agenda was "the very thing I have been hoping for."

Hillaire's enthusiasm was shared not only among the leaders of small, nearly landless tribes in Washington and Wisconsin, but by similarly embattled and forgotten groups across the country. These included the allotted Omahas, Poncas, and Winnebagos of Nebraska, the Mississippi Choctaws, the scattered Ojibwe communities of northern Michigan, Ute and Shoshone communities in Nevada and Idaho, and the Seminoles of Florida.

Collier and the Critics

It is difficult to discern a clear pattern of tribal acceptance or rejection of the IRA and other New Deal reforms. Most tribes were absorbed in local problems—land acquisition, establishing stable leadership, gaining legitimacy before state and federal agencies—and local perspectives shaped reactions to the new administration. Collier's Indian critics usually shared common concerns: suspicion of federal power, rejection of communal landholding, and discomfort with official support for traditional culture. As the Indian New Deal gained visibility, many of the commissioner's most outspoken critics came forward to join forces. At the end of 1934 they gathered in Gallup, New Mexico, to form the American Indian Federation (AIF), electing Joseph Bruner president of the new group and Jacob Morgan first national vice chairman. The AIF claimed a membership of 4,000, which included Thomas Sloan, an Omaha attorney who had once headed the Progressive Era Society of American Indians; the Cahuilla leader Rupert Costo; Fred Bauer, vice chief of the Eastern Band of Cherokees; Alice Jemison, a Washington lobbyist for the New York Senecas; and O. K. Chandler, a prominent Cherokee attorney.

The AIF quickly allied itself with Collier's political enemies. Bruner, Morgan, and Jemison made regular appearances at hearings called to review the Indian Office budget requests and Collier's administration of Indian affairs. Mennonite missionary Jacob Morgan was particularly appealing when he testified in his business suit. Carrying a briefcase and speaking in cultured tones, he could be counted on to rail against the commissioner's arrogance and duplicity. Over the course of the decade, Morgan formed a political alliance with New Mexico Senator Dennis Chavez who, despite his Democratic Party affiliation, was an ardent foe of both Collier and Secretary Ickes. Alice Jemison regularly called for the abolition of the Indian Office and a return to policymaking based on treaties. Her positions brought her close to Collier critics, including Senator Burton Wheeler of Montana and Congressman Alfred Beiter of New York. She applauded enthusiastically, for example, when Wheeler and his allies introduced legislation in 1937 to repeal the IRA.

Joseph Bruner was the most outspoken of the group. Willing to form alliances with Nazi sympathizers in the German American Bund, the Oklahoman grew increasingly strident over the course of the 1930s. He argued that Collier's membership in the American Civil Liberties Union, the presence of numerous Jews in his inner circle, and his admiration for modern dancer Isadora Duncan proved his Bolshevik and anti-Christian views. These attacks won the support, not only of many conservative New Deal opponents, but also of

Republican isolationists who supported the AIF's right-wing allies. In 1938, attacks from Bruner and Jemison surfaced in hearings before the newly created Committee on Un-American Activities.

Collier and Congress Extend the New Deal

Despite the opposition of Bruner and his colleagues, Collier solidified his position and expanded his list of legislative and bureaucratic victories. In 1936 Congress passed the Oklahoma Welfare Act, which extended the broad provisions of the IRA to the Indians in that state. Native American Oklahomans realized that by remaining outside the act, they could not qualify for federal loans and other benefits being made available to IRA tribes. Some small communities were eager to organize tribal governments to represent their concerns in Washington, but others opposed reconstituting their tribal governments. Allotted Indians did not like the idea of creating communally owned tribal property, while others scoffed at Washington's new-found enthusiasm for traditional Native ways. John Loco, a member of the Apache group at Fort Sill, Oklahoma, for example, asked why the Indian Office "brings us up like white people and then [when] we come up like white people they don't like it."

The 1935 Oklahoma Welfare Act extended the right to organize tribal governments to all Native American groups in the state. These tribes would be permitted to apply for federal loans and grants, but reflecting the power of the state's congressional delegation, state courts would continue to have jurisdiction over probate cases despite the exposure of numerous instances of fraud and neglect over the years. Oklahoma would also be allowed to continue levying a "production tax" on oil and gas pumped from Indian lands. Despite these drawbacks, thirty-one Oklahoma communities decided to accept the new law and redefine themselves as modern tribes.

In June of 1936 Congress extended the Collier's New Deal regime to Alaska by passing the Alaska Reorganization Act. This measure granted Native villages and groups throughout the territory the right to organize themselves under constitutions and corporate charters and to apply to the revolving credit fund for support. During the next decade forty-nine Alaskan communities, from Metlakatla,

a prosperous, Presbyterian-dominated Tshimsian fishing village in temperate southeast Alaska, to isolated Point Hope on the Arctic Ocean, organized under the new law.

Finally, Collier's ceaseless personal lobbying succeeded in maintaining the flow of federal funds from New Deal agencies to Native American communities. In addition to helping tribes secure grants from the Works Progress Administration and the Public Works Administration, he persuaded the Resettlement Administration (later the Farm Security Administration) to assist in the acquisition of new tribal land. Between 1933 and 1935, $45 million of emergency funds were spent in Indian communities. Many of these projects created important symbolic centers for Indian communities. In addition to the Navajo tribal headquarters built with New Deal funds in Window Rock, Arizona, crews of Crow construction workers built a tribal dance hall in the center of the tribe's Montana fair grounds, while workers employed by the National Youth Administration built the Tonawanda Community House on the Seneca reservation in western New York (the house was dedicated by Eleanor Roosevelt at a public ceremony in 1939), and WPA crews built a new dock at the Fort Madison Squamish reservation on Puget Sound.

During the Collier years the newly created Indian Arts and Crafts Board promoted Native arts, but many other federal agencies also subsidized individual artists. WPA projects often employed Native painters and sculptors on construction projects or employed Indians to record and preserve tribal arts and traditions. For example, the Navajo capital at Window Rock was decorated with murals by Navajo artist Gerald Nailor. Other projects subsidized an entire community. One of the most ambitious of these was the Seneca Arts Project, organized by anthropologist Arthur Parker, a founder of the Progressive Era Society of American Indians, who in the 1930s was director of the Rochester (New York) Municipal Museum. Supported by a grant from the WPA, Parker commissioned about 100 Seneca artists to produce more than 5,000 works of art from woodcarvers, basket makers, silversmiths, beadworkers, and painters on the Tonawanda and Cattaraugus reservations.

As a young man John Collier had written that American Indian communities were a "Red Atlantis," a hidden world whose revival would en-

PEOPLE, PLACES, AND THINGS

Crow Indian Round Hall

Crow Indian Round Hall

Constructed by CCC workers during the Depression, this dance hall was opened in 1937 and later named for Ivan Hoops, one of the first Crow soldiers to be killed in World War II. The hall is beautifully described in the excerpt below by Peter Nabokov. It has served as a venue for dances, hand games, and community events marking important holidays and celebrations.

In the 1870s, the Hidatsas conveyed a dance called "tawlissua" or Hot Dance to their old kinfolk, the Crows. During this transfer, the Crows paid handsomely, turning over nearly 600 horses and other property. A few decades later they erected dance houses (or "annissuashe"—"the house where they danced") for sheltering the ritual. Over time, these houses served other functions. By World War I each of the reservation's four major districts featured a dance hall maintained by Hot Dance clubs. In the 1930s, the convergence of a new, more relaxed official attitude towards traditional culture and the presence of new government employment programs, prompted the construction of this round house near Crow Agency, the reservation headquarters. Named for the first Crow soldier to fall in World War II, the Ivan Hoops Hall opened in 1937 on the tribe's fairgrounds near the Little Big Horn River. Cut from forests in the Big Horn mountains and carried more than seventy miles to this site, the hall's ridge poles covered a wider dirt floor than any previous Hot Dance structure. Before long the new dance hall also reinforced Crow Agency's centrality on the reservation, sheltering powwows, Tobacco Society adoptions, weddings, council meetings, dances, medicine bundle openings, clan feasts, veteran-honoring occasions, and the annual hand game tournament. Today the building is tended like an aging grandfather who enjoys his declining days sitting in the sun but who, at key moments in the Crow festival calendar, is still expected to creak back to work.

Adapted from Peter Nabokov, "Hidden Blueprints," *North Dakota Quarterly*, Fall 2000. Reprinted with permission.

rich and redeem an industrialized America that had lost its way. By the end of the 1930s it was clear that the commissioner had fallen far short of his ambitious goals. Collier's reluctance to work cooperatively with Indian communities had alienated many potential allies. Veering between bold public pronouncements and backroom deal-making, he had produced an innovative new law, the IRA, that held out significant promise but that also engendered suspicion and resentment. The nation's largest tribes—the Navajos and the Sioux—had rejected or publicly attacked his new law, and his other programs won mixed reviews. Congressional critics derided the commissioner as a romantic (and possibly un-American) social worker, while many tribes, especially the smallest and most desperate, embraced his programs.

In the decades following the Collier era, scholars have continued the debate over the commissioner's legacy. Captivated by his rhetoric and idealism, many have praised the Indian New Deal's dramatic shifts in policy and applauded Collier's public support for Indian culture and Indian leaders. Others have been more skeptical. Upon closer examination, the commissioner appears to have suffered from a lifelong habit of working alone and behind the scenes in moments of crisis. And Collier's programs appear not to have lived up to his enthusiastic promises. For example, while Collier urged tribal leaders to adopt the IRA because it would allow them to control their own communities, the final version of the law was so different from his original proposal that once in place the new governments had little ability to alter or oppose orders from Washington, D.C. In a benign administration like Collier's this weakness might be inconsequential, but in a more hostile time, the weakness of IRA tribal governments would be deeply frustrating to reservation leaders.

Nevertheless the Indian New Deal changed Indian country. New legislation and new contacts between tribal leaders and federal agencies insured that politically organized Native communities would be enduring features of the American landscape. The Indian Office had shifted from being an enemy of tribal life to its defender. The Indian New Deal shared some of the paternalism and short-sightedness of earlier reforms, but the change in tone at the Bureau of Indian Affairs energized many Native communities and marked the start of a new era of activism. At the same time, the infusion of federal dollars into tribal communities, however inadequate, signaled the advent of wage labor and a consequent move away from the isolated, subsistence existence of the pre-Collier era.

WORLD WAR II

During the 1930s, critics of the New Deal argued that John Collier's support for tribal reorganization threatened to separate Indian people from the American majority. It is ironic, then, that Collier spent the last four years of his record-setting tenure promoting Native American patriotism and urging the integration of Native Americans into the global struggle against fascism. For Americans, the actual fighting began on December 7, 1941, when the Japanese attacked Pearl Harbor, but the mobilization for World War II really had started in 1940 when Franklin Roosevelt had called for massive aid to Britain and Congress approved the first peacetime draft in American history. On the morning the Japanese dropped bombs on American battleships in Hawaii, 4,000 American Indians were already serving in the rapidly expanding American armed forces. One of those Native servicemen, Henry Nolatubby, a young Choctaw man from Oklahoma serving on the U.S.S. Arizona, was among the first to die that day.

Indians at War

World War II brought Indians and other Americans together as never before. Twenty-five thousand Indians served in the American military, but nearly twice that many (at least 40,000) left home during the war years to work in defense plants or to make new homes near loved ones. Remarkably, these tribal members—both military and civilian—were generally welcomed into white society. Unlike African-Americans, Indian soldiers fought in integrated units. While frequently viewed as stereotypical "warriors" and "chiefs," recruits were usually accepted and promoted on the same basis as their peers. (Among the heroes of the war were Admiral Joseph "Jocko" Clark, a Cherokee, the first Native American to attend Annapolis, and General Clarence Tinker, an Osage graduate of Haskell who was a commander of Air Force units in Hawaii when he was shot down and lost during the Battle of Midway.)

Native American civilian workers lived in integrated housing and were generally accepted socially. And in both military and civilian settings, Indians appeared to relish their new experiences and take special pride in their achievements. Native Americans responded to the call to arms with much the same enthusiasm they had shown in World War I. The peacetime draft, which began in October 1940, generated a few highly publicized incidents of Indian resistance, but most draftees cooperated with the authorities. The most significant objections to the draft came from a small Tohono O'odham village near the Mexican border and from Iroquois elders at Onondaga, New York. At the Tohono O'odham village of Toapit, a leader named Pia Machita insisted his community did not recognize the Gadsden Purchase and was therefore outside the boundaries of the United States and exempt from the draft. Confronted by the FBI, Machita fled into the desert where he eluded capture for seven months. Despite protests from John Collier and civil liberties groups, Pia Machita was eventually sentenced to eighteen months in prison for "denying the sovereignty of the United States."

Clinton Rickard, Jesse Lyons, and other Iroquois leaders made a similar claim, noting that their treaty with the United States set them apart from American citizens. Collier disagreed with their position, noting that "even aliens must register with the draft board." Undeterred, in early 1941 the Iroquois challenged the induction of Warren Green, an Onondaga man, into the army. After a hearing, the government prevailed and Green was ordered to serve. The Iroquois continued to protest their inclusion in the draft until their leaders approved their own declaration of war against Germany and Japan in June 1942. The only other examples of significant Indian draft resistance came in the South where Virginia Rappahannocks, North Carolina Cherokees, and Mississippi Choctaws refused to report to segregated induction centers established for African-Americans. The Cherokees' protests were ultimately successful, but the members of other southern groups were given no choice but to follow orders. Many dark-skinned Native Americans from the South therefore served with black troops in segregated units and were largely confined to noncombat roles.

Most Indians enlisted in the war effort with their white neighbors. The Indian Office newsletter, "Indians at Work," declared in February 1942 that "Indians are ready to defend America on all fronts." Readers saw stories describing Sioux men clamoring to join the Army in South Dakota, Pueblo communities appointing air raid wardens, and the Jicarilla Apache tribal council's decision to purchase a $100 war bond every week with the profits from its community enterprises. In the Kashaya Pomo community near Stewarts Point in northern California, tribal members formed a home guard and established a listening post to watch for Japanese warships. Similar units were staffed by Indians in Washington State and Wisconsin. Other stories in the national press emphasized the enthusiasm with which Native Americans approached the conflict.

The Minneapolis *Journal* reported in March 1942 that fifteen young men from the Turtle Mountain reserve enlisted in the Navy, two of them wearing feather headdresses and carrying tomahawks. A Montana newspaper quoted a young Flathead man who announced, "I'll scalp the Japs if I get near one," as he left for induction at Fort Lewis, Washington. Also in March the Arizona press noted that more than eight thousand Navajos had already registered for the draft and five hundred had been inducted. The public reacted to these news stories with enthusiasm. Indian patriotism seemed to confirm the common view of Indians as hardy warriors. "The red soldier is tough," the American Legion magazine observed; "usually he has lived out doors all of his life." The *Saturday Evening Post* added, "We would not need the Selective Service if all volunteered like Indians."

While tales of Native American soldiers were often colored by racist stereotypes, World War II generated a great many Indian heroes. Tales of Indian valor surfaced early in the war when it became known that among the members of the former Oklahoma and Arizona National Guard units that were serving with General MacArthur's beleaguered troops on Bataan were three hundred Indians. These men fought gallantly alongside their white comrades, and they endured the "Death March" that followed the Army's surrender. (One Choctaw soldier eluded the Japanese and led a Filipino resistance unit during the next three years.)

In the European theater, the Forty-fifth Army Infantry Division, initially organized in Oklahoma, included hundreds of Indians. The men of the Forty-fifth wore a thunderbird symbol on their uniforms (the image of a traditional Indian spirit being). They endured 511 days of combat in North Africa, Sicily, Italy, and southern France and won dozens of battlefield commendations. One of these was the Congressional Medal of Honor, which was awarded in 1944 to Lieutenant Ernest Childers, a Creek from Broken Arrow, Oklahoma. Childers was decorated for leading an uphill assault on an entrenched German position near Oliveto, Italy, in April 1943. Ignoring his own injuries, Childers killed five enemy soldiers and captured one other while eliminating a machine gun nest that had blocked the American advance.

The most celebrated individual Native American hero in the war was Ira Hamilton Hayes, a young

Pima man who had worked for the New Deal CCC before enlisting in the Marines in 1942. Hayes became a paratrooper and was sent to the Pacific theater. He served with distinction in the Solomon Islands and the assault on Bougainville, but he did not win public notoriety until he landed on Iwo Jima with the Twenty-Eighth Marine Division in February, 1945. In the bloody struggle to dislodge the Japanese from the island, Hayes took part in the assault on an enemy stronghold atop Mount Suribachi. On February 23 a party of Marines planted a small American flag at the mountain's summit; the next day a detachment of six other soldiers, including Hayes, was sent to erect a larger one. An Associated Press photographer captured an image of this second flag-raising that quickly became an icon of wartime patriotism. Three of the six flag-raisers were killed in subsequent fighting on Iwo Jima, but the remaining three were catapulted into the national spotlight. Returned to the states with his two comrades, Hayes spoke at rallies and memorial ceremonies across the country. The flag-raising image soon appeared on a new postage stamp and, after the war, was the inspiration for the World War II Marine memorial.

A group of Navajos made the most famous—and unique—Native American contribution to the nation's military success in the war. In World War I groups of Native soldiers had used their tribal languages to confuse the enemy and communicate without being detected. At the outset of World War II similar programs were launched that involved Oneidas, Ojibwes, and members of the Sauk and Fox tribes, but Philip Johnston, a missionary's son who had been raised on the Navajo reservation, proposed something more ambitious. Early in 1942, Johnston suggested to the commanders of the Marine Corps that they create an all-Navajo signal unit that would communicate in a code that used their famously complicated tribal language. Johnston pointed out that this Athapaskan language was extremely difficult to learn and that German anthropologists had never studied it. More important, he felt the language could be adapted easily into a military code. The Marines authorized a trial and by September 1942 a group of thirty Navajo men had been recruited into the program. They began learning and memorizing a list of 413 military terms that had been translated into the Navajo language. Fighter plane became "Hum-mingbird," for example, and machine gun became "fast shooter."

The first Navajo "code talkers" landed with the Marines at Guadalcanal in early 1943 and quickly won high praise for their bravery and reliability. Their code appeared impenetrable and it did not require time-consuming translation. Soon other Marine units requested "code talkers" and the Navajo signalmen moved on to Bougainville and other Pacific battle sites. The Navajos never served as a single unit, but were dispersed across the six Marine divisions that were fighting in the Pacific. By war's end over four hundred Navajo men had participated in the program, and their performance as efficient and inscrutable radiomen had become a staple of both the real battlefield and its many Hollywood re-creations.

The Home Front

While they generated few stories in the press, the Native Americans' civilian contributions to the war were often as dramatic as tales of battlefield heroism. As many as forty-six thousand Indians—nearly twice the number of those who served in uniform—left home during the war to take jobs in war industries or to work near family members in the service. While many of these individuals, particularly skilled male and female graduates of government boarding schools, traveled alone to major cities to take jobs at airplane factories, shipyards, and assembly lines, others traveled in groups to military posts or construction sites adjacent to their reservations. For example, three thousand Navajo and Pueblo workers constructed and maintained the Fort Wingate Munitions Depot not far from Gallup, New Mexico, and the Bellemont Depot near Flagstaff. Three hundred Tohono O'odham men and women worked at the Phelps-Dodge copper mine in Anjo, Arizona, and in upstate New York dozens of St. Regis Mohawks worked at the Aluminum Corporation of America's new plant on the St. Lawrence River. In Clearfield, Utah, crews of Pueblo laborers managed a massive Navy supply depot.

In Indian communities the war also offered women unprecedented opportunities. In addition to the 800 women who joined the armed services, at least 8,000 others left home between 1941 and

1945 to seek employment close to servicemen in their families. As many as one in four Native American women were involved in wartime industries. Among these "uprooted" women were some who took up traditionally male occupations on assembly lines and factories in faraway cities and others who pitched in locally, such as the Menominee women who staffed their tribe's famous sawmill, the Pueblo women who worked as truck drivers, and the many others who filled in as clerks and teachers with the Indian Office.

Both the draft and the new employment opportunities generated by the war effort transformed reservation life. With as many as half the available men working away from the reservations, unemployment rates plummeted. While rationing and shortages presented transportation problems, rising prices stimulated an increase in agricultural production. Farm sales increased from $9 million to $21 million during the war; timber sales also rose. Demand for tribal resources also boosted tribal income from mineral and oil leases. One thousand such leases were approved in 1944 alone.

The war had a more direct impact on one reservation. In 1942 at the Colorado River agency, the War Relocation Authority created a camp for Japanese-Americans who had been forcibly removed from their homes on the West Coast. The Indian Office had hoped this camp at Poston, California, would provide new buildings and irrigation facilities for local Indians to use once the war was over, but only a portion of the potential land was developed for agriculture and most of the camp's buildings were torn down in 1945, following the release of the 20,000 Japanese-Americans confined there.

But even as daily life on the reservations improved during the war, the long-term prospects for these largely rural communities seemed dim. With off-reservation wages rising to as much as three times the level paid back home, Native American men and women saw their future in cities rather than on their traditional homelands. A 1944 study of the Sisseton, Potawatomi, Navajo, and Pueblo communities, for example, revealed that as many as 25 percent of the reservation population had moved away during the war. Significant urban communities arose both in small, regional cities such as Flagstaff, Arizona, and Rapid City, South Dakota, and in larger urban centers such as Los Angeles, Denver, Minneapolis, and Seattle. In 1940 only twenty-five thousand Indians (8 percent of the total) lived in cities; by 1950 that figure had more than doubled. More significant, only half the number of Indians who identified themselves as farmers at the beginning of the war still claimed that occupation at war's end. And those who continued to farm during the war found the gap between themselves and their white neighbors increasing steadily. In South Dakota, for example, white farms were 40 percent larger and 200 percent more valuable before the war; afterward, the process of land consolidation and increased investment in machinery caused those differences to grow dramatically.

Despite the economic dislocations it caused, however, World War II generated an enormous sense of pride in Indian communities. Battlefield heroes like Ernest Childers and Ira Hayes returned home to celebrations that included both Indians and whites. Many tribes welcomed their veterans with proud revivals of old war ceremonies. These took place with little concern for the opposition of missionaries or government officials. The Kiowas, for example, revived their Black Legs society to incorporate its newest warriors into the tribe's ritual life, while Cheyennes, Crows, Navajos, and others held victory dances and cleansing rituals to welcome veterans back. "We dance for the benefit of the relatives who may be afflicted, for the dear ones in the armed services, and for the safe return of those dear ones," a Crow elder declared at one such celebration.

Sacrifice for the war effort also made it easier for tribal leaders to speak out about injustices suffered by their communities. In 1944, for example, the Navajo tribal council protested to the Interior Department when it learned that workers at the Fort Wingate Munitions Depot received lower wages than whites. That protest was unsuccessful, but in Alaska a campaign against segregation in public accommodations produced dramatic change. In 1945, following protests sparked by the arrest of Alberta Schenck, a young woman of mixed Inuit and white ancestry, for sitting in the "whites only" section of a Nome movie theater, the territorial legislature approved Alaska's first antidiscrimination law.

In 1940, on the eve of World War II, John Collier had declared, "[T]he future of the Indian depends on the fate of his land." By war's end, however, the Indians' future appeared to lie elsewhere. War service had brought Native Americans unprecedented public endorsement. Wartime employment continued the relentless transition from subsistence to a cash economy. Congress reduced federal appropriations for the Indian Office by 15 percent during the war and showed little interest in restoring these cuts once the conflict ended. Support for such New Deal dreams as cooperative farms, tribal cattle herds, and ambitious conservation and land management programs had disappeared. Even Collier, the visionary of the "Red Atlantis" and champion of reservation development, conceded that many Indians now rejected rural life. "Should economic conditions after the war continue to offer employment opportunities in industry," he wrote in 1943, "many Indians will undoubtedly continue to work away from the reservations."

CONCLUSION

Despite John Collier's high-profile reforms and the headlines celebrating the exploits of Native America's wartime heroes, the most profound events in Indian communities in the New Deal and World War II eras took place away from the glare of publicity. Like D'Arcy McNickle, who had labored to fit his sense of Indian history into the form of a novel, most Native American men and women in the 1930s and early 1940s struggled to live in ways that would give allegiance both to their tribal past and to their future as members of the larger American society. And for the first time, thanks to a new attitude in Washington, the rise of a new generation of leaders, and the impact of events outside the Indian world, it began to seem possible that these two previously separate worlds—traditional Indian culture and modern America—might finally be bridged. The struggle to link them took many forms. It occurred as reservation communities wrestled over whether or not to participate in John Collier's reform programs. It took place as artists decorated new WPA-financed buildings with images of a tribal past. It took place as Navajo stockmen and women balanced their individual economic interests against their reverence for their

landscape and traditions. It took place as well as young men and women went off to war—and as they returned to homecoming rituals that were older than living memory. But whatever the setting, these struggles signaled the birth of a new chapter in the history of North American Indian culture—a chapter in which tribes could adapt to modern conditions without surrendering Native lifeways.

Just as D'Arcy McNickle's private odyssey eventually bore fruit with the publication of *The Surrounded*, many of the individual and community upheavals generated by the New Deal and World War II produced movements and leaders who together would create and define a new, "modern" Indian identity. These individuals demonstrated that one could be actively engaged in modern warfare, politics, or business while remaining linked to ancient traditions. The New Deal and World War II provided the crucible that forged much of this new Indian identity. It would take the political turmoil of the 1950s and 1960s to reveal the full impact of this new identity on Indian people and their communities, but it was clear already at the end of World War II that a fundamental reorientation was underway. Two indications of this new Indian identity appeared in 1944, just as the victory over Germany and Japan grew certain. They illustrate the beginning of the process by which the changes taking place within the Native American community during the New Deal era would soon be communicated to the larger American public.

First, Ella Deloria, a fifty-five-year-old Yankton Sioux linguist, published a powerful manifesto of modern Indian identity. *Speaking of Indians* appeared while wartime patriotism was reaching a crescendo. Countering this trend of American nationalism, Deloria reminded her readers that Native Americans were not candidates for the American melting pot. She noted that Indians "belonging to the great human family, have the same innate powers, inborn intelligence, and potentialities as the rest of mankind." But she pointed out that Indians had a collective culture and identity that set them apart from whites. "[Indians] have imagination and inventiveness. . . . They differed in their habits and outlook simply because they were not exposed to the influences of outside cultures. Otherwise, they were just some more of earth's peoples climbing." She described the central elements of Native culture—language, kinship, religion, community values, and systems of education—while arguing that Indians shared a common humanity with whites. Her argument complimented McNickle's gripping novel.

Ella Deloria was an ideal author for this primer on Indianness. The daughter of Philip Deloria, one of the first Native Americans to be ordained an Episcopal priest, she had grown up in South Dakota and attended mission schools before pursuing a college education in the East. She studied at Oberlin College and Columbia University, where she encountered and began working with anthropologist Franz Boas. Following her graduation from Columbia in 1914, Deloria had worked as an assistant to her father and a teacher at the Haskell boarding school. In 1927 she returned to New York to pursue her linguistic studies with Boas, gathering and translating texts in all three dialects of her native Sioux language (Lakota, Dakota, and Nakota). Throughout her career Deloria also lectured on various aspects of Indian culture and consulted with tribal groups and public agencies on Indian issues.

"What can I do . . . to help you understand the Indians?" Deloria asked her readers. First, she proposed to describe her own Sioux heritage in order to communicate the "powerful inner force that is in habitual operation, dictating behavior and controlling the thought of all who live within its sphere." Deloria described the web of family obligations that determined individual behavior in Sioux societies, the cooperative spirit that permeated traditional camp life, the spiritual traditions that oriented individuals toward the environment and the cosmos, and the ethic of reciprocity (the latter she called "giving to get") that insured both harmony and survival in hunting communities that often veered from feast to famine. She wrote that these elements produced, "a scheme of life that worked." Deloria argued that for too long Indians "had been supervised and taken care of" by arrogant and paternalistic officials. "Let's face it," she declared, "and start correcting it now."

In November 1944, a few months after the publication of the Dakota linguist's little book, representatives of more than fifty tribes gathered in Denver to create the National Congress of American Indians (NCAI). The group's constitution opened with the bold declaration that in the future, tribal leaders—not exemplary individuals like

Charles Eastman—would be at the center of Indian affairs. "We, the members of Indian tribes of the United States," the charter began, "in order to secure to ourselves and our descendants the rights and benefits to which we are entitled . . . to enlighten the public toward a better understanding of the Indian race; to preserve Indian cultural values . . . to secure and to preserve rights under Indian treaties . . . and otherwise to promote the common welfare of the American Indians . . . do establish this organization."

The idea for the National Congress of American Indians had emerged during World War II from conversations among three American Indian employees of the Bureau of Indian Affairs: D'Arcy McNickle; Archie Phinney, a Nez Percé linguist whom Collier had appointed superintendent of the Northern Idaho Indian Agency; and Charles Heacock, a graduate of the University of Nebraska who was originally from the Rosebud Sioux reservation. Based on their experiences at the Bureau and with Congress, the three were convinced that Native Americans needed to develop a powerful and unified voice in order to be heard in the years to come. They also believed that the membership of this new organization should be limited to Indians. Beginning in January 1944, McNickle, Phinney, and Heacock began discussing their plan with BIA colleagues; by May, they decided to issue a call for a meeting in Denver in the fall.

McNickle, Phinney, and Heacock's appeal struck a responsive chord. While most delegates to the Denver meeting had previous ties to the Indian Office and only 10 percent of them were women, the gathering attracted a diverse group of leaders from Oklahoma and the northern Plains. The group's membership appeared to be widely representative of several competing constituencies: elders and young leaders, "full-bloods" and "mixed-blood," and those who were college or boarding school educated as well as those who were not. Napoleon Johnson, a Cherokee member of the Oklahoma State Supreme Court, was elected president of the new organization, while Edward Rogers, an Ojibwe attorney from Cass County, Minnesota, became vice-president and Dan Madrano, a Caddo member of the Oklahoma state legislature, secretary. In addition, the delegates elected an eight-member council that included tribal chairs from the Cheyenne River, Pine Ridge, Flathead, and

Papago reservations, plus Phinney; McNickle; Howard Gorman, a Navajo leader; and elder statesman Arthur Parker, a Seneca.

Before they adjourned the Denver meeting, the NCAI delegates adopted a series of resolutions calling for greater tribal authority in decision making, civil rights for all Indians (three states—Utah, Arizona, and New Mexico—still barred Indians from voting), and the establishment of a claims commission to hear tribal grievances against the federal government. Uniform support for this agenda demonstrated that despite internal differences, Indians in the postwar world would share a common commitment to defining a role for themselves in American social and political life. Native Americans would organize and agitate like other ethnic and racial groups; they would define their distinctive interests and make known their special claims on the American majority. And they would not retreat from their traditions or their past.

Speaking through their publications and outspoken declarations, Ella Deloria and the members of the NCAI signaled the arrival of a dramatic new moment in Native American life. No longer objects of pity or curiosity, American Indians could shift from defense to offense. Instead of struggling to define a space for themselves within American life, they could now announce that they intended to participate in—and even to lead—the development of a prosperous and progressive postwar world.

SUGGESTED READINGS

Bernstein, Alison. *American Indians and World War II: Toward a New Era in Indian Affairs.* Norman: University of Oklahoma Press, 1990.   A description of Native Americans during World War II that emphasizes the changes that both the war experience and events at home prompted in the conditions of American Indian life.

Biolsi, Thomas. *Organizing the Lakota: The Political Economy of the New Deal on the Pine Ridge and Rosebud Reservations.* Tucson: University of Arizona Press, 1992.   An anthropologist's view of the impact of New Deal reforms on two reservations in South Dakota that focuses on conflicts between different generations of leaders.

Deloria, Vine, Jr., and Clifford Lytle. *The Nations Within: The Past and Future of American Indian Sovereignty.* New York: Pantheon, 1984.   A history of the "Indian New Deal" by a Native American scholar who places John Collier's reforms in the context of an ongoing struggle by Indian people to regain control over their lands and resources.

Hauptman, Laurence. *The Iroquois and the New Deal.* Syracuse: Syracuse University Press, 1981.   The Iroquois generally opposed New Deal reforms, but some New York reservations became centers for change in the 1930s. Historian Hauptman explains this complex historical situation.

Kersey, Harry A., Jr. *The Florida Seminoles and the New Deal, 1933–1942.* Boca Raton: Florida Atlantic University Press, 1989.   A description of the mixed reception John Collier's reforms received among Native peoples in south Florida.

Parker, Dorothy R. *Singing an Indian Song: A Biography of D'Arcy McNickle.* Lincoln: University of Nebraska Press, 1992.   Scholarly study of a Native American author and activist who was one of John Collier's principal assistants during the New Deal years.

Parman, Donald. *The Navajos and the New Deal.* New Haven: Yale University Press, 1976.   A history of the impact of the New Deal on Navajo life and Navajo politics; explains why the Navajos chose to reject John Collier's reforms.

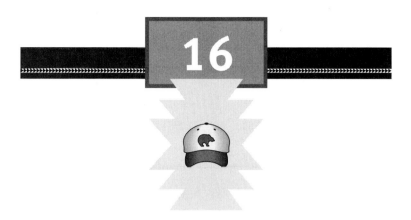

Fighting to Be Indians, 1945–1970

Before World War II, the Indians who lived in Minneapolis, Minnesota, nearly all knew each other. Census takers counted only 397 Native Americans in Minneapolis in 1930, and while that figure grew to nearly 2,000 by the outbreak of the war, the city's Indians continued to believe that they formed a tight-knit village within a modern metropolis. They gathered in churches, social clubs, and political organizations led by longtime, mostly middle-class residents like Amabel Bulin. Raised in a Dakota Sioux community in southern Minnesota, Bulin had attended the Tomah boarding school in Wisconsin before coming to the Twin Cities. A devout Catholic, she functioned as a one-woman social welfare agency, helping newcomers to the city find homes and jobs. She also maintained ties to white community leaders by participating in the General Federation of Women's Clubs; she eventually became the director of the Women's Clubs' "Indian Division."

During World War II Amabel Bulin began to notice a shift in city life. Testifying before a congressional investigating committee in the summer of 1944, she reported that "there are a lot of Indian people coming down [to the city] . . . and they are being pushed down into the slums." She noted that there were now more than 5,000 Indians in Min-

neapolis and St. Paul. Thanks to the wartime labor shortage, these newcomers had little trouble finding jobs, but the population had grown large and diverse. Indians no longer settled in integrated neighborhoods or socialized together in clubs and churches. Instead, immigrants from the reservations congregated in overcrowded ghettoes, forming intertribal friendships and often becoming involved with bootleggers and criminals. She urged federal authorities to appoint a full-time social worker to address these conditions. State officials were no help, she declared. "They think the Indian Bureau should take care of them," she told the committee. "They always think that." She added wearily that educating white Minnesotans about Native American issues was "a hopeless task."

Ignatia Broker was one of the people Bulin described. She arrived from a northern Ojibwe community in 1941, found work in a defense plant, and moved into a rented room with six other women. "Employment was good," Broker later recalled, "but Indian people faced discrimination in restaurants, nightclubs, retail and department stores . . . and worst of all in housing." Despite these hardships, Broker believed the wartime migration was "a good thing. . . . [I]t brought us to a brotherhood . . . we became an island from which a revival of spirit began."

Bulin's testimony and Broker's memory describe the birth of a new urban Indian community, one that was dependent on non-Indians for jobs but that nevertheless remained invisible to most city dwellers. In 1944 the Dakota activist was one of the few who could see what was happening; by 1970 this new reality was inescapable. Working-class communities of Indians would become a feature of city life across the country. More important, these new Indian communities would begin to wield unprecedented political and cultural power. While the post–World War II era was filled with dramatic public events and controversial new laws and leaders, the quiet shift Bulin first identified in 1944 would play a powerful role in every area of American Indian life, both on and off the reservations. Ignatia Broker confirmed this view in 1983 when she published her memoirs under the pen name Night Flying Woman. She reported that in the city "new fangled types of Indian people came into being: those demanding what was in our treaties, those demanding service to our people . . . and all reaching back for an [Indian] identity."

INDIANS ON THE MOVE

The twenty-five years following World War II produced profound changes in the size and character of the American Indian population. Beginning with the dislocations caused by the draft and the war effort's unprecedented demand for unskilled labor, Native Americans left their traditional homelands in record numbers, settled in cities and towns where few Native people had lived before them, and routinely worked alongside non-Indians. By 1970 this movement had altered the face of Native America.

Population Increases and a Rise in Intermarriage

Between 1950 and 1970 the population of American Indians in the United States more than doubled. In 1950, the Census Bureau counted 357,000 American Indians, only 15,000 more than it had counted twenty years earlier. Twenty years later that figure had risen to 793,000. Part of this increase can be explained by a change in census procedures—individuals now stated their own race rather than relying on enumerators to classify them on the basis of appearance—but it was also clear in 1970 that after decades of small increases, the Indian population had begun to explode.

There were many reasons for this rapid rise. First, modern health care became a universal feature of Indian life. The Public Health Service took over responsibility for reservation medical care from the BIA in 1955, ushering in a new era of professional management and increased appropriations. (Federal funding of Indian health rose by 300 percent between 1955 and 1965.) Public health education, widespread vaccination, and the migration of many Indians to cities where health care was more widely available also reduced the incidence of infectious diseases that had decimated reservation communities earlier in the century.

Improved health meant fewer deaths among Native American children, and a decline in the incidence of tuberculosis (TB) and other infectious diseases meant longer life expectancies. In the decade following 1955, the Indian infant death rate fell by 50 percent and the incidence of TB declined by two-thirds. Life expectancy among Native Americans rose from 51 in 1940 to 61 in 1960 and 65 in 1970. In 1940, life expectancy for whites was more than 13 years longer than for Indians; by 1970 that gap still existed, but it had been cut in half.

The improvement in Native American health and population size in the postwar era was accompanied by a stunning increase in the rate of intermarriage between Indians and members of other ethnic groups. Of course sexual relations between Indians and whites were as old as the frontier itself, but as late as 1900 a clear majority of all Indians counted by the federal census had no ancestors other than Indians. This figure varied considerably from tribe to tribe. In Oklahoma, for example, where thousands of outsiders had infiltrated Indian lands and where former southeastern tribes like the Cherokees and Creeks had a long tradition of intermarriage, only about a third of the Indians in the state in 1900 had no non-Indian ancestors. More than two-thirds were mixed-bloods. By contrast, in Arizona, an area long isolated from the non-Indian population centers of the East and home to the relatively homogeneous Navajos, Hopis, and Apaches, the Census Bureau reported in 1910 that only 14 percent of the state's Indians were of mixed ancestry.

Census statistics can tell us of improving health and declining isolation, but it is difficult to trace the impact of these trends on gender relations and family life. When large numbers of men and women experienced city living and integrated workplaces, or when people established new homes in unfamiliar places, new behaviors were bound to occur. Similarly, when these Native men and women returned to their reservations, they often found the old ways less attractive. The uniqueness of each tribe seemed less obvious and marriage to someone from "home" less important. In 1940, 88 percent of Indian men and 85 percent of Indian women were married to other Indians; by 1970, those figures had dropped to 65 percent and 60 percent, respectively. In 1970 at least a third of Indians were marrying outside their group and producing offspring of mixed ancestry. Not surprisingly the rate of intermarriage among the Indians who left reservations and moved to cities was nearly twice as high as the rate for those who continued to live on rural reservations.

Migration to the Cities and the Rise of Wage Labor

More significant than population increases and a rise in intermarriage—and a clear indication that Indians were literally on the move—was the fact that for the first time in their history, large numbers of Native Americans were becoming city dwellers. In 1926, 10,000 Indians—approximately 3 percent of the group—lived in cities; in 1956, that total had risen to 160,000 (30 percent of the total). In 1970 the federal census reported that more than 40 percent of all Indians—340,000 people—had made the transition to urban life. The move to the city encouraged other changes. In addition to fostering higher rates of intermarriage, cities also allowed greater access to education, widened exposure to new political systems, access to better health care, and the opportunity to interact with Indians from other tribes. As Night Flying Woman's memoir noted, city living also meant the rise of Indian ghettoes, new forms of poverty, and frequent encounters with alcohol and racial prejudice. All

of these changes loosened the ties binding urban Indians to tribal elders and reservation homelands.

Like the "Okies" who crowded Route 66 to California in the 1930s, thousands of Indians in the 1940s and 1950s headed for the nation's industrial cities in search of work and new homes. And the gap between reservation and urban incomes continued to grow. In 1949, for example, the average income of reservation residents was 80 percent of the figure for urban Indians. Twenty years later, reservation income had dropped to 57 percent of the amount earned by Indian city dwellers. Accompanying this income difference was a shift in occupations. In 1940, for example, the federal census reported that 50 percent of all Indian men were "farmers." By 1970 this figure had dropped to 2 percent. During the same period, the percentage of Indian workers listed as "skilled" or "semiskilled" rose from 10 percent to 50 percent. This phenomenon was taking place on reservations as well as in cities. On the Navajo reserve, for example, the percentage of tribal income from agriculture dropped from 58 percent in 1940 to 10 percent in 1958 to 2 percent in 1974.

Relocation

Despite the appeal of cities and wage labor in the postwar years, the movement of Indian people from rural farms to urban factories was not only the result of the "pull" of steady jobs, high wages, and a new life. Indians were also "pushed" to the cities by federal officials who devised a program of "relocation" as a remedy for reservation economies they believed would never be viable. In the aftermath of World War II, government officials assessing the reforms of the New Deal era noted that while the Collier administration's focus on tribal "reorganization" had brought some improvement to reservations, most of the jobs that had been created had been part of federal work projects. Few tribal industries had emerged and a new era of budget-cutting and administrative caution discouraged experts from expecting significant improvements. Finally, the imminent return of thousands of veterans and defense workers also prompted both tribal leaders and BIA officials to look for new sources of employment.

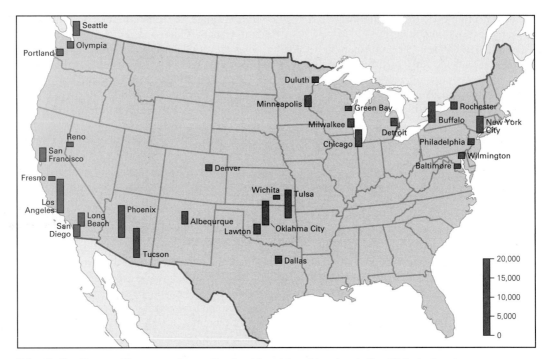

Urban Indian Communities, 1970. *Source: Reprinted from* Atlas of American Indian Affairs *by Francis Paul Prucha by permission of the University of Nebraska Press. Copyright © 1990 by the University of Nebraska Press.*

In 1948 a BIA pilot program provided assistance to Navajos seeking jobs in Denver, Los Angeles, and Salt Lake City. Relocation offices in those cities offered tribal members employment counseling and housing assistance, while tribal officials—assisted in many instances by traders and missionaries—actively recruited Navajo families to move. In 1950, the success of the Navajo program prompted Commissioner Dillon Myer (who, ironically, had supervised the internment of Japanese-Americans during World War II) to create a national program of "relocation." By 1960 there were BIA offices in eleven additional cities: Chicago, St. Louis, Oakland, San Francisco, San Jose, Dallas, Cleveland, Oklahoma City, Tulsa, Phoenix, and Albuquerque.

The government's program typically included three elements. Posters, films, and speakers advertised the appeal of city living and encouraged young Indian families to seek their fortunes away from the reservation. Second, small grants covered travel costs and a few weeks of living expenses for those who volunteered to relocate. Finally, the BIA's of-

fices in the relocation cities assisted with job placement, training, medical care, and housing. After 1957, relocating Indians were eligible for up to two years of vocational school and other benefits. At first this voluntary program seemed successful: 2,600 people were placed in 1953; four years later, the Bureau reported the largest annual relocation when nearly 7,000 Indians left their reservation homes with government help. By 1960, 33,000 people had gone through the government's program. Among them was the family of Charlie Mankiller, a Cherokee man with eleven children who left Oklahoma in 1957 for a job on San Francisco's docks. Charlie's daughter Wilma, eleven at the time of their move, later recalled that "[w]e went from living in a place with no phone, no TV, no plumbing, to downtown San Francisco. . . . We didn't know what to expect," she remembered, "no idea at all."

As Mankiller's memories suggest—and as Amabel Bulin had seen during the wartime boom in Minneapolis—many Indians who relocated under

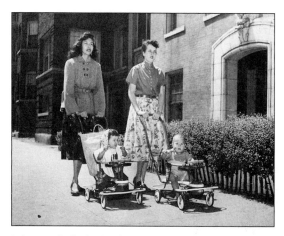

Urban Assimilation in Chicago Two neighbors take a walk with their children. City life opened new doors and formed new habits for recent arrivals from reservations.

government sponsorship discovered that urban living required drastic changes in habits and expectations. Cities were busy places, attuned to individuals who could travel on buses and subways, conform to the demands and timetables of a factory or office, and separate their work and private lives. By the 1960s, as the shift to a service economy began, these cities were also starting to lose skilled industrial jobs, so that even when they were prepared to take on a new occupation, some migrants found their factory had closed and they were compelled to train themselves for another new occupation. It was also true that city neighbors and employers did not always understand the demands of family or clan or the rhythms of a seasonal or ceremonial calendar. Cities could be lonely—and they operated on cash. Everything, from food to rent to recreation, required money; city streets and factories did not encourage sharing, barter, or gift-giving. Finally, cities offered Indian immigrants new (and often destructive) forms of escape: alcohol (still banned on most reservations), crime, and flight. Thousands of Native Americans like Charlie Mankiller and his wife mastered this challenging environment; they settled into steady jobs, learned new skills, and raised their families in a prosperous and stimulating environment. But oth-

ers were overwhelmed and they returned home, disappeared to new cities, or sank into crime and despair. The *Atlantic Monthly* reported in 1956 on the case of an enterprising Creek family that had become "slum dwellers in Los Angeles, without land or home or culture or peace."

The BIA's relocation program also carried an authoritarian edge. In a poor reservation community, government "encouragement" to a young family to relocate could easily become coercion, and an official "recommendation" of a job or apartment in the city could sound suspiciously like an order that had to be obeyed (particularly if the BIA official making the recommendation also controlled rent subsidies and vocational training scholarships). Nevertheless, it would be wrong to attribute the massive Indian migration to the city during the 1950s and 1960s solely to government coercion. Most Native Americans—perhaps as many as 75 percent of them—who moved to the city between 1950 and 1970 did so without government encouragement or assistance. And despite the failures and tragedies that accompanied this migration, most Indians chose to remain in their new homes rather than return to the reservations they had left behind.

New Communities and New Patterns of Life

Indians on the move in the postwar era created new communities and new patterns of life. California, for example, became a mecca for migrating Native Americans. In 1900 there were so few Native Americans in California that the state was not even listed among those with significant Indian populations. But the advent of large military installations and the rise of the aerospace industry after World War II soon catapulted California ahead of the rest. The state's Native American population rose from 48,000 in 1930 to nearly 70,000 in 1960 and 93,000 in 1970. Similar increases occurred in Colorado, Texas, and Illinois, as migrants flocked to Denver, Dallas, and Chicago in search of work.

The urban immigrants of the 1950s and 1960s found that they were often pioneers in places where few Indians had settled previously. Most cities had a small Indian community, but none was prepared for the massive population shift that soon got underway. Long Beach, California, for example,

PEOPLE, PLACES, AND THINGS

Chicago American Indian Center

Founded in 1953, this institution was one of the first urban Indian centers established in the United States. Initially the center served newly relocated Indian people who came to Chicago from the Dakotas, Minnesota, Michigan, and Wisconsin. Today the center is a social gathering place, an educational organization, and a place where Native American concerns are raised and articulated. Its programs attract Native Americans from the city and its suburbs, and it plays a major role in educating the public about Indian concerns.

Chicago community leaders Angeline DeCorah, Susan Power, and Joe Podlasek (*left to right*) with a dancer at the American Indian Center (*far left*).

counted barely 1,000 Indians in 1940; by 1980, 50,000 Native Americans had settled there. Chicago's Native population rose from 274 in 1940 to 6,500 in 1970. And the twin cities of Minneapolis and St. Paul, which counted 6,000 Indians at the end of World War II, contained more than three times that number by 1970. In each of these cities, as in Oakland, Denver, Los Angeles, and elsewhere, Native Americans created new institutions and new patterns of behavior. Encountering one another at BIA offices, in their churches, and in the workplace, migrants from different tribes formed friendships and began to seek out ways to socialize together. Their associations gradually produced a series of Indian centers and friendship houses that provided facilities for athletic events, community celebrations, and powwows. In 1953, the largely Sioux and Ojibwe migrants to Chicago opened the city's first Indian center with the assistance of the local BIA relocation office and the American Friends Service Committee. Chicago's American Indian Center hosted clubs, social events, and athletic teams in its rented rooms in a downtown office building. In 1954 the center sponsored its first powwow. This event, which culminated in the crowning of Miss Indian Chicago, quickly became an annual tradition. Similar groups soon formed in Oakland, Minneapolis, Milwaukee, Los Angeles, and Dallas.

In the 1950s the prospect of moving to the city was particularly appealing to young people. Better

educated than their parents and frustrated by limited employment opportunities in reservation communities, young families and single men and women were drawn to the prospect of new homes and higher incomes in the city. During the 1950s more than half of those who applied to the BIA for relocation assistance were single. Of the single migrants seeking BIA help, approximately 25 percent were women—many in this group were single mothers of small children. As had been true for earlier immigrants from Europe and the American South—and for their mothers and older sisters in World War II—cities offered Indian women more job opportunities and the chance to live free from the constraints of family and community scrutiny. The continuing appeal of the cities to young Native Americans was confirmed by a 1970 study that revealed that one-third of all urban Indians were in their twenties, as compared with one-quarter of rural Indians.

Changes in Reservation Communities

The social disruptions that transformed Indian life in the postwar era were not confined to cities. As reservation agriculture declined, Native Americans still living on reservations faced similar struggles to adapt to new economic realities and to create new forms of community. A Ute woman from Randlett, Utah, captured the essence of the economic up-heavals on postwar reservations when she told an interviewer in 1967 that the landscape of her child-hood had largely disappeared. She recalled that in the 1920s, the houses near her home "got gardens and haystacks and cattle and horses and every-thing. . . . Everything just look fine," she observed. "Nowadays," she complained, "you just see the houses, the barest kind. They don't have no hay, nothing." Lulu Brock worried that her neighbors in 1967 were "too lazy," but the gardens and hay-stacks did not disappear because of a sudden onset of poor Indian work habits; they vanished because of a dramatic shift in the American economy. As farmers struggled to compete in an increasingly in-ternational marketplace, many marginal areas such as the arid Northern Ute pasturelands in Utah or the prairies of western Nebraska were simply aban-doned. In an industrial economy, Indian-owned land was simply a commodity. If it could not be de-veloped profitably, or if its cultivation required ex-pensive machinery and chemicals, then Indian farmers were better off working for wages or re-ceiving welfare payments. If they chose to stay, they would have to endure the barren poverty Lulu Brock described.

The industrialization of the Western landscape came swiftly. In the fifteen years following World War II, the federal government spent $150 billion in the region. This investment in dams, highways, irrigation projects, and military installations cre-ated new urban centers and forged new links tying the region to the national economy. The Colorado and Columbia rivers, for example, now generated electricity for factories in Los Angeles and Seattle. Booming regional cities like Phoenix and Denver shipped goods produced in new factories to cus-tomers across the country.

These changes also stirred new visions of the In-dians' future. Amidst generous federal spending and expanding new industries, western politicians like Elmer Thomas of Oklahoma and South Dakota's Harlan Bushfield urged the Indian Office to drop the trust restrictions that exempted Indian lands from local taxes and prohibited land sales without Interior Department approval. Believing that Indians could share in the new prosperity in the West, these politicians argued that tribes should have full control of their property so that they could develop it (or borrow money, using land as collateral) on their own. Their arguments echoed Henry Dawes and other nineteenth-century re-formers who had promised prosperity for those who would "free" themselves from tribal life.

Some Native Americans agreed with the advo-cates of greater freedom, petitioning for the re-moval of trust restrictions on allotments in record numbers. In Oregon, Wade Crawford led a group of Klamath Indians who wanted federal authori-ties to remove the restrictions on the tribe's timber resources. Crawford and his colleagues condemned tribally owned land as "communistic." In Mon-tana, Blackfeet officials repeated this plea, arguing that the tribal council was well qualified to manage community pasturelands and oil reserves.

Some tribes responded to the move towards greater freedom by becoming more entrepreneurial. At Hoopa Valley in northern California, for ex-ample, the income from family-operated farming operations could not compete with the income to be derived from selling tribal timber. In response, from 1950 to 1970 the tribe leased mill sites to eleven separate logging operations and issued per-mits that authorized the removal of between 11 and 40 million board feet of timber annually. Tim-ber interests generally hired Hoopa labor, pump-ing millions of dollars into the local economy, but when the timber harvest was over, the tribe faced both barren hillsides and a mounting rate of un-employment among its members.

On the Plains, where Indian farmers decided it had become impossible to compete with their highly mechanized white neighbors, tribes leased their lands to large cattle interests, and former farmers turned to "cowboying" for wages. At the Pine Ridge reservation in 1955, 42 percent of family incomes came from wage labor; only 13 percent came from the profits of Indian-run agricultural operations.

Farther south, mechanized producers leased To-hono O'odham lands in Arizona. In 1957, as young tribal members left for wage work in nearby Phoenix and Tucson, tribal leaders negotiated long-term leases with local corporate growers for 12,000 acres of reservation farmland. By 1970 only half the Tohono O'odham people lived on the reserva-tion, and they survived primarily by working for white leaseholders on corporate farms carved from the tribal homeland.

As the West prospered, Indian mineral resources also grew more accessible and more attractive. U.S.

consumption of natural gas rose 50 percent between 1945 and 1950, for example, bringing exploration and pipeline companies to the Navajo reservation in record numbers. In 1960, when a new pipeline was completed across tribal land linking New Mexican producers to markets in California, the number of oil wells on the reservation rose to 860. Uranium mines opened in the Navajos' Chuska Mountains as well as on nearby lands adjoining Laguna and Acoma pueblos. These increases in production raised annual Navajo tribal income from $445,000 in 1950 to more than $14 million in the 1960s. Other communities received similar infusions of new cash. In 1955 the total income for all tribes stood at just under $30 million; a decade later that figure had more than doubled, with six tribes receiving nearly half this revenue: Navajos, Jicarilla Apaches, Blackfeet, Wind River Arapahos and Shoshones, and the tribes at Fort Peck and Fort Berthold. But the impact of oil drilling and mining was generally superficial and short-lived. Most of the new dollars went to tribal governments to cover operating expenses or modest payments to tribal members; little of it was invested in new businesses.

The most dramatic examples of the Indians' continuing marginal status in an increasingly prosperous West grew out of the ambitious dam projects launched across the region in the decades after World War II. Dams were constructed on the Columbia River, for example, to generate electricity and improve transportation. These dams also destroyed the last remaining major Indian fishing sites on the river; yet they contributed little to the development of new tribal enterprises. In Arizona, projects along the lower Colorado River inundated lands at the Yuma agency, offering local tribes little in return.

The most destructive dam project was launched along the Missouri River where five postwar dams destroyed 550 square miles of tribal land and dislocated more than nine hundred families. These dams were intended to provide irrigation for North and South Dakota agriculture, but their construction flooded and eradicated hundreds of Indian farms. Hardest hit was the Fort Berthold agency near Bismarck, North Dakota, where water stored behind the Garrison Dam drove 80 percent of the Indian families from their homes along the river. In the East, a similar project, the Kinzua Dam, destroyed 9,000 acres of Seneca lands in western New York, including the site of the Cold Spring Longhouse, a ceremonial center that had been functioning without interruption for more than 150 years. The affected tribes received cash for their losses, but few Indians shared in the economic benefits of these projects. As a consequence, more Indian families were set in motion, migrating to cities or seeking work on the white-run farms, ranches, and fishing boats that had just nudged them out of business.

Religious and Political Changes

The forces that disrupted the reservations' subsistence economies and spurred on greater migration and wage labor also disrupted traditional relations between men and women. On the Navajo reserve, for example, postwar changes undermined the economic autonomy and social prestige women had traditionally enjoyed in tribal life. With no herds of sheep and goats to draw on as an independent source of wealth, with families no longer living in rural communities dominated by clan mothers in their hogans, and with Navajo girls now considering schools and occupations away from their family responsibilities, the basis for female identity seemed to have been eliminated. A similar process unfolded in the Pueblo communities of the Southwest, where wage labor drew women away from traditional pursuits and opened options for them outside their villages.

The disruptions of the postwar era also encouraged a number of religious innovations. The Native American Church, which had been incorporated in Oklahoma during World War I, had spread during the 1920s and 1930s to tribes in the Midwest and Southwest and even into Canada. In the period after World War II, however, its practitioners dramatically expanded their influence and won vital legal protection for their rituals. The religion's focus on moral conduct and abstinence from alcohol made it ideally suited to displaced individuals engaged in wage labor. Its willingness to embrace members from a variety of tribes also attracted urban Indians living in multitribal neighborhoods.

The Navajo reservation was the site of dramatic confrontations over the new faith in the postwar era. Alarmed by the early popularity of the peyote ritual at Taos and other southwestern communities, Navajo leaders adopted a tribal resolution in June 1940 that outlawed the use of the plant on the reservation. Church members soon challenged the order, setting off an internal political struggle that did not end until 1967 when the tribe lifted its ban. By the 1970s, it was estimated that 40 percent of the tribe belonged to the Native American Church.

The church's flexibility even enabled it to spread to urban communities. In the 1950s and 1960s, peyote groups formed in Chicago, Los Angeles, and other relocation centers. These groups often held their meetings in the countryside near the city. The San Francisco group, for example, met in a hogan church in Sonoma County north of the city. The Los Angeles group was led by a man who worked during the week as an "Indian chief" at Disneyland. During these same years the ritual also spread to Denver, Tacoma, Washington, and Dallas, Texas.

Expanding legal protection also helped the Native American Church to spread into new areas. Most prominent in this regard was a 1964 decision from the California supreme court, *People* v. *Woody*, which ruled that the prosecution of a Native American for possession of peyote was an unconstitutional intrusion into private religious worship. "In a mass society, which presses at every point toward conformity," the court declared, "the protection of a self-expression, however unique, of the individual and group becomes ever more important. The varying currents of the subcultures that flow into the mainstream of our national life give depth and beauty."

The Native American Church was not the only Indian-oriented religious group to benefit from the disruptions of the 1950s and 1960s. Many Christian mission groups also experienced remarkable success during these years. The Latter Day Saints, or Mormons, for example, launched a concerted missionary campaign on the Navajo reservation in the 1950s, establishing forty-seven new congregations over the next two decades. Fundamentalist Protestants also made significant headway. In addition to their zeal, many fundamentalist groups were eager to recruit Native Americans as church leaders. With few formal requirements for clergy, Assembly of God congregations, Pentecostals, and independent Baptists recruited Native Americans— largely men—to be pastors in both urban and reservation communities. Again, the Navajo reservation

offers the most dramatic evidence. Between 1950 and 1977, the number of Baptist congregations on the reservation rose from one to sixty-two, while the Assembly of God created thirty-two churches, and the Pentecostal Holiness group established twenty-four.

Changes in Indian political liberties also created an arena of disruption and change. Even though they had been granted citizenship in 1924, Native Americans continued to experience discrimination that restricted their interaction with non-Indians. For example, federal regulations had long banned alcohol on Indian reservations. While established in the nineteenth century largely to police the behavior of unscrupulous traders, this ban had persisted into the twentieth century as a form of federal protection. Returning World War II veterans had been among the first to protest this paternalistic tradition, but their cry for "equal treatment" was soon picked up by the National Congress of American Indians and tribal leaders. In 1953 Congress repealed the federal prohibition (leaving tribes the option of passing their own bans), and it took the additional step of repealing other outdated laws such as one making it illegal to sell firearms and ammunition to Indians.

In the years before the modern Civil Rights movement, states largely determined who would vote. Some western states had prevented Indians from voting until the mid-twentieth century, but in the postwar era these last vestiges of frontier life passed from the scene. In Arizona, for example, state officials had considered reservation residents to be people "under guardianship" and did not allow them to vote. A 1948 Arizona Supreme Court decision overturned this position. Five other states— Idaho, Maine, Mississippi, New Mexico, and Washington—barred Indian voting because Indian trust lands were not taxed. Four of those states lifted their bans voluntarily, but New Mexico continued its restriction until it was challenged successfully in 1948. (Non-Indian New Mexicans continued to challenge the right of Native people to vote until 1962.) Finally, in 1956 Utah became the last state to accept Indians as voters when it dropped its practice of classifying Indian residents of reservations as not technically state residents. Several states, including Arizona, continued to use literacy tests to bar Indians from voting, but these were largely outlawed by the 1965 Voting Rights Act.

In the 1940s and 1950s the National Congress of American Indians and the Association on American Indian Affairs led the campaign to eliminate restrictions on Indian voting as well as other forms of discrimination. At their founding convention in 1944, NCAI members passed resolutions calling for the protection of Indian civil rights. Both the NCAI and the association's lawyers participated in the legal challenges to the Arizona and New Mexico voting regulations as well as in protests against both states' refusal to allow Indians to receive Social Security benefits. These two advocacy groups also protested against restrictive covenants that prevented Indians from buying homes in "whites only" sections of major cities.

Just as the postwar era offered middle-class Americans new vistas of mobility and affluence, so it promised Native Americans the opportunity to pursue their futures in new settings and in new ways. The growth and movement of the Indian population, together with the social and religious changes that took place within Indian communities, signaled a shift to a new style of life and promised new ways of relating to the American majority. Unfortunately, however, the promise embedded in these years of movement and change was obscured for most Indians by a countertrend of hostility and fear. For almost as quickly as American Indians began to enter major cities in significant numbers, their political opponents began to argue that the national government had fulfilled its legal and moral obligations to them. The time had come, these leaders declared, to end all "special treatment" for Indians and to "terminate" all ties between Native communities and the United States. This movement endangered all forms of federal support for tribes and sent a dark wave of fear through Indian America.

TERMINATION TAKES SHAPE

Two groups joined forces to produce the termination movement. First, dedicated opponents of the New Deal wanted to eradicate the reforms of the Collier era. They proposed to repeal the Indian Reorganization Act, disband the tribal governments formed in the 1930s, end Indian education, and,

ultimately, eliminate the Indian Office. Led by Oklahoma Senator Elmer Thomas and Joseph O'Mahoney of Wyoming, these critics claimed that the Roosevelt administration had tried to establish socialistic Indian communes and prevent tribal members from participating in the national economy. A second group wanted to extend the patriotic nationalism of the war years to Indian affairs. In their view, restricting the sale of Indian lands, applying separate rules to Indian citizens, and recognizing partially autonomous tribal governments undermined national unity. "Firm and constant consideration" for the Indians, Utah Senator Arthur Watkins declared, "should lead us all to work diligently and carefully for the full realization of [the Indians'] national citizenship."

It took several years for these two opponents of federal policy to formulate a clear plan for termination. They began by attacking the New Deal and pointing out how little the IRA and other dramatic reforms had altered conditions in Indian communities. Perhaps, the critics reasoned, the problems lay not in the reservations' inadequate schools and primitive economic infrastructure but in their isolation and overpopulation. A report in *Time* magazine in 1947, for example, noted that Indians were suffering because their herds were small, their farms were unproductive, and they lacked any long-term plan for economic development. A year later an Interior Department report on the Navajo reservation repeated this view. It declared that even the "maximum" development of all reservation resources would support only half of the tribe's sixty-five thousand members. The implication of this finding was that it was hopeless to expect reservations to become prosperous. Perhaps federal dollars would be better spent in an effort to integrate Indians into the national economy rather than promoting separate development.

This pessimistic view found ready endorsement in 1949 when the final report of a blue-ribbon Commission on the Organization of the Executive Branch, chaired by former president Herbert Hoover, singled out the Bureau of Indian Affairs for special comment. Echoing the bureau's congressional critics, the commission declared that tribal institutions had long been "smashed" by history and that only a "handful" of Indians remained. Given this circumstance, there was no alternative but to dissolve all tribal governments, transfer social service programs to the states, and integrate all Native Americans as taxpaying citizens of the country. While criticized by prominent Democrats on the commission, as well as by tribal leaders and former commissioner Collier, the Hoover Commission's report gave added power to the terminationists' arguments.

The Indian Claims Commission

The first step in the terminationists' campaign was winning approval for the Indian Claims Commission Act in August 1946. Proposed originally during the Collier administration and widely supported by tribal leaders, the claims commission—which would hear all Indian complaints against the federal government—had originally been viewed as a way to give all Indian groups "their day in court." When it reached the floor of Congress, however, the proposal contained a number of technical provisions that limited its effectiveness and shifted its goals.

The Indian Claims Commission Act would enable tribes to file claims against the United States for failing to enforce treaties, mismanaging resources, or violating common standards of "fair and honorable dealing." Earlier suggestions that tribes could bring forward a wide range of claims—including broad "moral claims"—were dropped from the new statute. Congress also declared that claims could only be filed for lands the government had purchased. Tribal domains that had been seized without payment—such as the Cherokee lands in Georgia—could not be the subject of a suit. The claims process was also undermined by an obscure provision in the new law that allowed judges to deduct money spent by the United States "for the benefit of the claimant" from any award. These deductions (which the government's attorneys called "offsets") could drastically reduce the amount a tribe might receive. (Faced with a judgment ordering payment to a tribe of $10 million, for example, government officials would be allowed to total up the cost of educational, health, and other services—however inadequate—as deductions from the award. Such creative bookkeeping could reduce even very large awards to insignificance.) Finally, all tribal claims would have to be filed within five years and all

awards would be delivered as cash. There would be no return of land or stolen property.

The law that reached President Truman's desk in 1946 created a mechanism for the final accounting of all Indian grievances against the United States. It therefore appealed to everyone who wanted to end the relationship between Indians and the United States. Even President Harry Truman, who considered vetoing the law because of its potential cost, embraced the measure as a prelude to the day when the government could remove itself from Indian affairs. He announced that the new statute would help tribes "take their place without handicap or special advantage in the economic life of the nation and share fully in its progress."

The Truman administration's approach to the new law convinced tribal leaders that the government was embarking on a program of "final settlements" rather than the resolution of past grievances. First, for example, the president passed over NCAI president Napoleon Johnson and the other Indian lawyers proposed to him for membership on the new Indian Claims Commission. Instead he appointed three white male political loyalists. Second, the attorney general announced that only those groups recognized by Congress could apply to the new commission, thereby making the concerns of more than one hundred thousand largely eastern Indians ineligible for consideration. Third, the commission announced that it would not conduct investigations of its own but would operate passively like a court, relying on expert witnesses and attorneys to present their competing arguments. This decision made skilled legal representation essential and helped remove the entire claims process from the hands of tribal leaders. Fourth, the ICC would not add interest to tribal awards (a practice familiar to any taxpayer who has ever paid a penalty to the IRS). Awards would be made on the basis of the value of the land or property in question at the time of the sale. Finally, the commission's awards, even when approved by Congress, were paid only after federal authorities had approved a tribe's plans for the use of the funds. In some cases, negotiations over final payment of a claim resembled blackmail as a tribe would be required to accept conditions (such as the termination of federal services) in exchange for an award.

Even though the ICC was to have a ten-year life span, the large number of cases brought before it and its protracted, legalistic proceedings prompted Congress to extend its life until 1978. Over this thirty-two-year period, the commission received 850 separate claims. Of these cases, 366 were either dismissed or combined with others; only 484 cases were decided. Of these, 285 were decided in favor of the plaintiffs, generating awards totaling $657 million or less than $1,000 per Native American in 1970. The United States was the first industrial nation to establish a tribunal to hear complaints by indigenous people, but the idealistic hope that the claims commission would deliver justice to Native Americans and restore Indian communities to economic independence remained unfulfilled.

Continuing Pressure for Termination

Termination dominated Indian affairs after the Republicans took control of Congress in 1946. Early in 1947, for example, the Senate Civil Service Committee issued a subpoena to Acting Commissioner William Zimmerman, one of Collier's old lieutenants, demanding that he provide a list of tribes ready to be released from federal supervision. Zimmerman complied, presenting the committee with three lists. The first, which contained groups with a combined population of 53,000, included reservations that had requested an end to federal supervision and that had minimal contact with the Indian Office. These included the Flathead, Iroquois, Klamath, Menominee, and Turtle Mountain communities. Zimmerman's second group of 75,000 people belonged to tribes that, he argued, operated with "minimal supervision" and might be released in two to ten years. Among these "semi-acculturated" tribes were the Blackfeet, Crows, Cheyenne River Sioux, and Winnebagos. Finally, Zimmerman listed tribes whose 250,000 members should remain under federal supervision indefinitely. These included Indians living at the Cheyenne and Arapaho, Hopi, Red Lake, Seminole, and Yakama reservations.

While Congress did not respond immediately to Zimmerman's subpoenaed testimony, his presentation seemed to confirm that some tribes were "ready" for the withdrawal of federal services. Statements from both NCAI leaders and a number of tribal officials also appeared to make this point. At its 1947 and 1948 annual meetings the NCAI

passed resolutions calling for the eventual abolition of the BIA. In addition to groups of Klamaths who had long wanted to control their own timber reserves, prosperous leaders among the Blackfeet and Menominees argued that they could do better on their own. And nationally prominent Indians such as Will Rogers Jr. often made a similar point by assuring the public that their people did not want to live permanently as government wards. Most Indian leaders continued to believe that federal protections on Indian land should remain, but there was widespread support—particularly from wealthier Indians—for giving tribes more freedom from federal control.

While Truman's surprise victory in November 1948 dampened enthusiasm for some Republican initiatives, congressional support for Indian "independence" continued. The catalyst for a new initiative came in 1950 when President Truman appointed Dillon Myer, the former director of the War Relocation Authority, the agency that had managed the incarceration of 120,000 Japanese-Americans during World War II, as Indian commissioner. An energetic administrator and ardent critic of the New Deal reforms, Myer moved quickly to establish a series of "withdrawal programs" that would lead Indians, in his words, "out of the shadow of federal paternalism and into the sunlight of full independence."

Myer formally established the federal relocation program to encourage Indians to leave reservations for cities and created a new "Division of Programs" within the Indian Office to develop specific plans for the termination of federal services to tribes. He also encouraged the work of the Governors' Interstate Indian Council (GIIC), an organization supported by states with major Indian population centers that advocated the incorporation of reservations into the states. In his two years in office Myer closed dozens of BIA schools, loosened regulations governing the sale of allotments, and expanded the agency's foster care program, which placed Indian children with non-Indian families. He also pressed tribes he believed were candidates for termination to develop specific plans for separation from the Indian Office. His proposal was approved by the small Siletz community near Portland, Oregon, as well as by the neighboring Grande Ronde agency, but tribal leaders among the Mission Indians of California, the Oregon Klamaths,

George Gilette, chairman of the Fort Berthold Indian Tribal Council, covers his face and weeps in Washington on May 20, 1948, as Secretary of the Interior J. A. Krug signs a contract to buy 155,000 acres of North Dakota's best Indian land for a dam and reservoir on the Missouri River.

and the Menominees of Wisconsin rejected the commissioner's overtures.

Despite the hostility of most tribal governments to termination, many prominent Indians, as well as the heads of the NCAI and the Association on American Indian Affairs, were ambivalent. NCAI Vice President Ben Dwight, for example, was active in the Governors' Interstate Council, as were fellow officers Napoleon Johnson and Frank George and the prominent Episcopal priest from South Dakota, Vine Deloria. At first many of these leaders supported Myer because he insisted his ultimate aim was to enable tribes to function independently within the American economy. Over time, however, they grew more skeptical. Myer ran roughshod over tribal interests in Alaska, interfered in local leadership disputes among the Mescalero Apaches, and undermined the Pyramid Lake Paiutes' efforts to gain control over the water in

the Truckee River. Still, tribal leaders were drawn to the antiestablishment rhetoric of Republicans who criticized the paternalism of the Indian Office and seemed to favor tribal rights. In 1952, for example, 95 percent of Navajo voters supported the pro-termination Republicans, providing Dwight Eisenhower with his margin of victory in New Mexico and making him the first Republican to carry the state since 1928.

But despite support for the victorious Republicans, two measures passed during the first months of the new administration quickly persuaded Native American leaders that termination would be dangerous. Both were approved in August 1953 with little input from tribal leaders and with no regard for Indian public opinion. First, House Concurrent Resolution 108, a nonbinding measure that Eisenhower signed on August 1, declared it to be the policy of Congress "to make the Indians . . .

subject to the same laws . . . as are applicable to other citizens [and] . . . to end their status as wards of the United States." The resolution went on to list many of the tribes mentioned previously as "ready" for termination (Flatheads, Klamaths, Menominees, Iroquois, and others) and to declare that "at the earliest possible time" these groups would be "freed from Federal [sic] supervision and control. . . ." Two weeks later Eisenhower signed a second measure, Public Law 280, which unilaterally extended state civil and criminal jurisdiction to Indian communities in Minnesota, California, Nebraska, Oregon, and Wisconsin. With the stroke of a pen the president had effectively abolished tribal courts and police systems on all reservations in these states. (New York State had acquired jurisdiction over tribal communities by special legislation approved in 1948.)

Both of these measures captured ideas that had been promoted by terminationists for most of the previous decade. Pushed most enthusiastically by Utah Republican Arthur Watkins, chair of the Senate subcommittee on Indian Affairs, and South Dakota's E. Y. Berry, his counterpart in the House, the two statutes (together with the Indian Claims Commission Act and the administrative changes instituted by Commissioner Myer) reflected the view that tribal communities were artifacts of the past that must be dissolved. Moreover, advocates argued, the Indians' service in the war, their recent movement into wage labor, their migration to cities, and their improving general health all indicated that they were destined for a future alongside other American citizens. From the perspective of these white, mostly western politicians, it made no sense to spend federal funds to subsidize overcrowded, economically depressed reservations. Termination would allow Indians, in Watkins's phrase, to "grow and develop as they should."

BATTLING BACK

Ironically, Watkins's rhetoric, while successful in the short run, ultimately doomed the termination movement. His contempt for tribes and their traditions so galvanized Indian opposition and so energized the NCAI and its allies that by the end of 1953 Native Americans were speaking out in opposition to the new policy with unprecedented vehemence and unity. At the 1953 NCAI convention (advertised with the theme "Crisis in Indian Affairs") opposition to termination was nearly unanimous. Frank George, the Nez Percé executive director who had sympathized with many of Dillon Myer's withdrawal proposals, was replaced by Helen Peterson, a Sioux social worker who was fiercely opposed to the new policy. D'Arcy McNickle, who had recently resigned from the Indian Office, rallied the delegates behind the new leadership when he declared that "the battle for civil rights may not yet be won, but the battle for the right to be culturally different has not even started."

NCAI Opposition to Termination

Early in 1954, when Watkins, Berry, and their allies announced hearings on twelve separate termination bills, the NCAI called an "Emergency Conference" in Washington, D.C. Organized hastily by Peterson, McNickle, and Cherokee activist Ruth Muskrat Bronson, the gathering mounted a vigorous lobbying effort in opposition to the termination bills. The campaign won widespread (and positive) press attention and effectively derailed the congressional hearings held to build support for the new measures. Representatives from forty-three tribes in twenty-one states and Alaska expressed opposition to the government's coercive new stance. Congress also heard from several major church and reform organizations, including the ACLU, the American Legion, the General Federation of Women's Clubs, and the National Council of Churches. In the end, Watkins won approval for six termination bills (affecting the Klamaths, Menominees, Alabama-Coushatas of Texas, and Ute and Paiute bands in Oregon and Utah), but the Utah Republican's commanding moment was over. The NCAI had managed to shift the public's attention from "assimilation" to the government's high-handed methods.

Later in 1954 the NCAI used its new visibility to help block the termination of the Salish-Kootenai community in Montana, as well as the Turtle Mountain Chippewas, Colvilles, and Seminoles. The next year the Democrats took control of Congress, effectively ending immediate threats to new tribes. Three

INDIAN VOICES   Alice Jemison Speaks Out Against Termination

Alice Lee Jemison (1901–1964) was born in Silver Creek, New York, near the Cattaraugus reservation. Married at eighteen (the same year she graduated from high school) and separated from her husband nine years later, Jemison supported herself and her two children through wage labor and freelance journalism. As the member of a powerful Seneca family, Jemison was deeply committed to the tradition of Iroquois political independence. She believed the treaties negotiated by her ancestors in the wake of the American Revolution should govern relations between Indians and whites and that neither state legislators nor Bureau of Indian Affairs officials should dictate to the tribe. As a consequence, Jemison supported Carlos Montezuma's campaign to abolish the BIA and opposed John Collier's New Deal reforms. In opposing Collier, Jemison foolishly appeared on the same platform as right wing extremists and Nazi sympathizers who shared her opposition to the New Deal, but she was not herself a fascist. Her single commitment was to Seneca sovereignty as reflected in the tribe's treaties with the United States.

In 1948, Senator Arthur Watkins and other advocates of termination attempted to enlist Jemison's support for one of their proposals: the transfer of criminal jurisdiction from tribal courts to local New York State authorities. Because Jemison frequently appeared before Congress on legislation affecting the Senecas, she asked for a chance to respond. It is fascinating to read Jemison's explanation for her opposition to the measure and to consider how closely her position resembles the call for self-determination that began to emanate from the National Indian Youth Council and other groups in the 1960s.

> There is a lot that can be said against the passage of these bills, but I would confine my statement to the treaty rights, which I believe is the fundamental question before this committee. Before I discuss those treaty rights, I would like to review just a little bit of the history of the Senecas and the other Six Nations Indians, and how it happened that we have these treaty rights.
>
> In proposing legislation for the Six Nation Indians of New York State, this committee is dealing with Indians who have been in constant contact with the white race since colonial days, and who played a very significant part in the early history of our country.
>
> When the white man first came to the Hudson River Valley in the early 1600's the Iroquois had a democratic, representative form of government, woman suffrage, and a league of nations which was then well over 100 years old. We were a powerful people, controlling vast areas of territory which extended from the Hudson to the Mississippi, and from along the St. Lawrence River Valley south as far as Tennessee.
>
> Our friendship was sought and courted by both the French and the British. We inclined to the British colonies, partly because Champlain was the first man to ever fire a gun upon us. We held the French at bay north of the Great Lakes and the St. Lawrence River. We formed a bulwark behind which the English colonies prospered and grew powerful.

When the revolution came to the colonies they sent emissaries to sit in council with the Six Nation Indians and ask them to remain neutral in this war with the mother country. The chief sat in council and said that the tribes themselves would not enter the war, but it was difficult to hold the young warriors from the warpath. Subsequently one tribe fought with the British, two of the tribes remained neutral, and three tribes were allies of the United States.

In the last grim winter at Valley Forge Washington was starving. General Schuyler came to the Oneidas asking food, and the Oneidas from their own slender stores sent 600 bushels of grain to Washington.

At the close of the Revolutionary War no provision was made in the treaties of peace for the Indians. The French and the British to the north of us constantly harassed us and urged us to rebel against the infant United States, which we did, and General Sullivan came up the Hudson and nearly annihilated some of our tribes. Washington then said that he would make treaties with us.

Three treaties were made, the final one being the treaty of Canandaiuga in 1794. That treaty assured to these Indians of New York State the right of self-government. The treaty said that they would have free use and enjoyment of their lands.

Washington, in his wisdom, recognized us as human beings, and under the same principles of the Constitution of the United States entitled to the same rights and privileges, the pursuit of happiness. These treaties guaranteed the boundaries of vast tracts of land, and these lands were to remain ours until we decided to sell to the United States.

The Indians have progressed under this system. They have taken their own time in doing it. They have kept their shares of the treaties. They have never made war against the United States. They have never claimed any other territory. In the War of 1812 the Six Nation Indians declared war independently against Great Britain and fought as allies of the United States. In the Civil War the Indians did not break their treaties, as did some others. They fought with the United States.

In the First World War when it was not legal to draft Indians our boys volunteered, and in this last World War we did not resist the draft, and out of a total number of approximately 2,700 Seneca Indians who occupied two reservations in New York State, there were approximately 500 Indians serving in the recent World War.

We did this because this is our country and we love it. We did this because we recognized this Government as being our Government as much as it is the Government of every State in this Union.

We too have contributed to the development and progress of this country. Now these bills have been introduced which by their very nature would violate every provision of our treaty for self-government. No Indian asked for the introduction of these bills. I don't know who asked that these bills be introduced. I do know that down through the years there has been a constant effort to remove the Indians from the little land that they do now own either to other lands or to force them to live under the laws of the white man.

We have kept our shares of the treaties, and we are here to ask that you keep yours. . . . So long as we are peaceful we should be left alone to enjoy what little rights we do now have, and the rights of which we are sure. We do not know what would happen to us under these bills. Other bills have passed and they did not always work out as they were supposed to. We know we have our treaty rights. We know that for 154 years we have lived in peace and harmony with the people of the United States and that we have been getting along all right. Those things we know. We do not wish to accept the uncertainty of these changes.

U.S. Congress. Senate. Subcommittee of the Committee on Interior and Insular Affairs. "Statement of Alice Lee Jemison." Hearings of S. 1683, S. 1686, S. 1687: New York Indians. 80th Congress, 2nd Session (Washington: Government Printing Office, 1948), 22–25.

years later Interior Secretary Fred Seaton declared that the unilateral termination of tribes had become "unthinkable." Termination was not over, however. Several small groups fell victim to the policy in the decade ahead. Three virtually landless Oklahoma tribes—Wyandotte, Peoria, and Ottawa—were terminated in 1956, the California Rancherias were terminated in 1959, the South Carolina Catawbas were terminated in 1959, and the 442 members of the Ponca tribe were terminated in 1962.

Following the success of its "Emergency Conference" the NCAI pressed its advantage by arguing that all tribes deserved protection until they themselves decided that they might want to disband. In 1954 the organization elected a forty-four-year-old Coeur d'Alene war veteran, Joe Garry, as its president. Former head of the Affiliated Tribes of the Northwest and a direct descendant of the nineteenth-century chief Spokane Garry, the new president was an articulate tribal leader who had come of age in the Collier era. The same convention that elected Garry also adopted a Point Nine program for reservation development that was modeled on the American Point Four program then in place to aid underdeveloped countries. Shifting to a more aggressive stance, the NCAI also began an ambitious voter registration drive and expanded its ties to the National Council of Churches and other civil rights groups.

Termination for the Klamaths and Menominees

For most tribes, termination was an abstract threat, but for the Menominees of Wisconsin and the Klamaths of Oregon, the cutoff of federal services was an immediate possibility. Because the Klamaths owned nearly 1 million acres of productive timberland, Senator Watkins and other conservative legislators believed tribal members would receive a large enough individual share of the community's assets to support their transition to a new life as independent citizens. Watkins also insisted that a $2.6 million judgment from the Court of Claims be held up until the tribe agreed to accept its new status. But despite the terminationists' optimistic predictions, the 1954 Klamath termination law proved

National Congress of American Indians President Joe Garry, holding his daughter Priscilla at a gathering in Spokane, Washington, in 1954. Pictured with Garry are his father, Isadore (far left), and Cleveland Kamiamkin (center), the son of the chief who had led the Yakama resistance against the United States a century earlier.

disastrous. More than 70 percent of the Klamaths opted to accept $43,700 each in exchange for their share of the tribal estate. Once they received their shares, Klamath people moved from rural reservation villages to nearby towns and used their new wealth to buy homes and cars. Few had the education or assistance necessary to invest their new wealth for future income. Within a few years, many Klamaths were living in poverty; in the process many of their community traditions disappeared.

Because there was no longer a Klamath tribe, children born into the community could not be enrolled as members. Few people could manage to obtain medical insurance, and rates of alcoholism and domestic violence skyrocketed. Those who could not find work near their old homes drifted to Portland, San Francisco, and other nearby cities. By 1972 only 42 percent of tribal members still lived near the former reservation. In the 1970s a group of Klamath leaders began to lobby for a restoration of their tribal government. They were finally successful in 1986, but the resurrection of their tribal government could not erase the misery of those who had suffered through the termination years.

The Menominees, with 3,270 members, were the largest tribe to be terminated. As with the Klamaths, large timber reserves on tribal land created the impression that this Wisconsin tribe would prosper once "free" from federal supervision. The Menominees also operated a sawmill that produced additional income for tribal members. But while the Klamaths had been divided over termination, most Menominees opposed the idea. They acknowledged that the tribal sawmill employed 550 people but pointed out that almost one-third of the tribe remained on welfare. The tribe also suffered from an infant mortality rate that was more than two times the state average, and tribal members lagged far behind their white neighbors in education and life expectancy. But Senator Watkins and his congressional allies were unmoved. As with the Klamaths, he insisted the tribe was eager for "freedom." As he had with the Klamaths, Watkins blocked a multimillion-dollar award to the tribe from the Indian Claims Commission, insisting that it be disbursed only after the Menominees agreed to dissolve their tribal status.

Menominee termination went into effect in 1961. The former reservation became a Wisconsin

Ada Deer Campaigning for Menominee Restoration

county, local BIA schools became part of the public system, and the tribe's Indian Health Service hospital closed. The Menominee homeland quickly descended into poverty, ill health, and despair. At the end of the 1960s Menominee County was the poorest in the state, no medical doctor practiced there, and half the population was on welfare. Even more discouraging, 69 percent of the local high school students dropped out before graduation, and unemployment ranged as high as 40 percent. By the early 1970s more than half the tribe had drifted away to Milwaukee, Chicago, and other cities in search of work. Interestingly, the effort to restore the tribe's government began among tribal members who had fled to urban areas. Rallying around an organization called DRUMS (Determination of Rights and Unity for Menominee Shareholders) and its principal spokesperson, a young social worker named Ada Deer, tribal members in Milwaukee and other Midwestern cities embarked on a tireless campaign to reverse their tribe's death sentence. They succeeded in 1973 when Congress approved a statute restoring the group to tribal status.

The End of Termination

During the 1960s, advocates of termination continued to argue that Indian tribes were inappropriate in a modern nation. Their persistence in the face of Indian opposition encouraged other enemies of Indian lifeways—people who had never reconciled themselves to the New Deal reforms of a generation earlier—to revive their attacks on Native religions and ceremonial customs. State officials continued to insist that Indian communities should submit to local authorities, and many missionaries—particularly Mormons and the surging groups of fundamentalist Protestants—were outspoken in their opposition to traditional culture. Conflicts arose between missionaries and officials in several tribes. At Isleta Pueblo in New Mexico, Governor Andy Abeita handcuffed the resident Catholic priest and escorted him out of town. And even though the drive for termination cooled during the decade, relocation and the adoption of Indian children by non-Indians continued unimpeded. Federal authorities did not formally renounce the termination policy until 1970 when President Richard Nixon sent a special message to Congress calling for a repeal of HCR 108.

Rejecting the idea that tribes could function in the modern world, and insisting that white people knew what was best for Native Americans, supporters of termination had offered Indians a modern version of the choice first put before them nearly a century earlier: conform to the white majority or perish. Once again they were being invited to "kill the Indian" to save the "man" who would become a member of the American majority. This choice, leaders like Joseph Garry and Helen Peterson insisted, was false. They argued, instead, that Indians could be both tribal and modern. They declared that adversaries like Senator Watkins might operate on good intentions, but they nevertheless represented paternalism, not "civilization."

The Indian response to terminationist arguments was an explicit theme of an innovative summer program that D'Arcy McNickle organized in 1956

with the assistance of the University of Chicago. The Workshop on American Indian Affairs offered American Indian college students an intensive introduction to anthropological theory and Indian history through readings and presentations by McNickle, Cherokee scholar Robert K. Thomas, and faculty members from Chicago. The instructors emphasized the parallels between U.S. Indian policy and European colonialism; they urged students to think beyond their tribal communities and to imagine a collective Native American response to termination. Thomas in particular insisted that the students reject the idea that they had to choose between "remaining a proud but poverty-stricken people or becoming imitation white men."

At the end of the 1960s, as they emerged from their struggle against termination, Native American leaders like Helen Peterson and Robert Thomas were prepared to make a powerful new case for the value of Indian traditions and the viability of Indian communities in modern society. At the same time, a growing number of people in Indian communities across the country found themselves connected to organizations and political allies that were eager to bring their message to the American public.

GAINING RECOGNITION

The first national forum for an aggressive defense of Indianness was a conference held in Chicago in June 1961. Initiated by anthropologist Sol Tax, encouraged by the NCAI, and supported by a grant from the Schwartzhaupt Foundation, the Chicago Conference was a unique event. It brought together the largest and most diverse group of Native American leaders ever assembled. The conference was planned by an all-Indian steering committee, and its 467 official participants (representing ninety tribes) were selected at nine regional meetings held earlier in the year. Because the conference organizers had also welcomed "self-identified" Indians to attend the regional meetings, delegates attended the June conference from urban Indian communities, from a number of smaller eastern tribes, and from groups that were not formally recognized by the Indian Office. These included the Lumbees and

Haliwas of North Carolina, and the Tunica-Biloxis and Houmas of Louisiana. The conference also attracted the participation of the Abenakis, Pequots, Mohegans, Narragansetts, and Wampanoags—all New England tribes who operated without formal ties to the BIA.

The American Indian Chicago Conference

With as many as 400 additional Indians present as observers and members of Chicago's burgeoning urban community offering daily powwows and other social events, the conference was a spectacular success. It produced a Declaration of Indian Purpose that demanded an end to termination and a central role for Indians in future government policymaking. Presented formally to President John Kennedy at a White House ceremony in June 1962, the declaration insisted on a new attitude on the part of Washington policymakers: "What we ask of America is not charity, not paternalism . . . we ask only that the nature of our situation be recognized and made the basis of policy and action." This action should support rather than undermine reservation communities, the delegates declared, because modern Indians "mean to hold [these] scraps and parcels as earnestly as any small nation or ethnic group was ever determined to hold to identity and survival."

The Chicago conference also offered an unprecedented opportunity for Indian leaders to form new alliances. Alabama Creek leader Calvin McGee spoke for many when he observed that in Chicago he had discovered "so many Indians in the same boat." This sense of common circumstance inspired new ties among small eastern communities who shared the ambiguous status of "non-recognized tribes," a common agenda for urban leaders from different parts of the country, and alliances of traditional religious leaders who felt harassed by missionaries and insensitive bureaucrats. The most outspoken participants at the gathering were the young college-educated delegates who criticized its cautious tone. Melvin Thom, a young Paiute veteran of the NCAI's summer workshops, noted that despite their idealistic declaration, conference leaders such as D'Arcy McNickle—whom he called "Uncle Tomahawks"—were ineffective: "fumbling around, passing resolutions and putting headdresses on people." Thom and his allies (and fellow workshop alumni) Clyde Warrior, a charismatic Ponca from Oklahoma; Navajo Herbert Blatchford; and Shirley Hill Witt, a Mohawk from New York, criticized the leadership during the meeting and then gathered in Albuquerque a few months later to form a new, more outspoken organization, the National Indian Youth Council. "It was time," Thom declared, "to raise some hell."

In 1961 hell-raising lay largely in the future, however, as tribal communities continued to battle against termination or struggle for greater public sympathy and support. Despite the improving atmosphere brought on by the new civil rights movement in the South, most Americans remained either ignorant or indifferent when it came to Indian affairs, and most government officials continued to believe they knew what was best for tribal leaders. Even John Kennedy, while agreeing to meet with representatives of the Chicago conference in the Rose Garden of the White House in 1962, had little to offer. The handsome young chief executive mingled briefly with the delegates before passing them off to meet with his vice president, Lyndon Johnson.

President Johnson's War on Poverty

The Chicago delegation's meeting with Johnson turned out to be fortuitous. Following Kennedy's death in November 1963, the new president embarked on an ambitious campaign to create a Great Society in which federal dollars would provide citizens with the education, health care, and legal protection necessary to overcome whatever hardships they had encountered in life. The first step in this campaign was an "unconditional war on poverty in America" to be directed by a new federal agency, the Office of Economic Opportunity (OEO), which would help direct funds to the areas of greatest need, bypassing existing bureaucracies when necessary.

Proposed by Johnson in early 1964, the OEO would support "community action programs" that would address social problems in the poorest communities in America. These social programs, Johnson argued, should operate with the "maximum feasible participation" of the people they were intended to serve. In developing his ideas, President

Johnson had first imagined the problems of urban ghettoes and the rural South, but thanks to the fortuitous meeting with tribal leaders in 1962, he was also thinking about Indians.

The new president met with the NCAI leadership at the White House in January 1964 and told them, "I have directed that in our attack on poverty program we put our Indian people in the forefront." Finding the Bureau of Indian Affairs relatively uninterested in Johnson's initiatives (BIA officials simply requested additional funding for existing programs), Indian leaders and their allies within the administration pressed their case directly on Capitol Hill. Richard Schifter, president of the Association on American Indian Affairs, for example, testified that tribes should be centrally involved in planning and directing antipoverty programs.

In May 1964, during a break in the hearings on Johnson's OEO proposal, the Episcopal Church and several other smaller reform groups organized the "American Indian Capitol Conference on Poverty" in Washington, D.C. The conference attracted nearly nine hundred participants who spoke out about the need for federal assistance that could go directly to Native communities without being controlled by paternalistic bureaucrats in the BIA. Many in Congress opposed this idea, but with the support of sympathetic westerners (notably Senator Lee Metcalf of Montana and South Dakota's George McGovern) Native leaders managed to insert their views into the final language of the antipoverty bill. When Johnson officially created the OEO in August 1964, groups within Indian communities were already preparing to apply to the new agency for support. Within three years sixty-seven independent Native American community action agencies were administering OEO antipoverty programs on 170 reservations. By 1970, $70 million in OEO funds had been spent to create reservation industrial parks; improve road, water, and sanitation systems; and build tribal businesses.

In many ways President Johnson's War on Poverty followed the pattern of the New Deal a generation before. New federal dollars flowed directly to Indian communities from a new federal agency. As had been the case with public works projects in the 1930s, these new dollars were "antipoverty" funds; they were not part of a Bureau of Indian Affairs initiative. Like the New Deal, the War on Poverty gave Native communities an alternative to the Indian Office. But Lyndon Johnson's War on Poverty differed from the New Deal in one fundamental way: it insisted that federal dollars be administered by community-based organizations that encouraged "maximum feasible participation" of Indian people. As a consequence, the initiatives launched in the 1960s encouraged the work of a new group of Native activists who were neither BIA administrators nor tribal officials.

New Leaders Emerge

The War on Poverty spawned a number of new programs. These included the Job Corps, Head Start, Upward Bound, VISTA ("the domestic Peace Corps"), and the Economic Development Administration (EDA). In addition, existing federal agencies such as the Small Business Administration, the Department of Housing and Urban Development (HUD), and the Legal Services Administration established "Indian desks" to extend their programs to Indian communities. These agencies produced an array of new social service programs on reservations and in Indian city neighborhoods, many led by educated young Native Americans and none dependent on BIA approval. Peter MacDonald, for example, a young engineer who had relocated to Los Angeles to work in the aerospace industry, returned to the Navajo reservation to direct the tribe's antipoverty program. Ladonna Harris, a Comanche community leader, formed Oklahomans for Indian Opportunity and organized community development projects that served several Native communities in that state. On the Salt River Reservation in Arizona a number of women who organized the local Head Start program became political leaders and council members. Vine Deloria Jr., the son of a widely respected Sioux Episcopal priest and nephew of linguist Ella Deloria, became executive director of NCAI in 1964. "For the first time," the younger Deloria observed, "tribes can plan and run their own programs for their people without someone in the BIA dictating to them."

The economic impact of Johnson's innovative programs was mixed. Conditions on several reservations improved, but few new business enterprises were successful. Imaginative new projects such as the Bottle Hollow Resort on the Uintah reservation in Utah or the computer assembly facility at

Zuni were built with federal assistance, but most suffered from poor planning, nepotism, and inexperienced management. New industrial parks were built, but they often sat empty; new shopping centers often fell into disrepair. But the shift to Native leadership continued, profoundly affecting the future of Indian policymaking.

In 1966, when Indian Commissioner Philleo Nash resigned, Johnson replaced him with Robert Bennett, an Oneida. The first Native American to hold the post in nearly a century, Bennett was a career BIA bureaucrat who had little opportunity to make dramatic changes. Nevertheless his appointment marked a historic shift; every commissioner since Bennett has been Native American. In Congress, sophisticated Indian lobbyists now blocked efforts to terminate federal services on reservations. Even the secretary of the interior was forced to adjust. In April 1966, Secretary Stewart Udall attempted to hold a closed-door planning meeting with key congressional leaders to discuss future Indian legislation. Such meetings had been routine for decades. Outside this gathering, however, sixty-two tribal leaders hastily assembled by Vine Deloria at the NCAI stood guard, eager to speak to the press. Embarrassed and outflanked, Udall announced that he would no longer discuss new policies without consulting tribal leaders. Deloria called the incident a "watershed."

Victories in Congress and the Courts

At the same time that the new call for "self determination" was gaining recognition among legislators and bureaucrats, the nation's courts were also beginning to take tribal governments seriously. Despite John Collier's promises in the 1930s, the tribal councils created by the Indian Reorganization Act did little more than administer government programs handed to them by Congress. They lacked the power to change budget allocations, remove BIA personnel, or overturn settled policy. Nevertheless, a growing number of local Indian politicians believed tribal governments had the potential to become the modern heirs of the powerful groups that had signed treaties with the U.S. government in the eighteenth and nineteenth centuries. They argued that since the IRA had officially "recognized" tribal governments, reservation leaders should claim the same legal status as their treaty-making ancestors.

In the 1930s and 1940s this viewpoint was translated into legal terms by Nathan Margold and Felix Cohen, two New Deal lawyers who had first come to Washington at the invitation of Interior Secretary Harold Ickes. Working in the legal office of the Department of Interior, Margold and Cohen developed the legal concept of *reserved sovereignty*. The term proved to be a crucial element in the campaign to strengthen tribal governments.

According to Margold and Cohen, the term *reserved sovereignty* embodied three separate elements. First, tribal governments exercised sovereign powers that were independent of federal authority. These powers were indigenous; they flowed from the Indians' ancient residence in North America and their former status as free and independent entities. Second, when the United States extended its sovereignty over tribes, it had required them to surrender certain specific elements of their governmental powers. Once defeated in war, for example, tribes signed treaties that pledged them to peace. By signing these treaties, tribes had surrendered their inherent sovereign power to make war. But they ceded nothing else. Cohen and Margold pointed out that whatever powers the tribes had *not* surrendered were retained by them. This was the third element of their theory: tribes could assert their remaining sovereign power over any domain they had not explicitly surrendered in previous agreements or treaties. Cohen and Margold believed that the concept of reserved sovereignty applied to all recognized tribes, regardless of their exact historical circumstance.

Bold as it was, the doctrine of reserved sovereignty had little impact on judicial opinion until 1959 when the Supreme Court decided *Williams* v. *Lee*, a case brought in Arizona Supreme Court by a non-Indian against a Navajo man who owed him $281 for food bought on credit. The Navajo's attorney argued that Arizona courts had no jurisdiction over such suits; he argued the case should have been filed in tribal court. He observed that the Navajos had never surrendered their authority over civil disputes arising in their territory. To the surprise of many, the Supreme Court agreed. The justices reasoned that the government's policy of protecting and promoting tribal government required anyone suing an Indian for the recovery of a debt should bring the complaint to a tribal court. Allowing the state action to proceed would "undermine" the tribal courts, which functioned not as branches of the BIA or some other federal agency, but as features of Navajo sovereignty.

This recognition of reserved sovereignty was repeated often during the next ten years. The Supreme Court declared in 1962, for example, that trading posts on reservations were not required to collect state sales taxes because another government—a tribe—had authority there. The court also ruled that tribal police could enforce their authority on privately owned land within a reservation, that tribal governments along the Colorado River—like the states of Arizona and California—were entitled to a portion of the water that flowed past their borders, and that the Menominee tribe was entitled to treaty-based hunting and fishing rights even *after* it was formally "terminated" by Congress. These were opening salvos in a battle between tribes and local governments over the limits of tribal power that proliferated during the 1960s. Growing numbers of young Indians began to consider law school, and in 1967 a federally supported Indian law program opened at the University of New Mexico. One of its first students was John Echo Hawk, a young Pawnee who would later become director of the Native American Rights Fund. The following year federally funded legal services offices were operating on ten reservations.

Encouraged by the courts' receptivity, tribal leaders pressed their advantage in both the courts and Congress. Beginning in 1962, for example, Native activists in the Puget Sound area tried to bring the decades-old dispute over fishing rights to a head by holding "fish-ins" along the Nisqually, Puyallup, and Columbia rivers. Indians arrested there for fishing out of season defended themselves by claiming they were exercising their rights under the 1855 Treaty of Point Elliott. Supported by the NIYC, the National Association for the Advancement of Colored People, and celebrities such as Marlon Brando and Episcopal canon John Yaryan, the protestors pressed their claims in hopes of winning a favorable ruling from the federal courts. At the same time the Oneidas and other Iroquois communities revived their long-standing land claims case against the State of New York and prepared new legal challenges to non-Indian land titles.

"Indian reform" also became a popular topic on Capitol Hill. Beginning in 1966, Senator Sam Ervin of North Carolina embarked on a series of hearings to investigate how well tribal governments protected the rights of Indians. Many tribal leaders protested this intrusion into local customs, but Ervin's committee also raised the visibility of an important tribal institution. In the end Ervin fashioned a proposal that became the 1968 "Indian Civil Rights Act." The new law imposed much of the U.S. Constitution's Bill of Rights on the tribes, but it also made some concessions to tribal custom. Because religious leaders held leadership positions in many communities, for example, the new law declared that the Constitution's prohibition against the establishment of religion was waived for Indian tribes.

As the 1960s drew to a close, Native Americans were becoming more visible actors in policy decisions affecting tribal communities. No longer politically silent or confined exclusively to reservations, Indians were beginning to make progress against the paternalistic thinking that for centuries had defined them as "savages" who could not participate in American life until they had abandoned their backward ways. Men and women who had defeated termination or managed antipoverty programs in their communities presented themselves as both "Indian" and "modern"—people who were tied to distinctive cultural traditions yet fully capable of participating in the social and cultural life of a space-age democracy.

Recognition in Literature and the Arts

The most significant event in the 1960s for Native American artists was the awarding of the 1969 Pulitzer Prize for literature to N. Scott Momaday's *House Made of Dawn*. The Kiowa author's story of a World War II veteran from Jemez Pueblo captured this recognition just as a generation of young Native authors began to find audiences for their work. Inventive and sophisticated, Momaday's novel carried its readers through the many realms Indians had explored during the previous quarter century: World War II, life in the city, and the reservation homeland. Other authors quickly joined this "renaissance" in Native literature. James Welch, a Blackfeet/Gros Ventre poet and novelist, graduated from the University of Montana in the early 1960s. He published his first book of poetry, *Riding The Earthboy 40*, in 1971 and his first novel, *Winter in the Blood,* in 1974. Leslie Marmon Silko, from Laguna Pueblo, followed a similar path, graduating from the University of New Mexico in 1969, publishing a book of poetry in 1974 and a popular novel, *Ceremony,* in 1977. Gerald Vizenor, an Ojibwe graduate of the University of Minnesota, worked as a reporter for the Minneapolis *Tribune* before publishing his first book of poetry in 1965 and his first collection of prose writings in 1972. Vizenor later went on to an academic career, publishing novels, essays, and literary criticism. Momaday's award helped create an audience for these new authors while it also provided them with a model for their own careers.

Aside from Momaday, the most popular American Indian writer of the 1960s was Vine Deloria Jr., whose scathing analysis of Indian-white relations, *Custer Died for Your Sins: An Indian Manifesto*, was published to wide acclaim in 1969. The son and grandson of Yankton Sioux missionaries, Deloria had earned a master's degree from the Lutheran School of Theology before turning to Indian politics and, later, to the law. Most of the material for *Custer Died* was drawn from Deloria's years in Washington when he served as executive director of the National Congress of American Indians. From his proposal to rename the Washington monument the national Indian monument ("Because we always get the shaft"), to his description of the spring arrival of anthropologists as part of an annual weather cycle marked by rain and flood, Deloria mercilessly prodded non-Indians to understand that Native people were fellow humans who could laugh at themselves and others and who were weary of paternalistic white people bearing promises of salvation. "Everyone else has problems," Deloria declared, "why do Indians have a plight?" His second book, published in 1970, captured his impatience in its title: *We Talk, You Listen.*

The growth of an American Indian literary community during the 1960s was a remarkable innovation. Native visual artists were more familiar to the non-Indian public, as Indian painters, sculptors, and weavers had been marketing their wares

since the early twentieth century. But the Indian writers' concentration on issues of identity and the problems associated with balancing tradition and modernity were also evident in the work of a new generation of painters and sculptors. Chief among these were three instructors at the Institute of American Indian Arts, a BIA school founded in 1962 to preserve indigenous artistic traditions. In their classrooms, Charles Loloma, a Hopi jeweler; Allen Houser, an Apache sculptor; and Fritz Scholder, a Luiseño painter, encouraged their students to interpret their tribal pasts with new techniques. Each instructor offered a model for this assignment. Loloma, for example, used unusual materials to fashion jewelry that captured themes drawn from Hopi history, while Houser experimented with monumental bronze pieces and Scholder exhibited brightly colored canvases that mocked popular stereotypes of Indians. Between 1966 and 1968 a major exhibition of work by artists affiliated with the institute toured the United States, Europe, and South America, attracting huge audiences to its display of "modern" Indian art.

Despite the growing stature of Native American artists and writers, most non-Indians in the 1960s continued to form their impressions of Native people at the movies or while watching television. These forms of mass entertainment were largely indifferent to the changes taking place within the Indian community—their goal, after all, was to sell tickets and advertising to white people, not to educate them—but even here Native Americans began to have an impact. For decades filmmakers had churned out popular films that pitted hardy white cavalrymen and cowboys against disorganized, cowardly Indians, but rising public sensitivity to racial issues after World War II began to change that standard script. *Duel in the Sun* (1946), *Fort Apache* (1948), and *She Wore A Yellow Ribbon* (1949) all contained scenes calling old stereotypes into question. The most innovative film of this period was *Broken Arrow*, released in 1950, which presented a western lawman and an Apache chief working together as allies, combating frontier racism and lawlessness.

Stereotypes continued to appear in Hollywood films, but a number of more complex and sympathetic portrayals appeared in the wake of *Broken Arrow*. Film biographies of Jim Thorpe (1951) and war hero Ira Hayes (*The Outsider*, 1961) presented remarkable men whose lives were undermined by white prejudice, while *Apache* (1954) and *Cheyenne Autumn* (1964) offered filmgoers case studies of Indian tribes dispossessed and mistreated by American settlers. In this same vein, *Tell Them Willy Boy Is Here* (1969) was a moving retelling of a massive desert manhunt for a troubled southern California Indian in the early twentieth century. The high point of this trend toward greater sympathy and complexity in presentations of Indians came in 1970 with the release of Arthur Penn's *Little Big Man*. Starring Dustin Hoffman as a white captive raised by Cheyennes who shuttled back and forth across the nineteenth-century frontier, the film punctured stereotypes, lampooned western icons such as George Armstrong Custer, and featured dozens of previously unknown Native American actors. (The Hollywood practice of casting heavily made up non-Indians such as Anthony Quinn, Tony Curtis, or Sal Mineo as Indians largely ended with *Little Big Man*.)

Television presentations of Native Americans followed a similar, if less dramatic arc of improvement. Over the course of the 1950s and 1960s sympathetic presentations of Indians appeared with increasing frequency amidst a sea of stereotypes and non-Indian faces. Hollywood veteran Jay Silverheels, a Mohawk, was perhaps the most visible TV figure of the era as his Tonto character rode alongside the Lone Ranger through dozens of thirty-minute adventures. While Silverheels's character was sympathetic, the program rarely addressed racial themes and the actor never faltered in his role as the white hero's "faithful Indian companion." Indians rarely appeared in the period's most popular westerns such as *Gunsmoke* and *Bonanza* and were almost completely invisible in other programming.

The single exception to this pattern of television neglect came in a 1958 news special. The television pioneer Edward R. Murrow had called on his colleagues to reject "phony Hollywood Indians," but few responded until the broadcast of *The American Stranger*. Produced by Robert McCormick of NBC, *Stranger* offered a caustic examination of termination, juxtaposing smug government officials with footage of rural poverty and ruined classrooms. *The Exiles*, a portrait of relocated Indians in Los Angeles, was broadcast in 1962, but few others followed.

NEW VOICES

Two new organizations emerged at the end of the 1960s, marking the dramatic shift that had taken place in Native American life in the years since World War II and suggesting a path Indian people would follow in the future. These new organizations welcomed members from all tribes and demanded that non-Indians recognize the tribes' claim to justice and fair treatment. They were less interested in education and employment than they were in recognition of Native American dignity and cultural persistence.

The American Indian Movement (AIM)

The first group emerged in Minneapolis, the city where Ignatia Broker had come seeking work in 1941 and where Amabel Bulin had detected the beginnings of an Indian "slum" in 1944. As both women observed, migration to the Twin Cities of Minneapolis and St. Paul continued during the postwar years, so by 1960 the south Minneapolis neighborhood where they congregated had come to be labeled "the reservation." In the summer of 1968 a small group of young Indian men, most of them first-generation city residents who had survived repeated run-ins with the police, formed a group to follow squad cars through their part of town to monitor the officers' behavior and prevent incidents of brutality. The patrols of the new American Indian Movement (AIM) were inspired by the tactics of the Black Panthers, a militant African-American group that had started working against police brutality in Oakland, California, a few years earlier. George Mitchell and Dennis Banks, the founders of the group, and Clyde Bellecourt, who soon joined them, were all Minnesota Ojibwes. Soon, however, members of other tribes joined them. Banks was ambitious and appealing. He told reporters he wanted to "straighten this country out."

Outspoken and colorful, AIM's leaders quickly attracted the attention of journalists, television camera crews, and government leaders. They lobbied local antipoverty agencies to channel funds to Indian organizations, organized educational programs (eventually founding a new school, The Little Red School House) to counter insensitive local schools, and spoke openly of their disdain for Christianity and their reverence for traditional tribal religions. Banks and Bellecourt made no apologies for their prison records. Their swagger and success inspired leaders in other cities to form AIM chapters, transforming the Minneapolis group into the leaders of a national organization. Media attention followed and inspired a series of new tactics that underscored their assertion that they were advocates of the "Indian" cause who felt little allegiance to the United States. On Thanksgiving Day 1970, AIM leaders received national coverage when they captured *Mayflower II*, a replica of the pilgrims' sailing ship, in Plymouth, Massachusetts. The following year they attacked another icon of national patriotism, Mount Rushmore, to protest the "desecration" of the Black Hills. AIM's leaders declared that they cared little for "equal rights" and "self-determination"; their real goal was complete Indian "sovereignty" over tribal lands and resources.

Indians of All Tribes Seizes Alcatraz

A second organization burst onto the scene in November 1969 when seventy-eight Native Americans, mostly young college students, took control of the abandoned federal prison on Alcatraz Island in San Francisco Bay. The group called themselves Indians of All Tribes. Their leader was Richard Oakes, a Mohawk who had drifted to California a few years earlier and had recently enrolled in the new Native American Studies program at San Francisco State University. Oakes was supported by Adam Nordwall, a "relocated" Ojibwe businessman who chaired the United Bay Area Council of American Indian Affairs (and who had organized a brief protest on the island in 1964).

As they settled into their new home, Oakes, Nordwall, and the protestors found themselves at the center of an international media event. They encouraged this attention by inviting sympathizers and the press to a grand open house on Thanksgiving Day, welcoming visits by Anthony Quinn, Jane Fonda, and other celebrities, and sending representatives to appear on late-night talk shows. The rock band Creedence Clearwater Revival gave the occupiers a boat to help with the shipment of supplies, and a Berkeley radio station offered Indians

Indians Protesting at Alcatraz. The early weeks of the Alcatraz occupation were marked by celebrations and spontaneous gatherings of Indian people from California and beyond. These occasions provided many opportunities for dramatic images of protesters posed before the famous profile of the island's prison buildings.

of All Tribes a half hour of broadcast time each day. Hosted by an articulate young Sioux activist, John Trudell, *Radio Free Alcatraz* was soon being rebroadcast on "alternative" stations in New York and Los Angeles. After several weeks the group began negotiating with federal officials, proposing to build an Indian cultural center or museum at the site. But as the occupation stretched into 1970, public interest waned, the island's leadership divided, government officials stalled, and conditions on the island deteriorated. Oakes left Alcatraz, and differences arose between students, activists, and older Bay Area leaders like Nordwall. Public attention shifted to other events in Southeast Asia and to the nation's college campuses; the population on the island dwindled. Finally, in June 1971, federal marshals removed the handful of remaining occupiers.

The significance of the Indians of All Tribes' occupation of Alcatraz, like the significance of the formation of AIM a year earlier, lay less in the immediate achievements of the new group than in the way it rallied Native Americans from all backgrounds to demand public recognition of Indian traditions and their historical claims. The events on Alcatraz not only captivated the California press, but they attracted hundreds of Indian visitors to the island. Among these were people who had been "relocated" to cities in the 1950s and 1960s, as well as those who had remained on their reservations. Wilma Mankiller arrived from her home in San Francisco. Energized by her visit, she would later return to Oklahoma to lead her tribe. George Horse Capture, then a sheet metal inspector in Oakland, reconnected with his Gros Ventre heritage during his time at Alcatraz. He returned to Montana and eventually became a distinguished scholar and museum curator. Thomas Benyaca, a Hopi elder, came to Alcatraz from Arizona to offer spiritual guidance, and Lenny Foster, a young Navajo college student, traveled to the island simply to participate in what he saw as the "spiritual rebirth" of his people.

CONCLUSION

The postwar era had begun with celebrations of individual heroism; it ended with celebrations of a people's common history and collective identity. Transformed from an isolated, rural people whose lives had been dominated by missionaries and government officials, Native Americans now demonstrated their ability to articulate a powerful national agenda and to speak out with one voice. Forced by the struggle against termination to devise ways of gaining access to political institutions, schools, media outlets, and the courts, Indians now demanded a central role in policymaking and showed themselves capable of promoting their demands before the public. Most important, once

they had captured the spotlight, Native Americans made it clear that they now rejected the choice between progress and Indianness that whites had been offering them for a century. In the years to come, Indians would pursue both goals simultaneously. They would struggle to improve conditions in urban and reservation communities while maintaining their allegiance to ancient traditions and cultural unity. They would pursue their goals but reject paternalism and assimilation.

One final event illustrated this new stance. At the end of 1970, the tiny Pueblo community of Taos, supported by the National Council of Churches and other reform groups, persuaded officials of Richard Nixon's White House to support the return of Blue Lake to tribal control. The lake, not only a source of water for their pueblo but also the location of important tribal shrines, had been transferred to the jurisdiction of the U.S. Forest Service in 1906 and kept there over tribal protests by federal officials who insisted that the tribe was not capable of managing the land properly. Tribal leaders argued that ownership of the lake should not be decided on the basis of bureaucratic efficiency, but on the religious and moral claims of the Taos people. When the tribe rejected a $10 million Indian Claims Commission award for the lake and insisted instead on the return of their sacred land, it was clear that the stalemate would continue indefinitely. The impasse was finally broken in December 1970 when legislation returning the lake and forty-eight thousand acres of surrounding forest passed Congress and was signed by President Nixon.

SUGGESTED READINGS

Castile, George Pierre. *To Show Heart: Native American Self-Determination and Federal Indian Policy, 1960–1975.* Tucson: University of Arizona Press, 1998.   An account of the emergence of new policies in the 1960s aimed at allowing tribes to manage their own federal assistance programs. The narrative also includes a description of the occupation of the Bureau of Indian Affairs building in 1972 and other events in the early years of the Red Power movement.

Deloria, Vine, Jr. *Custer Died For Your Sins: An Indian Manifesto.* New York: Avon, 1969.   The key Indian statement of the Red Power era; a critique of mainstream American attitudes towards Indians and a call for action.

LaGrand, James B. *Indian Metropolis: Native Americans in Chicago, 1945–1975*. Urbana: University of Illinois Press, 2002. A comprehensive history of Native American migrations to Chicago and the formation of an American Indian community in that city.

Lazarus, Edward. *Black Hills, White Justice: The Sioux Nation Versus the United States, 1775 to the Present*. New York: Harper Collins, 1991. A history of the Sioux struggle to reclaim the Black Hills following their seizure in 1877 by the United States. The book traces the claim from the nineteenth century to the U.S. Supreme Court decision on the matter in 1980, but a great portion of the narrative describes the actions of the Court of Claims and the Indian Claims Commission during the 1950s and 1960s.

Philp, Kenneth R. *Termination Revisited: American Indians on the Trail to Self-Determination, 1933–1953*. Lincoln: University of Nebraska Press, 1999. A history of Indian policymaking that traces the struggle of various tribes to reduce federal paternalism without losing the support of federal agencies.

Rosier, Paul. *Rebirth of the Blackfeet Nation, 1912–1954*. Lincoln: University of Nebraska Press, 2001. A close-up view of a major plains tribe in the first half of the twentieth century. A unique local perspective on national Indian policy changes, and an excellent profile of tribal leaders.

Stewart, Omer C. *Peyote Religion: A History*. Norman: University of Oklahoma Press, 1987. A history of the peyote ritual in the twentieth century that traces its spread from Mexico and the Southwest to Oklahoma and beyond.

Voget, Fred W. *The Shoshoni-Crow Sun Dance*. Norman: University of Oklahoma Press, 1984. A modern anthropologist's description of the reintroduction of the Sun Dance among the Crows in the 1940s and 1950s.

Acting Sovereign, 1970–1990

The surge of activism at the end of the 1960s was infectious. Indian people who had felt alone in strange cities or ignored by government officials found themselves engaged in a common cause; they suddenly sensed a kinship with counterparts from distant tribes. Spurred on by the enthusiasm of the Alcatraz occupation, the protesters looked for new battlegrounds. In March 1970, for example, several veterans of the San Francisco takeover—including Richard Oakes, one of the original organizers—helped climb the fences surrounding an abandoned army installation near Seattle, Washington. Within a year, following skirmishes with state police officers and local politicians, the occupiers gained title to the base. Fort Lawton became the Daybreak Star Cultural Center.

During 1970 Native Americans occupied BIA offices in Denver, Chicago, Cleveland, Minneapolis, Sacramento, and Santa Fe to protest inadequate services for urban Indian communities. Pit River Indians from northern California occupied land in Lassen National Forest in an effort to win back tribal territory. Mohawks camped on islands in the St. Lawrence River, claiming jurisdiction over their ancient territory. All of these events occurred while AIM leaders threatened to capture Ellis Island and the Statue of Liberty and to settle permanently on top of Mount Rushmore.

As the Indian protests and occupations spread outward across the American landscape, their impact was felt with increasing intensity. Each confrontation raised new possibilities. In California, for example, two Native American teachers at the University of California, Davis, who were veterans of the Alcatraz occupation, noticed that a nearby air force installation had closed. Inspired by their experiences in San Francisco Bay, Jack Forbes, whose ancestors were Lenapes from the East but who had been raised in southern California, and David Risling Jr., a member of that state's Hoopa tribe, led a group of forty students onto the former base, announcing that they would not leave until federal authorities deeded the six-hundred-acre property to a new Indian-run college. In January 1971, as federal authorities prepared to evict the last remaining protesters from Alcatraz, officials of the Department of Health Education and Welfare (later Health and Human Services) announced that Deganawidah/Quetzocoatl University, named for heroes of both the Iroquois and the Aztec cultures, would receive title to the land. Forbes, Risling, and their supporters quickly raised $300,000 from antipoverty agencies and the Ford Foundation and opened their school.

The transformations set in motion by the protests at Alcatraz and in Minneapolis also drew recruits to the Indian cause. The new activism captured the imagination of young people like Anna Mae Pictou, a young Mi'kmaq woman from Nova Scotia who, like many from her tribe, had migrated to Boston in the early 1960s to escape the poverty of her home reserve and to search for work. When Alcatraz was occupied and the AIM protests began, Anna Mae was a single mother struggling to support her two children and maintain her ties both to her home community in Canada and to other Indians in Boston. The twenty-five-year-old Pictou was thrilled with the new spirit of protest. She became an active member of the Boston Indian Council and urged fellow members—urban immigrants drawn from communities across the United States and Canada like herself—to support AIM and the Alcatraz occupiers. She also joined in when AIM organized a protest at Plymouth Rock during Thanksgiving in 1970. Soon afterwards, Anna Mae found work in an experimental Indian school in Maine, but in 1972 she returned to Boston. She soon met an Ojibwe artist, Nogeeshik Aquash, and the two began living together. Pictou enrolled in a teacher training program at a local college, but she and Aquash continued to be active in the burgeoning Indian protest movement. When AIM and other organizations announced protests or occupations, the young couple was often among those who responded.

Many of those who were mobilized by the activism of the 1960s would spend the next two decades exploiting their initial successes and broadening avenues to power in cities and rural communities across the nation. Veterans of Alcatraz and other similar actions formed the core of a new generation of aggressive Indian leaders who turned from the goal of "self-determination" to the pursuit of "sovereignty." People like Richard Oakes, Jack Forbes, and Anna Mae Pictou were less interested in administering programs and ideas handed to them by non-Indian social workers and politicians than they were in initiating and controlling projects of their own. It seemed in the 1970s and 1980s that tribes and urban Indian communities were beginning to live out one of the American Indian Movement's central slogans. During the early years

of the organization, AIM leaders would fire up their audiences with the challenge, "If you want to be sovereign, you have to *act* sovereign." The Alcatraz generation was eager to respond to this call.

RED POWER

During the turbulent 1960s, protest groups frequently insisted that their objective was not reform but power in some form. African-Americans sought Black Power, Latinos and Chicanos, Brown Power, while peace advocates insisted that they opposed the nation's military and struggled to return power to the people. In this atmosphere of insurgency, Native American calls, first for self-determination, and, later, for sovereignty, came to be labeled a struggle for Red Power. "Red power means we want power over our own lives," Vine Deloria Jr. declared.

When it was first invoked by Indian activists and the press, Red Power had no real definition. During the 1960s the term had been used by the organizers of the National Indian Youth Council when they separated themselves from the stuffy atmosphere of the 1961 Chicago Conference as well as by tribal leaders lobbying for antipoverty funds. But as the confrontations proliferated following the Alcatraz occupation and new activists came forward to join the cause, Red Power came to be equated with militant demands and direct action.

Late in 1971, Vine Deloria Jr. proposed uniting all Indians into a single political organization. The newly minted lawyer, who had witnessed the quickening pace of Indian politics during his term as executive director of the National Congress of American Indians from 1964 to 1967, suggested a formal agreement among the NCAI, the NIYC, AIM, and the newly formed National Tribal Chairman's Association to pursue a common agenda. Deloria imagined that NCAI would act as a Washington lobby group, NIYC would organize youth programs, tribal chairs would focus on pressuring the BIA bureaucracy, and AIM would provide the "activist punch." He believed a common commitment to enhancing the power and resources available to tribes and urban communities would hold the four organizations together. While no one formally rejected Deloria's plan, it was soon overtaken by an unprecedented sequence of dramatic and highly publicized American Indian protests.

AIM Takes Center Stage

Two features of modern American life made the new protests' intense drama possible. First, communications technology both publicized Indian actions and allowed activists to communicate with one another across vast distances. Second, Native Americans were now dispersed across the American landscape. Thanks to a generation of urban migration, by 1970 every major American city contained a multitribal Indian community that was generally sympathetic with the "Indian cause." Events in one location would find audiences in many others, and activists would always find allies, even when they operated far from home.

During 1972 two chains of events—one beginning in South Dakota and the other in California—intersected, generating a wave of publicity for AIM and the cause of Red Power and transforming local incidents into international confrontations. The first chain began in February 1972, with the death of Raymond Yellow Thunder, a fifty-one-year-old Sioux man, in Gordon, Nebraska, near the Pine Ridge Sioux reservation. Gordon was a typical reservation border town: filled with bars and liquor stores and run by white merchants who thought little of gouging their mostly Indian clientele. One night, a group of white cowboys had beaten Yellow Thunder, forced him to dance half-naked at an American Legion party, and then tossed him out into a frigid winter night. He died of his injuries and exposure. When local authorities failed to respond to family members who questioned the circumstances of Yellow Thunder's death, the young man's relatives began searching for help.

One of Yellow Thunder's relatives recalled that a local Indian family, the Means, who had moved to California years earlier, had a son who belonged to the American Indian Movement. The relatives made contact with Russell Means and within a few days, fourteen hundred Indians from eighty tribes descended on Gordon to demand that Yellow Thunder's killers be brought to justice. Within a few weeks five men were arrested in connection with the murder, town officials suspended a local police officer, Gordon created a human rights commission, and both the governor of Nebraska and the U.S. secretary of the interior had offered to help. The speed of AIM's response—a vivid contrast to the apparent indifference of local tribal officials—electrified the reservation. Young city Indians, dressed in jeans and leather vests and wearing braids and dark glasses, had put the elected tribal council and local BIA officials to shame.

The Gordon protests linked AIM to dissatisfaction with the Pine Ridge reservation leadership. The tribal council's inability to help Yellow Thunder's family underscored the weakness of the "recognized" BIA government. Resentments that had circulated since the campaign to ratify the IRA in the 1930s resurfaced. These resentments grew in April 1972 (two months after Yellow Thunder's murder), when an outspoken, hard-drinking Lakota politician, Richard Wilson, was elected tribal chair. Oblivious to the new currents running through his community, Chairman Wilson immediately set to work installing friends and family in tribal jobs and passing out government contracts to his allies.

During the summer of 1972, as the story of the Gordon protests spread and resentment of Wilson grew, support for the AIM militants deepened at both Pine Ridge and neighboring Rosebud. In August, Means and other AIM leaders participated in a Sun Dance at Rosebud that was sponsored by critics of the elected reservation leadership. One of those critics, former Rosebud chair Bob Burnette suggested dramatizing the group's concerns by marching on Washington, D.C.

In September 1972, just as the idea of a Washington march was surfacing in South Dakota, Richard Oakes, the Mohawk leader of the Alcatraz occupation, was shot and killed after an argument with a security guard at a northern California YMCA camp. Because Oakes had participated in numerous land occupations in California as well as the occupation of Fort Lawton and the fish-ins in Puget Sound, his funeral attracted dozens of activists from along the Pacific Coast. At that gathering Hank Adams, a leader of the fishing rights movement who had also worked with Martin Luther King and the Poor People's Campaign a few years earlier, called for a major demonstration as a memorial to Oakes. Someone suggested a gathering in Washington, D.C. The West Coast group soon

Occupation of the BIA, 1972   Native Americans taking part in the Trail of Broken Treaties protest in Washington, D.C. Fearing a possible police attack and angry at the administration's apparent indifference, the assembled activists refused to leave the BIA building.

learned of the AIM planning taking place in South Dakota and the two groups decided to join forces. They planned that three caravans of cars would begin in Los Angeles, San Francisco, and Seattle in mid-October and rendezvous in Minneapolis on October 23. The united group would proceed to Washington, arriving in early November, just as the presidential election campaign was reaching its climax.

Hank Adams drafted a list of Twenty Points that the group planned to deliver to the White House, and Burnette, the Sioux leader who first proposed the idea of the march, was named co-chairman. Adams's Twenty Points called for a return to treaty making, increased funding for housing and health care, and the abolition of the BIA. They called their protest the Trail of Broken Treaties.

The caravans that began to arrive in Washington on November 1 seemed to have gathered together all the elements of the Indian protest movement: West Coast fishing rights advocates, veterans of Alcatraz and Fort Lawton, urban Indians unhappy with the BIA, people from reservations who had given up on their tribal governments, and the media-savvy leaders of AIM. This volatile mix of people soon faced an unexpected crisis. Organizers learned that the accommodations they had been promised in Washington did not exist. The caravan had nowhere to gather or sleep. With little forethought, the entire group suddenly decided to seek help at the office building housing the Bureau of Indian Affairs. On the afternoon of November 2, while protesters gathered on the building's first floor and BIA officials upstairs scrambled to find a solution to the protesters' housing crisis, the waiting crowd grew impatient. Negotiations seemed to be proceeding well when suddenly a detachment of police officers arrived and ordered the Indians who now filled the entrance way to vacate the building. Provoked and frustrated, the protesters suddenly decided to stage a takeover. They barricaded the building's doors and erected a hastily drawn sign over the main entrance: "Native American Embassy." A new protest had begun. Among the group who rushed to join the occupation were Anna Mae Pictou and Nogeeshik Aquash.

The occupation of the BIA headquarters lasted six days. Eager to avoid bloodshed and bad publicity on the eve of a presidential election, Nixon administration officials resisted calls to clear the building by force. Eventually, $66,000 in cash was handed over to AIM leader Vernon Bellecourt on the day after Nixon's reelection. Bellecourt promised that this "travel money" (officially an antipoverty grant) would enable the protesters to leave town. The departing caravan left behind vandalized offices and took with them two truckloads of documents on the theory they would reveal government mismanagement. While some editorial writers expressed sympathy for the protesters, most mainstream press reports focused on the damage to the building and its contents. But among Native Americans the reaction was quite different. While a number of tribal leaders condemned the destruction of the BIA building, Russell Means and Dennis Banks, the telegenic AIM leaders who had taken command during the occupation, were suddenly insurgent heroes. Banks exulted, "We have destroyed the BIA." Calls for "treaty rights" and a restoration of "tribal sovereignty" had become a staple of the evening news.

Occupying Wounded Knee

Within four months sovereignty was back in the headlines. Again, AIM members led by Russell Means and Dennis Banks were the most visible members of a protest with irresistible drama and public appeal. This second event began in February 1973, when Means, Banks, and their local supporters attempted to intervene in the prosecution of a white man in Custer, South Dakota, who was accused of murdering Wesley Bad Heart Bull, a Sioux man from Pine Ridge. Once again, AIM had stepped into an ugly local dispute that local political leaders had avoided. Quiet diplomacy involving local county leaders and the AIM leadership

seemed to be effective at first, but suddenly a negotiating session between the principals held at the Custer courthouse exploded into a pitched battle between the police and the protesters. Before it ended, several members of each side were injured, the courthouse had been set ablaze, and thirty-seven Indians were in jail

The Custer "riot" drove Pine Ridge chairman Wilson and the BIA into an uncomfortable alliance. Distressed by Wilson's passivity in the face of interracial conflicts as well as his ongoing contempt for democratic procedures within the tribal government, Indian Office officials nevertheless welcomed his adamant opposition to AIM. The BIA even approved a $62,000 grant to Wilson's government to support an "auxiliary" police force to maintain order on the reservation. Quickly labeled the "goon squad" by his enemies, Wilson's force operated as the chairman's personal militia.

The Pine Ridge community, long divided along class and political lines, grew increasingly polarized. Wilson's supporters tended to be relatively well-off tribal members who were reservation ranchers or BIA employees. Many Wilson backers were also people of mixed (Indian and white) ancestry who lived in the village of Pine Ridge. His opponents were largely rural families with fewer ties to the cash economy and more interest in maintaining the tribe's traditional culture. One group saw the chairman as a bulwark against "outside agitators"; the other dismissed him as a puppet of the BIA and the wealthy ranchers who leased the bulk of the tribe's lands. A group of Wilson's critics organized themselves into the Oglala Sioux Civil Rights Organization (OSCRO) and brought impeachment proceedings against him. When this effort failed, protests intensified. The climax finally came on February 27, 1973, when Russell Means and other AIM leaders attended an OSCRO meeting where a group of traditional elders urged them to "take a stand" at Wounded Knee, the site of the 1890 massacre.

That night, Means and elders Frank Fools Crow and Pete Catches led a caravan of cars to Wounded Knee and quickly took control of the town. Within a few hours the group announced that they wished to reestablish the nineteenth-century treaty system. They declared, "We are operating under the provisions of the 1868 Sioux Treaty. This is an act of war initiated by the United States." Federal and tribal authorities responded to the Wounded Knee occupation by throwing up road blocks and sealing off the village from the outside world. Soon, pictures of long-haired insurgents encircled by heavily armed federal marshals flashed across television screens around the world. Within forty-eight hours of the initial occupation, both of South Dakota's U.S. senators had arrived to meet with the occupiers. Means and Dennis Banks welcomed visiting reporters, and federal authorities added to the frenzy by bringing in armored personnel carriers and allowing Chairman Wilson to add his road-blocks to their own. The protesters called on supporters from across the country to join them and began digging bunkers for protection; they insisted they would stay and die for their cause.

The Lakota elders who instigated the Wounded Knee occupation soon joined in declaring the village to be the Independent Oglala Nation. Means ordered any unauthorized entry into the village to be considered "an act of war." Veterans in the group led the construction of a network of bunkers and trenches. The publicity accompanying the occupation bore predictable results. Supporters began to arrive. Young Indian and non-Indian volunteers began carrying supplies overland, avoiding the roads patrolled by federal officials and Wilson's police. Representatives of the Vietnam Veterans Against the War arrived, as did Chicano and Asian political activists, idealistic college students, and a delegation from the Grand Council of the Iroquois. Anna Mae Pictou and her boyfriend Nogeeshik Aquash arrived within a few weeks. Captivated by the idea of occupying part of an "independent" nation, the two also decided to marry at Wounded Knee. Wallace Black Elk conducted the ceremony. In the end, nearly 350 Indians joined the occupation, roughly half of them from Pine Ridge and nearby Rosebud. A similar number of federal officers surrounded the village.

Resolving the crisis proved difficult. The occupiers had a number of targets—Chairman Wilson, the BIA, the Nixon administration, and Congress—and their rhetorical claims had grown so broad that there was little federal authorities could do to satisfy them. Negotiations stopped and started during March and April, but the standoff continued. Dug into their positions, the two sides fired thousands of rounds at each other. In March an FBI agent was seriously injured and in April two In-

dian protesters, Buddy LaMonte and Frank Clearwater, were killed. Finally on May 8 the two sides agreed on a settlement. Administration officials promised to investigate conditions at Pine Ridge and to meet with traditional leaders. The occupiers agreed to disperse and face prosecution for crimes committed during the occupation.

The Aftermath of Wounded Knee II

While the 1973 occupation of Wounded Knee, which quickly became known as Wounded Knee II, succeeded in winning a massive audience for Native American grievances, it marked the high point of Indian activism. Never again would the lines between groups seem so clear and never again would the militants win such wide support. In Wisconsin, for example, a group of Menominee activists led by two men who participated in the Wounded Knee occupation seized a shuttered Aleixan Brothers Novitiate on New Year's Day 1975 and demanded that it be "returned" to the tribe. Their action had a dubious legal basis (the Alexian's property was outside the boundaries of the Menominee reservation) and it came at a time when tribal officials were attempting to reorganize their government and reestablish ties to state and federal agencies. The male activists called themselves warriors (and demanded that the new Menominee council bar women from membership). Tribal officials led by Ada Deer (the leader of the recent tribal restoration effort), quickly denounced their action and urged the group to end their occupation. The warriors gave up in early February and the Alexian Brothers subsequently sold their facility to the tribe for $1, but tensions between Indians and whites in the area remained.

Similar tensions surfaced at Pine Ridge. In 1974 tribal chair Richard Wilson defeated AIM leader Russell Means in a reelection campaign marred by charges of vote buying and fraud. Wilson presented himself as a supporter of "law and order" and attacked Means as an outsider. Wilson's victory did not end the tension, however, as the tribal leader continued to direct his auxiliary "goon squad" to harass and intimidate opponents and the FBI appeared to ignore his actions. The resulting "reign of terror" resulted in dozens of mysterious deaths. Opponents charged that sixty-nine AIM members

INDIAN VOICES   Russell Means Advocates Reviving Indian Traditions

Russell Means was born in 1939 on the Pine Ridge reservation in South Dakota but his parents migrated to California during World War II and he was raised in Vallejo, near San Francisco. While he often performed well in school, Means was frequently in trouble with the police. After graduating from high school in 1958, Means had no particular focus for his talents until he participated in a short-lived occupation of Alcatraz Island in 1964. He then began participating in political activities, both in California and South Dakota. He worked briefly in a reservation antipoverty program in 1967 before moving to Cleveland, Ohio, where he worked as an accountant before becoming executive director of the city's new American Indian Center. When he joined the American Indian Movement in 1970, his good looks and forceful speaking style quickly won him national attention.

Means spent most of the 1970s as an AIM activist, participating in the occupation of both the BIA headquarters and Wounded Knee. He also spent a good deal of time in court, fighting various charges brought by federal authorities, and was imprisoned on two occasions. During the 1980s Means led a series of protests in the Black Hills, illegally occupying a protest "village" on federal land and giving a number of speeches on behalf of Sioux land claims and in opposition to mining both there and on Indian reservations across the United States. He turned to acting and writing during the 1990s, appearing in *The Last of the Mohicans* (1991), lending his voice to an animated version of *Pocahontas* (1995), and publishing his autobiography, *Where White Men Fear To Tread* (1995). He remained an outspoken critic of federal Indian policy throughout his career. The following excerpt from a speech he gave in the Black Hills in the summer of 1980 reflects Means's view that Red Power challenged European culture and the entire structure of relations between Native Americans and their fellow citizens. Means insisted that he and his fellow protesters were engaged in an anticolonial struggle aimed at replacing imposed European ideas with revived American Indian traditions.

It takes a strong effort on the part of each American Indian *not* to become Europeanized. The strength for this effort can only come from the traditional ways, the traditional values that our elders retain. It must come from the hoop, the four directions, the relations; it cannot come from the pages of a book or a thousand books. . . . A master's degree in "Indian Studies" or in "education" or in anything else cannot make a person into a human being or provide knowledge into the traditional ways. It can only make you into a mental European, an outsider. . . .

The European materialist tradition of despiritualizing the universe is very similar to the mental process which goes into dehumanizing another person. And who seems most expert at dehumanizing other people? And why? Soldiers who have seen a lot of combat learn to do this to the enemy before going back into combat. Murderers do it before going out to commit murder. Nazi SS guards did it to concentration camp inmates. Cops do it. Corporation leaders do it to the workers they send into the uranium mines and steel mills. Politicians do it to everyone in sight. And what the process has in common for each group doing the dehumanizing is that it makes it all right to kill and otherwise destroy other people. . . . the trick is to mentally convert the victims into nonhumans. . . .

In terms of the despiritualization of the universe, the mental process works so that it becomes virtuous to destroy the planet. Terms like *progress* and *development* are used as cover words here, the way *victory* and *freedom* are used to justify butchery in the dehumanization process. . . .

[Means goes on to condemn Marxism and other European revolutionary doctrines as no less destructive to Native Americans than capitalism.] There's a rule of thumb which can be applied here. You cannot judge the real nature of a European revolutionary doctrine on the basis of the changes it proposed to make within the European power structure and society. You can only judge it by the effects it will have on non-European peoples. This is because every revolution in European history has served to reinforce Europe's tendencies and abilities to export destruction to other peoples, other cultures, and the environment itself. I defy anyone to point out an example where this is not true. . . . Revolutionary Marxism is committed to even further perpetuation and perfection of the very industrial processes which is destroying us all. It offers only to "redistribute" the results—the money, maybe—of this industrialization to a wider section of the population. It offers to take wealth from the capitalists and pass it around; but in order to do so, Marxism must maintain the industrial system.

I do not believe that capitalism itself is really responsible for the situation in which American Indians have been declared a national sacrifice. No, it is the European tradition; European culture itself is responsible. Marxism is just the latest continuation of this tradition, not a solution to it. . . .

There is another way. There is the traditional Lakota way and the ways of other American Indian peoples. It is the way that knows that humans do not have the right to degrade Mother Earth, that there are forces beyond anything the European mind has conceived, that humans must be in harmony with *all* relations or the relations will eventually eliminate the disharmony. . . .

All European tradition[s], Marxism included, [have] conspired to defy the natural order of all things. Mother Earth has been abused, the powers have been abused, and this cannot go on forever. No theory can alter that simple fact. Mother Earth will retaliate, the whole environment will retaliate, and the abusers will be eliminated. . . . American Indians have been trying to explain this to Europeans for centuries. But . . . Europeans have proven themselves unable to hear. . . . It is only a matter of time until what Europeans call a "major catastrophe of global proportions" will occur. . . .

This leads me back to address those American Indians who are drifting through the universities, the city slums and other European institutions. If you are there to learn to resist the oppressor in accordance with your traditional ways, so be it . . . . But retain your sense of reality. Beware of coming to believe the white world now offers solutions to the problems it confronts us with. Beware, too, of allowing the words of native people to be twisted to the advantage of our enemies. Europe invented the practice of turning words around on themselves. You need only look to the treaties between American Indian peoples and various European governments to know this is true. Draw your strength from who you are. . . . Europeans have long since lost all touch with reality, if ever they were in touch with it. Feel sorry for them if you need to, but be comfortable with who you are as American Indians.

From Russell Means, "Fighting Words on the Future of the Earth," *Mother Jones* 15, no. 10 (December 1980): 22–38. Reprinted with permission of Russell Means.

and supporters had died by 1976, and they were convinced that the FBI had either assisted in the killing or failed to investigate fully the circumstances surrounding them.

The contest between AIM and the FBI grew more desperate in June 1975 when two FBI agents were killed in a shootout with a group of movement activists at Pine Ridge. Both sides disputed the circumstances surrounding the firefight (which also resulted in the death of AIM member Joseph Stuntz). AIM claimed government provocation; the FBI called it an ambush. As at Wounded Knee, the government spared no expense in its pursuit of the alleged murderers. After a wide-ranging manhut, four activists were charged with the agents' deaths; three were brought to trial. Two of the accused were acquitted in 1976, but the third, Leonard Peltier, an Ojibwe man who had been active with AIM in the Pacific Northwest, was convicted in a trial marred by charges of coerced testimony and government misconduct. In 1977 Peltier was sentenced to two consecutive life terms.

One of the most mysterious deaths to occur at Pine Ridge came in the closing days of 1975. At the end of February 1976, the partially decomposed body of a young woman was found in a rural area of the reservation. It was Anna Mae Aquash. She had returned to the East after the 1973 occupation but had been drawn back to AIM, working to raise funds and recruit new members. After the killing of the two FBI agents, she had been detained and questioned. Worried for her own safety, Aquash had disappeared in late 1975, hoping to elude both the government and AIM members who now hinted she might be an FBI informant. After a BIA-hired pathologist announced Aquash had died of exposure, her family won a court order to have her remains exhumed and re-

examined. The second autopsy revealed Aquash had died of a gunshot wound to the back of her head. AIM leaders accused Wilson and the FBI of the murder; others, including Aquash's family and AIM leader Russell Means, claimed that she was killed by fellow activists. In 2003, twenty-eight years after the crime, two former AIM members, John Gresham, a non-Indian Canadian, and Arlo Looking Cloud, a Lakota, were indicted for the crime. Looking Cloud was tried as an accomplice to the murder and convicted in February 2004. Gresham, the alleged murderer, resisted extradition to the United States.

Wilson's counterattacks weakened AIM's support at Pine Ridge, but the Justice Department's prosecution of the organization's leaders was far more effective in breaking up the organization. In the wake of the Wounded Knee occupation, federal officials brought charges against 562 people involved in some way with the incident. The subsequent trials stretched over two years and several Midwestern states, emptying AIM's treasury and absorbing all of its attention. Even when cases were dismissed, as they were in a highly publicized proceeding against Banks and Means in Minneapolis in 1974, the expense and effort involved left AIM severely damaged. The Wounded Knee trials also revealed that the FBI had infiltrated AIM. Most prominently, Douglass Durham, director of security and a close aid to Dennis Banks, announced in 1975 that he had been working for the FBI for two years.

While cleared of charges stemming from the Wounded Knee occupation, Dennis Banks was convicted in 1975 of "inciting" the violence at the Custer County courthouse in 1973. He fled to California and New York, but he ultimately surrendered in 1984 and served eighteen months in a state prison. Means, who was also cleared of federal charges brought against him, was ultimately convicted on charges arising from the Custer "riot" and served a term in a South Dakota prison.

Women and Red Power

One group of activists seemed largely invisible to federal prosecutors. While women had been involved in all of the protests and occupations from the fish-ins onward, few of them became movement leaders or subjects for federal prosecution. Lanada Boyer, a Shoshone-Bannock student from the University of California, Berkeley, had been an important leader at Alcatraz, but as AIM grew more prominent in the Red Power movement, women like her received less attention. Many women charged that the AIM leaders were caught up in the image of themselves as "warriors" and therefore resisted recognizing the work of their female colleagues.

Few women were in public positions during the occupation of the BIA even though a large percentage of the people involved in the takeover were female. At Pine Ridge, older reservation women were a vital part of AIM's support. Sarah Bad Heart Bull, the mother of the man whose murder sparked the protests at the Custer County courthouse, helped lead the demonstration there in early 1973, and several other women—most prominently Gladys Bissonette and Ellen Moves Camp—played a key role in persuading the anti-Wilson forces to occupy Wounded Knee. During the occupation, women were usually assigned to the role of supporting the males charged with defending the village's perimeter. Many women (including Anna Mae Aquash) helped dig defense bunkers and took their turns on patrol, and they resented the assumption that they were only qualified to prepare meals or take care of children and the elderly. Lorelai DeCora, a Lakota woman from Iowa, helped supervise a clinic that treated colds and fevers as well as gunshot wounds. She was assisted by many women, including Connie Martinez, an officer of the Chicano group, La Raza Unida. In March, the African American activist Angela Davis attempted to join the protesters, but was turned away by federal officials.

A member of the American Indian Movement (AIM), left, offers a peace pipe to Kent Frizzell, right, assistant U.S. attorney general, in a tepee at Wounded Knee, S.D., during a ceremony Thursday, April 5, 1973, ending the standoff between AIM and federal authorities. Beside Wallace Black Elk, kneeling, are AIM leaders, from right: Russell Means, Dennis Banks (headband), and Carter Camp (vest). (AP Photo/Jim Mone)

Ironically, the fact that women faced relatively little persecution after the dramatic events of the early 1970s meant that their ranks were not decimated during the aftermath to Wounded Knee. As a consequence, Native women became increasingly prominent in Indian politics during the 1970s. The formation of Women of All Red Nations (WARN) in 1974 by Phyllis Young, a Lakota AIM supporter, and other women was only the first step in this new political activism.

Red Power Declines

The period of intense Red Power activism came to an end in 1978 when a group of veterans of earlier protest movements—Alcatraz alumni, AIM activists, students, and reservation-based critics of the BIA—organized the Longest Walk to affirm their allegiance to traditional Native cultures and to dramatize their common concern for tribal rights. Beginning in San Francisco in the spring and ending in Washington, D.C., in July, the walk lacked the angry edge of earlier protests. Marchers insisted at rallies that they were on a spiritual mission to win the sympathy of the American majority. A final rally drew one thousand people to the Capitol Building to hear leaders call for greater recognition of tribal sovereignty.

The events at Alcatraz, Wounded Knee, and elsewhere in the early 1970s dramatized an ambitious new agenda. Protest leaders focused on the rights and privileges guaranteed in nineteenth-century treaties and thereby raised public awareness—among both Indians and non-Indians—of these issues. As the decade unfolded, however, other groups emerged to extend and broaden the rhetorical claims of Red Power leaders. For example, the National Indian Education Association was formed in 1969 as a forum for Native American teachers and school administrators who were concerned about curricular and school reform. The group became an early advocate of Indian-controlled schools and culturally sensitive texts, and its annual meeting provided a platform to publicize educators' concerns. The Native American Rights Fund, founded in Boulder, Colorado, in 1970 with support from the Ford Foundation, quickly took up the causes of tribes seeking to protect their property and natural resources. Finally, the National Tribal Chairman's Association was formed in 1971. While originally organized with support from the BIA to provide a voice for "responsible" elected tribal leaders, the NTCA refused to follow the government line. The group often criticized occupations and sit-ins, but its leaders were careful to speak out in defense of tribal rights and to express sympathy for frustrated Native Americans who believed their protests were being ignored.

At the same time that new organizations were forming, new publications were providing avenues for Indian writers to reach the public. The American Indian Historical Society, organized by Jeanette Henry and Rupert Costo, published *The Indian Historian* beginning in 1964, while the National Indian Youth Council's lively newsletter, *A.B.C.: Americans Before Columbus,* offered irreverent commentary on national politics. The *American Indian Law Review* began publishing in 1973, reporting on the growing number of court decisions affecting Native Americans, and the following year two academic journals appeared: the *American Indian Quarterly* and the *American Indian Culture and Research Journal.*

More than one thousand Indian journals, newsletters, and newspapers began publishing in the 1970s and 1980s. While many of these were supported by antipoverty grants that had a limited lifetime, this scale of production signaled the beginning of a Native American press community. The American Indian Press Service began operations in 1970, supplying extensive coverage of events to tribal newspapers and often taking a critical stance toward elected leaders. *Akwesasne Notes*, a newspaper launched by Jerry Gambill, an activist at the St. Regis reservation in northern New York in 1969, had the largest circulation during the decade. It attracted nearly eighty thousand readers with its vivid reporting and insurgent tone. In 1974 *Notes* published *Voices from Wounded Knee*, a compilation of pictures and quotations from the occupation that sold tens of thousands of copies and remained in print for many years.

During the 1970s many communities either began or greatly expanded their own newspapers. The *Navajo Times,* begun by the Navajo tribal council in 1959, was the largest of these. It was reorganized as an independent (though subsidized) entity in 1972 and commenced daily publication in 1984. Others in this diverse group of community publications ranged from the *OKC Camp Crier* (1974), published by an intertribal group in Oklahoma City, to the *Tundra Times* (founded in Fairbanks in 1962), to the *Red Cliff News* (1975), the newspaper of the Ojibwe community in Red Cliff, Wisconsin.

VICTORIES IN CONGRESS AND THE COURTS

Between 1970 and 1990 Congress passed more significant Indian legislation and the courts decided more cases involving Native Americans than during any comparable period in American history. The U.S. Supreme Court alone handed down sixty-five Indian law decisions between 1970 and 1985; the lower courts decided dozens more. During this same period, Congress focused more attention on

Native Americans than it had at any time since the 1930s. Some of this activity came in response to highly publicized protests. Other actions were inspired by a series of exposés of conditions on reservations and in urban Indian communities. The first of these came from the Senate Subcommittee on Indian Education, chaired first by Robert Kennedy and, after his assassination in 1968, by his brother Edward. The committee's final report released in 1969 called the nation's efforts to educate Indians "A National Tragedy" and recommended both increased appropriations and greater control by parents and local communities. Five years later in 1974 in the wake of the Wounded Knee occupation, Congress established the American Indian Policy Review Commission to investigate all aspects of federal policy. While overshadowed by the events surrounding President Nixon's resignation, the bipartisan commission and its largely Native American staff produced a list of more than two hundred recommendations for change.

The structure of congressional committees and the nature of policymaking in the 1970s and 1980s also influenced the pace of legislation. In the past, major changes in Indian policy began when the Interior Department made a recommendation to Congress. In the 1970s this pattern was reversed. This shift occurred both because of the decline in the Indian Office's stature within the federal government and because congressional activists seized the initiative.

Both houses of Congress reorganized their approach to Indian affairs. In the House of Representatives, Morris Udall of Arizona chaired the Committee on Interior and Insular Affairs from 1977 to 1989 and took personal command of legislation affecting Native Americans. He established close ties to Native American leaders and intervened frequently to win approval of key legislation. In the Senate, James Abourezk, an activist South Dakota attorney whose Lebanese immigrant parents had once operated a store on the Rosebud reservation, became chairman of the Senate subcommittee overseeing Indian legislation. Abourezk's personal engagement produced a torrent of new legislation. In 1977 he also succeeded in winning approval for the reestablishment of a standing committee on Indian Affairs, with himself as chair. Following the South Dakotan's departure from the Senate in 1979, Daniel Inouye, a Japanese-American from Hawaii, joined the committee, becoming chair in 1987. Inouye was the first nonwhite person to hold the committee chairmanship position and the first in nearly a century who was not from a state with a large Native American population. The tenor of the congressional committees changed even more dramatically in 1986 when Ben Nighthorse Campbell, a Northern Cheyenne, was elected to Congress. Campbell became a senator in 1992, assuming the chairmanship of the Indian Affairs Committee in 1997.

Congressional Reforms

The first significant congressional victory of the 1970s was the Alaska Native Claims Settlement Act (ANCSA). This measure emerged initially because the nature and extent of the Native titles to lands in Alaska had never been defined by Congress. The United States never signed treaties with the Indians, Inuits, and Aleuts of the territory, and neither the Organic Act of 1884 (setting up a territorial government) nor the statehood act passed in 1959 had defined which areas in the state would be recognized as "Indian country." When Alaska joined the union, the federal government had promised the state it would receive title to 102.5 million acres of the public lands there, but no administration had specified the boundaries of this mammoth grant.

By the late 1960s, the ambiguity of land titles in Alaska was producing an economic and political crisis. The discovery of large oil and gas deposits suddenly made it essential that federal authorities define land titles (and terms of ownership) for every corner of the state. At the same time, Alaska state officials were unilaterally laying claim to areas they wished to set aside for future development. The Alaska Federation of Natives, an organization formed in 1966 to represent Native interests, challenged many of these state claims, charging that they violated the customary titles of Native villages and tribal groups. In an effort to avoid a confrontation between Natives and the state, the secretary of the interior ordered a halt to any further state acquisition of public land. Faced with this standoff, the contending parties turned to Congress for a settlement.

All three groups—state officials, the Interior Department, and the Alaska Federation of Natives—agreed that a settlement should set aside land for Native Americans and offer tribal groups compensation for previous losses. They differed on the amounts to be offered and the nature of the Native title. Ultimately, the persistence of the AFN leadership and their Washington lobbyists (among them former Supreme Court Justice Arthur Goldberg), together with pressure from energy companies to reach a settlement quickly, produced the final bill. It granted Alaska's Native people 40 million acres of land and $962 million in compensation in exchange for all remaining claims to other parts of the state. According to the law, the 40 million acres would be divided among twelve regional corporations and a thirteenth corporation created for nonresident Natives. The corporations would manage resources in their areas and invest the compensation funds in new businesses. The residents of each region would be stockholders in their corporation.

The second major piece of legislation passed in the 1970s, the Indian Self-Determination and Educational Assistance Act, was signed into law by President Gerald Ford in January 1975. The act extended the self-determination concept first described during Lyndon Johnson's War on Poverty to all Indian programs. It declared that the federal government had an "obligation" to assure "maximum Indian participation in the direction of . . . federal services to Indian communities."

The new law directed the Interior Department and the Department of Health and Human Services to respond to tribal requests by entering into contracts that would permit tribes to "plan, conduct and administer" any program currently authorized for an Indian community. It also contained a special section outlining the process under which tribes could form school boards that would contract with the BIA for the education of the community's children. The law even provided for federal grants to tribes to assist them with planning projected contracts and with developing staffs to administer them. Theoretically at least, it would now be possible for a tribe to administer every federally funded program on its reservation.

Almost immediately, the leadership of the National Congress of American Indians and the National Tribal Chairmen's Association complained that the self-determination act was being undermined by "paternalistic" BIA administrators and stingy congressmen. They charged that agency bureaucrats insisted on unrealistic professional standards and cumbersome planning documents. Despite these objections, however, the new law had a profound impact on reservation life. In 1980, five years after its passage, 370 tribes had contracted for $200 million worth of federal services. The following year the BIA made 480 separate grants to tribes that were engaged in planning for new contracts.

The self-determination act marked a fundamental shift in both policy and the dynamics of reservation life. The new law allowed local tribal councils to take responsibility for housing, health care, education, and law enforcement. And equally significant, the proliferation of tribally administered programs moved the center of power in Native communities away from the local BIA superintendent and toward tribal councils.

This shift in power was particularly meaningful in the area of health care as protests arose during the 1970s against the sterilization of Native American women at government clinics. Publicized first by Constance Redbird Pinkerton-Uri, an Indian Health Service physician, this disturbing practice attracted national attention and, with Senator Aboureszk's assistance, the subject of a Government Accounting Office study. This study revealed that between 1973 and 1976, 3,406 women, or 3 percent of all Indian women of childbearing age, had been sterilized. Women's health became a central concern of the new, tribally administered clinics, as well as of Women of All Red Nations (WARN).

After the passage of the self-determination act, reservation governments gradually took control of the federal dollars being spent in their communities. Tribal governments began to function as local governments with both the resources and the legal standing to exercise significant control over schools, resources, and social services. The extent of this new authority became particularly evident at the end of the 1970s when Senator Aboureszk's new Indian Affairs Committee produced four major pieces of legislation that helped institutionalize the power of tribal governments.

In August 1978, Congress approved a joint resolution declaring it to be national policy to

Janine Pease, Founding President of the Crow Tribe's Little Big Horn College Beginning in 1980 with a tiny budget that often caused her to mop classroom floors herself, Janine Pease drew faculty and staff to an enterprise that soon became the envy of the nation's more than two-dozen tribal colleges.

"protect and preserve for American Indians their inherent right of freedom to believe, express, and exercise the traditional religions of the American Indian, Eskimo, Aleut and Native Hawaiians." The American Indian Religious Freedom Act (AIRFA) promised protection to Native people seeking access to sacred sites, and it assured them that their ceremonies and their use of sacred objects would be undisturbed. The resolution did not specify exactly which traditional practices would be protected, nor did it explain how far federal authorities should go in protecting access to sacred sites (questions that

would later be the subject of Supreme Court decisions), but it did constitute a new benchmark in public respect for Native American beliefs.

Two months after the approval of AIRFA, Congress adopted the Tribally Controlled Community College Assistance Act. A decade earlier, in 1968, funds from the Office of Economic Opportunity had enabled the Navajos to open a tribally controlled grammar school at Rough Rock, New Mexico. The tribe opened the Navajo Community College in 1969, and in 1971 a special congressional appropriation had enabled the tribe to build a permanent campus for the new school in Tsaile, Arizona. The 1978 Tribal College Act promised federal assistance to any tribally chartered postsecondary educational institution that was governed by a majority-Indian board of trustees and organized to "meet the needs of Indians." While federal appropriations never reached the levels originally projected in 1978 and tribal colleges often found themselves constrained by the requirements of accrediting agencies and donors, the new law signaled a remarkable commitment to the development of reservation institutions. By 1990, more than twenty tribally chartered colleges were operating on reservations from Michigan to Arizona.

In November 1978, Congress approved the American Indian Child Welfare Act. Concern for the large number of Native American children who were being transferred to non-Indian homes had been growing for more than a decade. The Indian Office had started encouraging the transfer of children to foster and adoptive parents in the 1950s on the assumption that this practice was benevolent; government officials believed it would be preferable for an Indian child to be raised in a middle-lass white home rather than a poor Native American one. By the late 1960s this widespread belief encouraged state welfare agencies to add their placement services to those offered by the BIA. The result, Senator Aboureszk declared, was a pattern of "unchecked, abusive child removal." One study made public in 1974 indicated that 25 to 35 percent of all Indian children were currently separated from their families and placed in foster or adoptive homes or sent to government boarding schools.

In the 1960s Congress was untroubled by the policy of placing Native American children with white families, but in the 1970s, amidst growing sympathy for tribal governments and tribal traditions, it was not difficult for Aboureszk to persuade his colleagues to act. Despite opposition from the Mormon Church, which operated an active adoption program on several reservations, the American Indian Child Welfare Act won widespread support. The new law declared that it would now be "the policy of this Nation . . . to promote the stability and security of Indian tribes and families." It implemented this policy by granting tribes exclusive jurisdiction over child custody proceedings involving their tribal members. The law also stipulated that Indian family members could intervene in state court proceedings in an effort to keep adopted children in Native American households. Tribes were authorized to create child and family service programs on reservations and "Indian organizations" were granted similar powers in urban areas.

The final major victory in this period of congressional activism came in 1980 when President Jimmy Carter signed the Maine Indian Claims Settlement Act. The new law was drafted in response to a court challenge the Passamaquoddy and Penobscot tribes and the Houlton Band of Maliseet Indians had raised to nineteenth century state land purchases that had been made without congressional approval. (The Trade and Intercourse Acts first approved by Congress in 1790 had stipulated that no state could purchase Indian land without federal approval.) The tribes' lawsuit had created turmoil in Maine because it called local property titles into question, threatening both the real estate market and the ability of local governments to issue bonds to finance their operations. Rather than embark on an extended legal battle against the tribes, the Carter administration decided to negotiate. The act's provisions reflected that negotiation. In exchange for the tribes' agreement to drop their lawsuit, the United States granted them $27 million and created a $54.5 million fund from which they could draw to make land purchases.

As the 1970s ended and the 1980s began, it became clear that Indian tribes had developed an entirely new relationship with congressional lawmakers. No longer viewed as relics of the past or barely competent advisory bodies, tribal councils and their leaders were now partners in policymaking. The extent of this shift in congressional outlook was made clear both in the new legislation

that was passed in the 1970s and 1980s and in the legislators' reversal of several termination decisions that had been made in the 1950s and 1960s. In addition to restoring the Menominees and Klamaths to tribal status in 1973 and 1986, respectively, Congress reestablished formal ties between the Indian Office and the Siletz of Oregon; the Modocs, Wyandots, Peorias, and Ottawas of Oklahoma; the Paiute bands of Utah; the Cow Creek Band of Umpquas of Oregon; the Poncas of Oklahoma; and the Catawbas of South Carolina. In 1978 Congress also authorized the establishment of a Federal Acknowledgment Project, a program that by 2000 had resulted in the recognition of the Jamestown Clallam Tribe of Washington, the Wampanoags of Martha's Vineyard, Massachusetts (now Aquinnah Wampanoags), and thirteen other groups. (Fifteen additional groups were denied recognition during the same period and 55 other cases remained under review. In all, 250 different groups expressed an interest in gaining federal recognition between 1978 and 2001.)

By 1980, legislators assumed that tribal cultures deserved protection and they viewed tribal governments as the logical organizations to administer services to Native Americans. They fashioned legislation in consultation with tribal officials and the leaders of national Indian organizations, and they viewed Indian affairs as a permanent federal responsibility. Representatives in Congress were no longer interested in "getting out of the Indian business," as their colleagues had been a generation before.

Victories in Court

During the 1980s, one prominent legal scholar who reviewed the remarkable string of recent legal victories noted that the courts had come to see treaties as "real promises" that, when ratified, had become "real laws." He added, "My sense is that most judges cannot shake that." In the 1970s and 1980s federal courts took treaty "promises" seriously and were generally sympathetic to tribal governments. The first and most dramatic of these decisions came in the state of Washington in 1974, when District Court Judge George Boldt responded to a petition from a group of fourteen Puget Sound tribes by declaring that these groups were entitled to harvest as

Walter Echo Hawk After growing up in the Pawnee community of Oklahoma and attending Oklahoma State University, Walter Echo Hawk received his law degree in 1973, one of the first graduates of the University of New Mexico Law School's Indian Law program. For most of the 1980s and 1990s, Echo Hawk was a senior attorney at the Native American Rights Fund, representing many tribes and playing a leading role in the development of national policies affecting American Indian religious freedom and the respectful treatment of cultural property and human remains.

much as 50 percent of the salmon that migrated through the state's waters.

In 1854 and 1855, the leaders of Washington's Indian tribes and territorial governor Isaac Stevens had signed a series of six treaties that granted land to the Americans while reserving for the Indians both reservations and the right to "fish in common with the citizens of the Territory." The tribes agreed to this exchange in large part because they de-

pended for their livelihood on the astonishing runs of salmon and steelhead that passed through the rivers of Puget Sound and the Columbia River basin. Access to these fish was more important to the Washington tribes than the size of their tribal domains. In the ensuing century, state encroachment on the Indians' fishing grounds, together with the growth of the commercial fishing industry, had reduced the tribes' share of this extraordinary resource. The Indians protested the erosion of their rights and the courts had generally sympathized with their pleas, but until the Boldt decisions no one could say exactly what it meant to fish "in common" with other Washingtonians. Everyone had agreed that tribal members could continue to fish from traditional sites within the boundaries of their new, small reservations, but the treaties had not indicated what should happen if the harvest of fish was reduced by commercial fishing (as it had been in the early years of the twentieth century) or eliminated by the construction of hydroelectric dams (as had occurred beginning in the 1930s). And the treaties had not indicated clearly who would regulate Indian fishers—the tribes or the state government? The fish-in protests of the 1960s—in which Native Americans purposefully violated state fish and game laws—created tests of these questions. Following a series of inconclusive rulings in both Oregon and Washington, federal authorities and the fourteen tribes brought all their complaints to Judge Boldt and asked for a definitive judgment.

After nearly four years of testimony and study, Boldt issued a ruling that linked the fishing rights controversy to the principles of Indian law and policy that had emerged in the 1960s and 1970s. He pointed out, for example, that the nineteenth-century treaties were not grants made by the United States *to* the Indians "but a grant of rights *from them*, and a reservation of those [rights] not granted." This basic insight—an insight which had been pointed out by earlier judges and had formed the basis for the doctrine of "reserved sovereignty"—made it clear that the privileges granted by the treaty should more properly be understood as treaty *rights*. "The mere passage of time has not eroded, and cannot erode, the rights guaranteed by solemn treaties," Boldt declared. While acknowledging that the state might issue regulations for conservation purposes, Judge Boldt ruled that the Indians' *right* to their share of the annual harvest would be protected by federal authorities and that the tribes were generally not subject to Washington's fishing laws.

Boldt's decision stunned Washington's non-Indian politicians and commercial fishermen. Protesters challenged the ruling in court, hanged the judge in effigy, and even distributed bumper stickers that read "Nuts to Boldt." More worrisome, state officials stirred memories of southern resistance to school desegregation by threatening to ignore the federal court's ruling. Their actions forced Judge Boldt to assert the national government's authority on behalf of the tribes—he issued a court order mandating the Indians' portion of the annual harvest. In 1978, after years of state resistance and the failure of several compromise attempts, the U.S. Supreme Court agreed to review Boldt's decision. The state urged the high court to overturn what they felt was an unwarranted federal intervention into local affairs, but the justices refused. Their ruling, issued on July 2, 1979, settled the matter permanently: "In our view," the six-member majority wrote, "the purpose and language of the treaties are unambiguous; they secure the Indians' right to take a share of each run of fish that passes through tribal fishing areas." After nearly a century of struggle, the Washington tribes were victorious.

The Washington fishing rights decision became an important precedent for similar cases brought before the federal courts in later years. In the nineteenth century, Ojibwe bands in Michigan, Wisconsin, and Minnesota had made agreements with the United States that resembled those in Washington Territory. The Indians granted land to white settlers in exchange for a recognition of their right and to continue their traditional hunting and fishing practices. As in the Northwest, the expansion of non-Indian settlements and an increasingly aggressive commercial and sport fishing industry gradually diminished the Indians' ability to exercise their treaty rights. The tribes refused to surrender their position, however, and during the 1960s had become increasingly assertive about their rights. These Great Lakes challenges began to come before the federal courts in the wake of the Washington fishing rights campaign. The Midwestern tribes were successful first in Michigan in 1979 and later in Wisconsin and Minnesota.

Victories in the fishing rights cases encouraged other tribal leaders, because they underscored the enduring power of the "promises" embedded in treaties and other federal pronouncements. During the 1980s, the Supreme Court recognized the power of these promises in two significant land issues. First, the justices sided with the Sioux and other signatories of the 1868 Fort Laramie Treaty in their complaint against the United States for the unlawful seizure of the Black Hills that had been carried out by a fraudulent treaty in 1877 (see Chapter 13). Capping a legal struggle that had begun nearly a century earlier, the Court majority declared that the United States had "an obligation . . . to make just compensation" for the land it had taken. Because the tribes involved rejected the Court's $100 million award—they insisted on a return of the hills rather than a cash payment—their landmark victory produced a stalemate rather than a resolution of the dispute. Nevertheless, the Court's decision represented a major vindication of a tribe's tenacious struggle for justice.

Land claims brought by the Oneidas against the state of New York were also acted upon favorably by the courts during the 1980s even though this dispute also remained unresolved. The Oneida claim arose from land purchases made by the state of New York in the early nineteenth century that (like similar purchases in Maine) violated the Trade and Intercourse Act. After a preliminary Supreme Court ruling in 1974 recognized the Court's responsibility to hear the tribe's complaint, the case returned to the lower courts for trial. It made its way to the high court again in 1985 when the justices ruled on the substance of the issues raised. The most significant aspect of this later ruling was the Court's declaration that treaty rights do not expire. The Supreme Court announced that when Indians sought the enforcement of federally guaranteed property rights, no time limit exists. The Court urged the state to negotiate a settlement with the Indians, but New York authorities were reluctant to act and the claim remained unresolved.

While the Supreme Court of the 1980s recognized fishing rights and land titles that were guaranteed in treaties, it was not so decisive when the "rights" claimed by tribes were not spelled out precisely in official agreements. In the area of water rights, for example, the courts had held from 1908 onward that when tribes granted land to the United States in a treaty while retaining specific areas for themselves, one should assume that the tribe also retained a right to enough water to make their tribal lands productive—even if water rights were not mentioned specifically in official documents. This principle of *implied* water rights was vitally important in the arid West where non-Indian settlers and local governments operating upstream often tried to divert water before it reached reservation communities. In the 1970s and 1980s the federal courts reaffirmed these tribal claims to water. In a series of decisions beginning in 1963, the Supreme Court insisted that Native American communities along the Colorado River be included when that watershed's resources were being divided between Arizona and California. In 1981 the Court also upheld the rights of Paiutes at Nevada's Pyramid Lake to retain sufficient water to maintain their fisheries.

But as litigation over the allocation of water grew more intense—tribes filed more than fifty lawsuits over water rights between 1970 and 1990—the courts became increasingly receptive to state pleas that it intervene in the water allocation process on behalf of non-Indians. Particularly worrisome for the tribes was a 1976 decision entitled *Colorado River Water Conservation District v. U.S.*, which recognized a state's interest in regulating water flowing through a reservation. Following that decision, the federal courts became more deferential to state interests even though they insisted they had not abandoned their role as guardians of tribal resources. Worried enough about the Supreme Court's commitment, many tribes negotiated agreements with state authorities rather than take their chances in court. In the Southwest, for example, the Tohono O'odhams and the Ak-Chin community decided to negotiate settlements with the state of Arizona that guaranteed the tribes specific amounts of water in exchange for the withdrawal of their legal claims.

The pattern of federal protection and state encroachment was also evident when tribes exercised the powers of their newly reinvigorated governments. With some significant exceptions, federal courts were willing to recognize the Indian community's desire to operate tribal governments without interference from state and federal authorities. The first clear statement of this position came in 1973 when the Supreme Court struck down Arizona's attempt to collect state income taxes from Navajos living on their reservation. Writing for the majority, Justice Thurgood Marshall declared that the recognition of the Navajo reservation by the United States in a treaty document "was meant to establish the land as within the exclusive sovereignty of the Navajos under general federal supervision." The courts applied this principle of "exclusive sovereignty" in a number of arenas, upholding tribal taxes on businesses operating on reservations, recognizing the jurisdiction of tribal courts over non-Indians in personal injury and other civil matters, and permitting tribes to regulate reservation hunting and fishing by non-Indians.

The most successful defense of the power of tribal governments came in 1978 when a case arising from the Santa Clara Pueblo reached the Supreme Court. Julia Martinez, a member of the pueblo, had sued her tribe for sex discrimination because it refused to enroll her children as members solely because their father was a Navajo. (Because the children of men who married women from outside the Pueblo were not denied membership in the tribe, Martinez claimed her children were being discriminated against by a sexist tribal law.) In its decision, the high court ruled against Martinez, noting that like all sovereign governments, tribes could not be sued without the existence of a specific law authorizing such action. While noting that Congress had the power to intervene to require tribes to follow all civil rights laws and to permit suits based on gender discrimination, the Court held that Congress had never passed legislation authorizing such suits. Until Congress acted, the Court declared, tribes possessed the same immunity "traditionally enjoyed by sovereign powers."

Ironically the Supreme Court dealt tribal governments the greatest blow of the modern era within a few weeks of announcing its decision regarding Julia Martinez. In March 1978, the justices decided that tribal governments do not have jurisdiction over non-Indians who violate criminal laws within an Indian reservation. The case arose in the state of Washington in August 1973, after Mark Oliphant, a young white man, was arrested by Port Madison tribal policemen for assault and battery. Oliphant, one of thousands of non-Indians attending the reservation's Chief Seattle Days celebration, quickly applied to the federal courts for a writ of habeas corpus, claiming that the tribal law-and-order code did not apply to him. Even though the Oliphant case provoked intense interest from anti-Indian activists and was addressed by the lower courts during the Washington fishing rights controversy, both the local district judge and justices of the appeals court denied the young man's claim, noting that the tribe's criminal jurisdiction was the same as "any governing power." These courts turned aside Oliphant's claim that he had no voice in tribal affairs by pointing out that this situation would also exist if he were arrested for speeding in California or Idaho. But when the Oliphant case reached the Supreme Court, a majority of the justices reached a different conclusion. Led by future Chief Justice William Rehnquist, the majority asserted that tribes were not like "any governing power" but were simply creatures of Congress that exercised limited power. The Court's decision in *Oliphant* turned the concept of "reserved sovereignty"—a position first outlined during the Collier era and followed with increasing regularity by the courts in the 1960s and 1970s—on its head. Instead of asserting that tribes were "sovereigns" that had all the powers they had not surrendered, Rehnquist declared tribal governments had *no* powers except those given to them by Congress. Tribes, the majority opinion ruled, could not wield powers that were "inconsistent with their status."

While tribes continued to win victories in the aftermath of the *Oliphant* decision, political pressures fueled by non-Indian resentment of the tribes' hunting and fishing rights victories, together with the increasingly conservative cast of the Supreme Court, raised concern among tribal leaders and their attorneys. Treaty language continued to be persuasive in many instances, but when controversial cases engaged issues beyond the specific language of a treaty or placed Native Americans in conflict with non-Indians on issues arising outside the boundaries of their reservations, Native Americans often found they had the support of only a minority of the high court's justices.

In 1988, for example, the Supreme Court was asked to review an appeals court decision that barred the United States Forest Service from building a logging road through an isolated part of the Six Rivers national forest in northern California. The ban had been sought by a group of Native Americans who claimed that because the proposed road (called the GO Road) entered areas used for traditional rituals, its construction would violate the American Indian Religious Freedom Act's prohibition against government actions that disrupted the practice of Native religions. Before siding with the Indians, the appeals court had balanced the GO Road's destructive impact against its "compelling" value to the economy of the Northwest. The appeals court justices concluded that the logging road's marginal economic significance was less important than the plaintiffs' ability to practice their religion without disruption.

The Supreme Court's decision in the GO Road case (officially *Lyng v. Northwest Indian Cemetery Protective Association*) demonstrated how vulnerable Native Americans' rights could be. Without a treaty title to the land in question and with only the broad language of the Religious Freedom Act to support their position, the Native American plaintiffs argued simply that the GO Road would make it impossible for them to follow their traditional religious rituals. The Court majority was unmoved. The justices chose instead to see the case as a confrontation between federal authority and a group of citizens who wished to have "a veto over public programs." From this perspective the Court would not stop the Forest Service construction program: "Whatever rights the Indians may have," the high court's decision concluded, "those rights do not divest the Government of its right to use what is after all, *its* land." In an angry dissent, Justice William Brennan charged that the Court's decision reduced American Indian religious freedom to "nothing more than the right to believe that their religion would be destroyed." He charged that the Court had made "a mockery" of the 1978 religious freedom act.

A second major defeat for Indian religious freedom claims occurred two years after the GO Road decision. In 1990 the Supreme Court upheld the state of Oregon's denial of unemployment benefits to Alfred Smith because Mr. Smith, a Klamath Indian, had been fired from his job for using peyote at a meeting of the Native American Church. Under Oregon law, workers fired for "misconduct" were ineligible for unemployment payments. As in the GO Road case, Mr. Smith's complaint did not arise from events on a reservation and were not based on treaty guarantees. Smith argued that he was being penalized for the "free exercise" of his religion, a right guaranteed under the First Amendment. Justice Antonin Scalia, appointed to the Court by Ronald Reagan in 1986, wrote the majority opinion that began by dismissing peyote as "a drug." Scalia insisted that recognizing the Native American Church's use of peyote would be "courting anarchy." Writing for a public increasingly concerned with the national "war on drugs," Scalia concluded that the nation could not "afford the luxury" of exempting Alfred Smith from Oregon's drug laws.

As insensitive as the Rehnquist Court could be with regard to Indian issues, it was not always hostile to broad assertions of Native American rights. Most notably in 1987, the Court (with Rehnquist in the majority) decided *California v. Cabazon Band of Mission Indians*, a case arising from the state of California's attempt to control bingo games sponsored by Indian tribes. In the 1970s the Florida Seminoles had been the first tribe to hold bingo games. When their operations survived legal challenges (the courts declared games of chance to be "civil activities" that tribes could sponsor without accepting state regulation), other tribes quickly followed suit. Because California was the first state to attempt to regulate Indian gaming with criminal statutes (and because Congress, in Public Law 280, had extended California's criminal jurisdiction to Indian communities; see Chapter 16), state authorities there were optimistic that they would prevail in the courts. After several police raids on Indian gaming halls in San Diego and Riverside counties in the early 1980s, the Cabazon and Morongo bands filed suit in federal court.

In February 1987, the Supreme Court ruled in favor of the Cabazon and Morongo plaintiffs, noting the importance of respecting Indian sovereignty and the "overriding goal" of promoting "tribal self-sufficiency and economic development." The same Court that worried that the exercise of Indian religious rights might produce "anarchy" viewed the popular and profitable Indian gambling enterprises as an acceptable form of tribal sovereignty. Congress followed this decision by passing the Indian Gaming Regulatory Act in 1988. The new law established ground rules for tribal gaming operations as well as procedures for states and tribes to follow when negotiating agreements between themselves regarding oversight and regulation.

SOVEREIGNTY ON THE GROUND

During the 1970s and 1980s, Native American activism created a new language for the discussion of Indian affairs. The struggles over Indian education, fishing rights, gambling, and dozens of other issues created an environment in which tribes could imagine the restoration of much of their power and authority and Native American people could aspire to a level of cultural freedom and political influence they had not enjoyed in 150 years. But as a new policy structure began to emerge in the 1970s, Native American communities faced an ongoing set of daily concerns—economic development, political stability, and cultural renewal—that threatened to undermine or destroy the goal of self-determination. These persistent problems hampered tribal communities as they struggled to implement a modern version of their historic sovereign status.

Economic Development

In the 1970s, every tribal government was concerned with reviving its economy and creating jobs for its members. While conditions varied from region to region, tribes faced the common tasks of creating an economic infrastructure in communities that had been neglected for decades and of fostering business growth for people whose local resources had long since been seized and exploited by outsiders. In the arid West, for example, large-scale mechanized farms and ranches had replaced the tiny homesteads that had dotted the prairies in the nineteenth century when the government had dreamed of making Native Americans into independent yeomen. Over the course of the twentieth century most communally owned tribal lands had been either purchased or leased by non-Indians. By 1970, only 2 percent of Native Americans were farmers, and few of these men and women had access to the capital necessary to buy the machinery, hybrid seed, and quality livestock that were essential for modern agricultural operations. The Ak-Chin community of Tohono O'odhams and Pimas constituted one noteworthy exception to this pattern. By agreeing to give up some of its treaty claims to water in Arizona, this group was able to raise sufficient capital to cultivate high-grade cotton on thousands of acres of tribal land. But most

---

American Indian and Alaska Native Population by Tribe: 2000

This table shows data for American Indian and Alaska Native tribes alone or in combination of tribes or races. Respondents who identified themselves as American Indian or Alaska Native were asked to report their enrolled or principal tribe. Data shown here reflect the written tribal entries reported on the questionnaire. Some of the entries (for example, Iroquois, Sioux, Colorado River, and Flathead) represent several reservations.

American Indian and Alaska Native Tribe	Number	American Indian and Alaska Native Tribe	Number
Total persons[1]	4,119,301	Paiute	13,532
Apache	96,833	Pima	11,493
Blackfeet	85,750	Potawatomi	25,595
Cherokee	729,533	Pueblo	74,085
Cheyenne	18,204	Puget Sound Salish	14,631
Chickasaw	38,351	Seminole	27,431
Chippewa	149,669	Shoshone	12,026
Choctaw	158,774	Sioux	153,360
Colville	9,393	Tohono O'odham	20,087
Comanche	19,376	United Houma Nation	8,713
Cree	7,734	Ute	10,385
Creek	71,310	Yakama	10,851
Crow	13,394	Yaqui	22,412
Delaware	16,341	Yuman	8,976
Iroquois	80,822	Alaskan Athabascan	18,838
Kiowa	12,242	Aleut	10,548
Latin American Indian	180,940	Eskimo	54,761
Lumbee	57,868	Tlingit-Haida	22,365
Menominee	9,840		
Navajo	298,197		
Osage	15,897		
Ottawa	10,677		

[1] Includes other tribes not listed here and all people who reported at least some of their racial ancestry as Native American. Note that 2.5 million people listed their principal racial identity as Native American.
Source: U.S. Census Bureau, The American Indian and Alaska Native Population: 2000, Census 2000 Brief (C2KBR/01-15), February 2002.

---

tribes were not so fortunate. In 1990 the Interior Department reported that 58 percent of Indian farms were smaller than 140 acres and that each generated less than $10,000 annually in sales.

In other businesses, the story was essentially the same: tribes lacked the resources to develop modern fishing fleets, mechanized mining operations, or manufacturing plants that would enable them to compete with well-financed white neighbors. Mining on Indian land was typically carried out by large corporations that leased tracts of reservation land. On the Navajo reservation in the 1980s, for example, the Peabody Coal Company employed 850 tribal members in surface mines, but paid royalties of less than $0.50 per ton on coal worth $21 a ton. In the Pacific Northwest, Indian-owned fishing boats competed with local corporations as well as with giant Russian and Japanese trawlers that could capture and process fish far out in the Pacific.

Several tribes found that tourism provided an alternative to farming, fishing, or leasing their lands to energy developers. Arizona's Mescalero Apaches and the Confederated Tribes of the Warm Springs

Reservation in Oregon, for example, used federal antipoverty funds to build inns and cultural centers on their reservations. Between 1967 and 1978 the Commerce Department's Economic Development Administration made sixty-three grants totaling $61 million for such projects. In this way the tribes were able to develop a set of well-paying jobs and launch businesses that did not threaten the reservation environment. Unfortunately, despite the publicity that accompanied successful operations such as the White Mountain Apaches' ski resort, tourism proved to be a high-risk enterprise. It seemed that for every success story, such as the Swinomish tribe's marina on Puget Sound, there was at least one abandoned project, such as the Standing Rock tribe's Chief Gall Lodge. Constructed on the banks of the Missouri River in the early 1970s, the lodge steadily lost money and was closed in 1977.

By 1980 it was clear that despite the tribes' growing legal and political power, their governments could do little to alter the economic circumstances created by allotment and decades of leasing and BIA paternalism. Most tribal governments were dependent on congressional appropriations or private investment capital from outside their community. Indian leaders might be successful lobbyists for policy reform in Washington, D.C., but their followers continued to migrate to cities in search of work. As a consequence, the percentage of the population living away from reservations continued to rise; in 1990 at least half of the 1.8 million Native Americans counted by federal census takers lived in cities—an absolute number higher than the entire Indian population of the United States in 1960. Only a quarter of the national Native American population actually lived on an Indian reservation.

Reservation leaders continued to draw on federal antipoverty funds to develop local businesses. During the 1960s and 1970s economic development grants fueled the construction of nearly fifty tribal industrial parks (plots of land with water, sewer, and electrical service that were expected to draw investment to the reservations like magnets), as well as individual tribal enterprises: the Bighorn Carpet Mill (which operated on the Crow reservation from 1968 to 1974), a Blackfeet pencil factory, and a Navajo enterprise that manufactured tennis shoes in Mexican Hat, New Mexico. Between 1966 and

1979, the Economic Development Administration spent $500 million on such projects.

While the Blackfeet pencil factory continued as a successful enterprise for many years, few other businesses survived the economic upheavals of the 1970s or overcame cultural barriers that prevented rural Native Americans from becoming successful factory workers. And despite the tribes' ability to attract development funds to their communities, Indians found it difficult to sustain their operations through economic hard times. In 1975, for example, an assembly plant operated on the Navajo reservation by the Fairchild Semiconductor Corporation responded to declining profits by laying off 140 reservation workers. When Navajos protested the reductions and a group of activists occupied the Fairchild factory, the company simply announced it would close its facility and leave the reservation.

But some antipoverty programs were successful. In central Mississippi, the determined chairman of the Choctaws, Phillip Martin, managed to attract corporate clients to a government-financed industrial park. The tribe built its twenty-acre park in 1973 with a $150,000 grant from the Economic Development Administration; in 1978 a second grant financed Chata Enterprise's first business venture. A tribal corporation, Chata Enterprises contracted to buy materials for automobile components from a subsidiary of General Motors with the understanding that the automaker would buy back the completed parts once the Choctaws had assembled them. With firm management and a steady supply of customers, Chata Enterprises turned a profit and began to grow. The company employed fifty-seven people in 1979; by the mid-1990s Chata Enterprises, with more than nine hundred employees, was one of the largest employers in Mississippi. Growth and profitability enabled the tribe to borrow money for new plants, tribal housing, and a shopping center. The Mississippi Choctaws' success demonstrated the importance of strong leadership as well as an accessible location and fortuitous timing—their tribal businesses profited from the economic resurgence of the 1980s.

During the 1970s and 1980s economic development projects based on the development of tribal manufacturing enterprises often ran counter to the shift in the national economy toward service industries. In the field of energy development, however, the tribes benefited from a national energy crisis and a rapid rise in prices. In this atmosphere, Native Americans were often able to translate their rising political power into economic success.

In the early 1970s, the rise of the OPEC oil cartel and the 1973 fuel shortage focused public attention on national energy resources. Tribal leaders learned that more than a third of the nation's uranium and 30 percent of its western coal reserves lay beneath reservation lands. Tribes with oil and gas reserves such as the Oklahoma Osages and New Mexico's Jicarilla Apaches had long relied on leases with energy companies to supplement other sources of income, but relatively few Native American coal and uranium reserves had been exploited.

Several tribes began to assert themselves in the mineral leasing process. In 1973 the Northern Cheyenne Tribal Council canceled all mining permits on its reservation. That same year tribes at the Fort Berthold agency declared a moratorium on future oil, gas, and coal development. In 1975 the Montana Crows filed suit against the Department of the Interior, charging that the government had signed away their resources for "quick sale" prices.

This discontent soon coalesced into united action. In 1974 twenty-six northern Plains tribes began meeting to devise ways of wielding more control over their energy resources. The following year the Plains groups, joined by the Navajos and other energy tribes from the Southwest (Hopi, Laguna Pueblo, Acoma Pueblo, and others) as well as a number of other western tribes (including the Uintah and Ouray Utes, Yakamas, and the Nez Percés of Idaho) gathered in Washington, D.C., to consider how to help one another counter the power of the energy companies. In Washington, they met with Ladonna Harris, a Comanche who had earlier founded Americans for Indian Opportunity, a group that had been working to promote Native economic development. Harris galvanized the group by declaring that Indian tribes were the "biggest private owners of energy in the U.S." She persuaded the delegates to form a new organization—Council of Energy Resource Tribes (CERT)—and to lobby the new Department of Energy for assistance.

Despite objections from the Bureau of Indian Affairs, a seed grant from the U.S. Department of Energy—and the founders' own enthusiasm—enabled the CERT tribes to form an effective organization. CERT staff members compiled accurate information about the tribes' energy resources and developed model leasing agreements that maximized the tribal role in energy development. The organization's leaders, particularly Navajo tribal chairman Peter MacDonald, who served as president of CERT from 1976 to 1982, helped revise the laws governing reservation leasing so tribes would play a larger role in negotiating more lucrative contracts with energy developers. By 1982 the tribes were earning nearly $400 million annually from royalties. As the energy boom began to fade, however, income from oil and coal contracts plummeted and the tribes' bargaining power fell with it. By the end of the decade the group was an important resource for its members, but it had not lived up to its grandiose claims. Forty-three tribes belonged to CERT, but fewer than half that number were significant oil producers.

One arena where tribal income became large enough to subsidize expansions in tribal governments was the field of Indian gaming. Congress passed the Indian Gaming Regulatory Act (IGRA) in October 1988, soon after the Supreme Court in *California v. Cabazon Band of Mission Indians* had recognized the right of tribal governments to operate gaming enterprises outside state regulations.

The Indian Gaming Regulatory Act contained a number of protections for tribal members. It required that gaming revenue go to tribes rather than to private companies or individuals, as is the case with casinos in the non-Indian world. In addition the law stipulated that tribal governments have the "exclusive right to regulate gaming activity" on their reservations and that outside investors would be prohibited from taking a controlling interest in a tribal gaming enterprise. The act affected all reservations in states where gambling was allowed in some form.

The most controversial part of the gaming act was the fact that while it permitted high-stakes bingo games to continue without state or federal regulation, it ordered tribes sponsoring any other game of chance—card games, slot machines, and casino operations—to negotiate "compacts" with state officials "governing the conduct of gaming activities." In effect, tribes were being required to gain state approval for the most profitable forms of gambling. While this requirement clearly diminished the sovereign authority of tribes, it insured that once a compact had been signed with a state, gaming could be a major feature of reservation economies. Some groups resented this qualification of tribal autonomy, but the common desire of both Indians and their white neighbors to reap the economic benefits of gaming carried the day. Negotiations over tribal-state compacts were soon underway in several states.

By the end of the 1980s the impact of the IGRA on Native American economic life was promising, but its ultimate impact remained uncertain. In 1987—the year preceding the passage of the act—the Bureau of Indian Affairs reported that 113 tribes had taken in approximately $225 million from bingo operations. By 1991 that figure had risen to 130 tribes whose income was estimated as nearing $1 billion. While this near-fivefold growth was dramatic, continued expansion into the 1990s was beyond the imagination of most leaders. The Seminoles, who had begun their bingo games in 1979, were the most successful group in the 1980s. Earning more than $45 million in 1987, they had few rivals; at the other extreme, the isolated Turtle Mountain Community in North Dakota reported revenues of only $60,000. In 1990 fewer than twenty state compacts were in force, and the following year Indian gaming accounted for less than 2 percent of all wagers placed in the United States. Income from high-stakes games was therefore insignificant. "The single most common gaming activity on Indian reservations," one expert reported in 1992, "is bingo."

Building Tribal Governments

Just as Indian communities struggled to enhance their own power by developing strategies to overcome poverty and economic dependency on reservations, so tribes also struggled during the 1970s and 1980s to establish themselves as a "third" level of government, functioning alongside federal authorities and the states. This assertiveness created an unprecedented demand for local administrative expertise and often set off fierce competition within tribes for control of their rapidly expanding governments.

Following the passage of the 1975 Indian Self-Determination and Educational Assistance Act, tribes were eager to take control of educational and social programs that previously had been adminis-

tered by the Indian Office. Elected leaders began negotiating contracts with federal officials to administer their own school systems, operate their own health clinics, develop tribal housing authorities, and staff their own police departments and tribal courts.

As tribes gained more control over the instruments of local government and social services, they were eager to employ tribal members as teachers, administrators, social workers, housing officials, and law enforcement officers. Establishing effective sovereignty frequently depended on how quickly and effectively governments could recruit people to fill these new jobs. This shift in social service agencies from BIA to tribal sponsorship meant that a number of jobs were suddenly under the control of local leaders. For the first time, tribal officials had significant numbers of jobs to distribute to constituents. As tribal governments took on new responsibilities, therefore, they also became the major employers in many reservation communities. At the same time, political disputes within these economically disadvantaged communities often involved competition between groups for access to government jobs.

A second consequence of the growing power of tribal governments derived from the fact that many of the tribes' new functions—education, health care, and social service administration—encompassed traditionally "female" occupations: teaching, nursing, counseling, and clerical work. As the tribal governments grew during the 1970s and 1980s, Indian women entered the tribal workforce in unprecedented numbers. At the same time, these women became involved in public issues related to their new jobs. Women such as Josephine Kelly (Sioux) and Christine Quintasket (Colville) had served as tribal leaders earlier in the century, but the 1970s generation was larger. Wilma Mankiller, for example, who had migrated to San Francisco as a child, returned to Cherokee country in Oklahoma in 1977 to work for her tribe in an antipoverty program. By 1983 her success had won her wide acclaim and she was elected deputy chief; the resignation of the Cherokee chief in 1984 led to her elevation to his position. Her experience was not unique. A study of the twelve tribal councils in the Pacific Northwest revealed that women held 45 percent of elected positions in the 1980s, a dramatic increase over previous decades.

A similar process operated in urban Indian communities. Women were central to educational programs, health care, services for the elderly, and other activities that fit both the traditional definition of their social role, and they responded to the demand for new employees. But these same activities, linked as they were to government funding and community politics, also drew women into public life and leadership. Ada Deer, the leader of the campaign to restore Menominees to tribal status, was employed as a social worker in Milwaukee in the 1960s, but she rose to prominence because her work with fellow tribespeople drew her into political issues in the Menominee community. Following her success in the restoration effort, she ran unsuccessfully for Congress and in 1993 was appointed by President Clinton to head the Bureau of Indian Affairs, the first woman to hold that office.

Older Indian women encouraged this growing engagement with politics. On the Navajo reservation, Annie Wauneka, the daughter of former leader Chee Dodge, had long served as the sole woman on the tribal council. Throughout the 1950s she had been a firm advocate of greater tribal control over education and social services on the reservation, and she had been a tireless campaigner for better health care. In 1975 she was a leader of a commission on the status of Navajo women. Viewed suspiciously by male tribal leaders (who told her at one point that "[w]e men, we take care of their problems"), the commission organized public forums for Navajo women across the reservation. Wauneka helped organize the first Navajo Women's Conference in 1976 and served as the group's keynote speaker. She argued in her speech that the imposition of western bureaucratic institutions had undermined the influence women had traditionally played in Indian life, and she urged her audience to "become more active in politics and . . . aware of the educational opportunities open to Native American women." Wauneka's position won wide endorsement in the new Indian press as well as in mainstream periodicals such as *Ladies Home Journal,* which voted her a woman of the year. Hundreds of women became involved in tribal governments during the 1970s and 1980s. In 1980, 12 percent of the nation's nearly five hundred tribes and native villages were headed by women.

As the scale of tribal government expanded and more tribal members participated in politics, com-petition for political leadership inevitably intensified. While the disputes at Pine Ridge that led to the 1973 Wounded Knee occupation had complex historical roots, for example, it was significant that in the five years preceding that crisis the tribe's annual budget had risen from $100,000 to more than $3 million. Elsewhere during the 1970s, new groups within a tribe—among them women, traditional rivals of entrenched leaders, younger and better educated members—arose to seek political power. A number of new political leaders emerged from this process. Quinault leader Joe DeLaCruz, for example, who had left his Northwest Coast reservation in the 1950s to serve in the military and, later, to administer a federal antipoverty program in Portland, Oregon, returned home in 1967 to campaign for tribal chair. Once elected, DeLaCruz asserted his tribe's sovereignty over the Pacific beaches that formed the western boundary of its reserve. New tribal ordinances barred clam diggers from entering the reservation and even prohibited surfers from riding the waves on Quinault beaches. Frequently challenged by both tribal critics and non-Indians, DeLaCruz survived as tribal president from 1971 to 1993. Wendell Chino, an ordained minister in the Dutch Reformed Church, followed a similar path. After leaving the Mescalero Apache reservation to attend college and seminary, Chino returned and was elected chairman in 1964. Chino, who died in 1998, battled federal bureaucrats and energy company executives throughout his twenty-four years in office.

Best known of the new tribal leaders of the 1970s and 1980s, however, was Peter MacDonald, born Hoshkaisith Begay in 1928, and renamed while a student at a BIA boarding school. MacDonald was a grand nephew of Deshna Clah Chescilgi, an early advocate of oil leasing who served as chair of the Navajo Tribal Council in 1928. After serving in the Marines at the end of World War II, MacDonald earned an engineering degree at the University of Oklahoma and worked at Hughes Aircraft in Los Angeles. He returned home to Arizona in 1963 to direct the Office of Navajo Economic Opportunity. In 1970, after seven years of building rodeo grounds and community centers across the reservation and establishing links to activists from many families and regional groups, MacDonald ran successfully for tribal chair. Between his inauguration in 1970 and his first departure from office in 1982 (he was re-elected to a fourth term in 1986), the Navajo tribal budget rose from $18 million to $160 million.

As the Navajo government expanded and Mac-Donald's power grew, his political opponents began to complain that the chairman was becoming increasingly authoritarian. In 1975 these opponents began to insist on a careful audit of tribal accounts. Several tribal officials were indicted following these investigations, but MacDonald remained above the fray until 1988 when a federal inquiry—prompted by the work of a young Shoshone-Bannock reporter named Mark Trahant, who wrote a series of investigative articles in the Arizona *Republic*—revealed a pattern of systematic payoffs and bribes. Investigators learned that the Navajo leader had accepted hundreds of thousands of dollars in payments as well as dozens of free trips, all-expenses-paid shopping sprees, and money for his family and cronies. MacDonald insisted that accepting extravagant gifts from non-Indian business associates was "a Navajo tradition," but the tribal council suspended him from office in early 1989. He was later convicted of bribery by both tribal and federal courts and sentenced to a term in federal prison.

Emerging Cultural Homelands

Finally, as political activism fueled the growth of ambitious and assertive tribal governments, reservations came to be perceived widely as cultural homelands. Encouraged both by the passage of the American Indian Religious Freedom Act and by the modern, ecumenical outlook of the major Christian denominations, Indian communities turned increasingly to the public celebration of traditional religious and cultural rituals. Largely freed from the authoritarian control of the Indian Office, the intrusion of state adoption agencies, and BIA educators who had long dominated their classrooms, reservation communities were now able to develop their own approaches to issues of family life, education, and cultural identity. As a result, by the 1990s Indian people on reservations as well as in urban areas felt comfortable asserting their identity as a distinctive group of Americans who shared a unique history and deserved the respect of their fellow citizens. This willingness to celebrate one's

traditions proudly and openly before the American public was unremarkable for most ethnic and racial groups in the United States; for Native Americans it was unprecedented.

On the Teton Sioux reservations of Pine Ridge and Rosebud, the 1970s saw an explosion of interest in traditional religious ceremonies. The Sun Dance, which had been forbidden for half a century and then gradually reintroduced in the 1940s and 1950s, suddenly became a seasonal phenomenon, with groups organizing dances on an almost weekly basis throughout the summer months. At the same time, growing numbers of families turned to sweat lodges, public naming ceremonies, and elaborate "giveaways" (where household goods and food are given to guests to honor an event or person) to celebrate major milestones in their lives or their communities. This revival, one group of scholars has observed, offered Native Americans the opportunity to "rediscover and reproduce an Indian culture and society."

Similar patterns were evident in other Native communities. Among the Navajos, a decades-long effort to suppress the peyote ritual was formally lifted by a vote of the tribal council in 1967. Following that action, the Native American Church was able to function openly and to expand its missionary activities. By the 1970s it was reported that 40 percent of the tribe participated in the rite. At the same time, Navajos from a variety of religious backgrounds turned to traditional ceremonies conducted by holy men or "singers." Navajo "medicine men" were even added to the faculty of the tribe's community college. While fewer tribal members held exclusively to traditional ways, a growing segment of the community added these ceremonies to Christian or Native American Church rituals. In one Navajo settlement, for example, researchers found that two-thirds of the residents were affiliated with two or more religious groups.

Cultural revivals occurred in eastern Indian communities as well. Among the Wisconsin Oneidas, for example, traditional longhouse religious rituals were reintroduced in the 1970s, nearly fifty years after they had last been practiced. This revival strengthened links between Iroquois groups who had remained in New York during the removals of the 1830s and those who had migrated to other parts of the United States, including the Seneca-Cayuga community in Oklahoma. Delega-

PEOPLE, PLACES, AND THINGS

Indian Governments at Work

As tribal governments have expanded their authority, they have taken over many tasks that were previously the responsibility of the Bureau of Indian Affairs. Most tribes now operate their own police departments. This officer, a member of the Sandia Pueblo Police, was photographed while on that northern New Mexico reservation.

The Indian Self-Determination Act and the rising strength of tribal political institutions have made it possible for reservation communities to control and administer a wide array of government programs. Today tribes operate schools and housing offices, and issue automobile license plates and hunting permits. Tribal officials frequently cooperate with state and federal authorities to manage forests, wildlife habitats, and parks. In some communities these agencies have negotiated "memorandums of understanding" that have formalized a partnership among three governments: federal, state, and tribe.

---

tions from both Oklahoma and New York met each summer to jointly celebrate the traditional "green corn ceremony." Other groups rekindled tribal bonds. The Eastern and Western Cherokees, who had been separated by force during the removals of the 1830s, staged an elaborate reunion and tribal celebration in 1984.

In the South, the Alabama Coushatas, who had been terminated in the 1950s, reestablished their federal recognition in 1973. The South Carolina Catawbas, who had been terminated in 1962, also lobbied for re-recognition. (They would not be successful until 1993.) Two other groups, the Poarch Creek Band of Creeks and the Tunica-Biloxis of Louisiana, successfully petitioned federal authorities for recognition by the BIA as Indian tribes, while several others gained recognition from state authorities. Among the latter were Haliwa and Waccamaw communities of North Carolina and several other small groups in Virginia, Alabama, and Louisiana. By 1990, thirty-eight southeastern groups were petitioning the federal government for recognition.

No event better marked this nationwide rise in cultural self-consciousness than the passage in 1990 of the Native American Graves Protection and Repatriation Act (NAGPRA). Enacted by a bipartisan group of sympathetic legislators who had been moved by tribal complaints regarding the storage of Indian skeletons in museums and the sad history of unscrupulous collectors who had often made off with a Native community's sacred objects, the new law required all of the nation's museums to compile inventories of their collections and to distribute these to the groups whose cultural artifacts they were. In addition, the new law ordered museums to return (or "repatriate") any of a tribe's human remains, sacred or ceremonial objects, or significant "objects of national patrimony" once these had been requested by the relevant tribe. Finally, as the NAGPRA law took final form, Congress also established a new museum devoted to Native American culture (to be called the National Museum of the American Indian) as part of the Smithsonian Institution. Tribal leaders and their congressional supporters imagined that both the new museum and the new repatriation act would reverse the drain of cultural artifacts from Indian communities to non-Indian museums while providing support for those who wished to preserve and sustain indigenous cultures. Completely reversing the policy that had dominated federal action for most of American history, government officials were now engaged in an effort to protect, restore, and nurture Native American traditions.

CONCLUSION

Looking back on the upheavals of the 1970s, Louis Bruce, the Mohawk businessman who had served as Indian commissioner during the occupation of the BIA building in 1972, noted that "not in this century has there been such a volume of creative turbulence in Indian country." He added that the "will for self-determination" had become "an irreversible trend, a tide in the destiny of American Indians that will eventually compel all of America once and for all to recognize the dignity and human rights of Indian people." The events of the 1970s and 1980s seemed to confirm this view. Sovereignty and self-determination generated an "irreversible trend" that prompted Indians across the continent to challenge the settled prejudices and practices of their non-Indian neighbors.

By 1990 the slogans of Alcatraz and Wounded Knee had been picked up by hundreds of thousands of Native Americans eager to implement the call for cultural renewal and political sovereignty. Dozens of newly minted Indian lawyers explored the meaning of treaty "rights" while congressional staffers worked with tribal leaders and their professional lobbyists to fashion laws that would give Native Americans greater political autonomy and raise tribes to a more prominent place within the federal system. Community leaders struggled to identify economic strategies that would foster growth and prosperity without sacrificing tribal prerogatives. And religious leaders, educators, and tribal officials worked to define Red Power in each of their realms. Indians were acting sovereign, but the exact form and shape that sovereignty would take was not yet clear.

SUGGESTED READINGS

Ambler, Marjane. *Breaking the Iron Bonds: Indian Control of Energy Development*. Lawrence: University Press of Kansas, 1990.   A journalist's account of Indian efforts to reclaim control over their mineral resources during the "self-determination" years of the 1970s ad 1980s.

Benedek, Emily. *The Wind Won't Know Me: A History of the Navajo-Hopi Land Dispute*. New York: Alfred A. Knopf, 1992.   A history of the century-long struggle between Hopis and Navajos over the proper placement of a border between their reservations. The book includes vivid descriptions of the public protests that erupted during the 1980s over the U.S. government's attempts to resolve the dispute.

Berger, Thomas R. *Village Journey: The Report of the Alaska Native Review Commission*. New York: Hill and Wang, 1985.   A firsthand description of the impact of the Alaska Native Claims Settlement Act and an assessment of the 1971 law's ability to alter fundamental economic relationships in the forty-ninth state.

Cornell, Stephen. *The Return of the Native: American Indian Political Resurgence*. New York: Oxford University Press, 1988.   A sociologist's study of the rise of American Indian activism in the 1970s that pays special attention to the rise of Indian organizations and their increasingly sophisticated tactics for winning national attention.

Fowler, Loretta. *Tribal Sovereignty and the Historical Imagination: Cheyenne-Arapaho Politics*. Lincoln: University of Nebraska Press, 2002.   A study of tribal politics on the Cheyenne-Arapaho reservation in Oklahoma during the twentieth century that pays special attention to the impact of the government's "self-determination" policy of the 1970s on community life.

Johnson, Troy, Joane Nagel, and Duane Champagne. *American Indian Activism: Alcatraz to the Longest Walk*. Urbana: University of Illinois Press, 1997.   A collection of commentaries and memoirs by activists that presents an overview of the Red Power era.

Josephy, Alvin, Jr., Joane Nagel, and Troy Johnson. *Red Power: The American Indians' Fight for Freedom*, 2nd ed. Lincoln: University of Nebraska Press, 1999.   An edited documentary history of the activism of the 1970s and beyond that spans religion, politics, education reform, and economic development.

Nesper, Larry. *The Walleye War: The Struggle for Ojibwe Spearfishing and Treaty Rights.* Lincoln: University of Nebraska Press, 2002.   An anthropologist's narrative of the fishing rights controversy in Wisconsin in the 1970s and 1980s.

Shoemaker, Nancy. *American Indian Population Recovery in the Twentieth Century.* Albuquerque: University of New Mexico Press, 1999.   A population history of Native America in the twentieth century. The author explains both the reversal of population decline that occurred in the first decades of the century and the reasons behind the rapid increases of later years.

Smith, Paul Chaat, and Robert Allen Warrior. *Like a Hurricane: The Indian Movement from Alcatraz to Wounded Knee.* New York: The New Press, 1999.   A gripping account of the beginnings of the Red Power era by two Native American scholars.

Indians in the New Millennium

In the fall of 2000, two young Indians commanded a national audience of citizens and decision makers; their efforts revealed the influence of Native Americans on American public life at the dawn of a new century and a new millennium. One of these leaders was a government official working in Washington, D.C.; the other was a political activist based on a Minnesota reservation. One spoke at a ceremony at the headquarters of the Department of Interior; the other, a third-party candidate for vice president of the United States, appeared at rallies of young people and environmental activists. But despite their different audiences, Kevin Gover and Winona LaDuke shared a common ability to express Native American concerns in ways that mobilized people far beyond the Indian community.

Kevin Gover, a member of the Pawnee tribe of Oklahoma, spoke on September 8 in Washington, D.C., at a ceremony marking the 175th anniversary of the founding of the Bureau of Indian Affairs. The 45-year-old lawyer had been appointed to head the bureau in 1996 by President Bill Clinton. Raised in a poor family in Lawton, Oklahoma, Gover had been educated first at Princeton University and then in the Indian law program at the University of New Mexico Law School. In 2000 he presided over the lavish anniversary event and gave the day's major address. With the secretary of the interior looking on, Gover stunned his audience by announcing that he saw in the department's anniversary "no occasion for celebration." Instead, he announced, it was "a time for sorrowful truths to be spoken. . . ." Gover went on to describe the sad history of the Bureau's actions. In the early 1800s it had organized the removal of eastern tribes from their homelands through the use of "threat, deceit and force." Later in the century it had "participated in the ethnic cleansing that befell the western tribes." The result of these and other actions, Gover noted, was "tragedy on a scale so ghastly that it cannot be dismissed as merely the inevitable consequence of the clash of competing ways of life." Gover added that his agency once "forbade the speaking of Indian languages, . . . outlawed traditional government, and made Indian people ashamed of who they were." The time had come for the bureau to recognize and apologize for its actions. Gover declared that the Indian Bureau now accepted its "legacy of racism and inhumanity" as well as "the moral responsibility of putting things right."

The *New York Times* gave Gover's statement a prominent place in its September 9 edition, calling his "remarkable" speech a "milestone" in the history of Indian affairs. It reported as well that Secretary of the Interior Bruce Babbitt welcomed the Pawnee official's attack on government-sponsored racism. The former Arizona governor noted that the Indian Bureau "now belongs to the Indians." Babbitt called on the agency's ten thousand employees (most of whom are Native Americans) to speak out on behalf of racial justice. "May you prosper, grow, advocate, get under people's skins," the secretary declared.

At the same time Gover was speaking at the Indian Bureau, Winona LaDuke was deeply engaged in her campaign to become vice president of the United States on the Green Party ticket. LaDuke had also been the Greens' 1996 vice presidential standard-bearer, but in 2000 she received significantly more attention as the running mate of Ralph Nader, the environmental activist who brought so much new attention to the ticket that it threatened to undermine the Democratic candidate's slim lead over Republican George Bush. Born in Los Angeles in 1959 to an Ojibwe father and a non-Indian mother, LaDuke had been raised in Ashland, Oregon, before going east to study at Harvard University in 1978. She won public attention while still an undergraduate at Harvard. After working with an antinuclear group in Nevada during summer break, LaDuke began pointing out to other environmentalists that two-thirds of the nation's uranium was mined either on or close to Indian lands. She persuaded environmental groups like Greenpeace that support for Indian sovereignty was an essential element in any antinuclear campaign. Speaking before thousands of activists at the 1980 Black Hills Survival Gathering (the event where Russell Means delivered his attack on European cultures), she had offered a detailed indictment of corrupt tribal governments who colluded with energy companies to despoil their traditional homelands. Labeled "No Nukes LaDuke," she became a tireless campaigner for greater community control over businesses and, in the process, greater tribal control over mining and resource development.

During the 1990s LaDuke shifted her focus to Minnesota's White Earth Reservation, her father's boyhood home and the headquarters of the tribe where she was enrolled. White Earth was an impoverished stage on which to try out her ideas for locally responsible economic development. Now a mother, she worked for the recovery of lost tribal lands and encouraged Indians to form coopera-

Winona LaDuke Winona LaDuke, raised in the West, educated in the Northeast, and committed to community development on her father's home reservation at White Earth, Minnesota. LaDuke was among the first activists to articulate the links between tribal sovereignty and environmental reform.

tive microbusinesses to produce and market indigenous foods and tribal handicrafts. "Someone has to speak up for community work and community people," she declared. She founded the White Earth Land Recovery Project, an organization committed to regaining title to reservation land lost during the allotment era, and traveled widely to speak and mobilize support among both Indian and non-Indian audiences. During the 2000 presidential campaign her stump appearances featured what one supporter labeled her "tired mother speech." LaDuke would reach out to her audiences by describing the fatigue she felt as a young mother confronting an uncaring and environmentally destructive government. "I'm tired of worrying my sons will be sent off to a war not worth fighting," she declared. "I'm tired of worrying about pesticides that get into my children's food."

In the end LaDuke and Nader polled 2.7 percent of the national vote. The Green ticket won widespread attention because the closeness of the race between the Republicans and Democrats often meant that Nader and LaDuke tipped the balance from Al Gore to George Bush. Most tribal leaders had endorsed the Democrat Al Gore, and they urged their constituents to stick with the major party candidate. LaDuke was pleased with the publicity generated by her campaign, but she criticized the media for patronizing her as "just some Indian chick from some reservation." She promised to keep up the fight. "I am going to work on a campaign for corporate accountability," she promised in a postelection interview.

Gover and LaDuke illustrate the impact Indians had on the modern American political system in the opening year of the twenty-first century. A skilled attorney like Gover could not only rise to command the Indian Office in Washington, D.C. (in fact every head of the BIA since 1970 had been Native American), but he could also reshape the agency's identity by linking it to major public concerns such as racial injustice. Similarly, LaDuke—articulate, charismatic, and uncompromising in her beliefs—could build a tie among environmental activists, political reformers, and Indian communities, drawing new constituencies to her campaign and enlarging the set of issues normally classified as either "Indian" or "environmental." Neither leader was limited by their heritage, by their membership in a single tribe, or by the institutions within which they maneuvered.

But despite the success of remarkable individuals such as Gover and LaDuke, the beginning of the twenty-first century was also marked by continuing problems in Native America that meant the future would remain uncertain. Native Americans facing the new millennium encountered several areas where nagging problems and ongoing controversies persisted without solutions. These areas of difficulty were not new, for they grew out of the long struggle of Native Americans to build new lives and new communities within the boundaries of the United States. Their efforts over five centuries had produced astounding victories and

breathtaking innovations, but Native people and their communities continued to suffer because of both the ignorance and neglect of the American majority and the uncertainty and division among Native Americans themselves. Not only could American Indians be neglected or forgotten in a large, multiracial industrialized democracy, but a rapidly growing and widely diverse Indian community was not always sure of the path it should follow into the future. In addition to achieving an impressive set of clear successes, it seemed that Indian people had also managed to define a series of new dilemmas.

In the decade of the 1990s, American Indians celebrated their unprecedented successes in their campaign to secure a place for "the people" in the nation's future even as they confronted new and more complex versions of old struggles. This mixture of success and frustration underlay much of Native American life at the beginning of the new millenium. Indian people faced the future with a mixture of pride, hope, and despair.

Five difficult questions confronted Native America.

First: *What does sovereignty mean?*

In the last decades of the twentieth century, tribes had come to be recognized as governmental units representing the interests of reservation Indians. But how much independent power would tribes exercise? If tribes were separate government units, could they act independently without regard for state or federal authority? Where would tribal powers end and the powers of counties, states, and the federal government begin? And equally important, how might conflicts between tribes and other governments be resolved—by laws passed by Congress, by the federal courts, or by new treaties?

Second: *How can Indian health be improved?*

Despite unparalleled growth in Native American population in the second half of the twentieth century, most Indian communities continued to be marked by low life expectancy, high rates of alcoholism and diabetes, and poor health care. What might be done to reverse some of the deeply destructive health patterns apparent both on reservations and in urban settings? And could new patterns of community health care be made compatible with both Indian traditions and tribal sovereignty?

INDIAN VOICES   Joy Harjo Writes About Indian Life

Joy Harjo was born in 1950 to Creek (Muscogee) parents in Tulsa, Oklahoma. She grew up there and attended the Institute of American Indian Art and the University of Iowa where she received an MFA degree in 1978. She has taught at the universities of Colorado, Arizona, New Mexico, and California and has published several books of poetry. Harjo is also an accomplished jazz musician. She plays the saxophone and her band, *Poetic Justice*, has toured the United States. Harjo now lives in Hawaii.

Harjo's poems and stories are both personal and historical. She reflects on her childhood in Oklahoma ("We were a stolen people in a stolen land. Oklahoma meant defeat."); on her experiences at the Institute of American Indian Art in Santa Fe, New Mexico, during the exciting years of artistic renewal during the 1960s and 1970s; and on her relationships with men, her children, and her grandchildren. As she has commented on her life and the lives of other Indian people who came of age in the generation of Red Power and the assertion of tribal sovereignty, she has focused on the many ways the power of outsiders has affected and changed Native American life. She has also written about the enduring strength of Indian cultural traditions and family ties. Harjo presents herself as both comfortable in the modern world and deeply suspicious of its future—a not unreasonable position for a Native person in the new millennium.

The Psychology of Earth and Sky

It is just before dawn. The mango tree responds to the wind's fierce jostling. A rooster stridently marks the emerging light. We are alerted and our spirits trek back through night and the stars to awaken here in this place known as *Honolulu*. Clouds harboring rain travel fast over the city and now a trash truck beeps as it backs up for collection. And dawn arrives, no matter the struggle of the night and how endless that night might be.

We are part of an old story and involved in it are migrations of winds, ocean currents, of seeds, songs and generations of nations.

In this life it seems like I am always leaving, flying over this earth that harbors many lives. I was born Indian, female and artist in the Creek Nation. It is still gray out as I follow the outline of memory. Over there is my teenage self getting out of a car, still a little drunk, waving good-bye to friends. We've been up all night, singing into the dark, joining the stars out on the mesa west of the Indian town, Albuquerque.

"When the dance is over sweetheart I will take you home in my one-eyed Ford. Wey-yo-hey-ya Hey-yah-hah. Hey-yah-haha."

That song was destined to become a classic.

The shutting of the car door echoes and echoes and leads to here. I always hear that door when I return to that memory. It's a holographic echo, turning over and over into itself. I am leaving. I am returning.

I turned to walk to my apartment in the back. All of us lived in the back of somewhere in that city where we were defining what it meant to be Indian in a system of massive colonization. It was a standing joke. A backdoor joke. The world was suddenly condensed by the shutting of the door, the sweet purr of the engine as the car drove off and the perfect near silence of the pause in the morning scramble of sparrows, the oohing of doves. I can still breathe it, that awareness of being alive part of the ceremony for the rising sun. I often lived for this moment of reconciliation, where night and morning met. It didn't matter that I didn't quite know how I was going to piece together what I needed for tuition, rent, groceries, books and childcare, how I was going to make sense of a past that threatened to destroy me during those times when I doubted that I deserved a place in the world. The songs we sang all night together filled me with promise, hope, the belief in a community that understood that the world was more than a contract between buyer and seller.

And that morning just as the dawn was arriving and I was coming home I knew that the sun needed us, needed my own little song made of the whirr push of the blood through my lungs and heart. Inside that bloodstream was born my son, my daughter. I was born of parents who would greet the dawn often in their courtship with their amazing passion driven by love, and later heartbreak.

Dawn was also the time my father often came home after he and my mother were married, had four children, dropped off by friends, reeking of smoke, beer and strange perfume. And I am his daughter. How much do we have to say in the path our feet will take? Is it ordained by the curve of a strand of DNA? Mixed with the urge to love, to take flight? My family survived, even continues to thrive, which works against the myth of Indian defeat and disappearance.

My daughter's house is near the First National Bank building in Albuquerque, a landmark from the sky as I climb toward the dawn in a jet. She is still asleep, the youngest curled in her arms. Her oldest is sleeping with her mouth open next to the three other beauties who also call my daughter *mother*. Anytime I left as she was growing up she missed me terribly. Even now as I fly away from her yet once more I feel the tug of her heart as it still questions the time of my next return, as if I left her at some point in the deepest roots of her memory and never came back. I want to tell her I will never leave her, and I send this poem to her and the girls as a guardian spirit.

Source: from *A Map to the Next World: Poems and Tales* by Joy Harjo. Copyright © 2000 by Joy Harjo. Used by permission of W. W. Norton & Company, Inc. (New York: Norton, 2000), 14–15.

Third: *What is the solution to Indian poverty?*

In the twenty-first century, despite decades of education and federally subsidized "community development," Native communities continued to rank among the poorest and least well housed groups in the nation. Indians were still poor. Could this pattern be altered—and what might be the cultural consequences of improved economic conditions? Would prosperity require tribes to abandon their culture?

Fourth: *Are casinos the answer?*

The one area of economic vitality in Native communities in the 1990s and afterward appeared to be Indian gaming. Would tribally sponsored casinos and other forms of entertainment deliver jobs and prosperity to Indian communities? And could the wealth enjoyed by the small number of successful tribes have an impact on the more numerous and less fortunate communities that had been unable to profit from tribally sponsored gaming?

What would be required to transfer wealth from some Native Americans to others?

Fifth: *Who is an Indian?*

Over the course of the twentieth century the definition of "an Indian" became unclear. Tribes maintained inconsistent standards for membership; at the same time the Census Bureau and other national organizations adopted their own unique definitions of Indianness. Individuals are "Indians" in some settings and not in others. Could this confusion be resolved? How? And by whom?

As the new millennium began there were no simple answers to these questions. There were, however, a variety of opinions regarding each of them and no widely accepted means of reaching a resolution. It was also clear that Native Americans would continue to debate these issues and would eventually develop strategies for addressing each of them. The answers that emerge from this process of debate will ultimately define the nature of American Indian life in the decades to come.

TRIBE OR NATION?

During the 1990s the outcome of two contests taking place in separate but related arenas defined tribal sovereignty for individual Indian communities. In the first arena, tribal governments pressed local, state, and federal authorities for greater recognition of their authority over reservation life and resources. Citing treaties and federal statutes, Indian leaders asserted sovereign authority over their own communities and challenged non-Indian governments who threatened to undermine tribal institutions. Tribes are nations, these leaders insisted, and deserve to be respected as such. But while tribes vastly expanded their powers, legislators and judges continued to insist that the national government established the "supreme law of the land." As a consequence, the balance between the competing claims of tribal, state, and federal sovereignty remained uncertain.

In the second arena, tribal members in the 1990s—even as they expressed their enthusiasm for community autonomy—pressed their own leaders to administer reservation governments fairly and efficiently. In the course of internal disputes on a number of reservations, many tribes adopted more democratic procedures and improved both the stability and the authority of their governments. In this process, Indian communities came to resemble the larger American society that surrounded them. While autonomous in many respects, tribal governments would not separate themselves entirely from the culture of constitutional democracy in the United States.

As a consequence of these two struggles, the term "tribal sovereignty," a phrase that had been central to policymaking in the 1970s and 1980s but had always been subject to a variety of interpretations, developed a more precise meaning as the new century began. The exact balance between a community's aspirations for independence and its obligations both to its members and to the nation surrounding it remained undefined.

In the 1990s tribal governments served their communities in a variety of ways. Tribal schools and colleges, tribal housing authorities, tribal police departments, tribal fish and game officials, more than 140 tribal courts, and dozens of tribal family welfare offices provided services and responded to local needs. Some branches of tribal government, such as housing authorities, administered federally funded programs; others, such as the tribal courts, operated independently under procedures established by federal statutes and local tribal councils. Under the tradition of tribal sovereignty, tribal governments were organized in a variety of ways. In some communities tribal judges were elected, for example, while in others they were appointed. Of necessity, however, all tribal offices and agencies came into contact with other governmental bodies. For example, tribal schools and colleges not only lobbied for funding from Congress but established ties to state education boards and responded to local teacher certification requirements. Police departments developed agreements with their local counterparts as well as with federal agencies such as the FBI. Increasingly, these interactions produced disputes regarding the extent of tribal authority.

Law enforcement provided the most intense confrontation between tribal authorities and other government agencies. In Todd County, South Dakota, for example, where 7,700 Rosebud Sioux Indians lived alongside 1,500 whites, a series of disputes arose over which government—the tribe or the county—was responsible for certain aspects of law and order. In 1971 the Rosebud tribal council passed an ordinance establishing its authority over liquor sales on the reservation. The target of this action was a municipally owned liquor store in the town of Mission, a largely white village occupying privately owned land within the reservation boundaries. The Mission Liquor Store rejected the tribe's ordinance (the store reported more than $400,000 in sales in 1975) and federal officials brought suit against it on behalf of the tribe. In 1984 the federal courts upheld the tribe's position and the liquor store was closed.

Just as the dispute over liquor sales was being resolved, however, Rosebud tribal officials brought another suit asking the federal courts to bar South Dakota authorities from arresting or prosecuting Native Americans on the highways of Todd County, all of which lay within the boundaries of the Rosebud reservation. Other South Dakota tribes filed briefs in support of the Rosebud authorities. Despite the state's vigorous objection to what it considered an intrusion on the power of the state to police its highways, an appeals court decision issued in 1990 affirmed the tribe's position; South Dakota's appeal to the Supreme Court was denied the following year. In the wake of these decisions the tribe began issuing its own license plates to tribal members.

The ongoing disputes in Todd County are a dramatic illustration of how assertions of tribal authority met local resistance and produced new, sharper definitions of tribal sovereignty. Supported by federal laws that recognized the significance of reservation borders and the power of tribal governments within them, Indian leaders were able to overcome local white opposition and extend the reach of their institutions and the scope of their community's sovereign authority. Because of ongoing white resistance to this authority, however, the Rosebud example also makes clear that the underlying tensions between aggressive tribal governments and non-Indians will likely continue to shape the debate over the future of tribal governments. Neither the tribes nor outside authorities will be able to define the meaning of tribal sovereignty alone.

A second dramatic illustration of the struggle between tribal governments and non-Indian authorities took place in 1999 in the Pacific Ocean, off the coast of Washington. There, near the northwestern tip of an arm of land that bends westward

from the Olympic Peninsula, lies the home of the Makah tribe. The Makahs had been seafaring whalers for centuries before they signed a treaty with the United States in the nineteenth century that granted land to the Americans in exchange for a reservation and a guarantee that tribal members could continue to harvest the seas for food. Following the adoption of this agreement, the Makahs lived peacefully alongside the white settlers who soon came to settle near them. By the 1920s the Makahs had given up whaling because the gray whale on which they had long depended was becoming extinct and the tribe could no longer sustain its hunting traditions.

The Makah whaling tradition lay dormant until the 1980s when international efforts to protect gray whales produced the news that a dramatic rise in their population was taking place. As the number of whales increased, commercial whale hunting revived under the supervision of an International Whaling Commission, which issued permits to member countries. Hundreds of whales were now being taken legally each year from the global gray whale population. In 1997, after learning of this reversal of the whale population's decline, the United States government, acting on behalf of the Makah tribe, applied for permission to hunt whales from the herd that migrated near their Washington reservation.

In 1998 the International Whaling Commission granted the U.S. request. It gave the Makahs permission to kill up to twenty whales for local consumption (not for sale) over a four-year period. While excited members of the tribe worked to reconstruct a whaling canoe, revive hunting rituals, and train a new generation of paddlers and harpoon men, environmentalists and editorial writers condemned the Makahs' plans. They complained that a revival of tribal traditions was taking place at the expense of "innocent whales." They were also disturbed that the whaling crew planned to harpoon an animal and then kill it with a .50 caliber rifle. Some protests grew hateful and threatening. In one particularly ugly example, the head of the tribe's whaling commission found twenty-five messages on her answering machine one day; each consisted of the sound of a gun being cocked and fired.

In May 1999, after a year of training and several unsuccessful voyages out into the Pacific, the

Makah whaling crew was finally successful. A team headed by Wayne Johnson managed to harpoon a whale, kill it, and tow it to shore before a gathering of supporters from neighboring Puget Sound Indian communities. The tribe's chairman, Ben Johnson told the crowd, "The Makah made history today," but public reaction to their success—beamed to television screens across the globe—ran strongly in the opposite direction. The *Seattle Times* reported comments running 10 to 1 against the tribe, the governor of Washington announced his disapproval, and one environmental group posted a banner headline on its website that read, "Damn the Makah forever." The tribe stoutly defended its action as consistent with its treaty agreements with the United States, and most Indians appeared to agree. Again, a confrontation had helped define an aspect of tribal sovereignty, but for the Makahs the victory was uncertain. In the aftermath of the Makahs' successful hunt, some Indian leaders expressed the fear that continued assertion of this particular treaty right might undermine public support for other claims to fish and water or harm tribal efforts in the areas of law enforcement, economic development, or education. The debate over tribal governments, therefore, began to take place both as a part of a confrontation between the tribe and its non-Indian neighbors and as a subject for debate within the Indian communities themselves. In the Makahs' case, while they continued to defend their right to hunt gray whales, they did not immediately seek to repeat the success of their 1999 hunt.

During the 1990s Native Americans were also debating the rules governing the behavior of tribal officials and the powers of tribal governments. While reservation leaders were frequently absorbed in extending the reach and power of their authority, their constituents came to worry about procedures and the rights of dissenters within the community. Tribal members were eager to see their governments grow, but they worried that their leaders were losing touch with—or worse, ignoring—the wishes of their constituents.

The most dramatic example of an aggressive, but disconnected, leader was Peter MacDonald, the talented, but ultimately corrupt, chairman of the Navajo tribal council. One of the most troubling aspects of the MacDonald crisis was that the evidence of his wrongdoing came from a federal in-

quiry. The tribe's organic code did not provide for the impeachment or removal of the chief executive. When the tribal council, outraged by the chairman's unwillingness to accept any responsibility for his actions, voted to strip MacDonald of his powers and place him on "leave," MacDonald simply ignored them, charging that they were enemies of tribal sovereignty. His supporters staged a sit-in in the chairman's offices and cheered when MacDonald appointed a new set of tribal judges who quickly ordered him reinstated. The Navajo Supreme Court ultimately upheld the council's original dismissal, but for a time the nation's largest reservation was ruled by two competing sets of leaders, one appointed by MacDonald and the other by the council.

Once MacDonald had been dispatched to federal prison, the Navajos reorganized their government. The chairman was replaced by a president who could veto legislation but who no longer presided over tribal council meetings or appointed council committees. The new "speaker of the council" presided over the council and played a central role in committee assignments and managing legislation. This new separation of powers not only would allow for disagreements and even impeachments to occur in the future, but, more importantly, would enable a variety of political interests to vie with one another for power. The Navajos were no longer limited to one powerful leader. One Navajo politician called the event "a political awakening." MacDonald's release from prison in 2001 revived bitter memories of the past, but the new structure of tribal government appeared well able to contain the ongoing rivalry between his supporters and his critics.

Other tribes have challenged the authority of powerful leaders, revealing both the weakness of governments that do not allow for the separation of powers and the difficulty of establishing the legitimacy of governments that reservation residents often dismiss as puppets of the Bureau of Indian Affairs or powerful corporate interests. When faced with corrupt or incompetent leaders in the 1990s, tribal members often found that their tribal courts or councils were dominated by the chief executive and were therefore unable to act. In 1997, for example, beleaguered Cherokee chief Joe Byrd managed to elude his critics by impeaching and removing from office the tribal court justices who had ordered him to surrender financial records to investigators. At the same time, insurgent groups on the Pine Ridge and Crow reservations with similar complaints found themselves caught between powerful political opponents who controlled the entire machinery of tribal government and apathetic tribal members who were reluctant to become involved in a "nontraditional" and alien governmental institution.

Disputes over civil liberties have also caused confrontations between tribal members and tribal governments. In 2000 only 68 tribes had adopted written constitutions that explicitly recognized press freedom on reservations. This number represents less than 25 percent of the 280 tribes and communities that publish newspapers. Because of the tribes' sovereign status, their governments are also exempt from the 1967 Freedom of Information Act. Tribal reporters are therefore hampered in their efforts to ferret out embarrassing information from tribal officials when trouble arises. The 1968 Indian Civil Rights Act provides for a guarantee of free speech and a free press, but it is not clear how that provision applies to tribally owned publications. Most reservation newspapers are owned by tribal governments. As a consequence, refusing to print a story or removing a particularly troublesome reporter can be defended by tribal authorities as a business decision, not a government intrusion on free speech. Civil rights laws prohibit governments from interfering with privately owned publications; the Constitution defends an individual's right to speak out, but it does not guarantee that a reporter's story will be printed or job will be secure.

During the 1990s a number of disputes arose between tribal governments and their newspapers. In 1994, for example, the Hopi tribal council shut down the *Hopi Tutuvehni* because the newspaper did not present "balanced" coverage of local politics. That same year Robin Powell was fired as editor of the *Turtle Mountain Times* after she began running a large blank space in the paper to protest the tribal council's refusal to make public the minutes of its meetings. "This space reserved for the tribal minutes," was printed in the blank space. Three years later Cherokee chief Joe Byrd, while battling investigations of his financial affairs, laid off the entire staff of the inquisitive *Cherokee Nation* newspaper. Other battles were less public. Sharon Tom, editor of the Salt River–Pima–Maricopa newspaper near

Phoenix managed to cover recall elections and controversial local issues, but pressure from tribal leaders to stick to feature stories finally caused her to quit after three years on the job. "There is no separation of powers between the tribal government and the press," she announced later. "With tribal media, it's one and the same."

As in other areas of political conflict, the struggle between Native American reporters and their tribal employers will certainly continue in the new millennium. The Native American Journalists Association publicizes instances of censorship and lobbies for press freedom guarantees in tribal constitutions. Local reporters are also supported by a small group of independent publications that cover national Indian affairs and do not rely on tribal subsidies. These include an irreverent newspaper, *News From Indian Country* and *Native Peoples*, a slick, full-color magazine. The outcome of these disputes remains unclear, but as with the effort to extend the power of tribal governments or to restructure tribal institutions, the discussion of these issues will surely continue, defining in the process the precise meaning of tribal sovereignty for twenty-first century Native America.

INDIAN HEALTH

The 2000 census reported a Native American population of 2,475,000. These figures indicate that over the course of the twentieth century the Indian population of the United States had increased ten times. While a number of theories have been proposed to explain this dramatic growth, including a growing tendency of individuals to reclassify themselves as American Indians, these figures also reflect a general improvement in Indian health. The life expectancy of Indians, for example, rose from 65.1 years in 1969 to 71.1 in the early 1980s. While still lagging behind the white life expectancy of 74.4, this figure is twenty years higher than the 1940 figure of 51.0. Native Americans made similar dramatic gains in the areas of infant mortality (the number of infants who die soon after birth) and maternal mortality (the number of mothers who die from complications associated with childbirth). By the mid-1980s, the infant mortality rate had dropped to 9.8 per 1,000, down from 62.7 per 1,000 just thirty years earlier, a reduction of more than 80 percent. The maternal mortality rate dropped even more dramatically, from 82.6 per 100,000 in the 1950s to 8.8 per 100,000 in the 1980s.

With access to health clinics and hospitals, many of them run by tribes, Native Americans in the twenty-first century could expect to live longer and healthier lives than had their parents and grandparents. In 1990 the Indian Health Service (which in 1954 had been transferred from the Bureau of Indian Affairs to the Department of Health and Human Services) operated 50 hospitals and 450 outpatient facilities for Native clients. More than half of all Indians lived in cities where services and salaries were generally higher than in rural areas and virtually all of them attended school. (The overall educational level of American Indians doubled between 1940 and 1980.)

Despite these advances, however, the state of American Indian health in the new millennium was uncertain. In 1991 the Indian Health Service reported the rate of Indian alcoholism was more than four times the rate among the population at large. Alcoholism's consequences became an increasing preoccupation of Indian leaders during the 1990s, with tribes taking steps to end liquor sales in reservation communities and acting to educate their members about the health risks associated with drinking. Among the latter, fetal alcohol syndrome (FAS) became a special area of concern following the publication in 1989 of Michael Dorris's *The Broken Cord*. A Native American author and educator at Dartmouth College, Dorris described the learning and developmental problems that affect children whose mothers drink excessively while pregnant. Several reservation health workers claimed that a significant percentage of Indian children exhibited symptoms of FAS, and some communities even considered incarcerating pregnant mothers who refused to stop drinking.

Infectious and chronic diseases associated with poverty also continued to afflict Native American communities in the 1990s. Tuberculosis infection was four times greater among Native Americans than among the American majority population, and diabetes mellitus afflicted more than twice the number of Indians as it did all others. In addition, there were nearly a third more deaths from pneumonia and influenza among Indians than among the population at large. During the 1990s health professionals also worried that the infection rate for sexually transmitted diseases (STDs) among Native Americans was consistently measured at double the rate found among whites. While not a serious health risk in itself, STDs are a major indicator of susceptibility to AIDS. Despite the fact that there were fewer than five hundred AIDS cases reported among Native Americans in 2001, the number of cases appeared to be rising rapidly.

Health studies also revealed a disturbing trend among Native American children and youth. The U.S. Centers for Disease Control and Prevention reported in 2003, for example, that between 1989 and 1998 accidental or violent injuries accounted for 75 percent of all deaths among Indian and Alaskan Native children under the age of eighteen. This rate was twice the national average. The study also reported that during the 1990s homicide and suicide rates for Indian youth were far higher than among comparable groups of young whites. The situation appeared particularly grim on rural reservations. In the Dakotas, Nebraska, and Iowa, for example, the suicide rate among Native American children under nineteen was more than six times the national average.

Despite vastly improved overall statistics, then, Indian people in the new millennium continue to be inordinately affected by alcoholism, infectious diseases, and violence. And tragically, these causes of death took their greatest toll among young people. The death rate for Indians ages 15–24 was 60 percent higher than for the overall American population in that age category; for those aged 25–44 the rate was 80 percent higher. As a consequence, the Native American community in 2000, while growing in size and life expectancy, was clearly a group whose health was at risk.

The solution to this troubling situation was not clear, for the level of health care and health-related education available to Indian communities in 2000 appeared roughly equivalent to what was available to other groups. Moreover Indian communities themselves had become increasingly involved in health-care delivery. The quality of neonatal and pediatric care approached national norms. But conditions within Native communities seemed to undermine the efforts of health-care workers and educators. The rates of disease, preventable infections, and violence remained inexplicably high, cutting down too many otherwise healthy young people and endangering the future of the entire Indian community.

How could American Indians reduce rates of alcoholism, diabetes, and pneumonia and eliminate the uncomfortable presence of violent and early death? Observers seeking answers to these questions frequently looked beyond clinics and hospitals and examined the social and economic conditions that shaped Indian communities. When they did so, they were forced to confront the enduring reality of Indian poverty. The task of improving Indian health quickly led to the related question of how best to alleviate economic hardship and social isolation. And discussions of how best to proceed in this arena inevitably raised questions of who should direct health-care policy in "sovereign" communities as well as how much health services could hope to accomplish in communities with multiple problems and uncertain economies. As important a goal as it had been for a generation, tribal sovereignty alone seemed unable either to solve the problem of disease and violence or to eradicate the enduring handicaps produced by Indian poverty.

STRUGGLING ECONOMIES

During the 1990s, tribes continued to seek ways of maximizing the return on tribal resources and expanding the capacity of community business enterprises. Many of these efforts were successful. The Mississippi Choctaws, for example, continued to develop their industrial park and to develop assembly plants for Ford, Chrysler, AT&T, Xerox, and other industrial giants. The tribal corporation, Chata Enterprises, provided so many jobs for the six thousand enrolled Choctaws in the state and for non-Indians in the surrounding region that the tribe became one of the largest employers in the South. At the Warm Springs agency in central Oregon, tribal enterprises ranging from a power plant to a luxury resort employed twelve hundred people by 1993 and were generating nearly $100 million

in revenues. Other tribes developed tribal farms, shopping centers, convenience stores, banks, and truck stops, and a National Indian Business Association established an active presence in Washington, D.C.

Despite these advances, however, few tribal enterprises—or even the increasingly profitable tribal leases with energy developers—proved capable of employing entire Indian communities. None of the decade's tribal development projects generated resources that would enable groups to support the growing portion of their members who chose to live away from reservations. Even though individual income among Mississippi Choctaws rose dramatically during the 1980s, for example, a Harvard University economic survey revealed that a third of the tribe continued to earn less than $7,000 per year.

In a similar vein, the Alaska Federation of Natives (AFN) reported in 1989 that even though there had been tremendous growth in health and educational levels during the 1980s, they could hold out little hope for the multimillion dollar tribal corporations that had been created in 1971. According to the AFN, these corporations, which lawmakers had hoped would bring prosperity to the North, faced "the geographic and economic barriers that constrain rural economic development." While noting that some corporations had been successful, the AFN concluded that there was "little likelihood that Native corporations will be able to expand the private sector economy significantly in rural Alaska." While progress was being made, the goals of full employment and a living income for the region's Native Americans continued to appear unreachable.

The U.S. Census Bureau confirmed this pessimistic view in 2002 when it released a report on poverty rates among American racial groups based on surveys conducted in the last years of the 1990s. Native Americans remained the group with the highest percentage of its members below the poverty line—nearly 26 percent—but even more disturbing, the Census Bureau report noted that the boom years of the late 1990s apparently had had no impact on Indians. While poverty rates among African-Americans and Hispanics dropped by up to 10 percent in the last three years of the decade, the rate among Native Americans actually rose slightly.

Tapping America's Potential

President Bill Clinton's visit to Pine Ridge, South Dakota, in 1999 was criticized by many as a one-day publicity stunt. Nevertheless, the attention focused on this Lakota Sioux reservation during the president's visit brought the persistence and the intensity of Native American poverty sharply into focus.

The impact of ongoing poverty on Native Americans is not difficult to imagine. BIA police reported in 2000, for example, that as many as six thousand Native American young people belonged to one of 520 gangs that it had identified as operating on the nation's reservations. That year the Navajo tribe began work on the first youth correctional facility to be constructed on an Indian reservation. At the same time as these depressing statistics were being collected, Native Americans were being assaulted by an ever-increasing array of images from the American majority that emphasized its wealth and mobility. Television, popular music, Hollywood movies, and nearby shopping malls communicated the enormous gap separating Indian and middle-class communities. This onslaught could only further discourage Indian community leaders and those dedicated to reviving Native languages and traditions.

In the summer of 1999 President Clinton helped illustrate the tragedy of Indian poverty when he brought the national spotlight to the Pine Ridge reservation in western South Dakota. The first president to visit an American Indian community in more than sixty years, Clinton noted that the twenty-five thousand residents of Pine Ridge had few jobs, limited health-care facilities, and only sixty-two miles of paved roads. The dot-com boom that was then filling the nation's business pages was nowhere to be found on the windswept Dakota pasturelands.

Perhaps more discouraging than the poverty the president encountered in 1999 was the fact that Clinton had little to offer his Sioux hosts in the way of encouragement. Ever since the end of the War on Poverty twenty years earlier, federal officials had stressed the themes of self-reliance and tribal development rather than massive government investment. Despite Clinton's sympathy for his Lakota hosts, his recommendations were indistinguishable from those that had come from his immediate Republican predecessors, Ronald Reagan and George Bush. He promised support for tribal enterprises, but he did not mention direct assistance. He told his audience at Pine Ridge that he had come to learn "what you want to do and to tell you we will give you the tools." He offered federal loans and tax credits for new businesses; he did not offer schools, teachers, roads, or public works projects.

At the end of the twentieth century, with direct subsidies unlikely and tribal enterprises supplying at best only a portion of the jobs and income Native Americans required, it was difficult to imagine a solution to the problem of Indian poverty. Over the course of the previous two centuries, the resources on which tribes had relied for their welfare—land, water, access to game—had been seized by the American majority and used to benefit non-Indians. Hampered by inadequate education and health-care systems, and lacking access to investment capital, Indians had rarely managed to compete with outsiders in business or the professions. In the last half of the twentieth century, tribes and individuals had managed to improve living standards and develop a series of successful enterprises by leasing their resources to outsiders or operating businesses on the margins of the national economy. They had also gained sufficient political influence to reverse the power of outsiders to control reservation mineral and water resources and to reaffirm tribal rights to fish, hunt, and otherwise regulate economic life within the community. Still, poverty remained and no one—Indian or non-Indian—could offer a comprehensive solution to its destructive presence.

Are Casinos the Answer?

Indian casinos were the most glamorous—and unexpected—aspect of American Indian life in the 1990s. When the American Indian Gaming Regulatory Act (AIGRA) won congressional approval in 1988, few expected the law to have a significant impact on Native life. Most observers hoped that small-scale "bingo parlors" and modest casinos would sprout up on reservations situated near large population centers, providing jobs for tribal members and possibly anchoring modest resort developments. The financial, security, and administrative challenges associated with the creation of large, Las Vegas–style casinos seemed beyond the capacity of tribal governments. And even if tribes did manage to construct and manage large gambling centers, it seemed inevitable that political opposition from non-Indians and the lurking presence of organized crime would probably bring them to ruin within a few years. As one pessimistic economic development expert recalled years later, "I saw nothing but failures."

Ten years after the gaming law's passage, it was clear that the experts had been wrong. Two hundred tribes operated casinos and bingo parlors, drawing nearly $10 billion in revenue from the American public and supporting a work force of two hundred thousand nationwide. (Experts estimate that this work force is 75 percent non-Indian.) Twenty-nine states had negotiated the compacts with tribes that AIGRA had stipulated was a prerequisite to opening casinos. These agreements regulated the size, nature, and location of gaming operations and defined the state's share of the winnings. (The state's payment was defined in several ways, either as a fixed figure or as a percentage of slot machine or other gambling revenue.) Forty-six gaming establishments operated in Oklahoma alone. While it was difficult to know precisely the net profits generated by Indian casinos, most estimates in the first years of the new century put this figure at approximately $2 billion, larger than the annual appropriations for the operations of the Bureau of Indian Affairs. In short, in the space of ten years, a source of income had arisen that generated more dollars for Native Americans than the federal government annually appropriated for their welfare. This phenomenal development raised two questions: how did this success arise? And could casino profits provide the answer to Indian poverty?

There were three reasons why AIGRA proved so successful. First, thanks in large part to the legal and political struggles of the 1970s and 1980s, tribal leaders in the 1990s were prepared to move aggressively to exploit the new gaming law. Second, once successful, gaming tribes moved rapidly into the political arena, supporting friendly candidates, organizing public relations campaigns in support of their interests, and lobbying state and federal legislators. Third, local non-Indian politicians, impressed by the success of Indian casinos

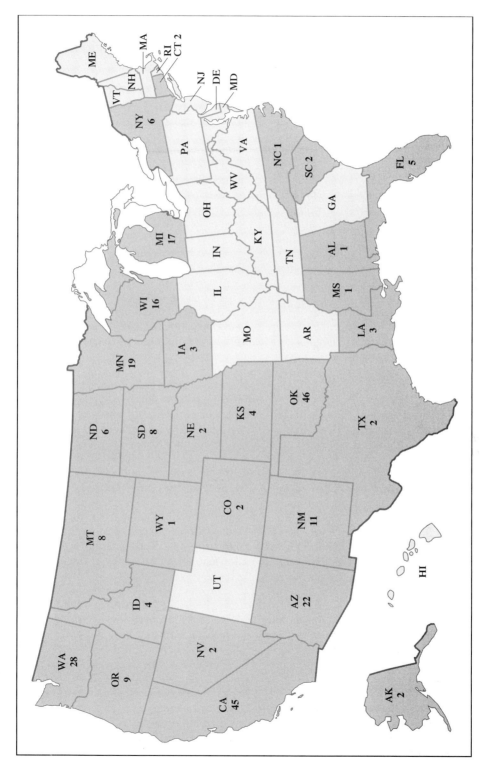

American Indian Tribal Casinos (For a list of tribal gaming establishments by state, see Appendix G.)

and limited by the anti-tax sentiments of their constituencies, saw tribal gaming not only as a painless source of state revenue but also as an instrument for economic development. While worried about their inability to control sovereign tribes, these state politicians gradually embraced and encouraged the tribes' ambitions.

The most prominent and aggressive leader of a gaming tribe in the 1990s was Richard (Skip) Hayward, tribal chairman of the Mashantucket Pequots. Hayward, a former welder at the Electric Boat shipyard in Groton, Connecticut, had spent the 1970s encouraging his relatives to protect the Pequot's two-hundred-acre state reservation, which was all that remained of the tribe's former holdings. In addition to leading an effort to set up homes on the reserve, Hayward had also made plans for tribal enterprises that could draw on the federal government's rising interest in reservation development. Unfortunately, during the 1970s Hayward's ambitions were stopped by the fact that the Pequots were recognized as a tribe only by the state of Connecticut—not by the federal government—and were therefore ineligible for many of the economic development programs sponsored by the Bureau of Indian Affairs.

The Pequots' status changed in 1983 when Hayward and his attorneys persuaded federal authorities that Connecticut had taken tribal lands in the past without federal authorization. Acting with the support of the state's congressional delegation—led by maverick Republican Senator Lowell Weicker—Congress in late 1983 passed a special bill that granted the Pequots federal recognition and awarded them $900,000 for new land purchases as compensation for past damages. In 1986 Hayward and the Pequots opened a high-stakes bingo game on the Pequot reservation. Earlier tribal enterprises such as a pizza parlor and a firewood business had been only marginally successful, but the Pequots' proximity to the large, urban populations of New York, Providence, and Boston helped the tribe fill its new bingo hall with a thousand visitors a day. Two years later, when Congress approved AIGRA, Hayward began working to replace the tribe's modest bingo operation with a full-fledged casino. By 1991 the Pequots had successfully negotiated a compact with the state authorities that promised 25 percent of all slot machine royalties to Connecticut and had secured a $60 million loan from Malaysian entrepreneur Lim Goh Tong. Foxwoods Casino opened on February 15, 1992; more than ten thousand people squeezed through its doors that first day. Within weeks it was clear that Foxwoods would be the most successful casino in North America.

The success of Foxwoods established a model for other tribes to follow. In the 1990s, large casinos featuring big name entertainers and mammoth gaming rooms opened on Oneida lands in upstate New York; at Prior Lake, Minnesota; at the Mohegan Sun resort near Stonington, Connecticut; and at reservations in Oregon, New Mexico, and Arizona. Financed by outsiders eager to share in the casinos' remarkable profits (but owned by the tribe in accordance with AIGRA), operated by sophisticated managers and security personnel, and guarded by skilled tribal attorneys, these resorts drew hordes of mostly non-Indian visitors to its card games and slot machines. Many casinos expanded quickly, adding golf courses, new hotels, and convention facilities. (The Pequots built a $180 million tribal museum, which opened in 1997, adjacent to Foxwoods.)

The Pequots' success was clearly a function of Chairman Hayward's vision and energy, but it was also made possible by the cooperation of Connecticut authorities. In the decade following the passage of AIGRA, other tribes recognized that political support from state officials was crucial to their success. The benefits of working with state politicians were demonstrated most amply in California. At first California officials had tried to bar local tribes from opening casinos. They refused to negotiate gaming compacts with the state's Indian leaders, hoping to hold the line at low-stakes bingo parlors. In retaliation, the tribes began setting up slot machines in their bingo halls (according to AIGRA these machines could only be installed after a state compact had been negotiated). State officials condemned the Indian action as illegal; the tribes responded that they were eager to reach an agreement with the state but that California authorities were being obstructionist.

Republican Governor Pete Wilson negotiated a modest compact covering slot machines in 1998, but the California tribes were not satisfied. They launched a campaign for a ballot initiative that would permit Las Vegas–style casinos on all of the state's reservations. This campaign emphasized the economic benefits of gaming, particularly for rural areas, and began to win broad support. While successful at the polls, the 1998 initiative was later struck down by the state supreme court. Undeterred, in 2000 the tribes launched yet another campaign for a ballot initiative that would overturn the state supreme court's decision. Thanks in part to a $21 million advertising effort sponsored by the tribes that again emphasized the economic benefits of gaming for the entire state, that initiative was approved in March 2000.

Following the 2000 vote, Democratic governor Gray Davis (himself the beneficiary of a $650,000 campaign contribution from gaming tribes) moved quickly to approve compacts with California tribes and to facilitate the expansion of their gaming operations. By 2002 there were forty-five Indian gaming operations open in the state, with twenty more anticipated for the future. Tribes in other states followed a similar pattern, taking their cases to the general public in television and radio campaigns and ensuring their access to elected leaders by making campaign contributions to both individuals and political parties. Tribal officials also learned the benefits of making charitable contributions to local schools and hospitals, and casino operators made a point of being prominent members of local chambers of commerce and other business organizations.

Finally, state politicians began to see tribal gaming as an instrument for economic development. Connecticut authorities had long been interested in the Pequots' impact on the depressed economy of the eastern part of their state where idle shipyards and declining heavy industry had produced poor schools and highways and left the area with an aging, depressed population. According to a study conducted at the University of Connecticut, by 1998 the Pequots' overall business activity had generated 41,000 new jobs in the region, adding more than $1 billion per year to the state's economy. In upstate New York, government officials saw the Oneidas' Turning Stone Casino create more than 3,000 jobs in an area marked by rural poverty and population decline and decided to take the initiative for expansion themselves. Rather than wait for a tribe to approach him, New York Governor George Pataki *offered* a casino compact to the Seneca tribe in hopes that a Seneca casino would stimulate business in the depressed Buffalo-Niagara area. Pataki even offered the Senecas the use of the state-financed Niagara Falls Convention Center for its first gambling hall. The governor estimated that the state's compact with the Senecas would generate $830 million over ten years.

While resistance to Indian gaming continued in New York and elsewhere, political leaders across the country increasingly saw casinos as potential boosters of economic growth and tribal officials as businessmen and women who shared their commitment to "the system." This vision of Indian casinos as an alternate source of revenue for the states grew more powerful as economic conditions worsened during 2002 and 2003 and states faced growing deficits. Several governors approached tribes offering new casino agreements in return for payments to their state treasuries.

Despite its growth, however, the rise of the Indian gaming industry produced a number of difficult questions for Indians and non-Indians to ponder. Much of the income from gaming was concentrated in the hands of a few tribes and, unfortunately, most of the best-known gaming tribes are very small. The Pequots, for example, whose casino generates revenues approaching $1 billion per year, count fewer than 500 members. Two hundred tribes participated in the gaming business, but only about two dozen of these produce more than half of all gaming income. California provides a vivid illustration of this phenomenon. There, only about 10 percent of the state's 300,000 Indians belong to local tribes (the rest are immigrants from other states) and of these 30,000 people, fewer than 3 percent are members of groups who operate casinos. The nation's largest reservation, the Navajo Nation, did not approve the construction of a casino until 2001, and this was a relatively small operation far removed from the tribe's population center. By one 1998 estimate, gaming income affected only 8 percent of the entire Native American population.

In addition to gaming's limited reach, many tribes were troubled by a business that ultimately relied on the greed of gullible (although willing) tourists and retirees and had little relevance to indigenous cultures. Even leaders who supported gambling as a necessary instrument for economic independence regretted that the business required their communities to obscure and minimize their histories and distinctive ways of life. Hosting Las Vegas entertainers and housing busloads of travelers seemed inconsistent with ancient tribal lifeways. While some tribal members reveled in their

Elder Housing at Mohegan Tribal Headquarters The Fort Hill Community for Elders is only one example of how casino revenue has been used to improve the lives of Mohegan Indians. Such projects are important both to build internal support for gaming and to improve the tribe's public image.

newfound wealth and influence, others worried about the consequences of embracing the white world's cash and greed.

The success of Indian gaming signals the tribes' remarkable strength and creativity. But gaming also raises serious questions to be debated in the future. How can gaming income be used to develop businesses that are more culturally appropriate and that promise more long-term benefits for tribal workers and their families? Most gaming tribes have developed plans for alternate uses of gaming income, but none has developed businesses that can generate comparable quantities of cash. Second, can the avalanche of dollars generated by relatively few casinos somehow have an impact on the desperate economic conditions under which many Indians live? Can the political influence enjoyed by gaming tribes work to benefit Native Americans in distant and underserved communities like Pine Ridge? As the twenty-first century began, no clear answers emerged to any of these questions.

WHO IS AN INDIAN?

The final question with which Native Americans struggled during the 1990s and the onset of the new millennium was the definition of Indianness itself. As the group grew more politically powerful, more aware of its needs, and more jealous of its rights and prerogatives, it has become increasingly important for Native Americans to define who is an Indian and who is not.

At the same time, as Indians have become more deeply involved in the majority culture of the United States, Native people have had increased opportunities to live away from tribal areas and to marry non-Indians. In the decades since the 1940s when the population shift away from rural reservations began, large urban communities have emerged that contain thousands of individuals with both multitribal and multiracial heritages. At the same time, as non-Indians have come to view Native American traditions with greater interest and sympathy, it has become more attractive for individuals who belong to other racial groups to recognize an affiliation with Indian people. Some individuals who had previously obscured or hidden their Indian ancestry now recognize and promote their ties to the Native past. Others, such as the popular writer Jamake Highwater or the Hollywood actor "Iron Eyes" Cody, have simply invented an Indian ancestry out of an intense desire to become part of Native American life.

In the midst of these movements—of Indians to new homes, of non-Indians into Indian families, and of non-Indians into invented identities—tribal leaders, sympathetic whites, and Indian policymakers have asked an increasingly difficult question: Who is an Indian?

The 2000 census reported that approximately 2.5 million Americans listed their racial identity as American Indian or Alaskan Native. In addition, because the Census Bureau in 2000 for the first time allowed individuals to list more than one racial identity, it reported that another 1.6 million people reported a mixed racial heritage, combining American Indian with one or more other races. The 4.1 million people who reported themselves as wholly or partially American Indian in the 2000 census lived in every section of the United States, although 43 percent lived in the West and only 9 per-

Iron Eyes Cody. Originally a Hollywood actor, Iron Eyes Cody was featured in a series of television advertisements in the 1970s that condemned American air and water pollution. Cody posed as an Indian chief, shedding tears over the desecration of his homeland. Most viewers were not aware that none of "the chief's" ancestors were Native Americans.

years, the pace of American Indian population growth suggests otherwise. By 1940 the American Indian population had risen only to 345,000. A decade later in 1950 the census reported an increase to 357,000, a rise of only 4 percent. During the decade of the 1950s, however, the population figure rose by 46 percent and in the 1960s the rise was 51 percent. Both of these remarkable increases were surpassed in the 1970s when the American Indian population rose by 72 percent to 1.3 million. The rise in the 1980s was a relatively modest 38 percent, to a total of 1.8 million reported in the 1990 census. Interestingly, the rise in 2000 to 2.5 million people who reported *only* American Indian ancestry repeated the 38 percent rate of increase from the 1980s.

While Indian communities experienced improvements in health care and general prosperity during the last half of the twentieth century, the surge in population during those same years—an increase of more than 2 million between 1950 and 2000—indicates a shift in "self-identification," that is, the race individuals reported to census takers during the process of compiling each ten-year report. In 1960 the Census Bureau changed its method of enumeration from a system in which census personnel assigned racial designations to individuals to a system of self-identification. The largest rates of increase came after that shift.

Confirming the hypothesis that people shifted their affiliations in the censuses of the late twentieth century is the fact that analysis of those the censuses described as belonging to the "Indian" community in 1990 reveals dramatic differences from the identical group described in the 1960 census. The 1990 group was more than twice as "urban" as those who were identified as Indians in 1960. In addition, more than three times as many of the 1990 Indians were intermarried with whites as the 1960 Indians had been thirty years earlier. Finally, most of the growth in the census populations of the 1970s and 1980s occurred in states that historically had very small Indian communities.

The 2000 census further complicates the nature and definition of "Indian community." In addition to reporting a group of 4.1 million people, more than one-third of whom identify themselves with a second racial group in addition to American Indians, the 2000 census revealed that more than 1 million of the 2000 Indian group did not identify

cent of them lived in the Northeast. The majority of the group lived in cities, with New York (87,000) and Los Angeles (53,000) containing the largest concentrations of urban Indians. Native Americans made up the majority in 26 U.S. counties and comprise 19 percent of the population of Alaska (the highest percentage of any state).

A century earlier, in 1900, the Census Bureau had reported 237,000 Indians in the United States. While it may be possible for a group of that size to grow to ten times its original size in one hundred

PEOPLE, PLACES, AND THINGS

National Museum of the American Indian

The National Museum of the American Indian (NMAI), which opened on the mall in Washington, D.C., in September 2004, provides a home for more than one million artifacts of the indigenous civilizations of the Americas. The museum is also a platform for the study of Native American peoples and their histories and a place where Native artists and scholars can present their work to the public. Located at the foot of Capitol Hill and nestled alongside the Smithsonian Institution's other cultural storehouses, the NMAI symbolizes the American Indian community's visibility in modern America, as well as the many questions Native Americans generate, both for themselves and for others.

Senior Smithsonian administrator Sheila Burke, Senator Daniel Inouye (D-Hawaii), Director Rick West, Senator Ben Nighthorse Campbell (R-Colorado), and Secretary of the Smithsonian Lawrence M. Small celebrate at the ceremonies opening the National Museum of the American Indian on September 21, 2004.

themselves as members of any specific tribe. Of those who did, 730,000 identify themselves as Cherokees and 181,000 as "Latin American Indians." (The Cherokee tribe itself reported 175,000 members in 1996.) According to the 2000 census, modern Indians do not necessarily belong to tribes. Because of this fact—and the fact that most Indians live in urban areas—it is also apparent that as of 2000 a relatively small number of American Indians—approximately one million—live on reservations. And because the trend towards urban living and intermarriage is unlikely to reverse itself in the decades ahead, it seems safe to assume that the trend towards multiple racial identities, fewer people identifying with a single tribe, and a dwindling percentage of people living on reservations will continue in the twenty-first century.

One possible source of clarity in this complex swirl of identities could be tribal membership. Regardless of how census takers or the general public might define the boundaries of the Indian community, one might argue that "real" Indians are members of tribes. After all, historically Indians have functioned as tribal members and tribes themselves have become important political enti-

ties. If someone is not affiliated with a tribe, he or she cannot function in American political or social life as an Indian. But there are two problems with using tribal membership to determine Indianness. First, there is no common qualification for tribal membership. As a matter of law, tribes—as sovereign entities—determine their own membership requirements. Neither the Bureau of Indian Affairs nor Congress has ever dictated membership criteria to the tribes. As a result, many tribes—the Pequots, the Sault St. Marie Chippewas, and the Cherokees, for example—do not require a particular degree of tribal ancestry in order to be included as a member of the group. Others, such as the White Mountain Apaches, require as many as half of one's ancestors to have been tribal members. As a result, an individual with substantial Indian ancestry might not qualify as an "Indian" among the White Mountain Apaches while in other groups, this same person could be considered a model "Indian" citizen.

A final layer of complication arises from the question, "What is a tribe?" While the Bureau of Indian Affairs recognizes more than 500 "tribes" (these include Alaskan Native villages), there are 150 additional groups who have sought—but failed—to acquire the same legal status. Fifty-five of these applicants have petitioned the Indian Bureau's Branch of Acknowledgement and Research, an office created in 1978 to study the applications of people wishing to gain federal recognition (see Chapter 17). To date, fewer than half of these petitions have been acted on positively. More than 100 groups insist that they are tribes even though they remain "unrecognized" by federal authorities and most other Native American communities.

There are also groups that have avoided the recognition process altogether because their histories do not conform to the requirements of the Bureau of Indian Affairs. These are often communities who first gathered as refugees in the wake of white expansion or who have come from a variety of tribal backgrounds to form a new group identity. Most prominent among these amalgamated nonrecognized groups are the Lumbees of North Carolina, a community of Indian people with no single tribal ancestry that has long occupied lands in Robeson County, North Carolina (see Chapters 11 and 13).

For more than 150 years the Lumbees have defined themselves apart from both the white and black communities of that state. While counting more than 40,000 members and operating with the recognition of both their non-Indian neighbors and state authorities in North Carolina, the Lumbee Indians are not a federally recognized tribe and are not likely to become one because they cannot document a treaty relationship with the United States or a consistent set of ethnographic traditions coming down to them from an aboriginal past. As an alternative, Lumbee leaders have sought a congressional declaration to win them recognition equivalent to what the Pequots gained in 1983. To date, however, opposition from recognized tribes and their supporters has prevented this action from taking place. Among the Lumbees' most outspoken opponents have been the federally recognized Eastern Cherokees who also live in North Carolina. When lobbying against Lumbee recognition, Eastern Cherokee leaders have dismissed the Robeson County group as people who experienced "extensive intermarriage with various races."

It is unlikely that a single definition of "who is an Indian" will emerge from this complex and rapidly shifting social reality. Some definitions may suffice for government health and education programs, others may best apply to Bureau of Indian Affairs efforts to support reservation development, and still others may work for private aid groups. Indian organizations may employ still other criteria when organizing community support for a political campaign. What will be crucial in the decades to come will be that groups clarify their definitions and the reasons for them, and that Native Americans themselves have an opportunity to create their own definitions of Indianness rather than be forced to accept categories and membership requirements invented by others.

CONCLUSION

The pace of change in Native America has rarely slackened since the invasion of the Europeans began five centuries ago. This colonization process disrupted every aspect of the indigenous cultures, from social relations to health to politics and to ways of making a living. But through these centuries of upheaval and loss, American Indian communities have demonstrated a constant—almost miraculous—ability to adapt and persevere. The challenges that lie ahead in the new millennium are among the most difficult that Indian people have yet faced, and yet if the story of the past five centuries teaches anything, it is that inventive and unexpected answers are certain to emerge in the years to come. Somehow in the future, as in the past, "the people" will endure.

SUGGESTED READINGS

Biolsi, Thomas. *Deadliest Enemies: Law and the Making of Race Relations On and Off Rosebud Reservation.* Berkeley: University of California Press, 2001.   A history of recent legal battles between Indians and non-Indians in rural South Dakota that criticizes the courts for inflaming racial conflict and creating political polarization.

Bordewich, Fergus M. *Killing the White Man's Indian: Reinventing Native Americans at the End of the Twentieth Century.* New York: Doubleday, 1996.   A journalist's account of contemporary Native American life that includes descriptions of legal battles, social problems, economic development programs, repatriation, and casinos that are often critical of Indian leaders and community activists.

Colton, Larry. *Counting Coup: A True Story of Basketball and Honor on the Little Big Horn.* New York: Warner Books, 2000. A profile of Sharon LaForge, a Crow Indian high school basketball star, and the world of Indian basketball in Montana.

Dorris, Michael. The Broken Cord: *A Family's Ongoing Struggle with Fetal Alcohol Syndrome.* New York: Harper and Row, 1989. A Native writer's description of the struggles of his adoptive son and the impact of fetal alcohol syndrome on American Indian families.

Fromson, Brett. *Hitting the Jackpot: The Inside Story of the Richest Indian Tribe in History.* New York: Atlantic Monthly Press, 2003. A history of the Pequots and their immensely profitable casino in Connecticut by a financial reporter.

Nagel, Joane. *American Indian Ethnic Renewal: Red Power and the Resurgence of Identity and Culture.* New York: Oxford University Press, 1996. A sociologist's study of the impact of the Red Power movement on ethnic pride and the revitalization of Native communities.

Ortiz, Simon. *Speaking for the Generations: Native Writers on Writing.* Tucson: University of Arizona Press, 1998. Interviews with some of the most articulate spokespeople for contemporary Native American communities.

Sullivan, Robert. *A Whale Hunt: Two Years on the Olympic Peninsula with the Makah and Their Canoe.* New York: Scribner, 2000. A white journalist's account of the Makah tribe's campaign to reestablish their whale-hunting tradition and the white backlash that followed the killing of their first whale in 1999.

Wilkins, David E. *American Indian Politics and the American Political System.* Lanham, MD: Rowman and Littlefield, 2002. A comprehensive guide to the modern political structure of tribes and their relationship to federal and state governments and agencies.

Appendix A

CHRONOLOGY

c. 12,500 BCE	Oldest confirmed settlement in Western Hemisphere at Monte Verde, Chile
c. 8800 BCE	Lindenmeier site, Colorado, utilized by Paleo-Indian bands
7000 BCE	Earliest maize cultivated in Western Hemisphere in central Mexico
3000 BCE	Earliest arrivals of Aleut and Inuit peoples in Alaska
c. 1500 BCE	Earliest maize grown in southwestern and eastern North America
c. 100 BCE–400 CE	Hopewell culture flourishes in areas of eastern North America and Plains
c. 1100–1200	Chaco Canyon and Cahokia flourish as regional centers in Southwest and Midwest, respectively
c. 1200–1300	Severe drought disrupts Native American societies in Midwest, Plains, and Southwest
c. 1400	Iroquois and Huron confederacies formed
1492	Columbus lands among Tainos
c. 1500	Apaches and Navajos arrive in Southwest
1519	Cortés crushes Aztec empire
1528–34	Cabeza de Vaca and companions live among Karankawas
1540–41	De Soto defeated by Native Americans in Southeast
1542	Coronado abandons colonization effort in Southwest
1543	Cartier abandons effort to colonize on St. Lawrence River
1565–1601	Native Americans from Florida peninsula to Chesapeake Bay resist Spanish colonization
1580	Native American–French trade begins on St. Lawrence
1585–1590	Roanokes and Croatan prevent establishment of English colony at Roanoke
1598	Oñate crushes uprising at Ácoma Pueblo, establishes Spanish colony of New Mexico
1609	New France allies with Hurons and St. Lawrence Valley Indians against Five Nations Iroquois; beginnings of Indian-Dutch trade on Hudson River
1616–19	Deadly epidemic strikes coastal Native Americans in New England
1633–34	Smallpox epidemic devastates Native Americans throughout Northeast
1637	Pequot War in southern New England
1643–45	Kieft's War in New Netherland
1646	Virginia crushes final military resistance by Powhatans and allies
1648–57	Five Nations Iroquois wage Beaver Wars against Hurons and other Native peoples in eastern Great Lakes region
1647	Apalachees revolt in Florida
1656	Timucuas rebel against Spanish rule in Florida
1675–76	King Philip's War in southern New England; Bacon's Rebellion in Virginia
1677	First Covenant Chain treaties between Five Nations Iroquois and English colonies
1680–92	Pueblo Revolt in New Mexico; Spanish driven from colony
1689–1713	Eastern Native Americans drawn into European imperial wars (War of League of Augsburg and War of Spanish Succession)
1690s	English and French traders become active among Native peoples on northern Plains
1700	French establish trade ties with Caddos on Red River
1701	Iroquois Grand Settlement with England and France
1711–13	Tuscarora War in North Carolina
1712–50	Mesquakie Wars with New France and its Native American allies
1715–16	Yamasee War in South Carolina
1722	Tuscaroras become sixth nation in Iroquois Confederacy
1722–27	Anglo-Abenaki wars in northern New England

1729–30	Natchez uprising against French rule in Louisiana
c. 1730	Eastern Shoshones introduce horses in northern Plains
1734	"Walking Purchase" of Delaware lands by Pennsylvania
1738	Establishment of direct French-Indian trade ties on upper Missouri River
1742	Dakota Sioux make peace with French and latter's Indian allies
1746–50	Choctaw civil war
1750s–1760s	Russian traders permeate Aleutian Islands and enslave Aleuts
1754	Spanish officials broker temporary peace among Comanches, Apaches, and other southwestern tribes
1754–61	Eastern Native Americans drawn into Anglo-French war (in Europe, Seven Years War, 1756–63)
1763	French withdraw from North America; Pontiac's rebellion; Royal Proclamation by Britain to establish a boundary line between Native Americans and colonists
1768	First Treaty of Fort Stanwix
1769	Franciscans begin mission system in California
1775–83	Eastern Native Americans drawn into American Revolution
1780–82	Smallpox epidemic spreads among Native Americans throughout western North America
1781	Quechans evict Spanish from Colorado River
1783	Treaty of Paris grants independence to rebellious British colonies without providing for affected Indian allies of Britain
1786	Peace treaty between New Mexico and western Comanches
1790s	Western Cherokees begin the migration to Arkansas and southern Missouri
1790	Congress passes first Indian Trade and Intercourse Acts designed to regulate economic and political relationships between U.S. citizens and tribes
1791	St. Clair's Defeat: U.S. suffers greatest military loss to Indians; over 640 soldiers killed; confederacy led by Little Turtle inflicts fatal casualties on over one-third of the standing army of the U.S.
1794	Battle of Fallen Timbers: Anthony Wayne defeats Indian confederacy in Ohio
1795	Treaty of Greenville: Midwestern confederacy cedes much of Ohio to U.S.
1799	Handsome Lake and Longhouse religion emerge among the Senecas. Russian-American Company organized to monopolize fur trade in Alaska.
1803	U.S. obtains Louisiana Territory from France
1804–1806	Lewis and Clark visit the western tribes in the newly acquired Louisiana Territory, and in the Pacific Northwest
1805	Tenskwatawa (Shawnee Prophet) emerges among Shawnees and begins religious revitalization that Tecumseh later (1807–08) will transform into a political movement
1807	Manuel Lisa builds American Fur Co. post at mouth of the Big Horn River; American trappers permeate northern Rockies and trade with neighboring tribes
1811	Battle of the Tippecanoe: Wm. Henry Harrison defeats Shawnee Prophet and destroys Prophetstown; Tecumseh recruiting tribes in the South
1812–1815	War of 1812: Tecumseh and midwestern tribes fight with British against U.S.
1813	Tecumseh killed at the Battle of the Thames in Canada
1814	Creek War in the South ends with the Red Sticks' defeat at Horseshoe Bend, in Alabama
1818	First Seminole War: Andrew Jackson invades Spanish Florida. Dine Ana-aii settle near Zunis and Acomas
1819	U.S. acquires Florida in Adams-Onis Treaty
1820	Mexico becomes independent; Anglos begin colonization of East Texas

1821	Sequoyah formulates the Cherokee syllabary. William Becknell starts Santa Fe trade
1824	Secretary of War establishes first Office of Indian Affairs within the War Department. British Hudson Bay Co. opens trade with Tlingits.
1824	Chumash revolt in southern California
1825–1840	Rendezvous emerge and function as trading fairs for Rocky Mountain tribes, trappers, and traders. Anglo trappers settle at Taos and Santa Fe.
1827	Red Bird Uprising among the Ho-Chunks in Wisconsin. Cherokees adopt a written constitution
1828–29	Yokut uprising in central California
1830	Indian Removal Act passed by Congress
1830s	Chihuahua and Sonora pass bounty laws on Apache scalps.
1831	*Cherokee Nation v. Georgia:* U.S. Supreme Court defines tribes as "domestic dependent nations."
1832	Black Hawk War in Illinois and Wisconsin. *Worcester v. Georgia:* U.S. Supreme Court rules that state laws do not extend to Indian owned territory
1833	Mexican government secularizes missions in California. Potawatomi removals begin in Illinois and Indiana. Bent's Fort established on Arkansas River to trade with Southern Cheyennes and Arapahos.
1835–1838	Second Seminole War; Osceola captured in 1837, dies in 1838
1836	Creeks removed to Indian Territory
1837–1838	Smallpox decimates Mandans, Arikaras, and Hidatsas
1837–1840	Chickasaws removed to Indian Territory
1838–1840	Cherokees removed over "Trail of Tears"; Texas Cherokees forced to withdraw to Indian Territory
1841	Cherokee and Choctaw nations establish public schools in Indian Territory
1845	Wildcat leads part of Seminoles to Mexico
1846	Treaty of Guadalupe Hidalgo transfers Southwest from Mexico to U.S. Miami removals begin in Indiana.
1847	Pueblos attack Americans in Taos Revolt
1848	Gold discovered at Sutter's Mill in California, non-Indians flock to region
1851	First Treaty of Fort Laramie: most Plains tribes to remain north of the Platte and south of the Arkansas rivers; Cheyennes and Arapahos to hunt in western Kansas, eastern Colorado. Cherokee Nation establishes male and female seminaries.
1853–1855	Rogue River War in Oregon
1854–1855	Gov. Isaac Stevens purchases Indian lands in Washington Territory
1855	Chickasaws establish separate nation in Indian Territory
1861–1865	Civil War
1862	Santee Dakota uprising in Minnesota
1863	Mescalero Apaches forced onto Bosque Redondo reservation in New Mexico. Kit Carson conducts campaign against Navajos.
1863–1867	Red Cloud's War: Lakotas and Cheyennes defend Powder River country against miners and U.S. army; (1866) Lakotas led by Crazy Horse defeat Fetterman
1864	Sand Creek Massacre in Colorado. Navajos forced on "the Long Walk" from Arizona to Bosque Redondo
1865	Stand Watie is the last Confederate general to surrender to the Union
1867	U.S. purchases Alaska from Russia
1867–1870	Additional tribes (Osages, Shawnees, Pawnees, Delawares, Oto-Missourias, et al.) resettled in Indian Territory

1868	Second Treaty of Fort Laramie: Lakotas to occupy lands between Missouri River and Big Horn Mountains; army to keep non-Indians from Lakota lands. Bosque Redondo abolished; Navajos return to Four Corners region
1868	Grant's Peace Policy initiated
1871	Congress decides that federal government will sign no more treaties with tribes
1872	Western Apaches assigned to reservations in Arizona
1872–1873	Modoc War in California
1874	Red River War ends with the defeat of southern Plains tribes at Palo Duro Canyon
1876	Battle of the Little Big Horn
1877	Crazy Horse murdered. Chief Joseph and Nez Percé flee Idaho for Canada. Government representatives coerce Sioux leaders into accepting a treaty that transfers Black Hills to the United States.
1878	Paiute, Bannock, Sheepeater War in Oregon and Idaho
1878–1879	Cheyennes flee reservation in Oklahoma attempting to return to northern Plains ("Cheyenne Autumn").
1879	Ute War in Colorado. Victorio flees reservation, killed in Mexico (1880). Indian Industrial School opens at abandoned army barracks in Carlisle, Pennsylvania.
1882	Indian Rights Association established in Philadelphia, PA.
1884	Sarah Winnemucca publishes *Life Among the Piutes*, an account of her life and her tribe's encounter with American expansion.
1885	North Carolina legislature recognizes "Croatan Indians" and approves separate schools for their children.
1885–1886	Geronimo leads Apache resistance
1887	General Allotment Act, sponsored by Massachusetts Senator Henry Dawes, becomes law.
1889	Sioux agree to sell 9 million acres in western Dakotas, breaking up "Great Sioux Reserve" and creating several smaller reservations. Nelson Act establishes White Earth reservation in northwestern Minnesota as reservation for Ojibwe bands; 1,000 tribal members relocate there. Skolaskin, a prophet on the Colville reservation, sent to military prison on Alcatraz Island for opposing government "civilization" programs.
1890	Ghost Dance spreads to Lakotas. Sitting Bull murdered at Standing Rock reservation. Wounded Knee massacre at Pine Ridge reservation.
1898	Curtis Act establishes timetable for dissolution of tribal governments in Indian Territory.
1903	Supreme Court declares in *Lone Wolf v. Hitchcock* that Congress may violate Indian treaties.
1907	Congress ignores Indian petitions to create state of Sequoyah, unites Indian Territory and Oklahoma Territory in new state of Oklahoma.
1911	Society of American Indians founded in Columbus, Ohio.
1912	Jim Thorpe wins gold medals in decathlon and pentathlon at Olympic games in Stockholm, Sweden. Alaska Native Brotherhood and Alaska Native Sisterhood organized.
1916	Charles Eastman publishes autobiography, *From The Deep Woods to Civilization*.
1917	United States enters World War I; 12,000 Native Americans join armed services.
1918	Native American Church in Oklahoma organized as a nonprofit corporation.
1922	All Pueblo Council meets and adopts resolutions opposing New Mexico Senator Holm Bursum's bill to settle titles to tribal land. Navajo Tribal Council organized.
1924	Congress grants U.S. citizenship to all Native Americans not previously enfranchised by earlier legislation.
1928	Meriam Report on conditions among American Indians delivered to Secretary of Interior.

1933	President Roosevelt appoints John Collier Commissioner of Indian Affairs.
1934	Congress approves Indian Reorganization Act. American Indian Federation organized to oppose Collier policies.
1935	D'Arcy McNickle publishes *The Surrounded*. Klamaths, Crows, Navajos, and Iroquois tribes reject Indian Reorganization Act.
1936	Congress extends Indian Reorganization Act to Alaska and Oklahoma.
1939	Tonawanda Community House, built with Works Progress Administration support, dedicated by Eleanor Roosevelt.
1941	United States enters World War II; 25,000 Native Americans join armed services; at least 40,000 Indians leave home to take war-related jobs.
1942	U.S. Marines establish special code talker unit using bilingual Navajo volunteers.
1944	National Congress of American Indians organized in Denver, Colorado.
1945	Ira Hayes welcomed home as a war hero after participating in the raising of the American flag on Mount Suribachi on the Pacific island of Iwo Jima.
1946	Congress approves Indian Claims Commission Act.
1950	Commissioner of Indian Affairs Dillon Myer announces national program of relocation to help Indian families move to cities to take advantage of economic opportunities away from reservations.
1953	Congress approves resolution calling for termination of federal ties to tribes and adopts Public Law 280, unilaterally extending state criminal jurisdiction to reservations in five states (Minnesota, California, Nebraska, Oregon, and Wisconsin). Chicago American Indian Center founded; first urban Indian center in the United States
1955	Indian Health Service transferred to Department of Health, Education and Welfare (later Health and Human Services).
1961	Menominee Tribe terminated; Menominee reservation becomes a county; federal support withdrawn. (Congress reversed itself by restoring tribal status to Menominees in 1973.)
1962	Tribal leaders formally present "Declaration of Purpose" resolution, adopted the previous year in Chicago, to President John Kennedy.
1964	Deciding the case, *People v. Woody*, the California Supreme Court ruled that prosecuting an Indian member of the Native American Church for possession of peyote is unconstitutional.
1968	Congress approves American Indian Civil Rights Act. American Indian Movement founded in Minneapolis.
1969	Kiowa author N. Scott Momaday wins Pulitzer Prize in literature for *House Made of Dawn*. Former NCAI Executive Director Vine Deloria, Jr., publishes *Custer Died For Your Sins: An Indian Manifesto*. Community activists seize abandoned federal prison on Alcatraz Island in San Francisco Bay.
1970	Nixon administration formally cancels national policy of termination.
1971	Congress approves Alaska Native Claims Settlement Act.
1972	"Trail of Broken Treaties" protesters occupy Bureau of Indian Affairs offices in Washington, D.C.
1973	AIM activists occupy Wounded Knee, South Dakota.
1974	Coalition of some three dozen tribes form Council of Energy Resource Tribes.
1975	Two FBI agents killed in gun battle with AIM members in South Dakota. Anna Mae Acquash murdered. Congress approves American Indian Self Determination and Educational Assistance Act
1978	Congress approves American Indian Religious Freedom Act and American Indian Child Welfare Act.

1979	U.S. Supreme Court upholds lower court decisions affirming Columbia River and Puget Sound tribes' treaty-based fishing rights.
1980	President Carter signs Maine Indian Claims Settlement Act. U.S. Supreme Court upholds Sioux tribe's claims for compensation for seizure of Black Hills. Tribes refuse to accept the reward, declaring, "The Black Hills are not for sale."
1988	In the "Go Road decision," the U.S. Supreme Court refuses to recognize an Indian petition to prevent logging of sacred areas within a national forest. Congress approves the American Indian Gaming Regulatory Act.
1990	Congress approves Native American Graves Protection and Repatriation Act.
1992	Mashantucket Pequot tribe opens casino in Connecticut.
1996	Winona LaDuke runs as vice presidential candidate of the Green Party. She repeats this effort in 2000.
1999	Makah hunters kill whale under authorization from the International Whaling Commission.
2000	Kevin Gover issues formal apology for Bureau of Indian Affairs' legacy of "racism and inhumanity."

Appendix B

State and Federally Recognized Tribes

The following is a state-by-state listing of Indian tribes or groups that are federally recognized and eligible for funding and services from the Bureau of Indian Affairs (BIA). The list also includes Indian tribes or groups that are recognized by the states. State recognition acknowledges their status within the state but does not guarantee funding from the state or the federal government. State-recognized Indian tribes are not federally recognized; however, federally recognized tribes may also be state-recognized.

This list was compiled by the National Conference of State Legislatures (http://www.ncsl.org/programs/statetribe/tribes.htm) and is current as of August 2005.

Alabama

Federally Recognized

Poarch Band of Creeks

State-Recognized

Mowa Band of Choctaws
Echota Cherokees
Cherokees of S.E. Alabama
MaChis Lower Alabama Creek Tribe
Star Clan-Muscogee Creek Tribe
Cherokees of N.E. Alabama

Alaska

Federally Recognized

Village of Afognak
Native Village of Akhiok
Akiachak Native Community
Akiak Native Community
Native Village of Akutan
Village of Alakanuk
Alatna Village
Native Village of Aleknagik
Algaaciq Native Village (St. Mary's)
Allakaket Village
Native Village of Ambler
Village of Anaktuvuk Pass
Yupiit of Andreafski
Angoon Community Association
Village of Aniak
Anvik Village
Arctic Village (See Native Village of Venetie Tribal Government)
Native Village of Atka

Asa'carsarmiut Tribe (formerly Native Village of Mountain Village)
Atqasuk Village (Atkasook)
Village of Atmautluak
Native Village of Barrow Inupiat Traditional Government (formerly Native Village of Barrow)
Beaver Village
Native Village of Belkofski
Village of Bill Moore's Slough
Birch Creek Village
Native Village of Brevig Mission
Native Village of Buckland
Native Village of Cantwell
Native Village of Chanega (Chenega)
Chalkyitsik Village
Village of Chefornak
Chevak Native Village
Chickaloon Native Village
Native Village of Chignik
Native Village of Chignik Lagoon
Chignik Lake Village
Chilkat Indian Village (Kluckwan)
Chilkoot Indian Association (Haines)
Chinik Eskimo Community (Golovin)
Native Village of Chistochina
Native Village of Chitina
Native Village of Chuathbaluk (Russian Mission, Kuskokwim)
Chuloonawick Native Village
Circle Native Community

Village of Clark's Point
Native Village of Council
Craig Community Association
Village of Crooked Creek
Curyung Tribal Council (formerly Native Village of Dillingham)
Native Village of Deering
Native Village of Diomede (Inalik)
Village of Dot Lake
Douglas Indian Association
Native Village of Eagle
Native Village of Eek
Egegik Village
Eklutna Native Village
Native Village of Ekuk
Ekwok Village
Native Village of Elim
Emmonak Village
Evansville Village (Bettles Field)
Native Village of Eyak (Cordova)
Native Village of False Pass
Native Village of Fort Yukon
Native Village of Gakona
Galena Village (Louden Village)
Native Village of Gambell
Native Village of Georgetown
Native Village of Goodnews Bay
Organized Village of Grayling (Holikachuk)
Gulkana Village
Native Village of Hamilton
Healy Lake Village
Holy Cross Village
Hoonah Indian Association
Native Village of Hooper Bay
Hughes Village

Huslia Village

Hydaburg Cooperative Association

Igiugig Village

Village of Iliamna

Inupiat Community of the Arctic Slope

Iqurmuit Traditional Council (formerly Native Village of Russian Mission)

Ivanoff Bay Village

Kaguyak Village

Organized Village of Kake

Kaktovik Village (Barter Island)

Village of Kalskag

Village of Kaltag

Native Village of Kanatak

Native Village of Karluk

Organized Village of Kasaan

Native Village of Kasigluk

Kenaitze Indian Tribe

Ketchikan Indian Corporation

Native Village of Kiana

Agdaagux Tribe of King Cove

King Island Native Community

King Salmon Tribe

Native Village of Kipnuk

Native Village of Kivalina

Klawock Cooperative Association

Native Village of Kluti Kaah (Copper Center)

Knik Tribe

Native Village of Kobuk

Kokhanok Village

New Koliganek Village Council (formerly Koliganek Village)

Native Village of Kongiganak

Village of Kotlik

Native Village of Kotzebue

Native Village of Koyuk

Koyukuk Native Village

Organized Village of Kwethluk

Native Village of Kwigillingok

Native Village of Kwinhagak (Quinhagak)

Native Village of Larsen Bay

Levelock Village

Lesnoi Village (Woody Island)

Lime Village

Village of Lower Kalskag

Manley Hot Springs Village

Manokotak Village

Native Village of Marshall (Fortuna Ledge)

Native Village of Mary's Igloo

McGrath Native Village

Native Village of Mekoryuk

Mentasta Traditional Council (formerly Mentasta Lake Village)

Metlakatla Indian Community, Annette Island Reserve

Native Village of Minto

Naknek Native Village

Native Village of Nanwalek (English Bay)

Native Village of Napaimute

Native Village of Napakiak

Native Village of Napaskiak

Native Village of Nelson Lagoon

Nenana Native Association

New Stuyahok Village

Newhalen Village

Newtok Village

Native Village of Nightmute

Nikolai Village

Native Village of Nikolski

Ninilchik Village

Native Village of Noatak

Nome Eskimo Community

Nondalton Village

Noorvik Native Community

Northway Village

Native Village of Nuiqsut (Nooiksut)

Nulato Village

Native Village of Nunapitchuk

Village of Ohogamiut

Village of Old Harbor

Orutsararmuit Native Village (Bethel)

Oscarville Traditional Village

Native Village of Ouzinkie

Native Village of Paimiut

Pauloff Harbor Village

Pedro Bay Village

Native Village of Perryville

Petersburg Indian Association

Native Village of Pilot Point

Pilot Station Traditional Village

Native Village of Pitka's Point

Platinum Traditional Village

Native Village of Point Hope

Native Village of Point Lay

Native Village of Port Graham

Native Village of Port Heiden

Native Village of Port Lions

Portage Creek Village (Ohgsenakale)

Pribilof Islands Aleut Communities of St. Paul and St. George Islands

Qagan Toyagungin Tribe of Sand Point Village

Rampart Village

Village of Red Devil

Native Village of Ruby

Village of Salamatoff

Organized Village of Saxman

Native Village of Savoonga

Saint George (See Pribilof Islands Aleut Communities of St. Paul and St. George Islands)

Native Village of Saint Michael

Saint Paul (See Pribilof Islands Aleut Communities of St. Paul and St. George Islands)

Native Village of Scammon Bay

Native Village of Selawik

Seldovia Village Tribe

Shageluk Native Village

Native Village of Shaktoolik

Native Village of Sheldon's Point

Native Village of Shishmaref

Shoonaq' Tribe of Kodiak

Native Village of Shungnak

Sitka Tribe of Alaska

Skagway Village

Village of Sleetmute

Village of Solomon

South Naknek Village

Stebbins Community Association

Native Village of Stevens

Village of Stony River

Takotna Village

Native Village of Tanacross

Native Village of Tanana

Native Village of Tatitlek

Native Village of Tazlina

Telida Village

Native Village of Teller

Native Village of Tetlin

Central Council of the Tlingit and Haida Indian Tribes

Traditional Village of Togiak

Native Village of Toksook Bay

Tuluksak Native Community
Native Village of Tuntutuliak
Native Village of Tununak
Twin Hills Village
Native Village of Tyonek
Ugashik Village
Umkumiute Native Village
Native Village of Unalakleet
Qawalangin Tribe of Unalaska
Native Village of Unga
Village of Venetie (See Native
    Village of Venetie Tribal
    Government)
Native Village of Venetie Tribal
    Government (Arctic Village and
    Village of Venetie)
Village of Wainwright
Native Village of Wales
Native Village of White
    Mountain
Wrangell Cooperative
    Association
Yakutat Tlingit Tribe

Arizona

Federally Recognized

Ak Chin Indian Community
Cocopah Tribe
Colorado River Indian Tribes
    (Arizona and California)
Fort McDowell Yavapai Nation
Fort Mojave Indian Tribe
    (Arizona, California, and
    Nevada)
Gila River Indian Community
Havasupai Tribe
Hopi Tribe
Hualapai Indian Tribe
Kaibab Band of Paiute Indians
Navajo Nation (Arizona, New
    Mexico, and Utah)
Pascua Yaqui Tribe
Quechan Tribe (Arizona and
    California)
Salt River Pima-Maricopa Indian
    Community
San Carlos Apache Tribe
San Juan Southern Paiute Tribe
Tohono O'odham Nation
Tonto Apache Tribe
White Mountain Apache Tribe

Yavapai-Apache Nation
Yavapai-Prescott Tribe

California

Federally Recognized

Agua Caliente Band of Cahuilla
    Indians
Alturas Indian Rancheria
Augustine Band of Cahuilla
    Mission Indians
Bear River Band of the
    Rohnerville Rancheria
Berry Creek Rancheria of Maidu
    Indians of California
Big Lagoon Rancheria
Big Pine Band of Owens Valley
    Paiute Shoshone Indians
Big Sandy Rancheria of Mono
    Indians
Big Valley Band of Pomo Indians
Blue Lake Rancheria
Bridgeport Paiute Indian
    Colony
Buena Vista Rancheria of
    Me-Wuk Indians
Cabazon Band of Cahuilla
    Mission Indians
Cachil DeHe Band of Wintun
    Indians of the Colusa Indian
    Community
Cahuilla Band of Mission Indians
Cahto Indian Tribe
Campo Band of Diegueño
    Mission Indians
Capitan Grande Band of
    Diegueño Mission Indians
Barona Group of Capitan Grande
    Band of Mission Indians
Viejas (Baron Long) Group of
    Capitan Grande Band of
    Mission Indians
Cedarville Rancheria
Chemehuevi Indian Tribe
Cher-Ae Heights Indian
    Community
Chicken Ranch Rancheria of
    Me-Wuk Indians
Cloverdale Rancheria of Pomo
    Indians
Cold Springs Rancheria of Mono
    Indians

Colorado River Indian Tribes
    (Arizona and California)
Cortina Indian Rancheria of
    Wintun Indians
Coyote Valley Band of Pomo
    Indians
Cuyapaipe Community of
    Diegueño Mission Indians
Death Valley Timbi-Sha Shoshone
    Band
Dry Creek Rancheria of Pomo
    Indians
Elem Indian Colony of Pomo
    Indians of the Sulphur Bank
    Rancheria
Elk Valley Rancheria
Enterprise Rancheria of Maidu
    Indians
Fort Bidwell Indian
    Community
Fort Independence Indian
    Community of Paiute Indians
Fort Mojave Indian Tribe
    (Arizona, California, and
    Nevada)
Graton Rancheria
Greenville Rancheria of Maidu
    Indians
Grindstone Indian Rancheria of
    Wintun-Wailaki Indians
Guidiville Rancheria
Hoopa Valley Tribe
Hopland Band of Pomo Indians
Inaja Band of Diegueño Mission
    Indians
Ione Band of Miwok Indians
Jackson Rancheria of Me-Wuk
    Indians
Jamul Indian Village
Karuk Tribe
Kashia Band of Pomo Indians of
    the Stewart's Point Rancheria
La Jolla Band of Luiseño Mission
    Indians
La Posta Band of Diegueño
    Mission Indians
Los Coyotes Band of Cahuilla
    Mission Indians
Lower Lake Rancheria
Lytton Rancheria
Manchester Band of Pomo
    Indians

Manzanita Band of Diegueño
 Mission Indians
Mechoopda Indian Tribe
Mesa Grande Band of Diegueño
 Mission Indians
Middletown Rancheria of Pomo
 Indians
Mooretown Rancheria of Maidu
 Indians
Morongo Band of Cahuilla
 Mission Indians
Northfork Rancheria of Mono
 Indians
Paiute-Shoshone Indians of the
 Bishop Community
Paiute-Shoshone Indians of the
 Lone Pine Community
Pala Band of Luiseño Mission
 Indians
Paskenta Band of Nomlaki
 Indians
Pauma Band of Luiseño Mission
 Indians
Pechanga Band of Luiseño
 Mission Indians
Picayune Rancheria of
 Chukchansi Indians
Pinoleville Rancheria of Pomo
 Indians
Pit River Tribe (includes Big Bend,
 Lookout, Montgomery Creek,
 and Roaring Creek Rancherias
 and XL Ranch)
Potter Valley Rancheria of Pomo
 Indians
Quartz Valley Indian Community
Quechan Tribe (Arizona and
 California)
Ramona Band or Village of
 Cahuilla Mission Indians
Redding Rancheria
Redwood Valley Rancheria of
 Pomo Indians
Resighini Rancheria (formerly
 known as the Coast Indian
 Community of Yurok Indians
 of the Resighini Rancheria)
Rincon Band of Luiseño Mission
 Indians
Robinson Rancheria of Pomo
 Indians

Round Valley Indian Tribes
 (formerly known as the Covelo
 Indian Community)
Rumsey Indian Rancheria of
 Wintun Indians
San Manual Band of Serrano
 Mission Indians
San Pasqual Band of Diegueño
 Mission Indians
Santa Rosa Indian Community
Santa Rosa Band of Cahuilla
 Mission Indians
Santa Ynez Band of Chumash
 Mission Indians
Santa Ysabel Band of Diegueño
 Mission Indians
Scotts Valley Band of Pomo Indians
Sheep Ranch Rancheria of
 Me-Wuk Indians
Sherwood Valley Rancheria of
 Pomo Indians
Shingle Springs Band of Miwok
 Indians
Smith River Rancheria
Soboba Band of Luiseño Mission
 Indians
Susanville Indian Rancheria
Sycuan Band of Diegueño
 Mission Indians
Table Bluff Reservation—Wiyot
 Tribe
Table Mountain Rancheria
Torres-Martinez Band of Cahuilla
 Mission Indians
Tule River Indian Tribe
Tuolumne Band of Me-Wuk
 Indians
Twenty-Nine Palms Band of
 Mission Indians
United Auburn Indian
 Community
Upper Lake Band of Pomo
 Indians
Utu Utu Gwaitu Paiute Tribe
Washoe Tribe (Carson Colony,
 Dresslerville Colony,
 Woodfords Community,
 Stewart Community, and
 Washoe Ranches) (California
 and Nevada)
Yurok Tribe

Colorado

Federally Recognized

Southern Ute Indian Tribe
Ute Mountain Tribe (Colorado,
 New Mexico, and Utah)

Connecticut

Federally Recognized

Mashantucket Pequot Tribe
Mohegan Indian Tribe
Schaghticoke Tribal Nation

State-Recognized

Golden Hill Paugussett Tribe
Paucatuck Eastern Pequot Tribe
Schaghticoke Bands

Delaware

State-Recognized

Nanticoke Indians

Florida

Federally Recognized

Miccosukee Tribe of Indians
Seminole Tribe (Dania, Big
 Cypress, Brighton, Hollywood,
 and Tampa reservations)

Georgia

State-Recognized

Georgia Tribe of Eastern
 Cherokee
Lower Muscogee Creek Tribe
Cherokee of Georgia Tribal
 Council

Idaho

Federally Recognized

Coeur D'Alene Tribe
Kootenai Tribe
Nez Percé Tribe
Shoshone-Bannock Tribes

Iowa

Federally Recognized

Sac & Fox Tribe of the
 Mississippi

Kansas

Federally Recognized

Iowa Tribe (Kansas and
  Nebraska)
Kickapoo Tribe of Indians
Prairie Band of Potawatomi
  Nation
Sac & Fox Nation of Missouri
  (Kansas and Nebraska)

Louisiana

Federally Recognized

Chitimacha Tribe
Coushatta Tribe
Jena Band of Choctaw Indians
Tunica-Biloxi Indian Tribe

State-Recognized

Caddo Indian Tribe
Choctaw-Apache of Ebarb
Clifton Choctaw
Louisiana Choctaw
United Houma Nation

Maine

Federally Recognized

Aroostook Band of Micmac
  Indians
Houlton Band of Maliseet Indians
Passamaquoddy Tribe
Penobscot Tribe

State-Recognized

Passamaquoddy Tribe
Penobscot Nation

Massachusetts

Federally Recognized

Wampanoag Tribe of Gay Head
  (Aquinnah)

State-Recognized

Hassanamisco

Michigan

Federally Recognized

Bay Mills Indian Community
Grand Traverse Band of Ottawa
  and Chippewa Indians

Hannahville Indian Community
Huron Potawatomi, Inc.
Keweenaw Bay Indian
  Community of L'Anse and
  Ontonagon Bands of Chippewa
  Indians
Lac Vieux Desert Band of Lake
  Superior Chippewa Indians
Little River Band of Ottawa
  Indians
Little Traverse Bay Bands of
  Odawa Indians
Match-e-be-nash-she-wish Band
  of Potawatomi Indians
Pokagon Band of Potawatomi
  Indians
Saginaw Chippewa Indian Tribe
Sault Ste. Marie Tribe of
  Chippewa Indians

State-Recognized

Burt Lake Band of Ottawa and
  Chippewa Indians
Gun Lake Band of Grand River
  Ottawa Indians
Swan Creek Black River
  Confederated Ojibwe Tribes
Grand River Band of Ottawa
  Indians

Minnesota

Federally Recognized

Lower Sioux Indian Community
  of Minnesota Mdewakanton
  Sioux Indians
Minnesota Chippewa Tribe (Six
  component reservations: Bois
  Forte Band [Nett Lake],
  Fond du Lac Band, Grand
  Portage Band, Leech Lake
  Band, Mille Lacs Band, and
  White Earth Band)
Prairie Island Indian Community
  of Minnesota Mdewakanton
  Sioux Indians
Red Lake Band of Chippewa
  Indians
Shakopee Mdewakanton Sioux
  Community
Upper Sioux Community

Mississippi

Federally Recognized

Mississippi Band of Choctaw
  Indians

Missouri

State-Recognized

Northern Cherokee
Chickamauga Cherokee

Federally Recognized

Eastern Shawnee Tribe of
  Oklahoma

Montana

Federally Recognized

Assiniboine and Sioux Tribes
Blackfeet Tribe
Chippewa-Cree Indians
Confederated Salish and Kootenai
  Tribes
Crow Tribe
Fort Belknap Indian Community
Northern Cheyenne Tribe

Nebraska

Federally Recognized

Iowa Tribe (Kansas and
  Nebraska)
Omaha Tribe
Ponca Tribe
Sac & Fox Nation of Missouri
  (Kansas and Nebraska)
Santee Sioux Tribe
Winnebago Tribe

Nevada

Federally Recognized

Confederated Tribes of the
  Goshute Reservation (Nevada
  and Utah)
Duckwater Shoshone Tribe
Ely Shoshone Tribe
Fort McDermitt Paiute and
  Shoshone Tribes (Nevada and
  Oregon)
Fort Mojave Indian Tribe
  (Arizona, California, and
  Nevada)

Las Vegas Tribe of Paiute Indians of the Las Vegas Indian Colony
Lovelock Paiute Tribe of the Lovelock Indian Colony
Moapa Band of Paiute Indians
Paiute-Shoshone Tribe
Pyramid Lake Paiute Tribe
Reno-Sparks Indian Colony
Shoshone-Paiute Tribes
Summit Lake Paiute Tribe
Te-Moak Tribes of Western Shoshone Indians (Four constituent bands: Battle Mountain, Elko, South Fork, and Wells)
Walker River Paiute Tribe
Washoe Tribe (Nevada and California) (Carson Colony, Dresslerville Colony, Woodfords Community, Stewart Community, and Washoe Ranches)
Winnemucca Indian Colony
Yerington Paiute Tribe
Yomba Shoshone Tribe

New Jersey
State-Recognized
Rankokus

New Mexico
Federally Recognized
Jicarilla Apache Nation
Mescalero Apache Tribe
Navajo Nation (Arizona, New Mexico, and Utah)
Pueblo of Acoma
Pueblo of Cochiti
Pueblo of Jemez
Pueblo of Isleta
Pueblo of Laguna
Pueblo of Nambe
Pueblo of Picuris
Pueblo of Pojoaque
Pueblo of San Felipe
Pueblo of San Juan
Pueblo of San Ildefonso
Pueblo of Sandia
Pueblo of Santa Ana
Pueblo of Santa Clara
Pueblo of Santo Domingo

Pueblo of Taos
Pueblo of Tesuque
Pueblo of Zia
Ute Mountain Tribe (Colorado, New Mexico, and Utah)
Zuni Tribe

New York
Federally Recognized
Cayuga Nation
Oneida Nation
Onondaga Nation
Seneca Nation
St. Regis Band of Mohawk Indians
Tonawanda Band of Seneca Indians
Tuscarora Nation

State-Recognized
Poospatuck
Shinnecock

North Carolina
Federally Recognized
Eastern Band of Cherokee Indians

State-Recognized
Coharie
Haliwa-Saponi
Lumbee
Meherrin
Waccamaw-Siouan

North Dakota
Federally Recognized
Spirit Lake Tribe (formerly known as the Devil's Lake Sioux Tribe)
Standing Rock Sioux Tribe (North and South Dakota)
Three Affiliated Tribes of the Fort Berthold Reservation
Turtle Mountain Band of Chippewa Indians

Oklahoma
Federally Recognized
Absentee-Shawnee Tribe of Indians
Alabama-Quassarte Tribal Town

Apache Tribe
Caddo Indian Tribe
Cherokee Nation
Cheyenne-Arapaho Tribes
Chickasaw Nation
Choctaw Nation
Citizen Potawatomi Nation
Comanche Nation
Delaware Tribe of Indians
Delaware Nation
Eastern Shawnee Tribe
Fort Sill Apache Tribe
Iowa Tribe
Kaw Nation
Kialegee Tribal Town
Kickapoo Tribe
Kiowa Indian Tribe
Miami Tribe
Modoc Tribe
Muscogee (Creek) Nation
Osage Tribe
Ottawa Tribe
Otoe-Missouria Tribe
Pawnee Nation
Peoria Tribe
Ponca Tribe
Quapaw Tribe
Sac & Fox Nation
Seminole Nation
Seneca-Cayuga Tribe
Shawnee Tribe
Thlopthlocco Tribal Town
Tonkawa Tribe
United Keetoowah Band of Cherokee Indians
Wichita and Affiliated Tribes (Wichita, Keechi, Waco, and Tawakonie)
Wyandotte Tribe

Oregon
Federally Recognized
Burns Paiute Tribe
Confederated Tribes of the Coos, Lower Umpqua, and Siuslaw Indians
Confederated Tribes of the Grand Ronde Community
Confederated Tribes of the Siletz Reservation
Confederated Tribes of the Umatilla Reservation

Confederated Tribes of the Warm
   Springs Reservation
Coquille Tribe
Cow Creek Band of Umpqua
   Indians
Fort McDermitt Paiute and
   Shoshone Tribes (Nevada and
   Oregon)
Klamath Indian Tribe

Rhode Island

Federally Recognized

Narragansett Indian Tribe

South Carolina

Federally Recognized

Catawba Indian Nation (Catawba
   Tribe)

State-Recognized

Pee Dee Nation
Waccamaw Indian People

South Dakota

Federally Recognized

Cheyenne River Sioux Tribe
Crow Creek Sioux Tribe
Flandreau Santee Sioux Tribe
Lower Brulé Sioux Tribe
Oglala Sioux Tribe
Rosebud Sioux Tribe
Sisseton-Wahpeton Sioux Tribe
Standing Rock Sioux Tribe
   (North Dakota and South
   Dakota)
Yankton Sioux Tribe

Texas

Federally Recognized

Alabama-Coushatta Tribes
Kickapoo Traditional Tribe
Ysleta Del Sur Pueblo

Utah

Federally Recognized

Confederated Tribes of the
   Goshute Reservation (Nevada
   and Utah)

Navajo Nation (Arizona, New
   Mexico, and Utah)
Northwestern Band of Shoshoni
   Nation (Washakie)
Paiute Indian Tribe
Skull Valley Band of Goshute
   Indians
Utc Indian Tribe of the Uintah
   and Ouray Reservation
Ute Mountain Tribe (Colorado,
   New Mexico, and Utah)

Virginia

State-Recognized

Eastern Chickahominy
Chickahominy
Mattaponi
Monacan
Nansemond
Pamunkey
Rappahannock
Upper Mattaponi

Washington

Federally Recognized

Confederated Tribes of the
   Chehalis Reservation
Confederated Tribes of the
   Colville Reservation
Confederated Tribes and Bands of
   the Yakama Nation
Hoh Indian Tribe
Jamestown S'Klallam Tribe
Kalispel Indian Community
Lower Elwha Tribal Community
Lummi Tribe
Makah Indian Tribe
Muckleshoot Indian Tribe
Nisqually Indian Tribe
Nooksack Indian Tribe
Port Gamble Indian Community
Puyallup Tribe
Quileute Tribe
Quinault Tribe
Samish Indian Tribe
Sauk-Suiattle Indian Tribe
Shoalwater Bay Tribe
Skokomish Indian Tribe
Snoqualmie Tribe
Spokane Tribe
Squaxin Island Tribe

Stillaguamish Tribe
Suquamish Indian Tribe
Swinomish Indians
Tulalip Tribes
Upper Skagit Indian Tribe

Wisconsin

Federally Recognized

Bad River Band of the Lake
   Superior Tribe of Chippewa
   Indians
Forest County Potawotomi
   Community
Ho-Chunk Nation
Lac Courte Oreilles Band of Lake
   Superior Chippewa Indians
Lac du Flambeau Band of Lake
   Superior Chippewa Indians
Menominee Indian Tribe
Oneida Tribe
Red Cliff Band of Lake Superior
   Chippewa Indians
Sokaogon Chippewa Community
St. Croix Chippewa Indians
Stockbridge-Munsee Community
   of Mohican Indians

Wyoming

Federally Recognized

Arapahoe Tribe
Shoshone Tribe

**Source (federally recognized
   tribes):** *Federal Register, Friday,
   July 12, 2002.*
Source (state-recognized tribes):
   National Indian Law Library;
   Various State Commissions on
   Indian Affairs.
© 2005 National Conference of
   State Legislatures, All Rights
   Reserved
Denver Office: Tel: 303-364-7700,
   Fax: 303-364-7800, 7700 East
   First Place, Denver, CO 80230
Washington Office:
   Tel: 202-624-5400,
   Fax: 202-737-1069, 444 North
   Capitol Street, N.W., Suite 515,
   Washington, D.C. 20001

Appendix C

Most Populous Tribes

This information is derived from the U.S. Census publication "The American Indian and Alaska Native Population: 2000" based on the 2000 U.S. census data. It is available at http://www.census.gov/prod/2002pubs/c2kbr01-15.pdf. The data reflect responses by those persons reporting that they belong to one tribe.

Tribe	Population
1. Cherokee	281,069
2. Navajo	269,202
3. Sioux	108,272
4. Chippewa	105,907
5. Choctaw	87,349
6. Pueblo	59,533
7. Apache	57,060
8. Lumbee	51,913
9. Eskimo	45,919
10. Iroquois	45,212
11. Creek	40,223
12. Blackfeet	27,104
13. Chickasaw	20,887
14. Tohono O'odham	17,466
15. Potawatomi	15,817
16. Yaqui	15,224
17. Tlingit-Haida	14,825
18. Alaska Athabascan	14,520
19. Seminole	12,431
20. Aleut	11,941

Appendix D

Largest Landholding Tribes

Tribe	State	Tribal Trust Land (acres)	Individual Trust Allotments (acres)	Total Indian Land (acres)
Navajo	AZ, NM, UT	14,715,093	717,077	15,432,170
Tohono O'odham	AZ	2,773,850	320	2,774,170
Pine Ridge	SD	749,883	1,314,624	2,064,507
Cheyenne River	SD	1,150,546	872,843	2,023,389
San Carlos	AZ	1,826,541	0	1,826,541
Wind River	WY	1,710,169	101,196	1,811,365
Rosebud	SD	1,135,230	641,009	1,776,239
White Mountain Apache	AZ	1,664,972	0	1,644,972
Hopi	AZ	1,560,993	220	1,561,213
Crow	MT	408,444	1,107,561	1,516,005
Standing Rock	ND, SD	422,512	825,822	1,248,334
Fort Berthold	ND	596,257	604,409	1,200,666
Yakima	WA	904,411	225,851	1,130,262
Colville	WA	1,023,641	39,395	1,063,036
Uintah & Ouray	UT	1,007,238	14,318	1,021,556
Hualapai	AZ	992,463	0	992,463
Blackfeet	MT	302,072	635,630	937,702
Fort Peck	MT	391,769	512,914	904,683
Jicarilla	NM	823,580	0	823,580
Warm Springs	OR	592,143	51,348	643,491
Flathead	MT	581,907	45,164	627,071
Fort Belknap	MT	235,595	385,376	620,971
Ute Mountain	CO	588,825	8,483	597,308
Red Lake	MN	564,452	0	564,452
Fort Hall	ID	260,837	229,041	489,878

Sources: Annual Report of Indian Lands, BIA office of Trust Responsibilities, September 30, 1985; BIA area offices in Aberdeen, South Dakota; Billings, Montana; and Phoenix, Arizona.

Appendix E

SUGGESTED GENERAL REFERENCE WORKS

Cambridge History of the Native Peoples of the Americas. 3 Vols. Cambridge Eng. and New York: Cambridge University Press, 1996–2000. The two-part volumes include authoritative, comprehensive essays by scholars summarizing current interpretations and debates on the histories of indigenous peoples in North America, Mesoamerica, and South America, respectively.

Columbia Guides to American History and Culture. New York: Columbia University Press, 2001-. Each volume in this series of guides is authored by a highly respected scholar, and the individual volumes focus on geographic regions. In 2006 three volumes were in print (Theda Perdue and Michael Green, Southeast; Kathleen Bragdon, Northeast; and Loretta Fowler, Plains). The volumes briefly survey the history of the tribes of the region, and include a chronology, a section on "People, Places, and Events," and suggestions for further reading.

Davis, Mary B., ed. *Native America in the Twentieth Century: An Encyclopedia*. New York: Garland Publishing Inc., 1996. A comprehensive reference to Native Americans in the twentieth century, with entries focusing upon political, cultural, economic, religious, and medical subjects. The volume also contains entries on specific tribes but not on specific individuals.

Deloria, Philip J. and Neal Salisbury, eds. *A Companion to American Indian History*. Malden, MA: Blackwell Publishers Ltd., 2002. This volume contains twenty-five essays which explore past and current scholarship on major themes in Native American history. The essays are written by acknowledged specialists in the field.

Hoxie, Frederick E., ed. *Encyclopedia of North American Indians: Native American History, Culture, and Life from Paleo-Indians to the Present*. Boston: Houghton Mifflin, 1996. A one-volume reference work with entries on culture areas, tribes, major events in Native American history, prominent individuals, contemporary issues, and major controversies. Indexed by subject, tribe, and author, the encyclopedia's entries were prepared by academic experts as well as community members. Many authors are Native American.

Josephy, Alvin M. Jr., ed. *America in 1492: The World of Indian Peoples Before the Arrival of Columbus*. New York: Alfred A. Knopf, 1992. Produced with the assistance of the D'Arcy McNickle Center for the History of the American Indian, at the Newberry Library, this volume contains essays by major scholars assessing the state of various Indian cultures throughout the Americas in 1492. Other essays focus on Native American art, religion, languages, kinship systems, and concepts of science and technology.

Kappler, Charles J., comp and ed. *Indian Affairs: Laws and Treaties, Vol. II, Treaties*. Washington: Government Printing Office, 1904. Reprinted by Amereon House (Mattituck, NY, 1972). This indispensable volume contains the verbatim texts of all ratified treaties and subsequent "agreements" negotiated between the United States and the Indian tribes, 1778–1883. The treaties are arranged chronologically and contain the names of those Native Americans who signed them.

Nabakov, Peter, and Robert Easton. *Native American Architecture*. New York: Oxford University Press, 1989. Profusely illustrated, this volume surveys the broad spectrum of buildings utilized by Native American people resident in the continental United States and Alaska.

Prucha, Francis Paul. *Atlas of American Indian Affairs*. Lincoln: University of Nebraska Press, 1990. This atlas contains useful maps illustrating demographics, land cessions, reservations, and military posts, and several maps focusing upon events such as the Black Hawk War, Indian Removal routes, and the Little Big Horn confrontation.

Prucha, Francis Paul. *A Bibliographic Guide to the History of Indian-White Relations in the United States*. Chicago: University of Chicago Press, 1977. Compiled by a meticulous scholar, this volume lists the major sources (manuscript collections, records, documents, government publications, books, articles, and other works) that were available for research or published prior to 1975. A major research tool, this guide has an excellent index.

Prucha, Francis Paul. *Indian-White Relations in the United States: A Bibliography of Works Published 1975–1980*. Lincoln: University of Nebraska Press,

1982.   This volume extends the coverage of materials listed in the previous volume to 1980. The Newberry Library's D'Arcy McNickle Center for American History organized two additional volumes to extend Prucha's bibliographies to cover material published through 1990. These volumes are: William Swagerty, ed., *Scholars and the Indian Experience* (Bloomington: Indiana University Press, 1984; and Jay Miller, Colin Calloway, and Richard Sattler, *Writings in Indian History, 1985–1990* (Norman: University of Oklahoma Press, 1995).

Sturtevant, William C. ed., *Handbook of North American Indians*. 20 vols. Washington: Smithsonian Institution Press, 1978-.   This multi-volume reference remains the definitive reference work on Native American people. By 2006 thirteen of the proposed 20 volumes had been published. Most volumes have a geographical focus (Northeast, Northwest Coast, Plains, etc.) with a discussion of tribes occupying those regions. Others focus on subjects such as languages, Indian-white relations, biography, etc. The entries are detailed and written by acknowledged scholars. An indispensable research tool for serious scholars.

Tanner, Helen Hornbeck, ed. *Atlas of Great Lakes Indian History*.   Highly praised by scholars, this atlas contains a good textual discussion and superb maps of tribal history in the Great Lakes region from the pre-Columbian period through the late nineteenth century.

Thomas, David Hurst, Jay Miller, Richard White, Peter Nabakov, and Philip J. Deloria. *The Native Americans: An Illustrated History*. Atlanta: Turner Publishing Inc., 1993.   This beautifully illustrated "coffee-table" book, written by leading scholars, not only provides a popular account of Native American history, but it also features hundreds of vivid illustrations suitable for classroom use or PowerPoint presentations. An excellent resource.

Tiller, Veronica Velarde, comp. and ed.. *Tiller's Guide to Indian Country: Economic Profiles of American Indian Reservations*. Albuquerque: BowArrow Publishing Co, 2005.   An excellent resource for information on contemporary Native American communities. The volume contains data on tribal membership, tribally held lands, governments, education, per capita income, tribal enterprises, web sites, etc.

Wright, Muriel H. *A Guide to the Indian Tribes of Oklahoma*. Norman: University of Oklahoma Press, 1951.   This illustrated volume remains one of the best reference works for the Oklahoma tribes, particularly after the removal period, or during their residence in Oklahoma.

Appendix F

Films and Videos

Another Wind Is Moving: The Off-Reservation Indian Boarding School. Produced by Donald D. Stull and directed by David Kendall. Kickapoo Nations School and Summit Street Productions. 58 mins. 1985. An examination of the history of off-reservation schools from the late nineteenth century to their phasing out in the late twentieth century.

Atanarjuat, the Fast Runner. Produced by Paul Apak Angilirq, Norman Cohn, and Zacharias Kunuk. Igloolik Isuma Productions Inc. 172 mins. 2001. Canada's first feature-length fiction film written, produced, directed, and acted by Inuits, *Atanarjuat* is an exciting action thriller set in ancient Igloolik. The film unfolds as a life-threatening struggle between powerful natural and supernatural characters. It presents a wonderful evocation of pre-contact tribal life.

Black Hawk's War. Produced by Gary Foreman. The History Channel/Arts and Entertainment Network. 50 mins. 2000. This excellent docu-drama examines the events surrounding the Black Hawk War and appraises the role of both Black Hawk and Keokuk. The film illustrates that the conflict was caused by miscalculations on both sides.

Black Indians: An American Story. Produced by Rich Heape. Rich Heape Films Inc. 60 mins. 2000. Narrated by James Earl Jones, this film focuses upon Native Americans of mixed Indian–African American ancestry. It provides insights into modern definitions of "race" and Native American identity.

Broken Treaty at Battle Mountain. Produced and directed by Joel L. Freedman. Cinnamon Productions. 59 mins. 1984. This film examines the struggle of traditional western Shoshones to recover lands guaranteed to them by treaty in 1863, but subsequently lost.

Cahokia Mounds: Ancient Metropolis. Produced by the Cahokia Mounds Museum Society. Approx. 55. min. 1994. The film provides an excellent survey of the rise, flowering, and fall of Cahokia and its Mississippian inhabitants. It is filmed on site at Cahokia, utilizes artistic re-creations, and amply illustrates the sophistication and complexity of Mississippian society.

Captives. Produced by Gary Foreman. The History Channel/Arts and Entertainment Network. 50 mins. 1998. A perceptive docu-drama that illustrates that many white captives adapted readily to Native American culture and were adopted into the tribes. The film also indicates that many captives were reluctant to return to white society.

Contrary Warriors: A Story of the Crow Tribe. Produced by Connie Poten and Pamela Roberts. Rattlesnake Productions. 58 mins. 1985. Narrated by Peter Coyote, this film offers an excellent look at reservation life in the first seven decades of the 20th century. It focuses on the life of Robert Yellowtail, a Crow leader who worked within the system to protect Crow lands and resources.

The Dakota Conflict. Narrated by Floyd Westerman and Garrison Keillor. KTCB-Minneapolis-St. Paul. 60 mins. 1992. This film provides an excellent, balanced documentary account of the Minnesota Santee Dakota uprising in 1864.

Fallen Timbers. Produced by Gary Foreman. The History Channel/Arts and Entertainment Network. 50 min. 2000. An excellent docu-drama focusing upon the life of William Wells and the post-revolutionary struggle for the Ohio country, the film also discusses Harmar's Defeat, St. Clair's Defeat, and the Treaty of Greenville.

Gathering Up Again: Fiesta in Santa Fe. Produced and directed by Jeanette De Bouzek. Quotidian Independent Documentary Research. 47 mins. 1992. Documents the celebration in Santa Fe of the three hundredth anniversary of the Spanish "re-conquest" of New Mexico and the bitter ethnic conflicts that emerged among Anglos, Hispanics, and Pueblo Indians.

Geronimo and the Apache Resistance. Produced by Neal Goodwin. WGBH-Boston. Part of *The American Experience* series. 60 mins. 1990. An excellent documentary on Geronimo and the Apache resistance, the film also traces the subsequent fate of Geronimo and his followers in Florida and Oklahoma.

Incident at Oglala: The Leonard Peltier Story. Produced by Arthur Chobanian. Miramax Films. 90 mins. 1992. This film examines the incidents surrounding the murder of two FBI agents on the Pine Ridge Reservation in 1975, and the subsequent trial and imprisonment of Leonard Peltier.

Indian America: A Gift from the Past. Produced and directed by Karen Thomas. Media Resource Associates, Inc. 60 mins. 1994.   Recounts the late twentieth-century archaeological discovery of the Makah village of Ozette, buried in a mudslide on the Olympic Peninsula five hundred years earlier, and how evidence found at the site has contributed to a strengthening of Makah culture and identity.

Indians, Outlaws, and Angie Debo. Produced by Barbara Abrash. WGBH-Boston. Part of *The American Experience* series. 60 mins. 1989.   Focusing upon the life of Angie Debo, an Oklahoma historian who exposed the frauds through which tribes in eastern Oklahoma lost their land, this excellent documentary provides insights into the shortcomings of the Dawes Act and its allotment of tribal land.

In the Light of Reverence. Produced by Christopher McLeod and Malinda Maynor. Earth Island Institute. Approx 70 mins. 2001.   This documentary illustrates Native American attachments to the land, or specific locations, and focuses upon tribespeople's attempts to protect Devil's Tower in Wyoming, Mt. Shasta in California, and sacred sites in the Southwest.

In the Spirit of Crazy Horse. Produced by Michael Dubois and Kevin McKiernan. *Frontline* – PBS. 60 mins. 1990.   This documentary offers insights into the rise of the American Indian Movement and focuses upon clashes between activists and federal (and tribal) officials in South Dakota during the 1960s and 1970s.

In the White Man's Image. Produced by Christine Lesiak. PBS. Part of *The American Experience* series. 55 mins. 1990.   Focusing upon Carlisle Indian School and the students who enrolled at the institution, this documentary examines federal attempts to change the cultural perspective of Native American students. Interviews with alumni are featured.

In Whose Honor: Native American Mascots. 46 mins. 1997.   This excellent documentary examines the controversy over the use of Native American mascots and focuses upon Charlene Teters, a graduate student at the University of Illinois, and her fight against Chief Illiniwek. Other mascots (Washington Redskins, Cleveland Indians, Atlanta Braves) also are discussed.

Ishi—The Last Yahi. Produced by Jed Riffe. Rattlesnake Productions. 60 min. 1990.   An excellent documentary account of Ishi, the last "wild" Indian who walked out of the California wilderness in 1911. The film provides good coverage of Ishi's response to living in San Francisco in the early twentieth century.

Last Stand at the Little Big Horn. Narrated by Scott Momaday. WGBH-Boston. Part of *The American Experience* series. 60 mins. 1992.   This documentary presents the most balanced account of the Battle of the Little Big Horn and discusses these events from both the U.S. Army's and Native Americans' perspectives.

Mashpee. Produced by Mark Gunning and Maureen McNamara. 59 mins. 1984.   An in-depth exploration of the issues and surprising outcome of the Mashpee Indians' unsuccessful effort in 1976 to recover tribal lands.

My Hands Are the Tools of My Soul. Narrated by Gerald Vizenor. Texture Films. 54 mins. 1978. This superb and haunting film illustrates how Native American artistic expression reflects Native American culture. This film has an almost mystical quality.

Navajo Code Talkers: The Epic Story. Produced by Brendan Tully and Francine M. Reznik. Brendan Tully Productions. Approx. 55 min. 1993.   This documentary focuses upon the Navajo Code Talkers, their experiences during World War II, and their continued influence among the Navajo people.

The Peyote Road. Produced by Gary Rhine. Kifaru Productions. 59 mins. 1993.   Documenting Native Americans' traditional use of peyote for religious purposes, this film focuses upon the Native American Church and its struggle to retain peyote as a sacrament, particularly in response to legal challenges by state governments.

Pontiac. Produced by Gary Foreman. The History Channel/Arts and Entertainment Network. 50 mins. 1996.   An excellent docu-drama focusing upon Pontiac's Revolt, this dramatic account traces the rise of Indian resentment in the Great Lakes following the Seven Years War and features historically accurate clothing, uniforms, weaponry, and personal adornment.

The Return of the Navajo Boy. Produced by Jeff Spitz and Bennie Klain. Groundswell Films. 52 mins. 2000.   A Sundance Film Festival 2000 selection, *The Return of the Navajo Boy* chronicles an extraordinary chain of events, beginning with the appearance of a 1950s film reel, which lead to the return of a long lost brother to his Navajo family. The film touches on media portrayals of Indians as well as the impact of uranium mining on the Navajos.

Smoke Signals. Produced by Larry Estes and Scott Rosenfelt. Miramax Films. 89 mins. 1998. Based on Sherman Alexie's short stories about life on the Spokane Indian reservation, and directed by Chris Eyre, this story focuses on the experiences of a young Indian "nerd" who travels to Arizona with a friend to retrieve the friend's father's remains. This Native American "road" movie is filled with observations about Indian stereotypes, and insights into definitions and problems of Native American identity.

Tecumseh. Produced by Gary Foreman. The History Channel/Arts and Entertainment Network. 50 mins. 1996. Another excellent docu-drama by Foreman which presents a relatively well-balanced account of the rise of Tecumseh and the Shawnee Prophet. The film presents a biographical study of Tecumseh through his death at the Battle of the Thames.

The War that Made America. Produced by Eric Stange and Ben Loetermann. WQED-Pittsburgh and French and Indian War 250 Inc. 240 mins. 2006. The first two hours of this four part docu-drama focusing on the French and Indian War (Seven Years War) examine the important role that Native Americans played in colonial politics and warfare during the middle decades of the 18th century. Excellent teaching materials for discussing these events are available from www .thewarthatmadeamerica.org.

Those Who Came Before. Southwest Parks and Monument Association. 60 mins. 1997. Focusing upon the Anasazi culture, this documentary provides an in-depth look at major ruins at Bandelier, Canyon de Chelley, and Mesa Verde, and what excavations at these locations tell archaeologists about the Anasazi people. This film presents a favorable perspective of archaeology.

When the Forest Ran Red. Senator John Heinz Pittsburgh Regional History Center and the Smithsonian Institution. 59 min. 2001. This excellent docu-drama examines the role Native Americans played in the coming of the Seven Years War to North America. It vividly illustrates that tribal leaders successfully manipulated both the British and French. Violent, but recommended.

Where the Spirit Lives. Produced by Paul Stephens. Amazing Spirit Productions Ltd. and the Canadian Broadcasting Corporation. 97 mins. 1991. This heart-rending dramatization of life in a Canadian boarding school during the 1930s is very applicable to Native American boarding schools in the U.S. It illustrates the physical, emotional, and sexual abuse endured by Native American students. This is a fictitious account, but tragically, one that is based on real circumstances.

Who Owns the Past? Produced by Jed Riffe. Jed Riffe Productions. 58 mins. 1999. A well-balanced examination of the controversy over the exhumation and control of Native American human remains and burial goods. The film discusses NAGPRA and Kennewick Man.

Appendix G

List of Tribal Gaming Operations

From http://indiancasinodirectory.org as of December, 2005.

Alabama

Creek Bingo Palace
    Atmore, AL

Alaska

KCAGaming/Bingo
    Klawock, AK
Native Village Barrow Pulltab
    Barrow, AK

Arizona

Apache Gold Casino
    San Carlos, AZ
Bluewater Casino
    Parker, AZ
Bucky's Casino
    Prescott, AZ
Casino Arizona at Indian Bend
    Scottsdale, AZ
Casino Arizona at Salt River
    Scottsdale, AZ
Casino Del Sol
    Tucson, AZ
Casino of the Sun
    Tucson, AZ
Cliff Castle Casino
    Camp Verde, AZ
Cocopah Bingo and Casino
    Somerton, AZ
Desert Diamond Casino Nogales
    Tucson, AZ
Desert Diamond Casino Pima
    Sahuerita, AZ
Fort McDowell Casino
    Fountain Hills, AZ
Golden Ha San Casino
    Ajo, AZ
Harrah's AkChin Casino
    Maricopa, AZ
HonDah Resort, Casino and
    Conference Center
    Pinetop, AZ

Lone Butte Casino
    Chandler, AZ
Mazatzal Casino
    Payson, AZ
Paradise Casino
    Yuma, AZ
Spirit Mountain Casino
    Mohave Valley, AZ
Vee Quiva Casino
    Laveen, AZ
Wildhorse Pass Casino
    Chandler, AZ
Yavapai Casino
    Prescott, AZ

California

Agua Caliente Casino
    Rancho Mirage, CA
Barona Casino
    Lakeside, CA
Black Bart Casino
    Willits, CA
Cache Creek Indian Bingo
    and Casino
    Brooks, CA
Cahuilla Creek Casino
    Anza, CA
Casino Morongo
    Cabazon, CA
Cher-Ae Heights Casino
    Trinidad, CA
Chicken Ranch Bingo and Casino
    Jamestown, CA
Chumash Casino
    Santa Ynez, CA
Colusa Indian Bingo and Casino
    Colusa, CA
Crystal Mountain Casino
    Placerville, CA
Eagle Mountain Casino
    Porterville, CA

Elk Valley Casino
    Crescent City, CA
Fantasy Springs Casino
    Indio, CA
Feather Falls Casino
    Oroville, CA
Gold Country Casino
    Oroville, CA
Golden Acorn Casino and Travel
    Center
    Campo, CA
Golden Bears Casino
    Klamath, CA
Havasu Landing Resort and
    Casino
    Havasu Lake, CA
Hopland and Shp-ka-wah
    Casino
    Hopland, CA
Jackson Rancheria Casino
    Jackson, CA
Konocti Vista Casino and Bingo
    Lakeport, CA
Lucky 7 Casino
    Smith River, CA
Lucky Bear Casino
    Hoopa, CA
Mono Wind Casino
    Auberry, CA
Paiute Palace Casino
    Bishop, CA
Pechanga Entertainment Center
    Pechanga, CA
Pit River Casino
    Burney, CA
Red Fox Casino and Bingo
    Laytonville, CA
Rincon Casino
    Valley Center, CA
Robinson Rancheria Casino and
    Bingo
    Nice, CA

San Manuel Indian Bingo and
Casino
Highland, CA
Shodakai Coyote Valley Casino
Redwood Valley, CA
Sierra Springs Casino and
Restaurant
Big Pine, CA
Soboba Casino
San Jacinto, CA
Spa Resort and Casino
Palm Springs, CA
Susanville Casino
Susanville, CA
Sycuan Casino
El Cajon, CA
Table Mountain Casino and
Bingo
Friant, CA
The Palace Indian Gaming Center
Lemoore, CA
Trump 29 Casino
Coachella, CA
Twin Pines Casino
Middletown, CA
Valley View Casino
Valley Center, CA
Viejas Casino
Alpine, CA
Win-River Casino Bingo
Redding, CA

Colorado

Sky Ute Casino and Lodge
Ignacio, CO
Ute Mountain Casino
Cortez, CO

Connecticut

Foxwood Resorts Casino
Ledyard, CT
Mohegan Sun
Uncasville, CT

Florida

Miccosukee Indian Gaming
Miami, FL
Seminole Indian Casino—
Brighton
Okechobee, FL

Seminole Indian Casino—
Hollywood
Hollywood, FL
Seminole Indian Casino—
Immokalee
Immokalee, FL
Seminole Indian Casino—Tampa
Tampa, FL

Idaho

Clearwater River Casino
Lewiston, ID
Coeur D'Alene Casino Resort
Hotel
Worley, ID
It'se Ye-Ye Casino
Kamiah, ID
Shoshone Bannock High Stakes
Bingo
Fort Hall, ID

Iowa

Casino Omaha
Omawa, IA
Meskwaki Bingo Casino Hotel
Tama, IA
WinnaVegas Casino and Bingo
Sloan, IA

Kansas

Casino White Cloud
White Cloud, KS
Golden Eagle Casino
Horton, KS
Harrah's Prairie Band Casino
Mayetta, KS
Sac and Fox Casino
Powhattan, KS

Louisiana

Cypress Bayou Casino
Charenton, LA
Grand Casino Coushatta
Kinder, LA
Paragon Casino Resort
Marksville, LA

Michigan

Bay Mills Resort and Casino
Brimley, MI
Big Bucks Bingo
Baraga, MI

Chip In's Island Resort and
Casino
Harris, MI
Kewadin Casino Christmas
Christmas, MI
Kewadin Casino Hessel
Hessel, MI
Kewadin Casino Manistique
Manistique, MI
Kewadin Casino, Hotels and
Convention Center
Sault Ste. Marie, MI
Kewadin Shores Casino
St. Ignace, MI
King's Club Casino
Brimley, MI
Lac Vieux Desert Resort Casino
Watersmeet, MI
Leelanau Sands Casino
Suttons Bay, MI
Little River Casino
Manistee, MI
Ojibwe Casino Resort
Baraga, MI
Ojibwe II Casino
Marquette, MI
Soaring Eagle Casino Hotel
Mt. Pleasant, MI
Turtle Creek Casino
Williamsburg, MI
Victories Casino Entertainment
Center
Petoskey, MI

Minnesota

7 Clans Casino and Hotel
Thief River Falls, MN
Black Bear Casino and Hotel
Carlton, MN
Fond du Luth Casino
Duluth, MN
Fortune Bay Resort Casino
Tower, MN
Grand Casino Hinkley
Hinkley, MN
Grand Casino Mille Lacs
Onamia, MN
Grand Portage Lodge and Casino
Grand Portage, MN
Jackpot Junction Casino and
Hotel
Morton, MN

Lake of the Woods Casino and
  Bingo
  Warroad, MN
Little Six Casino
  Prior Lake, MN
Mystic Lake Casino
  Hotel
  Prior Lake, MN
Northern Lights Casino
  Walker, MN
Palace Casino Hotel
  Cass Lake, MN
Prairie's Edge Casino and
  Resort
  Granite Falls, MN
Red Lake Casino and Bingo
  Red Lake, MN
Shooting Star Casino
  Mahnomen, MN
Treasure Island Resort and
  Casino
  Red Wing, MN
Treasure Island Resort and
  Casino
  Welch, MN
White Oak Casino
  Deer River, MN

Mississippi

Silver Star Resort and Casino at
  Pearl River
  Choctaw, MS

Montana

Charging Horse Casino and
  Bingo
  Lame Deer, MT
Discovery Lodge Casino
  Cut Bank, MT
Four C's Casino
  Box Elder, MT
Ft. Belknap Casino
  Ft. Belknap, MT
Glacier Peaks Casino
  Browning, MT
KwaTaqNuk Casino
  Polson, MT
Little Big Horn Casino
  Crow Agency, MT
Silver Wolf Casino
  Wolf Point, MT

Nebraska

Ohiya Casino
  Niobrara, NE
Rosebud Casino
  Valentine, NE

Nevada

Avi Resort and Casino
  Laughlin, NV
Moapa Tribal Casino
  Moapa, NV

New Mexico

Camel Rock Casino
  Santa Fe, NM
Cities of Gold Casino
  Santa Fe, NM
Dancing Eagle Casino
  Casa Blanca, NM
Inn of the Mountain Gods and
  Casino Apache
  Mescalero, NM
Isleta Casino
  Albuquerque, NM
Oh Kay Casino Resort
  San Juan Pueblo, NM
San Felipe Casino
  Hollywood
  San Felipe, NM
Sandia Casino
  Albuquerque, NM
Santa Ana Star Casino
  Bernalillo, NM
Sky City Casino
  San Fidel, NM
Taos Mountain Casino
  Taos, NM

New York

Akwesasne Mohawk Casino
  Akwesasne, NY
Mohawk Bingo Palace
  Hogansburg, NY
Seneca Nation Bingo-Allegany
  Salamanca, NY
Seneca Nation Bingo-Cattaraugus
  Irving, NY
Seneca Niagara Casino
  Niagara Falls, NY
Turning Stone Casino Resort
  Verona, NY

North Carolina

Harrah's Cherokee Casino
  Cherokee, NC

North Dakota

4 Bears Casino and Lodge
  New Town, ND
Big O Casino
  Wahpeton, ND
Dakota Magic Casino
  and Hotel
  Hankinson, ND
Prairie Knights Casino and Lodge
  Ft. Yates, ND
Skydancer Casino and Hotel
  Belcourt, ND
Spirit Lake Casino and Resort
  St. Michael, ND

Oklahoma

7 Clans Casino
  Red Rock, OK
Ada Gaming Center
  Ada, OK
Ardmore Gaming Center
  Ardmore, OK
Border Town Bingo
  Wyandotte, OK
Bristow Indian Community Bingo
  Bristow, OK
Checotah Indian Community
  Bingo
  Checotah, OK
Cherokee Casino
  Catoosa, OK
Cherokee Casino
  Roland, OK
Cherokee Casino
  Siloam Springs, OK
Cheyenne and Arapaho Bingo
  Clinton, OK
Choctaw Downs
  Grant, OK
Choctaw Gaming Center, Durant
  Durant, OK
Choctaw Gaming Center,
  McAlester
  McAlester, OK
Choctaw Gaming Center, Pocola
  Pocola, OK

Choctaw Gaming Center,
  Stringtown
  Stringtown, OK
Cimarron Bingo Casino
  Perkins, OK
Comanche Red River Casino
  Randlett, OK
Creek Nation Casino
  Tulsa, OK
Creek Nation Muscogee Bingo
  Muskogee, OK
Creek Nation Okmulgee Bingo
  Okmulgee, OK
Davis Gaming Center
  Davis, OK
Delaware Bingo Casino
  Anadarko, OK
Eufaula Indian Community Bingo
  Eufaula, OK
Fire Lake Entertainment Center
  Shawnee, OK
Goldsby Gaming Center
  Norman, OK
Kaw Nation Bingo
  Newkirk, OK
Keetoowah Bingo
  Tahlequah, OK
Lucky Star Bingo
  Concho, OK
Madill Gaming Center
  Madill, OK
Marlow Gaming Center
  Duncan, OK
Miami Tribe Entertainment
  Miami, OK
Newcastle Gaming Center
  Newcastle, OK
Ponca Tribal Bingo
  Ponca City, OK
Quapaw Casino
  Miami, OK
Seminole Nation Bingo
  Seminole, OK
Seneca Cayuga Bingo
  Grove, OK
Sulphur Gaming Center
  Sulphur, OK
Thlopthlocco Tribal Town
  Gaming Center
  Okemah, OK
Thunder Bird Entertainment Center
  Norman, OK

Tonkawa Casino
  Tonkawa, OK
Touso Ishto Gaming Center
  Thackerville, OK
Choctaw Casino, Broken Bow
  Broken Bow, OK

Oregon

Chinook Winds Casino
  Lincoln City, OR
Indian Head Casino
  Warm Springs, OR
Kla Mo Ya Casino
  Chiloquin, OR
Seven Feathers Hotel and Casino
  Resort
  Canyonville, OR
Spirit Mountain Casino
  Willamina, OR
The Mill Casino Hotel
  North Bend, OR
The Old Camp Casino
  Burns, OR
Three Rivers Casino
  Florence, OR
Wildhorse Resort and Casino
  Pendleton, OR

South Carolina

Catawba High Stakes Bingo
  Rock Hill, SC
Golden Buffalo Casino
  Lower Brute, SC

South Dakota

Agency Bingo and Casino
  Sisseton, SD
Dakota Magic Casino and Resort
  Hankinson, SD
Dakota Sioux Casino
  Watertown, SD
Fort Randall Casino and Hotel
  Wagner, SD
Grand River Casino
  Mobridge, SD
Lode Star Casino
  Ft. Thompson, SD
Prairie Wind Casino
  Pine Ridge, SD
Royal River Casino, Bingo and
  Motel
  Flandreau, SD

Texas

Lucky Eagle Casino
  Eagle Pass, TX
Speaking Rock Casino
  El Paso, TX

Washington

7 Cedars Casino
  Sequim, WA
Chewelah Casino
  Chewelah, WA
Clearwater Casino
  Suquamish, WA
Coulee Dam Casino
  Coulee Dam, WA
Double Eagle Casino
  Chewelah, WA
Emerald Queen Casino
  Tacoma, WA
Lil Chief's Casino
  Wellpinit, WA
Little Creek Casino
  Shelton, WA
Lucky Dog Casino
  Skokomish Nation, WA
Lucky Eagle Casino and
  Bingo
  Rochester, WA
Makah Tribal Bingo
  Neah Bay, WA
Mill Bay Casino
  Manson, WA
Muckleshoot Indian Casino
  Auburn, WA
Nisqually Red Wind Casino
  Olympia, WA
Nooksack River Casino
  Deming, WA
Northern Quest Casino
  Airway Heights, WA
Okanogan Bingo Casino
  Okanogan, WA
Point No Point Casino
  Kingston, WA
Puyallup Tribe's Bingo Palace
  Tacoma, WA
Quileute Tribe Casino
  LaPush, WA
Quinault Beach Resort and
  Casino
  Ocean Shores, WA

Shoalwater Bay Casino
Tokeland, WA
Silver Reef Casino
Ferndale, WA
Skagit Valley Casino Resort
Bow, WA
Swinomish Northern Lights Casino
Anacortes, WA
Tulalip Casino and Bingo
Marysville, WA
Two Rivers Casino and Resort
Davenport, WA
Yakama Legend's Casino
Toppenish, WA

Wisconsin

Bad River Casino and Lodge
Odanah, WI
DeJope Bingo and Entertainment
Madison, WI

Grindstone Creek Casino
Hayward, WI
Ho-Chunk Casino
Baraboo, WI
Hole in the Wall Casino and
Hotel
Danbury, WI
Isle Vista Casino
Bayfield, WI
LCO Casino, Lodge and
Convention Center
Hayward, WI
Majestic Pines Casino Bingo and
Hotel
Black River Falls, WI
Menominee Casino, Bingo and
Hotel
Keshena, WI
Mohican North Star Casino and
Bingo
Bowler, WI

Mole Lake Casino and Hotel
Crandon, WI
Oneida Bingo and Casino
Oneida, WI
Potawatomi Bingo and Casino
Milwaukee, WI
Potawatomi Bingo, Northern
Lights Casino
Wabeno, WI
Rainbow Casino and Bingo
Nekoosa, WI
St. Croix Casino and Hotel
Turtle Lake, WI

Wyoming

789 Bingo
Riverton, WY

Photo Credits

Chapter 1

P. 4, Reproduced by permission of the Ohio Historical Society; p. 9, Richard Alexander Cooke III; p. 16, The Nelson-Atkins Museum of Art, Kansas City, Missouri. Purchase: the Donald D. Jones Fund for American Indian Art, 2003. 11. Photography by Jamison Miller; p. 17, Courtesy of the Robert Dechert Collection, Department of Special Collections, Van Pelt/Dietrich Library Center, University of Pennsylvania, Philadelphia. Retouched by Matthew C. Robbins; p. 19, Courtesy of the Santa Barbara Museum of Natural History; p. 23, Field Museum of Natural History, Chicago; Werner Forman/Art Resource, N.Y.

Chapter 2

P. 30, Firenze, Biblioteca Medicea Laurenziana ms. Laur. Med. Palat. 220, c 460v, Su concessione del Ministero per i Beni e le Attività Culturali. E vietata ogni ulteriore riproducione con qualsiasi mezzo; p. 37, Stapleton Collection/CORBIS; p. 41, Prints and Photographs Division, Library of Congress; p. 44, © George H. H. Huey; p. 48, National Archives of Canada.

Chapter 3

P. 57, Courtesy of the Robert Dechert Collection, Department of Special Collections, Van Pelt/Dietrich Library Center, University of Pennsylvania, Philadelphia; p. 67, Drawing from John Underhill's News from America; p. 70 I.N. Phelps Stokes Collection, Miriam and Ira D. Wallach Division of Art, Prints and Photographs, The New York Public Library. Astor, Lenox and Tilden Foundations; p. 73, Tradescant Collection, Ashmolean Museum, Oxford University. Bridgeman Art Archive; p. 76, Prints and Photographs Division, Library of Congress; p. 78, Photograph by John K. Hillers, Courtesy Palace of the Governors (MNM/DCA), Neg. #16096.

Chapter 4

P. 85, Rochester Museum & Science Center; p. 86, Library Company of Philadelphia; p. 92, Mackinac State Historical Parks Collection; p. 98, Courtesy of the British Public Record Office, CO700/Carolina 21. National Archives Britain; p. 101, Burgerbibliotek, Bern; p. 103, David Muench/CORBIS.

Chapter 5

P. 118, From William Verelst, *Trustees of Georgia* (1734–35). Courtesy, Winterthur Museum. 56.567; p. 123, Courtesy of the Boston Public Library, Print Department; p. 125, Peabody Museum, Harvard University, photo 41–72–10/20T2377; p. 131, Segesser I, detail. Courtesy Palace of the Governors (MNM/DCA); p. 132, From the Collection of the Gilcrease Museum, Tulsa, Oklahoma.

Chapter 6

P. 136, National Anthropological Archives, Smithsonian Institution, 087469.24; p. 141, Bettmann/CORBIS; p. 144, William L. Clements Library; p. 147, Fenimore House Museum, New York State Historical Association, Cooperstown, N.Y. Photo by Richard Walker; p. 153, Library of Congress.

Chapter 7

P. 165, Reproduced by permission of the Ohio Historical Society. SC 404; p. 169 (upper and lower), Tippecanoe County Historical Association. Lafayette, Indiana; p. 170, Reproduced by permission of the Chicago Historical Society. Object x 0269; p. 182, Special Collections Department, Georgia State University Library; p. 184, Bettmann/CORBIS.

Chapter 8

P. 193, Buffalo Bill Historical Center, Cody, Wyoming. Gift of Mr. William J34E. Weiss; 21.70; p. 199, Historical Picture Archive/CORBIS; p. 202, Amon Carter Museum, Fort Worth, TX #1961.195; p. 206, Beinecke Rare Book and Manuscript Library, Yale University, EEcd 815D; p. 208, National Geographic Image Collection.

Chapter 9

P. 214, Burstein Collection/CORBIS; p. 219 (upper and lower), Tippecanoe County Historical Association, Lafayette, Indiana; p. 228, painting by Robert Lindneux, Woolaroc Museum, Bartlesville, OK; p. 234, Prints and Photographs Division, Library of Congress; p. 237, painting by John Clymer; National Archives neg# 127-G 10H-306073A.

Index

A

A.B.C.: *Americans Before Columbus* (newsletter), 435

Abeita, Andy, 415

Abenakis: captives of, 46, 81; cultivation of food crops and, 64; English and, 65; heavy casualties of, 65; in praying towns, 89; efforts to remain independent, 95; Anglo-French colonization and, 113–114; in Ohio Valley, 115, 138; military service by, 122; recognition and, 416. *See also* Penobscot Abenakis

Abourezk, James, 436, 437, 438–439

Absentee Shawnees, 275

Acadia, French colony of, 113

Acomas: origin of, 10; Spanish and, 44, 77, 106

Acorn Bluff, 213

Acuera Timucuas. *See* Timucuas

Adams, Cassily, 305

Adams, Hank, 427, 428

Adams, John: Indian policy under, 220

Adams, John Quincy: Indian policy under, 224, 231

Adams-Onis Treaty (1819), 236

Adena culture, 13, 15

Adoption, 82, 91. *See also* Captives

Affiliated Tribes of the Northwest, 413

African Americans: Seminoles and, 245–246. *See also* Slaves

Agriculture: bean cultivation in, 6, 8, 14, 40; food production and, 6, 12, 14–15, 18–19, 24, 40, 64; maize cultivation in, 6, 8, 14, 15, 24, 40, 49; squash cultivation in, 6, 8, 14, 40; irrigation in, 8, 30; green corn ceremonies and, 14–15; tobacco production in, 74–75, 90. *See also* Farming

Ahhaton, Sarah, 68–69

AIDS, 463

Aix-la-Chapelle, Treaty of (1748), 114

Ak-Chin community: water rights and, 442, 447–448

Akimel O'odhams (Pimas), 6, 7–8, 10–11

Akwesasne Notes (newspaper), 435

Alabamas: in Texas, 252

Alarcón, Hernando de, 43, 45

Alaska: Indians in, 204–205; Russian fur traders in, 205–209; British traders in, 207–210; American traders in, 209–210

Alaska Federation of Natives, 436–437, 464

Alaska Native Brotherhood (ANB), 363

Alaska Native Claims Settlement Act, 436

Alaska Native Sisterhood (ANS), 363

Alaska Packers Association, 368

Alaska Reorganization Act (1936), 388

Albany: trading at, 94

Albuquerque, 264; relocation of Indians to, 400

Alcatraz, 317; seizure of, 422–423, 425, 426, 452

Alcohol: effects on Native Americans, 58, 143, 180, 182, 221, 463

Aleixan Brothers Novitiate: seizure of, 430

Aleuts (Unangans), 24–25; language of, 3, 24; fur trade and, 204–207; farming by, 206–207; hunting by, 207

Algonkins, 49, 55, 58, 63

Algonquian language family, 18, 19, 49, 71, 91, 92

Aliquippa, 116

Alligator, 236, 237, 245–246

All-Pueblo Council, 361, 363

Altaha, Wallace, 368

American Athletic Union (AAU), 355

American Board of Commissioners for Foreign Missions, 178, 261

American Civil Liberties Union (ACLU), 379, 387; termination and, 410

American Friends Service Committee, 402

American Fur Company, 210; steamboat of, 198

American Horse, 304, 327

American Indian Capitol Conference on Poverty, 417

American Indian Chicago Conference (1961), 416, 426

American Indian Child Welfare Act (1978), 438, 439

American Indian Culture and Research Journal, 435

American Indian Defense Association (AIDA), 375, 377, 379

American Indian Federation, 387

American Indian Gaming Regulatory Act (AIGRA), 466–468

American Indian Historical Society, 435

American Indian Law Review, 435

American Indian literary community: growth of, 420

American Indian Magazine, 363

American Indian Movement (AIM), 421–422, 426, 431; in center stage, 427–429

American Indian Policy Review Commission, 436

American Indian Press Service, 435

American Indian Quarterly, 435

American Indian Religious Freedom Act (AIRFA), 438, 443, 450

American Legion: termination and, 410

American Point Four program, 413

American Red Cross, 375

American Revolution, 166; Eastern Indians and, 141–149

Americans for Indian Opportunity, 446

The American Stranger, 421

Amherst, Jeffrey, 141, 142, 145

Amherstburg, 185

Anaica, 33

Anasazis (ancestors of modern Pueblo Indians): Chaco Canyon and, 8–9; refugees of, 10; farming by, 11; trade for shells, 20

Ancient Society (Morgan), 324

Andrés, 161

Andros, Edmund, 89, 91, 93

Anglo-Powhatan wars, 71, 74

Anishinaabe. *See* Ojibwes

Anthony, Scott, 288

Antipoverty programs, 446

Antonia, Doña, 38

Anza, Juan Bautista de, 154, 157

Apache (movie), 421

Apaches: in Southwest, 11, 131–132, 154, 155; ancestors, 22; and Coronado, 43; and Pueblos, 77;

raiding, 77, 102, 106–107, 263, 265, 315–319; and Spanish, 79, 151–152; migrations, 121–132; smallpox among, 135; in Texas, 253; lifestyle, 280; oppose Mexico, 280–281; Mexican bounty on, 281; oppose Carleton, 282–283; flee reservations, 315–319; raise cattle, 368; intermarriage among, 399. *See also* Chiricahuas; Jicarilla Apaches; Kiowa Apaches; Lipan Apaches; Mescalero Apaches; Mimbreno Apaches

Apalachees, 98; as coastal people, 17; Spanish and, 33; baptism of, 75; in Florida, 75–76; new tribes among, 97; lands vacated by, 148

Appamattucks, 74

Aquash, Anna Mae (Pictou), 433, 434. *See also* Pictou, Anna Mae

Aquash, Nogeeshik, 426, 429, 430

Arapahos, 24; lifestyle of, 192, 193–194; at rendevouz, 211; and intertribal warfare, 243, 287; sign Treaty of Ft. Laramie (1851), 287; raids against Americans, 287–290, 292, 298–301; at Sand Creek Massacre, 288–289; sign Treaty of medicine Lodge Creek, 292; sign Treaty of Fort Laramie (1868), 293; at Battle of Rosebud, 302–303; rituals among, 352; mineral revenues, 404; and termination, 408

Archiah, James, 356

Arikaras, 23; oral traditions of, 3; farming by, 130, 195; smallpox and, 135, 198; lifestyle of, 192, 198; Lewis and Clark expedition and, 194–195, 197, 204; horses and, 198; fur trade and, 210; intertribal warfare and, 287

Armijo, Manuel, 264, 265

Arosen, 82

Arroyo Hondo, 266

Art: rock, 8, 21; of Native Americans, 420–421

Asah, Spencer, 356

Assateagues: resistance to English by, 120–121

Assembly of God: Native Americans and, 405

Assiniboines: fur trade and, 92–93, 210; Dakotas and, 128; French

trade with, 128; buffalo hunting by, 129; Lewis and Clark expedition and, 195–196; smallpox and, 198; intertribal warfare and, 287; relocation of, 287; resent Sioux arrival in Canada, 308; land allotment and, 327

Association on American Indian Affairs, 379, 406, 409, 417

Astor, John Jacob, 210

Atchison, Topeka and Santa Fe Railway, 352

Athapaskans, 22–23; language family of, 3, 11, 19, 22, 392; missions for, 207

Atkins, John, 326–327

Atkinson, Henry, 234

Atsina: Lewis and Clark expedition and, 203

AT&T, 464

Attakullaculla (Little Carpenter), 117, 140, 147

Augusta, Georgia, 96

Augusta, Treaty of (1773), 146

Austin, Mary, 356, 361, 375

Austin, Stephen F., 250

Austrian Succession, War of (1740–1748), 114, 115, 116

Awashunkes: abandonment of Metacom by, 89; surrender of, 89

Aztalan, 16

Aztecs, 29, 30–31

B

Baca, Francisco, 283

Bacon, Nathaniel, 90

Bacone College, 352

Bacon's Rebellion, 90–91, 119

Bad Axe, Battle of, 234

Bad Heart Bull, Sarah, 434

Bad Heart Bull, Wesley, 429

Baffin Island, 25

Bahamas, 29; Tainos on, 29

Bailey, Mildred, 357

Baltasar, 160

Baltimore, Lord, 90

Banks, Dennis, 421–422, 429–430, 433, 434

Bannocks: fur trade and, 210; rendezvous and, 211; warfare and, 304; rebellion against reservation life, 312–314; land allotment and, 327

Baptist Cherokee Association, 352

Baptist Church's Home Mission Board, 352

Baptists: missions of, 178, 215; Native Americans and, 352, 405

Baranov, Alexander, 206, 208, 209

Barboncito, 284

Barlowe, Arthur, 40

Barnett, Jackson, 369

Bashaba, 65

Baskets: Chumash, 19

Bataan, 391

Bat Cave (New Mexico), 6

Bauer, Fred, 387

Baylor, John, 251

Baylor, John R., 251, 282

Beans: cultivation of, 6, 8, 14, 40

Beauharnois, Charles de la Boische de, 127, 128, 130

Beaver Wars (1648–1657), 63–64, 72, 91, 93, 115; refugees from, 97

Becknell, I. William, 264

Beecher's Island, Battle of (1868), 298

Beiter, Alfred, 387

Bella Coolas, 21

Bellecourt, Clyde, 421–422, 429

Bellemont Depot, 392

Bender, Charles, 355

Bennett, Robert, 418

Bent, Charles, 266

Bent, William, 264–265

Benteen, Frederick, 303, 304

Bent's Fort, 193

Benyaca, Thomas, 423

Beothuks: Norse and, 25, 28; encountering strangers from across Atlantic, 46; kidnapping of dozens of, 46

Bering Sea, crossing of, 24

Bering Strait, crossing of, 2

Berkeley, William, 74, 90

Berry, E. Y., 410

Bertrand, Madeline, 219

Big Foot, 339

Big Hole, Battle of (1877), 311

Bighorn Carpet Bill, 446

Big Meadows, Battle of, 262

Big Tree, 299, 300

Biloxi Bay, 99

Bison: hunting of, 4, 5, 6, 22, 191–193, 211, 242–243, 287, 300

Bitterroot Mountains, 200, 203

Black Buffalo, 189, 194

Black Cat, 196–197
Black Coyote, 339
Black Dog, 242
Black Elk, Wallace, 430, 434
Blackfeet, 24; trade with Europeans, 29, 203–204; horses and, 90–91; fur trade and, 93, 210; Shoshone and, 129–130, 135; smallpox and, 135, 198; Lewis and Clark expedition and, 200, 203; rendezvous and, 211; warfare and, 303; resent Sioux arrival in Canada, 308; land allotment and, 327; rituals of, 352; Indian Reorganization Act and, 385–386; economic issues for, 403; mineral revenue for, 404; termination and, 408. *See also* Piegan Blackfeet
Blackfeet Confederacy, 192
Blackfeet Pencil Factory, 446
Blackfeet Reserve, 359
Black Hawk, 233–235
Black Hawk War, 233–235
Black Heart, 340–341
Black Hills, 359–360
Black Hills Survival Gathering (1980), 455
Black Hills Treaty Council, 360, 362
Black Hoof, 220
Black Kettle, 288, 289, 298
Black Legs society, 393
Black Panthers, 421
Black Pawnees. *See* Wichitas
Black Warrior River, 40
Blatchford, Herbert, 416
The Blessing Way, 283
Bloods: Lewis and Clark expedition and, 203
Bloody Island Massacre, 257
Blue Jacket, 170–171
Blue Lake: return of, to tribal control, 423
Boarding schools, 178, 215–216, 247–249, 274, 334–335, 355, 397. *See also* Carlisle Indian Industrial Training School; Education
Board of Indian Commissioners, 370, 377
Boas, Franz, 395
Bodega Bay, 206
Bodmer, Karl, 198, 199
Boggy Depot, 247

Boldt, George, 439–441
Bonanza (television show), 421
Bonfire Shelter site, 5
Bonnin, Gertrude Simmons, 356, 365, 369
Bosomworth, Thomas: marriage to Coosaponakeesa, 110–111
Bosque Redondo, 282, 284, 286; Navajo exile at, 284, 285, 286
Boston Indian Council, 426
Boston Latin School, 249
Bottle Hollow Resort, 417–418
Boudinot, Elias Cornelius, 227, 243, 270, 330
Boudinot, Frank, 358
Bou-ge-te Smokey, 356
Bowlegs, Billy, 238
Boyer, Lanada, 434
Boy Pioneers, 355
Boy Scouts, 355
Bozeman Trail, 289–290, 292; government abandonment of, 268
Braddock, Edward, 138, 139, 140
Bradley, L. P., 295
Brainerd, David, 124
Brainerd, John, 124
Brainerd Mission, 178, 216
Brando, Marlon, 419
Brant, Joseph, 146–147, 148, 149, 150–151, 167, 171, 180–181
Brazos Reserve, 251
Brennan, William, 443
Bressani, Father, 62
Brims, 110, 117; death of, 118
British East Indian Company, 206
Brock, Lulu, 403
Broken Arrow (movie), 420
The Broken Cord (Dorris), 463
Broker, Ignatia, 397–398, 421
Bronson, Ruth Muskrat, 410
Brothers Three (Oskinson), 373
Browning, government agency at, 327
Bruce, Louis, 452
Bruner, Joseph, 380, 387–388
Buckskin Charley, 347
Buffalo. *See* Bison
Buffalo Horn, 313
Buffalo Medicine, 189

Buffalo Soldiers (African American troops), 298
Bulin, Amabel, 397–398, 400–401, 421
Bull Bear, 298
Burke Act (1906), 366
Burnett, William, 219
Burnette, Bob, 427, 428
Bursum, Holm O., 361, 362
Bursum bill, 363
Bush, George H. W., 455, 456, 466
Bushfield, Harlan, 403
Butterfield Stage Company, 282
Byington, Cyrus, 247
Byrd, Joe, 461–462

C
Cabeza de Vaca, Alvar Nuñez, 42
Cabot, John, 46
Cabrillo, Juan Rodriguez, 44–45, 157
Caddos: language family of, 23; establishment of new province among, 108; acquisition of horses and guns, 130; Spanish and, 152; in New Mexico, 154; in Texas, 250, 251; on Brazos Reserve, 251; lifestyle of, 251; Civil War and, 270, 272; land allotment and, 326, 327. *See also* Natchitoches Caddos
Cadillac, Antoine de la Mothe, 124
Cahokia: social structure of, 15–16; exchange networks of, 16, 17; peak and decline of, 16, 17
Cahokias, 26, 231. *See also* Illinois Confederacy
Caldwell, Billy, 232
Calendar: Cahokian, 15
California, 253–260; Indians in, 18–20, 44–45, 155–162, 255–256, 257, 259–260; Spanish settlements in, 44–45, 156–157; missions in, 156, 255; Gold Rush in, 257, 258–259
California v. *Cabazon Band of Mission Indians*, 444, 447
Call, Richard, 236
Calos, 14
Calumet, 91, 124
Calusas: abandonment of farming by, 14; chiefdoms of, 17; Spanish and, 31, 35–38; captives of, 36
Calvert, Leonard, 71
Cameahwait, 200

Campbell, Ben Nighthouse, 436

Campbell, William, 172–173

Camp Fire Girls, 355

Camp Grant Massacre, 316

Camp Holmes Treaty, 243

Camp Verde, 316

Canarsee Munsees, 69. *See also* Munsees

Canary Islands, 29

Canby, Edward, 309–310

Cáncer de Barbastro, Luis, 35–36

Cañon del Muerto, Arizona, 44

Canyon de Chelly, 283, 284, 286

Cape Breton Island, 49

Cape Cod Indians. *See* Wampanoags

Cape Girardeau, 231

Cape Hatteras, 41

Captain Jack Kintpuash, 308–310

Captives: spread of disease and, 36; treatment of, 59, 169–170, 279–280; Williams, Eunice, as, 81–82, 83, 95, 142, 169; adoption into Native American families, 82; Rowlandson, Mary as, 88; Gyles, John, as, 95; lives of, 142

Caribou, 4

Carleton, James, 282, 283, 284, 285, 286, 315

Carlisle Indian Industrial Training School, 300, 322, 331, 333–335, 340, 354. *See also* Education

Carlos, 37–38

Carson, Christopher "Kit," 282, 284, 314

Carson, Hampton L., 359

Carter, Jimmy: Indian policy under, 439

Cartier, Jacques, 47, 49

Casa Grande, 8; emergence of, 7

Casinos, 458–459, 466–470

Cass, Lewis, 218, 223

Castaño de Sosa, Gaspar, 43–44

Catawbas, 40, 137, 141, 145; British policy and, 100; and Yamasee War, 100, 101; and Iroquois, 101, 114, 120; population of, 119; and English colonists, 120; in Civil War, 277; rights of, 331; termination and, 413; recognition of, 439

Catches, Pete, 429

Cather, Willa, 361

Catherine the Great, 207

Catholicism. *See* Christianity

Catití, Alonso, 105

Catlin, George, 198, 199, 291

Caudi, 104

Cautantowwit, 15

Cayugas, 17, 21; warfare among, 83; treaties with, 84; American Revolution and, 147, 149; leadership of, 180; arrival of, in Indian Territory, 276. *See also* Iroquois

Cayuses: Whitman massacre and, 241–242; western settlement and, 261; reservations for, 337

Cèleron de Blainville, Pierre-Joseph, 116

A Century of Dishonor (Jackson), 332

Ceremony (Welch), 420

Chaco Canyon, 9, 20, 26; Anasazi culture and, 8–9

Champlain, Samuel de, 55–56

Chandler, O. K., 387

Charbonneau, Touissant, 200

Chartier, Peter, 116

Chata, 317

Chata Enterprises, 446, 464

Chatahoochee, 98

Chavez, Dennis, 387

Chekilli, 110

Chequamegon Bay: Indian villages at, 91

Cherokee Advocate, 247, 274

Cherokee Female Seminary, 248–249, 274

Cherokee Light Horse, 216

Cherokee Male Seminary, 249, 274

Cherokee Nation, 462

Cherokee National Council, 216–217, 227, 248

Cherokee Nation v. Georgia, 226–227

Cherokee Outlet, 226, 273, 274

Cherokee Phoenix, 227, 243

Cherokee Rifles, 270–272

Cherokees, 26, 40, 71, 140–141, 145; stories of, 1–2, 7; traditional spiritual beliefs of, 2; language, 97; in Yamasee War, 100–101; relations with other tribes, 114, 117, 119, 218, 242; in Ohio Country, 115, 137, 166–167; crowning of Moytoy, 117; and South Carolina, 117; in American Revolution, 147–148; Chicka-maugas split from, 148; mission-

aries among, 178, 216–220, 227, 243, 247; removal of, 214, 222, 226–230, 243; education of, 215–216, 248–250, 274; men's roles, 215–216; planter elite among, 215–216, 269; government of, 216–217; women's roles, 216–217, 246, 247–249, 272; syllabary, 217; slavery among, 246–247, 270; in Texas, 253; in Civil War, 270–272, 277; and Reconstruction, 272–274; and land allotment, 327, 329; Eastern Band of, 387; and draft resistance, 391; marriage patterns, 398; and membership criteria, 472

Chert, 15

Cheyenne Autumn (movie), 421

Cheyenne River Sioux, 338; termination and, 408

Cheyennes, 24; oral traditions of, 3; migration of, 130; lifestyle of, 192–194, 352; and intertribal trade, 195; and intertribal warfare, 243, 287; in Indian Territory, 276; assigned lands at Ft. Laramie Treaty (1851), 287; at Sand Creek Massacre, 288–289; warfare with Americans, 288–289, 290, 292, 296, 298, 300, 301–304, 306; flight from Oklahoma, 308; lands allotted, 326, 360; conditions on reservation, 332; education, 333; raise cattle, 368; in World War II, 393; termination, 408

Chicago: relocation of Indians to, 400, 401; opening of urban Indian center in, 402; American Indian Conference (1961) in, 416, 426

Chicago, Milwaukee, and St. Paul Railroad, 327

Chicago American Indian Center, 402

Chicago and Northwestern Railroad, 327

Chickahominies, 64, 74; American Revolution and, 148; rights of, 331; community of, 352; rituals of, 353

Chickamaugas: American Revolution and, 148; split from Cherokees, 148

Chickasaws: resist Spanish influence, 35, 38; form confederacy, 40, 97; and intertribal warfare, 96, 126, 140–141, 243; relations with French, 99, 124; relations with British, 112, 145; in American Revolution, 148; missionaries among, 178; mixed-lineage planters among, 215, 269; and removal, 223–224; government of, 245; women's roles among, 246; slavery among, 246–247; lifestyle among, 247, 269; in Texas, 252; in Civil War, 270, 272; in Reconstruction, 272; and land allotment, 329

Chicora, Francisco de, 31

Chiefdoms: principal difference between confederacies and, 39

Chief Gall Lodge, 446

Chihuahua, 319

Childers, Ernest, 391, 393

Chino, Wendell, 449

Chinooks, 21; Lewis and Clark expedition and, 201, 202; fur trade and, 204; missions and, 261

Chippewyans, 22

Chiricahuas (Apaches), 282; Spanish and, 152; Civil War and, 282–283

Chivington, John M., 288, 289

Choctaw Academy, 247

Choctaw National Council, 247

Choctaws, 40, 95, 173; form confederacy, 97–98; relations with French, 99, 124–125; civil war among, 111–112, 126–127; and British policy, 145; in American Revolution, 148; missionaries among, 178, 247–248; removal of, 214, 222–223; women's roles among, 215, 246; and intertribal warfare, 243; tribal government, 245; slavery among, 246–247; education, 247, 249; in Texas, 252–253; planter-elite among, 269; in Civil War, 270, 272; and Reconstruction, 272; and land allotment, 329; and Indian Reorganization Act, 387; and draft resistance, 391; and economic issues, 446, 464

Choptanks: resist English, 120–121

Choris, Louis, 159

Chota: as center of anti-English bloc, 117; 1776 conference at, 147

Chouteau, Auguste, 242

Chouteau, Pierre, 242

Christianity: Guales and, 38, 75; Pueblos and, 43, 77–78, 103, 104, 105, 106–107; Powhatans and, 50, 74; Pocahontas and, 54; conversion of Hurons to, 57; Massachusetts and, 68–69, 123; Timucuas and, 75, 76; Apalachees and, 75–76; Iroquois and, 81, 85–87; among Mohawk Iroquois, 81; at Kahnawake and, 86; beautification of Kateri Tekakwitha, 86–87; Nipmucs and, 88; Wampanoags and, 88, 123; on "middle ground," 91, 92; Illinois and, 92; Caddos and, 108; adoption of, 112; Abenakis and, 113, 114; Mi'kmaqs, 113, 114; conversion of Native Americans to, 122–124, 215–216; eastern Indians and, 123; Delawares and, 123–124; Apaches and, 132; Indians in California and, 155, 157–162. See also Franciscans; Jesuits

Christian Reformed Church, 352

Chumashes, 19–20, 45; 1824 revolt of, 160–161

Chupu, 160–161

Church, Benjamin, 89

Cibola, 42–43

Cipriano, 162

Citizen Band Potawatomis (Citizen Potawatomi Nation), 275

Civilian Conservation Corps (CCC), 379

Civil War, 259, 268–293; in Indian territory, 269–272; Eastern Indians in, 276–277; Apaches and, 280–283; in Southwest, 280–286

Clans, 197

Clark, George Rogers, 148

Clark, Joseph "Jocko," 390

Clark, William, 189, 191, 194–204, 261; return home, 203–204

Clatsops: Lewis and Clark expedition and, 202–203; western settlement and, 261

Clearwater, Frank, 430

Clearwater Reservation, 312

Clermont, 242

Cleveland: relocation of Indians to, 400

Cleveland, Grover, 335

Clinton, Bill, 449, 454; visit to Pine Ridge Reservation, 465–466

Cloud, Henry Roe, 370, 378

Clovis points, 4

Clum, John, 316

Coahuila, 246, 253

Coahuilatecans: in Texas, 250

Cochise, 281, 282, 316, 318

Cockacoeske, 90

Cody, Iron Eyes, 470, 471

Cody, William F. (Buffalo Bill), 299, 340–342

Coeur d'Alene: desire for horses, 130; western settlement and, 261

Cofitachequi, 16–17, 33, 35, 39, 96

Cogawea (Quintasket), 356

Cohen, Felix, 418

Colbert, George, 175

Colbert family, 223

Cold Spring Longhouse, 404

Collier, John, 361, 370, 374–383, 385–390, 393–394, 399, 407, 411, 418

Collins, Caspar, 290

Colorado, Mangas, 281; death of, 283

Colorado River Water Conservation District v. U.S., 442

Colorado Trail, 287

Colter, John, 210

Columbian Exposition (Chicago), 340, 344

Columbia River Indians, 337

Columbus, Christopher, 28, 30, 31; Tainos and, 29–30

Colville Reservation, 312, 337; and termination, 410

Colyer, Vincent, 316

Comanche Peak, 251

Comancheros, 264

Comanches, 107; as traders, 111–112, 131–132, 264; acquire horses and guns, 131; acquire livestock, 131, 192–193, 297; warfare of, 131–132, 242–243, 250–253, 263, 296, 298–300; smallpox among, 135–136; and Spanish, 151–152; in New Mexico, 153–155; and Civil War, 270, 290; and land allotment, 326; and peyote, 349. See also Parker, Quanah; Penateka Comanches

Commercial fishing: in displacing Northwest Indians, 328–329

Commission on the Organization of the Executive Branch, 406–407

Committee of One Hundred, 370

Concentration, government policy of, 268–269, 292

Concord, battle at, 146

Conestogas: Susquehannocks known as, 94

Confederated Tribes of the Warm Springs Reservation, 445–446

Congregationalists: missions of, 178; efforts to convert Indians, 215. See also Puritans

Connecorte, 117

Conoco, 369

Conoys: migration of, 121

Conquering Bear, William, 289, 355

Cook, Sherburne, 19, 158

Coolidge, Calvin, 370

Cooperators, 296

Coosaponakeesa (Mary Musgrove), 117, 118; marriages of, 110–111, 117; role among the Creek, 119

Coosas, 16–17, 35, 38, 39, 40

Cooswootna (Juan Antonio), 255

Copala, 104

Coquilles: western settlement and, 261

Cornell University, 462

Cornett, Edward, 251

Cornplanter (Seneca chief), 181

Cornplanter, Jesse, 365

Cornstalk, 147

Coronado, Francisco Vásquez de, 42–43

Cortés, Hernán, 44–45; Aztecs and, 30

Costo, Rupert, 387, 435

Council of Energy Resource Tribes (CERT), 446

Council of Nine Agencies, 360

Council Springs, Treaty of, 251

Coureur de bois, 218

Court of Indian Affairs, 379

Coushatas, 451; in Texas, 252; termination and, 410

Couture, Guillaume, 61

Covenant Chain system of alliances, 87–90, 91, 93, 94, 114, 115, 140, 145, 146–147

Cow Creek Band of Umpquas: recognition of, 439

Coweta, 98, 110

Crawford, Wade, 378, 403

Crazy Horse, 290, 301, 302–303, 304, 308, 320, 323, 359; death of, 295–296, 322

Crazy Snakes, 358

Creedence Clearwater Revival, 422

Creeks, 40, 97, 98–99; trade among, 92–93, 98, 174–175; confederacy, 98–99, 174–175, 235; in Yamasee War, 110; British influence among, 111, 117; clans, 111; women's role among, 111; French influence among, 117–118; Spanish influence among, 117–118; relations with Cherokees, 140–141; in American Revolution, 148; politics and government, 174–175, 224, 245, 269; missionaries among, 178; Red Sticks among, 185–186; removal, 214, 224, 226; planter-elite among, 215, 269; in Creek War of 1836, 226; and inter-tribal warfare, 226, 242, 243; flee to Florida, 235; slavery among, 246–247; in Texas, 253; in Civil War, 270, 272; and Reconstruction, 272–273; and land allotment, 329; marriage patterns, 398. See also Lower Creeks; Ochese Creeks; Upper Creeks; Yamacraw Creeks

Crees: Dakotas and, 128; French trade with, 128; buffalo hunting by, 129; rebellion against reservation life, 308

Croatoans, 40, 41; schools for, 331

Crook, George A., 302, 304, 313, 315, 316, 317, 319, 327, 338

Crow Dance, 353

Crow Feather, James, 360

Crow Indian Round Hall, 389

Crows, 24; medicine shield, 23; desire for horses, 130; smallpox and, 135; lifestyle of, 192; Lewis and Clark expedition and, 195–197, 200; fur trade and, 210; hunting for bisons by, 210–211; rendezvous and, 211; intertribal warfare and, 287; relocation of, 287; post Civil War and, 293; warfare among, 301, 302; land ownership and, 324–325; land allotment and,

327, 359–360; peyote use by, 349; Montana, 359; tribal governance system of, 385; World War II and, 393; termination and, 408

Cuerno Verde, 154

Cuk Su:dagi (Black Water), 7

Cultural revivals, 450–451

Cuming, Sir Alexander, 117

Cupenos: in California, 255; Gold Rush and, 259

Curley Headed Doctor, 309

Curtis, Tony, 421

Curtis Act (1898), 329–330

Custer, George Armstrong, 290, 292, 298, 301, 303–304, 421

Custer Died for Your Sins: An Indian Manifesto (Deloria), 420

Cuzco, 30

D

Dade, Francis, 236

Dakotas: French and, 124, 128–129; warfare and, 127, 242; intertribal warfare and, 242; Santee Dakota Rebellion (1862), 278–280. See also Santees; Sioux

Dale, Thomas, 54

Dallas: relocation of Indians to, 400, 401; powwows in, 402

The Dalles (Columbia River), 21–22, 201–202

Dancing Rabbit Creek, Treaty of (1830), 222, 223

Danger Cave, 24

Darlington, Brinton, 299

Davis, Angela, 434

Davis, Gray, 469

Davis, Jefferson, 282

Dawes, Henry, 325–327, 329, 403

Dawes Commission, 357

Dawes General Allotment Act (1887), 326–327, 330, 386

Daybreak Star Cultural Center, 425

Deaf Man, 170

Declaration of Indian Purpose, 416

DeCora, Lorelai, 434

Deer, Ada, 414–415, 430, 449

Deerfield, Massachusetts, 95; raid on, 81

Deganawidah (Peacemaker), 18, 60

Deganawidah/Quetzocoatl University, 425–426

DeLaCruz, Joe, 449

Delawares (Lenni Lenape), 18, 69–71, 91; Pennsylvania and, 93–94; anti-European resistance by, 112; in Ohio Country, 115, 116, 137, 138, 168; sale of land by, 115; Christian, 123–124; British and, 139–140, 145; Seven Years War and, 142; smallpox and, 143; fireworks display and, 164; missions for, 178; colonists and, 179; alcohol and, 180; relations with other tribes, 218; removal of, 230–231, 233; intertribal warfare and, 242; in Texas, 251, 252; arrival of, in Indian Territory, 274; Civil War and, 286; mistreatment of, 332

Delaware Valley: settlement of, 114

Deloria, Ella, 394–395, 396, 417

Deloria, Philip, 395

Deloria, Vine, Jr., 409, 417, 418, 420, 426–427

Democratic Party: under Andrew Jackson, 221

Denes, 11, 22

Denver: relocation of Indians to, 400, 401, 402

Deshna Clah Chescilgi, 449

DeSmet, Pierre Jean, 292–293

de Soto, Hernando, 33–35, 36, 38, 39, 40, 43, 96, 97

Detroit: established by French, 94; violence at, 94; British control of, 142, 167; siege of, 143

Devil's Lake Reservation, 352, 359

DeWitt's Corner, Treaty of (1777), 148

Diggers, 312–313

Dine-Ana-aii, 283

Diphtheria: impact on Indians, 119, 158

Diseases: impact on Native Americans, 28, 57, 90. See also specific diseases

D-Mouche-kee-awh, 219

Doak's Stand, Treaty of (1820), 222

Doaksville, 247, 272

Doaksville, Treaty of (1837), 245

Dodd, Robert, 365

Dodge, Chee, 449

Dodge, Henry L., 283

Dodge, Mabel, 361

Doegs: killing of Englishman by, 90; peaceful trade with, 90

Dog Soldiers (Cheyennes), 288, 299

Doniphan, Alexander, 265–266, 283

Donnacona, 47

Dorantes, Andrés, 27

Dorchester, Lord, 171

Dorris, Michael, 463

Draft resistance, 391

Dragging Canoe, 147–148, 166–167

Drake, Sir Francis, 41, 45

Dream Dance, 352, 353

Dreamers, 310, 337

Drew, John, 270

Drouillard, George, 194

Drum Dance, 352

DRUMS (Determination of Rights and Unity for Menominee Shareholders), 414–415

Duel in the Sun (movie), 420

Dull Knife, 304, 308

Dummer's War, 113

Duncan, Isadora, 387

Dundy, Elmer, 332

Dunlap's Station, 170

Dunmore, Lord, 146

Durham, Douglass, 433

Dutch: exploration and settlements of, 55, 59, 64, 65–66, 69–71, 72, 83. See also Netherlands; New Netherland

Dutch West India Company, 58, 59

Duwali, 252–253

Dwight, Ben, 409

Dysentery: impact on Indians, 42, 119, 158

E

Eastern Abanakis. See Abenakis; Penobscot Abenakis

Eastern Band of Cherokees, 387

Eastern Woodlands: farmers in, 11–18; kinship in, 82

Eastman, Charles, 350, 351, 356, 370, 395

Easton, Pennsylvania: treaty conference at, in 1758, 139, 140

Eaton, John, 222–223

Echo Hawk, John, 419

Echo-Hawk, Roger C., 3

Echo Hawk, Walter, 440

Economic Development Administration (EDA), 417

Edmunds, Newton, 290

Education, 333–335; of Cherokees, 215, 216, 248–250, 274; of

Choctaws, 247, 249; of Lakotas, 322; of Croatans, 331; of Lumbees, 331. See also Boarding schools

Edwards, Haden, 252–253

Eisenhower, Dwight D., 354; Indian policies under, 409–410

El Caydi, 105

El Chato, 105

Eliot, John, 68, 88

Elliott, Matthew, 167

El Paso, 106

El Saca, 103, 105

Emistisigno, 148

Empresarios, 250, 252

Encomenderos, 78

Encomienda, 78

England: commercial rivalry between France and, 92; war with Spain, 118.

English: in Roanoke, 40–41; in Northeast, 45; in Newfoundland, 46; in Jamestown, 53–54; in Virginia, 53–54, 72–75, 91; in New England, 65–69, 87–90; in Chesapeake, 71–72, 90–91; New Netherland and, 84; in Pennsylvania, 93–94; in Carolinas, 95, 100–102; in Southeast, 95, 96–99; enslavement of Indians by, 96–97; Indian policy of, 143–146, 176

Epidemic diseases: impact on Indians, 28, 29, 36, 39, 45, 82. See also specific diseases

Eries, 50, 63, 64, 71; migration of, 96–97

Ervin, Sam, 419

Eskiminzin, 316

Eskimos. See Inuits (Eskimos)

Esopus Munsees, 70–71. See also Munsees

Esopus Wars (1658–1660 and 1663–1664), 70–71

Espejo, Antonio de, 43

Estanislao, 161–162

Esteban, 27–28, 42; death of, 42

Eufaula, 247, 326, 358

Evans, John, 287–288

Exchange networks, 41; transformation of, 13. See also Trade networks

The Exiles, 421

Extension Act (Alabama, 224, 1829)

F

Factory system: expansion of, 176–177

Fairchild Semiconductor Corporation, 446

Fall, Albert, 361, 362

Fallarone Islands, 206–207

Fallen Timbers, Battle of, 164–165, 171–173, 182

Fancy Dance, 353

Farming: in Southwest, 6; Hohokam, 7; Anasazi, 8; in Eastern Woodlands, 11–18; religion and, 14–15; in eastern Plains, 23; in Great Basin, 24; Aztec, 30; Timucua, 37; Abenaki, 64; English, 87, 90; subsistence level and, 112; among Delawares, 178; among Five Southern Tribes, 178, 215, 217, 222, 235, 246–247, 272–274; among Miamis, 178; among Shawnees, 178; among Senecas, 181; among Arikaras, 195; among Hidatsas, 195; among Mandans, 195; Aleut, 206–207; among Pomos, 207; among Caddos, 251; among Wichitas, 252; among Santee Dakotas, 279; among Navajos, 283–286. See also Agriculture

Farm Security Administration, 388

Feast of the Dead, 58

Federal Acknowledgment Project, 439

Felipe, Don, 38

Fertility: embodiment of, in supernatural beings, 15

Fetal alcohol syndrome, 463

Fetterman, William J., 290

Field, Robert, 252–253

Fields, Richard, 215

First Anglo-Powhatan War (1610–1614). See Powhatans

Fish-ins, 419

Fitzpatrick, Thomas, 289

Five Civilized Tribes. See Five Southern Tribes

Five Nations Iroquois Confederacy. See Iroquois Confederacy

Five Southern Tribes, 274, 329; socioeconomic divisions among, 245–247; membership rolls, 357

Flathead Reservations, 359; Indian Reorganization Act and, 385

Flatheads. See Salish

Florida, 33, 39, 42, 118; artifacts in, 12; Indians in, 14, 17, 31–32, 36–38, 75–76, 96, 97, 98, 99, 148; colony of, 31, 37; Spanish in, 31–32, 37–38, 50, 75–76, 95, 98, 99; French in, 36–37; attacks in, 96, 97, 99.

Folsum, David, 222

Folsum, Peter, 247

Fonda, Jane, 422

Font, Pedro, 7

Fools Crow, Frank, 429

Forbes, Jack, 425–426

Forbes, John, 140–141

Ford, Gerald: Indian policy under, 437

Ford Motor, 464

Forsyth, George, 298

Forsyth, James, 339

Fort Abraham Lincoln, 302

Fort Apache (movie), 420

Fort Atkinson, 287

Fort Belknap, 327

Fort Berthold Indian Reservation, 198; economic issues for tribes at, 404, 446

Fort Bowie, 282

Fort Buford, 308

Fort C. F. Smith, 268, 290, 293

Fort Canby, 284, 285

Fort Caroline, 36, 37

Fort Clatsop, 201, 203

Fort Coffee, 247

Fort Colville, 327

Fort Cumberland, 138

Fort Dearborn, 185

Fort Defiance, 173, 283

Fort Duquesne, 117; British attack and capture of, 137, 138, 139, 140; Washington's assault on, 140

Fort Ellis, 302

Fort Fetterman, 302

Fort Finney, 167; Treaty of, 167

Fort Gibson, 245; Indian removal and, 230

Fort Gibson, Treaty of, 236

Fort Goodwin, 317

Fort Greenville, 171

Fort Hall, 327

Fort Hall Reservation, 314

Fort Harmar, 168; Treaty of (1789), 168

Fort Jackson, Treaty of (1814), 186

Fort Jefferson, 171

Fort King, 236

Fort Klamath, 310

Fort Laramie, 268, 287, 289, 292

Fort Laramie, Treaty of (1851), 289

Fort Laramie, Treaty of (1868), 268, 293, 297, 302, 327, 360, 386, 441

Fort Lawton, 425; occupation of, 427, 428–429

Fort Lewis, 391

Fort Loudoun, 140; surrender of, 141

Fort Lyon, 287–288

Fort Madison Squamish Reservation, 388

Fort Manuel, 210

Fort Marion, 237, 300

Fort McIntosh, 167; treaty of, 167

Fort Meigs, 185

Fort Miamis, 171, 172

Fort Michilimackinac, 185

Fort Mims, 186

Fort Missoula, 311

Fort Mitchell, 226

Fort Moultrie, 237

Fort Niagara, 138; French erection of, 114; siege of, 143

Fort Orange, 58, 66; trade at, 58, 59, 69

Fort Orleans: French establishment of, 130–131

Fort Oswego, 138; British erection of, 114; capture of, 138, 139

Fort Peck, 327; economic issues for tribes at, 404

Fort Phil Kearney, 268, 290, 293

Fort Pierre, 289

Fort Pitt, 142; British control of, 139, 140; siege of, 143

Fort Randall, 308

Fort Rankin, 289

Fort Recovery, 171

Fort Reno, 268, 293

Fort Rice, 289

Fort Richardson, 299

Fort Ridgley: assaults on, 279

Fort Robinson, 295, 308, 322, 323

Fort Rock Cave, 24

Fort Rosalie: French construction of, 125

Fort Ross, 206, 207

Fort Sill, 298–299, 299, 319

Fort Smith, 271

Fort St. Dionysius, 209

Fort Stanton, 282

Fort Stanwix: Treaty of (1768), 145–146; Treaty of (1784), 167, 181

Fort Supply, 298

Fort Toulouse: construction of, 117

Fort Union, 198

Fort Vermilion, 204

Fort Wallace, 292, 298

Fort Washington, 168, 171

Fort Wayne, 185

Fort Wayne, Treaty of, 182

Fort William Henry: capture of, 139

Fort Wingate, 284; Munitions Depot, 392, 393

Fort Wise, 287–288

Fort Wise, Treaty of (1864), 288

Fort Yates, 365

Forty-fifth Army Infantry Division, 391

Foster, Lenny, 423

Foxes. *See* Mesquakies

Foxwoods Casino, 468

France: commercial rivalry between England and, 92; in Treaty of Paris (1763), 142. *See also* French; New France

Francis, Josiah, 186

Franciscans: missionary activities of, 38, 43, 75–78, 95, 98, 102, 103, 106–107, 156; life and death in missions established in, 157–162

Francis I, King of France, 47

Frankfurter, Felix, 377–378

Franklin (state), 173

Fraser River, 21

Fredonia, Republic of, 252–253

Fredonian Revolt, 252–253

Freedom of Information Act (1967), 462

French: Native Americans and, 36–37, 55–64, 93–95, 113–114, 124–129, 132; exploration of Northeast, 45–49; in Northeast, 46–49, 81, 83, 84–87; fur trade and, 48–49, 92–93; in Chesapeake, 50; New England and, 64, 65; warfare and, 81, 94; in Great Lakes/Ohio Valley, 91–93, 94–95; Five Nations and, 93–95; in Detroit, 94; Iroquois conflict with, 94; in Louisiana, 99–100; in Mississippi Valley, 108, 124–129; on the Plains, 108; in Acadia, 113; forts established by, 125,

130–131. *See also* France; New France

Frizzell, Kent, 434

From the Deep Woods to Civilization (Eastman), 351, 356

Fundamentalist Protestants: Native Americans and, 405

Fur trade, 48–49, 57, 87, 92–94, 204–211, 261

G

Gabrielino, 45, 156; traditional religion of, 160

Gadsden Purchase (1853), 282, 391

Gall, 304

Gallay, Alan, 101

Gambill, Jerry, 435

Garland, Hamlin, 375

Garland, John, 222

Garra, Antonio, 255, 259

Garrison Dam, 404

Garry, Joe, 413, 415

Garuwundi, 252–253

General Allotment Act (1887), 366

General Council of the Indian Territory, 273

General Federation of Women's Clubs, 375, 379, 397; Indian Division of, 397; termination and, 410

Gentile, Carlos, 363

George, Frank, 409, 410

George II, King of England, 117

George III, King of England: Proclamation of 1763, 144–145

Georgia, 173; Spanish in, 38; trade with Indians in, 110; Coosaponakeesa in, 110–111; founding of, 110–111; land ownership in, 111; Indian raids on, 147; Indian removal and, 222; gold in, 226

German American Bund, 387

Germans: immigration to Pennsylvania, 114

Geronimo, 296, 316, 317, 318, 319, 320, 347

Ghent, Treaty of, 186

Ghost Dance, 338–340, 341, 350, 352

Gibbon, John, 302, 303, 304, 311

Gibson, A. M., 249–250

Gila River/Valley, 6, 8

Gill, Joseph, 95

Gist, George, 217

Gnadenhütten: founding of, 123

Godefroy, Thomas, 62

Godfroy, Francois, 218, 232

Gold: Spanish interest in, 29, 30, 33, 42–43, 77; in Georgia, 226; in California, 257–259; in Washington, 262; in Colorado, 287; in Montana, 289; in the Black Hills, 301–302

Goldberg, Arthur, 437

Gonzalez, José, 264

Goodman, Benny, 357

Gopher John, 253

Gordon, Nebraska: death of Raymond Yellow Thunder in, 427

Gore, Al, 456

Gorman, Howard, 396

GO Road case, 443–444

Gover, Kevin, 454–455

Governors' Interstate Indian Council (GIIC), 408, 409

Graffenreid, Cristoph von, 100

Gran Apacheria, 152

Grand Council of the Iroquois, 430

Grande Ronde Reservation, 262, 408

Grand Settlement (1701), 94, 114

Grange, Red, 354

Grant, Ulysses S.: in Civil War, 272, 276–277; Peace Policy of, 296, 299, 310; Indian policy under, 304, 316

Grass, John, 327

Grass Dance, 353

Grattan, John, 289

Gray Bird, 279

Great Awakening, 123

Great Depression, 374, 375

Greater Antilles: Tainos on, 29

Great Lakes Reserve, 352

Great Sioux Reserve, 327

Great Sioux Uprising, 280

Greeley, Horace, 220

Green, Warren, 391

Green Bay: Indian villages at, 91

Green Corn Festivals, 14–15, 246

Greenland, 46; Norse colonization of, 25

Green Party, 455, 456

Greenpeace, 455

Green Peach War (1881), 273

Greenville, Treaty of (1795), 165, 173, 176, 179

Greenville Treaty Line, 180

Gresham, John, 433

Grey Lock's War, 113

Griffin, Edward, 110

Gros Ventres: fur trade and, 93; French trade with, 129; Lewis and Clark expedition and, 203; rendezvous and, 211; intertribal warfare and, 287; relocation of, 287; land allotment and, 327

Groton, Connecticut, 120

Guadalcanal, 392

Guadalupe Hidalgo, Treaty of (1848), 257, 361–362

Guales, 17, 38, 75; revolt by, 75; in Florida, 75–76; Westos' capture of, 96; enslavement of, 97

Guanahani, 29

Gulick, Charlotte, 355

Gulick, Luther, 355

Guns: among Iroquois, 59, 64; after Pueblo Revolt, 106; among Plains Indians, 129, 130, 131, 132

Gunsmoke (movie), 421

Guyon, Joe, 354

Gyles, John, 95

H

Haida: fur trade and, 207

Hale, William K., 369

Haliwas: recognition and, 416, 451

Hampton Institute, 333, 386

Hamtramck, John, 168

Hancock, Winfield Scott, 290

Handsome Lake, 180–181

Hanis: western settlement and, 261

Hardin, John, 168

Harding, Warren G.: administration of, 362

Hares, 22

Hariot, Thomas, 40

Harjo, Chitto, 344, 358, 359, 364

Harjo, Joy, 457–458

Harlem Globetrotters, 355

Harmar, Josiah, 168, 170

Harney, William S., 289, 292

Harris, Ladonna, 417, 446

Harrison, Carter, 375

Harrison, William Henry, 177, 179, 182

Hartford, Treaty of (1638), 67–68

Harvey, Fred Company, 355; tourist hotels, 367

Hasanai: in Texas, 251

Haskell Institute, 334, 390

Haudenosaunee. *See* Iroquois Confederacy

Hawikuh, 27, 42, 43; encounter of Esteban and Zunis at, 27, 28

Hayes, Ira Hamilton, 391–392, 393, 420

Hayes, Lucy Ware Webb, 333

Hayward, Richard, 468

Heacock, Charles, 395

Head-Smashed-In, 22

Head Start, 417

Heckewelder, John, 168

Henderson, Alice Corbin, 356

Henderson, Richard, 146; Henderson's Purchase, 146

Hendrick, 115

Henry, Jeanette, 435

Herrero (headman), 285

Hewett, Edgar, 356, 361

Hickok, Wild Bill, 340

Hickory Ground, 358, 364

Hicks, Charles, 175

Hicks, George, 229

Hidatsas, 23; farming by, 130; smallpox among, 135, 198; lifestyle, 192; trade, 195, 204; Lewis and Clark expedition among, 195–197, 201; government and politics, 196–197; group identity, 197; religion, 197; horses among, 198; cattle herding, 368; Hot Dance of, 389

Highwater, Jamake, 470

Hillaire, Joe, 387

Hispaniola: Tainos on, 29

Hitchcock, Ethan A., 358

Hoag, Enoch, 273

Hochelaga, 47, 49

Ho-Chunks (Winnebagos): Siouan-speaking, 91; warfare and, 127; Dakotas and, 128; removal of, 214, 231; as entrepreneurs, 219; as entrepreurs, 219; resistance to removal, 233–234; use of peyote by, 349; Indian Reorganization Act and, 387; termination and, 408

Hoffman, Dustin, 421

Hogup Cave, 24

Hohokams, 20; culture of, 6–8; farming by, 7; refugees and, 10

Hokeah, Jack, 356

Holiday, Billie, 357

Homicide rates, 463

Honatteniate, 62

Honey Springs, 247

Hooker Jim, 309, 310

Hoopa, 425–426

Hoops, Ivan, 389

Hoover, Herbert Clark, 374, 375; Indian policy under, 406–407

Hopewell culture, 13–14, 15; ceremonial centers of, 13, 22–23

Hopis, 106; oral traditions of, 3; formation of, 10; Spanish and, 106–107, 156; Navajo conflicts with, 283; Snake and Antelope ceremony, 352; intermarriage among, 399; termination and, 408; *Tutuvehni*, 462

Horse Capture, George, 423

Horses: Native American acquisition of, 59, 64, 130–131; effect on Indians, 107, 129–132; arrival of, 190–191, 192; women as benefactor of, 191; life on the Plains and, 197–198

Hot Dance, 389

Houma: recognition and, 416

House and Urban Development, U.S. Department of, 417

House Made of Dawn (Momaday), 419

Houser, Allen, 420

Houston, Sam, 251, 253

Howard, Oliver, 310–312, 313, 316

Hudson, Henry, 58

Hudson's Bay Company, 203, 206, 209, 260–261; trading posts established by, 92

Hump, 290

Hunkapapas (Lakota): lifestyle of, 192; warfare among, 301; warfare and, 303. *See also* Dakotas; Lakotas

Hunter, Robert, 369

Hupas, 19, 22

Hurons, 18, 47, 49, 50, 55–58, 59, 72; relations with other Indians, 18, 59, 63–64; conversion to Catholicism of, 57, 59, 63; Jesuit missionaries and, 57–58; captives of, 81; language of, 91; in Ohio Country, 94, 115; trade with Europeans, 94. *See also* Wyandots

Hurtado, Albert, 257

I

Ice Age: movement of first Americans and, 2–3; climatic warming and, 5

Ickes, Harold L., 375, 377, 387, 418

Illinois Confederacy: Algonquian-speaking, 91; Five Nations attack, 93; and French, 124; warfare, 127; removal, 231. *See also* Cahokias; Kaskaskias; Peorias

Implacables, 358

Incas, 29, 30–31

Ince, Tom, 357

Indentured servants: disease and malnutrition among, 73; Native Americans as, 121

Independent Oglala Nation, 430

Indian Arts and Crafts Board, 388

Indian Boyhood (Eastman), 356

Indian Civil Rights Act (1968), 419, 462

Indian Claims Commission, 407–408, 410, 414, 423

Indian Claims Commission Act (1946), 407

Indian Gaming Regulatory Act (1988), 444, 447–448

Indian handicrafts: popularity of, 355–356

Indian health, 370, 375, 462–464; improvement in, 398–399, 456

Indian Health Service, 463

The Indian Historian, 435

Indian Industrial Training School, 322

"Indianisme," 122

Indian Knoll, 12–13; shell goods at, 12–13; social ranking of, 13

Indian removal, 213–238; in the Southeast, 222–230; in the Old Northwest, 230–233; armed resistance to, 233–238

Indian Removal Act (1830), 221, 222, 223

Indian Reorganization Act (1934), 377, 379–382, 382, 387, 406, 418

Indian Rights Association, 332–333, 340, 358, 359, 369, 374, 377, 379, 380

Indian Self-Determination and Educational Assistance Act (1975), 437, 448

Indian Shaker movement (1882), 350

Indian slave raids, 148

Indian slave trade: rise of, 96–97

Indians of All Tribes: seizure of Alcatraz by, 422–423

Indian Springs, Treaty of (1825), 212, 224, 226

Indian territory, 243–250; Civil War in, 269–272; Reconstruction in, 272–276; land allotment and, 327; breaking up, 329–330; end of, 357–359

Indian Treaty Keeping and Protective Association, 332

Indian voting, 405–406

Infant mortality, 463

Influenza: impact on Indians, 28, 57, 119, 125

Inkpaduta ("Scarlet Point"): Santee Dakota Rebellion and, 278

Inouye, Daniel, 436

Institute for Government Research, 370

Institute of American Indian Arts, 420

Intermarriage, 91, 218; increase in, 398–399

International Olympic Committee, 355

International Whaling Commission, 460–461

Inuits (Eskimos), 24–25; language of, 3, 24; fur trade and, 204–207

Inupik, 24

Iowas: migration of, 130; lifestyle of, 192

Ipai, 44–45, 157; Gold Rush and, 259

Iroquois: oral traditions of, 2, 3; consolidation of, 17; confederacy council of, 18; relations with other tribes, 18, 59, 63–64, 93–94, 114; Europeans and, 47; French and, 55–64; alliance with Netherlands, 58; mourning wars of, 58–59; rise of, 58–59; acquisition of guns, 59; kinship in, 82; wampum for, 83–84; iconography of, 85; language and, 91; neutrality in Northeast, 94–95; colonists and, 111; in Ohio Country, 115; American Revolution and, 148; missions and, 261; land allotment and, 330; termination and, 408, 410. *See also* Cayugas; Iroquois Confederacy; Mingos; Mohawks; Oneidas; Onondagas; Senecas; Tuscaroras

Iroquois Confederacy, 17, 49, 50, 55, 59, 64, 72; power of, 55; pro-tocols of, 60; neutrality of, 83; New France and, 84–86, 93; mourning wars of, 93; diplomacy and, 111; formal recognition of, by British, 114; war with Catawba, 120; Tuscaroras as sixth nation in, 121; American Revolution and, 149. *See also* Iroquois

Iroquois League: loss of leadership by, 180–181

Irrigation, 30; Hohokam, 8

Isaacs, Captain, 186

Isparhechar, 273

J

J. R. Williams (Union Steamboat), 271

Jack, Stonewall, 88

Jackson, Andrew, 186; Indian policy under, 220–221, 223, 224, 227; Seminole Wars and, 235–236

Jackson, Helen Hunt, 332

Jacobson, O. B., 356

Jake, Chief, 326–327

James, Darwin Rush, 340

James, Frank, 271

James, Jesse, 271

James I (King of England), 72

Jamestown, 74; settlement of, 53–54; problems at, 72–73

Jamestown Clallam Tribe, 439

Janos: uprising among, 106

Jay's Treaty, 173

Jefferson, Thomas, 324; on the American republic, 149; civilization program under, 177; Indian policy under, 179–180, 220, 222; Louisiana Purchase and, 187, 194

Jeffords, Tom, 316

Jemez pueblos, 77

Jemison, Alice, 387–388, 411–413

Jemison, Mary, 142, 169

Jerome, David H., 329, 358

Jesuits, 59, 63; as missionaries, 50, 55, 57, 64, 71, 84, 85–86, 92, 95, 261; Hurons and, 57–58, 63; witchcraft and, 58, 59, 63; colonist-Indian relations and, 91, 113; missions of, 261

Jesup, Thomas S., 236–238

Jewett, George, 365

Jicarilla Apaches: Comanches and, 131; Spanish and, 152; lifestyle of, 193; Civil War and, 280;

support for Indian Reorganization Act, 382–383; mineral revenue for, 404. *See also* Apaches

Joaquin (headman), 283

Joara, 39; alliance between Pardo and, 39

Job Corps, 417

Jogues, Father, 62

Johnson, Ben, 461

Johnson, Jimmy, 354

Johnson, Lyndon: War on Poverty under, 416–417, 437, 465

Johnson, Molly, 150

Johnson, Napoleon, 395, 407, 409

Johnson, Pauline (Tekahionwake), 356

Johnson, Richard M., 247

Johnson, Wayne, 461

Johnson, William, 145, 150

Johnson-O'Malley Act, 382

Johnston, Philip, 392

Jolliet, Louis, 99

Jones, Robert, 247

Jones, William, 366, 370

Jornada de Muerto, 281

José, Nicholas, 160

Josecillo El Manco, 152

Joseph, Chief, 203, 308, 310–312, 316, 320, 331, 337

Joseph, William, 258–259

Juanillo, Don, 38

Juh, 316, 317

Jumanos, 23, 42, 43; raids of, 107

Jumper, 236, 237

The Jungle (Sinclair), 369

K

Kabotie, Fred, 356

Kadohadachos: in Texas, 251

Kahnawake, New France, 81, 82, 86, 93, 94, 95, 113, 138

Kakima: as an entrepreneur, 219

Kalapoolas: western settlement and, 261

Kalispels, 21

Kamiakins, 262; western settlement and, 262

Kansas (Indians); 23, 130, 274, 286

Kansas (state), 286

Kansas (territory), 269

Kansas-Nebraska Act (1854), 269

Karankawas, 42; La Salle establishment of small colony among, 108; in Texas, 250

Kashaya Pomo, 391

Kaskaskias, 91; removal of, 231. *See also* Illinois Confederacy

Kautz, August, 316

Kawarahki Pawnees, 23

Keam's Canyon School, 335

Kearney, Stephen W., 265–266

Keetowahs (Cherokees), 270–271, 358, 362; oposition to removal, 243; Reconstruction and, 273, 274; antiallotment cause and, 338

Kekionga, 168

Kelsey, Henry, 129

Kennard, Motey, 270

Kennedy, Edward, 436

Kennedy, John: Indian policy under, 416

Kennedy, Robert, 436

Ken-Tuck, 169

Keokuk, 233

Keokuk, Moses, 275

Kiala, 128

Kickapoos: Algonquian-speaking, 91; warfare and, 94, 127; in Ohio Country, 115, 168; relations with other tribes, 218; removal of, 231; resistance to removal, 234; in Coahuila, 246; in Texas, 252, 253; arrival of, in Indian Territory, 275

Kicking Bear, 338, 341

Kieft, Willem, 69–70

Kieft's War (1643–1645), 69, 70

Kills, Bert, 379

Kincaid, 16

King, Martin Luther, 427

King, William, 374

King George's War, 114

King Philip's War (1675–76). *See* Metacom's War

Kingsbury, Cyrus, 178

King William's War (1689–97), 93, 94

Kinzua Dam, 404

Kiowa Apaches, 22, 152, 193, 290; at Treaty of Medicine Lodge Creek, 292

Kiowa Five, 349

Kiowas, 152, 276, 287, 290; migration, 192; characterized, 193; warfare, 242–243, 264, 298–300; trade, 264; at Treaty of Medicine Lodge Creek, 292; own large horse herds, 297; lands allotted,

326–327, 358–359; and peyote, 349; dance at powwows, 353; revive Black Legs Society, 393

Kirkland, Samuel, 147

Kittamaquund, 71

Kiva, 6

Klamaths: reservation for, 308–309, 313; Indian Reorganization Act and, 383; economic issues for, 403; termination and, 408, 410, 413–415

Knights of the Golden Circle, 270

Knox, Henry, 168

Kodiak Island, 206, 207, 208

Kootenais: Indian Reorganization Act and, 385; termination and, 410

Koster site, 11–12, 13

Kuskuskis, 116

Kutenais: arrival of horses and, 190; treaties with, 262

L

Lac du Flambeau, 352

La Demoiselle, 116

LaDuke, Winona, 454, 455–456

LaFlesche, Francis, 345

La Follette, Robert, 367–368

Lagunas, 106

Lake Champlain, 55; battle of, 64

Lake George, 138, 139

Lake of the Woods, 128

Lake Okeechobee, 238

Lakotas: and Lewis and Clark expedition, 189–190, 195–197, 198, 200; and horses, 192; and lifestyle, 192, 194, 296–298; migrate to plains, 192; as traders, 194–195, 297–298; smallpox among, 198; at fur trade rendezvous, 211; warfare among, 235, 242, 289–290, 296. 300–308, 312; and Bozeman Trail, 268; sign Ft. Laramie Treaty (1851), 287, 289; sign Ft. Laramie Treaty (1868), 292–293; and education, 322; Ghost Dance among, 338–340. *See also* Brulé Lakotas; Dakotas; Hunkapapas; Minneconjous; Oglalas; Santees; Sioux

Lalawethike, 181–182

Lamar, Mirabeau B., 251, 253

Lame Deer, 308

La Montagne, 86

LaMonte, Buddy, 430

Lancaster, Burt, 421

Lancaster, Massachusetts: Indian attack on, 88

Lane, Franklin, 367

Lane, James, 272

Lane, Ralph, 40

Langlade, Charles, 116

Language families, 3; Aleut-Inuit, 3, 24; Athapaskan, 3, 11, 19, 22; Algonquian, 18, 19, 49, 71, 91, 92; Caddoan, 23; Siouan, 23, 91; Muskogean, 33, 97, 110

L'Anse aux Meadows, 25

Lapointe, Sam, 386

La Purísima, 161; uprising at, 161

La Raza Unida, 434

La Salle, Rene-Robert Cavelier, 99, 108

Lassen National Forest: occupancy of land in, 425

The Last of the Mohicans (movie), 431

Latter Day Saints: missionary campaign of, 405

Laudonnière, René de Goulaine de, 36

La Vérendrye, Pierre Gaultier de Varennes, sieur de, 128, 130

Lawrenceville Academy, 249

Leader, Otis, 365

League of Augsburg, War of, 93

Le Borgne, 196–197

Lee, Robert E., 272, 276

Left Hand, 288

Legal Services Administration, 417

Le Gris, 164

Lehner Ranch Arroyo (New Mexico), 4

Lenni Lenape. *See* Delawares (Lenni Lenape)

Leupp, Francis, 366

Levi, John, 354

Lewis, Meriwether, 189, 191, 194–204, 261; return home, 203–204

Lewis and Clark expedition, 187, 189, 191, 194–204, 261; Sacagawea and, 200–201; journals of, 203

Lexington, battle at, 146

License plates, tribal, 451

Life Among the Piutes (Winnemucca), 344

Life expectancy: for Native Americans, 398, 462–463

Like a Fishook Village, 198

Lim Goh Tong, 468

Lincoln, Abraham, 280

Lindenmeier site, 5–6

Lipan Apaches: Comanches and, 131; Spanish and, 152; lifestyle of, 193; in Texas, 250; Civil War and, 280; peyote use by, 348–349. *See also* Apaches

Lisa, Manuel, 210

Little Big Horn, Battle of, 302–306, 308, 327

Little Big Man, 295

Little Big Man (movie), 421

Little Carpenter. *See* Attakullaculla (Little Carpenter)

Little Crow, 278, 279, 280

Little Ice Age, 25

Little Plume, 347

The Little Red School House, 421–422

Little Turtle, 164–165, 168, 170–171, 182

Little Wolf, 304, 308

Locke, Victor, 365

Loco, John, 317, 388

Lodge Grass, 352

Logan, 146

Logan, Benjamin, 167

Logstown, 116; Virginia delegates at, 116–117

Loloma, Charles, 420

Lolo Trail, 200

Lone Ranger, 421

Lone Star Republic, 251, 253

Lone Wolf, Delos, 358

Lone Wolf v. *Hitchcock,* 359–360, 366

Long Beach, California: relocation of Indians to, 401–402

Long Earrings, 283

Longest Walk, 434–435

Long Island, 70

Long Island of the Holston, Treaty of (1777), 148

Long Walk, 383

Lookout, Fred, 369

Lorette, 95

Los Angeles: relocation of Indians to, 400, 402; powwows in, 402

Los Pinos Agency, 315

Louisiana: establishment of, 95; Indian-Imperial War and French, 99–100; Natchez uprisings in, 124–125

Louisiana Purchase, 187, 194

Love, Robert, 246

Lower Brulé Sioux agency, 382

Lower Creeks, 98, 99; anti-English sentiment among, 118; British policy and, 145; American Revolution and, 148; in Southeast, 174. *See also* Creeks

Lowrie, Henry, 276

Lozen, 318–319

Luhan, Antonio, 361

Luhan, Mabel Dodge, 356

Luiseños: Gold Rush and, 259

Lumbees, 41; in Civil War, 276; schools for, 331; recognition and, 415–416, 473

Lummis: commercial fishing and, 329, 368

Luna y Arellano, Tristán de, 38–39, 40

Lyng v. *Northwest Indian Cemetery Protective Association,* 443–444

Lyons, Jesse, 391

Lysine, 6

Lyttleton, William, 141

M

Mábila, 35, 39

MacArthur, Douglas, 391

MacDonald, Peter, 417, 446, 449–450, 461

Machita, Pia, 391

Mackenzie, Ranald, 300

Madrano, Dan, 395

Mahicans, 55, 58, 71; killing by, 84; move to Ohio Valley, 115. *See also* Stockbridge Mahicans

Maidus: gold rush and, 257

Maine Indian Claims Settlement Act (1980), 439

Maize: cultivation of, 6, 8, 14, 15, 24, 40, 49

Makahs, 20; fur trade and, 204; western settlement and, 261; whaling and, 460–461

Malacate, Antonio, 103

Malachi, 110

Malaria: impact on Indians, 158

Malheur River Reservation, 313

Malinche, 30

Mammoths, 4; extinction of, 4–5

Mandans, 23; farming by, 130; lifestyle of, 192, 196–199;

trade and, 195, 204; Lewis and Clark expedition and, 195–197; politics and, 196–197; group identity of, 197; religion of, 197, 201, 204; horses and, 198; small-pox and, 198; earth lodges of, 199

Manhattan Island, 69

Mankiller, Charlie, 400–401

Mankiller, Wilma, 400, 423, 448–449

Manteo, 40, 41

Manuelito, 284, 336

Many Horses, 191

Margold, Nathan, 377–378, 418

Marguerie, Francois, 62

Marquette, Jacques, 99

Marshall, John, 226–227

Marshall, Thurgood, 442

Martin, Eben, 360

Martin, John, 247

Martin, Phillip, 446

Martin del Valle, Francisco, 133

Martinez, Connie, 434

Martinez, Julian, 355, 442

Martinez., Maria, 355

Maryland: founding of, 71; trade and, 71; Native American resistance in, 120–121

Mascoutens: warfare and, 94, 127; move to Ohio Valley, 115

Mashantucket Pequots, 468; resistance of, 120. *See also* Pequots

Mashpees: lands of, on Cape Cod, 330; powwows of, 353. *See also* Wampanoags

Massachusetts (colony), 66, 68, 72

Massachusetts (Indians), 65, 66–67, 68, 120, 123; in Metacom's War, 88

Massacre Cave, 283

Massasoit, 65

Massaw, 119–120

Mastodons, 4; extinction of, 4–5

Matador Land and Cattle Company, 368

Matagorda Bay, 108

Maternal mortality, 463

Mattaponis, 90

Matthews, John Joseph, 365, 373

Mayflower, 65

Mayflower II: AIM takeover of, 422

McCormick, Robert, 421

McCoy, Isaac, 179, 221

McCullough, John, 142

McGee, Calvin, 416

McGillivray, Alexander, 149, 174–175

McGovern, George, 417

McIntosh, Chilly, 270

McIntosh, Daniel, 270

McIntosh, Roley, 243, 245

McIntosh, William, 213–214, 224, 226, 245, 270

McIntosh-Checote-Perryman faction, 273

McKee, Alexander, 167

McKenney, Thomas, 221

McKinley, William, 335

McLaughlin, James, 339

McNickle, D'Arcy, 373–374, 376–378, 394, 395, 396, 410, 415, 416

McQueen, Peter, 186

Means, Russell, 427, 429–430, 431–433, 434, 455

Measles: impact on Native Americans, 28, 57, 158, 242

Medfield, Massachusetts: Indian attack on, 88

Medicine Lodge Creek, 22

Medicine Lodge Creek, Treaty of (1867), 293, 297, 358–359

Medicine Tail Coulee, 304

Meeker, Nathan, 314, 315

Meherrins: migration of, 121

Membertou, 49, 64

Memeskia, 116

Menawa, 213–214

Mendoza, Antonio, 42

Menéndez de Avilés, Pedro, 37–38, 50, 51

Menominees: remain in Wisconsin, 231; rituals of, 352; economic enterprise of, 367–368; termination and, 408, 409, 410, 413–415. *See also* Deer, Ada

Meriam, Lewis, 370–371, 374, 378

Meriam Report, 370–371, 374, 377

Mescalero Apaches: Comanches and, 131; Spanish and, 152; attacked by Carleton, 282; at Bosque Redondo, 282, 284, 286; measles among, 286. *See also* Apaches

Mesquakies (Foxes), 91; at Detroit, 94; wars of, 94–95, 112, 127–128; removal of, 214; as entrepreneurs, 219; women's roles

among, 220; resistance to removal, 233, 234–235; intertribal warfare and, 242; arrival of, in Indian Territory, 275; World War II and, 392

Metacom, 88, 89

Metacom's War (1675–1676), 88, 89, 90, 95

Metcalf, Lee, 417

Methodists: efforts to convert Indians, 215

Métis, 218, 232

Metlakatla, 388

Mexican-American War (1846–1848), 245, 253, 265, 281

Mexico: Aztecs in, 30–31; Indians in, 253; U.S. war with, 253, 265; independence of, 253–254; granting of citizenship to Indians, 263

Mexico City: smallpox epidemic in, 136

Meyers, John, 355

Miamis: Algonquian-speaking, 91; Five Nations attack on, 93; in Ohio Country, 94, 115, 167, 168; trade with English, 94; warfare and, 127; French and, 139; American Revolution and, 148; captives of, 169; missions for, 178; leadership of, 181; women's roles in, 220; alcohol and, 221; removal of, 232–233; arrival of, in Indian Territory, 276

Miantonomi, 87

Micanopy, 236, 237, 238, 245–246

Michilimackinac: Indian villages at, 91; British withdrawal from, 167

Mico, Eneah, 174, 226

Mico, Hoboithle, 174, 175, 179–180

The Middle Five (LaFlesche), 345

Middle Plantation, Treaty of (1677), 90

Mikhailovosk, 208

Mi'kmaqs, 46, 64, 66; kidnapping of dozens of, 46; French and, 49, 65; Anglo-French colonization and, 113–114; military service by, 122

Miles, John, 299

Miles, Nelson, 304, 312, 319

Milk Creek, Battle of, 315

Miller, Carl, 386

Mills, Anson, 304

Miluks: western settlement and, 261

Mimbreno Apaches: Mexican War and, 281; Civil War and, 282–283. *See also* Apaches

Mineo, Sal, 421

Mineral resources: accessibility of, 403–404, 445

Mingos: in Ohio Country, 115–116, 116, 137, 138; Seven Years War and, 142; Delaware Indians, 143

Minneapolis: Native Americans living in, 397, 421; powwows in, 402

Minneconjous: lifestyle of, 192; warfare and, 303, 304; Wounded Knee and, 339. *See also* Dakotas; Lakotas; Sioux

Miss Indian Chicago, 402

Missionaries, 68–69, 74, 88, 123–124, 143, 147, 177–179, 181, 215. *See also* Franciscans; Jesuits

Mission Dolores: Ohlones gambling at, 159. *See also* Mission San Francisco

Missions: Franciscan, 38; Jesuit, 55, 57, 64, 71, 84, 85–86, 95, 261; life and death at, 157–160; rebellion at, 160; Protestant, 178, 215, 261; schools at, 178–179. *See also* Franciscans; Jesuits; *specific missions*

Mission San Carlos, 160

Mission San Francisco, 160. *See also* Mission Dolores

Mission San Gabriel, 157, 160

Mission San José, 161–162

Mission Santa Cruz, 160

Mississaugas: American Revolution and, 149

Mississippians, 15–18, 45; confrontation with de Soto, 33–35; resistance of, 38; Spanish and, 39–40

Missouri Fur Company: fur trade and, 210

Missouris, 23; migration of, 130; Lewis and Clark expedition and, 194; arrival of, in Indian Territory, 275

Mitchell, George, 421

Miwoks, 45; horses and, 161; in California, 255; gold rush and, 257

Mobile, 99

The Moccasin Maker (Johnson), 356

Moctezuma, 30

Modocs: arrival of, in Indian Territory, 276; rebellion against reservation life, 308–310; recognition of, 439

Modoc War, 310

Mogollon, 8

Mohawk-Mahican War (1624–1628), 58, 69

Mohawks, 17, 49, 59, 71, 72; captives of, 81; religion of, 81; kinship in, 82; warfare among, 84; relations with colonists, 89; land encroachment on, 115; in Anglo-French War, 138; Cherokees and, 141; American Revolution and, 146–147; Spanish and, 156; leadership of, 180. *See also* Iroquois

Moheag, Abigail Speen, 121–122

Mohegans, 66–67, 68, 276; in Metacom's War, 88; recognition and, 416

Momaday, N. Scott, 419, 420

Montagnais, 48, 49, 55, 58, 64

Montauks: Christianity and, 123

Montcalm, 138–139

Monte Verde, 3

Montezuma, Carlos, 363–364, 411

Montmagny, 91–92

Montreal: Iroquois attack on, 93; Mohawk attack on, 115; French surrender of, 140

Mooney, James, 1

Moore, James, 99

Moore, W. L., 331

Mopope, Stephen, 356

Moravians: Native American conversion to, 123–124; as missionaries, 178, 215

Morgan, George, 168

Morgan, Jacob C., 352, 385, 387

Morgan, Lewis Henry, 324–325

Mormon emigrants, 286, 289

Moses, 337

Moultrie Creek, Treaty of (1823), 236

Moundville, 16–17, 40

Mountain men, 210

Mountains, 22

Mount Rushmore: AIM attack on, 422; threats to settle on, 425

Mourning Dove, 356

Mourning wars, 58–59, 101, 114

Mouto (Madeline Bertrand), 219

Movies, 356–357, 420–421

Moytoy, 117

Mt. Pleasant (Michigan), 218, 220

Munsees, 58, 69–71, 70; Canarsee Munsees, 69; Esopus Munsees, 70–71; removal of, 231

Murrow, Edward R., 421

Musgrove, John, 110, 117

Musgrove, Mary. *See* Coosaponakeesa (Mary Musgrove)

Mushalatubbee, 243

Muskogean language, 33, 97, 110

Myer, Dillon, 400, 408, 410

My People The Sioux (Luther Standing Bear), 356

Myrick, Andrew, 278

Mystic, 67

N

Nachez, 316, 317, 319

Nader, Ralph, 455, 456

Nailor, Gerald, 388

Nakaidoklini, 317

Nampeyo, 355

Nana, 318, 319

Nanipacana, 39

Nansemonds, 74; migration of, 121

Nanticokes: English resistance by, 120–121; migration of, 121; rights of, 331

Nantucket: Wampanoags on, 119

Napochies, 39

Naranjo, Domingo, 106

Naranjo, Pedro, 103, 104–105

Narbonna, 283

Narragansett Bay, 46

Narragansetts, 15, 18, 46–47, 65–67; colonists and, 88, 89, 111; in Metacom's War, 88; land allotment and, 330; recognition and, 416

Narváez, Pánfilo de, 31, 33, 42

Nash, Philleo, 418

Natchez, 39; French and, 15, 124; uprisings by, 124–125

Natchez Sun (grand chief), 125

Natchitoches Caddos: French and, 108; in Texas, 251. *See also* Caddos

Natick, Massachusetts, 120, 123

National Association for the Advancement of Colored People, 419

National Board of Indian Commissioners, 299

National Catholic Basketball Tournament, 355

National Congress of American Indians (NCAI), 395–396, 405, 406, 407, 409, 410, 420, 426, 437; Emergency Conference of, 410, 413; opposition to termination, 410–413

National Council of Churches, 413, 423; termination and, 410

National Indian Education Association, 435

National Indian Youth Council, 411, 416, 426, 435

National Museum of the American Indian, 451–452, 472

National Tribal Chairman's Association, 426, 435, 437

National Youth Administration, 388

Native American Church, 348–357, 404–405, 444, 450. *See also* Peyote

Native American Graves Protection and Repatriation Act (NAGPRA), 451

Native American Journalists Association, 462

Native American Rights Fund, 419, 435, 440

Native Americans: oral traditions of, 1–3, 7; effects of alcohol on, 58, 143, 180, 221; slave trade and, 96–97, 101–102; mass migrations of, 112; resistance to English authority, 120–121; slavery of, 121; indebtedness of, 121–122; cultural identity of, 122; in military service, 122; spirituality of, 122–124; in Mississippi Valley, 124–129; captives of, 169–170; missionaries among, 177–179; intermarriage among, 218, 398–399; women as entrepreneurs, 219–220; in Civil War era, 268–293; in popular culture, 353–357; life expectancy for, 398; population increases in, 398–399; migration to the cities, 399; wage labor among, 399; relocation of, 399–401; new patterns of life for, 401–402; changes in reservation communities, 402–404; religious and political changes for, 404–406; termination and, 406–415; recognition for, 415–421; new voices for,

421–423; defining who is Indian, 459, 470–473. *See also specific tribes*

Navajo "code talkers," 392

Navajo Community College, 438

Navajos (Diné): raid Pueblos, Spanards and Mexicans, 77, 102, 106–107, 263, 265, 283; in Southwest, and Pueblos, 77, 102, 106, 263; in Southwest, 154–155; cultural change among, 283, 367; attacked by Americans, 284; and Long Walk, 284; at Bosque Redondo, 284–286; education among, 333; peyote use among, 349, 404–405; and Indian Reorganization Act, 383, 385–386; mineral revenue, 404; tribal council, 449, 461; casino, 469

Navajo Times, 435

Navajo Women's Conference, 449

Neapope, 233

Necotawance, 74

Neighbors, Robert, 251

Nelson Act (1889), 328

Nemattanew, 74

Neolin, 143

Neopit, 368

Nespelems: reservations for, 337

Netherlands: Iroquois alliance with, 58. *See also* Dutch; New Netherland

Neutrals, 63

Neve, Felipe de, 159

New Albion, 45

New Amsterdam, 69

New Archangel, 207

New Bern, 100

Newcastle Land and Livestock Company, 368

New Deal, 378–379; Indian reactions to, 382–390; Indian extension of, 388–390

New Echota, 227

New Echota, treaty of (1835), 227, 228

New England: exploration and settlement of, 64–69; Metacom's War and the Covenant Chain in, 87–90; racial hierarchies in, 91

Newfoundland: English in, 46

New France: Indians and, 55–64, 83, 84–86, 91–92; emergent refugee communities and, 91–92. *See also* French

New Haven, 68

New Helvetia, 255–256

New Hope Academy, 247

New Light Christianity, 123–124

New Mexico: Indians in, 77, 104–107, 153–155; Spanish in, 106–107; defending lands of, 361–362

New Netherland, 69, 70; beginning of, 58; trading activities, 65–66; population of, 70; English conquest of, 84. *See also* Dutch; Netherlands

New Orleans: smallpox epidemic in, 136–137; Battle of, 221

Newport, Christopher, 72, 73

News from Indian Country, 462

New Sweden: settlement of, 70, 71–72

New Ulm: Santee attacks on, 279

New York, Treaty of (1790), 175

Nez Percé, 21, 316, 331; horses and, 130; Lewis and Clark expedition and, 200–201, 201, 203; guns and, 204; trade and, 204; fur trade and, 210, 261; hunting for bisons by, 210–211; rendezvous and, 211; western settlement and, 242, 261; missions and, 261; arrival of, in Indian Territory, 275; rebellion against reservation life, 308; Chief Joseph and, 310–312; reservations for, 337; rituals of, 353

Nicaagat (Jack), 314–315

Night Flying Woman, 398. *See also* Broker, Ignatia

Nighthawks, 358

Nipissings, 63

Nipmucs, 87; conversion of, 88; in Metacom's War, 88; migration of, 121

Nisenans: in California, 255; gold rush and, 257

Nisquallies: western settlement and, 262

Nixon, Richard: Indian policy under, 415, 423, 429

Niza, Fray Marcos de, 42–43

Nolatubby, Henry, 390

Nootkas: fur trade and, 204

Nootka Sound Crisis (1789), 174

Nordwall, Adam, 422–423

Norridgewock: burning of, 113

Norse colonization, 25, 28, 46

North, Frank, 299

North Carolina Home Guard, 276

Northeast: French exploration and settlements in, 45–49, 55–64; Indian-European relations in, 45–51; Iroquois in, 55–64, 83–95, 114–115; Anglo-French colonization of, 113–114

Northeastern Oklahoma State College, 248

Northern Cheyenne Tribal Council, 446

Northern Pacific Railroad, 328

Northern Plains: Native Americans of, 129–130; Indian warfare on, 301–308

Northern Rockies: tribes of, 210–211

North Fork Town, 247

Northwest: Indian tribes in, 20–21, 260–263; Indian Removal in, 230–233; commercial fishing by Indians in, 328–329

North West Company, 203

Northwest Federation of American Indians (NFAI), 363, 387

Northwest Passage, 50

Nottaways: migration of, 121

Nova Scotia: British control of, 113; attack on British in, 114

Numic-speaking, 24

O

Oakes, Richard, 422, 425, 426, 427

Oakland: relocation of Indians to, 400, 402; powwows in, 402

Oaxaca, 6

Occoneechees: peaceful, 90

Ochese Creeks, 38–39, 98, 101. *See also* Creeks

Office of Economic Opportunity (OEO), 416–417

Ogden Land Company, 233

Oglalas: warfare among, 301, 303. *See also* Lakotas; Sioux

Oglala Sioux Civil Rights Organization (OSCRO), 429

Oglethorpe, James, 110, 111; return to England, 118

Ohio Country: Indian refugees in, 115–117; colonist-Indian relations in, 166–173

Ohiyesa. *See* Eastman, Charles

Ohlones (Costanoans), 45; missions and, 159, 160

Ojibwes, 14, 64; Algonquian-speaking, 91; at Detroit, 94; and French, 94, 124, 128; lifestyle, 192; remain in upper Midwest, 231–232; in Civil War, 276; peyote use among, 349; rituals, 352–353; economic enterprises, 367–368; and Indian Reorganization Act, 387; in World War II, 392; migrate to urban areas, 402; and American Indian Movement, 421

Okanagons, 21; reservations for, 337

OKC Camp Crier, 435

Okhotsk, 205

Okipa Ceremony, 197

Oklahoma: removal of Indians to, 222–224, 226; land runs in, 329; Cheyennes in, 353; creation of, 358; intermarriage in, 398. *See also* Indian territory

Oklahoma City: relocation of Indians to, 400

Oklahomans for Indian Opportunity, 417

Oklahoma's Poor Rich Indians (Bonnin), 369

Oklahoma Territory: creation and settlement of, 329–330

Oklahoma Welfare Act (1936), 388

Oklahombi, Joseph, 365

Okmulgee Constitution, 273

Old Briton. *See* La Demoiselle

Old Hop, 117

Old Indian Days (Eastman), 356

Old Toby, 200

Oliphant, Mark, 442–443

Olleyquotequiebe, 157

Olsen-Chubbock site, 5, 22

Omaha Dance, 353

Omahas, 23; migration of, 130; lifestyle of, 192; Lewis and Clark expedition and, 194; Indian Reorganization Act and, 387

O'Mahoney, Joseph, 406

Oñate, Don Juan de, 44, 77, 78; search for gold by, 77

One Eye, 196

Oneidas, 17, 56; treaties with, 84; American Revolution and, 147, 149; removal of, 231; served with 37th Wisconsin Volunteers, 276; support for Indian Reorganization Act, 382; Indian Reorganization Act and, 386; World War II and, 392; land claims of, 441. *See also* Iroquois

Oneidas' Turning Stone Casino, 469

Onondagas, 17, 93, 100; warfare among, 83, 84; treaties with, 84; artifacts of, 85; captives of, 93; American Revolution and, 147, 149; effect of disease epidemic, 147; as Tuscarora Company, 276. *See also* Iroquois

Onontio, 91–92, 94

Oorang: sports and, 355

Opatas, 42, 43

Opechancanough, 74

Opothle Yaholo, 224, 226, 245, 270–272

Oral traditions: Native American, 2–3, 7

Oregon Donation Land Use Law (1850), 261

Oregon Trail, 286, 287, 289

Organic Act (1884), 436

Orontony, 116

Ortiz, Alfonso, 107

Ortiz, Juan, 33, 36

Osages: trade and, 111; impact of horses and guns on, 129, 130–131; relations with other tribes, 218; intertribal warfare and, 242; western settlement and, 242–243; arrival of, in Indian Territory, 274, 276; land allotment and, 326; reservation of, 357; petroleum reservoir on reservation of, 368–369

Osceola, 236, 237, 238

Oskinson, John Milton, 373

Ossossané, 63

Other Day, John, 279

Otoe-Missouria: arrival of, in Indian Territory, 275; Civil War and, 286. *See also* Missouris

Otos, 23; acquisition of horses and guns, 130; migration of, 130; lifestyle of, 192; Lewis and Clark expedition and, 194

Ottawas, 64, 276; Algonquian-speaking, 91; fur trade and, 92–93; French and, 94; in Ohio Country, 94, 138, 168; Dakotas and, 128; fireworks display and, 164; women, 220; removal of, 231, 232; arrival of, in Indian Territory, 276; termination and, 413; recognition of, 439

Ouray, 314, 315

Outer Banks, 40

Outing, 334

The Outsider (movie), 420–421

Overhill people, 166–167

Owen, Robert, 330

Owl, Lula, 364

Owl Woman, 264–265

Ozette, 20

P

Paha Sapa, 308

Paiute-Bannock War (1878), 314

Paiutes: rebellion against reservation life, 312–314; water rights and, 409, 442; termination and, 410; recognition of, 439

Paleo-Indians: projectile points of, 4; kill sites of, 4–5; earliest, 4–6; campsites of, 5; shift in hunting habits, 5; sites of, 22

Palma, Salvador, 157

Palmer, Joel, 262

Palouses: western settlement and, 262; reservations for, 337

Pamunkeys, 74; peaceful, 90; colonists and, 111; land sale by, 121; in Civil War, 276; rights of, 331

Pancoast, Henry, 332

Panton and Leslie (British trading firm), 174–175

Papagos. *See* Tohono O'odhams (Papagos)

Papoonan, 142

Pardo, Juan, 39, 40; alliance between Joara and, 39

Parenteau, Isidore, 373

Paris, Treaty of (1763), 142

Paris, Treaty of (1783), 149, 166, 167, 173

Parker, Arthur, 370, 388, 396

Parker, Ely S., 276–277

Parker, Quanah, 301, 329, 347, 349

Park Hill (Indian Territory), 247

Partisan, 189, 194

Passapegh, 73

Passamaquoddies: activism and, 439. *See also* Abenakis

Pataki, George, 469

Paul, William, 363

Pawnees, 23, 43; origination of calumet by, 91; acquire horses and guns, 130; and French, 132; attacked by Lakotas, 192, 301;

lifestyle, 192; warfare with eastern immigrant tribes, 243; trade among, 264, 286; arrive in Indian Territory, 274–275; meet American travelers, 286–287; steal horses, 287; assist army, 299, 304; lands allotted, 326

Payne, Scott, 315

Payne's Landing (Treaty of), 236

Peabody Coal Company, 445

Peach War (1655), 70

Pea Ridge, Battle of (1862), 271

Pecos: resistance of, 43

Pelota, 75

Peltier, Leonard, 433

Pembroke State College for Indians, 331

Penateka Comanches: in Texas, 251–252. *See also* Comanches

Pend d'Oreille: missions and, 261; western settlement and, 261; treaties with, 262

Penn, Arthur, 421

Penn, William, 93

Pennsylvania: settlement of, 93–94, 114–115

Penobscot Abenakis: villages of, 49; signing of treaty with British, 113–114; activism and, 439. *See also* Abenakis

Pensacola, Treaty of (1784), 174, 175

Pensacolas, 17; flight of, 39

Pentecostals: Native Americans and, 405

Penutian language, 21

Peo-Peo-Mox-Mox, 262

People v. *Woody,* 405

Peorias: removal of, 231; arrival of, in Indian Territory, 276; termination and, 413; recognition of, 439. *See also* Illinois Confederacy

Pequots, 65–68, 276; in Metacom's War, 88; recognition and, 416, 473; economics and, 468; membership criteria and, 472. *See also* Mashantucket Pequots

Pequot War (1637), 67, 87, 88

Peralta, Don Pedro de, 77

Perez, Albeoni, 264

Perry, Oliver, 183, 185

Peters, Susan, 356

Peterson, Helen, 410, 415

Petroglyphs: in Columbia Plateau, 21–22

Petuns, 63; Iroquoian-speaking, 91; move to Ohio Country, 94, 115

Peyote: Native American use of, 348–349, 404–405, 444. *See also* Native American Church

Peyote Road Man, 349

Phelps-Dodge copper mine, 392

Philippine Islands: Spanish control of, 45

Phillips Petroleum, 369

Phinney, Archie, 395, 396

Phoenix: relocation of Indians to, 400

Piankashaws: arrival of, in Indian Territory, 276

Pickawillany, 116

Pickleweed seeds, 24

Pictographs: in Columbia Plateau, 21–22; Navajo, 44

Pictou, Anna Mae, 426, 429, 430. *See also* Aquash, Anna Mae

Picurís, 106

Piegan Blackfeet: effect of smallpox on, 136; horses and, 190–191; Lewis and Clark expedition and, 203. *See also* Blackfeet

Pierce, Bemus, 354

Pierre's Hole, 211

Pike, Albert, 269–270

Pilgrims, 65

Pimas. *See* Akimel O'odhams (Pimas)

Pine Ridge Reservation, 308, 338, 339, 352, 359, 386, 450; wage labor on, 403; AIM militants in, 427; activism and, 430, 433; Clinton visit to, 465–466

Piros: uprising among, 106

Piscataways, 64; Jesuit mission to, 71; in Upper Chesapeake, 71–72; migration of, 121

Pitchlynn family, 222

Pit-houses: building in Great Basin, 24

Pit River Indians: occupancy of land in Lassen National Forest, 425

Pizarro, Francisco, 30–31, 33

Plague: impact on Indians, 28

Plains: tribes on, during Civil War era, 286–292; cultural change on the, 296–298; Indian warfare on Southern, 298–299; Indian warfare on Northern, 301–308

Plains Indians, 22–24; Lewis and Clark expedition and, 194–198

Plenty Kill, 322, 323, 324, 331, 333, 334, 340, 356. *See also* Standing Bear, Luther

Plymouth, 65–66, 68

Plymouth Bay, 65

Plymouth Rock: protest at, 426

Pneumonia: impact on Indians, 119, 158

Poarch Creek Band of Creeks, 451

Pocahontas, 72; marriage of John Rolfe and, 53–54, 73; visit to England of, 73

Pocomokes: resistance to English by, 120–121

Pocumtucks, 87

Poetic Justice, 457

Point Elliott, Treaty of (1855), 419

Point Hope, 388

Point Nine program, 413

Pokagon, Simon, 344

Polelonema, Otis, 356

Political changes: among Native Americans, 404–406

Pomeroy, Samuel, 272

Pomos, 45; Russians and, 207; Gold Rush and, 257; Indian Reorganization Act and, 383

Poncas, 23; arrival of, in Indian Territory, 275; warfare among, 301; land of, 331–332; mistreatment of, 332; Indian Reorganization Act and, 387

Ponce de León, Juan, 31

Pontiac, 145; assassination of, 145

Poor People's Campaign, 427

Popé, 103, 104–105, 106

Popo Agie (River), 211

Popular culture: Indians in, 353–357

Port Royal, 64

Portuguese: in Northeast, 45

Posey, Alexander, 344

Post, Christian Frederick, 139

Poston, California: War Relocation camp at, 393

Potawatomis, 64; Algonquian-speaking, 91; warfare among, 127; in Ohio Country, 138, 168; in American Revolution, 148; captives among, 169; alcohol among, 180, 221; as entrepreneurs, 218–220, 286; women's roles among, 220; removal, 232–234; warfare against plains tribes, 242–243; arrive in Indian

Territory, 275; emergence of Citizen Band (Citizen Potawatomi Nation), 275; in Civil War, 286; rituals, 352; in World War II, 393

Potlatches, 20–21, 209

Poverty, 464–466; problem of, 369–371; solution to, 458; diseases associated with, 463

Poverty (Hunter), 369

Poverty Point, 13; social ranking at, 13

Powder River Country, 268

Powell, Robin, 462

Powhatan, 51, 53–54, 73–74; mantle of, 73; death of, 74

Powhatan Confederacy, 51; defeat of, 96

Powhatans, 18, 50, 64, 73, 74; resistance by, 40, 50–51; Virginia settlement and, 53–54, 72–75; visit to England by, 54; First Anglo Powhatan War, 73; clothes worn by, 122

Powwows, 353

Prairie du Chien, Treaty of (1825), 231

Pratt, Richard, 300, 324, 325, 333, 335, 340, 354

Praying towns, 68, 69, 86, 89, 95, 123

Presbyterians: boarding school of, 178; as missionaries, 215

Press, freedom of, 462

Price, Hiram, 352

Price, Sterling, 266

Prince of Wales Island, 207

Prince William Sound, 207

Proclamation of 1763, 144–145, 146, 176

Proctor, Henry, 183, 185

Projectile points, 4

Promyshlemniki, 205, 206

Prophetstown, 182, 185

Protestants: missions of, 178, 215, 261. *See also specific denominations*

Public Health Service: responsibility for reservation medical care, 398–399

Public Works Administration (PWA), 379, 388

Pueblo Bonito, 9

Pueblo Indians, 41; oral traditions, 2; origins, 10; impact of Spanish on, 43–44, 77–78, 112; belief in

harmony, 77; trade with Apaches and Navajos, 77; Franciscans among, 77–78; languages, 79; conversion to Christianity, 102; epidemic disease among, 102, 135; revolt against Spanish, 102–107; retain indigenous religion, 103, 131, 156; revolt against Mexican government, 264; revolt against Americans (Taos Revolt), 265–266; and Indian Reorganization Act, 285; peyote use among, 349; festivals and celebrations, 352; in World War II, 393

Puerto Rico: Tainos on, 29

Puget Sound: societies of, 20; commercial fishing in, 368

Puritans: missionary efforts by, 68–69

Putnam, George Haven, 375

Puyallups: western settlement and, 262; Indian Reorganization Act and, 387

Pynchon, John, 87–88

Pynchon, William, 68

Pyramid Lake Paiutes: water rights and, 409. *See also* Paiutes

Q

Quaabe, Paul, 121

Quakers: missionaries of, 178, 181

Qualla Boundary (Eastern Cherokee) Reservation, 277

Quallatown, 277

Quantrill, William, 271

Quapaw Agency, 310

Quapaws: arrival of, in Indian Territory, 276

The Quarterly Journal, 363

Quebec, 55, 63; English in, 57, 140; French in, 57

Quechans (Yumas), 45; and Spanish, 157; Gold Rush and, 259

Queen Anne's War (1702–1713), 94, 99

Queppish, Eben, 363

Quinaults: western settlement and, 261

Quinkent (Douglas), 314

Quinn, Anthony, 421, 422

Quintana, Andrés, 160

Quintasket, Christine, 356. *See also* Mourning Dove

Quinton, Amelia Stone, 332

R

Radio Free Alcatraz, 422

Raleigh, Sir Walter, 40–41

Râle's War, 113

Ramsey, Alexander, 279

Ranked village societies: formation of, 19

Rappahannocks: draft resistance and, 391

Reagan, Ronald, 444, 466

Rebolledo, Diego de, 76

Reciprocity, 2, 12, 23, 27, 28, 29, 45, 72

Reconstruction: in Indian territory, 272–276

Redbird Pinkerton-Uri, Constance, 437

Red Bird Uprising, 231

Red Cliff News, 435

Red Cloud, 268, 290, 293, 301, 304, 308, 336, 360

The Redeemed Captive Returned to Zion (Williams), 81–82

Red Lake: termination and, 408

The Red Man, 333

Red Power, 426–435, 431, 452, 457; women and, 434; decline of, 434–435

Red River: French-Caddo trading post at, 108

Red River War, 299–301

Red Shirt, 341

Red Shoes. *See* Shulush Houma

Red Star, 308

Red Sticks: Creeks and, 185–186

Red Vermillion, 220

Rehnquist, William, 443

Reifel, Ben, 378

Relocation, 399–401

Rendezvous, 211

Reno, Marcus, 303–304

Repartimiento, 78

Reservation communities: changes in, 402–404

Reserved sovereignty: doctrine of, 418–419, 440–441

Resettlement Administration, 379, 388

Revitalization movements, 179–182, 185–186

Reynolds, John, 234

Rhoads, Charles, 374

Rhode Island, 68; establishment of, 66; Great Swamp in, 88

Richardville, Jean Baptiste, 218, 220, 232

Richelieu River, 55

Rickard, Clinton, 391

Ridge, John, 227, 243

Ridge, Major, 227, 243

Ridge family, 227, 228

Riding The Earthboy 40 (Welch), 420

Rio Grande, 41, 77

Risling, David, Jr., 425–426

Roanoke: English colony, 40–41, 72

Roanokes, 40–41

Roberval, Jean François de La Rocque, sieur de, 47

Robinson, Alexander, 232

Rochester (New York) Municipal Museum, 388

Rock art, 8, 21

Rockefeller, John D., 352

Rockefeller, John D., Jr., 370

Rocky Mountain Fur Company, 211

Rocky Mountain House, 204

Rodríguez, Agustín, 43

Rogers, Edward, 395

Rogers, Will, Jr., 408

Rogue River tribes, 261–262

Rogue River War, 262

Rolfe, John: marriage of Pocahontas and, 53–54, 73; visit to England of, 73

Rolfe, Thomas, 54

Roman Nose, 298

Roosevelt, Eleanor, 388

Roosevelt, Franklin Delano: election of, 375; signing of Indian Reorganization Act by, 380; Indian policy under, 406

Roosevelt, Theodore (Teddy), 322, 358, 366; inauguration of, 347

Rosebud, Battle of (1876), 302, 327

Rosebud Reservation, 308, 322, 335, 338, 340, 352, 359, 386, 395, 450, 459–460; AIM militants in, 427

Ross, John, 227–230, 243, 245, 247, 270, 271, 273

Ross, Lewis, 246–247

Ross, Quatie (John Ross's wife), 230

Ross, William Potter, 273

Rouensa, Marie, 92

Rowlandson, Mary: capture of, 88

Royer, Daniel, 338–339

Runaway slaves: Seminoles and, 235; in Texas, 253

Rusk, Thomas Jefferson, 253

Russian American Company, 206, 207, 209

Russian Orthodox priests: in Alaska, 207

Russians: fur trade by, 205–207; Tlingits and, 207–209

Ryan, W. Carson, 374

S

Sacagawea. *See* Sakakawea

Sagadahoc, failure of, 65, 72

Sahaptin language, 21

St. Augustine (Florida), 31, 38, 75, 148; founding of, 76

St. Clair, Arthur, 168, 170–171

St. Genevieve, 231

St. Joseph's Society, 350–351

St. Lawrence-Great Lakes Interior: trade and upheaval in, 49–50

St. Lawrence River, 64; French expedition to, 47; Mohawk occupancy of islands in, 425

St. Louis: French at, 152; relocation of Indians to, 400

St. Mary's Society, 350–351

St. Peter's (Steamboat), 198

St. Regis Mohawks, 392

Saint-Denis, Louis Juchereau de, 108

Sakakawea, 200–201, 202

Salamanca, 330

Salishes, 21; language of, 21; Lewis and Clark expedition and, 200–201; desire for guns, 204; fur trade and, 210; rendezvous and, 211; missions and, 261; treaties with, 262; land allotment and, 327; termination and, 410

Salt Lake City: relocation of Indians to, 400

Salt River-Pima-Maricopa newspaper, 462

Salt River Reservation, 417

Salt River/Valley, 6, 8

Samaria Indian Baptist Church, 352

San Antonio: Apache raid on, 131–132

San Buenaventura, 161

San Carlos Apache agency, 382

San Carlos Mission, 158

Sand Creek, 288–289; massacre at, 290

San Diego: settlement of, 155

Sandoval, Cebolla, 283
Sandoval, U.S. v., 361–362
Sands, Oktarsars Harjo, 273
Sands Rebellion (1870–1872), 273
Sandusky: settlement of, 115
San Felipe: pueblo of, 104
San Francisco: relocation of Indians to, 400
San Jose: relocation of Indians to, 400
San Juan Bautista: Spanish post of, 108
San Juan River, 8, 9
San Mateo, 37
Sanpoils: reservations for, 337
San Salvador, 29
Sans Arcs (Lakota): lifestyle of, 192; warfare and, 303. *See also* Lakotas; Sioux
Santa Ana, 264; pueblo of, 106
Santa Barbara, 161
Santa Barbara Channel, 19
Santa Catalina Island, 45
Santa Clara Pueblos: Indian Reorganization Act and, 385
Santa Elena, 38–39
Santa Fe, 103, 106; construction of capital at, 78; "Fiesta," 356
Santa Fe Trail, 264, 287
Santa Rita del Cobre, 281
Santa Ynéz, 161
Santee Dakota Rebellion (1862), 269, 278–280
Santee Normal Training School, 350
Santo Domingo, 44
Saponis: Christianity and, 123
Sarsis: Lewis and Clark expedition and, 203
Sassacus, 67
Sassamon, John, 88
Satank, 299
Satanta, 299, 300
Saturiwa, 36
Saukemapper, 135, 136
Saukenuk, 233
Sauks: warfare and, 127; removal of, 214; resistance to removal, 233, 234–235; intertribal warfare and, 242, 243; arrival of, in Indian Territory, 275; World War II and, 392
Sault St. Marie Ojibwes: membership criteria and, 472

Sault Ste. Marie: Indian villages at, 91
Savannahs, 99; attack of Westos by, 97; Shawnees known as, 97; English and, 100
Save the Babies campaign, 370
Scalia, Antonin, 444
Scarface Charley, 309
Schaghticoke, New York, 89, 95, 113
Schenck, Alberta, 393
Schifter, Richard, 417
Scholder, Fritz, 420
Schools. *See* Education
Schurz, Carl, 315, 333
Schuyler, John, 81–82
Scots-Irish: immigration to Pennsylvania, 114
Scott, Winfield: Indian removal and, 228, 236
Scurvy, 47
Sea mammals: hunting, 24
Seaton, Fred, 413
Second Anglo-Powhatan War (1622–1632), 74
Secotan, 40
Seger, John, 241
Self-determination, 411, 426, 452
Sells, Cato, 366
Seminoles: and American Revolution, 148; resist removal, 233, 235–238; and African-Americans, 235–238, 245–246, 272; in Mexico, 246, 253; in Texas, 246, 253; in Civil War, 270, 272; and Reconstruction, 272; and land allotment, 329; and Indian Reorganization Act, 387; and termination, 408, 410
Seminole Wars, 235–238
Senate, U.S.: Civil Service Committee, 408; Indian Affairs Committee, 436, 437; Subcommittee on Indian Education, 436
Seneca Arts Project, 388
Senecas, 17, 59, 93; warfare among, 83, 84, 127; treaties with, 84; French attack on, 93; in Ohio Country, 115, 168; American Revolution and, 147, 149; Handsome Lake and, 180–181; on reservations, 181; removal of, 233; arrival of, in Indian Territory, 276; as Tuscarora Company,

276; economic enterprise of, 367–368. *See also* Iroquois
Sequoyah (Cherokee scholar), 217
Sequoyah (proposed Indian state), creation of, 358
Serra, Junípero, 157–158
Seventh Cavalry, 339
Seven Years War, 111, 120, 137; Eastern Indians and, 137–141; capture of colonists in, 142
Sewall, Samuel, 122
Sexually transmitted diseases, 463; syphilis, 28; impact on Indians, 158 *See also Venereal disease*
Shaker rituals, 350
Shakopee, 280
Shawnee Prophet, 182, 185
Shawnees: known as Savannahs, 97; in Ohio Country, 115–116, 137–138, 167–168; and British, 120–121, 145; in Seven Years War, 142; relations with other tribes, 143, 218; in American Revolution, 147–149; captives among, 169; missionaries among, 178; and alcohol, 180; government and politics, 181–182; and religious revitalization, 181–182; an intertribal warfare in west, 218, 242; removal, 231, 233; in Texas, 252–253; arrive in Indian Territory, 274–276; and immigrants, 286
Sheepeaters, 313–314
Sheepeater War (1879), 313
Shelikov, Gregory, 206
Sherman, William Tecumseh, 276, 292, 299, 300, 310, 340
She Wore a Yellow Ribbon (movie), 420
Shingas, 138, 139
Short Bull, 341
Shoshones, 24; and Blackfeet, 129–130, 135; meet Lewis and Clark expedition, 200; and fur trade, 204, 210; hunt bison, 210–211; at rendevouz, 211; and intertribal warfare, 287; assist U.S. army, 301–302, 304; lands allotted, 327; and peyote, 349; and Indian Reorganization Act, 387; receive mineral revenue, 404
Shulush Houma (Red Shoes), 127
Sibley, Henry, 279
Sihaspas, 192

Siksikas: Lewis and Clark expedition and, 203. *See also* Blackfeet

Sikyatki, 355

Siletz: reservation for, 262; recognition of, 439

Silko, Leslie Marmon, 420

Silverheels, Jay, 421

Simcoe, John Graves, 171

Simons, Nelson Drew, 363

Sinclair, Upton, 369

Siouan, 23, 91

Sioux: hunting by, 22; trade and, 92–93, 111, 112; land allotment and, 327, 360; mistreatment of, 332; education of, 333; rituals of, 352; urban migration of, 402; Rosebud, 459–460. *See also* Dakotas; Hunkapapas; Lakotas; Minneconjous; Oglalas; Sans Arcs; Santees; Sissetons; Teton Sioux; Yankton Sioux

Sioux Dance, 353

Sioux Travellers, 355

Sissetons (Lakota): World War II and, 393

Sitka, 208, 209

Sitting Bull, 301, 302, 304, 306, 308, 312, 320, 339, 340, 359

Six Nations Iroquois Confederacy. *See* Iroquois Confederacy

Skidi Pawnees, 23

Skilloots: Lewis and Clark expedition and, 201

Skolaskin, 337

Skullyville, 247

Slaves: Native Americans as, 20, 67–68, 96–97, 99, 100, 101–102, 121; Africans as, 30, 31, 101, 121; escaped, and the Seminoles, 235; runaway, 235, 253; ownership by Indian planters, 246–247. *See also* African Americans

Slave trade, 42, 68; Indian, 95–97, 99, 100, 101–102

Slaveys, 22

Sloan, Thomas, 387

Slocum, Frances, 169–170

Slocum, John, 350

Small Business Administration, 417

Smallpox: impact on Native Americans, 28, 29, 30, 47, 57, 58, 66, 76, 77–78, 84, 114, 119, 125, 135–137, 139, 143, 158, 192, 198

Smet, Pierre Jean de, 261

Smith, Alfred, 444

Smith, Jedediah, 210

Smith, John, 53, 54, 72

Smith, Redbird, 358

Smoholla, 310, 337

Snake Dance, 352–353

Snake River, 21

Snaketown, 6

Society of American Indians (SAI), 363, 369, 387, 388

Solar observations: Anasazi, 8; Poverty Point, 13; Cahokia, 15

Solovief, Ivan, 205

South Carolina: Spanish in, 38; local Indians in, 96; expansion of, 97; Cherokee discontent with, 117

Southeast: Spanish expansion in, 75–76; Indian slave trade in, 96–97; emergence of Indian confederacies in, 97–99; efforts to defend autonomy in, 173–175; Indian removal and, 222–230

Southern Pacific Railroad, 355

Southern Rights Party, 270

Southwest, 263–266; advent of farming in, 6; Hohokam culture in, 6; Anasazi culture in, 8–9; new societies in, 10–11; Spanish in, 42–43, 77–79; struggles for power in, 151–155; Civil War in, 280–286

Sovereignty: meaning of, 456; defining tribal, 459–462

Spalding, Eliza, 261

Spalding, Henry, 261

Spanish: conquest of Aztecs and Incas, 28–31; Tainos and, 29–30; in Florida, 31, 33, 75–76, 95; in Southeast, 31, 33–40, 75–76, 95–99; Mississippians' confrontation with, 33–35; colonization efforts of, 36, 38–39, 75–78; in Southwest, 41–45, 77–79, 102–108; Karankawas and, 42; slave trade and, 42, 131; Zunis and, 43; in Northeast, 45; in Chesapeake, 50–51; in New Mexico, 77–79; enslavement of Indians by, 96–97; Pueblo revolts and, 102–107

Spanish Armada, 41

Spanish Succession, War of (1702–1713), 94, 99, 108

Speen, Robin, 68

Spencer Academy, 247

Spirit Lake Massacre, 278

Spokane Garry, 413

Spokanes, 21; western settlement and, 261, 262

Spotted Tail, 292, 301, 304, 306, 322

Spotted Tail, Steve, 365

Spotted Tail Agency, 304

Springer, William K., 358–359

Squanto, 65

Squash: cultivation of, 6, 8, 14, 40

Squaxon: western settlement and, 262

Stadacona, 47, 49, 55

Standing Bear: Kiowa, 326; Ponca, 331–332, 345; Luther, 340, 356, 357

Standing Rock Reserve, 338, 359

Starved Rock, 91

Statue of Liberty: threats to occupy, 425

Steck, William, 281

Stereotypes in movies, 420–421

Stevens, Isaac, 262, 440

Stillman, Isaiah, 234

Stillman's Run, Battle of, 234

Stockbridge Mahicans: Cherokees and, 141; removal of, 231; service with 37th Wisconsin Volunteers, 276; Indian Reorganization Act and, 386–387. *See also* Mahicans

Stokes Commission (1833), 242

Stomp Dance, 246

Stoneman, George, 316

Stories: Cherokee, 1–2, 7; origin, 3

Street, James, 234–235

Stuart, John, 145, 148

Stung Serpent, 126

Stuntz, Joseph, 433

Sturgis, Samuel, 311–312

Stuyvesant, Peter, 70

Suicide rates, 463

Sullivan, John, 148, 167

Sully, Alfred, 289, 290

Sumas: uprising among, 106

Summit Springs, Battle of, 299

Sun Dance, 336, 352, 450

Sundown (Matthews), 373

Supreme Court, U.S., cases: *Cherokee Nation v. Georgia*, 226–227; *Worcester v. Georgia*, 227; *Lone Wolf v. Hitchcock*, 359–360, 366; *People v. Woody*, 405; *Williams v. Lee*, 418–419; Indian law decisions in, 435–436; *Colorado River Water Conservation District v. U.S.*, 442; *Lyng v. Northwest Indian Cemetery Protective Association*, 443–444; *California v. Cabazon Band of Mission Indians*, 444, 447

The Surrounded (McNickle), 373–374, 394

Susquehanna Valley: settlement of, 114

Susquehannocks, 50, 64, 90; in Upper Chesapeake, 71–72; warfare among, 83; known as Conestogas, 94; migration of, 121

Sutter, John, 255–256

Swat the Fly campaign, 370

Swedish colonists, 70, 71–72

Swimmer, 1

Swinomish: Indian Reorganization Act and, 383

Syphilis, 28

T

Table Rock, Treaty of (1853), 261

Tac, Pablo, 159–160

Tadoussac, 49

Tahchee, 252

Tahlequah, Oklahoma, 247, 248, 249, 271, 274

Tainos: Columbus and, 29–30; death of, 31; warfare and, 106

Tall Bull, 299

Tamaulipas, 253

Tanaghrisson, 116–117, 137

Taos Pueblo, 77, 103, 104, 105; trade fairs at, 11, 132, 153; winter ceremonials at, 361; return of Blue Lake to tribal control and, 423

Taos Revolt, 263, 266

Tarabal, Sebastián, 157

Tatamy, Tunda (Moses), 124

Tatobem, 66

Tatum, Lawrie, 299

Tax, Sol, 415

Tax issues: landownership and, 403

Taylor, Zachary: Indian removal and, 237–238

Taza, 316

Tazcaluzas, 35, 39; resistance of, 38

Tecumseh, 173, 181–185, 233, 247

Teepees, 291

Tejas, 108

Tekakwitha, Kateri, 86–87; beatification of, 87

Television presentations, 421

Teller, Henry, 328

Tell Them Willy Boy Is Here (movie), 421

Tenochtitlan, 30

Tenskwatawa, 182

Termination, 406–410; Indian Claims Commission and, 407–408; continuing pressure for, 408–410; National Congress of American Indians opposition to, 410–413; for the Klamaths and Menominees, 413–415; end of, 415

Terry, Alfred, 292, 302, 303, 304

Tesuque: pueblo of, 104

Teton Lakota Parasol, 342

Teton Sioux: migration of, 128, 130; lifestyle of, 192; Lewis and Clark expedition and, 194. *See also* Lakotas; Sioux

Tewanima, Louis, 355

Tewas, 106

Texas: Indian tribes in, 42, 250–252; emigrant Indians in, 252–253

Texas Rangers, 251, 299

Texas Republic, 253

Texas Revolution, 250, 253

Thames, Battle of the (1813), 247

Thayendanegea, 150. *See also* Brant, Joseph

Theyanoguin, 115

Third Colorado Cavalry, 288

37th Wisconsin Volunteers, 276

Thom, Melvin, 416

Thomas, Elmer, 403, 406

Thomas, Robert K., 415

Thomas, William Holland, 277

Thomas's Legion of Indians and Highlanders, 277

Thompson, Wiley, 236

Thornburgh, Thomas, 314–315

Thorpe, George, 74

Thorpe, Jim, 354–355, 420

Tibbles, Thomas Henry, 332

Tilamoks: western settlement and, 261

Tilini, 104

Timber rights, 328, 403

Timucuas, 33, 34, 36, 37–38; in Florida, 75–76; enslavement of,

97; slave raids on, 97; missions and, 99; lands vacated by, 148

Tinker, Clarence, 390

Tippecanoe, Battle of (1811), 182, 185

Tishimingo, 247

Tleume, 104

Tlingits: fur trade and, 207–210; as woodworkers, 209; regional organization of, 362–363

Tobacco, 73, 74

Tocobagas, 33

Tohono O'odhams (Papagos), 10–11, 316, 392; village of Toapit, 390–391; leasing of, 403; water rights and, 442, 447–448

Tohopeka, 186

Tolowas, 19

Tom, Sharon, 462

Tomahas, 241

Tomah boarding school, 397

Tonawanda Community House, 388

Tonkawas: service to the Republic of Texas, 250–251; arrival of, in Indian Territory, 275

Toogaloo, 101

Topinbee, 232

Totem poles: on Northwest Coast, 20; of the Tlingits, 207

Tourism, 445–446

Toypurina, 160

Trachoma, 42

Trade and Intercourse Acts, 176, 177, 220–221, 439

Trade networks: Anasazi in, 8, 9; Hohokams in, 8; Mississippian, 23. *See also* Exchange networks

Trahant, Mark, 450

Trail of Broken Treaties, 428

Trail of Tears, 228, 229–230, 243. *See also* Cherokees

Treaty Winnebagos: removal of, 231

Treviño, Juan Francisco, 103

Tribal governments: power of, 442–443; building, 448–450

Tribally Controlled Community College Assistance Act, 438

Troup, George M., 224, 253

Trudell, John, 422

Truman, Harry: Indian policy under, 407, 408

Truteau, Jean Baptiste, 192

Tsagigalal, 21–22

Tsa Toke, Monroe, 349, 356

Tshimshians: fur trade and, 207; regional organization of, 363; Indian Reorganization Act and, 388

Tsireh, Awa, 356

Tuberculosis: impact on Indians, 119, 158

Tulsa: relocation of Indians to, 400

Tundra Times, 435

Tunica-Biloxis, 451; recognition and, 416

Tupatú, Luis, 103, 106

Turk: death of, 43

Turtle: effigy of, 85

Turtle Mountain Ojibwe: reserve, 391; termination and, 410; community, 448

Turtle Mountain Times, 462

Tuscarora Company, 276

Tuscaroras: migration of, 121; American Revolution and, 147, 149. *See also* Iroquois

Tuscarora War, 100, 102, 117

Tustennuggee, Etomme, 213

Two Kettles, 192

Two Moons, 305–306

Tyler, John: Indian policy under, 238

Typhoid: impact on Indians, 42, 158

U

Udall, Morris, 436

Udall, Stewart, 418

Uintahs: reservation for, 417–418

Umatillas, 21; western settlement and, 261; reservations for, 313, 337

Umiak, 25

Umpquas: western settlement and, 261; recognition of Cow Creek Bank of, 439

Unangans. *See* Aleuts (Unangans)

Uncas, 66

Uncle Tomahawks, 416

Uncompahgre Utes, 315

Union Pacific Railroad: construction of, 301

Union Party, 273

United American Company, 206

United Bay Area Council of American Indian Affairs, 422

United States citizens: Indians as, 357–358

U.S. Bureau of Indian Affairs (BIA), 221, 262, 283, 284, 286, 299, 340, 357, 375; mismanages Indian removal, 223, 226, 228, 230, 232–233, 236; mediates Choctaw-Chickasaw land dispute, 245; has limited influence in Texas, 251; urges policy of concentration, 268–269; resettles northern tribes in Indian Territory, 274–276; mismanages Santee agencies, 278; mismanages Bosque Redondo, 284–286; quarrels with army, 289–290; orders all Sioux to agencies, 302; and Modocs, 309; and Utes, 314–315; establishes Apache reservations, 316–317; expansion of, 335–336; pressure for change and, 374; support for allotment, 375; communications and, 376–377; development of new agenda for, 379; relocation program of, 400, 401, 402; critics of, 406; occupancy of, 425, 428; anniversary of founding of, 454; Indian Arts and Crafts Act (1935), 382

Unmak, 205

Upper Creeks, 98, 99; British policy and, 145; American Revolution and, 148; in Southeast, 174. *See also* Creeks

Upward Bound, 417

Utes, 24, 79; raids on Pueblos, 106; depredations by, 107; raids of, 107; Comanches and, 132; in New Mexico, 154; Spanish and, 156; rebellion against reservation life, 314–315; land allotment and, 327; use of peyote by, 349; Indian Reorganization Act and, 387; termination and, 410

Ute War (1879), 314–315

Utina: French and, 36–37

Utrecht, Treaty of, 113; formal recognition of, by British, 114

Uturituc, 7

V

Valeriano, 160

Vallejo, Mariano, 162

Van Buren, Martin: Indian policy under, 233

Van Curler, Arent, 59

Vann, David, 215

Vann, James, 175

Vann, Joseph, 227

Vargas, Diego de, 106–107

Vaudreil, Philippe de Rigault de, 127

Velasco, Don Luis de, 50–51

Vélez Cachupin, Tomas, 132–133

Venereal disease: syphilis, 38; impact on Indians, 158. *See also* Sexually transmitted diseases

Veniaminoff, Ivan, 207

Verrazzano, Giovanni de, 46–47

Victorio, 316–317, 318

Vietnam Veterans Against the War, 430

Vincennes, 148

Vinland, 25

Virginia: settlement of, 53–54, 72–75, 96; Anglo-Powhatan warfare in, 71; Bacon's Rebellion and, 90–91; racial hierarchy in, 91; Indian raids on, 147

Virginia Company, 73

Virgin Islands: Tainos on, 29

VISTA, 417

Vizenor, Gerald, 420

Voices from Wounded Knee, 435

Voting Rights Act (1965), 405

W

Wabanaki Alliance, 113–114

Wabokioskiek, 234

Waccamaws: recognition of, 451

Wagon Box Fight, 290

Wahoo Swamp, 236

Wahpekute: Santee Dakota Rebellion (1862) and, 278. *See also* Santees

Waiilatpu Mission: Whitmans killed at, 241–242

Walapais: Spanish and, 156

Walker, Francis, 300

Walker, Robert J., 269

Walker, Tandy, 272

Walking Purchase, 115, 117

Walla Wallas: Lewis and Clark expedition and, 201; western settlement and, 261; reservations for, 337

Wampanoags, 18, 46–47, 65, 87, 363; British and, 88, 89, 119; in Metacom's War, 88; forced labor of, 121; Christianity and, 123; recognition of, 416, 439. *See also* Mashpees

Wampum: exchange for goods and, 50, 65–66, 67, 68–69; supply to Iroquois, 83–84

Wampum belts, 18
Wanapams: Lewis and Clark expedition and, 201
Wanchese, 40
Wannamaker, John, 332–333
Wannas, 71
Warner, Glenn S. (Pop), 354
War of 1812, 176–177, 178, 185, 186, 204, 214, 215, 217, 220, 221, 224
War on Poverty, 416–417, 437, 465–466
War Relocation Authority, 393
Warrior, Clyde, 416
Warrior (steamboat), 234
Wascos, 21; Lewis and Clark expedition and, 201; western settlement and, 261
Washakie, 336
Washani Creed, 337
Washington, George, 363; French and, 117; in Ohio River Valley, 137–138; assault on Fort Duquesne, 140; on government trading posts, 176; championing of rational experiments, 177; Indian policy under, 220
Washington, Second Treaty of, 226
Washington, Treaty of (1826), 224
Washington March (1972), 427
Washita, Battle of, 298–299
Wassaja (newsletter), 364
Watie, Stand, 243, 270–272, 273
Watkins, Arthur, 406, 410, 411, 413, 414
Waubansee, 232
Wauneka, Annie, 449
Wayne, Anthony, 164–165, 170, 171–173
Webster, Daniel, 282
Weicker, Lowell, 468
Welch, James, 420
Wells, William, 170
Welsh, Herbert, 332, 335, 340, 341
Wendats. *See* Hurons
Weroances, 18
Wessells, Henry, 308
West, J. R., 282
Western Settlement: Indian-American interactions in, 241–267
Westos, 96–97; regrouping of, 98
Wewoka, 272
Weyanock, 74
Whales, 19; hunted by Makahs, 460–461

Wheeler, Burton K., 380, 387
Wheeler-Howard Act (1934). *See* Indian Reorganization Act
Wheelock, Eleazar, 123
Where White Men Fear To Tread (Means), 431
Whipple, J. S., 330
White, Andrew, 71
White, John, 40–41
White, Richard, 60, 92
White Bird, 312
White Bird Hill, Battle of, 311
White Earth Land Recovery Project, 455
White Earth Reservation, 455
White Eyes, 147
Whiteman, Paul, 357
White Mountain Apache Reservation, 368, 382
White Mountain Apaches: membership criteria and, 472
Whitman, Marcus, 261; death of, 241–242
Whitman, Narcissa, 261; death of, 241–242
Whitman mission, 241–242, 261, 310–312; massacre, 241–242
Wichitas, 23, 43, 250; acquisition of horses and guns, 130; and Apaches, 131–132; allied to French, 132; relations with Spanish, 152, 154; lifestyle, 192, 251–252; and intertribal warfare, 242, 252; in Mexico, 246; on Brazos Reserve, 251; in Texas, 251–252; in Indian Territory, 252, 276; allies of Confederate States, 270
Wigwam Evenings (Eastman), 356
Wilbur, Ray Lyman, 375
Wildcat (Seminole), 237, 245–246, 253
Wild West Show, 340–342
Williams, Eunice, 81–82, 83, 95, 142, 169
Williams, John, 81–82
Williams, Roger, 66
Williams v. *Lee*, 418–419
Wilson, Florence, 248–249
Wilson, Jimmie, 142
Wilson, Pete, 468–469
Wilson, Richard, 427, 429, 430, 433
Wilson, Woodrow, 367

Window Rock, AZ, 385, 388; community center in, 379
Wind River Arapahos: mineral revenue for, 404. *See also* Arapahos
Winema, 309–310
Wingina: assassination of, 40
Winnebago Prophet, 234
Winnebagos. *See* Ho-Chunks (Winnebagos)
Winnemucca, Sarah, 313, 343–344
Winter, George, 169, 170, 219
Winter in the Blood (Welch), 420
Wishrams, 21; Lewis and Clark expedition and, 201; western settlement and, 261
Wissler, Clark, 336
Witt, Shirley Hill, 416
Wiyots, 19
Women: role as mother, 4; food production role of, 6, 12, 14–15, 18–19, 24, 40; as religious healers, 12; land ownership by, 111; Seneca, 181; as beneficiaries of horses, 191; Cherokee, 216–217, 246; Mesquakie, 220; Miami, 220; Ottawa, 220; Potawatomi, 220; Chickasaw, 246; Choctaw, 246; Red Power and, 434; in tribal workforce, 448–449
Women of All Red Nations (WARN), 434, 437
Women's Christian Temperance Union, 332
Women's National Indian Association, 332
Woodcraft League, 355
Woodward, Henry, 96
Wool, John, 262
Worcester, Samuel, 227
Worcester v. *Georgia*, 227
Work, Hubert, 370
Workshop on American Indian Affairs, 415
Works Progress Administration (WPA), 379, 382, 388
World War I (1914–1918), 360, 370, 392; Native Americans in, 364–365
World War II (1939–1945), 390–394; Indians in, 390–392; home front in, 392–394
Wounded Knee, 339–340; massacre at, 350, 352; occupancy of, 429–430, 436, 452; aftermath of, 430, 433

Wovoka, 338, 350

Wrangell, Baron von Ferdinand, 209

Wrangell Island, 209

Wraps Up His Tail, 338

Wyandots: in Ohio Country, 115, 116, 167, 168; leadership of, 181; arrival of, in Indian Territory, 276; termination and, 413; recognition of, 439. *See also* Hurons

Wynkoop. Edward, 288

X

Xerox, 464

Y

Yakamas, 21; desire for horses, 130; Lewis and Clark expedition and, 201; western settlement and, 261, 262; reservations for, 313–314, 337, 408; termination and, 408

Yakutat: Russian settlement at, 207

Yamacraw Creeks, 110; anti-English sentiment among, 118. *See also* Creeks

Yamasees, 99; slave raids of, 97; conflict with English, 100–101; destruction of village of, 117

Yamasee War, 1, 102, 117, 119, 121; end of, 110, 111

Yankton Sioux: migration of, 128, 130; lifestyle of, 192; Lewis and Clark expedition and, 194. *See also* Lakotas; Sioux

Yaryan, John, 419

Yavapais, 316

Yazoo Strip, 174, 222

Yellow Bird, 339

Yellow fever, 119

Yellowknifes, 22

Yellow Robe, Chauncey, 365

Yellowtail, Robert, 360, 370, 375, 377, 378

Yellow Thunder, Raymond, 427

Yokuts: horses and, 161–162

York (Clark's African-American slave), 194

Young, Phyllis, 434

Younger Brothers, 271

Young Hawk, Joe, 365

Yuchis, 98

Yumas. *See* Quechans (Yumas)

Yupiks, 24

Yuroks, 19

Z

Zacatecas, Mexico, 39

Zemis, 29

Zia: pueblo of, 106

Zimmerman, William, 408

Zitkala Sa, 356. *See also* Bonnin, Gertrude

Zoar, 352

Zunis, 10, 27, 42, 77; ceremonies calling for rain, 27; encounter with Esteban, 27–28, 42; Spanish and, 43, 106; 1703 uprising in, 107; Navajo conflicts with, 283